The Macintosh BIBLE

7th Edition

SHARON ZARDETTO AKER

Peachpit Press

The Macintosh Bible, 7th Edition
Sharon Zardetto Aker

Peachpit Press
1249 Eighth Street
Berkeley, CA 94710
510 524-2178
800 283-9444
fax 510 524-2221

Find us on the Web at http://www.peachpit.com

Peachpit Press is a division of Addison Wesley Longman

Editors Cheryl Applewood and Nancy Davis
Production coordinator Kate Reber
Proofreaders Carol Burbo, Becky Morgan, Carroll Proffitt
Manufacturing coordinator Ren Thompson
Compositors Jerry Szubin, Sharon Zardetto Aker
Series and interior design Mimi Heft
Part opener art Carol Aiton, Parallax Design
Indexer Valerie Robbins

ISBN 0-201-87483-0

0 9 8 7 6 5 4 3 2 1

Printed and bound in the United States of America

Dedication

Dedicated, with love, to my in-laws.

The Wolfsons

Arnold & Ethel
Steven & Claudia

The Ostroves

Al & Naomi
Neil & Connie
Jeff & Michelle, Max, Alissa

The Gersteins

Allen & Thelma
Rob & Sandy, Emily
Dave Jay

Table of Contents

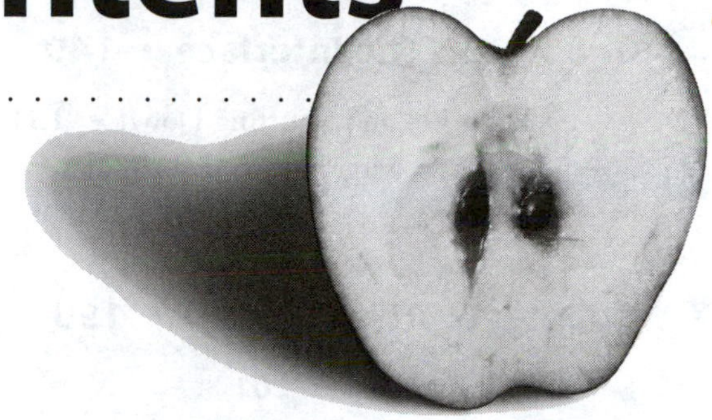

Part 3: The Operating System

Part 4: Other System Elements

Part 5: Productivity Software

Part 6: Creativity Software

Part 7: Special Areas

Part 8: Connections

Part 9: Appendices

Foreword

If you're new to *The Macintosh Bible*, welcome. And if you're not, welcome back, to this Seventh Edition. I've come back, too, after having written the Third Edition, way back when, and then gone off to do other things. After having been asked to contribute some chapters to the last edition, I realized that what I really wanted was to do the whole darn thing again, start to finish. It took a lot of lobbying, but the powers-that-be at Peachpit Press finally agreed—with some trepidation, of course, seeing as how the last two editions had umpteen editors and a cast of thousands as contributors.

If you're one of the tens of thousands of readers who have bought many editions through the years, you'll notice a big change in this edition—and it might be a familiar one. What I've done with this version is bring it back more to what the earlier editions were: heavy on the tips, tricks, and shortcuts—especially for desktop and other interface elements—and much less in the way of software reviews and general, not-so-Mac-specific background information.

This book is for any and every Mac enthusiast. Whether you're a beginner or an experienced user, you'll find many things throughout the book that you didn't know before—or perhaps knew, but not quite as thoroughly as you thought!

If you'd like to be a part of the next edition, or offer feedback on this one, drop by *thetipster.com!*

Sharon Zardetto Aker
North Caldwell, NJ

July, 1998

Acknowledgments

At Peachpit

Nancy Ruenzel, Head Honcho. For succumbing to persistent, severe arm-twisting and finally handing this project over to me.

Cheryl Applewood, Editor. For jumping into the fray just in the nick of time.

Mimi Heft and Kate Reber, Design and Production. For putting up with (and responding to) my "but couldn't we just change this part a *little*..."

On the Home Front

Doffie Hochreich, tech reader and copy editor. A labor of love, much appreciated.

Rich Wolfson, tech reader and chapter editor. And, of course, so much more <g>.

Jerry Szubin. Layout artist extraordinaire.

Carol Aiton. Because I said, "I wish I had different Part Openers," and she granted the wish.

The "Graphics Team." Jerry and Carol, and Marilyn Rose, John Luttropp, and Tommy Ricotta. For previewing and reviewing the Fonts, Graphics, Page Layout, and Printing chapters with me—and all I had to do was provide them with Sunday brunch now and then.

thetipster.com

Binky Melnik. For pulling together and maintaining the Tipster web site for me because I had no time to do it myself. (And thanks to Mike Hetelson for hosting it.)

About This Book

System Software. This book assumes you're using at least OS 8; everything was written and tested for 8.0 and 8.1. However, the operating system is a moving target, with 8.5 scheduled to release when this book hits the shelves. Chapter 11 is an overview of 8.5, written with only a (late) beta copy of 8.5 available—consider it a beta chapter (many of the "screen shots" are faked).

Bylines. With only a few exceptions, the initials you'll see after some entries identify the people who worked on the material in previous editions (although everything was checked and updated for this one). The contributors are identified, chapter by chapter, in Appendix A.

Web addresses. When a company is mentioned in the text, its URL is noted in the margin to save you the trouble of looking it up in Appendix B or online. We've dispensed with the URL prefix of *http://www;* not only can we assume, reasonably safely, that you know enough to handle the simple form of the address, but current browsers don't even insist on your typing in that part. (And if you're not familiar with URLs, you could read Chapter 27 first.)

Icons. Margin icons are a Macintosh Bible tradition. But along with the total redesign of the book, there are new icons this time around.

Top Tip. Something especially important or interesting, or just downright nifty.

Product Pick. Software that the author particularly likes, and you probably will, too.

Just for Fun. This icon is, as you may have noticed, an Easter Egg—the phrase used to describe a hidden joke in software.

World Wide Web. The web address for a company mentioned in the text.

The Macintosh Bible Doesn't End Here! Most computer books are out of date a few months after they're published. But not *The Macintosh Bible*. To keep the information in it current, free access to a readers-only companion Web site is included in the price of the book. At this site, you'll find live links to all the Web sites mentioned in the book, clarifications and corrections, online resources, and more. We'll also post a major update in the fall of 1999 filled with new tips, tricks, shortcuts, and product reviews. The companion site is located at **`www.macbible.com`.** Note that you must own this book to get access to this readers-only site. It's password-protected, and the password is hidden inside these pages, so make sure you have your book on hand when accessing the site.

PART 1

For Beginners Only

Part 1 At a Glance

1

Welcome to Macintosh

In This Chapter

On the Desktop

The Pointer and the Mouse

The screen. When you first turn on your Macintosh, you see the famous Mac desktop, the home base for all your computer activities. At the top is the menubar, displaying individual menu titles. The little pictures on the desktop are icons; there are miniature icons in the menubar, too.

The program that actually provides the desktop and its operations is the *Finder*, so the terms *desktop* and *Finder* are used pretty much interchangeably.

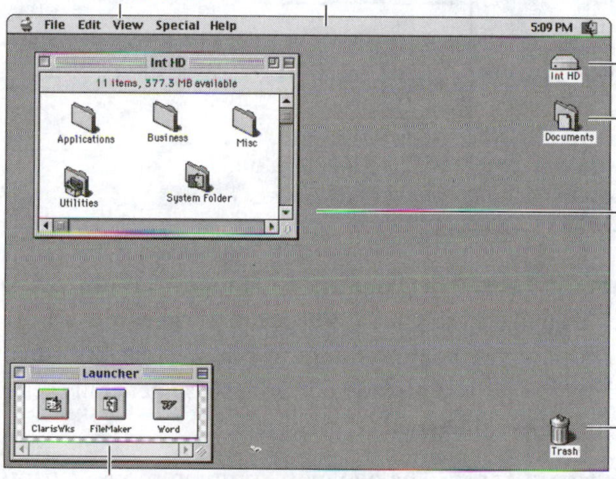

The Mac desktop, with its menubar and icons—and various windows—is what you see when you first start the computer.

Your desktop probably looks different. There are lots of reasons your initial desktop screen won't look like the one shown here, and none of them is anything to worry about. If, for instance, your Mac's been used (and it probably has been), there may be no windows, or many different windows, on the desktop; and it's unlikely your Launcher buttons—if your Launcher window is open—will match the ones here.

But if the icon in the far right of the menubar is different from the ones you see here, you're running a different version of the system software. The picture here shows, from top to bottom, OS 8's Finder application icon and menubar clock; System 7.5's clock and Help menu icon, with its Finder application icon; and System 7's Help menu and Finder icon. If there's no Help menu at all, and a different icon for the Finder, the Mac is running some version of System 6.

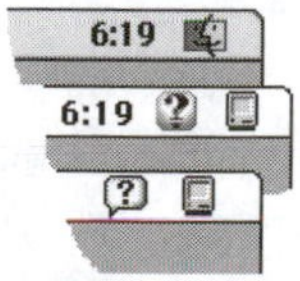

Your menus might be different. With the advent of OS 8, the Finder comes in two flavors: simple and a little less simple. When your desktop is in Simple Finder mode, the menus list only the most essential of commands. Simple Finder is turned on and off through a checkbox in the Preferences dialog, accessible through the Preferences command in the Edit menu. If your Finder menus don't have as many commands as appear in pictures here and throughout the book, you need to uncheck the Simple Finder checkbox. (I haven't introduced menus, or commands, or even checkboxes for that matter, but thought I'd mention this now in case you were wondering.)

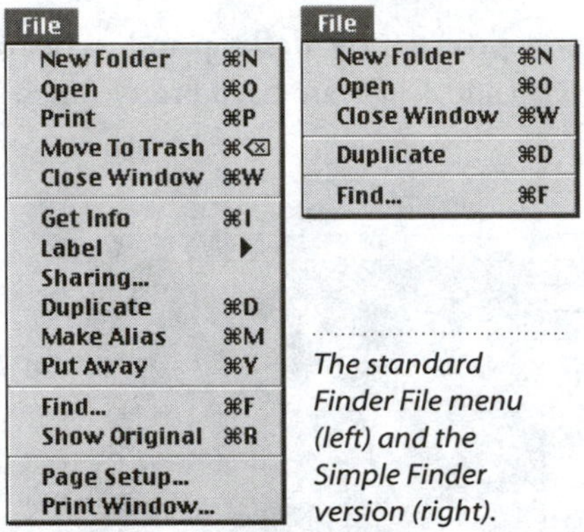

The standard Finder File menu (left) and the Simple Finder version (right).

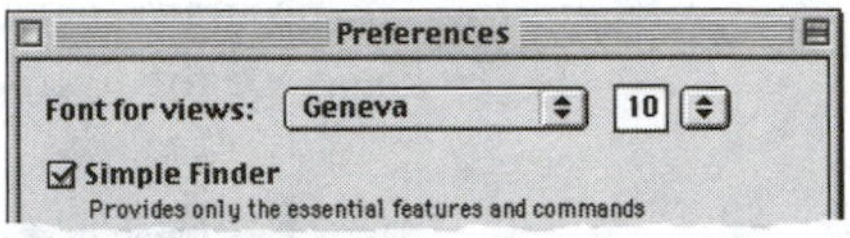

Turn the Simple Finder on and off in the Preferences dialog.

Pointer, cursor. When you move the mouse around on your desk, an arrow moves around on the screen. The arrow is called the *pointer,* reasonably enough, since you point to things with it. But it takes other shapes, too, and you don't always just *point* with it, so it's also generally referred to as the *mouse cursor,* or simply the *cursor*.

Common cursors. The two most common mouse cursors are the pointer and the *text* (or *I-beam)* cursor that appears when you're dealing with text. But you'll see an amazing variety of cursors as you work with the Mac, since the shape of the cursor usually indicates what you're able to do at any point in using a program. Even the Finder provides four special new cursors in OS 8, to go along with four of its new desktop capabilities.

The pointer and the I-beam (top) are the most common mouse cursors. The OS 8 desktop includes four new cursors (middle). The watch and the beachball (bottom) are "wait" cursors that tell you the Mac is busy.

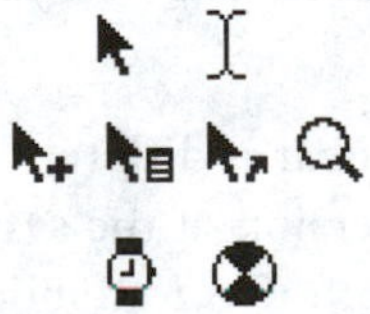

A "wait" cursor tells you the Mac is busy and you'll have to wait until it's finished. It was originally a static wristwatch, later replaced by one with spinning hands so you could tell if the computer was really working on something or if it had frozen up for some reason. The spinning "beachball" is another system-level wait signal.

Mouse moves. There are six basic mouse actions:

- **Pointing** is simply rolling the mouse to move the cursor to a specific spot, usually so that it points to an item.
- **Pressing** is holding the mouse button down while pointing to something; you press on a menu title to open a menu.
- **Clicking** is a quick press-and-release of the mouse button; you usually click *on* something, which means you point to an object before you click.
- **Double-clicking** means clicking twice in a row, at just the right speed and without moving the mouse in between (so that the Mac doesn't interpret it as two single clicks).
- **Click-and-a-half**—new to OS 8—is clicking the mouse button twice, but keeping it down on the second click; this lets you do some special things with icons on the desktop.
- **Dragging** means keeping the button down while you move the mouse. Sometimes you actually drag an item; sometimes the drag operation doesn't move anything but is used to define an area of the screen.

There are other "mouse moves," too. Some programs—including the Finder—let you perform special operations by combining the basic mouse moves with the press of key. So, holding down ⌘ (the Command key) while dragging a desktop icon (a "command-drag") makes the icon snap to the invisible desktop grid when you let it go; holding down Option while you drag an item (an "option-drag") usually makes a copy of the item in the new location.

Getting help. On the Mac, help is never more than a few mouse moves away. The Help menu (the last menu title in the Finder, and in most applications) has not one, but two kinds of help: Balloon Help, which was introduced in System 7, and Mac OS Help, introduced as Apple Guide in System 7.5.

Turn on Balloon Help by choosing Show Balloons in the menu. Then point to something—you don't even have to click the mouse—to get information about it, which shows up in a little balloon. The information in the balloon comes from the program you're using, so the actual helpfulness of Balloon Help really depends on the programmer's thoroughness.

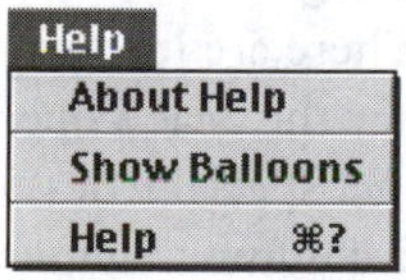

The Help menu is always available as the last menu; it lets you access both the Balloon help and OS Help systems.

When Balloon help is on, pointing to any item gets you an information-filled balloon.

OS Help is an interactive help system that not only lets you look up information, but can even walk you through necessary steps, opening menus and windows and control panels, showing you what to do—it even draws a big red circle around any item that it wants to bring to your attention! You access it by choosing Help from the Help menu, or by pressing ⌘?. When you're in applications, the Help menu may have more selections, depending on what the program provides in the way of help.

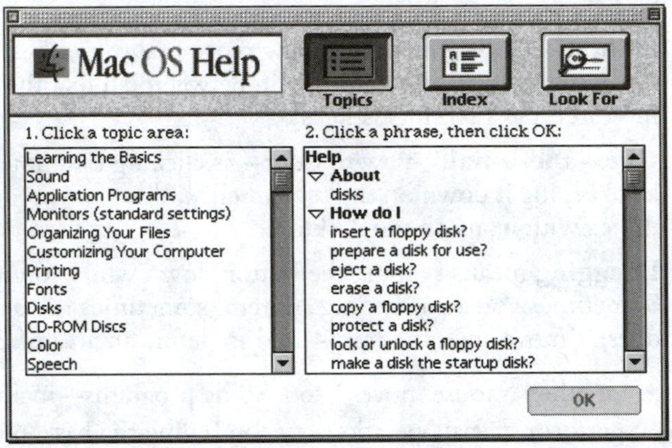

OS Help lets you look for help in several ways: according to topics, through an index, or by using a search feature. You can look up facts or get a demonstration.

Working with Desktop Icons

Icons. Icons represent various things on your desktop, like disks, folders, and files. (A *file* is any discrete collection of information—a program like a word processor, a memo you wrote with the word processor, or a component of the system software.)

There are many different types of icons on the Mac. There are icons to represent each kind of disk you use (a hard disk, a floppy, a CD) as well as for other types of storage. Each application has its own distinctive icon, and a document icon is usually visually related to the "parent" application. If the Mac can't figure out which application created a document, it uses a *generic* icon, which represents a piece of paper with its upper-right corner turned down. Then there are folder icons, which you use to organize the other icons on your desktop. There are lots of special folders and files used by the Mac's operating system, and most get special icons. There is, for instance, a common element in the design of all control panels, and of all extensions.

A document icon is usually visually related to the application that created it. When the Mac doesn't know about the "parent" application, it uses a generic document icon for the file.

The icons at the left are all control panels, and include the "slider" control in the icon design. Those in the middle group, using the puzzle-piece design, are all extensions. The group at the right consists of special system folders—notice the slider and puzzle-piece themes are carried through for the Extensions and Control Panels folders.

Folders. A *folder* can hold files and other folders, so you use folders to organize what's on your disks. You create a new folder with the New Folder command in the File menu. You can put folders within folders within folders to your heart's content—whatever you need to organize your work and make things easy to find.

Selecting icons. To select an icon, click on it; it's darkened, and its name is highlighted, to show that it's selected.

You can select more than one icon at a time by clicking on one and then shift-clicking (hold down Shift while you click the mouse button) on the others. Or, drag a rectangle around the icons you want: point to an empty spot in a window, press the mouse button, and drag. You'll see a thick gray line defining the rectangle, and any icon even partially inside the rectangle will be selected.

To *deselect* an icon, simply select something else, or click where nothing will be selected.

> ***You know you're a Mac Addict when you refer to the Macintosh Bible as "The Good Book."***
> *Michael Fields, submitted to Mac Addict magazine*

Renaming icons. To rename an icon, first select its *name* by clicking directly on the name (not on the picture); a selected name is highlighted inside an editing rectangle. There's a brief delay from the time you click to the time the editing rectangle appears, so be patient. (If you click a second time too soon, the Mac thinks you've double-clicked and will open the icon.)

Clicking on the name of an icon puts an editing rectangle around it (and selects the icon); when the cursor is inside the rectangle, it changes to the text cursor.

Basic text-editing techniques work in the editing rectangle. You can use icon names of up to 31 characters, and include any character except the colon (:).

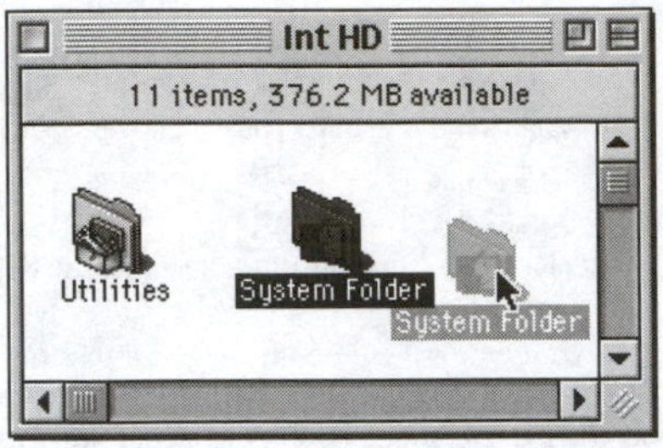

When you drag an icon, a ghost of the item moves with the pointer; when you let go of the mouse button, the icon moves to the new spot.

Moving icons. Move a standard icon by dragging it to a new position. (Button icons are a little trickier to move—you have to grab them by their names.) A "ghost" of the icon moves along with the pointer until you release the mouse button, at which point the icon jumps to its new location.

Dragging an icon from one place to another on the same disk just changes its location. But dragging an icon from one disk to another leaves the original intact and puts a copy onto the other disk. So, dragging a file from a floppy disk or CD to your hard drive means there are then two copies of the file: the original and a duplicate on your hard drive.

When you're dragging one icon into another—putting something into a folder, or into the Trash—the "target" icon darkens when you've moved the cursor (and the icon) into the right position.

When you're putting one icon into another, the "target" darkens when you're in the right area. In the picture on the left, the document won't be in the folder if the mouse button is released, but the one on the right will.

Opening icons. The basic way to open an icon is to double-click on it. You can also select an icon and then choose Open from the File menu or press ⌘O. An opened icon is filled with a dark dotted pattern to show that it's open. Finder windows also have a special "button" view which turns a window's icons into buttons that need only a single click to open them.

What happens when you open an icon depends on what the icon represents: opening a disk, a folder, or the Trash opens a window; opening an application

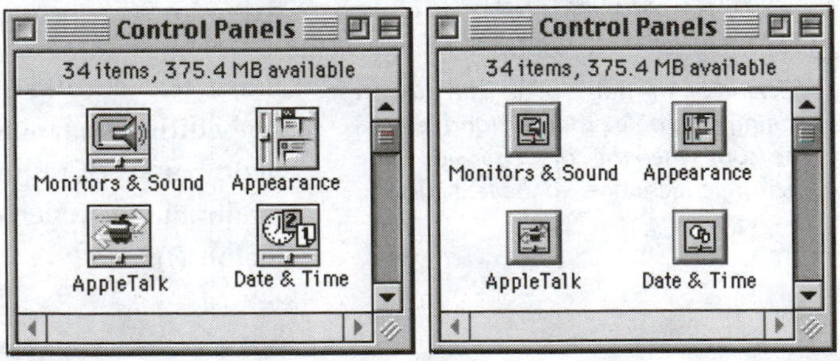

Standard icons (as on the left) need a double-click to open them. Using the button view for icons (as on the right) means you need only a single click to open them.

icon launches the program; opening a document icon launches its parent application and then opens the document inside it.

Using the Trash. To erase a file, you drag it into the Trash can. But items just sit in the Trash until you use the Special menu's Empty Trash command. You'll know when the Trash needs emptying because its lid comes off, and the contents stick out, whenever there's something inside it.

To take something out of the Trash before it's erased, double-click on the Trash icon to open it, and drag the file out of the Trash's window. Or, just select the icon in the window and use the Put Away command from the Special menu—the icon zooms back to wherever it was before you trashed it.

Ejecting disks. To eject a floppy disk or CD, select its icon on the desktop and choose the Eject command from the Special menu. Or, you can drag the disk icon to the Trash; don't worry—nothing will be erased! But the icon disappears from the desktop and the disk is ejected from the drive.

Working with Windows

Windows. When you open something on the desktop—a disk, a folder, or the Trash—you get a *window* that shows what's stored inside. Opening a document in an application displays the contents of the document in a window. Windows are your work areas on the Mac, and although Finder windows have some special properties to make file-handling easier, most Mac windows behave in the same way and have common controls.

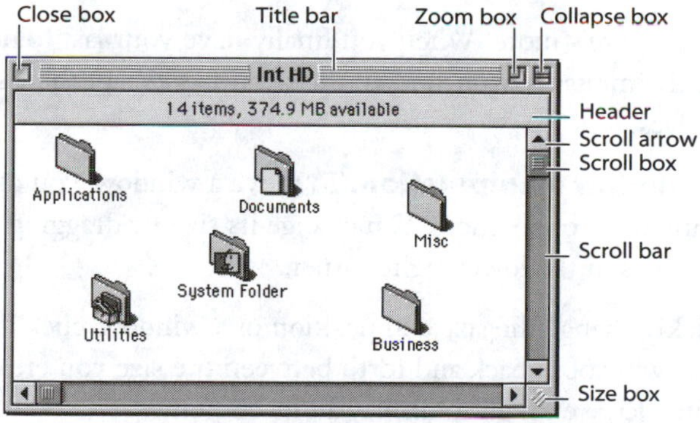

All Finder windows, and most document windows, share the same basic "parts" and controls (although the header is a Finder-only window component).

Opening and closing. When a window first opens on the desktop, it's active: it's on top of any other open windows, and any window commands, like "Close," apply to only to this window. Only one window is active at a time; you can tell which it is by its striped title bar. If you want to activate a window that's already open, all you have to do is click anywhere in it.

To close a window, click its *close box* at the left end of the title bar. Or, choose the Close command from the File menu or press ⌘W.

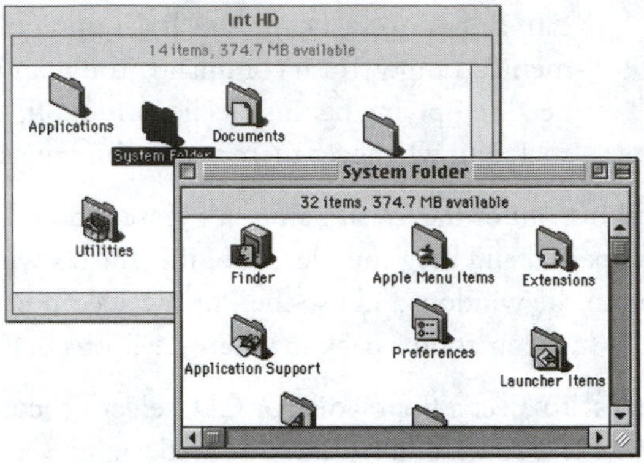

The active window—shown in the front here—has a striped title bar and visible scroll controls. An inactive window, like the Int HD window in this picture, has a blank title bar and scroll areas. The System Folder icon in the background window is darkened because it's opened—that's the window that's in the foreground.

Spring-open folders. OS 8 introduced a special way to access an item inside a series of folders. Instead of opening each of the nested folders with a double-click, you can use the new "spring-open" folder option. With a click-and-a-half (click once, then click again immediately, keeping the mouse button down on the second click) on a disk or folder icon, the mouse cursor changes to a magnifying glass. Hold the mouse button down, and the icon opens. With the mouse button still down, move the cursor over the next folder you want opened, and it springs open; find the next folder you want, put the cursor over it, and it opens, too. As long as the mouse button is down, the folders keep opening.

But wait, there's more! When you finally have your last folder open, you release the mouse button, and all the windows except the last one neatly close themselves!

Basic window manipulation. To move a window, you drag it by its *title bar* or by any of its outer edges. You change its size by dragging the *size box*—the triple stripes in the lower-right corner.

To quickly change the size and position of a window, click in its *zoom box:* the window will zoom back and forth between the size you created and a size that's just large enough to display all its contents.

If your screen is cluttered with windows, click in the *collapse box* to collapse it into just its title bar; another click snaps the window open again.

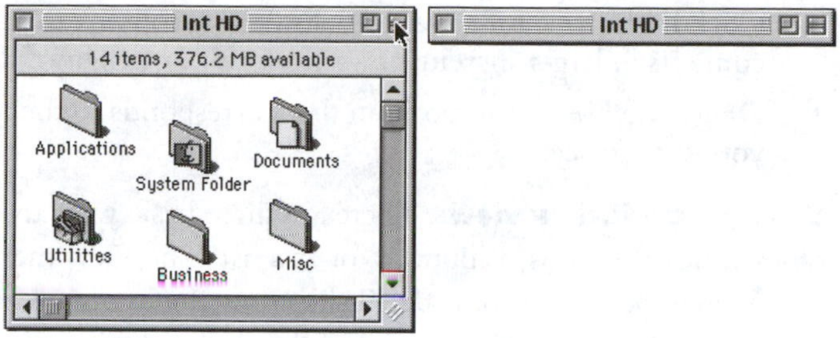

Click in a window's collapse box to shrink it down to just its title bar.

Another way to get desktop windows out of the way without closing them is to turn them into tabs at the bottom of the screen: grab a window by its title bar and drag it all the way to the bottom of the screen. (Or, use the As Pop-up Window command in the View menu to turn the active window into a tab.) You'll get a tab with the window's name on it. Once a window is a tab, you can click on the tab for the window to pop up to show its contents; click on the tab again to send the window back to the bottom of the screen. To turn it back into a regular window, just drag it up onto the desktop again, or use the View menu's As Window command.

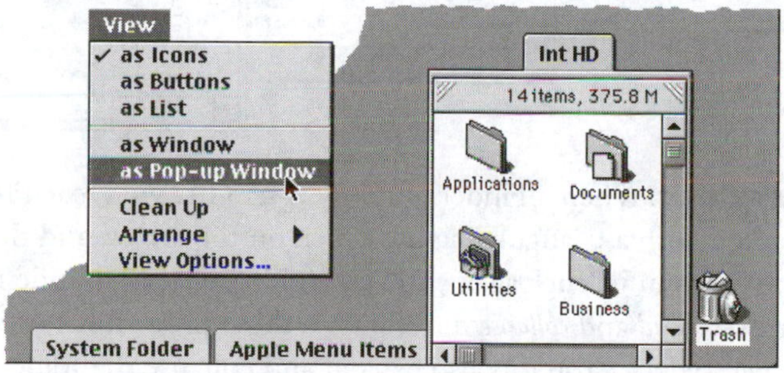

You can turn windows into pop-up tabs at the bottom of the screen; click on a tab, and the window pops up, like the Int HD window here.

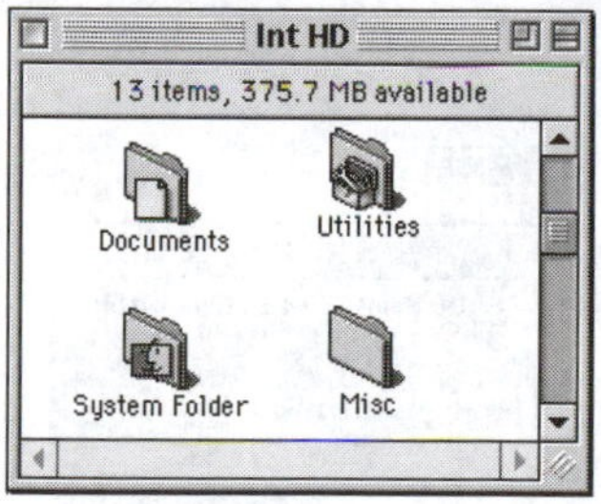

The vertical scroll bar here is dark gray, which means there are items above and/or below the ones displayed. Since the horizontal scroll bar is light and missing a scroll box, there are no items to the left or right of the ones that are showing.

Scrolling windows. Light gray scroll bars in an active window mean everything that's in the window is showing. When either or both scroll bars are a dark gray, there are items in the window that aren't displayed.

The position of the scroll box in the scroll bar indicates what part of the window you're looking at: If it's at the top, for instance, you're viewing the uppermost items in the window.

- Click on a *scroll arrow* to scroll the window in that direction; press on an arrow (that is, keep the mouse button down) for continuous scrolling.

- Click in the *scroll bar* above or below the scroll box to scroll the window contents in larger increments—the width or height of the window itself.
- Drag a *scroll box* into a position that corresponds to the area of the window you want to see.

Changing window views. There are three basic ways to view the contents of a window: as icons, as buttons, or as a list. The View menu lets you choose the view, as well as set some details like how the items are organized (alphabetically, or by size, for instance) and the size of the icons or buttons.

The techniques you use on icons (like double-clicking to open, clicking to select, dragging to select multiple items) work on items in list views, too.

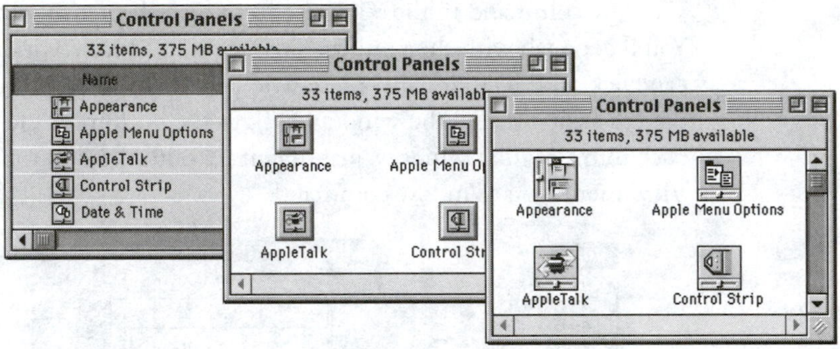

The same window in list, button, and icon views.

List views. When a Finder window is in a list view, each folder in it is marked with a triangular arrow. Click on the arrow, and the folder *expands* to list what's in it; click again, and the folder *collapses* to hide its contents. (The terms *expand* and *collapse* differentiate these procedures from *opening* and *closing* folders.) You can also expand and collapse the folders inside the expanded folders to as many levels as you want.

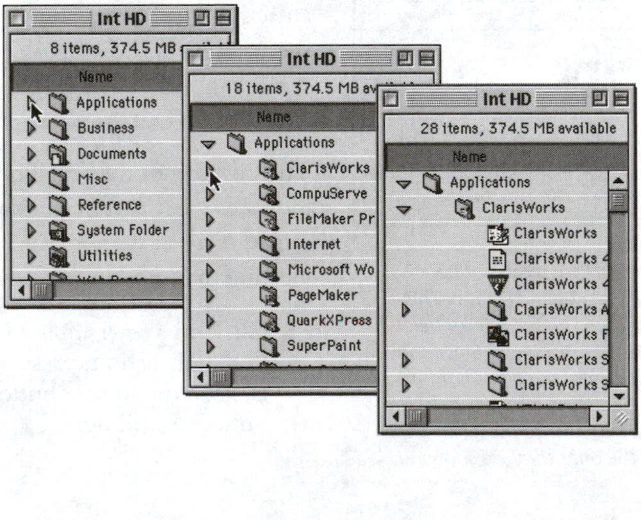

Clicking on a folder's arrow in a list view (on the Applications folder in the left-most window, and on the ClarisWorks folder in the center window) expands the folder, listing what's inside.

Menus and Dialog Boxes

Menus

Using menus. Using menus is a cinch: you press on the menu title to open the menu, slide the pointer down to the command you want (each command is highlighted as you touch it), and release the mouse button. If the menu's open and you decide you don't want any of the commands, simply move the pointer off the menu and let go—you don't have to go back up to the menu title.

To select from a menu, press on its title, slide down to the command you want, and then let go of the mouse button.

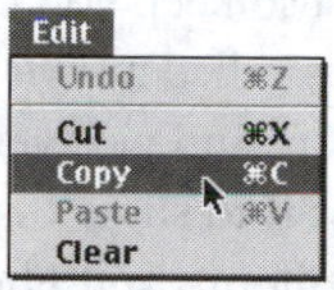

OS 8 introduced *sticky menus*: click briefly on a menu title, and the menu stays open even though the mouse button is released. To choose a command from a "stuck" menu, just click on it.

Dimmed commands. Sometimes a command is *dimmed* in the menu—its name is gray instead of black, like the Paste command in the last picture. A dimmed command can't be used because it doesn't apply to the situation at the time you open the menu. (In the case of the dimmed Paste command, there was nothing *to* paste.)

Application and system menus. Most menu titles are words, and "belong" to whatever application you're working in. You'll see these titles in the menubar change as you move from one application to another (although most programs include a File and Edit menu). There are some *system* menus, however, that stay on the menubar no matter what program you're in—they're system-wide rather than application-specific. Most system menus are icons, although the Help menu is an exception to that. The basic system menus are:

- The menu at the far left lists whatever you put in the Apple Menu Items folder inside the System Folder. (Arthur Naiman, author of the original edition of *The Macintosh Bible*, pointed out that this is called the *Apple* menu, since so few people can pronounce .)
- The Application menu at the far right lists all open applications so you can easily switch from one to another.
- The Help menu that appears as the last menu title, to the right of all the application menus.

Utility programs can put their own icon menus in the menubar, too, so that you'll be able to access them no matter what application you're working in.

System menus are usually little icons, although the Help menu is also a system menu.

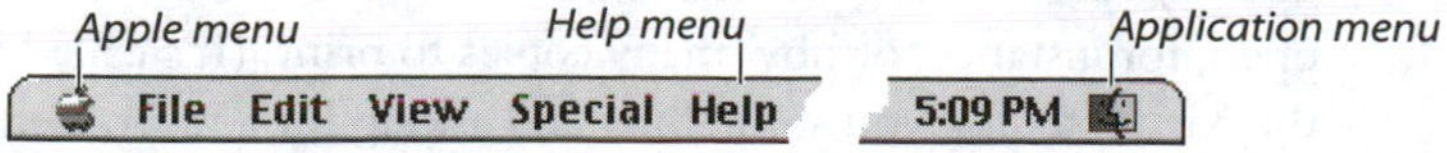

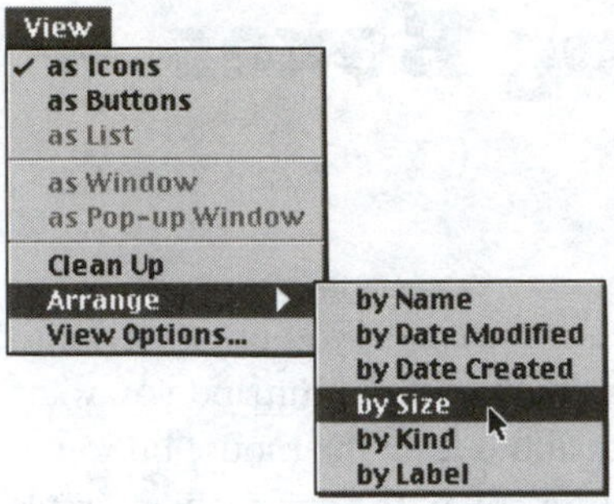

The arrow to the right of a menu command indicates a submenu.

Submenus. A triangular arrow to the right of a menu item means there's a submenu; pause on the main menu command, and the submenu appears. To choose from the submenu, slide the pointer into it, to the command you want.

Toggle commands. Some "commands" are actually choices that stay in effect until you turn them off—a Bold command in a Style menu, for instance, will turn selected text bold but can also keep you typing in bold text until you turn it off. This kind of command is called a *toggle* because if you choose it when it's turned off, it gets turned on, and vice versa. A toggle command sometimes has a check mark in front of it to show that it's in effect, although some change wording, like Show Balloons and Hide Balloons.

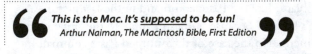

> "*This is the Mac. It's supposed to be fun!*"
> *Arthur Naiman, The Macintosh Bible, First Edition*

Not all checkmarks in a menu are toggles. The View menu, for instance (shown in the last picture to illustrate submenus) puts a check mark in front of the current window view; you don't choose it to turn it off—you choose a different view, and then *that's* the checked item in the menu.

Keyboard commands. Many menu commands have *keyboard equivalents*, which means you can give the command without opening the menu at all, but just by holding down [⌘] while you press a letter (whatever's listed in the menu next to that command). So, pressing [⌘][O] is the same as choosing Open from the File menu. (The [⌘] key—on some keyboards there's no apple on it, but just the cloverleaf squiggle—is called the *command* key.)

Keyboard commands are often simply [⌘] plus the first letter of the command name. Sometimes other *modifier keys* in addition to [⌘] (like [Shift], [Option], and even [Ctrl], alone or in combination) are used so you'll have more keyboard combinations available.

Although the letter listed in a menu for a keyboard command is in uppercase, you don't press [Shift] to use it—in fact, adding [Shift] to the combination can change the command entirely.

Dialog Boxes and Alerts

Dialog boxes. Choosing a command with an ellipsis after it (those three dots…) opens a *dialog box* where you enter information—which document to open, for instance, or how many copies to print. (It's called a dialog because the Mac is telling you something and asking for a response.) Dialog boxes have all sorts of "controls"—buttons, boxes, lists, and menus—that let you easily input information and give commands.

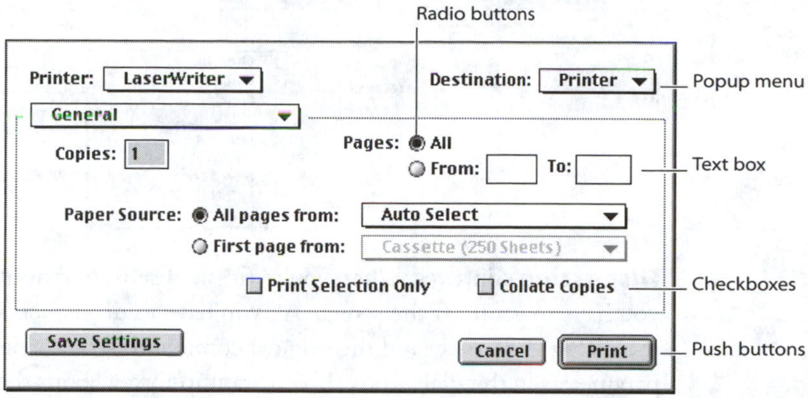

A typical Mac dialog box and its standard components.

Text boxes and lists. A *text box* is a frame where you type in information, like the name for the document or the number of pages you want to print. To move from one text box to another, you can click in the box you want, or press [Tab] to move to the next box.

A *list box* has a scrollable list from which you make a choice by clicking on the item, or sometimes by typing one or more letters to identify the item you want.

Buttons. Buttons are the quickest way to input dialog box information. There are three basic types:

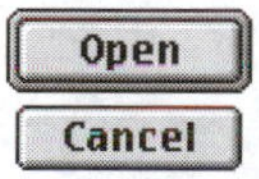

- Standard buttons, called *push buttons,* are rounded rectangles with commands inside them; click a button to execute the command. When a button is highlighted with a border around it, it's the *default* button: pressing [Return] or [Enter] works the same as clicking the button.
- *Radio buttons* come in groups, for options that are mutually exclusive: choosing one of them means you can't have any of the others. When you click on a radio button (it fills in to show it's been selected), the previously chosen button is deselected.
- *Checkboxes* can be used singly, but often come in groups for items that are *not* mutually exclusive: you can check any, all, or none of the checkboxes in a group. Clicking in the box puts a checkmark in it, which indicates the option is "on"; clicking in it again turns it "off."

Pop-up menus. You'll find a variety of *pop-up menus* when you're working with the Mac: menus that show up someplace other than in the menubar at the top of the screen. In dialog boxes, the standard pop-up menu has a double arrow at its right. (If you've turned off the "platinum windows" option in the Appearance control panel, pop-up menus revert to the older-style shadowed box with a downward-pointing arrow at the right.) Press on a pop-up menu, and it—well, it pops up, and lets you select something by dragging the mouse up or down.

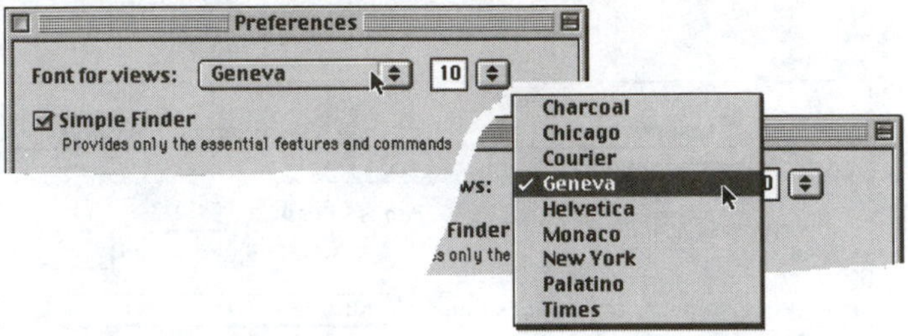

Using a pop-up menu.

Dismissing dialogs. When you're finished setting options in a dialog box you have to get it off the screen. All you have to do is click an OK button for the dialog to go away and the original command to be carried out using the parameters in the dialog box. If you want to forget about the whole thing, you can go back to where you were before you chose the command that opened the dialog: click the Cancel button in the dialog (or press ⌘., which most dialogs interpret as a Cancel command).

Alerts. An *alert* is a special kind of dialog box, one with just a statement or a warning in it, like: *Using Revert will cancel all the changes you've made since you opened the document.* (An alert is more of a monologue than a dialog.) Alerts have a minimum of buttons—usually just OK and Cancel, or sometimes just the OK button so you can acknowledge the warning and dismiss the dialog.

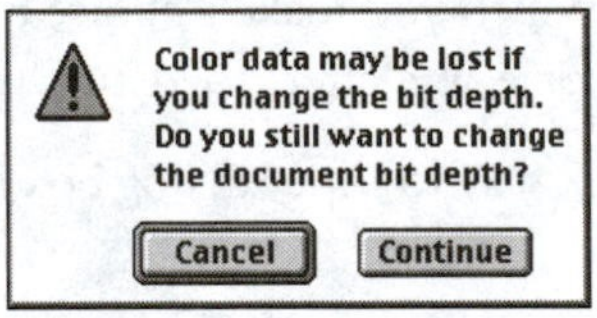

An alert warns you about something you're about to do, providing minimal options from that point.

Beyond the Desktop

Applications and Documents

Applications and their documents. *Applications* are programs that enable you to get work done; *documents* are the files you create with applications. So, a word processor is an application; when you write the first chapter of the Great American Novel, or a brief memo—those are documents.

Launching and quitting applications. To use an application, you *launch* it, which is another way of saying you open it. Opening an application (the same way you open any desktop icon) gives you a whole new environment to work in, where the basic rules you've learned still apply but a wealth of other capabilities await you.

Every application provides a Quit command in its File menu, and its keyboard equivalent (⌘Q) won't vary from program to program. Quitting an applica-

Macintosh OS 8.5 Support

Farallon supports Macintosh OS 8.5 with all it's current products. The following Farallon products have been tested in our labs:

- PN990 Fast EtherTX-10/100 NuBus Card
- PN990a Fast EtherTX-10/100 NuBus Card
- PN995 Fast EtherTX-10/100 CardBus
- PN996 Fast EtherTX-10/100 PCI Plus Card
- PN998 Fast EtherTX-10/100 Comm Slot II Card
- PN994 Fast EtherTX-10/100 3Com drivers
- PN593 EtherMac PCI Card*
- PN893 EtherWave PCI Card*
- PN595 EtherMac PC Card for Powerbooks
- PN595a EtherMac PC Card for Powerbooks
- PN591 EtherMac PowerBook 1400 Card
- PN590a EtherMac II-C NuBus Card
- PN890 EtherWave NuBus Card
- PN592a EtherMac LC-C LC/PDS Card
- PN892 EtherWave LC Card
- PN598 EtherMac LC Comm Slot Card
- PN898 EtherWave LC Comm Slot Card

There are no known problems with any Farallon products that are not listed.

*The Farallon driver for the PN593-C/PN893 will fail under System 8.5 due to a problem with Apple's ENet driver:

> **Problem:** Installing System 8.5 on a Mac using the Farallon PN593-C /PN893 PCI card will fail to load the driver correctly. The user will not be able to select the Ethernet Slot-X driver in the Appletalk Control Panel. They will get an error message if they try to do so.
>
> **Situation:** This is due to the way Apple's driver works with 10 meg PCI cards based on the DEC chip. The Apple driver will be loaded rather than the Farallon driver. This puts the Farallon card into the wrong mode. Apple has acknowledged this problem and will try to fix it in future System versions.
>
> **Solution:** The user should go to the Extensions Manager and disable the Apple ENet extension and reboot. Or move the Apple ENet extension from the System folder and reboot. This will force the machine to use the Farallon driver in the correct mode.

tion automatically closes any open documents, first giving you the option to save any changes you might have made.

The Launcher. While double-clicking on an application icon is an easy way to launch it, sometimes it's not so easy to get to the icon—it might be buried in one, two, or even three (or more!) folders. The Launcher window is an easy way to launch programs that you'd otherwise have to open folders to get at. You simply click once on the icon button in the Launcher window to open the program.

You click on a button in the Launcher window to launch the item that the button represents.

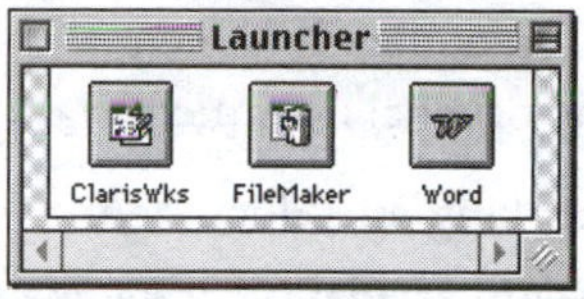

To open the Launcher window, open the Launcher control panel; you can make it open automatically on startup by checking the Show Launcher at System Startup button in the General Controls control panel. To add a button to the Launcher, just drag a program icon right into its window; the program won't really move there, but a button will be created for it.

Moving between applications. As long as you have enough memory, you can run more than one program at a time. The Application menu at the far right of the menubar lists all applications that are open; selecting one from the list moves you to that program.

The Application menu lists all the open applications. Choosing one from the menu moves you into that program.

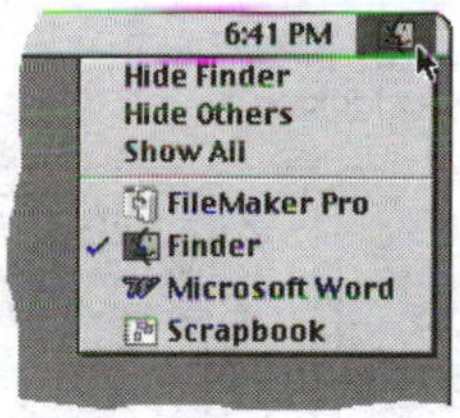

Any windows that belong to inactive but open applications hang around in the background, coming forward when the application is selected from the menu. Clicking anywhere in a background window is another way to move into an application. If you don't want the background applications' windows showing while you're working, use the Hide/Show commands in the Application menu.

Opening and creating documents. To open a document, use the Open command from the application's File menu. If you're on the desktop, you can double-click on the document: the application that created it launches and opens the document. If the application is already running, the Mac switches from the Finder to the application and opens the document.

Selecting the New command gives you a new, blank document in any application.

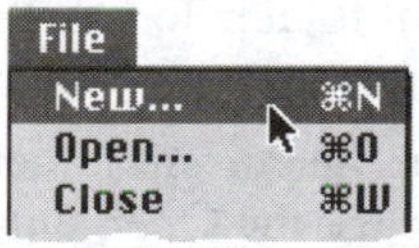

Most applications start up with an empty document window for you to work in. But if you don't have an empty window, or if you've used the initial one, you can get a new blank document by using the application's New command.

Saving and closing documents. A document exists only in the computer's memory and disappears when you close it unless you've stored it on the disk, using the application's Save command. Changes to an existing document also have to be explicitly saved.

When you use Save on a new document, you'll get a Save dialog where you can name the document and show where on the disk you want it stored. When you use Save on a document that's been saved before, no dialog appears—the Mac just goes ahead and saves the edited version of the document, replacing the previous version on the disk. Most applications provide a Save As command so you can save an edited document as a separate document, with a different name, so the original document stays intact.

Don't wait until you're finished working on a document to save it; instead, save every five or ten minutes to guard against mishaps like a power failure or a computer crash that could cause you to lose the work you've done.

The Open and Save dialogs. The dialog boxes you'll see when you're opening or saving documents (cleverly referred to as the Open and Save dialogs) have many features in common, since both let you navigate around disks and through folders. A Save dialog, though, has to provide at least one more option—that of naming the current document. The dialogs in the following figure are the basic ones; many programs provide extra controls, like checkboxes and pop-up menus, depending on the features the program provides. You might, for instance, be able to specify what kind of files will show in the list, or a special format in which the document will be saved.

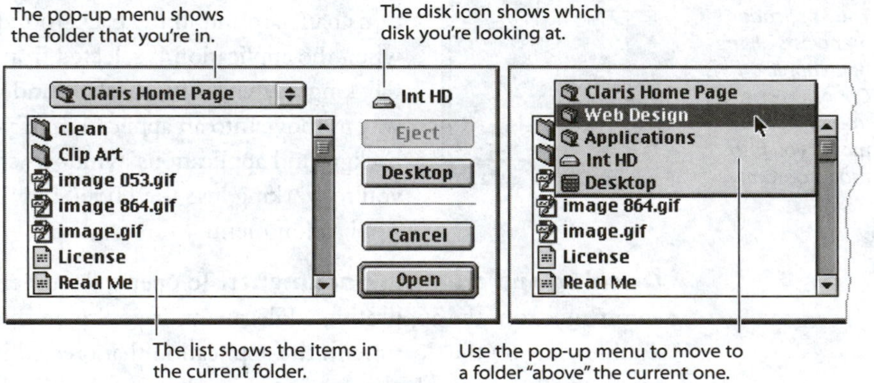

The basic Open dialog box lets you navigate through the folders of your disk to find the document you want to open.

In the Open box:

- The **pop-up menu** shows the current folder. To move "up" to one of the listed folders, select it from the menu.
- The **list** shows the files and folders in the current folder. To open something in the list, click on it and then click the Open button, or just double-click on the name in the list.
- The **disk icon** shows which disk the current folder is on.
- The **Eject** button is available when the current folder is on a floppy disk, or other removable media.
- The **Desktop** button jumps you right up to the top level, listing the files and folders that are out loose on the desktop.

- The **Cancel** button dismisses the dialog without opening anything.
- The **Open** button (since it's the default button, you can press Return instead of clicking it) opens the item you've selected in the list.

The basic Save box has three additional features:

- The **text box** is where you type the name of the document you're saving.
- The **New Folder button** (it doesn't say "Folder," but uses an obvious icon) lets you create a new folder inside the current folder.
- The **Save button**, which you click after you've picked a location for the document and given it a name, changes to Open if you've selected a folder in the list.

The basic Save dialog lets you name your document and choose a place for it to be stored.

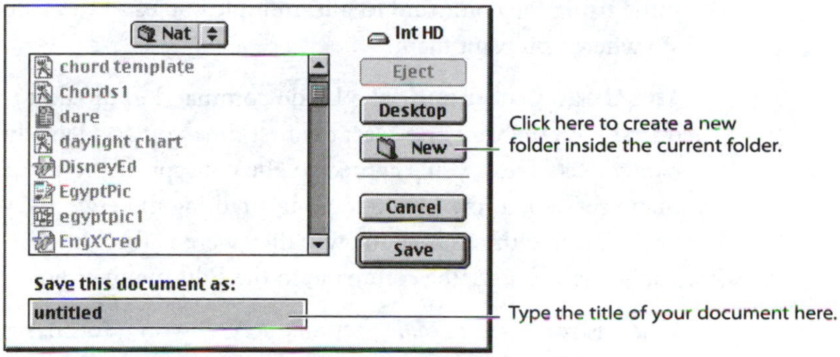

Cutting, Copying, and Pasting

The Clipboard. One of the most elegant and useful tools on the Mac is the *Clipboard*—a temporary holding place for material that you *cut* or *copy* from one place to *paste* in another. The Clipboard can hold material of almost any length, and it's an easy way to move material inside a document, between documents, or even between applications.

Nearly every Edit menu starts with these four commands, and the keyboard equivalents for them never vary.

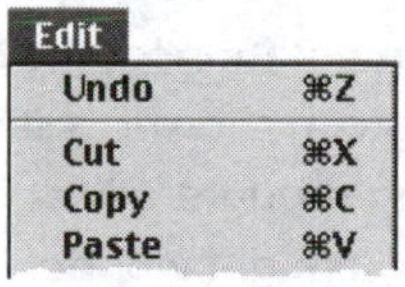

You'll find Cut, Copy, and Paste commands in the Edit menu of every Mac program. The keyboard shortcuts for these commands are practically sacred and don't change from one program to another as other keyboard equivalents do: ⌘X is Cut, ⌘C is Copy, and ⌘V is Paste. Together with the ⌘Z shortcut for the Undo command, these four fixtures of the Edit menu use the first four keys on the bottom row of the keyboard.

The Cut, Copy and Paste commands. Using Cut or Copy on selected material places the selection on the Clipboard; with Cut, the selection disappears from the document, while Copy leaves the original in place. If you want to delete a selection from a document without moving it someplace else, there's no need to put it on the Clipboard: just press Delete.

To put something from the Clipboard into a document, you use the Paste command. If you're working with text, the pasted material appears at the insertion point or replaces selected text. In graphics programs, a pasted item usually appears in the center of the window and stays selected so you can move it wherever you want.

Tempo, tempo. The Clipboard is a *temporary* holding place in two ways. First, because it can hold only one item at a time, putting something new on the Clipboard replaces what was there before. Second, the Clipboard contents disappear entirely when you shut down the computer.

On the other hand, using Paste doesn't empty the Clipboard, so you can continue using the command to put multiple copies of the Clipboard contents anywhere you want them.

The Undo Command. The Undo command in the Edit menu was introduced with the very first Mac; the first time you accidentally delete ten paragraphs of text, you'll appreciate the concept. If you use the Undo command twice in a row (without doing anything in between), you can undo the undo, putting things back the way they were before the first undo. In fact, after you've used Undo, the command in the Edit menu often changes to Redo.

Undo is restricted to *editing* actions, so you won't, for instance, be able to undo saving a document or opening a new window. It's also restricted to a single action, the last one you took; so, use it immediately or lose the opportunity for a quick fix. Some programs implement a "multiple undo" feature, so you can reverse, step by step, the work that you've done.

IN THE BEGINNING

The early Macs had rocker switches on their backs to turn them on and off instead of keyboard power control. The documentation for the original Macintosh showed a serious young man staring thoughtfully at his Mac screen. But you might wonder just what his thoughts were as he concentrated on a blank screen. Only the back of the Mac showed in the photo, but the rocker switch is very obviously—to those of us who for years reached around to the back of the Mac to switch it on and off—in the off position.

PART 2

Hardware

Part 2 At a Glance

2

Basic Hardware

In This Chapter

Inside and Outside

Processors

A chip off the old silicon block. A *chip* is a little silicon wafer with microscopic circuits etched into it; it's more formally called an *integrated circuit,* or *IC, chip.* You don't see or handle these chips; they're encased in plastic or ceramic

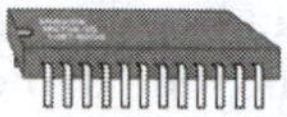

blocks with metal connectors protruding from them. These little insectoid blocks are also usually referred to as chips.

The processor chip. At the very heart of the computer is (to mix a metaphor) its brain, the *central processing unit,* or *CPU.* It's also referred to as the *microprocessor, processor chip, processor*, or simply *chip*, although there are many other kinds of chips, including memory chips.

Just what does a processor chip process? Instructions. Many millions are sent to the chip every second by system software and applications.

CPU and CPU. While *CPU* does stand for *central processing unit*, ever since the modular Mac II came out way back in the Middle Ages, "CPU" has also referred to the actual box that holds the CPU (and the motherboard, and slots, and other things).

The two processor families. Macs can be divided into two groups: those that use a Motorola 68000-series processor chip (all the Macs from the original one up through the Quadra), and those that use the IBM/Motorola PowerPC chip.

We often have to differentiate between these two major categories of Macs for both convenience and practical reasons. So, we refer to the older Macs as being the *68K models*, the K standing for the *kilo* prefix that indicates 1,000. The *PowerPC models* are either referred to just that way, or, more commonly, as PowerMacs—even though several Performa models are PowerPC-based.

The PowerPC processor. Current Macs use the PowerPC chip made by IBM and Motorola. These chips use a special technology called *RISC (reduced instruction set computing);* they have more raw power than the previous chip technology, *CISC (complex instruction set computing).* There are several different PowerPC chips in use:

- **601:** The first generation of this chip runs at 60 to 80MHz; the last goes to 120MHz.
- **603:** The 603 was designed to be inexpensive and energy efficient. It's actually slower than the 601: a 75MHz 603 works at about the same pace as a 66MHz 601.

- **603e:** Even smaller than the 603 (which was smaller than the 601—that's why it was cheaper), the 603e also gives off less heat, making it perfect for the first round of PowerPC PowerBooks. But it's faster than the 603 because its cache is twice the size. With clock speeds of up to 200MHz, it's great for the low-end desktop Macs, too.

Clock speeds and cache
Later this chapter

- **604:** The 604 is an improvement over the 603e in the area that counts the most: speed. Part of that comes from the more efficient way the cache works.
- **604e:** A small name change, but a big performance boost because the 604e cache is twice the size of the 604's, and it can handle many more instructions in the same time frame. (Of course, the time frame is in milliseconds when you're talking about chips.)
- **750:** This chip is so special, it gets a name (sort of) instead of a just number: the G3. It also gets an entry of its own, coming right up.

The G3 processor. A few years into the PowerPC-chip series, which began as a standard for use by more than one operating system, somebody finally decided to tweak the chip's performance for the only OS that was really using it: the Mac OS. The result is the PowerPC G3 which, despite its superior performance, actually costs less to make. Apple is so proud of the development that they named a new line of computers after it, the G3 series.

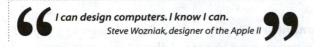

> ***I can design computers. I know I can.***
> *Steve Wozniak, designer of the Apple II*

The 68000 family. The Mac started out using the Motorola 68000 chip itself, but later models used subsequent chips in the series: the 68020, 68030, and 68040. The PowerBook 190 was the last model to be manufactured with a Motorola 68000-series processor. (The 68000 chip was so named because it had 68,000 transistors etched on it. Does the 68040 have forty more transistors? No—it has almost forty *times* as many: around 1.2 *million*!)

The 68000 chip is called the "sixty-eight thousand," but other chips in the series aren't pronounced as their numbers; the 68020, for instance, is "sixty-eight oh-twenty." But that's a mouthful, so the chips are abbreviated, in writing and speaking, to the numbers that differentiate them: '020 ("oh-twenty"), '030 ("oh-thirty"), and '040 ("oh-forty"). If you're referring to a 68000-series chip without meaning any specific one, you use the number *680x0* or the abbreviation *68K*.

A quick look at some of the capabilities of the chips in this family shows how technology continually improves and speeds a computer's performance. You can skip this list if you hate the technical stuff (you'll find all the terms explained later in this chapter).

- The **68000** was used for the first Macs. Although considered a 32-bit chip, it handles only 16-bit chunks of information internally.

- The **68HC000** is a special low-power version of the 68000 chip. ("Low-power" refers to the electricity needed to keep it running, not to its capabilities; it was used in the battery-powered PowerBook 100.)
- The **68020**, introduced in the Mac II, deals with 32-bit chunks internally and has a 256-byte instruction cache to hold frequently accessed information.
- The **68030** includes a 256-byte data cache in addition to the instruction cache and provides two 32-bit data paths instead of one so it can handle twice the information traffic. The '030 includes a *paged memory management unit,* known as a PMMU, something that's necessary for using virtual memory.
- The **68040** has instruction and data caches sixteen times larger than the ones in the '030, and has built-in capabilities for most of the functions of the math coprocessor that had to be added separately to earlier machines.
- The **68LC040** is a special, low-cost version of the 68040 that doesn't include the math coprocessor functions.

newertech.com

GURU. A terrific guide to the specs of all the Macs is **GURU**: GUide to Memory Updates, from Newer Technology. Despite its name, and its original intent as a memory guide, you'll get information about the CPUs, too, and all sorts of details. Selecting a model from the main palette gives you a window with three tabs of information about that machine. It's available for free from Newer—you can download it from their web site.

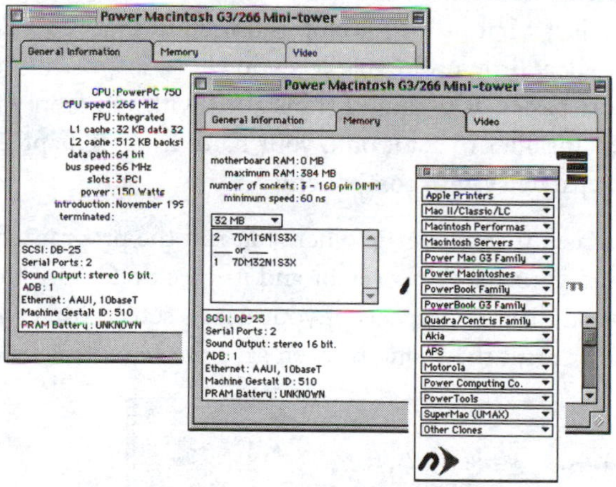

GURU's palette (top) and two tabs of information from one of the model windows.

Caches, Clocks, and Coprocessors

Cache as cache can. A memory *cache* (pronounced "cash," not "ca-shay" or "catch") speeds a Mac's performance by storing frequently used instructions in special high-speed memory that's faster than regular RAM. A *level 1* cache is built into the processor; a *level 2* cache—also referred to as a *secondary cache,* and abbreviated *L2*—is an external one installed in a slot on the logic board. Most PowerMacs come with secondary caches.

The newest term in caching is *backside cache,* the type of cache used for G3 processors. The speed at which information passes between a processor and a level 2 cache is limited by the speed of the system bus—the internal route for moving information around. A backside cache is connected to the CPU so they can talk directly back and forth, at a rate limited by on the processor's speed rather than the bus speed; that can double the transfer rate, although not all backside caches work at that top limit.

Caches vary in size from one CPU and Mac model to another. A larger cache provides faster overall performance.

Clock speed. Information marches through a processor chip to the beat of a very special drum: a quartz crystal that vibrates in response to an electric current. The pulses are so rapid that they're measured in *megahertz*—millions of cycles per second. This crystal "clock" determines the *clock rate,* or *clock speed,* or, simply, the *speed* of your processor. A 200MHz clock beats 200 million times a second. To put that in perspective: if your heart beat as many times as a 200MHz clock beats in a *single minute*, you'd be over 300 years old.

You can't compare clock speeds from one computer to another if they're using different processors; a more advanced chip often outperforms an older chip that has a faster clock rate. A PowerMac 6500 running at 300MHz, for instance, is only half as fast as a PowerMac G3 at 266MHz.

Speed (and other) checks. Don't know exactly what your clock rate is? Wondering just what processor chip is buried in that box? The Apple System Profiler is a neat little utility that lets you check lots of your system's hardware and software basics. If it didn't get installed with OS 8 on your computer, you can run the Installer to get it onto your hard drive. (Chapter 8 talks about installing separate system components.)

The first screen that shows up when you run the program identifies, among other things, your Mac's processor and its clock rate. Use the Select menu to get reports on different aspects of your Mac's setup; you can just view them on-screen, or print them out, or even save the reports as text files.

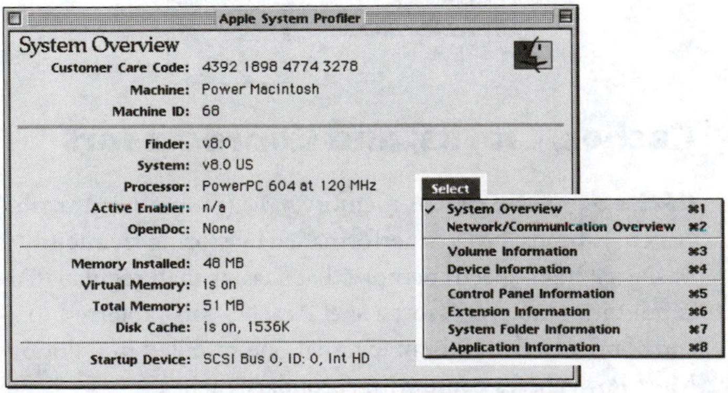

The Profiler utility lists, among other things, your Mac's processor and its clock rate. Its Select menu lets you look at other informative roundups.

connectix.com

The software speed bump. Accelerate your Mac without changing its hardware: install **Speed Doubler 8** ($50, Connectix). While the name is a slight exaggeration—you won't *double* the speed of your machine—you will see a significant increase in its performance, depending on just which activities you're measuring.

Speed Doubler 8 has changed from a small extension that did only behind-the-scenes speed-ups to a collection of utilities to make your Mac work faster. Its main module, as always, boosts the speed of non-native code (instructions written for the 68K-based Macs instead of for the PowerPC chip) for applications that haven't been completely rewritten. With all major, and most smaller, applications having been optimized for PowerPC, Speed Doubler's core technology is less important than it was, the addition of other items was almost a necessity. Speed Doubler 8's extra components provide: faster disk performance by improving Apple's disk caching feature; faster file copying on the desktop, even (and especially) across networks; file synchronization for PowerBooks; and basic backup capabilities.

In all, though, you'll most benefit from Speed Doubler if you have an older Mac and software.

Speed bump. Accelerate your Mac without touching the hardware—just install Connectix' **Speed Doubler** ($100).

Speed Doubler's main module is for Power Macs; it boosts the speed considerably. Since even the Finder is still not entirely native for PowerPC Macs, Speed Doubler helps even users who are using native applications. The speed increase you get depends on your Mac, and your software, but you can generally assume you'll be bumped up a little past the capabilities of the model that's one step beyond yours; so, a PowerMac 6100 with Speed Doubler can perform a little better than a PowerMac 7100.

Speed Doubler also includes a module for 68K Macs that increases their performance, although not as impressively as on the PowerMac side.

Coprocessors. A *coprocessor* is a secondary processor that specializes in a specific kind of computation, speeding up the tasks it's specifically designed for and relieving the main processor of some work. PowerMacs, for instance, use DMA (direct memory access) chips to supervise the exchange of information between memory and disks and other devices.

The 68K coprocessors. When the Motorola 68000 series was the standard Mac processor, it often got a boost from coprocessors:

- **FPU:** The most commonly used processor was a math coprocessor, the *FPU (floating point unit).* It didn't help straightforward math much (although it let the Mac work with 18 decimal places of accuracy instead of 14) but accelerated calculation-intensive processes like three-dimensional modeling and animation. The Mac II and '030 Macs used FPUs; the chip's functions were built into the '040 Macs.

- **PMMU:** The functions of a *PMMU (paged memory management unit)* were built into '030 and later chips. But because the Mac II (the first color Mac) was a 68020, and System 7 needed a PMMU for certain functions, the PMMU used to be a big deal.
- **DSP:** A *DSP (digital signal processor)* was used in AV Macs to help speed data transfers, necessary for handling sound and images.

shareware.com

FPU emulation. Some older applications absolutely insist on finding an FPU chip—they won't run at all without one present. This presents a problem on machines whose FPU functions are built into the processor ('040 and later Macs). The shareware **SoftwareFPU** can trick almost any program into thinking there's an FPU in the Mac. There's even a special version written in native PowerPC code.

Busses and Slots

Boards, mothers, and daughters. Chips are attached—sometimes just snapped in, sometimes soldered—to *boards* that are printed with metal tracings to serve as circuits (hence the full phrase *printed circuit board).* The *logic* board is the main board in a computer; it has the ROM chip on it. The main board is also called the *motherboard;* continuing the matriarchal metaphor, boards attached to the main board are *daughterboards.* There are also boards that are installed separately from the logic board; sometimes they're referred to as *cards.*

Slots and cards. An expansion *slot* is a connector inside the Mac where you plug in a card or board. Metallic spots or pins along the board's edge make contact with the connectors inside the slot when you install it.

Most Macs offer specialized slots for things like memory or an internal modem. In addition, they offer several slots of one "generic" type that accept boards for things like video output, video or processor acceleration, DOS-compatible computing, or special networking capabilities.

Sometimes getting at a slot is an exercise in frustration. The more paranoid among us might think that Apple is punishing us for begging for an "open Mac" all those years ago (you couldn't always open a Mac's case, and it didn't always offer slots). Just to install memory in a 7100, for instance, requires removing the power supply, the internal hard drive, the floppy drive, and the CD-ROM drive—not a process for the faint-of-heart!

The data bus. Information travels inside the Mac on its *data path*, or *data bus.* The wider the path, the faster the machine works for a given processor and clock speed, just as more cars can stream by when there are more lanes on the highway. The data path is measured according to how much information can be moved in one chunk; 68K Macs have 16- or 32-bit paths, while PowerMacs use 64-bit paths.

A narrow data path can cripple a computer, no matter its speed. For example: The LC had an '020 processor running at 16MHz, and the LC II had a much-improved '030 processor at 16MHz. The LC II should have been faster because of its better processor, but the two machines had almost identical performance because they both had 16-bit data buses.

The two bus routes. The first expandable Macs, and years of subsequent ones, used *NuBus* slots for internal expansion. The size and number of these slots varied from one model to another; some models need 7-inch NuBus cards, others take 14-inch ones. The revolutionary glory of the "NuBus architecture" was that it was *self-arbitrating:* the Mac knew which cards were installed, which had priority at any given time, and so on. This was wonderful in comparison to PC operations, where every time you installed a new board you had to fiddle with little switches and jumpers and hope you had it right so the information flow on the data bus didn't come to a screeching halt as one card's demands clashed with another's.

But, NuBus has served its purpose and can no longer keep up with the demands of the fastest Mac models. The current expansion slot standard is a *PCI (Peripheral Component Interconnect)* slot; it, too, is self-arbitrating and has become a cross-platform standard.

Hopping another bus. Apple never produced a Mac that used both PCI and NuBus slots, although it would have eased the transition to new machines for many users. PowerComputing sold a model with both types of slots when PCI was a new standard. So, if you move from a NuBus to a PCI machine, you won't be able to take your NuBus cards with you.

Off the bus route. There are several other common slots inside various Mac models:

- PDS, or *processor direct slot*, with a direct connection to the processor.
- A communications slot (CS) for an internal modem.
- Memory slots for RAM.
- Video slots for video cards that run monitors.

The PDS slot. Some Macs have a *PDS (processor direct slot)*, a direct connection to the computer's processor. A Mac can have only a single PDS. ("PDS slot" is an accepted phrase, but it actually translates to "processor direct slot slot"!)

There are different kinds of PDS cards, named for the machines in which they first appeared—SE PDS, LC PDS, and LC III PDS, for instance. In some models, using a PDS card blocks one of the NuBus slots; then again, some models have a PDS slot that takes an adapter so you ccan plug in a NuBus card instead.

Expansion bay and PCMCIA slots. PowerBooks have two special expansion capabilities not found on desk Macs: the expansion bay and the PCMCIA slot. The expansion bay is *not* the same thing as a "storage bay" in tower-design desk Macs, which is merely a space (and waiting cables) to add internal storage devices. Both the bay and PCMCIA are covered in the PowerBook chapter.

I/O Ports

Ins and outs. You don't need to open the Mac to add hardware. In fact, the most common and useful hardware add-ons are, by their very name—*peripheral*—outside the Mac: modems, printers, keyboards, scanners, and so on. The socket where you plug in a peripheral's cable is called a *port,* and there's a wide variety of them on the back of the Mac. They're sometimes referred to as *I/O* ports, for Input/Output.

Serial and parallel. Ports can be divided into two general categories: *serial*, where the information travels in a stream of data pretty much single file, one bit at a time; and *parallel*, which is more like a multi-lane highway, letting the information march along at least eight bits abreast. Parallel, of course, is a much faster connection; the Mac's modem and printer ports are serial, while the SCSI port is parallel.

The basic ports. Not all Macs have all the ports listed here; in fact, if you include PowerBooks, there are some Macs that have only two ports. But most Macs provide about a half-dozen ports for standard peripherals. Only the modem and printer ports accept the same cable, so it's hard to attach something incorrectly; besides, every port is labeled with an icon to help you figure out what goes where.

- The **ADB** port (*Apple Desktop Bus*—remember, a bus is something that information travels on in a computer) is for your keyboard and mouse, and anything that replaces one or the other—a trackball, for instance. Most Macs have a single ADB port, since you can plug the keyboard into it and then plug the mouse into the keyboard.
- The **printer** port not only accommodates printers but also serves as the main network connector.
- The **modem** port is used, of course, for modems, but can also handle other serial devices, like some printers.
- The **SCSI** port is for external SCSI devices like hard drives, CD-ROM drives, removable storage (like Zip and SyQuest), and scanners. Desk Macs use a 25-pin SCSI connector; PowerBooks use a more compact one called HDI-30.
- The **display**, or **monitor**, port, is on Macs that provide support for a monitor. But keep in mind that there are different levels of "support": few models can run an extra-large display from their internal video, and many are limited in the number of colors they can display on even a standard-size screen.

- **Video-in** and **video-out** ports are included on all AV and many later PowerMac models. The video-in port lets you hook up a camcorder or VCR to play into a window on the Mac. The video-out port (not to be confused with the monitor port) lets you send a video signal to a standard TV or a VCR.
- The **sound out** port, available on most Macs, lets you plug in headphones or small speakers that use a standard miniplug (like Walkman headphones). All Macs already have built-in speakers.
- The **sound input** port accepts an Apple microphone (some models just have built-in mikes so you wind up pretty much talking to the screen). Some Macs have, in addition, **stereo sound input**, with separate ports for left and right input.
- The **Ethernet** port, available at least as an option on most new Macs, is for Ethernet network connections.
- There's a separate **headphone** port on some later Mac models, conveniently located on the front of the case rather than on the back.

SCSI styles. The external SCSI port on all Macs so far is the standard SCSI that's been used on Macs since they first had SCSI ports. Many newer models offer two separate SCSI busses: the standard one for external devices, which often includes the default internal drive, and a second, faster SCSI bus for multiple internal devices in tower-case models. The old standard SCSI might eventually be referred to as SCSI-1, since newer standards are labeled SCSI-2 and SCSI-3. There's lots more about the SCSI standards in the *Wonderful World of SCSI* section of Chapter 4.

Catching the newest bus. The release of the iMac introduced the Mac world to the latest and greatest of I/O schemes: USB (Universal Serial Bus). On the iMac, the USB is used in lieu of SCSI, ADB, *and* standard serial ports! In the larger computer world, the USB is expected to become a standard for many devices, including drives, keyboards, mice, modems, printers, scanners, cameras, and even monitors.

A USB-capable machine can support up to 127 USB devices, although each needs it's own connector. You won't find more than two or three connectors on any machine, but there are USB *hubs* that connect to the computer and provide multiple USB ports. In fact, the iMac's keyboard is a hub, and you can plug both the mouse and another USB device into it.

Unfortunately, while USB is inexpensive and fast for a few devices, it slows down with multiple devices—not a big deal for a keyboard or floppy drive, but a problem for high-capacity storage.

Video port or video port. The name of the port for built-in monitor support has been gradually evolving; it's generally called the *video port*, although sometimes it's called the *monitor port.* Apple began referring to it as the *display port* when it introduced Macs with ports for hooking up video equipment like

TVs and camcorders. If you see or hear the term *video port* or *video support*, you'll have to judge from the context whether it's referring to a monitor display or the more general video capability.

The GeoPort. The GeoPort isn't a separate port at all, but a specialized version of a serial (modem or printer) port. This port provides extra speed, so that it can be used for multiple purposes—send a fax, print a document, maintain a network connection—all at the same time. The modem ports on AV models are GeoPorts, as are both the modem and the printer ports on most PowerMacs.

GeoPorts provide room for a nine-pin connector instead of the standard eight-pin serial connector, so you usually can tell something is a GeoPort just by looking at it. That ninth hole provides electricity to Apple's GeoPort Adapter, if you get one. But the GeoPort approach has never caught on. A combination of lack of user understanding, initial modem speeds easily eclipsed by stand-alone modems for not much more money (or, at some points, for *less* money), and other minor but annoying hardware and software drawbacks kept it from becoming any kind of standard, even on a computer that's used to setting its own.

Luckily, since the GeoPort difference is an extra hole, it can still function as a standard serial connector.

Not always a GeoPort. The external difference between a GeoPort and a standard serial port is the presence of a ninth pin. The PowerMac 5200 and the Performa 5200 and 6200, however, have a ninth pin on their modem ports—but they are *not* GeoPorts.

The high-density display port. Many PowerPC-based Macs have a special, over-sized display port called the *AV* or *high-density* port. The AV port is actually a combination monitor, ADB, sound, and video port that was designed for multimedia monitors like Apple's AudioVision 14 Display, which has built-in speakers, a microphone, and places to plug in a keyboard and other peripherals. It supports monitors up to mid-size or portrait, but not large 19- to 21-inch models. You need a $30 **PowerMac Display Adapter** to connect any other monitor to an AV high-density port. —JK

Memory Chips

Rich Wolfson was the special contributor for this section, though his initials aren't on the entries.

Measurements

A common measuring stick. Both memory and storage space use the same units of measure: bits, bytes, kilobytes, megabytes, and so on. This probably accounts for the beginner's frequent confusion between the room on the hard drive and available memory (*"What does this dialog mean, there isn't enough memory? I have 500 megabytes available on my hard drive!"*).

These units are based on the binary numbering system that's at the heart of the computer's processor, in contrast to the human-friendly *decimal*, or *base 10,* system.

A little bit. The smallest unit of information a computer deals with is a *bit*, a word that comes from the phrase *binary digit*. A bit, like the binary digits 1 and 0, can represent one of only two possibilities: 1 or 0, black or white, on or off. Eight bits together make a *byte*. A byte is still very small when it comes to representing information: a single alphabetic character, for instance, is usually represented internally by a byte—and that doesn't include any font or styling information. (Old hands at programming also have a special word for a group of four bits—a half-byte: a *nybble.*)

Beyond bytes. The measurements we use after bits and bytes are a sometimes confusing blend of binary numbers and the words we use in our decimal system of numbering.

The prefix *kilo*, for instance, stands for *thousand*, but a *kilobyte* is not 1000 bytes: it's 1024 bytes, the closest "round" number to a thousand in binary. The kilobyte, abbreviated as *K*, is something you're probably familiar with as a unit measurement for file sizes.

With *mega* standing for million, a *megabyte* is roughly a million bytes. Just as 1,000,000 in decimal is actually 1000 thousands, the megabyte (abbreviated *MB)* is 1024 kilobytes. The amount of memory in your computer and the size of many hard drives are usually given in terms of megabytes, or *megs.*

The next unit is the *gigabyte*, which—as you may have anticipated—is 1024 megabytes. The term is often shortened to *gig,* and is abbreviated *GB.* Most hard drives now offer a gig or more of storage (and 500MB drives are sometimes referred to as a "half gig" or .5GB).

Here's a quick review:

8 bits	=	1 byte
1024 bytes	=	1 kilobyte (1K)
1024K	=	1 megabyte (1MB)
1024MB	=	1 gigabyte (1GB)

What's next? Well, it'll be a while before you can find a drive that offers a terabyte of space, but when you do, you'll know it's 1024 gigs.

Memory Basics

RAM. *RAM (random access memory)*, or just *memory*, is where your computer stores information when it's on. RAM holds part of the system software, and part or all of the applications and documents you're working on, so the amount of memory in your Mac limits the size and number of applications and documents you can have open at one time.

But *RAM* isn't just a nebulous electronic cavern that gets filled with information as you work. It's a series of tiny electronic switches that keep track of information by being in either On or Off positions. The switches, packed like minuscule sardines into a memory chip, are held in position by a constant flow of electricity; so, turn off the computer, and you lose whatever's in RAM.

All Macs come with some RAM, but you can buy and install more. All Macs also have limits as to how much RAM they can actually use; as system software and application demands increase over the years, the RAM limitation in older Macs is usually what makes owners consign them to a closet.

IN THE BEGINNING

Hoping to make it easier for beginners, the Mac system originally calculated a kilobyte as an even 1000 bytes. Apple gave up this particular swim against the tide and switched to the 1024-bytes-to-a-K system in 1986 when it released System 3 (which, by the way, came with Finder 5).

But here's what happened to those of us caught in the transition: Before the system update, the then-standard 400K disk showed 400K available for storage. You updated your system, put the disk back in, and found that the disk had 391K available. Where did that 9K go? Nowhere: 400 "old" K's equaled 400,000 bytes, while 391 "new" K's equaled 400,384 bytes, the true capacity of the disk.

ROM. ROM stands for *read-only memory.* Despite the word *memory* in its name, it's not at all the kind of memory people are referring to when they talk about a computer's memory. It's the *read-only* part that makes it so different: you can use the information stored in it, but you can't change it or add to it. As the Mac developed, its ROMs grew: the original Mac had 64K of information in its ROM, while the first PowerMacs had 4 *megs:* sixty-four times as much! There's a move away from ROM-based information in Macs, with more information stored on disk and in RAM; this makes Macs cheaper to produce and easier to upgrade.

Clean and dirty ROMs. Starting with the Mac II, Macs were theoretically able to address more than 8 megabytes of memory. But it was only in theory for that model, as well as for the Mac IIx, IIfx, IIcx, and SE30 because of their ROMs—later to become known as "dirty" ROMs. For these machines to use more than 8MB of RAM, you need an extension called *Mode32.* (This is covered in more detail in Chapter 13.)

On-board and add-in. The earliest Macs had memory that was soldered onto the motherboard along with everything else. Current Macs have no RAM soldered on, just slots for memory cards. Along the way, there were models with both soldered-in memory and memory slots. When you see a reference to "on-board" memory, that refers to RAM that's soldered to the motherboard.

SIMMs and DIMMs. The chips that make up your computer's RAM are attached to little boards to create a *memory module. SIMMs (single in-line memory modules)* and *DIMMs (dual in-line, etc.)* are the two main types of memory boards used in Macs. The *single* and *dual* parts of the their names (both terms are pronounced as words, not as initials) refer to how their I/O contacts are designed, with the dual setup being able to transfer information more quickly.

Older Macs use SIMMs, while the newer ones use DIMMs. The iMac uses *SODIMMS: small outline dual in-line memory modules,* which are smaller than the standard DIMMs.

PowerBooks don't use SIMMs or DIMMs because there's not enough room inside; they use something that's referred to generically as *memory modules*.

A typical memory module, a SIMM.

Since most of the information in this chapter refers to both SIMMs and DIMMs, I'm going to use the abbreviation S/DIMM to refer to both types.

Size isn't *size*. The *size* of a S/DIMM isn't its physical dimensions, but its *capacity*, also sometimes called its *density*—the amount of memory on the board. Originally, SIMMs were 256K, so you needed four of them to upgrade your Mac Plus with an additional meg of memory; later, the SIMM standard size was 1MB, so four of them gave you four megs. Over the years, the SIMM size increased as, luckily, the relative price dropped. Now you can buy DIMMs for your PowerMac in 16- and 32-meg sizes. (Did you notice that S/DIMM sizes use that ever-popular binary numbering system: 1, 2, 4, 8, 16, 32, and so on?)

Memory speed. A S/DIMM is rated by the speed at which its memory can be accessed. The speed is measured in *nanoseconds*, abbreviated as *ns*.

Lets take a few whole seconds to think about this scale. A nanosecond is a *billionth* of a second. How small is that? Well, start with a *millisecond*, a thousandth of a second: electricity can travel the length of Manhattan in less than a millisecond. In a nanosecond, electricity can travel from about the back of your heel to the tip of your toe. (The next unit is a *picosecond*, which is a trillionth of a second; electricity travels from one side of the period at the end of this sentence to the other in a picosecond.) Now, back to S/DIMMs.

The speed rating of a S/DIMM is given in terms of how long it takes to do something, rather than some miles-per-hour type of rating. So, a lower number means a faster rating: a 100ns SIMM is faster than a 120ns SIMM.

The RAM barrier. The amount of memory you can put in your Mac depends on the number of slots available for S/DIMMs, and how large a S/DIMM the slot can accommodate. There are also rules, which we'll cover later, that limit your choices as to how much RAM you can put in at a time—you can't just say, *Well, I can afford three megs this month, and I'll get two more as soon as I can.*

Most important, however, is the overall RAM limit in a Mac, which varies from one model to another.

A Little Beyond the Basics

Pseudo, and so on. The basic RAM chips that make up your computer's memory is more completely referred to as DRAM, *("D-ram")* with the D standing for *dynamic*, because its contents change. The phrase comes in handy, since sometimes we need to differentiate between this kind of memory and the other kinds of memory chips in your computer:

- **VRAM**. *("V-ram")*. *Video RAM* is specialized high-speed RAM used—you guessed it—for the video display. (Early Macs grabbed screen memory from the DRAM, which wasn't such a problem back when Mac screens were black-and-white, 9-inch displays.)
- **PRAM**. *("P-ram")*. *Parameter RAM* is a small amount of memory in your Mac that's powered by an internal battery. It keeps track of various control panel settings like the mouse tracking speed, the virtual memory setting, and the time and date. (That's how the Mac remembers what time it is even if you unplug it.)
- **Static RAM, SRAM**. *("S-ram")*. *Static RAM* doesn't need constant refreshing to keep its information; it holds it until you change it.
- **Pseudo-static RAM**. Pseudo-static RAM takes only a very little electrical power to keep its switches set in place, so it's used in PowerBooks, where power draw is always a concern. It's also a lot less expensive than true static RAM.
- **Flash RAM**. Despite its name that connotes a short-lived flash-in-the-pan attitude, flash RAM actually holds its information even without any electrical current available—for as long as ten years. Flash RAM is available for some PowerBooks, on insertable cards that serve as extremely fast hard drives.

EDO and EDON'T. There are two types of DRAM DIMMs. EDO (pronounced as separate letters) is *extended data output* and is five to twenty-five percent faster than the other kind. The "other" kind, which is often just referred to as "standard" or "regular" DIMMs, is *fast page mode,* or FPM. Some PowerMacs need EDO DIMMs; others can't use them; still others can use either—but may not benefit from the extra EDO speed. The biggest caveat: the PowerMac 7200 can be damaged if you use EDO DIMMs in it. The EDO information is rounded up on the next page.

And now, SDRAM. You know all about a computer's clock speed—the metronome that keeps things moving through the processor. But memory access has always had a different timing scheme, based on the memory chips themselves. Because the memory is *asynchronous*—it's timing has nothing to do with the speed or needs of the processor's cycles—there are periods of

PowerMacs and EDO DIMMs

Model	FPM	EDO (no speed benefit)	EDO with speed benefit
6100, 7100, 8100	●	●	
4400	●		●
5200, 5300, 6200, 6300	●	●	
5400, 6360, 6400 (no Zip drive)	●	●	
6400 with internal Zip drive	●		●
7200	●	✖	✖
7300, 7500, 7600, 8500, 8600, 9500, 9600	●	●	

✖ Using EDO in the 7200 can ruin the motherboard

inactivity ("wait states") for the processor. Standard DRAM, as described two entries ago, is asynchronous.

But *synchronous DRAM*, or *SDRAM*, uses a clock that synchronizes with the processor's clock and eliminates the wait state, resulting in speeds up to twenty percent faster than EDO RAM. SDRAM is used in the G3 Macs.

Translation. If you're looking at memory specs, or at the S/DIMMs themselves, you may see markings like *1 x 8-40* or *4 x 32-80*. First of all, the pronunciation is "one by eight, forty." Next, it's relatively easy to interpret the numbers.

The first two numbers—*a x b*—describe the total amount of memory on the board, with *a* being the amount of memory in each chip, and *b* the number of chips. But of course it's not quite that straightforward, since the chip memory is described in terms of mega*bits*.

With binary numbers, *mega* actually stands for 1,048,576, so that's how many bits there are in a megabit. You can divide that by 8 to find out how many *bytes* there are—131,072—and divide *that* by 1024 to find that a megabit is 128K. So, for a 1 x 8, there are 8 chips of one megabit each: a total of 1,024K, or one meg. For the 4 x 32, the chips are four megabits each (512K); with 32 of them, that's 16,384K, or 16 megs.

The second number also provides a clue as to whether the module is a SIMM or DIMM, and how many pins it has: 32 is a 72-pin SIMM, 8 is a 30-pin SIMM, and 64 is a DIMM. The number after the hyphen is, as you've probably guessed, simply the memory's speed.

thechipmerchant.com

If you want to get even more technical, go for it. In fact, go on the Web for it. The Chip Merchant, an excellent place to buy memory, has all sorts of background information on its web site.

Don't read this entry about refresh rates. Unless you're really a techie, a techie-wannabe, or really, really curious.

You may see specs on a DIMM that refer to its *refresh rate*. It all harks back to the issue of RAM, or DRAM, needing a constant supply of electricity to keep its switches set—to "remember" things. That's not exactly accurate, although it's the party line because nobody wants you to think the RAM contents can survive a shutdown. But the truth is, the chips don't need a constant flow of electricity; they work perfectly well with little zaps at regular intervals. RAM chips (the real chips, the tiny things inside that black block we also call a "chip") are arranged in tiny rows and columns; each row gets a new zap of electricity (or is "refreshed"), and then the next row gets zapped, and so on. The refresh rate refers to the number of zaps it takes to get all the rows juiced—in other words, how many rows can be zapped in a single "refresh cycle." A 2K refresh rate handles 2000 rows of chips in a single cycle. Which, of course, is measured in small fractions of a second. So, if you can turn off your Mac and get it back on again in that time frame, your RAM contents will be there waiting for you.

SIMM (and DIMM) City

Pin count. SIMMs come in 30-pin and 72-pin styles; DIMMs come as 168-pin models. The "pins" are the tiny metallic strips at the edge of the board that make contact with the connectors when you slide the board into the memory slot. The oldest Macs use the 30-pin SIMMs, while the later 68K models use the 72-pin model. The earliest PowerMacs also used 72-pin SIMMs, but all subsequent ones use DIMMs.

Bank on it. A *bank* is a group of memory slots that accommodate 30-pin SIMMs, although it's not always clear how many slots make a bank: four slots might be a single bank, or two banks of two slots. The bank system varies from one model to another.

The important thing about banks is that you have to treat them as an entity when you install SIMMs: each bank has to be totally filled or totally empty, and each slot in a bank has to have the same size SIMM. Some Macs have individual "banking" requirements, like needing one bank filled before the other if you're using only one, or one should hold the lower-density SIMMs if you're putting different sizes in each bank.

Whether a bank is two or four slots for 30-pin SIMMs depends on which Mac model you're using and how it handles information internally. A 30-pin SIMM handles 8 bits of information at time. Most Macs use four slots to a bank because they handle 32 bits of information at a time, grabbing a "layer" of 8 bits from each of the four SIMM banks simultaneously. In a model like the LC, which handles 16 bits of information at a time, a SIMM bank is only two slots because it can grab only two 8-bit chunks of information at a time. The banks are usually identified (as A and B) right on the logic board.

But the whole banking business (so to speak) in 30-pin Macs is nearly moot now because the price of memory has dropped so precipitously: it's a reasonable cost to fill all slots in all banks with the highest possible SIMM size.

Self-banking for 72-pin SIMMs. A 72-pin SIMM can hand off information in 32-bit chunks at a time, just what later-model 68K Macs require. So, there's no need to deal with banks of slots; a 72-pin SIMM is, to all intents and purposes, a bank all by itself. As a result, you can add 72-pin SIMMs one at a time; you can put a SIMM in any available slot; and, you can put any size SIMM in any slot in any order

PowerMacs and SIMMs. The earliest PowerMacs used SIMMs, not the DIMMs that later models used. Since PowerMacs move 64 bits of information around at time, and their 72-pin SIMMs provide 32-bit chunks, many PowerMacs require you to install *pairs* of SIMMs, so the computer can get at 64 bits of information at a time. Some models that don't *require* it still *recommend* it for best performance. On the other hand, in some models, it makes no difference at all!

> ***One of my nerdy friends has a megabyte of linear RAM in his Macintosh. What's he do with it? He installs six applications in Switcher. What's he doing with the applications? Not much… Everybody needs a hobby.***
>
> *Doug Clapp, MacUser, February 1986*

PowerMacs and DIMMs. Once Apple created a machine that handled 64-bit chunks of information internally, it needed memory modules that matched so we wouldn't have to worry about pairing SIMMs to get things to work. Luckily (well, maybe not all that luckily—somebody probably did some research and planning), DIMMs came along. With its 168-pin connector, a DIMM can receive and send 64-bits of information at a time, just what a PowerMac needs.

You might be surprised at first to find that DIMM speeds don't seem all that much faster than the SIMMs used in PowerMacs: 70ns DIMMs and 80ns SIMMs, for the most part (remember, a lower number is a faster speed). But keep in mind that the DIMMs are moving twice as much information for every tick of that really tiny clock the computer uses: 64 bits versus a SIMM's 32 bits. So the DIMM is already moves information twice as fast as a SIMM with the same speed rating.

Interleaving: speeding up even more. Even though information zips around inside a PowerMac at speeds only dreamt of a few years ago, engineers look to tweak every little aspect they can think of to increase the speed (and therefore the performance). The special tweak for PowerMac DIMM memory is something called *interleaving,* which lets the Mac "read and write" to multiple spots in memory at the same time.

For machines that support memory interleave (basically the 7500, 8500, and 9500 series), you have to install pairs of same-sized DIMMs in the correct slots so the Mac can look at them both at the same time.

What are the correct slots for the pairs? The slots are labeled with letters and numbers: A1, A2, A3, and so on, and B1, B2, and B3, and on. Start with the highest number of each letter (A6 and B6, or A4 and B4 for most models) and put the matching DIMMs in them. Use the next-highest pair of slots for the next two DIMMs, and so on.

Some non-PowerPC Macs with 72-pin SIMMs also use interleaving to speed performance, but it's easier to figure out where the SIMMs should go to make interleaving kick in: put pairs of same-size SIMMs in adjacent slots.

IN THE BEGINNING

The cost of computer memory has gone down over the years, with only a few occasional upward blips along the way. And it's a good thing, too, considering how much memory we need to run a system and an application or two these days.

The original Mac had 128K of memory. An upgrade to the "Fat Mac" total of 512K cost $1000, for just that extra 384K of memory—which comes out to over $2600 per meg! At that rate, the 128 megs in my current Mac would be worth over $332,800.

But it could be even worse. A year after the first personal computer, the Altair, was available, you could buy a RAM upgrade for $150—for a 4K board. (That's not a typo: K, not meg.) At *that* rate, my 128 megs would be worth, at about $38,400 per meg, $4,915,200!

Buying and Installing Memory

Where to get memory. There are three basic ways to buy memory:

- Bring your computer to a computer superstore and pay them not only for the memory, but for the installation. This is the most expensive option, as you'll be paying premium prices for the memory as well as for the labor. You could buy the memory there and then install it yourself at home, but between the store-display packaging cost and the store's markup, you'll still spend more there than anywhere else.
- Order from a multi-purpose vendor like **Newer Technology** that provides full service: they'll know what chips you need, they'll provide installation instructions, and they do a little bit of hand-holding, too. This kind of vendor is less expensive than going to a computer store.

- Buy from a memory-only vendor like **Chip Merchant**, which will know exactly what you need and provide the S/DIMMs but no instructions. The chips are guaranteed, and they even buy back ones you may not need anymore.

newertech.com
thechipmerchant.com

There are other vendors who can be trusted to know what they're doing, but Newer and Chip Merchant have wonderful reputations in the Mac community and I can recommend them both from years of personal experience.

Installing (and removing) S/DIMMs. It's not difficult to install memory in your computer, although some models make it difficult to get at the memory slots by putting all sorts of things in the way. You don't have to be a techie to do it; as long as you're not all thumbs, you'll be okay. For years now, Macs have come with memory installation instructions. Make sure you look through your manual to see how to open the Mac's case and get at the memory slots. In general:

1. Unplug the Mac and any attached devices.
2. Carefully remove the cover and any components obstructing the memory slots.
3. Before handling the memory, touch the Mac's power supply. This will discharge any static you and/or the Mac have built up.
4. Install the memory boards, keeping these guidelines in mind:
    - S/DIMMs go in only in one direction! For SIMMs, look for the little hole in the one end of the SIMM, and make sure it matches the SIMM bracket on the motherboard.
    - Older Macs have little clips that hold the SIMMs in place; they're easy to break and difficult to replace. The clips usually release the SIMM when you push the top edge of the SIMM at an angle; sometimes you have to use a fingernail or small screwdriver to get the clips to let go.
    - Once the clips are open, or if there are no clips, it's usually difficult to just pull the board straight out. Older Macs need the board angled before you can pull; in most Macs, you may find that alternating gentle tugs at each end of the board, pulling from the top edge, will get it out.
    - Never force the boards into position; you can damage both the board and the socket. Position the S/DIMM, then push firmly but gently on the top edge to slide it into the socket. On most older Macs, you have to insert the board at an angle (if that's the way it came out) and then straighten it; if there are clips, make sure they snap into place when the board goes in. —SZA/RT

Speed signs. You can tell the speed of a SIMM just by looking at it: the speed is printed somewhere on the chip. Of course, it would be much too easy if the actual speed rating were printed on the board. For 60ns and 80ns chips, you'll see those numbers, but triple-digit speeds are often marked with only two digits: 10 for 100ns, 12 for 120ns, and so on.

Use faster memory, but not slower. Using faster memory than what your Mac is rated for won't speed anything up, but it won't hurt, either. On the other hand, using memory that's slower than what your Mac can handle does slow down the whole system. The chart at the end of this chapter lists the memory speed requirements for all the Mac models.

> *To cope with the fact that many new programs have outgrown [512K of memory in] the Macintosh, some Mac owners are installing memory upgrade boards [that] can boost the amount of RAM to as much as 2 megabytes. Many of the upgrades void the Apple warranty, however.*
>
> *Macworld, February 1986*

Avoid composite memory. A composite S/DIMM has double the usual number of chips on it because the chips themselves are of a lower density—and therefore less expensive. So, for instance, a composite 16MB SIMM has sixteen 1MB chips instead of eight 2MB chips. Some composite S/DIMMs have timing problems in working with the Mac's processor, with pleasant side effects like frequent, random system crashes. Sometimes you'll get composite SIMMs to work, but it depends on the SIMMs and how they're manufactured, and on which Mac you're using, since some are more tolerant of the timing problems. But even if you get a few to work, adding a few more may bring the whole thing crashing down—even though the new ones might work all by themselves, too. Since you'll never be able to tell which composites might work and which won't, it's best to avoid them completely and pay a little extra for a sure thing.

Current (and Recent) Models

The PowerMacs

About PowerMacs. The PowerMac line was launched in March 1994 as the first branch of the Mac family to use the new, more powerful RISC technology of the PowerPC processor chips. The first group of machines (the 6100, 7100, and 8100, using the 601 chip) was barely in the stores before they were each upgraded to faster speeds. The next round (the 5200, 6200, and 7200) included two machines with the less-expensive 603 PowerPC chip instead of the 601. Subsequent models, including the 7500, 8500, and 9500 series only a year later used the 604 chip, while the 7600, 8600, and 9600 series that followed soon after went to the 604e. The PowerMacs don't have a lock on the PowerPC processor: Many Performa models use it, too.

The G3 series. The computers based on the "G3" 750 PowerPC chip (hmm… it just occurred to me that perhaps that stands for third generation) are called G3 computers. The approach Apple has taken for the G3 line is that you pretty much have your choice of two form factors and two feature sets.

The form factors are the shape: a tower or the common, flatter CPU box (which Apple refers to as "a sleek, low-lying desktop model"). The feature sets are meant to appeal to two different types of users: the general Mac user (business and education) and the graphic designer/multimedia honcho who needs more power. For the latter group, there's a faster chip, a higher RAM limit, a larger hard drive, and 24-bit video input/output ports.

All the initial G3 models use IDE drives of at least 4GB capacity and come with built-in Zip drives. (The 8600, released at the same time, offered the same but used an internal SCSI drive.)

Because iMacs are just being launched as I write this, go to macbible.com for our exclusive iMac supplement. (For even more specific iMac info, look for the forthcoming* The Little iMac Book, *by Mac expert Robin Williams, also from Peachpit Press.)

The iMaginative iMac. The introduction of the new iMac (it's been introduced, but it's not yet available as I write this) puzzled many Apple watchers. Not because of the design—although that raised many eyebrows—but because of what's included, and not, with this unit, supposedly the first of a new line of consumer-level Macs.

First, the design. It's George Jetson-ish, from the rounded lines of the partly translucent case to the curved keyboard and strange mouse. The colors are "ice" white and "Bondi" blue (Bondi is a surfer beach in Australia); even the mouse is translucent, and its half-blue, half-white ball seems to be mesmerizing people as they work with it. But why aren't they looking at the 15-inch built-in screen (with its ultra-high refresh rate of 117Hz) instead of the mouse?

But the iMac is famous for what it *doesn't* have. No built-in Zip drive. No PCI slots. No SCSI port. No ADB connectors. No floppy drive! This Mac seems to be an island. What it *does* have is a USB (Universal Serial Bus) connector, the coming thing in computer connectivity. Unfortunately, it's not coming as fast as the iMac, so you'll be hard-pressed to find USB devices (floppy drives, modems, Zip drives) for a while. It's possible to connect a non-USB device by using a special adapter, but then you'll need a special driver from the manufacturer of the USB device in order for the Mac to "see" the peripheral anyway.

What's the *i* in *iMac*? It's for *internet*, of course. But don't be fooled by the buzzword (or, in this case, the buzzletter): the first round of iMacs will ship with System 8.1, and the iMac has no more internet ease-of-access or features than other Macs with the same system software.

Native and emulation modes. A PowerMac can work in two different modes: *native,* which means it's using software made to take advantage of the PowerPC chip, and *emulation,* which means it's pretending to be a 68000-based machine, running software made for earlier Macs. These modes are invisible to the user: The Mac works in whatever mode is necessary to get the job done, switching back and forth without your telling it to—in fact, without your even knowing.

PowerMacs and memory. Every product line seems to have a few quirks when it comes to memory requirements, and the PowerMacs are no exception.

- The **4400**, which needs EDO DIMMs, doesn't support interleaved memory. The first socket can accommodate only up to a 32MB DIMM; the other two can use 64MB DIMMs.
- Using EDO DIMMs in the **7200** series can damage not only the DIMMs, but also the Mac's logic board.
- Apple approved 70ns DIMMs for the **8600** series, but many users found problems with those; 60ns or faster DIMMs seem to work better.
- Some versions of the **Performa 6330** logic board fully support EDO memory, and others don't—although using EDO won't harm anything. So, use EDO just in case your particular machine can benefit from it!

PowerMac AV's. PowerMac AV models (mostly variations of the x100 models—6100, 7100, and so on) include an AV card in the PDS slot instead of an accelerated display card. The AV card provides a second display port and video-in and video-out ports; it gives you (not surprisingly, considering its name—the AV stands for *audio-visual)* all the special video capabilities of a 68K AV Mac, but on a faster machine. There's no DSP chip on the card (as there is in the AV's) because the PowerPC chip can handle all its functions at speeds rivaling that dedicated chip. But there is a DAV slot on the AV board that you can use to add cards that extend the audio and video capabilities of the computer. Note that many PowerMacs come with video-in and video-out ports even though they're not AV models. —SZA/JK

IN THE BEGINNING

Apple's award-winning introductory commercial for its new Macintosh computer aired only once: during the 1984 SuperBowl. Its theme: why 1984 (the year) wouldn't be like 1984 (the book). Hundreds of brain-washed workers trudged into an auditorium to listen to a televised lecture, until the screen was smashed by a slow-motion sledge hammer throw. Most people have no idea just what propaganda was being spouted by that talking head, but here it is. You can download a copy of this on the web at apple/whymac/ads.html.

Each of you is a single cell in the great body of the State. And today, that great body has purged itself of parasites. We have triumphed over the unprincipled dissemination of facts. The thugs and wreckers have been cast out. Let each and every cell rejoice! For today we celebrate the first glorious anniversary of the Information Purification Directive. We have created, for the first time in all history, a garden of pure ideology where each worker may bloom secure from the pests purveying contradictory and confusing truths. Our unification of thought is more powerful a weapon than any fleet or army on earth. We are one people. With one will. One resolve. One cause. Our enemies shall talk themselves to death, and we will bury them with their own confusion. We shall prevail!

Silence isn't golden. If you have external speakers connected to a PowerMac 5500 or 6500 at startup and then disconnect them while the computer's running, the internal speakers won't make any sound. You have to restart the computer to get the internal speaker working correctly.

The 5xxx and 6xxx mystery problem. If your Mac is from the PowerMac or Performa 5200, 5300, 6200, or 6300 series and you're experiencing continual freezes, there's a special utility on your system CD that you should run. You'll find it in the CD's Utilities folder; it's called the 5xxx/6xxx Tester. You run the test, and if a message tells you a problem was found, you call Apple and they do a free repair. (Of course, your problem could be just software-based, in which case the Tester won't diagnose anything.) The 6360 model (PowerMac and Performa) is exempt from whatever problem seems to plague the others in the family.

Freezes and other problems
Chapter 24

5xxx/6xxx Tester 1.1

Any Mac in any of these series (excepting the 5260, 6320, and 6360) won't be able to run OS 8 if it's suffering from this unnamed hardware problem, so make sure you run the tester.

Performas

About Performas. Performas were originally marketed as Apple's consumer machine: bottom of-the-line power, pre-packaged with a keyboard and not-so-great monitor, bundled with software, given a special set of "extra-easy" system software, and sold through general stores like Sears and K-Mart. In fact, to get around Apple's original agreements with its dealers, which prevented it from selling Macintoshes except through them, these machines were named "Performa" with no "Macintosh" anywhere in the name.

But everything changes. Later Performa models weren't under-powered by any means; they matched other mainstream Macs' capabilities, used standard Mac software, and even had an official name change to "Macintosh Performa."

Performa names. Performa model names are probably the worst of any in the Mac family. Sometimes the only difference from one model to another is the inclusion of a CD-ROM drive or a modem; sometimes it's an even simpler matter of the size of the hard drive. So, we wind up with model numbers like 460, 466, and 467, and 5200, 5215, and 5216! Who can keep track? We've put the important specs in the chart at the end of the chapter, combining similar machines (mostly into "series" groups, like the 5200 series, for instance) into single entries.

In general, the last number of a three-digit model number (460, 466, 467) means a minor difference like a hard drive or modem, while the major components—processor, speed, slots—are the same. For a four-digit model number, the last two digits (6200, 6215) are the ones that indicate minor component differences.

The most important clue you can glean from a Performa name, however, is whether it's a PowerPC machine: to date, all 3-digit Performa models are 68K Macs, and 4-digit models use the PowerPC chip.

Performa system software. Performa models up until the 580 (in the spring of 1995) were released with a special version of the system software, the "P" version of System 7 and System 7.1. The major differences between the P and standard versions were the inclusion of At Ease (a Finder replacement), a special Launcher window, and a different General Controls control panel. But even early Performas are still Macs, and you can install the standard, later system software on them; and the Launcher and the special General Controls control panel became part of later system software versions.

No HFS Plus startup. Performa models based on the '040 chip can't make full use of the Extended format option for hard drives introduced with OS 8.1. (This special formatting option is covered in detail in Chapter 4.) An '040 machine can't start up from an HFS Plus drive, nor can it store virtual memory files on one. It can, however, access disks formatted for HFS Plus.

Performa equivalents. Because of the original marketing idea for Performas (mainstream vs. Apple dealer), many of the early Performa models are basically the equivalent of some other Mac:

Performa	*Other Mac*
200	Classic II
400	LC II
405, 410, 430	LC II (plus modem and larger drive)
450	LC III
460, 466, 467	LC III (with faster clock speed)
550, 560	LC 550
575, 577, 578	LC 575
600, 600CD	IIvx (without cache card and FPU)
630	LC 630
630 DOS	LC 630 DOS

And, for balance, many of the recent Performa models are almost exactly the same as the PowerMac model with the same number (like a 6100). —SZA/JK

The missing modem port. Performas with built-in modems still have a modem port—but it's covered with a little plastic cap because it's dead, blocked by the internal modem. You can resurrect it if you need it for an external modem (because you bought one that's faster than the internal) or for some other serial-port device. Open the Performa case and take out the internal modem. That's it. Oh, and take off the plastic cap.

The 5300/100 LC heat sink. If you're adding or removing a SIMM from the slot next to the processor on a 5300/100 LC board, you have to (I hate to tell you this) remove the heat sink on the logic board first, and then replace it when you're finished. You'll have to pry off the four corner tabs of the heat sink on the back of the board, then remove it from the top of the board. Install or change the SIMM, and then replace the heat sink.

Not Your Mainstream Mac

Ephemeral Macs. Did you ever hear of the Mac TV? An all-in-one design, 32MHz-'030 with an 8MB RAM limit, a CD-ROM drive, a 14-inch color monitor, stereo speakers—and a TV tuner, all in a consumer-electronics black casing? It was an odd animal, with very limited availability during its short lifetime, so don't be surprised if you never knew of its existence.

There are other Mac models whose names are sometimes bandied about, yet it's hard to find solid information about them. This is usually because the model was strictly for the overseas market. The IIvi, for instance, was basically the same as the IIvx; the Color Classic II was a slightly improved version of the now-defunct compact unit; and, the 5300 (not to be confused with the PowerBook 5300) was a 100MHz Performa 5200.

The Anniversary Mac. Jerry Seinfeld wasn't the only one with this Mac model (it replaced his earlier one, also apparently unused, back in the corner of his TV living room), but he was one of only a few. This 250MHz 603e machine's chief appeal was its sleek black styling, but it came with lots of special stuff, like a Bose sound system (including integrated stereo speakers and subwoofer), a TV and radio tuner, and a special keyboard with detachable touchpad. Nearly everyone was put off by the incredibly high price tag.

The somewhat confusing name—the Twentieth Anniversary Mac—referred to Apple's birthday, not the Mac's.

> ***The Mac, some Mac, any Mac that's any good will be cloned.***
>
> *MacUser, June 1988*

Mac clones. In early Mac days, a "clone" was definitely a Bad Thing: an illegal (and therefore behind-the-times and/or very glitchy) copy of the Mac's ROMs and supporting hardware in a cheaper setup than you could get from Apple. After a decade or so, a clone became a Good Thing, with Apple licensing its technology so other companies could build Macs by any other name.

Now, a clone is a non-existent thing: Apple changed its strategy to boost its own sales and save the company from a slow, painful death by canceling all licensing agreements. Whether the strategy succeeds remains to be seen. Clones that came and went include PowerComputing, Daystar, Radius, APS, and UMax. The specs for clone machines aren't in the charts in this book, but you can find them in Newer's GURU guide (described earlier) and on various Mac-related web sites.

The Servers. Any Mac can work as a file server on a network, but Apple has provided two lines of machines specifically for that purpose. Workgroup Servers and Network Servers come without monitors or keyboards, but with hardware enhancements like support for up to 20 (Workgroup series) or 70 (Network series) SCSI devices. Some also come with various workgroup/network administration software. The first Workgroup server was basically a Quadra with a tape backup drive, but subsequent models are all PowerPC-based, and the latest are G3 models. There's a chart at the end of the chapter that lists the Server models.

Macintosh DOS and Windows. Mac models with "DOS Compatible" in their names are two, two, two computers in one. The PowerMac 6100/66 DOS Compatible, the LC 630 DOS Compatible, and the Performa 630 and 640CD DOS Compatibles each came with a 486DX2 processor on a separate card inside.

But that processor is to the PC world what the '040 is to the Mac world (and, heaven knows, there's *no* parallel to DOS in the Mac world). Later Compatible models include a Pentium processor instead, and their names use the phrase *PC Compatible.*

Creating a hybrid. You don't have to buy a DOS or PC Compatible Mac model: you can make one. Apple's not the only manufacturer making Pentium-based PCI cards that let you put another computer inside your computer. Besides the Apple **PC Compatibility Card**, there's the **Détante** from Radius and the **OrangePC Coprocessor** from Orange Micro. The cards range in price from $700 to $1200, depending on which processor and speed you're buying.

But you can buy a low-end or mid-range Pentium machine for the same price (or less), so you'll have to decide if you'd rather have two or two-in-one. Sure, you'll save on needing two monitors if you opt for the card route, and it'll save desk space, too, but you'll have to share the hard drive and add more memory.

When you need access to a PC, the hardware route has a big advantage because it's the "real thing"; software emulation, however, is handy for just an occasional foray to the other side when speed isn't critical. (You'll find information on PC emulation in Chapter 8.)

Older Macs

Quadra and Centris

Centris and Quadra. The short-lived Centris line debuted in early 1993, in the midst of a veritable explosion of new Mac models; they were the first to use the '040 processor. Within a year, these models were sucked into the Quadra line in Apple's effort to streamline its offerings.

The Quadras derived their name from the '040 chip. They introduced the "tower" style case that offers bays for extra internal storage devices; they were also the first Macs to include Ethernet network connections.

The Quadra/Centris combo. The Centris 650, introduced with a 25MHz processor, got a boost to 33MHz and was re-christened the Quadra 650 less than a year later. So, you'll often see the name Quadra/Centris used to refer to it and to the 610, which was also renamed a Quadra after a speed boost to 25MHz.

For some Quadra/Centris models, like the 650, there are minor differences between the two, like whether or not an FPU was standard or optional. Other Quadra/Centris models, like the 660AV, are absolutely identical.

No HFS Plus startup. Although Centrises and Quadras can run OS 8, they can't make full use of the Extended format option for hard drives introduced with OS 8.1. (This special formatting option is covered in detail in Chapter 4.) An '040 machine can't start up from an HFS Plus drive, nor can it store virtual memory files on one. It can, however, access disks formatted for HFS Plus.

The AV models. The Quadra and Centris AV models were the first aimed at multimedia and other audio and video mavens. Their DSP processor helps speed data transfers (sound and video are hefty packages of data). They can output directly to TV or tape using NTSC, PAL, or S-video signals, and can record and play back video and CD-quality stereo sound.

Greenish-screen fix. If you're using the Apple Basic Color Monitor on a Centris or Quadra, you may find the screen is greenish or washed-out blue. Use the Apple Basic Color Monitor extension to clear it up.

Quadra 950 display problem. If you use the built-in video card and set the monitor to millions of colors, you may find that many graphics images don't display correctly. Use the 950 Color Addition extension to clear it up.

Centris and Quadra memory interleaving. For Quadra and Centris models 610, 650, and 800, you can get up to a ten percent speed boost by installing SIMMs in the correct order because they support memory interleaving (discussed earlier in the chapter). Keep SIMMs in pairs in adjacent slots; for instance, 8-meg SIMMs in the first two slots and 4-meg SIMMs in the next two, instead of alternating SIMM sizes in the four slots.

The Quadra 900/950 conundrum. When you check the table at the end of the chapter, you'll see that the Quadra 900 is listed as using a maximum of 64MB of RAM, while the 950's max is 256. Whether or not that's actually true is debatable, depending on the source of your information. I, of course, checked with Apple for you—but that was little help. Their deep-level memory guideline treats both computers the same, but these are the specs: 16 slots to handle 1, 4, 8, or 16MB SIMMs; 8 and 16-meg SIMMs are not "officially supported" on either platform since they were not part of the test cycle; 256MB maximum RAM limit. Those facts don't fit together: use the largest approved size and you get a 64-meg limit (16 banks of 4-meg SIMMs, with nothing on the logic board).

Okay, so maybe 256MB is the theoretical limit. But check other Apple literature—made for "the masses" instead of the techies—and you'll see the machines listed differently: a 64MB maximum for the 900, and 256MB for the 950. So, that's what's in our chart.

The Cache Switch control panel. The Cache Switch control panel is strictly for '040 Macs—Quadra and Centris models—because they have built-in caches that act independently of the disk cache. The radio button choices in the control panel aren't exactly helpfully labeled.

Click the Faster button to use the full speed of your machine; use the More Compatible button if you're having trouble running software that's even older than your Mac, even though you may find its speed cut in half. (That is, in fact, the reason for the Cache Switch—when the Quadras first came out, software that didn't strictly adhere to Apple's programming guidelines often had trouble working at all.)

The buttons are actually labeled *Faster (Caches Enabled)* and *More Compatible (Caches Disabled)*. Note the use of the plural *caches*. These machines have two caches, one for instructions and one for data, that are switched on and off together.

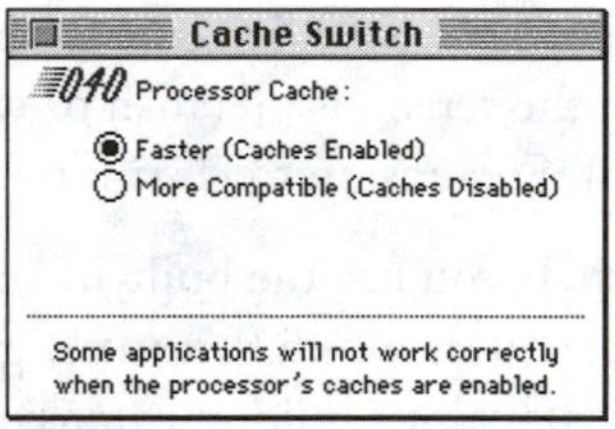

Unlike most control panel settings, you don't have to restart the computer for the settings in Cache Switch to take effect.

Golden Oldies

The II Line. The Mac II line started with—what else—the Mac II, which was the first *modular* Mac. It had no built-in screen but came with slots so you could add a video card of your choice (not that there was much choice then) and other cards as they became available. The Mac II was the first to go beyond the 68000 processor chip; it uses the 68020, while all the other Macs in the line use the '030 chip.

During the five-year life span of the II line, six other models came out:

- The **IIx** introduced the '030 chip and included an FPU; it also was the first to use 1.4MB floppy drives.
- The **IIcx** was a slightly faster IIx, with three NuBus slots instead of six.

- The **IIci** ran at 25MHz instead of its predecessors' 16MHz, and was the first Mac to have a built-in video card and a cache card slot.
- The **IIsi**, meant as a low-cost alternative to the ci, introduced the "pizza box" case, RAM on the motherboard, and a sound input port with a microphone.
- The **IIvx** replaced the IIci, and provided a now-standard innovation: an internal CD-ROM drive.
- The top of the II line was the **IIfx**, with its 40MHz processor and six NuBus slots.

IN THE BEGINNING

There used to be some logic behind the Mac naming conventions. Not a lot, but some.

The second and third Mac models were named simply 512 and 512e (although the popular name was *Fat Mac*). The Mac Plus had a lot of pluses, with its 800K drive, SCSI port, and a full meg of memory; the Mac SE was apparently named for *system expansion* because it had an expansion slot; the SE/30 was an SE with an '030 processor.

In the meantime, there was the Mac II line which started with, of course, the Mac II and then added the Mac IIx, whose capabilities extended beyond those of the II.

But that's where all the problems began. The important difference between the SE and the SE/30 was that '030 processor; the move from the II to the IIx was the same. But you couldn't call it the Mac II/30 because at the time two numbers with a slash between them, like 4/40, indicated memory and hard drive capacity and II/30 would be way too confusing. And why couldn't they use the II/IIx convention for the SE upgrade? Well, if they added the x to the SE…

The LC line. The LC line was meant to be the low-cost alternative to other Macs (that's what the "LC" stands for) and they were, for a while. But once the Performas—that other low-cost alternative—were no longer limited to stores like Sears, the LC family became an educational-institution-only line before it just faded away. (Its LC cognomen lives on in some PowerMac models.)

The LC models range from the original LC with its 16MHz '020 chip to the later '040 models, but they're all severely limited in expansion possibilities, with no NuBus or PCI slots.

Classics. The first Mac Classic was a throwback in more than just the return to a compact case: it also returned users to a 9-inch black-and-white screen and the poky 68000 processor, with no FPU and a 4-meg RAM limit—hardly better than the long-dead Mac Plus. The Classic II bettered the situation with a 16MHz '030 chip and the ability to address up to 10 megs of memory. The Color Classic finally put a color screen into a classic case, allowed for an optional FPU, and provided a PDS slot. But to no avail: Performa models were finally offered as all-in-one units with larger screens, and no one wanted a compact after that!

Ancient history. How can we not mention, at least in passing, the Mac that started it all, and its immediate successors?

- The original Mac, which we retroactively refer to as the 128K, was ground-breaking in concept, design and execution—all in 128K of memory, with a single, 400K floppy drive. The so-called Fat Mac, with quadruple the memory (all of 512K), was introduced about ten months later. That's over $2600 per meg!) The 512Ke, released the following year, offered an 800K drive.

- The Mac Plus came out two years after the first Mac, with an 800K floppy drive, a SCSI port for a hard drive (even though there was no hard drive available), and a full megabyte of memory, expandable to 4MB.
- The Mac SE showed up more than a year after the Plus, with an internal slot (that you couldn't get at), the ADB connector for keyboard and mouse, and a second floppy or an internal hard disk; later production models included the SuperFloppy drive. The SE/30 introduced the '030 chip and the FPU, and was the first compact Mac to break the 4-meg RAM barrier.

Memory and Mac II line. Here's what you should know about memory and the Mac II models:

- The Mac II and IIx require a special type of SIMM if you're using larger than 1-meg modules. Be sure to specify your model when ordering SIMMs and make certain the vendor knows the difference. They have to be PAL *(programmable logic array)* SIMMs that have one chip beyond the usual eight on a SIMM.
- In the Mac II, you can't put SIMMs larger than 1MB in Bank A. And, if the Bank A SIMMs are larger than the ones in Bank B, the memory won't be recognized.
- If a Mac II is upgraded to use a SuperDrive, which includes new ROM chips, the model's inherent memory problems (mentioned earlier in this entry) are solved. You'll be able to use standard instead of PAL SIMMs, you can use large SIMMs in Bank A, and it doesn't matter which bank the larger set of SIMMs is in.
- To take advantage of more than 8MB of physical RAM, the Macintosh II must have a PMMU installed and Apple's 32-bit System Enabler or MODE 32.
- The Mac IIfx uses SIMMs different from any other Mac: it needs special 64-pin SIMMs.
- On a IIci using its internal video card, keep Bank A (the one closer to the drive) filled with the smaller SIMMs if you're using different densities in

the two banks. The ci's built-in video steals RAM from the first bank; with this SIMM arrangement, you can keep things from slowing down any more than necessary.

Speeding up the IIci and IIsi. Upping the cache amount in the Memory control panel on a Mac IIci or IIsi boosts their performance considerably because of the way these two models use regular RAM to help their video displays. On a IIsi with color or gray set to four levels or higher in the Monitor (or Monitors and Sound) control panel, set the cache to 768K. This keeps the cache and video-dedicated RAM in the main memory chips on the motherboard instead of in SIMMs, resulting in much faster performance. To get the same benefits for a IIci set to four or more grays or colors, there are two additional conditions: there should be 5, 9, or 11 megs of RAM installed; and the four 256K SIMMs that make the odd-number total of RAM must be in Bank A (the one closest to the disk drive).

Both models will show significant speed increases if you use a separate video card instead of the built-in one.

And, for the IIci only:

- If you're using the internal video and have different-density SIMMs in each bank, keep Bank A filled with the smaller SIMMs.
- For an all-round, but small, speed increase, keep 32-bit addressing turned on in the Memory control panel even if you don't have more than 8 megs of memory.
- Finally, if yours is an early IIci that doesn't have a cache card, see if you can get one—they were originally $70 but if you can find one at all, it will only be about $20 now. It's well worth it if you're sticking with the ci for a while. It's easy to see if you have one: Open the case and look at the motherboard—the cache slot is right in the center.

Sound on the IIsi. The IIsi has a finicky connection between the motherboard and the speaker; sometimes the sound output quits until you restart. Here are some things you can do about it: Open the Sound control panel, set the volume to maximum, and then reset it to the volume you want. Or, attach an external speaker to the sound port, since the problem is the connection to the internal speaker. Or, open the case, unplug the speaker cable, clean the contacts, and plug the cable back in.

Catch LCII. The LCII can address a maximum of 10 megs of memory. It has 4MB on board, and two slots; you have to put the same size SIMMs in each slot. So, putting a 4-meg SIMM in each slot gives you a total of 12 megs with the on-board memory. But the LCII can see only 10 of them. (Now do you get the pathetic pun in the entry title?)

Classic and Classic II memory expansion. The Classic came with one meg of RAM soldered to the logic board. If you want to add RAM, you have to use Apple's **Macintosh Classic 1MB Expansion Card**. It has an additional meg of memory, and two SIMM slots (the 1MB in the title refers to the on-board memory—you fill the slots to get more than the 1MB). Since the Classic can handle only 4MB of RAM, you can put only 1MB SIMMs in each slot.

The Classic II also uses the expansion card, but the card came with the machine. Classic II specs note 2MB of on-board memory, but that refers to one on the logic board and one on the expansion card. Since the Classic II can handle 10 megs of memory, you can put two 4-meg SIMMs in the slots.

For the Plus and SE. The Mac Plus and SE have four SIMM slots that are paired in two banks. These models can't address any more than 4 megs of memory, so you'll want to put a 1-meg SIMM in every slot; you don't have to worry about the banks at all.

But you do have to worry about the special attention these two machines need if you're adding memory. Not only are they difficult to open, but they also have special jumpers or resistors on their motherboards that need to be adjusted if you want to install their four-meg maximum memory. This is not a do-it-yourself job unless you really know what you're doing yourself. That doesn't necessarily mean you need a professional (in fact, few shops would know much about these relics); you might find an old hand in a user group who's done this before.

The rare ROM disk. The Classic has a unique feature: a *ROM disk* that lets you start up the machine with the built-in System 6.0.3 without any disk. To access it, you startup while holding down [⌘][Option][X][O].

When you have nothing better to do.... There are lots of nifty little things hidden in the older Mac models. (Maybe there are things in the newer Macs, too, but we haven't found them yet.)

- The IIci has a picture of its design team buried in it. Set the Mac's date to 9/20/89, set the monitor to 256 colors, and restart while holding down [⌘][Option][C][I]. Restart by using the reset switch.
- The IIfx design team left its picture inside, too: Set the clock to 3/19/89, the monitor to 256 colors, and then restart holding down [⌘][Option][F][X]. Restart by using the reset switch.

In each case, restart the Mac by using the reset switch.

- There's a secret message in the Mac Plus. Press the interrupt switch at the left side of the computer. Type *G 40E118* (type the space and use a zero, not the letter O), then press [Return].
- The SE has the same secret message. Press the interrupt switch and type *G 40E118* and press [Return].
- The SE also has a built-in slide show. Press the interrupt switch, type *G 41D89A*, then press [Return].

- For the SE/30's secret message, press the interrupt switch and type *DM 4082E853 20* (type both spaces!) and press Return. (You want to know the message. *What are you staring at?* No, I know you're reading the book—that's the message.)

Buying Hardware

Being a Smart Consumer

Lead time. Magazines and newspapers set up their advertising in advance, and things often change between the time the ad was designed and when you see it. For magazines, the lead time is at least a month—that's why so many ads for things with volatile prices, like memory chips, say "call for price." As for local newspapers and stores, ads usually go in on Thursday for the Sunday paper—so if Apple announces a new machine or price cut on Friday, it won't be reflected in the ad. And supplemental circulars are prepared *months* in advance, so the prices on older models might be entirely different by the time you see the ad.

You don't need a MAP. Apple, and some other vendors, restrict their resellers with something called *MAP—minimum advertised price*. That means that no matter what the store might be willing to sell the computer for, they can't advertise below Apple's set price. How does knowing this help you?

- The price in the store might be lower than the one advertised in the newspaper; don't compare prices based just on ads.
- A store may make up a "bundle," or offer a great price on a second, non-MAP item, when you buy the computer at the advertised price.
- The salesperson, or the manager, might be willing to sell it for less than the marked price; it can't hurt to ask.

Roll your own bundle. The profit margin on Macs is relatively small, and so there may not be much bargaining room when you start with its sticker price. But smaller items usually have larger profit margins, so you might suggest a roll-your-own bundle that includes cables, printer paper, and some software, at 20 to 30 percent off their sticker prices.

This is also a good reason to plan to buy lots of stuff all at once instead of the computer first, and peripherals and supplies later.

Money-back guarantee. Don't buy from a store that doesn't offer a money-back guarantee for hardware, no questions asked, for two weeks to a month. And make sure you check the "fine print" on that guarantee:

- Items like printers are often excluded from this guarantee because once you try them, they're used and can't be resold.

- Are you going to be charged a "re-stocking" fee if you return the item?
- For mail order: Do they pay the shipping on the return? Do they reimburse you for the original shipping? Is there a "handling fee" separate from shipping, and is it non-refundable?
- If you pay by check originally, will you have to wait weeks for a cash refund?

Get price protection. Shop at a store that offers 30-day price protection. That means if the price drops within 30 days of your purchase, you can be refunded the difference. Make sure you keep your receipts, and check the price just before the 30-day period is up. (This is hardly worth the effort on a $30 piece of software that drops by a few dollars. But when your new Mac's price drops $200 immediately after you buy it...)

Even if a store doesn't advertise this policy, you may find that they're willing to do it—especially if they offer a return policy, because otherwise you could return the item at the original, high price and just buy another box at the new, low price. (Sometimes it helps to point this out to sales or management!)

Already-opened boxes. If the box you're buying has obviously been opened and re-closed, don't take anybody's word for its being because of some "stock" or "check" procedure. Assume the box has been opened and emptied: Open the box in the store, make sure the inner packaging is in shape and that everything, including cables, manuals, and registration cards, is still there.

Which brings us to another point: Often items are returned to stores simply because a customer changed his mind, or didn't like it, or decided on something even better—it's not necessarily because there's something wrong with the item. You can ask if there's any returned merchandise available at a discount—the store can't always return it to Apple, nor can it sell it as brand-spanking new, and is often willing to sell it at some discount.

store.apple.com
maconnection.com
macwarehouse.com
smalldog.com
outpost.com

Mail-order and online merchants. For years I've bought software and small hardware (memory, drives) through mail-order but recommended "real" stores when it came to the computer itself. With Mac sales down in the world-at-large, computer stores stock only a few models and have even fewer knowledgeable sales people. Buying the Mac itself through mail order or on the web is a good approach, and even Apple has opened an online store for sales, imaginatively named The Apple Store. In addition, here are a few places I can recommend from experience: MacConnection, MacWarehouse, (print catalogs with web sites), Small Dog Electronics, and Cyberian Outpost (web-only).

A few more points. A few final admonitions:

- If the price seems too good to be true, it probably is. Dealer costs are almost always the same. Check the fine print.
- An Apple warranty always applies to a new Mac no matter where you buy it, but service and support vary from one store to another.
- Avoid shopping at crowded, rushed times: weekends, holiday sales, the hour before closing. When the store is crowded, you can't get undivided attention or bargaining time.
- If a salesperson says an item is out of stock and he doesn't know when it will be available, that's the truth—Apple never tells when back orders will be filled. If you get the reverse ("We'll have it next week" or "It will be three months"), don't count on it.
- Using a credit card for the purchase is always your best defense, no matter where you're shopping, since you can stop a disputed payment. Using anything other than a credit card for mail-order merchandise is the height of foolishness.

Buying a New Mac

Falling prices. Computer prices are always falling. There's always a new model just around the corner. If you focus on these two facts, you'll never buy a computer.

tidbits.com

So, other than watching the timing in regard to Apple's releasing new models (which usually drops the price of the current models), when you're ready, go get a computer. Check your favorite web sites for up-to-date information; the electronic newsletter TidBITs is a good source of information about upcoming new releases.

The penultimate Mac. Unless you're doing high-end video or multimedia, you don't need a top-of-the-line Mac. Second from top can save you hundreds of dollars and will probably still be more than you need. A model just recently discontinued (as long as it's not dead-end technology, like a processor chip that won't run the next operating system) is always a bargain.

Hidden costs for the second-time buyer. When you already have a Mac and want to buy a new one, take into account all the non-obvious costs of upgrading. The memory you added to your old Mac to boost it to 48MB might not fit in the new model—and the buyer of your old Mac may not want all that memory. If you have a video card for a large monitor, that may not fit in the new machine either, and you'll need a new one—and, once again, your buyer may not want that card or large monitor. Finally, your software: if you're switching from a 68000-based Mac to a PowerPC-based one, you may need different versions of your basic software packages to run on the new machine.

The three-year plan. Or two. My father's car-buying philosophy was to buy a new car every three years—before the current one started having trouble and/or had racked up enough mileage to really drop its trade-in value.

My computer-buying philosophy was the same for a long time, because a three-year-old machine brought in a decent sum—it's not *that* out of date, and there will always be new computer buyers on a tight budget. In the past few years, I've changed that recommendation to keep closer to a two-year plan, because as the price of a new computer drops, so does that of used computers.

I also put the trickle-down theory into practice: when I get a new computer, the kids get mine, and theirs gets sold. It keeps them upgraded, and I have a reasonably new machine to fall back on if something happens to my main one. (Oh, okay, you might as well know: my husband's Mac is also in the house—he has another one at work—and we have three PowerBooks, too. It's not likely I'll be Mac-less for a second of my current existence.)

Buying a Used Mac

Is an old Mac usable? Well, it depends, of course, on how old the Mac is and what you want to do with it. After all, an eight-track tape player is usable if it comes with all the tapes you'll ever want to listen to. Likewise even the oldest Mac, if it has its original software, is still usable. You could type in the original MacWrite, play in MacPaint, and print on an ImageWriter printer. But you couldn't get support for those programs or the system software if you have a problem, and you couldn't run any new software on it. And you couldn't share information with any other users with newer Macs—the disks they're using won't work in your machine and, in all likelihood, you're not using software that's compatible anymore, either.

Older Macs have many problems for someone who wants to stay even reasonably current on the software front. Newer software, even if it's not written strictly for a PowerPC-based Mac, needs lots of memory and there are 8- and 10-meg limits on older machines. And if the software runs on a non-PowerPC machine, it may run so slowly that it's practically unusable, especially on something less than an '040 machine. Then there's the absence of a CD-ROM drive, and relatively small internal hard drive to consider.

In general, if you can get a Mac that will do what you need, don't worry about "better and faster" unless that's in your budget. But even if you're on a tight budget and buying used equipment, don't buy more than one (or possibly two) generations behind the current models. And, finally, don't worry about buying a discontinued model: just because the line's discontinued, that doesn't mean the Mac stops working.

Buying used. Buying a used computer isn't like buying a used car. You're not getting something with high mileage and components ready to fall apart; most faulty hardware problems show up in the first couple months of use, while under warranty and in the original owner's possession. Still, there are many things to consider if you're not buying new.

- **The CPU**. It's not just a matter of PowerPC versus non-PowerPC processors, nor is it just *"Oh, I don't mind if it's going to be slow—I'm not all that swift myself."* Lots of software, and OS 8 itself, won't run on less than an '040 chip.
- **Memory**. Choose About this Computer or About this Macintosh on the Apple menu to make sure you're getting all the RAM you think you are.
- **Hard drive**. If the machine starts up, you'll be able to see the hard drive and verify that it's working. But check the size: if it's around 100MB or less, you'll need to get a new drive—the OS 8 System Folder alone can run upwards of 90MB.
- **Keyboard**. Check every single key, and the supporting feet that hold the keyboard up at an angle. Wiggle the cable at both ends (the computer and the keyboard) and make sure that doesn't cause a problem with the connection. It's easy to buy a new keyboard, but it will run you about another $100.
- **Mouse**. Roll it around and make sure the cursor on the screen moves accordingly. Wiggle the cable at both ends while you're using it. If the performance is erratic, pop out the ball and make sure there's not a lot of dirt inside causing the problem.
- **Floppy drive**. Make sure it can read a variety of disks—bring your own. Format a disk, too, and make sure that works without a problem.
- **Screen**. Middle-aged monitors start losing their brightness. You may not even be able to identify a "faded" monitor unless you're next to, or used to, a very bright one. You don't have to avoid the purchase if it's less than shiningly bright, but make sure you can live with it. (Don't forget to try the brightness controls!) A really old monitor might have some burn-in; turn it off and see if there's a ghost of the menubar on the blank screen. If there is, either don't buy it or use it as a bargaining point on the price.
- **Video card**. If there's a separate video card in the Mac, use the Monitors control panel to see what it is. If it's strictly a black-and-white affair, you'll certainly notice without the control panel, but it's hard to tell, just by looking, whether you've got, say, 4 or 16 shades of gray, or 256 or thousands of colors, or thousands or millions of colors. The list in the control panel will be clear. Clicking the Options button in the control panel will identify the specific video card in use.

Buying old and upgrading. Don't. Buying a used Mac that needs further upgrading is not usually a good idea. Spend a few hundred on the Mac, another hundred or so on memory, around two hundred for a big hard drive—and you've got the cost of a new, low-end Mac. Or at least certainly the cost of a newer used Mac!

Buying a used PowerBook. If you're shopping for a used PowerBook (which can be a great bargain if all you need is a traveling word processor and e-mail machine), there are some additional things to keep in mind:

- The oldest PowerBooks have small hard drives, severe restrictions on memory, and laughable 2400-baud modems. Figure in the cost of a new modem and possibly another hard drive; you can't do much about memory limitations.
- Rechargeable batteries aren't immortal; if the PowerBook is two years old or more, you're going to need a new battery (or two). You may also want to buy a newer, more efficient power adapter if yours is an older model.

See the PowerBook chapter for more details.

Used versus reconditioned. Buying a *reconditioned*, or refurbished, Mac is not the same as buying a used one (and buying a *factory*-refurbished unit is different from buying one refurbished by a third party). When someone buys a Mac and returns it either because there's a problem or he just changed his mind, a store can't legally sell it as new.

Apple gets these items back eventually. If there was a problem, the component is replaced; then, everything is wrapped just like new, with all the interior packaging, manuals, and so on. Then it's sold at a discount. I've been recommending refurbished units to people on a budget who don't need cutting-edge setups (refurbished units are usually a step behind the current models), and there's not been a single problem with any of the units I've been involved with.

smalldog.com
store.apple.com

Most resellers on the Web have refurbished units available at least occasionally. Try Small Dog Electronics, the User Group Connection, and the Apple Store.

Upgrades

PowerMacs

G3: Gee whiz! Writing about almost any product in a book is like shooting at a moving target, but when it comes to hardware upgrades, the targets are moving even faster than usual. As I write this, G3 upgrade cards are just coming out; the companies providing them are playing leapfrog, each pushing the speed envelope a little further with each product, and the prices are stratospheric for the top-end cards. So, while the general advice in this entry (and others in this section) will remain sound, the particulars—product availability, product specs, and, especially, prices—will be changing on at least a monthly basis in the early stages of the game.

Upgrading a "standard" PowerPC to a G3 can be a really good move; how good a move it is can depend on the price, and the price often depends on what machine you're starting out with. In addition, there's a vast difference in price depending on the speed of the processor on the upgrade card, and the size and speed of the backside cache that comes along with it. (Backside cache? Didn't you read the entire chapter up to this point? We covered that quite a while ago.)

For instance, Newer Technologies' **MaxPowr Pro G3** upgrades offer several different choices in processor speeds, and a variety of cache sizes and speeds. As you can see (the current-as-of-this-writing prices are used here), a high-end upgrade is three times the price of a low-end one—and costs more than a brand-new low-end G3 machine!

Processor speed	***Cache size***	***Cache speed***	***Price***
220 MHz	512K	110 MHz	$540
250 MHz	512K	125 MHz	$680
266 MHz	1MB	133 MHz	$980
300 MHz	512K	150 MHz	$980
300 MHz	1MB	150 MHz	$1330
300 MHz	1MB	300 MHz	$1930

powerlogix.com
totalimpact.com
newertech.com

Newer isn't the only vendor offering a variety of G3 upgrades. Total Impact's **PowerUP 750** boards range from a 250MHz processor with a 125MHz, 512K backside cache to a 275MHz processor with a matched-speed 1MB cache. PowerLogix's **PowerForce** cards offer processor speeds of 250 and 275MHz, both with 275MHZ, 1MB caches.

Which PowerMacs can you upgrade with the cards? The list varies slightly from one vendor to another, but you can pretty much count on being able to upgrade a Mac from any one of these series: 7300, 7500, 7600, 8500, 8600, 9500, and 9600.

G3-ing an x100 Mac. At this point, there's only one vendor offering a G3 upgrade for your 6100, 7100, or 8100 Mac, and it's a bargain. Newer has two versions of its **MaxPowr G3** card for your 6100: 210MHz ($500) and 240MHz ($700). For the 7100 and 8100, the prices are a hundred dollars higher.

The 604e upgrade. If a G3 upgrade isn't in your budget, perhaps you can treat yourself to a fast 604e PowerPC processor (speeds from 150 to 250 MHz) upgrade card, doubling or even tripling your Mac's performance. **MAXpowr Citation** from Newer, **PowerUP 604e** from Total Impact,

DayStar's upgrade card, and **PowerBoost** from PowerLogix can supercharge your 7300, 7500, 7600, 8500, or 9500 for $200-$450.

All these companies provide benchmark comparisons so you can see how much of a speed boost you might get from this kind of upgrade; you can also check the reviews in the "back issues" of magazines like Macworld that keep their information on their web sites. But for a less-than-technical evaluation, here's what happened when I put a 200Mhz 604e card in my 7600, replacing its 120Mhz 603 processor (not coincidentally, I did it while writing this chapter), with times given in minutes and seconds:

	Before	*After*
Startup	2:24	2:00
Launch Word 6	:28	:18
Completely expand System Folder to list all 2500 items	1:10	:50
Scroll through completely expanded System Folder	4:27	3:50

As far as I'm concerned, the minor speed boost was not worth a $200 upgrade. Make sure your step up in an upgrade is a big enough leap to make it worth the money—moving up from a 601 to a 604e, for instance, makes sense.

The collateral upgrade costs. Check carefully as to what else on your Mac system will have to be changed if you upgrade your processor. When I went from a 603 to a 604e, for instance, I had to change the cache card ($50) that had come with the Mac because it had some timing problems, and replace my 70ns memory with 60ns memory ($200). Together, that cost more than the upgrade card! (Not to mention, as a side issue, that I ordered the card from MacWorks and it didn't work, and they insisted on a re-stocking fee as well as extra shipping charges for both the return of the card and its replacement (which I told them I didn't want)… and on and on. Thank goodness my bank let me stop the charge card payment—and it's still in dispute months later because, despite their verbal agreement to forgo the re-stocking fee because the card was defective, MacWorks won't credit my account!)

Then came the G3 card. The surprise expense there was also extra memory. I got past the first hurdle, which is having just the right type and speed of RAM—I already had that. But you can't use virtual memory on a PowerPC Mac that's upgraded to a G3 because it's too slow and causes crashes from timing problems. Since programs use so much more memory if there's no virtual memory turned on (as detailed in Chapter 12), I had to add another 64 megs of memory to my Mac so I could continue working on this book (which has me keep Word, FileMaker, Photoshop, QuarkXPress, and Explorer open at all times!).

Reset the logic board. If you replace the processor card in your Mac, make sure you reset the motherboard. There's a little red button on most PowerMac motherboards (on my 7600, the button was gray and *very* difficult to see); if you swap processor cards, press the button before you put the CPU case back together. You'll find that this also resets the internal clock for time and date.

Use a cache. If your PowerMac has an optional cache, and you didn't opt for it, change your mind! Installing a cache can give you an immediate speed boost of ten to fifteen percent. (You won't see the same significant improvement if you simply upgrade a 256K cache to a 512K one.)

Older Macs

To upgrade or not to upgrade. At this point in Mac development, it doesn't pay to upgrade a non-PowerPC Mac. If you need more speed and better performance, there's nothing you can do for the older machines that will make you happy. Accelerators that replace one 68K chip with another won't get you where you want to go; a clock boost for an existing chip is unreliable at best and still won't perform well enough. Even replacing the logic board with a PowerPC logic board (if you can find a compatible one) is a questionable move: you'll still need more memory and a larger hard drive, you'll be stuck with NuBus slots instead of PCI, the internal bus speed will slow things down—and you'll have spent enough on the upgrades to pay for a new low-end PowerPC, or a used model that's still lots newer than yours.

If you can't move to a new machine yet, adding memory and getting a larger hard drive is a reasonable stopgap measure: memory's cheap, a hard drive can go with you to the next machine, and you'll reap immediate benefits from either improvement. If that just won't do it, consider buying a used Mac that's better and faster than the one you're using—there are some incredible bargains out there.

shrevesystems.com
smalldog.com
preowned.com

Getting upgrade components for the oldest Macs is becoming more and more difficult. Your best bets for older parts and upgrades are Shreve Systems, Small Dog Electronics and Pre-Owned Electronics.

PowerBook upgrades
Chapter 23

Apple 68K CPU upgrades. Apple no longer provides logic board upgrades for older Macs, except for some PowerPC upgrades. If you're buying or dealing with used equipment whose owners insist that there's a different machine "inside" than that identified on the outside, this list of past Apple CPU upgrades might be helpful:

Original model	*Changed to this*	*With part number*
Mac Classic	Mac Classic II	M1545LL/A
Mac LC or LC II	Mac LC III	M1386LL/A
Performa 400, 405, 410, 430	Performa 450	M0375LL/A
Mac II or IIx	Mac IIfx	M1330LL/A
Mac IIvx, Performa 600, 600CD	Quadra 650	M1421LL/A
Quadra 900	Quadra 950	M6940ZA

Tables

Rich Wolfson was the special contributor for this section, though his initials aren't on the entries.

The charts. There are three charts here, for different groups of Macs. The entire Mac family could be broken down in many different ways: desk models versus compacts; PowerPC versus non-PowerPC; 68K models divided into '030, '040, and others; separate charts for separate model lines. But the breakdown we're using is:

- PowerPC-Based Macs
- '040 Macs
- Older Macs

PowerBook spec charts

Chapter 23

A separate list for PowerPC models needs no explanation. But there's a good reason for a separate '040 list: they're the only non-PowerPC Macs than can run OS 8, so they are still usable in a way the other 68K machines aren't. All the rest of the machines are grouped into the final chart, which includes, for old-times' sake, the original compact Macs along with everything else.

This division does present a few problems for someone looking up a model: Performas, for instance, are in all three charts, and LC models are in two of them. But there's a quick look-up guide in another entry coming up.

The models. There's little sense in listing every single Mac model ever made; the differences from one model to another are sometimes as minor as the inclusion of a CD-ROM drive. Other times, everything's the same except that the processor runs at a different speed—which is worth noting, but not worth giving a model another whole line in the chart!

Whenever models are nearly identical, they're combined into a single entry; so, for instance you won't find an entry for a Performa 5215 or 5216, since all the pertinent information is listed for the 5200. (Although in some instances, for clarity, multiple model names are listed on a single line—as for the Performa 400, 405, and 410.) Differences that warrant a separate entry are things like a different chip, a different internal drive standard, and different memory capacities. Differences that don't warrant a separate entry are, first of all, things that aren't even included in the chart (like the size of the original hard drive, an internal CD-ROM drive, or how much memory a model came with initially), as well as simply the speed of the processor chip.

As a general rule, the last two digits of a four-digit model number aren't listed separately in the chart, nor is the last digit of a three-digit model. There are exceptions where necessary: the 5260, for instance, uses a different chip from the rest of the 5200 series, so it needs a separate line. Other models rolled together are those like the 7600/120 and the 7600/132: since their only difference is the processor speed, the different available speeds are simply listed under the processor speed.

Where's my Performa/LC? Because Performa and LC models evolved quite a bit during their model lifetimes, you'll find them in more than one of these charts, based on their processor chips. Here's a quick roundup, by model number groups, of where they can be found:

	PowerPC-Based Chart	'040 Models Chart	Older Macs Chart
Performas			
2xx			all
4xx		47x	all others
5xx		57x	all others
6xx		all others	600
5xxx, 6xxx	all		
LC's			
LC, LC II, LCIII			all
4xx		all	
5xx		all others	520, 550
6xx		all	

The specs. The Spec Charts here try to be thorough without succumbing to the gotta-have-everything-listed syndrome. So, the columns in the chart list processors and their speeds, L2 caches (for PowerPC models), slots, and memory specification—the stuff you really need to know about.

- **Chip** and **Speed:** On the PowerPC chart, all the chips are, of course, PowerPC chips. On the other charts, all the chips are 68000-based Motorolas. When a model series had machines with different speeds, like the 6100/60 and 6100/66, the two different speeds are noted in the Speed column, but the machine is treated as a single model.
- **L2 cache:** This is only on PowerPCs; the chart notes whether one was standard or optional.
- **Internal drive:** IDE or SCSI is noted.
- **Slots:** The number of PCI or NuBus slots is noted, along with a list of other internal slots.
- **Memory:** For PowerPC models, the memory type (SIMM or DIMM) is noted; all SIMMs are 72-pin. For non-PowerPC models, all memory is SIMM-based, with the number of pins noted.

PowerPC-based Macs

	PROCESSOR			SLOTS		
Model	**Chip**	**Speed (MHz)**	**L2 cache**	**PCI**	**NuBus**	**Other**
G3 Models						
Tower models	750	266/300	●	6	-	-
Desktop models	750	233/266	●	3	-	CS
iMac	750	233	●	-	-	CS
PowerMac						
9600	604e	300/350	●	6	-	-
9500/200	604e	200	●	6	-	-
9500/180MP* 2CPU	604e	180	●	6	-	-
9500	604	120/132/150	●	6	-	-
8600	604e	200/250/300	●	3	-	-
8500	604	120/132/150/180	●	3	-	-
8100	601	80/100/110	●	-	3	(PDS filled)
7600/120	604	120/132	●	3	-	-
7500/100	601	100	opt	3	-	-
7300	604e	166/180/200	●	3	-	-
7200	601	75/90/120	opt	3	-	-
7100	601	66/80	opt	-	3	(PDS filled)
6500	603e	225/250/275/300	●	2	-	-
6400	603e	200	opt	2	-	CS, TV, video in/out
Anniversary Mac	603e	250	opt	1	-	-
6100	601	60/66	opt	-	1*	* NuBus *or* PDS
5500	603e	225	opt	1	-	CS, TV, video in/out
5400	603e	120/180/200	opt	1	-	CS, TV, video in/out
5300/100 LC	603e	100	●	-	-	LC, CS, TV, video in/out
5260	603e	100/120	●	-	-	LC, CS, TV, video in/out
5200/75 LC	603	75	●	-	-	LC, CS, TV, video in/out
4400	603e	160/200	●	2	-	-
Performa						
6400/200	603e	200	●	2	-	CS, TV, video in
6400/180	603e	180	opt	2	-	CS, TV, video in
6360	603e	160	opt	-	-	LC, CS, TV, video in/out
6260CD	603e	100	●	-	-	LC, CS, TV, video in/out
6300CD	603e	100/120	●	-	-	LC, CS, TV, video in/out
6200CD	603	75	●	-	-	LC, CS, TV, video in/out
6110CD	601	60	opt	-	1*	* NuBus *or* PDS
5400CD	603e	120	opt	1	-	CS, TV, video in/out
5260CD	603e	100	●	-	-	LC, CS, TV, video in/out
5300CD	603e	100	●	-	-	LC, CS, TV, video in/out
5200CD	603	75	●	-	-	LC, CS, TV, video in/out

		MEMORY					
Model	**Int. drive**	**Max**	**On-board**	**Slots**	**SIMM (72)**	**DIMM**	**Speed (ns)**
G3 Models							
Tower models	IDE	768	-	3	-	●	60
Desktop models	IDE	384	-	3	-	●	60
iMac	IDE	128	-	2	-	●	60
PowerMac							
9600	SCSI	768	-		-	-	
9500/200	SCSI	768	-	12	-	●	70
9500/180MP* 2CPU	SCSI	768	-	12	-	●	70
9500	SCSI	768	-	12	-	●	70
8600	SCSI	512	-	8	-	●	60
8500	SCSI	512	-	8	-	●	70
8100	SCSI	264	8	8	●	-	80
7600/120	SCSI	512	-	8	-	●	70
7500/100	SCSI	512	-	8	-	●	70
7300	SCSI	512	-	8	-	-	70
7200	SCSI	256	-	4	-	●	70
7100	SCSI	136	8	4	●	-	80
6500	IDE	128	-	2	-	●	60
6400	IDE	136	8	2	-	●	70
Anniversary Mac	SCSI	256	-	2	-	●	60
6100	SCSI	72	8	2	●	-	80
5500	IDE	128	8	2	-	●	70
5400	IDE	136	8	2	-	●	70
5300/100 LC	IDE	64	-	2	●	-	80
5260	IDE	64	-	2	●	-	80
5200/75 LC	IDE	64	-	2	●	-	80
4400	IDE	160	-	3	-	●	70
Performa							
6400/200	IDE	136	8	2	-	●	70
6400/180	IDE	136	8	2	-	●	70
6360	IDE	136	8	2	-	●	70
6260CD	IDE	64	-	2	●	-	80
6300CD	IDE	64	-	2	●	-	80
6200CD	IDE	64	-	2	●	-	80
6110CD	SCSI	72	8	2	●	-	80
5400CD	IDE	136	8	2	-	●	70
5260CD	IDE	64	-	2	●	-	80
5300CD	IDE	64	-	2	●	-	80
5200CD	IDE	64	-	2	●	-	80

'040 Macs

MODEL	PROCESSOR		SLOTS		MEMORY					
	Chip	Speed (MHz)	NuBus	Other	Internal Drive	Max (MB)	Onboard (MB)	Slots	# pins SIMMs	Speed (ns)
Performa										
475, 476	68LC040	50	-	LC PDS	SCSI	36	4	1	72	80
575, 577, 578	68LC040	66	-	LC PDS, CS	SCSI	36	4	1	72	80
580CD	68LC040	66	-	LC PDS, CS	IDE	52	4	2	72	80
630/630CD	68LC040	66	-	LC PDS, CS	IDE	36	4	1	72	80
630CD DOS Compatible	68LC040	66	-	CS	IDE	52	4	2	72	80
631CD	68LC040	66	-	LC PDS, CS	IDE	52	4	2	72	80
635CD	68LC040	66	-	LC PDS, CS	IDE	36	4	1	72	80
636/636CD	68LC040	66	-	LC PDS, CS	IDE	36	4	1	72	80
637CD	68LC040	66	-	LC PDS, CS	IDE	36	4	1	72	80
638CD	68LC040	66	-	LC PDS, CS	IDE	36	4	1	72	80
640CD DOS Compatible	68LC040	66	-	CS	IDE	52	4	2	72	80
Quadra/Centris										
Quadra 605	68LC040	50	-	LC III PDS	SCSI	36	4	1	72	80
Centris 610	68LC040	40	1	PDS	SCSI	68	4	2	72	80
Quadra 610	68040	50	1	PDS	SCSI	68	4	2	72	80
Quadra 610 DOS Compatible	68040	50	-	PDS	SCSI	68	4	2	72	80
Quadra 630	68040	66	-	LC PDS, CS	IDE	36	4	1	72	80
Centris 650	68040	50	3	PDS	SCSI	132	4	4	72	80
Quadra 650	68040	66	3	PDS	SCSI	136	8	4	72	80
Quadra/ Centris 660AV	68040	50	1	PDS	SCSI	68	4	2	72	70
Quadra 700	68040	50	2	PDS	SCSI	20	4	4	30	80
Quadra 800	68040	66	3	PDS	SCSI	136	8	4	72	60
Quadra 840AV	68040	80	3		SCSI	128	-	4	72	60
Quadra 900	68040	50	5	PDS	SCSI	20	-	16	30	80
Quadra 950	68040	66	5	PDS	SCSI	256	-	16	30	80
LC										
LC 475	68LC040	50	-	LC III PDS	SCSI	36	4	1	72	80
LC 575	68LC040	66	-	LC PDS, CS	SCSI	36	4	1	72	80
LC 580	68LC040	66	-	LC PDS, CS	IDE	52	4	2	72	80
LC 630	68LC040	66	-	LC PDS, CS	IDE	36	4	1	72	80
LC 630 DOS Compatible	68LC040	66	-	CS	IDE	52	8	2	72	80

Older Macs

MODEL	PROCESSOR		SLOTS		Internal Drive	MEMORY				
	Chip	Speed (MHz)	NuBus	Other		Max (MB)	Onboard (MB)	Slots	# pins SIMMs	Speed (ns)
Performa										
200	68030	16	-	-	SCSI	10	2	2	30	100
250	68030	16	-	LC PDS	SCSI	10	4	2	30	100
400, 405, 410, 430	68030	16	-	LC PDS	SCSI	10	4	2	30	100
450	68030	25	-	LC III PDS	SCSI	36	4	1	72	80
460, 466, 467	68030	33	-	LC III PDS	SCSI	36	4	1	72	80
550, 560	68030	33	-	LC PDS	SCSI	36	4	1	72	80
600, 600CD	68030	32	3	PDS	SCSI	68	4	4	30	80
The LC Models										
LC	68020	16	-	LC PDS	SCSI	10	2	2	30	100
LC II	68030	16	-	LC PDS	SCSI	10	4	2	30	100
LC III	68030	25	-	LC III PDS	SCSI	36	4	1	72	80
LC 520	68030	25	-	LC PDS	SCSI	36	4	1	72	80
LC 550	68030	33	-	LC PDS	SCSI	36	4	1	72	80
The II Line										
II	68020	16	6	-	SCSI	20	-	8	30	120
IIx	68030	16	6	-	SCSI	32	-	8	64	120
IIcx	68030	16	3	-	SCSI	128	-	8	30	120
IIci	68030	25	3	-	SCSI	128	-	8	30	80
IIsi	68030	20	1	PDS	SCSI	17	1	4	30	100
IIvx	68030	32	3	PDS	SCSI	68	4	4	30	80
IIfx	68030	40	6	PDS	SCSI	128	-	8	-	80
Compact Models										
Classic II	68030	16	-	-	SCSI	10	2	2	30	100
Color Classic	68030	16	-	LC PDS	SCSI	10	4	2	30	100
Classic	68000	8	-	-	SCSI	4	1	2	30	120
SE/30	68030	16	-	SE/30 PDS	SCSI	32	-	8	30	120
SE	68000	8	-	SE PDS	SCSI	4	-	4	30	150
Plus	68000	8	-	-	SCSI	4	-	4	30	150
512K	68000	8	-	-	SCSI	512K	512K	-	-	-
128K	68000	8	-	-	SCSI	128K	128K	-	-	-

3

Peripherals

Keyboard and Mouse

Monitors

Tablets and Scanners

In This Chapter

Keyboard and Mouse

Easy as ADB

The other bus. Most people are at least vaguely aware that there's a "bus" in the computer—usually they're thinking of the SCSI bus, the wires along which SCSI information travels. But there's another very important Mac bus: the *Apple Desktop Bus*, or *ADB*, that's used for basic input devices: the keyboard and the mouse, mouse substitutes like trackballs and trackpads, and even some scanners.

ADB chains. You can create a *chain* of ADB devices—a keyboard, a trackball, and a mouse, for instance. But since the mouse presents a dead end, it always has to be the last device. There are T- and Y-connectors available that let you branch two items (a mouse and a trackball, for instance) from a single ADB connector. And many devices, especially trackballs, come with "pass-through" connectors so you can plug in the new device and then the mouse.

There's a theoretical limit of sixteen ADB devices for the Mac, since there are sixteen different "addresses" that can be assigned internally to ADB devices to keep track of them. But you can really use only three or four in a chain (which, face it, ought to be plenty) because with more than that, the signal from the last device is too weak to reach the Mac. That's probably because the other ADB chain limitation kicks in—the total length of the chain shouldn't exceed five meters (about sixteen feet).

Live ADB unplugging. Although it's generally believed that plugging or unplugging an ADB connector while the Mac is turned on is a dangerous thing, it was a problem only on some early Mac models.

There was nothing inherently dangerous about the ADB on these machines, but the design of the logic board was such that a minor flexion of the board could occur if the ADB plug was inserted or removed a little too vigorously—resulting in a short from the ADB power line to the metal shielding on the inside of the case. Zap! And goodbye to the ADB fuse! Later Macs have thermal, self-resetting fuses which prevent this problem.

But you are left with this minor annoyance: If you have to connect your mouse after the computer's on, it's going to move the cursor very slowly, and using the Mouse control panel to reset the tracking speed isn't going to help much. You need to restart the Mac to get the mouse to behave correctly. —SZA/DR

The Plus's minus. The Mac Plus does *not* use the ADB standard for its keyboard or mouse, so you can't buy a new keyboard or mouse for it.

Getting along. If your keyboard wire is too short, get a different one. Computer supply catalogs and web sites offer six-foot ADB cords in coiled and uncoiled varieties. My keyboard cable is attached to the back of the Mac CPU, then snakes around the back of a corner desk and under it, into the slide-out keyboard drawer. Try that with the standard cable!

ADB cable. The ADB cable used on the Mac is the same as Super VHS cabling (S-video)—even the connectors are the same. So if you want an extra-long or extra-short custom ADB cable, you can get one at a local electronics store.

Keyboards

Evaluating keyboards. When you buy a modular Mac, the keyboard usually isn't included. Most people will automatically buy an Apple keyboard, even though there are others on the market that might suit a particular purpose much better. There are two major considerations for a keyboard:

- **Key feel**: Every keyboard has a slightly different feel. Do you prefer a hard, solid keystroke or a softer, mushier one? You'll need to do some hands-on testing to decide.
- **Ergonomics**: Using a keyboard a lot can also put you at risk for various injuries, some of which can become permanent disabilities. If you're constantly typing, you should seriously consider getting one of the specially built ergonomic keyboards on the market.

There are additional items to keep in mind, although since there aren't *that* many keyboards out there, you may not be able to get the exact combination of features you want.

- **Extra keys:** Make sure the keyboard you get has function keys along the top and a separate numeric keypad. You can use the function keys in various programs for all sorts of shortcuts (not to mention programming them for macros), and you'll love the ease of entry a numeric keypad provides. We also highly recommend "extended" keyboards that include a separate grouping of the cursor-control keys (←→↓↑) and a cluster for moving around in your document (Page Up, Page Down, and so on).
- **Built-in trackballs:** Some keyboards have built-in trackballs, which save you the expense of buying one separately if you want one. But don't assume the keyboard's trackball will work the same way as others you might have used; built-ins tend to be smaller and harder to control.
- **Built-in trackpads:** A few keyboards provide built-in trackpads so you can work the way you would on a PowerBook keyboard (but less cramped).
- **Key arrangement:** Some keyboards have unique layouts you may find either very convenient or very annoying. The basic alphanumeric keys are always in place, but the placements of the Power key, and ⌘, Control, and Option vary.

- **The ADB connection:** A thoughtfully designed keyboard has two ADB connections, one on each side or at each end of the back so you can plug in the mouse on either side. Some, though, are hard-wired for the Mac connection, and a wire sticking out from the center back of a keyboard can keep you from storing it against the base of the Mac or in a small keyboard drawer. —SZA/JK/JC

Some basic keyboards. There's a variety of keyboards around for you to choose from if you're not looking for anything fancy.

- Apple's **AppleDesign** ($90) and the **Apple Extended Keyboard II** ($160). They're virtually identical except the AppleDesign has a nice contoured shape and the Extended II includes a plastic template that fits over the row of function keys that serves as a reference for shortcuts.
- Datadesk was one of the first companies to make Mac keyboards, and it still does. The **Mac101E** ($120) is lighter yet more satisfying to the touch than Apple's or other companies' offerings.
- MacWarehouse's "house brand" **PowerUser 105 Extended** ($50) has a durable design and a one-year warranty, but has no height adjustment, pressing the keys down required some extra effort, and it has an uncomfortably small Delete key.
- Another model worth checking out is MicroSpeed's **Keyboard Deluxe Mac** ($70). —SZA/JK/JC

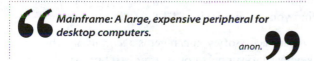

> ***Mainframe: A large, expensive peripheral for desktop computers.***
>
> *anon.*

Ergonomic keyboards. An "ergonomic" keyboard is one that is friendly to your wrists and fingers, letting them stay in a more natural position while you type. If you spend unbroken hours at your keyboard, you need one of these. Ergonomic keyboards have the alphanumeric keys split down the middle so your hands can be further apart; the two key sections are at a slight angle to each other, and the keyboard is generally humped in the middle, with a built-in wrist rest. All together, these details add up to a less painful typing experience. (As I can attest to: when I first started having problems—chronic tendinitis in my hands and wrists—my doctor told me to wear wrist braces, which helped considerably. But after a few weeks of the braces, with a standard keyboard, my shoulders were killing me because I had to squeeze my elbows in so close to my body while my wrists were being kept straight. A natural keyboard, combined with the wrist braces, made this book possible.)

The finger-friendliest ergonomic keyboard for the Mac is Adesso's **Tru-Form** ($90), which I use—although I dislike the placement of the Power On key, right between Option and Control to the right of the spacebar. I am very grateful to the system feature that traps the press of that key, asking me if I really want to shut down!

Get on your feet! Does your keyboard have feet? Let me tell you a true story that has nothing to do with keyboards: A young married couple, who shall remain nameless, bought a sleek, modern, wood-and-glass coffee table that they really loved, although they were disappointed that, while the showroom model rolled around easily, theirs sat immovable on it wooden base. Years later, as they moved from their apartment to their first house, the coffee table was being lifted onto the van and they saw that underneath, tucked up in the wooden base, were the casters, safely wrapped in a plastic bag.

Okay, back to the keyboard: did you ever look at the bottom of yours? Most keyboards have feet or ledges that can be raised or lowered to change the angle of the keyboard for more comfortable typing.

datadesk.com

Trackball keyboards. If you like a trackball instead of (or in addition to) a mouse, you don't have to get a separate unit. Datadesk offers several keyboards with built-in trackballs: **TrackBoard** ($150), **SmartBoard** ($100), and **Lil' BigBoard** ($80). Don't forget that the feel of a built-in trackball, which is usually much lighter than a separate unit, differs greatly from the external trackballs.

Trackpad keyboards. Your best bet for a keyboard with built-in cursor control is **TouchBoard** ($180, Datadesk) which features a touch-sensitive pad similar to those on PowerBooks. The pad offers better, more accurate control of the mouse than a built-in trackball. It lacks a numeric keypad but you can add one for $70 if you find you really miss it. —SZA/JC

Wrist rest. The best keyboard accessory you can get is a *wrist wrest*, which fits against the front of the keyboard to support not your wrists, but usually the heel of your palm; this keeps your hands from bending at the wrist at an unnatural, straining angle as you fingers touch the keys but the base of your hand rests near or on the desk surface, below the height of the keyboard.

Mouse and Substitutes

Ergonomic mice. Apple's basic mouse has gone through several redesigns over the years. The current one, the ergonomically designed **Desktop Bus Mouse II** ($80) is molded to fit into your hand and requires less effort to click the mouse button, which helps prevent injury from repetitive motions.

For a fraction of the price, Kensington's **Mouse in a Box** ($40) gives you a design and shape similar to Apple's but comes with a five-year warranty and an amazing 90-day no risk trial.

kensington.com

The Kensington folks also make the two-button **Kensington Mouse** ($60) and the programmable, four-button **Thinking Mouse** ($90); both have a symmetrical shape and allow their buttons to be configured to reduce repetitive tasks. —SZA/JC

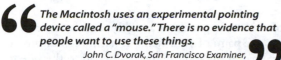

> *The Macintosh uses an experimental pointing device called a "mouse." There is no evidence that people want to use these things.*
> John C. Dvorak, San Francisco Examiner, February, 1984

Chopping off the mouse's tail. There are several cordless mouse models available, which can work on the desktop or for presentations when you want to be further away from the Mac.

- Logitech's **Cordless MouseMan** ($70) uses radio signals sent to a receiver that's plugged into the keyboard's ADB port. The battery-powered mouse has three buttons, and can be used up to six feet away from the receiver.
- Logitech's second offering is **TrackMan Live** ($150), which uses the same software for its three programmable buttons, and also uses a radio receiver, but you can get 30 feet away from the Mac.
- The **Port Presentation System** ($130, Port) also uses a receiver that plugs into the keyboard, but it uses infrared light (like television remotes) to transmit information; you can be up to 45 feet away, as long as you have pretty good aim. As its name implies, it's meant for presentations, so it has five programmable buttons to trigger whatever effects you've set up for your screen presentation.
- The **GyroPoint Desk** ($70, Gyration) works both on the desktop and in mid-air. It's not cordless—it has a nine-foot (!) wire—but it's good for presentations because its gyroscopic innards let you wave the mouse in the air and get true cursor movement on the screen. (If you tend to talk with your hands, of course, this could be a problem.)

Trackballs. Trackballs are like upside-down mice: you roll a ball that sits inside a stationary holder. Trackballs take less desk space and provide more precise control over the cursor on the screen, which is particularly important for graphics. They all have at least two buttons: one that's like a normal mouse button, and one that can lock in the down position so you can drag objects or menus without holding the button down with your finger.

- The **TurboMouse** ($110) from Kensington is the best-known Mac trackball; year after year, Mac magazines give it top review ratings and "Best Of" awards and it remains one of our favorites as well. Its ball is much larger and heavier than other trackballs, so it has more inertia. The size, position, size, and feel of the four buttons are excellent; they require enough pressure that they keep you from clicking accidentally, without making you press very hard. Kensington includes its own software that has many advanced features; you can, for instance, select spots on the screen and make the pointer jump to them by clicking both TurboMouse buttons and rolling the ball in the proper direction.
- CoStar's **Stingray** ($100) has a small ball that's easy to control; its two buttons take the form of a pair of sloping wings which surround the ball. They're so sensitive you have to be careful not to click them accidentally. You can alter pointer speed and select which button you want to use as the normal click and which to use as the click-lock—a boon to lefties.

- Microspeed's **MacTRAC** ($70) is comfortable to use, and sports a built-in sloped wrist rest.
- The **Trackman Marble** ($100, Logitech) is a highly ergonomic trackball that fits comfortably into the palm of your hand. It has three buttons at the end of a large, curved palmrest, and the trackball is off to the side for your thumb to control. You can program two of the three buttons using the MouseKey software for custom shortcuts. —SZA/BB/JC

Trackpads. Trackpads were introduced in PowerBooks, but it didn't take long for them to migrate to the desktop, first as add-ons and then as an integral part of a keyboard design. Using a trackpad means just sliding your finger lightly around on its surface: they're easy to use, but take a lot of getting used to. As with most PowerBook trackpads, you can just tap or double-tap the pad instead of clicking or double-clicking a button. The most popular trackpad add-on is the **GlidePoint** ($80, Alps), with its three programmable buttons. —SZA/JC

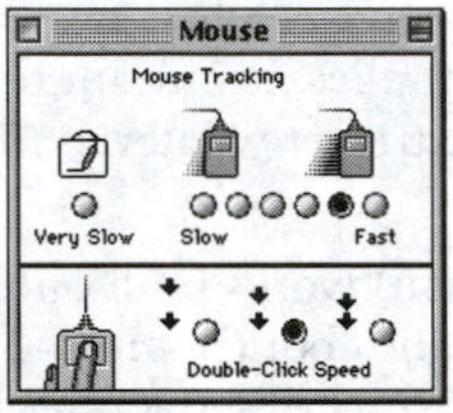

The Mouse control panel. There's not a lot to customizing the mouse, but the two options—tracking speed and double-click speed—are important. They're covered in detail in Chapter 5.

Monitors

Monitor Basics

Pixels and resolution. The tiny dots that make up the images on your screen are *pixels,* a term cobbled from the words *picture elements.* The smaller the dots are, the finer the lines that can be drawn; the *more* dots there are, the more information can be displayed.

The word *resolution* is used in two different ways when it comes to monitors. It can refer to the number of pixels that fit in an inch: the *dots per inch*, or dpi of a monitor—which, of course, also describes the size of the dots. A higher number means higher resolution; a lower number gives lower resolution, with sometimes chunky-looking lines and text. Mac monitors started out at 72 dpi, but have dropped as low as 64 dpi (on the awful 12" color monitor); most Apple monitors offer resolutions from 72 to 80 dpi.

Another way *resolution* is used—the more common usage, which we'll stick to for the rest of this chapter—is to describe how many pixels are displayed across and down the screen: a standard monitor has a 640 (horizontal) by 480 (vertical) resolution, while a double-page monitor's resolution is usually 1,024 by 768.

Monitors of different sizes can have the same screen resolution: the Apple 14-inch color monitor and the 9-inch PowerBook Duo screen both display 640 by 480 pixels, for instance. The pixels on the Duo display are much smaller, of course, in order to fit that many in that space—the Duo has a 85-dpi display, compared to the monitor's 69 dpi.

Live long and phosphor. Computer monitor screens are coated on the inside with phosphors; a gun at the back of the monitor shoots a stream of electrons at the screen, and the phosphors glow when they're "excited" by the electrons. The combination of glowing and dim phosphors combine to give you the images on your screen.

For black-and-white monitors, the phosphor coating is white, so you see either black or white where the phosphor spots are glowing or not. For a grayscale monitor, the electron gun shoots with varying intensities to provide gray shades. For color monitors, each pixel on the screen is actually made of three dots together—red, green, and blue; the electron gun (or three guns, sometimes) fires at one or more of the dots and they appear as a single colored dot on the screen.

Scan rates. The electron gun inside the monitor shoots at the screen (and at *you!)* starting in the upper left corner, tracing a horizontal line to the other edge of the screen, then snapping back to the left side and drawing another line beneath the first. After it zigzags its way to the bottom of the screen, it jumps back up to the top to start again—and it has to get there before the phosphor fades from the top line, or the image will flicker.

The speed at which the gun works is called its *scan rate* or *refresh rate;* the rate is measured in *hertz* (cycles per second), abbreviated *Hz*. Larger monitors need faster refresh rates; a monitor with a higher resolution also needs a faster refresh rate. If you can switch your monitor's resolution, you'll see the different refresh rates noted for the resolutions in the Monitors & Sound control panel.

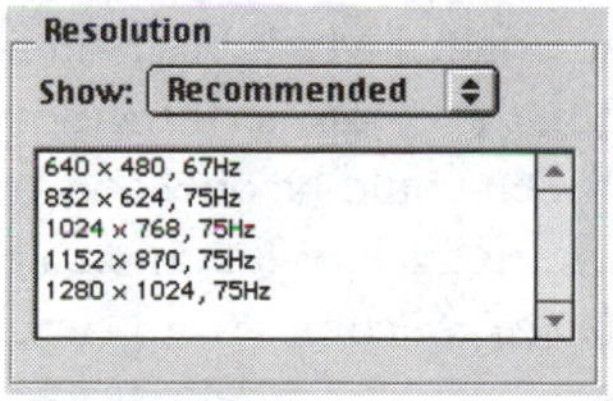

The scan rate changes to accommodate different resolutions on the display.

Multisync. Many monitors can be set up to display several different resolutions—depending on the capabilities of the Mac they're hooked up to—so you either cram more information onto the screen or blow everything up to a more readable size. They're called *multisync* (or, occasionally, *multiscan)* monitors and can usually be used with PCs as well as Macs.

You might need a special adapter plug from the monitor's manufacturer (it's inexpensive, and sometimes even free) to make a particular resolution work, but if you've installed a display card you should be able to make the switch through the Monitors & Sound control panel. —SZA/JK

Monitors and memory. The original Mac display's resolution was 512 by 384; because it was black and white and needed only a single bit of memory for each of its nearly 200,000 pixels, it needed a total of only about 24K of memory to take care of the display.

> *[The future "appliance Mac" features...] The monitor will be a separate unit allowing a choice for those affluent enough to take advantage of it. The basic monitor will be a black-and-white, portrait-format, page-size box.*
>
> *Steve Bobker, MacUser, June 1988*

Compare that to the memory cost for the larger and more colorful displays: a standard 14" monitor at 640 by 480 resolution uses 256K of RAM for 8-bit color (256 colors); it needs twice that (not surprisingly) for 16-bit color; and a full meg of memory is needed to provide millions of colors. A larger monitor—a double-page display for instance—needs four megs of memory to work with the millions of colors that 24-bit color provides.

Keep this in mind: a bigger screen needs more memory, and so does greater color depth.

In the original Macs, and for some time into the product line, the RAM needed for video display was just grabbed from the standard system memory. As monitors and their memory requirements grew, separate RAM—*video RAM*, or *VRAM* ("vee-ram")—chips were added to support the monitor. VRAM can also be installed on a separate video card, if that's what you're using to connect your monitor to the Mac.

In many cases, the VRAM in your Mac or on a video card is upgradable, so if you're not getting millions of colors but want them, adding VRAM may be all you need.

Not out of your depth. On the original Mac's black-and-white screen, each pixel corresponded to a single bit in the computer's memory. Since the pixel could be only black or white, and a bit could be only one or zero, one bit of memory per pixel was enough to keep track of things on a black-and-white display. (That's where the word *bitmapped* comes from—each pixel is *mapped* to a single bit in memory.)

On a color (or grayscale) screen, you need more than a single bit of memory per pixel, so that each pixel can be one of several colors. If you double the memory allotment, the two bits provide four different choices (because, in binary, two digits can represent numbers from zero to three). With four bits of memory, you can do 16 colors; eight bits gets you 256 colors, and so on:

1-bit = 2 colors	8-bit = 256 colors
2-bit = 4 colors	16-bit = 65,536 colors
4-bit = 16 colors	24-bit = 16.7 million colors

You can refer to a monitor setup in regard to the number of colors it can display ("256 colors") or by identifying its *bit depth* ("8-bit color"), which refers to how much memory is allocated to each pixel.

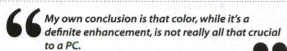

> ***My own conclusion is that color, while it's a definite enhancement, is not really all that crucial to a PC.***
>
> *David Bunnell, Macworld, January 1986*

Video support. The earliest Macs came with built-in displays, and the early rounds of modulars supported only Apple monitors. Some current models still support a built-in display, and others provide built-in video circuitry so all you have to do is plug in a separate monitor; in most cases, the built-in support can be upgraded with VRAM to provide support for larger monitors or more color depth. On any Mac with slots, you can add a video card so you can plug a monitor into it, replacing or supplementing the built-in video support.

Miscellaneous terminology. Here's a list of other terms used in relation to monitors:

- **RGB:** The three primary colors on a monitor (finger paints and Play Doh notwithstanding) are red, green, and blue—because you're mixing light, not pigments. *RGB monitor* is an almost archaic term at this point, since color is the standard.
- **CRT:** The electron guns at the back of early monitors (and TVs) was a *cathode ray tube,* so we had *CRT monitors* for a long time. The term is archaic now, even if the technology hasn't changed much.
- **Dot pitch:** Three colored dots—red, green, and blue—make up each pixel on a color screen; the distance between the dots is the *dot pitch,* measured in millimeters. A smaller dot pitch gives a higher-resolution display (*resolution* meaning the size of the pixels, not the number of pixels on the screen).
- **Interlace:** Mac monitors draw their images one line at a time, from top to bottom. Television screens, and some monitors for other computer systems, draw alternate lines on the screen: the odd-numbered lines are drawn on one pass, while the even-numbered lines are drawn on the next. Drawing alternate lines is called *interlacing*, and it reduces flicker on systems that aren't as fast as the Mac's *non-interlaced* setup.
- **Degaussing:** Does your monitor have automatic or manual degaussing, and what the heck is it? If you move your display and put it down a little roughly, or just bump into it, you may find that the colors change because the jarring might shift the magnetic field. Degaussing corrects the colors by resetting the field.
- **Convergence:** This is a way to focus the three color beams to work together. A monitor that lets you adjust convergence without having to open up the casing is a Very Good Thing.
- **VGA, SGVA:** The CGA (color graphics adapter) standard in the PC world was replaced by VGA (video graphics array) and SVGA (super

video, etc.); they're generic terms that refer to monitors designed for PC computers, but most are usable on the Mac.

- **ELF, VLF:** The electromagnetic emissions produced by your monitor—extremely low frequency and very low frequency radiation. Although some health concerns were raised in recent years, no conclusive evidence was ever produced to link this radiation to cancer or other health concerns.
- **NTSC:** The signal that runs a monitor is nothing like the one that's used by a TV—the NTSC (National Television Standards Committee) signal. You can use special hardware to turn the Mac output into an NTSC signal that can go to a videotape to be played on a television.
- **Energy Star:** The program set up by the Clinton administration that required all computers bought by the government to use low power consumption when idle. An Energy Star-compliant monitor sleeps or otherwise cuts down its power draw when not in use.

Monitor manufacturers. Apple monitors are excellent (most use Sony tubes), but there's not a wide enough variety for serious shoppers. As with so many peripherals, and especially in categories where we share hardware with the PC world, specific models come and go rather quickly. So, here are the monitor brands that have consistently received high ratings in the Mac community (you'll have to check current Mac publications, or the manufacturers' web sites for specifics): Apple, Radius, Sony and NEC.

More About Monitors

Measuring a monitor. A standard monitor measurement (14" color, 15" portrait, and so on) is a diagonal one, like the one for televisions. But it hardly tells you *anything* helpful. For one thing, the measurement is unlikely to be the actual *display area*—the part that shows things, not including the black rim—up to a quarter-inch or more—surrounding the picture. For another, the diagonal measurement alone doesn't give a clue as to the *orientation* of the screen: you'd think a 15" monitor would be a little bigger than a 14", but when the first is a portrait display and the second is a standard "landscape" display, there's a big difference as to what you'll be able to see on each one. And, finally, the measurement doesn't tell you anything about the resolution—how many pixels will be displayed horizontally and vertically. And it's that pixel count that really counts (not the overall number—which still doesn't tell you the size or shape of the screen—but the resolution). When you're monitor shopping, check all the specs.

72 dots to the inch. Always. No matter how many pixels your monitor packs into an inch, the basic Mac measurement is still 72 dots per inch. Huh?

Every 72 dots on the screen equals an inch in a printout. If you're using a program with a ruler in it, the ruler's inch marks will be at every 72 dots, no matter what the true on-screen measurement is. As odd as it might sound, this quirky rule of measurement ensures that as you move from Mac to Mac, or change monitors on your own system, what you intended to design in your document stays the same. It also means that the higher your monitor's resolution, the smaller the 72-dot inch measurement. On an 86-dpi screen, for instance, a ruler inch actually measures about .84 inches; on a 65-dpi screen, a ruler inch's actual measurement is about 1.11 inches.

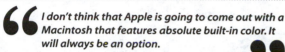

> *I don't think that Apple is going to come out with a Macintosh that features absolute built-in color. It will always be an option.*
>
> *Neil Shapiro, MacUser, April 1987*

16.7 million colors. Always. A Mac can always "think" in millions of colors (16.7 million, to be more exact). The color limitations of 256, or thousands, for a video display refers to the number of colors that can be shown at *one time.* The colors come from the overall collection of 16.7 million. There's a basic "system palette" of 256 colors, for instance, that the Mac uses on the desktop. But if you're in a graphics program, you can switch to a palette of pastels, or a palette of saturated hues—any set of 256 colors at a time is possible.

Not the scan rate. A monitor's *refresh rate*—how often it redraws the image on the screen—helps determine how steady and solid the image looks. But don't confuse the refresh rate with the screen's ability to keep up with the mouse when you move a graphic around on the screen; the latter depends on the speed of the Mac and its graphics acceleration, if it has any. —JK/AN/BB

My friend flicker. There's no reason you would want make your screen flicker, except that in describing how to do it, I get to pass on an important piece of Mac lore.

Find yourself a hard candy (Life Savers are the traditional choice). Don't let it melt in your mouth: crunch it, biting down sharply while staring at the screen—preferably out of the corner of your eye, but a good crunch will let you look at it straight on. The tiny but sudden jarring to your vision caused by the crunch will put your vision out of sync with the monitor's scan rate, and you'll see the screen flicker. While you're at it, get Wintergreen Life Savers and do the flicker trick in the dark with a friend so you can parallel process, doing a second test at the same time: see if those candies really do emit a spark when they're crunched.

Grayscale limitations. True grayscale monitors (as opposed to a color monitor that can run in a "black and white" mode) can produce only shades of gray, and only up to 256 of them, because the shades are produced by an electron beam of varying intensities. So, while limited VRAM can keep you to fewer than 256 shades of gray, extra VRAM can't push you beyond that number.

Old monitors sometimes die... But first they fade away. A monitor's brightness fades over time, so gradually that you won't notice it until you're looking at a new one. But keep that in mind if you're buying a used unit, figuring that you'll eventually replace the CPU but keep the monitor.

Catch the wave. If you find that the image on your monitor is sort of swimming or shimmering, there may be nothing wrong with it—it could be the environment at fault. Low-frequency magnetic waves interfere with the image, and guess what? Monitors produce low-frequency magnetic waves. So, a double-monitor setup is particularly prone to a little wave action, as are monitors set back-to-back in a shared office space; but you might also find interference from power lines coming into the building near where your monitor is set up.

Monitors include shielding (some more than others) but you may need some external shielding in some cases. A steel sheet set between the monitor and the source of the interference can do the trick; the thicker the metal, the better it will work. But it has to be the right kind of steel, too, since certain alloys work better than others: stainless steel is the least effective, while an alloy made specifically to shield magnetic fields works best. An alloy called Mumetal is one that's made to solve interference problems; it's a little expensive, but worth every penny when your monitor is making you seasick. One supplier is Magnetic Shield Corporation.

magnetic-shield.com

The Control Panel

Monitors & Sound. The Monitors & Sound control panel lets you set the number of colors you want displayed on the screen, and choose a resolution if your monitor provides more than one. The picture here shows the basic choices for an Apple 14" color monitor running from a Mac's internal video port.

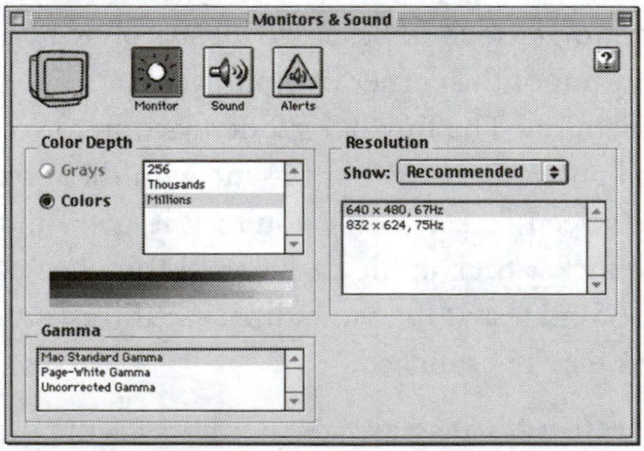

The settings. The number of grays or colors available in the Color Depth section depends on three factors: the monitor, the monitor support (internal or add-on card), and the amount of VRAM available. The color bars beneath the list of choices change to show you what you'll get at different color depths.

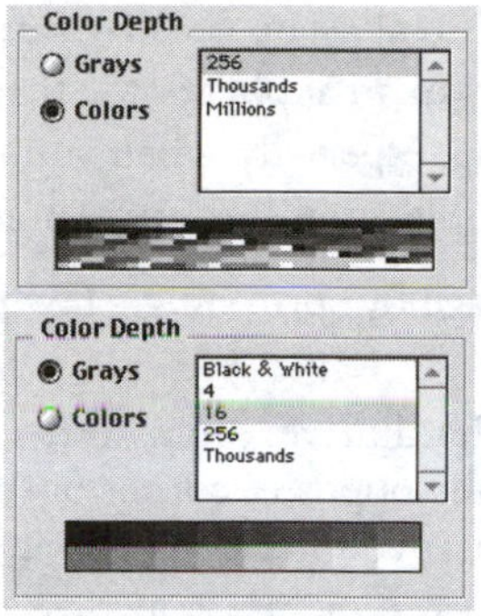

The color bars show a sample of the color depth you've chosen.

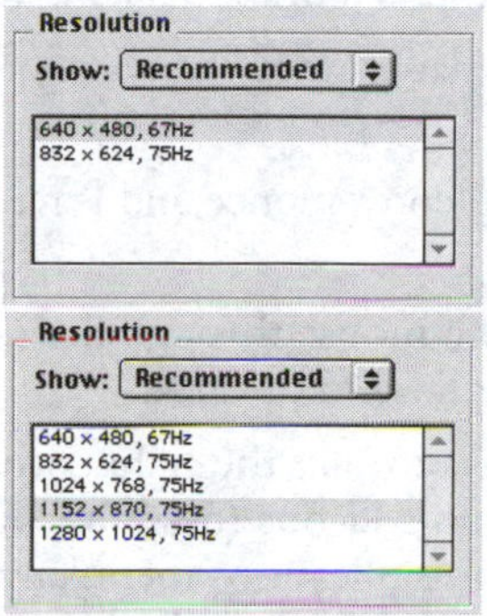

Two different monitors on the same Mac offer different resolution choices: a standard Apple 14" monitor on internal video support (top) and an Apple 20" display on an added video card (bottom).

To select a new resolution, just click on one of the choices in the list. The choices vary from one Mac and monitor to another. I have two monitors on my Mac, and they provide different resolution options; yours may be completely different—and might offer none but the default setting.

The most puzzling of the control panel choices is the Gamma setting. You may have only one choice—which is, of course, no choice at all—so you don't have to worry about it. Or, you may be faced with up to three choices: Mac Standard Gamma, Page-White Gamma, and Uncorrected Gamma. A click on each one will show you the changes: Standard is brighter than the uncorrected Gamma setting, while Page White affects the white areas of the display rather than the mid-range of colors that the other choices correct. Unless you're having problems, leave it at the Mac Standard setting.

By any other name. Apple renamed its AppleVision 750 and 850 displays ColorSync Displays. The Monitors & Sound control panel in OS 8.1 identifies the monitors by their new names, but you can keep using the 750 or 850 ColorSync profiles, since they're identical.

> ***We recommend you take an x-acto knife, remove the offending page from the magazine, shred it, and hoover up the pieces. Then reward yourself with a coke and a twinkie from the frigidaire. (You might want to xerox this page for future reference.)***
>
> *MacUser, 1988 (Reply to E-Machine's complaint that their trademark The Big Picture had been used as a title for an article about big-screen displays.)*

Monitors, no sound. Some video devices can't be accessed using OS 8's Monitors & Sound control panel. But you can usually use the old Monitors control panel instead to adjust settings. You'll find it stored in the Apple Extras folder on your hard disk if you did a regular system install; otherwise, you can find it on your system CD.

Using Large or Double Monitors

The full-monty monitor. If you do page layout work, a double-page display (a 20" or 21" monitor) is worth every extra penny, even including the price of the video card and VRAM you'll probably need to run it. Being able to see facing pages side-by-side is more than a convenience: it's a design necessity.

Big monitor strategies. The extra real estate on a large monitor is great for big and multiple document windows in an application—that's why you got it. But it also calls for a little re-thinking, especially when you're working on the desktop. (All of these apply for multiple-monitor setups, too, of course.)

- Cut down on extra mouse mileage by sprinkling a few trash can aliases around.
- Create an alias of your internal hard drive, or any other volumes that are usually mounted, and put it in the opposite corner of the screen, in case you're in that neighborhood when you need to open it.
- If you never used the Launcher (described in Chapter 12) because there wasn't much room on the desktop, it's time to take it out.
- Set up your most-used windows as window tabs across the bottom expanse of the screen.
- Create aliases for drag-and-drop convenience and leave them right out on the desktop.
- Increase the tracking speed of the mouse through the Mouse control panel—a big screen takes a long time to traverse.
- The Applications menu is far away, up in the right corner of a large monitor. Several contextual menu add-ons (described in Chapter 6) let you pop up the equivalent of an Applications menu anywhere on the screen. I like Window Monkey (described in Chapter 12) because its application/window menu can be appended to the end of the other menus in the menubar, putting it roughly in the center of a large monitor.

The double monitor setup. Lots of people (like me) wind up with two monitors because they start with a standard size, then later spring for a two-page display. For graphics and layout, you can't beat this setup: the large monitor for the main work, and the smaller one for tool palettes and other support items, or for extra document windows.

To run two monitors, you'll need a video card for one of them, because very few Mac models provide internal video support for two monitors. But that's really all you need, because the Mac was designed to support multiple monitors.

When both monitors are running, they're treated as one large virtual monitor: the mouse cursor glides from one to the other, and you can easily drag things back and forth. One monitor is designated as the *main* monitor; it gets the menu bar, and it's where applications open their windows by default.

The new, dead monitor. When you first hook up a second monitor and turn everything on, the new monitor will stay blank until you open the Monitors & Sound control panel; at that point, the Mac looks around and realizes you have an extra monitor, and the monitor comes on.

The control panel. When you're working with two (or more) monitors, the Monitors & Sound control panel changes to provide the extra options available for multiple-monitor setups. When you open the control panel, you'll get two nearly identical windows, one on each monitor; to set the resolution, or any of the monitor-specific options, click in the window on the monitor you want to adjust.

The control panel window on the main monitor offers more controls: the sound buttons, for one, but also the Arrange button that lets you define the relationship between the two monitors. When you click the Arrange button in the control panel, you'll see two monitor icons in the window, with a list of options above them.

- You can drag the mouse directly from one monitor to the other when you have two, but you have to tell the Mac their relative positions by dragging the monitor icons to the right spots.
- If your monitors are the same size so you're not sure which icon stands for which monitor, press the *Identify the monitors* button. A number will appear on each monitor (both the real ones and the icons) so you can see which is which. Although the button looks like a standard push button, it works differently: the numbers stay on the screen only as long as you keep pressing the button.
- To set the main monitor—the one that will have the menu bar on it—drag the miniature menu bar to the monitor icon of your choice.
- To set the startup monitor—the one that will get the Welcome to Macintosh screen—first click the *Identify the startup screen* button. You'll see a smiling Mac appear on the current startup monitor; leave it there or drag it to the other monitor.

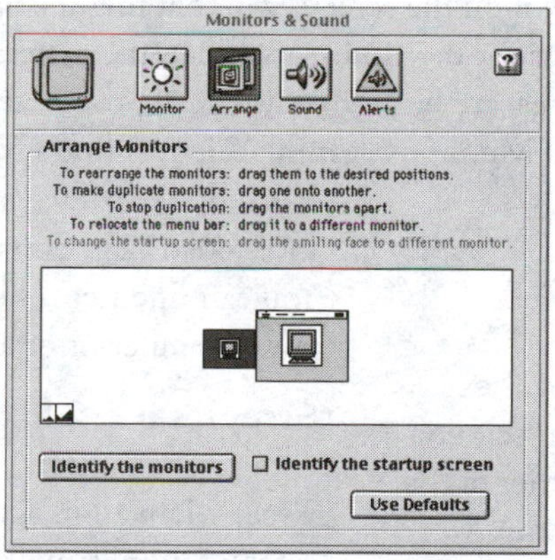

The multiple-monitor setup options in the Monitors & Sound control panel.

- The zoom buttons in the lower left work but are useless, since the zoom levels they provide make absolutely no difference to what you have to do in this window.

Closing the Monitors & Sound control panel window on either monitor closes them both.

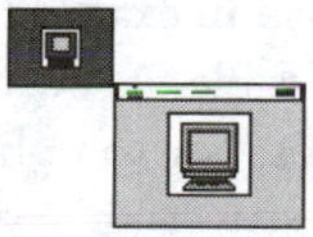

Preventing flyover. If you want to keep your mouse cursor from sliding over to the other screen too easily, you can set up the icons in the Monitors & Sound control panel as shown here. (Personally, I'd rather have a few accidental flyovers than have to go to only a single spot to get across.)

Video mirroring. Although the default multiple-monitor setup lets you use the two displays as a single, large one, there are time you might want to set up *video mirroring,* where both monitors display the same information. (This is usually for presentations, or in educational settings—and for some PowerBooks, it's the only way you can use an attached monitor.) Use the Arrange button in the Monitors & Sound control panel to set up mirroring: just drag one monitor icon on top of the other. If the monitors are different resolutions, the smaller screen appears centered on the bigger monitor with a black border around it.

When mirroring is set up, you can prevent the mouse cursor from showing up on the "slave" monitor by clicking the *Hide pointer on this monitor* checkbox in the control panel window on the target monitor; you'll find it not in the Arrange "screen" of the control panel, where it logically belongs, but back on the main screen you see when you click the Monitor icon at the top of the control panel window.

Caring for a Monitor

Keeping it clean. You may have noticed that a quick wipe of a dusty screen with something like a tissue doesn't help much—in fact, sometimes it makes things worse because the static build-up from the swipe attracts more dust.

A screen needs a damp wiping to do any good—but that's *damp,* not wet. You should use a special monitor-cleaner solution, because the glare-reduction coating on most screens can be damaged by any abrasive cleaner. And if you're using a spray, don't spray it on the screen, where it might drip down into the casing; spray the cloth. As for the cloth—the finer, the better: cloths made for monitors, or for eyeglasses, are best. My favorite approach, though, is also simple: I keep a container of Monitor Cleaning Wipes (mine's from Kensington) at hand; like baby wipes, they're "pre-moistened" and pop out one at a time. You can find items like these in almost any computer or office supply store.

Screen savers. In the early days of computer monitors, "burn-in" was an issue: when an image stayed on the screen too long, with the screen's phosphor coating constantly being refreshed in exactly the same spots, it was possible to "burn" the image into the phosphor so a ghost of it would always stay vaguely visible no matter what else you did.

IN THE BEGINNING

Berkeley Systems entered, and then owned, the screensaver market with a package, and on-screen theme, called Flying Toasters (the grandfather of the Flying Toilets in their Totally Twisted package). A copy-cat program, Bill and Opus, came out soon after; Berkeley Systems sued, and won.

Then, Jefferson Starship (née Airplane) sued Berkeley Systems for stealing their flying toasters from *30 Seconds Over Winterland.* Jefferson won. Pretty slick, huh?

While the time needed to really burn in an image wasn't something normal users would run into, the whole idea spawned the software category of screen-saver utility: a program that would kick in if the computer was idle for too long, constantly changing the display until you came back to work. Modern monitors aren't candidates for screen burn-in, but the fun of screensavers has been burned into the collective users' consciousness, so they're here to stay. (Your monitor goes to sleep to save energy, not to preserve the phosphor coating.)

berkeley.com

The first Mac screensaver was Pyro, which put simple fireworks on the screen. But the standard is Berkeley System's **After Dark** ($25-$40 per package), which comes in so many flavors it's staggering. Whether you want the old standbys that include Boris the Cat and Flying Toasters, or something thematic like Star Trek (original and The Next Generation), Marvel Comics, Looney Tunes, Disney characters, the Simpsons, or the Totally Twisted collection, you can have it. And you'll find plenty of other modules on-line for downloading. Each package provides not only ready-made screens, but also the ability to edit them and combine features from different scenes. After Dark isn't the only screensaver around, but it's the standard by which all others are measured: other screensavers can run After Dark modules, and make sure that their modules work with After Dark.

The Shock Clock and Toxic dump selections from the Totally Twisted collection.

Tablets and Scanners

Scanners

In general. *Scanners* are devices that convert images—photographs or other artwork—into digital form so they can be stored and manipulated by computers. When used in conjunction with *OCR* (optical character recognition) software, they can also convert a page of text into an editable document on your computer. Mac-compatible scanners range in price from a few hundred dollars to thousands of dollars. (The really high-end equipment is needed for demanding jobs like color photographs in slick publications.)

The scanner models on the market change frequently and there are often variations even between one individual unit and another, so make sure you're familiar with scanner features and capabilities before you start shopping. —JM

How scanners work. During scanning, light is reflected off (or passed through) the artwork and focused onto *CCDs* (charge-coupled devices—basically, light sensors) that convert the light energy to electricity. Color scanners use colored filters (or sometimes a prism) to read red, green, and blue values separately, and then combine the three single-color scans to yield a full-color image. Though the principle is the same for all scanners, units differ in several ways: how many readings per inch they take (the scanner's resolution); how much color information they capture at each reading (the scanner's bit depth); whether they take separate passes of the light source to read the red, green, and blue values (three-pass scanners) or take all the readings in a single pass (minimizing the chance for mis-registration and speeding up the scanning process); and the quality of the scanning software that comes with the machine. —JM

Bit depth. One-bit scanners read all sample points as either black or white. There aren't very many of these around anymore. Most people use 8-bit grayscale scanners (for 256 shades of gray) or 24-bit color scanners (256 shades each of red, green, and blue, for a total of more than 16 million colors).

Some scanners read 36 or 48 bits of information at each sample point, even though their final product is a 24-bit file. Doing this reduces the amount of *noise* (inaccurate data) that CCDs inherently produce. (The less noise there is in relation to total data collected, the more usable information the scanner can deliver.)

This extra information doesn't go to waste. A common problem when you alter scans is that you lose information—if you brighten colors, for example, you might lose image detail. But when you scan 48 bits, you can tell the scanner to digitally convert only the brightest 16 million colors, say, so that its final 24-bit image contains the best information. —JM

IN THE BEGINNING

Here's a peripheral you never heard of!

Back in the really early days, a "fat" Mac was one with 512K of memory, the computer case was sealed, and SIMMs (memory modules) hadn't been invented. But you *could* add memory—as an external peripheral, the *DASCH* (Disk Acceleration/Storage Control Hardware). It connected to the printer or modem port, and you could string together multiple units to get up to 16 megs of RAM! Here's a comment from the October 1985 issue of MacUser:

> *And the price is pretty reasonable. DASCH comes in three versions. The 500K version lists for $495, the 1 MB version is $975, and the 2MB monster is $1785.*

Resolution. A scanner's resolution refers to the number of sample points per inch it's capable of capturing (often expressed as *dpi*, although *spi* is more accurate). Some scanners are also rated in terms of total resolution, the maximum number of points they can sample. To compare these two figures, divide the total resolution by each dimension of your intended output, then average the two figures. For example, a scanner whose total resolution is 2,000 by 3,000 dots can output a 5- by 7-inch image at a resolution of about 415 dpi (2,000/5 = 400; 3,000/7 = 428.6; (400+428.6)/2 = 414.3). —JM/AN

Types of scanners. The two most common types of scanners are:

- **Flatbed scanners**. These operate like photocopiers; you place the artwork on a glass surface, and a scan head and light source move across it under the glass. Flatbeds can scan almost anything that has at least one flat side—even a slab of marble. Most of them can't scan transparencies or slides, but some manufacturers offer attachments for that purpose. All flatbeds will scan up to at least 8.5 by 11 inches, and some go up to 11 by 17 inches.
- **Transparency scanners**. As their name suggests, transparency scanners scan transparent materials such as 35mm slides, negatives, and larger photographic transparencies (4 by 5 inches or 8 by 10 inches). —JM

Evaluating scan quality. You can't evaluate the quality of a scanned image for a printout by looking at it on the screen. Scans that look dull on a screen may actually contain better data for printing than those that look bright and colorful. It usually isn't possible to make a scan and then print it on the output device you're planning to use, but you can at least avoid some of the most obvious and common problems by making a few test scans and analyzing them with Photoshop's Levels chart (other image-editing programs have similar capabilities).

In the end, the quality of your scans will depend just as much on your skill in processing them as on how good a scanner you used. Just about every scan needs to be brightened and sharpened in software, and no scanner program can take the place of a good image-editing program like Photoshop (which comes bundled with many scanners). Also remember that, for most people, differences in quality won't matter as much as differences in convenience. Small color imbalances probably won't bother you if you're producing newsletters, but a slow scanner will annoy you every time you use it.

The scanner should provide a Photoshop plug-in or some other software that enables you to scan directly into your image-editing package. Because most scans need correction, most people find this the most convenient way to work. —JM

Which one? Perhaps because there are so many scanners out there, models seem to come and go faster than Mac models do. Dependable, reputable manufacturers whose scanners have consistently received good reviews are La Cie, Epson, Hewlett-Packard, Nikon, Microtek, and Apple. You should check current Mac publications for information and reviews about current products.

The PaperPort alternative. Neither a flat-bed nor a transparency scanner, the **PaperPort** ($150, Visioneer) is a tiny (about 12 by 4 inches) unit that accepts paper through its rollers. It's perfect for OCR scanning (it includes OmniPage Lite software), business cards (with the included Corex CardScan), and graphics—as long as you're not doing high-end graphic work.

visioneer.com

The PaperPort Strobe offers the same tiny footprint, a updated sleek design, and color scanning for only $250. It also handles documents as small as business cards, and 8.5" wide paper up to 30 inches long.

The OCR solution. If you scan a page of text, it comes in as a graphic—that is, it's just a picture of the text, not editable words. With OCR (optical character recognition) software, however, you can scan a page of text and it turns into editable text.

OmniPage

It's easy to get good OCR software: just buy OmniPage ($100, Caere). Its intelligence consistently amazes users, correctly interpreting different fonts and handling multiple-column layouts with ease.

caere.com

Expanding serial ports. If you're running out of places to plug in serial devices (such as modems, additional printers, scanners, or graphics tablets) you have a couple of expansion options.

The least expensive route is an A/B switch box (about $25, and $10 for an additional serial cable), which allows the connection of one additional serial device on one of the Mac's two serial ports. The only disadvantage is that you can use only one of the two devices at a time. You could also potentially run into a problem with any system extensions or control panels that need to communicate with the particular serial device you've switched off on the A/B box.

An entirely different solution is a card that supplies additional serial ports, along with software that lets your Mac take advantage of the extra outlets. Prices range from $230 to $725 for cards with two, four, or eight ports; most cards provide four ports for a mid-range price. Some of your choices are: **Lightning-PCI** (Creative Solutions), **Romulus** (Megawolf), and the **SX-4** (Keyspan). Check the specs carefully before you buy an expander like this: some can't handle specific peripherals like a MIDI unit, or a QuickCam, or certain printers. —SZA/JC

creative-solutions-inc.com
megawolf.com
keyspan.com

Graphics Tablets

The tablet alternative. Sometimes a mouse just doesn't cut it. Especially when you want to really *draw,* using a pencil or pen. The solution is a pressure-sensitive tablet that lets you use a special pen to draw on its surface, with the motions translated into "mouse moves." Other than a "driver" for the tablet, you don't need any special software—once the tablet is up and running, you can use it any graphics (or other) program you want.

The pens that accompany tablets have gone from being wired-on to wireless but battery-powered to wireless and battery-free. But wired or not, the artistic freedom a tablet provides is invaluable for someone who has to argue with the mouse when trying to work in a graphics program.

wacom.com

The Wacom way. Wacom, the industry leader in graphics tablets for some time, has a full line of **ArtZ** tablets (ranging from 6 by 8 to 12 by 18 inches, from $300 to $850). The ArtZ can interpret as many as 256 pressure levels; its featherweight stylus, the **UltraPen**, has a programmable switch you can use to assign different functions. The best thing about the ArtZ tablets is that you can completely customize the performance of the stylus and the tablet, and save different sets of preferences for each program you work with, so you don't have to waste time switching them back and forth. My favorite adjustment is the Custom Pressure Curve, which lets you control the tablet's response to different pressure levels, so you can, for example, obtain a softer and more sensitive "brush." —SZA/AC/JC

calcomp.com

DrawingSlate II. The CalComp **DrawingSlate II** features a cordless stylus, and although it's a little heavier than the Wacom's, it's very responsive, and the tip has a great feel to it. The stylus has two buttons for defining actions or commands that, together with the 18-function menu on the tablet, make DrawingSlate a useful tool for working with macros. The models range from 4 by 5 inches ($100) to 12 by 18 inches ($500). —SZA/AC/JC

Tracking speed. The Mouse control panel lets you set the *tracking speed* for the cursor: the relationship between how fast you move the mouse and how far the mouse cursor travels on the screen. When you're using a graphics tablet, you'll want to set the tracking to the special very-slow tracking setting so you can sketch in a more natural movement on the pad—there's no difference, at that setting, between the distance you move on the tablet and the distance the cursor moves on the screen.

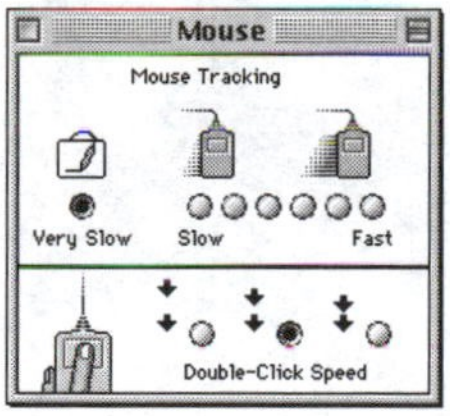

4

Storage

About Disks

Floppy Disks and Drives

Hard Drives

Other Storage Media

The Wonderful World of SCSI

In This Chapter

About Disks

The Basics

Some basic terms. There are a few terms used in this chapter, and throughout the book, that don't sound at all Mac-ish (not surprisingly, since they pre-date the Mac), but they're very useful and we have no alternatives.

A *volume* is a disk or anything that's treated like a disk on your desktop: a floppy, a CD, a disk partition, a removable disk like a Zip or a SyQuest, a file server, or even a folder that's shared separately across a network. When a volume's icon appears on your desktop, it's *mounted.* Removing the icon is *unmounting* (not *dismounting).* When the Mac is getting information from a disk, it's *reading* from it; when it's putting information onto the disk, it's *writing* onto it.

Bits, bytes, and K
Chapter 2

The magnetic storage standard. The bi-polarity of magnetism, where everything is either north or south, happily coincides with the binary language of computers, where everything boils down to either zero or one. A disk surface is covered with iron oxide, which is easily magnetized. So, the standard storage media—floppies and hard drives—use the north/south orientation of tiny magnetized particles to represent the ones and zeros of a computer's mother tongue.

But just how small are those small magnetic particles? Consider a Mac floppy, which isn't nearly the densest storage medium available. It stores 1.4 megabytes of information. That's 11,744,051 *bits* of data, so there's nearly 6 million bits on each side of the disk. (That number refers to only *your* data; there's other, invisible, stuff that the Mac stores on every disk.) The surface area of a 3.5" disk, after subtracting the center hub, is about 8.5 square inches. That comes to about 706,000 bits of information, or magnetic particles, *per square inch.* And that's nothing compared to disks that pack things in much more closely!

> ***"Computer people spend their time worrying about whether magnetized particles are standing up or lying down."***
> *Gantz & Rochester, The Naked Computer*

Tracks and sectors. A disk's surface is divided into concentric rings called *tracks;* the tracks are subdivided into areas called *sectors.* These divisions aren't physically present on a disk; the entire surface has an iron oxide magnetic coating. When you first format a disk, the operating system creates the dividers—little magnetic fences—so it will be able to use the disk. (And different systems need different track/sector setups—that's why there's a difference between a Mac-formatted disk and one formatted for that other kind of computer.)

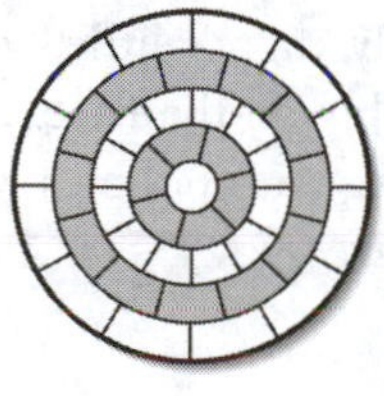

A disk surface is divided into concentric tracks that are subdivided into sectors.

Read-write heads. On the inside, drives and disks basically work somewhat like record players (remember those?). Instead of a needle, the "tone arm" has electromagnets on it that check and change the information on the disk; the magnets, and the whole arm assembly, are called *read-write* heads. Instead of traveling inward in a spiral groove as a tone arm does on a record, the read-write head moves in towards the center and out towards the perimeter of the disk; this motion combined with the spinning of the disk lets the read-write head get at every last particle on the surface area.

Mounting two volumes with the same name. Normally, you can't have two items with the same name on the desktop, but you can have two disks with identical names. The Mac assigns each mounted volume a unique ID number, and uses that number internally to refer to the disk.

A Little Beyond the Basics

No trespassing! A portion of every disk is reserved for the Mac's use. There are several invisible files the Mac uses to keep track of things on a disk; the larger the disk, the larger the file. Storage space for the invisible files is set aside when a disk is initialized. That's why you'll never, ever, start with an empty disk that reports every last K available; even a newly initialized floppy reports at least 1K as being used even with no items on the disk.

Do you know where your files are? You think you do, but you don't. You think they're in folders on your disk, but those folders are nothing more than graphical metaphors to help us puny little humans find the files we need.

File fragmentation
Later this chapter

When you save a file, it's stored in as many sectors on the disk as are needed to accommodate it. Sometimes the sectors aren't even next to each other. And even if several files are stored in contiguous sectors, it's unlikely that every file that you have "in" a folder is actually stored next to, or anywhere near, the other files in that folder.

The Mac uses a special database to keep track of where files and *pieces* of files are stored. This invisible file is stored on the main level of a disk, and acts as a kind of table of contents; instead of chapter titles and page numbers, it stores filenames and sector numbers. But imagine reading a book the same way the Mac reads a file! It would go something like this: *Chapter 2 starts on page 37 and continues for four pages. Then jump to page 123 and read ten pages. Next, go to page 7 and read two pages.*

Formatting versus initializing. Actually, there's little "versus" about these two terms, since they're used interchangeably on the Mac. For some reason, *initialization* is used most often when dealing with floppies, while *formatting* seems to be the term of choice for hard drives.

Initializing or formatting erases files from a disk and builds the little magnetic fences that divide the surface into tracks and sectors. The process also blocks out any bad segments of a disk so they won't be used, and reserves certain spots for special data like startup information and file locations.

Recovering trashed files
Chapter 24

Emptying the trash doesn't erase files. When you drag something to the trash and empty it, the file isn't actually erased. Instead, the file's name is erased from the disk's invisible directory, and the sectors that it used are marked as available; for most intents and purposes, the sectors are empty.

But since files aren't immediately erased, and sectors aren't always immediately re-used, that means the files are still recoverable, with the right software tools.

How many files can dance on the platter of a drive? The Mac's original filing system (*MFS, Macintosh Filing System*) choked on as few as 400 files: that's how many you could keep on a disk. Then *HFS* (*Hierarchical Filing System*) came along, and upped that limit considerably: its 32-bit system for keeping track of disk contents allowed 2,147,483,648 bytes of information on a disk: 2 gigs.

System 7.5 pushed that barrier so that the Mac could see drives as large as 4 gigabytes, although space wasn't used too efficiently. OS 8 didn't change much about disk formatting, but its first update did: OS 8.1 introduced *HFS Plus*, described in more detail in the next section.

IN THE BEGINNING

When the Mac operating system moved from MFS to HFS to accommodate more files per disk, there was a simple way to tell whether a disk had been initialized as an MFS or an HFS volume (we're talking about floppy disks here, since that's all there was). The picture here shows the difference between the windows on one kind of disk and on the other. Can't see it? The HFS window is on the right: it has a single dot at the far left of the double line at the bottom of the window header. Really.

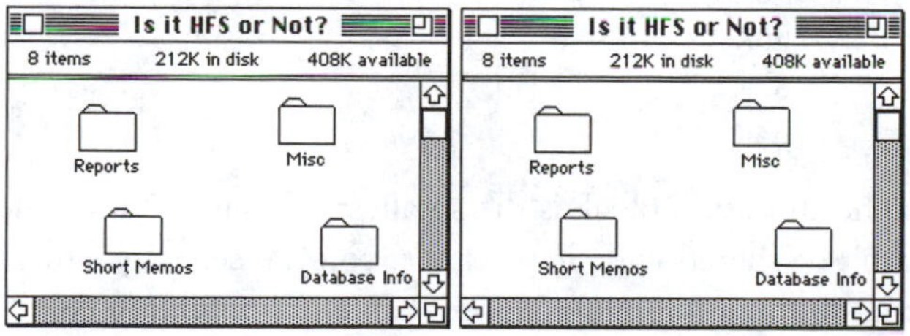

Allocation Blocks

Forks and resources
Chapter 12

Allocation blocks. This is one of my favorite topics. It's so ridiculous to have to worry about things like allocation blocks, but understanding them helps you understand some other disk issues.

As you already know (if you've read this chapter so far), a disk is divided into tracks and sectors. But there's another division, too, known as an *allocation block*. It's not a physical section on the disk; instead, it's a "logical" division, a way the Mac can treat a group of sectors as a single unit.

The allocation block is the smallest unit the Mac works with when storing a file. A block can't store two different files; if it isn't completely filled by a file (or a part of a file that's spilled over from its other storage blocks), the remaining space stays empty. Putting a very small file into a very large block wastes a lot of space, and the problem is compounded by the fact that most Mac files consist of two *forks,* one for data and one for resources, and the forks are stored in separate allocation blocks no matter how small they are. But there's nothing you can do about it, since the Mac's operating system defines the allocation block size.

A file is larger on a larger disk. Once you've got the concept of allocation blocks down pat, you're ready for this mind-boggling corollary: the larger the disk, the more room a file takes. Try it. Make an alias on a floppy disk and get Info on it; the size is reported as 1K. Drag it to your hard drive and check the size. What do you get? It might be 2K, it might be 8K, it might be 64K—it all depends on the size of your hard drive.

The actual size of an allocation block depends on the size of the disk; larger disks have larger blocks, because a disk can be divided into only 65,535 blocks at most. Disks under 60MB use 1K for each allocation block; for every 32MB of disk capacity, the size of an allocation block grows by .5K. So, you get a progression like this (I've skipped a lot of steps):

Disk Size	*Allocation Block Size*
(floppies)	1K
128MB	2K
256MB	4K
384MB	6K
1GB	20K
2GB	32K
4GB	64K

Keeping in mind that the allocation block is the smallest "container" for a file, and that extra space can't be shared with another file, you can see why a tiny file like an alias can take 1K on a floppy and more than 64K someplace else. (In fact, a 1K file can take 128K of space on a 4-gig drive because it needs two blocks to store its two separate forks.)

Get Info for physical and logical sizes. It's easy to find out how large (or small) a file really is without regard to the allocation blocks it's using up. The Get Info window for a file lists its size: both its true ("physical") size and the allocation block ("logical") size. In fact, Get Info makes the difference very clear, as you can see in the pictures here. The size is first given in terms of how much room it takes on the disk (it might be reported in K or MB, depending on the file's size); then, parenthetically, it gives the number of "bytes used"—that's the physical size of the file.

So, the larger file (at the top of the picture) is reported as 2.3MB on the disk, with an actual size of 2,469,996 bytes—numbers that are reasonably close to each other. The alias, however, is only 538 bytes (about half a K) in physical size, but takes 20K on the disk—a space about forty times larger than it needs. (And here's a trick with which you can amaze your family and friends: with just the information in an Info window for a small file, you can identify the size of the drive it's on. The one in the picture, for instance, is 20K; using the chart from a few entries ago, you can see that a 20K allocation block is used on one-gig drives, ergo…)

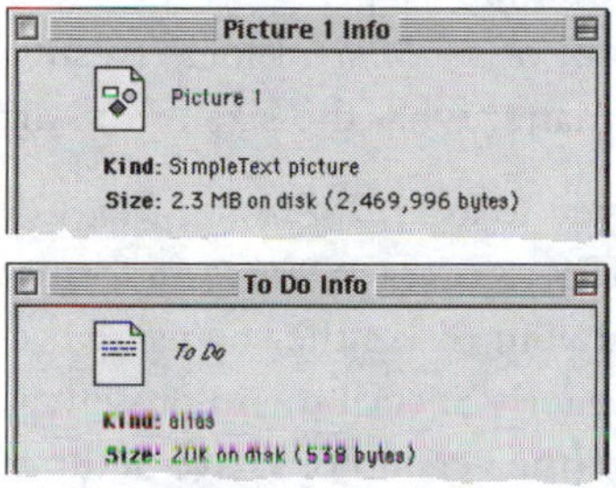

Comparing the size a file takes on disk to its actual size in bytes.

You might be wondering, for the file pictured at the top, how something that's about 2.47 million bytes seems to be taking *less* room then necessary, at 2.3MB. If you are wondering, then you've forgotten the binary rules of computer sizing, where a K is 1024 bytes and a meg is 1024K. So, the file at 2.46 million actual bytes is about 2.3MB.

Not a total waste, but a waste. When you consider, say, the 20K allocation blocks on a 1GB drive, and that a 1K file uses an entire block, it's easy to start feeling that 19 out of every 20K is wasted. But that's not the case. If you have a 21K file, it's going to fill an entire block, and overflow to the next, where it uses only 1 of the 20K. And if your file is just shy of 1MB, it's going to completely fill 51 blocks and spill over perhaps only 1K to the fifty-second block, where it wastes 19K. So, the most you can waste on a 1GB drive is 19K *per file*. And it's unlikely that in every instance of a partially filled block only 1K will be used; on average, 10K per file wasted on a 1GB disk.

As the disk gets larger and the allocation blocks get bigger, the numbers for the average number of files and the average waste per file increase. When you reach 2GB drives, the percentage of wasted space on a drive is significant, and by 4 gigs it's ridiculous. The table on the next page gives you an idea of how the problem increases with the size of the drive.

If most of your files are very large, the total number of files on your drive is smaller and so the waste factor is lower; of course, for tons of small files, the situation is even worse than in the chart. In other words: a small number of large files uses space more efficiently than a large number of small files.

Wasted Drive Space

Drive size	Allocation block size	Average waste per file	Average number of files (filled drive)	Total average	Percentage of drive wasted
500MB	17K	8.5K	7,500	62MB	12%
1GB	20K	10K	15,000	146MB	14%
2GB	32K	32K	30,000	469MB	23%
4GB	64K	64K	60,000	1.88GB	47%

HFS Plus: Extended Format

HFS Plus to the rescue. Starting with OS 8.1, the larger disk/larger file size problem was licked. The update to OS 8 introduced a new file structure that allows many more allocation blocks per disk. Instead of the former 65,536-block limit, it has a limit of 4.2 *billion* blocks, resulting in smaller allocation block sizes: 4K no matter what the size of the drive.

The new file structure is referred to as *HFS Plus*, or *Mac OS Extended* format (making the older structure *HFS* or *Mac OS Standard* format). To make use of it, you'll to have to reformat your disk either by using the Erase Disk command from the OS 8.1 Finder's Special menu or with a formatter that understands the new structure (the version of Drive Setup that comes with OS 8.1, or an updated version of your favorite third-party formatter). Reformatting your disk means wiping it out completely, so you'll have to back up everything someplace else and then restore the contents. But reformatting the drive isn't enough: you also have to use OS 8.1 itself to avail yourself of the new, compact file format.

You can use OS 8.1 without reformatting your drive—it can work with previous file formats. That's a good thing, since floppies and CDs remain standard HFS file structures!

Why 4K? The actual file structure of HFS Plus allows allocation blocks to be as small as 512 bytes—half a K. So why does it work with something eight times larger?

As you work with files and they grow and shrink in size, they use a different number of blocks; additional blocks don't usually wind up being next to the originals, and the more you change the files, the more fragmented they become. The smaller the application blocks are on a disk, the more likely it is that a file will eventually be chopped up into lots of tiny pieces instead of fewer, larger pieces. That extra fragmentation slows down a disk's performance.

Despite HFS Plus's ability to use .5K allocation blocks, Apple settled on 4K as a balance between too-large allocations that waste space and too-small allocations that increase file fragmentation and degrade drive performance.

Your mileage may vary. With Extended formatting, you'll be able to store more on your hard disk, but how much more depends on the size of the disk you started out with and the size of your files. Under Standard formatting, the "wastage" is higher on larger drives and for smaller file sizes; your savings will be relative to what you were wasting before.

The Plus is optional. Because there are some compatibility problems with HFS Extended Format—the major one being that disks formatted that way can't be used on systems lower than OS 8.1—using the format is an option. When you erase a disk with the Finder's Erase command, you'll be able to choose between the formats, as you can see in the picture here. The option shows up for any volume larger than 32MB, which is the threshold for HFS Plus advantages.

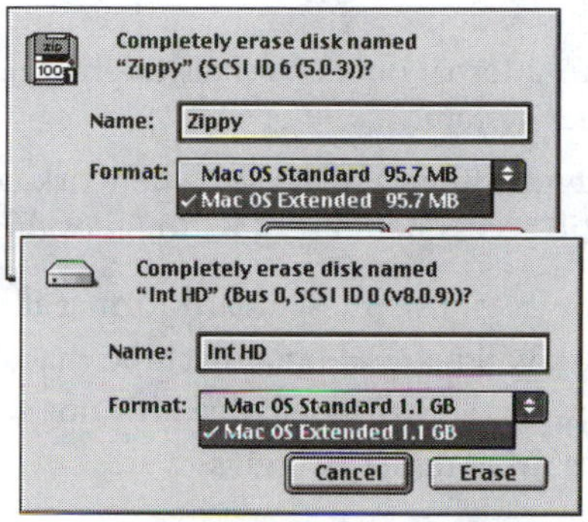

Choosing between Standard (HFS) and Extended (HFS Plus) formats when erasing disks—a Zip (top) and a hard drive (bottom).

HFS minus. An Extended format disk can be read only by OS 8.1 and later. Hook up an HFS Plus disk to an earlier system, and you won't be able to get at its contents. All you'll see is a single file named—well, you can see in this picture what it's named. It's a SimpleText document that explains to the uninitiated (that's not you, since you've been initiated here) that the disk can be read by OS 8.1 and later systems.

Don't jump to HFS Plus right away. Before you move to OS 8.1 and its HFS Plus formatting, make sure that you have updates for your important disk and file recovery utilities; older versions won't be able to work with the new file structure. And make sure you know the difference between a utility's compatibility with OS 8.1 and its working with HFS Plus. Norton's Utilities version 3.5.2 will work under 8.1, for instance, but it can't diagnose or repair HFS Plus volume problems; so, it's fine for a standard-format drive under 8.1, but not for the new format.

When should you move to the extended format, then? If your disk utilities are updated for the new format, you can use it on your internal hard drive (as soon as you find time to completely reformat it, that is). Here are some other considerations:

- The disk should be at least a gig in size before you bother with HFS Plus. For smaller disks, the percentage of waste is relatively minimal, especially compared to the bother of backing up, reformatting, and restoring the contents.

- The disk must be greater than 32MB or an Extended-format initialization will fail.
- If you're partitioning a newly formatted drive with Drive Setup, you can format some partitions as Standard and Others as Extended.
- The majority of your files should be on the small side. If your documents are mostly from word processing, spreadsheets, databases, programming, or web pages, your disk is a good candidate for HFS Plus. If you do high-end graphics, sound, or video, your large files aren't wasting that much space to begin with.
- The disk should be an internal one; externals might need to be used on a Mac running an earlier system.
- You can share an Extended format drive on a network, and Macs using earlier systems can still access it and read all the files on it.

As for externals and removables: use the standard format if there's even the *slightest* chance that the disk will be used on a machine that's not running OS 8.1 or later. Also be guided by the size of the disk: it's not worth using the HFS Plus for formatting a drive under two gigs in size.

The hidden extension support. If you're using Extended format disks, you need a special extension and support files in your System Folder: the Text Encoding Converter extension and its folder of support files. These get installed automatically with OS 8 and later, but make sure you don't delete them (even if they have no obvious purpose).

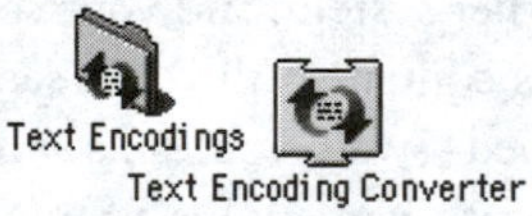

PlusMaker and PlusMaximizer. Alsoft quickly pounced on the HFS Plus bandwagon by offering, just *before* OS 8.1 came out, two utilities related to the new disk formatting feature. Alsoft's **PlusMaker** ($30) lets you set up your drives to use small allocation blocks *without* having to reinitialize them, by futzing with the disk directory instead of manipulating the files themselves; it takes about 20 minutes to process a larger hard drive (instead of the several hours for a real reformat). **PlusMaximizer** ($30) lets you get even more out of a true reformat, by allowing allocation blocks of .5K instead of the 4K that Apple settled on for the block size.

alsoftinc.com

Third-party drives and formatters. If you're using a non-Apple drive and its formatter doesn't offer the HFS Plus option, you can still get it: in most cases, you can format the drive, then restart under OS 8.1 (but not with the drive as the startup!) and use the Erase command from the Special memory to set up the drive with Extended format.

No all-round Plus for '040 Macs. OS 8 and its descendants won't run on any 68K Mac except for those with '040 chips, like Quadras. But an '040 machine can't start up from an Extended format drive, nor can it store virtual memory files on one. But when running OS 8.1, it can access other HFS Plus volumes.

Floppy Disks and Drives

Basics

Floppy disks and drives. The first Mac had a single, internal floppy drive whose disks stored 400K of information; a few months later, an external floppy drive became available—and it seemed such a luxury to have one floppy to hold the system software and an application, and a second one to hold documents! About two years later, the double-sided floppy and drive were introduced, with an astounding 800K of storage available on a single disk. (Now the Mac comes standard with an internal drive that holds more than a thousand times that amount of information.)

Since 1990, the standard floppy drive has used floppies that hold 1.4MB of data. They've been standard for so long that they no longer need a name to differentiate them from their predecessors, but Apple officially called the drive *FDHD* (floppy drive, high density); less formally, the drive and disks were referred to as the *SuperDrive* and *super floppies*.

Why are those little hard-cased things called *floppy?* Because the inner material is a disk of magnetic media (much like the material used as audio cassette tape), and it really is floppy. And, prior to the 3.5" plastic-encased disk that the Mac made popular, there were 5.25" and 8.5" disks covered in cardboard, for which the *floppy* nomenclature made sense.

Backwards compatibility. Millions of Mac users will live their whole computing lives without ever seeing a 400K disk; some won't ever run across an 800K disk, either. But if you do, don't worry: the current drive can read all three sizes of disks.

How can you tell the difference among the three? The disk case is usually stamped somewhere with "single-sided" or "double-sided" and/or "double-density" or "HD" (for *high density)*. You can, however, tell a 1.4MB floppy at a glance because it has a square hole in the corner of the case, across from the hole that serves as a lock. And, of course, you can just slap the disk into the drive and see how much information is stored on it.

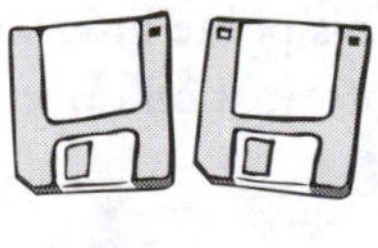

1.4MB floppies (right) have an extra hole in the disk case.

Buying floppies. If you buy floppies, you don't have to buy made-for-Mac floppies—in fact, you'd be hard-pressed to find them. A box of floppies labeled *double sided, double density* or *HD* is all you need. In many cases, the *double density* label may be missing, so just check that the capacity of the disk is around 1.4MB. For a little extra money, you can buy pre-formatted disks; you'll have to be the judge as to whether or not a few extra dollars is worth a few minutes formatting time.

Pre-formatted disks come in two flavors—Mac and PC. It's hard to find Mac-formatted disks in computer or office stores, although Mac catalogs carry them. If the only thing you can find is PC-formatted disks, you can buy them and just reformat them for your Mac, which can handle both formats equally. My husband buys IBM-formatted disks and uses them as-is; the Mac can read and write to them with no problems, and he can easily hand them to a Windows-based colleague without worrying about whether *they'll* be able to read the disk.

IN THE BEGINNING

When the first Mac came out, you could buy a box of Sony-manufactured but Apple-labeled floppy disks: $50 dollars for ten of them. Within months, the price plummeted to $35 for ten: only $3.50 each for 400K disks! Later, of course, prices truly plunged. (And, just for fun, compare even the best floppy storage price to a Zip disk, which isn't physically much bigger but stores 100 megs of information at about 10 cents per meg as of this writing.)

	400K disks		800K disks		1.4MB disks	
	Price per disk	Price per MB storage	Price per disk	Price per MB storage	Price per disk	Price per MB storage
Mar 84	$3.50	$8.96	-	-	-	-
Nov 85	$1.99	$5.09	-	-	-	-
May 88	$1.09	$2.79	$1.39	$1.78	-	-
Apr 92	-	-	.90	$1.15	$1.50	$1.07
Jun 94	-	-	.80	$1.02	$1.20	.86
Mar 98	-	-			.50	.36

Initializing a floppy disk. Initializing a new floppy disk is so easy, it's hardly worth mentioning, except that there are some options in the main dialog.

When you insert a new disk that's never been formatted, you'll get a dialog telling you the disk is unreadable and asking if you'd like to initialize it (see, there's that initialize/format thing again). This polite little stopgap is just in case the disk is already formatted and has information on it that you need, but for some reason is currently unreadable.

If you want to initialize the disk, you can type in a name for it (or leave it at *untitled,* and name it later), and choose a format: Macintosh 1.4MB, the default; DOS 1.4 MB for DOS and Windows machines (this choice is available if you have the PC Exchange control panel running); and ProDOS 1.4MB for Apple II computers. (If you're working with an old 800K disk, the choices in the menu will be Macintosh 800K, DOS 720K and ProDOS

800K.) Then click the Initialize button; you'll see a series of dialogs as the disk is being processed, and in a minute or two you'll have the disk ready to go.

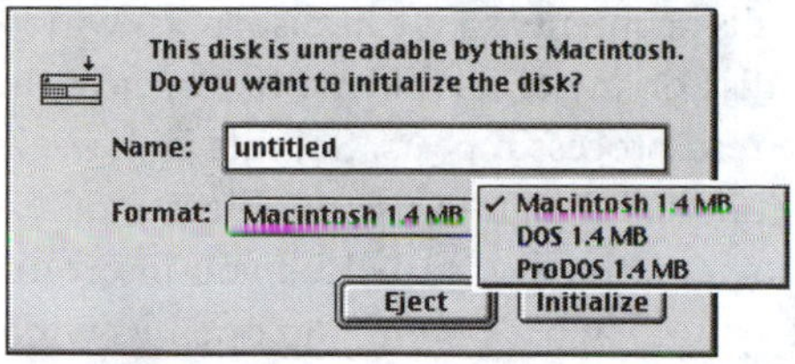

The disk formatting dialog provides three options in its menu (inset).

Care and feeding. Floppies are not delicate little creatures. While pouring sticky liquids all over them or sticking a pin through the media after opening the protective shutter is bound to cause problems, you don't have to be overly careful. (In fact, I've taken apart poured-upon floppy cases, cleaned everything off, put them back together and used them. Of course, that was back when I had important stuff on floppies, and two small children.)

And, while anything that stores information magnetically is prone to problems from magnets, it takes a *lot* of magnetizing to scramble a disk's information. I couldn't find a non-initialized disk when I wanted to do some screen shots for this chapter, so I tried to ruin a disk by rubbing it with a magnet. It was still readable. I tried a small rare-earth magnet, which is stronger. It was *still* absolutely readable!

So, be reasonably careful when handling disks, but don't worry about it.

Using Floppies

Ejecting a floppy disk. You have several choices when it comes to ejecting disks:

- Select the icon and choose Put Away (⌘Y) from the File menu.
- Select the icon and choose Eject (⌘E) from the Special menu.
- Drag the icon to the Trash.

In OS 8, using the Eject command finally works completely: it both ejects the disk and removes its icon from the desktop. Previously, the icon would remain in a "ghost" state even though the disk itself was ejected.

These options also work for any removable media, like Zip cartridges.

Leaving a ghost behind. If you like the way the Eject command used to work, leaving the floppy's ghost icon on the desktop, you can still have it that way: holding Option while opening the Special menu changes the Eject command to Eject and Leave Behind.

Ghost icons **Chapter 6**

I'm not sure why you'd ever want to do this; leaving a ghost disk behind triggers an annoying "Please insert the disk" dialog at frequent intervals. When you insert a disk, the delay before it appears on the desktop is due to the Finder's reading the disk contents so it can display its windows as soon as you double-click on the disk or any of its folders. If you eject the disk normally, then re-insert it, the read process repeats. So, this is the only scenario that I can think of where you might want to use the Eject and Leave Behind option: There's nothing written on the disk's label, so you insert the disk to see what's on it. You open its windows, then temporarily eject the disk so you can write on the label before you forget what's there. Then you reinsert the disk to copy or use the files. By leaving the ghost behind when you eject the disk, there's no delay when you re-insert it.

Holding down Option changes the standard Eject command.

Emergency eject. You can eject a floppy in an emergency situation by pressing ⌘ Shift 1. Or, in a *real* emergency, you can poke a straightened paper clip into the little hole by the floppy drive to push the disk out. (There's a similar hole by the CD tray, for the same reason.) When you eject a floppy manually, its "ghost" icon remains on the desktop.

Erasing the disk. Erase a floppy with the Special menu's Erase Disk command. You'll get a dialog similar to the one for blank disks; click the Erase button and the process continues as it does for a newly initialized disk.

Erasing a disk with the Erase Disk command takes longer than just dumping the disk's contents into the trash and emptying it, but there are good reasons for doing it the long way:

- Everything on the disk is erased, including invisible files that may be taking up needed space.

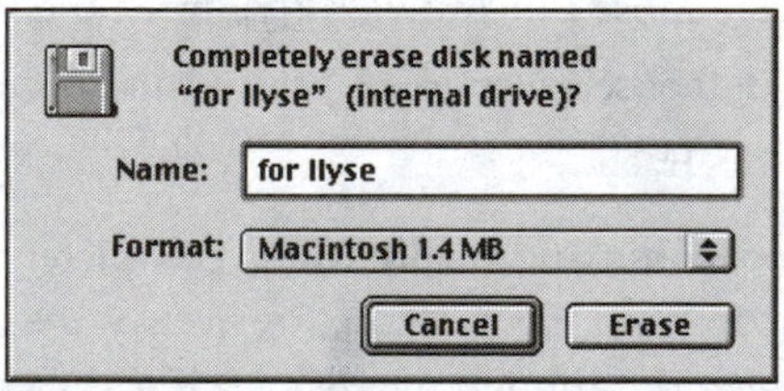

The Erase dialog is nearly identical to the Initialize dialog.

- The invisible Desktop file is re-created from scratch, with old icons purged from it, freeing up more room on the disk.
- The initialization process checks the entire disk for any flaws, so you can be more sure of the disk's reliability.

Erase dialog shortcut. If you're absolutely sure you want to erase a floppy and don't need to check its contents beforehand, you can have the Erase dialog appear automatically: hold down ⌘ Option Tab as you insert the disk.

Locking a floppy. Lock a disk by sliding the plastic locking tab so the hole is open. (Doesn't that feel backwards? When the hole is open the disk is locked, and when it's closed the disk is unlocked.) Any windows belonging to a locked disk display a little padlock in their headers.

You can't change anything on a locked disk. You can copy files from it, but not to it. You can open the locked disk's windows and even move its icons around, but those changes are only in the Finder's memory and won't be stored on the disk; the next time you insert the disk, its windows and icons will look the same as the last time you inserted it.

A locked floppy (top) has an open tab.

Copy a file that's "too big." If you have a floppy disk that shows 14K of remaining space, go ahead and copy a 40K file to it—it's likely the file will fit with no problem. In fact, you might be able to copy a 1.5MB or 1.6MB file to a floppy with a standard capacity of 1.4MB. Because of the allocation block issue described earlier—which makes files take more room on larger drives—how "large" a file can be dragged to a floppy depends on how large the disk is where the original file is stored.

Disk labels. You don't have to peel off a disk label in order to put on a fresh one: you can just layer them three or four deep if you want. Just make sure that the small edge that wraps around to the bottom of the disk is pressed on firmly so it won't interfere with the drive mechanism.

> ***The whole notion of computing takes a quantum leap when you discover that information can be stored in one place rather than scattered over hundreds of little disks.***
>
> *Macworld, July 1985*

If you peel off a label and the disk has adhesive residue on it, rubbing it with a cloth moistened with a little WD-40 oil (or lighter fluid, or rubber cement thinner) will take it off.

Or, try erasable labels: the **LabelOnce** kit for floppies comes with a special pen and eraser and 25 labels for about $9; "refills"—a set of 50 labels—are $7. The felt-tip markers make for quick-drying, legible writing that can later be erased. (Of course, you can write on a standard label with a pencil so that's it's easily erased—but it's not so easily read!) Kits for other types of disk labels (Zip, Jaz, Syquest, and so on) are also available; you can check them out through the **APS** catalog or web site.

apstech.com

Floppy-to-floppy copy. If you want to copy the contents of one floppy to another, use the hard drive as a go-between. Copy the floppy to the hard drive by dragging its icon right onto the hard drive icon or into its window. The Mac will create a folder with the same name as the floppy disk, and put all the disk contents in the folder. Eject the disk, insert another one, open the folder that was created for the floppy contents, and drag the folder contents to the new floppy. This is lots faster than trying to swap two floppies in and out of a single drive.

The Disk Copy utility
Later this chapter

This *doesn't* work for special floppies, like installation disks, that have invisible files on them for both practical and copy-protection purposes.

Working with PC floppies. Macs can read from, write to, and even format floppies that DOS/Windows machines use—as long as you have the PC Exchange control panel installed. As long as PC Exchange is in your system, you don't have to do anything special. The PC-formatted disk will appear on your desktop like any other floppy, but with a PC stamped on the icon. To format a disk as a PC disk, just select that option in the Initialize dialog.

Exchange

Keep in mind, though, that being able to read a *disk*, and being able to read the *files* on it, are two different things. (File translation issues are covered in Chapter 12.)

The PC floppy slowdown. While the Mac has no trouble working with PC-formatted disks, it does take longer to read from and write to that format than its own format. So, if you have a choice, stick with Mac-formatted floppies; don't be lazy and skip reformatting a PC disk because you think it's exactly the same as using a Mac disk.

More Floppy Info

Floppies and the trash. If your trash can's lid pops off when you insert a floppy disk, something was dragged from the floppy to the Trash the last time the disk was used, but the Trash wasn't emptied; so, the file is still on the disk.

Trying to copy files to a disk that has trashed but not yet erased files gets you a dialog offering to empty the trash—if erasing those files will actually provide enough room for the copied file.

Making more room on a floppy. When I started this seventh edition project, I decided it was time to drop some really old stuff that's been carried through several editions. I assumed that not too many people used floppies too often, and that all the little hints and tips we've used forever were perhaps a little stale, and not all that useful.

Then, while I was working on this chapter, one of my husband's colleagues called: she needed to transfer a file from her PowerBook to her Performa and, for various reasons, her only option was using a floppy. But the file, at its smallest, was still 50K too big to fit on the floppy. I suggested a trick that amazed her: I had her insert the floppy while holding down ⌘ and Option. Like magic (sort of), she was then able to copy the file to the floppy.

Rebuilding the desktop
Chapter 24

As described earlier, the Mac keeps invisible files on every disk to keep track of things. One of the files is a database that stores the icons of the files on the disk. When you erase the files, the icons remain in the database; the more different icons that have lived on the disk, the larger the database is. When you "rebuild the desktop" by holding ⌘ and Option when a disk is inserted, the file is purged of all the icons that aren't being used by files still on the disk.

Since her invisible file was almost 150K, and rebuilding made it only 1K, there was plenty of room to copy the file to the disk.

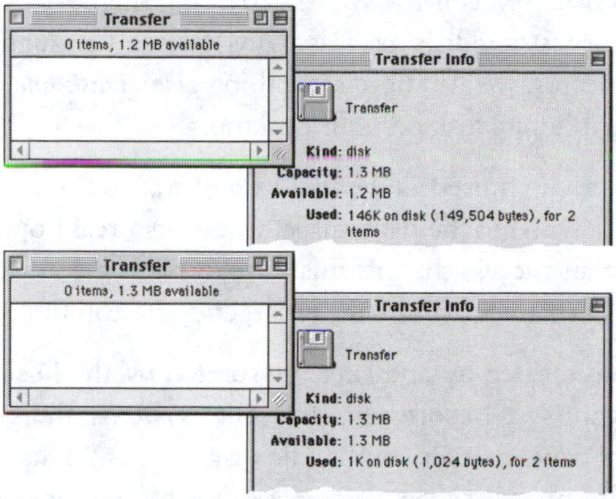

Top, the main window for an "empty" floppy disk that shows zero items, yet only 1.2MB available. The Get Info window reports 146K used by two items—invisible desktop files. After rebuilding the desktop, the same disk (bottom) shows zero items but 1.3MB available; its Info window shows only 1K used by two invisible files.

Where do all those K go? You put in a floppy, there are no files on it (or you erase the files), but there's hundreds of K still reported as being used. This table shows where they might be, and what to do to recover them. (You don't have to guess at which of these is the problem; using the Erase Disk command erases trashed files and invisible ones, rebuilds the desktop file, and checks for any bad sectors.)

The Missing K

Why they're missing...	How to get them back...
There are files dragged to the Trash, but not yet erased.	Use the Empty Trash command.
The desktop file is bloated with old icons that have been used for files on this disk)	Re-insert the disk while holding down ⌘ and Caps Lock to rebuild the desktop file.
There are invisible files on the disk (besides the desktop file) that were put there by some utility or program.	You can delete invisible files with the correct utility but it's easier to just reformat the disk.
There are some bad sectors on the disk that were set aside as unusable when the disk was formatted.	There's nothing you can do about this.

The "minor repairs" offer. If you insert a disk and get a dialog that says something like: *This disk needs minor repairs. Do you want me to repair it?*, go ahead and click the OK button. If you don't, you won't be able to read the disk contents; if you do, the process won't erase anything on the disk.

No more floppy info. Starting with OS 8, you can't enter comments into the Get Info window for a floppy. The space that used to be allocated for that is now used to keep track of the extra view settings for the disk and its folders.

Disk Images

Rich Wolfson was the special contributor for this section, though his initials aren't on the entries.

The virtual floppy. As if RAM disks (treating memory as disk space) and Virtual Memory (using disk space as RAM) weren't enough in the way of computer concepts, we also have something else: a *disk image*, which provides a sort of virtual floppy disk on your desktop.

RAM disks and virtual memory
Chapter 13

Disk images are often used as the medium of transfer for software downloads from web sites: you get the disk image, put it on a real floppy or mount it as a virtual floppy, and access the information. You'll find some disk images on your OS 8 CD that help you make emergency startup floppies.

A disk image is created by, and later interpreted by, the Disk Copy utility that comes with your system software. (In earlier systems, there was a Mount Image control panel that let you handle disk images.) The file that Disk Copy makes and interprets is called a *disk image file.* Its icon looks like a document (with the turned-down corner) with a floppy icon on it.

Disk Copy can also be used to make copies of, and copy information to, actual floppy disks.

Mounting a disk image. With Disk Copy anywhere on your hard drive, mounting a disk image is a single-step process: double-click on the image file. Disk Copy opens, mounts the image, and quits—and all you see is a dialog or two flashing by as Disk Copy does its work, and then the disk image on the desktop, looking just like a real floppy.

You can also mount a disk image "manually," by first running the Disk Copy program. Then, you either use the Mount Image command to open the image file, or just drag the image file into the Disk Copy window.

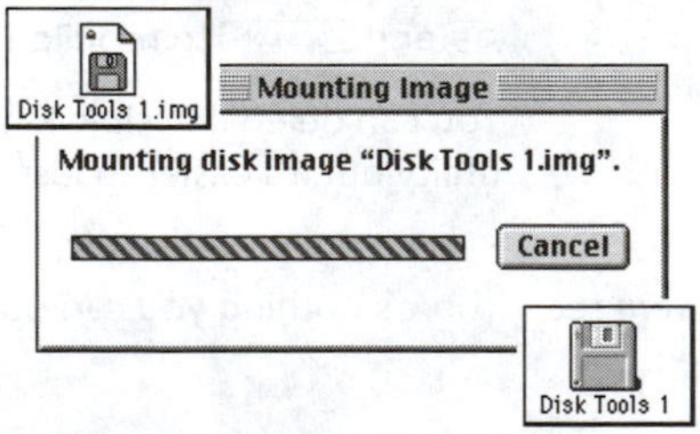

Double-click on the image file (upper left) and Disk Copy does its work, mounting the disk image (lower right).

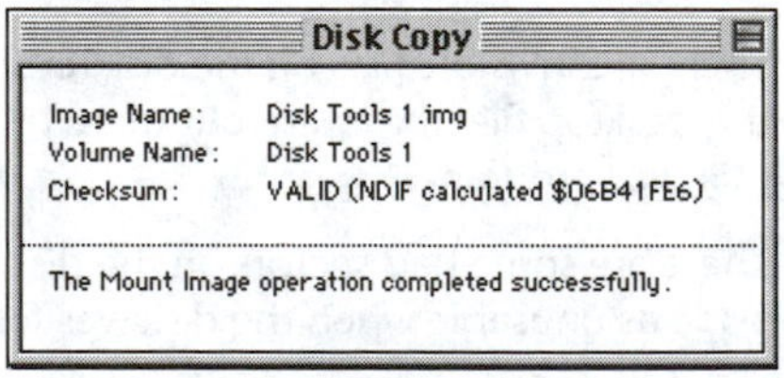

You can mount images manually by first running the Disk Copy utility.

Using a disk image. Once a disk image is mounted, you can treat it like a standard floppy disk. If it was created as a read-only image, you'll see a lock icon in each of its windows and you won't be able to copy anything to it—just as with a real disk. When you want to get rid of the disk image, drag it to the Trash or use the Eject Disk or Put Away command.

Thanks for the (extra) memory. Disk Copy's default memory allocation lets it easily mount disk images, but isn't always enough for making copies to a floppy disk, an operation that often needs more memory. You should set its Preferred memory size to 2 megs (2048K) if you're going to make real floppies.

Memory allocations
Chapter 13

Creating a disk image. You can easily create disk images from folders or from other disks with Disk Copy. Simply use one of the three Create commands from the Image menu and follow the prompts. (The Create New Image command was added in the 6.2 version; it lets you create a blank disk image which, when mounted, lets you copy things to it.) You'll have to choose one of the three disk image formats: Read/Write (the only one available for blank images), Read-Only, and Read-Only Compressed.

If you use the Read/Write option, you'll be able to write information to the mounted disk image; when the disk is unmounted, the information is written back to the image file, so that the next time it's mounted, the new information will be there. The Read-Only option creates disks that are locked when they're mounted.

Starting with version 6.1.2 of Disk Copy, which shipped with OS 8, inserting a floppy, or even a CD, while Disk Copy is running in the foreground automatically triggers the Create Image from Disk command.

The ever-changing version number. Disk Copy 6.1.2 shipped on the first OS 8 CDs, and 6.2 on the first OS 8.1 CDs; somewhere in-between, there was a 6.1.3 update, too. All these little number changes add little features. The major changes from the OS 8 version to the OS 8.1 version are: the ability to create blank read-write images; support for Macintosh Extended format volumes; support for segmented images; and, now Disk Copy will launch without the ObjectSupportLib extension active, although it's necessary for AppleScript control of Disk Copy.

Converting disk images. Disk Copy's Image menu includes a Convert Image command that lets you change an image's format (Read/Write, Read-Only, Read-Only Compressed) from its original state to the one you want. You can also use the Convert command to change the old Disk Copy 4.2 images to the newer format.

Disk images for backups. I use Disk Copy as another way to back up my hard drive at work: I make a compressed disk image that can be stored on the file server. If I run into a disaster with my hard drive, I can easily restore it with the weekly "snapshot" that Disk Copy takes.

Making a *real* floppy. To create a full-fledged floppy from a disk image, you run Disk Copy and use the Make a Floppy command. You'll be asked to select the image file for the procedure, and to insert a disk; there are settings you can alter regarding whether or not you get warned if there's already information on the disk.

You can also start the copy-to-floppy process by double-clicking on the image file with Option down. If Disk Copy is already open, you can drag the image file into the window while you hold down Option, which will send the data to the floppy rather than mounting the image.

Option-dragging an image into the Disk Copy window is a little tricky. When an application is open and you Option-click on the desktop or any of its icons, the system interprets that as your wanting to move to the desktop and hide all the windows of the current application. With the Disk Copy window active, the Option-click on a desktop disk image (when you grab it for dragging) means the Disk Copy window disappears! To avoid this problem, just start dragging the disk image into the Disk Copy window without any keys down; just before you let go of the mouse button, press and hold Option.

Working with old image files. If you have disk image files from previous versions of Disk Copy, you'll be able to use them by first running Disk Copy, and then manipulating the images. Here are the things that *won't* work if you have old image files and the new Disk Copy:

- Double-clicking on the image file to get the disk image to mount.
- Option-double-clicking on the image file to start the copy-to-a-real-floppy process.
- Option-dragging the file into the Disk Copy window to start copying to a floppy.

If you want these capabilities for older image files, run them through OS 8's Disk Copy, using the Convert command to change them to the new format.

Where *is* that floppy image? I've never used disk images except briefly when I've downloaded them from Apple's system software support site. So I never thought much about them until I started writing this section. And then I started wondering: where exactly does an image "live" when it's mounted? It doesn't get its own memory allocation, and it doesn't use up any of the system's memory allocation, as does a RAM disk. Aha, I thought, it's an invisible file on the startup drive! A little investigation proved that wrong, too.

The disk image is nothing more than a fancy kind of alias that points to the original image *file.* The disk image lets you manipulate the information on your virtual disk, but it's just a way of manipulating the information in the image file. The disk image, temporarily stored on your startup drive, takes no more room than does an alias (a few K) no matter what's "on" it; the image file, on the other hand, uses about 1.4MB of space—the size of a floppy disk—on whatever disk it's stored on.

And where's that image *file*? If you've lost track of an image file and for some reason want to get to it while the image is mounted, do a Get Info on the disk image. The Where information identifies the volume that stores the image, though not the enclosing folder path. The file's name is always the same as the image's, with *.img* added to it, so you can use Find File if you have to.

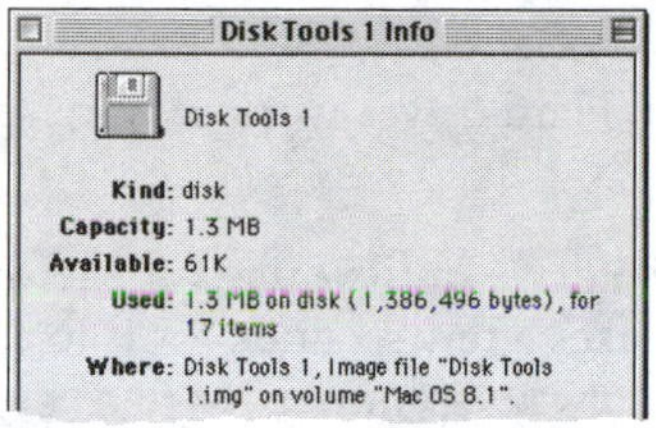

Aloha. Choose the About command from under the Apple menu while Disk Copy's open, and ⌘-click on the copyright symbol; hold down the mouse button to see what happens. Then try it with ⌘ and Option down—and then you'll understand the title of this entry.

Scripted procedures. Disk Copy is very AppleScriptable: a program can be written in AppleScript which is then executed by Disk Copy. The Disk Tools folder on your system CD holds a good example of this: when you click on the Make Disk Tools Floppies icon, you're prompted to insert a floppy, and the information is copied directly to the floppy. But the icon is just an AppleScript that tells Disk Copy what to do. If you wanted to actually mount the disk images to take a look at them, you'd just double-click directly on the disk image files instead of on the Make Floppies icon.

The Make Disk icon on your system CD is simply an AppleScript that directs Disk Copy to make actual floppies. If you want to mount an image, double-click on it directly.

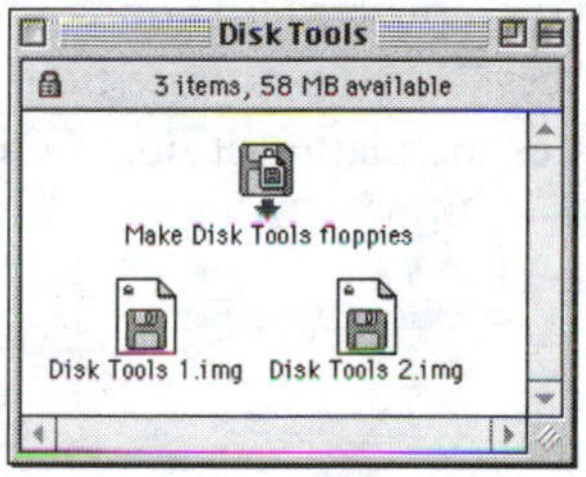

ShrinkWrap for special needs. Aladdin Systems' **ShrinkWrap** used to be miles ahead of the disk-image options provided with the Mac system software. It's still a little ahead, with better compression/decompression, and faster mounting and copying, but unless you're going to be handling lots of disk images or disk copying, it's hard to beat the freebie that comes with the system software. In fact, Aladdin now categorizes this product under "Developer Technology" for those distributing software.

aladdinsys.com

Hard Drives

About Hard Drives

Hard drives. The difference between a disk (the storage *medium)* and a drive (the *mechanism)* is easy to see when you're talking about floppies. But a *hard drive* is the medium and the mechanism in one, sealed unit; understandably, the terms *hard drive* and *hard disk* are interchangeable.

The basic internal mechanism of a hard drive is like a floppy drive on steroids: there are multiple platters coated with magnetic particles, and a read-write head for every platter.

Why hard drives are faster. Hard drives work at warp speed compared to floppies for a number of reasons:

- A floppy disk sits still in the drive until you ask for its attention, at which point it starts spinning; it takes a few seconds for it to come to full speed. The hard drive platters are always spinning.
- The hard drive platters spin lots faster than a floppy: ten to twenty-five times faster.
- The information on a hard drive is packed together more tightly than it is on a floppy. As a result, the read-write heads don't have to travel as far to get from one piece of information to another.

The mighty mote. Hard drives are sealed shut because even a tiny speck of dust can cause disaster in a mechanism that works at high speeds and small tolerances. How tiny is tiny? A smoke particle could be a problem (that's *smoke,* not ash); leave a fingerprint on a platter and you could have a problem. And just how small are the tolerances? The read-write head in a hard drive, unlike that in a floppy, never touches the platter; it floats a few *microns* above the media (far less than the width of a human hair).

IN THE BEGINNING...

There were no hard drives available when the Macs first came out; the only storage device was a single 400K floppy drive. The first Mac hard drive from Apple was an external 20MB model. It cost $1500 and, although you could eventually run the Mac from a System Folder on the hard drive, you couldn't start up from it. You had to start up with a special floppy and then turn control over to the system on the hard drive.

Fragmentation. Whenever you put something on a disk, the Mac tries to save it in contiguous blocks. If it can't find a large enough space, it divides the file into pieces and puts them wherever it can. This is usually referred to as *fragmentation,* or *disk fragmentation* (even though its the *files* that are actually fragmented). Fragmentation can slow down your hard disk because it takes longer to gather up all the fragments of a file when you want to open or copy it.

Fragmentation also occurs as you edit files: a document may have been in one spot on the disk when you first created it, but if later editing makes it larger, and there isn't any empty space next to its original blocks, it saves the "spillover" in some other, possibly far away, location.

Fighting fragmentation *Defragmenters,* or *optimizers* (because they optimize disk performance), are utility programs that work by analyzing your disk and shuffling fragments of files around until each forms a neat, contiguous whole.

alsoftinc.com
lacie.com
symantec.com

The best of the bunch has always been Alsoft's DiskExpress; the current package is **DiskExpress Pro** ($50), which needs to be updated to 3.0.1 at least to work with OS 8. (If you have version 3, you can download a minor update patch from Alsoft's web site). DiskExpress can do its thing on command or whenever your Mac is sitting idle, any time or during hours you specify. Besides defragmenting, it can track what files you use most often and group them at the most accessible parts of the disk. Altogether, it's a great tool for the compulsive hard-disk jockey.

You'll find a simpler optimizer in the leading disk utility, Symantec's **Norton Utilities**; there's also an optimization command in La Cie's **Silverlining** disk formatter.

All of the optimization programs take precautions to ensure your disk won't be scrambled if there's a crash or a power outage during the defragmentation process, but it's always a good idea to make sure you have an up-to-date backup before letting an optimizer loose. Also, as of this writing, none of these utilities work with HFS-Plus formatted disks, although they should by the time you read this. —SZA/HN/JC

Drive maintenance
Chapter 24

Don't fight it. All the information in the last entry is accurate. Accurate—but perhaps misleading. I can't really recommend you add defragmentation to your arsenal of drive maintenance procedures. The time you save in accessing files won't add up to the time it will take to do a precautionary backup and the defrag itself. A drive that's used a lot should be, every year or so, just completely wiped and reformatted anyway; that keeps files from being severely defragmented.

Formatting and Partitioning

The Apple formatter. Your internal Apple hard drive comes already formatted, but if you need to reformat it, use the Drive Setup utility that comes with your system software. (Remember: formatting not only readies the drive for use by mapping out tracks and sectors, but also sets aside any bad sections of the disk so data won't be stored in an unreliable spot.)

For nearly a decade, the formatting software that came with Apple's system software was HDSC Setup, with the *SC* standing for SCSI. When Apple started selling Macs with IDE drives, that didn't quite cut it, so they came out with a utility called Internal HD Format (since only internal drives are IDE's). You don't have to worry any more about what drive you have and which utility to use, since OS 8's Drive Setup can handle both kinds of drives.

Third-party formatting software. Apple's formatter works only on Apple's drives. For other drives, you use either the software that comes with the drive or a "universal" hard disk formatter to set up the drive and install or update the disk driver (covered in the next entry). Third-party disk formatters work for almost any kind of drive, including Apple's, and also for removable media. (Apple's formatter is slated to handle third-party drives soon, so check for updates before you worry about getting some other software.)

fwb.com
lacie.com

Two companies head the pack when it comes to Mac drive formatting. FWB Software offers **Hard Disk ToolKit Personal Edition** ($50), which provides all the basics, and **Hard Disk ToolKit** ($130), which includes all sorts of extras like file and folder protection, heavy-duty encryption security, and the ability to format multiple drives simultaneously. (The Personal Edition is all most people need.) **Silverlining** ($100, La Cie) has long been a Mac favorite. Both publishers update their products regularly.

Disk drivers. A *driver* is a piece of software that regulates how the Mac interacts with a peripheral device. The icons for various printers in your Extensions folder, for instance, are printer drivers. A hard drive needs a driver, too, but you won't find it in your Extensions folder. A *disk driver* is quietly tucked into its own invisible partition on a hard drive when you format it. It loads into memory every time you start up, and mounts the disk's icon on the desktop.

The driver can be updated separately at a later date without your having to reformat the drive. When you upgrade the operating system, it's important to also update the driver. It won't affect the data on the drive, so you can update the driver without moving your files away to a safe place. (Although it's recommended you do a backup before an update "just in case," I don't know anyone who ever has, nor anyone who's ever had a problem with lost data.)

You update the driver with disk formatting software. For Apple drives, use the Drive Setup utility: select the drive in the Setup window, and choose Update Driver from the Functions menu. For third-party drives, you use whatever formatting software you used for the drive. You'll be able to update the formatting software, if necessary, by downloading the latest version tweak from the publisher's web site.

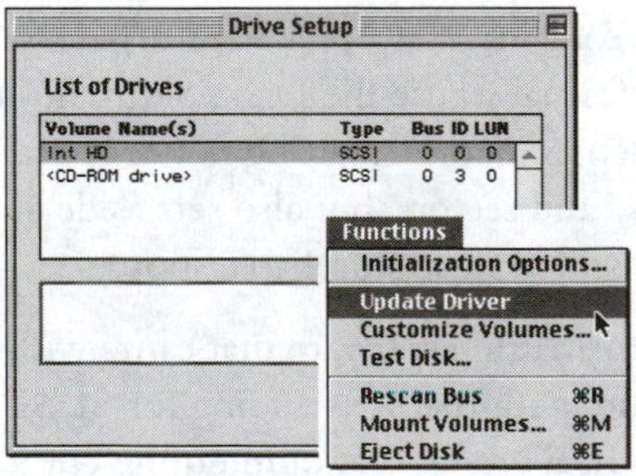

Updating a disk driver with Drive Setup.

Keep in mind that you can only update a driver with the most recent version of a drive utility: you can't, for instance, update a driver for OS 12.5 with the drive utility that came with OS 12.

The disk icon. The standard hard drive icon you see on all the screenshots throughout this book are the Apple icons, which are automatically used by all

Apple hard drives. But when you buy a third-party drive, and format it with third-party software, you'll get a different default icon; some formatters let you choose from among several icons for the disk. (You can also paste in your own icon, as described in Chapter 6).

Low-level and zeroing options. The Drive Setup utility offers two unexplained options when you're formatting a drive: *low-level format* and *zero all data*. A standard initialization doesn't erase information on a drive—it just erases the directory that keeps track of where files are stored. The low-level format wipes the drive clean—and it can take a couple of hours for a large drive, so be sure you have the time, even though you won't usually have the need for it. The zeroing option replaces every bit of data on the drive with zeros, obliterating the information so even a file-recovery program can't retrieve anything. If you work for the CIA (or against it, for that matter), you'll want to zero things out.

The interleave ratio. Because older Macs couldn't digest data as fast as it could be read off a hard disk, you had to tell your formatting software to go through some special tricks to give the Mac a little time to catch up between each bit it read from the disk. This process was called setting the *interleave ratio*, or just the *interleave*.

Using an interleave of 3:1, for example, makes the Mac skip two sectors and read only every third sector on the disk. This gives the Mac enough time to swallow the data before the next sector passes underneath the read-write head.

The Mac Plus required an interleave ratio of 3:1; for the SE, the Classic, and the PowerBook 100, the requisite ratio is 2:1. All later Macs however, have been able to handle a 1:1 ratio, which makes performance much better. An interleave of 1:1 means that every consecutive sector is read with no "digestion time" required.

Most formatters now suggest or automatically set the optimal ratio, so you shouldn't have to think about the issue at all—if you confront a choice, just leave it at 1:1 unless you're working with one of the early Macs. —HN/JC

When the driver doesn't fit. Okay, I already reassured you that updating a disk driver doesn't mean you have to reformat your drive, but on very rare occasions, that's just what you'll have to do. For instance: disk drivers used prior to System 7 took a 16K partition, but with System 7, they grew to need more space—a partition of 32K, where it remains now. You can't update a pre-System 7 driver without reformatting the drive because you can't change partition sizes without reformatting. And, sometime in the future, the 32K partition isn't going to work anymore either, and everyone will be reformatting drives to accommodate a 64K partition.

Partitioning. *Partitioning* is dividing a single disk into multiple "logical" volumes—sections that the Mac treats as completely separate disks. Here are some reasons why you might want to partition a large drive:

- If you work with mostly small files (word processor documents or spreadsheets) and your hard drive is a gig or more in capacity, you waste lots of space if you're working with a system (and drive formatting) prior to OS 8.1; this "allocation block" problem was described in detail earlier in the chapter. A smaller partition gets smaller allocation blocks, and utilizes space more efficiently.
- If you share your hard drive with kids or a coworker, or use it for distinctly separate purposes (business and home), you can mount disk partitions only when necessary and protect the important ones with passwords.
- You can keep extraneous volume partitions from mounting at startup, which saves time (because the Finder has to read through the disk contents at startup) and desktop space until you really need to use the volumes, at which point you can manually mount them.

You can partition a drive only when you're formatting it, so it's something you have to do either right at the beginning or you'll have to be willing to erase your disk and start again. Apple's Drive Setup utility doesn't provide extra options like password protection, but most third-party products do.

Creating partitions. Partitioning a hard drive with Apple's Drive Setup is easier than it was with the HDSC Setup utility:

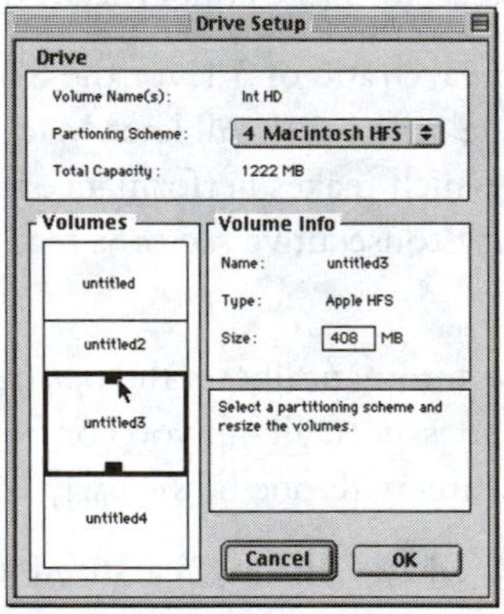

Partitioning a drive with Drive Setup. When you drag on the "handle" of a selected partition, the partition size changes.

1. Launch Drive Setup.
2. Select the target drive in the window.
3. Click the Initialize button.
4. Click the Custom Setup button.
5. Select the number of partitions you want from the Partitioning Scheme pop-up menu. (Use one of the HFS choices; the ProDOS choices at the bottom of the menu are for Apple II computers.)
6. Manipulate the "map" in the lower left corner of the window to adjust the relative sizes of your partitions. You'll see the exact size in megabytes listed at the right.
7. Click OK to start the partitioning process. (You'll get to name the partitions when they appear on the desktop.)

Since Drive Setup works on only Apple drives, and Apple provides only internal drives, the only time you'll be using Drive Setup for partitioning is if you reformat your internal drive. So, you'll be running the Drive Setup utility from a different disk: the OS CD, or an external hard drive or removable that can also work as a startup.

Selecting a small partition. If you have a relatively small partition in the Drive Setup map when you're creating partitions, it's hard to select it by clicking on it. But if you press Tab, it will select volumes in turn, so you'll get to the tiny one sooner or later.

Working with partitions. While my startup disk (the internal Apple drive) is over a gig in size, I've left it unpartitioned. But my second internal drive is a good example of how handy, and easy, it is to use partitions once they're set up.

I have six partitions on the 4GB drive. There's 120 megs each for three different system software versions, which I think of in a Dickensian sort of way as past, present, and future: System 7.6; a straight-vanilla current OS 8.x with no third-party extras; and an OS 8 "plus" for beta, and, later, genuine but still test versions of OS 8 updates. None of these mounts automatically at startup. There are three other partitions that do mount at every startup: a reasonably large partition for applications that I need available, but don't use all that often; my backup volume; and, my Warehouse volume that holds all sorts of stuff.

When I want to mount one of the unmounted partitions, I simply open the APS Mounter utility I keep in my Apple menu (the disk is from APS, although as you can see in the picture, it's a Quantum mechanism), select the partition in the list and click the Mount button. Unmounting is a simple matter of selecting something and clicking Unmount; automatically mounting (or not) at startup is a simple checkbox in an Info dialog.

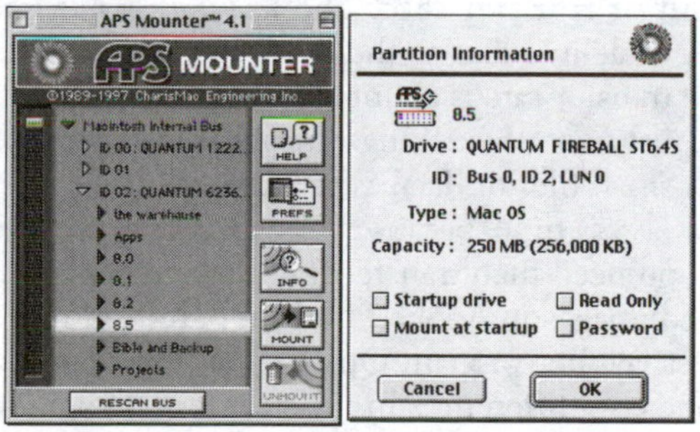

The mounting utility for a partitioned APS drive.

A partition as a startup. As noted in Chapter 5, you can set an individual partition as the startup device, since partitions appear as separate drives in the Startup Disk control panel.

But it's important that you set that partition to be mounted at startup, through whatever software you use to manipulate your partitions. It's easy to overlook this. You might manually mount a partition during a work session and later assign it as the startup drive before you shut down. At the next startup, the Mac will try to start up with that partition but will usually choke part way through the process because the lack of an auto-mount setting interferes with the Mac's using that partition at all.

Choosing a Hard Drive

Speeds and specs. When you buy a hard drive, the three main considerations are capacity, price, and a dependable vendor. Except for ultra-high-end video and multimedia development where every nanosecond counts, you don't have to worry much about the down-and-dirty specs. But here's what it all means:

- **Form factors.** Drives are categorized by two physical dimensions: the diameter of the platters inside and the height of the entire sealed mechanism. The diameter is measured in inches. The height is referred to as *full-height*, *half-height*, or *low-profile*, although the small PowerBook drives are measured in millimeters. So, a drive might be referred to as a half-height three-and-a-half-inch mechanism, or a low-profile two-and-a-half-inch device.
- **Seek and access times**. *Average seek time* is how long it takes the heads to move to the desired track. *Average access time* is that figure plus an additional amount for *latency*, the average wait for the desired sector to come around under the heads once they get to the right track. Unfortunately, many vendors are sloppy and inconsistent in their use of these terms; some will even tell you they mean the same thing. If milliseconds (ms) matter to you, be sure you're using the same standard when comparing products: a drive with an average *access* time of 12 ms is actually faster than one with an average *seek* time of 8 ms.
- **Throughput or transfer rate**. The *data transfer rate* is a measure of how fast a drive can deliver data to the Mac once it gets to the sectors it's looking for. The transfer rate is counted in megabytes per second (or sometimes, just to confuse things, mega*bits* per second). If you deal mostly with small files or database records, transfer rate is less important than seek or access time, because your drive will spend more time getting to the data you need than transferring it to the Mac. But if you work with large scanned images in Adobe Photoshop, for example, or big QuarkXPress layouts, or giant QuickTime files, transfers actually take whole seconds, so differences in the transfer rate matter—much more than a difference of a few thousandths of a second in seek or access time.
- **Burst transfer.** There's a difference between *burst transfer rates* and *sustained transfer rates*. The former measures how fast a drive can pump out a small amount of data loaded into memory buffers on the drive controller; the latter is how fast it can deliver larger amounts, even after the buffers are empty. Burst rates are much higher, so some vendors focus on those, but for most purposes the sustained rate is more important.
- **Spindle speed**. The standard *spindle speed*—the rate at which a hard disk's platters rotate—used to be 3,600 rpm. In the last few years drive manufacturers delivered drives that spin at up to 10,000 rpm. The extra

rotation speed reduces latency, but its main value is to boost sustained transfer rates: the faster the disks are spinning, the faster the drive should be able to read in all the data it's after. You'll notice the difference mainly with big files. —SZA/HN/JC

> ***"Average users can store all their programs as well as a year's worth of files on a 10-megabyte hard disk—and theoretically never have to look at a floppy again."***
>
> *David Bunnel, Macworld, July 1985*

Mean times. Real mean. A hard drive is one of the few computer components with mechanical parts—and those parts perform at high speeds and with small tolerances. Drive manufacturers use a reliability rating referred to as MTBF—*mean time between failures.* Now, there's a term about as accurate as "life insurance," which we all know is actually *death* insurance. The MTBF rating, given in hours, is not really the time *between* failures, but the time *until* a failure. And since the failure is usually some component entirely giving out, it's really a measure of PLS: probable life span. That said, however, MTBF is pretty much a useless figure, with ratings for most drives these days from 500,000 to a million hours. Even if you keep the drive on for twenty-four hours a day, that's around a hundred years. (I guess we can safely assume that those figures are extrapolated from laboratory tests and not calculated from actual field data!)

Warranty. The length of time a drive is covered by warranty is extremely important; most offer one- or two-year coverage. Should the drive mechanism or any components inside an external case fail (power supply, fan, and so on), the vendor will typically replace the drive at no charge. They will not, however, cover the cost to recover or re-create any data lost as a result of a drive failure, so be sure you back up religiously. —HN/JC

The bus slowdown. No matter how fast a hard drive is, you won't get the benefits of its speed unless your Mac can receive information at a speed at least as fast. Pre-Quadra desktop models, PowerBooks up through the 500's, and Duos are limited to about 1.5MB a second, despite the fact that basic SCSI specs call for a transfer rate of 5MB a second. You can use faster disks with these machines, but you won't see the extra speed. Since the Centris/Quadra, the Mac's SCSI bus handles 5MB per second; recent models with two SCSI busses have a fast, 10MB-per-second internal bus and the standard 5MB per second for external devices; some of the latest models handle twice *that* speed, for a 20MB-per-second rate.

All guts, no glory. Most of the hard drives you see aren't manufactured by the companies whose names are on the outside of the case. Instead, drive companies buy the innards from a handful of suppliers, referred to as *OEMs*—(it's pronounced as separate letters and stands for *original equipment manufacturers)*: Quantum, Seagate, and IBM are among the best and the most popular. The drive vendor puts the mechanism in a case, adds a power supply and then sells it with or without warranties, software, cables, and so on.

A few more points. Here are a few more things to keep in mind when you're buying a hard drive:

- **The price**. Of course, I didn't have to tell you that. And you already know that a high price doesn't guarantee high quality. But keep in mind that the price-per-meg of storage goes down as the capacity goes up, since there's a relatively fixed cost for the case, power supply, and cables for each unit.
- **The case.** Do you need a small unit for transportability from, say, home to work? Do you want one that sits flat, or stands on end—or one that can be used either way?
- **Cables.** Does the drive come with a high-quality cable? (Cables, and their quality, are covered in the SCSI section.) Does it come with the *right* cable for your Mac and other peripherals? Sometimes you get a choice of which cable will be included—one that connects the drive to the Mac or one that connects it to other SCSI devices.
- **Termination.** Is it internally terminated? Actively terminated? Unterminated? Check the termination section later in this chapter—but active termination is the best.
- **Software.** Forget the gazillion megabytes of shareware games, because you can get that anywhere. Get a drive with formatting software if you can—software that's supported with frequent updates by the manufacturer.
- **For internal drives.** Internal drives are cheaper than external ones because you're not paying for the case or cables, or power supply. Make sure you get the right size for your Mac model, and check whether you need to order cables or brackets for the drive, or if they're ready and waiting in your Mac already.

APS Drives

Brand-name buying. Assuming that you're reading this book for some concrete recommendations as to which products to buy, here are two outright recommendations: **APS Technologies** and **La Cie**. When I first wrote this, they were separate companies, but before the book was finished, La Cie bought APS (although they are operating separately). You get mail-order and web-order availability of top-notch products from Mac-oriented companies; APS's "extras," like cables, are high-quality items.

apstech.com
lacie.com

These aren't exclusive recommendations: shop around, read ads and reviews, check with friends, and then buy from a company that's been around for a while, since that's the best indicator for its being around for awhile longer.

The RAID approach. RAID stands for *redundant array of inexpensive disks,* which sounds a little silly, since the disks aren't all that inexpensive—and were lots more expensive back when the phrase was coined. (Sometimes the setup is just referred to as an *array.)* RAIDs are multiple disks attached to your Mac and used in either of two special ways: for *striping* or as *mirrors.*

> **“*Given Apple's history ... the hard disk is nice, but the price is phenomenal! It's realistic, reasonable, responsible, affordable, and most of all, totally uncharacteristic.*”**
>
> *MacUser, January 1986*
> *(in regard to Apple's first hard drive, 20 megs for $1500)*

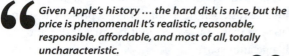

In striping, the disks are used as a single disk, with information split across the drives; with two read-write heads working at the same time, storing data takes less time. Its disadvantage is that if you lose one disk, you've effectively lost both, and all your data. With mirroring, the same information sent to both drives at the same time; you have two copies of your data at all times, making backups as you go along. The drawback is that it takes longer to store the two copies.

Recycling an old internal drive. If you decide to replace an older SCSI internal hard disk with a larger-capacity drive, you don't have to use the old internal as a paperweight. One good use for a former internal drive is putting it in a LaserWriter that can accommodate its own disk for font storage (although not all drives fit inside LaserWriters).

Hard drive inside LaserWriters
Chapter 15

A great way to recycle an older internal drive is to turn it into an external drive. You need a case and a power supply, available from companies like APS Technologies.

Hard-wiring an ID number. Internal hard drives are set to ID 0, which never presents a problem—until you use the tip in the last entry and turn an old internal disk into an external one. You'll wind up with an external drive set to ID 0, and the new internal which must also be set to ID 0.

Internal drives, and the replacement you buy, use pins and jumpers on their circuit boards to indicate the ID number. The pins come in three sets of two, and the jumpers between them (or lack thereof) add up to the ID number, using a pattern that works with binary numbers, as shown in the picture here. The jumpers themselves usually come in a little package along with the drive, and they're not difficult to install.

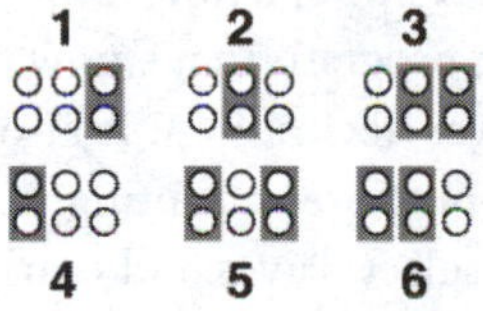

Jumper combinations for SCSI ID numbers.

Other Storage Media

Removable Media

In general. *Removable media* refers to high-capacity storage systems that let you change disks or cartridges; the most popular types are CD-ROMs, Zip disks, and SyQuest cartridges.

Removables are SCSI devices, which presents a problem: the Mac checks the SCSI chain at startup to mount disks, and then doesn't look at it again. So it doesn't notice when you insert a disk because it's not looking at empty SCSI devices. And while a removable disk will be mounted if it's present at startup, the Mac has no way of knowing that you've ejected it because it doesn't expect SCSI devices to change after startup.

At this point, you may be wondering what I'm talking about, because you've inserted and ejected CDs on your system with no problem. But there are extensions in your Extensions folder that take care of this—chiefly, the Apple CD-ROM extension. And that's just what you need for any type of removable: an extension (and/or a control panel) that lets the Mac understand the comings and goings of other kinds of removable disks. When you buy a removable disk system, you'll get the software you need to handle its media, although the Iomega extension for Zip disks even comes with Apple's system software now.

The fixed disk that ain't broke. If you hear the phrase *fixed disk,* it's not referring to a repaired item. It's simply the generic term for drives/disks that don't have removable cartridges.

A removable as startup. You can set a removable disk to be the startup by using the Startup Disk control panel. The device appears in the control panel as long as *any* disk is inserted—it doesn't need a system folder on it to show up. Later, as long as there's an actual system startup disk in the drive, it will be used as the startup.

newertech.com
shareware.com

After-mount. If you insert a removable disk and it doesn't show up on the desktop, you may be missing the proper extension, or the extension might be incompatible with the system software you're using. Several utilities can mount SCSI-device disks after they've been inserted, but you can't beat **SCSIProbe**, a long-time Mac favorite freeware program that's now distributed by Newer Technology. It also serves as a general-purpose mounting utility, since it lets you select drives and mark them (and their partitions) to mount automatically at startup; and, if a fixed disk fails to mount for some reason, SCSIProbe will let you get at it. Another nifty, free mounting control panel is **Mt. Everything** by Horst Pralow, who asks nothing more than a postcard in payment for his efforts.

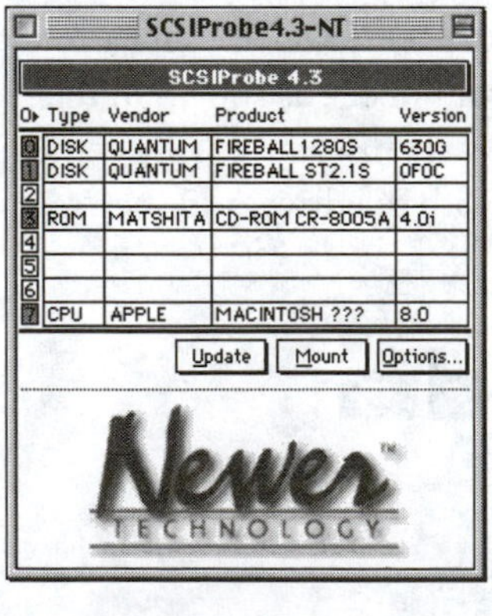

SCSIProbe can mount disks that aren't mounting automatically.

Auto-mounting removable media. If you don't have the right driver for a removable disk to be mounted on your desktop, and you don't have a utility for after-the-fact mounting, restart the Mac with the disk already in the drive—it will be mounted like any other SCSI disk. You'll have to shut down the Mac to remove the disk.

Removable drivers on the disks. Just as a hard disk needs a driver installed in order for it to mount on the desktop, so does a removable disk; the removable's driver is installed when you format the disk. Occasionally you'll find an old removable disk or cartridge with a driver that's much older than the mounting software or the system software expects to find. Sometimes that means the disk just won't show up on the desktop. But you can usually mount it either with something like SCSIProbe or with the utility that came with your removable drive; the drive utility can also usually update the driver on the disk. Very old cartridges might have to be reformatted before the driver can be updated, if the new driver needs a larger partition than the old one did.

Removable technologies. Here's a roundup of removable media types, excluding the popular Zip and Jaz drives, which get entries of their own.

- **SyQuest** drives were the first popular removable-media devices for the Mac, and they ruled the roost for a long time. A SyQuest cartridge is like a hard disk except there's only one platter, in a plastic cartridge. Insert the cartridge in the drive, and its shutter opens to give the read-write heads access—much the way a floppy disk behaves. The original SyQuests had a capacity of 44MB; it took several years to move to 88MB cartridges, but not long afterwards, it jumped to 200MB. Each offered "backward compatibility," the ability of the drive unit to read earlier formats.
- **Flopticals**. Magnetic storage technology was stuck in a awkward rut for a while: the relatively ungainly heads had a hard time getting to just the right spot as the magnetic particles were made smaller and packed together more tightly to provide more storage capacity. The cleverly named *floptical* (floppy/optical) disks and drive addressed the issue by using a laser to accurately position the magnetic read-write head. But a floptical isn't truly an optical storage technology because the laser isn't involved in reading or writing the data.
- **Magneto-opticals**. Beyond the positioning problem solved by floptical technology, the standard magnetic head can't focus on a small enough area of a disk, so particles have to be spread out in order not to be accidentally flipped—leading to lots of wasted space on standard magnetic disks. In magneto-optical (MO) technology, lasers are an integral part of the read-write process. In a write operation, the MO's plastic disk is attacked from both sides at the same time. On one side, a laser heats up a spot to a point (the Curie point, as a matter of fact) where the media's crystals become susceptible to a magnetic field. On the other side, a magnetic write head aligns the crystals in one direction or the other for a one or a zero. This dual approach solves the problem of a magnetic head's not being able to focus on a small enough area. The read process in an MO drive is solely optical, as a less-intense laser hits the data and is reflected back at an angle dependent on the alignment of the crystals it hits.

  One of MO's biggest advantages originally was the stability of its media, with a 30-year shelf life for stored data. But the drives are slower than magnetic removables because their heads are larger and heavier, and because a separate erase pass is needed before new information can be written to the disk. While MO technology has advanced from painfully slow to just plain slow, it has lost its edge as a basic storage or even archive medium: other formats (Jaz, CDs) offer more storage per disk, at lower cost per meg, and CDs offer shelf-life at least as long as the MO medium.

- **Bernoulli drives.** You probably recognize the name Iomega in relation to its Zip and Jaz cartridges, but it was known first for another kind of removable media: Bernoulli drives. Named after the eighteenth-century mathematician who observed and quantified air pressure phenomena, a Bernoulli drive is based on the same principle that keeps an airplane up in the air. The two flexible disks inside a Bernoulli drive are lifted towards the read-write heads because of the negative air pressure caused by their spinning. Bernoulli technology never caught on in the Mac market. It's not at the head of the class for price, performance, or capacity; its main claim to superiority—its immunity to serious head crashes—has been obviated by the improved technology of standard magnetic media.
- **DVD.** What's more compact than compact discs? DVD disks. It's too early to write much about them (since they're not available as I write this) but keep your eye out for this ultra-high-density storage option. —SZA/HN/JC

Zip 100

Zippity do-dah. When Iomega introduced its **Zip** drive ($150), evolutionary in design and revolutionary in price (initially, $200), no one uttered the phrase "removable hard drive"; perhaps its removable cartridges are just too much like floppies to warrant the connotation of some big, clunky design. With a "head-to-disk interface" different from the SyQuest approach, using the somewhat forgiving heads of a hard drive (usually paired with rigid disks) and a slightly flexible media (usually paired with the rigid heads of a floppy drive), the Zip drive exploded onto the market offering 100MB of data on a floppy-sized disk, for a price anyone can afford. And, not least of all, its speed is closer to a hard drive than to other removable media.

The original Zip drive has some annoying design features: you're limited to selecting only 5 or 6 as its SCSI ID number; there's no power switch—if it's plugged in, it's on; the curved top surface means you can't put anything on top of it, even a lightweight modem of about the same size; the dark blue case sticks out like a sore thumb on almost any setup, without the saving grace of being at least an *interesting* color.

The **Zip Plus** ($200), introduced in early 1998, offers an on/off switch, the ability to hook up to either a Mac or a Windows machine (the original had two different versions), and a universal power supply that can be used if you're traveling outside the U.S.. (My guess is that the older units will be available only until existing supplies run out, since there's no reason to offer both models concurrently.) But not long after their introduction, some disk-access problems were discovered, and the only solution was to keep the Zip Plus drive as the only external SCSI device. We're awarding it an Editor's Product Pick anyway because of how special it is, but you should check on the status of that problem before you get one.

Zip drive

In all, Zips became so standard so quickly that unless you need a removable that offers more than 100MB on disk (to store huge graphics or multimedia files), the Zip is the only sensible way to go: it's great for backups and archives, and it works well as a transfer medium because so many people have Zip drives. The drives are even an option on some G3-series Macs; and, there's a removable drive available for PowerBooks that accept swappable floppy and CD units.

iomega.com

All that Jaz. Inspired by the success of the Zip technology and the problem of high-end designers not being able to use the disks because their file sizes often exceed 100MB, Iomega created the Zip's big brother: the **Jaz** drive ($400) and its gigabyte-capacity disks. Jaz didn't take over the market the way Zip did—but then, it cost twice as much and was targeted to a smaller group of users, most of whom already had some kind of high-capacity removable storage and backup solutions.

Then SyQuest announced its SyJet 1.5GB system (that's in the next entry) and Iomega upped the ante with the **Jaz 2GB** ($650) system in early 1998. The new model doesn't leave early adopters out in the cold, since it can read the 1GB cartridges, too.

The SyQuest answers. SyQuest was a little late on the miniaturization bandwagon, resting on the laurels of its standard cartridges for a little too long. When the Zip drive came out, people gladly tossed their clunky, lower-capacity SyQuests.

SyQuest's reply, the **EZ135** technically beat the Zip at its own game: the small cartridge stored 30 percent more than Zip disks, at a faster speed, for a lower price per megabyte of storage. But Zip was first out of the gate and the EZ135 never caught up. So, SyQuest moved to its **EZFlyer** ($150) model with 230MB cartridges (and a copycat blue design) as its lower-capacity device. To offer competition against Iomega's Jaz, there's the **SyJet** ($300), which provides 50 percent more storage than the original Jaz, at 1.5GB per cartridge.

syquest.com

Both EZFlyer and SyJet beat Iomega's offerings in technical aspects. But EZFlyer has an almost impossible task, considering the Zip's market penetration. The SyJet, on the other hand, still has a chance to own the higher-capacity removable market.

If you need mostly personal backup and storage capacity, and won't be exchanging disks with others, give the SyQuest offerings serious consideration.

CD-ROMs

CD-ROM drives. Unlike floppies and hard drives, which let you both store your information and get it back, a CD-ROM drive offers a one-way capability, evidenced in its very name: *compact disc read only memory.* A CD stores about

600MB of information. (Did you notice that CDs are *discs* and other, computer-only items, are *disks?)*

A CD-ROM drive is not a magnetic storage medium. A disc is produced with smooth *land* areas and little bumps called *pits.* Instead of a read-write head, a CD-ROM drive uses a laser directed at spots on the disc. A laser beam hitting a pit is scattered, but when it hits a smooth area, the beam is reflected directly back at a sensor: together, they provide the binary feedback of computer storage.

CD Disc

Caddy shack. Older CD-ROM drives, including those built into the first Macs to offer that option, use a *caddy* to hold a CD. You put the disk in the caddy, then insert the caddy into the CD-ROM drive opening.

Playing audio CDs
Chapter 22

The newer approach has been used for years: press a button on the drive and a tray slides out to accept the CD; a gentle push slides the tray back in. In all, it's very much like an audio CD mechanism in a stereo setup. If you have a choice (if you're buying a used unit, say), avoid the caddy systems—if nothing else, you can be sure the unit is very slow compared to current offerings.

External drives. If yours is an older Mac without a built-in CD-ROM drive, you can add an external one, hooking it to the SCSI port the same way you add an external drive. But if you're trying to update a really old Mac, be careful: a friend of mine planned to buy an external CD drive for the old LC that her pre-school granddaughter "inherited," since all the decent kid's stuff comes on CD. But a quick look at a dozen or so packages proved the futility of that move: every one required at least an '040 Mac (the LC is an '030) and/or more memory than the LC, with its 10MB RAM limit, could provide.

CD-ROM drives are one of the few peripheral devices that Apple makes—and one of the even fewer whose price is reasonable compared to third-party offerings. Other reliable CD-ROM drive brands include APS, La Cie, Sony, and Panasonic.

CD speed. The original computer CD-ROM drives worked at the same speed as audio CDs, with a transfer rate of about 150K per second. Subsequent models have increased the spin rate considerably, a great relief to anyone who's taken upwards of five minutes to dig down through a folder hierarchy on a CD.

The speed of a CD is given in terms of the speed of that original technology: a 2X unit (also referred to as *double speed)* is twice as fast; 4X units (also referred to as *quad speeds* or *quads)* are four times faster, and so on. Not all the increments doubled the speed: next came 6X and 8X models, then 12X and 16X; as of this writing, there are new G3 Macs that include 24X units, and at least one manufacturer is offering 48X models. (After the quad speed units, people stopped using descriptive words, and stuck with just the numbers; you won't hear anything about *hex-speed*, *oct-speed*, or *dodeca-speed* drives. The speeds are referred to with their numbers and the letter X, so you say *"12 X,"* not *"twelve times.")*

Feel the burn. Despite their read-only nomenclature, CDs can indeed be written to, and the cost of the technology has dropped so sharply that it's in the realm of upscale computer users. The general term for the technology, and sometimes the units, is CD-R, for CD *recordable*, but the units are also general referred to as "burners," for their ability to burn information into a blank CD. (Although what's really happening inside is not the industrial "burning" of pits: instead, the writer deposits tiny splotches of material to dull the reflectivity of certain spots.) Pinnacle, Microtek, La Cie, and others all make dependable units.

IDE and CD burns. Creating a CD with a recordable unit usually involves setting up the CD contents on a hard drive, and having the information written to the CD from the drive. Most IDE drives perform too slowly for this to work correctly, so make sure you'll be able to do the transfers from a SCSI drive. (SCSI and IDE are described later in the chapter.)

Starting up from a CD. When you want to start up from a CD that has a System Folder on it, you have two choices. You can insert the CD while the computer's on, select it in the Startup Disk control panel, and restart; or you can put in the CD and start up by holding down the C key.

Of course, if the computer's off, you can't put the CD in because the tray won't open. But here's how you do it: start the computer and immediately press the button to open the CD tray. As soon as it opens, slap in the CD and give the tray a little push, and get that C key down immediately. It's not so hard to get it all done while the Mac is still going through its basic startup process, before it even looks for a system disk.

The CD-DVD clash. From the strange-but-true file: if you have a DVD ROM drive and you start up your Mac with a bootable CD in the CD-ROM drive *but* the CD isn't the startup disc, you might not be able to see any DVD disks. You can start up with a non-bootable CD in the drive, or you can start up with the CD itself, and you'll be able to access the DVDs.

Shortcut to a CDs inner folders. Say you have a CD of clip art. On its top level, it may have two folders, one for art and one for some sort of catalog. The art folder might be divided into types of graphics files, and each of those folders might be divided into topics. Further in, maybe there are subtopic and sub-subtopic folders, and then, perhaps, folders for alphabetical groupings. *You* keep accessing a sixth-level folder for the icons you like to use on your web page designs.

You don't have to click your way through all the folders (or use the spring-loaded folder option) to get to the inner folder—it can take a long time to open folders on a relatively slow CD-ROM drive. Instead, make an alias of the folder you use often, and leave it on the desktop, in the Apple menu, or any place on your hard drive that's easy to get to. Double-click on the folder alias while the CD is in the drive, and its window appears—without the outer folders opening at all.

If you want to be able to select from several inner folders on a CD without opening the outer ones, put an alias of the CD itself into your Apple menu. Whenever the CD is in the drive, the item in the Apple menu will show submenus for all of the folders.

Using Zips

Zip disks. Soon after Zip drives were introduced, the disks settled down to a standard $15 per disk. Within a year or so, buying a 10-pack and getting the long-lived rebate brought the price down to $10 per disk. If you need only a few disks, buy a 10-pack anyway, because the price is much better—it's easy enough to find someone to split the pack with you. Zip disks come pre-formatted for Macs or PCs; if you can't find Mac disks, get the PC disks and reformat them on your system.

But don't go out and buy a carton of a hundred or so disks unless you're going to use them all within a few months. Why? Because although Iomega's zealously and jealously guarding its rights to be the sole producer of Zip-compatible cartridges, they've practically lost that battle in Europe as of this writing, and the U.S. monopoly probably won't hold. Iomega's profit margin on the disks is phenomenal—the disks cost about a dollar to produce—and they could easily cut the price in half and still make lots of money whenever some competitor starts selling discounted disks. (Did you ever wonder why the drives are so inexpensive? It's like Gillette practically giving away razors because you'll have to buy the blades.)

Power down. The newer Zip drives have power on/off buttons, but the originals don't; to turn off power to the original drive, you have to unplug it. But you don't have to reach under your desk to get at the plug: just disconnect the power supply from the side of the drive. (You think that's obvious, don't you? Well, then, I won't reveal the names of any of the people I mentioned this to who said "Gee, I never thought of that!")

Accessories. Zip disks haven't spawned a cottage industry of accessories, but there are quite a few things available; as you might guess, they vary in usefulness. Some are available from Iomega, and some from other vendors:

- **Power cords**. If you constantly use your Zip in two locations, getting an extra power cord so you can leave one at each site is a great convenience. Iomega offers the standard power cord that comes with the drive as a separate item. If you bought an early Zip drive, you can buy the newer power cord that includes an international power supply if you need it for your travels.

- **Carry cases**. You'll find there are two sizes: one is barely larger than the Zip drive itself, while the other accommodates the power supply, cable, and a handful of a disks. One or the other is a necessity if you bring your Zip back and forth between locations.
- **Storage cases**. Zips don't fit in holders made for floppies. While their individual plastic cases protect the disks themselves, a stacking holder makes them easier to see and access.
- **Battery pack**. If you're using an external Zip drive with a PowerBook and need to run it without plugging it in, you can get a separate battery pack to power the Zip.

The bi-platform Zip Tools disk. The Zip drive comes with a Zip Tools disk that includes: the extension you need for the Mac to acknowledge inserted disks; a special program that lets you mount and unmount Zips even without the extension running; a formatter for formatting Zip disks with options like write verifies and password protection; a utility to ease Zip-to-Zip copies; a utility that catalogs what's archived on each removable disk; and the obligatory folder of shareware games.

Although the Zip drive you buy for a Mac is different from the one you buy for a PC, the Zip Tools disk is the same; however, as soon as you use it once, from then on it works only for a PC or Mac—whichever was its first experience. Spooky.

Check out the Tools utility. If you buy formatted Zips, you may never open the Tools utility to format a disk, and you'd never know that it offers options like password protection for reading from or writing to a disk. It also lets you set options for the Zip drive, including whether or not to verify every write operation (which takes a little longer, but further ensures data integrity) and how long the sleep interval should be (a disk spins down if you're not using it for a certain length of time.)

Be my guest. The Tools disk includes a utility called Iomega Guest that lets Zips be mounted and unmounted even if the Iomega extension isn't installed. Use the Guest program and you get exactly the same support as when the extension is running—you just have to run it manually each time you start up the Mac.

This helps in two situations. First, if you bring your Zip with you to another Mac, you can just run the Guest program and you'll be able to insert and eject Zips. But the Guest program can be very useful at "home," too: if you're troubleshooting and have to start without extensions, but you need to access a Zip disk (perhaps the extension conflict is one that's preventing you from seeing the Zip), running the Guest program is a good workaround.

Don't erase from the Finder. Erasing a Zip disk with the Finder's Erase Disk command will erase the information on the disk, but the disk won't be checked for bad spots the way a floppy is when you use that command. You should take the time to erase a Zip with the Tools utility, and choose the option *Surface Verify* which can repair bad spots on the disk. Note that the Quick Erase option in the Tools utility is the same as using the Finder's Erase command.

The emergency eject. That little round eject button on the front of the Zip drive doesn't normally work on Mac systems, where you have to eject the disk from the desktop or from within a utility program. If you've inserted a disk that doesn't mount, the eject button usually works.

But in an emergency—like when the power's off—you can use the emergency paper clip ejection tool. Old Mac hands know all about this, as it's the same way you can get a disk out of a floppy drive or, now, a CD-ROM drive. But you may not have realized that the Zip has a paper-clip hole—it's at the *back* of the unit.

Using a Zip as a startup. You can make a startup disk on a Zip and use it to run your Mac in a pinch. What kind of pinch? Well, my sons have one program that just won't run under OS 8 and they still need to use it, so they have System 7.6 on a Zip that can run the Mac when they need that program. You might consider a clean (no third-party extensions) OS 8 Zip disk as insurance against when your own cluttered System Folder temporarily collapses under its own weight.

SCSIProbe
Earlier this chapter

To make a Zip startup, just use the OS Installer (covered in Chapter 8). Use the Startup Disk control panel to set the Zip as the startup device and restart the Mac. If you want to be able to use the Zip startup in an emergency when your Mac won't start up (and so you can't set the Zip as the startup disk), make sure you include a copy of SCSIProbe on the Zip disk. Then, you can start the Mac while holding down ⌘ Option Shift Delete, which makes it ignore the internal drive. Finally, use SCSIProbe to mount the internal drive.

apstech.com

PowerBook hookup. To connect a Zip drive to a PowerBook, you need a special adapter to provide a 25-pin SCSI connector for the Zip cable. Iomega makes such a PowerBook adapter, but APS's **SCSI DOC** ($30) does that and also provides the capability to switch to a SCSI-mode connection. (See the PowerBook chapter for further details on all that.)

PC-formatted Zips. If you use the PC Exchange control panel that comes with your system software, you'll be able to mount and use PC-formatted Zips the same way you can use PC-formatted floppies. However, Iomega recommends that you do this only when it's necessary to transfer files between platforms, and not as a standard operational procedure: storing Mac files on PC-formatted Zips risks losing data from those files. So, if you buy PC-formatted Zips, reformat them to the Mac format.

You can't use the Erase Disk command in the Finder to erase a Zip and format it to another standard (PC to Mac, or Mac to PC); for that, you have to use Iomega's Tools utility.

The Wonderful World of SCSI

The Basics

The scuzzy standard. SCSI stands for *small computer system interface.* It's pronounced *scuzzy,* which has an appropriately derogatory ring to it considering the problems it often causes.

SCSI is the *bus* that handles the electrical signals flowing from one device to another on your computer setup, back and forth between the Mac and peripheral devices like hard drives, CD-ROM drives, other removable storage devices, and scanners.

Subsequent scuzzy. As quirky as SCSI can be, its 5MB-per-second transfer rate was so much faster than other available options that it became the standard. But everything changes in time, and computers change in record time.

The SCSI-2 standard encompasses three variations: *Fast,* with double the speed of standard SCSI because the data is traveling faster; *Wide,* with double the speed of standard SCSI because twice as many wires are used; and *Fast and Wide,* with—you guessed it—both faster transfers and more wires, for quadruple the standard speed.

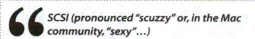

> ***SCSI (pronounced "scuzzy" or, in the Mac community, "sexy"…)***
>
> *Michael D. Wesley, MacUser, September 1986*
> *(The alternate pronunciation never caught on.)*

Then there's SCSI-3, long proposed but just implemented as of this writing. The current incarnation, known as *Ultra SCSI,* uses double the normal SCSI bus clock rate of 10MHz to speed transfers; while SCSI-2's top speed is 20MB per second for the Fast and Wide option, SCSI-3 can hit 40MB per second.

The Mac's standard for external SCSI devices is still the original SCSI. But many later-model Macs offer two separate SCSI busses, one for inside the machine and one for external devices—with the internal bus a SCSI-2 bus that supports the 10MB-per-second Fast (but not Wide) standard.

To get the benefits of an advanced SCSI bus, however, you have to buy devices that are capable of making use of the bus: SCSI-2- or SCSI-3- *capable* devices.

The SCSI chain overview. Since Macs have a single SCSI connector on the outside (some have a second, strictly internal one), if you want to add multiple SCSI devices, you have to link one to another in a series referred to as a *daisy chain.* But you have to worry about more than simply finding cables with the right connectors: a SCSI chain is an inherently unfriendly setup, guaranteed to cause more problems as you add more devices.

The basics you have to consider when setting up a SCSI chain are: the number of devices, the ID number of each device, the total length of the wiring used in the chain, and proper termination of the SCSI signals. All these issues are covered in detail in the next few sections.

PCI and slots in general
Chapter 2

After-the-fact SCSI 2 and 3. If your Mac has only a single, plain old standard SCSI bus but has PCI slots, you can add faster SCSI. Adaptec's **PowerDomain** SCSI accelerator cards provide a new, faster SCSI bus for your Mac. The **2940UW** ($350) or the **3940UW** ($550) can be a good investment if your computing activities are disk-intensive (as with high-end graphics and video).

adaptec.com
atto.tech

The **SiliconExpress IV** ($650, ATTO) provides fast and wide SCSI for NuBus PowerPCs and Quadras. But if you're so in need of speed that you're considering a faster SCSI bus, it's unlikely that the speed of your NuBus-based Mac is good enough, and your money should be invested in a new Mac rather than in a pricey SCSI upgrade.

Combining SCSI types on a chain. If you have a SCSI-2 bus, you can add standard SCSI devices to it. If you're mixing devices on a chain, put the SCSI-2 devices first so that they'll work at their faster speed. Then, where you want to add the standard SCSI device to the chain, use a special adapter that converts the 68-pin wide SCSI bus to the standard 50-pin connector. APS offers several options along these lines for $20-$30, depending on whether you're stepping down from SCSI-2 or SCSI-3, and its adapters include special termination for those 18 pins that are no longer being used on the chain.

The IDEs of drives. In a cost-cutting measure, Apple began several years ago using IDE *(Integrated Drive Electronics)* internal drives instead of SCSI models in the lower-priced models of each of its lines. The IDE drives, which are cheaper and offer higher capacity for their physical size than SCSI devices, have been available in the PC world for a long time.

Why don't all Macs use IDE drives and devices, then? Because, although newer models offer ever-increasing speed, they lag behind their SCSI counterparts. SCSI devices have their own microcontrollers; an IDE device needs the CPU's help for transferring data, which can result in quite an overall performance hit. More importantly, you can have only two IDE devices on a chain, which severely limits both internal and external expansion.

Macs with IDE drives still offer a SCSI port for other devices. If you use third-party formatting software instead of Apple's, you'll have to make sure it knows how to deal with IDE drives and not just SCSI ones.

Firewire. *Firewire* is a proposed industry standard that would allow about 60 devices to chain to a single, six-pin port. You'll be able to add and remove devices from the chain without shutting things down, you won't have to worry about termination, you could use cables that are less expensive... a dream come true. We'll see.

The SCSI Chain

SCSI Probe
Chapter 24

Number of devices, and ID numbers. A SCSI chain can consist of up to seven devices (eight, if you count the Mac itself, which acts as the "host" for the chain). Each device needs a unique ID number, from 0 to 6—computers like to start counting at zero, not one. Apple's internal hard drives are always set to 0, and the Mac is assigned 7, so you use numbers 1 through 6 for everything else.

Most external devices have simple switches that let you easily change the ID number. Some models make you push little buttons that combine to stand for a number (like one switch up and three down stands for 1), and other, older designs actually have internally set IDs; avoid both!

Default ID numbers. With the exception of 0 (used by the internal drive) and 7 (used by the Mac), you can use any available SCSI ID number for your devices. The ID numbers you assign don't have to be related in any way to the order in which the devices are attached. But there are certain numbers almost always used by certain items, so you should stick with the conventions:

- **ID 0** is assigned to the internal hard drive. You don't usually have to worry about this, since that's the way the computer comes. But if you buy a new, larger hard drive to replace the original, it needs to be set to 0.
- **ID 1** is used for factory-installed internal Duo Dock drives, so it's good to stick to that if you add one of your own to a Dock. A PowerBook in SCSI disk mode defaults to ID 1, although that's easily changed through a control panel. Using ID 1 for a second internal hard drive in a desktop Mac is a good approach, since it's unlikely to conflict with other standards unless you occasionally hook up your PowerBook as an external drive on your desktop system.
- **ID 3** is used for Apple's internal CD-ROM drives, so it makes sense, if you're using only an external CD unit, to set it to 3.
- Zip drives are limited to being set to **ID 5** or **ID 6**.

The startup scan. At startup, the Mac scans the SCSI bus for a device with a System Folder on it. It doesn't care what's connected where; if it can't start from the internal hard drive, it checks other SCSI devices in reverse order of their ID numbers, with the highest number getting start-up priority.

Checking SCSI ID numbers. You don't have to peer around to the back of your Mac's peripherals to check their ID numbers, or rip open the case to check the settings for internal devices. Just do a Get Info for the drive (or, for removables, insert a disk/cartridge and Get Info on it). The Info window notes the SCSI ID number of the device.

There's another piece of system software that will show you SCSI ID numbers even if you don't have anything inserted in the removable devices: the PC Exchange control panel. Click its Options buttons and you'll see a list of attached devices.

A drive's Info window (left) and the PC Exchange control panel (right) both tell you the SCSI ID numbers of your devices.

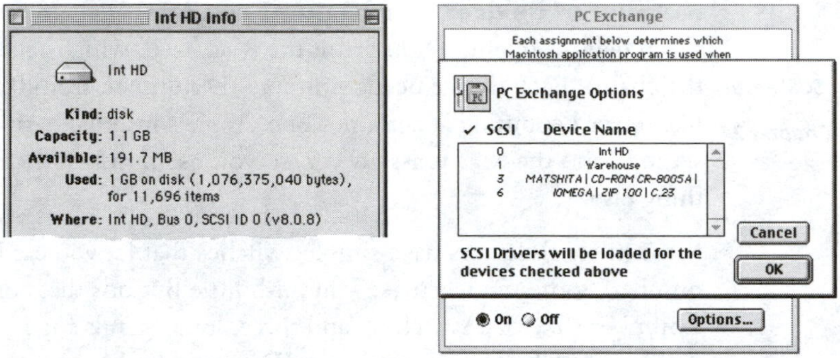

Keep all devices on. The general rule is that all SCSI devices on the chain should be on, whether or not you're using them. You'll find people who claim they keep one or more devices switched off and their chain works just fine, but more often than not an unpowered SCSI device on the chain—even on the very end of it—can cause problems up and down the entire chain.

Double your pleasure. If you have a double SCSI bus on your new PowerPC-based Mac, you get to have up to 14 devices hooked to your Mac: seven on each chain, with the Mac acting as the eighth device for both chains. No doubt you'll be doubling your chances of SCSI problems, too.

Cabling

Basic ports and cables. Desktop Macs have a 25-pin connector for SCSI devices. Since most SCSI devices have 50-pin SCSI connectors, you need a cable with a 25-pin connector at one end and a 50-pin connector at the other, both male; Apple's basic *SCSI system cable* provides this setup.

When you're adding more than one external device, you have to connect their 50-pin connectors by a cable with two male 50-pin connectors; Apple calls this cable its *SCSI peripheral interface cable.* For an external device that uses a 25-pin connector, however, you need a cable with two male 25-pin connectors; most such devices come with the cable so you won't have to buy it separately.

You can get any of these cables from any computer supplier; they don't have to be Mac vendors. The standard connectors are referred to as *Centronics,* so you can buy a 50-pin male to 50-pin male Centronics SCSI cable, and you'll have the equivalent of Apple's SCSI peripheral interface cable.

PowerBooks, of course, have their own SCSI connector, smaller than that at the back of desktop Mac. It's called the HDI-30 (high-density interface, 30 pins), and uses a cable called the HDI-30 SCSI System Cable to attach SCSI devices to the PowerBook.

More ports in the SCSI storm. If you go beyond the original SCSI standard, you'll have to also move beyond the basic cables and connectors. Most SCSI-2 adapter cards, for instance, use a special high-density 50-pin connector (HD-50) because the standard 50-pin SCSI connection is too large to fit on the edge of the card.

For wide or fast and wide SCSI setups, there's an entirely different connector to accommodate the different number of wires; the connector is has 68 pins.

SCSI chain lengths. If your SCSI chain is too long, signals may be too weak to be received clearly and you could wind up with a variety of problems. Theoretically, the chain can extend up to 7 meters (about 23 feet), measured from your computer to the last device in a SCSI chain—including all internal ribbon cables (figure 4-10 inches inside each device). Apple recommends a maximum of 6 meters (about 20 feet). A general rule: The shorter, the better—for both the total chain and individual cables. Standard SCSI cables are 2 to 6 feet long, but you can get 12" cables that can save many feet in a multi-device setup.

Note that the length of a cable includes the connectors, which are usually at least an inch and a half deep, adding three inches to the overall measurement. You may look at a cable and estimate it to be 8 or 9 inches long because you're looking at the *wire* portion, but in reality it's probably a 12-inch cable. —SZA/HN

Cable quality. The quality of your cables can make the difference between constant hassles and a bus that hums along smoothly. It may seem silly to spend $20 to $50 for a foot or so of wire, but if you're building a complex SCSI chain, this is not the place to economize. Look for double-shielded cables; they're usually thick and heavy because they have lots of shielding around the separate wires inside the cable to minimize the possibility of signals on one line generating noise on another, as well as shielding around the whole bundle just under the outside layer. Look for a good, strong connection between the cable and the connector, and for gold-plated pins on the connectors, too. —SZA/RS/HN

Cable care. Cables aren't overly delicate, but you should be kind to them. Don't bend them more than necessary. Don't push the devices against a wall so that there's a 90-degree bend in the cable right after the connector. When attaching or removing them, push straight in or pull straight out—don't wiggle them back and forth. Use the snap-in or screw-in fasteners to keep the connection tight.

The no-cable setup. If you have multiple external drives, getting them all from the same vendor can help, because companies like APS and La Cie make special SCSI connectors for stacking their drives; the connectors are more like clamps than cables, and let the SCSI signal travel the shortest distance between the two devices.

Hot plugging. *Hot plugging*, which means adding or removing a SCSI device while the Mac is turned on, is not something you should contemplate. Or, go ahead and contemplate it, but don't do it. If you don't insert or remove the SCSI connector evenly so that all the pins make or cease contact at the same time, you can blow the connection—and the device, and your Mac. It's usually easy enough to do a smooth connect or disconnect, but it's hardly worth the risk. (An early scene in *Raiders of the Lost Ark* comes to mind: Indiana *very* carefully replaces the golden idol with a sack of sand so the weight on its pedestal remains constant. And you know what happened *then!)*

Termination

Termination. The electrical signals that race up and down your SCSI cables generate electrical echoes, or noise. If they're not suppressed, these reflections can be strong enough to confuse devices on the bus. That can cause all sorts of problems, including slowdowns, data errors, drives refusing to appear on the desktop, and crashes. A *terminator* (also called a *resistor)* keeps signals from echoing back on a SCSI chain.

A terminator requires a small amount of electrical power—*termination power*—that's usually provided by the SCSI device itself. The only time "term power" is an issue is if you hook up a device with no termination power to a Mac that provides no termination power. All Macs except the Mac Plus and PowerBooks (and the Portable) provide termination power. Without termination power, the SCSI chain can't work, so hooking up a PowerBook as an external SCSI device to a Mac Plus turns into a problem. —SZA/HN

Terminators. A terminator looks somewhat like the connector on a SCSI cable, but has no cable attached. Some terminators are dead-ends: a 50-pin connector on one side, and a blank wall on the other. Others are *pass-through* terminators with 50-pin connectors on both sides (one male, one female) so you can connect a cable to it, although you can use a pass-through connector at the end of a chain the same way you'd use a blank one.

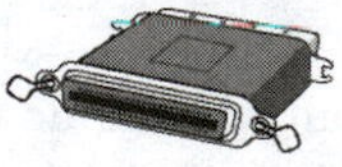

A pass-through terminator.

Self-termination and active termination. Back when every Mac that had an external device had only a single one—a hard drive—it made some sense to have the termination for that drive inside the drive itself. With termination needed at the end of the SCSI chain, and the external hard drive always being at the end of the chain, there wasn't much problem. But now this kind of device—referred to as *internally* or *self terminated*—is a real pain in the chain.

The better solution is a device that has *active* termination: internal termination that can be turned on or off as needed. Many hard drives are now actively terminated, which is a real boon. But watch the terminology: *self-termination* has slipped a little in its meaning and is sometimes used to describe an active-termination device. If something is described as self-terminated, double check whether it has standard termination built-in (you don't want it because you have to open the case to adjust it) or has active termination (you do want it).

Basic termination. There are termination *guidelines* rather than *rules* because you can follow all the standard termination advice and still have SCSI-chain problems. For most systems, with no or few additional SCSI devices, the standard setup works. For systems with lots of devices, especially problematic ones like scanners and SyQuests, sometimes the standards just don't work, and you have to play around until you find a winning combination of device order and termination control.

The general guideline is simple: the first and last devices in the chain should be terminated. The internal hard drive is terminated with resistors on its circuit board, so you don't have to worry about that end. If you add a single external device, it should be terminated; if you add multiple devices, the last one should be terminated. —SZA/HN

Additional termination. When the basic termination-at-both-ends doesn't seem to be working, it's time to start considering additional termination somewhere else along the line, or an alternate placement of the second terminator. My favorite first-step solution is to put the second terminator *before* the last device; sometimes a terminator both before and after the last device is what you need. For a long SCSI chain, a third terminator somewhere in the middle is often helpful; general guidelines call for a terminator at every 10 feet along SCSI cabling (remember to include the invisible cabling inside the device itself).

When there's no internal hard drive. For a Mac without an internal hard drive, terminating the drive itself is usually sufficient; if it's not actively terminated internally, you can use one of its connectors to attach it to the Mac and the other for a terminator.

If you're connecting more than one device to a Mac without an internal hard drive, you should use one terminator *before* the first hard drive, and another at the end of the chain. This means you need a pass-through terminator that connects to the back of the drive and lets you hook up the cable from the Mac. A standard terminator on the last device takes care of the other end of the chain.

SCSI Sentry

SCSI Sentry. If you had any idea of how many times I've recommended that people buy **SCSI Sentry** ($40, $20 for optional power adapter) or **SCSI Sentry II** ($70) over the years, you'd think I was getting kickbacks from APS Technologies.

apstech.com

SCSI Sentry is not much larger than a standard terminator; it can be used as an end or pass-through terminator. It has several lights on it that let you know what's going on in the SCSI chain—when information is being requested, and when it's being provided. Checking what lights are on or off can help determine what the SCSI problem is: a bad or loose cable, a problem in the Mac itself, a lack of power, an ID conflict. But you won't have to worry much about what's going on, since SCSI Sentry adjusts the termination on the chain as needed. The optional power cord lets you provide termination power along the chain, too—an option often needed in PowerBook setups. SCSI Sentry II is all that and more, with termination power included with an international power supply.

Special Macs, special termination. Some older Mac models have special termination considerations:

- The internal SCSI drive on the **Quadra 950** should remain unterminated because the termination is on the motherboard for the internal SCSI bus.
- The **Mac IIfx** follows the general rules above, but it requires a special terminator at the end of the chain because it uses a special SCSI chip. Apple calls it the SCSI Terminator II, but everyone else refers to it as the *black terminator*.
- Because the **Mac Plus** has no internal SCSI connector, your first external device (the one closest to the Mac) is considered the first device and should be terminated, as should the last device on the chain. If you have only one drive on the chain, it should be terminated.

PART 3

The Operating System

Part 3 At a Glance

5

The Interface

Starting Up and Shutting Down

Mouse and Menus

Windows and Dialogs

The Clipboard

Using the Keyboard

System Sounds

In This Chapter

Starting Up and Shutting Down

Turning on the Mac

Turning it on. Depending on your Mac model, you turn it on with either the Power key on the keyboard (the one with the leftward-pointing triangular arrow) or, for older models, the switch at the back of the machine. On some models the monitor might have to be switched on separately.

Peripherals like modems and printers, and even monitors, can be turned on after you've started the Mac. Almost everything else (external hard drives, CD-ROM drives, Zip drives, scanners) will be attached through the SCSI port and should be turned on before the Mac.

Booting. *Booting,* or *booting up*, is another term for starting up the computer; *rebooting* is, logically enough, restarting it. The origin of the term is not yet lost in the mists of time. Early computers used a series of small "loader" programs to get going, since nothing at all was built in; each did its own little job and then loaded the next program. This was referred to at first as *bootstrapping,* from the old saying "pulling yourself by your own bootstraps" and was later shortened to *booting.*

The startup disk is always the one at the top—the Int HD in this picture.

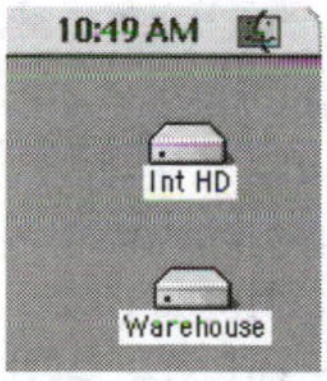

The startup disk. When you turn on the Mac, it looks for a disk with a System Folder on it. Any disk with the System and Finder files on it is a *system disk;* the one the Mac uses is the *startup disk.* The internal hard drive is almost always the startup disk. If it can't find a startup disk, the Mac displays a floppy disk icon with a blinking question mark in it.

If there's more than one system disk available to the Mac (say, on an internal hard drive, and external hard drive, and an inserted CD), it's easy to tell which is running the Mac: the startup disk icon is always in the top right corner of the screen.

The startup procedure. When you first turn on the Mac, you'll see the famous "Happy Mac," an icon of a smiling Mac. Then you get the friendly

"Welcome to Mac OS" dialog box with the Mac OS logo. Next comes a "progress bar" labeled *Starting Up* that replaces the Welcome statement; the bar gives you some idea of how far along the Mac is in its startup procedure, and how much farther it has to go. You'll see a series of icons appear across the bottom of the screen—the extensions and controls panels that are loading into memory. (This part is referred to variously as the *icon parade* or the *init march*—"init" being an old term for "extension.") Finally, you get to your desktop.

There's lots going on during a normal Mac startup before you even see that Happy Mac. When you hit the Power key, the CPU gets to work and looks to a special spot in the ROM for instructions as to what to do next. It follows those instructions, running some hardware self-diagnostics; if everything checks out, it looks for a startup disk.

Once the CPU finds the startup disk, it reads part of the System file into memory. It's a selfless act: the first information it reads in is the part of the operating system that controls the CPU. At that point, the operating system takes over, leaving the CPU to simply follow whatever orders it receives from the system. (There's lots more going on that we mere mortals don't need to know; this is about all we need to keep us happy and informed.)

The extra-happy Mac. Sometimes the Happy Mac stays on your screen a lot longer than usual. This happens on PowerMacs for the first startup after a system crash, because the Mac is taking time to check the integrity of all the files on the disk—some may have been harmed if open when the crash occurred. The larger your hard drive, and the more files on it, the longer the Happy Mac will be smiling at you during startup.

The not-so-happy Mac. The Happy Mac's evil twin is always waiting in the background. The Sad Mac shows up at startup on some models when things are going *really* wrong. Sometimes his appearance is triggered by corrupted system files, sometimes by mild or severe hardware problems. He's accompanied by some heart-sinking sounds like arpeggiated chords (fondly referred to as the *chimes of doom)* or car-crash sound effects. The Sad Mac, and other startup problems like general crashes and freezes are covered in Chapter 24.

More memory, longer startup. One of the self-diagnostic procedures during startup is checking out the installed memory. So, the more memory you have, the longer your startup takes. You probably won't notice anything unless you add more memory and then the startup takes longer than you're used to.

Restarting. Restarting is not the same as shutting down the Mac and then turning it on again; it's a separate procedure, using the Restart command in the Special menu.

Why would you want to do this? Sometimes you make some changes in a control panel that won't take effect until the next time you start up the Mac, and you might want to start it up right away. Or, sometimes you'll be having some intermittent problems due to possible memory fragmentation, and you'll want to start all over with a restart.

Another way to use the Restart command is to simply hit the Power key on the keyboard; this is actually a shutdown procedure, but you'll get a dialog asking you if you want to shut down or restart.

Restarting is also sometimes referred to as a *reboot,* or any of several phrases containing the word "warm," implying that the machine's still warm from being used: *warm start, warm restart, warm boot, warm reboot.*

Auto startup. The Energy Saver control panel (which works on current and recent Macs and systems) lets you set an automatic time for your Mac to start up. Click the Scheduled Startup & Shutdown button, and enter the time you want the Mac to start up on its own. Giving the Mac a head start at startup means you won't have to twiddle your thumbs through what can be a lengthy warm-up. You can even set it for only weekdays, or only weekends, or a specific day of the week by using the pop-up menu.

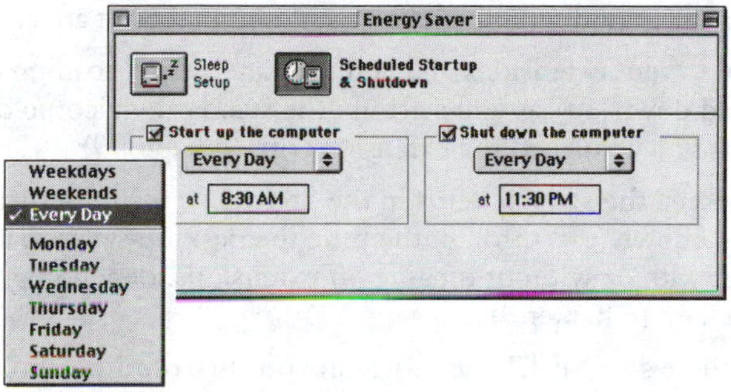

Use the Energy Saver to make the Mac turn itself on; you can even pick specific days from the pop-up menu.

The hardware restart. Sometimes your Mac freezes up and you'd like to restart it, but you can't because it won't recognize anything you do with the mouse—even clicking in a button that says Restart. There's more about this in Chapter 24, but here's the way out of that particular pickle: press ⌘ Control and the Power key all at the same time. This works for all current and recent Mac models.

Use a power strip. If you have a lot of peripherals, use a power strip to turn them all on at the same time by using the switch on the power strip. **Kensington** makes a terrific color-coded power strip, where each outlet is framed in a different color. It comes with matching color tabs you can attach to the far end of each power cord (near the device); you can tell which plug is for what peripheral without having to trace along its length to see where it winds up. You won't pull the plug on the wrong device! There are also power strips that put lots of space between the outlets so that a chunky AC adapter won't block an extra hole. In my setup, a telephone, an answering machine, a Zip drive, and an external modem all need adapters and crowd standard power strips.

PRAM **Chapter 13**

But don't plug the Mac itself into a power strip. The internal battery that keeps PRAM charged while the Mac is off is itself trickle-charged by the power supply; keeping the Mac unplugged, or its equivalent by turning off a power strip that it's plugged into, means the battery won't last as long.

Startup Options

Startup keys roundup. There are lots of different key combinations that you can press at startup to do something to (or with) the Mac's operating system. Here's a roundup—you'll find details on most of these items in the chapters noted.

- To start with a neat desktop, with all its windows closed no matter how you left them, hold down Option. You don't have to hold it through the entire startup procedure—pressing it after the extensions have loaded is usually time enough. This closes *all* windows—including any you've turned into pop-up windows, so their tabs won't be at the bottom of the screen anymore. (There's a little interface breakdown here, since using other close-all-windows options on the desktop doesn't affect window tabs.)
- To prevent extensions and control panels from loading during startup, hold down Shift as you start up; the standard welcome dialog will note that you've turned the extensions off. (Chapter 9)
- To keep the startup items in the Startup Items folder from launching, hold down Shift through the time the desktop starts to appear; you can do this with or without turning off extensions, depending on when you press the key. (Chapter 9)
- If there's a QuickTime movie in your Startup Items folder but you don't want to see it for the umpteenth time, press ⌘. to cancel it.
- If you're using the Extensions Manager that came with the system software, holding down Spacebar at startup opens the Extensions Manager before everything else loads so you can specify which extensions you want to use for a work session. (Chapter 9)
- Turn off virtual memory temporarily by holding down ⌘ during the startup procedure. (Chapter 13)
- Hold down ⌘ Option to rebuild the desktop. (Chapter 24)
- Press ⌘ Option P R to zap the PRAM. (Chapter 24)
- Bypass the internal hard drive by holding down ⌘ Option Shift Delete. (Chapter 24)

Starting from a CD. If you have a system CD in the drive—that is, a CD with a system folder on it—some Macs will automatically give precedence to the CD as the startup drive. When you want to force the Mac to use the CD as the startup (of course, only when there is a system on the CD), hold down C at startup.

Create startup items. If you want something to open automatically at startup—an application, a specific document, or even a folder, put it or its alias in the Startup Items folder inside the System Folder. (If you've checked the *Show Launcher at startup* button in the General control panels, the system puts an alias of the Launcher control panel in the Startup Items folder.)

There's lots more information about startup items in Chapter 9, including tidbits like having sound, or even a movie automatically play at startup.

The startup screen. Replace the boring "Welcome to Mac OS" box at startup with a graphic of your choice. Take any PICT-type graphic (graphic file types are covered in Chapter 19) and name it StartupScreen; capitals don't matter, but be sure to leave out the space between the two words. Some graphics programs provide an option to save a document as a startup screen, which not only sets the correct type for the file but often also gets rid of extra white space around the image and/or centers it on the page. Drop the file in your System Folder *(not* in the Startup Items folder); the file gets a cute little Happy Mac icon and, if you didn't use capital letters when you named the file, it's automatically edited to *StartupScreen.*

StartupScreen

The next time you start up, you'll see your picture instead of the standard welcome dialog.

Here are a few other things you should know about the startup screen:

- The startup screen is only a temporary picture, to replace the Welcome dialog, and is not the same as a background picture for the desktop.
- If the startup picture is bigger than the screen, it's displayed starting at the upper left corner.
- If you use the wrong type of graphics file as the startup screen, it may be ignored, or you may wind up with a very strange display graphic on startup. It might look like your computer is *really* messed up—you'll probably get a random dotted pattern—but the startup procedure will continue.
- When you use a startup screen, you won't get the Welcome to Macintosh—which, of course, you can live without. But you also won't get the progress bar that shows how much of the system has loaded in, and you might miss that quite a bit, even though you'll still see all your extensions marching across the bottom of the screen.

Ejecting a floppy. If you shut down with a floppy in the drive, you can eject it during the startup process by holding down the mouse button as the Mac starts up. This used to be a great way of spitting out a floppy startup disk so you wouldn't waste time starting up just to close down again so you could insert another floppy startup. The chances of your using a floppy as a startup are so slim these days, that this is probably the last time this particular piece of information will remain in an edition of the Bible!

Multiple Startup Devices

Startup order. The icon in the upper right corner of your desktop is that of the *startup disk,* the one with the System Folder on it; usually, it's your internal hard drive. But you might have more than one device with a System Folder available to the Mac at startup—a floppy disk, a CD, an external hard drive, and so on. Here's the order in which the Mac scans its devices for a startup folder—the first one it finds "wins"!

1. Floppy drives: first, the internal, then a second internal drive, and then an external drive. (There were days when a system could actually fit on a floppy!)
2. The device identified in Startup Disk control panel.
3. The internal hard drive.
4. External SCSI devices, starting with the one with the highest ID number.
5. A second check on the internal hard drive.
6. Back to the floppy drive (in case you didn't get that disk in fast enough at startup!).

When the Mac can't find a startup disk at all, it puts up a disk icon with a flashing question mark in it.

The Startup Disk control panel. You can override the normal startup order by specifying a startup disk in the Startup Disk control panel; all you have to do is click on the disk you want used as the startup. The control panel isn't all that bright—it will list all disks currently available to the Mac, whether or not there are System Folders on them. (It won't list a floppy, since that's the default first startup disk anyway.)

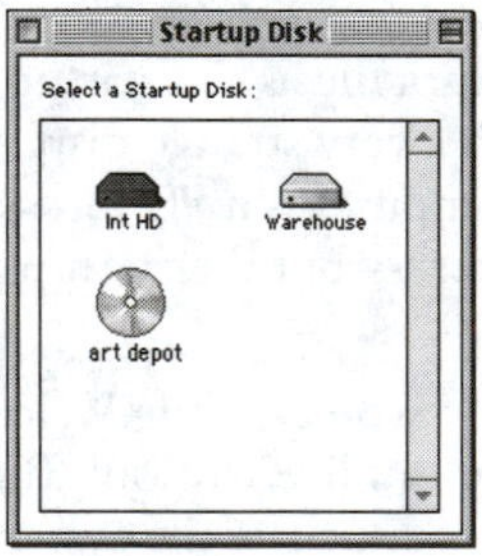

The Startup Disk control panel lists all mounted volumes, whether or not they have System Folders on them.

Clicking in the white area of the Startup Disk control panel's window so that no icon is selected sets the startup disk to the one with the highest SCSI ID number.

Startup partitions. If you have a hard drive divided into several partitions, each partition shows up in the Startup Disk control panel as a separate drive. In older systems, choosing a partition as a startup didn't always work. The only thing the Mac noted was the device's SCSI ID number, and used it to set the startup; the first partition it found on that drive was used as the startup no matter what you might have selected in the control panel—and "first" partition could be the first alphabetically or the first created.

SCSI IDs and partitions **Chapter 4**

This is no longer a problem: the partition you select is the one that will be used as a startup as long as it has a working System Folder.

Ignoring the control panel. If you're starting your Mac and realize that you want the startup to default back to your internal drive but something else is selected in the Startup Disk control panel, you can start up with ⌘ Option held down: that zaps the PRAM and makes the Mac "forget" the Startup Disk control panel settings.

Zapping
Chapter 24

Where *is* that other drive? When an external hard drive doesn't show up on the desktop because it wasn't ready—you didn't turn it on in time—when the Mac looked for it, restarting the system will mount it. But you can also force the drive to show up on the desktop without a restart by using a special utility like SCSIProbe, as described in Chapter 24.

Sleeping

Perchance to dream. Starting up the Mac can take pretty long these days; and, if you're working in multiple applications on large and numerous documents, getting back to where you left off isn't worth shutting down the Mac if you're only on a long lunch break. But leaving everything up and running seems like a waste of electricity, not to mention all those little photons smashing themselves against the phosphor coating on your screen for no good reason. With later-model Macs, Apple has finally been able to provide something less drastic than shutdown: the Sleep mode that PowerBook owners have long been able to use.

There are two aspects to sleeping: one that turns off the screen, and one that spins down the hard drive. You can separate these functions so that, for instance, your screen will sleep (dim) but the hard drive will stay on in case someone needs to access it on a network.

To put your computer to sleep, use the Sleep command in the Finder's special menu. (In computer-speak, *sleep* is also a verb: *"Sleep the computer if you're going to leave it on by itself."*) To wake up the Mac, just hit any key on the keyboard.

When you wake your Mac—by simply pressing any key—you'll find it exactly as you left it, with applications and documents and windows open. Unlike with the Shutdown command, which prompts you to save documents before shutdown, sleeping triggers no warnings. While the sleep mode itself won't cause any work to be lost, who knows what might happen if you're away from your computer for too long. Even if you're leaving the documents open, make it a habit to save your work any time you walk away from your computer.

Putting your Mac into sleep mode saves energy.

When you install OS 8, the Energy Saver control panel is automatically installed and set to put your computer to sleep after a certain idle interval (as long as it's a model that can sleep). Since this can be really confusing to beginners—coming back to a blank screen when they thought they left the computer on—there's a startup notice on *every* startup about the sleep function and the control panel. The notice continues until you've reset the control panel manually, at which point the Mac figures you know enough about it to not be worried about a seemingly comatose machine.

Triggering sleep from the keyboard. If you want to put your computer to sleep immediately without going to the Finder to use its Sleep command, press the Power key on the keyboard. The dialog asks if you really want to shut down (since that's what the key is really for), but one of the buttons in the dialog also provides a sleep option instead. You can click the button or just press S (with no ⌘) to trigger it.

Automatic napping. You can set the Mac to go to sleep if you're away from it for too long—after all, what's it going to do without you around, anyway? Use the Energy Saver control panel to set the "idle time": how long it should wait with no activity before going to sleep. Click the Sleep Setup button in the control panel, and move the slider to the time interval you want. If you move the control to the *Never* setting, the computer won't sleep when you leave it alone.

If you want the computer to shut down when you've been away too long, click the *Shut down instead of sleeping* checkbox.

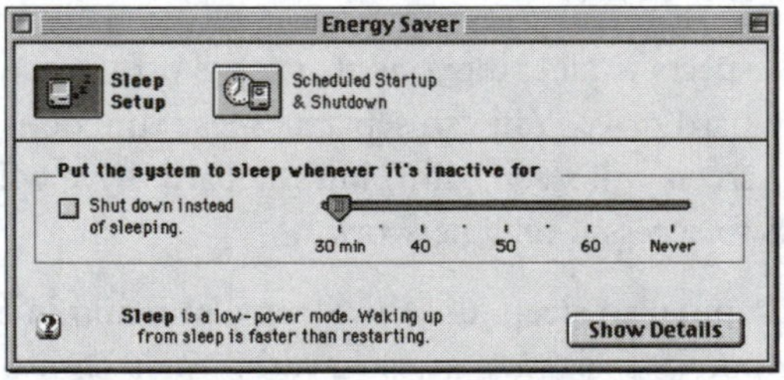

Use the Sleep Setup button in the Energy Saver control panel to set the idle interval, and to choose between sleeping and shutdown when the Mac's been inactive.

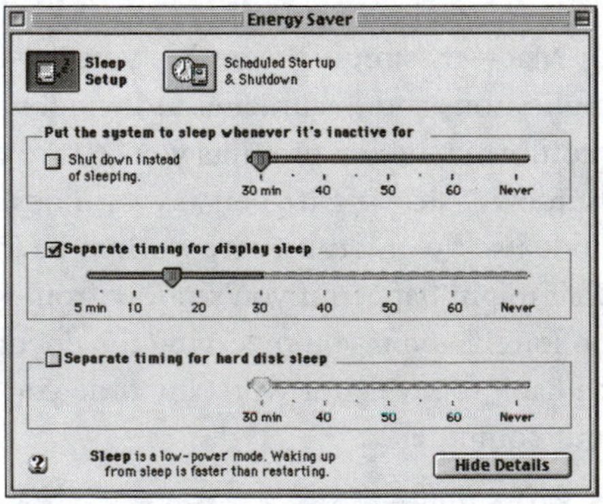

The full Energy Saver control panel provides separate controls for display and hard disk sleep intervals.

Details, details. Using the Show Details button in the Energy Saver control panel expands the box so you can set the screen and disk sleep modes separately. You'll find that, logically enough, you can't set a component to sleep at a larger interval than you set the whole system to sleep. You'll even get some nice interface feedback about the situation: as you can see in the picture here, although the display sleep is set to about fifteen minutes, its control bar is shaded to the point where the system sleep is set—you can't drag the control past that spot.

When not to fall asleep. If your Mac is getting ready to perform a time-intensive task like a low-level disk format, set the hard drive sleep to Never. Otherwise, it's possible that the drive will spin down while the Mac is "thinking" for a little while, and the process might stop entirely, reporting an error that you won't really be able to identify.

Screen sleep only. If you want to set only your screen to sleep and leave the drive running at all times (perhaps because others will need to access it on a network), slide the system sleep control to Never, since it's the overriding control. Then you can set the hard disk sleep to Never, too, and leave the display sleep at whatever time you want.

Shutting Down the Mac

Shutting down isn't turning off. The Mac uses a special shut down procedure when you use the Shut Down command in the Finder's Special menu, and it's not the same as just flipping an Off switch on the Mac or a power strip.

The most obvious thing the Mac does when you shut down "properly" is check if there are any unsaved documents hanging around and ask if you want to save them. It also quits each of the programs in turn, which means any temporary files an application creates for itself while it's running get erased instead of remaining on the drive.

But on the desktop, there are things that you *think* you've done, because *you've* done them—but the Mac hasn't. The Mac has merely stored the changes in its memory so they can be done at a later, more convenient, time; this makes things seem to work faster while you're doing them. If you shut off the computer without any warning, the Mac never transfers the information from memory to the disk. As a result, you may find that the window you opened and reorganized is closed and still disorganized when you start the Mac again; an annoying, but not earth-shattering, problem.

Finally, if you abruptly shut down, nothing in your Shut Down Items folder will run. What? You don't have anything there? Maybe you do without realizing it. If you've set up something to do automatic backups, or virus or disk-integrity checks at shut down, that might get triggered at shut down time. And some software and/or extensions run special routines at shutdown—and if they don't know the computer's being shut down, they can't run. A shutdown routine might be as simple as one that empties the Trash, but it might be as important as one that takes care of disk security, file recovery, or backup information.

Shut down with the Power key. When you want to manually shut down, you don't have to use the Finder's Shut Down command. Just hit the Power key, and you'll get the dialog shown here, giving you the option of truly shutting down or restarting or going to sleep—or canceling the whole thing. (I for one am extremely grateful for this dialog. I use a special ergonomic keyboard, and it has some odd key placements—including the Power key's being in between Option and Control, so I occasionally hit it by mistake.)

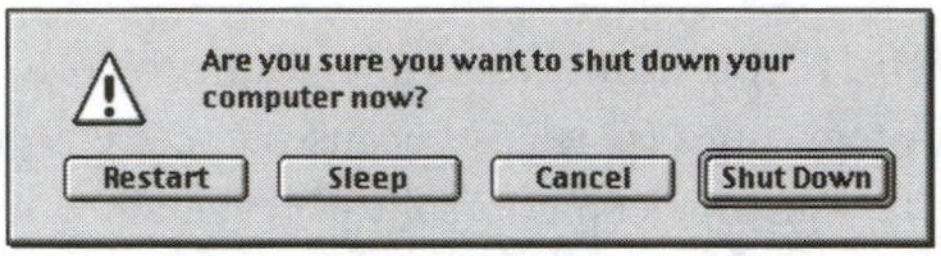

Pressing the Power key opens this dialog.

There are several keyboard equivalents for the buttons in the Shutdown dialog:

Shut Down:	Return or Enter	Sleep:	S
Cancel:	Esc or ⌘ .	Restart:	R

Leaving it on. The general consensus of professional opinion has always been (and perhaps still is) that leaving your computer on for long periods of time is less stressful on the components than turning it on and off. I used to leave my Mac on for days at a time (hey, if you start at seven in the morning and work on and off till midnight, it hardly seems worth shutting off!), but that was in the early days with an early Mac that didn't draw all that much power.

While leaving your Mac on is unlikely to do it any damage, there is the electricity to think about—the *really* hidden cost of a large Mac setup. My current approach (no pun intended) is: on first thing in the morning, and off last thing at night, even if I'm gone for hours in the middle of the day. Luckily, with the sleep option now available on desktop Macs, I don't have to leave it on all the way when I'm not there.

Shut down automatically. You can set the Mac to shut down automatically using the Energy Saver control panel. Click the Scheduled Startup & Shutdown button, and enter the time you want the Mac to shut down. If you happen to be working around the shutdown time, you'll get a fifteen-minute warning dialog with the option to cancel the shutdown entirely or put it off for an hour. You can even set the startup/shutdown choices to work only on weekdays. If you set an auto shutdown but leave some open, unsaved documents around, don't worry: it won't shut down and ignore the documents.

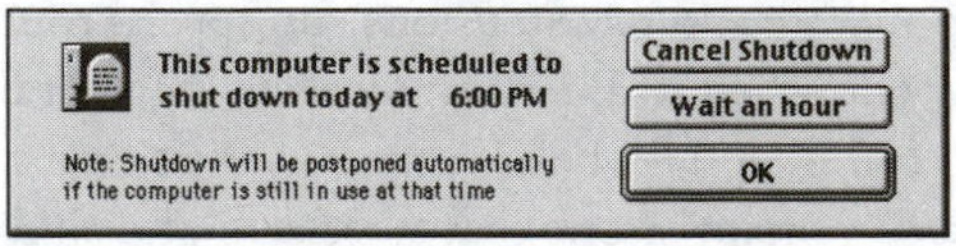

You'll get a warning if you're still working when the automatic shutdown time approaches.

But all through my System 7.6 year, and in all my time with OS 8 so far, I have found Energy Saver to be very undependable. Somehow the shutdown time is erratic—sometimes it shuts me down in the middle of the afternoon instead of late at night, no matter how many times I check the settings of both the system clock and the Energy Saver. And, if the Mac is sleeping when the shutdown time rolls around, it won't shut down—and I always have the sleep setting on. So, I just manually shut down most of the time.

The CPU's power button. Current and recent Macs have power buttons on the CPU box; in most cases, the button has a circle with a straight line in it. This functions the same as the on-off switches on older Macs—if you hit it while you're working, it's as if you'd pulled the plug out of the wall socket. The Mac turns off without saving anything at all.

Wake up and shut down. If you set your Mac to automatically shut down, but the computer's sleeping when the shutdown time arrives, here's what will happen. You come back to your computer and press a key to wake it up; maybe you even press the Power key because you think it's shut down. In any case, it wakes up, and you see a dialog on the screen asking if you want to save some document that you left open and unsaved. You click OK. The document gets saved, the application quits, and the computer shuts down—much to your surprise, because it's supposed to ignore the shut down when you're working.

But once the shutdown sequence begins, the Mac doesn't pay any attention to how it was triggered; it behaves as if you had selected the Shut Down command. So, even though you're sitting there waiting to get back to work, the Mac shuts down. (It's a little like the countdown in a self-destruct sequence without Captain Kirk/Picard/Janeway around to stop it.)

Oddly enough, when you don't have any unsaved documents waiting and the auto shutdown rolls around while the computer's sleeping, you can come back, wake it up, and get back to work—the shutdown time has come and gone with no effect at all.

The adding-insult-to-injury dialog. If you don't shut down the Mac properly—which means you've pretty much pulled the plug, literally or figuratively—you'll see this dialog when you start up again. It's so ridiculous, and insulting—I know how to shut this thing down—the only time I can't do it correctly is when the Mac crashes and I have to shut it off. Oddly enough, the dialog doesn't even mention the Finder's Shut Down command but only the Power key.

Luckily, you can prevent this dialog from showing up by unchecking the *Warn me* checkbox in the General Controls control panel.

This computer may not have been shut down properly the last time it was used. To turn off this computer, always press the Power key on the keyboard.
OK

One of the most annoying of all Mac dialogs.

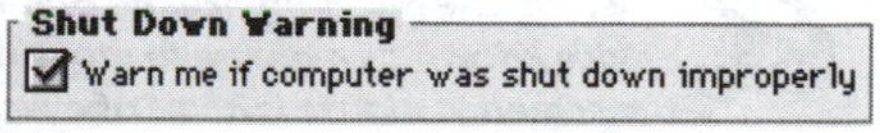
Shut Down Warning
Warn me if computer was shut down improperly

You can turn off the improper shutdown dialog through this setting in the General Controls control panel.

Mouse and Menus

The Mouse

The hot spot. The most important part of any cursor is its *hot spot:* the one spot (a single pixel in size) that "counts" when you're using the cursor. On the pointer, the hot spot is the tip of the arrow, and that's the spot that has to be touching the item you're pointing to. The entire arrow doesn't have to be inside the object you're selecting; on the other hand, if everything *except* the tip is inside the object, it won't do any good at all.

It's tip of the arrow that "counts" and has to be touching a disk icon if you want to select it.

New system cursors. The mouse pointer, or cursor, can take on a wide variety of shapes. Some of them are system cursors, used on the desktop and available to any program that needs them; others are specific to the application you're using.

OS 8 has added four new cursors for use on the desktop. One is a subtle reminder for when you're dragging an icon that's going to be copied instead of just moved: there's a little plus sign appended to the pointer. The other three show up when you use the new features added in OS 8, contextual menus, drag-aliasing, and spring-loaded folders.

The four new desktop cursors.

The "wait" cursors. There are some cursors, generally referred to as "wait" cursors, that are animated—they spin or change to let you know that the Mac hasn't frozen up while some tedious operation is taking all its attention. An animated cursor (the spinning hands on the watch, the spinning beachball, counting fingers, or spinning globe) is actually a series of cursors displayed one after the other.

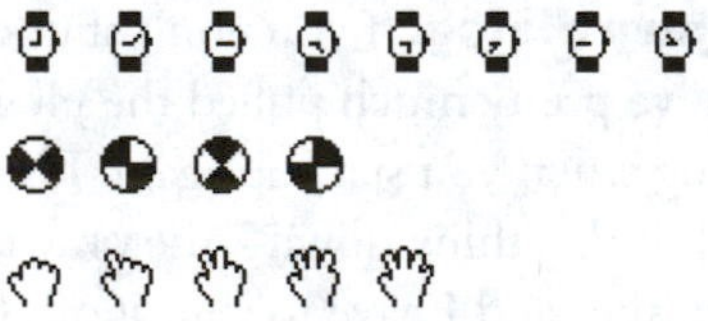

Animated cursors are actually stored as separate cursors that are used in sequence.

Double-clicking as Open Sesame. A double-click of the mouse almost always opens something. It usually substitutes for a single click to select something and a subsequent Open command from a menu or button. Double-click on a folder icon on the desktop to open the folder; double-click on an application icon to open—or *launch*—it. Even double-clicking on an item in a list in an Open dialog works instead of clicking on the item and then clicking the Open button.

The major exception to this rule is that double-clicking on text usually selects an entire word.

> ***"The Lisa [the Mac's immediate predecessor] uses a device known as a mouse to move a pointer around the screen. A mouse is a sort of executive joystick. If you want to file something, you move the pointer to a picture of a little folder and push a button. Business, then, becomes a computer game."***
>
> *Peter MacWilliams, The Word Processing Book, 1983*

The click-and-a-half. OS 8 added a new term to the mouse lexicon: *click-and-a-half.* It's like a double-click but instead of releasing the mouse button at the end of the second click, you keep holding it down. It's used for drilling down through folders on the desktop.

The double-click speed. The only difference between a double-click and two single clicks is the amount of time between the clicks. But *you* get to set the length of that interval (slow, medium, or fast) by using the speed settings in the Mouse control panel. Since a click-and-a-half might also be a click followed by a *press,* the double-click speed setting affects that operation, too.

Adjust the double-click and mouse tracking speeds in the Mouse control panel.

The double-click speed setting also affects the "rename delay" for a desktop icon: the time it takes for the editing rectangle to appear around an icon's name after you click on it.

Tracking speed. The Mouse control panel also lets you set the *tracking speed* for the cursor: the relationship between how fast you move the mouse and how far the mouse cursor travels on the screen.

Setting the tracking at Very Slow means there's no difference between the mouse and cursor "mileage": moving the mouse three inches moves the cursor three inches, no matter what your speed. At other settings, the mouse and cursor distances match if you move the mouse very slowly. But when you move the mouse quickly, the cursor can move from about twice the mouse distance (at a slow settings) to about five times the mouse distance.

Coruscating cursors. If you're bored with black-and-white cursors, there is a cure; in fact, there are two cures. DublClick's **ClickChange** and Nova Development's **Zonkers** utility packages, described more fully later in this chapter, let you change the drab basic system cursors into eye-catching little works of art. A steaming coffee cup instead of the spinning wristwatch. A pulsing red wedge instead of the arrow—or a shimmering rainbow pointer. If you want something other than what's supplied with the package, use the included cursor editor to design your own.

Menu Basics

Menu blink control. A menu item blinks when you select it (it's subtle but appreciated feedback). You can turn off the blink entirely, or choose one, two, or three blinks as the feedback in the Menu Blinking section of the General Controls control panel.

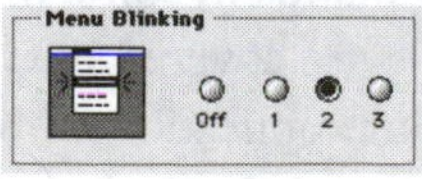

Don't backtrack. If you've opened a menu and dragged to a command and then change your mind, you don't have to backtrack up to the menu name to get out without triggering a command. Just slide the mouse cursor off the menu anywhere (you'll see that the highlight disappears from the menu command) and then let go of the mouse button. This works in submenus as well as main menus.

For further info.... When a menu command is followed by an ellipsis (three dots, like this…) that means the Mac needs more information before the command can be executed, so a dialog box opens when you select the command.

Key symbols in menus. The ⌘ symbol is easy to display in a menu because it's also a symbol on the keyboard. But the other modifier keys—Shift, Option, and Ctrl—need special symbols in a menu because they appear as words on the keyboard. The cryptic symbols Apple picked are shown here.

Modifier keys, and non-printing keys, use the special symbols shown here when they appear in a menu.

⌘	Command	⇥	Tab
⇧	Shift	↩	Return
⌥	Option	←	Arrow Key
^	Control	⌦	Forward Delete
␣	Spacebar	F9	Function Key
⌤	Enter	⌨9	Keypad Number

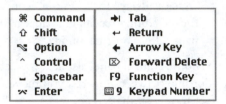

And what happens when a keyboard command involves some other nonprinting key (like Tab, Enter, or Return) that has to show in a menu? They, too, have their own symbols.

Highlight color. Back in the dark ages (or, more precisely, the black-and-white ages), menus were white, their commands black, and dimmed commands were a black-and-white checkerboard that looked sort of gray; the highlight as you selected a command was a simple white-on-black reversal. With color Macs and later systems, the menus were still black-and-white, but dimmed commands were actually gray letters, and the selection highlight was also gray.

Welcome to the more colorful world of OS 8. Menus now have a gray background, as does the menubar (though I confess I prefer the white) and the highlight when you select a command is… whatever you want it to be. When you use the Appearance control panel to set the Accent Color that's used for dialog box and window components, as described in later in the chapter, the color is also used for menu highlighting.

Two commands for the press of one. To give two or more keyboard commands in a row, you can keep the ⌘ down while you press the other keys you need. For instance, if you want to save a document, then close it, then quit the program, you don't have to press ⌘S, then ⌘W, then ⌘Q. Just hold down ⌘, then press S, W, and Q in turn.

Menus and keyboard modifiers. Holding down Option or Shift (or sometimes both) can change one or more commands in some menus. The Finder offers several examples of this feature (they're covered in Chapter 6), but always remember to experiment in all your applications. I blush to admit that it wasn't until after a year of use that I realized that holding down Shift while opening Word's File menu changes the Close command to Close All.

More Menus

Submenu selection. When you want something from a submenu, you don't have to make a ninety-degree turn from the main menu into the submenu. If you move fast enough (you don't have to be *really* speedy), you can slide diagonally from the main menu command directly to the submenu command without the submenu's closing.

You can drag directly to a submenu command (right).

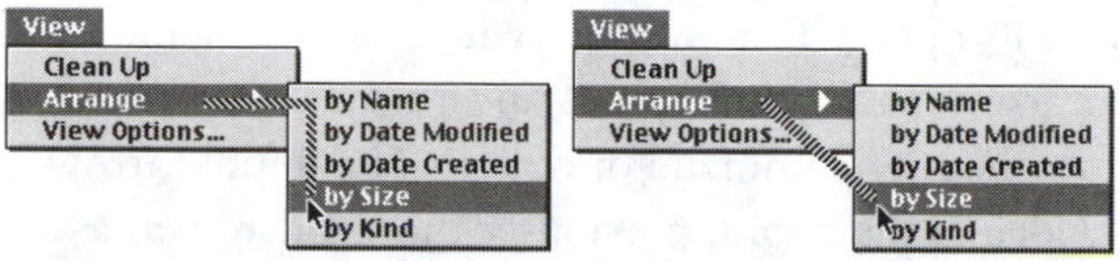

A menu with too many items to display at once has an arrow at the bottom (left). Hold the pointer at the bottom of the menu, and the menu scrolls; an arrow appears at the top of the menu to show that it can scroll in that direction, too (right).

Scrolling menus. When a menu has so many items on it that they can't all fit on the screen, the menu can scroll to show you all the choices. A downward-pointing arrow at the bottom of a menu indicates that there are items off in that direction; slide down to the arrow, and the menu starts to scroll. Once it's scrolling, there'll be an upward-pointing arrow at the top to show that there are now choices off in *that* direction; slide the pointer back up to scroll in that direction.

You don't have to put the cursor on a scrolling menu's arrow to make it scroll up or down; anywhere along the bottom (or top) edge of the menu will do. In fact, you can even hold the cursor below the menu and keep it scrolling as long as you slide out through the bottom of the menu and not its side.

It's hard to catch the item you want as it scrolls by, but you don't have to worry about that: once you see it, just slide the pointer back into the menu and the scrolling stops so you can get to the item you want.

Speed scrolling. If your scrolling menus are incredibly long (as can happen with font menus), you might find it handy to adjust the scrolling speed—either faster so you can get through it, or slower so you can better see the names as they scroll by. Position the cursor anywhere in the body of the scroll arrow for medium-speed scrolling. To slow it down, keep the point of the cursor just outside the scroll arrow, just past its base. Put the cursor at the pointed tip of the scroll arrow to make the menu scroll faster.

Pop-up menus. When pop-up menus first started popping up in the Mac interface, there wasn't much in the way of standardization. Sometimes a pop-up was simply a rectangle with a drop shadow, sometimes it had an arrow in or near it; sometimes the current menu choice showed as the menu's "title," and sometimes the title hovered above it.

In OS 8, though, pop-up menus seem to have settled down. You'll see a rounded rectangle that includes the current menu choice and a double-headed arrow at its right. Click on it (anywhere on the menu—you don't have to click on the arrows) and you'll get a standard square-cornered menu from which you can choose a command or option. The double arrow is a nice detail to have added to the menu; previously, the standard was a downward-pointing arrow, but pop-up menus tend to pop *up*, or in both directions, at least as often as they open downward.

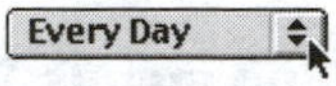

Old-style pop-ups. If you turn off the "platinum windows" option in the Appearance control panel, pop-up menus revert to the older-style shadowed box with a downward-pointing arrow at the right.

Sticky menus. Another new OS 8 feature is *sticky menus.* Just click on a menu title in the menubar and the menu stays open even if you release the mouse button. You can even slide the mouse cursor away from the menu and it stays open.

To select a command from an open menu, just click on it. To close the menu without choosing a command from it, click anywhere on the screen, or press ⌘ .. (Or, you could sit there and do nothing for a while—stuck menus close themselves after about 15 seconds.)

Switching sticky menus. Once a menu is "stuck" open, you can open a different one by sliding the mouse cursor (remember, you're finger's not on the button at this point) over to another menu title. The original menu closes and the new one sticks open for you.

Stuff sticks all over the place. Sticky menus work everywhere—at least everywhere I could think to try it so far. You might expect them to work from the menubar in every application (and they do), but it's nice to find that they work on pop-up menus in dialog boxes (like the Open and Save dialogs) and even on contextual menus that pop up anywhere on the screen that you need them—just click to open the menu and it stays open until you use it or click elsewhere.

Teflon-coated menus. If your sticky menus don't work exactly the way you'd like them to, try the freeware **Teflon**, a control panel that lets you disable sticky menus (odd that Apple didn't provide that capability), or adjust their behavior: they can drop down and stick without your even clicking the mouse button, or you can adjust the amount of time that defines the difference between a *click* and a *press* on a menu title (since that's the difference between a stuck menu and one that goes away when you release the mouse button).

Contextual menus. OS 8 introduced a special kind of pop-up menu: the *contextual* menus that pop up when you hold down Control and press the mouse button. There's lots more about these in Chapter 6, because although this is a system-wide feature, it's most fully implemented on the desktop at this point. As soon as developers jump on this particular bandwagon, you'll have pop-up contextual menus everywhere. (There have been pop-up contextuals in several programs already—Microsoft products and FileMaker Pro 3 come to mind—but they've been strictly application-specific and will have to be re-done to comply with the system's contextual menus.)

The System font. The font used for menus and dialogs changed from our beloved Chicago to the slightly more angular Charcoal for OS 8. You can switch back by using the Appearance control panel and setting the System font to Chicago.

You might have been disappointed to find only two fonts in the Appearance control panel. However, the Appearance control panel is ready to use five other fonts: Capitals, Gadget, Sand, Textile, and Techno. I'm sure they'll all be available well before you read this book.

Use the Appearance control panel to switch system fonts.

Windows and Dialogs

About Windows

The new look. OS 8's windows have a new, three-dimensional look referred to as "platinum." With the new shading, the stripes in the title bar look like ridges, the close box looks somewhat concave, and there's a rolled rim around the sides and bottom of each window, outside the scroll bars. The size box in the lower right, though still officially designated as such, is no longer a box—it's a triple stripe. And, there's a new control in the upper right, the collapse box, that takes over for the old Window Shade control panel. (After a decade of clicking in the upper right of a window to zoom it, I keep hitting that collapse box instead—couldn't they have kept the zoom box in the corner and put the collapse box on the inside?!)

Window basics **Chapter 1**

windows **Chapter 6**

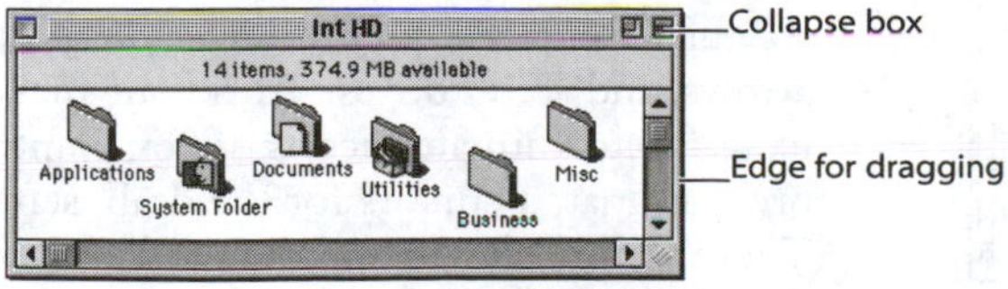

The new window look and some new window parts.

The uni-directional zoom box. The Finder's About box is the only place I've found this so far, but there's obviously a special window control built-in to the system for programmers to hook into. The About box can be resized only vertically, and its zoom box acknowledges the fact by using a slightly different design. (The Find File application, which also allows only vertical resizing, still uses a standard zoom.)

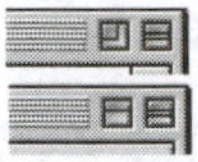

The standard zoom box (top) and the vertical zoom box (bottom).

Controlling the new look. You can change the basic look of your windows—and some of their behaviors—through the Appearance control panel.

With the Color option selected, you can choose an accent color that will be applied to scroll boxes in windows and parts of dialog boxes, like progress bars. (The same accent color will be used for your menu selection highlight.)

Clicking the Options button in the control panel lets you set the behavior for collapsing windows, change the system font (used in menus, dialog boxes, and window titles) from the new Charcoal font back to good ol' Chicago, and set the 3-D platinum window option for only the desktop, or for all your applications, too.

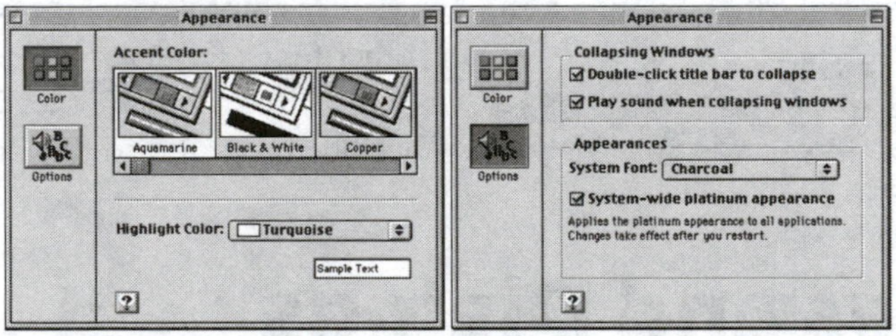

The two faces of the Appearance control panel lets you control the new window looks and system font.

Getting the old look back. If you turn off the system-wide platinum windows in applications, you'll get the standard System 7 windows. You'll lose not only the "look," but also the collapse box, and the rim around the outside of the window that lets you drag the window around. The collapse *function* is still available if you leave *Double-click title bar to collapse* checked in the Appearance control panel; you'll just have to access it by double-clicking on title bars instead of using a collapse box.

A different new look. If the platinum look just isn't enough for you, you can take the years of development that went into the elegant Mac interface and ruin it in just minutes.

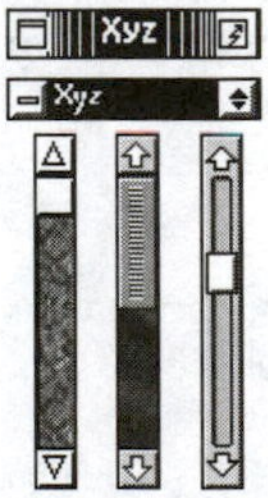

A very small sampling of possible title and scroll bars from ClickChange.

- **ClickChange** ($58, DublClick Software) lets you control just about every facet of the Mac look. Windows, for instance: move the title to one end or the other instead of leaving it centered; pick a new style of title bar, scroll arrows, and scroll boxes. Turn your menu titles into icons—into animated icons, if you want. Substitute colored, animated cursors for the drab, static system version. There's more slicing and dicing than is worth listing here (including adding double scroll arrows and assigning sounds to various system events).

- **Kaleidoscope** ($20, shareware) is a terrific collection of interface-twisting capabilities brought to you by the folks who made the shareware packages Greg's Buttons and Aaron Lite (and Heavy). Select a "color scheme" and it changes the color and look of window components; you can also assign colors to the background of Finder windows, and even change the font used in menus and dialogs (beyond the choices the Appearance control panel provides). If you look around online, you'll find color schemes that other people have designed that you can add to your Kaleidoscope folder; you can use Kaleidoscope's tools to create your own color schemes.

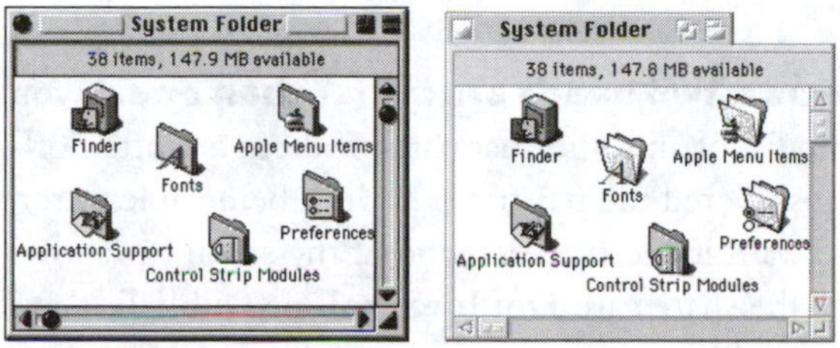

Two Kaleidoscope window fashions, Sherbet (orange flavor) and BeBox varieties; with the latter, even system icons change.

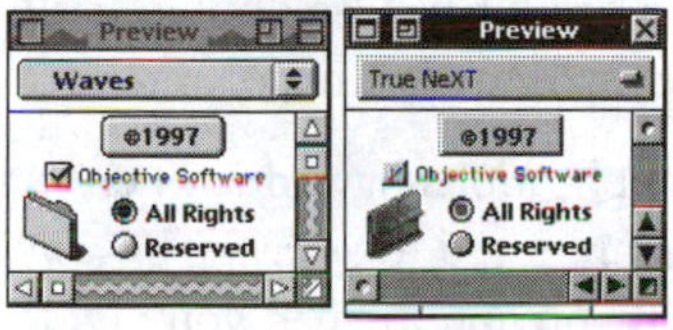

A few of Niji's window choices.

- **Niji** ($20, shareware) is Japanese for "rainbow" and that's what you get for your windows: a rainbow of colors and designs to apply. The pictures here don't do the designs justice. Niji changes the whole look of your menus, too.

- **Zonkers** ($25, Nova Development) suggests you can turn your Mac into a virtual theme park with all its interface alterations, including window color and styles, buttons, animated cursors, background pictures and icons.

Live scrolling. The "live scroll" feature that was introduced in OS 8 works on the desktop, and in any application that's aware of the capability and allows its use. What's live scrolling? As you drag the scroll box, the contents of the window move so you don't have to guess where you should let go in order to see a specific spot in the document.

Some applications, like Netscape Navigator, provide the live scroll feature as a standard, or an option, separate from OS 8's provision.

Why windows scroll backwards. Scroll controls seem to work backwards when you're new to the Mac. (Of course, scrolling becomes second nature in a very short time, so it hardly matters how it feels at first!) But here's why a click in a down arrow scrolls things upwards, a click in the left arrow scrolls things to the right, and so on: You're not scrolling the contents, you're moving the *window.* Conceptually, although not physically, a click in the down arrow moves the window *down,* which makes the relative position of its contents move up. The picture on the next page explains it better than any more words can.

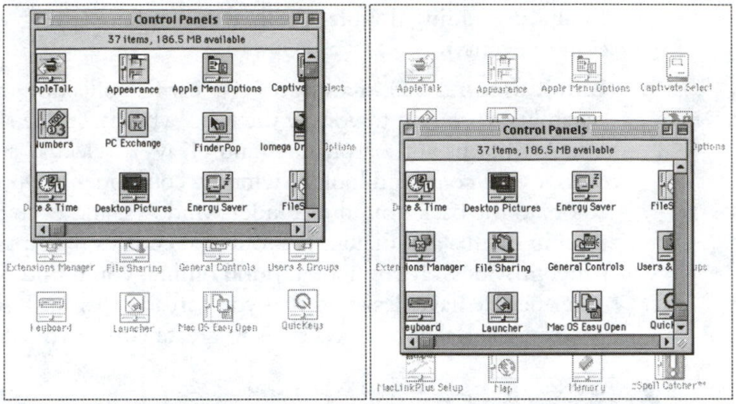

Clicking in a scroll arrow conceptually moves the window, not the contents. With the Control Panel window supposedly moving down when you click the down arrow, the contents, relatively speaking, move upwards.

Scroll arrows: two heads are better than one. If you move your windows around a lot and find that parts of them are often off-screen, you've probably discovered the frustration of not being able to scroll your window to where you want it because each end of the scroll bar shows only *one* scroll arrow. Use the shareware **DoubleScroll** or DublClick's **ClickChange** to turn every scroll arrow into a two-headed beast so you can scroll in both directions from either end of a scroll bar. Use double scroll arrows for just a little while, and you'll realize Apple made a major interface omission.

Splitting windows. Some applications have document windows that can be split into separate areas, usually referred to as *panes*, by a *split bar*, a thick black line next to the scroll arrow. By moving the bar, you divide the window into two parts, each with its own scroll controls. Splitting a window lets you look at two different parts of your document at the same time. In a word processor, for instance, you could work on any part of the document while keeping your

introductory comments in view at all times. In a spreadsheet, you can usually split a window both vertically and horizontally, giving you four independently scrolling areas on the screen.

Windoids. Okay, hardly anyone calls them windoids anymore. These special kinds of windows are variously referred to as *floating windows* or *palettes.* Most applications refer to them as *tool palettes* and you hardly even think of them as windows. But palettes are windows, special ones that defy the general rule that the frontmost window is the one that's affected by your actions. While you work in your standard document window, a palette floats on top of it so you can reach tools and commands, or see information about what you're doing.

The floating issue aside, most palettes follow basic window rules amongst themselves—when you have more than one open, for instance, and they're overlapping, the one you've clicked in most recently is on the top. A few palettes have resize boxes; most have title bars, although the bars are thin, have a different pattern in them, and can be at the top or side of the palette. And, almost all have that all-important feature: a close box so you can get it off the screen.

Manipulating Windows

Moving and resizing. The standard way to move a window is to drag it by its title bar. With OS 8, finally, there's an additional option: you can grab a window by any of its outer edges in order to drag it around. (As long as you keep the Platinum option turned on in the Appearance control panel—that's what gives windows the extra edge.)

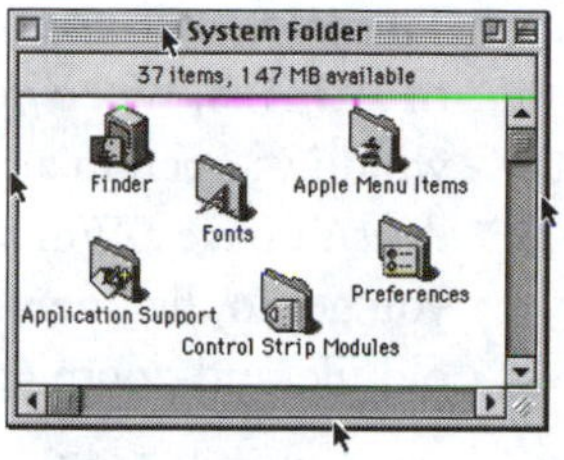

You can drag a platinum window by any of its four edges.

Change a window's size by dragging the *size box* in the lower right. Of course, in the Platinum world, it's not really a box anymore: it's a triple-stripe affair in the corner of the window.

To quickly re-size a window, click in its *zoom box.* This toggles the window's size and shape between the one you created and a full-screen size.

Getting windows out of the way. There are many ways to manage a screenful of windows, keeping most of them out of the way while you work with the most important ones. You can:

Hiding windows that belong to applications in the background .... *Chapter 12*

- **Close** some or all of the windows you're not using.
- **Collapse** unused windows down to their title bars.
- **Hide** windows that don't belong to the application you're currently using.
- Turn the window into a **tab** at the bottom of the screen on the desktop.

Moving inactive windows. You can move an inactive window *without* making it the active one by holding down ⌘ as you drag the window by its title bar or outer edge. This works in most programs, though not all; it's been a Finder feature for a long time. If you have multiple applications open, you can't move windows that belong to another application without bringing that application to the front; the ⌘-drag works only for windows within an application.

Full-size versus full-size. When it comes to windows, the definition of "full-size" varies according to where you are.

On the desktop, clicking the zoom box to open a window to its full size opens it only far enough to display all the items in it. The largest zoomed size, no matter how many things are in the window, is the size of the screen *less* a strip along the right edge so disk icons and the Trash are always visible. (This is a thoughtful touch—you can zoom the window open for maximum access but still drag things from it to the Trash or another disk.)

In other programs, the zoom toggle will certainly switch between two sizes, but the "full-size" is open to interpretation. And if you have a large monitor, or a two-monitor setup, zooming is an adventure. On my 20-inch monitor, in various applications, a full-screen zoom can be: the full screen; the full height, but not the full width of the screen; just enough to show the window contents; or only as large as the memory partition for that program can handle. And, since I use a double-monitor setup, sometimes clicking the zoom box in a window on one screen zooms it over to the other screen where the menubar is; zooming a window that's straddling the two monitor screens sometimes keeps it on the screen where the zoom box is, and sometimes sends it to the screen that "owns" the larger portion of the window when I click it.

IN THE BEGINNING

Mac windows weren't born with zoom boxes; they weren't added until the advent of the Mac Plus in 1986. Maybe that's why there's still some confusion as to exactly how the zoom toggle should behave.

The tile-and-zoom method for multiples. When you have several windows open in an application that doesn't have a Windows menu to help you get to the one you want, use the old tile-and-zoom approach.

First, *tile* the windows—arrange your windows so you can see all of them completely. For four windows, give each a quarter of the screen; for three, set them each to take a third of the screen horizontal, and so on.

To work in a window, click its zoom box; it zooms to fill the screen. Zoom it down when you're finished, and zoom up the next one. This way, you can always easily see a little of each window so you can tell which one you want—something you lose when you collapse a window down to its title bar. And, if the application provides window-to-window drag and drop, you'll be able to move selections from one place to another.

Collapsing Windows

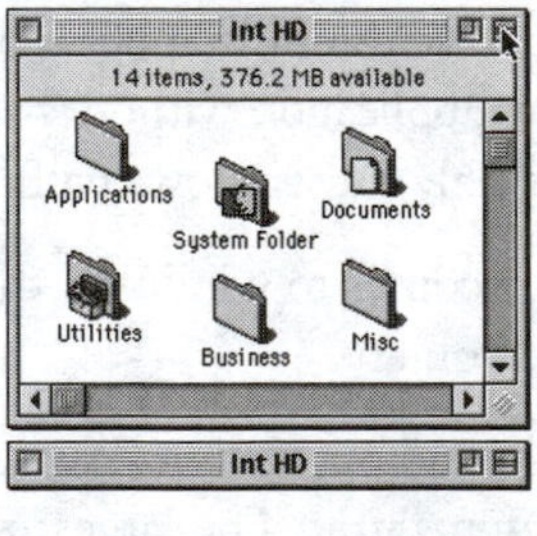

Click in a window's collapse box to shrink it down to just its title bar.

No more WindowShade. The WindowShade control panel that came in System 7 is already gone, replaced by a window-frame control: to collapse a window down to its title bar, all you have to do is click in its collapse box.

You can still double-click directly on the title bar of a window to collapse it instead of clicking in the collapse box. Use the Appearance control panel to turn the double-click option on and off, and to keep or squelch that cute little *pffft* sound during the collapse/expand procedure. (The bigger your window is, the longer the expand sound lasts. Really. A little window goes *pfft,* but a large one goes *pfffffft.)*

No platinum, no collapse control. As mentioned briefly earlier in the chapter, if you turn off the *System-wide platinum appearance* option in the Appearance control panel, you'll lose not only OS 8's 3-D look for windows, but also the new window controls, including the collapse box. You'll still be able to collapse windows as long as you leave the double-click option on in the control panel.

Use the Appearance control panel to turn the double-click and sound options for collapsing on and off.

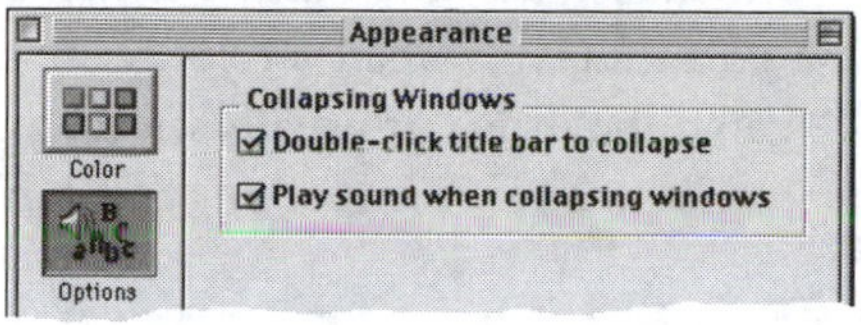

The complete collapse. Hold Option while you click in a window's collapse box, and you'll collapse all an application's windows at once (this works for all Finder windows, too.

The expand-zoom combo. The zoom box remains on a collapsed title bar and still functions as it should, although perhaps not exactly as you'd expect.

If you collapse a small window and then click its zoom box, you won't get a title bar zooming to another size: you'll get the window zooming open to its full size. If you collapse the full size window, clicking the zoom box opens the smaller version of the window. So, the zoom box both opens the window *and* zooms it to the other view—handy when you're going from a tiny title bar to a full-size window. Not so handy to shrink it down again, since it takes two clicks: one for the zoom box, then one for the collapse box—which has moved away from your mouse cursor after you clicked the zoom box.

The title bar is still a window! The title bar is still a window, even if most of it is hidden from view. So, you can still use commands on it that you would if it were expanded: you can close it, for instance, with the close box or a keyboard or menu command, and you can save the document without having to actually see the contents—just as long as the title bar itself is active.

Dialog Boxes

Modal dialogs. Most dialog boxes are *modal*: you can't do anything else until you've dealt with them—you're stuck in that mode. You have to put away the dialog before you can get back to your application. If you click outside the dialog, you'll just get a beep. Some dialog boxes are obviously modal because they're totally unmovable, without even a title bar you could use for dragging. Other dialogs *seem* non-modal because they have title bars—but that's only because the program is being nice and letting you move it on the screen in case you need to see something behind it to make your dialog decisions.

Alerts. An *alert*, as noted in Chapter 1, is more of a monologue than a dialog, since it's just a statement or warning, with only an OK or Cancel button (or both) for your feedback.

There are three standard icons used in alert boxes, for situations of varying intensity. *Note* is a talking head; *Caution* is an exclamation point in a yellow triangle whose color and shape were obviously inspired by roadside warning signs; and the red *Stop,* which also uses the traffic theme. Take that stop sign seriously, because if you go ahead with whatever you were doing that triggered the dialog, it usually means you're about to do something really important that can't be undone.

IN THE BEGINNING

The Mac has always had three basic alert icons, with the same basic meanings. But the icons were not always so easily differentiated. In fact, only one is still the same (except, of course, for the addition of color and now OS 8's 3-D look).

All three of the original icons were talking heads, in keeping with the "dialog" theme. As you can see, it was difficult to figure out the level of urgency—which is more serious, an exclamation point or an asterisk?

Missing close controls. Some dialogs (like the About boxes or opening screens for some applications) have no close controls—neither a close box in the window nor Cancel or Close buttons. Clicking in the dialog often closes it; usually pressing Return, Enter, Esc—or sometimes any key at all—works.

Selecting from lists. To select something from a scrolling list in a dialog, you can scroll until you see the item you want, and then click on it. But in most dialogs, you can type a few letters of the item's name to jump to it, and in some you can use the arrow keys (↑ and ↓) to move up and down in the list.

There's no standard for dialogs that have more than one scrolling list. In some, you can click on or tab to the list you want, and then type to select your item; sometimes the "active" list is surrounded by a frame to show it's the one that's "accepting" the typing. Other dialogs let you type to select from only one list, or from the most recently used list, or just ignore your typing.

Multiple selections in a list. Some dialogs let you select more than one item from a list at one time. But there's no indication of which lists allow multiple selections, and the way to do it varies from one application to the next.

Try a multiple selection in a list by holding down Shift as you click on different items. This is the most commonly available option, but it doesn't always work the same way. Sometimes the Shift-click selects the single item you clicked on, adding it to the selection, as when you select icons in a desktop window. Sometimes Shift-clicking selects everything from the original selection to the place you're clicking, like when you're working with text.

Sometimes holding down Shift will let you drag across parts of the list, adding all the items you touch to the selection.

When a Shift-click won't let you select non-contiguous items in a list, try clicking with ⌘ down (a fairly common option), or Option.

Keyboard controls for buttons. The default button in any dialog used to be surrounded by a heavy, clunky frame; in OS 8, the default button has a more elegant rim around it. Hitting Return or Enter almost always triggers the default button. For a Cancel button, especially when it's not the default, ⌘. or Esc usually works.

You'll notice that a well-designed Mac program has the correct button as the default in a dialog; depending on the situation, the "correct" button might be OK or it might be Cancel—or any other button. It should always be the conservative, you-can-take-it-back choice that's the default so you don't hit it by mistake. If the question is *Ok to erase the entire hard drive?* or *Delete all 1,345 records from the database?* you don't want OK to be the default!

The framed default button is triggered by pressing Return.

Dialog tabs. Some dialog boxes ask for *lots* of information. To keep the dialogs from getting too large, options are broken down into groups that you can look at one at a time. While some dialogs offer a pop-up menu to select what group you're looking at (as in Print dialogs) and some give you icons along the side to click in (as in the Appearance control panel), the idea of *tabs* is gaining ground. You can see all the tabs all the time (which makes them better than pop-up menus) and they don't take as much room as icon buttons. You move from one group of options to another by clicking a tab.

In Microsoft products, both the tab that you click on and the screen of information it reveals are referred to as *tabs,* and the terminology will probably creep over to the Mac OS while we're not looking.

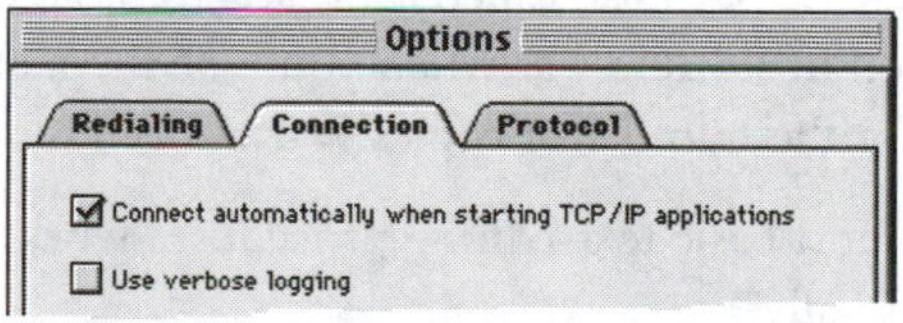

The Options dialog for the PPP control panel uses tabs to divide its information into smaller chunks.

Buttons and Text Boxes

The new look. The OS 8 Platinum 3-D appearance has affected buttons as well as windows: everything has a gray (oh, all right, *platinum*) patina to it and a slight 3-D effect. Radio buttons are particularly interesting, with the shadows giving a real pushed-in look to the button. Checkboxes have gone from having an X in the middle to having a real checkmark.

Push buttons are like menu commands. Of the three types of buttons—push, radio, and checkbox—the push button is the one used to execute a command rather than select an option. Because it's so much like a menu command, a push button often exhibits menu-command-like behavior: you may find an ellipsis (these three dots…) in its label, meaning a dialog will open; it can be dimmed when the current situation wouldn't allow that command to be carried out; and it can even have a command-key equivalent listed right in the button.

IN THE BEGINNING

Ever wonder why those little round ones are called "radio" buttons? It has to do with how clicking on one deselects the previously clicked one in the group. On old car radios that let you push buttons in to select a radio station, pushing in a button popped out the previously pushed-in one.

Don't click on the little buttons. When it comes to radio buttons and checkboxes, you don't have to click right in the little circle or box: clicking anywhere on the button name works just as well.

The mixed checkbox. Checkboxes are gray blanks when an option isn't selected, and have a checkmark in them when it is. But you'll occasionally see a dark gray in-between state, too.

Say you've selected some text that is a mixture of formats—some is italicized and some is not. You open a text-formatting dialog that has checkmarks for turning formats on and off. Will the Italic box be checked or not? Some programs ignore mixed formats and set the boxes to match the beginning of the selection. But smarter ones darken the checkbox to indicate that it applies to some, but not all, of the selection.

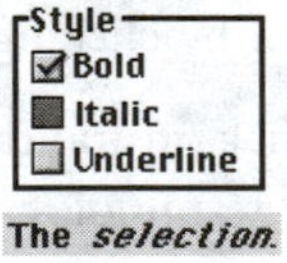

The Italic checkbox is darkened because some, but not all, of the selection is italicized.

Clicking on a dark gray checkbox will cycle it around from checked to unchecked to darkened again.

Text-box basics. A *text box* (also called a *text field,* or *field,* or *box)* is where you type information in a dialog—as when you type the name of a document in the Save dialog, or the number of copies you want in the Print dialog.

Keep in mind that most basic text-editing procedures work in most dialog text boxes, so you can usually:

- Double-click to select a single word.
- Use the arrow keys (←→) to move the insertion point.
- Type to replace selected text (so, if the text is already selected, you don't have to hit Delete before you start typing).
- Paste something into, or copy it from, a text box with the Paste or Copy commands.

Moving around. You can move from one text box to another in a dialog by clicking where you want to go, or by using Tab to move to the next box and Shift Tab to move to the previous one. The tabbing is circular: if you hit Tab when you're in the last box, you'll wind up in the first box.

When you move to a box by clicking, you usually wind up with the text insertion point at the spot that you clicked; when you use Tab to move to a box, the entire contents of the box are selected.

Tabbing is generally a better way to move around, not only because the keyboard is faster than the mouse for this operation, but because with the contents selected, you can just type to replace them. If you want to only do a minor edit on text-box contents, clicking in the box exactly at the spot you want to edit can be quicker because the blinking insertion point will appear exactly where you click.

If you're a keyboard whiz, even minor editing may be accomplished more quickly from the keyboard. You can tab to the box, then use ← or → to move to the beginning or the end of the selection; a few more arrow-key presses will get you to the spot you want.

When the last shall be first. You can jump to the last text box in a dialog when it first opens by hitting Shift Tab. Since most dialogs open with the first text box already selected, moving to the "previous" box puts you in the last one in the dialog.

Using Tab when there's only one text box. If you use Tab in a dialog with only a single text box, sometimes the contents of the box will be selected. This can be handy. Say you've done a search for the word *movie* in your document, and come up with nothing. The Find dialog is still open, with the blinking cursor at the end of the word *movie.* To replace it with *film*, you have to either backspace five times and then type, or go for the mouse, double-click to select the word, hit Delete to erase it, then type. In dialogs that let you use Tab, you can just hit Tab to select the box's contents, then type the new word to replace it.

A snappy little utility. I'm not sure what amazes me more: that Apple left out some minor interface details they should have thought of, or that someone else always remedies such oversights. The freeware utility **SnapTo** places the cursor over the default button in a dialog box no matter where it was when the dialog was called up. Dismiss the dialog, and the cursor snaps back to where it was before you started. It's a minor convenience on standard screens, and a major one on large screens and multiple monitor setups.

The Clipboard

About the Clipboard

The Clipboard. The Clipboard doesn't actually exist except as a concept—it's not a desk accessory or utility that you can open. But it works as a transfer medium for text, graphics, and even sound, from one place to another within a document, between documents, and between applications.

The four important things to keep in mind about the Clipboard are:

- The Clipboard holds only one item at a time (although the item can be very large).
- When you put something on the Clipboard, it replaces the item that was there.
- Pasting an item from the Clipboard doesn't take it off the Clipboard; the item remains on the Clipboard until it's replaced by something else or until you shut down the computer.
- Clipboard contents are held in RAM—the part of memory that's erased when the computer is shut off.

Using Cut, Copy and Paste. The commands you use in dealing with the Clipboard are all gathered into every application's Edit menu. The Cut and Copy commands place selected material on the Clipboard; Cut removes the selection from the document, while Copy keeps the original in place.

The Paste command places the Clipboard contents into your current document. Where the pasted material appears depends on the type of document. In a word processor, for instance, the pasted material appears at the insertion point or replaces a selection. In a graphics or layout program, the pasted item is usually an object that appears at the center of the window, selected, so you can move it where you want.

Using Paste doesn't clear the Clipboard of its contents—you can use the Paste command over and over for multiple copies, in various places, of whatever's on the Clipboard.

The Clear command. Along with the Cut, Copy, and Paste commands, most Edit menus include a Clear command that deletes a selection without placing it on the Clipboard—it's the same as pressing Delete.

Inter-application copy and pastes. Sometimes what you copy in one program is not exactly what gets pasted into another program. This isn't a Clipboard limitation: it's because some applications don't understand all the formats used by other applications. For instance, if you create a FileMaker layout that has an icon button with an attached script, you can copy the button to the Clipboard and paste it into another layout, and the script goes along with it. But paste that icon into a graphics program, and you'll get the icon alone—the graphics program doesn't understand the format of a script attached to a button. Each application does its best to interpret the Clipboard contents as completely as possible, extracting all the information it understands.

The one and only Clipboard. There's no such thing as a *system Clipboard* and an *application Clipboard*. There's only one Clipboard, but some people use these phrases to refer to the way using the Clipboard preserves all the formats of an item while you're inside an application, but might not transfer everything to another program.

Restoring Clipboard contents. If you cut or copy something and then realize you still need what was previously on the Clipboard, use the Undo command. When it undoes the Cut or Copy command, it also restores the Clipboard to its previous state.

Remembering the keyboard commands. The keyboard equivalents for Cut, Copy, and Paste don't lend themselves to mnemonics, although of course, the C for Copy is easy, and the X for Cut is somewhat like a pair of scissors.

But it's easy to remember the series of commands as they appear in almost all Edit menus: the keyboard equivalents for Undo, Cut, Copy, and Paste are ⌘ with Z, X, C, and V, the first four keys in the bottom row of the keyboard.

In some Edit menus, ⌘B is the keyboard equivalent for the Clear command. That's left over from when the Mac keyboard had a Backspace key instead of a Delete key.

Function key equivalents. The function keys F1, F2, F3, and F4 are single-key commands for Undo, Cut, Copy, and Paste in almost all programs. (It's amazing how much easier that can be than a two-keys-at-a-time shortcut!)

Undoing

I take it back! I didn't mean it! There are many things about the Mac that I wish I could have in my "real" life. One of them is the ability to add more memory. The other is an Undo command. On the Mac, Undo is an escape mechanism of sorts. When you change your mind about something you've just changed in your document—whether it's making a title bold or deleting the first five paragraphs of your novel—choosing Undo "undoes" it.

Undo is meant only for *editing* commands—changing styles, cutting or pasting, or typing, for instance; you can't Undo something like saving a document.

Undoing the Undo. The basic Undo command is a one-trick pony: it undoes only the most recent editing action (typing is an editing change). Try using Undo twice in a row in most programs, and the second Undo undoes the first undo. (Did you follow that sentence? The second Undo acts as a Redo command, restoring what you had before you used Undo the first time.) Some applications actually provide a Redo command in the menu, with the name changing to help you figure out what you might be redoing: Redo Typing, Redo Formatting Change, and so on.

On the other hand, some applications provide multiple levels of Undo: choosing Undo eradicates the last editing procedure, another Undo selection undoes the change before that, and so on. To get the Redo function in these programs, you have to choose a separate Redo command.

The ultimate Undo. The ultimate Undo command isn't in any menu, but it works even when an Undo command wouldn't be available. Before you make a major change to your document that you might want to "take back," save your document. Then make the change. If you don't like it, open the saved version of the document. Some programs actually offer this function as a File menu command; usually, it's called Revert or Revert to Last Saved.

A very few programs—FileMaker, for instance—save changes to the disk as soon as you make them, so you won't be able to revert to the previously saved version. If a program doesn't have an explicit Save command in the File menu, it's saving changes automatically.

Back to the Clipboard

Checking the Clipboard contents. When you use a Show Clipboard command (like the one in the Finder's Edit menu), you get a "view-only" window that shows you what's on the Clipboard—you can't select it or edit it in any way. But you can usually scroll and/or resize the window to view all the contents.

The Scrapbook side trip. If you'd like to check just what's *really* on your Clipboard, you can paste it into the Scrapbook, which accepts almost anything—text, graphics, sound, and movies. You'll get not only a report as to the size of what you pasted, but a list of what kind of *resources*—special file types or formats—are included.

In the picture on the next page, text was copied from Microsoft Word and pasted into the Scrapbook at the left. You can see the types listed: DSIG, CLAP, styled text, and RTF. The very same selection was pasted into ClarisWorks, copied, and pasted back into the Scrapbook at the right. The only type that's left is styled text. Look at the size of the two selections, too: 2K for the Word paste, and 429 bytes (less than half a K) for the ClarisWorks paste. All the application-specific formats that Word copies to the Clipboard (and that the Scrapbook preserves) are lost if you paste the selection into ClarisWorks. This makes perfect sense, of course; Word's styles (that is, paragraph styles as opposed to bold/italic character styles) wouldn't work in ClarisWorks anyway.

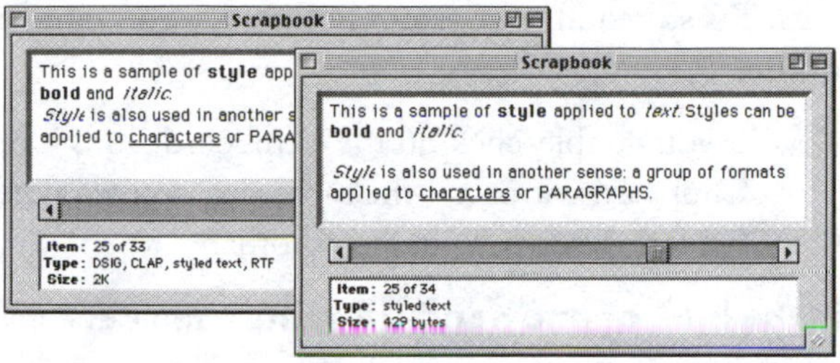

The Scrapbook notes the types of information that were pasted in from the Clipboard. Word's formats (left) are significantly different from ClarisWorks' (right), although they look the same on the surface.

Flushing the Clipboard. Since the Clipboard contents are held in memory, when you copy a large item to it, there can be a significant amount of memory tied up. You may find your application running a little more slowly. Since pasting from the Clipboard leaves the contents intact, it's not immediately apparent how you can clear the Clipboard if you don't need the large item there anymore.

But you can "flush" the Clipboard to free up memory. You can't actually empty it without restarting the Mac, but you can put something smaller on it. Copy a single letter (or, if you're in a graphics program, a very small graphic item) to the Clipboard—twice. The first time you do it, the new item is on the Clipboard, but the old contents are being held in reserve in case you use the Undo command, which would undo the copy procedure and place the old contents back on the Clipboard.

A bulging Clipboard slows you down. A full Clipboard can slow you down as you launch applications or move from one to another. When you "enter" a program, whether you're moving there from another one or just launching it, the application takes a look at the Clipboard and interprets its contents as best it can, figuring out which of the stored types of information it can handle. Depending on your Mac's inherent speed, a switch to another program might take up to 30 seconds or more instead of three to 10 seconds when you have a full Clipboard. So, if you don't need what's on the Clipboard, flush it before you move to another program.

A bulging Clipboard can slow you down within a program, too, not because of any translation process but because it might be using up a big chunk of memory that would otherwise be used for other things in the application. If you notice a slowdown, flush the Clipboard; if you need the contents for something, you can temporarily paste it somewhere else in your document, or in a temporary document you create just for that purpose.

The Clipboard file. Okay, I lied. I told you that the Clipboard contents are kept in memory, but that's not always entirely true. Sometimes what you put on the Clipboard is just too large to be held entirely in RAM, so the information gets dumped to the disk, to be retrieved when necessary. There's no difference from the user's point of view—you don't save or open the Clipboard file, and you'll lose it when the computer shuts off.

The file itself is stored in the System Folder; its icon, not surprisingly, is a Clipboard.

If you double-click on the Clipboard icon, it opens into the Clipboard window—the same one you get when you use the Finder's Show Clipboard command.

What is the look of one hand clapping? You can copy sounds within and between certain programs, which means they're on the Clipboard at some point. And you can look at the Clipboard contents—if not in the program, certainly from the Finder. That means you can look at the sound on your Clipboard. But you won't see much. In earlier systems, what you'd see is the generic Mac sound icon, but now you get something handier: a Play Sound button that lets you *hear* what's on the Clipboard.

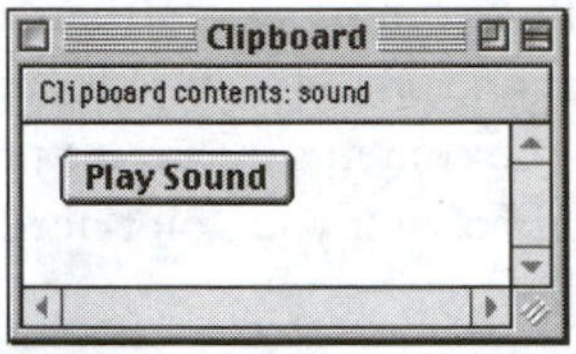

You can play a sound that's on the Clipboard, in the Finder if not in other applications.

When the Paste command won't. Sometimes transferring information from one application to another via the Clipboard becomes a problem that has nothing to do with the format of the item that's on the Clipboard. Sometimes you just get a little glitch that doesn't seem to transfer the Clipboard contents into another program: you use Paste, and you get what used to be on the Clipboard (or there's a dimmed Paste command and you don't get anything at all). You move back to where you came from, check the Clipboard contents and, sure enough, there's the new material after all. Move back to where you trying to paste, and, somehow, those Clipboard contents are gone. (In my experience, Microsoft Word is often a culprit in this area, but then I use Word more than anything else, so that's not exactly a statistically valid observation.)

In any case, here are a few things you can try when your copied material doesn't seem to "stick" to the Clipboard between applications; they've all worked for me at one time or another.

- Repeat the Copy command at the original location and try again.
- Hold Option while you choose the Copy command from the Edit menu.
- Paste the material inside the original application before switching to the other one.
- Go through the Finder: Move to the desktop, check the Clipboard with the Show Clipboard command, and if the material is there, move to the second application.
- Use the Scrapbook as a last resort. From the original application, go to the Scrapbook and paste the material there. Then move to the second application; sometimes you can do a direct paste at this point, without having to copy the material out of the Scrapbook. But if the paste doesn't work, move back to the Scrapbook, Copy or Cut the material, and then paste it into the second application.

Oddly enough (although there are philosophies that claim there are no such things as coincidences), as I was working on this tip, my friend Carol called and complained that she couldn't paste something that she copied from PageMaker into QuarkXPress. I made all the above suggestions, reading them right off the screen. No dice. I tried it myself: sure enough, Quark won't accept anything that carries PageMaker's *ALD6* format type along with it—and we're talking just selected text here, not anything fancy. Frankly, I think it's a plot, not a bug.

Applications can run out of memory. Not all programs put large Clipboard contents on the disk. If you get any Out of Memory messages *(Can't complete operation—out of memory; Can't Undo—not enough memory; Running low on memory—save your document and quit the application)* it might be because a huge Clipboard is taking up a lot of room. Flushing the Clipboard sometimes alleviates the out-of-memory problem, at least temporarily. You should plan to quit the program as soon as possible and allocate more memory to it for the next work session.

Allocating memory
Chapter 13

Optional preservation on quitting. Some programs ask if you want to preserve the Clipboard contents when you're quitting. If you don't need what's there, tell the program to get rid of it. If there's a lot on the Clipboard and you don't need it, but the program isn't smart enough to ask you, flush the Clipboard yourself.

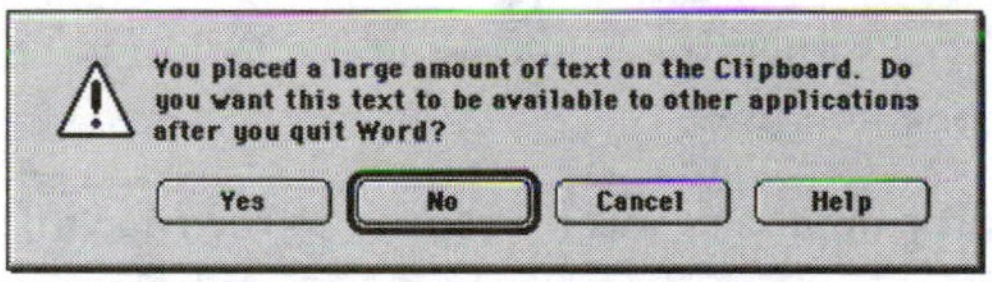

Put the Clipboard in the Apple menu. You can make a generic Show Clipboard command for the Apple menu so you can use it whenever an application doesn't provide one of its own. Make an alias of the Clipboard file that's in the System Folder; rename it *Show Clipboard* and put it in the Apple Menu Items folder.

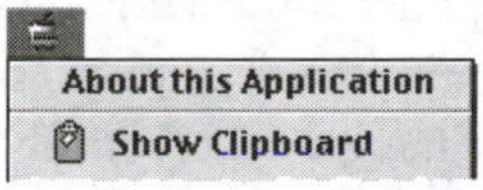

Make a Show Clipboard command for the Apple menu.

When you want to check the Clipboard, select the "command" from the Apple menu; it will even have a neat little Clipboard icon that came from the original. You'll be switched to the desktop and the Clipboard window will open.

Option-copying to the Clipboard. Most programs that generate PostScript artwork provide a special copying option so you can either copy all the PostScript information to the Clipboard to be pasted in another PostScript-savvy program/document or copy just the QuickDraw information so that almost any program can use that information. Most of the programs work this way: use the Copy command, and the PostScript information in the selection is copied to the Clipboard; hold down Option while you choose Copy and only the QuickDraw information is copied. The figure here shows what gets pasted down into a non-PostScript-savvy program with each of those procedures.

Left, the paste result from a standard copy; right, the paste result from an option-copy.

Not the Clipboard: Drag and Drop

Drag and Drop. When Apple introduced the phrase *drag and drop* with System 7, it referred to the ability to drag a desktop document icon and drop it onto an application icon, and have the application launch with the document opened in it. There was some mild confusion because Microsoft had introduced a drag-and-drop editing feature in its programs that meant you could simply drag a selection from one spot to another in your document without using the Clipboard.

When System 7.5 was announced, Apple's drag-and-drop philosophy had fallen more in line with Microsoft's: you could just drag a selection from one place to another, skipping the Cut, Copy, and Paste commands.

But an application has to be designed to use the system-level drag-and-drop capability, so you don't automatically get this nifty feature. If you want to see what it's like, you can use two of Apple's desk accessories, the Scrapbook and the Note Pad. Type something in the Note Pad, select it, and then drag it right into the Scrapbook window.

The drag-and-drop approach was first added to the Mac interface as extensions throughout System 7 releases: Macintosh Drag-and-Drop, Clipping Extension, Drag Manager Extension, Dragging Enabler—all came and went as they were eventually rolled into the system. They're all an intrinsic part of OS 8.

Drag and drop within applications. If you can do drag and drop in an application, even from one document window to another, that doesn't necessarily mean that the application is using Apple's drag and drop technology. What's the difference? When it's the application itself, you can use drag and drop only within the application; when it's Apple's, you can use it for moving things from one application to another (and to and from the desktop).

Droppings...whoops, I mean *clippings*. When you don't have two applications open and can't drag and drop between them, you don't have to store the transfer material in an interim application or desk accessory like the Scrapbook: You can just drop the selection onto the desktop. Later, you can drag it (the icon itself) into the document where you want it.

A dropped selection is called a *clipping;* its icon is that of a page torn out of a notebook, but changes according to whether the clipping is text, graphics, or a sound. The default name is simply *text clipping,* or *picture clipping*, so you should rename it right away in order to keep track of what it really is. Double-clicking on a clipping icon opens a window that displays the text or graphic (double-clicking a sound clipping merely plays it).

If you find yourself creating and using clippings, there's no need to clutter your desktop: clippings can be dragged into the Scrapbook for easy storage and viewing—and most things that can be dragged to the desktop can be dragged directly to the Scrapbook to begin with.

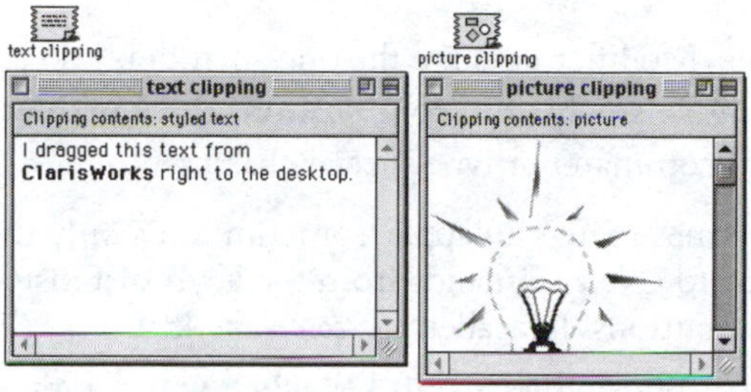

Clipping files on the desktop, and their display windows.

Copying a clipping. If you have a clipping that you want to use in a document but that application doesn't support drag and drop, open the clipping window and copy the contents so you can paste it into your application. (If you do that more than once or twice, though, you should just be dropping selections into the Scrapbook to begin with.)

You don't have to select the contents of the clipping window before you copy them; in fact, you *can't* select anything in the window. But the Copy command in the Edit menu works on the whole window even though nothing's selected.

Dragging a copy versus dragging the original. When you drag a selection from one application to another, or between an application and the desktop, the original stays in place, so the drag is actually a copy-and-paste operation. However, when you drag a selection within an application, whether it's within or between documents, the drag almost always moves the original to the new location—the equivalent of a cut-and-paste. Using Option as you drag usually lets you drag a copy of the selection to the new spot.

Using the Keyboard

A Keyboard Tour

The Mac keyboard is not a typewriter. There are a lot more keys on a computer keyboard than on a typewriter. The letters and punctuation are the same, but you also get: function keys (like F1 and F2); modifier keys (⌘,

Option, Control); cursor and window-scroll controls (↑↓←→, Home, End, Page Up, Page Down); and special keys like Help and ⌦ (Forward Delete). And, of course, you have the convenience, on most keyboards, of a separate numeric keypad for number entry.

Keyboards
Chapter 3

Some keys that look like standard typewriter keys—Caps Lock, for instance—behave differently on a computer keyboard. In fact, even the so-called standard letter keys act differently because, instead of providing only two characters per key (upper and lowercase), the Mac keyboard provides four characters per key in most situations.

Modifier keys. Modifier keys are the ones that don't do anything by themselves, but are used, singly or in combination, along with other keys to either give a keyboard command or type special characters.

- ⌘ (sometimes there's an apple, sometimes it's only the cloverleaf symbol) is used to give commands from the keyboard instead of by using menus and buttons. It's called the *command* key.
- Shift acts like a typewriter's shift key when you're typing, changing most characters to uppercase. But paired with other modifiers, it provides more key combinations for either typing special characters or for giving keyboard commands.
- Option acts like a second Shift key when you're typing, letting you type special characters from each key. Like Shift, it can also be paired with ⌘ for keyboard commands.
- Control doesn't have a specialized function, since it's a relative newcomer to Mac keyboards. Sometimes it serves as an alternative ⌘ key (so ⌘O can do one thing and Control O another) or an additional modifier for a keyboard command. On some keyboards the key is too small for the whole title, so it's spelled Ctrl.

The modifier keys are often used in combination, as you've already seen in many entries in the book: ⌘Option or Option Shift, for instance.

The numeric keypad and NumLock. The numeric keypad makes number entry more convenient, with all the numbers, a period for the decimal point, and standard mathematical operators clustered together. (* is for multiplication, / is for division).

The Num Lock ("numeric lock") key is for toggling the keypad between two different functions in programs that let you use the keyboard not only for number entry, but also for something like cursor control. Most keyboards have a numlock light which might or might not be coordinated with the programs you use.

But the numeric lock function of that key is actually the lesser of its functions: its major function (based on the relative sizes of the word printed on the key) is as a Clear key. What does it do? Sometimes it triggers the Clear command, if there is one in the Edit menu—a way of deleting something without cutting or copying it to the keyboard. But it offers a handy option in applications like spreadsheets: if you have multiple cells selected, pressing Delete erases only the contents of the active cell, while pressing Clear empties all the selected cells.

Function keys. The *function keys* along the top of the keyboard, F1 through F15, perform different functions in different programs. In some programs, they don't do anything at all (except for, if you're lucky, the system-level Cut, Copy, and Paste commands as noted in the next entry). This is probably because the whole function-key concept never really sank into the collective Mac programming consciousness, since the keys weren't available on Mac keyboards for years.

But they're really handy. Most high-end programs use them for built-in or user-assigned shortcuts. Most of all, though, they're handy for when you make your own keyboard shortcuts with a macro utility, as discussed in Chapter 10.

A function key is not the same as an *FKEY*, which is something old Mac hands know about—a special kind of "resource" that can be called up with certain key combinations starting with ⌘Shift and including a number, like the screen-dump option described in Chapter 10.

Hard-wired Cut, Copy, and Paste. The F1 through F4 keys act as single-key commands for Undo, Cut, Copy, and Paste. Because this is a system-level feature, it's available in most programs, or at least it *should* be.

Delete back and forwards. On older keyboards, the Backspace key moved the text insertion point backwards one character at a time, erasing characters in its path. It was, of course, named for the same key on typewriter keyboards, whose function it mimicked to some extent. But since the key also erased the letters, and served to erase selected text and graphics, somebody finally realized it should have a new name; hence, the Delete key.

But a key that's almost as handy is ⌦ (Forward Delete), in the cluster of keys that include Page Up and Page Down. As you might expect, it erases characters to the right of the insertion point. If you force yourself to use it (it's easy to ignore!), after a while you'll wonder how you lived without it. In most programs, it also serves as a general delete control, erasing selected text and graphics.

Help! I need somebody... The Help key has finally settled down, in OS 8, to a specific function controlled by the system: it triggers the main Help item in the Help menu—the same as pressing ⌘?.

You can go home again. The Page Up, Page Down, Home, and End keys don't work consistently from one program to the next. Home and End sometimes move you to the beginning and end of a document, as they should, but sometimes they merely move you to the top and bottom of the screen instead. Page Up and Page Down sometimes move you to the top and bottom of a screen, and sometimes to the ends of what would be a printed page. With all four keys, sometimes it's just the view that shifts from one part of a document to another, and sometimes the insertion point is also moved to a new spot.

Once you learn how they work in the applications you use most often, however, you'll find them very handy.

IN THE BEGINNING

The Mac's keyboard has evolved along with the Mac itself. Not only did the early keyboards have no function keys, the earliest ones—for the original Mac and the Fat Mac—didn't have arrow keys, either. Steve Jobs was fanatically adamant about the mouse's being the main device for selecting and moving things on the screen and wouldn't allow arrow keys on "his" keyboard. The third Mac, the Mac Plus, had a keyboard with arrow keys, much to the relief of those of us who wanted to be able to move a character or a line at a time in text without reaching for the mouse.

Oh—and as long as we're talking about keys on the keyboard: What *is* that shape on the Command key? A cloverleaf? A butterfly? No, it's a symbol that's a Swedish campground trail marker that stands for "remarkable feature." How's that for trivia?

The great escape. As with so many keys that weren't on the early Mac keyboards, the Esc key performs various functions, or sometimes has no effect at all. The only standard for this key is that it (almost) always works to trigger the Cancel button in a dialog box.

Keyboarding

Caps lock isn't Shift lock. On a typewriter, there's a Shift-lock key: it mechanically locks the keyboard into a mode where all the shifted characters are typed without your having to hold down the Shift key itself. On a computer keyboard, Caps Lock is just what it says: it locks the keyboard for capital letters, not for *shifted* characters. The difference? You can type a number from the top row of keys and really get the number, not the punctuation; you can type commas and periods instead of < and >, and so on, yet still get all the uppercase letters when you use the alphabetic keys.

Return versus Enter. Sometimes Enter is just an alternative for Return, and sometimes it performs a different function—it depends what application you're in. Most of the time, they're the same—you can use either, for instance, to "click" the default button in a dialog. But spreadsheets and databases, for instance, consistently treat the keys differently: Return enters information into a cell and also moves you into the next cell while Enter enters information without changing the active cell.

The key repeat and delay. When you hold down a key that types a character, you wind up with a whole string of those characters typed into your document. The speed at which the characters are typed is the *key repeat rate;* if it's too fast, you won't be able to remove your finger from the key at just the right time—with just the right number of characters having been typed. (Or, more commonly, with just the right number of characters *erased*, since most people use the repeat-key capability for Delete and ⌦.) But before the repeating starts, there's a slight delay, to give you time to get your finger off the key; without a reasonable delay, you might be typing liiiikke tthiiiss.

You can set both the repeat rate and the delay timing in the Keyboard control panel, which provides slider controls for both. The Off setting for the Delay doesn't turn off the delay (which would mean there's no delay and every key press release would be a race between you and the computer); it actually turns off the *repeat.* Turning off the repeat completely is helpful for young children and for people with physical limitations for keyboarding.

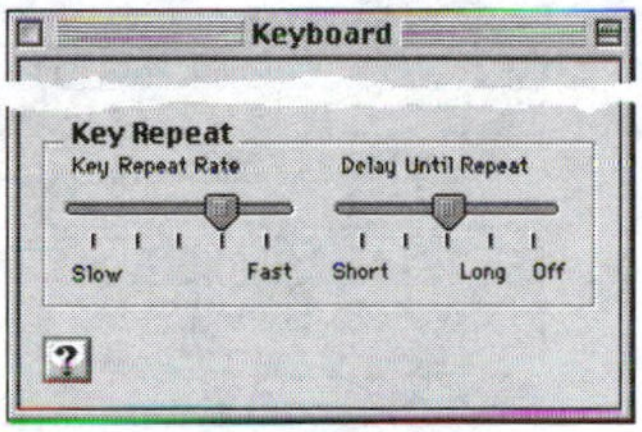

Use the keys at the bottom of the Keyboard control panel to adjust key repeat speeds and delays.

Typing ahead. If you start typing while the Mac is busy doing something, like opening a dialog box, up to ten keystrokes go into a buffer that the Mac reads when it gets a chance. Hit ⌘S for Save, and you can start typing the name of document before the dialog appears; or, hit ⌘F for Find, and start typing the word you're looking for before that dialog shows up.

The buffer works for more than just typing letters—other keys, and keyboard commands, are stored, too. You could hit ⌘F, type *book,* and hit Return all before you see the dialog and you'll start the search for that word as if you had waited to click the default button in the dialog.

Typing ahead doesn't *always* work; sometimes the Mac is busy and when it comes back to you, one of the first things it does is empty the keyboard buffer without paying any attention to what's in it. This can be an important feature in many cases, because it keeps inappropriate keystrokes from being passed on to another program, say, or to the wrong part of the program you're in. In other cases, of course, it's simply annoying.

The most important keyboarding tip of all. Learn to type! Whatever time you put into learning and practicing will be paid back a hundredfold during your computing hours. Even if you don't deign to learn that pesky top row of numbers—learn those letters and basic punctuation! Some typing software is covered in Chapter 25.

Foreign Character Sets

Using foreign keyboards. The Keyboard control panel lists quite a few foreign languages, along with cute little icons that pretty much represent a country's flag. You can select one or more keyboards beyond the default U.S. by checking them in the list. (You can't uncheck the U.S. keyboard; it will always be in the keyboard menu.)

And then what? Well, first of all, everything that's checked gets listed in a special Keyboard menu that appears on the far right of the menubar as soon as you close the control panel. It's a system menu, so it'll be available no matter what application you're working in.

Typing accented characters
Chapter 14

Choosing a keyboard from the menu changes the characters that are available from each key. Luckily, the Key Caps desk accessory reflects the changes you've made so you can keep track of things.

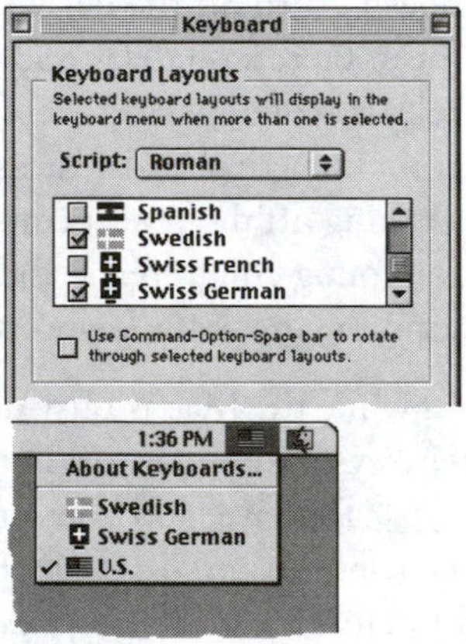

Checking a keyboard in the list (top) will add it to the Keyboard menu (bottom).

The Keycaps desk accessory can show you what the new keyboard layout looks like. These are the unshifted (top) and shifted (bottom) layouts for the French keyboard.

Keyboard resources. The keyboard layouts listed in the Keyboard control panel exist as *resources* inside your System file. (There's more information about resources, and your System file, in Chapter 8.)

It's easy to add or remove keyboard resources. Double-click on the System file suitcase icon, and it opens to show you the user-modifiable resources. You'll see keyboards and sounds. Just drag out the keyboards you no longer want.

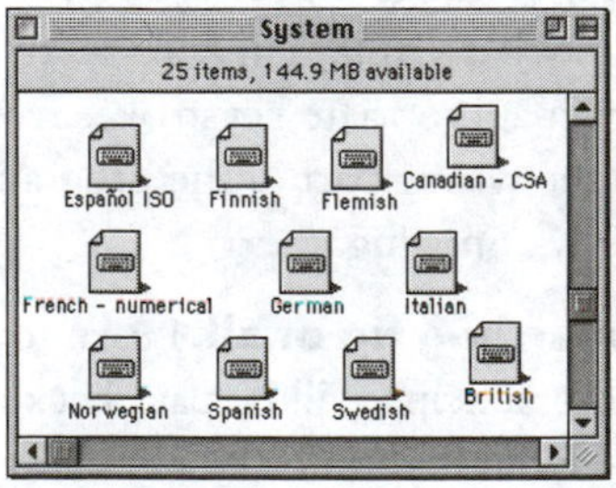

Keyboard resources in the System file.

To add a keyboard resource, you can drag it into the closed System file—but not into the closed System *Folder*, which won't know how to route it to the correct spot.

Using Dvorak. Some readers may recognize that name as belonging to a computer-industry columnist, but that's not who we're talking about. We're referring to the man (the columnist's uncle or great-uncle, if I recall correctly) who redesigned the standard QWERTY keyboard layout so your fingers wouldn't have to travel so far as they type. The Dvorak layout puts the letters you type most often right under your fingers instead of in the most awkward spots. (The current arrangement was designed to keep very old mechanical typewriters from jamming by not letting anyone type too quickly.)

The Dvorak layout.

The Dvorak layout keyboard resource is readily available almost everywhere online, so if you want to try it you can download it and install it. Prepare to be *very* confused for a while.

Easy Access

The Easy Access control panel. The Easy Access control panel was designed to help those whose physical limitations might be interfering with typing multiple-key combinations. With Easy Access, you can use a single finger to type shifted characters and combinations like ⌘ Option O. And you can bypass the mouse entirely, using the numeric keypad to do mouse moves. These little feats of magic are performed through Easy Access's three components: Mouse Keys, Slow Keys, and Sticky Keys. Easy Access is not part of a standard OS installation, but if you need it, you can go back and install it separately in OS 8.0 (customized and partial installs are covered in Chapter 8); in OS 8.1, you'll find it in the Universal Access folder inside the CD Extras folder on the system CD.

Mouse Keys. To control the mouse cursor from the keyboard, turn on the Mouse Keys section of Easy Access. Once the mouse control is turned on, the keys surrounding 5 on the keypad move the cursor in any of eight directions. The 5 key itself acts as the mouse button for clicks and double-clicks; 0 locks down the mouse button so you can use menus and drag things on screen, while . unlocks it.

Pressing one of the cursor-control keys moves the cursor a single pixel on the screen; holding the key down keeps the cursor sailing slowly in that direction. The *Initial Delay* setting in the Easy Access window defines how long it takes for that initial key press to be interpreted as a key being held down. The *Maximum Speed* setting sets the speed limit for the cursor once it gets going.

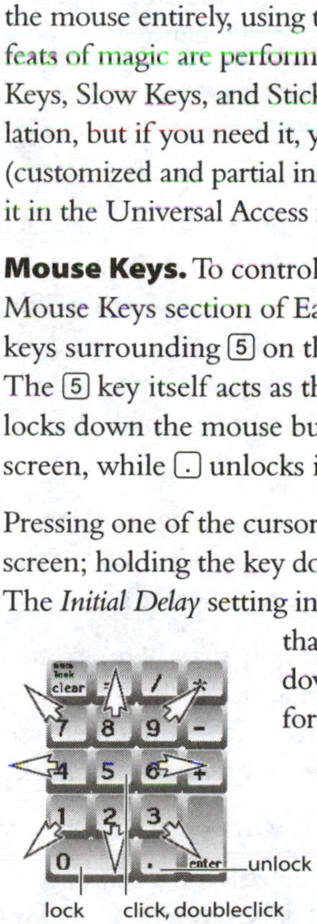

The Mouse Keys actions for the keypad.

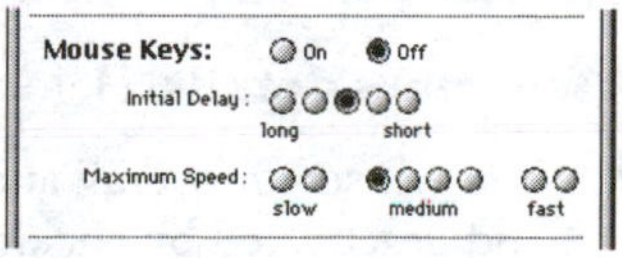

Slow Keys. The Slow Keys option adds a delay to each key press so an accidental press won't register; you can turn it on and off, and set how long the delay should be. When Slow Keys is active, keys don't repeat no matter how long you hold them down.

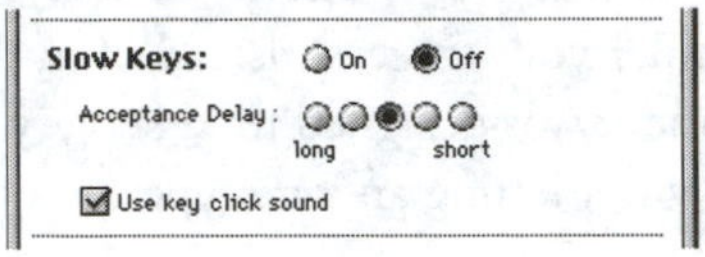

The optional "key click" sound for Slow Keys blips at the end of the delay period (just before the key registers), and again as the character is typed. (The blip itself seems to have been taken from the video game Pong. Remember that?)

Sticky Keys. Sticky Keys lets you type a combination like ⌘O or ⌘Option N by pressing one key at a time instead of all at once. You can "stick" a modifier key down for just a single subsequent key press (the way you'd want to for a capital letter (Shift L) or a simple command combination (⌘O), or keep it stuck down so you can type something like ⌘Shift Option K.

Turn Sticky Keys on and off by using the buttons in the control panel or by pressing Shift five times in succession. When Sticky Keys is on, a little bracket (which is supposed to represent a depressed key) appears in the right corner of the menubar.

To set a modifier key for a single further keystroke, just type it. The Sticky Keys icon in the menubar changes to show the modifier is locked down. Type the next key, and it will be combined with the modifier.

Top, the bracket icon that shows Sticky Keys is activated; middle, a modifier is set; bottom, a modifier is locked.

To lock down a modifier for multiple key presses, just press the modifier twice; the bracket icon fills in to show the modifier is locked. Then type the other modifiers and characters you need. The modifier lock lets you type something like ⌘Shift Option K one key at a time, or do something like set both Bold and Italic text style by locking down ⌘ and then pressing B and I in turn.

To unlock a modifier, press it twice in a row again. (If you want to "unset" a modifier without using it, you have to press it a total of three times—once to set it, once to lock it, and once more to cancel it.)

The icon in the menu bar indicates only that there's something set or locked; there's no indication as to which modifier, or how many modifiers, are actually in use. But you can get audio feedback as modifiers are set, locked, and canceled by checking the *Beep when modifier key is set* checkbox.

A few more details. Here are a few more handy details about Easy Access:

- You can set an overall audio feedback for when Easy Access is activated and deactivated by clicking the Use On/Off Audio Feedback button at the top of the control panel. You'll get a little ascending *brrrp* when it's turned on and a descending one when it's turned off.

- Activate Mouse Keys from the keyboard by pressing ⌘ Shift Option Clear.
- Two additional ways to turn off Sticky Keys are: pressing any two modifier keys at the same time, or pressing ⌘ . . (*Really* pressing ⌘ . , both keys at the same time.)
- Perform a Shift-click operation by locking the Shift key down with Sticky Keys and then manipulating the cursor and clicking the mouse button with Mouse Keys.

The nudge command. Most programs that let you move objects in a document provide a "nudge" command to move a selection one pixel at a time. If the program you use doesn't, use Mouse Keys. It often takes less time to activate and use Mouse Keys even for a single nudge than to repeatedly reposition an item, missing the exact placement you want.

System Sounds

Basic Beep and Barely Beyond

Beep beep. The *system beep,* or *alert sound*, is that beeping sound you get with an alert box, or *as* an alert by itself when you're doing something that's not quite allowed. The beep doesn't have to be a beep at all, although it's still *called* a beep no matter what sound it makes. There are several different alert sounds included with your system; you can add others, and even create your own. In addition, you can set the volume for the beep or turn it off altogether.

To select a new sound, click on the Alerts button in the Monitors & Sound control panel, and click on one of the listed sounds; you'll hear a sample as soon as you click. Change the volume by dragging the slider control by the little speaker icons. Sliding it all the way to the left turns the sound off completely; instead of beeping, the Mac will flash the menubar as an attention-getter.

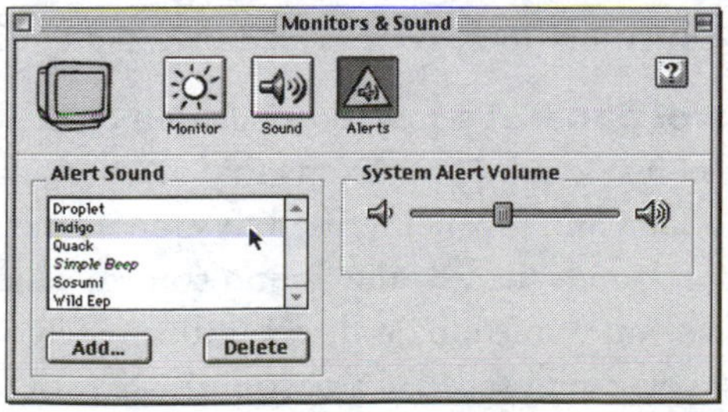

Change your alert sound, and its volume, in the Monitors & Sound control panel.

Adjusting the volume. To change the volume of your alert sound, click the Sound button in Monitors & Sound, and use the slider control in the Computer Speaker Volume area to set the volume.

If you click the Mute button, there will be no alert sound at all. Instead, the menubar will flash to get your attention. (This controls both the alert sound and any audio CD you play; it doesn't affect the startup sound.)

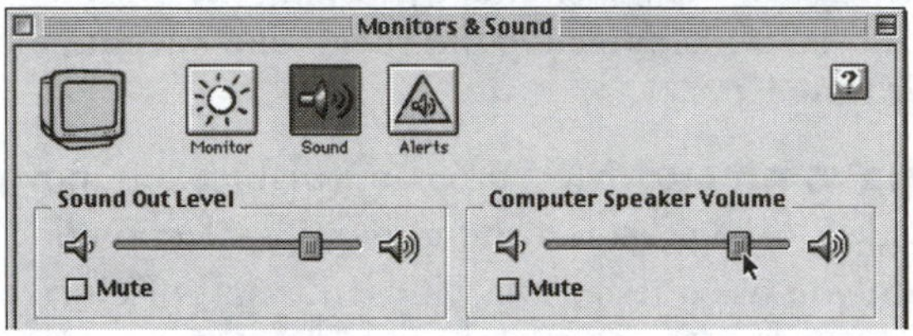

Adjusting the alert volume.

IN THE BEGINNING

The Mac always had sound. At its debut, it actually talked—that was back in the days when Steve Jobs knew how to put on a show. MacinTalk speech aside, the Mac could always at least beep from day one—which sounds like no big deal, but the "other" personal computer didn't have any built-in sound capability. But all you could do at first was adjust the volume of the Mac's single-sound vocabulary. When the Mac II was introduced, it had special controls for setting the system beep, which no longer had to be a beep; this capability became part of the system software in 1988, with System 6.0.

Taking sounds out of the control panel. There are two ways to take a sound out of the Alert sound listing in Monitors & Sound. The first, easiest, way is to select the sound in the list and click the Delete button. The other way involves dealing with the System file itself, which is covered a little further on.

It's not a control panel. The Monitors & Sound control panel isn't a control panel, despite its icon and its residence in the Control Panels folder. It's actually an application, which you can see if you do a Get Info on it. So, if you're having any trouble recording sounds and get out-of-memory messages, try allocating more memory to it, as described in Chapter 12.

The Sound control panel. A standard installation of OS 8 puts the old Sound control panel inside the Apple Extras folder. I thought at first that, since the Monitors & Sound control panel refused to support the Cut, Copy, and Paste commands for sounds the way the Sound control panel did, that Apple left it around in case you wanted to do that. Unfortunately, while you can use it to Copy sounds, you can't use it to Paste sounds—so you're left putting existing sound files into the System file only by dragging them there directly.

Creating and Collecting Sounds

Recording an alert sound. All recent Macs come with a microphone, either built in or as an accessory that plugs into its own port. You can use it to record sounds that you can put in various places—including the Monitors & Sound control panel!

Here's how to record a sound (you can test it by saying something):

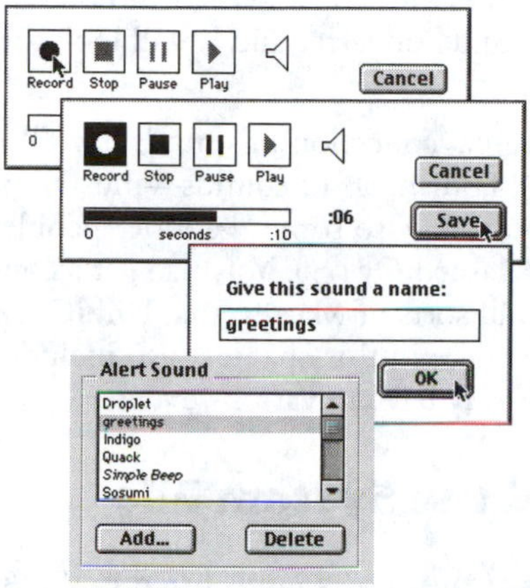

Adding a new sound to the control panel.

1. In the Alerts section of the Monitors & Sound control panel, click the Add button.
2. The small dialog that opens provides basic recording controls: Record, Stop, Pause, and Play. Click the Record button. If you're finished with the sound before the progress bar reaches the end (you have 10 seconds), click the Stop button.
3. Click the Save button.
4. Name the sound.

You'll find your new sound listed in the control panel, and already selected.

Record from an audio CD

Chapter 22

But you don't have to record sounds yourself to use as alert sounds. Everyone else already has, and half of them have posted their collections somewhere in cyberspace. If you're surfing the web or hanging out on AOL, you'll be able to find all sorts of sounds for your system.

Keep it short even if not sweet. Although you can record up to ten seconds of sound for an alert, you don't *want* to record ten seconds of sound. First, sounds load completely into memory before they're played. So, a long sound takes longer to load, and eats up memory. And you'll get *really* tired of long alert sounds in no time at all!

Master of your sound domain. If you're into system sounds, here are some items you should take a look at:

- **Kaboom!** ($30, Nova Development Software) lets you take total control of system sounds on your Mac—not just *the* system sound (the alert beep), but all sorts of sounds. With Kaboom! you can assign a sound to any of a zillion events—inserting a disk, emptying the trash (the favorite among adolescents everywhere—making it sound like a flushing toilet), zooming or even scrolling a window. But wait, there's more! Along with the 150 sounds that come with the package, you get a sound editor that lets you tweak those and other sounds: play them backwards, chop them up, add echoes. It's a great time waster (and I mean that in the nicest possible way).

- **SoundMaster** ($15, Bruce Tomlin) served as the basis for the commercial package Kaboom! With it, you can assign sounds to events like startup and shutdown, emptying the trash, and inserting a disk.
- **Snd2SysBeep** (part of MiniGrinders utilities, freeware, Steve Smith and Apple Computer) extracts sounds from files and converts them to separate sound files that you can use as system sounds. So, drag a sound clippings file onto SndConverter, or a sound page right from the Scrapbook, onto SndConverter, and you get a sound resource file you can put into your System file. Or, drag any file that contains a sound—even an application—onto SndConverter and it will look through the file for any extractable sounds.
- If you want to buy a great collection of sounds, try **ClickTrax** ($40, DublClick Software). Four megs of sounds—mostly impersonations of the rich and/or famous, but also some "generic" people sounds (there is, for instance, a folder named *Oy vey*). You also get a control panel that lets you assign sounds to all sorts of Mac events. DublClick's ClickChange utility, described elsewhere in this chapter, also includes the ability to assign sounds you already have to various events

Sound Files and the System File

Sounds and the System file. The sounds listed in the Alert sound list are actually *resources* stored in your System file. If you double-click on your System file in the System Folder, you'll see icons for each of the sounds in the list. You can drag sound resources in and out of the System file as long as no applications are running. The additions and deletions will be reflected in the alerts list in Monitors & Sound.

Of course, if you want put a sound file *into* the System file, it had to be just the right kind of sound. There are many different kinds of sound files in use on the Mac, and not all can be system sounds. The sounds that work are files or resources of the type *snd*, also referred to as "System 7 sounds," since the file type changed from System 6 to System 7. But it's easy enough to find out what works: drag a sound file into the System file window, or, more conveniently, into the closed System file, and if it goes in, it's the right type.

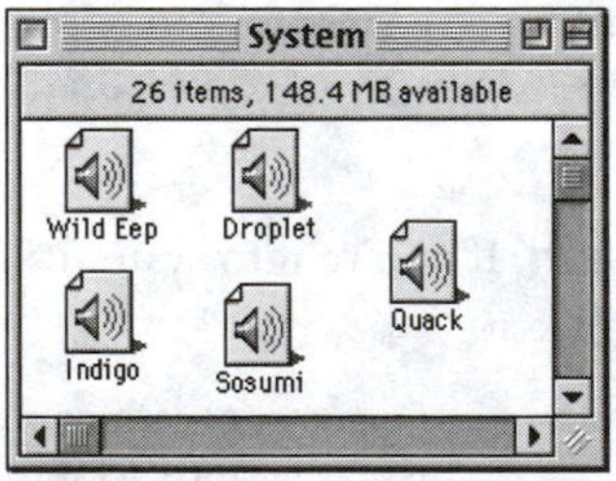

Sounds in the System file.

Renaming a sound. You can rename a sound while you're in the opened System file—it's the only type of resource whose name you can change while it's inside the System file.

Using a system sound elsewhere. There's no obvious way to move a system sound into another program that uses sound. But you can often do it this way:

1. Open the System file and drag out the sound (or drag out a *copy* of the sound by Option-dragging it out of the System file's window).
2. Drag the sound file directly into the Scrapbook window.
3. Copy the sound from the Scrapbook.
4. Paste the sound into the application.

Startup Sounds

A new startup sound. You can't alter the basic startup chord that your Mac uses when it starts up. But you can easily add another startup sound of your own for when the desktop appears: put a sound file or its alias into your Startup Items folder. As long as the sound plays when you double-click on it, putting it in the folder will "open" it at startup—which plays the sound.

Killing the startup sound. Changing the volume or clicking the Mute button in the Monitors & Sound control panel doesn't affect the startup chord. If you want to dampen it, you have to plug something into the audio port on the back of the Mac. If you use earphones (to keep your coworkers from realizing you're playing CDs or games!), that will keep the startup chord from being audible. If you just want to get rid of the sound, get a "miniplug" from an electronics store—it's the little plug that's at the end of earphones, and plug that into the audio port. But then you won't hear *any* sounds, including alert sounds.

6

The Desktop

In This Chapter

On the Desktop

The Basics

Finder/desktop. The *Finder* is the application that gives you your desktop and takes care of all the file-handling procedures (copying, re-naming, deleting) you do on your desktop. *Finder* and *desktop* are pretty much interchangeable terms, except in a few nuanced instances. You can, for instance, "move to" the desktop or the Finder, or "work" *in* the Finder or *on* the desktop; but, while you can put something on your desktop, you don't put anything "on" or "in" the Finder. (There are other almost-always interchangeable terms on the desktop, like *icon* and *file*, and *folder* and *window.)*

The desktop is both a general place where you work, and the actual background of the screen while you're working there (*"click on the desktop"*).

The desktop itself is a solid surface (metaphorically speaking, of course). If you're in an application and want to switch back to the Finder, you don't have to click on one of its icons or windows: you can click on any exposed desktop surface. (This wasn't always the case; prior to System 7, you couldn't click on the desktop surface and get switched into the Finder.)

Activating desktop. The desktop itself can be active, so that selecting an icon with a keyboard command can be done for "loose" icons scattered around. If all Finder windows are closed, the desktop is active by default. But you can activate it while windows are open, too, with any of these:

- Click on the actual desktop—the pattern or picture. (You used to have to click on a desktop icon—clicking the desktop itself didn't work if there were any open windows.)
- Click on an icon that's on the desktop.
- Press ⌘Shift.

Shared and shared alike. While the desktop is created and maintained by the system on your hard drive, loose icons out on the desktop don't necessarily belong that hard drive. The desktop is shared by every disk that you're using at one time—which could be, say, your internal hard drive, a second hard drive, a floppy, and a CD.

This can cause confusion at first. You drag a file from a floppy onto the desktop, thinking you've copied it to your hard drive but, when you eject the disk, the icon disappears. (And when you reinsert the disk, the icon comes back.) That's because the file is still stored on the floppy disk—still "belongs" to the floppy—and is just being displayed out on the desktop where you dragged it.

Get Info command
Later this chapter

There's no way to tell just by looking at an icon whether it "belongs" to your hard drive or another mounted volume, but you can use the Get Info command to see where it's actually stored.

What's new on the menu. OS 8's Finder has changed its menus around. And, reversing a "no submenu" policy that Apple OS engineers crossed only for the Apple menu until now, some of the menus actually sport submenus.

- The Label menu has disappeared, sucked into the File menu as a submenu.
- The File menu includes two new commands: the long-awaited Move to Trash and the handy Find Original.
- The Edit menu now includes a Preferences command, which sets some desktop-wide options; it replaces some control panels, like Views.
- The View menu has been completely re-organized into a more logical set of commands, to accommodate new window capabilities in the Finder.
- The Special menu has lost its Clean Up command, which has moved over to the View menu where it more logically belongs.

What looks like a new menu on the desktop—Help—is the new system approach to the Help menu; it's no longer a question-mark icon menu at the right of the menu bar.

The Simple Finder option. There are two versions of the Finder: the standard one you get by default when you install the system software, and a Simple Finder option you can turn on through the Preferences command in the edit menu.

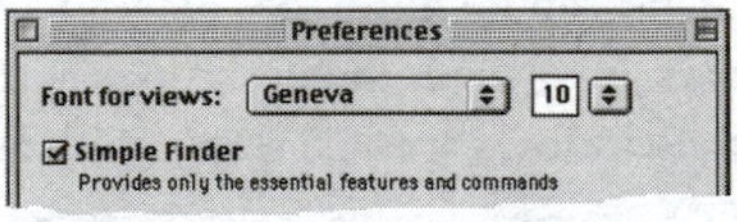

Turn the Simple Finder on and off through the Finder's Preferences command.

The Simple Finder cuts down on the number of menu commands available, as shown in the picture here, and disables some other desktop capabilities like pop-up contextual menus and pop-up windows, file sharing setup, making aliases, changing the options in windows for things like icon and button size, and all keyboard equivalents for menu commands.

Of course, you'll be such an expert when you're done with this book that you won't need Simple Finder, but you might want to set it on for young kids, or beginners who you're helping out.

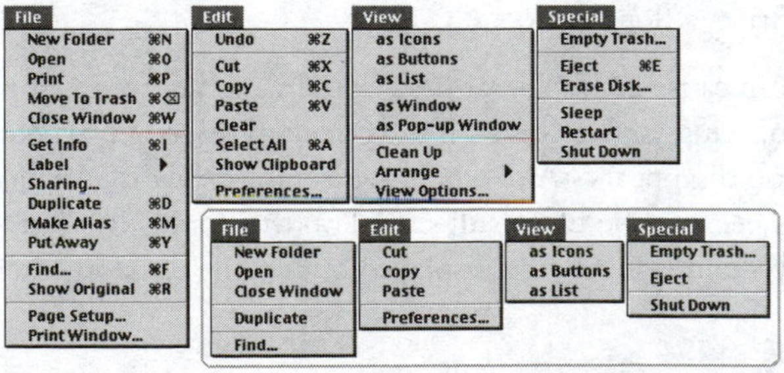

The full Finder menus (top) and the Simple Finder menus (bottom, framed).

Sticky stuff. As explained in Chapter 5, OS 8 offers a feature called Sticky Menus: you can simply click on a Finder menu and it stays open without your having to hold the mouse button down. To select a command, click on it once; click anywhere outside the menu to close it without using a command.

All types of menus stick now, including pop-ups in dialog boxes and desktop contextual menus.

The About Command

The About Command. The About This Computer command in the Apple menu gives basic information about your Mac's hardware configuration, its system software, how its memory is allocated, and which applications are running. (The command changes to *About [Whatever]*, depending on the application that's running.)

In early systems, this command used to be About the Finder. Later, it changed to About this Macintosh. Then, in an effort to encompass clone-makers in the fold, the command changed to About this Computer. At this writing, Apple's pulled back all its cloning licenses; I'd expect the command to be changed back to About this Macintosh in subsequent system software.

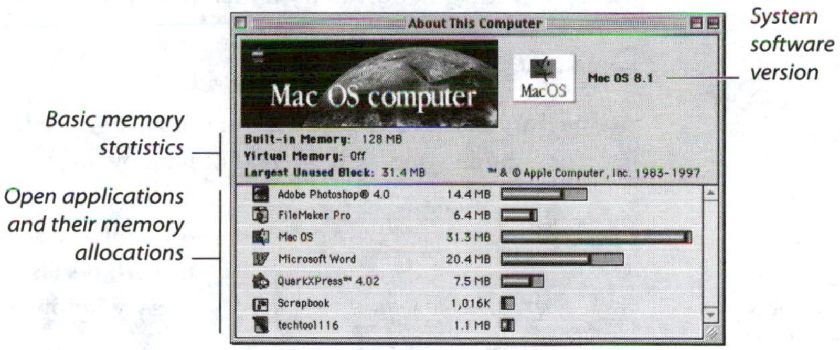

The About command in the Finder provides a dialog box with lots of important information.

Opening a listed program. The About box, while offering important information, has always been limited in interactive capabilities. Wouldn't you think that as long as you've got a list of running applications, you could just double-click on one and switch to it? Every time a new system comes out, it's one of the first things I check. So, when OS 8 came out, I clicked and double-clicked to no avail—and then I remembered: contextual menus! Sure enough, Control-clicking on one of the listed applications (or anywhere in its memory bar) popped up a menu with three choices: Help, Open and Get Info. Choosing Open sends you to the program. (Quibble: why *Open?* If it's in the box, it's already open. Why not *Go to,* or *Switch to,* or *Bring to Front?* And why can't it be the *first* item?) Unfortunately, choosing Get Info invariably gets a non-fatal error dialog, at least in OS 8's initial release.

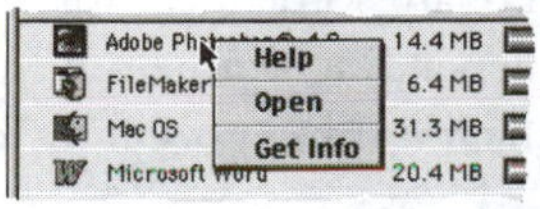

Control-click on the icon, name, or memory-use bar of a listed item, and use the Open command to move to the application.

More about the memory allocation bars. The dark-versus-light areas in the bars for each running application refer to the memory allocated and the current memory used. Turn on Help balloons, point to a bar, and you'll get a balloon that tells you how much memory is actually being used. (There's more about this, and other application memory issues, in Chapter 13.)

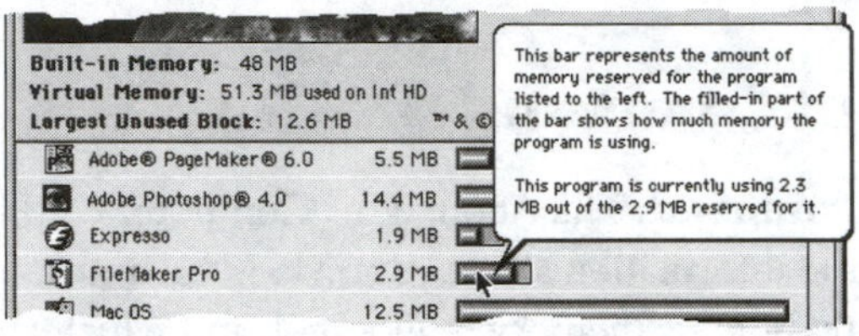

Using Help Balloons in the About box.

The old Finder picture and credits. For a trip down memory lane—more or less—hold Option while opening the Apple menu. The command changes to the older *About the Finder* command, and the dialog that opens is a paean to the original Finder dialog which was a black-and-white mountain affair. Wait five to ten seconds for a scrolling list of credits. (Unfortunately, the old trick of holding Cmd Option when you choose About, which used to get you a smiley-face cursor with an animated tongue, has been dumped. Maybe they'll put it back in—it won't hurt to try it each time you update your system.)

Desktop Details

Adjusting the window font. You can change the font that's used for labeling icons and in window headers (not window *titles)* through the Preferences command in the Edit menu. Just pick the font and size, and the change is instant; it's also global, applying to every window, and to the desktop itself.

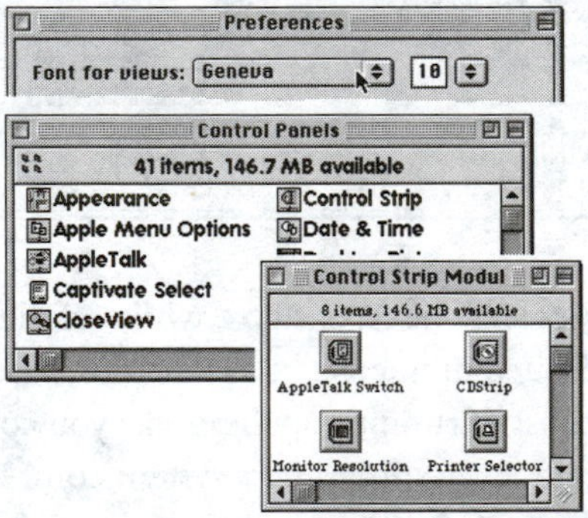

Use the Preferences command to change the font used for icon names and window headers.

The *system font,* which is set through the Appearance control panel, is something different: it's the one that's used in window title bars, menus and dialog boxes.

Create a little clutter. Although even the standard monitor these days provides a lot more real estate than the original nine-inch Mac screen, it's easy to clutter up the desktop. But keeping often-used icons out on the desktop makes sense because it's easier than drilling down through folders or even sliding through the Apple menu. Here are some ideas for what you might want to leave out on your desktop, depending on the way you work. Don't forget that you don't have to leave the *real* thing out on the desktop—you can use an alias.

- A **project folder** that you open every day—or several times a day.
- A **calendar** or **To Do** document that you use constantly.
- The **System Folder** so you can easily install fonts, control panels, and extensions by just dragging them in without having to open the drive's main window.
- The **Apple Menu Items folder** so you can drag things into (and out of) your Apple menu with no fuss.
- **Drag and drop utilities** for various handy operations: StuffIt Expander, for instance, or perhaps your word processor to force documents to open in it by dropping them on the icon.
- **Trash aliases** so you don't have to drag things too far to get rid of them.

The Desktop Folder. Yes, the desktop is actually a folder. Sort of. The things out on your desktop are actually stored on your hard drive, of course, even though they're not in the hard drive's window or any of its folders. The solution to this seeming conundrum is the ephemeral Desktop Folder. If you put an alias of a disk into your Apple menu, and then look at the first submenu, you'll see an item named Desktop Folder; look at its contents, and you'll see the items that are out on your desktop.

You'll also see a Desktop Folder if you're networked to another Mac; the remote machine's icon will have a Desktop Folder on it that contains its desktop icons. If you open the folder, the arrangement of icons in the window will duplicate the arrangement of the icons on the other computer's desktop.

Browsing your way through the Finder. For an alternative view of the Finder, try **greg's browser** (shareware, $20). It doesn't replace the Finder, but works as a separate window of multiple columns. Select an item in one column and see its contents in the next, and so on. You can install buttons at the top of the window for instant-open folders, and you can manipulate any of the items you see: move them from one place to another, open them, or even send them to the trash.

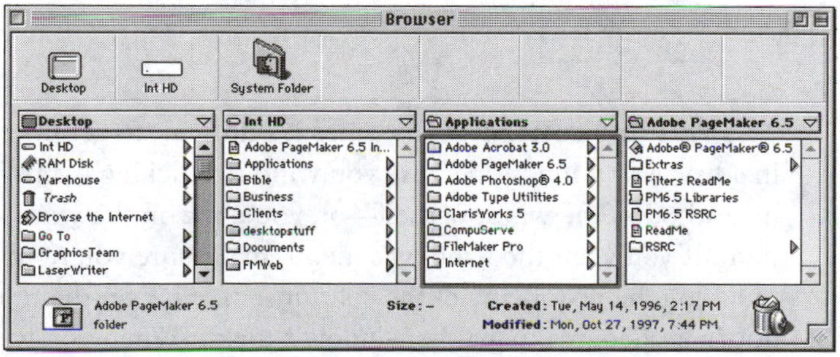

The out-of-memory Finder report. The Finder, being an application somewhat like other applications, works in a certain amount of memory.

When memory's tight, you may get an out-of-memory message asking you to close windows and try again whatever it was that choked the Finder—a copy, for instance, or opening another window. Complying with the close-window request (you can close them all at once by pressing ⌘ Option W) should let you get on with your work. But you should restart the computer at your earliest convenience, just in case there's something mixed up about the memory allocation, which will cause a more serious problem if you keep working.

Rebuilding your desktop. The phrase *rebuilding your desktop* has nothing to do with arranging icons or selecting a new desktop background picture. It's a trouble-shooting procedure described in Chapter 24.

Contextual Menus

Contextual menus. OS 8's new desktop "contextual menus" are great: hold down Control and click on something—anything—and a menu pops up with commands that can be used on that item. As soon as you press Control, the cursor changes to show you can get a contextual menu with the click of a button: a tiny menu is appended to the usual mouse pointer. The pictures here show some of the contextual menus available in the Finder.

To get a menu for an open window, you can Control-click on its title or header, or on any empty spot.

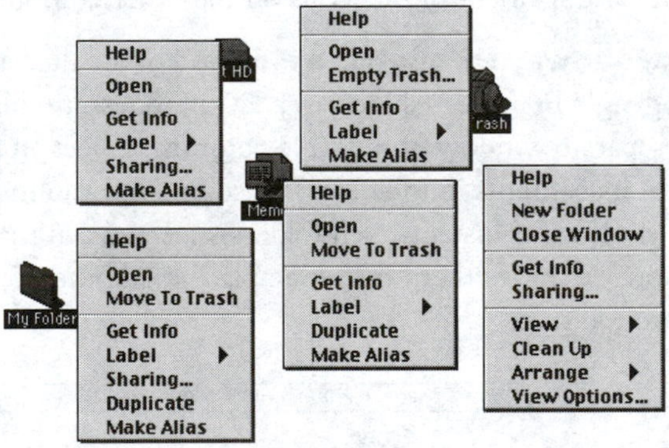

The contents of the contextual menu depend on what you're pointing to; the menu at the far right is the one for windows.

The window context. Sometimes it's difficult to get the right pop-up menu in a list-view window, because you wind up clicking on an item in the list instead of on the window itself—or, you click on the window instead of the item. If you want the window's menu, make sure you're not on an icon or touching the text in any of the columns; or, click on the title bar or the window's header area to get the window's menu. When you want the icon's menu, clicking anywhere along its row won't work—you have to click on the icon itself, or on any of the text in its row.

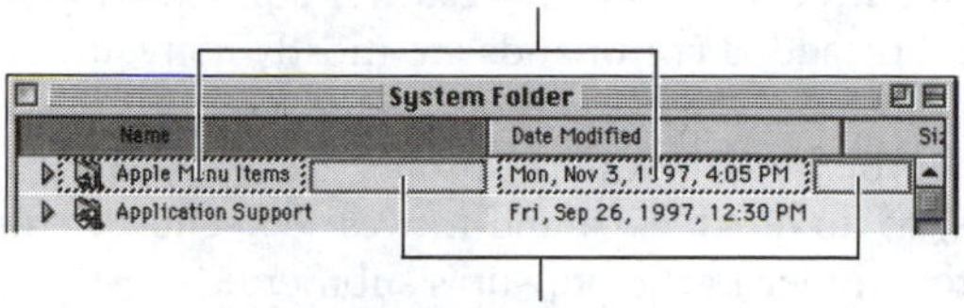

In the first row in this window, Command-clicking anywhere inside one of the striped areas will pop up a menu for the folder; Command-clicking inside one of the gray boxes will pop up the window contextual menu.

The desktop menu. When I said you could get contextual menus everywhere on the desktop, I really meant *everywhere*: click on the bare desktop and you get a menu with basic View commands, as well as New Folder and Change Desktop Background, which opens the Desktop Pictures application.

Don't select first, just click. The handiest little trick when it comes to contextual menus on the desktop is that you don't have to select the item before you click on it for the menu: Control-clicking on an item selects it and pops up the menu at the same time.

Work on multiple selections. If you have more than one item selected, you can use a contextual menu to do something to all the items at once—just Control-click on any one of the selected icons. If you select icons of different types, the pop-up menu will be limited to the commands that can work on every item in the selection.

Watch for widgets. Contextual menus are an extensible part of system software: Apple left "hooks" in the feature so other people could not only put contextual menu menus in their programs, but add to ones that already exist. When you see utilities beginning with the letters CM or CMM (contextual menu manager), that's a clue they're related to this feature.

Contextual Menu Items

If you add any CM utilities or plug-ins, you'll find a Contextual Menu Items folder added to your System Folder; it's automatically given a special icon, as are the other special System Folder subfolders. It will often have subfolders of its own to hold items needed by other utilities.

Contextual menu extensions. Here are a few shareware suggestions for tweaking your contextual menus:

- If you don't want to have to hold down Control to get the pop-up menu (and it's amazing how annoying a two-handed option can get), **Look Mom, No Hands** ($9) lets you get at contextual menu single-handedly; all you'll have to do is hold down the mouse button for about two seconds, and the contextual menu will pop-up. Nifty idea, but it's expensive for a one-trick pony—especially when there are multi-trick ponies available for the same price, or less—or for free.

- **PowerMenu** ($15) provides a pop-up menu anywhere, not just on the desktop; it adds commands to whatever contextual menu the application provides. The added commands are mostly convenient navigational tools; it lists, for instance, all open programs so you can move from one to another. In the Finder, you can use its "target" folders (you choose the list of targets) to do quick copy and moves: ⌘-click on an item and copy or move it to a folder in the pop-up's submenu.
- **CMTools** (freeware) is a little confusing to set up, but once you've got it going, it's great. You put application and folder aliases inside subfolders in the CMTool Configuration folder; the items you put in the subfolders appear as submenus in your pop-up. So, you Control-click on an item and slide to the Copy To command, and you have a choice of the folders whose aliases you've placed in the Copy To folder: the Apple Menu Items folder, for instance. With folders like Launch, Compress, Set File Type To, and Open Using, CMTools' functionality soon becomes a real crutch.
- **FinderPop** (freeware) is an extremely elegant presentation of some needed functions in the Finder, added right to the Finder's pop-up menus. You'll get: a list of running programs, along with a note about the largest free block of memory; a hierarchical list of the contents of any disk or subfolder you click on; a list of all open Finder windows; and a list of loose desktop icons. Just having these lists available is handy, since you can choose anything and it will open or activate—move to an application, for instance, or open a buried folder. But choose something from a menu while you're clicking on an item, and the item is moved there: it's opened into an application, or moved or aliased into a folder. In addition, you can control the font for the pop-up menus; last, but nowhere near least, you can drop the necessity for the Control key entirely and just press the mouse button to get the menus.

More File Info

- **More File Info** ($10, shareware) pops up all sorts of info about the file you're pointing to. Its features are detailed later in the chapter, in the Get Info Command section.

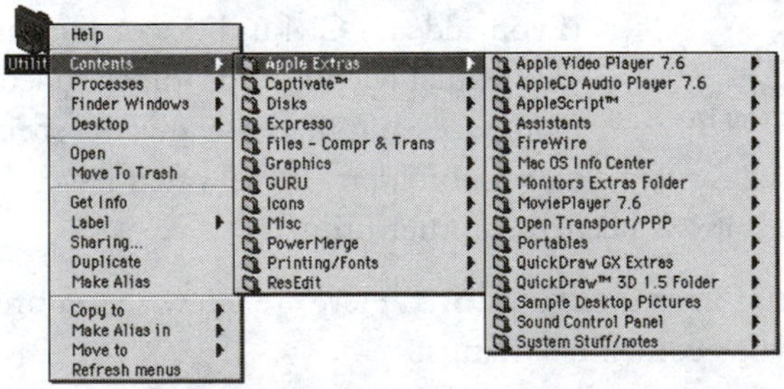

FinderPop's alterations to Finder contextual menus include a Contents command for folders and disks, as well as a choice of fonts and sizes for the menus themselves.

Desktop Patterns and Pictures

The Desktop Pictures application. The Desktop Pictures application, which is placed in your Control Panels folder (so you probably think it's a control panel, but it's not), lets you change your desktop's background to a different pattern or to a picture. It replaces the old Desktop Patterns control panel, and the even older approach of changing patterns in the General Controls control panel.

Since you can do all the basics of changing patterns and pictures inside Desktop Picture's window, you might not even notice that it has menus. The File menu is a skimpy Close and Quit list. The Edit menu has predictable but welcome Undo, Cut, Copy and Paste and Clear commands that work on patterns but not on pictures. The two final commands in the Edit menu, one each for the pattern and picture modes, are covered separately, below.

Memory allocations

Chapter 13

Desktop Pictures can run short on memory. If you're working with lots of patterns or complicated pictures, it's possible you'll get an out-of-memory message from Desktop Pictures. Close the window, open the Control Panels folder, select the Desktop Pictures icon, and Get Info on it. Add an extra 100K or so to its 400K default memory allocation.

Where are the patterns and pictures? The default patterns that come in Desktop Pictures are stored in the application itself. When you add patterns, they're stored in the Desktop Pictures Prefs file that's in the System Folder's Preferences folder.

The original pictures available as desktop backgrounds are in a folder named Sample Desktop Pictures inside the Apple Extras folder. But the pictures you add to Desktop Pictures can be stored anywhere on the drive. If you don't remember where you put the file that you added to Desktop Pictures, use the Show Picture File In Finder command from the Edit menu. You'll be switched to the Finder, the file's folder will be opened, and the picture file selected.

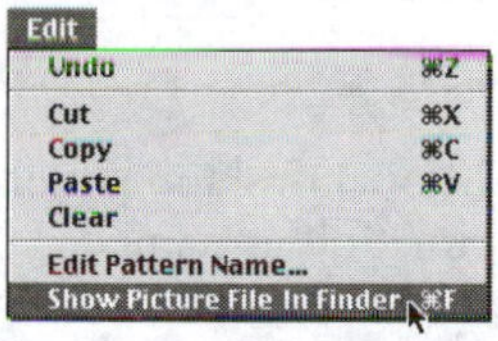

If you don't remember where you stored the desktop picture, let the Mac find it for you.

Changing your desktop pattern. To change the desktop pattern, open Desktop Pictures and click the Pattern button in the left panel. Use the scroll bar to browse through the included patterns; you'll notice that each pattern has a name, and the size of the base pattern for the repeat is also noted. If you'd like to see a larger sample of the pattern without putting it on the desktop, you can make the window larger. When you find a pattern you like, click the Set Desktop button.

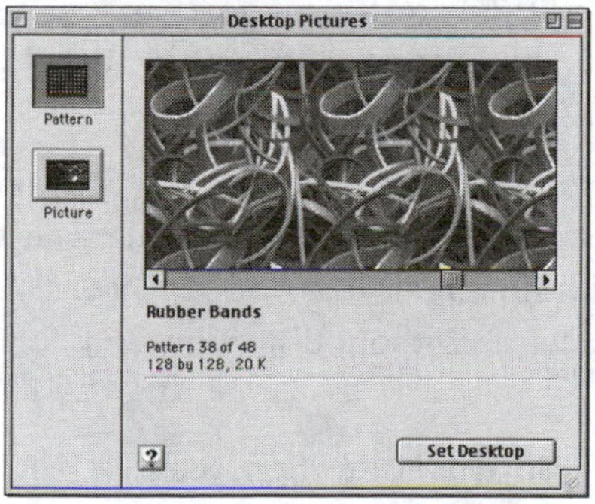

Using Desktop Pictures to choose a background pattern.

Keyboard and mouse shortcuts. In Pattern mode, use ← and → to browse through the samples; double-clicking on the sample is the same as clicking the Set Desktop button.

In Picture mode, you can get a contextual menu by holding down either ⌘ or Control and clicking on the sample picture. The menu that pops up is a combination of the window's Position pop-up menu, the Find Picture command in the menu, and the Remove button.

Adding patterns. You can add patterns to the 48 that come as default choices by pasting or dragging them in. Desktop Pictures can accommodate up to 226 patterns; if for some reason you have so little else to do that you actually add that many and then try one more, you'll get a dialog that pretty much tells you to cease and desist.

To paste in a pattern, copy any picture or design to the Clipboard, and then paste it into the Desktop Pictures sample pattern window. The image will be repeatedly tiled to fill the screen, although there may be some distortion if the image doesn't start out at the right size or with the right proportions.

You can also just drag a pattern into the Desktop Picture window from any drag-enabled application. For instance, try dragging a picture straight from the Scrapbook into the patterns sample window. You can even drag a picture file right from the desktop window (or one of its windows) into the patterns sample window, as long as the file is a type that Desktop Pictures "understands": PICT, JPEG, GIF, or Clippings. (These file types are covered in Chapter 19.) Once the new pattern is in the window, use the Edit Pattern Name command in the Edit menu to name the pattern.

Where can you get ready-made patterns?

- The OS 8 CD has a folder of additional desktop patterns—in a file named *Additional Desktop Patterns*, in a folder named *Additional Desktop Patterns.* The only problem is that the file is, of all things, a *Scrapbook* file. Chapter 10 explains how to deal with Scrapbook files so you can access the extra patterns.
- Since the desktop pictures that come with the system are in JPEG format, and you can use JPEGs as desktop patterns, you can turn a desktop picture into a smaller, repeating pattern just by dragging it into the pattern window.

Creating patterns. Creating patterns for the Mac desktop is a minor art form. Aside from aesthetic considerations, there's the issue of not letting the background interfere with finding or using desktop icons. And beyond that, there's getting the image to tile without distortion, and, for textural patterns, getting seamless tiles.

First, the distortion issue. To avoid distortion, the base pattern for tiling has to measure a multiple of eight, from 8 to 512 pixels, on each side (that's 8, 16, 32, 64, 128, 256, or 512). Although most people think in terms of *square* tiles, you can use an image that's, say 16 by 64 pixels and still avoid distortion. If you use either of the largest sizes for the image, you'll be limited as to how large the second dimension can be. You can have 512 by 32 or 256 by 64, so the largest *square* tile you can use is 128 by 128. If you use an image that's not the right proportions, it will be shrunk or stretched to fit the nearest allowable tile size.

As for seamless tiling of textures, that takes *lots* of work. You have to make sure that the top edge absolutely matches the bottom, and the left one matches the right. It takes time and patience, and an enlarged view in your favorite graphics program.

Restoring the system patterns. To remove a default pattern from Desktop Pictures, you use the Edit menu's Cut or Clear command when the pattern's displayed in the window. Once you've deleted default patterns, there's no way to get them back individually. You might think that reinstalling Desktop Pictures itself would do the trick, but it won't.

When you "delete" a default pattern, it's not actually removed at all. It's still a part of the Desktop Pictures application; it's just no longer displayed in the window. While the patterns themselves are in the application, the record of what you've deleted from the displayed samples is stored in the Desktop Pictures Prefs file, along with the user-defined patterns. So, to restore all the system patterns, all you have to do is remove the record of having deleted them: remove the Desktop Pictures Prefs file from the Preferences folder, and restart the Mac. The next time you open Desktop Pictures, it will create a new Prefs file.

You'll lose any of your own patterns that you've added to Desktop Pictures, since they're stored in the file. If you want to save them, drag them one at a time either into the Scrapbook or right onto the desktop; after the Prefs file is recreated, you can drag them back in again.

The bloated Prefs file. The file that stores your extra patterns and the record of what you've done to the system patterns just grows and grows. You may add a few patterns and then delete them; later, you may add a few more and eventually delete some of them. But the deleted patterns, although no longer available, are still in the file.

Changing the desktop picture. To use a picture instead of a pattern for your desktop, click the Picture button in the left panel. Use the Select Picture button to choose from among the pictures supplied with your system; you'll get a dialog box that lets you select pictures from anywhere on your disk.

Use the Position menu to choose how a smaller-than-the-screen picture will be displayed: centered, tiled, scaled, and so on. Then use the Set Desktop button to apply the picture to the desktop.

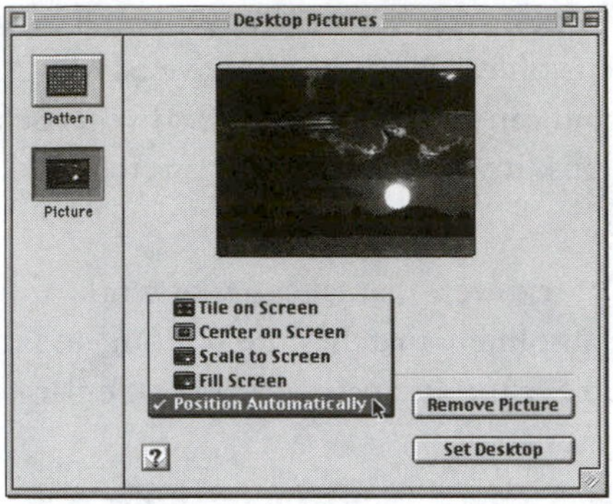

Using Desktop Pictures to set a background picture; the pop-up menu lets you define how the picture should be used to fill the screen.

To remove a picture from the desktop, use the Remove Picture button. If you want to change desktop pictures, you have to first remove the current one, then select the next.

Extra pictures. The OS 8 system CD has a folder in it that contains 22 extra desktop pictures. Just copy them to the folder that holds your desktop pictures on your hard drive (the system installation puts them in a folder named Desktop Pictures inside the Apple Extras folder).

Adding pictures. Any image of the right graphics type can be used as a desktop background. You can use JPEG or GIF images, although JPEGs better lend themselves to being scaled to fit the screen.

The pictures can be stored anywhere on your hard drive. I like to tuck them away in a Desktop Pictures folder in the Preferences folder inside the System Folder.

Randomizing the background pictures. You can make the Mac randomly choose a background picture each time you start up the Mac from a folder. First, fill a folder with usable pictures—or just use the ones that came with OS 8. Position the folder icon so you'll still be able to see it when the Desktop Pictures window is open. Open Desktop Picture, grab the folder full of pictures, and drop it right into the sample picture window.

When the desktop picture is set to random, there's a note in the window, beneath the picture's name that says: *picked randomly from folder Sample Desktop Pictures* (or whatever the name of the folder is).

To end the random factor, click the Remove Picture button, or select the more appropriately named Remove Folder command from the pop-up menu.

For multiple monitors. If you use a multiple-monitor setup, you can put a different picture on each screen, or leave one with the desktop pattern and put a picture on the other, but you can't use two different patterns at the same time.

When you have two monitors, the Picture mode of Desktop Pictures will show two sample screens representing your monitors. Click on a sample to activate it and then use the Select Picture and Set Desktop buttons. You can drag a picture from one sample screen to the other to change the monitor on which it appears.

One on the desktop is worth two in the bush. Find any plain PICT file and rename it *secret about box.* Then open the Desktop Patterns control panel and drag the PICT file into the preview window. (Open the Desktop Patterns window to the size of your screen to better see what results.)

Icons

Basics

Icons. The icons on your desktop fall into five main groups:

- **File icons** for things like applications and documents. A *file* is any discrete collection of information, so file icons also include things like fonts and sounds.
- **Volume icons**, for disks and other types of storage (like file servers).
- **Alias icons** that stand in for any other icons on the disk.
- **Folder icons** for storing and grouping other icons.
- **The Trash** icon, used for deleting files from disks.

The term *icon* sometimes refers to only the picture that you see (*"change the icons to a smaller size"*) and sometimes to the item the icon represents (*"Copy the icon to another disk"*). The meaning is usually clear from the context.

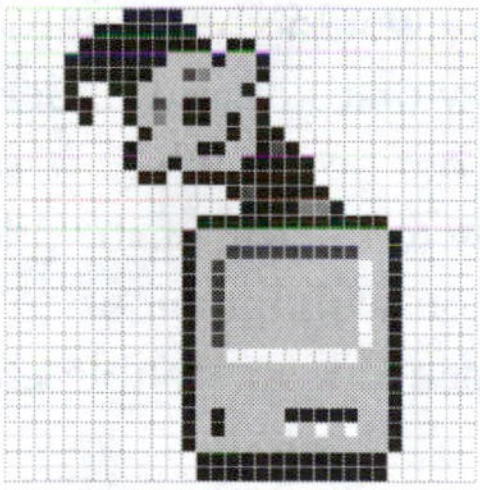

Even icons that don't look square are designed in a square grid.

The standard Finder icon is a specific size: a 32-pixel square. Even icons that don't look square live within a 32 by 32 grid.

The overall look of icons has changed in OS 8, with everything getting a 3-D look. Even volume icons, which were still black-and-white all through System 7's various versions, are finally colorized in OS 8.

Opening icons. There are more ways to open an icon than you probably want to know about, but here goes:

- Double-click on it if it's a standard icon; for button icons, a single click will do the trick.
- Select it and use the Open command in the File menu.
- Control-click on it and use the Open command in the contextual menu (this works whether or not you select the item first).
- Select it and press ⌘O.
- Select it and press ⌘↓. (This seemingly strange combination actually falls in with a set of keyboard commands on the desktop, covered in detail a little later in the chapter.)

What "open" means. You can open any desktop icon, but what "open" means depends on what the icon is. When you open:

- **a disk, folder, or the Trash**, a window opens showing you what's inside.
- **an application**, the program launches.
- **a document**, the program that created it launches, and the document opens inside it.
- **a control panel**, it opens.
- **a font file**, a window opens showing font information and samples.
- **a sound file**, the sound is played.
- **the System file**, a window opens showing the resource files that are user-installable.
- **a suitcase file**, a window opens showing the suitcase contents.

Visual clues to icon states. The way an icon appears lets you know its "state": selected or not, and opened or not. A selected icon has a dark gray mask superimposed on it—you'll still be able to see its features and colors, but they'll be dulled. An opened icon is simply an outline filled with a dotted pattern; you won't be able to see any of the icon's details. An icon that's both selected and opened is a much darker version of the dotted pattern.

Opening an open icon. If an icon is already opened, you can still double-click on it as if it weren't open yet. Why would you want to? It might be the easiest way of finding a folder's window that's buried under some other windows—you can see the opened folder, but not its window, so double-clicking on the opened folder brings its window to the top of the pile. Or, you might want to switch into a running application without choosing it from the Application menu: if you can see its opened icon, double-clicking on it sends you to the program.

Generic icons. A generic icon is one that doesn't have any special identifying features except for its general type; you can tell the icon is an application, or a document, or a folder, but you can't tell which application or which document.

Tiny generic icons, available in list-view windows, indicate only the general type of the file.

Tiny generic icons are used to label items in list-view windows when you choose the smallest size for icons.

When full-size generic icons show up, it can be due to any of several reasons:

- There's no other icon available. Programmers have to design icons for their programs and documents; if they don't, the Mac uses a generic icon. For an application, that's a diamond shape with a writing hand in it; for a document, it's a rectangular "piece of paper" with its corner folded down.

- You don't have the application that created the document. If you have a Microsoft Word document but you don't have Word, the document icon will be generic. That's because the icon isn't stored with the document; the document keeps track of which application created it, and the Finder looks up the "parent" to see what its documents should look like—but if the application isn't around, the Finder can't look it up. If you used to have Word on your drive, though, you might get the correct icon; the Finder stores that kind of information until you rebuild the desktop.
- You have a small problem with some documents losing their connection to their parent applications. Rebuilding the desktop (Chapter 24) can take care of the problem, restoring the icons.
- You have a large problem with your disk or operating system which may require re-installing the system software (Chapter 8), repairing the drive (Chapter 24), or both.

Size options on the desktop. This is mentioned elsewhere under other topics, but keep in mind that OS 8 finally lets you change how loose icons appear on the desktop. They don't have to stay as full-size icons anymore: you can change their size, and you can even use the new button icon option.

An open-and-shut case. Hold [Option] while you double-click an icon, and the window that's holding that icon closes as the icon opens. This is especially useful when you're opening a control panel, since you don't usually want the Control Panels window left open on the desktop.

Icon Names

Editing icon names. You have to select an icon's name to change it, and there's a slight difference between selecting an icon and selecting its name.

Selecting an icon's name.

Clicking on an icon selects it; clicking on the icon's *name* selects the name. When the name is selected, the icon itself is also selected—it goes gray—but there's an editing rectangle around the name.

Basic editing techniques work inside the editing rectangle: click to put the insertion point at a specific spot, use [Delete] and [⌦] (finally, in OS 8, the Forward Delete key works on the desktop!), double-click to select a word, use [←] and [→] to move in the rectangle; type to replace selected text, and so on.

The rename delay. It goes by various names—the editing delay, the rename delay—but it's the same thing: there's a delay between the time you click on an icon's name and when the editing rectangle appears. (I call it the Mac minute, in honor of the New York minute: the time between a traffic light's turning green and the people behind you beeping their horns. The rename delay is a little longer.)

The rename delay can be up to a full two seconds; that may not sound like a lot, but in practice it is. In fact, it's a problem because you click on the name to select it, it doesn't activate, so you click on it again—and the Mac thinks you've double-clicked, and opens the file! The length of the rename delay is controlled by the double-click speed setting for the mouse in the Mouse control panel. Strange, but true. A slower double-click speed means a longer rename delay!

Avoiding the rename delay. To avoid the rename delay altogether when you're using the mouse, click on the icon's name and then immediately move the mouse. You may need a little practice: move the mouse too soon, and you'll drag the icon; too late, and the editing rectangle would be appearing anyway. The best method is to click somewhere in the name away from the spot you want to edit, and just move immediately to the spot you want. Or, click on the name and immediately move the mouse down a little, away from the name.

Keyboard name selection. If an icon's already selected, typing Return or Enter will select its name. Combining keyboard selection techniques with name-selection techniques lets you do almost anything without a mouse. (That's a heretical statement from a Mac die-hard, but the truth is, I can type *awfully* fast!)

You can't edit some icon names. When you click on an icon's name but the editing rectangle doesn't appear, it's usually because the icon is locked (through its Info window)—locking a file keeps you from changing both the contents and the name. This applies to locked disks and to CDs, which are by definition locked from any changes.

The system also prevents some icons from being renamed—a shared volume on a network, for instance: just think of the mess it would cause if you tried renaming a disk or folder after it's already been mounted on someone else's desktop on a network! You don't actually have to be on a network to run into this little problem: if File Sharing is on (in the File Sharing control panel) and a disk or folder is set to be shared (with the Finder's Sharing command), you won't be able to change the icon's name.

The name game. There are only a few rules when it comes to naming icons:

- The name can't be longer than 31 characters, except for disk icons, which are limited to 27 characters.
- There's no difference between upper- and lowercase letters for file names. MY FOLDER, *My Folder,* and *MY folDER* are all the same as far as the Mac's concerned.
- You can't have two items of the same name in the same folder (or out on the desktop unless they belong to different disks).

- You can't use a colon (:) in an icon's name. A colon is reserved by the system for a file's full *path name*—the one that starts with the volume it's on, lists all the folders it's in, and ends with the file's name, like this: *Int HD:System Folder:Control Panels:Appearance.* Using a colon would really confuse things!

You can't break these rules even if you wanted to. Try typing a colon in an icon's name on the desktop, and the Mac types in a hyphen instead; try using a colon when you're naming a file in a Save box, and nothing at all gets typed.

Copying and pasting an icon's name. You can use the Copy and Paste commands on icon names. You can use the Copy command on a selected icon—the name itself doesn't have to be selected. But to use the Paste command, the name itself has to be selected.

Using Copy and Paste on multiple icons. You can use the Copy command on a multiple icon selection, and all the icon names are copied to the Clipboard. There used to be a limit of 255 characters for this operation, but that's a thing of the past; so, you can Select All, and then Copy, and paste the resulting list in any word processor or text processor (like SimpleText), and print out a list of a window's or a disk's contents. This is often easier than using the Finder's Print command, which is slower because it prints icons along with the text. On the other hand, the order in which items are copied to the Clipboard is confusing; it's not related to how things are sorted in the window, but instead seems to be based on when each item was put into the window.

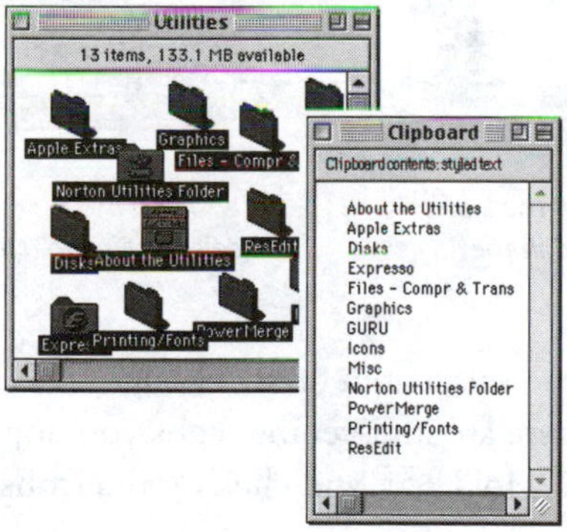

A Copy command on selected icons places their names on the Clipboard.

If you have expanded folders in a list view, the information is copied to the Clipboard in an odd way: first, it lists all the main-level items; next, all the second-level items (in groups according to the folders they belong to); then, the third-level items (again, in groups according to their enclosing folders), and so on.

Name extensions. When an icon's name ends in a period followed by three letters (like *guides.sit* or *DiskUtil.sea)*, that usually indicates something special about the file. (Yes, this was borrowed from the DOS world—the pre-Windows Microsoft environment—but let's not quibble over provenance.) It's a handy way to identify a type of file without having to check the icon itself. The two most common name extensions are *.sit* and *.sea.* The first is for *StuffIt*, indicating a stuffed, or compressed, file; the second is for *self-extracting archive*, another type of compressed file. Both of these are covered in Chapter 28.

Selecting Icons

Selecting and moving button icons
Later this chapter

Selecting an icon. Select an icon by clicking on it. To select an item in a list view, you can click on the icon or anywhere along the line where there's text—but you have to click on the text, not on the space between, say, the icon's name and its modification date. BUT—you don't want to click on its name, because that will select the name for editing rather than select the icon.

Deselect the icon by selecting something else, or by clicking someplace that won't select anything. If, for some reason you can't find an empty spot to click on, holding Shift and clicking on a selected icon will deselect it.

Selecting multiple icons. If you want to select everything in a window, use the Select All (⌘A) command in the Edit menu.

To select more than one icon at a time, you can drag the mouse in a window to draw a rectangle (you'll see a gray line as you drag); anything even partially in the rectangle will be selected. You can drag a rectangle in both icon and list views.

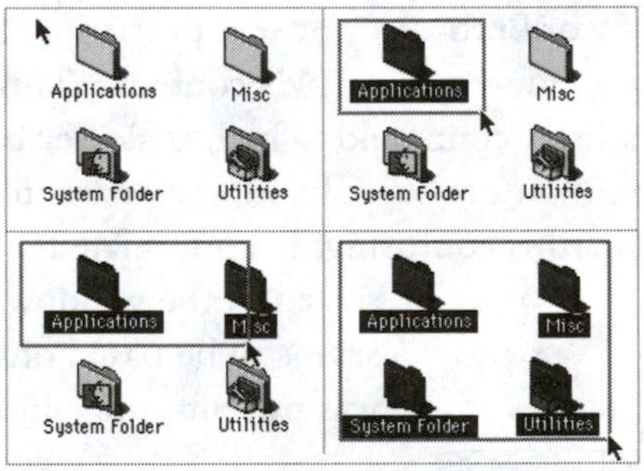

Dragging a rectangle selects all the icons that are even partially enclosed in the rectangle.

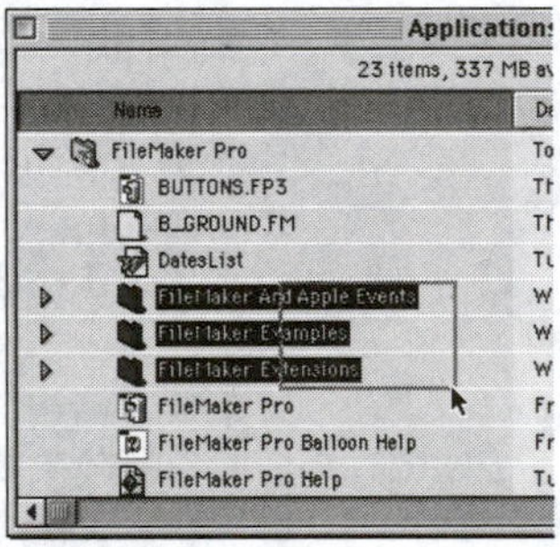

You can drag a rectangle to select items in a list view, too.

When the icons you want to select aren't near enough to each other to use a selection rectangle, or there are intervening icons you don't want selected, use the Shift-click method. Hold Shift and click on the icons you want.

You can combine the selection methods: select a bunch of icons with a rectangle, then Shift-click to select one or two others that aren't nearby. Or, drag a rectangle around one group, hold Shift and drag around another group—both groups are selected.

You can deselect an icon in a selected group by Shift-clicking on it. This is handy when you've made a new folder inside a window and want to drag everything except one file (and, of course, the new folder itself) into it: do a Select All, then Shift-click on the new folder and excepted file, then drag everything into the new folder. You can also deselect a group of icons by Shift-dragging around them.

Selecting icons from different folders. You can select icons from different folders (to open documents, apply labels, make copies, and so on) by keeping a parent window open in a List view, expanding the folders, and Shift-clicking on the files you want.

Selecting icons with the keyboard. There are three ways to select icons from the keyboard:

- Type the icon's name. You have to type only enough letters to differentiate it from everything else in the window, so using one or two letters is usually enough.
- Use Tab to move to the next icon alphabetically, and Shift Tab to the previous alphabetical icon. This works no matter how your icons are arranged, or how your list is sorted. If no icon is selected, Tab selects the first alphabetical icon and Shift Tab the last one.
- Use ↑↓←→ to move from the currently selected icon to the one in the direction of the arrow (only ↑ and ↓ work in list views). If no icon is selected, ↑ and ← select the first (uppermost) icon and ↓ and → the last one.

When you're in a list-view window and some of its folders are expanded, using the typing or Tab approaches can be confusing. They select items without regard to their position in the hierarchy, so you may jump from an item in the main level to one several levels down in a far-away folder if it happens to come next alphabetically and is in an expanded folder.

Moving Icons

Ghosts instead of outlines. When you drag an icon to move it to a new position, a ghost of the icon travels along with the cursor until you let go, making the original jump to the new position. The ghost is a relatively new feature; in earlier systems, it was a simple outline that moved with the cursor, not a ghost.

When you want to move an icon that's in a list view, grabbing it by the tiny icon in front of its name is the easiest and most obvious way. But you can grab it anywhere along its line of information, as long as you're actually touching some text (even its modified date, for instance) and not the blank space between the columns; you can even drag it by its name without the name's being activated for editing.

Dragging in OS 8 uses a ghost instead of an outline.

Moving versus copying. Moving an icon within a window simply changes its position in the window. Moving it from one window to another, or between a window and the desktop, changes its location, but there's still only that one copy of the icon on disk.

Moving an icon from one disk to another, actually *copies* the file so that the original remains in the first location, and an exact copy is placed in the new location. The Finder will give you a clue when this is going to happen: drag an icon to a spot where it will be copied (onto another disk icon, or onto a folder icon or any window that belongs to another disk) and the arrow cursor change to a special copy cursor—an arrow with a plus sign attached. And, of course, you'll see the copy dialog while the copy's being made.

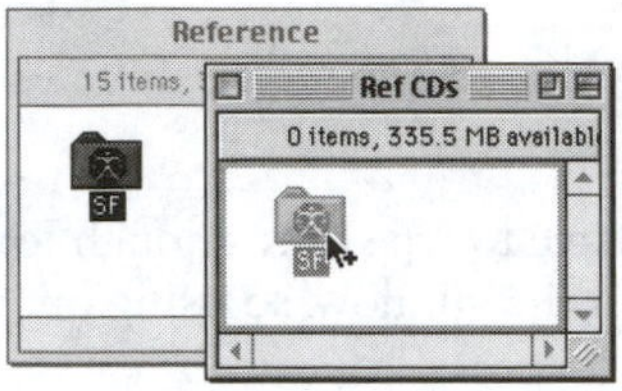

Dragging this icon from its original window to the second one gives the "copy" cursor because the second window belongs to another drive.

Moving icons into other icons. To put one icon into another one (into the Trash, into a folder, onto a disk icon), drag one right on top of the other. The target icon highlights when the pointer is over it, so you'll know when you're in the right spot. (If you have a bunch of icons surrounding your Trash icon, you've been missing the target.)

When the "target" darkens, the icon you're moving will land inside it.

You can also put an icon into something by dragging it into the other's open window.

Drag one, drag all. When multiple icons are selected, moving one of them moves them all. With a multiple move, it's the position of the pointer that counts for the destination: don't worry if, as you're moving items from one window to another, some of the ghosts of the items aren't in the destination window. As long as the mouse cursor is positioned in the destination when you let go of the button, all the items will be moved there.

Using the grid. Both icon and button window views allow you to keep items snapped to invisible grid points inside the windows. Set the grid snap on through the window's View Options dialog (from the View menu or the pop-up menu), and every time you let go of an icon, it snaps to the nearest grid point. (Note that until OS 8, the grid snap was a global setting for all windows; now it's turned on and off for individual windows.) When the grid snap is on, a little grid icon appears at the left of the window's header to remind you that it's on.

You have to be careful where you drop an icon, though: drop it too close to a grid point where there's already an icon, and it will snap to the same point, hiding itself behind the icon already there. Even though you don't see the first icon darken, it sure feels like you've dropped one icon into another, because the one you've just moved disappears from view.

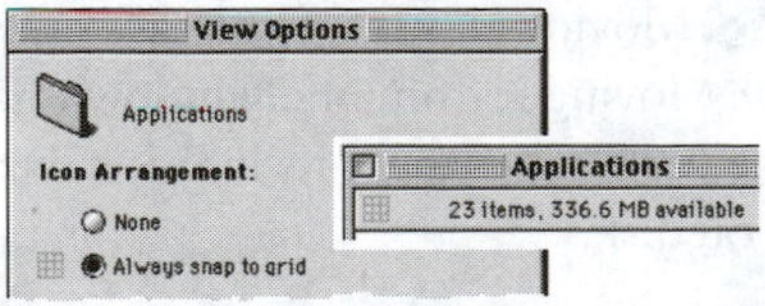

Set the grid snap on for a window through its View Options dialog; when the grid is on, there's a grid icon in the window's header.

Changing the grid size. To alter the grid size, use the Finder's Preferences command from the Edit menu. You can choose between tight or wide spacing, but the old option of a staggered grid is no longer available. (Which is a real shame—wouldn't it be nice to be able to choose a combination of tight/wide and straight/staggered?)

Set the grid spacing with the Finder's Preferences command.

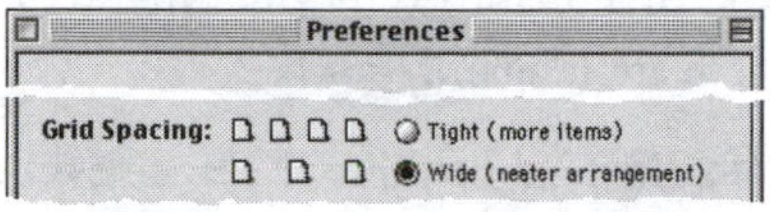

Reversing the grid-snap setting. If you have the grid-snap on for a window but want to place an icon or button off a grid point, hold ⌘ while you drag the icon. Conversely, if the grid snap is off, you can snap a dragged item to the grid point by holding ⌘ while you drag it.

This temporary snap-to-grid function is handy when you're dragging multiple files into a window that's not set to use the grid automatically. The dragged icons can be all bunched up during the drag (based on wherever they came from) but if you hold Control before you let go of the button, they'll all spread out to grid points.

Putting things into list-view windows. Dragging an icon into a list-view window can be tricky, especially when there are expanded folders showing. If you drop an item just anywhere in the window, it might wind up in an inner folder accidentally, rather than in the main level of the window.

The best way to make sure something lands in the main level of a window is to let it go anywhere in the window "frame": at the top (that's the title bar, header, and column titles); at the side or bottom, in the scroll bars; at the left side, on the little edge that you use to drag the window. The inner part of the window highlights in acknowledgment when you're in the right spot.

If you drag an icon into the inner part of the window, you have to let it go in a "bare" spot for it to land in the main window level. The empty area at the bottom of a list works, as does any spot where you're not actually touching an icon or text that belongs to a folder.

If you want something to land inside an inner folder in the window, you don't have to drag it to the folder icon. Drag it so that it's touching any column of text that's in the row that describes the folder; you'll see the folder highlight, telling you the icon will go into it. If the folder is expanded, you can drag the icon to touch any of the inner documents; the enclosing folder will still highlight. But you have to avoid letting it go while it's touching a folder that's inside the one you're aiming for.

Finally, if you're dragging something out of an expanded folder in a list window and want it relocated to the main level, drag it up into the window header or title.

Dragging from an inactive window. Here's how most people drag an icon from an inactive background window (let's call it Window Two) into the current active window (we'll call it Window One): click in Window Two to activate it; grab the icon and drag it into Window One, which is now inactive; click in Window One to activate it again.

But you can do it in one step instead of three, because ever since System 7, you can grab something from a background window and drag it into the active window without activating the background window. The Finder knows the difference between a click that selects an item or window, and the click that actually begins a drag operation.

Copying and Duplicating Icons

Copy-over warnings. When you move an icon into a window where an icon of that name already exists, the Finder warns you that you're about to replace an existing file (since you can't have two items with the same name in the same folder).

The warning comes in several flavors; the one you get depends on which of the files is older. When the one that's going to be copied over is older, the notification includes a polite "Do you want to replace… ?" question. If the one that's going to be replaced is newer, the warning asks, in a subtly stronger tone: "Are you sure you want to… ?" When the items are the same (at least, according to their modified dates), or can't be easily compared (as when a folder is replacing a folder), you get a neutrally worded dialog.

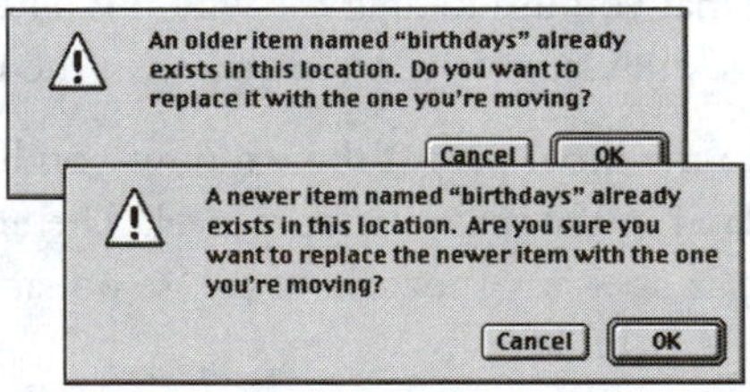

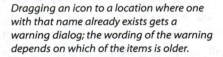

Dragging an icon to a location where one with that name already exists gets a warning dialog; the wording of the warning depends on which of the items is older.

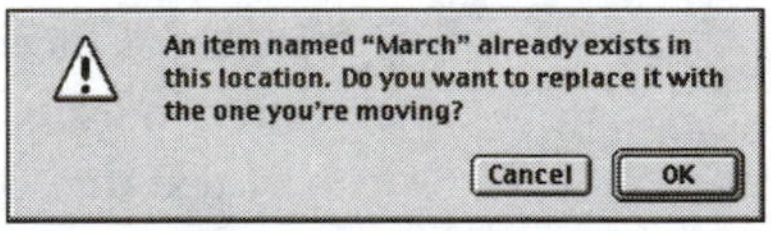

When modified dates aren't available, you get this neutrally worded dialog.

When you're dragging multiple icons from one place to another and only one item is in danger of being replaced, you'll see the same dialog as if you were dragging only one item: the one that tells you if the item is older or newer. If more than one item is going to be replaced, you get just a general warning that refers to "some items" without naming the items. You don't even get a chance to copy the non-duplicate items. You have to go back and check the files you're working with to figure out which ones are the duplicates.

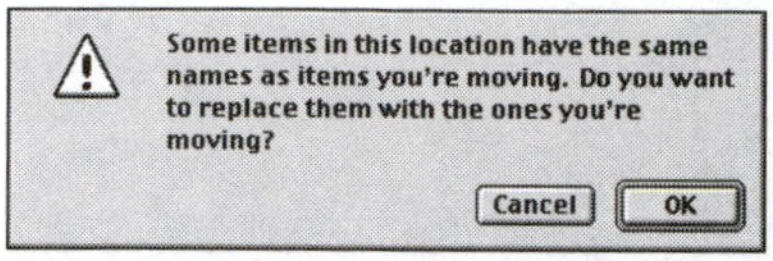

Copying over multiple files gets this warning, which doesn't tell you which items are the duplicates.

The pre-flight check. When you move or copy an item from one place to another, the Finder compares what you're moving to what's already stored in the destination; that's how you get the warnings that you're about to copy over an existing file.

When you're moving one or only a few items at a time, or moving to a place with few or no items already there, the comparison doesn't take very long, so you don't even know it's going on. But if you drag lots of files at a time into a folder that already has lots of files, there can be a considerable delay before the copying starts, while the Finder double-checks all the files it's juggling. But now that you know what's going on in the background, the delay won't worry or annoy you.

The Copy dialog. Whether you're making a copy by dragging an item or by using the Duplicate command, the OS 8 Finder provides a nifty new Copy dialog that keeps you posted on the details of the procedure.

First, if there's a lot of background checking before the copy, as described in the last entry, you get a dialog that lets you know there's some preparation going on. Its progress bar is a control known as a barber pole (and with OS 8's 3-D look and assignable colors, you can make it really look like a red-striped barber pole).

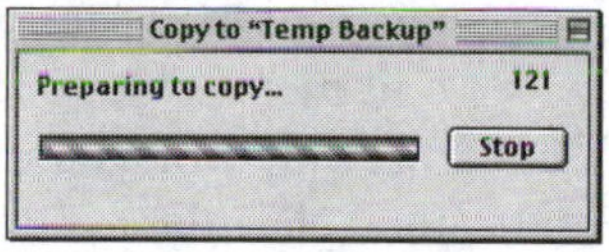

Before the Copy dialog.

The main copy dialog gives you an idea of how long the copy operation is going to take—not only with the usual progress bar, but with an actual time prediction. Clicking on the arrow in front of the Time Remaining report gives you a fuller dialog, with information about exactly which file of a group is being copied at the time.

Click the arrow to get a more complete report on the copy procedure.

You can't always count on the time as reported in the Copy window. When you're working on local volumes, it's reasonably accurate, but it seems to get confused when it comes to copies across networked volumes. The dialog shown on the next page, for instance, showed up when I was copying a 500K file, which actually took less than a minute.

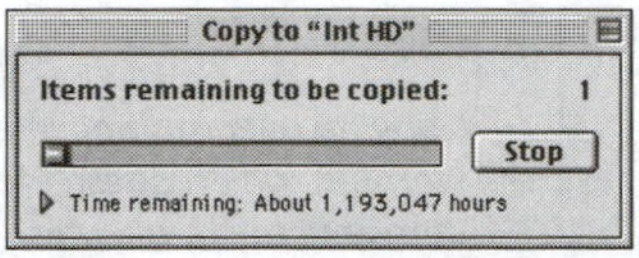

The occasionally erroneous time report.

Copying is a background procedure. While a desktop copy is going on, you can go on, too—you don't have to sit and watch the progress bar. Since copying is a background procedure, you can work in an application while the Mac does the grunt work behind the scenes.

Under System 7, this background procedure still limited you in what you could do—you couldn't, for instance, double-click an icon to launch a program during a copy (although you could launch it from the Apple menu!). In OS 8, you won't find any such restrictions.

Stopping the copy procedure. You can stop the copy process at any time by clicking the Stop button or pressing ⌘. or Esc. If any folders or files have already been completely copied to the new destination, they'll be there, but the rest of the items won't be copied. Even if you stop the procedure right at the beginning, you may find a new folder at the destination that matches the folder you were going to copy, even though the new one may be empty.

The Duplicate command. To copy of a file or folder, you can use the File menu's Duplicate command—not the Edit menu's Copy command, since that only work's for an icon's *name.* Just select the icon(s) and choose Duplicate or press ⌘D. You'll get a copy dialog on the screen as the copy is made. The copy is exactly the same as the original—including the created and modified dates—except that its name has the word *copy* appended to it.

If you make another duplicate of the file, *copy 1* is appended to the name of the newest duplicate (in keeping with a computer's habit of starting counting at zero instead of one). Interestingly enough, whether you copy the original a second time or copy the duplicate, the new file is named *copy 1.* (It's a little less amazing when you play around for a while and discover that a duplicate of any file with the word *copy* at the end is duplicated as *copy 1* even if it's an original; the same holds for any *copy x* at the end of an icon's name.)

Duplicating folders. Duplicating a folder duplicates everything inside of it—files, and subfolders and their subfolders. But the names of the items inside the folder don't change to have *copy* after them.

IN THE BEGINNING

The Duplicate command in early Mac systems didn't bother with numbering the copies it made. Instead, it added *Copy of* as a prefix to the duplicate's name. The second duplicate would be prefixed *Copy of Copy of,* and the next would start with *Copy of Copy of Copy of.* Not only did that mean your copies were not alphabetically sorted anywhere near the originals, but you ran into the filename length limit pretty quickly, even on the earliest systems that let you use 256-character names.

Copying over folders. When you copy or move a folder from one place to another, and there's already a folder with the same name in the destination, you get only the standard "Do you want to replace… ?" dialog. The Finder doesn't know or care that the two folders have entirely different contents. If you OK the replacement, the folder you're moving will replace the other folder *and all its contents*.

Whenever you're dealing with two folders that have the same name, it's better to open them and drag their contents back and forth.

The folder versus file copy. The Mac doesn't care what kinds of files you replace with others of the same name: if you name a document *PageMaker* and then copy it into that application's folder, you'll be asked if you want to replace one with the other—and your application's gone.

But there's no way the Mac is going to let you do something *really* stupid like replace a whole folder of stuff with a single file just because you happened to give both the same name; it won't let the reverse happen, either. You'll get one of the dialogs shown here if you ever try.

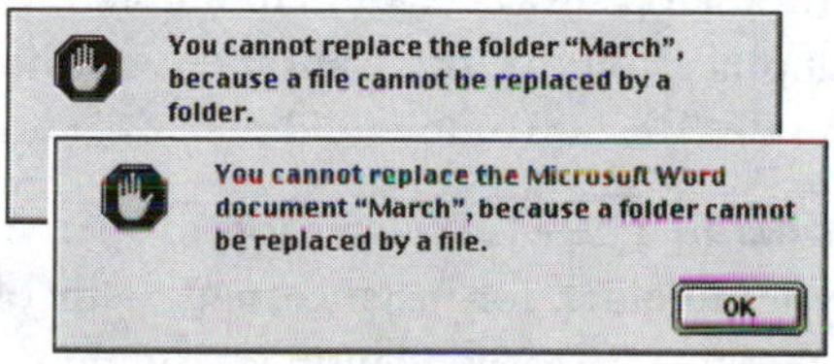

You can't replace a file with a folder, or vice versa.

The option-drag copy. Dragging an icon from one spot to another merely changes its location. If you'd like to make a copy of the item instead of just move it, you don't have to use the Duplicate command (which means you'd have to change its name to get rid of the *copy* suffix, and you can imagine how long that takes!). Instead, hold Option while you drag the icon to a new location and you'll get an exact copy in the destination. The mouse cursor changes to the copy cursor while you're dragging to let you know what's going to happen. And you don't have to be quick on the keyboard: as long as you press Option before you let go of the icon, you'll get a copy.

Auto-copy from locked volumes. When you're using a CD, or logged onto a file server, you can't make any changes to the location of files belonging to those volumes—including dragging items to the desktop. If you drag something from a window on a locked volume onto your desktop, the Finder automatically makes a copy of that item on your system disk and leaves it on the desktop. (I think this is awfully presumptuous; in previous systems, you'd get a dialog asking if you'd like a copy made since you couldn't move the original.)

Folders and Disks

Create a new, untitled folder with the New Folder command.

Creating folders. The New Folder command in the File menu creates a new folder; it shows up as *untitled folder*, with its name selected for editing. Use folders to organize your desktop icons, grouping them however makes the most sense to you.

> ***Just because you have a folder on your desktop named Empty Folder, that doesn't mean there's nothing in it. Whenever you create a new folder… its default name is Empty folder. Putting something in it doesn't change its name. [Many users throw it away by mistake.] Apple should change the default name of new folders to something less misleading, like Untitled folder.***
>
> *Sharon Zardetto Aker,*
> *The Macintosh Bible, Third Edition*

Creating a folder out on the desktop. A new folder is created in the active window. If you want to create a folder on the desktop, activate the desktop first by clicking on it or by pressing ⌘ Shift. (Of course, if you're going to click on the desktop to activate it, you might as well Control-click on it, which will pop up a contextual menu with a New Folder command in it.)

A folder created on the desktop always belongs to the startup disk. If you want to make a folder for another volume, but want it out on the desktop, you have to first create it in that disk's window, and then drag it out to the desktop.

Well, aren't they *special!* The Mac creates lots of special folder icons for special folders: the System Folder, for instance, and many of its subfolders have special icons so that they're easily identified. But you'll also find that folders named Utilities, Applications, or Documents kept on the main level of the disk also get their own special icons. In some cases, the system creates the folders; in others, you can create a folder with the correct name and the system will just take over and make the icon after you've made the folder.

Organizational skills. Folders are an organizational tool that everyone uses in different ways. You can put folders within folders within folders as far as you want. Accessing deeply nested folders and files isn't the problem it once was, what with all the navigational tools we have at our disposal now: aliases, the Apple menu, the Launcher, spring-loaded folders, and hierarchical capabilities in list-view windows.

Nonetheless, some general guidelines and suggestions may help:

- Keep an application and its support files and folders in the same folder—unless those support files are shared by other applications.
- Keep applications together in one Applications folder. (I've been recommending this since before the system made an Applications folder for

you!) If you have a lot of applications, you can subgroup them in inner folders (all graphics programs together, for instance, or all the applications you use for the Internet); or, you can make primary and secondary folders for applications you use a lot and not so often.

- Put utilities together in a single folder. I keep subfolders in my Utilities to group utilities for disks, for graphics, for file compression, and so on.
- Make a project folder for each project. This works much better than having separate folders for *types* of documents, like word processing, graphics, and so on.
- Make a Desk Accessory folder to group those little utilities together (the Calculator, Scrapbook, and so on) instead of leaving them loose in the Apple menu.

Suitcase icons and their contents *Suitcases* are a special type of file that hold special information called *resources.* The System file is a suitcase file, as are the files that hold fonts. I'm mentioning them here because it's easy to confuse a suitcase with a folder—each holds other things, you can open them to see what's inside, and you drag things into and out of them.

But suitcases differ from folders both in what they can hold and how things are moved into and out of them. The System file holds special keyboard and sound resources, and font suitcases hold fonts. At first, moving things into and out of a suitcase seems exactly the same as with a folder: you double-click to open it, and drag out an icon. But with a folder, the icon you drag out is simply relocated. With a suitcase, the icon is *copied* to the new spot and removed from the suitcase—you'll even get a Copy dialog. This is because a folder holds items that are already files all by themselves. A suitcase is actually a file, and its resources are part of the file; dragging out a resource removes part of the suitcase file—it's as if you dragged a paragraph out of a word processor document. The copy procedure takes the resource and makes it a stand-alone file instead of part of the suitcase file.

There's more about working with suitcase files in both the System Folder and Fonts chapters.

IN THE BEGINNING

There wasn't always a New Folder command in the File menu. In fact, there wasn't a New Folder command anywhere in the first Macintosh system. There was an Empty Folder on the desktop, and you had to duplicate it and then rename it in order to create a new folder.

Volume icons. First, a little terminology. When a disk icon appears on the desktop, it's *mounted.* Hard drives, floppies, CDs, disk partitions, file servers on a network—any icon that represents a discrete storage device is referred to as a *volume.* When you double-click on a volume to open it, you're looking at the *disk window,* the *main window* or the *root level* of the volume.

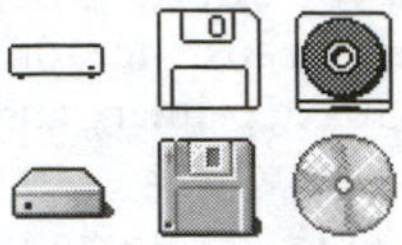

Basic disk icons were black-and-white (top) until OS 8 (bottom).

Okay, now back to the icons. Even though color Macs have been around a *long* time now, OS 8 is the first system that provides color icons for volumes. (That is, as defaults—we've been able to edit individual icons since System 7.)

Ejecting disks. There are several ways to eject a floppy, CD, or any other "removable" volume:

- Select the icon and choose Put Away (⌘Y) from the File menu.
- Select the icon and choose Eject (⌘E) from the Special menu.
- Drag the icon to the Trash.

I've always enjoyed demonstrating that last one to new users and watch them cringe, expecting their disks to be erased. (Other than that, I'm a pretty nice person.)

In OS 8, using the Eject command finally works completely: it both ejects the disk and removes its icon from the desktop. Previously, the icon would remain in a "ghost" state even though the disk itself was ejected.

Copying floppy disk contents. You can copy an entire floppy disk to your hard drive by simply dragging the icon of the floppy onto the hard drive or into any of its windows; you'll get a folder named after the disk, with everything from the disk inside. You think this isn't worth mentioning? Hah! You weren't around in the beginning, when this procedure would replace the entire contents of the hard drive with the contents of the floppy. Really!

Labels

Basics. Applying a *label* to an icon gives it an extra attribute that you can use for finding or sorting; you can see labels by turning on the Label column in List views. Applying a label also gives the icon a sort of color wash so you can tell what the label is when you're in an icon or button view.

The idea of labeling is basically a handy one. Every file on the Mac has certain intrinsic attributes: it's a specific size; it was created at a certain time and date, and so on. But there's no unifying attribute for all the files concerned with, say, a certain project that you're working on. But, by applying a label, you can add an attribute that lets you gather things together or sort them by some characteristic you think is important rather than what the Finder thinks is important.

Why aren't labels used, then, except for about five percent of the time by two percent of users? Because there are only six of them, they change when you might not expect them to, and you can apply them only while working on the desktop—not while saving a file, where it would be the most convenient.

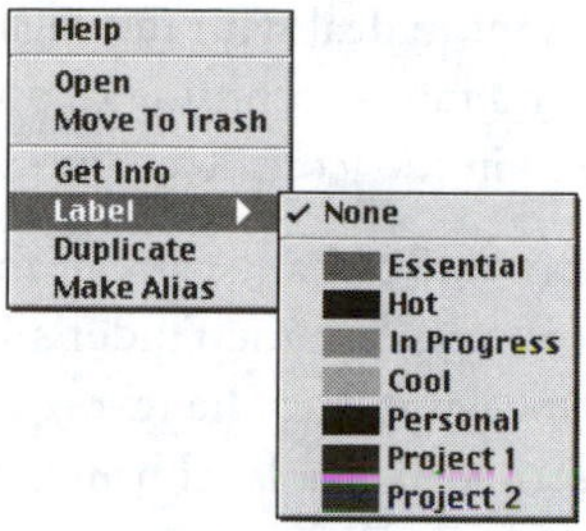

You can get to labels through the contextual menu for icons.

To apply a label, select the icon and use the Label submenu in the File menu. Or, use the contextual pop-up menu when you're pointing to an item; it has a Label submenu, too. To remove a label, select the item and choose None from the Label submenu.

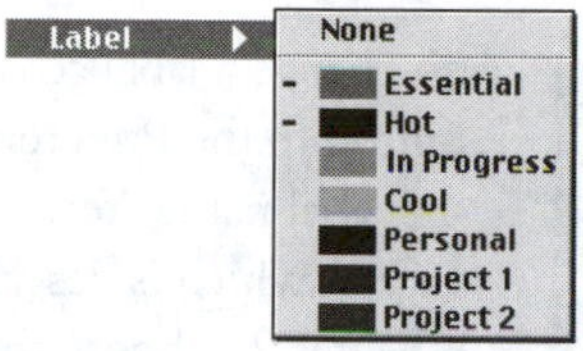

A hyphen indicates that some of the icons in the selection have that label applied.

The Label menu hyphen. A checkmark next to a label in the Label menu means, of course, that the selected icon has that label. But if you see a hyphen next to a label, that means you've selected multiple items with various labels—the hyphen means that some of the items in the selection have that label.

Sorting by label. When you sort a window by label, items are sorted according to the labels' order in the Label menu—not alphabetically by label, or by light-to-dark label color, or by some intuited label value (*Important* before *Do This Later*).

This isn't really much of a problem, since if you use labels, being able to group items according to their labels is more important than the order of the labeled groups.

Labels on duplicated files. If you copy (by dragging) or duplicate (with the Duplicate command) a labeled icon on the desktop, the new copy has the same label as the original. When you make an alias of an icon, the alias inherits the original's label, too.

But if you use the Save As command from within an application on a document that had a labeled assigned to it, you'll be creating an entirely new document and it won't have the original's label on it.

Volatile label names. Icons aren't indelibly stamped with the labels that you assign to them. Once you edit label names and colors (as described on the next page), the labels you've already assigned change.

All the Finder cares about is where on the Label menu an icon's label belongs. If your first label is *Personal* and you assign it to your checkbook files and later you change the first label to *Top Priority Business,* your checkbook files will change to the Top Priority Business label. This can be especially confusing when you've archived files with certain labels attached, and six months later you look at them and their labels seem to have changed. And, as for checking the labels of icons that have been transferred from one Mac to another—don't get me started on that one!

Label alternative. If you don't want to deal with the vagaries of labels, but would like to be able to group or find items according to projects, or importance, try using the Comments field in the icons' Get Info windows.

Changing label names and colors. To change any of the seven default label names, use the Preferences command in the Finder's Edit menu. In the Preferences dialog, just type the new name into the text box for the label. There's nothing to prevent you from leaving a label blank, or using the same name multiple times, if you really want to confuse yourself.

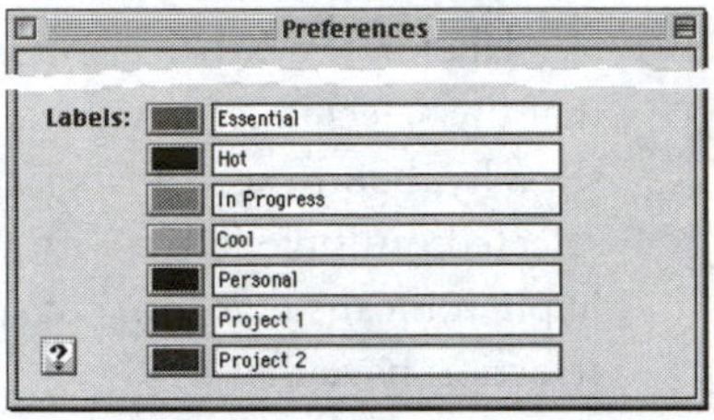

Change label names by editing them in the Preferences dialog. Change the colors by clicking a color button.

To change a label color, click on the color button in the Preferences dialog next to the label name. You'll get the Color Picker, which is described in detail in Chapter 9. Choose the new color, click OK, and your label has the new color.

Labels without colors. If you want to assign text labels to icons but not change their colors because you like your colored icons the way they are, change the label colors to black or white—they won't show when applied to a colored icon.

Back to defaults. If you've changed your labels and would like to reset them to their defaults, here's a chart of the names and the color values as assigned in the RGB Picker section of the Color Picker.

Label	*Color*	*Red*	*Green*	*Blue*
Essential	Orange	100	39	1
Hot	Red	86	3	3
In Progress	Pink	95	3	52
Cool	Light Blue	1	67	92
Personal	Dark Blue	0	0	83
Project 1	Green	0	39	7
Project 2	Brown	34	17	2

Suggested label uses. Because labeling is a vague sort of thing, I use it for only one long-term use, but I do use labels often for short-term help.

First, the long-term use: when I install or reinstall a system, I mark all the Apple system extensions and control panels by labeling them. It makes no difference what label I use—the name or color can be changed at any time—because I just don't use that label for anything else in those folders. It makes it quite easy to separate the Apple-provided system extensions from others. I also mark all the Microsoft extensions with another label for easy grouping.

As for short-term use, I use labels when I'm cleaning up a hard drive, or transferring a large number of files from one place to another. So, if I have to reformat a hard drive, first I copy all its files someplace else. Instead of just restoring everything when the drive is ready, I put things back in stages, and use labels on the backup copies for things like: *Need right away, Add second, Probably don't need,* and so on—it's amazing how much junk accumulates without your even knowing about it.

You could also use labels to mark everything that belongs to a certain project; that way, if you don't keep it all in one folder, you can still round them all up with the Find command. Or, even within a folder, you can mark some items as draft copies, and so on.

As long as you don't have to use too many labels, and you don't expect to need items labeled permanently, you can make use of the Label attribute.

The Info Window

The Get Info command. You can use the File menu's Get Info command on any selected icon on the desktop. The Info window that appears lists all sorts of information about the icon (some of which can also be displayed in a list view). Info window information and options vary depending on the type of icon you've selected, but most include:

- **Kind**: Whether it's a document, an application, a disk, a folder, and so on.
- **Size**: In K or in megabytes, whichever makes more sense for the size of the file, as well as a parenthetical note as to the size in bytes.
- **Where** the file is—in which folders on what disk.
- **Created** and **Modified** dates.
- A **Comments** box you can type notes in.

Because the information in an Info window depends on what kind of icon you've selected, the specifics of each one are covered elsewhere. But the picture on the next page shows the various forms of the Info box. As you can see, other information includes:

- A **Locked** checkbox box for documents and applications.
- A **Stationery Pad** checkbox for documents.
- **Memory** allocation information for applications.
- The **Version** information for applications.
- The **Warning** checkbox for the Trash.

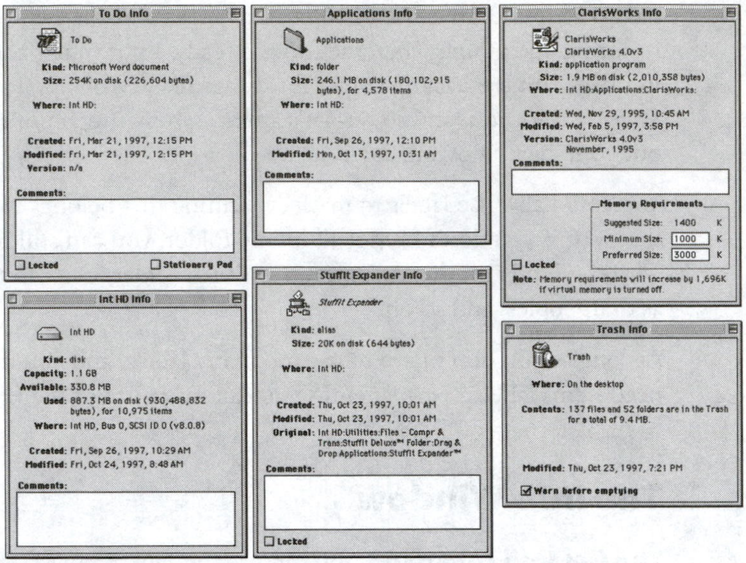

The Info window changes based on the type of icon you've selected: document, folder, application, disk, alias, or the Trash.

The Comments box. Since you can both search for and sort by information typed into a Comments box, this feature can be really useful if you train yourself to use it.

You're limited to about 210 characters in the box, most of which show all at once. There's no scroll bar, but you can drag through the text to make it scroll. And the text is always 10-point Geneva, even if you change your desktop font.

Long-lived comments. The comments in an Info window survive a desktop rebuild procedure. That's worth mentioning, since until System 7.5.3, comments were deleted when you rebuilt the desktop. (Rebuilding the desktop? That's a fix-it procedure described in Chapter 24.)

The size in bytes. The file size reported in an Info window is given, parenthetically, in bytes. Why isn't the K or MB size enough of a report—and why don't those measures match the byte report? (As detailed in Chapter 2, there are 1024 bytes in a K and 1024K in a meg.)

The room allotted on a disk for a file (the first measurement, as noted in the Info window—"on disk") is hardly ever the size of the file. A disk is divided into small blocks, like cubbyholes, and a file gets an entire block to itself, even if it doesn't fill that block. If it's bigger than the block, it spills over into another block—but that entire block is allocated to the file whether it needs it or not. (There's lot more about block allocations and file sizes in Chapter 4.)

The byte measurement of a file in an Info window is the most accurate measurement of file size you'll get from the Finder. In list-view windows, the size reported for a file or folder is the total number of blocks it takes.

Complete item counts for folders. It's not easy to figure out how many items are in a folder, counting everything in all its subfolders. In an icon view, you get just the number of icons on the top level. In a list view, the window header reports only how many items are "exposed," counting things inside folders only if the folders have been expanded in the list. And in both views, you get a report on only how much space is left on the disk, not how much is stored in the folder. But if you use Get Info, the size reported in the Information window will tell you how many items there are *including* all subfolders, and also how much room the folder takes on the disk.

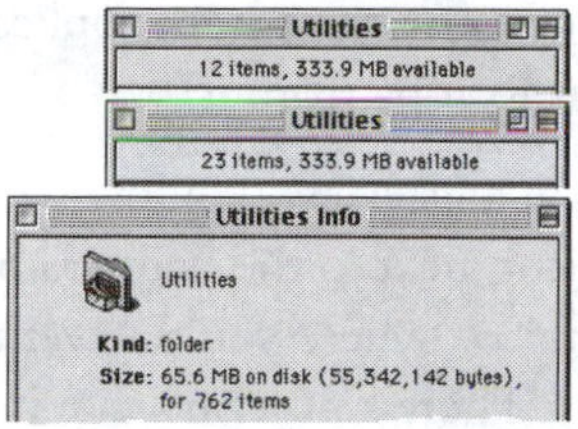

Top, the icon view reports 12 items; middle, a list view reports 23 items because some inner folders are expanded in the list; bottom, the real info, from the Info window.

The hard disk Info window. The Info window for a hard drive offers quite a bit of valuable information. You can get a complete report of how many items are on it, and how much room they take. But you can also find out, next to the *Where* label, what the drive's SCSI ID number is, and what version of what drive formatter was used to set up the drive. (The picture here shows an Apple drive, so no formatter name is listed.)

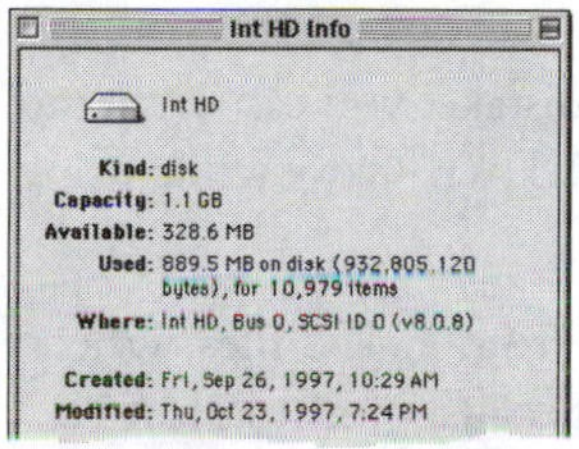

There's lots of important information in a drive's Info window.

The created date in a drive's info window isn't the day it rolled off the assembly line; it's the date the drive was formatted.

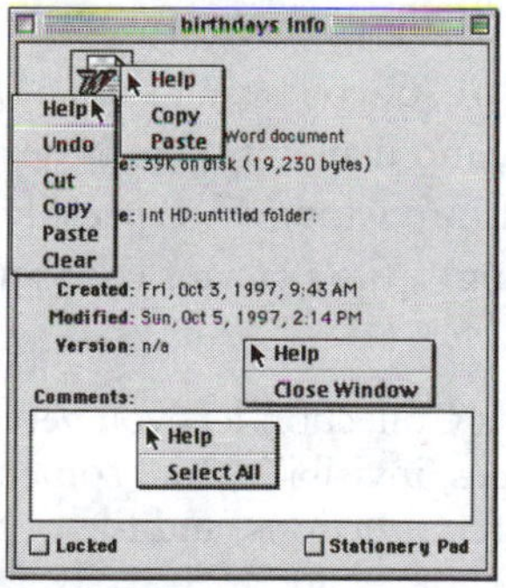

The two menus that are by the icon show the difference between clicking on an already edited icon (left) and the file's true icon (right), which can't be cut or cleared.

The Info window's contextual menus. There are quite a few pop-up menus available in an Info window, depending where you Control-click, as you can see in the picture here. The two different menus for clicking on the icon depend on whether it's the default icon or an edited one—there's more about editing icons later in this chapter.

Getting Info on the current window. If you use the Get Info command from the File menu when a window is open but nothing's selected in it, sometimes you'll get info for the open window, and sometimes you'll get info for one of its parent windows up in the hierarchy—it all depends on which windows in the hierarchy are open and which are closed.

But to get the Info for an open window, you don't have to go back and find its folder, select it, and Get Info on the folder. Just use the contextual menu on any spot in the window and choose Get Info from it.

Locking items. You can lock an application or document by checking the Locked box in its Info window; unlocking, of course, is simply unchecking the box. (Other icons, like folders and disks, don't have Locked checkboxes.)

You can't alter a locked file: you can't change its name, edit its icon, or modify its contents (although you can change its label). You can, however, open a locked document to read it; depending on the parent application, you'll probably also be able to make selections to copy from it.

A locked file has its name marked in a list-view window with a little padlock. Thankfully, OS 8 had moved the icon next to the name rather than at the far right end of all the columns in window, where you'd never really see it.

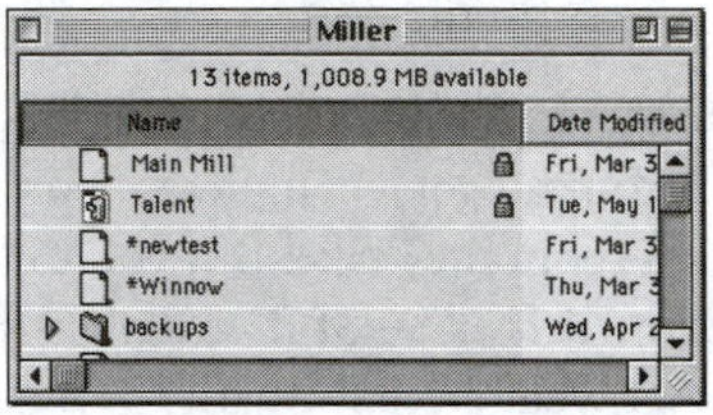

Locked files get little padlocks next to them in list views.

There's no visual cue in an icon view as to whether an icon is locked. But a quick check, without having to open an Info window, is to click on the icon's name: if the editing rectangle doesn't appear, the file is locked.

A locked icon can't be erased by mistake: you can drag it to the Trash, but it won't be erased unless you hold down Option while using the Empty Trash command.

(A locked disk is entirely different from locked files. When you lock a disk, you can't change anything on it because nothing can be written to the disk. But the files themselves aren't locked, so you can copy them to your hard drive and alter them from there.)

Other ways to get info. There are, of course, all sorts of little utilities that let you get info on a desktop item, and many of them better the information available through the Finder's Get Info window—especially when it comes to displaying (and sometimes changing) a file's creator code and file type. These three are all shareware:

- DiskTools, from the DiskTools Collection lets you get and set information like creator codes, file types, invisibility, and some things you never heard of! (It also provides search functions, and file-copying features.)
- More File Info is a contextual menu add-on that lets you get more info on a file simply by ⌘-clicking on it.

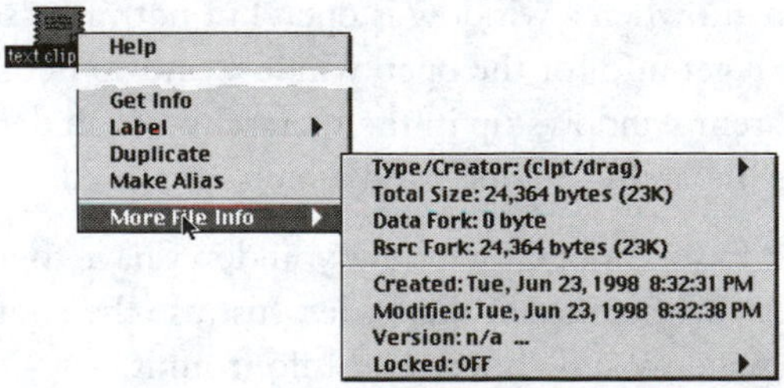

More File Info's contextual menu provides a little more info in a very handy form.

- Drop•Info provides basic file information, including file type and creator code, for any icon you drop onto it.

Editing Icons

Basics. You can change the icon of any file, folder, or disk:

1. Create a new icon in any graphics program, and copy it to the Clipboard.
2. Select the icon you want to change, and choose Get Info from the File menu.
3. Click on the picture of the icon in the Info window; when it's selected, it's surrounded by a frame.
4. Choose Paste from the Edit menu.

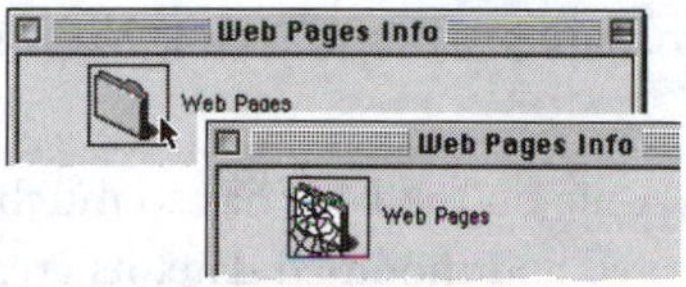

Select the icon in the Info window, and paste a new icon over it.

The change to the icon itself occurs immediately. (To copy an existing icon, open its Info window, click on the icon picture, and choose the Copy command.)

Reverting to the original icon. The original icon is always lurking behind the edited one. To revert to the original, select the icon in the Info window and press Delete or choose Cut or Clear from the Edit menu.

Getting the right size for an icon. An icon is exactly 32 dots by 32 dots square. If you use a tiny picture for an icon, it gets pasted into the center of the icon area. If you use a larger picture, it gets squeezed down to fit.

One of the hardest things to do is to get a new folder icon placed correctly in the icon area. If you start with a standard icon as a template, the top-to-bottom placement is fine, since OS 8 folders, unlike their predecessors, are a full 32 pixels tall. But they're only 30 pixels wide, and nudged up against the left edge of the icon area. If you simply alter the folder, copy it, and then paste it back into the Info window, you'll get a folder that's not in line with other folders. If you care enough to keep things correct, you have to select the white area to the right of the folder in your graphics program so that it's included in the icon design that you'll paste in.

Little things. Here are a few more things to remember when you're editing icons:

- Pressing Tab alternately selects and deselects the icon in the Info window, so you can do an open-select-copy/paste-close completely from the keyboard: ⌘O, Tab, ⌘C or ⌘V, and ⌘W.
- You can't change the icon of a locked file, although you can select the icon in the Info window to copy it for pasting onto another icon.
- Some special system icons are locked, even though the items themselves are not—the special folders inside the System Folder, for instance, can be

copied but not altered. The Trash icon, oddly enough, can't even be selected for editing.

- If the color of the icon in the Info window doesn't match the color of the icon on the desktop, the desktop icon has a label attached to it.
- Light colors in an icon often disappear unless completely surrounded by a darker color, to protect the desktop or window background from "leaking" through and obscuring the light color.
- Pasting a completely white region into an icon makes the icon completely disappear (a neat affect, when you want to do it on purpose).
- If you edit the icon of an item that's shared on a network, other users won't see the new icon until they've logged off and then back on again.
- The Open and Save dialogs show only generic icons, not any special system or edited icons. If you want to be able to see your edited icons in these dialogs, try the shareware program **Dialog View** detailed in Chapter 12.

Where the icon is stored. A file on the Mac has so much specialized information stored with it—its created and modified date, its creator and file type, a label (maybe), its basic icon—that there's no problem in slapping in a little more information: the icon information is added to the list of "resources" stored along with the file and its contents.

But when it comes to folders and disks, that's not the case—there's no place to put the edited icon, because folder and disk information are stored differently. So where does that icon get stored? A special invisible file, named *Icon*, is placed inside the folder, or on the root level of the disk; it holds the icon information. (Oddly enough, if you delete the custom icon, the invisible file remains.) This approach used to cause some odd problems—like inaccurate reporting of the number of items in the Trash—but OS 8 has cleaned up its approach, and no longer counts that invisible icon as an item, since you can't see it.

Leave a list on the desktop. You can keep a list of items on your desktop—no icons, just names. Paste a blank icon (a plain white blob) in each item's Get Info window to make it invisible, and then stack the items on top of each other so it looks like just a list of names. You can create folders with dashed lines as names to use as dividers in the list. By locking each of the aliases in Get Info, you can be sure that a double-click will always open the original—a little hesitation won't select the name for editing, since a locked file can't be renamed. And, you can still drag things onto any of the items, just by dragging the icon(s) right into the name.

Leave a list out on the desktop, including dividers.

Instant icons. You don't have to spend hours hand-tooling custom icons. Others have already done that, so you can buy the fruits of their labors.

- For instant custom folders, try the terrific little shareware program **Folder Icon Maker** by Greg Robbins (whose email name is the Lord-of-the-Rings-ish *grobbins*). Just drop an icon onto the Folder Icon Maker application, and it makes a folder with a miniature version of the icon stamped on it—especially great for your application folders! But don't be fooled by the drag-and-drop convenience—there are many little options in this program that you won't see unless you double-click on the application and run it to see its menus. You can, for instance: set the basic folder to one of several types; have the folder created inside the current one, or apply the icon to the enclosing folder; adjust the position of the miniature icon in relation to the folder; and send the folder icon to the Clipboard rather than have a new folder created automatically.

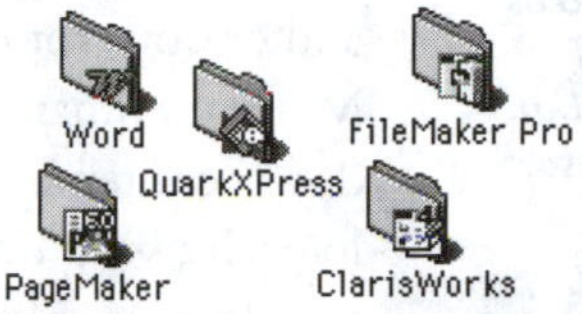

- For instant icons of any kind, try **Zonkers** ($25, Nova Development); you can choose from over 2500 included icons (through a handy icon browser), or use its full-featured icon editor to create your own.

novadevcorp.com
dublclick.com

- **IconMania!** ($40, DublClick) also provides a zillion icons for you to choose from, a browser to help you plow through them, and a full-featured icon editor. You also get a nifty "thumbnail" capability: drag any graphic file onto IconMania! and the file's icon changes to match the contents of the file.
- And, of course, all you have to is surf the Web or wander around AOL and you'll find thousands of custom icons that you can use on your system.

Windows

Finder Window Basics

The Platinum look. Finder windows certainly look different under OS 8, but it's not just Finder windows: it's *all* windows that get the new "platinum" look and features like the collapse box and the frame that lets you drag a window by any edge (details are in Chapter 5).

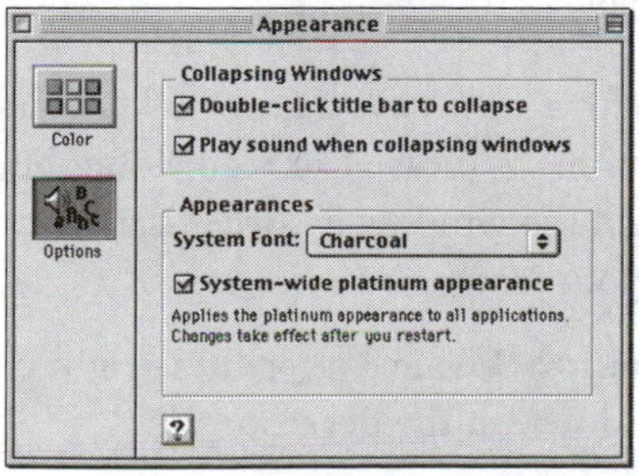

You can turn off the platinum windows for everything but the Finder by unchecking the System-wide option.

Although I just said that *all* windows get the new treatment, that really means that by default they all get the new look. You can turn off the platinum appearance for everything but the Finder: open the Appearance control panel, click the Options button, and uncheck the *System-wide platinum appearance* option.

The new point of view overview. The total reorganization of the Finder's View menu in OS 8 provides two basic types of commands: those that change the way a *window* looks and behaves, and those that change how the *contents* of the window look and behave.

For the windows themselves, there's a choice between standard and pop-up windows. For contents, there are three basic choices (icons, buttons, or list) and options for each of those choices. Menu commands regarding a window's contents are divided more logically, with one group for how they should be displayed (*as* icons, finally, instead of *by* icons, for instance) and another for how they should be sorted.

> ***The commands in the View menu really ought to be divided into two groups. The first two commands are which icon view you'd like—standard or small. (In fact, the commands ought to be as Icon and as Small Icon, since the "by" denotes some sort of order.) The other commands are all list views, but they're not just a type of view: the commands sort the contents of the window according to the category you choose in the menu.***
>
> *Sharon Aker, The Mac Almanac*

Window versus folder. On the desktop, the terms *window* and *folder* are often synonymous. Although some windows, like the Trash and the main level of a disk, aren't folders, the majority of windows show you what's inside a folder. So, we can refer to opening folders, or opening windows, and it's almost always the same thing. A more generic reference is to open an *icon*—which embraces disk icons and the trash, too.

The new header. The header for Finder windows has changed. Aside from the fact it's now gray instead of white, the information about how much room is already used on the disk has been dropped. The reports on the number of items used and how much room is left on the desk have been moved from the outer edges of the window header to the center. Why? To make room for the new little icons that show up in the window header to indicate how you've set various window options.

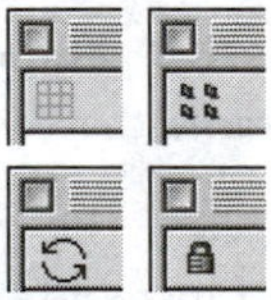

Header icons indicate window status. Top: The autogrid feature, and the keep arranged option. Bottom: the moving arrows that tell you all the information isn't displayed in the window yet, and the padlock that means the window belongs to a locked disk.

In addition, list-view windows now have a gray background, with white lines dividing items in the list to make it easier to read along the rows of information. The column by which the window is sorted is a darker gray, so you always know what order your icons are in.

Automatic window closing. Using Option in the right circumstances helps to automatically close windows on the desktop.

There are three basic ways to close a desktop window, and adding Option to any of them closes *all* the desktop windows:

To close a window:	***To close all windows:***
Click in a window's close box	Click in a window's close box while holding Option
Choose Close Window from theFile menu	Hold Option while opening the File menu; the command changes to Close All
Press ⌘W	Press ⌘ Option W

In addition, if you're opening an icon, holding down Option while you open it (by double-clicking or using the Open command from the menu or keyboard) closes the window as the item is opened.

And, finally, using Option while opening items from a window's Path menu closes the window, too—more about the Path menu a little later.

Close all windows *except* this one! If your desktop is cluttered with opened windows and you'd like all of them closed except for the one you're working in, drag the working window to the bottom of the screen so it turns into a window tab, use ⌘ Option W to close all the opened windows (it won't affect the tab), and then drag the tabbed window back out onto the desktop.

The directional sort. When I first wrote this chapter, I was working in OS 8 and right about here, I lamented the fact that sorting in Finder windows was still in a single direction, with no choices given to the user—gee, sometimes I want to sort with the *oldest* item at the top of the list!

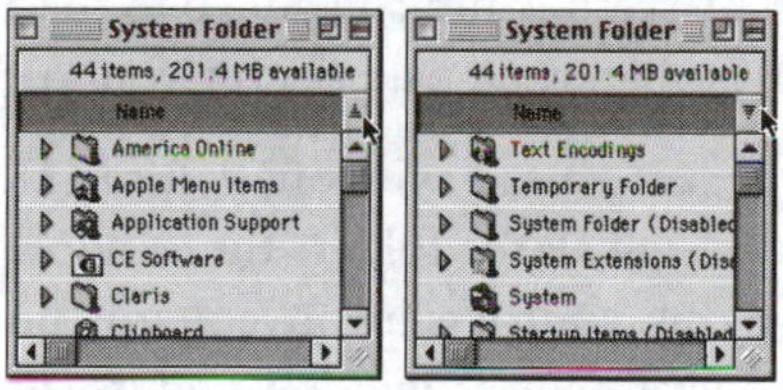

Click in the sort direction arrow to change the sorting order from ascending (left) to descending (right).

By the time I came back to edit this chapter, 8.1 was out with its minor but greatly appreciated new Finder window feature: the sort direction arrow, at the top of the vertical scroll bar. Click on the arrow to change the basic ascending sort to a descending sort, and back again.

Force to full-size. When you zoom a desktop window, it toggles between the size you defined and one just large enough to display its contents, rather than one that fills the screen. To zoom a window to full-screen size, hold down Option when you click in the zoom box. Even at full-screen size, you'll have a clear inch at the right edge of the screen so you can still see the Trash and disk icons.

Moving a background window Hold down ⌘ and drag an inactive Finder window to move it without activating it. This comes in handy when, for instance, a window is blocking the disk that you're trying to drag an icon to; without the command-drag option, you'd have to activate the window that's in the way, move it, then activate the first window again. In the meantime, if you'd made a selection in that first window, it would be gone and you'd have to select it again before you could drag the items to the disk icon.

The title bar is still a window! The title bar is still a window, even if most of it is hidden from view. So, you can still:

- Use the close box, or any menu or keyboard close command on it if it's the active window. When you reopen the window, it opens as a standard, expanded window.
- ⌘-click on its title to get the Path menu.
- Control-click on the title bar to get the contextual window menu, or use Finder menu commands on the window while it's active: you can change windows views (even though you can't see them), set the sort order, and so on. If you choose New Folder, the window snaps open so you can see the folder and give it a name.
- Drop an icon into the title bar. The icon just seems to disappear, but it's in the window once you let go; it will land in the main level of the window, ignoring any subfolders.

Changing window backgrounds. Don't like that pinstripe-gray list-view Finder window background that comes with the rest of the Platinum appearance?

Window Monkey ($20, shareware) offers several enhancements for navigating windows and folders—detailed in Chapter 12—but also lets you set the background of any Finder window to a color or pattern. With Window Monkey running, there's a Pattern command added to the Finder's View menu; its submenu displays colors and patterns for you to choose from.

tigertech.com
shareware.com

When you apply a color or pattern to a window, you can choose whether or not to have it "cascade" through all the folders the window contains, and their subfolders, although this control is inconveniently buried in the control panel. But you'll find that "stamping" a window and its subfolders with a special color or pattern can provide a handy visual clue when you're working on the desktop.

Kaleidoscope, a utility described in the last chapter, can also change the window background color.

Scrolling

Live scrolling. New in OS 8, Finder windows offer "live" scrolling: as you drag a scroll box, the window scrolls. No more guessing where to let go in order to see the items you're looking for.

Scroll while dragging. When you drag an icon to the edge of a window, but not outside it, the window will scroll as soon as the cursor comes to within 16 pixels of the window's edge (that's about the width of a scroll bar). Of course, this only works if the window can be scrolled in that direction anyway, as indicated by the gray scroll bars.

Variable-speed scrolling. You can scroll a Finder window without using the scroll controls or dragging an icon. Draw a line with the mouse cursor, starting just inside the edge of the window and dragging to a point just a few pixels into the scroll bar, header, or left edge. (It's not really a line that you're drawing—it's a very skinny rectangle, and if you hit any icons as you scroll by, they'll be selected.) The window slowly scrolls its contents by.

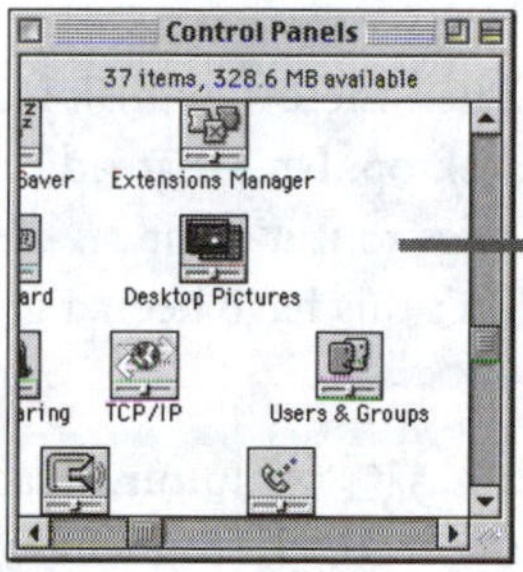

Drag a skinny rectangle beyond the edge of the window for fast scrolling; if you drag to within the scroll bar area, the scrolling is slower.

Now, the variable-speed part: the further you drag away from the main window area, the faster the window scrolls. You can even drag way outside the window; as long as you keep the mouse button down, the window remains active, and scrolling.

Diagonal scrolling. There are "hot spots" in the outer corners of each Finder window that make it scroll both horizontally and vertically at the same time. Just press the mouse button while you're inside the window, drag into any of the hot spots, and the window will scroll diagonally. (Once again, if you hit any icons as they scroll by, they'll be selected.)

The further out you drag, the faster things will scroll: variable-speed diagonal scrolling!

Drag-scroll in list view. Dragging an icon scrolls a list-view window, too, but only in vertical directions. This is particularly convenient when you want to put an item into a folder that's not currently displayed in the list: drag the icon up or down, pausing in either the window's header or the bottom scroll area.

Keyboard window scrolling. Scroll desktop windows vertically without touching the mouse: using Page Up or Page Down is like clicking in the vertical scroll bar above or below the scroll box, while pressing Home or End is like dragging the scroll box to the top or bottom of the scroll bar.

Folders and Paths

The Path menu. To see a window's "path"—which folder it's in, and which folder *that* one's in, and which folder *that* one's in, all the way back to the disk—point to the window's title, hold down ⌘, and press the mouse button. (You have to point to the window title itself, not just the title bar, and this works only on the active window.) This Path menu should look familiar—it's the one you see in Open and Save dialogs.

To move to any window listed in the menu, just select it in the menu. The window opens (if it's not already open) and comes to the top of whatever other windows are opened on the desktop.

Command-click on a window title to see the Path menu that tells you the "path" back up to the hard drive.

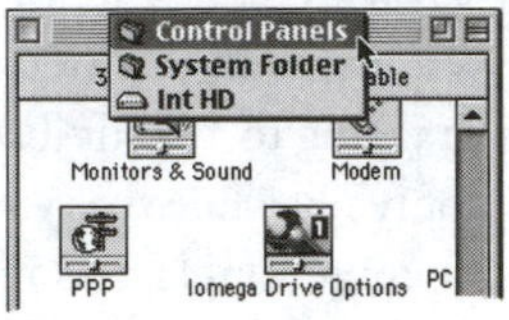

You can get a Path menu for a pop-up window, but only when it's popped up, not when it's a tab at the bottom of the screen. (There's more about pop-up windows, and window tabs, at the end of this chapter.)

When the disk icon is missing. When there's no disk icon at the top of the Path menu, the folder is out on the desktop. Isn't that ridiculous? It's already difficult to tell what disk a folder belongs to if it's out on the desktop and you have multiple disks mounted—wouldn't this have been a great way to find out where that folder belongs?

Closing windows behind you. Just as Option automatically closes windows in other desktop situations, you can use it for closing windows while you're using the Path menu. Just hold Option when you select something from the Path menu and the current window closes as the new one opens.

Keyboard commands for navigating paths. You can open, close, and activate windows from the keyboard as if you were using the Path menu:

- ⌘↓ opens a selected folder. (Of course, so does ⌘O, but the ↓ option is also available in order to match the other keyboard commands described here.)
- ⌘Option↓ opens a selected folder while closing its "parent."
- ⌘↑ activates the parent of the current window, opening it if necessary.
- ⌘Option↑ activates the parent while closing the current window.

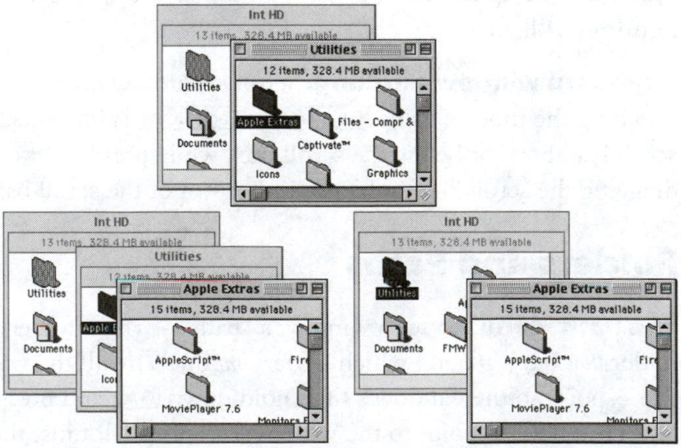

With the Apple Extras folder selected (top), Command-down opens it (bottom, left), and Command-Option-down opens the folder and closes the window that it's in (bottom, right).

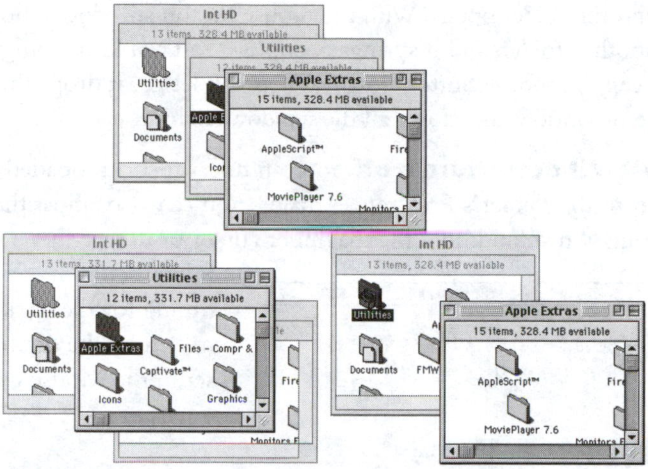

With the Apple Extras folder window active (top), Command-up activates its parent (bottom, left), and Command-Option-up activates the parent and closes the current window (bottom, right).

Spring-Loaded Folders.

The basics. One of OS 8's little joys is the way you can drill down through layers of folders without having to double-click your mouse to death and leave a trail of open windows behind you.

To use the desktop's "spring-loaded" folders, you use another new-to-OS 8 feature, the click-and-a-half: click the mouse button, release it, and click it again, keeping it down the second time. When you do this while you're on a folder, you'll see the pointer change to a magnifying glass; the folder will blink, then open. As long as you keep the mouse button down, you can hover over the next folder for a second or two, and it opens, and so does the next, and so on. The great thing about this feature is that the folders spring closed, too: as soon as you let go of the mouse button, all the windows except the final one close.

Some things to keep in mind:

- Once the folder springs open and you want to drill down further, but you can't see the next folder you want, hold the cursor at any edge of the window, or on a scroll control, to make the window scroll.
- If a folder you're drilling through is already open, its window will move to where you're holding the mouse cursor.
- If you drag the cursor out of the window area, the window closes and you'll be back in the previous window.
- If you try to look up "spring-loaded folders" in the Mac's help system, you won't be able to find it there. In an apparent terminology snit, it's listed as "spring-open" folders.

The spring-open drag. The handiest aspect of spring-loaded folders is that you can trigger it without a click-and-a-half. Just drag an icon over a folder as if you were going to drop it in, but don't let go; keep the mouse button down, and the folder opens. With the mouse button still down, hold the icon over another folder, and it springs open, too. You can keep going as long as you keep the mouse button down. When you let go, it drops the icon into the current window and closes all the windows behind it.

Slow it down, turn it off. You can turn off spring-loaded folders completely from the Finder's Preferences dialog. You can also adjust the delay for how long you should hold the magnifier cursor or dragged icon over a closed folder before it springs open. (The timing for the click-and-a-half is controlled by the double-click time that's set in the Mouse control panel.)

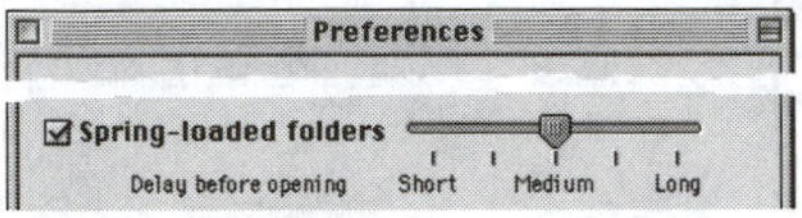

Window Views

The View Options dialogs. The View menu (and pop-up desktop windows) have a View Options command that opens a dialog with various choices for how the contents of a window are displayed. The choices in the dialog depend on how you've set the window view: as Icon, as Buttons, or as List. The pictures here give you an idea of the differences among the dialogs. As you can see, the icon and button view options are very similar, while the list-view options are completely different.

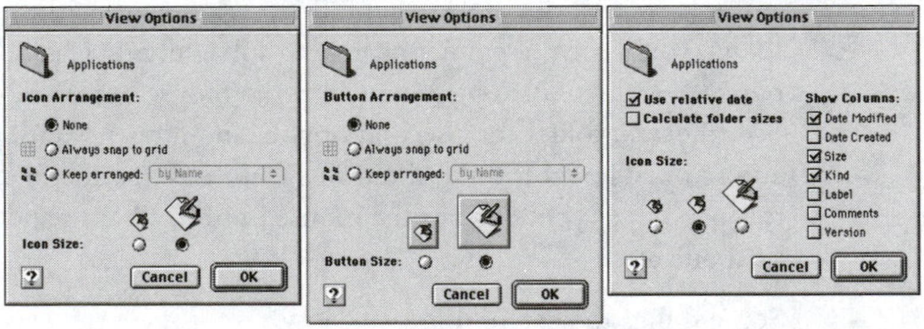

These are the three View Options dialog for the same window, based on how the window's view has been set: as icons, as buttons, or as a list.

Arranging things. No matter which type of window view you choose—icons, buttons, or list—you can arrange the window contents according to any of the usual criteria. In a nice piece of attention to detail, the View menu has the command Arrange By for icon and button views, and Sort By for list views, since you're stuck with the columnar arrangement in a list view. The submenu for Arrange By lists all the possibilities; the Sort By submenu lists only those columns that are displayed in the current window. (If the Arrange or Sort command is dimmed, it's because the window is set, through the View Options command, to the Keep Arranged option (described in the next section).

Desktop icons. Here's a new OS 8 feature that you might never notice because most people don't look at the View menu when there's no window open. But now you can change the look of loose icons on the desktop. You can change their type (icon or button, small or large), snap them to the grid (okay, that was always available), and keep them arranged by name, date, and so on. (Changing the size and icon type affects both volume and trash icons; arranging things by name or date affects everything *except* volume icons and the trash.)

Window by window instead of global. There's no more Views control panel. In previous systems, it let you: set the font for the desktop, turn the snap-to grid on and off, set the size of list-view icons, and define which columns would appear in list views. With the exception of setting the desktop font, which is accessed through the Appearances control panel, all these options are now set on a window-by-window basis instead of globally, using commands in the View menu.

Using "seed" folders. When you create a folder, it inherits all the options you've set for the window in which you created it. If your window is set to be viewed as a list of only two columns (name and date, say), sorted by name, and to use large icons, any folder you create inside it will have the same options as defaults. It can take a long time to set all the details of a window to your specifications. Despite some complaints about how these settings are no longer global, it's handy to be able to have different window setups. If there are a few setups you use more than others (say, a two-column sorted-by-name list, a small-icon button view that stays arranged by name, and a standard-sized icon no-grid window), you can make "seeds" from which you can create as many like-designed folders as you want.

Create your seed folders with descriptive names (*2-col Name List, Small buttons, Free Icons)* and set them to appropriate options. Gather them together in a Seed folder, set them to be small buttons, and make the Seed folder pop-up window.

> ***And it's possible to build the [Mac II's} RAM up to two gigabytes by filling the slots with RAM cards. Those numbers are so staggering that they made me break out laughing when I first read the specs. what could anyone possibly do with two gigabytes of RAM?***
>
> *Michael D. Wesley, MacUser, April 1987*

Whenever you need a folder of a specific type, click the Seed tab, click the folder button (the Seed window closes automatically) and make the new folder inside that window. Drag the new folder to the location you want. This all takes seconds and is lots easier than setting all the options every time you need a special type of folder.

Icon and Button Views

Icons versus buttons. The new choice for icons in OS 8 is the button view: turn every icon in a window into a button by using the View menu's As Button command. The difference between standard icons and buttons is that you need a double-click to open a regular icon but it takes only a single click to open a button. (When we refer to "icons" in this and other chapters, that usually encompasses both standard and button icons.)

Both button and icon views offer two sizes in their View Options dialog. Choosing the smaller of the two icon views puts the icon's title to the right of the icon instead of beneath it. The smaller of the two button options is about the size of a standard icon; the large button option is giant-size, to accommodate the full-size icon. The size settings are independent of each other: move from a standard icon size and view to a button view, set the buttons to small, move back to the icon view—and you won't see small icons, but the standard size you had the last time you used that view.

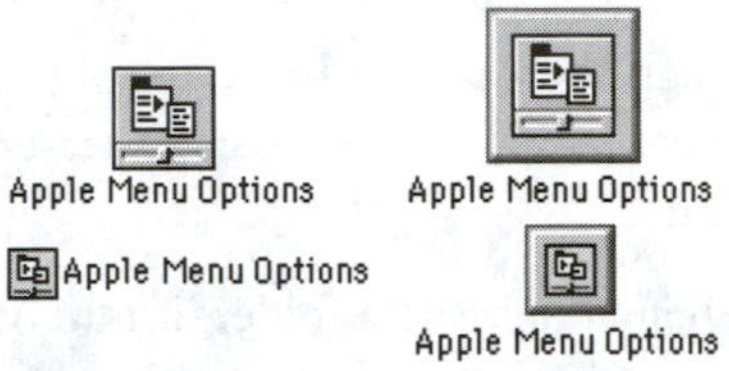

Large and small icons (left) and buttons (right.)

Using small icons on the desktop saves a lot of room.

Use small desktop icons. If you're leaving out a bunch of icons on the desktop for easy access, there's no sense in taking up more room than necessary. Use View Options for the desktop and change the icons to a smaller size. You get the added benefit of the icon name's being to the side of the icon rather than beneath it, making it easier to stack them.

Arranging things. Use the View menu's Arrange submenu to organize icons in a window according to their names, dates (created or modified), size, kind, or label. To quickly straighten things if you don't have auto-grid on while you're moving things around, use the Clean Up command to position all the icons at the same time—although you might not be so happy when things zoom to grid points away from the spots you want them to be. When you Clean Up, icons are reorganized not only to fill empty grid points, but also so that you'll have to scroll in only one direction to see them all—they get stacked vertically in as many columns as the width of the window can accommodate.

Auto-arranging things. A window arrangement lasts only as long as you don't move anything in it or add anything to it. If you'd like a window *always* arranged, use the Keep Arranged option in View Options for that window. Click the button and select how you want things arranged from the pop-up. Then try dropping things into the window: you'll find that everything shuffles around so the new item can be positioned correctly. In addition, if you resize the window, everything is reorganized so that you'll always be able to see the first few ordered items at the top of the window—as with the Clean Up command, you'll have to scroll only vertically to see the rest of

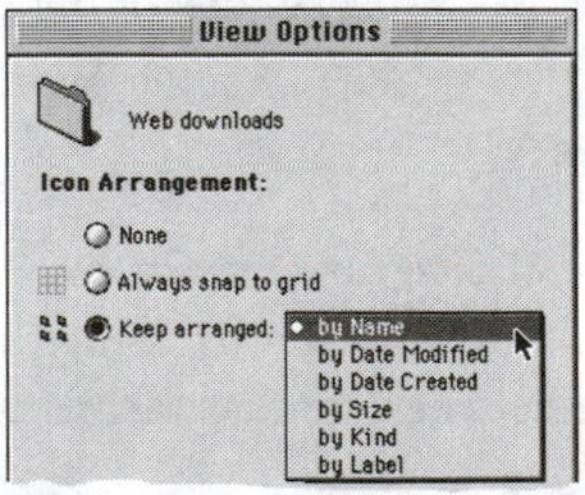

Making a permanent arrangement.

the items in the window. A window with the Keep Arranged setting active has a little icon in its header (matching the one in the control panel) to show that the setting's active.

As disconcerting as it can be when you resize a Keep Arranged window and everything jumps around to fit the new window size, keeping icons arranged in a window is a very efficient approach.

Any time you want things to stay alphabetical but easily available, and yet don't want a list view (the Control Panels folder, for instance, or the System Folder), you can use the Keep Arranged option. Or, you might want your document folder to always come up with its icons sorted by date.

Working with button icons. The button-icon view introduced in OS 8 is handy but not always intuitive.

- At first, it seems that you can't move the buttons inside a window, except perhaps by using a Clean Up command: when you press the mouse button to drag the icon button, it's interpreted as a click and opens the button. But if you drag the button by its *name*, you can re-position it in the window.
- It also seems at first that you can't select a button icon without selecting its name for editing, because the only place to click on it without clicking the button itself is on its name. But there are two ways to select a button icon without selecting its name. One way is to drag a rectangle around it (as if you were going to select multiple icons). Actually, you don't really have to draw a rectangle: just sort of drag the mouse right through the icon. Or, hold down Shift and click on the button to select it without triggering it. The only indication of a button icon's selected state is the fact that the name itself is selected, but not activated for editing.

Selecting a button icon without triggering it.

- It doesn't "feel" as if it would work, but you can drag an item right onto a button as if it were a standard icon. The icon inside the button (not the entire button) darkens as it would if it were a standard icon.
- You can't trigger the spring-loaded option on a folder that's a button, because you can't ever get to the click-and-a-half you need: the first click triggers the button. But if, while you're drilling down from a higher folder, you encounter a folder button, you can hold the magnifying glass cursor over it and it will spring open. And, if you drag an item onto a folder button and hold it there a second or two, the folder springs open just as a standard folder icon would.

The List View

The new List views. OS 8's new List views looks familiar enough to be comfortable to work in with no extra learning effort, but there are a few changes that make working with lists a little easier.

The most obvious change is the gray approach, which allows for tiny white dividing lines for the rows; while I don't like the gray background, I do appreciate the horizontal divisions that make reading a row easier.

One of the best changes is the column headers: no longer plain-text labels that most people didn't realize acted as buttons for sorting purposes, the column headers look like the buttons that they are. And instead of a subtle underlined title to indicate which column the window's sorted by, now we have the entire column darkened.

The other best change is the sorting arrow at the top of the vertical scroll bar that lets you choose ascending or descending sorts in the window.

The columns. There can be up to eight columns of information in list-view window: Name, Date Modified, Date Created (new in OS 8), Size, Kind, Label, Comments, and Version. The Name column is always present, but the others can be turned on or off for each window through the View Options dialog. You'll find that the Sort List submenu in the View menu changes to accommodate only those columns showing—which is a shame, because it sure would be convenient to sort things by, say, label, without having to keep its column showing.

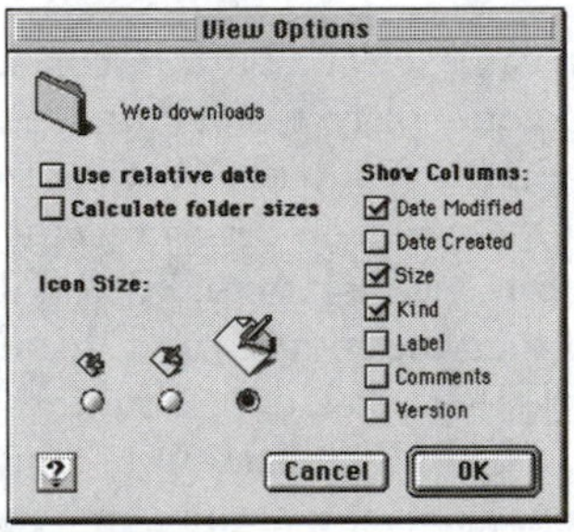

Control the columns in a list window by checking or unchecking them in the View Options dialog.

Unfortunately, we *still* can't re-order the columns in a list-view window, or adjust their sizes (that's for OS 8.5!). The size of the name column changes its width automatically to accommodate a full name, at whatever font size you've chosen in the Appearance control panel.

Icon size in list views. The View Options for list views provides three choices for icon size; in the dialog, there doesn't seem to be much difference between the smallest and the middle one, but that's because the icons themselves in the button labels are misleading.

You really have only two size choices for icons in the list view: standard and small. The third choice—the tiny one in the dialog—actually switches the icons in the dialog to generic icons that indicate only what type of file something is (folder, application, document) without any of the identifying artwork that tells you which application or what kind of document.

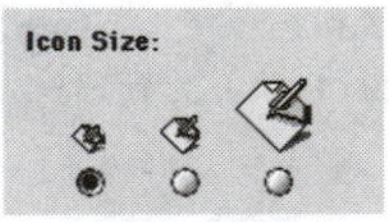

Selecting the smallest of the icon sizes gives you generic icons in a list view.

Folder sizes. Folder sizes are not listed in the Size column of a list-view window unless you turn on the *Calculate folder sizes* option in the View Options dialog. It may seem that this slows things down in the Finder, since the folder sizes get filled in rather slowly when you first open a window that lists folder sizes. But if you keep in mind that you don't have to wait for the sizes to be filled in before you do something else—you can work in the window, or outside of it while the Mac does the calculations. You can even work in an application while the Finder keeps churning away in the background. (Of course, if you want to check relative folder sizes, you'll just have to wait for all of them to be listed.)

Yesterday and today. Most people are pleasantly surprised to find that the dates on their files are sometimes stamped *Today* or *Yesterday.* (After all, how many times have you stopped to figure out what today's date is—and then

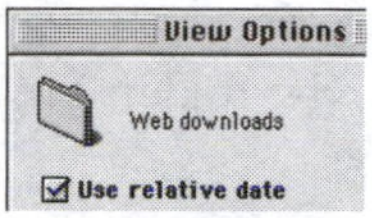

how many times do you wind up clicking on the menubar clock for just that information?) But if you want the actual date instead of the relative one, uncheck the *Use relative date* option in the View Options dialog for any window.

Yesterday and today aren't the only relative dates available. Use the Date & Time control panel to set the date ahead by a day, then create and save a document. Set the date back to the correct day, and take a look at the date on that document.

Smart modified dates for folders. A folder is considered modified, and its modified date is altered, when you move something into or out of it, just as it was in earlier systems. OS 8, however cleans up the worst of the old modified-date problems: if you alter a file in a folder, the folder's modified date changes, keeping the folder with your most recent work in it at the top of the modified list. (That sounds logical, but it didn't used to happen that way.)

Another situation where the OS 8 Finder is smarter is in regard to temporary files. Some applications create temporary files while you're working and then erase them when you quit. In previous systems, a folder holding temporary files was "modified" both when the files were created and when they were erased; back in the Finder, the folder had a new modified date/time even though its contents were the same as before. In the situations I was able to test, the temporary application files didn't affect the folder's modified date.

Keep in mind that the modified date of a document sometimes gets altered by an application even if all you've done is *looked* at a file and closed it again without making any changes. If a document's modified date changes, so does its folder.

Live updates for open windows. In previous systems, saving a file to a folder whose window was open on the desktop didn't always work correctly because the modified date for the saved file wasn't updated for a long time—or sometimes, at all, until the window was closed and re-opened. It works fine now!

Working with Hierarchical Lists

The hierarchical list. The list view lets you see a hierarchical outline of your folders and files by *expanding* and *collapsing* folders in the list to see their contents. (It's important to stick with the terms *expand* and *collapse* so as not to confuse those operations with *opening* or *closing* a folder.)

To expand a folder, you click on the arrow in front of it; the contents of a folder are listed beneath it, indented beneath the folder's name. To collapse it, you click on the arrow again. The arrow changes its direction when a folder is expanded or collapsed. (If you double-click on an arrow by mistake, the second click will be ignored—a very subtle, very nice touch.)

A folder "remembers" how far you expanded its contents, so if you collapse it and later expand it again, the contents are listed the way you left them. And if you close a window and re-open it, the folders are expanded to the level that you last used in that window.

A folder in a list with no arrow in front of it is merely an alias of a folder—you can't expand it because an alias opens its original, and nothing else. A downward-pointing arrow in front of a folder with nothing expanded beneath means the folder is empty.

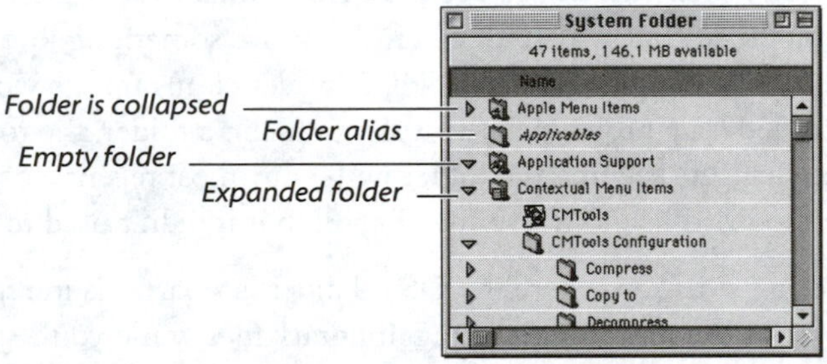

The direction of the hierarchical arrow, and what's listed under a folder, tell you about the folder and its contents.

Expanding and collapsing inner levels. Folders that are listed beneath other folders can be expanded or collapsed independently, so you can expand the hierarchical list as far as you need it. To have all of a folder's contents expanded as far as possible, hold Option as you click on the folder's arrow to expand it. This saves your having to click separately on all its inner folders and their inner folders, and so on.

Holding Option while you click on an arrow to collapse a folder collapses all the inner folders, too, so that the next time you expand it you'll see only the top level of its contents.

Expanding folder interactions. What happens when you try to expand a folder that shows in a list, but it's already opened as either a standard or pop-up window? A folder that's already opened is still listed in its parent folder's list view, with an arrow in front of it; its icon is darkened, just as its full-size icon would be darkened to indicate that it's open.

You can't both expand and open a folder, so as soon as you click on the arrow, the opened window closes—whether it was a standard window or a pop-up window. Click the arrow again, and the folder's list merely collapses—it doesn't turn back into a window.

Conversely, if you have a folder expanded in a list view and then open it, its window opens but its list collapses in the parent window. Closing the folder's window doesn't automatically expand it again.

Expanding and collapsing with the keyboard. You can use these keyboard commands to expand and collapse folders. (And, since you can select folders from the keyboard, too, you don't need the mouse for manipulating Finder windows.) Notice that adding Option to the sequence affects the inner folders, just as it does when you're clicking on the folder arrows.

- ⌘→ expands the first level of the selected folder.
- ⌘Option→ expands all the levels of the selected folder.
- ⌘← collapses the selected folder without affecting the expansion level inside it.
- ⌘Option← collapses the selected folder, and also collapses all the folders within it.

You can collapse all the folders inside a list-view window by holding down ⌘ while pressing A and then ←. This triggers the Select All command (⌘A) and then the collapse command (⌘←).

Sorting in List Views

Sorting lists. There are two ways to sort the items in a list-view window: use the Sort List submenu (in the View menu or in the pop-up menu) or simply click on the column name in the window. The currently sorted column in a window is always a darker shade of gray.

Use the direction arrow at the top of the vertical scroll bar to set the sorting order to ascending or descending; the direction of the arrow itself tells you which is the current order.

Most sorting is actually grouping. Sorting a list by anything other than Name actually groups items, not sorts them, since only an item's name is unique—you can have many items with the same Kind, or Date Modified, or even Comments. When items are grouped together by the criterion you've chosen, they'll be subsorted automatically by name—that is, they'll be listed alphabetically within the group.

Sorting criteria. Here's a quick roundup of the sorting criteria in list-view windows, assuming the default, ascending sorting order:

- **by Name** sorts alphabetically by the item's name.
- **by Date Modified** sorts with the most recent date on top.
- **by Date Created** sorts with the most recent date on top.

- **by Kind** sorts alphabetically according the item's type (application, document, folder, and so on).
- **by Size** sorts the list so that the largest item is at the top.
- **by Label** sorts the items according to the order that the labels appear in the Label submenu.
- **by Version** sorts by version numbers with the lowest—(that's usually the oldest)—on top. Version numbers are used mainly for applications and system files like extensions and control panels. But because version numbers are a strange mixture of numbers, multiple decimals, and letters, you won't always get what you expect. Some of the items in my Extensions folder sort in this version order: 1.0, 1.0.1, 1.0.3, 1.0a, 2.0.1, 2.0.8, 2.06, 4.0.1, 4.0b.
- **by Comments** sorts items alphabetically by the first few words in the Comments field of their Get Info windows.

The Mac alphabet. File names are alphabetized both in list-view windows on the desktop and in Open and Save dialogs. If you know the Mac's alphabetizing rules, you can force a document or folder to the top or bottom of a list by changing its name.

- There's no difference between capitals and lowercase letters: *file, FILES,* and *Filet* would be sorted in exactly that order.
- Numbers come before letters: *9* comes before *A*, and *folder 1* comes before *folder A*.
- Numbers are sorted alphabetically. Just as *B* comes after *AA*, *2* comes after *11* because the first character is the one that counts in the alphabetization.
- Punctuation marks come before, between, and after letters and numbers. With the exception of the carat (^) and the @ sign, the symbols on the keyboard's number keys, and the plus and minus signs, come before both letters and numbers. Other punctuation symbols sort between the numbers and the letters; some are sorted after the letters of the alphabet. Here's a quick roundup of the sorting order for characters that show on your keyboard:

  [space] ! " # $ % &' ( ) * + , - . /
  0, 1, 2... 9
  ; < = > ? @
  A, B, C... Z
  [\ ] ^ _ ` { | } ~

- Option characters (the ones you type with Option), like punctuation, sort before, between, and after numbers and letters. The ones most often used in icon names (•, §, ∞, ™, *f*, ®, and ©) are sorted at the end, after numbers, letters, and punctuation marks.

If all this seems difficult to remember because it makes no sense, rest assured: it *is* difficult to remember, but it *does* make sense. The symbols are sorted according to their ASCII codes (covered in Chapter 12) except for the fact that upper- and lowercase letters are considered equal for Mac sorting.

Getting numbers to sort where you want them. If you use numbers in folder or file names, whether at the front of the name or inside it somewhere, it's relatively easy to make the numbers sort correctly: just add leading spaces before the numbers. If the highest number you're using is double-digit, you need only a single leading space in front of the single-digit numbers. If your numbers go into three digits, you'll need two spaces in front of single digits and one space in front of double digits to keep everything sorted correctly.

No leading spaces	*Leading spaces*
Chapter 1	Chapter 1
Chapter 10	Chapter 2
Chapter 2	Chapter 3
Chapter 3	Chapter 10

Folder sizes in sorting. When you sort by Size, folders are clumped together at the bottom of the list unless the *Calculate folder sizes* option is turned on.

Sort-of inherited sorting. When you select a sorting order for a list-view window, the sorting order is also used by any folder you expand in that window—it doesn't matter if the folder is expanded before or after you do the sort. Change the sorting order for the window, and the sublist(s) change their order, too. But a subfolder doesn't inherit the sorting order (or even the list view, for that matter) if you open it into a separate window. This applies to the direction of the sort, too.

Pop-up Windows

Pop-up window basics. Use the As Pop-up Window command in the View menu to turn the active window into a pop-up window that sits at the bottom of the screen, with its name in a tab at the top of what used to be the title bar. Click in the tab to collapse the window down to *just* a tab at the bottom of the screen. Click the tab again to pop the window back up.

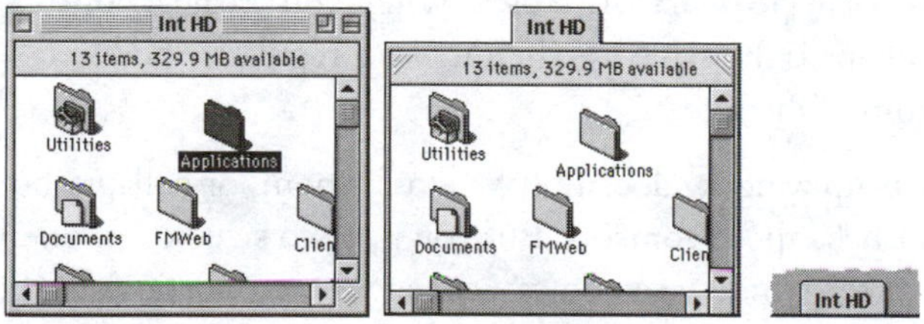

A standard window, its pop-up version (which is glued to the bottom of the screen), and its tab-only mode.

To turn the pop-up back into a standard window, use the View menu's As Window command when the window is popped up.

As you create pop-up windows, the tabs are neatly arrayed from left to right across the screen, with the tabs just large enough to display the name of the window. There's only so much room at the bottom of your screen, of course, and you can't make a second row of tabs. You'll get a dialog telling you to make some room if you try to make another tab when there's no room left.

Closing pop-up windows. This is getting a separate entry because I want to be sure you notice it! You can spend the rest of your desktop life clicking on the tab of an opened pop-up window to pop it back down, and that will work just fine. But you should realize that clicking *anywhere* outside the pop-up window closes it automatically, because a popped-up window has to be the active window. If you click on another tab, in an opened window, or even on the desktop, the window turns back into a tab.

In addition, any command that closes a standard desktop window also pops down a popped-up window: using the File menu's Close command, a contextual menu's Close command, pressing ⌘W, or using one of the Close All options like Shift Option W.

The drag method. Drag any window down to the bottom of the screen, and it automatically turns into a tab. There are two advantages to this method: it's a single step (using the View menu, you have to create the pop-up window, then close it down to a tab); and you can put the tab anywhere along the bottom of the screen instead of its taking the next available spot.

Dragging a popped-up window away from the bottom of the screen (you don't have to drag it by the tab—any edge will do) turns it back into a standard window.

Where have all the folders gone? Well, unfortunately, they haven't gone anywhere. The folders whose windows you turn into tabs in the hopes of reducing desktop clutter remain wherever they were, just as they do when you double-click on one to open its window. In fact, a folder whose window is a tab has its icon darkened exactly the way it is when you've opened its window. So, a folder stays on the desktop or in its parent folder even while it exists as a tab at the bottom of the screen.

Re-sizing pop-up windows. When you create a pop-up window, its size and shape is the same as when it was a regular window; it's just stuck at the bottom of the screen.

A pop-up window doesn't have close, zoom, or collapse boxes because you don't need those controls. But you get two size boxes, one in each *upper* corner of the window so you can change the proportions of the window.

You won't be able to drag the edge of the window in further than the edge of the tab, so at first it seems that you can't have a window any narrower than its name. But if you make the window narrow before you turn it into a pop-up, you can get a smaller-than-the-name tab, with the end of the name truncated.

A long window name uses a wide tab by default (left); resizing the window before you turn it into a pop-up gives you a smaller tab with a truncated name (right).

And, of course, you don't have to keep the tab centered on the window just because that's the way it starts out. Put the tab on the left or right side by dragging that edge of the window inward.

Moving tabs. You can re-position a window tab by dragging it horizontally along the bottom of the screen to a new spot. But this works only when the tab is just a tab; if the window is popped up, you can't move it at all except to turn it into a regular window.

Editing tab names. When you turn a window into a tab, the tab is sized to accommodate the length of the name. If you edit the folder's name, it changes on the tab, but the tab doesn't change size. So, you can wind up with a longer window name truncated on a tab, or a very wide tab with only a few letters in the center. The only way to adjust it is to change the pop-up window into a standard one and then back again into a pop-up.

Kind of a drag. When you click on a tab to pop up a window, it jumps to its full height. If you'd rather have a shorter view, you can drag the window up by the tab just as far as you want it, although there are two problems with the drag method. First, if you drag too far, you'll have ripped the window away from the bottom of the screen and turned it back into a standard window. The other problem is that you won't have the bottom scroll controls available. But if you know the item you want is right at the top of the window, maybe a little drag is all you need.

Clicking on the tab of a half-popped window like this pops it back down, not up to full height.

Pop-up menus for pop-up windows. You can Control-click directly on a window tab to get the window's contextual menu; you don't have to open the window first. This is handy especially if you want to use the As Window command from the View menu, which would require you to pop the window up first so that it's the active one.

The more you know... Here's a short list of a few more things you should know about pop-up windows:

- You can't exactly drag something into a window tab, as convenient as that would be. If you try, you'll see that the window pops up to its full size as soon as you touch the tab, no matter when you let go of the icon you're dragging. Unless you're *very* quick, the new icon lands at the bottom of the window; if you manage to let it go sooner, *you'll* still wind up at the bottom of the window, where the mouse cursor is.
- When you double-click on the folder of a window that's a tab, the window pops up.

- If you expand the folder of window that's a tab, the tab disappears. Collapsing the folder doesn't put the tab back—that's a manual operation.
- Using the Close All command (adding Option to a standard Close Window command) pops down any opened pop-up window.
- If you start the Mac holding down Option, which closes all its desktop windows, all window tabs will disappear.

IN THE BEGINNING

Macs, like so many other kinds of products, are assigned code names while they're under development. Here's what some of them were:

Mac Plus	Mr. T
Mac SE	Aladdin, Chablis
Mac 30	Green Jade
Mac Classic	XO
Mac II	Milwaukee, Paris
Mac IIx	Spock
Mac IIcx	Aurora
Mac IIci	Aurora II, Pacific
Mac IIsi	Ericson, Raffica
Mac LC	Elsie
Mac LC II	Foster Farms
Quadra 700	Shadow
Quadra 900	Darwin
Mac Portable	Esprit, Laguna, Malibu
PowerBook 100	Derringer, Rosebud
Duos	BOB
PowerMac 7100-66	BHA
PowerMac 8100-80	Cold Fusion
PowerBook 500 series	Blackbird

Bob?? That stood for Best of Both Worlds, for the laptop Duo and its deskbound Dock. And what about that BHA code name for one of the PowerMacs? An additive for breakfast cereals? Nope. It stands for *Butt Head Astronomer*, after the astronomer in question found out that the original code name was *his* name; he objected to the use of his name on a product, even one under development, without his permission or endorsement. I won't use his name in vain, but Apple probably hoped to sell billions and billions of the machine.

Make a GoTo folder. My favorite navigational aid is what I call a GoTo folder which, while "invented" primarily for moving around from within Open and Save boxes (covered in Chapter 12), also helps out on the desktop.

Make a folder that contains aliases of the other folders you use the most: the System Folder, the Fonts folder, the Control Panels folder, whichever application and/or project folders you use a lot. You'll be able to jump to your most-used folders without opening, or drilling down through, lots of other folders first. I've used this approach for a long time, ever since aliases were available in System 7. But with OS 8, it's even handier, because pop-up windows and icon buttons make it work even better.

Create your GoTo folder and put the aliases in it. Set the window to be viewed as buttons, and use the View Options command to make the buttons small. Arrange the icons in a vertical line (you can use the Clean Up command, but that leaves them too far apart, so you'll still have to do a little dragging), and zoom the window so it snaps to a tall, narrow shape; you might have to widen it a little manually so you can see the entire window title. Finally, drag it to the bottom of the screen or use the As Pop-up Window command to turn it into a tab. (You can put the actual folder icon any place; for instance, tuck it into your Utilities folder.)

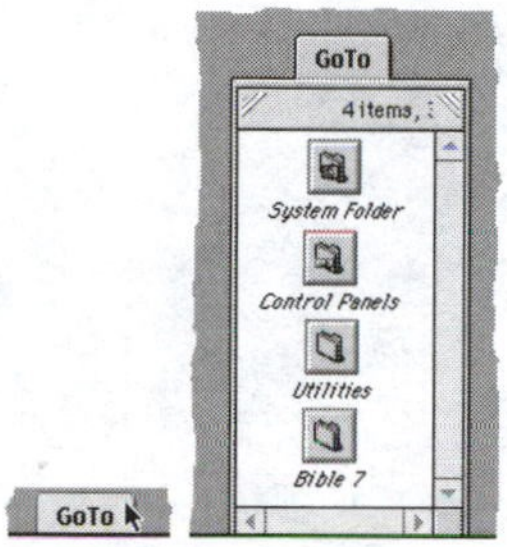

A single click on the tab opens the window; a single click on a button opens that folder and pops the window back down.

What's great about this approach is that the folder is out of the way yet readily available. Click the tab to see your column of buttons; a single click on a button opens that folder. As a bonus, the GoTo window immediately collapses back down into a tab because a pop-up window stays popped up only while it's the active window—and opening another folder makes *it* the active one.

The Launcher can't be a pop-up window. One of the first things I did on my OS 8 desktop was drag the Launcher window down to turn it into a tab. Whoops! Despite its "feel," the Launcher isn't a Finder window, so it doesn't turn into a tab. But you can use several of OS 8's new features to create your own, better, Launcher.

The Launcher control panel
Chapter 12

7

More Desktop

The Trash

Aliases

Find File

Printing from the Desktop

In This Chapter

The Trash

Trashing Items

The new trash can. When you drag something into the empty trash icon, the icon changes—its lid comes off. (Never mind that you should take the lid off *before* you try putting something in it....) Items dragged to the trash stay in it until you use the Special menu's Empty Trash command.

The Move to Trash command. There's a new command in OS 8's File menu: Move to Trash. Finally! You don't have to drag stuff to the trash to get rid of it! Just select an icon—or multiple icons—and choose Move to Trash. Even better, you don't need to use the menu command: send a selected item to the trash by pressing ⌘Delete. This keyboard command is listed in the File menu next to Move to Trash, but the standard menu symbol for Delete is used, so you might be a little confused as to what key it refers to.

> *Don't you think we're all old enough now to have a Delete command that would let us erase a selected icon without having to drag it to the Great Trash Can in the Corner??*
>
> *Sharon Aker, The Mac Almanac, 1994*

Using the contextual menu. The other way to send an item to the trash without the menu command is to use the contextual menu that pops up when you Control-click on an item. The advantage to using this is that you don't even have to select the item first: just Control-click on it and choose the Move to Trash command. If you have items already selected, Control-clicking on one of them and using the command sends all of them to the trash.

The warning dialog. When you use the Empty Trash command, you get a warning dialog asking if you're sure you want to permanently delete the items in the trash. Personally, I like that dialog: it tells me how many megs of space I'm about to free up on my drive. (It's still amazes and amuses me that the contents of my trash usually take up more space than the entire capacity of my first hard drive.) But the dialog annoys lots of users, who don't seem to realize they can turn it off. Select the trash icon and choose Get Info from the File menu, then uncheck the *Warn before emptying* option. The trash's Info window provides lots of handy information about your trashed items, too: how many there are, what kind they are, and how much room they take on the disk.

The trash warning can be turned off by unchecking the setting in the Info window.

Reverse the warning. If you like the trash warning, as I do, you can leave it on and just bypass it occasionally by holding Option as you choose the Empty Trash command. Even the ellipses after the command goes away temporarily.

If you'd like the opposite effect—keeping the warning off as the default and only occasionally turning on to see the results of some major disk-cleaning before the trash is emptied—Option works for that, too, because the key actually reverses the trash Warning setting.

Checking the warning setting. You can check the trash warning setting without opening the trash's Info window: just look at the command in the menu. If it has the ellipses (Empty Trash…), the warning's on; without it (Empty Trash) the warning's off. Isn't that elegant? The ellipsis that signifies a dialog will open if you select a command goes away when there won't be any dialog.

Retrieving Items

Retrieving from the trash. It's easy to take something out of the trash: just open the trash by double-clicking on it, and drag the item you want out of the trash window. (Of course, if you've emptied the trash, you won't find the item there.)

The Put Away command. The File menu's Put Away command zips an icon back to where it came from. Selecting an item in the trash and choosing Put Away sends the item back to the folder it came from. You can even drag an item from the trash to the desktop, and later use the Put Away command on it.

(Put Away's not only for trashed items—it works when you've put something on the desktop from a folder, or even from the Find File utility: just select the items and choose Put Away.)

Trashed items aren't erased. When you use the Empty Trash command, the items in the trash are not actually erased from the disk. What happens is that the item's entry in the disk's directory (the invisible file that keeps track of what's on the disk) is erased, and the parts of the disk where the item was stored are marked as available for re-use. As long as that part of the disk isn't used, the file is actually still there. That's how "recovery" software works—it can find parts of files in apparently unused disk sectors and piece them back together.

When you empty the trash by mistake. Stop! Immediately! Don't do anything except run a trash-recovery utility.

File recovery
Chapter 24

If you work with any documents at all, or copy anything to your disk after you empty the trash, you run the risk of re-using the sectors where the file you want back was stored—and once you do that, there's no hope of recovering the information.

You may think that working on an existing document couldn't possibly affect the recently vacated disk sectors because, after all, the current document already exists on the disk. Well, it does, but editing it may change the file size and "spill over" into another sector—just the one you need preserved for your file recovery program.

Some users make the mistake of running out for file-recovery software, copying it to their hard drives, and then running it to get the erased file back. Guess what? Sometimes the recovery software is written to the disk right on top of the files it was supposed to rescue.

Trash Tidbits

The communal trash can. Like the desktop itself, the trash is communal property, used by all the volumes you can see on your Mac. You can't erase just the items trashed from, say, the internal drive while leaving the ones from the external drive.

Trash in Apple menu. If you like to check out what's in your trash (which is much more socially acceptable than digging through someone else's garbage), put an alias of your trash in the Apple Menu Items folder. You'll get a submenu listing the items in the trash, and it's always available to you even if you're not in the Finder.

Since the trash is actually something of a glorified folder from the Finder's point of view, if you put an alias of your hard drive in your Apple menu, you'll see the trash listed in its submenu, with its own submenu of contents.

The trash window reports 106 items, but the Info window gives the more accurate count because it includes items inside folders.

Counting trashed items. The item count in the trash window is calculated the same way as for other desktop windows: a folder in the window counts as one item no matter how many items it might hold. If you want a more accurate count, use Get Info on the trash—it counts the items *inside* other items.

The Rescued Items folder. Sometimes a Rescued Items folder shows up in the trash. The files inside the folder are the temporary files an application makes while you're working; if the Mac crashes, the temporary files get dumped into the Rescued folder in the trash. Sometimes you can open these files and recover some of the work you perhaps forgot to save before the crash.

Now isn't that just *wonderful?!* Files preserved at the very last minute, files perhaps containing information that you thought was gone for good, files that might save your very hide… and they're hidden in the trash—where you probably never look—because, of course, why would you? The only things in there are the things you put there because you didn't want them anymore, right?

In any case, if you crash while you're working and you've lost some work, the trash is the first place to check when you restart.

The Trash and Removable Disks

Now you see it... When you drag an item from a floppy or other ejectable disk into the trash, and then eject the disk, the items disappear from the trash. But that's not because they're automatically erased (as was true in some early Mac systems); it's just that they're in an invisible trash folder on the disk they came from in the first place. When you reinsert that disk, they'll pop right back into your trash.

Making room on a floppy. If you're going to erase items from a floppy or other ejectable (like a Zip cartridge) to make room for something new you want to copy to it, you don't have to trash the items, empty the trash, then drag the new items over. Skip the middle step: drag the old items to the trash and then drag the new items to the disk. You'll get a dialog telling you that you can't do that unless you empty the trash first—and it offers to empty it. Saves about three seconds every time!

If the Mac doesn't offer to empty the trash for you in this situation, and you get only the dialog telling you there's not enough room on the disk, that means that there wouldn't be enough room even if the items in the trash were erased.

IN THE BEGINNING

Just some notes on the evolution of the trash can:

- The trash can didn't always react when you put something in it. The bulging trash can was added in 1987 with System 5.4/Finder 4.0.
- The trash-as-folder approach was introduced in System 7.
- In the old days, if you dragged a floppy to the trash to eject it, and there were items you had dragged from the disk to the trash, those items would be erased before the disk was ejected.
- In the earliest systems, dragging an empty folder to the trash would make the folder disappear completely.

Ejecting disks. It goes against all common sense. It's totally counter-intuitive. But it's true. Dragging a floppy or other ejectable disk to the trash ejects it. (Hey, I remember when that feature was introduced and we all loved it as a shortcut for the Eject Disk command; Apple wouldn't dare dump the feature now. I hope.)

The drag-to-trash as an eject mechanism is actually even more general than that. It's not so much an *eject* mechanism as it is an *unmount* mechanism; so, dragging the icon of a shared network volume to the trash breaks the network connection to that volume.

Tiny Trash Troubles

Trashing locked icons. Normally, a locked icon can't be erased; if you put it in the trash and use the Empty Trash command, you'll get a dialog telling you so. If there's a mixture of locked and unlocked items waiting to be trashed, the dialog simply notes that it can't erase locked items and asks if you want the other items erased.

It may seem at that point that you'll have to manually open the trash and unlock the locked file(s) in order to erase them, but that's not the case. If you try to empty the trash when it has *only* locked files in it, you'll get a more helpful dialog, one that provides the solution for erasing locked files even when they're mixed with others. The dialog tells you to hold down Option while choosing Empty Trash if you want to erase a locked file. So, stay a step ahead and hold down the key whenever you want to erase locked files.

(Now, why do you suppose that the dialogs can't be even more helpful? Instead of just telling you to hold down Option, why doesn't the dialog offer to go ahead and erase them for you? Why doesn't the first dialog, for that matter, give you the option (no pun intended) of erasing the locked files?)

The Mac refuses to erase locked files when they're mixed in with others (foreground) but tells you how to do it when there's only locked files in the trash (background).

The Option clash. If you've been paying attention in this trash section, you may have noticed a potential clash: holding Option while selecting Empty Trash erases locked items in the trash—but it also reverses the Warning setting. This causes a slight problem in one of the four possible combinations of your warning setting and using Option.

If you have the warning off, but hold down Option to turn it on (say you wanted to see how much room you're about to free up on your drive), and there's nothing in the trash except locked files, everything gets erased with no further ado. No dialog about the contents of the trash, even though you wanted it. No dialog telling you there are locked files in there, so you've accidentally bypassed a built-in safety measure.

Trashing items with the same name. The trash can't hold two items with the same name. You probably won't ever notice this, since if you drag something into the trash, and an item with the same name is already there, the first one in is quietly renamed without your ever being notified.

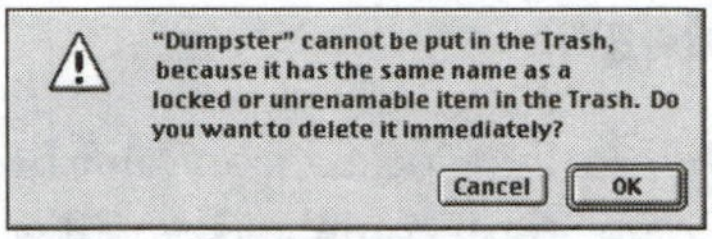

The trash offers instant erasure for some items.

If the file that's already in the trash is locked, however, it can't be automatically renamed. In that case, you'll get the dialog shown here.

Files in use. You can't erase a file that's in use. You can put it in the trash, but you won't be able to erase it: you'll get a dialog telling you it's in use and couldn't be erased.

This all seems reasonable and logical—erasing a document that's still open in an application, or an extension that's still running in the background would wreak all sorts of havoc. But sometimes the "in use" definition isn't all that obvious—and sometimes it's bogus. Occasionally a document that was used during the current work session won't be released from its "in use" status until you quit the application—even though you've closed the document. Situations like a corrupted font file can also trigger the "in use" dialog.

When you get the "in use" refusal to empty the trash, don't worry about it. Try emptying again just before shutting down, when all your applications are closed. If that doesn't work, try again when you start up the Mac. If *that* doesn't work, try starting up the Mac without extensions and then empty the trash.

Trash Tricks

Take it to the edge. It's likely that you'll find yourself dragging items to the trash for months until you get used to the fact that there are keyboard options to send things into the trash. So, as long as you're dragging, wouldn't it be nice to be able to just drag an item off the right edge of the screen and have it wind up in the trash? You can. Simply open the trash window, size it to the full height of your screen, and drag it almost completely off the screen so only its left edge shows at the right edge of the monitor. Drag anything to the edge of the screen, and it winds up in the trash window.

Extra trash cans. If you have a large screen or multiple-monitor setup, make aliases of your trash can and scatter them around. On my two-monitor setup, the 20-inch main screen has a second trash can at the top right (next to the drive icon), and two more cans at the top and bottom of the second screen, at the right edge, where it butts against the larger monitor.

Each alias you make will have the name *alias* appended to it, so you'll wind up with *trash alias, trash alias alias, trash alias alias alias,* and so on. When you rename them, you can't name them all *trash* because you can't duplicate names on the desktop. If you don't feel creative (*Recycle, Wastebasket, Garbage Bin, Dumpster*), you can just leave different numbers of leading and/or trailing spaces around the word *trash* so they'll all look like they're named the same.

Holding tank. Don't you just hate to throw things away because you always realize you need it just right after you've gotten rid of it? You can make a *Hold for trash* folder to act as an interim stopping place for items you think you want to throw away. Occasionally sort the items by date, and if they've sat in the folder, untouched, for months, drag them to the real trash. You can put the folder right next to the trash, or move the trash somewhere else and put the holding folder in the trash's spot.

Eject icon. If it bothers you to drag disks to the trash icon to eject them (but you still like the drag-eject option), make an alias of the trash and change its icon to look like a disk drive opening. In fact, you can edit the icons of two or three trash aliases and place them side by side to make a larger eject target. Name two adjacent aliases *Eject* and *Disks*, or name three of them *Drag* and *here to* and *eject.*

Dumpster. For some unfathomable reason, you can't paste your own icon onto the trash icon—you can't even select it to copy it, although you can both copy and paste over icons on trash aliases. And, of course, the trash actually has two icons anyway, one for empty and one for full (and maybe its unalterableness isn't so unfathomable in light of that). If you want a change-of-trash, though, try the shareware **Dumpster** which lets you choose from hundreds of different trash can icons, and even offers a randomize function so you'll never know what trash receptacle you'll be working with when you start up. All the icons, like the samples shown here, come in empty and full versions.

Aliases

About Aliases

Alias, not a copy. An alias is not a copy of a file, although it's sort of like a copy of the file's *icon*—the alias is a "pointer" to the original file. It exists for one thing, and one thing only: to let you open the original item. When you "open" an alias, it's the original that opens. If you erase an alias or copy it to another disk, it's only the alias that's erased or copied, not the original; if you rename the alias or edit its icon, it's only the alias that changes.

You can alias anything: a document, an application, a folder, even a disk. Why would you want to? Because it lets you access a file from many different locations: in both an Applications folder and the Apple Menu Items folder for instance, or both in the System Folder and on the desktop. An alias is very small, so you won't waste a lot of space with multiple aliases for a single item.

How small? Well, on a small disk an alias takes only a single K of space; on large drives, it can take up to 20K—but that's still very small on a 1GB or greater drive. (Chapter 4 covers the whole issue of how files sizes change with disk sizes.)

I'd like to point out that when my younger son was eleven, he came up with the idea of aliases before Apple did. His internal hard drive was full (games took up a lot of room in pre-CD days), and he asked if he couldn't just put "a picture" of each of the games that were on the external drive onto the internal drive so he wouldn't have to open the second drive's icon. I should've shipped him off to Apple right away; I believe, due to his age, his salary would have been turned over to me.

Making an alias. To make an alias, select an icon and choose Make Alias from the File menu. The alias icon will match the icon of the original; its name will be the same, with *alias* appended to it. Alias' names are always in italics, which makes them easy to spot, and to differentiate from the original.

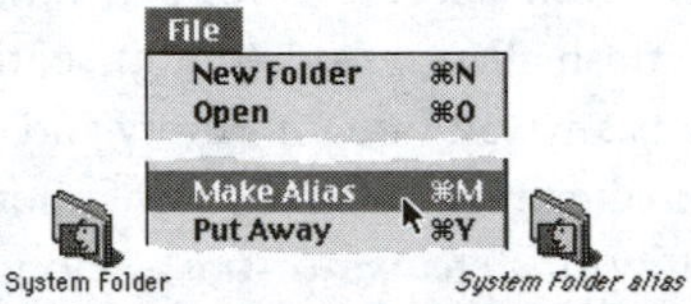

Making an alias.

You can alias more than one item at a time: select as many icons as you want and choose the Make Alias command.

What a drag it is getting aliased. You can create an alias simply by holding down [⌘] and [Option] and dragging an item. If you let go in the same location, the name of the alias will be the standard: the name of the original plus the suffix *alias.* But if you drag it to a new location while you're creating the alias, the Finder is smart enough to leave off the *alias* tag. You'll see the arrow cursor change to the special "make alias" cursor as soon as you press the keys.

Rename the alias. Take that *alias* suffix off your aliases—you don't need a bunch of things in your Apple menu like *Microsoft Word alias* and *ClarisWorks alias.* In most cases you'll want the alias to have the same name as the original.

The quickest way to rename an alias is as you're making it. A new alias has its name selected when it appears, so it's easy to rename it then—all you have to do is type. But if you want it named the same as the original, you don't have to re-type the name:

- Select the icon you want to alias.
- Press [⌘][M] to make the alias.
- Press [→] to move to the end of the editing rectangle.
- Press [Delete] five times, or just hold it down, to erase the word *alias.*

You have to leave the space that was between the icon's name and the word *alias*, because two items can't have exactly the same name in the same folder or on the desktop. (I have a QuicKeys macro in the Finder that does all this whenever I press ⌘M, the Finder's standard Make Alias command; there's more about macros in Chapter 10.)

Renaming the alias or the original. Once you make an alias, you can rename the original file, or move it elsewhere on the disk, and the alias will still find it. You can also rename or move the alias, and the items will still be linked. The only thing that breaks the link is erasing either the original or the alias. (It's a til-death-do-us-part kind of relationship.)

This magical connection is possible because every file and folder you create on a disk has its own unique ID number, assigned and catalogued by the Finder. An alias looks up its original in the Finder's directory according to its ID number, not its name or location.

Finding the original. Getting to the original of an alias is no longer a procedure that requires opening the alias's Info window, as in previous systems. In OS 8, selecting the alias and choosing Show Original from the File menu (or pressing ⌘R) finds the original item.

The one-trick pony. Aliases are only, only, only for opening the original. I'm repeating this because I've seen so many people copy an alias to another disk, then erase the originals, thinking the information was copied to the disk along with the aliases—and being quite surprised, or proud, that the "copies" took so little room. The only thing you copy when you drag an alias to another disk is the alias itself.

Using Aliases

Folder aliases. Aliasing a folder means you can keep it wherever it logically belongs (or is required), no matter how deeply nested, and yet keep it easily accessible by keeping the alias on the desktop, in the Apple menu, or somewhere else more near to the surface.

When you alias a folder, its contents aren't aliased. The most important thing to remember: copying a folder alias to another disk does NOT copy the contents of the original folder there!

Make an alias of a folder, and you get an alias that's permanently glued shut: try to open it, and the original opens (which is, of course the whole point). The folder's window even zooms open from wherever the original folder is, not from the alias. In a list view, a folder alias doesn't even have an arrow that lets you expand its contents (because it doesn't *have* any contents).

Put something into a folder alias, and it instantly winds up in the original folder. For you Star Trek fans and physicists out there, the alias is pretty much a worm hole; for the rest of you, an alias is a little like a chute in Chutes and Ladders.

Desktop alias suggestions. Here are some handy aliases to keep out on the desktop:

- Make desktop aliases for any application or utility that you use with the drag-and-drop method. The instant gratification you get from many drag-and-drop setups fades when you have to open a window or two to access the program. I keep an alias of Word hanging around so I can drag text files into it; and everyone I know keeps an alias of StuffIt Expander out where it can be accessed easily.
- Alias any deeply nested folder that you want to be able to drop things into easily.

Aliases and the Apple menu
Chapter 9

- An alias of the System Folder out on the desktop is especially convenient: any time you want to install a new font, extension, or control panel, all you have to do is drag it into the System Folder alias and it gets routed to the correct spot.
- Put extra trash cans around to save dragging time.
- Alias your hard drive icon if you have a large monitor, or two monitors. You'll be able to double-click on it without traveling so far.

Trash aliases. A trash alias doesn't plump when you put something in it, because you never really put anything in it—things go right to the original trash.

You can also put a trash alias inside a window, which is something you can't do with the regular trash can. This can be a handy way to trash things from a busy folder, although OS 8's Move to Trash command is even handier.

Accessing inner folders on CDs. You can use aliases to speed up retrieval of items from CDs, which are still the slowest of the various storage mediums we use on the Mac. Instead of wading through a series of nested folders to get to the item you want, make an alias of the final, inner folder you usually head for, and keep it on your hard drive. Double-clicking on the alias will open the real folder (or file, for that matter) from the CD without your having to wade through folders there. If the CD isn't inserted at the time, a dialog will tell you which CD you should insert.

Aliases in Open/Save dialogs. When you "open" a folder alias in an Open/Save dialog, it's the same as opening the real thing. This is great, because you can jump from one place to another without traveling through the real hierarchy of folders. If your application always defaults to its own folder for the initial Open or Save command, for instance, you can put an alias of the folder you use for your documents inside the application folder; open the alias, and you move to the real folder.

Opening the alias of a file in an Open dialog, of course, opens the real thing.

The jump-to-folder alias trick. The standard way of using aliases in Open/Save dialogs is handy, but the niftiest trick is using the Option option.

Hold down Option while you "open" an alias in the dialog's list, and you're transferred to the folder that contains the alias; this works whether the alias is for a file or a folder.

You can use the Option option with any of the methods for opening an item in the list:

- Hold Option while you double-click the alias name.
- Select the alias and hold Option while you click the Open button.
- Select the alias and press ⌘Option O.
- Select the alias and hold down Option while you press Return to trigger the default Open button.

Back-and-forth folders. If you move back and forth between two specific folders frequently, keeping an alias of each one in the other one saves time. I find that I often switch between the Control Panels folder and the Extensions folder, for instance; with an alias of one in the other, I don't have to go back up to the System Folder to move from one to the other.

The Go To folder. Create a folder and name it *Go To* (or something similar), but make sure you put a space as the first character in its name so it always percolates to the top of a list. Leave it on the desktop.

A Go-To desktop pop-up window
Chapter 6

Put aliases of your most often used folders inside the Go To folder—your projects, the System Folder, whatever. No matter what application you're working in, and no matter where the Open/Save dialog puts you, it's simple to get where you want to go: Type ⌘D to get to the desktop, type Spacebar to move to the Go To folder, type Return to open it, type a letter that will select the folder you want, and type Return once more to move to the folder. (It takes less time to do it than to read about it). I find this setup incredibly convenient because no matter what I'm doing, the places I need to be most often are readily accessible.

A Show Clipboard command. If you double-click on the Clipboard file in the System Folder, a window opens showing what's on the Clipboard. Some applications include a Show Clipboard command, but you can make one that's always available:

Make an alias of the Clipboard file, and name it Show Clipboard. Put it in the Apple menu. That's it—select the "command" from the Apple menu any time you want to check the Clipboard.

Cataloging files. If you sometimes have trouble remembering which floppy disk or cartridge you've backed up a file onto, here's an easy way to catalog them. Make aliases of every file on the backup disk and put them in a folder on your hard disk. When you double-click on one of the aliases, the Mac will ask for—by name—the disk that contains it. (Be sure you label your backup disks with the name that they use on the desktop.)

Be careful when you set up aliases for items that are stored off-line. You can't start with files on your hard drive, alias them, move the originals to a floppy, delete the originals from the hard drive, and expect the aliases to find the files that went to the floppy. (Well, you can *expect* it, but....) Because, of course, what's on the floppy are *copies* of the original files; the aliases point to the *original* originals, which you've erased.

For off-line storage, you have to make the aliases *on the disk where the originals are stored.* Then you drag the aliases back to the hard disk. You can delete the aliases from the floppy; the ones on the hard drive are exact duplicates and don't need the "first generation" aliases to find the files. —SZA/NL

Off-line compression aliases. If you want to keep track of files which are going to be stored in combined, compressed archives on a removable disk, it makes more sense to alias the separate files before you compress them into one package. That way, you can double-click on the alias for *Chapter 1* and be directed to a disk that holds the combined archive for the *Great American Novel.*

However, you have to create the aliases on the removable media, not on the hard drive, and if the files are large, you're not going to be able to move them—or at least all of them—to the other disk before the compression. Here's how to get around the problem: create empty folders on the removable disk named for the items inside the compressed package. Alias the folders, copy them to the hard drive, and then delete the empty folders from the floppy (or leave them—they don't take much room). When you double-click on the folder alias, it will prompt you to insert the disk that holds the original file, even though that file doesn't exist separately anymore.

Mounting shared disks. Normally, mounting a shared disk or folder on your Mac is a multi-step process through the Chooser. But once the item's mounted, if you make an alias of it, double-clicking on the alias will automatically re-mount the item with no more than a click in an OK button. —CR

Alias Tidbits

Lock your folder aliases. You can't lock a folder, but you can lock its alias. Why would you want to? When it's locked, you can double-click anywhere on it to open it—including on its name, which would otherwise be selected for editing.

Alias of an alias. If you make an alias of an alias, double-clicking on the second alias still opens the original; at least, that's what it looks like. What's actually happening is that the second alias is opening the first alias, which opens the original. What difference does that make? If you erase the first alias, the second alias won't work, because it was never pointing directly to the original. So, if you want multiple aliases for an item, make them all directly from the original.

Custom icons on aliases. The relationship between aliases and custom icons (covered in the last chapter) is a little fickle.

- If you alias an item that has a custom icon, the alias gets the same custom icon.
- If you change the original item's icon, the alias's icon is updated to match it the next time you use the alias to open the original. (Unless you drag and drop something into the alias to open it—that doesn't count, and the icon won't change.)
- If you change the alias' icon separately, it won't be updated to match any change to the original's icon.

Finding orphaned aliases. There's no built-in, high-tech way to find "orphaned" aliases—aliases whose originals are no longer around. But you can use Find File (covered later in this chapter) to find all the aliases on your drive, or in certain folders—say, everything except your System Folder, and scroll through the list for likely candidates to be dumped.

Losing the link to the original. When you use an alias for an item that's been deleted from a disk, you'll get a dialog telling you the original can't be found. This occasionally happens even when the original is still around; sometimes it's because you've rebuilt the desktop and some links broke, though sometimes rebuilding the desktop *fixes* broken links. (Hey, I only report the news.) In any case, don't panic, assuming that you've actually lost the original: use the Find command to track down the original.

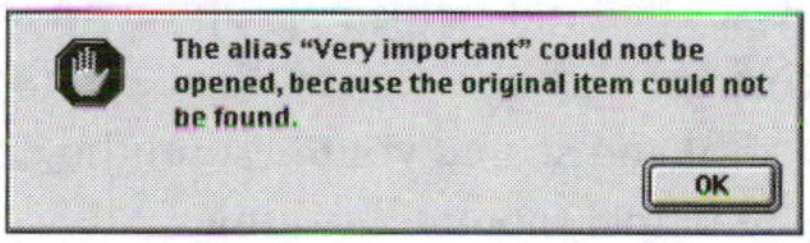

The re-wired alias. Say you have an alias to a document you use every day—a To Do document—and you keep the alias out on the desktop to make it easy to get to the original. At some point, you create another document called To Do and decide that's the one you want to access from the desktop. So, you trash the original and drag the new To Do document into the same folder. As you've already guessed, the alias won't work for the new document.

But wait! You *can* make the old alias open the new document! And you can save the step of deleting the original document, too. Drag the new To Do document into the folder while the original is still there. You'll get the "Do you want to replace the file" dialog. (Or, save the new To Do into that folder directly from the application where you create it—that also triggers the "Do you want to replace" dialog.) As long as the Finder officially replaces the original with the new document, with your permission, the alias you made opens the new document!

Find File

Jerry Szubin was the special research assistant for this section. Most of the tips here are the result of his contributions.

Using Find File

The Find command. The Find command in the Finder's File menu launches the Find File utility that lets you search an entire hard drive for a file, even if you can't remember its complete name. And if you strike out on the name, you can search by all sorts of criteria. If, say, you created a report in ClarisWorks some time in the middle of last week, you can set up the search criteria to be "file type" of CWWP (that's the ClarisWorks word processor file type) and a date "within 2 days of" the date you think you last modified it—that should be enough to pinpoint the file. Find File has an almost bewildering number of options and hidden features; it's practically worth a little book all by itself.

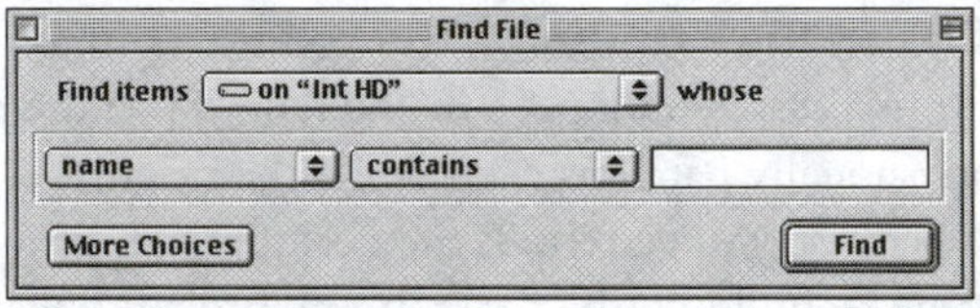

Set the search area. Use the Find Items pop-up menu at the top of the window to set the search area. The choices are divided into three areas on the menu: combinations of local and shared volumes; on the desktop and in desktop selections; and the individual mounted volumes.

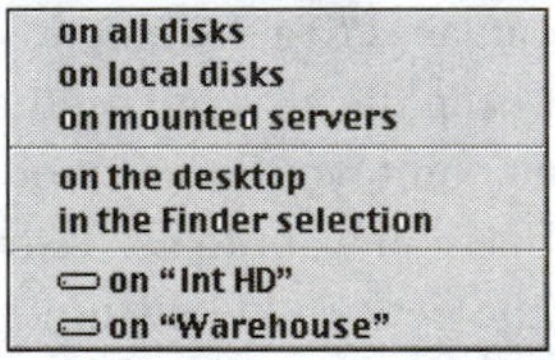

- **on all disks** looks at all mounted volumes
- **on local disks** looks at non-network volumes
- **on mounted servers** looks at network volumes only
- **on the desktop** looks at loose items on the desktop, and inside desktop folders
- **in the Finder** selection looks at selected items and inside any selected folders
- **on [volumename]** lets you select a specific volume to be searched

Search criteria. You can tell Find File what to look for in a variety of ways, filling in the details using pop-up menus, fill-in text boxes, and occasional arrow controls. When you make a choice from the first menu, the other options change so they relate to your choice. The table on the next page shows all the basic choices. (The available options sometimes change with even a minor system update, so make sure you go through the menus whenever you update your system.)

Find File Search Criteria

Search for a file whose...	Choices	Match*
name	contains starts with ends with is is not doesn't contain	[text]
size	is less than is greater than	[number]K
kind	is is not	alias application clipping file control panel document extension folder font letter sound stationery
label	is is not	None (label list)
date created	is: before/after/not is within 1/2/3 days of is within 1/2/3 weeks of is within 1/2/3/6 months of	[month/date/yr]
date modified	(same as date created choices)	[month/date/yr]
version	is is not	[text]
comments	contain do not contain	[text]
lock attribute	is	locked unlocked
folder attribute	is is not	empty shared mounted
file type	is is not	[text]
creator	is is not	[text]

*Item in [brackets] is what you fill in

Multiple criteria. To use multiple criteria for a search, use the More Choices button in the Find File window; you can keep clicking the button for more choices until there's a row for each one of the available options. It's a great way to narrow down the search: looking for something whose *kind* is document, was created in a certain time range, and whose name contains "memo" will give you a shorter list of candidates than if you just go for the name.

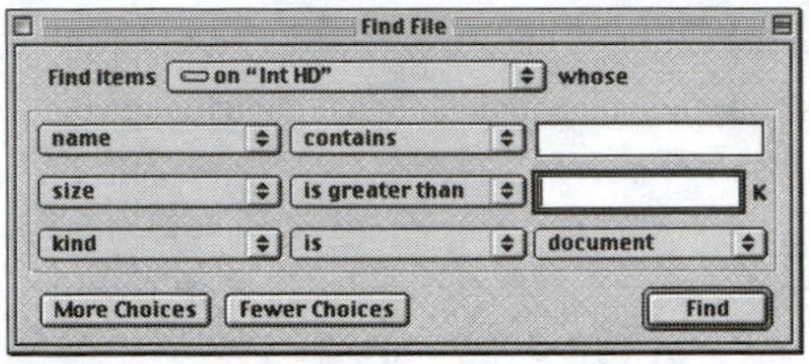

Use multiple criteria for a search by clicking the More Choices button.

The hit list. After Find File searches for your file, it opens the Items Found window. In the upper area, it lists the "hits"; the lower area shows the complete path to the item you've selected in the upper pane.

Find File provides an amazing number of options once you've found the file: Look through its menus and you'll see commands for opening, printing, and even getting Info on a selected item, as well as for opening the folder that the selected item is in. If all you want to do is open a found item, you can double-click on it in either the upper or lower pane, and it opens.

You can change the size of the Items Found window in only a vertical direction with its size box. You can change the relative sizes of the upper and lower panes by dragging the double line between them up or down. (In a cute little interface nicety, the grabber hand cursor closes around the lines when you drag them.)

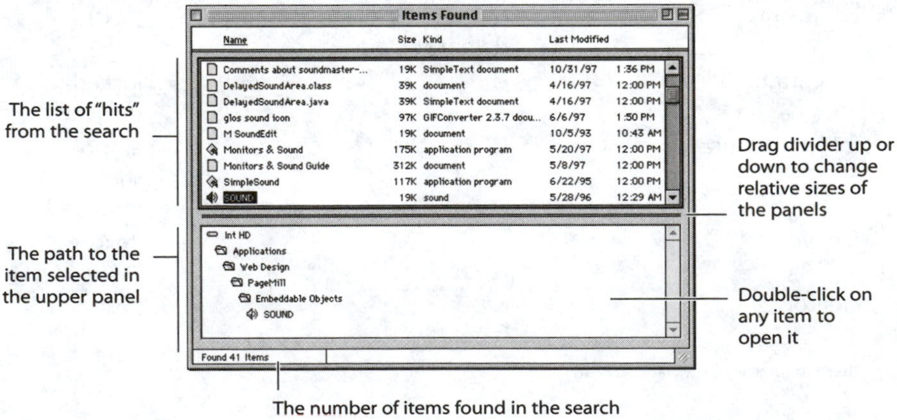

Give Find File some room. Even though the Find command is built into the Finder's menus, Find File itself is still an application. If you're going to do vast searches that might compile large lists of hits, give Find File more memory through its Info window. (Allocating memory is covered in Chapter 4.)

A ton of tidbits. Here's a bunch of little-but-handy things you should know about Find File:

- You can use the Edit menu's Preferences command to change the lists in the Found window to a different font or size.
- Press ⌘ when you click the Find button, and the bottom of the Find window expands to report on the search progress: which volume is currently being searched, and the name of the last item found.
- If you stop an in-progress search, you'll get a dialog asking if you want to see all the items found so far. If you know you want to see them (and most of the time, that's what you'll want), hold Option while you click the Stop button; that bypasses the dialog and goes right to the list.
- The search looks at files, not *in* files. You won't be able to find a font or sound resource that's inside a suitcase file. (Suitcase files are covered in Chapter 9.)
- If you Option-double-click on an item in the list, the Found Items window closes as the item opens. (This mimics that same capability in Finder windows.)
- If an ejectable volume is showing in the Find Items menu, you can hold down Option and drag the menu to the trash, and the disk will be ejected.
- When you Option-drag an ejectable disk to the trash, its name stays displayed in the Find Items menu. Insert another disk, and its name automatically appears as the selected volume.
- If you hold Option while choosing Find File from the Apple menu, the Find window opens in the center of the screen no matter where you had it positioned when you last closed it. (Pressing Cmd Option F doesn't do anything for the positioning.)
- If you want the Items Found window to open centered below the Find window, hold down Option as you click the Find button, or immediately afterwards. (Actually, as long as you get the button down before the window opens, this will work.)
- In case you're trying, you're trying in vain: System 7.x let you bypass Find File and use the old Find command by holding Shift when you chose the Find command, but OS 8 has only Find File.

In the Find Window

Keyboard shortcuts. There are some handy keyboard shortcuts for working in the Find File window:

- To cycle through the mounted volumes in the Find Items pop-up menu, use ⌘1, ⌘2, ⌘3, and so on.

- When there's more than one text field showing with multiple criteria, Tab moves to the next one and ShiftTab moves to the previous one.
- Use CmdM instead of clicking the More Choices button and CmdR for the Fewer Choices button.

Deleting a criterion row. If you've set up multiple criteria for your search, then decide that, for instance, the second of your five criteria isn't one you want to use, you don't have to delete the later ones with the Fewer Choices button and start again. Just Option-drag the whole row to the trash; you have to grab it from the right or left edge, or anywhere in between the pop-up menus and text boxes.

(If you drop the row on the desktop, it will turn into a useless clippings file containing the phrase *"deleted Find File search criterion."*)

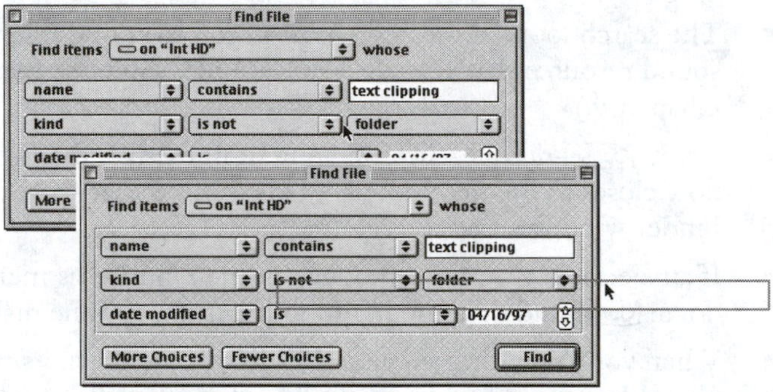

Dragging a row out of the Find dialog.

Returning to a single criterion. If you're working with three or more criteria for a search, and then need only a single criterion for the next search (or you've decided not to be quite so specific), you don't have to repeatedly click the Fewer Choices button to get rid of the extra rows. Just Shift-click on Fewer Choices or press CmdShiftR; or, hold ShiftOption as you drag any row to the trash.

Use a sample for criteria. You can use any icon as a "sample" for the criteria you're building in the Find File window: select the criterion you want, then just drag the icon right into the Find File window, into the criteria area.

This method is especially convenient when you're using the Creator or File Type choices, since most people don't know any of the special codes. But drag, say, a Word document into the window when Creator is selected, you'll see MSWD entered into the text box.

But keep in mind that *all* the criteria for the dragged item will be entered into any criteria rows showing in the window. If you want the icon's file type and kind, but not it's created date, you either have to drag it into the window before you click More Choices for the date, or adjust the date after you've dragged the icon in.

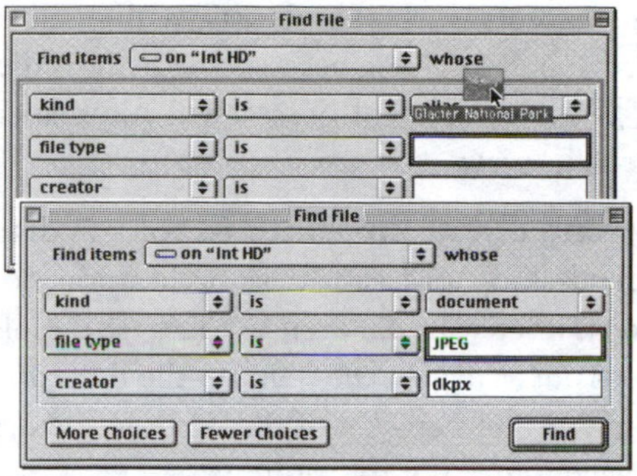

Dragging an item into the criteria area fills in the rows with the item's specs.

Just look through these. If you want to search certain mounted volumes but not others, but the group you want to search isn't a pre-defined one like *local volumes*, just select the icons of the volumes you want to search (Shift-click on each in turn) and drag the group into the Find Items menu in the window.

If you'd like to search through several folders, just select them and drag the group into the menu.

Non-ejectable volumes only. To search through all the mounted volumes *except* for ejectables like floppies or CD-ROMs, start with *on all volumes* or *on local volumes* from the pop-up menu, but instead of just clicking the Find button, Shift-click on it.

Working in the Items Found Window

Sorting in forward and reverse. You can sort the list in the Items Found window by any of its four columns: Name, Size, Kind, or Last Modified. Choose the column from the View menu, or click on the column name in the window.

But you can also sort in reverse order by adding Option: hold it while you choose from the menu, or Option-click on the column title.

Working with the lists. Select an item in either list by clicking on its icon or the text in any of its columns. To select multiple items, Shift-click on them; to select them all, use the Select All command in the Edit menu.

There are also some keyboard shortcuts for scrolling the lists and selecting items:

- Use Tab to alternately select the top or bottom list. The currently active list will have a black frame around it.
- You can use the ↑↓ keys to move up and down in the list, selecting the item above or below the current one. If nothing's selected, using the arrow keys selects the first (↑) or last (↓) item.
- Use Page Up and Page Down to scroll through the list; Home and End jump to the top and bottom of the list.

All these keyboard shortcuts work in both lists, with one exception: if the bottom pane has no scroll bars showing because the path to the selected item is brief, using Page Up, Page Down, Home, or End will automatically activate the upper pane and scroll its view.

Dragging something out of the window. You can drag an item from the top pane right to the desktop, or to any desktop location (to a folder, onto an application icon, to another volume, even to the trash). Holding down Option while you drag it out puts a *copy* of the item on the desktop; holding down ⌘ while you drag it out puts an *alias* of the item on the desktop. This works only for single selected items, not for multiples.

Dragging multiple items to the trash. You can't drag multiple items to the trash from the Items Found window. But you *can* drag multiple items to an *alias* of the trash, which, of course, sends them to the trash. Go figure. In fact, you can drag multiple items from the Found window to *any* alias, even though you can't drag them to a regular folder. (This is so obviously a bug that it will certainly be fixed eventually—so double-check that your version of Find File still won't do this before you start using this work-around.)

Making a list. Select any or all of the items in the Found window, and use the Copy command to copy the list to the Clipboard; paste it into text or word processor, and you'll get a list of the names of the items found.

To get all the columns of information showing in the window, drag selected items (or the whole selected list) to any drag-enabled text processor (like SimpleText, the Note Pad, or even a Stickies note). You wind up with a tab-delimited list of information, with all the details that show in the Found window (the size, kind, modified date, and so on). There really are tabs there—but neither the Note Pad or Stickies can handle tabs, so they're treated as spaces, as you can see in the picture here.

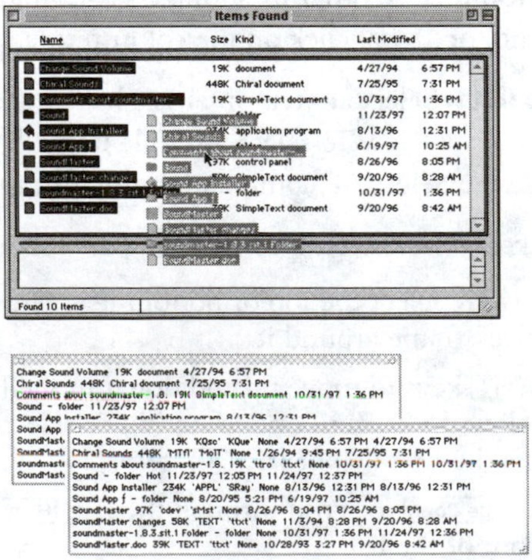

Drag selected items into a drag-enabled text processor to get all the columns of information (Stickies notes are shown here). An Option-drag copies even more information, as you can see in the foreground Stickies note.

Hold Option while you drag and you get two extra columns of information for each item: the file type and creator codes.

What if you want all those columns of information but your word processor doesn't support drag and drop? Drag it into the Note Pad or Stickies, copy it there, and paste that into your word processor document.

Power User Options

More info. Use the Preferences command in the Edit menu to get more complete information about the found items. Check the *Use full descriptions for found items* option and you'll get descriptions like "Word document" instead of just "document." (Searching for things with this option on slows down the search.)

Simultaneous searches. If you're a really A-type personality, you can get the Mac to look for more than one thing at a time. You might already know that finding things is a "background task": while Find File does its job, you can go on and do other things. (And if you didn't know, you know now.)

You can make a copy of the Find File application (it's in the Apple Menu Items folder) and give it another name. Then, you can get one search going with one copy and use the other copy to do another search at the same time.

The hidden search criteria. Hold down Option when you pop up the first menu in a row (the one that defaults to Name), and you'll get four additional search criteria, shown in the table here.

Find File's Hidden Search Criteria

Search for a file whose...	Choices	Match
contents	contain do not contain	[text]*
name/icon lock	is	locked unlocked
custom icon	is	present not present
visibility	is	invisible visible

*Item in [brackets] is what you fill in

Using the Contents search. The Contents option for searching makes Find File look *inside* files, at the text stored there. (That still doesn't let it look inside suitcases at fonts, by the way.) Find File ignores applications and certain other file types when you're doing a contents search.

When you're searching the contents of files, holding Option when you click the Find button makes the search go faster; this searches through the ASCII text of each file, and doesn't work for languages other than English.

No rummaging through suitcases. The Find command, even when you use a Contents search, can't look through Font suitcases, so you won't be able to find individual font files stored in their suitcases.

Printing from the Desktop

Printing Files from the Desktop

Printing from the desktop. To print a document from the desktop, select it and choose Print from the File menu (or use ⌘P). Both the document and its application open and the application's Print dialog appears so you can select options. (So make sure you're paying attention: don't just hit ⌘P and walk away.) The document prints, the application quits, and you're back on the desktop.

You don't get a chance to use the Page Setup command during this process, so if you need anything special, you'll have to open the document and use the application's Print command.

Printing multiple documents. Few applications provide an option to print more than one document at a time. But if you select them all on the desktop and use the Print command, you'll be able to print them all at once.

There's a single Print dialog when you're printing multiple documents, and its settings (number of copies, page numbers, paper tray, and so on) apply to all of the documents you're printing.

Printing from multiple applications. If the documents you select on the desktop belong to different applications, each application will open in turn, print its documents, and quit. You'll be presented with one Print dialog for each application, so this isn't a walk-away-from-it procedure.

Canceling a print job. If you click the Cancel button in the Print dialog, the print job gets canceled and the application quits. If you've selected multiple documents, the whole process is canceled.

Using ⌘. to cancel an in-progress print job cancels the job, all the other print jobs (if you selected multiple documents) and quits the application.

If you want to cancel the printing for just the current document, or for only one of the documents that have already been processed, try catching them in the Desktop PrintMonitor, where you can manipulate waiting print jobs. Deleting a document from that list won't affect the others waiting to go. (There's lots more about the Desktop PrintMonitor in Chapter 15.)

Printing Desktop Windows

Printing desktop windows. The Print Window command in the File menu prints the active window with its current settings for view, font, font size, and so on. It prints the entire contents of the window—not the contents of closed or unexpanded folders, but everything you'd see if you scrolled through the window. You get a page header that matches the window header (noting the number of items and room left on the disk) and a footer with a page number. If you print a list-view window, you'll get the gray buttons at the top of each column as column headers, although the rest of the page won't have the gray background (thank goodness!).

The Print Window command isn't at all the same as the Print command, which prints the current selection in a window, opening its parent application to do so. (That's covered in Chapter 15.)

But not on a DeskWriter. If you're using a Hewlett-Packard DeskWriter printer, don't try printing desktop windows. Or, go ahead and try—but you'll be sorry. The printer driver software for DeskWriters doesn't contain the information needed to print a Finder window.

Get single-page widths. The printout of a large window is "tiled" to as many pages as necessary. So, for instance, if a list view window has too many columns to fit across a single piece of paper, two pages will be printed—one for the left half of the window, and one for the right half. Here are a few ways to keep things down to one page in width:

- It's unlikely you'll be printing windows in button or icon views, but if you do, size the window to no more than the width of a sheet of paper, and use the Clean Up command to get all the icons organized—the command automatically places icons within the width of the window.
- Limit the number of columns in a list-view window so you get only what you need (just name, type, and modified date, for instance) and can keep it all on one page. Use the View Options command for the window to change the columns.
- Expanding folders in a list increases the width of the Name column; the more levels that are expanded, the wider the column. Keep folders collapsed if you don't need to see their contents so you don't bump the width of the printout to another page. (To collapse all the folders, press ⌘A and then ⌘←).
- Use the Finder's Preferences command to change the font (and, more importantly, the font size) in the window to squeeze a little more in on each page. (Using a PostScript font won't speed up the printing on a PostScript printer, however; it's those little icons that take a long time to print.)
- Use the Page Setup command to scale down the size of the page—even at 50 percent, it's pretty legible, and you can print more columns across the page.

8

System Software

About System Software

System Installation

Post-Install Procedures

Reinstalls, Deinstalls, etc.

In This Chapter

About System Software

In General

System software. The hardware components of your computer system aren't enough to make a working computer; it's the software that really makes things happen. Without software, a computer is like a terrific stereo system without CDs: you have the potential, but you don't have the music.

The most important software of all is the *system software*—the stuff that gets the computer working at its most basic level. The system software creates the desktop and provides across-the-board capabilities like cutting and pasting. The Mac's system software is inside the System Folder on your hard drive. When you buy a Mac, the most recent version of the system software is already installed on it, but you can continually upgrade it as new system releases become available.

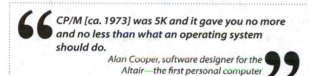

> ***CP/M [ca. 1973] was 5K and it gave you no more and no less than what an operating system should do.***
>
> *Alan Cooper, software designer for the Altair—the first personal computer*

The system software, together with the routines built into the Mac's ROM (which provide the lowest-level essentials like window- and menu-handling), make up the Mac's *operating system.*

What system you already have. There are two easy ways to check what system software a Mac is running. The easier is to use the About this Computer command from the Apple menu at the desktop; the other is to select the System file icon inside the System Folder and Get Info on it.

Two places to check the what's current system software version.

Processor chips
Chapter 2

Hardware requirements. Not every Mac can run every system, and it's not only a matter of having enough hard drive space or memory. To run OS 8, the Mac needs a PowerPC chip or an '040 processor (that's Centrises, Quadras, some PowerBooks, and some Performas).

Beyond that, you'll need at least 16 megs of memory. The system software alone will take 10 to 15 megs of memory depending on how you configure it, so 16 megs won't get you far: you'll be able to run a single program at best—and not a memory-hungry one at that. It's better to think of 20 or 24 megs as your starting point, and 32 to 40 megs as a comfortable amount for running two, or even three, programs of reasonable size at a time.

Space is relative. How much room you need on your hard drive for OS 8 or its immediate descendants depends on several factors:

- How large the drive is to start with. (That sounds like a bad circular reference, but files take more room on larger drives, as discussed in Chapter 4.)
- Whether or not the drive is formatted with HFS Plus under OS 8.1 (or later). This lets files take the same amount of room no matter what the size of the drive.
- How full an installation you perform: you can install just the standard options, or more or fewer of them.

Which Mac you're using also makes a small difference, since different models need a few different resources, but the size difference for that is minor compared to the other considerations.

It's also important to know that you need extra room during the installation itself, so you need more than just what will be the final size of the System Folder. A final consideration: if you're doing a clean install so that the old System Folder is being preserved instead of some of its contents being replaced, the "space needed" is in addition to that already used by the System Folder.

Here are the numbers for some situations, to give you an idea of what you might need. The drive sizes are for drives under regular HFS formatting, not the new formatting available with 8.1. The "Standard" system install refers to one that includes the default options set by the Installer; the "Conservative" system install is one that has all the optional items turned off.

Megabytes of Space Needed for OS 8

Drive Size	Standard Installation	Standard System Folder	Conservative Installation	Conservative System Folder
500MB	127	117	115	50
1GB	139	129	120	58
2GB	152	140	125	68
Any size, HFS Plus	132	122	118	56

The 5000/6000 flaw. Some Performa and PowerMac 5200, 5300, 6200, and 6300 series Macs have a hardware flaw that prevents them from using OS 8. The 5260, 6320, and 6360 models are not affected, but it's impossible to predict which specific machines otherwise included in those series are afflicted.

There's a special utility you can run to text your machine to see if it's okay or not: the *5xxx/6xxx Tester* is in the Utilities folder on the system CD. Run the test, and if it tells you the problem was found, you can call Apple for a free fix.

Don't upgrade. At least, don't upgrade right away. Wait three to six months after a major system release before you upgrade; by then, all (or almost all) of the bugs will have been worked out. And, applications and utilities that you like will be able to work with the new operating system.

That other operating system. If you need to be ambidextrous, so to speak, in your computing environment, you have several choices: get a Mac and a Windows machine; get a Mac and a card that puts a Pentium processor inside it; or, pretend you have a Windows machine by running an *emulator,* a software-based "shell" within which you can run Windows and Windows programs. One of the hardware routes is a better choice if you have a lot of Windowing to do; but for a single program, or occasional use, you should check out an emulator.

connectix.com
insignia.com

Connectix offers **Virtual PC** in three flavors: version 2 includes Windows 95, for $150; version 1.0 with Windows 3.11 is $100; and a version that has PC DOS, for $50. For the Windows 95 version, you need a PowerMac running at 180MHz or faster and at least 24 megs of RAM. Plan to allocate 150MB of hard drive space just for the software (VirtualPC with Windows), and enough space for the Windows programs you want to run.

SoftWindows from Insignia Solutions ($190), also comes with Windows 95; it wants 24MB of RAM and 200MB of disk space. The 5.0 version offers a 25 percent speed improvement over the previous version.

No matter which emulator you choose, the performance is better if your Mac is a fast machine.

Sticking with System 7

Hardware requirements. Whoops. You can't run OS 8 on your hardware. If it's just a matter of memory—go get some. If your processor won't handle it, though, what *can* you run? You should run the latest system that you can:

- System 7.6 needs 16 megs of RAM—but half of that can be virtual memory, so that's a bare minimum of 8 megs of physical RAM. You can't run 7.6 on these models: LC, Classic, IIcx, IIx, II, SE/30, SE, Mac Plus, or PowerBook 100.
- System 7.5.5 will work for the machines listed above, but not for the two original Macs—the very first, and the "Fat" 512K Mac.

Apple's recommended memory amount for System 7.5 and 7.6 is 4 megs for 68K Macs and 8 megs for PowerMacs; double that amount if you install

QuickDraw GX. While 4 and 8 megs are a little unrealistic (you can run the system software, but not much in the way of applications!), the important clue is the extra toll GX takes. Don't bother installing it—you won't be using it anyway.

Enablers. An *enabler* is a system file that enables system software to work with a Mac model that came out after the system software was introduced. Before enablers—that is, before System 7.1—a new version of the system software, with a second decimal number, had to be used for new machines. But this seemingly simple idea got confusing very quickly, with new enablers coming out all the time, and being replaced, updated, and combined—and with intuitive names like Enabler 131 (which, in some sort of mathematical joke, replaced Enablers 111 and 121). Finally, *all* the enablers for System 7.0 and System 7.1 were rolled into the main System 7.5 technology. But the calm was short-lived, as new machines introduced after System 7.5 required enablers of their own.

Enablers for System 7.5

Model	System	Enabler	Version
PowerMac 6100/66, 7100/80, 8100/100, 8100/110	7.5	PowerPC Enabler	1.1.1
PowerMac 5200, Performa 6200	7.5.1	System Enabler 406	1.0
PowerMac 7200, 9500	7.5.2	System Enabler 701	1.1
PowerMac 7500, 8500	7.5.2	System Enabler 701	1.2
PowerBook 190, 2300, 5300 series	7.5.2	PowerBook 5300/2300/190 Enabler	1.2.1

System Versions

System version numbers. System software, like other software, continually evolves, with higher numbers indicating later versions. A double-decimal system is used so that you can tell the difference between major and minor changes.

When the main number changes (like System 6 to System 7, or System 7 to OS 8), that indicates a major change, with totally new approaches to the system environment—so major that often older hardware can't handle it and older software can't run under it. A change in the first decimal place (like System 8.0 to System 8.1), usually means some significant component was changed or added, but you won't have to relearn anything or change your hardware or software.

A change to the second decimal place, like System 7.5.1 to System 7.5.2 (it's too early to know about OS 8 second-decimal changes), can mean one of two things. It can indicate that there were some bug fixes and/or enhancements to minor system components like printer drivers. Or it might be the newest version of the current system with a few minor tweaks so it works on Mac hardware that was developed after the system was released. Or, it can be a combination—a fix for existing Macs through an updater, while those fixes are rolled into the version of the system that's shipping on new Macs.

When there's an *x* in a version number, it's referring to any number in that (and later) spots. So, 8.x would refer to all revisions of OS 8 (as would the phrase *OS 8* itself).

This book assumes you're using OS 8 or one of its updates (that is, 8.x); we used OS 8 and 8.1 for all our testing, tips, and comments.

Oh say, can you say... Okay, so you want to sound like you know what you're talking about. (After all, you can actually know what you're talking about, but not *sound* as if you do, if you mispronounce things.) So, for system (and other) software, never say "zero"; say "oh"—and don't mention the decimal point. So, it's "eight-oh" and "eight-one" for 8.0 and 8.1; if there's something like OS 8.1.3, you'd say "eight-one-three."

Keeping track. How can you keep track of system software upgrades, updates, problems, and fixes? The easiest way is to let someone else do it for you: join a user group—there's *always* someone who has the latest information. Don't count on print magazines—information is three to four months old by the time you see it. Surfing and hanging around online is one of the best ways to keep abreast of system software changes. And, while you have to buy the system software, updates are free for the downloading.

apple.com

Different strokes for different models. When you install system software, one of the basics is a choice of system software "for this computer." Choosing this option installs a system for the Mac model that's doing the installation. Another choice is "Universal," which creates a system that will run *any* Mac (or, at least, any Mac that can support the operating system). What's the difference?

Different Mac models need different system software—and that's not referring to the fact that, say, an '030 machine can't run OS 8. As Macs evolve, later models have more information built into their ROMs. Systems on earlier machines need this information "patched" into their System files so the older machines can perform the same way (albeit more slowly) as their more sophisticated descendants. In addition, there are support files needed by some models that aren't needed by others because of some special hardware (this is especially obvious when you compare desk models to PowerBooks).

The OS 8 difference. The changes from System 7 to OS 8 are so major that the operating system needed not only a number change, but a variation in its "first" name as well. If you haven't used OS 8 yet, the best way to see the differences (which are far too numerous to even outline here) is to skim through Chapters 5, 6, and 7, which describe interface and desktop features, although the changes are not solely surface ones.

Updating system software
Later this chapter

The 8.1 update. The most major change introduced in the 8.1 update is one that's optional: the HFS Plus, or Extended Format, for large disks (which is covered in detail in Chapter 4). There are other minor changes, improvements, and fixes for printing, networking, and telecommunications, but most are invisible to the user.

The first 8.1 system CDs that were available offered an icon labeled *OS 8.1 Install*, but what it does is first install OS 8, and then run the OS 8.1 updater!

> ***"Other computers have operating systems, but that term was, until relatively recently, foreign to Mac users… there's lots of cross-over jargon, so you may hear or see references to the Mac's operating system, or the Mac OS. If you see the term Mac OS instead of system or Finder or desktop, you can be pretty sure that you're reading something meant for non-Mac users who wouldn't recognize the term Finder, or something that was written by someone who's come over (but not all the way) from the "other side."***
>
> *Sharon Aker, The Mac Almanac, 1994*
> *Editor's note: Well, it was true at the time!*

After 8.1. What's after 8.1? Well, when I started writing this chapter, 8.2 was scheduled to come out the month after the book went to the printer (which would be the month *before* it hit the shelves). Before I finished the chapter, 8.2 had morphed into 8.5 and had slipped two or three months—so it should be out about the time this book hits the shelves. Since I have a prerelease version of 8.5, and there are so many major changes in the desktop interface, I've devoted a chapter (which, despite its being Chapter 11, was the *last* written for this book) to rounding up the latest and greatest features. But the chapter itself is sort of a beta version, since some of it's based on best guesses—and faked screen shots!

The longer-term outlook has OS 9 being skipped entirely, in favor of what's labeled OS X (pronounced *ten*) about a year and a half down the road from this writing. It's scheduled to have all sorts of nifty things, of course, but beware: it's supposed to run on only G3 Macs.

Other updates. It's too early, at this writing, to say how various minor updates to OS 8 system software will be handled. You can read the *Sticking with System 7* section to see how tune-ups, updates, and enablers made life miserable, and brace yourself for what will come for OS 8.

So far, we've had the full 8.1 update and a few items, like Quicktime 3.0 and a new Drive Setup utility, released piecemeal. And one new PowerBook, released after 8.2, does have an enabler with its system.

System Installation

General Guidelines

Why you have to install system software. When you buy a Mac, there's a System Folder on the hard drive. But there are lots of times when you have to install system software yourself:

- You might reformat the hard drive and have to start with a completely new system.
- You might have to *reinstall* the same system version because yours has become corrupted.
- You might *update* the current system to fix some bugs or to move to a new system release.
- You might want to install an alternate, complete system on an external hard drive.

Time trials. When it's time to install new system software, make sure there's *plenty* of time! Even an easy, trouble-free install can take about two hours. If you're putting a stuffed-to-the-gills System Folder back together with all your third-party utilities, extensions, and control panels, you can easily spend about five hours getting everything going again—and that's if nothing goes wrong with the extensions you add back in!

The Installer. It's absolutely imperative that you use the Installer for putting a new or updated system on your hard disk—don't just drag a System Folder, or the System file or Finder, from the install disk and expect things to work. The Installer not only makes sure you have exactly what you need, it also does all the drudgery of putting things in the various folders where they belong.

You should also start up from the system CD when you do the install—you can't replace the system that's running your computer. If you're installing a system on an external disk, you can be running from your internal drive, insert the CD, and run the installer—but you should restart with all your extensions off (except the one that lets you see CDs).

System disk redux. We defined *system disk* back in Chapter 5 as one with a System Folder on it (with the *startup disk* being the one that's actually running the Mac at any given time). There's another meaning to *system disk*, because sometimes it's used as a short reference to a *system software disk*—one with system installation software on it.

System installation disks for OS 8 are CDs; they're also startup disks, so you can start your computer from the CD and install the system software onto your hard drive. (You can't, after all, start up with your hard drive's system and expect to be able to replace it while it's running the show).

System CDs prior to OS 8 included a way to make a set of floppy system disks for older Macs with no CD-ROM drive. If your Mac is too old to accommodate a CD, you are, in all likelihood, better off sticking with the last of the System 7 systems, System 7.5.5 or 7.6.1.

Keep it clean. The "clean install" philosophy should be your guiding principle for major upgrades and for reinstalls needed because you're having problems.

A clean install puts all your old System Folder contents in a separate folder and creates a new System Folder for the new system. Then, you get to check all your old non-Apple extensions, control panels, and other system files one at a time (or, more practically, in batches) to see if they work with the new system.

If you don't opt for the clean install, the "replacement" of your current System Folder isn't a wholesale replacement; anything you've added to it in the way of third-party utilities will still be there when you're done.

Automatic, Easy, and Custom installs. Most people are aware that the Installer provides a choice between an Easy Install (the default) and a Custom Install, even if they're not clear as to the benefits of either. But it's actually, and unfortunately, a little more complicated than that.

The Installer first offers an "automatic" installation of everything (and then some) that you need, although there is a choice as to which special components (Runtime for Java, Personal Web Sharing, and so on) you want included. Despite the surface level of customization, that's not considered a custom install. If you bypass this simplest level of installation, by using the unfortunately labeled Customize button, you've traveled into the a mode we'll refer to as "manual" to differentiate from the automatic installation. At this level, you once again get to choose the major components for the installation, although you have more options than in the previous window. When you make your choices and move to the next window, *that's* when you're offered the choice between an Easy or Custom install!

We'll cover all the details of all three methods in the rest of this section. But which one should you use?

- Use the **automatic** option offered early in the install procedure if you're a relative beginner, in a great hurry, or just don't care about details and want a system that runs your computer even if it might not be optimized for disk space and memory usage.
- Use the **Easy Install** offered later in the procedure if you'd like to block installation of certain components not listed in the automatic install screen, but don't want to be bothered with the details of your System Folder or decisions about every single component of your system software. At worst, you'll waste some hard drive space for system files that

you don't need (they won't interfere with your working system). You'd also use this option if you're reinstalling the main system software and don't want to reinstall every component.

- Do a **Custom Install** if you want to select both major categories and the nitty-gritty of files you want installed. If you have the patience, it's not all that difficult; you can always install a component if you're not sure whether you need it, and take it out later. (There's a category-by-category guide coming up soon.) The benefit to doing a custom install is that you'll use less space on your hard drive, and might also use less memory to run your system.

The Installer flow chart. For a company that designs beautiful interfaces and operating systems, Apple sure doesn't know how to design a friendly installer—and that was never more clear to me than when I tried organizing the information in this chapter and, especially, when I wanted to make a simple flow chart of how the Installer program works. First there's the problem alluded to in the previous entry: it's not just a matter of Easy versus Custom installation, and even the Easy (and, before that, the "automatic") installs offer some level of customization. Either-or choices that should be branches from a single window are missing; instead, you go from a window to one of the choices and have to move on from there yourself. Important options like clean installation and updating the disk driver are offered in odd places and presented in an inconsistent manner.

That said, it's not impossible to understand how the Installer works, and all the options it provides. But it sure is helpful if you familiarize yourself with the overall approach before you get down to particulars. The picture on the next page gives you a tour of the installer.

Before you install. System installation is no big mystery, but it takes time and effort; there are things you have to do before it even starts, and there are many items to attend to when it's finished.

Before you use the Installer:

1. Read the Read Me files that come with the Installer. The information in this chapter is life-saving, no doubt, and more thorough, but the Read Me file on most disks will be more current. It's the only place you're going to find out about special little problems.
2. If you have internet access, get your settings information from the three control panels involved: TCP/IP, PPP, and Modem. Write them down so you can enter the information again later. (Or take a screen shot and print it out—see Chapter 10 for screen-shot information.)
3. If you're installing a later version of the system software than you're currently using, make sure that all your software programs and utilities will work with the new system software. If you need to replace them, get the updates before you bother with the installation. This includes not only your major applications, but also the utilities you depend on the most.

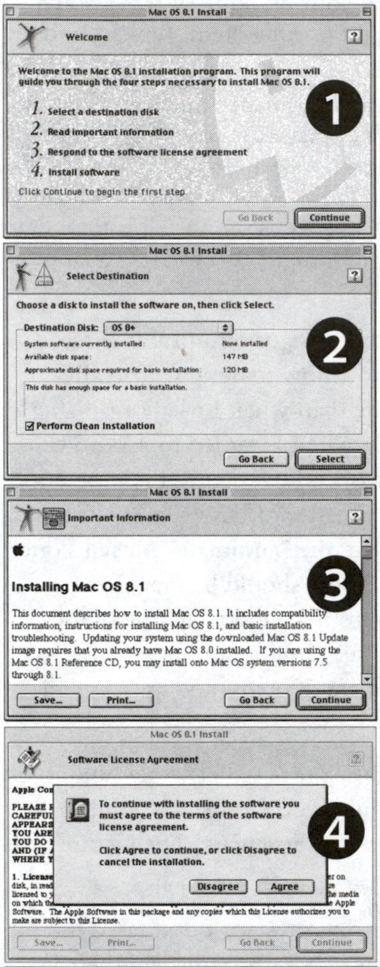

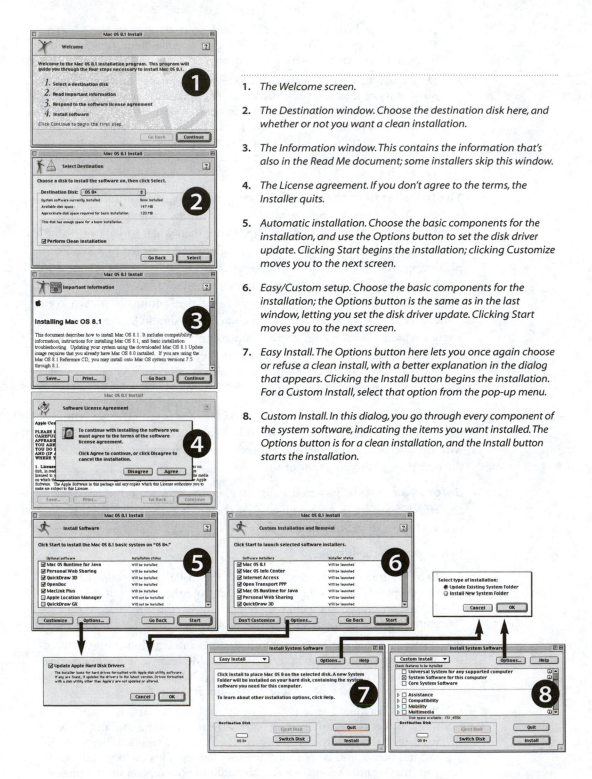

1. *The Welcome screen.*
2. *The Destination window. Choose the destination disk here, and whether or not you want a clean installation.*
3. *The Information window. This contains the information that's also in the Read Me document; some installers skip this window.*
4. *The License agreement. If you don't agree to the terms, the Installer quits.*
5. *Automatic installation. Choose the basic components for the installation, and use the Options button to set the disk driver update. Clicking Start begins the installation; clicking Customize moves you to the next screen.*
6. *Easy/Custom setup. Choose the basic components for the installation; the Options button is the same as in the last window, letting you set the disk driver update. Clicking Start moves you to the next screen.*
7. *Easy Install. The Options button here lets you once again choose or refuse a clean install, with a better explanation in the dialog that appears. Clicking the Install button begins the installation. For a Custom Install, select that option from the pop-up menu.*
8. *Custom Install. In this dialog, you go through every component of the system software, indicating the items you want installed. The Options button is for a clean installation, and the Install button starts the installation.*

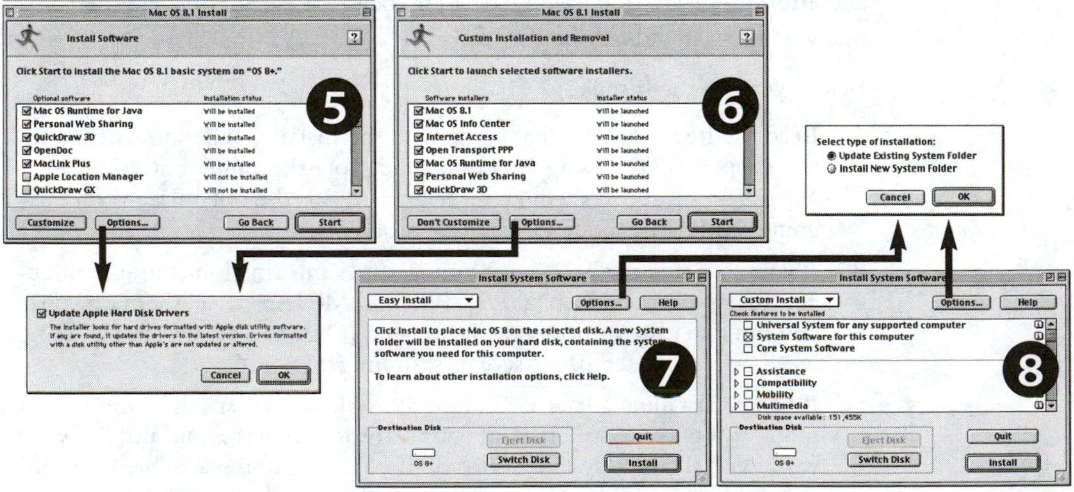

4. If the disk you're installing the system on isn't formatted with Apple software (the Drive Setup utility, which works only with Apple disks), get the latest version of your formatting software from its publisher or from the drive vendor. This is absolutely essential before you consider updating system software.

Disk First Aid **Chapter 24**

5. Run the Disk First Aid utility—use the latest version, on your new system CD—to check that the drive is in good shape. (If you use another, heavier-duty disk utility like Norton's Disk Doctor or TechTool Pro, this is a good time to run it, too.

Hard drive drivers **Chapter 4**

6. If you have a non-Apple disk, update its driver software with the latest version of the formatting software you use. (For Apple disks, this step is integrated into the installation process.)

During and after. Okay, now you can start the installation itself. It can be boiled down to three steps (but the middle step is a doozy):

1. Start up the computer with the system CD.
2. Double-click on the Installer icon and choose your options (as in the next thousand or so entries).
3. Restart the Mac.

But wait, there's more! Here are some of things you need to do when you restart (details are in later sections):

1. Answer the questions in the Setup Assistant that automatically launches on the first startup after installation; the Internet Assistant opens next; you can work with it right away or dismiss it and deal with it later.
2. Reset the defaults in the Memory control panel.
3. If you're going to label the Apple extensions and control panels before you add your own, now's the time to do it.
4. Get items from the CD that aren't included in the installation.
5. Reorganize all the folders that the installer put on your hard drive.
6. Set, or reset, your control panels and other "environmental" elements like the Apple menu and desktop pattern.
7. Depending on the type of installation you did, go through the Extensions and Control Panels folders, getting rid of things you don't need.
8. Look through the Old System Folder (created by a Clean Install option), and drag your non-Apple items into the new System Folder.

The Extra-Easy Way

The no-fuss method. The easiest way to install system software is the "automatic" method (which was screen 5 in the Installer flow chart on the previous page). Once you choose only a few basic options, the rest of the installation is performed without further ado. You'll get a system that will run the computer that's doing the installation (which means you can't do it this way if you're installing a system on an external or removable disk that will be used on other Macs). It won't be optimized for memory use or disk space, since it will assume you want all sorts of things (like OpenDoc, for instance) that in fact you may never use. But you can get rid of extraneous items later.

The destination disk. The first screen you get after the Installer's Welcome notice lets you select the drive you want to install your system on. You'll get a report as to how much space is available, and whether or not it's enough for the installation; because temporary files are written to the disk during installation, and then later erased, you're going to need more space (almost double) than just enough to accommodate the final system folder.

But the most important part of this screen is the Perform Clean Installation checkbox: make sure you check it before you continue. (If the button is dimmed, you've selected a drive that doesn't have a System Folder already on it—in which case, it's an extra-clean installation!)

When you click Continue, you'll get a screen of Read Me information. If you didn't read the Read Me's before (they're on the CD), read them now! With the next Continue button, you'll get the software license agreement, and not one, but *two* Agree buttons to click. My advice? Don't read—just click. No one's going to quiz you on the reading, and it's not as if you can install the software if you don't agree with the agreement!

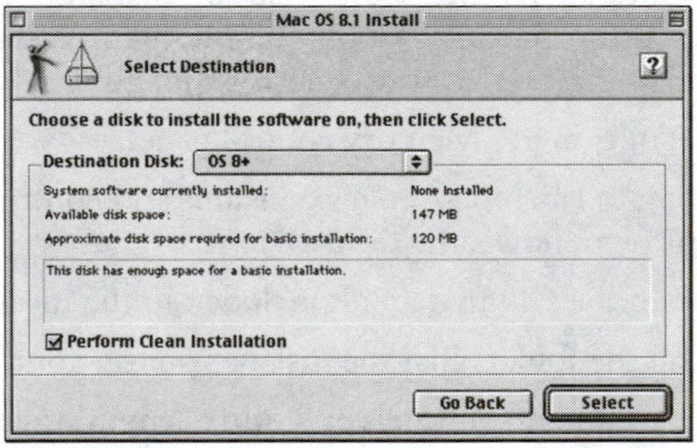

The driver update. Clicking the Options button in the Installer window provides only a single option: to update the disk driver. As the dialog explains, it works only with disks formatted with Apple disk utilities; currently, that's Drive Setup. By default, this option is turned on—and the whole thing is hidden behind the often overlooked Options button. This arrangement is probably in response to years of users forgetting to update drivers along with system software.

Turn off the Update option if you're installing onto a drive that wasn't formatted with Apple software, or if you're doing a reinstall or partial custom install and have already updated the driver. If you forget to turn it off, there's no harm done except a few minutes wasted: a new copy of the driver will be written over the old one if it's an Apple drive.

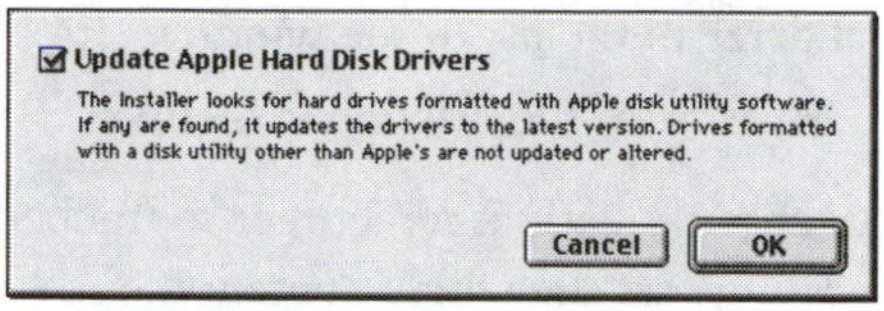

Non-Apple drives. If you forget to turn off the Update option and you're working on a non-Apple drive, it will look like the driver is being updated: you get a "Checking hard drive" dialog, followed by the "Updating driver" dialog with a progress bar. It takes a long time for a dialog to appear to let you know that the drive wasn't, after all, touched. The wait is long enough for this train of thought to roll by: *Whoops, I forgot to turn off that option. Wait—I'm doing the external drive, and that's not an Apple drive. Hmmm—I thought it wouldn't update non-Apple drives. Gee—I wonder if I should click that Stop button. Oooh—is it writing over the existing driver and then the drive isn't going to work at all? Arghh—I've really got a mess on my hands now.*

After toying with your emotions, the dialog box shown here appears, and it's not a comforting one; in fact, it's downright misleading. It tells you, right at the top, to stop the installation process, implying that you can't go on. But then you get an Ignore Warning button if you want to continue. How about a button that says "Go ahead, I already updated the drivers on this disk."? Nothing like scaring the less-informed!

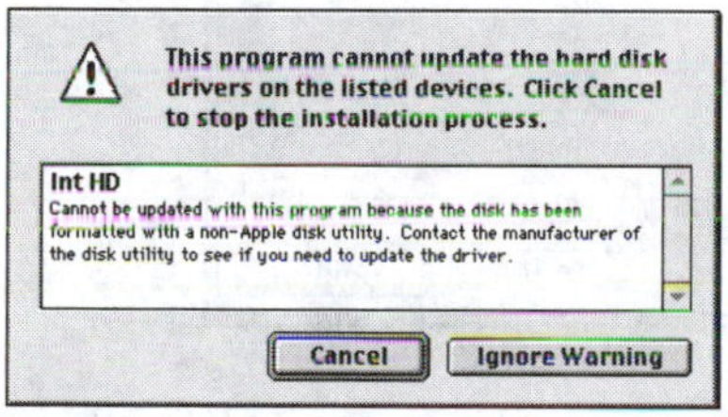

Partitions and driver updates. Just when I thought I had finished writing this chapter, a friend called with a problem: he was installing OS 8 on a friend's computer and had run into the non-Apple update dialog after the progress dialog seemed to indicate that the update was, indeed, being done. The dialog, however, listed a partition of the internal drive that wasn't getting the system installed on it. So, the driver was installed on the system partition and everything was okay, right? Wrong. The internal drive was a non-Apple drive, formatted and partitioned with non-Apple software. The dialog just didn't see any difference between one partition and the other (partitions share the same SCSI number since they're physically the same drive).

Updating the driver separately. The Installer checks all the drives connected to the Mac and tries to update all the drivers if you've left that option on. If you have an Apple internal drive that needs a driver update but a different brand as a second internal or an external drive, you'll have to wait through the Installer's attempt to update the non-Apple drivers. To avoid this, you can update the Apple drive's driver separately before you begin the install procedure:

1. Start up from the system CD.
2. Run the copy of Drive Setup you'll find in the CD's Utilities folder.
3. Select the internal drive in the list in the window.
4. Choose Update Driver from the Functions menu.

When you do your system installation, remember to uncheck the Update Driver option so you can bypass the whole operation.

The automatic installation. The Install Software screen in the Installer looks as if it's asking you to customize the installation, since there's a list of items for you to check for inclusion in the installation process, but that's not the case. At least, not entirely. You can go with the items that are checked by default, or check a few more (or uncheck some of the originals), but this isn't considered a custom installation—this is the "automatic" installation described earlier. The items listed for OS 8 and 8.1 installs are:

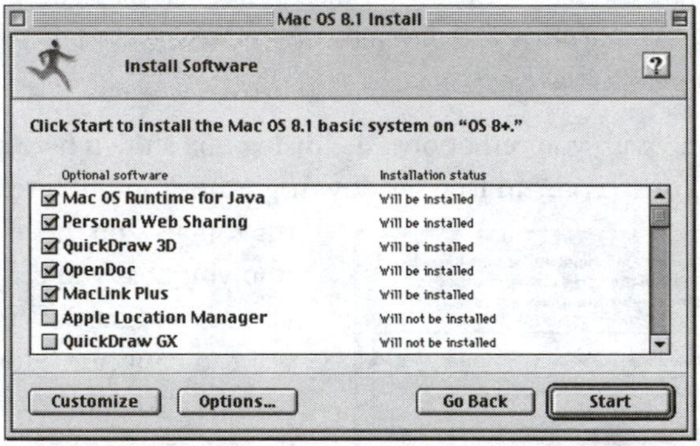

- **Mac OS Runtime for Java**: Go ahead and leave this checked on—you'll eventually use it while you're surfing the web.
- **Personal Web Sharing**: If you're not networked to another computer, don't bother. If you are networked but expect never to set up your machine to serve a few web pages to another computer, don't bother.
- **QuickDraw 3D**: Leave this checked on if you have a PowerPC Mac.
- **OpenDoc**: This should be unchecked by 99 percent of users, since it's a dead-end technology and it's unlikely you'll need it for any of your applications.
- **MacLink Plus**: Definitely leave this on.
- **Apple Location Manager**: Unless you're using a PowerBook, there's no need to even consider this one.
- **QuickDraw GX**: Another technology that didn't get much past getting off the ground. Most people can leave this off—but check out *Afterwards* section later in the chapter, which describes how to get some of the extras that come along with GX without installing GX itself.

- **Cyberdog:** This choice was on the OS 8 CD but not the 8.1 CD; yet another didn't-go-anywhere technology you don't need.
- **Text-to-Speech**: If you're not going to be working with this feature, you don't need its components.
- **Apple Remote Access**: You only need Remote Access software if you're connecting directly with another Mac, or one's connecting to you (as when you call the "home" computer with your PowerBook).

When you click the Start button, the actual installation begins.

The Easy Way

The non-custom customization. An Easy Install starts out the same way as the extra-easy, automatic install described in the last section: select the destination disk, mark the clean install option (or not), and set the disk driver to be updated (or not). But when you forego the automatic installation and click the Customize button instead of the Start button, you get only a slightly changed dialog.

In this window—titled *Custom Installation and Removal* rather than *Install Software*—you get additional items in the list of system components:

- Mac OS
- Mac OS Info Center
- Internet Access
- Open Transport PPP

All of these components are installed by default through the previous window. As to what you should select in this window, follow the guidelines in the previous entry, and add the four new items. The Options button here is the same as in the last window: it lets you set the Update Driver option.

Despite the phrase *Custom Installation* in the window's title, you're not at a Custom Install yet, and, in fact, when you click the Start button you merely move to another window—which is the Easy Install option!

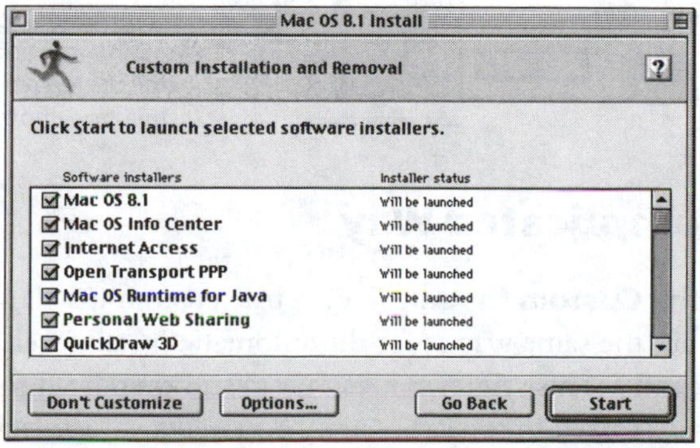

Yet another Easy choice. Just when you think you've started your customized system software installation by clicking the Start button, you get a dialog that tells you you're doing an Easy Install after all. If you click the Install button on this screen, the installation will actually begin, and continue without your having to do anything else. All the subcomponents of the system components you selected in the previous screen will be installed. As with the automatic installation, the system that gets installed is one that will run only the Mac that's doing the installation, so don't use this option on an external drive or removable that might be used on another Mac model.

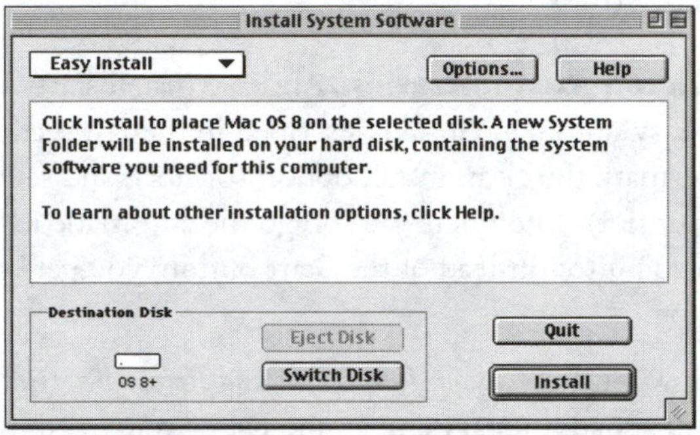

The second Options button. The Options button in this Easy Install window isn't a second chance at setting the update driver choice. Instead, it's a second chance at setting up a clean installation. The dialog is straightforward—in fact, much clearer than the Perform Clean Installation checkbox in the Destination dialog—but why the option is available in two spots, under two descriptions, is beyond my powers of explanation. The information in the Easy Install dialog changes to reflect your choice: in one case, it says *A new System Folder will be installed on your hard disk...* and in the other it says *Click Install to update the software on the selected disk.* In addition, the Install button in the dialog reflects the clean installation status: it will say either Install or Clean Install.

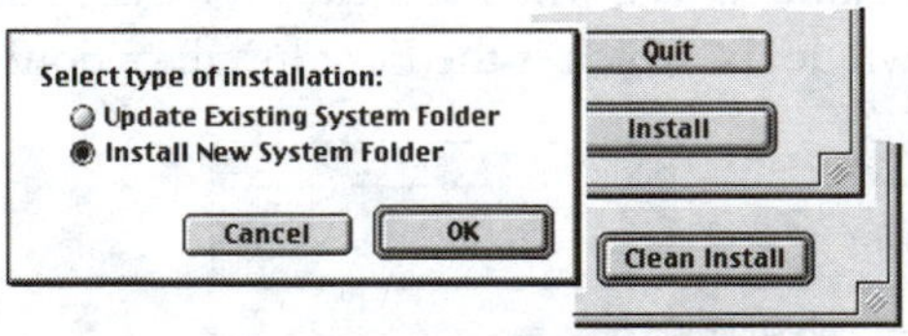

A second chance at choosing a clean installation, by clicking the New System Folder button. The Install button reflects the clean installation choice.

The Complicated Way

Finally, the Custom Install. To do a true custom install of system software, you start out the same way as for the automatic install (Welcome, Destination, Read Me, and License Agreement screens) and then head for the Easy Install option, as described in the last section. You make your selections in the

Custom Installation and Removal window and click the Start button, as you do for the Easy Install. But then, instead of clicking Install in the next window, you select Custom Install from its pop-up menu—and, finally, you're at the Custom Install window.

This Installer window displays a neat list collapsed into main categories. By expanding and collapsing the list (by clicking the arrows in front of the checkboxes) and checking and unchecking items in it, you select the specific software you want installed. Checking and unchecking a top-level box selects and unselects all its subitems.

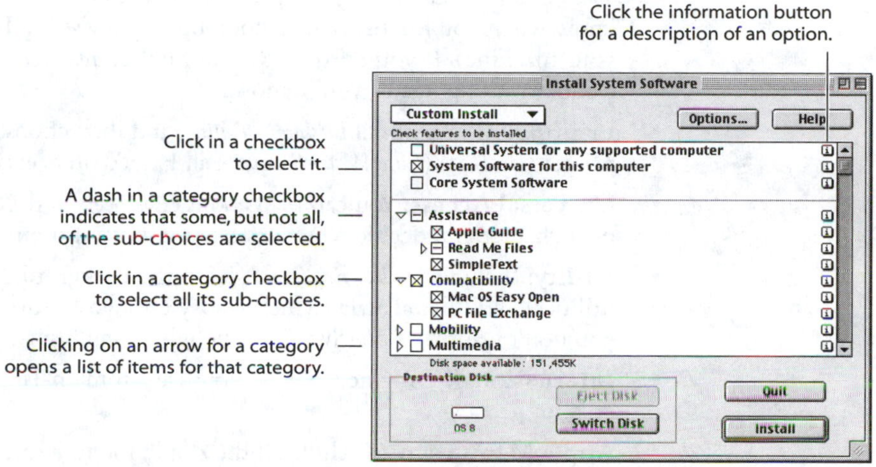

The really custom choices. There's a chart at the end of this section that lists all the choices in the OS 8.1 custom install list; while there are bound to be changes with various updates, it should serve as a handy guide as to what's available for you to pick and choose from. But here's some guidance in regard to each of the major categories:

- **System Software:** The first three selections are *Universal*, *System Software for this computer*, and *Core System Software*. You should almost always choose "for this computer"—it's what you need to run the computer you're using for the installation. The Universal system will run any Mac, so you might want to put it on an external hard drive or removable that might be used on another Mac as a startup; but there's no reason to use it for a single specific machine, especially since it adds about 7 megs to your System Folder. The Core System Software, formerly the "Minimal Install" makes a more compact version of the software specific to your computer. But, at about 11 megs, it's too big to fit on a floppy and too limited to really run your computer on a day-to-day basis, so there's not much reason for it to even be offered as an option.
- **Assistance:** As you can see in the chart, this includes *Apple Guide* and *SimpleText*. You should install both, but you might want to pick through the list of Read Me Files and dump any of the ones you're don't need.

- **Compatibility:** You should install both *Mac OS Easy Open* and *PC Exchange*.
- **Mobility:** The items here are strictly for PowerBooks, so you can skip the list if you're using a desktop model. (The Control Strip that's listed here is listed again in the Control Panel section, so don't worry if you want to include that in your installation.)
- **Multimedia:** You should include all of the subitems on this list, since the *Video Player* and even *MacinTalk* may be used by multimedia CDs (including kids' stuff) that you'll use.
- **Networking and Connectivity:** Include *Open Transport*, *Communications Tools*, and *File Sharing* (even if you're not on a network, since you never know when you might want to hook up, say, a visiting PowerBook to your machine). If you need *A/ROSE* or either *Token Talk* option for special networking needs, you'll know.
- **Printing:** Always install *Desktop Printing*, and then choose whatever type of printer you have (*LaserWriter 8* covers all LaserWriters except for the 300).
- **Universal Access:** You can read about *CloseView* and *Easy Access* in the next chapter and decide whether or not you want them.
- **Utility:** Include *AppleScript* (it's used in the background by lots of little utilities) and *Control Strip* (which is easy enough to turn off if you decide you don't want it). *ColorSync* is for people doing high-end color output.
- **International:** Only necessary if you use a foreign-language operating system.
- **Apple Menu Items:** Include all the Apple menu items.
- **Control Panels:** There's a long list of control panels for even basic installation; the chart at the end of this section marks which ones everyone should install. As for the other items, it depends on your setup. Some items (*PowerBook Display, Trackpad*) are obviously for PowerBooks, while some (*Infrared*, for example) are less obvious; for the most part, check the list under Mobility, and items listed both there and here are for PowerBooks. Other items are for other specific hardware setups: *Power Macintosh Card* is for '040 machines using a PowerPC card; *601 Processor Upgrade* lets you turn that upgrade card on and off; *Serial Switch* is for Quadra 950 Macs.
- **Extensions:** The installer presents a surprisingly short list of Extension options; the real surprise, I suppose, is the number of extensions not on this list that get installed anyway. But the setup actually makes sense: if you've selected the File Sharing control panel, the related extensions (File Sharing Extension, File Sharing Library) get installed automatically without your having to specifically select them. (And the reason you wind up with so many extensions is that you've selected items from elsewhere on the list that use multiple extensions; Open Transport, for instance, uses at least nine extensions.) From this short list, you should include *Color Picker. A/ROSE* is for special networking needs for some NuBus cards, and the other items are hardware-specific: *7200 Graphics Accelerator* is for the PowerMac 7200; *PowerPC Monitors* is for the

AudioVision 14 monitor on PowerPC Macs; *PrinterShare* lets you share non-network printers (like StyleWriters) across a network; *AppleVision* is for the AppleVision monitors; *Quadra Monitors Extension* and *Quadra AV Monitors Extension* work with the built-in video card for Quadra and Centris standard and AV models.

- **Fonts:** It's a short list of basic fonts; include them all.

Info. The Info button next to each item in the list can be a valuable tool, providing information that helps you decide whether you need to install the item. Or it can be totally useless, as you can see by the pictures here.

But it's even worse than useless in some cases. Let me quote Apple's Read Me from 8.1 on this one: "If you select the information button… the installer may report an earlier version number than the component that is actually installed. For example, the information button for Apple Video Player will report the version to be installed as 1.6.2… version 1.7.1 will actually be installed.

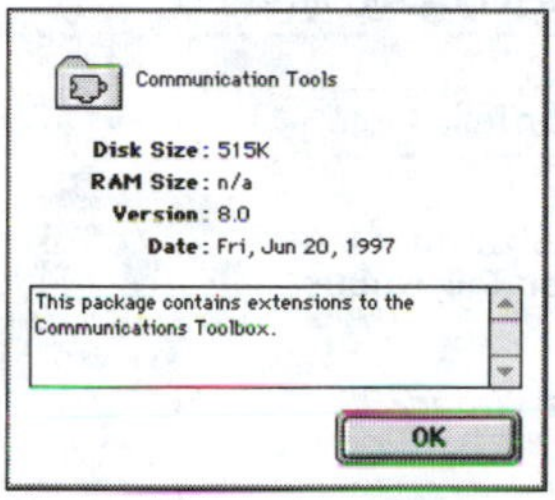

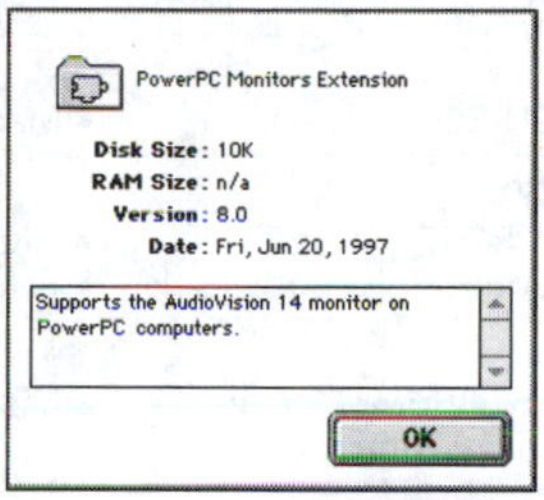

Some Info boxes are less than helpful (left), while others tell you just what you need to know (right).

The no-thinking-necessary chart. The No-Thinking-Necessary Custom Install Guide chart on the next page will help you through a custom install. The table lists all the items in the current Custom Install list; all you have to do is ignore the grey-bulleted items, and install the rest. (The major exception: PowerBook owners will want to install all or most of the items in the Mobility group, many of which are repeated under the Control Panels group.)

Don't walk away. When you've finished clicking your way through your choices, you click the Install button and watch the installation process: a slowly moving progress bar and a mesmerizing cursor of counting fingers. You get bored and leave to do something more interesting. You come back an hour later to find the installation complete.

Wrong! You come back an hour later to find a dialog waiting for you to click another Install or Continue button. And after some of the installation is done, you get another. And another. And another. Some dialogs offer Continue buttons that merely take you to the next dialog, which gives you an Install button.

Most of the main system components—the ones you selected way back in the window after you chose the destination disk—have their own welcome screens and/or install dialogs. Some even offer you Easy and Custom installs of their own. It's an incredibly ridiculous situation and Apple should be

The No-Thinking-Necessary Custom Install Guide

SECTION 1

- ***Universal System for Any Supported Computer***
- ***System Software for This Computer***
- ***Core System Software***

SECTION 2

Assistance

- Apple Guide
- Read Me Files
  - *About Apple Guide*
  - *About Automated Tasks*
  - *About Text-to-Speech*
  - *About FireWire*
  - *About Mac OS*
  - *About More Auto. Tasks*
  - *About Multiprocessing*
  - *About Open Transport*
  - *About Open Transport/PPP*
  - *About Portables Extras*
- SimpleText

Compatibility

- Mac OS Easy Open
- PC Exchange

Mobility (for PowerBooks)

- Apple IR File Exchange
- Auto Remounter
- Battery Recondition
- Control Strip
- File Assistant
- PC Card Extensions
- PowerBook
- PowerBook Display
- PowerBook Monitors Ext
- PowerBook Setup
- Trackpad

Multimedia

- Apple Video Player
- CD-ROM
- MacinTalk 3
- QuickTime

Networking and Connectivity

- Open Transport
- Open Tnspt Networking
- A/ROSE
- Communications Tools
- File Sharing
- Token Talk NuBus
- Token Talk PCI

Printing (include your printer)

- Desktop Printing
- ImageWriter
- StyleWriter Family
- LaserWriter 8
- LaserWriter 300

Universal Access

- CloseView
- Easy Access

Utility

- AppleScript
- ColorSync
- Control Strip

International

- WorldScript I
- WorldScript II

SECTION 3

Apple Menu Items

- Apple System Profiler
- AppleCD Audio Player
- Calculator
- Find File
- Graphing Calculator
- Jigsaw Puzzle
- Key Caps
- Note Pad
- Scrapbook
- Stickies

Control Panels

- 601 Processor Upgrade
- Appearance
- Apple Menu Options
- AppleTalk
- Auto Power On/Off
- Auto Remounter
- CPU Energy Saver
- ColorSync Sys Profile
- Control Strip
- Date & Time
- Desktop Pictures
- Energy Saver
- Extension Manager
- File Sharing
- General Controls
- Infrared
- Keyboard
- Launcher
- Mac OS Easy Open
- Map
- Memory
- Monitors & Sound
- Mouse
- Numbers
- PC Exchange
- Power Macintosh Card
- PowerBook
- PowerBook Display
- QuickTime Settings
- Screen
- Serial Switch
- Sound
- Startup Disk
- Text
- Trackpad
- Users & Groups

Extensions

- 7200 Graphics Accel.
- A/ROSE
- Color Picker
- PowerPC Monitors Ext
- Printer Share
- Quadra AV Monitors Ext
- Quadra Monitors Extension
- AppleVision

Fonts

- Chicago
- Courier
- Geneva
- Helvetica
- Monaco
- New York
- Palatino
- Times

ashamed of itself for the design. You'll have at least a dozen screens you have to click through to finish the installation, so you'll have to babysit the Mac all the way. (Okay, I've seen a worse installer—but it was for a Windows NT Server and I wasn't expecting elegance to begin with.)

One of the many useless interruptions of Custom Install.

Post-Install Procedures

Afterwards

It's not over till... Just because the Installer is finished with its job, that doesn't mean you're finished with yours. There are lots of details to contend with after you've put the new system on a drive, as listed in the *During and after* entry in the General Guidelines section. They include dealing with the Setup Assistant programs, resetting all your OS environmental choices, getting stuff from the system CD that doesn't get installed, putting your System Folder back together with all your third-party add-ons, and generally cleaning up after the Installer no matter which install option you chose.

Energy Saver. The first thing you get when you restart your Mac after a system installation for any new or recent Mac model is a dialog asking you to set your Energy Saver control panel; if you don't take care of it right away, you'll get the same dialog every time you start up your Mac. (There's more about this control panel in Chapter 5.)

The Assistants. The Mac OS Setup Assistant program automatically runs when you restart your computer after a system installation. It asks you questions about your computer's name, your name, and a password for network use. Just because you're not using a network that connects you to other computers doesn't mean you can skip this: if you use an AppleTalk printer (that includes most LaserWriters), you have a network—and if you don't complete the network questions, you won't be able to set up your printer easily. (As I learned to my chagrin when I bypassed the Assistant and spent hours trying to get a desktop printer set up for my LaserWriter.) But even if your network is your Mac and your printer, the Assistant won't continue unless you provide a password.

If you've passed up this small but important detail, you can run the Assistant later: you'll find it in the Assistants folder on the top level of your drive.

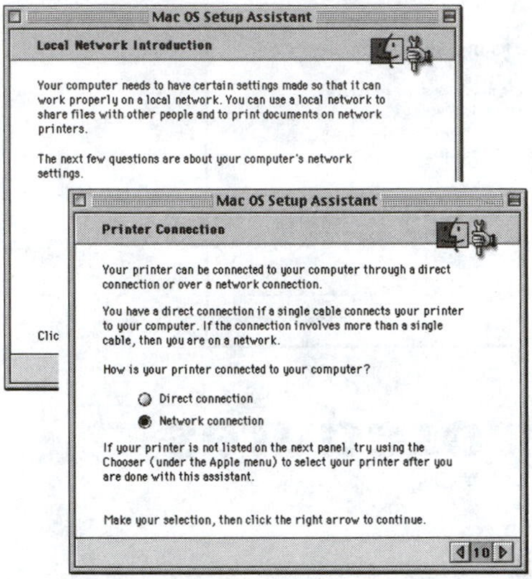

Internet Assistant and setup .... ***Chapter 27***

The Internet Assistant runs next; in order to answer its questions, you're going to need information at hand about your internet hookup from your service provider (or from the stuff you wrote down *before* you upgraded your system software). You don't have to run this Assistant; most providers' installation software takes care of putting all the right information in the right place.

Later assistance. If you don't cooperate with Setup Assistant when you first restart, but quit it so you can do it later, you'll find it in the Assistants folder that the Installer left on the top level of your hard drive.

The assistant information. You're not stuck with the names (yours and your computer's) and password you enter in the Assistant: you can access the same information through the File Sharing control panel, and change it there.

Set the defaults to change them. Open the Memory control panel and click the Use Defaults button to reset the disk cache to a more generous allotment than the initial 96K; for some odd reason, the initial default setting is not the same as what you get when you click Use Defaults. This will speed up Finder operations considerably, as discussed more fully in Chapter 13. You might want to restart immediately so you can do the rest of your post-installation chores with a faster Finder.

Stuff a "pure" System Folder. If you've got plenty of room on your hard drive, or on an external or removable, you can make a compressed version of your System Folder with a utility like **StuffIt** and keep it for future use (it

StuffIt and StuffIt Deluxe
Chapter 28

should squeeze down to about 40 percent of its original size). If you need to replace a few system components, it can be faster to unstuff the archive and grab what you need from it than to run the installer again (not even counting the time it might take to find your system CD!).

Colorize your system components. When you have a just-off-the-shelf System Folder (so to speak), it's a good time to "brand" all the system extensions and control panels so you can always tell them apart from the ones you add or that get installed along with other software. Select all the items in the Extension folder and use the Label submenu in the File menu to apply a label and color; repeat the procedure for the Control Panels folder. After you've added items to these folders, you'll be able to tell at a glance which are system items; or, you'll be able to add a Label column to either window so you can group things according to labels.

Labels and window views
Chapter 6

You might find it handy to rename one of the labels to something like "Apple's Stuff," using the Preferences command from the Finder's File menu.

Copy over Disk Copy. There's a Utilities folder on the system CD that contains the Disk Copy folder. This utility doesn't get copied to your hard drive in a standard install, so make sure you drag it over yourself into your Utilities folder, since it will come in handy.

Install some GX components. I've recommended that you not install QuickDraw GX (one of the top-level components you can check or uncheck in the Installer) because few people use it, and also because it eats up a lot of system memory. But when you install QuickDraw GX with OS 8, you also get Adobe Type Manager (ATM), which improves the look of fonts on your screen, and four extra fonts: Hoefler Text, Hoefler Ornaments, Tekton Plus, and Skia. Why turn down the opportunity for good-looking text and extra fonts?

Fonts and ATM
Chapter 14

Under *Adding Components and Items* in the *Reinstalls, Deinstalls, etc.* section, you'll find instruction on how to custom install separate components. If you customize a QuickDraw GX install, you can bypass the QuickDraw GX software itself, but still install ATM and the extra fonts.

With OS 8.1, it's easier: ATM and the extra fonts are in an Adobe folder on the system CD, and you can simply drag them to your hard drive.

Cosmetic Concerns

Clean up. No matter how you customize your installation, you're going to wind up with items you don't want or need in your System Folder. Go through the items in the subfolders with an eye towards getting rid of whatever you don't need. In some cases, you'll find things you thought you specifically excluded from the installation—and you did, but the Installer ignored you. In other cases, they'll be things you had no control over anyway—like the half-million translation files that come with MacLinkPlus.

If you have any doubts about what an item actually does, make sure you don't erase it: set it aside in another folder until you're sure you can live without it.

> ***"A fully loaded System Folder can easily weigh in at 200K, which doesn't leave much room for application programs and documents on disk.***
> *Adrian Mello, Macworld magazine, April 1985.*
> *(When there were no hard drives and a floppy held 400K.)"*

Easy install, then clean up. There are some things couples just never agree on, and in order to ensure household harmony, they just have to agree to disagree. Ann Landers (and/or Dear Abby—who can remember?) says one of the main issues is which way the toilet paper should hang. Another, although neither of the sisters knows about it, is how to install new system software. I always customize the installation, which takes time but cuts down on clutter. My other half insists on doing easy installs, and then just taking out the unnecessary items. He has a valid point, since a Custom install requires lots of babysitting and still requires some clean up. But I like the illusion of control it gives me. *Vive la différence!* (Gee, I gave this to my husband, who is always first in my line of tech readers, and he scribbled something next to that last sentence: "They should only know!" I have *no* idea what he means!)

Make your emergency disks. As long as you have your system CD out and you've just installed a fresh System Folder, you should go ahead and make an emergency floppy startup set with the disk images on the CD. (There's more information about this in Chapter 24.)

Environmental issues. Although it doesn't have to be done immediately, a new system often means you have to set up a new "environment": desktop backgrounds, the Apple menu, and so on. A minor change in system software won't change your settings—but a major one, like the leap from 7.x to OS 8, will set everything to system defaults.

While none of these is of pressing importance, getting some of them done early on lets you get to work more efficiently—even if the work you're doing is customizing your environment.

- Organize your Apple menu so it contains the items and submenus you want.
- If you use the Launcher, now's the time to set it up.
- Use the Desktop Patterns control panel to set your desktop background.
- Use the Appearances control panel to select a highlight color for selected text and a color scheme for windows.
- Use the Finder's Preferences command to set the font for icon and list views, select the Simple Finder if you want it, and for spring-loaded folder settings.

- In the General Controls control panel, uncheck the *Warn me if computer was shut down improperly* checkbox. While you're in there, you can set the other controls, too.

The really hard part. Once everything's back together and working smoothly, it's time to get to the real drudgery: putting your very own personalized System Folder back together. If you've done a clean system installation, you'll have a new System Folder, and your old one will have been renamed *Old System Folder* by the Installer. All your old third-party extensions, control panels, and odds and ends are in the old folder, and it's time to transfer them to the new one.

If you're the type who doesn't stroll through your System Folder at regular (or even irregular) intervals, you're in for a big shock: there's *lots* of stuff in there that you were unaware of! Here are some of the things you'll have to move, but don't take this list as a be-all and end-all guide—everyone's system is different. In the long run, you're going to have to open windows for your new System Folder and your old one side by side, and compare, item-by-item, what you used to have to what you have after a new installation.

Extension conflicts
Chapter 24

- **Extensions folder:** This is one of the hardest folders to update. There are a zillion system extensions from Apple, and a zillion more from other places. You'll be well aware of extensions you've added yourself, but you may not realize how many utilities and applications install extension components. You'll have to move all your non-Apple extensions into the new extensions folder. You can do this in batches, or all at once (with crossed fingers) and hope that you won't have to track down any extension conflicts. Don't forget to check inside the Extensions (Disabled) folder if you have one—you may have temporarily disabled a perfectly good extension before the system install.
- **Control Panels folder:** Same advice as for the Extensions folder, including looking in a (Disabled) folder.
- **Preferences folder:** Lots of people miss this one—and it's a big one. I just checked, and there are currently 126 items in my Preferences folder. Preferences files for utilities and applications may hold information as simple as where you like your windows opening on the screen, but they can hold important information, too, like the fact that the software's been registered, or your internet provider's connection information. After you've copied over all the things you think you need to, save everything else for weeks at least until you're sure you don't need any of the items. (Netscape's folder, with its all-important bookmark file, is a frequently overlooked item.)
- **Fonts:** You'll have to move all your own fonts into the new Font folder. This would be a good time to reorganize them if you've been meaning to do it but haven't found the time. If you've combined fonts and suitcases in your last system, don't forget: the basic fonts have been freshly installed, so don't copy over a suitcase that includes copies of the system's fonts.

- **Other subfolders:** Did you already have contextual menu items and control strip components in your previous systems? You'll have to add them to the new System Folder.
- **System Folder top level:** Some extensions are stored in the main level of the System Folder instead of in a subfolder; don't forget them.
- **Application folders:** Many applications make their own System Folder subfolders; sometimes the folder belongs to the publisher and works for all its products (like Claris and Microsoft folders). You'll have to move all these over, too.

Outside the System Folder

What else gets installed. But the Installer creates more than just a System Folder. Here are some of the other folders you might find (the specifics depend on how you've customized your installation) on your hard drive after an installation:

- **Apple Extras:** Contains subfolders for LaserWriter Software, AppleScript, FireWire, Mac OS Info Center, Mac OS Runtime for Java, MacLink Plus, Monitors Extra, Open Transport/PPP, Portables, QuickDraw 3D, Sample Desktop Pictures, and Sound Control Panel. Some of these folders, like AppleScript and MacLink Plus, contain applications and support documents; some have alternative (Sound Control Panel, Monitors Extras) or additional (LaserWriter, Java, Open Transport) system components. Almost all have Read Me files or other documentation.
- **Applications:** The ever-helpful SimpleText, and video-related components like the Apple Video Player and the Movie Player.
- **Assistants:** Mac OS Setup Assistant (just in case you didn't run it on the restart after installation) and an alias to the Internet Setup Assistant, whose original is buried down in the Internet folder.
- **Internet:** Odds and ends for internet use, like DropStuff and StuffIt expander; an Internet Applications subfolder containing Internet Explorer, Netscape Navigator, and Claris Emailer Lite.
- **Mac OS Read Me Files:** Basics on the basics: OS 8/OS 8.1, Extended Formatting, Printer Tips, and Open Transport Information.
- **Utilities:** The all-important Disk First Aid and Drive Setup utilities.
- **Web Pages:** Personal Web Sharing support files and samples.

Organize the top-level folders. Another after-installation housekeeping chore is organizing the folders the Installer leaves on the main level of the drive. The actual organization depends on how you work, and the actual folders depend on what you've chosen to install. The Assistants folder, for instance, with its two items, shouldn't have to stay in your main window, and it's unlikely you'll want to keep the Read Me Files and Apple Extras folders on that level either. In fact, you might want to relocate some of the Apple Extras items: many of its subfolders more logically belong in the Utilities folder, for instance.

CD Extras and other extras. Take a tour of your system CD after you've restarted your Mac with the fresh system software. There's more than just system stuff on it, even beyond the extra items installed on your hard drive. For instance:

- A **Utilities folder** that contains uncompressed copies of SimpleText, Disk First Aid, Drive Setup, and Disk Copy (as well as a few other items). They're uncompressed so you can use them directly from the CD before the installation.
- A folder of **Read Me Files** that provide information about various aspects of system software and Apple hardware.
- The **Disk Tools Images** folder that contains the images you need to create emergency startup floppies.
- An **Internet Extras** folder with various goodies, including **Internet Explorer** and **Netscape**—just in case you didn't install them initially.
- **CD Extras** is potentially the most interesting folder on the system CD. On the initial OS 8 CD, it included items ranging from practically necessary through interesting to hardly-anybody-would-need-this, as listed here.

Acrobat Reader 3.0	HyperCard Updates
Additional Desktop Patterns	Iomega Tools
Additional Desktop Pictures	Movie Player Extras
Additional Modem Scripts	Pointer Mode Control
Apple Telecom	QuickDraw 3D Extras
AppleCD Player	QuickTime Sample
At Ease Updaters	Spanish Text-to-Speech 1.5
Eric's Solitaire Sampler	

On previous system CDs, there have been interesting folders like extra fonts. The "extras" change from one system release to another, so make sure you look through everything.

Reinstalls, Deinstalls, etc.

Adding Components and Items

Why would you? Even if you use the easiest, "automatic," installation procedure, you have to choose the major system software components you want installed. At some point, you may want to add one of the components that you skipped the first time around. Say, for instance, you bypassed the opportunity to install the Personal Web Sharing software. Some months later, you get into web page design and want to try out the built-in web sharing capability that the Mac offers. Or perhaps you're reading through the next chapter and decide you'd like to try out the Easy Access control panel—but it's not part of an automatic *or* an easy install, so you're going to have to install that individual item to get it into your System Folder.

One other reason you might wind up installing an individual item or system component: if you throw something out by mistake or a specific file gets corrupted, you'll have to replace it with a fresh copy.

How far do you have to go? Most system component additions require your using the Installer, but just how you use it depends on what it is you're trying to install. Just as a full installation can be an automatic one, or an Easy or a Custom Install, so too can a component installation—you have to go far enough to find the component you need.

The pictures here, for instance, show two of the Installer screens; the first is the one whose Start button begins an automatic installation, while the second one takes you to the Easy versus Custom Install screen. If you want to, say, install Personal Web Sharing, you'll be able to just uncheck everything else in the list and click the Start button in the first screen. If you skipped installing the Mac OS Info Center the first time around and want to add it later, you're going to have to use the Customize button to move to the second screen, and uncheck everything from the list except the Info Center. From there, you'll be able to click the Start button for an Easy Install. These are the components available from the first screen, for an automatic installation:

- Mac OS Runtime for Java
- Personal Web Sharing
- QuickDraw 3D
- OpenDoc
- MacLink Plus
- Apple Location Manager
- QuickDraw GX
- Text-to-Speech
- Apple Remote Access

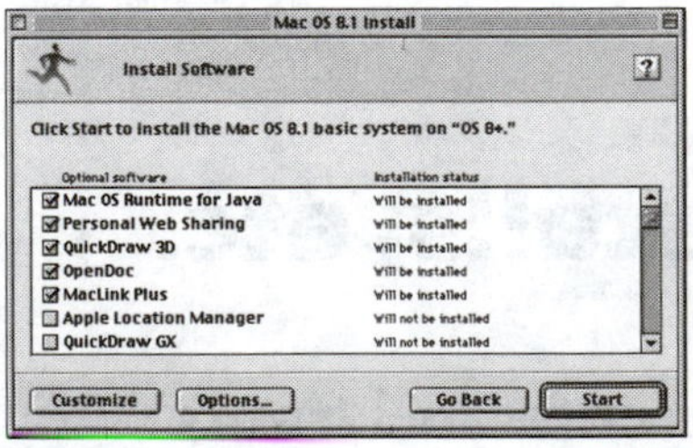

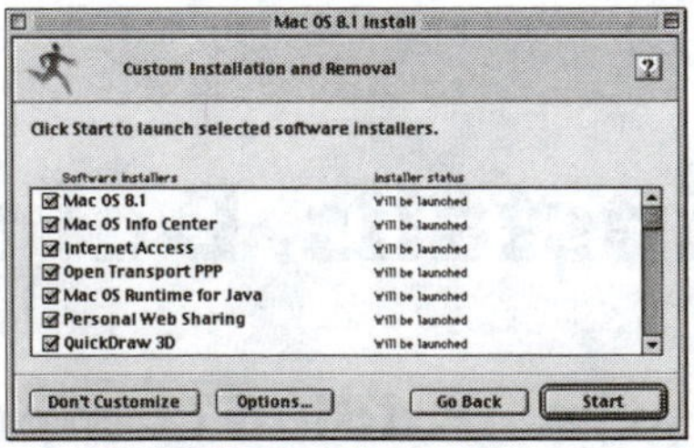

If you want to add the Personal Web Sharing component, or anything listed in the window on the left, you'll be able to do an automatic install by using the Start button in the window. To access some components, you have to go the next window, shown at right; from there, you can do an Easy or Custom Install.

The pre-reinstall concerns. When you're installing just a system component, you don't have to worry about the two important preinstall procedures: running Disk First Aid and updating the disk driver. In fact, you definitely don't want to bother with reinstalling the disk driver, so make sure you turn it off either with the checkbox in the Destination screen or the Options button in the later install screen. But you might run Disk First Aid even though it's not strictly necessary; it's a good thing to do at intervals, and using any installation process as a reminder is useful—sort of the way changing your clocks for Daylight Savings Time is supposed to remind you about changing the battery in your smoke alarms.

You should, however still start up from the CD. You can install some components from the CD Installer while you're actually running from your internal hard drive, but then you should at least restart with all your extensions off.

Adding a system component. Here's a quick run through of how to add a major system component like Personal Web sharing, or any of components available in the first Install window. (You might want to refer back to the Installer flow chart earlier in the chapter.)

1. Restart the Mac with the CD.
2. Run the Installer.
3. Select the hard drive in the Destination window (the second window of the Installer).
4. Uncheck the Perform Clean Installation checkbox. Once this is unchecked, you'll get an extra dialog at some point before the actual installation, noting that you already have system software installed and asking what you want to do. Click the Add/Remove button when the dialog shows up.

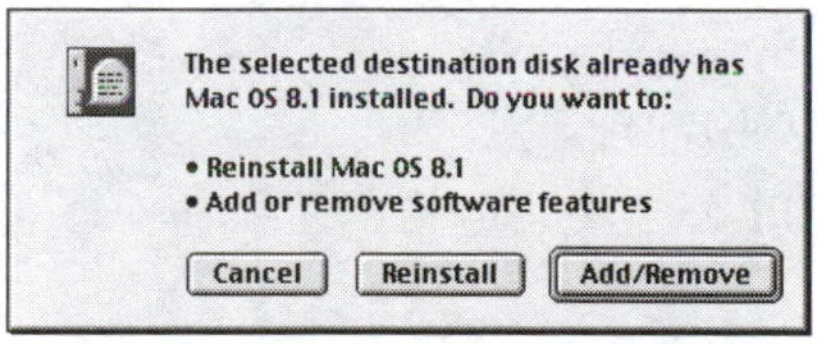

5. Click your way through the next two screens, until you get the main Install window.
6. Click the Options button and turn off the Update Driver option.
7. Check the Personal Web Sharing component, and uncheck all other items.
8. Click the Start button.

The Installer takes over and installs the various software components for Personal Web Sharing.

To perform an Easy Install of a component not listed in the first Install window (OS Info Center, Open Transport PPP, or Internet), use the first six steps above, then:

7. Click the Customize button.
8. Check the component you want in the list.
9. Click the Start button to move to the Easy Install window.
10. Click the Clean Install button.

Adding a single item. Adding a single item rather than a component that's listed separately (and usually consists of a group of support items) means you have to go "all the way" with the Installer, to the Custom Install screen. And, you have to know where the item is.

Most individual items that you'll be looking for are in the biggest component of all—the OS. The *No-Thinking-Necessary Custom Install Guide* chart earlier in the chapter will be a valuable reference for this procedure. Say you want the Control Strip control panel: you'll find it in three spots, under Mobility, Utility, and Control Panels—any one will do. Trashed your Stickies notes application and want to reinstall it? The chart shows it's in the Apple Menu Items category. Need a fresh copy of Apple Video Player? There it is, in the Multimedia section.

Once you know where the item is, here's how you get to it. Let's say you're going for the Control Strip control panel—and that you've followed steps 1-5 in the last entry.

1. Click the Customize button.
2. Uncheck everything except *Mac OS*.
3. Click the Start button.
4. Choose Custom Install from the pop-up menu.
5. Uncheck everything.
6. Expand the Utility category.
7. Check Control Strip.
8. Click Install.

Bypassing the main Installer. Many of the system software components have their own installers on the system CD; when you choose components through the OS installer, it merely launches the other installers as necessary. If there's a separate installer for the component you need, you can run it separately instead of through the main Installer. This means you'll bypass the Welcome and Destination screens, the Read Me, and, for most components, the "automatic install" screen. You won't have the opportunity to check the Clean Install button (a moot point for any but a system install, anyway) and there's no driver update done (also a moot point on a component install). You can indicate a drive other than the installing drive even though you skip the Destination screen, since there's a Switch Disk button instead (like the one used in application installers, described in Chapter 12.)

Most of the installers are inside a folder named *Software Installers,* which is buried inside another folder on the CD. It's easy enough to look around for it, even without using Find File. (Although if you can't find a folder by that name, do a search for the word Installer.) The picture here shows the individual installer folders on the 8.1 CD.

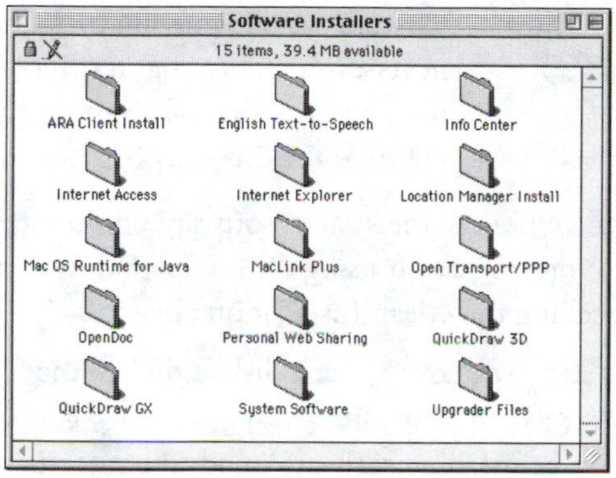

The system CD contains many installers, and you can run them separately for specific components.

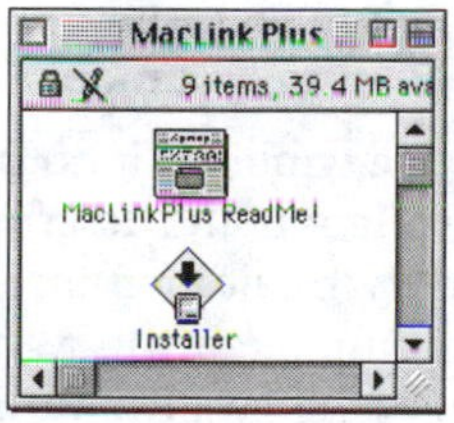

Run the component Installer by clicking on its icon.

To run the installer, open its folder, and simply double-click on the Installer icon. Most of these "sub-installers" give you a quick licensing agreement and then go directly to the Install window that lets you choose between an Easy and a Custom Install from a pop-up menu; some have only "automatic" installs that don't give you any choice about the sub-items that are included.

Bypassing all the installers. Before you go through all the bother of running any installer, check if the item you need is on the CD in an uncompressed form: use Find File to search for it. Disk utilities, for instance, are available in their full-blown versions; one install CD I have has the Easy Access and CloseView control panels uncompressed in a folder named Mobility.

Do the search while your hard drive is still running the computer—there's no need to start up from the CD. And if you find what you're looking for, you can just drag it over to your drive.

Removing Components

Manually removing system components. As you work with your Mac, you'll probably find that there are some control panels and extensions that you never use; you may not have even meant to install them, but sometimes the

Installer does whatever it wants in the way of little pieces. The easiest thing to do with these items is to simply switch them off with the Extensions Manager; they'll be placed in Disabled folders and after you're *sure* you don't need them (after more than a month goes by), you can trash them.

But other system components aren't so easy to get rid of, since they consist of more than a single item. That's when the Installer comes in handy as a deinstaller.

The Remove option. If you never do a full Custom install with the Installer, it's possible to never even realize that it offers a Remove function, because that option is in the same pop-up menu as the Custom Install choice.

When you want to remove some system software component, you run the Installer without worrying about using Disk First Aid first, or updating the disk driver, or checking the Clean Installation checkbox.

1. In the Destination window, select a disk and click the Start button.
2. If the Perform Clean Installation checkbox is checked, you'll get a dialog asking if you're reinstalling software or adding or removing it: click the Add/Remove button. (You can bypass the dialog by unchecking the checkbox; but the actual setting doesn't matter, since you're removing something so the whole idea of "clean install" is moot.)
3. The Installer skips the next two or three windows it normally displays, and you see the list of system components. Ignore the description above the list "*…launch selected software installers*" and its implication that you're actually installing something here; check the component you want to remove. The example in the picture is the removal of the Java Runtime components.

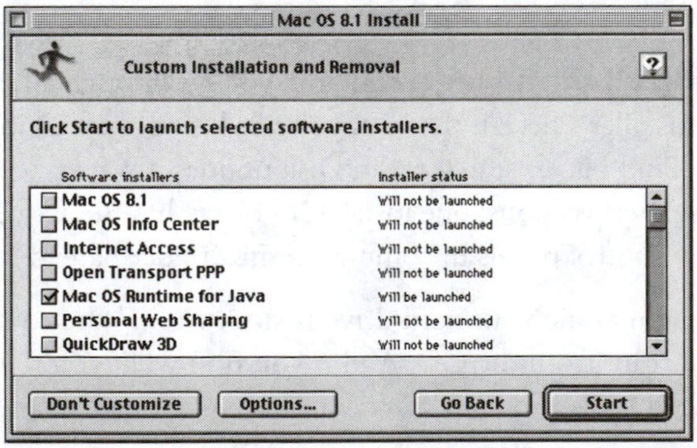

This familiar-looking window from install operations is also used for removing items.

4. Click the Start button.
5. In the next window (the Easy Install window), select Custom Remove from the pop-up menu.
6. Check the components to be removed, and click the Remove button.

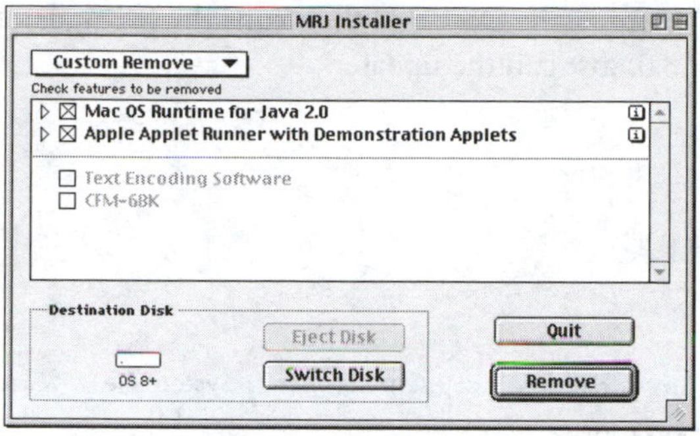

Select components and click the Remove button.

When it comes to removing items, the Installer actually shows some nice interface detail (finally!). As you can see in the picture, there are two dimmed items in the list. These items are installed with the Java runtime components, but they're also installed, and used, with other system components. So, while you can see that they go with Java Runtime, you can't remove them because they need to be available for something else in the system.

Updating Your System Software

Updating versus upgrading. There are only shades of meaning here, with an *update* usually referring to a minor change (from 8.0 to 8.1, say) and an *upgrade* connoting a major leap, as from system 7.x to OS 8. But the terms aren't strictly defined or clearly differentiated all the time.

In general, however, while a system upgrade demands a clean install procedure and that you check that all your old software will run under the new system, a minor update is just that—some minor changes to the stuff in your System Folder. It's important to read through the Read Me files, and check with online and other knowledgeable sources to determine when an update is minor or not: while OS 8 to 8.1 is minor, System 7.0 to 7.1 was not—so don't depend just on a number change for a clue as to whether or not an update is major.

Dirty-install updates. For minor updates of system software, you can skip the whole Clean Install procedure, with its concomitant get-stuff-from-the-old-System-folder operation. The worst you'll have is a few third-party extensions or control panels that might break under the update, and it's no more difficult tracking down those problems from a single new System Folder than by putting them in from the old System Folder.

The 8.1 update. If you already have OS 8 installed, you can move to 8.1 simply by running the 8.1 updater. This is available for downloading from Apple's web site (though it's a *looong* download on a standard modem).

If you have an 8.1 system CD, you can use it to simply update your existing, installed 8.0 system. You'll find two Install icons, one for an 8.1 system, and one for an 8.1 update. If you choose the 8.1 system install, what happens is that the CD first installs OS 8 and then runs the 8.1 updater—so if you already have 8.0, just run the updater.

IN THE BEGINNING

You think it's difficult keeping up with system software version numbers? Pity us poor pioneers: Apple didn't start using system "sets" until something called "System Tools 5.0"—which consisted of a System file version 4.2 and a Finder version 6.0.

Before that, we had the pleasant state of affairs shown here.

System number	*System file*	*Finder*
-	1.0	1.1
-	2.0	2.0g
-	2.0	4.1
-	3.0	5.1
-	3.1	5.2
-	3.2	5.3
-	3.3	5.4
-	4.0	5.4
-	4.1	5.5
5.0	4.2	6.0
5.1	4.3	6.0
6.0	6.0	6.1

Updating the driver. For even a minor system update, like 8.0 to 8.1, make sure you update the disk driver. You can do it as part of the system update through the Options button that lets you elect to update the driver, or you can do it by running the latest version of Drive Setup, as described earlier. If yours is a non-Apple drive, or an Apple drive formatted with non-Apple software, get an appropriate update from the software company that made your disk formatter.

Running the updater. When you run a system updater, which looks and behaves like the Installer, you should be running your Mac from a system other than the one you're updating. If you don't start up from a system CD, start from another volume with all extensions off.

For minor updates of system software, don't worry about setting up a clean install option. Older items will be replaced by the newer ones during the update.

Bug fixes and *that* kind of update. The only update available as I write this (8.1) offers improvements over the previous versions of OS 8 in some ways. But, historically, there have been interim updates of system software to take care of specific bugs or to cater to specific hardware needs of some Mac models. Usually these system versions have a second decimal number (like 7.5.3). Installation of these updates has never been by running anything that looked like an installer: sometimes you dropped something into the System Folder, and sometimes you ran a little updater utility that changed all the necessary items without your having to do any picking and choosing.

It's too early to tell how these kinds of updates will be handled in OS 8. But you can cehck the System 7 entries earlier in this chapter, checking the Tune-Up and Enabler entries to see how they've been handled in the recent past.

Reinstalling System Software

Reinstalls. When you reinstall a system because it's been giving you trouble (constant crashing, perhaps, or weird printing problems), make sure you do a clean install even though the new system is the same version number as the one you're already using. The Installer checks if you have the most recent version of a system file; it doesn't check to see if that file's intact. So, for instance, if it sees the current version of a printer driver, it won't replace it—and that might be the component giving you problems.

How to reinstall. When you reinstall system software because of problems, make sure it's a Custom Install—because you don't need all the stuff an automatic or Easy Install does. Start up from the CD, and run the Installer. Then:

1. In the Destination dialog, check the Perform Clean Install checkbox.
2. In the Custom Installation and Removal dialog, uncheck everything except *Mac OS*.
3. In the same dialog, use the Options button to uncheck the Driver Update option.
4. Click the Customize button.
5. Select Custom Install from the pop-up menu in the next window.
6. In the list, check *only* the following items: System Software for this Computer, Printing, Control Panels, and Extensions.
7. Click the Clean Install button.

By installing only the items listed, you can be sure of replacing 99.99 percent of the system components that might be causing problems or might have been corrupted due to the troublemaker.

After the reinstall, you'll have to put your specialized old System Folder items into the new System Folder. But that won't take as long as when you're installing entirely new system software, because you'll already know that your current third-party utilities work with this system software.

Newer versus older questions. When you're reinstalling a system, you may get a few (or a lot) of questions about which version of certain files should remain on the drive. These dialogs come in two flavors: one that lets you keep the older or the newer file, and one that only lets you keep the older version.

First of all, you wouldn't expect to see these questions during a clean install, because you're creating a new System Folder, so how can you have older files? But they seem to crop up anyway, so here's the guideline: when given a choice (as with the top dialog in the picture), keep the newer file; otherwise, let it keep the older file (the bottom dialog, as you can see, gives you no choice except to do that or stop the installation). In most cases, the Installer will overwrite the older file during the installation anyway.

Choose the Newer version when you have a choice, but Continue with the older one when you have to.

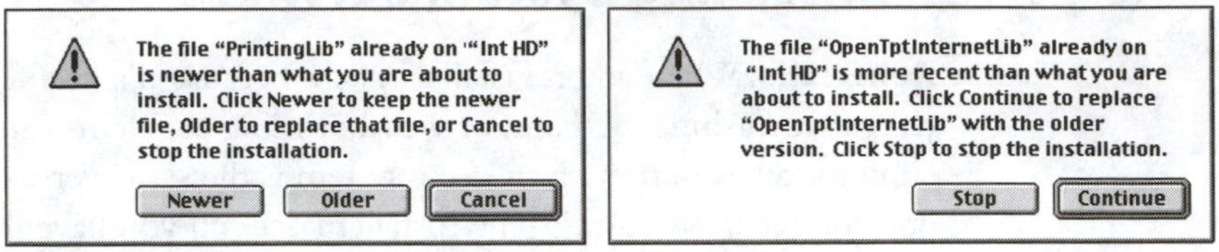

Getting it together. After you've installed the new system folder, make the Mac create a list of the extensions and control panels you were running before the installation but are now missing, so you'll have a guide as to what you have to add back into your new system folders.

Get the Extensions Manager preferences file from your old System Folder (there's a folder of Extensions Manager preferences—use the one from your main working set if there's more than one), and drag it into the new System Folder (inside the Preferences folder, in the Extensions Manager Preferences folder). Then, open Extensions Manager—which will tell you that the current set doesn't match your old set and offer to create a disk file listing the missing items.

9

The System Folder

In This Chapter

The System Folder

The System Folder and Files

The System Folder. The System Folder is the most important folder on your hard drive because it contains the software-based portions of the Mac's operating system. And just to prove that it's special, it's stamped with the OS icon. You'll find a few "loose" files in the System Folder, among them the System and the Finder. In addition, you'll find lots of special subfolders that hold other pieces of the system software. As you add third-party items (software from places other than Apple) that need to go in the System Folder, you'll find their files and folders in there, too.

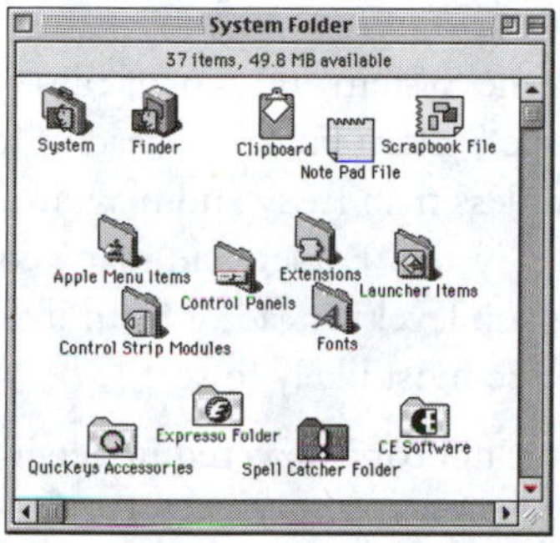

The System Folder holds a combination of files (top section), system subfolders (the middle section), and third-party software folders (bottom section).

By any other name. It doesn't matter what you name your System Folder. Any folder with the System and Finder files in it is the System Folder and will get stamped with the OS icon.

The System file. The System file contains the core of the software-based instructions that run the Mac; they work in conjunction with the hardware-based instructions in the Mac's ROM. (Many of the other files in the System Folder's subfolders also add to the Mac's operating system.) The System file has a suitcase-style icon because it's a special type of file—a suitcase file.

The size of the System file on the disk has little to do with the amount of memory your system uses when it's running. The only relationship between the System file size and the memory your system uses is that they both keep growing over time. Back in System 7.1, the System file hovered around 1 meg; the basic OS 8 System file is around 6 megs.

> ***"Primarily due to the bulkiness of a System file containing several fonts and desk accessories, hardly enough room remains in 512K for more than one program and an open document."***
> *Macworld, April 1986*

System, system. The word *system* in this chapter usually refers to your system software, but can be used in several different ways: the version of the system software you're using *(What system are you running?)*; your system software in general *(The system crashed)*; or your hardware configuration *(Which Mac system do you have?)*. The phrase *System file* (with a capital S) refers specifically to the suitcase-icon System file in your System Folder. Without the capital, *system file* refers to any file inside your System Folder or its subfolders.

Likewise, the *System Folder* (capitalized) is that special System Folder; a *system folder*, uncapitalized, refers to one of the System Folder's subfolders.

The Finder. The Finder file is what provides the Finder's capabilities; it's your desktop, with all its menus and abilities, that's squeezed into this file. While the Finder used to be more independent—before System 7, it was a separate application that you could allocate memory to, for instance—it has become more and more closely aligned with the System file; during System 6's reign, it was suggested that the Finder file would soon be rolled into the System file. But, apparently, not *too* soon.

Other "loose" files. Besides the System and Finder files, you may see several other files out "loose" in the System Folder instead of inside one of the subfolders. Some programs are less than fussy and may drop some preferences or support files right inside the System Folder, and many control panels and extensions can work from this top level instead of from inside their own folders. But here are the items you're most likely to see:

- **Clipboard**. Although the Clipboard (covered in detail in Chapter 5) is actually a RAM-based file, when memory's tight and you cut or copy something large to the Clipboard, the item is temporarily written to the disk, in this file.

Note Pad and Scrapbook files
Chapter 10

- **Notepad File** and **Scrapbook File**. These are the files that hold the material you put in those desk accessories.
- **MacTCP DNR**: This file is automatically created when you use your telecommunications software.

During System 7's reign, minor updates for bugs or new hardware were provided in the form of *enablers* and other files that were stored in the System Folder; it's too early to tell if OS 8 will take the same approach.

A single System Folder. You shouldn't keep more than one System Folder on your hard drive, even though it may seem like a good idea to have either two different versions of the system software, or both working and backup copies of the folder. The Mac can get a little schizophrenic if you offer it more than a single System Folder on a drive.

This is not as much of a problem as it used to be. Back when both an application and a System Folder could fit on a floppy disk, people with hard drives would copy the entire disk contents over—with one System Folder for almost every application. A basic troubleshooting procedure was checking for multiple System Folders and deleting all but one.

Subfolder Basics

The subfolders. The collection of folders inside your System Folder depends to some extent on which Mac you have, which system version

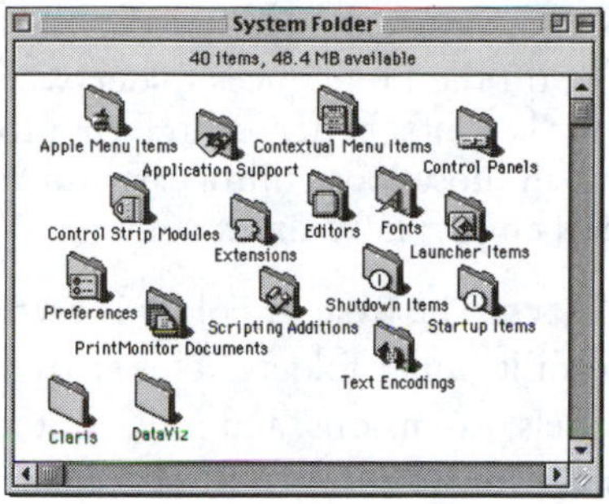

The common system subfolders.

you're running (and which components you've chosen), and what applications you use; all of these things can put special subfolders inside the System Folder. The picture here shows the basic system subfolders; you can see that most of them get special icons. Some of the subfolders (like Fonts) are described in detail in other chapters; some (like Apple Menu Items) have their own sections in this chapter; and some merit only a line or two of description. Here's a list of where you'll find information about the common subfolders:

Subfolder	*Chapter*	*Subfolder*	*Chapter*
Apple Menu Items	9	Scripting Additions	10
Fonts	14	DataViz	12
Application Support	9	Shutdown Items	9
Launcher Items	12	Desktop Printers	15
Contextual Menu Items	6	Speakable Items	22
Preferences	9	Disabled folders	9
Control Panels	9	Startup Items	9
PrintMonitor Documents	15	Extensions	9
Control Strip Modules	9	Text Encodings	9

Miscellaneous subfolders. Some of the System Folder's subfolders don't need (or, in some cases, deserve) lots of detail. Here are some that you won't find elsewhere in the book:

- **(Disabled) folders:** The Extensions Manager lets you choose which extensions and control panels you want running the next time you use your Mac. It doesn't turn these items on and off: it simply moves them in and out of the folders where they have to be in order to run. When you indicate that you don't want an item to run, it's moved into the *Extensions (Disabled)* or *Control Panels (Disabled)* folder until you want to use it again. You may find disabled folders for other system subfolders, like Fonts and Startup Items, too.
- **Text Encodings:** Holds documents used by the Text Encoding extension, allowing certain text conversions and translations to be done behind the scenes.
- **Third-party folders:** Many applications need all sorts of support files (dictionaries, glossaries, import/export filters, and so on) in order to work. Sometimes these are stored in the application's folder, but when a company makes more than one Mac product, shared support files are often stored in the System Folder instead; many utilities store their folders in the System Folder. My System Folder, for instance, has folders named CE Software, Claris, MS Internet, QuicKeys Accessories, and Spell Catcher.

- **Application Support:** This is a good idea that no one's using yet; it should take the pressure off the Preferences folder, where everything seems to get dumped for lack of a better, central spot for an application's miscellaneous files, and all those loose third-party folders described above. But so far, mine's empty; how about yours?

Auto-routing to subfolders. The System Folder is pretty smart—it can route certain items to some of its inner folders. This started in System 7, with auto-routing for control panels, extensions, and fonts, but includes many other types of files, so you get auto-routing to these folders:

- Control Panels
- Extensions
- Font
- Control Strip Modules
- Contextual Menu Items
- Apple Menu Items

What gets routed to the Apple Menu Items folder? Desk accessories. But not just any desk accessory—it has to be a *real* desk accessory. The Calculator and Key Caps, for instance, are real desk accessories; the Jigsaw Puzzle, Scrapbook, and Note Pad are actually applications, as you can see by checking their "Kind" in either their Info windows or in a list view. There are also some other routing capabilities that don't seem to be implemented completely (for Preferences files, for instance) but you may find them working in subsequent versions of the system software.

Dragging a "routable" item onto the System Folder's icon (*not* into its window) gets you a dialog asking if you want the item sent to the correct folder. If you drag a group of items at the same time, you'll get a dialog afterwards telling you what went where.

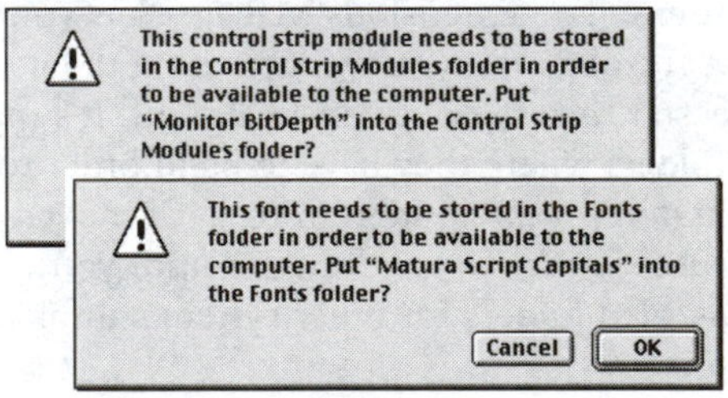

Dragging a special item onto the System Folder icon gives you a dialog offering to place the item in the correct subfolder.

Let auto-routing help you. If you're not sure where something belongs—not all extensions and control panels have icons that identify them as such—you don't have to resort to reading a manual! Dragging it to the closed System Folder might solve the problem for you. (Then again, it might just load up the top level of your System Folder with items whose destinations, and perhaps even purposes and origins, are unknown.)

Grand Central dispatching. To take advantage of the System Folder's routing capabilities, keep an alias of it out on the desktop so it's easy to get to.

Easy come, easy go. In most cases, a System Folder subfolder gets stamped with its special icon as long as it has the correct name and is inside the System Folder; sometimes it also has to have something (of the right type) inside in order to be tagged as special.

Drag your Fonts folder out of the System Folder, for instance, and create a new, empty folder. Name it Fonts, put a single font in it, and voilá: you have a new, stamped Fonts folder. (You'll also have a very short Font menu.)

When you drag a "routable" file to the closed System Folder, and the subfolder doesn't exist, the Mac still asks if you want it to go into the proper folder (Contextual Menu Items, say, or Control Strip Modules). When you say yes, it simply creates the subfolder and then puts the item inside.

The basic folders that always exist even if you don't use them, like Startup Items and Shutdown Items, are automatically recreated at startup if you've trashed them during a work session.

Suitcase Files and Resources

Fonts are in suitcases, too
Chapter 14

Suitcases aren't folders. The System file is a special type of file called a *suitcase*, not only because of the shape of its icon, but because of the way it behaves. A suitcase isn't the same as a folder, despite some surface similarities (you double-click on the icon to open its window, and you can drag things into and out of it).

Suitcases are actually *files,* not folders, and they hold *resources,* not other files or folders. While items in a folder still exist as separate files, when you put a resource into a suitcase it becomes an integral part of that suitcase file and is no longer a separate file on the disk. When you drag a resource out of a suitcase, a new, separate file is created on the disk. You'll even get a Copy dialog during the procedure, which is certainly not something you ever see when you're simply moving a folder's contents to someplace else on the same disk.

Note that the dialogs don't say that the Mac is *copying* something from one place to another; they say that something is being *moved.* Unlike a copy operation that puts a copy in a new location and leaves the original, a *move* makes the copy and then erases the original.

System resources. In addition to zillions of lines of programming code that you can't (and shouldn't want to!) get at, the System file contains many different kinds of *resources*—things like dialog boxes, cursors, and icons—that give the Mac its Macness. You can get at some of these resources with Apple's ResEdit utility (that's covered in Chapter 10), but there are a few types of resources that are easy for any user to install and remove.

To see these files, just double-click on the System file: a window opens to show the user-configurable resources. Depending on your system, you'll see any or all of these:

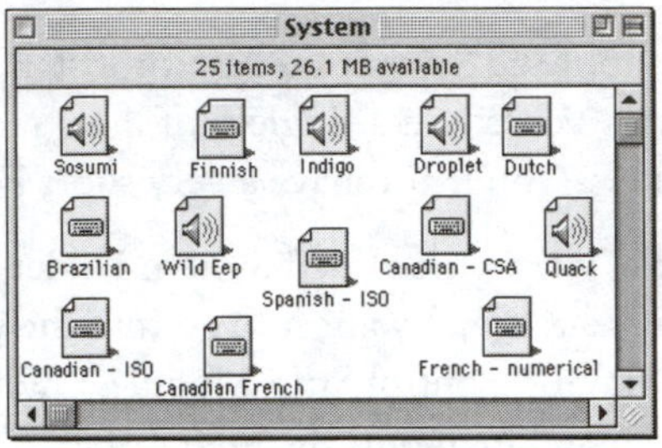

The opened System file displays user-configurable resources.

- **Sounds**: The basic system beep is built in so deeply that you can't get at it, but the other sounds are there as separate files.
- **Keyboard layouts**: You usually need only a single one—and the standard one is "buried" so you can't delete it—but you can add more. These are the layouts that are listed in the Keyboard control panel.
- **Language scripts**: You probably don't have any of these—they're for non-Roman-alphabet languages like Hebrew and Japanese.

Ins and outs. You add a resource to the System file by dragging it into the System file's opened window, its closed icon, or the closed System Folder. Dragging it to the closed System Folder gets you a dialog offering to put the item in its place (so to speak). To remove a resource, of course, you'll have to open the System file icon. You can't add or remove resources while any applications are running.

About Extensions and Control Panels

In General

Extensibility. Extensions *extend* the capability of the system software by loading into memory at startup, right there along with the system software. They're like little pieces of the System file that exist separately so you can add or delete them according to your needs. Extensions let you, in effect, build your own Mac operating system.

A certain (large) number of extensions come with your basic OS. Apple continually creates new extensions that tweak problems in the System file, provide communication with peripherals, and give older Macs some of the capabilities of the newer ones.

There are also a zillion or so third-party extensions that add capabilities to your basic Mac system. These range from silly and/or tiny (like eyeballs that watch your cursor) to as useful and complex as a macro utility that lets you automate many of your Mac operations

Extensions versus applications. An extension is available on a system-wide basis. It's always ready and waiting no matter what program you're in. A spell checker that comes with your word processor works in that program; a standalone utility spell checker has to be launched like any other program; but a spell checker that comes as an extension works anywhere you care to use it.

Extensions that provide special capabilities to only specific programs (the Finder, for instance) aren't system-*wide*, but they're still system-*level*, acting like built-in operations.

Extensions versus control panels. At first it seems easy to differentiate between extensions and control panels, because they're in different folders and because a quick definition says extensions load into memory and control panels change some system feature. But, in fact, the dividing line isn't always so clear.

Yes, an item is either an extension or a control panel; some utilities even have two components, one an extension and one a control panel. But some extensions—Chooser extensions for printer drivers, for instance—don't load into memory at startup. And some control panels have components that *do* load into memory at startup, which is why you'll see their icons during the "parade" at startup.

In this chapter, the term *extension* often includes any control panel that loads into memory at startup.

The icon parade. During startup, you see a parade of icons across the bottom of the screen; sometimes there are so many that they wrap up to a second line. These are the items that are loading into memory—extensions and control panels.

This icon display gives you something to think about while the Mac's starting up: *Gee, I wonder what that icon stands for? I don't remember installing anything with a rainbow on it.* For some reason, Apple hasn't seen fit to allow the icon names to be displayed during the march. But it's one of the pleasant extra features provided by Conflict Catcher, described more fully later.

What's an *init*? The pre-System 7 term *init (ih-NIT)* is often used instead of *extension,* but it also refers to control panels that load into memory at startup. It comes from the word *initialize,* because the program's information is placed into memory at startup, when all the computer's systems are initialized.

Extensions and memory. Since extensions load into memory, using lots of extensions eventually eats up lots of memory; you can't just keep adding extensions without eventually paying a price. And, since they load into memory at startup, when you add a new extension to your collection you have to restart the Mac in order for it to take effect.

Not the startup folder. Even though extensions and control panels load into memory at startup, they are *not* startup items, so don't put them in the Startup Items folder. If you do, the Mac will attempt to "open" them at startup (which is not the same as putting them into memory). "Opening" an extension doesn't do anything at all—try double-clicking on one in your Extensions folder. You get the ever-so-helpful dialog shown here (did they *have* to use "functionality" *twice?).* Put extensions in your Startup Items folder, and you'll get one of these dialogs for every single one of them at startup. As for control panels in the Startup Items folder: most control panels can't be opened unless they've already been loaded into memory, so you'll usually wind up with messages telling you just that. Sometimes you actually get the control panel with controls that seem to work, but the changes just won't register.

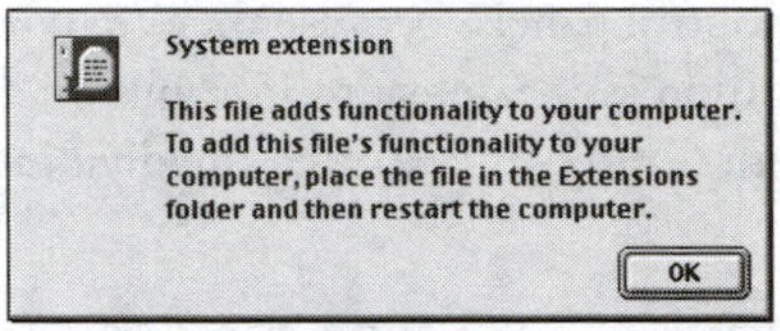

You get this dialog for an extension that's been misplaced in the Startup Items folder.

Making a list and checking it once. When you want to check your extensions and control panels—what you have, what's on and off—you can go through the folders in your System Folder, and even print their windows. But there are two much better ways, and which one you should use depends on the type of report you want.

The first, and more obvious one, is using the Extensions Manager control panel, which has a Save Set as Text command. You'll get a text file that lists the items in your Extensions folder, in the Extensions (Disabled) folder, in the Control Panels folder, and so on. You'll even have a report on the size, version number, and type and creators for each item.

The second way is to use the hidden little gem Apple System Profiler that by default is installed in your Apple Menu Items folder so it's accessible from the Apple menu. You can set it to show control panels or extensions, and then to show either all the items in each category, or just the Apple items, or just the non-Apple items. The list in the window puts a bullet in front of active items, and shows the location of a selected item. Use the File menu's Create Report command to create a file that contains lists of extensions, control panels, and/or other system items. Unlike the Extensions Manager report, this one lumps together all the control panels, then all the extensions, and so on, regardless of whether they're on or off; they're listed alphabetically, and a bullet indicates that the item is active. The only additional information is each item's version number—which is often all you need.

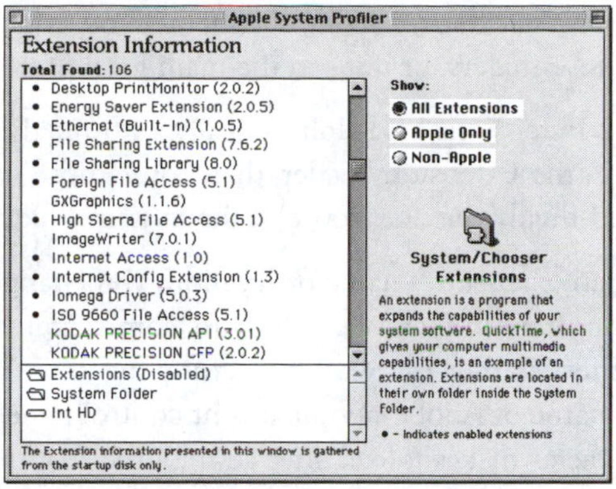

Use Apple System Profiler to get an overview of what extensions and control panels are available on your system, and which are activated.

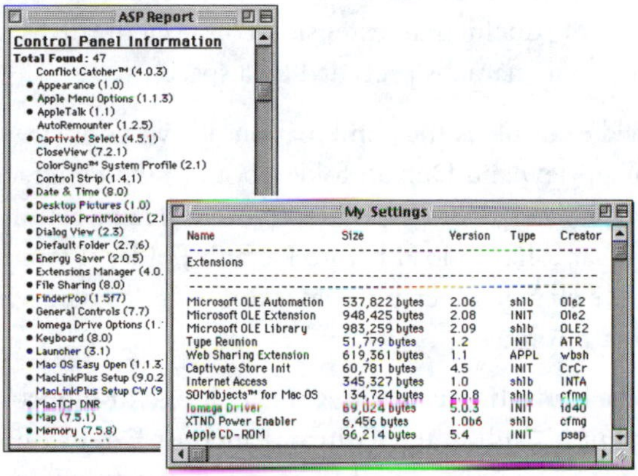

Create reports from Apple System Profiler (left) or the Extensions Manager (right).

Using Extensions and Control Panels

Installing extensions and control panels. You don't need an installer to take care of putting new extensions in your system, although they're handy when a utility provides several pieces, like a control panel, an extension, and a support folder. Just drag the pieces to the closed System Folder to route them to the right place. The important thing to remember is that you usually have to restart the computer for new extensions and control panels to work.

Trashing extensions. It's not so easy to trash an extension (or a control panel) because you're not allowed to erase any file that's in use; most extensions, since they load into memory at startup, are flagged as "in use" even if you're not using their particular capabilities at any given time.

So, trashing an extension is usually a two-step process. First, drag it out of the Extensions folder or use Extensions Manager to disable it. Then, after you restart the Mac, you can drag it to the Trash.

Where extensions and control panels live. Sure: extensions go in the Extensions folder and control panels go in the Control Panels folder. But that's not always the case. An extension/control panel will be loaded into memory if it's in either of those folders, or if it's in the main level of the System Folder.

Loading order. Extensions load alphabetically, in three different groups: first come the items in the Extensions folder, then come those in the Control Panels folder, and finally the ones loose in the System Folder.

So, by changing an extension's name or location, you change the loading order. This is important in many cases because some extensions need to be loaded before others so they can work peacefully together. You may have noticed that the name of Adobe's popular font control panel is ~ATM. The leading tilde character makes it load after all the other control panels, instead of first, where it would be based on its "real" name. Apple's Extension Manager control panel has an extension component, EM Extension, that has to load first—so its name is preceded by a space.

Another good example is the combination of two popular shareware control panels, Dialog View and Default folder, both of which affect Open and Save dialogs. Dialog View's documentation (you do read documentation, don't you?) notes that it has to load before Default Folder if you're using both of them. I simply changed Default Folder to Diefault Folder, and had no problem using both utilities.

X marks the icon. If you see an X through one of the icons, that means it's not loading but it's still in the Control Panels or Extensions folder: It may be turned off from within the control panel, it may be a demo that's reached its expiration date, or it might not be able to load because another extension that it depends on didn't load first.

Extension conflicts. An extension *conflict* occurs when two or more extensions (or control panels) can't work together, or when a single extension just can't work with the system software. Sometimes extensions fight over the same spots in memory; sometimes they're trying to manipulate the same system resources; sometimes their functions just clash. Whatever the reason, extension conflicts are probably the leading cause of problems on the Mac (although SCSI problems run a close second).

What kind of problems? The easiest to diagnose is the one that keeps your Mac from starting up—it freezes while the extensions are loading. Conflicts can also lead to intermittent system crashes while you're working, or all sorts of general weirdness in some or all applications.

Extension conflicts **Chapter 24**

Preventing extensions from loading. You can prevent a single extension from loading by moving it out of any of three folders that let it load (Extensions folder, Control Panels folder, and System Folder). Apple's Extensions Manager creates "disabled" folders for each type of extension (as well as for the Startup

Items folder and Shutdown Items folder); this is a good place to stick temporarily unwanted extensions, even if you're doing it manually. Some control panels provide Off switches that keep them from loading on the next startup without your having to actually move the icon to another folder.

To turn off *all* extensions, hold down Shift when you start up the Mac, and keep it down until you see the *Extensions off* subtitle in the opening dialog. (This also prevents items in the Startup Items folder from opening, unless you get your finger off Shift in time.)

The Shift effect. Using Shift to turn off extensions also affects virtual memory and the disk cache settings that were set in the Memory control panel. Virtual memory is temporarily turned off, and the cache is either turned off (on older Macs) or set back to its minimal size (on newer Macs that always need the cache on). While you'll be able to see that VM is off, as described in the last entry, there's no way to tell that the cache has been reset unless you happen to know how much your system usually takes for its memory allocation, and can see that the amount of the cache is no longer in the allocation. The cache setting in the control panel remains where you set it so that it will be used on the next startup; there's no visual clue as to the fact it's not currently on. You'll just have to trust me on this one.

IN THE BEGINNING

The number of control panels remained the same from the very beginning of the Mac right up through System 6. Can you guess how many there were?

One. Sort of. There was something named Control Panel, but it was desk accessory.

When you opened *the* Control Panel, you saw a scrolling list of icons at the left that were *control panel devices.* At the right, you got the controls for the selected control panel device. All in a neat little package. With the General device selected, you'd get all the things shown here (which have since been dispersed among the General Controls, Memory, Sound, and Date & Time control panels).

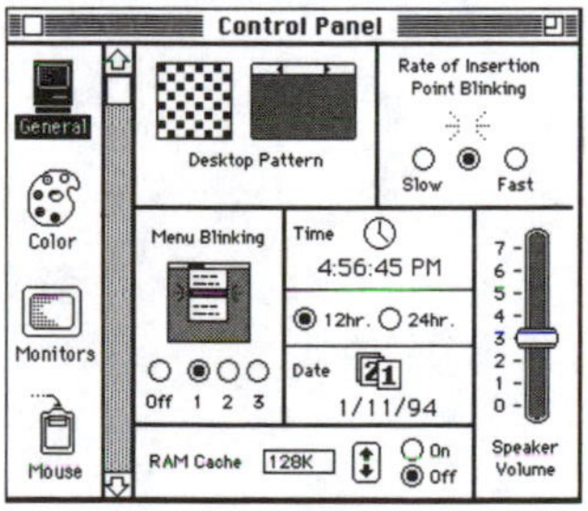

But even this modular control panel wasn't always on the Mac. It showed up in mid-1987, in System 4.0/Finder 5.4—a full three years into the Mac's life.

Turn off extensions for installations. When you install new software, you should turn off all your extensions first. Some programs don't install properly with certain extensions running; this is particularly a problem with virus-protection extensions, but you can never be sure which extension will get in the way. What might happen? Maybe nothing. On the other hand, maybe you won't be able to run the program, or maybe it will have printing problems or just crash unexpectedly.

I'd like to use an unnamed friend as an example here. He installed PowerPoint but couldn't get it to run, despite the fact it was the then-latest copy with the most recent system software. Suspecting an extension conflict, I asked him to start up with Shift down; when he saw the *Extensions off* notice he said "So *that's* what they meant in the installation instructions." Uh-huh. A correct re-install solved the problem.

The Extensions Manager

Rich Wolfson was the special research assistant for this section. Most of the tips here are the result of his contributions.

The Extensions Manager. Apple's Extension Manager, which first showed up in one of System 7's incarnations, keeps getting bigger and better. You use the Extensions Manager to control where all your extensions and control panels are: instead of dragging them in and out of folders manually, you work with the lists in the Manager's window, and it takes care of the background shuffling. You can also move things in and out of the Startup Items and Shutdown Items folders.

The Extensions Manager comes in two pieces, and they both need to be in place for it to work: the EM Manager in the Extensions folder, and the Extensions Manager itself in the Control Panels folder. (There's a third piece, in the Preferences folder, but it will be automatically recreated if it's missing.)

Viewing extension information. In the Extensions Manager, you can view all your extensions and control panels in three different ways, using commands in the View menu:

- **As Folders** gives you gives you hierarchical views for the folders similar to Finder lists.

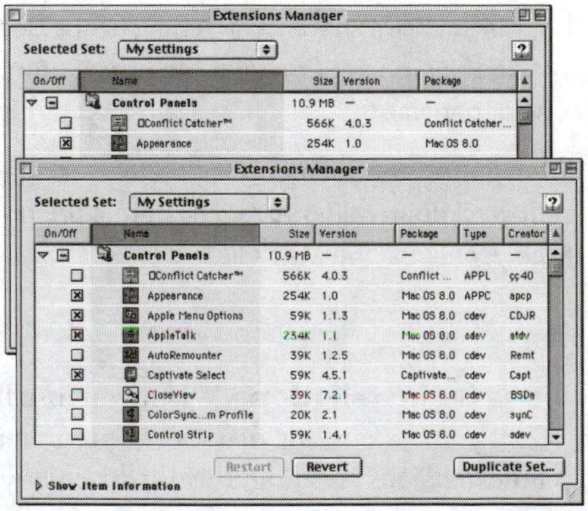

The Extensions Manager window in Folder view; the frontmost view shows the Type and Creator columns turned on.

- **As Packages** divides the items, irrespective of their locations, into groups based on their vendors or functions. (The package information is always displayed in the Package column in other views.)
- **As Items** presents a long list not broken down into any groupings at all.

The column headers at the top of the window are actually buttons which you can click to sort the list according to that column. And you can add up to two more columns: the Edit menu's Preferences command lets you turn on columns for Type and Creator codes.

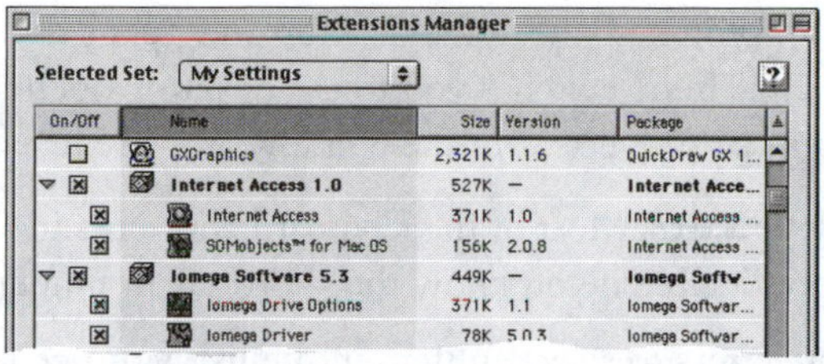

The Extensions Manager window in Packages view.

Details, details. To get details on any item in the list, click the Show Item Information arrow at the bottom of the window. You'll see the information for the selected item. (Unlike the sample picture here, more often than not you'll just get a message that says "There is no further information available for this item.")

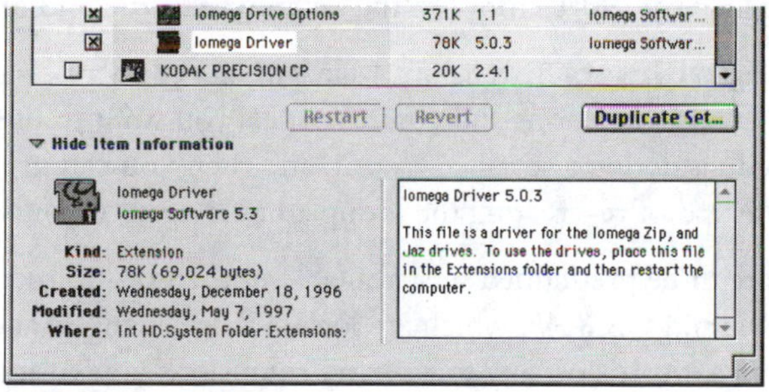

Open the bottom of the window to get detailed information for a selected item.

Manipulating items. To turn items on and off, simply check or uncheck their checkboxes. (Sometimes I have a little trouble with this: the X in the box, since it's neither an OS 8 checkmark nor a full, corner-to-corner X as in previous systems, sometimes feels like a mark that crosses out the item from the list—which is, of course, exactly the opposite of what it does.)

If you're looking at either of the hierarchical views—Folders or Packages—you can mark the main box on or off, and all its items will be marked or unmarked accordingly. A dash in a main box means that some of its sublist is checked, and some unchecked.

But keep in mind what's happening in the background: the items you check or uncheck are moved from one folder to another, depending on their new status. Items you turn on are moved into their folders; items you turn off move into the matching Disabled folders. The move is done as soon as you close the Extensions Manager (or, if you use its Restart button, just before the computer shuts down for the restart). The changes you make won't take effect until you restart, just as if you had moved the items manually.

Order from the menu. Don't overlook the four handy commands in the Edit menu. All On and All Off change the settings of all the items in one fell swoop. Get Info switches you to the desktop and opens the selected item's Info window. Find Item switches you to the desktop, opens the window for the selected item, and selects it in the window.

Keyboard shortcuts. Most of the keyboard shortcuts in Extensions Manager are predictable if you know the shortcuts in Finder windows:

- Type a few letters to select an item in the list; you need only as many letters as necessary to uniquely identify the item. An item that's hidden because its folder or package is collapsed can't be selected.
- Use ↑ and ↓ to select the next or previous item in the list.
- Use Tab and Shift Tab to select the next or previous item alphabetically, no matter how you have the items sorted in the window.
- Use Page Up and Page Down to move a "windowful" up and down in the list; use Home or End to move to the beginning or the end of the list.

Working with sets. Extensions Manager lets you work with "sets," special combinations extensions and control panels you want to use together. All you have to do is define a set once, save it, and then you can just select it from the menu instead of re-creating the group all over again if you need it.

There are three predefined sets, available in the pop-up menu in the window: *OS 8 Base* and *OS 8 All*, which are locked from changes, and *My Settings*. OS 8 All, since it turns off any third-party extensions you've added, is a handy trouble-shooting set. And when it doesn't work, OS 8 Base is even handier, since it turns off the least essential of the Apple-supplied extensions (such as those for personal web sharing, and MacLink translators).

The My Settings file is easy to change, and it's the way you set up your own working set of extensions and control panels. You don't have to save the changes you make in the window; that's automatic when you close it. If you change your mind, you can click the Revert button at the bottom of the window.

To make a new set, use the New Set command from the File menu; give it a name and make your changes. It's usually easier, however, to duplicate an existing set (with a menu command or the button in the window) and make changes from there.

Working behind the scenes. Extensions Manager won't always be the way you manipulate your extensions; in fact, there's no way to add or delete extensions from within the Manager. So, sometimes when you open Extensions Manager, the status of your extensions—what's in what folder—will be different from the set you last defined when Extensions Manager was open.

This doesn't confuse Extensions Manager, though its dialog might confuse you. Here are the choices:

- **Update**: Changes the definition of the current set to match what you've done to your folders since the last time you used Extensions Manager.
- **Revert**: Changes everything you've done to your folders to match the definition of the current set (that means you're undoing all the installations and changes you've done from the desktop).
- **Create New Set**: Usually the safest option. If you've added a bunch of new extensions and you run into problems, having created a new set means you'll be able to move back to your tried-and-true set without a lot of checkbox-tweaking.

After you've worked behind its back, Extensions Manager asks, in less than crystal-clear prose, what the heck you want it to do.

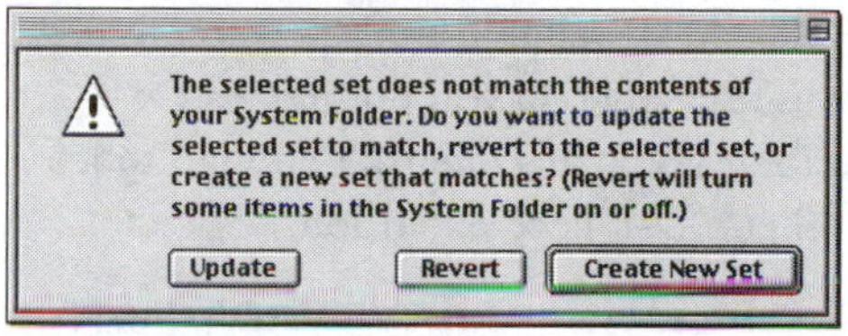

If you've deleted extensions since the last time you used Extensions Manager and then you restart, or select a set that used to include the now-deleted files, you'll get the second dialog shown here. If you click OK, you'll get a text file named *Missing Extensions* placed on the desktop.

If you've deleted extensions, Extension Manager can save a text file of the missing items.

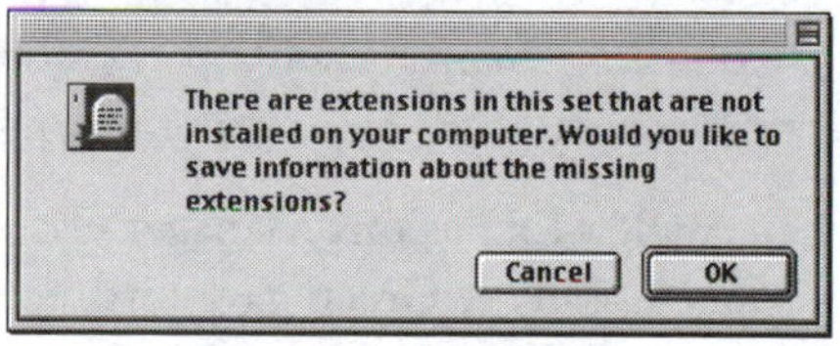

Handling duplicate files. It's easy to wind up with two copies of an extension or control panel, one in the standard folder and one in the disabled folder. Many QuickTime components, for instance, come with multimedia software as well as with the system. Install the software, and it puts copies of extensions in your Extensions folder even if you have the same thing already in your Disabled folder. The extension might be a newer or older version, or exactly the same, but you do wind up with two of them. If you turn off the newly installed one through Extensions Manager, you'll get the dialog shown here. In this case, the items are exactly the same, as you can see by the version numbers and created and modified dates. Check carefully when you get a

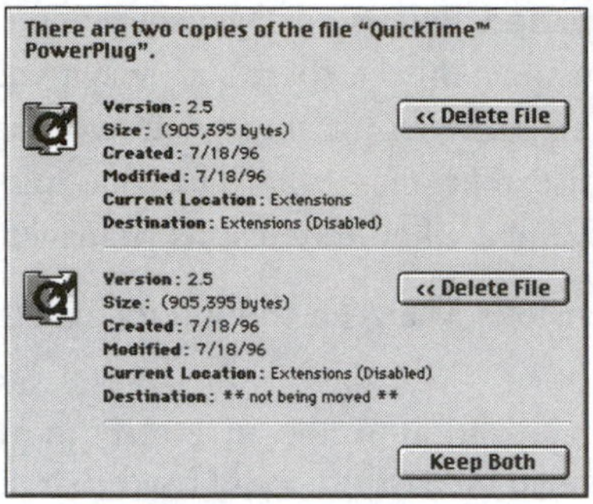

Extensions Manager checks for duplicate files and lets you decide what to do with them.

similar dialog: just because you have two versions, that doesn't mean the most recent one is the enabled version, nor does an identical version number always indicate identical files (go by the modified date). Delete the older of the two versions; if both versions are the same, trash the one in the Disabled folder. If you really want to keep both versions, you can click the Keep Both button.

A CD set for installs. Most software installations should be done with all your extensions off. The only problem is that you need certain extensions on or you can't install the software that comes on CDs—because without one or more of the CD extensions, you won't be able to see the CD.

Make a set for installing software by creating a new set and turning off everything with the All Off command in the Edit menu. Then look for and turn on the Apple CD-ROM extension in the extension folder. That alone should be enough to let you read any CD you put in. (As OS 8 grows, there may be further extensions for CDs; if this one isn't enough to let you read a CD, try turning on some other CD-related extensions.)

If your install CD is also a system disk that you can start up from, then don't worry about changing your extension set: the CD will be running the show, not the System Folder on your hard drive.

Selecting a new set at startup. If you're starting your Mac and realize you didn't select the proper startup set in Extensions Manager before you shut down—or you're not even sure which set is active—hold down Spacebar when you start the Mac. The Extensions Manager will open before the extensions load, and you can select the set you want before anything else happens.

Conflict Catcher

Conflict Catcher When Apple's Extensions Manager was an itty-bitty thing with only basic functionality, Casady & Green gave birth to Conflict Catcher, an extensions manager on growth hormones. Apple's Extensions Manager has grown to a level where it's a "real" piece of software that lets you actually manage your System Folder subfolder contents, but **Conflict Catcher** ($80) remains better.

casadyg.com

Conflict Catcher's main claim to fame, reflected in its very name, is that it lets you track down extension conflicts by turning groups of extensions (and control panels, of course) on and off to track down the one(s) causing system problems. But even if you never have to track down a conflict (which, of course, would put you in a small minority), Conflict Catcher's management capabilities are just far enough ahead of the Extensions Manager's to make it worth the price.

More than anything else, I love Conflict Catcher's ability to create groups of extensions/control panels that you can turn on and off in one click—like all of Microsoft's, for instance, or everything related to QuicKeys. Extensions Manager's "packages" function is supposed to let you do that, but the package idea isn't built into many of the items you use; Conflict Catcher lets you impose a definition of a set on any combination of items. You'll like the little touches, too, like being able to change the size of the icons that march across the screen at startup, and, more importantly, have the *names* displayed under the icons.

When OS 8.1 was first released, it seemed that Conflict Catcher itself was a problem; the compatibility problem was so bad that the Apple installer, at Casady & Greene's request, was designed to move Conflict Catcher into a disabled folder. A 4.1 update was rushed out to take care of the problem, which seemed to be that Conflict Catcher would erroneously identify several of the basic system files as corrupt. As it turned out, Conflict Catcher was right: some of the basic system files *were* corrupt (although didn't cause problems), as Apple discovered later. Just thought I'd set the record straight here.

In the Extensions Folder

Kinds of extensions. When we refer to extensions, we're usually talking about what's more accurately defined as a *system extension*—the kind that has, or should have, a puzzle-piece type of icon, and loads into memory at startup. But there are other kinds of extensions, and other things automatically stored in your Extensions folder. Just take a look at it in a list view and check the Kind column to see the variety.

- **Chooser extensions** are the items that show up in the Chooser for printing, networking, and faxing. Many of the Chooser extensions are named for various printers and have icons that look like little printers; these are the *printer drivers,* software that lets a Mac and a printer talk to each other. These items seldom load into memory at startup, but are added as selected in Chooser and used for printing.
- **Guide documents** (labeled simply as *documents* in the Kind column) are documents that store information used by the Mac help system. These are not loaded into memory, either.

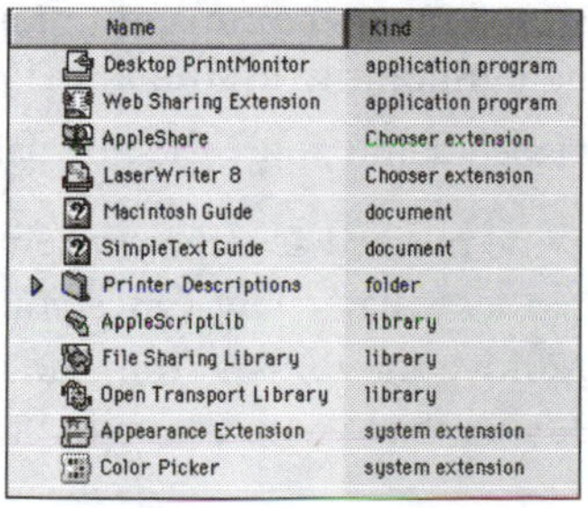

The Extensions folder actually holds many different types of files.

- **Libraries** are files of information shared by various system components and applications. Most are loaded, at least partially, into memory at startup.
- **Applications**, like the Desktop PrintMonitor and the Web Sharing Extension (despite its name), will route themselves to the Extensions folder but they are true applications.

- There are also **folders** of information—like printer descriptions—that are used by other items in the Extensions folder.

The puzzler. The basic extension icon is usually a puzzle-piece, which is fitting (no pun intended) for the system software components that few people can figure out—and often don't fit together. When it comes to extensions, it's unlikely that even anyone at Apple knows for sure what they all are and what they do.

Many items in your Extensions folder, though sometimes no less puzzling, have different types of icons. Printer drivers are little printers; most library items have two hands holding a rectangular icon; help documents have document icons with question marks in them.

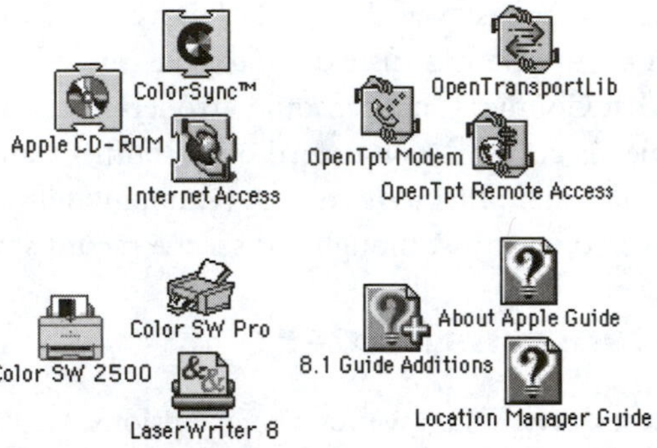

The basic extension icons: puzzle pieces, hand-held libraries, printer shapes, and help files.

Labels

Chapter 6

Keeping track of extensions, etc. If you've read the chapter about installing system software, you might recall that I suggested you "stamp" all the extensions and control panels with a label immediately after installation so you can always tell the Apple pieces.

Here's a variation: mark all your extensions and control panels (and maybe even fonts) just before you install any new software so you can easily see what the new product has added. If you want to coordinate this idea with keeping the Apple items marked separately, here's how you do it inside each folder you want to mark:

1. Add a label column to a list view with the View Options command.
2. Sort according to Label to separate the previously "stamped" Apple items from the other.
3. Optional: Use the Finder's Preferences command to rename one of the standard labels to something temporarily useful, like *Already in here*.
4. Select everything that's *not* labeled and apply the new label to it.

All the items in your folders will be marked as either system software items or *Already* so after the install you can see what's new. Once you're familiar with what's been installed, you can remove the *Already* from the non-Apple things, or apply it to the new arrivals. It's too bad we're limited as to the number of different labels available.

PowerBook extensions
Chapter 23

The OS 8 extensions. It's difficult to provide a complete list of the extensions that OS 8 uses, since the list varies according to your hardware and the system components you chose to install. Here are the basic OS 8 extensions, divided into logical groups (unfortunately, the Packages option in the Extensions Manager clumps many of them together as simply the OS 8 package.)

Printing
Apple Color SW Pro CMM
Desktop Printer Spooler
Desktop PrintMonitor
LaserWriter 8, ImageWriter, etc.
Printer Descriptions (folder)
Printer Share
PrintingLib
PrintMonitor

Communications
Internet Access
Internet Config Extension
Modem Scripts (folder)
Open Tpt AppleTalk Library
Open Tpt Internet Library
Open Transport Guide Additions
Open Transport Library
OpenTpt Modem
OpenTpt Remote Access
OpenTpt Serial Arbitrator
OpenTptAppleTalkLib
OpenTptInternetLib
OpenTransportLib
Serial (Built-in)
Web Sharing Extension

Network
AppleShare
Ethernet (Built-In)
File Sharing Extension
File Sharing Library

CD-ROMs
Apple CD-ROM
Apple Photo Access
Audio CD Access
Foreign File Access
ISO 9660 File Access
High Sierra File Access

Graphics, Sound, Video
°AppleVision
Apple QD3D HW Driver
Apple QD3D HW Plug-In
ATI Graphics Accelerator
Color Picker
ColorSync™
MacinTalk 3
QuickDraw 3D
QuickDraw 3D IR
QuickDraw 3D RAVE
QuickDraw 3D Viewer
QuickTime
QuickTime MPEG Extension
QuickTime Musical Instruments
QuickTime PowerPlug
QuickTime VR
Speech Manager
SystemAV
Video Startup

Help System
About Apple Guide
Apple Guide
Global Guide Files (folders)
Energy Saver Guide Additions
Macintosh Guide
SimpleText Guide

Miscellaneous
EM Extension
Appearance Extension
AppleScriptLib
AppleScript™
Color Picker
Contextual Menu Extension
Energy Saver Extension
MacLinkPlus for Easy Open
Memory Manager
Shared Library Manager
Shared Library Manager PPC
SOMobjects™ for Mac OS
Text Encoding Converter

Now you see them... And now you don't. Some extensions (and other system files) that you get used to seeing under one system version aren't necessary under another because they've been rolled into the main system software or replaced by something else. Then again, new ones keep cropping up all the time. Among the missing in OS 8 are: Clipping Extension, Desktop Printer Extension, Find File Extension, Finder Help, and Finder Scripting Extension.

Keeping up appearances. On some Mac models under OS 8 and 8.1, the computer won't start up without the Appearance Extension in the Extensions folder: you can take the Appearance *control panel* out, but not the extension.

If you turn off the extension and then can't start up, you have two escape routes. If you're using the Extensions Manager, hold down the Spacebar at startup to get the Extensions Manager to open so you can turn the Appearance extension back on. If that doesn't work, you'll have to start up with your system CD and put the extension back in place; you should find it in your Extensions (Disabled) folder.

The Color Picker

Indirect access only. The Color Picker extension provides a common interface for all sorts of programs to let you pick the exact shade of color you want for whatever you're doing. So, while you can't access the Color Picker directly, you'll see it through many other routes—including the Appearance control panel when you want to set a highlight color, and the Finder's Preferences dialog when you want to change label colors.

Peter Piper picks a pack of pickers. Because there are so many different ways to describe a color, the Color Picker actually provides six different pickers, with different approaches to color definition; click on an icon in the left panel and get the related controls.

- **CMYK Picker:** Colors defined by amounts of Cyan, Magenta, Yellow, and Black, the way it is for color printing.
- **Crayon Picker:** Just the fun approach to picking a color, familiar to most since toddlerhood.
- **HLS Picker:** Hue (the main color), Lightness (the amount of black/white mixed in), and Saturation (the intensity of the color) combine for the color definition. In OS 8, the Hue is the *Hue Angle* and can be defined as the number of degrees that represent the chosen color's position on the color wheel (which seems like an unnecessary complication to me).
- **HSV Picker:** Hue and Saturation again, but this time the third option is Value, which changes how light or dark the final color is; a very subtle difference from the HLS version.
- **HTML Picker:** With this picker, you can automatically limit choices to the "web-safe" colors (discussed in Chapter 21.)

- **RGB Picker:** Make colors from the light-based Red, Green, and Blue monitor primaries.

> *...someday a Mac or the equivalent of a Mac with color would be wonderful.*
> *Bill Gates, interviewed in Macworld, 1985*

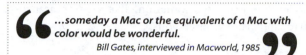

Using a color picker. With the exception of the Crayon Picker, each of the pickers provides either a color wheel or slider bar controls, or both, for you to adjust the color; the color values are noted by numbers as well as on the controls. There's also a swatch of the current color and the color you're creating, so you can compare them.

- The color wheel has a crosshairs marking the current selected spot. You can drag the crosshairs around, but it's easier to just click in a new spot—and then drag to find the *exact* shade you're looking for.
- Drag the markers on the slider controls to their new positions.
- The numbers reflect the settings you've made on the color wheel and sliders, but you can just type directly into the text boxes to change the numbers.

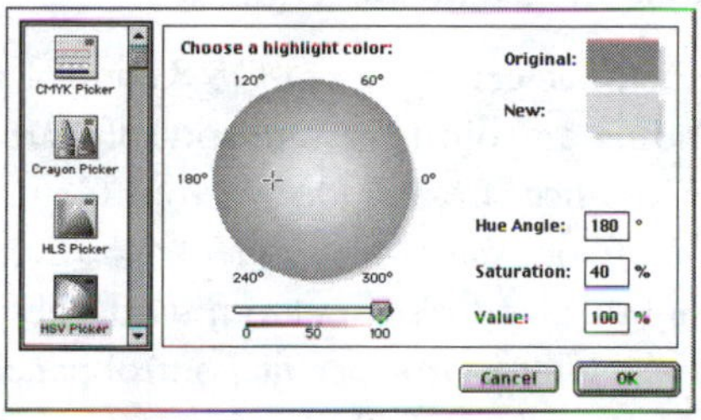

A typical color picker, with the color wheel, a slider control, numeric readouts, and sample swatches.

Grabbing a screen color. When the Color Picker is open, if you hold down the Option key, the mouse cursor changes to an eyedropper. Click anywhere on the screen (*anywhere*—outside the dialog, up in the menubar, from a document window in the background) with the eyedropper, and the color you click on is chosen as the new color.

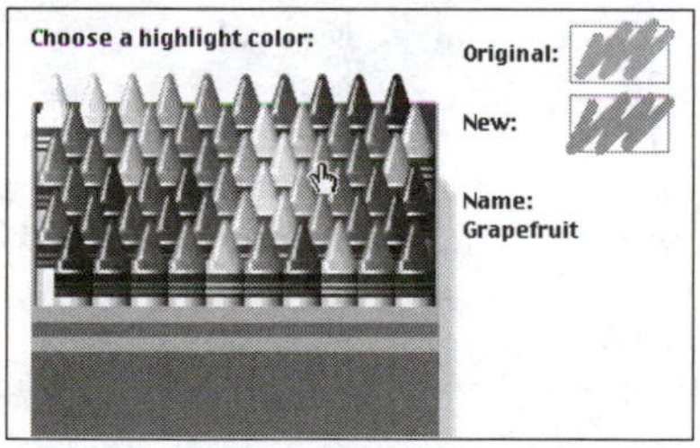

Clicking a crayon chooses its color.

The crayon picker. The Crayon Picker takes an entirely different approach to choosing colors: select a crayon by clicking on it, and it becomes the new color—and every color even gets a name.

When you use the eye-dropper trick (holding down the Option key) in the Crayon Picker, and click anywhere on the screen (say, along the lighter or darker edge of the crayon point), that color gets selected—and the color name takes a laid-back approach: you'll see things like *Pine-ish, Warm Marble-ish, Grapefruit-ish*, and so on.

Mom, I need new Crayolas. Why ever they included it, and who ever first ran across it, I don't know—but, boy, this buried trick is really cute. Use the Date & Time control panel to temporarily set your clock ahead a couple of years, then access the Crayon Picker through something like the Appearances control panel, and see what happens to your crayons.

In the Control Panels Folder

What's Where, What's What

PowerBook control panels
Chapter 23

OS 8 control panels. The number of system control panels is small only in comparison to the number of system extensions. Control panels come and go with system software versions and hardware models; sometimes their functions are rolled into other control panels or the basic system software, and sometimes their functions are just no longer needed.

The chart here shows the basic general set of OS 8 control panels; there are some differences depending on your hardware and software setup. *Editor Setup* and *OpenDoc Setup*, for instance, are included in your Control Panels folder when you install the OpenDoc system component; however, since we've recommended against doing that, and it's so seldom used, they didn't make it into this "basic set" list. And hardware-specific control panels like *Brightness* for the Classics and *Cache Switch* for '040 Macs aren't in this list, either.

Not all the control panels are described in this chapter, since most are detailed in context in other parts of the book. The ones that didn't fit anyplace else (like the Map) pretty much came home to roost in this chapter.

Control Panel	*Chapter*	*Control Panel*	*Chapter*
Appearance	5	MacLinkPlus Setup	12
Apple Menu Options	9	MacTCP	27
AppleTalk	26	Map	9
ATM	14	Memory	13
AutoRemounter	23	Modem	27
Close View	9	Monitors & Sound	3, 22
ColorSync System Profile	9	Mouse	5
Control Strip	9	Numbers	9
Date & Time	9	Password Security	23
Desktop Pictures	5	PC Exchange	12
Easy Access	5	PPP	27
Energy Saver	5	QuickTime™ Settings	22
Extensions Manager	9	Speech	22
File Sharing	26	Startup Disk	5
General Controls	9	TCP/IP	27
Keyboard	5	Text	9
Launcher	12	Users & Groups	26
Mac OS Easy Open	12		

The dear departed. Many of the old standards in the way of control panels have disappeared in OS 8, sucked into other parts of the system software or otherwise made obsolete.

- **Auto Power On/Off:** Replaced by Energy Saver control panel for most Macs.
- **Color:** Replaced by Appearances control panel.
- **Desktop Patterns:** Replaced by Desktop Pictures.
- **File Sharing Monitor, Sharing Setup:** Rolled into the single File Sharing control panel.
- **Labels:** Replaced by Finder submenu.
- **Monitors:** Replaced by Monitors & Sound.
- **Sound, Sound & Displays:** Replaced by Monitors & Sound.
- **Views:** Replaced by Finder's View menu and submenus.
- **WindowShade:** Built into system; settings in Appearance control panel.

Hardware-specific control panels. There's a handful of control panels that are installed on only a few Mac models because they address a specific capability or problem for those models.

- **Brightness:** Adjusts brightness of screen on Classic and Classic II models.
- **Button Disabler:** Disables sound and brightness buttons on Performa and LC 500-series models to keep "unauthorized" users (students, children) from changing the settings.
- **Cache Switch:** The Cache Switch control panel turns the '040 "processor caching" on and off so that older programs that aren't compatible with the caching operation can run on '040 (and 'LC040) machines. (This should only apply to older programs, but in fact Microsoft Internet Explorer 3 couldn't work on one of three Quadra 610's that I know until the cache was turned off.) Since the caching is something that speeds up the Mac, turning it off can cut its speed in half. If you Option-click on the Faster or More Compatible button, the changes take effect immediately instead of after restart.
- **Serial Switch:** For Mac IIfx and Quadra 950 only; you have to choose the *More Compatible* option when a program is having trouble accessing the printer or modem port.

A control panel is a Finder window. Really. If you're in a program and open a control panel from the Apple menu, you'll be switched to the Finder for the control panel to open. All the Finder menus are active, and the Finder is marked as the active application in the Applications menu at the right of the menubar. If you leave a control panel open, go to an application, and move back to the Finder, you'll see the control panel window come up to the front with all the other Finder windows you left open. Still don't believe me? Try Option-clicking in a control panel's close box: not only will all the open control panels close, all the Finder windows will close, too.

Auto-closing the control panels folder. If you're opening a control panel from inside the Control Panels folder window on the desktop, you can Option-double-click on the control panel icon to automatically close the window as the control panel opens.

But you should never have to open a control panel from a desktop window if you set up your Apple menu correctly. Those details are later in this chapter.

Delayed gratification. Some changes you make in some control panels (like General Controls, Mouse, or Desktop Patterns) take effect immediately, but most won't do anything until you restart the Mac. Most control panels politely inform you as to the situation.

The Control Strip

Control Strip basics. The Control Strip provides instant on-screen access to many control panel options, as well as to other functions. You can, for instance, choose a desktop printer without a trip to the desktop or to Chooser, set the sound volume, and change monitor settings. There's a Control Strip Modules folder inside the System Folder; every module in the folder appears as an icon in the Control Strip itself.

The Control Strip first shows up on the screen as a little tab down in the left corner; click on the tab, and the strip pops open. Click on an icon, and a menu or some sort of control pops up.

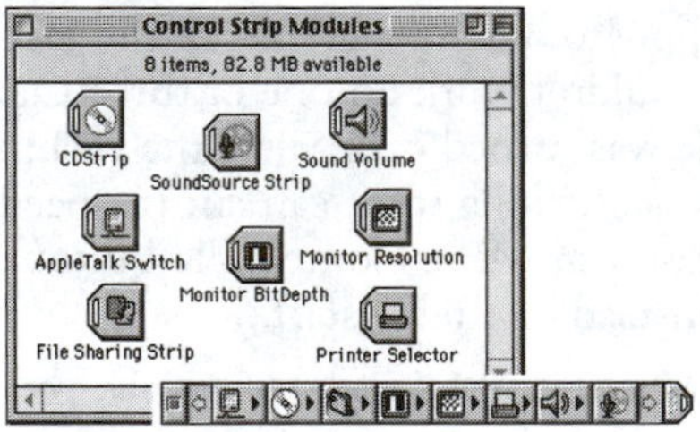

The Control Strip Modules folder, and the Control Strip created by the modules.

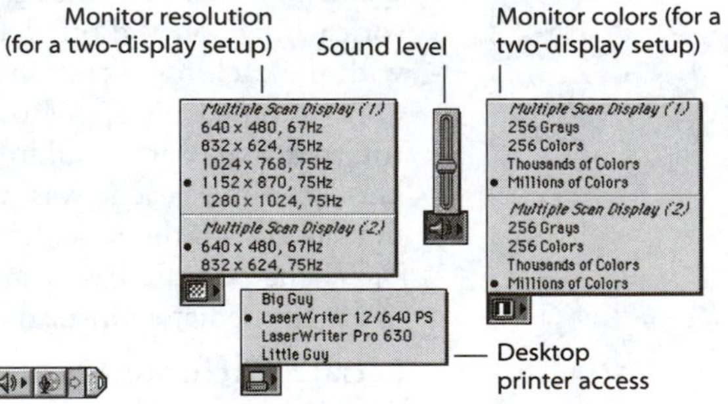

Some Control Strip controls.

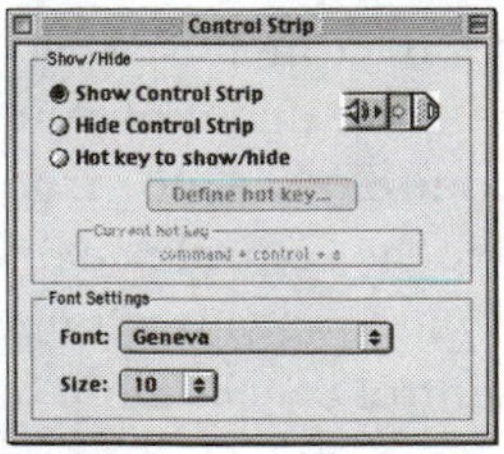

The Control Strip's master control is the Control Strip control panel.

The control panel. The Control Strip control panel lets you show or hide the Control Strip itself, set it to show and hide with a key combination (a "hot key"), and choose the font and size for the pop-up menus for the strip.

The Control Strip control panel has to be in the Control Panels folder at startup for you to be able to use the Control Strip. But as long as the control panel is active, using the Show and Hide commands affect the Control Strip immediately—there's no restarting just to make the strip come and go.

Controlling the Control Strip. The Control Strip seems permanently glued to the lower left edge of your screen, and its only two states seem to be completely open or completely closed. But that's not true: you can move it around, adjust its length and even reorder the items in the strip.

- Open the Control Strip by clicking on the tab. Once it's open, you can close it by clicking either on the tab or in the close box at the opposite end of the strip.
- Drag the strip to a new position by holding down Option and dragging it by the tab. The Control Strip always has to be attached to the left or right edge of the screen, so when you let it go it will snap to the nearest screen edge.
- Change the order of the icons in the strip by Option-dragging them into new positions.
- Change the length of the Control Strip by dragging the tab in or out. Once the strip is too short to display all its icons at once, the scroll arrows at each end of the strip are activated.

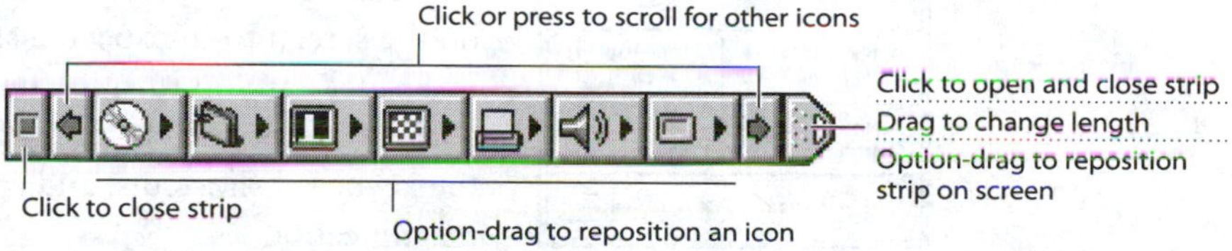

Adding and deleting items. To add a module to your Control Strip, you put it in the Control Strip folder; if you drag it to the closed System Folder, it will be routed correctly, just as extensions and control panels are. But, as with most extensions and control panels, you can't use the new module until after you restart—it won't even show up in the strip until then.

When you remove items from the folder, their icons stay on the strip (and you can keep using them) until you restart the Mac.

shareware.com

Control Strip add-ons. Because the Control Strip is modular in design, there are third-party items available as freeware and shareware. As with all modular system components, and all shareware, the quality of available items ranges from poor to fantastic, and their usefulness has the same wide range. For example:

- **OTT/PPP Strip:** Freeware pop-up control for PPP connections, with optional readouts for connect time, connect speed, and activity "lights." You'll never have to open the PPP control panel again except to set up a new configuration, which will then be added to the pop-up menu's list.

- **Mouser:** Constant readout of your mouse coordinates. ($5 shareware)
- **StripLaunch:** Lists up to 64 items in its menu (based on aliases you drop into the Control Strip Modules folder) so you can open them easily. ($5 shareware)

Other Control Panels

Brightness. Only a few Macs (the Classic and Classic II) use the Brightness control panel to control their screens. But there's a nice feature built into it: if you set the brightness lower than 4, the brightness is automatically reset when you restart—so you won't start up with a screen so dim you think it's dead.

CloseView. The CloseView control panel is meant for the visually impaired, but anyone can use it for some instant screen magnification. It's not installed as part of a standard installation, but you can go back and get it from the system CD if you want to try it out. (On the OS 8 CD, you have to do a custom install, described in the last chapter; on the OS 8.1 CD, you'll find it loose in the Universal Access folder inside the CD Extras folder.)

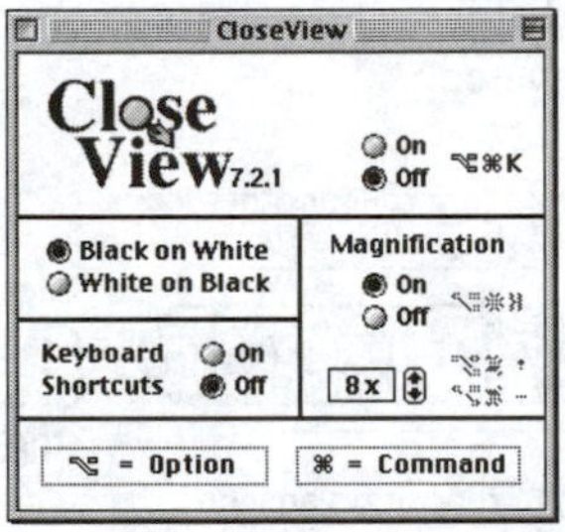

CloseView provides magnification up to 16 times normal and lets you reverse text windows to white on black (which also inverts all colors on the screen to unexpected shades). The control panel lets you turn its functions on and off with a "master switch" at the top, use or ignore the keyboard shortcuts, and set the level of magnification.

Once you've turned on CloseView, you'll get a large black frame surrounding your mouse cursor; it signifies how much of the screen will be displayed if you activate the currently magnification. (So, a high magnification level gets you a smaller black frame.) Turn on the magnification, and you zoom in for a close look—I mean, view—of the section in the frame.

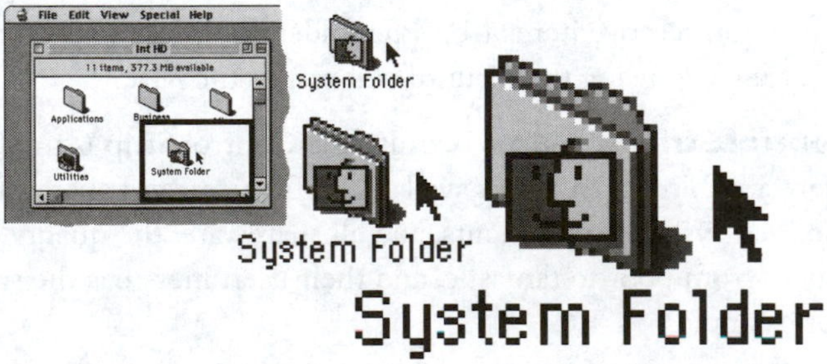

A black frame surrounds your cursor to show how much of the screen will be magnified (left). The magnified System Folders are 2x, 4x, and 8x views; CloseView can go up to a 16x view.

Date & Time. The Date & Time control panel lets you set the date, time, and time zone for your Mac's clock; you can also choose the date and time formats that will be used by the system.

But the handiest option in the control panel is the Menubar Clock, which puts a digital clock in your menubar; you can turn it on or off, specify the font, size, color and type of readout, and even set it to chime on the hour, half hour, or quarter hour.

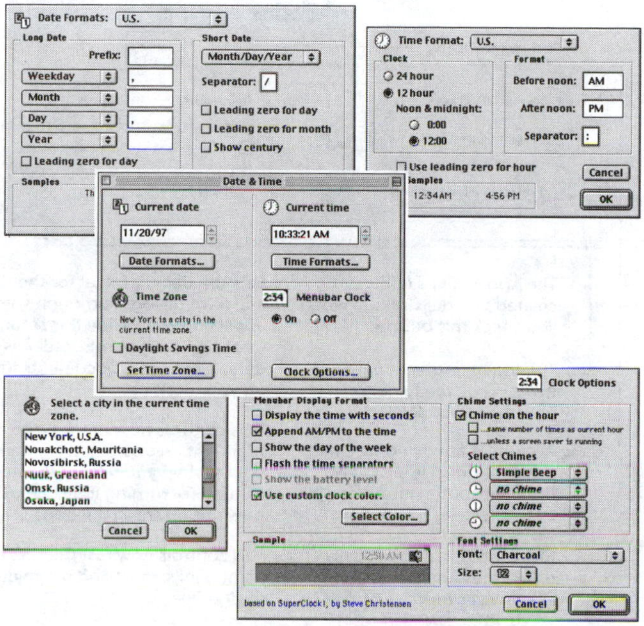

The Date & Time control panel and its four option dialogs.

Click-clock. Here are two hidden options for the menubar clock:

- Click on the time to see the date; the date stays for a few seconds, or you can click to immediately return to the time readout (if you can't stand not knowing what time it is for a few seconds).
- Option-click on the time to make it disappear from the menu; Option-click in the same area to make the time visible again.

On Powerbooks, the menubar clock has a special battery indicator; that's covered in Chapter 23.

General Controls. The current General Controls control panel first showed up in System 7.5; it was a total redesign that incorporated features first found in Performa system software, and banished the desktop patterns to a separate control panel. In fact, the only things left from the original version are the rates for the insertion point and menu blinks!

Unchecking this hides desktop windows and icons when you're in other applications; you won't be able to click on the desktop surface to move to the Finder, either. (If you use the Application menu's Hide command, the Finder's windows are hidden, but its icons are not.)

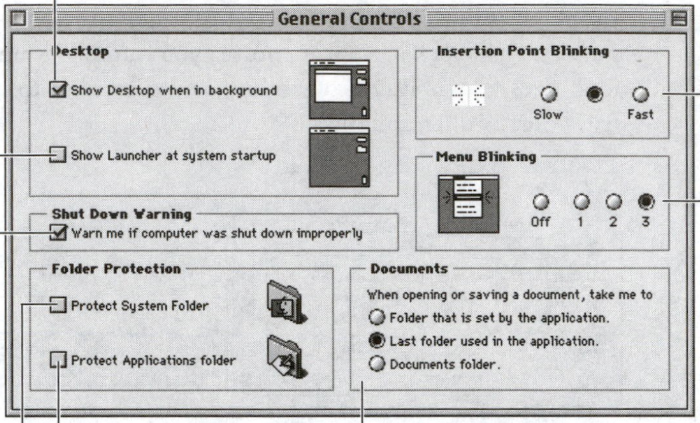

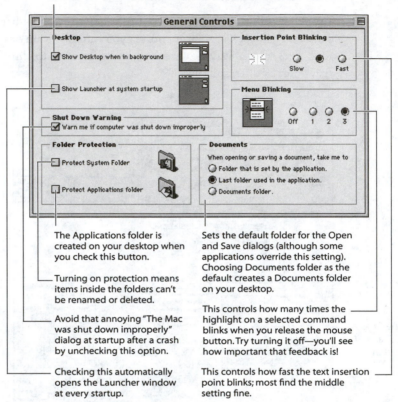

The Applications folder is created on your desktop when you check this button.

Turning on protection means items inside the folders can't be renamed or deleted.

Avoid that annoying "The Mac was shut down improperly" dialog at startup after a crash by unchecking this option.

Checking this automatically opens the Launcher window at every startup.

Sets the default folder for the Open and Save dialogs (although some applications override this setting). Choosing Documents folder as the default creates a Documents folder on your desktop.

This controls how many times the highlight on a selected command blinks when you release the mouse button. Try turning it off—you'll see how important that feedback is!

This controls how fast the text insertion point blinks; most find the middle setting fine.

MacTCP DNR. This is a really strange little animal. You won't find it in your Control Panels folder, but loose in your System Folder after you've used any software to jump on the internet. Drag it to the trash and it magically reappears the next time you go online. Even stranger is the fact that although its icon looks like a control panel and its "kind" is "control panel," it's not a control panel and you can't open it. MacTCP DNR (*TCP* from *TCP/IP* and *DNR* for *domain name resolver)* is a vestige from earlier systems, when the MacTCP control panel was stored in the main level of the System Folder. Some communications programs will look for information only from a specific source in a specific place—and MacTCP DNR is it. Look for this to eventually disappear (without reappearing) from the system software as other programs are updated.

Map. The Map control panel isn't very useful, when you come right down to it, but it's certainly packed with a lot of details, whether or not you need them. The twinkling dots are cities included in the Map's database. The larger blinking star marks the city that's currently selected, and the blinking cross is the "base" city from which distances and time differences are measured.

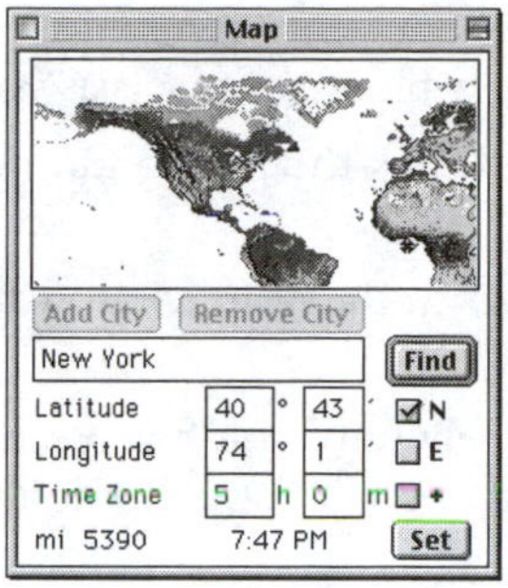

- To select a city, you click on it (or click and then drag the mouse until you hit the city—they're all very tiny).
- To set the base city, select it, and then click the Set button.
- To scroll the map, drag the mouse to any edge of the map (or to a corner to scroll diagonally). As with Finder windows, there's variable speed scrolling: the further you drag the mouse past the edge of the map, the faster it scrolls.
- When N is checked, the noted latitude is North; when E is checked, the noted longitude is is East. Unchecked, of course, they're South and West.
- The distance noted in the lower left corner is that between the base city and the current city. You can cycle through different units of measure—miles, kilometers, and degrees—by clicking on the measurement.

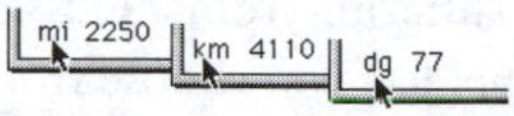

- There are three time readouts you can get in the Map window: the actual time in the selected city (assuming you've set the time for the base city correctly in relation to the time on your Mac's clock), the time zone that the selected city is in, and the time difference between the selected city and your base city. To switch between the last two, just click on the Time Zone/Time Different label. The + checkbox refers to the time difference: checked, it means the time noted is that many hours later than the base city, while if it's unchecked, the time is earlier than the base.
- To find a city on the map, type its name in the text box and click the Find button. You don't have to worry about capitalization, and you have to type only enough of the city's name to uniquely identify it. Typing *new,* for instance, finds New Delhi, but *new y* will find New York. Pressing Option when you click the Find button, or pressing ⌘Option will find the next city alphabetically after the one that's displayed.
- If you're a National Geography Bee winner, you can easily add new cities to the Map; otherwise, you'll need an atlas for the details. You have to click on the right spot, type the city's name, and click the Add City button. To remove a city, simply select it and click the Remove City button.
- You can paste any picture into the map window. But you'll lose the original, because in an unfriendly piece of programming, it's the internal resource of the Map control panel itself that gets replaced when you paste something in. If you can't resist but later regret your rash action, there's a spare map picture in the Scrapbook that can copied and pasted into the Map.

Okay, now the nonsense:

- You can get an enlarged map by holding down Shift when you open the control panel. You can get an even larger one by holding Option. And, yes, you can get an even *larger* one by hold Shift Option together when you open it. Unfortunately, all you get is an enlargement of the bitmapped original picture, with larger and larger blocks of pixels as you zoom in.

- Type *mid* in the text box and click the Find button—you can see where it takes you.
- Click on the version number in the Map window to see the name of the programmer.
- Scroll around the world slowly until you find a set of initials buried in the map. (I assume they belong to the artist, but I don't know; if you know, let *me* know!)

Numbers. The Numbers control panel, ushered in by System 7.1, lets you state preferences for how numbers are formatted on the desktop and in any application that looks to the system for guidance. So, you can remove the comma as the thousands separator and get 1024K reported in windows instead of 1,024K; or, replace it with an apostrophe for 1'024K. If that strikes you as very odd (as it does me), you're suffering from a U.S.-centric point of view; in fact, the Numbers control panel lets you choose from a list of countries to set the separator as well as the control panel's other settings: the decimal point and currency notation.

Password Security. Although the Password Security control panel was intended more for PowerBooks, it's functional on desktop Macs, too. (But it's detailed in the PowerBook chapter.)

When OS 8.1 was introduced, with its HFS Extended formatting option for drives, the version of Password Security that came with it didn't work with extended-format drives. There's no word at this point if it will be updated for use (although we can assume it will be); if you format your drive with the Extended option, don't use Password Security unless you have a version that Apple explicitly states works with HFS Plus.

Text. The Text control panel has two settings—scripting and sorting—whose behaviors are defined by the languages you choose from the pop-up menus.

The Apple Menu Items Folder

The Apple Menu Options Control Panel

The Apple menu. Except for the first, "About," command in the Apple menu, the items listed in the Apple menu are those inside the Apple Menu Items folder. A standard system installation starts with some basic desk accessories, control panels, and folders in the menu, but you can add anything you want; changes you make to the folder are immediately reflected in the menu. Setting up a perfect Apple menu is an art, tempered by personal preferences.

Selecting something from the Apple menu opens it: it's the same as double-clicking on the item itself on the desktop.

The Apple Menu Options control panel. The hierarchical Apple menu debuted as part of system software in System 7.5, courtesy of the Apple Menu Options control panel. Luckily, the early buggy version is long gone, and now it's a utility you shouldn't do without.

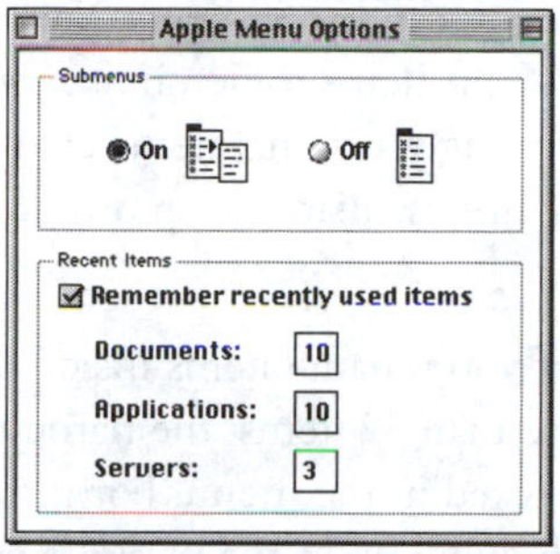

You can turn Apple Menu Options' two main features on and off separately.

The control panel provides two types of features: the hierarchical Apple menu itself, and three special "Recent" folders, for documents, applications, and servers. You can turn these two features on and off separately in the control panel, and set the number of items you want in each of the Recent folders.

The hierarchical option. With hierarchical menus option turned on, any folder (or folder alias) in the Apple Menu Items folder shows a submenu in the Apple menu. You can directly select any item from the submenu, or choose the folder name itself to open the folder. Hierarchical menus are shown down to five levels, so nested folders gives you submenus and subsubmenus, and so on. This feature was added awfully late to the system software, and it should be automatic rather than an option—but some good things take a long time.

Recent items. Apple Menu Options keeps track of recently used items in three categories: documents, applications, and servers. There's a checkbox that activates or deactivates all three categories; for each category, you can specify up to 99 items to be included in its submenu.

Using the recent items option creates three folders inside the Apple Menu Items folder, one for each category. As you open applications or documents, or log onto file servers, an alias for the item you use is placed in the appropriate folder, creating a submenu for the Apple menu.

To turn off a single category (like *Servers*, for instance), either delete the number next to it in the control panel, or type a zero.

The odd documents list. Until you use a Recent Documents folder, you don't realize just what the Mac OS considers a document. And, in fact, its definition is so weird as to make the Recent Documents list unusable for many people. You might find things like:

- Various windows from your e-mail software, like an Address Book, Define Address, and Edit Addresses (by whatever name).

- If you use QuicKeys, you'll find the QuicKeys window listed, as well as many of its subwindows, like Sequence Editor.
- When you use FileMaker, the Script Editor, each script, and many layout definition dialogs (Specify Button, Specify Field) are considered documents.

The Apple Menu Items Folder

The outer limits. The Apple menu can list 52 items. You can put as many items as you want in the Apple Menu Items folder, but only the first 52 alphabetical items will be listed. Interestingly, original items take precedence over aliases: when you exceed the maximum, aliases drop out of the menu first, regardless of their alphabetization.

It's also interesting to note that if you rename items inside the Apple Menu Items folder when there are more than 52 items, the name change is often ignored when it comes to being listed in the menu. For instance, if you have a folder named *Zebras* that's not showing up in the menu because it's the fifty-third item, renaming to *A Zebra folder* won't necessarily bump it up in the list and knock the next bottom-most item out of the menu.

To force an update of a crowded Apple menu, drag a few items out of the Apple Menu Items folder (it doesn't matter which ones—just so there are fewer than 52 left) onto the desktop; let them go so the Mac will update the menu; then, drag the items back into the folder and the menu is updated again. At that point, your menu will match your folder.

The self-alias shortcut. When you're first setting up your Apple menu, or whenever you decide to do some major reorganization, make life easier by putting an alias of the Apple Menu Items folder inside itself. That sounds odd, but you'll then see the Apple Menu Items folder listed in the Apple menu, where you can open it easily.

In later versions of System 7, this little trick gave you cascading Apple menus, each one coming out from the Apple Menu Items folder listing; OS 8, however, is smarter than that and refuses to provide a submenu for the Apple Menu Items folder alias.

Adding items. Most of the items you put in the Apple Menu Items folder will be aliases, not originals. Don't forget the "instant-alias" desktop trick: ⌘ Option-drag an icon into the Apple Menu Items folder to make an alias of it, and the *alias* suffix won't even appear in its name.

The "white-hole" shortcut. To drag something into the Apple Menu Items folder, you have to *get* to the Apple Menu Items folder, which is in the System Folder—which usually takes a long time to open because there's so much stuff in there. So, make an alias of the Apple Menu Items folder and leave it out on the desktop to make access easier.

In fact, take this one step further: rename the alias with multiple spaces so its name looks blank, and drag the icon to the top left of the screen, under the Apple menu. You can push the icon itself "under" the menubar so only the blank name shows. To put something into the Apple menu, drag it to this "white hole" and let it go. And remember—if you want to just have an *alias* of the item in the Apple menu, hold down ⌘Option as you drag it into the "hole."

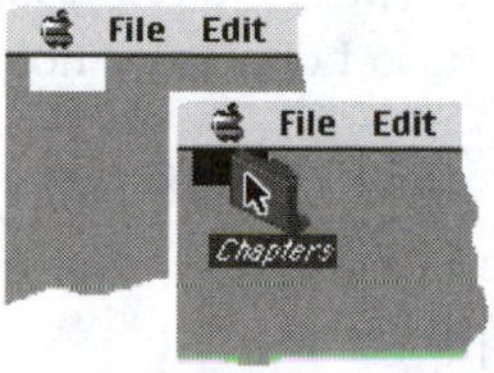

Dropping something into the special Apple Menu Items folder alias.

Organizing Your Apple Menu

Keep it short. To make the Apple menu work its best for you, keep it short: sure, it lets you list 52 items, but then you have to scroll through all of them to get to the bottom. Organize the menu items into folders so you can access them from submenus, cutting down on the overall travel time. And don't forget about sticky menus: just click on the apple icon to drop the menu and then roll your mouse to the right spot without having to hold down the mouse button.

The starting lineup. When you install OS 8, it starts with a collection of about 20 items in the Apple Menu Items folder—only half of which you'll probably use.

Your first step should be to create a Desk Accessories folder inside the Apple Menu Items folder, and put all the odds and ends inside it—how often are you going to take out the Jigsaw Puzzle or Graphing Calculator, anyway? And you can include Find File in that group, because although you'll use it a lot, you can open it with a simple ⌘F in the Finder.

Next, get rid of certain items (all of which are aliases, anyway, so the real things are still on your hard drive):

- **Automated Tasks:** The real folder is inside the Apple Extras folder that the Installer puts on your hard drive. This contains four simple AppleScripts, three of which are for file-sharing. The fourth is one that makes an alias of a selected icon and puts it into the Apple menu. Selecting a submenu command to create an alias is less convenient than ⌘Option-dragging it into an Apple Menu Items folder desktop alias, so if you keep the command around, move it out of the folder, to the main level of the Apple Menu Items folder.
- **SimpleSound:** It's unlikely you'll need this alternative to the Monitors & Sound control panel—and if you do, you should put the real thing in your Control Panels folder.
- **Apple Video Player:** Again, this is just an alias. Unless you use the player often, you don't need it in the menu; for occasional use, add it to the Desk Accessories folder.

If there are certain desk accessories you use all the time (the Calculator, for instance), it makes sense to leave them on the main level of the Apple menu so you don't have to open the submenu. (I use QuicKeys and keyboard commands to open the items I use the most, so I don't care how deeply they're buried in a folder.)

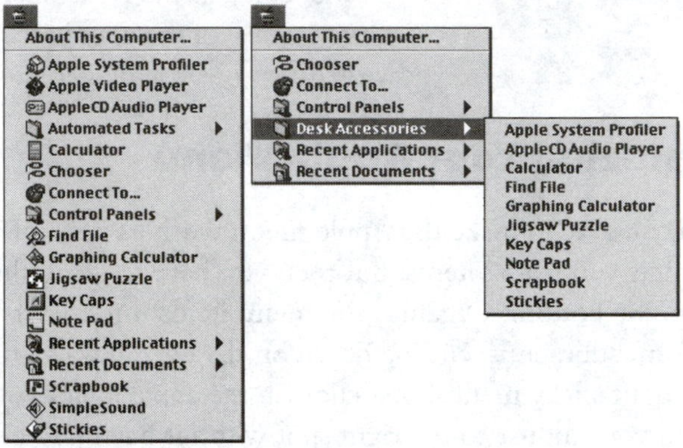

The installed Apple menu (left) and the first round of organization (right).

Rearranging the items. Since things are listed alphabetically in the Apple menu, rearranging them is a simple matter of renaming them, according to the same rules for desktop items (as discussed in Chapter 6): putting a leading character like a space in front of a name brings it to the top of the list, while a leading character like a bullet (on Option 8) sinks it to the bottom. (You can't rename the Recent folders that the Apple Menu Options control panel creates, or it will create new ones.)

An extra benefit of renaming things with special characters—using bullets, say, for folders, and hyphens for applications—is that the leading character serves to group the items, keeping them alphabetized within each group, as shown in the picture here (where a double bullet drops the *Connect To* choice to the very bottom of the menu). To adjust ordering within a group—say you want Photoshop at the top of the applications group, or the Fonts folder at the top of the folders group, just type a space after the leading character, before the item's name.

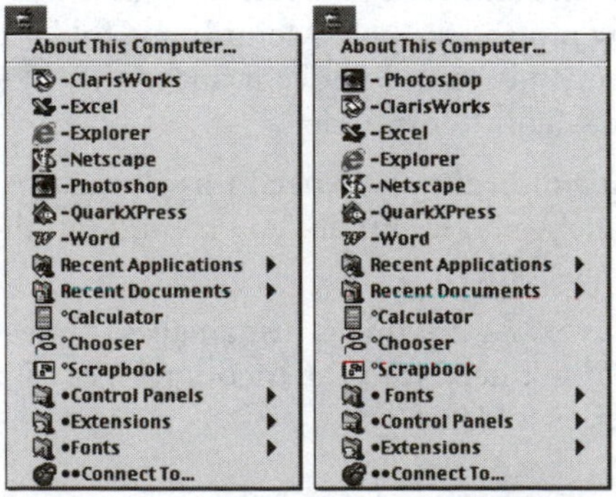

Leader characters divide these Apple menus into five groups: hyphens, no leaders, degree marks, bullets, and double bullets. A minor change to names within a group—putting a space before Photoshop and Fonts, in this picture—changes their positions in their groups (right).

What you see isn't always what you get. Because most people leave their system font at the default Charcoal and their desktop font at the default Geneva (not that there's anything wrong with that), most also overlook the fact that there are more characters available in Charcoal (and in Chicago, if you've refused to move to Charcoal) than in Geneva. If you type the Option and Shift Option characters in an icon's name, they might show up as boxes on the desktop but they'll be sorted according to the actual characters, and appear correctly in the menu. The picture here shows some of the characters available in Charcoal/Chicago that you might want as leader characters.

Available characters differ between Geneva and Charcoal/Chicago, so what you see in the Apple Menu Items folder (right) will look entirely different in the menu itself.

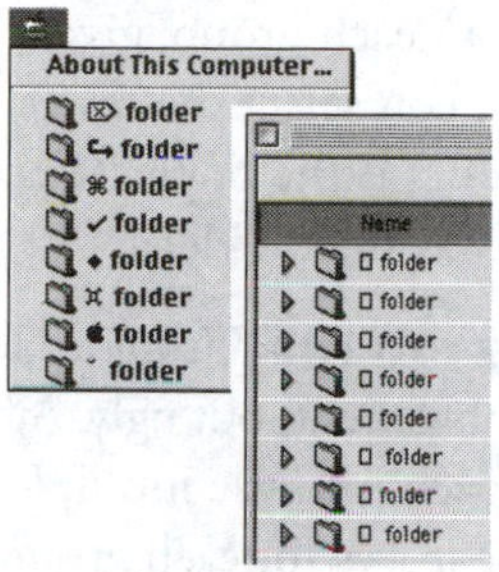

Chapter 14, the Font chapter, discusses where on the keyboard you'll find all these special characters. Some of the ones shown here, like the checkmark and the command-key symbol, are accessed only with the Control key—which you can't use to type while you're on the desktop. But you can open the Key Caps desk accessory, click the keys in there to produce the characters, than copy them out and paste them into the icon's name.

Divide and conquer. Grouping like items together isn't really enough for speedy Apple menu choices, since you still have to read reasonably carefully. But if you separate the items with special dividers, it's easier to zip right to the area you want. To make dividers:

1. Create empty folders, giving them names that consist of a string of hyphens, periods, or even underline characters. (If you use a tiny character like a period, you'll want to put spaces between them to stretch them out the width of the Apple menu; the 32-character limit for names keeps you from typing in a long string of periods.)

Make dividers by creating empty folders, naming them appropriately, and obliterating their icons.

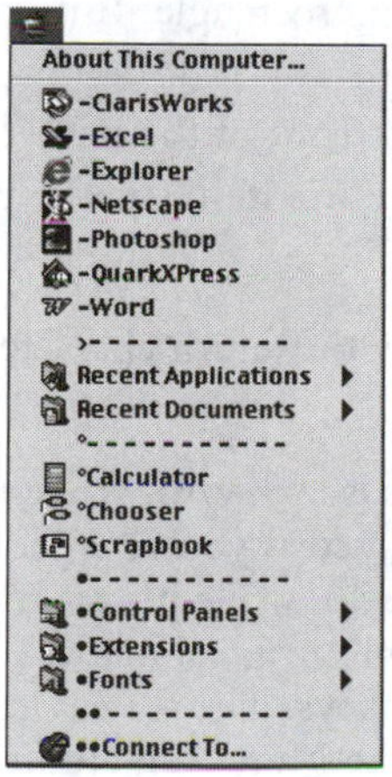

2. Force the folders to the correct spots in the menu by adding leader characters to match the groups you've created. Depending on the divider character you've chosen, the folder will sort to the top or the bottom of the group: hyphens and periods put the folder at the top of the group, while underscores drop it to the bottom. You may have to get creative if you're in a situation like the one illustrated here, where there was no obvious leader character to use for the divider between the hyphen group on top and the "bare" items that come next, since both a hyphen and a space jumped the first divider to the very top of the menu. A little experimenting showed that the greater-than symbol put the folder in the correct position.

3. Remove the folder icons from the menu by editing their icons in their Get Info windows: pasting in a plain white square will erase the icon. (That's all covered in Chapter 7.)

Slip-proof dividers. So, you like the divider idea and put a half-dozen in your Apple menu. The only problem is that you mistakenly select them a dozen times a day when you're aiming for the item above or below the divider—and you're returned to the desktop, where an empty folder with the strange name opens.

If you run into this problem, don't use blank folders as your dividers. Instead, make an alias of the last item in each group, give it the following divider's "name," and erase its icon. If you select the divider by mistake, you'll get the item before it. (Or, if yours is the opposite problem, you can alias the first item in each group to act as the divider.)

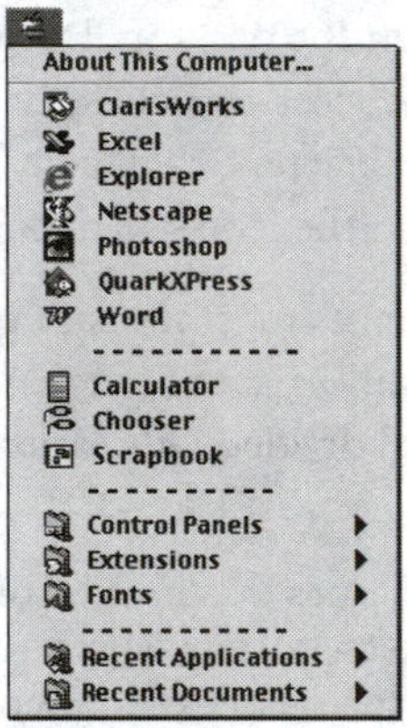

Using multiple spaces as leader characters works for a few groups.

Many happy returns. Using leader characters makes for a convenient, but ugly, Apple menu. An alternate approach is to use multiple spaces—a different number of spaces for each group—as the leader character. This makes for a much neater appearance, but if you have more than four groups, the gap in front of the names of the upper items becomes very obvious.

The alternative takes a little more work, but the results are perfect. Instead of using multiple spaces, use multiple Returns as the leader character. Names with more returns will sort on top of those with fewer Returns—but they'll be invisible in the Apple menu.

Of course, you can't actually type Return in an icon's name, since that's what activates and deactivates the editing rectangle. But you can type the Returns someplace else—like the Note Pad—and then copy and paste them into the icon's name, inserting them in front of the name. Once you paste in the Returns, you won't be able to see the item's name until you deselect the icon and/or the editing rectangle.

You'll find a few quirks when working with Return characters in Apple menu item names:

- Working with Returns in the names is awkward: while the editing rectangle is selected, you can't see the characters you've typed after the Returns—all you see is blank space. So, while it's relatively easy to paste multiple Returns in front of the icon's original name, editing it afterwards becomes guesswork with the arrow keys. The easiest thing to do is to copy the icon's name, paste it into the Note Pad, edit it there, and copy the whole thing (the Returns and the name) to be pasted back into the icon's editing rectangle.

An Apple menu with items grouped by multiple, invisible Return characters. Note that within some groups, a bullet leader character drops an item to the bottom.

- If you're looking through the Apple Menu Items folder in an Open or Save dialog (or in any dialog that's accessing the folder's contents) the items will be alphabetized the same way they are in the Apple menu; it will look like a standard list, but you won't be able to type letters to select items because they don't begin with letters—they begin with returns.
- If you've set up any macros that launch items in the Apple menu—the Chooser or Calculator, for instance—before you organize it, you'll have to re-record the macros because the names will have changed.

AMICO, amigo. Take the drudgery out of customizing your Apple menu's order with the nifty **AMICO** (Apple Menu Items Custom Order) extension ($10 shareware). With AMICO running, your Apple menu's appearance is controlled by the View and Arrange settings for the Apple Menu Items folder's window: arrange things by date or size in the window, for instance, and that's how you'll see them in the menu.

> ***It took a long time to get the first pull-down menus. At first they were across the top of each window as opposed to...at the top of the screen. We ran into all kinds of problems [like] what happens when...the menus are long and go off the bottom?***
>
> *Bill Atkinson*

Neither of those arrangements would be very helpful, of course, so AMICO echoes the arrangement of icons in an icon-view window: set up rows of icons in the window, start or end them with a folder whose name starts with a hyphen, and you've got groups of items in the Apple menu with dividers between. Rearrange the icons, and you've rearranged the menu—it's as simple as that. You can even put dimmed words or phrases anywhere in the menu to act as section labels.

AMICO

AMICO is almost perfect in what it does; the "almost" comes from the fact that the Apple menu isn't always immediately updated to reflect the shuffling you've done in the window. But just launching a program usually forces the update, and the whole thing doesn't cause any perceptible delay. (It makes me long for the halcyon days of System 7 when Apple menu utilities let you reorder submenus and even pick the fonts for the submenu display.)

The two-tier approach. The Control Panels folder that the Installer puts in your Apple menu is an alias to the real thing. It's convenient, but only to a point: if the control panels you use the most often are alphabetically towards the bottom of the list, you have a lot of scrolling to do before you get to the one you want.

Simply renaming the control panels to change their order doesn't work, since that also changes the order in which they load into memory at startup. Instead, try the two-tier approach:

1. In the Apple Menu Items folder, rename the Control Panels folder alias with a bullet in front of it.
2. Create a new folder in the Apple Menu Items folder named *Control Panels.*
3. Put the renamed Control Panels folder alias into the new Control Panels folder.
4. Open the real Control Panels folder (its alias is, conveniently, right in the window you're working in) and select the items you use the most. Hold down ⌘ Option and drag them to the new Control Panels folder you just made; this puts aliases of the items into the new folder.

That's all. What you're left with is a Control Panels folder listing in the Apple menu for the new folder you created. In its submenu, you'll find your control panel aliases listed first, with the alias to the real Control Panels folder at the bottom of the list (because of the bullet). If you want one of your popular control panels, you select it from the submenu; if you need something else, you go to the next submenu.

The two-tier approach puts aliases of the control panels you use the most at the top of the submenu and provides access to all control panels in the next submenu.

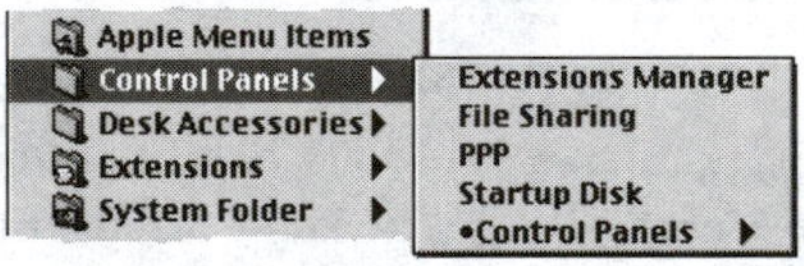

Applications. The Installer makes an Applications folder for you, but you probably were going to make one anyway; in fact, you might have made more than one if you have lots of applications and wanted to divide them into groups. Having an Application submenu in the Apple menu makes for easy program launching even if you're already in another program.

But just putting an alias of your Applications folder(s) into the Apple menu isn't the best approach; even if you don't have a lot of applications, the folder has a subfolder for each one, and the application isn't the only thing in its folder. So, you wind up having to go down to a second submenu and look through it for the application you want to open.

The shortcut to QuarkXPress, through the special Applications folder.

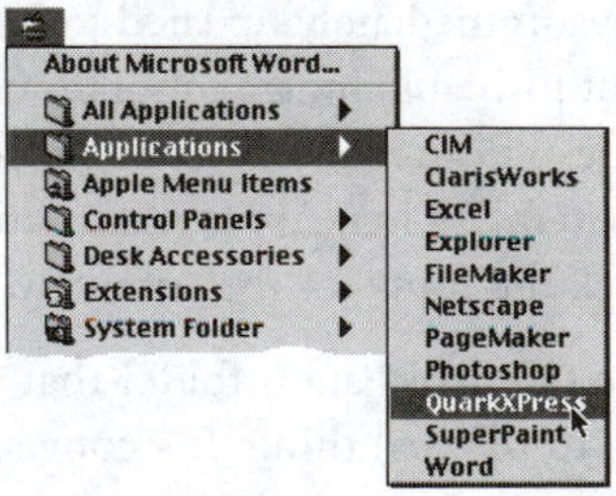

Instead of the two-tier approach used for control panels, I use two separate folders for applications in the Apple menu. One is the Applications folder alias, but it's renamed *All*

Applications. This shows everything in all the application folders, but I use it only occasionally. Instead, I created another Applications folder directly in the Apple Menu Items folder, and put aliases of my most often used applications in it. That means I can launch an application from a short submenu instead of wending my way through extra menus.

Things to put in your menu. Here's a quick round up of ideas about the things you might want to keep in your Apple menu; some of them are described more fully in other chapters.

- **Your hard drive(s):** You'll be able to access anything up to five folders deep without opening the folders themselves if you put an alias of your hard drive in the Apple menu.
- **The Desktop folder:** You'll get this as a submenu item if you put your hard disk in the menu; you'll be able to get at any loose desktop file or folder.
- **The System Folder and subfolders:** The Control Panels folder is aliased by default for inclusion in the Apple menu, but having the System Folder itself there is handy, too. I also keep an alias of the Extensions folder in my Apple menu—you can't ever open an extension, but it's an easy way to see what's running when you want to do a quick check.
- **Desk Accessory folder:** The real ones, like the Calculator, and the "wannabes" like the AppleCD Audio Player are more convenient as submenu selections than as main-level items that make the Apple menu too long, so make a folder for them.
- **Special subgroups:** You can keep, say, all the file-sharing control panels easily accessible by putting their aliases in a separate folder; or, divide your applications into major categories like *Graphics, Telecommunications,* and so on. These subfolders can go on the main level of the Apple menu or at the top of the appropriate submenu.
- **Removable disks and CDs:** Their submenus will show up only when they're actually mounted. (Chapter 4)
- **Launcher Items:** Put an alias of the Launcher Items folder in the menu so you can reach your launch items even when you're not on the desktop (or when you're on a very crowded desktop, with the Launcher window obscured). (Chapter 12)
- **The Clipboard:** An alias of the Clipboard icon that's loose in your System Folder lets you trigger the Finder's Show Clipboard command. (Chapter 5.)
- **Trash can:** An alias lets you see just how much garbage is piling up, without your having to go to the desktop or open the trash icon. (Chapter 7)
- **Desktop printer:** An alias of the desktop printer lets you open the desktop PrintMonitor. (Chapter 15)
- **Servers:** Log on to a server with a quick menu selection. (Chapter 26)

The delay. When you put an alias of a "large" item in the Apple Menu Items folder—something like the System Folder, or a hard drive or CD—it can take anywhere from many seconds to a full minute or more before you can do anything else, since the Mac has to build its submenus (and subsubs and subsubsubs) so you'll be able to access them quickly. This can be quite disconcerting because the mouse pointer doesn't turn into a wristwatch, and you'll hear your drive churning away as the Mac writes information to it—it sure *sounds* like something's going wrong. But be patient, and everything will get back to normal.

The invisible Desktop Folder. The Desktop Folder is an invisible folder that the Mac uses to "hold" all those items out loose on your desktop. If you put your hard drive in the Apple menu, you'll see the Desktop Folder listed in its submenu; in the folder's submenu will be all the things you have lying around on your desktop (the ones that belong to that drive, that is—not other volumes, or desktop items that belong to other items).

It's difficult to put the Desktop Folder in the main level of your Apple menu so you can get at desktop items more directly, because, after all, it's an invisible file and you can't make an alias of it. But if you have a network connection to another Mac, you'll be able to see your Desktop Folder from the other machine; make an alias of the folder while you're on the other machine (the alias will be made right on your drive) and then you can put the alias in your Apple Menu Items folder.

Connect To... what? I know the suspense is killing you; I left this till the last entry on purpose. Just what *is* that *Connect To* item that the Installer puts in your Apple menu?

If you open it, you get a tiny dialog box; you type in a web site address (URL) and click Connect, and the Mac launches your browser of choice to take you directly to that site. I ignored, and even eliminated, this little item for several months, thinking it offered absolutely no function since I had other ways to launch my browser and "go" places. But then I realized how handy it is: if your browser is set for a specific home page, that's where it always goes first—using Connect To bypasses the home page and take you directly to your destination.

Other Subfolders

The Startup Items Folder

The folder. Anything in the Startup Items folder opens when you start your Mac, right after the desktop appears. You'll want to put aliases, not original items, in the folder—it's an awkward place to store things.

That icon on the folder is meant to represent the power switch used on the first of the modular Macs—a round button with a vertical slash. (It's too bad the same icon is used for the Shutdown items folder—wouldn't you think they could've at least rotated the slash to a horizontal position?)

Startup Items

The items. The main candidates for the Startup Items folder are:

- One or more application aliases to launch them at startup.
- The alias of a document to open both it and its application—great for something like a To-Do list or calendar that you check first thing every day.

Other likely candidates include:

- Folder aliases for any windows you want opened on the desktop at startup but usually close during the course of working.
- A Launcher control panel alias—which is placed in the folder automatically by the General Controls control panel if you check the *Open Launcher at startup* option.
- A sound file (or alias) that you'd like played at startup.

The starting lineup. Items in the Startup Items folder are launched alphabetically, but in groups; within the groups, real items are given precedence over aliases (really!). This is the opening order:

1. applications
2. documents
3. sounds
4. folders
5. desk accessories

Since the order in which applications launch can have an effect on how memory is used when you quit them, you may want to rename the application aliases you put in the folder so they'll load in the order you want. (Remember, opening a document from the Startup Items folder also opens its application, so you don't have to open the application first—and you can control the order of application launching by renaming the document aliases.)

Back to the desktop? In OS 8 and 8.1, if you want a folder or two to open at startup but you also set either an application or a document to open, the desktop folder opens after the application launches, but it opens in the background—so you don't wind up back on the desktop. There's currently no way around this, but keep your eyes open for shareware solutions: in previous systems, a utility called *FinderToFront* used to get you back to the desktop at startup, but as of this writing, there's no OS 8 equivalent (and putting an alias of the Finder in the Startup Items folder, another old trick, doesn't work any more, either).

A special startup message. If you'd like to have a startup message on the screen (presumably on someone *else's* screen, since there's not much reason to write a note to yourself), you could make a SimpleText document, or write something in the Note Pad, and put their aliases in the Startup Items folder. But there's a better way to make a quick, application-less message:

1. Type the message in any drag-enabled application or utility, like the Note Pad.
2. Select the text and drag it to the desktop.
3. Name it something appropriate.
4. Put it in the Startup Items folder.

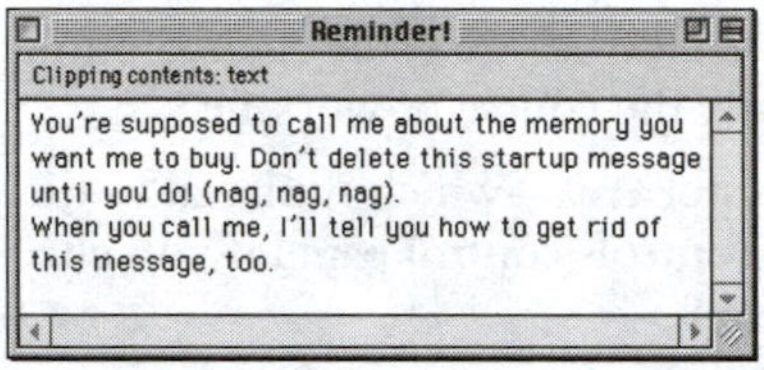

When you open a text clipping, all you see is the message—there's no application that opens to handle a "clippings document"; so, when it's opened as a startup item, all you have to do is close the window and everything's closed.

Bypassing startup items. When you hold down Shift to keep all the extensions from loading at startup and keep it down, you'll also prevent startup items from opening.

To quash the extensions but not the startup items, release the Shift key as soon as you see the *Welcome to Macintosh, Extensions off* dialog. To load extensions but bypass the startup items, press Shift after the extensions finish loading, before things show up on the desktop (about the time the menubar appears is when you should get the key down).

Shutdown items. You can probably guess what this folder is for, although you may not be able to figure out how to make use of it. Since anything in the Shutdown Items folder opens, or runs, when you use the Shut Down command, some utilities—especially ones that make automatic backups—place something in this folder to trigger an action when you use the Shut Down command.

If you know how to write AppleScripts, you might place a script in the Shutdown Items folder that would, for instance, empty the trash before you shut down.

But you don't have to get that fancy. If there's something you should do before you shut down your Mac, put the related document or program in this folder so it opens before the Mac shuts down: I have a PowerMerge document in there so I can do a backup at every shutdown. When you quit the program that was launched from the Shutdown Items folder, the Mac finishes shutting down—which can come as quite a surprise if you've worked for a while since you used the Shut Down command.

Preferences

The folder. The Preferences folder holds files that applications and utilities use to keep track of things like how you've set up their defaults, if you've registered and entered a serial number, what documents you were using last time you used the application, and so on. These files are generally referred to as *prefs* or *settings* files, and their names usually include the word *preferences, prefs, settings,* or *defaults.*

As applications get more complicated, a single preferences file isn't always enough, so many programs create folders inside the Preferences folder. Netscape and Explorer, for instance, keep not only program settings but also caches of web pages in the folders they place inside your preferences folder.

Corrupted preferences. Preference files for some programs are very susceptible to corruption, and a corrupted preferences file often keeps a program from launching or behaving correctly. One of the first things you should do when a program starts giving you grief when it always behaved before is get rid of its preferences file and try again—there's even a Finder Preferences file that occasionally needs to be trashed.

That said, be careful: some preferences files contain important information, like a registration number, that lets you run the program without, say, reminders to register. Your best bet is to pay attention to the next entry.

The forgotten backup. Preferences files aren't often included in piecemeal backups (as opposed to total-disk backups), but they should be. It doesn't matter if you have to rebuild your Finder Preferences file, but some preferences files contain important information that you don't want to lose. You should occasionally back up the preferences file of certain programs so you can replace them if they become corrupted.

10

Other System Stuff

Desk Accessories

Help Systems

Odds and Ends

For the Power User

Macro Editors

In This Chapter

Desk Accessories

In General

Once and future DAs. *Desk accessories* are little applications with narrowly focused capabilities. Prior to System 7, they were part of the System file itself; with System 7, they became stand-alone items.

In the early Mac days, DAs (as they're called) were a special solution to a special problem. You could run only a single program at a time, so you would have had to quit MacWrite just to take out a Calculator program. So, DAs like the Calculator, Alarm Clock, and Scrapbook were designed to run in a tiny chunk of memory and in a special "layer" that didn't require your quitting the one and only application you could use.

Those days are far behind us but the desk accessory nomenclature, and a little of its philosophy, remains. A *true* DA has a "kind" of desk accessory if you check it in a list-view window, and there are only three left in the system software: Chooser, Calculator, and Key Caps. Other items that *used* to be desk accessories, like the Scrapbook and Note Pad, or would have been desk accessories, like Stickies and the AppleCD Audio Player, are actually applications.

This section covers the actual, used-to-be, and would-have-been desk accessories that come in OS 8 (except for a few, like Chooser and Key Caps, that are covered elsewhere in the book in context of some other subject matter).

Auto-routing for the real thing. If you're dealing with a *real* desk accessory—one whose "kind" is desk accessory, like Key Caps—you can drag it into the closed System Folder and it will be routed to the Apple Menu Items folder.

Treated like an application. Even a real DA is treated like an application from the system's point of view for some things: it gets its own memory allocation, and, when open, it's listed in the Applications menu at the right of the menubar. But in other ways, it's still not an application: you can't, for instance, allocate more memory to it through its Get Info window.

Calculator

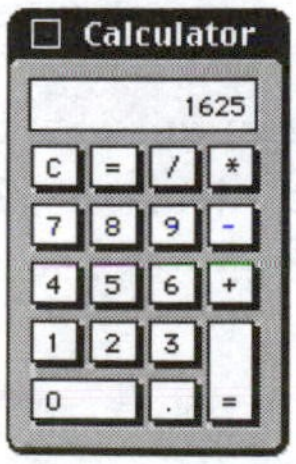

Calculator The Calculator is what it looks like, and its simplicity belies its usefulness for quick calculations (you don't always need Excel!). Enter numbers by clicking the Calculator's keys or by using your keyboard. The asterisk is for multiplication, and the slash is for division. To get the answer, you can click [=] on the Calculator or press [=] or [Enter] on the keyboard.

The Copy command copies the results in the Calculator's window to the Clipboard (you don't have to select anything first).

Priority of operations. What's 3+5*2? You probably answered 16, and the Calculator would agree with you; it works in strict left-to-right order for a calculation. But it's worth pointing that out, because spreadsheets give priority to certain operations—multiplication, for instance, is more important than addition and is performed first—so a spreadsheet's answer to that problem would be 13.

Off-site calculations. You don't have to click or type every problem into the Calculator; you can paste in something like *16*42+8* and have the operation performed automatically—you'll see the Calculator's buttons being "clicked," like a player piano's keys being depressed by ghost fingers. This is especially convenient when you're typing in more than two or three numbers, since the Calculator's C (clear) key clears everything, and not just the last number you entered. If you make a mistake, you have to start again—but typing the problem elsewhere first lets you make corrections.

What a drag. The Calculator is a special type of window that you seldom see on a Mac, with the black bar across the top and no real "edges." But you can drag it by more than just the title bar: the curved lower corners, if you grab just the right spots, serve as "handles" by which the Calculator can be dragged.

A word is worth a thousand numbers. If the Calculator's lack of number formatting makes it difficult to read long numbers because there are no commas, and you're comfortable reading scientific notation, you can switch the Calculator's readout to scientific notation by pressing E on your keyboard.

And, the Calculator can switch to a text readout for special occasions: type E, then 9999 and press Enter—the answer is *infinity.* Then try E9999/E9999 and see what happens.

Bigger and better calculators. If you need something a little stronger than the Calculator but you still don't need a spreadsheet, why don't you just build your own Calculator? Dubl-Click's **Calculator Construction Set** has been around for years, and its longevity may be due to its flexibility. You can create your own custom calculators using a toolbox similar to those found in painting programs. Your calculator can have time and calendar components, and you can start from scratch or just alter one of the many predesigned models it comes with.

dublclick.com

The DiskTools Collection, described elsewhere in this chapter and also in Chapter 6, includes two calculators: a scientific calculator (shown on the next page) and an RPN calculator. (That's *Reverse Polish Notation,* a setup for a joke if I ever heard one!)

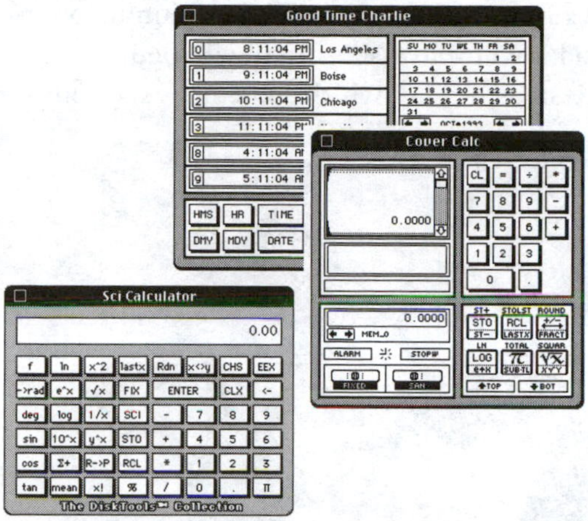

One of DiskTools' calculators, and two samples from the Construction Set

Graphing Calculator

Basics. The graphing calculator is one of those things that, if you don't need it, my explanation won't do you any good, and if you do need it, you don't need my explanation (you know what I mean?). The basic Graphing Calculator window is pretty straightforward, with an area in which you can type an equation and an area that displays the results. It's not always easy to type in or edit the equation—you certainly need the small or full keypad, and often you'll have to delete more than you'd like of an existing equation because it's difficult to click in it and insert characters or edit them—but there are also a few non-obvious capabilities in the window, described in the picture here.

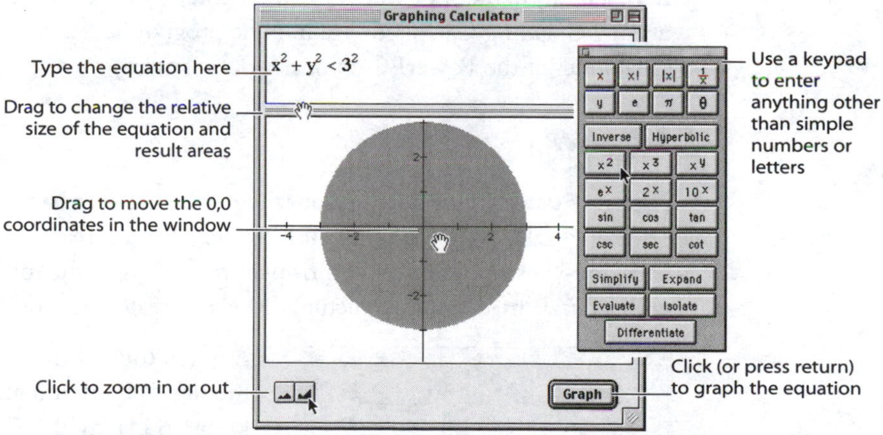

Interactive pictures. When you graph a 3-D picture, you can work with it interactively—grab it and move it around to get different views. The picture here, for the equation z=xy, is shown in four of its views. And here's something really special, which you'll discover by accident as you twist something around: give it a little push, and it will keep spinning on its own. Give it a bigger push, and it will spin faster. Try it with figures produced with equations like $(x^2 + y^2)\ 3^2$ or $x^2 + y^2 3^2$, which sometimes start out spinning.

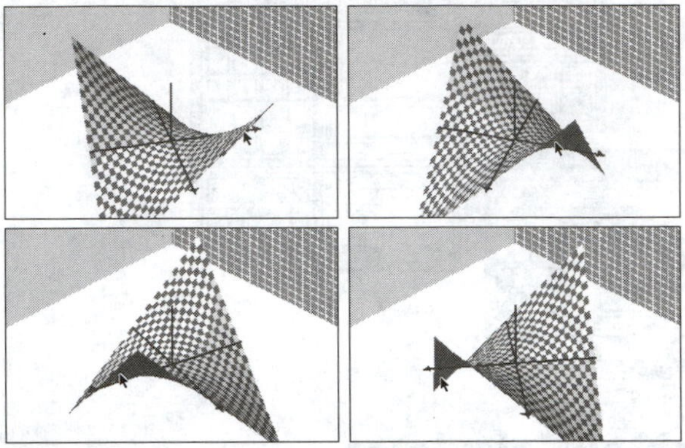

Four views of the same graph, dragged around by the mouse.

Help, I need somebody. Check the Credits through the Graphing Calculator's About command under the Apple menu, or through its Help window, and point to some of the people involved in the project while Balloon Help is turned on.

Save those pictures. You can grab a picture of any nifty result by using the Copy command, but you can also just drag and drop the picture from the Graphing Calculator's window into any drag-and-drop enabled program, or right onto the desktop as a clipping.

The Wow! demo. Choose Full Demo from the Demo menu and sit back. It's a lengthy demo, but worth every second of your time—even if you never use the Graphing Calculator again. (The program was written to show off the capabilities of the PowerPC chip, and does it ever!)

Jigsaw

Jigsaw Puzzle. This not-very-puzzling diversion isn't half as interesting as the original Puzzle, even if it looks a little better. If your preschooler isn't jaded by bells-and-whistles software (surprisingly, most aren't), she might enjoy playing with a puzzle made out of a picture that she's created in another program.

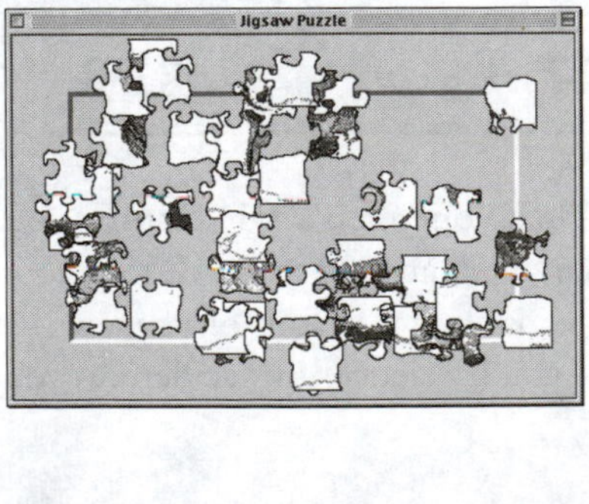

A quick tour of the Jigsaw Puzzle's menus will tell you all you need to know to play with it: use the Start New Puzzle command to break the picture into pieces, choosing the size of the pieces you want at the start. As you drag pieces into their spots, they'll snap into place if you're within a few pixels of where they belong. In fact, matching pieces will snap together, and move as a unit, without their having to be in the right spot.

A picture dragged in from the Scrapbook (left) and an imported PICT (right).

PICT file type
Chapter 19

Make your own. You probably already guessed you could make your own jigsaw puzzle, but maybe you didn't know there are three ways to do it:

- Paste a picture into the Jigsaw Puzzle window.
- Drag a picture in from a drag-and-drop capable utility like the Scrapbook.
- Use the Open command to import any PICT-type graphic.

Solving the puzzle. Okay, you're not likely to need help in solving this particular puzzle. But there are two "help" features that your little one can use—one for help, and the other for fun. The Show Picture command shows what the puzzle picture looks like. And the Solve Puzzle command puts pieces into place one at time with little sound effects—overall, something that young kids are happy to watch over and over.

Notepad

Note Pad. The venerable Note Pad was stuck in a time warp from the beginning of the Mac until System 7.5, when it was updated with things like: a 3-D look and sound effects when you flip a page; a resizable window; scrollable text on each page; your choice of font and size for (all) text; drag-and-drop capability; and a Find function. In OS 8, it has a 3-D look, but no additional features.

The Note Pad can come in handy for a few special, temporary purposes, like quickly storing a web address, but it's still not beefy enough to serve any practical purpose.

To flip between pages, click on the corner of the next page, or the upturned page corner, in the lower left of the Note Pad. For all its little improvements, the modern version lost a major one: you can't flip from page 8 (the last one) right around to page 1 anymore. (Although you can use the Go To command to jump to any page.)

Multiple files. If you do use the Note Pad but its eight pages aren't enough for you, you can work with multiple Note Pad files: duplicate the Note Pad File that's in the System Folder and name it whatever you want. When you double-click on a Note Pad file, it opens; if the Note Pad was already open, it just switches to the contents of the file that you double-clicked.

And if you really use multiple Note Pad files, you can put them all in a folder inside the Apple Menu Items folder, so you can easily open them just by selecting from a submenu.

DiskTools Collection

Note Pad replacement. If you like the *idea* of the Note Pad, but find it too limiting, you can use SimpleText or the old TeachText instead: create a document in either utility, name it Note Pad, and stick it in your Apple menu.

shareware.com

But neither of those relatively small applications provides the separate-page approach of the Note Pad, which give you the "feel" of separating your information by pages into some sort of free-form database. The perfect solution: **Phone Pad**, part of the **DiskTools Collection**—the whole collection is a $10 shareware collection (by Evan Gross, author of Spell Catcher) that's worth twice the price. The Phone Pad provides a thousand searchable pages, automatic dialing (which is probably not as convenient as it was years ago when people used the same line for their computers and voice calls), and a terrific index feature that lets you put any word from any page in a separate column and jump to that page simply by double-clicking on the word.

More about DiskTools
Chapter 6

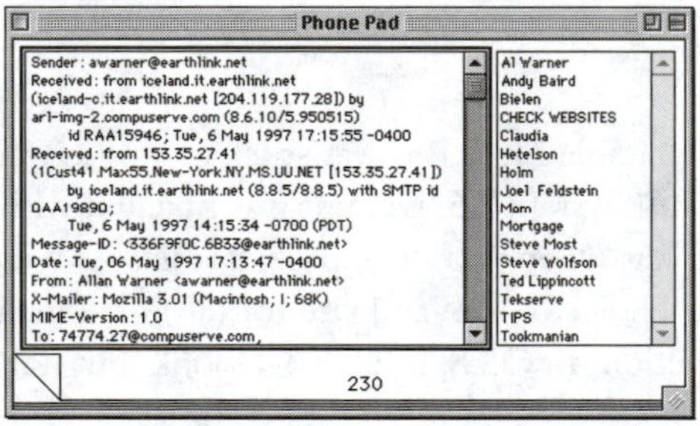

The PhonePad from DiskTools is a Note Pad on steroids. The column at right serves as an index—click on something in the list, and you jump to that page.

Scrapbook

The Scrapbook. The Scrapbook has been gradually improved over the years, making it a reasonably useful little utility for storing and transferring text, graphics of all types, sounds, QuickTime movies, and even application-specific items like FileMaker buttons with their scripts intact. In fact, I can't imagine why anyone would leave little desktop clippings around (from drag-and-drop procedures, described in Chapter 5) when you can neatly store—and view—all those items in the Scrapbook.

Clicking the Scrapbook's zoom box toggles the window between a size that accommodates a full-size version of the page contents (up to the size of the screen) and the last size you used. When the window's not large enough for a full-size version of the graphic, it shrinks the graphic to fit in the window, although what you copy out is still the full version. Clicking the scroll arrows or dragging the scroll box shows different pages; using ← and → or Page Up and Page Down also flips the pages.

The bottom of the Scrapbook window displays information about what's on the page, including its size (as if it were a separate file) and, for a picture, its dimensions. The *Type* information lets you know what kind of information is embedded in the stored item; it might be as simple as *picture* or *text*, or it might try to be more informative, as shown in the picture here, which is text pasted in from Microsoft Word.

In a Zen-like approach to unidentifiable items, if you paste something non-standard (like, say, a QuicKeys macro) into the Scrapbook, it's stored there but not displayed; instead, you'll get the notice: *This item has no text, picture, sound, or movie.*

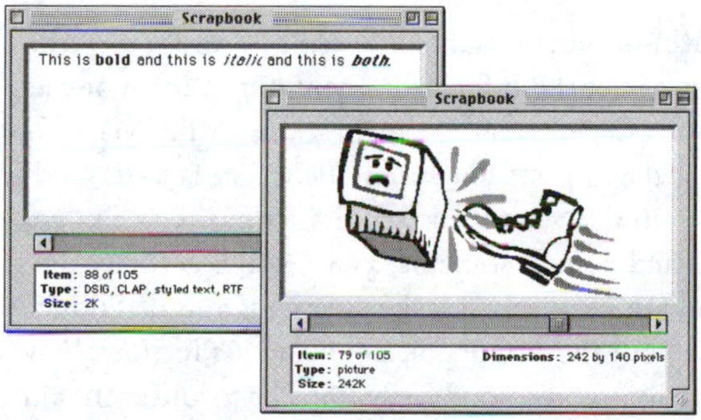

Information about each item is displayed at the bottom of the window.

Ins and outs. There are two ways to put something into the Scrapbook. The usual way is to copy something to the Clipboard and then Paste it into the Scrapbook; the item appears on a newly created page which is inserted before ("on top") of the page that's currently showing. The Scrapbook is also fully drag-and-drop capable, so you can drag things into it from any other drag-and-drop environment; you can even just drag loose clippings files right into it. (You should be able to drag multiple clippings files all at once, but I've found that doing that often creates multiple pages for one of the clippings, and none for the others.)

To get something from the Scrapbook, you simply display the page and use the Cut or Copy command; this is one of the few places you don't specifically select something before using those commands. You can drag a page out of the Scrapbook to place a copy either on the desktop (in a clippings file) or into a document. If you want to just get rid of a page, use the Edit menu's Clear command.

The unkindest cut. If you use the Cut command on a Scrapbook page, you can't Undo it. But you *can* just use the Paste command to put it right back.

IN THE BEGINNING

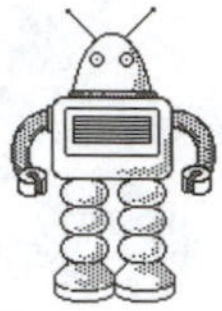

If you know what the Fish and the Robot were, you've been with the Mac for a long time. Here's what the two famous pictures in the original Scrapbook looked like.

The pink party hat with streamers and confetti has been in the Scrapbook for many years now, and it's getting pretty tired (or, rather, *we're* tired of seeing it). But the original Scrapbook had a party-theme picture, too, as you can see here.

Special items. The Scrapbook doesn't do any "converting" of information, so whether or not the information you put in from one application can transfer to another depends on the applications. A FileMaker button with a script can be copied and pasted between FileMaker layouts, and it can pasted in and retrieved from the Scrapbook with its script intact, but copy it from the Scrapbook and paste it someplace else, you'll get only the graphic part of the button and not its attached script (just as if you had done the copy and paste directly without the Scrapbook stopover). As for text, basic text styles (bold, italic, underline, and so on) easily transfer to and from almost any program; whether or not special information like style sheet and paragraph definitions can be transferred through the Scrapbook depends on where the text came from and where it's going.

The Scrapbook file. Since there's no Save or Open command, it's hard to remember that the Scrapbook is actually made of two items: the Scrapbook application, and its one-and-only "document," the Scrapbook file that's stored in the main level of the System Folder. Double-clicking on the Scrapbook file opens the Scrapbook. In fact, double-clicking on any Scrapbook file (if you have more than one—we'll get to that in a minute) opens the Scrapbook.

If there's no Scrapbook file in the System Folder when you open the Scrapbook itself from the Apple menu (where it's placed by default), it creates a new file for itself, and you'll get a page that says "Empty Scrapbook." (The early Scrapbook had less functionality, but more whimsy. An empty Scrapbook file provide this message in its window: “This space for rent.”)

Multiple Scrapbook files. Why would you wind up with multiple Scrapbook files so that you’d have to know how to handle them? Well, the OS 8.1 system CD has a folder in its CD Extras folder named *Additional Desktop Patterns.* And, in there you’ll find a file with the same name—and it’s a Scrapbook file.

The Scrapbook can handle only one file at a time. If you open the Scrapbook application, it automatically opens the file in the System Folder; on the other hand, if you double-click a Scrapbook file anywhere, the Scrapbook itself opens and displays the contents of that file. (If the Scrapbook is already open, it closes and then reopens to show the new file.) So, if you want to temporarily access an alternative Scrapbook file, just double-click on it. To make it your default, put it in the System Folder, either replacing the one that’s already there or first preserving the original by moving or renaming it.

Combining Scrapbook file contents is a multistep process, but it’s not difficult: open one of the files and drag each page to the desktop, creating a clippings file for each page. Open the other Scrapbook file and drag the clippings in; you can drag them all at once, and a page will be created for each clipping.

Desktop Pictures control panel
Chapter 6

If it’s the Additional Desktop Patterns file you open temporarily, you can just drag the patterns you want from the Scrapbook window into the Desktop Pictures control panel window.

A captivating Scrapbook replacement. My favorite Scrapbook replacement is **Captivate Store**, part of the Captivate utility ($80, Casady & Greene). Half of the package is devoted to taking screen shots (that’s discussed later in this chapter); the other half lets you retrieve not only screen shots that you may have taken, but anything else that you can put on the Clipboard and want to retrieve later. Captivate Store is perhaps best described as a hierarchical pop-up scrapbook. Its pop-up menu lists the folders and subfolders where you have items stored; pointing to a menu item pops out a sample of the item so you know what’s there. Selecting the item copies it to the Clipboard and automatically pastes it down in your current application. Captivate Store can handle text, PICT, sound, or QuickTime files that you’ve put in its folders from within the Finder; you can also paste just about anything into Captivate Store and it will create a file for that item.

Captivate

casadyg.com

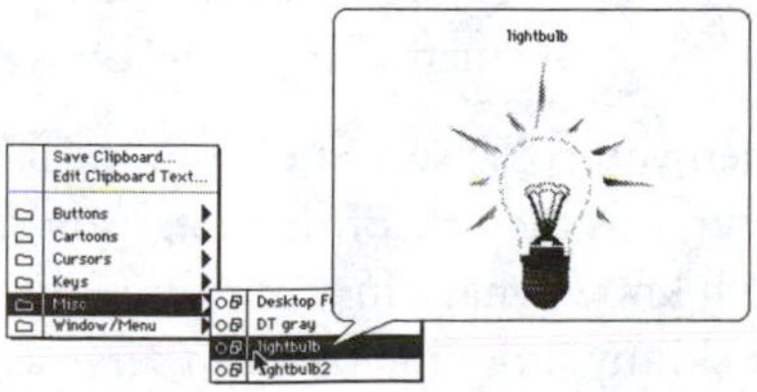

Captivate Store’s pop-up menu lets you choose text or graphics that you’ve previously stored; whatever you select is automatically pasted in your document.

Stickies

Stickies. Stickies is a little application, initially stored in the Apple Menu Items folder, that lets you make the electronic equivalent of Post-it® notes. It also lets you clutter up your screen, the same way you can with the paper version. A sticky memo is a little window with minimal controls (a title bar, close box, and zoom box). Use Stickies' menus to change the color of the note, and the font used in it.

Unfortunately, a note sticks to a spot on a screen, and not to anything particular, like a window or an icon. And, since Stickies is an application, it has to be the active one for its notes to show up on top of other windows on the screen.

Although Stickies don't have scroll bars, you can continue typing beyond what looks like the bottom of the note, and everything will scroll automatically; if you need to scroll a small note to see what's past the bottom edge, drag inside the text to make the window scroll.

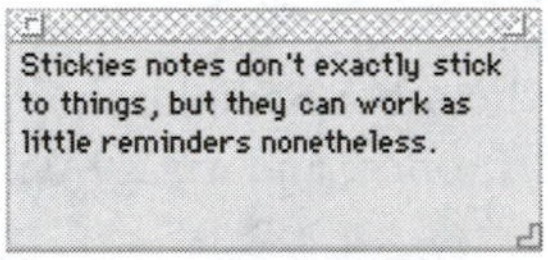

Stickies notes don't exactly stick to things, but they can work as little reminders nonetheless.

The nonstandard zoom box in the upper right corner works as you'd expect, but there's no collapse box as there should be for OS 8 windows. However, if you double-click on a note's title bar, you can collapse and expand the window. And, if you don't mind losing the zoom box functionality, you can use Stickies' Preferences command to change the zoom box to a collapse box.

Setting a default note. You can make your new notes start up with the color and text specifications you want by creating a note that you like and then using the Use as Default command while that note is active.

Setting up stationery. If you want to, in effect, set up several defaults for Stickies notes (say, yellow with 12-point Bold Geneva, and purple with 9-point Times), you can use this trick to create stationery:

1. Create and format a note the way you want it, leaving the actual note area blank. Make sure that the formatted note is the active window.
2. Choose Export Text from the File menu.
3. Click the Save as Stationery box and save it with an appropriate name.

Make stationery for Stickies notes.

Export several different formats, saving them in a subfolder in the Apple menu, and selecting one will open a blank note already formatted the way you want it.

Making note bars. When you collapse a Stickies note, its first line of text is moved to the title bar to serve as the title of the note. You can make use of this not only because you'll know what's in a note without opening its window, but also because the skinny little title bars can serve as reminders themselves: just type a line of text, collapse the window by double-clicking on the title bar, and use the resulting single-line note as a reminder.

The nontalking moose. Who the heck ever found this particular trick? Start a new stickie note, type *Antler!* (keep the initial uppercase letter, and the exclamation point) and press Return.

Help Systems

OS Help

The Help menu. In OS 8, the Help menu has been changed from a question-mark icon at the right of the menu bar to a Help menu (in text) that appends itself as the last menu on the menubar no matter what program you're in.

The contents of the Help menu change based on what application you're in. The first item is always an About command, usually for Balloon Help but sometimes for some aspect of the application's help system. The second item toggles from Show Balloons to Hide Balloons for the Balloon Help system. The remaining commands depend on what Help system is built into the currently active application. There may be tutorials, shortcut lists, full-blown interactive help, or even nothing at all.

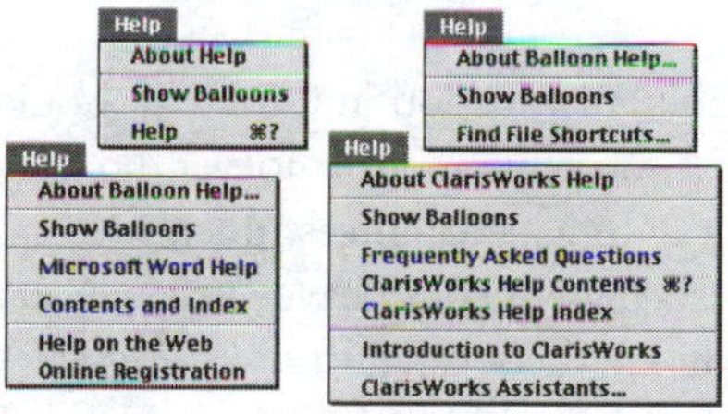

Help menus for: the Finder, Find File, Microsoft Word, and ClarisWorks.

General OS Help. In OS 8, the Apple Guide system has been rechristened Mac OS Help, but the actual system, accessed through the Help command in the Finder's Help menu, is still the same.

You can access Help information in three different ways, through the buttons at the top of the Help window:

- **Topics** shows a list of topics (in no discernable order) in the left pane, with specifics in the right pane.
- **Index** shows an alphabetical listing in the left pane; click or drag the pointer at the top of the scrolling list to jump to a specific spot.
- **Look for** lets you type a word or phrase in a box, and related items are listed at the right; you don't have to click on the arrow, as the instructions state, but you do have to at least click in the text box before you can type in it.

In each case, the right panel shows a scrollable, hierarchical list of topics. The lists are seldom too long to just scroll through, but you can use the triangle in front of the main topics to collapse and expand a long list.

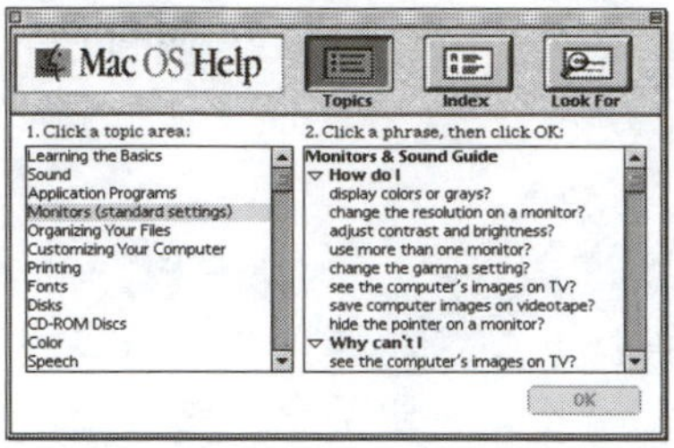

The Topics view in the Help system. (Notice the order of topics—none!)

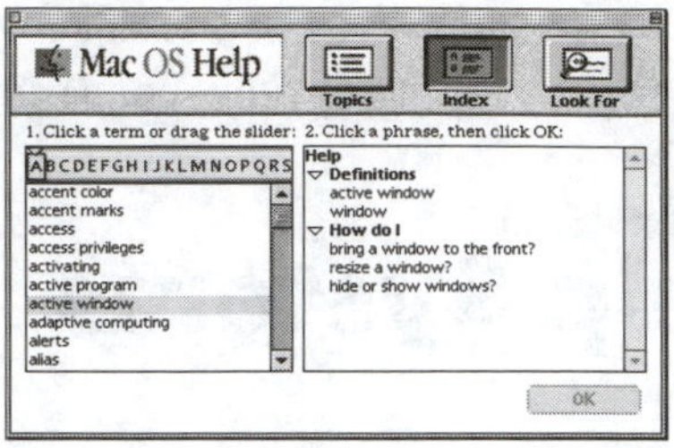

The Index view in the Help system. Click on the letter you want if you can see it, or drag the pointer to scroll the letters.

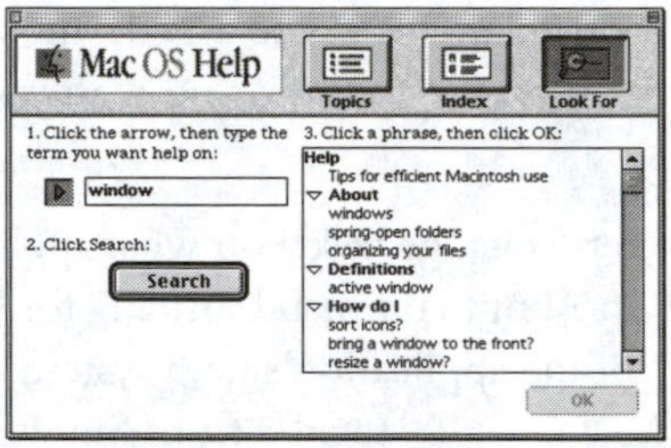

The lookup view in the Help system.

Lame lookups. The Look For function in OS Help should be the most useful approach to looking for something, but whoever did the database for it should be fired (not that the Index guarantees much success, either). One quick example out of oh-so-many I could have chosen: You're in the Finder's Preferences dialog and you see the setting for *spring-loaded folders*. You want to know more about them, so you type the phrase into Help's Look For. You get nothing—it doesn't know from spring-loaded with or without the hyphen, and with or without the *folder(s)*. But if you search just for *folder* (but why should you?), you'll see an item *spring-open folders* in the list that you can click on.

Tell me, show me. Once you've found a topic you want to explore in the Help system, you click the Start button. You'll get a dialog that may or may not be helpful, and may or may not be part of more information. When you hit the jackpot, you can get several screens of information as well as a mildly interactive tutorial.

The interactive part kicks in when the Help window tells you to do something (open a window, select a menu command) and you don't bother, but just click the "next" button: first, the Mac either circles the target (say, a menu title or item, or an icon in a window) in red, or draws a big red arrow pointing to it. Then, if you don't do anything, the Mac will do the next step for you, like open the window or execute the menu command.

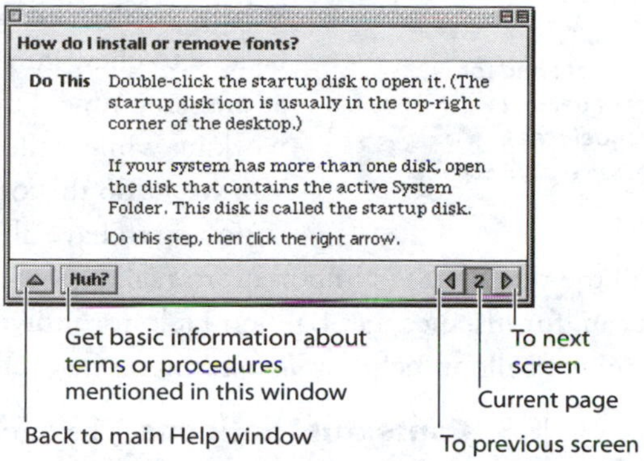

A basic Help information window.

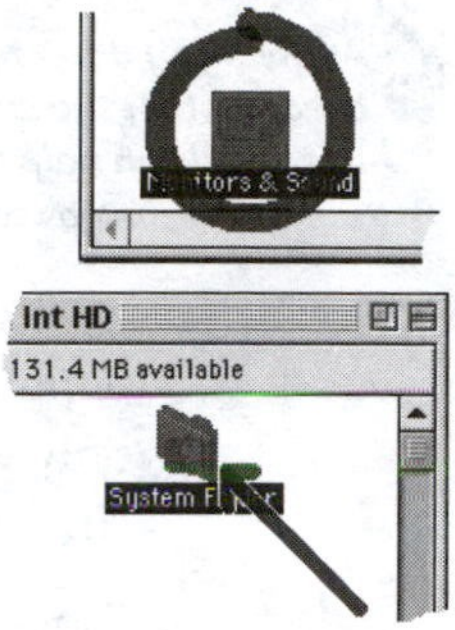

The Help highlights are more eye-catching in their native red.

Balloon Help

About balloons. The Mac's first built-in help system, Balloon Help, debuted in System 7; while it's been somewhat overshadowed by the OS Help system, and far too many people ignore it, there's nothing handier when you're faced with a dialog box providing a list of choices that you don't understand.

Turn on Balloon Help by choosing Show Balloons from the Help menu. (The command changes to Hide Balloons so you can turn the little buggers off.) Then point to something—you don't even have to click the mouse—to get information about it, which shows up in a little balloon. The information in the balloon comes from the program you're using, so the actual helpfulness of Balloon Help really depends on the programmer's thoroughness.

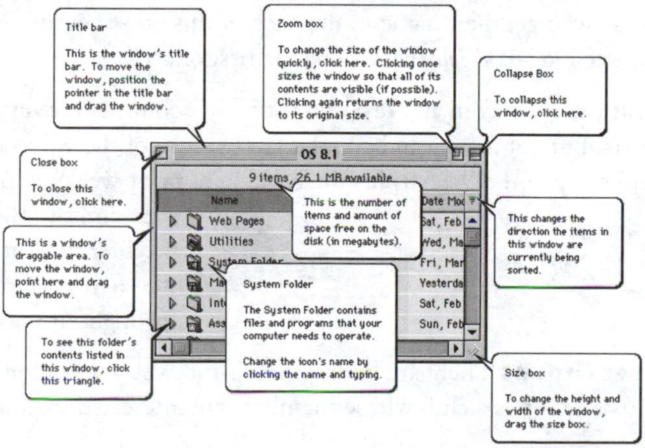

When Balloon help is on, pointing to any item gets you an information-filled balloon. This shows just some of the balloons available for Finder windows.

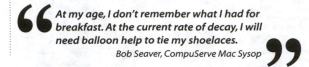

> ***At my age, I don't remember what I had for breakfast. At the current rate of decay, I will need balloon help to tie my shoelaces.***
>
> *Bob Seaver, CompuServe Mac Sysop*

While you're working. You may not be able to chew gum and click a mouse at the same time, but you can continue working while Balloon Help is on. You won't do this often, because it's annoying to have all those balloons popping out all the time, but it's important to realize you can do this: it's the only way you can, for instance, get Balloon Help for individual menu items. (In fact, you can get balloon help for *dimmed* menu items!)

Contextual balloons. The information in Balloon Help can change based on the status of the item you're pointing to. The picture here, for instance, shows two different balloons for the Trash can.

In the About box. When you use the Finder's About this Computer command to see how memory's being used, the bars that represent the memory for each running application use a darker color to show how much of the allocation is actually being used. If you want a specific number for memory use, point to the bar with Balloon Help on.

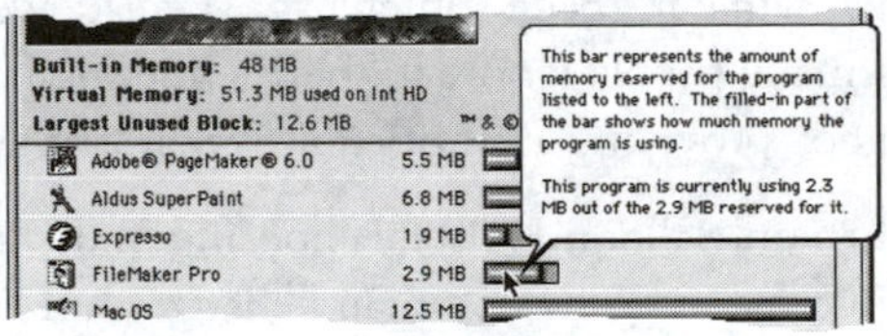

Getting Help from Other Sources

'Tis better to give than to receive. Before we list some of the places you can get help, let me list one where you can *give* help, and join the list of "tipsters" who get their name in the back of this book because they've sent in a tip (or tried to—it's *really* hard to be the first one!).

Visit thetipster.com and drop me a tip, or a comment. Everything will be read—but not many can be replied to because of the volume of e-mail! You'll find a Tip of the Week (plus the backlog of prior weeks), links to other Mac sites, links to the Editor's Choice product sites, and links to most of the shareware products mentioned throughout the book.

User Groups There are books, there's the Web—and then there are people. A user group is a club whose members are interested in computers in general, or in a particular kind of computer, or even specific software. They're typically nonprofit and independent of manufacturers and publishers.

Meetings are usually free. Membership, with its perks of a newsletter, access to shareware libraries, and sometimes even discounts on major products, usually runs $20-60 a year. Subgroups, called *SIGs* (special interest groups), meet for members who share a particular focus, like beginners or musicians.

To find a User Group near you, stop by Apple's web site: apple.com/usergroups/.

Reading material. Hey, this book is great, but it has a serious limitation: *time.* When you want more timely printed material, you need a monthly or weekly Mac publication—all of whom have web sites, too, where you can get more information about subscribing to the paper version:

Macworld	macworld.com
MacAddict	macaddict.com
MacWEEK	macweek.com

Then there's TidBITs (tidbits.com), a free electronic newsletter that covers the computer industry with an emphasis on the Macintosh and the Internet. It's distributed to about 150,000 readers each week on the Internet and on most commercial services.

On the Web. The Web is an incredible source of information for almost anything, but especially for computer information. Surf by these sites:

- *macintouch.com:* News and analysis, product coverage, system software notes.
- *macfixit.com:* Problems and solutions, updates (news about them, and sometimes the updates themselves) for utilities and software.
- *macdirectory.com:* Track down hardware and software info, seminars and events, and even job opportunities.
- *maccentral.com:* News, software downloads, sales.
- *evangelist.macaddict.com:* When you're feeling down… drop in to find out about the latest and greatest news, and how the Mac is still surviving. Subscribe to the Evangelist newsletter while you're there.

Don't forget the web sites for specific companies, where you can find out about the latest software update or hardware release, and often pick up technical information, too. Here are some of the Apple sites you might want to go to:

- Apple Computer: *apple.com*
- Apple Tech Info Library: *info.apple.com/til/*
- Apple Facts Online: *product.info.apple.com/productinfo/datasheets/*
- Apple Software Updates: *info.apple.com/swupdates/*

The online services. Both AOL and CompuServe offer extensive Mac support in the form of libraries, announcements, and thousands of other users, at least *one* of whom has already figured out whatever you're asking. This direct question-and-answer support, as yet unavailable on the Web, is the main reason you should consider subscribing to them (and accessing the Web through them) instead of getting an ISP only.

Odds and Ends

SimpleText

SimpleText. SimpleText replaced the venerable TeachText as the basic Mac text processor many years ago. Unlike its predecessor, it supports multiple fonts, styles, and sizes, multiple windows, can record and play back a single sound per document, and even has drag-and-drop editing. But more than anything else, it serves as a reader for ReadMe documents, those instructional little treatises that come with so many programs and utilities.

SimpleText is installed in the Applications folder on the main level of your hard drive. If you put it away in some folder (I stick it in Utilities) and later reinstall your system software, you'll get another copy back in the Applications folder. SimpleText also comes with many programs and may be installed in their folders. You should try using the Find command occasionally to weed out multiple copies of SimpleText.

Grabbing graphics. When a SimpleText document is composed solely of a graphic (as when you open a plain PICT file by double-clicking on it), you can use the Select All command, and then the Copy command, to put the whole thing on the Clipboard. But if you want only a section of the graphic, you can just drag across it—you'll see a rectangle where you drag—and use the Copy command for that.

You can't add a graphic to a SimpleText document without some serious gymnastics, using ResEdit; this is covered in the ResEdit section later in the chapter.

Editing a ReadMe. Don't you find it annoying that all those nifty ReadMe files can be only read or printed? You can't alter them, or even select an area to copy someplace else. You don't have to put up with that anymore.

There are two types of SimpleText files, with two different file types: *TEXT* and *ttro*. TEXT-type files are the ones you create when you save something from SimpleText. The ttro (TeachText read only) types are the ones you can't edit—unless you change the type to TEXT. Here are a few ways you can do the alteration:

- Use any utility that lets you change file types. **DiskTools**, **Drop•Info**, and **More File Info**, all covered in Chapter 6, can do the trick.
- Use the Color Menu (described in the next entry) utility to alter SimpleText itself.
- Use an AppleScript application (described later in this chapter) to do the dirty work.
- You can change file types in ResEdit, which is like using a hammer to kill a fly, unless you're already working in ResEdit for something else; the procedure is described later in this chapter.

File types and creator codes
Chapter 12

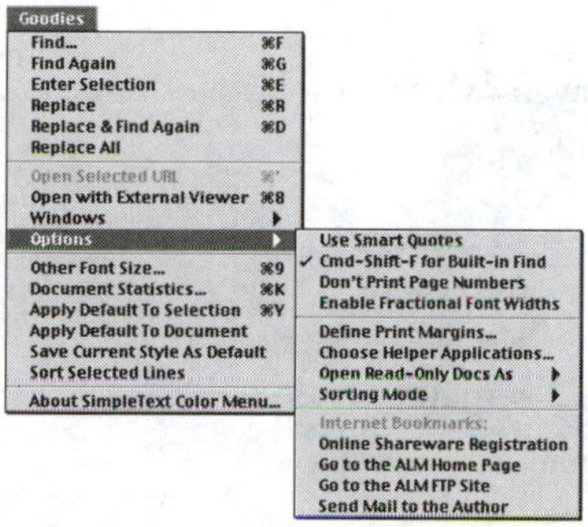

Even if you use only half of Color Menu's additions, it's worth the shareware fee.

Color Menu addition. A nifty little shareware utility called **SimpleText Color Menu** ($10) alters SimpleText so that it sports a Color menu that you can use to colorize text, and a Goodies menu that provides all sorts of little goodies (of course), like more powerful Find and Replace commands, sorting capabilities, and a way to set and apply user-defined default text styles. While it doesn't provide the single most-needed addition to SimpleText (an easy way to paste in a graphic), it does have the next most-needed command: a way to open a non-editable ReadMe file as an editable document.

shareware.com

Embedding graphics. You can view PICT files in SimpleText, but you can't paste a graphic into a document. Later in the chapter, I describe how to use ResEdit to embed graphics in a SimpleText document, but there is (as there is so often!) a shareware solution, too. **PICTInText** ($10) lets you open your text file in its special window and indicate where you want your PICT file to be inserted (it has to be a separate file to start with—you can't just paste something from the Clipboard); saving the files from the utility keeps it as a text file that SimpleText can open.

Screen Shots

They shoot screens, don't they? The Mac has a built-in way of taking *screen shots,* or *screen dumps*—a file that contains a picture of how your screen, or part of it, looks.

Press ⌘ Shift 3 and you'll hear a little click (it's supposed to be a camera shutter); a few seconds later, you'll find a file named *Picture 1* on the main level of your drive (subsequent shots have higher numbers). If you double-click on it, it will open in SimpleText, but you can open it in almost any graphics program.

Partial screen shots. There are two ways to take pictures of only part of the screen. If you want to select a rectangular section of the screen, press ⌘ Shift 4; you'll get a crosshairs cursor with which you can make the selection. But if you want a shot of a single window, it's easier to press Caps Lock and then ⌘ Shift 4. You'll get a bulls-eye cursor; click in a window with it, and that's the window whose picture will be saved to the disk.

Straight to the Clipboard. For any of the screenshot options—full screen, partial screen, or window—you can have the image placed directly on the Clipboard instead of in a disk file: add Control to the key combination you're using for the shot.

Keyboard roundup. Okay, now that you know there are all these screenshot variations, here's a roundup:

Press	***to capture***
⌘ Shift 3	full screen
⌘ Shift 4	a selected area
⌘ Shift Caps Lock 4	targeted window

Add Control to any combination to put the picture on the Clipboard

Screen shot problem on 7200's. On Mac 7200 models, the mouse pointer doesn't always appear in captured graphics. You'll find a special control panel, Pointer Mode, in the CD Extras folder on your system CD that takes care of this problem. Install the control panel (all you have to do is drag it from the CD), restart the Mac, open the control panel, and check the Standard Mode option. (If you find your mouse cursor flashes a lot when it's over graphics, you'll want to turn off this standard mode unless you're taking a screen shot.)

IN THE BEGINNING

The built-in screenshot capability was in the Mac since the very beginning, although you couldn't do anything besides the entire screen. (On the other hand, you had an option to dump it directly to the printer instead of to a disk file.) There wasn't any sound, either, except for the drone of the floppy drive as the file was written to it.

But the naming convention was different: the first was named *Screen 0* (because computers really start counting at zero, not one), the next *Screen 1*, and so on, through *Screen 9*. You couldn't take an eleventh picture because those were the only names available; but you usually couldn't take even ten pictures, because even though the black-and-white files didn't take a lot of room, the floppy disk had a system folder and an application on it—and maybe a few documents, too.

A better shot. If you need something more in regard to screenshots, there are commercial and shareware utilities available. Additional features include things like being able to: save the captured image to a disk file, the Clipboard, or even into the Scrapbook; grab pictures of opened menus; and include the cursor or not.

casadyg.com
beale.com
shareware.com

Casady & Greene's **Captivate** package ($80) has a good capture module, and the advantage of the terrific Captivate Store scrapbook-like utility described earlier in the chapter. **Exposure Pro** ($120, Beale Street Group) offers an incredible array of save options (in TIFF, GIF, JPEG, or PICT, for instance) and built-in editing tools, but you'd have to practically be in the business of taking screen shots for it to be worth the price. Beale also offers **ScreenShot** ($50), which is elegant and reasonably powerful, but a little pricey compared to the shareware offerings **Snapz Pro** ($20) and the terrific **FlashIt** ($15).

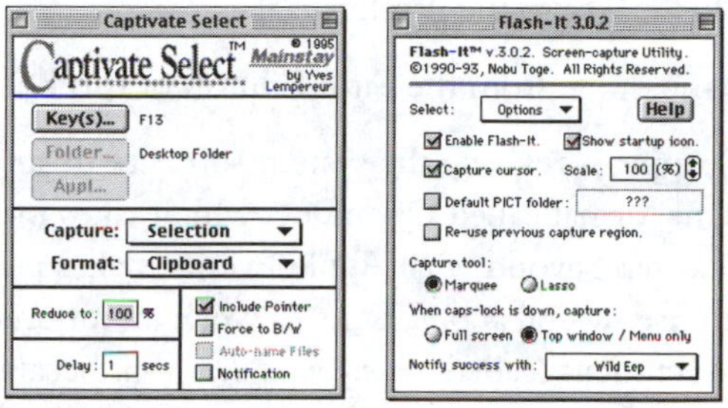

Control panels for Captivate and FlashIt.

Also...

Apple events. Apple Events are part of an underlying technology through which applications can communicate, and even control one another; an "event" is a command sent from one application to another. For this to work, an application has to be "aware" of events—it has to be designed to take advantage of Apple Events. Apple Events can work on one Mac, or between Macs on a network or over a modem line. AppleScript uses Apple events to control the Finder and other "pliable" programs. —SZA/JK/CR

WorldScript. The Mac has been able to write in different languages and alphabets for quite some time. But with WorldScript, the Mac provides programmers with a standardized approach to different alphabets and supports "double-byte" languages like Japanese and Chinese.

Although WorldScript is built into system software from version 7.1 on, to actually type something in a foreign alphabet you'll need one of Apple's Language Kits (about $250) and a program that supports WorldScript, like Nisus Writer. —EC

Publish and Subscribe. Publish and Subscribe, introduced in System 7, works like an automatic cut-and-paste feature, allowing you to link data so that changing it in one place also changes it anyplace else you've put it. The data is "published" from one document, creating a separate file, the "edition."

Another document "subscribes" to the edition and can be set to automatically update if the edition changes.

It's a great idea that didn't catch on, never getting the support from both users and software companies that it would need to become an important part of Mac computing. —SZA/CR/JK

QuickDraw. QuickDraw is the set of graphics routines built into the Mac's ROMs that control how things are drawn on the screen. "Drawn" doesn't mean just pictures, though—characters in fonts are "drawn" on the screen, too. This leads to the misnomer "QuickDraw printer" for a non-PostScript printer, since the Mac's QuickDraw routines do all the formation of letters and then send the images to the printer.

OpenDoc. Let me quote from the Fifth Edition of this book:

"At this writing, Apple is revising the system software to support a revolutionary new document format called OpenDoc, which takes interapplication communication a step beyond what Apple Events makes possible. OpenDoc will allow you to use several applications to work on different types of data within a single document (called a *compound document* because of the multiple formats it contains). Parts of a document that would normally be separate documents from different applications could be part of a single file, eliminating the need to cut and paste between applications or re-importing into a central document every time it needs editing."

Let me quote from the Sixth Edition of this book:

"It's interesting, or frustrating, to note that as I write this for the Sixth Edition, John's 'as I write this' from the Fifth Edition doesn't get changed. We're still waiting for OpenDoc; it's closer, but not here 'as I write this.'"

And here's the Seventh Edition comment: OpenDoc has officially been moved to the category of "unsupported" *as of this writing.* —SZA/JK

For the Power User

AppleScript Basics

About AppleScript. AppleScript isn't just a built-in macro capability; as with most things, its power and flexibility come with an ease-of-use tradeoff. AppleScript is an entire programming language and, except for a few instances (some of which I provide in the Projects section below), isn't practical for most users. The information in this section will help you decide if you should pursue it further, and the next two sections will give you tips on using the Script Editor and a few sample scripts to try.

The Script Editor is the crux of AppleScript, even for scripts that are simply recorded from the Finder. It shows the steps of the script and provides a way to alter them and then save the script so you can run it later. Unlike standard macro utilities, AppleScript provides no way to call up one of its scripts with a simple keystroke—probably one of the reasons the masses didn't take to it.

Macro utilities
Later this chapter

Scriptable versus recordable. Some applications are "AppleScript aware": they understand and respond to AppleScript commands so you can automate their use; these applications are *scriptable*. Some applications take this to another level: they're *recordable*—you can run the Script Editor and record actions taken in the other application, and the actions are turned into editable scripts. An application can be scriptable without being recordable (but it won't be recordable if it isn't scriptable!)

How can you tell which applications can be scripted? Well, most scriptable applications are proud of it, so its ads or documentation will point that out. But you can check it yourself with the Script Editor.

Use the Script Editor's Open Dictionary command to "open" an application. If the application isn't scriptable, you'll get a dialog telling you so. If it is scriptable, its *dictionary* will open—the list of AppleScript commands that it understands. To see if the application is recordable (which very few are), just try recording a simple step and see if anything shows up in the script window.

Script types. There are three ways to save a script from the Script Editor, and each gets a different desktop icon:

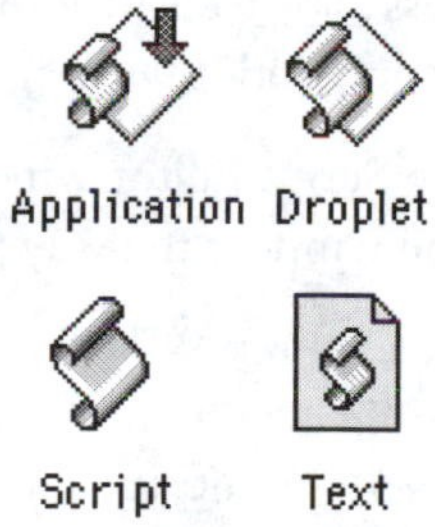

- **Application:** There are two types of AppleScript applications, each with its own icon. The first is a standard, double-clickable application. The second is a "droplet," an application that works when you drop icons onto it. (Unlike any old application that will open a document dropped onto it, a droplet is designed to *do* something to the items you drop onto it, not actually *open* them.)
- **Compiled Script:** This is a basic Script Editor document, which opens into Script Editor.
- **Text:** This is a text-only file that can be opened by any application that handles text files, but it gets a special icon, and if you double-click on it, it will open in Script Editor.

Where you put the scripts. If you put a scripted application in the Apple Menu Items folder, or in a subfolder that's in the Apple menu, you can run the script by simply selecting it from the menu. (In fact, when you install your system, it puts an alias to the Automated Tasks folder in the Apple menu; this is a folder that contains some basic AppleScripts that work on Finder items.)

Some scripts belong in the Startup Items folder or the Shutdown Items folder so that they'll run every time you start up or shut down the Mac. Droplets are left stored out on the desktop, for easy access.

Scripting Tips

Setting styles. When the syntax of a script is checked (whether because you've checked the Syntax button or because you've run or saved the script), formatting is automatically applied to the script to make it easy to read and follow. If you don't like the default styles, you can change them through the AppleScript Formatting command.

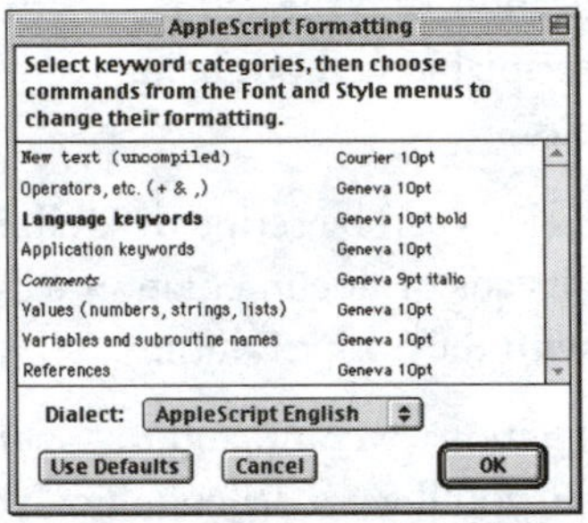

But if you want to highlight part of your script in a special way, you can use the commands in the Font and Style menus to override the default formatting.

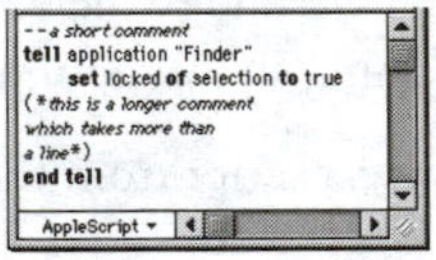

Constant comment. There are two ways to add comments (reminders or descriptions that aren't part of the script) to a script. For short comments, begin the line with two hyphens. For longer ones, where you'll want to press Return for multiple lines, begin the comment with (* and end it with *).

To be continued... Lines of code in the Script Editor window are infinitely long: they don't wrap to stay visible in the window the way word-processed text does.

To break a single line of code into shorter lines without interrupting the code itself and confusing the Script Editor, type the ¬ (Option L) character where you want the line to break, and then press Return. Or, to both enter the character and move down to the next line, use one of the Editor's friendliest little shortcuts: press Option Return.

Making a splash. When you save a script as an application, you have a choice as to whether or not running the script triggers a splash screen before the script itself is executed. (A splash screen is the first thing you see when you run an application—the "Welcome To" notice.) For scripts you're making for your own use, you won't want to be bothered with a splash screen, so make sure you turn it off: check the Never Show Startup Screen button in the Save dialog when you're saving the script.

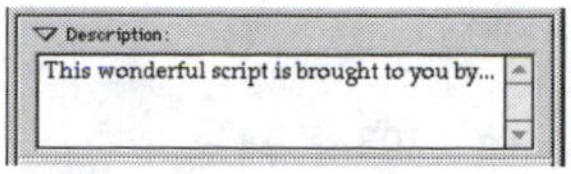

Customize a splash-screen message by putting it in the Description box.

But you might want a splash screen for scripts you give to others. To customize the message in the screen, type it into the Description box at the top of the Script Editor window.

AppleScript Projects

How to enter and save a project. To create any of the projects in this section, launch the Script Editor (it should be inside the AppleScript folder in the Apple Extras folder) and type the script lines. When you type them in the window, don't worry about the line indents or bold text that you see in these listings; the Script Editor applies those formats itself. You type everything in and then click the Syntax button, and the Editor checks everything you've typed—it's a great way to spot typos! (Pressing Enter "clicks" the Syntax button, too.)

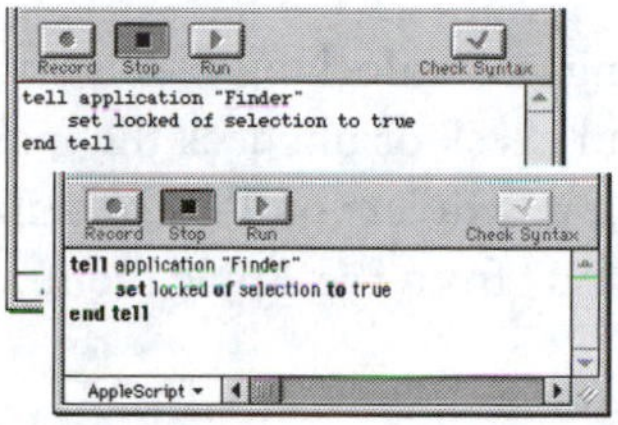

Before and after clicking the Syntax button.

Each of the brief projects described in this section has to be saved as an application. After you type in the script for a project, here's how to save it:

1. Use the Save command from the File menu.
2. Choose Application from the pop-up menu in the Save dialog.
3. Uncheck the Stay Open box.
4. Check the Never Show Startup Screen box.

Most of the projects here should be stored in the Apple menu or one of its submenus; when you select it from the (sub)menu, the script runs—it feels just like selecting a menu command.

Rearrange desktop at startup. I have four volumes that are always on my desktop, and no matter where I put them, they line up along the right edge of the screen on every restart. I don't *want* them there, but there's not much choice. At least, not without a script.

You can organize multiple volumes, too, just by recording the action of dragging them to their new positions. Here's how to record this particular script:

1. Arrange the desktop so you can see the volume icons and clear the space where you want to put them.
2. Run the Script Editor (make sure its window isn't in the way of what you want to do with your icons) and click the Record button.
3. Drag the icons to their new positions.
4. Click the Stop button in the Script Editor window.

That's all there is to it. Your script will look something like this:

```
tell application "Finder"
   activate
   select disk "OS 8"
   set position of selection to {1037, 11}
   select disk "OS 8.1"
   set position of selection to {1039, 46}
   select disk "Warehouse"
   set position of selection to {989, 22}
end tell
```

Save the script as an application, and put it in the Startup Items folder inside the System Folder so it runs at every startup.

Lock and unlock files. Locking and unlocking files is such a pain: you have to do a Get Info for each one and check or uncheck the locked box. A very simple AppleScript, and a variation, will let you lock or unlock single or multiple files with a simple "command" from the Apple menu.

Here's the script that locks files:

```
tell application "Finder"
   set locked of selection to true
end tell
```

And you could probably guess that this is how you unlock files:

```
tell application "Finder"
   set locked of selection to false
end tell
```

Save these as separate applications and put them in the Apple menu (or, better, in a folder in the Apple menu so they're in a submenu). Select an item, or multiple items, in a desktop window and then choose the "command" from the Apple menu. That's it.

Setting window views. Turning columns in a list view on and off is another annoying desktop procedure: you have to go through the View Options dialog and check and uncheck the items you want included. If you use only one or two standard views for most windows, you can automate the column display.

Here's a script for displaying only the first two columns—Name and Date Modified. It turns on the Date Modified and turns off all the others (the Name column is always on, so there's no command for it). The first command changes the window to a list view (in this case, the "name" view, which sorts it by name) because the columns can't be turned on and off when you're in an icon view. "Window 1" refers to the frontmost Finder window.

```
tell application "Finder"
   set view of window 1 to name
   set show modification date of window 1 to true
   set show size of window 1 to false
   set show kind of window 1 to false
   set show label of window 1 to false
   set show creation date of window 1 to false
   set show comments of window 1 to false
   set show version of window 1 to false
end tell
```

You could probably guess your way to making other column-display views, and I'm going to let you: just change the columns you want displayed to "true" and the ones you want hidden to "false" in the script. Save the scripts (I use three, named *TwoColumn, AllColumns,* and *MyColumns)* as applications and store them in your Apple menu.

Editable ReadMe's. As mentioned earlier in the chapter, most ReadMe files are saved in a special format so that you can't edit them. There are several ways around this problem, and here's another one: a script that changes the file's type so that it's editable. This is all it takes:

```
tell application "Finder"
   set file type of selection to "TEXT"
end tell
```

Save the script as an application and put it in your Apple menu. Select the ReadMe file or files, and choose the "command" from the menu.

If you'd rather have a droplet that you can drop ReadMe files onto, use this script; it lets you drop a single, or multiple ReadMe's onto the script icon:

```
on open (itemList)
   repeat with eachOne in itemList
         tell application "Finder"
               set file type of eachOne to "TEXT"
         end tell
   end repeat
end open
```

Using ResEdit

The resource editor. One of the nicest things about Macintosh software, and something that sets it apart from most PC software, is that the code that makes a program run is separate from the interface that's presented to the user—the dialog boxes, alerts, menus, icons, pictures, sounds, and so on, collectively known as *resources*. That means you don't have to be a programmer to futz around with the interface; all you need is a *resource editor*.

Apple's ResEdit program is a freeware utility that lets you get at resources. Used incorrectly, it can render your program (or your system, if you're working on the System file or Finder) inoperable. Make sure you *always* work on a copy, and in the case of system resources, make sure you have a disk you can boot up your Mac with, in case you damage the installed System.

You can change (or just copy) resources from practically any application, desk accessory, extension, control panel, or other nondocument file. A few programs, most notably those from Microsoft, cannot be looked at or tinkered with. (Spoilsports!)

What does all this mean? It means you can personalize your programs and the System and Finder by changing the wording of menu commands, adding keyboard shortcuts, and editing text and icons in dialogs and alerts. You can also transfer pictures and sounds from one program to another.

> ***"Apple is considering voiding the warranty for consumers who use ResEdit. Some factions at Apple wants to forbid sales entirely to anyone who's even heard of ResEdit. "Ever heard of a program called ResEdit? You have? Sorry, we can't sell you a Macintosh. How about an Amiga?"***
>
> *Doug Clapp, MacUser, 1986*

The next entry gives you a super-quick introduction to ResEdit itself, and the other entries in this section give you an idea of the kinds of things you can do with it. —SZA/EC

Three steps to happy ResEditing. If you follow these three steps (along with general Mac hygiene, like regular saves and backups) you should be able to modify your resources without fear.

1. **Always, but *always*, work on a copy.** That has already been said, but it bears repeating: Never work on the original or sole copy of a program or the System. Instead, make a copy of the program and alter *that*. It's easy to damage a file so that it will never run again, and unless you have a clean copy, you'll have lost it forever.
2. **Be careful what you touch.** There are many different kinds of resources; some are more difficult to alter than others, and some are downright dangerous to mess around with. Generally speaking, you should limit yourself to these resources:
   - **DITL**: dialog box contents, with corresponding DLOG or ALRT resource that stores the window size and title.
   - **MENU** and **CMNU**: menu resources
   - **STR#:** string resources attached to menus and dialogs
   - **PICT:** pictures used in the program
   - **CURS:** cursors in programs and the system

- **ICON, ics4, ic18** (and other resources beginning with IC): icon families
- **snd:** sound resources can't be altered easily but you can copy and paste them from one place to another

3. **Don't create, just modify.** Don't erase anything and don't create anything: only modify what's already there. Generally, you should stick to cosmetic changes—modifying a button's text, size, color, and shape is fine, but changing it from a button to a checkbox will probably cause the program to hang. —SZA/EC

Jumping around. Since ⌘O is used to open files, ResEdit lets you use Return and Enter to open practically everything else. Try it while you have a resource item selected in a list, or while you have a button selected in a dialog box, just to name a few spots. You can use ⌘W to close, and the ↑↓ keys to move up and down the lists. You can also type in a resource item number (or a name if it has one) to jump to that item. —EC

Hidden objects. Sometimes you'll find that various objects are piled up one on top of another in a window that holds DITL resources. Each item has a resource number that you can see by holding down Option, or by turning on the numbers with the DITL menu's Show Item Numbers command. To select an object that's underneath another, use the Select Item Number command in the DITL menu, enter the appropriate number, and press Enter. —SZA/EC

Close all windows. Changing a resource always means burrowing down through a series of windows. But you don't have to close them all one at a time. If you Option-click in a close box, all the "parent" windows for that window close along with it, not including the main window for the file you're editing. This is handy because you may be editing more than one type of resource, and the other windows will stay open.

When you want to close the entire file, you can just click in the close box of its main window, and all its windows will close, too.

Just say NO. Here's another really, really, *really* important reason to always work on a copy of the file you're editing: ResEdit makes changes to the file as you go along, despite the misleading "Save changes?" dialog when you close a window. If you say no, it deletes the changes and restores the file to its original state. So, if you crash while editing the file, there will be changes made to it without your okay—and they might be changes that make the file unusable.

ResEdit Projects

Adding a keyboard command to a menu. It's easy to add keyboard equivalents to menu commands for any application that stores its menus in the standard way (forget Microsoft products!). The following example adds the standard ⌘B to the Clear command in the Stickies desk accessory's Edit menu.

1. Open Stickies in ResEdit and double-click on the MENU resource icon.
2. Double-click on the picture of the Edit menu to open the editing window.
3. Click on the Clear command in the sample menu at the left of the window.
4. Type a B in the box labeled Cmd-Key. You'll see the keyboard equivalent immediately added to the picture of the menu. (The menu you're editing also appears in ResEdit's menu bar so you can pull it down and see what it looks like.)
5. Close all windows and click Yes when you're asked if you want the changes saved.

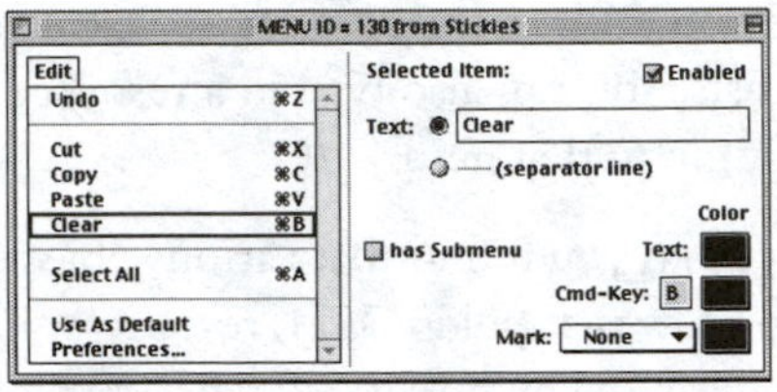

Type the letter B in the Cmd-Key box in the lower right to add the keyboard equivalent to the Stickies Edit menu.

Notice there are commands in this window to set the color of the command in a menu. And there's a Style menu in ResEdit's menu bar when you're working on menu items, so you can apply Italic or Bold or Underline to a menu command if you want to.

Grabbing a sound. You can move sounds from one application to another, or from an application into the Sound control panel so you can use it for your system beep. This example gets the xylophone sound that's used in the Jigsaw Puzzle desk accessory when you complete the puzzle, and puts it into the Sound control panel.

1. Open the Jigsaw Puzzle in ResEdit, and double-click on the *snd* resource.
2. Select the "CongratsSnd" line from the list of sounds in the window that opens.
3. Use Copy from the Edit menu.
4. Open the Sound control panel and select Alert Sounds from the pop-up menu.
5. Choose Paste from the Edit menu, and name the sound in the dialog that appears.

That's all—don't forget to close the Jigsaw Puzzle file in ResEdit.

Changing the sample font sentence. When you double-click a font file, you get a sample of the font; the sample changes from one system to the next, but usually includes all the letters of the alphabet and only a single capital letter. You can change the sample sentence by using ResEdit on the Finder itself; you might find it convenient to capitalize each of the words in the sentence so that your font samples display some uppercase letters.

Working on a *copy* of the Finder (which, once everything's okay, you can use as your *real* Finder):

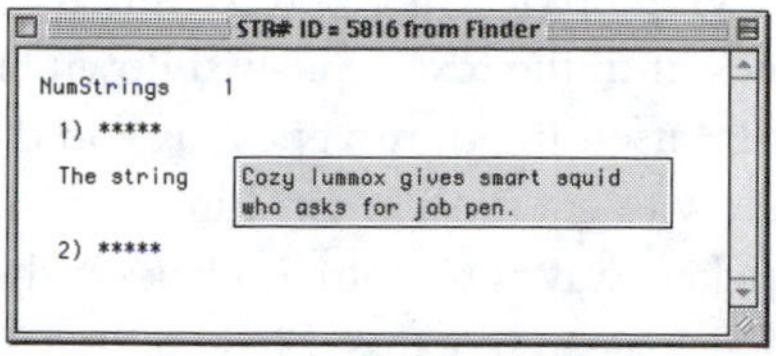

Accessing the Finder's font-sample sentence.

1. Double-click on the STR# resource.
2. Double-click on 5816.
3. Change the sample sentence to whatever you want.
4. Save the changes.

Add a graphic to a SimpleText document. Note that the name of this system application is *not* SimpleGraphic; if you want to embed a graphic (or multiple graphics) in a SimpleText document, you have to use ResEdit to do it. Here's how:

First, create and save the graphic(s) you want to use in the document. Make sure they're readily available for copying to the Clipboard, since they have to be pasted into ResEdit for this to work. (Sticking them in the Scrapbook is a good idea.) Then:

1. Create the basic SimpleText document in SimpleText.
2. Wherever you want to insert a graphic, type Option Spacebar. (Type it on a separate line, because you can't do any fancy layout here.)
3. Save the document.
4. Launch ResEdit and open the SimpleText document in it. (You can just drag the document onto the ResEdit icon.)
5. Get your first graphic on the Clipboard, and paste it right into the main window in ResEdit. If it's in an icon view, you'll see a new icon, labeled PICT, appear; if it's in a list view, you'll see PICT added to the list of the resources.
6. Continue pasting any other pictures directly into the main window. If you're using an icon view, you won't see any changes, since they'll be added to the new PICT resource category. If you're using a list view, you'll see the number of PICT resources change with each paste.
7. Double-click on the PICT resource to see thumbnails of the pictures. Select each picture in turn and press ⌘I for the Get Resource Info command.
8. For each picture, change the resource ID number. For the picture you want in the first Option Spacebar spot in your document, use ID 1000. For the next, use 1001, and so on.

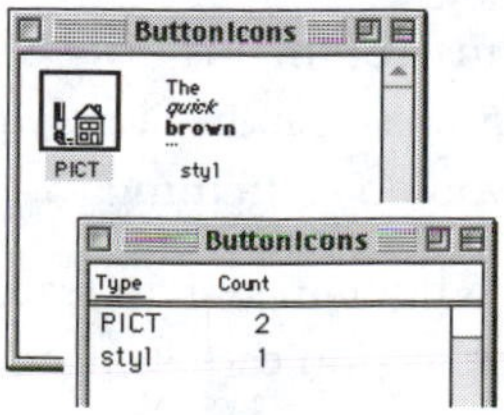

The PICT resources added to the icon-view window (top) and the list-view window (bottom).

Save all the changes you've made either with the Save command or as you close the file's windows.

But your work's not over, because SimpleText is really simple-minded, and you still have to get the text and pictures to work together. Open the document in

SimpleText, and you'll see the pictures floating over the text that's supposed to follow them. Click the text cursor at the beginning of the paragraph that's supposed to come *after* the graphic (it will be pretty much *under* the graphic), and press Return a few times until the text is pushed down far enough to get past the picture. The picture itself might disappear as you do this, and you'll have to "refresh" the window to get it back: scrolling or resizing the window usually works, but the quickest way is to double-click on the title bar to collapse it, and then double-click again to expand it.

When you have the text and graphics positioned properly, save the document again. If you'd like to make the document read-only, you can do it with DiskTools or Drop•Info, as described in the SimpleText section earlier in the chapter, or use ResEdit: open the document in ResEdit, select *Get Info for [document]* from the File menu, and change the file's type from *TEXT* to *ttro*.

Macro Editors

The tips in this section apply to all macro editors. While the rest of the macro tips in this chapter are for QuicKeys, you can go through them for ideas to use with your macro editor.

About Macros

What's a macro? A *macro* is a series of commands or actions that's invoked with a single key combination, menu selection, or button click. On a simple level, you can use a *macro editor* to assign a keyboard equivalent to a menu command that doesn't have one, or combine two menu commands into a single one—putting Save and Quit onto ⌘ Option Q, for instance.

But that doesn't even scratch the surface of a macro program's power. As I wrote this chapter, for instance, I put the figures and their captions in the Word document as footnotes. When I was finished, I used a macro that went to each footnote reference mark, cut out the related picture, put it into a Photoshop document, and saved it as a PICT file, asking me to name the document; next, it came back to Word, cut the caption out of the footnote, and put it into the body of the chapter, formatting it as needed for layout—applying the right style, typing "CAPTION:" in front of it, and marking it with the figure number.

I hope that description intrigues you, rather than frightening you away. Because although you can wind up doing some complicated programming-like list of commands for an intricate macro, the majority of macros—even those that play back a long series of actions—can be simply recorded by telling the macro editor to watch you while you do something.

While creating and using macros isn't a built-in system feature, it's such a system-*level* function, and the AppleScript section earlier in this chapter talks about automating things, that the whole issue fits better in this chapter than in any other in the book.

Macro editors. QuicKeys may pretty much own the Mac macro market, but that doesn't mean it's your only choice for automation.

cesoft.com
westcodesoft.com
binarysoft.com

- **QuicKeys** ($100, CE Software) is the standard in Mac macros. It's both the easiest to use on its surface level and the one you'll be able to build more complex macros in without worrying about some scripting language. (Although be warned: to make the most of its power, you'll have to spend some time learning its quirks and its more powerful features.) Even after all these years of reviewer (and, I would suppose, user) complaints, QuicKeys still sports a clunky interface that makes some of the simpler things look harder than they are: shortcuts are divided into categories (button clicks, file launching, "mousies," and more), each with its own icon and dialog boxes, and there are way too many subsubmenus. But it's still your best bet for simple and complicated macros to be called up by keystrokes, stored in a menu, or put into a palette.
- **OneClick** ($75, WestCode Software), as its name implies, focuses on palettes of buttons that contain scripts. The scripting language is powerful, but you'll need time to learn it, and the overall interface is a little clunky, requiring lots of steps through several dialog boxes for even relatively simple setups. And if you want a macro triggered by a keystroke, you still have to create a button for it first.
- At only half the price of the other macro utilities, **KeyQuencer** ($45, Binary Software) seems like a bargain, and it is, with its speed, low memory overhead, and easy-to-learn scripting language. But you're going to have to learn the scripting, because it has no recording capability, which is what makes most macro editors easy to use for beginners and for any-level user who just wants to cobble together a quick shortcut.

Two different numbers. When you're typing, the numbers at the top of the keyboard and the ones on the numeric keypad are the same—it doesn't matter which you use to enter the numbers.

But when you're assigning macros to keyboard combinations, the numbers *are* different—which is great, because with ⌘1 being different from ⌘ [keypad] 1, you have more key combinations available. (The symbols on the keypad are different from their main-keyboard counterparts, too.)

Don't forget that you can use the ↑←→↓ keys and also the navigation keys (Home, End, and so on).

Modifier key clusters. The way to stretch out the number of keyboard assignments you can make—aside from using the numeric keypad, as just described—is to use different combinations of the modifier keys ⌘, Option, Shift, and Control. Since they're grouped in the corners of the keyboard, it's really simple to hold down two, three, or four of them at the same time. In fact, there are so many possible combinations that you'll have trouble remembering what's assigned where. Which brings me to…

Plan ahead. If you, like most people, start out by creating a few macros that you know you want to use right away, and then later add a few more, and then lots later do even more, your keyboard commands are likely to bear little relationship to the macros they trigger, and none to each other.

Your keyboard commands will be easier to remember if you plan ahead and use some logic in their assignments, grouping like commands by using the same modifier keys for them. When I'm working in Word (with its own macro capability), for instance, I use Control Shift for procedures in outliner mode, so adding a number expands the outline to that level, and using the plus or minus sign expands or collapses the current level; Control Option plus a letter triggers a style; ⌘ Control plus numbers or arrow keys manipulates window position and size, and so on.

If you haven't started out like this, bite the bullet and go back and reassign better keys—you'll learn the new combinations in no time.

Labels R Us. Even if you plan ahead and use some logic to help you remember keyboard assignments, once you're past a couple dozen, it gets pretty impossible to keep track of the macros that you use less often than others.

There's one piece of hardware that I use to boost my Mac productivity that isn't even vaguely computer hardware: my Brother P-Touch labeler. I have about 60 macros, at least half of which are used many times every day. But there are only so many logical keyboard commands available, and although I find it easy to remember modifier key combinations, it's not always so easy to remember, say, which keypad number is assigned to which folder-opening macro. I just stick tiny labels on the keys; in fact, some keys have two labels on them. In different colors.

You can use regular labels cut down to size—Avery makes a vast collection in many colors. You can even, as I used to, pencil a few letters on the keyboard itself, just above and below the function keys if you're using them for launching programs. (I don't do it anymore because my ergonomic keyboard is curved in such a way I that can't see the keyboard edge beyond the function keys.)

Hot key hierarchy. A macro editor lets you create application-specific macros as well as "universal" shortcuts that work no matter where you are. When you're working with keyboard commands (as opposed to button palettes), you might find that you've assigned the same keyboard sequence to a universal command as to an application command—and it might already be used by the application you're in. Which one "wins"?

Most macro utilities use the same hierarchy. First, the macro always takes priority over the built-in application keyboard command. If you have both an application-specific and a universal keyboard command, the application-specific one takes precedence.

Multi-application macros. When you create or record a macro that involves more than one application, make sure you store it as the right kind of macro. If you're not careful, you'll wind up storing the macro by default with the application where you end it—which means you're not going to be able to trigger the macro where you need it. If the macro will always begin in a specific application, store it with the macros for that application rather than as a Universal macro.

Short-lived but sweet. Don't think of a macro as something you should create for a procedure that you do all the time, every day. If you have to repeat a procedure in a specific document just for the week you're working in it, or even for the three hours one afternoon that it needs polishing, it's still worth creating a temporary macro to save yourself some time. I always have about a half dozen short-lived macros in my list; I always include *temp* in their names so I know I can wipe them out and reuse the keyboard assignment for the next temporary macro.

QuicKeys: General Tips

Allocate more memory. If you're going to use QuicKeys for anything more than a few launch macros, you should allocate more memory to it. But you can't do that the way you usually allocate memory to a program. Instead, open the QuicKeys control panel and click the Configure button, then click one of the radio buttons for the Buffer size. You can also configure the QuicKeys buffer from within the QuicKeys editor, using the Configure command in the Options menu.

Use the direct approach. Whenever possible, build a macro from within the QuicKeys editor rather than recording it. When you record a macro, it becomes a "sequence" and is listed as such in the editor window. But very often that sequence consists of only a single step that is likely to be an option that can be created directly. For instance, you may have recorded the clicking of an OK button that could have just been a Button shortcut. If you work within the QuicKeys editor and use the shortcuts for single item, you'll be able to later sort the items by type, and also use them to build other macros.

Edit out unneeded steps. When you record a QuicKeys macro rather than build it "manually" in the Sequence editor, you'll get a lot of unneeded steps—usually Wait commands, either for fractions of a section or until a window opens. Always go back and edit your recorded sequences, getting rid of unneeded steps and delays.

Back up your quick keys. Your collection of QuicKeys shortcuts is one of those things that's easy to forget to back up if you, like most people, back up piecemeal rather than copying your entire hard drive someplace. Regularly copy the entire QuicKeys folder to a safe spot; don't copy just the Keysets folder, because that risks breaking the link between them and the Sequences.

Preferred extensions. There's a list of "loose" extensions in the Extensions submenu, above the submenus that list both repeats of the loose ones and others. If you don't use all those separately listed items, you can shorten the list by using the QuicKeys Extensions Manager, which you can open through QuicKeys' File menu; you can also add any item that you use often so you won't have to go through submenus. Use the Preferred checkbox for the items you want in the list, and uncheck the ones you want removed.

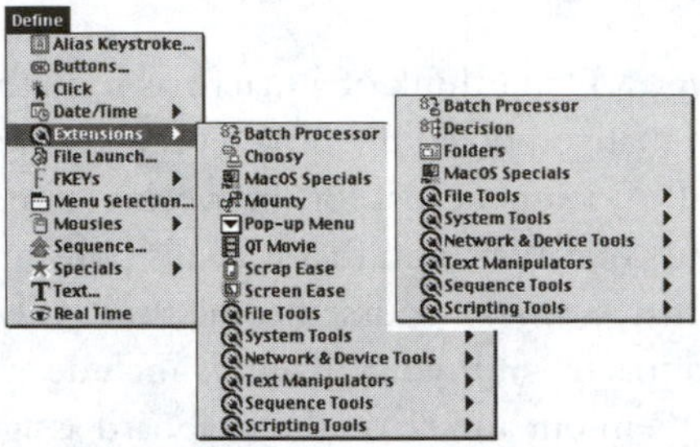

The original extensions list, and the altered one.

Reassigning a keystroke. When you want to rename or edit a macro, you can select it in the Editor's list and use ⌘M for Modify, or you can just double-click on it in the list. But if you want to change just the keystrokes that calls up the macro, you don't have to use the Modify command at all: just click on the keystroke in the list, and press the new key combination.

Moving to the Universal set. If you mistakenly save a macro as an application-specific shortcut but meant to make it universal, it's easy to move it: select it in the application's shortcut list, use ⌘X to cut it, click the Universal tab, and use ⌘V to paste it into the list.

QuicKeys: Universal Macros

Controlling control panels. If you work with certain control panels on a regular basis, you can record macros that take them out, adjust settings, and put them away again. (Note that QuicKeys has several built-in controls for monitor settings, printer selection, network volume mounting, and sound.)

For instance, I use two macros that control the PPP control panel: one to open the connection, and another to close it. Although most communication and internet software can automatically open the connection when you launch the program and close it when you quit, I found that didn't work for me: I often leave the program open for later use but need the connection closed, or I launch a second telecom program when the connection's already open.

Keyboard button presses. Record macros that let you "click" buttons in dialog boxes so you don't always have to reach for the mouse; these are especially convenient when it's a simple dialog that just presents a few buttons and no other controls. Make sure you save them as universal macros so that they'll work no matter what application you're in. Here's a list of suggestions which avoid the problem of assigning something like ⌘C for Configure when that combination is often built in for the Cancel button; in fact, even Control-C isn't a good idea for Configure because of the potential confusion. And, don't forget: Return and Enter always work for the highlighted button in a dialog, and ⌘. and Esc trigger the Cancel button.

Control-Y	Yes	Control-T	Options
Control-N	No	Control-K	Configure
Control-S	Save	Control-R	Revert
Control-D	Don't Save	Control-H	Help

Window swapping. One of QuicKeys' Special shortcuts is called Select Second Window. You might ignore it until you realize what it will really do: it will let you move back and forth between two document windows. How? Well, when you trigger the "second window" to come forward, the one behind the current one comes to the top, and the current window becomes the second window—which will come forward when you use the macro, and so on. So, you wind up toggling between two windows no matter how many are open. (I use Control-→ for this.) There's also a Select Back Window shortcut in case you want to manipulate all your windows, but it doesn't work reliably in all applications. (I use Control-← for this one.)

Jumping to folders. The File Tools extension lets you assign keystrokes to specific folders. If you trigger the macro while you're in an Open/Save dialog, the dialog jumps to the folder. The folder-opening macro has an option that makes it open the target folder if you're on the desktop, too—so take a look at the procedure described in *Macros on the Desktop,* later in this section.

The PrintMonitor macro. As explained in the Printing chapter, the desktop printer icon that lets you access the PrintMonitor is in many ways a special folder. And, since it's a folder, you can create a macro that opens it—so you'll have instant access to the Print Monitor no matter where you are.

One way to set up this macro works if you've set up access to the Monitor through your Apple menu by putting an alias of the printer icon in the Apple Menu Items folder, as discussed in the Printer chapter: you simply create a macro that selects the printer from the menu. You can also open it by recording a move to the Finder, activating the desktop, selecting the printer icon by typing its name, and then opening it. But here's the best way to create what's only a two-step sequence, with the fastest playback:

1. Create a sequence macro.
2. The first step has to move you to the Finder. If you've already made a move-to-Finder macro, you can use the Import Steps command to put it

in this sequence. Otherwise, use the Process Swap extension (it's in the System Tools group) to create the step.

3. For the second step, use the Folder extension (from the File Tools group) to select and open the desktop printer.

That's all you need. I've assigned Control Shift * to this, to keep it in line with the other folder-opening macros (described in the *Macros for the Desktop* section.)

QuicKeys: Launching and Switching

Launching applications. QuicKeys' File Launch option makes it easy to assign a key to a program or file launch, so all you have to think about is which keys to use. And the launch macro will work not only to launch the program initially, but also to move you to it if it's already open.

Use the function keys (F5, F6, and so on) at the top of the keyboard as single-key launchers for the applications you use most. Avoid the first four keys because they work as single-stroke Undo, Cut, Copy, and Paste commands in most programs. You can even reserve the last three keys (off in a group by themselves) for special functions (mine are assigned to trigger a screen capture, hide all background applications, and move to the Finder) and still have eight keys left for launching applications. And the way I use modifier keys, each key does double duty, providing sixteen launch keys.

I use the eight function keys, with modifiers, to perform different functions related to program launching:

- With no modifier, the key moves me to one of my programs if it's already open. (As described in the next entry, you may want to separate the launch macro from the "switch to" macro.) Since this is what I do more than anything else, that's the unmodified use of the key.
- With Shift, the key launches the program.
- With ⌘, the key triggers something extra (a *command* of some sort) relating to the application that's "wired" to the key: a special document opens in Word, the telecom program logs on for my e-mail, my database of Mac products opens in FileMaker, and so on.
- With Option, an alternate program (the *optional* one) opens from the key, giving me 16 launch keys. I assign related programs to the same key, like Quark XPress and PageMaker, and Netscape and Explorer.

There are more, logical combinations that can be assigned (like launching one of the secondary programs with a template automatically opening), but I haven't found that I need that level of automation with the secondary programs.

I don't use up the function keys on launching small items like desk accessories and the Chooser; instead, I use the cluster Ctrl Option Shift along with a keypad number to launch those.

Switching to an already-open application. If you use the basic launch macro and the application is already open, you'll be transferred into that program. That's pretty convenient, on the surface, but it poses a problem. A QuicKeys launch macro takes you through the Finder to the opened application. If it takes two to five seconds to switch from one program to another, you'll need four to ten seconds when you have to detour through the Finder; and, the more you have on the Clipboard when you do the switch, the longer it takes. It also takes time for opened Finder windows to be drawn on the screen, but the extra time isn't the issue: the Finder windows might interfere with something you set up where you want to see windows from two different programs at the same time (which happens to me *all* the time).

The solution is to ignore the launch macro, and create a separate macro for switching into an open program, using the Process Swap extension. First, you have to open the program for which you want to set up the macro. Then, from the QuicKeys Define menu, use these submenu items: Extensions>System Tools>Process Swap. In the Process Swap dialog, select the application from the pop-up menu.

For the Finder. Since you can't "launch" the Finder, most QuicKeys users set up a switch-to-Finder macro by selecting it from the Applications menu at the right of the menu bar. But the way to do it is to use this Process Swap extension.

Next and previous applications. Sometimes it's just easier to cycle through your open applications, moving back and forth between two or three programs instead of jumping to one with its Swap or Launch key. QuicKeys has built-in Next Application and Previous Application commands for this, in the Process Swap dialog; I put mine on Option Control ← and Option Control →. (Note that *Previous* refers to the order of the programs that you launched, not the last program that you *used.)*

You *can* jump back to the program you used immediately before you jumped to the current one with the Switch Back option in the Process Swap dialog. And, if you run a whole bunch of programs at one time and want to be able to use the keyboard to call up a list and select the one you want to go to, use the Switch To (From List) option: it opens a dialog listing all opened applications, and you can select from the list by typing a few keys. I put the Switch Back and Switch to List options on ⌘ Option Control ← and ⌘ Option Control →.

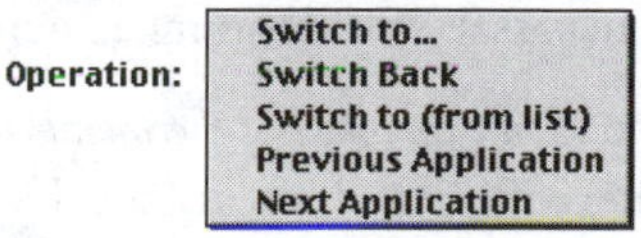

Use all the Process Swap options to really automate moving around in opened applications.

QuicKeys: Macros for the Desktop

Finder menu commands, Part 1. Create a macro for every Finder menu command—including its submenus. The handiest ones are the ones that take care of View menu commands like As List and As Icons, and the Arrange submenu commands like By Name, By Size, and so on. (All the recommended keyboard assignments in this section can be used—along with any recommended combinations in earlier sections—without clashing with each other or any built-in keyboard commands.)

There aren't enough alphabetic commands to go around—especially ones that make sense. But if you use ⌘ for the modifier for File and Edit menu commands—since those are the menus with most of the keyboard equivalents anyway—you can use ⌘ Option for the View menu commands, and add Shift for the commands in its Arrange submenu. That way you can reuse logical alphabetic keys without any clashes. If you're going to assign keys to the Special menu's commands, you can use ⌘ Shift (think: S for Special, S for Shift). But the Sleep, Restart, and Shut Down commands are available from the keyboard anyway, for systems on which pressing the Power key triggers the Shut Down dialog—you can just press the letter of the button you want in that dialog.

The chart on the next page suggests shortcut key combinations (the Finder's built-in commands are in bold), so you don't have to bother figuring out the assignments. (Why should *both* of us have to spend our time doing that?) When the first letter of a command was already used, sometimes its second or last letter is used, or the first letter from its second word. The Show Clipboard command gets the alliterative K alternate for C. There's absolutely nothing logical left for Print Window, so I use a slash—but I only use the command once in blue moon, anyway; there's no good letter key left for Preferences, either, but the equal sign is an easy one to remember for that. And ⌘ Shift W is out for the As Window command because it's the built-in command for Close All Windows.

Finder menu commands, Part 2. When you create macros for Finder menu commands, don't record them—use the Menu Selection option from the Define menu instead. When you record a menu choice, it's recorded as a Sequence QuicKey, instead of the more direct Menu Selection type. More importantly, in order to record the selection, you'll have to actually execute the command, while that's not necessary for defining a Menu Selection.

Finally, make sure you check the *Don't complain if the menu choice can't be found* option in the Menu dialog. Otherwise, if you press, say, the keys to sort by name but you're in an Icon view, you won't get a dialog saying the menu choice isn't available—nothing at all will happen.

Recommended Keyboard Commands for Finder Menus

File		
New Folder	⌘	**N**
Open	⌘	**O**
Print	⌘	**P**
Move To Trash	⌘	<
Close Window	⌘	**W**
Get Info	⌘	**I**
Label		
None	⌘	0 (zero)
Labels/Colors	⌘	1 through 7
Sharing	⌘	H
Duplicate	⌘	**D**
Make Alias	⌘	**M**
Put Away	⌘	**Y**
Find	⌘	**F**
Show Original	⌘	**R**
Page Setup	⌘	U
Print Window	⌘	/

Edit		
Undo	⌘	**Z**
Cut	⌘	**X**
Copy	⌘	**C**
Paste	⌘	**V**
Clear	⌘	B
Select All	⌘	**A**
Show Clipboard	⌘	K
Preferences	⌘	=

View		
as Icons	⌘ Option	I
as Buttons	⌘ Option	B
as List	⌘ Option	L
as Window	⌘ Option	D
as Pop-up Window	⌘ Option	P
Clean Up	⌘ Option	U
Arrange		
Name	⌘ Shift Option	N
Date Modified	⌘ Shift Option	M
Date Created	⌘ Shift Option	C
Size	⌘ Shift Option	S
Kind	⌘ Shift Option	K
Label	⌘ Shift Option	L
View Options	⌘ Option	V

Special		
Empty Trash	⌘ Shift	E
Eject	⌘	**E**
Erase Disk	⌘ Shift	D
Sleep	⌘ Shift	S
Restart	⌘ Shift	R
Shut Down	⌘ Shift	H

*Bold letters are built-in keyboard shortcuts

Making a better Make Alias command. The Finder's Make Alias command already has a keyboard equivalent, but you can improve upon the command itself, which creates the alias using the original icon's name with *alias* appended to it. To create an alias without that pesky suffix, record a macro that includes these steps (making sure you first select an icon that can be aliased):

1. Choose Make Alias from the File menu.
2. Press → to move the insertion point to the end of the alias's name (it's automatically selected when it's created).
3. Press Delete five times to erase the word *alias*.

That's all. By not erasing the space that comes before the word *alias,* the alias has a name that's different from the original's, so they can coexist in the same folder—which is where the alias is created. I use ⌘M to invoke this macro, since it replaces the Finder's Make Alias command (no sense in wasting a key assignment!).

Reverse sort. The little Sort Ascending/Descending button added to OS 8.1 windows can be triggered with a macro if you record it carefully. (The *what* button? Didn't you read Chapter 6 yet?? Immediately above the up scroll arrow in a list-view window is a little button that you can click to sort the window in ascending or descending order according to the current sorted column.) Here's how to do it:

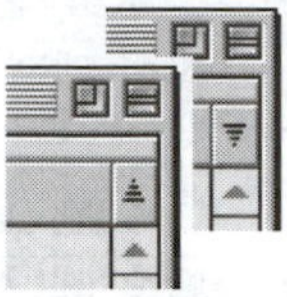

1. Open a Finder window and put it in a list view. (You should be able to do this with a previously recorded macro!)
2. Start recording.
3. Click the Sort button in the window.
4. Stop the recording.
5. In the Sequence window, name the macro and assign it a hot key (I use SortUpDown and Control↓.)
6. Double-click on the single Click step in the Sequence window.
7. In the Click dialog, click the Click button (really!).
8. In the next dialog, click the button in the upper-right corner of the sample window under Click Position.
9. OK your way out of all the dialogs.

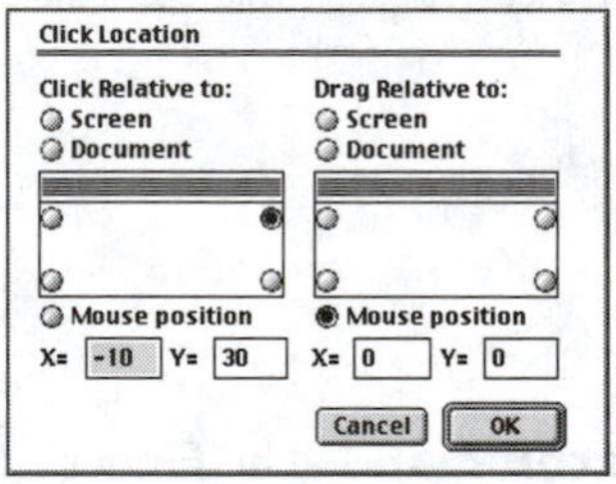

Set the relative click position.

Redefining the click to be relative to the upper-right corner of a Finder window ensures that the Sort button will be clicked no matter how you resize your windows. And, using Control↓ as the hot key coordinates nicely with the window-swapping macros described under *Universal Macros*.

Jumping to folders. The File Tools extension lets you assign keystrokes to specific folders. If you trigger the macro while you're in an Open/Save dialog, the dialog jumps to the folder. But when you're on the desktop, it can also open the folder itself—and being able to open, say, the System Folder or the Extensions folder with a keystroke is even more convenient than it sounds.

Because I use the shareware Default Folder to jump to folders in Open/Save dialogs, I don't use as many Folder shortcuts as I might otherwise. But I do still use them on the desktop to jump to certain folders without having to reach for the mouse. The keystrokes I use so as not to interfere with other desktop macros recommended in this section are listed here. The folders listed here are ones everyone has and might want to access; I actually use another half-dozen folder-opening macros for project folders that I access often. I keep all the folder macros clustered on the keypad, and trigger them with [Control][Shift]; there are sixteen unique keys available, not including [Num Lock] and [Enter].

System Folder	[Control][Shift][1]
Extensions folder	[Control][Shift][2]
Control Panels folder	[Control][Shift][3]
Apple Menu Items folder	[Control][Shift][4]
Fonts folder	[Control][Shift][5]
Desk Accessories	[Control][Shift][6]

Here's how to create the macro in the Editor:

1. Click the Universal or the Finder tab, depending on whether you want the macro to work in Open/Save dialogs or just on the desktop.
2. From the Define menu, select these submenu items: Extensions>File Tools>Folders.
3. In the Folders Extension dialog (shown in the picture here), name the macro, assign the keystroke, and click the Select Folder button.

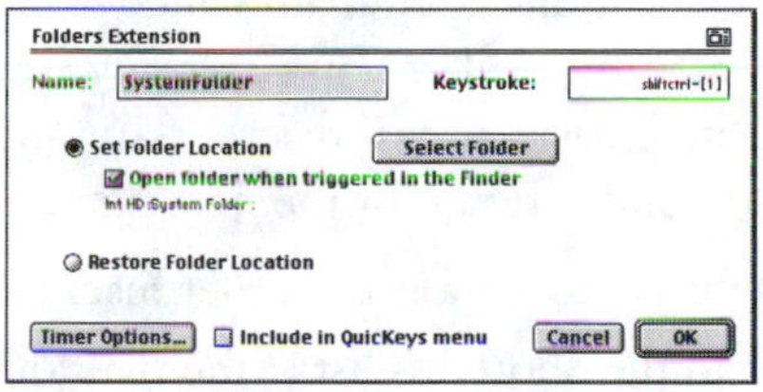

4. Find, *and open,* the target folder in the Open dialog.
5. Click the Select button.
6. Check the *Open folder when triggered in the Finder* button.
7. Click OK.

After you've made the first folder-open macro, it's easier to copy and paste it in the Editor window, and then edit the copies, than it is to create the new ones from scratch. (You can skip a few steps, including selecting from subsubmenus.) You double-click on the copy, change the name and keystroke and select the new folder—which will be near the last folder you selected, so you won't have to travel far in the Open dialog.

Opening volumes. Your internal hard drive, or any mounted volume, for that matter, counts as a "folder" because it has a desktop window, and you can use the Folder extension on it. If you have only a single hard drive, make a macro to open its main window the same way you open folders, as described in the last entry; assign [Control][Shift][0] (zero on the keypad) to keep it in line with the other key assignments.

If you always have several volumes mounted, you can make an "open main window" command for each one of them with the Folder extension, and assign them to Control Shift 1, Control Shift 2, and so on, using the standard number keys rather than the ones on the keypad.

Closing everything but the main window. The Finder has a built-in Close All Windows command, but often you'll want to close all the windows *except* for the main window of the internal hard drive. Create a sequence that closes all the windows, and then uses the "open volume" macro described in the last entry.

Building the sequence is much better than recording it, since recording it leaves extraneous Wait commands that you'll have to edit out.

1. Choose Sequence from the Define menu in the QuicKeys editor.
2. Choose Menu Selection from the Define menu in the Sequence editor.
3. Select the Close Window command from the Finder's File menu.
4. Double-click on the Close Window menu item in the sequence editor so you can edit it.
5. In the Menu dialog, check the Option button under *While selecting from menu, hold down* section; that changes the Finder command from Close Window to Close All windows.
6. Click OK to close the dialog.

At this point, you have to create an "open main window" macro for the volume as described in the last entry, unless you've already created it. Here's how to add the previously created macro to this macro, assuming the Sequence editor window is still open and is ready for the next step to be added:

7. Click the Import Steps tab to see a list of other macros you've created.
8. Click the Finder tab in the Shortcuts list at the right of the window.
9. Find the macro you made to open the main window of the disk, and drag it into the list at the left, which is the sequence you're creating.

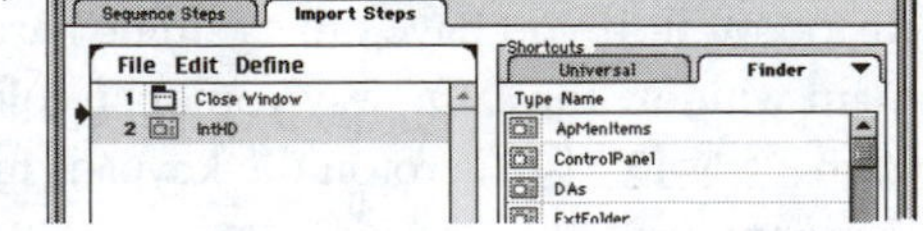

Dragging the previously created macro into the current sequence

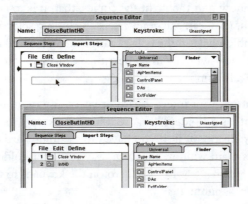

That's all you need for this macro; it's only two steps. You should use all four modifier keys (⌘ Shift Option Control) plus the numeric key you've assigned to open the disk's window as the hot key for this "close everything but" macro.

11

Intro to OS 8.5

On the Desktop

Finder Windows

Icons and Folders

Beyond the Desktop

In This Chapter

On the Desktop

This chapter was written with a beta version of OS 8.5, so consider it a beta chapter!

The Environment

The new (again) look. OS 8.5 makes some major interface changes to the desktop, as well as some subtle ones. On the major end, there's the variety of new looks for windows, including not only different title bars but also special scroll arrows and scroll boxes; on the subtle end, there are things like sounds that accompany certain desktop procedures and a pastel shading for the background of icon titles. And, in between, there are things like a slightly changed look for alias icons and a collection of new system fonts. In order to control these new items, there have been changes to some Finder commands and control panels, notably the Preferences command and the Appearance control panel.

The Preferences command now opens a three-tabbed dialog to control general window settings, window view options, and label names and colors.

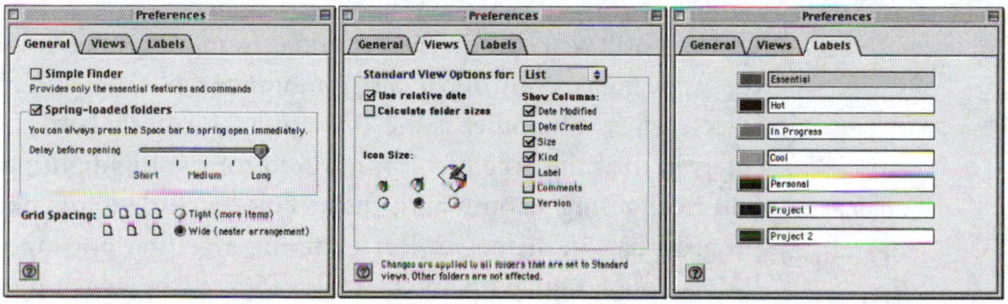

The three faces of the Finder's Preferences command.

The Appearance control panel has been completely overhauled. It still lets you set options that the previous control panel did, like the system font and highlight color. But it has also absorbed the functions of OS 8's Desktop Pictures control panel, and provides a way to deal with all the new desktop options. It presents all these options in a very clear way, through six tabs in the dialog.

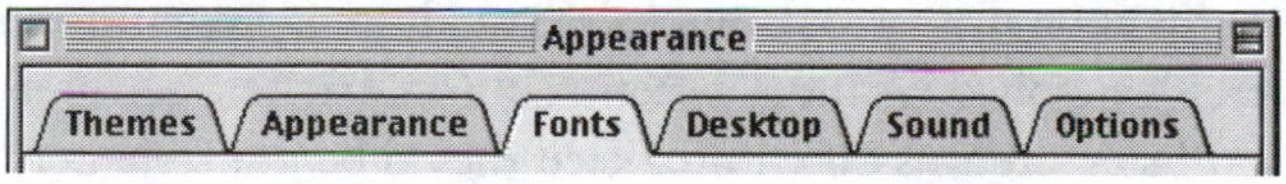

The new Appearance control panel has six tabs.

The window appearance. The Appearance tab of the Appearance control panel lets you set the type of window appearance (aren't you getting tired of that word?) for all your windows—not just the Finder. Instead of the staid, if elegant, platinum approach, you can choose from a variety of alternate lifestyles; the earliest versions of 8.5 include Gizmo and Hi-Tech. (I expect thousands of sets to show up within weeks of this system's release!)

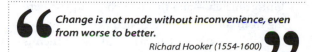

> ***Change is not made without inconvenience, even from worse to better.***
>
> *Richard Hooker (1554-1600)*

At press time, these features were removed from OS 8.5, but it is expected they will be included in a future update.

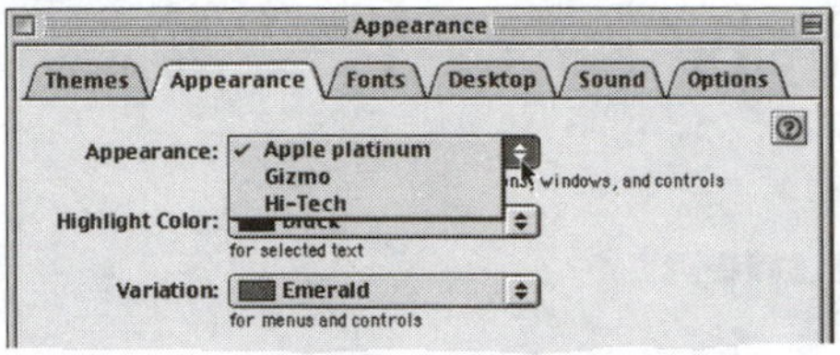

Selecting an appearance changes windows and also menus, dialog boxes, and standard icons, as you can see by the samples here. The changes aren't solely for Finder windows: they affect all windows in all applications.

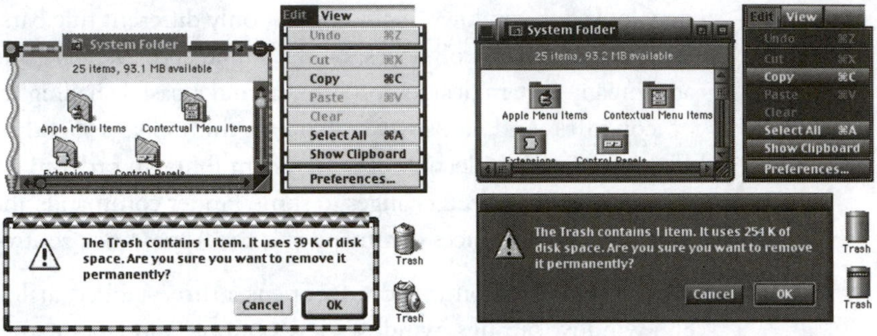

Sample window, menu, dialog, and empty and full trash cans from Gizmo (left) and Hi-Tech (right).

Color your world. You can set two different types of color choices through the Appearance control panel's Appearance tab. One is the highlight color for selected text. The other is the "Variation," formerly (and more sensibly) referred to as the accent color; it's used for the highlighting in menus when you're choosing a command, and to colorize little items like scroll boxes and progress bars in dialogs. Select a color from either pop-up menu, or use the Other option which opens the Color Picker so you can make your own color.

Color Picker
Chapter 9

Fonts

New system fonts. In OS 8, the Appearance control panel provided a choice between Charcoal and Chicago for use as the system font—the one that appears in menus and dialogs. Those who poked around in the system's innards soon discovered "hooks" for additional system fonts, though they weren't supplied with the system. (In fact, back in Chapter 5, which I wrote months before this one, I predicted they'd be available before you read this book—and here they are, practically available before I finish *writing* this book!)

System fonts
Chapter 9

Anyway, the new system fonts are Capitals, Gadget, Sand, Techno, and Textile, and you can choose from among them (and Charcoal and Chicago) in the Fonts tab of the Appearance control panel. The pictures here give you an idea of what they look like in menus and dialogs. Unfortunately—and this is such a surprise coming from the interface-oriented Apple—most of the fonts are not particularly readable in menus and dialogs.

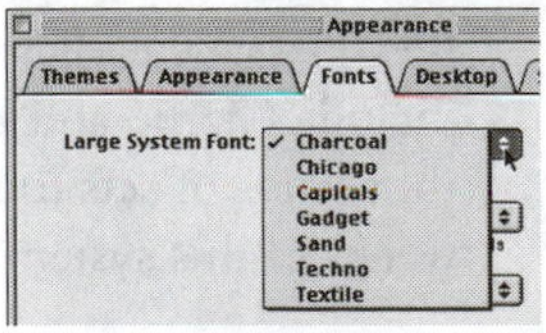

The new system fonts.

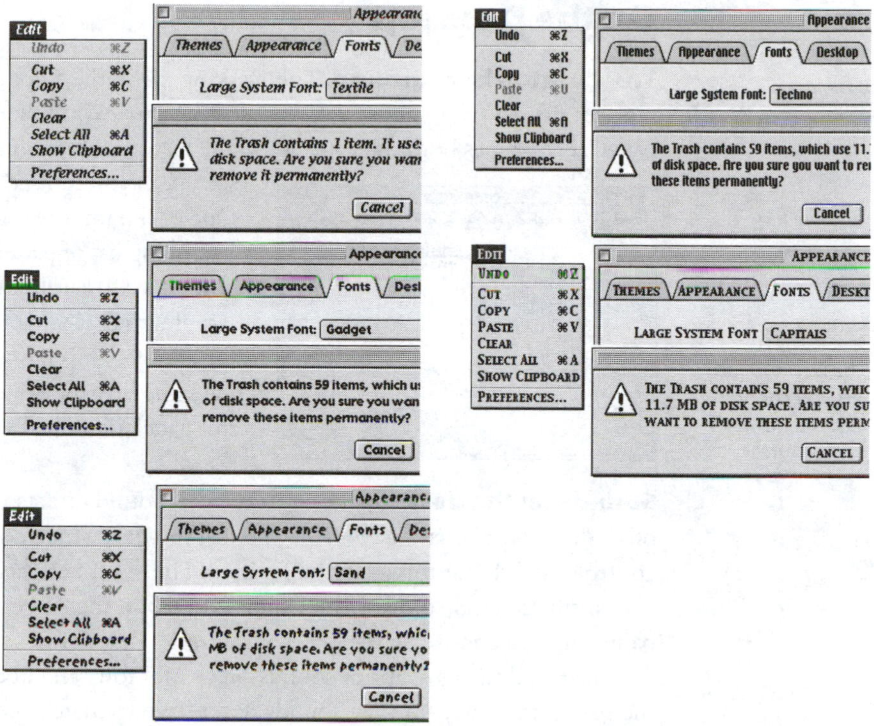

The small system font. We now have control over an aspect of system fonts that we couldn't touch before: the "small" system font, the one that's used for, as the Appearance control panel points out, explanatory text and labels. What are those? Just take a look at the picture here, which shows the standard Geneva and then Georgia as the small system font. The small font is always 10 points, so there aren't many fonts that work well in this capacity.

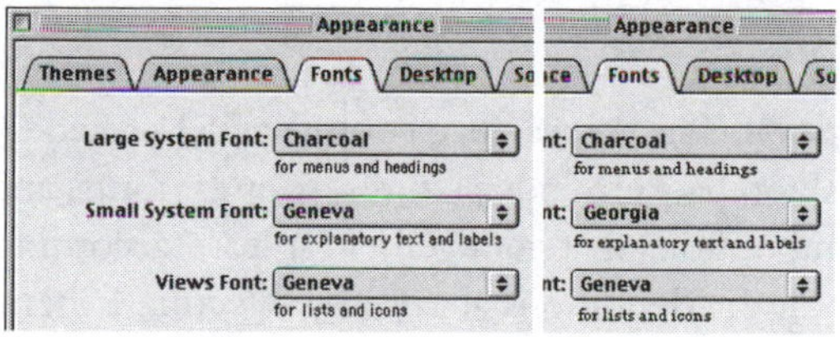

The small system fonts is used for descriptions in dialogs.

The views font. Previously available through the Finder's Preferences command, the "Views" font—the one used for labeling icons on the desktop and in Finder windows—is now set in the Fonts tab of the Appearance control panel.

Anti-aliasing. The final option in the Fonts tab is for turning "smooth fonts" on or off for font sizes above a certain size (you get to choose the certain size). Although the default size cutoff is 12 points (that includes the 12-point fonts in the aliasing), you'll probably want to set it higher if you turn on the option. Aliasing the 12-point size used for basic text entry and for menus and dialogs makes things look a little muddy.

On the Desktop

The desktop background. The Desktop tab in the Appearance control panel replaces the old (well, not so *old*—let's just say *previous)* Desktop Pictures control panel. It combines both the pattern and the picture access on a single, neat screen, as you can see in the picture here. One of the improvements is that you get a scrolling list of pattern names so you don't have to scroll through the pattern samples to find what you need. Except for the reorganization, the controls work the same way they do in the older control panel, described in Chapter 6.

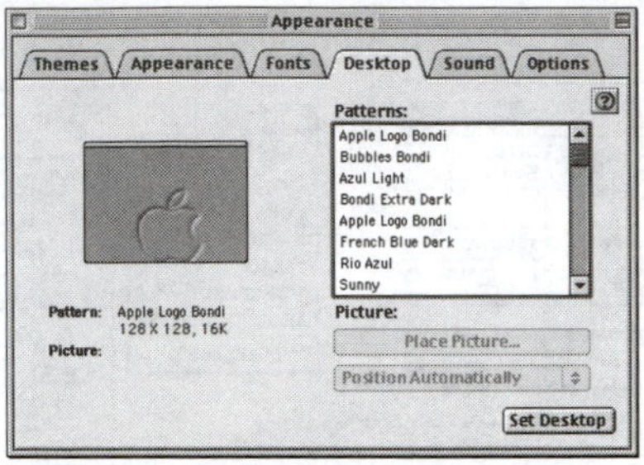

The Desktop tab lets you change desktop patterns and pictures.

Sounds on the desktop. You can turn on sound effects for desktop and other "events" like choosing from menus, moving windows, using window controls, and doing things in the Finder. (The sound effects are a variety of clicks, snicks, pffts, and brrps.) The Sound tab in the Appearance control panel lets you choose an overall "sound track" that defines the kinds of sounds you hear, and turn groups of sounds on or off. You can choose anything from the sound track pop-up; the sounds don't have to match the appearance or theme already selected in other control panel tabs.

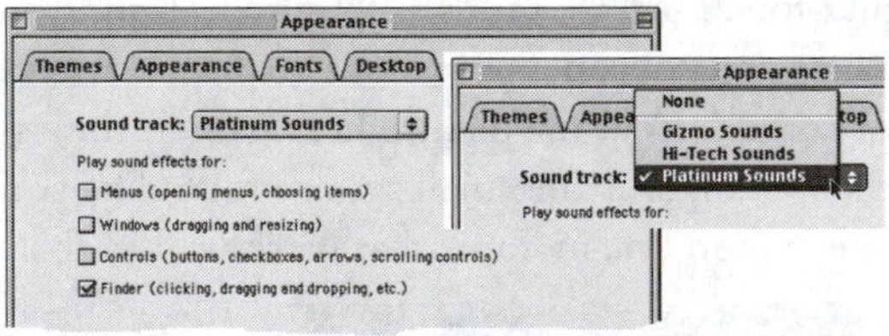

The Sound tab lets you turn sounds on and off for various activities, and select an overall "sound track" (inset).

The theme park. The Appearance control panel provides a set of *themes:* collections of desktop backgrounds/pictures, sounds, fonts, and window appearances and options that go together (at least, according to *someone's* taste). You can apply all the definitions at once by selecting a theme from the Theme tab. (Take a close look at the Roswell background in the picture here.)

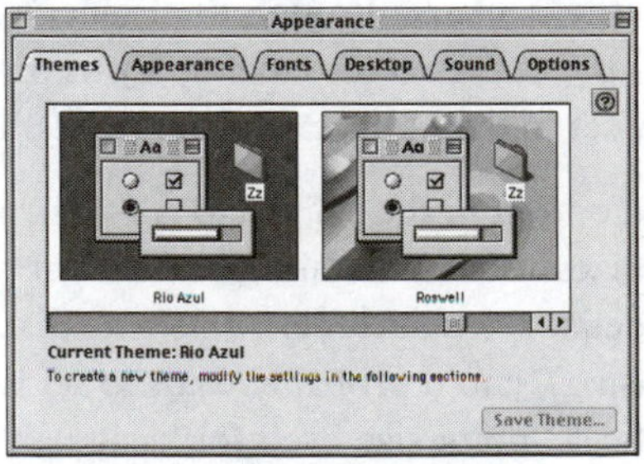

You're not stuck with every aspect of a theme package. You can select a theme and then modify any part of it by selecting options from the other tabs in the control panel. If you do, you'll get a notice at the bottom of the Theme tab that the current theme is "current settings."

Your personal theme park. You can create your own themes for reuse very easily. Just set all the options in the Appearance control panel—you can start with an existing theme or from scratch—and then go to the Theme tab and click the Save Theme button (or select it from the File menu). You'll get to name your theme, and a sample of it is added to the Theme tab.

To get rid of a theme you've created, select it in the Theme tab and choose Clear from the Edit menu.

About this secret... I don't know if this a beta-only trick, or will stay in the final version of 8.5, but hold down ⌘ Option Control and select the About command from the Finder's Apple menu and see what happens.

Find File

Find File
Chapter 7

The Find triumvirate. The Find File utility sports a new interface and three distinct types of searching: the standard, based on file attributes like name, size, and kind; searching through the *contents* of files; and searching the Internet. You'll notice the change right away, since the three functions are accessible through tabs in the Find File dialog.

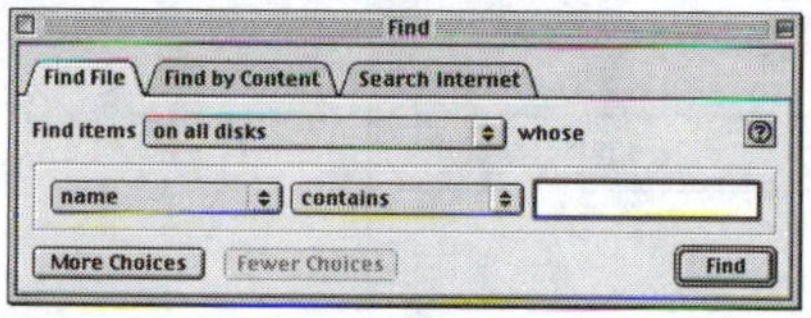

The new Find File takes a tabbed approach.

Finding files on disks. The Find File tab provides access to the familiar Find File dialog; little has changed except that the previously hidden "content" option isn't hidden anymore because there's a separate tab for it.

The Found Items window functions the same way, although it looks a little different, incorporating a lined list in the upper area that matches that of list-view Finder windows. And, as with 8.5's list views, you can adjust the size of the columns by dragging the line between the column titles (although you can't reorder the columns), and use the Sort button at the top of the vertical scroll bar to reverse the current sorting order.

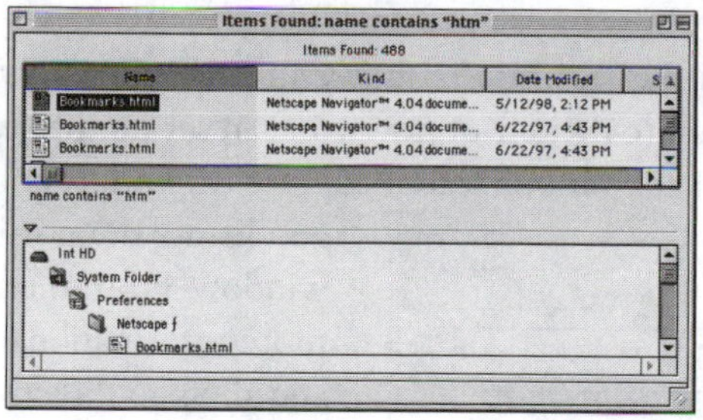

The Items Found window has a slightly different interface.

Searching through file contents. Searching through the contents of files on your disk is more sophisticated now than it was through the hidden feature in the older Find File (as described in Chapter 7), but it is also, as a result, more complicated. In order to be able to use the Find by Content tab in Find File, you have to *index* a disk first, compiling a list of its contents.

To index a disk, click the Index Volumes button in the Find by Content tab. In the next dialog, you select the volumes you want indexed. Make sure you're not in a hurry: it can take about a half hour to index a gigabyte worth of files. And, unfortunately, as soon as you change *anything* on the disk, you'll have to update the index or the new items won't be included in the search. On the other hand, an indexed search is *incredibly* fast, and you can schedule the indexing to be updated when you're away from your computer.

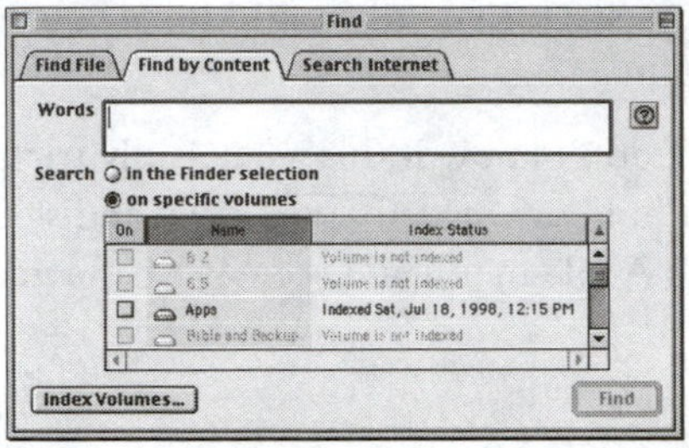

To use the Find by Content tab, you have to have indexed volumes. In this picture, only the Apps drive has been indexed and is available for selection.

When there's a group of found files, you'll get them listed in the Items Found window, sorted by relevance as the default.

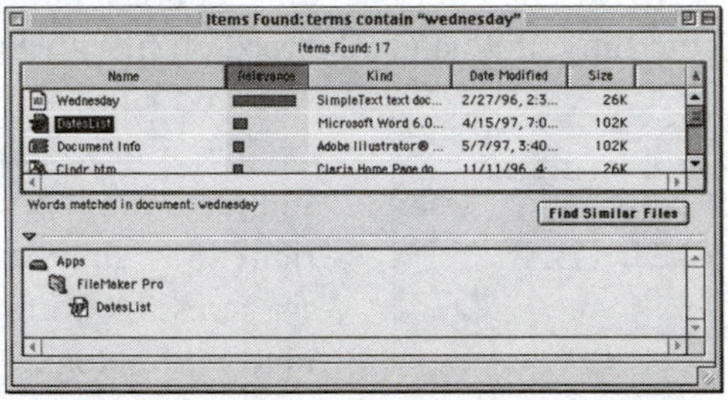

The Found items list from a Contents search includes a Relevance rating.

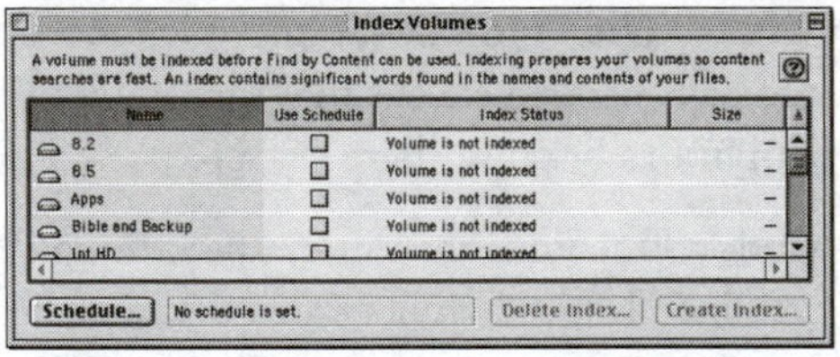

From the Index Volumes dialog, you can schedule a time for automatic indexing.

Searching the Internet. You probably already know how to search the Internet—once you're there. But now you can set up the search in Find File and let the Mac check various search engines for you, rounding up the "hits" and listing them in the Items Found window. From there, you can get more information about a found item and then go directly to the site in question. Use the Search list in the Search Internet tab to set which search engines should be included in the procedure.

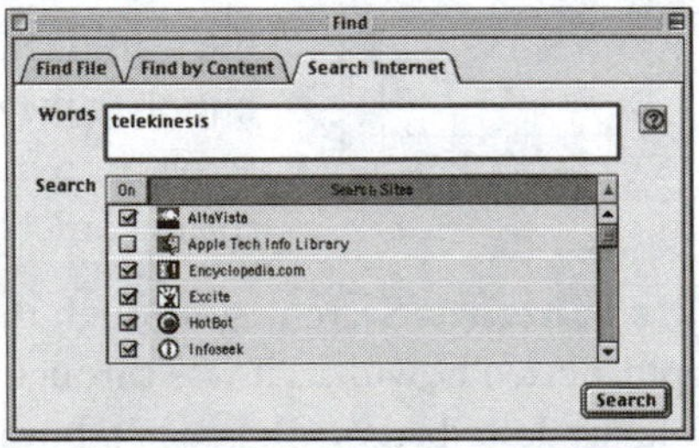

You can search the Internet, telling Find File which search engines to check.

Quick keyboard shortcuts. Once Find File is open (you can open it with ⌘F), you can switch among its tabs with keyboard commands: ⌘G is for Find by Content and ⌘H for Search the Internet. (There's no logic to the choice of letters in the commands—they're just alphabetical.) Using ⌘F activates the basic Find tab again.

Finder Windows

Defining Windows

Global window views. Those engineers at Apple listened to everybody who complained about OS 8's individual-window view options, which made it difficult to easily set a window's options (the size of its icons, which columns should be included in a list view, whether or not folder sizes should be calculated, and so on) to some sort of standard. And they provided a solution that didn't take away the ability to design a window the way you want it.

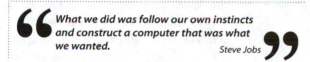

> *What we did was follow our own instincts and construct a computer that was what we wanted.*
> *Steve Jobs*

In 8.5, you get to define global settings for windows and then you can change them on a window-by-window basis; and, any time you want, you can reset a window to the standard settings.

To set the global window options:

1. Choose Preferences from the Edit menu.
2. Click the Views tab in the dialog box.
3. Use the pop-up menu to see the options for List, Icon, and Button views, and select the options you want.

When you put away the Preferences dialog, the options you chose become the definition of a "standard" window.

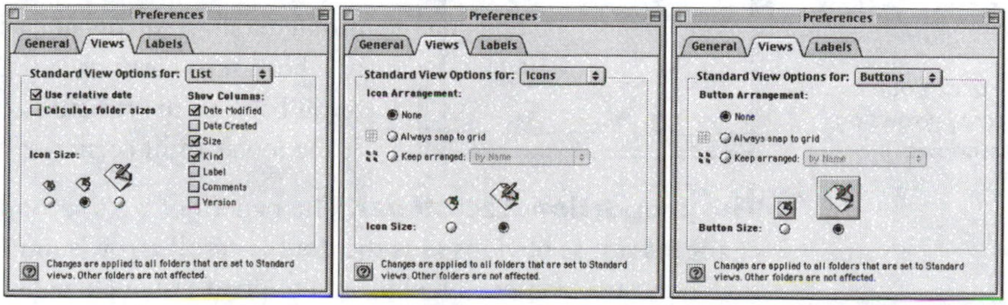

The three sets of view options in the Preferences dialog.

Applying the standard settings. To return any altered window to the defaults settings:

1. Make sure the window you want to change is the active one.
2. Use the View Options command from either the View menu or the contextual menu that pops up when you hold down the Control key and click in the window.
3. In the View Options dialog, click the Set to Standard Views button.
4. Click OK.

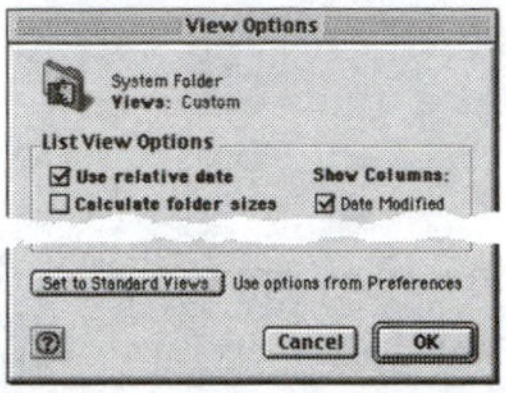

The Set to Standard Views button returns a window to default settings.

Note that resetting a window to a standard view doesn't change the order or width of columns that you might have changed manually, although any column not included in your Standard definition will disappear.

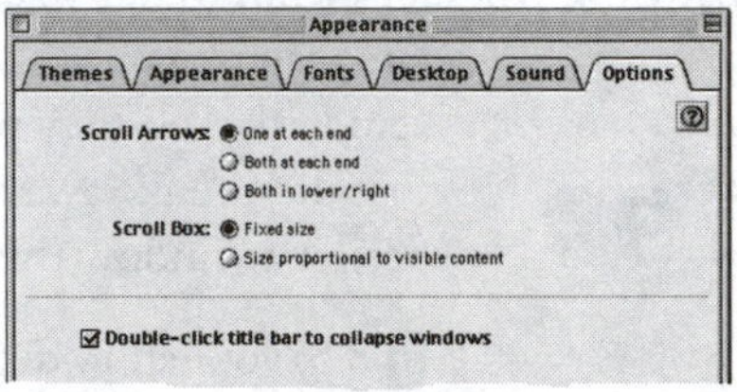

The Options tab of the Appearance control panel.

The Options tab. The options tab of the Appearance control panel provides a way to redefine your scroll arrows and scroll boxes for all windows (not just for the Finder). The *Double-click title bar to collapse windows* option also makes a surprise appearance in this tab.

At press time, the double scroll arrows had been deleted from OS 8.5. It is expected that they will reappear in a future OS update.

Double your pleasure. One of the best-ever window interface improvements is one that up to now has been available only through third-party add-ons: double scroll arrows. Once you've worked with this feature, you won't know how you lived without it. A double scroll arrow puts both directional arrows on each end of the scroll bar. You won't have to travel so far with the mouse to scroll a window; and, if part of the window is off the screen, you won't have to move the whole window just to scroll its contents.

Handy double scroll arrows on windows.

The Options tab in the Appearance control panel provides three different options for scroll arrows: the standard (but soon to be made obsolete) single arrow at each end of the scroll bar; both scroll arrows at both ends of the scroll bars; or the ridiculous both arrows only at the lower right corner of every window.

The proportional scroll bar. The benefit of 8.5's second subtle window change is not as obvious as is the double scroll arrow's, but the *proportional scroll box*, once you get a feel for it, is a great visual clue about the unseen contents of a window.

When you turn on proportional scroll boxes in the Options tab of the Appearance control panel, scroll boxes in both horizontal and vertical scroll bars change size in proportion to how much of the window's contents are visible. So, if you're looking at a Finder window and the horizontal scroll box nearly fills its scroll bar (as in the picture here), you'll know that that most of the window contents are already on display.

The scroll box is proportional to *everything* in the window, not just the currently visible items. So, although you can see all the icons in the picture here, the scroll box doesn't fill the bar because some icon somewhere along the right edge has a name that's too long to fit in the window. (And, since the box is proportional to the size of the scroll bar, it changes size when you change the size of the window.)

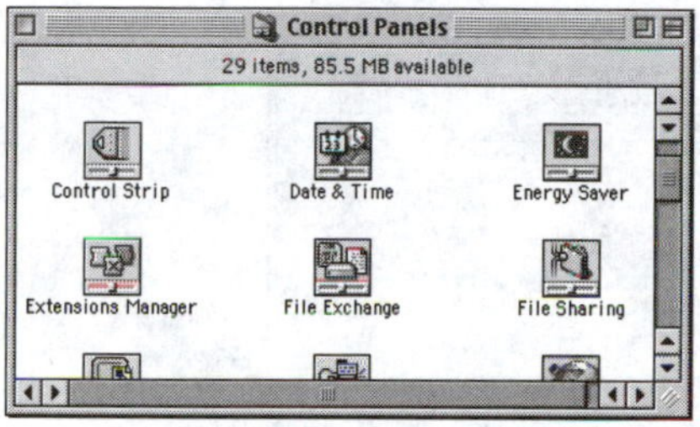

The large horizontal scroll box here indicates that there's little left to be seen in that direction (in fact, it's only a few letters of some of the longer names that aren't within the viewing area). Vertically, about 25 percent of the window contents is displayed at one time, based on the proportionate size of the scroll box.

Working in List Views

Moving and resizing columns. Finally! Column control in list-view Finder windows! 8.5 lets you both reorder the columns and change their widths. To change the column order, just drag the column title to a new position. And if you've ever used a spreadsheet, you won't have to think twice about how to change the width of a column in a list-view window: just drag the line between the column labels to the left or right. You'll even get the same cursor that's used by most spreadsheets for the same operation. (The columns that are actually available in a window depend on what you've set with the View Options command.)

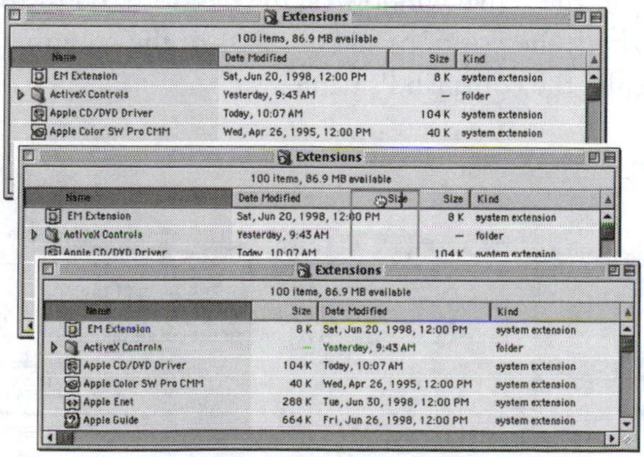

Dragging the Size column to a new position.

Smart resizing. The best thing about resizable columns is that they're very smart. Narrow down the Date Modified column, for instance, and you'll see the day drop out, and then the date switches to a MM/DD/YY format (which takes less room), and then the time drops out, as shown in the picture here. When you're tightening up the name column, the text for longer names gets a little squished before the middle of the name drops out (since it's almost always easier to identify a file if you have the beginning and the end of the name to work with).

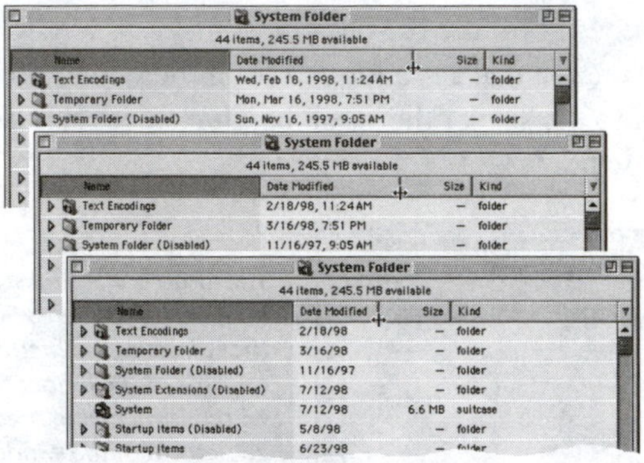

Making a date column narrower first changes the way the date is represented, and then drops out the time.

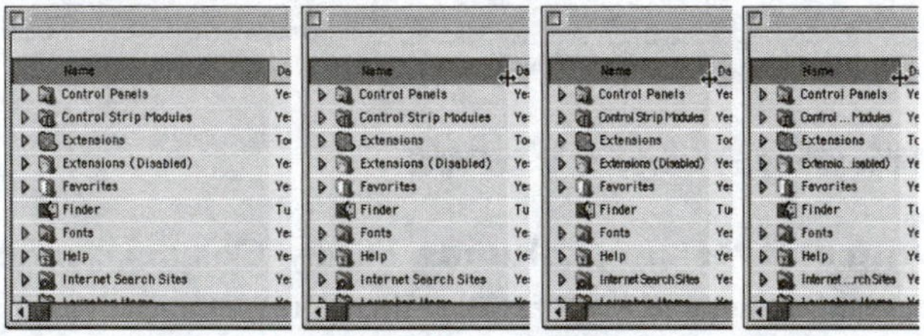

Making the name column narrower. Left to right: the default column, a narrower column with no changes to the file titles, a column with condensed type, and a column with "ellipsized" names.

Resetting the columns. If you want to return the columns in a window to their defaults, use the Reset Column Positions command in the View menu (it will apply to the active window on the desktop). As the dialog box will inform you, both the positions *and* the sizes of the columns will return to defaults, despite the command's name.

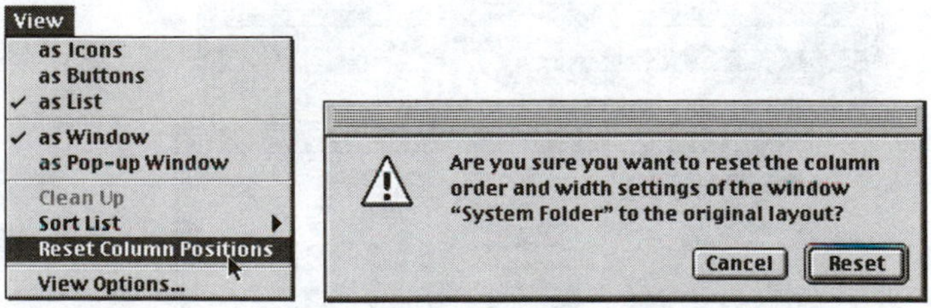

The Title Bar Icon

The title bar addition. You'll notice right away that Finder windows have little icons in the title bars that indicate whether they're folder or disk windows (or anything else—like the Trash). But they're not there solely for identification purposes; they represent a totally new, and terrific, function in 8.5. You can manipulate the folder (or disk or whatever) that the window represents by dragging the icon right off the title bar.

Say you check the contents of a folder and then decide you want to throw the folder away. What do you have to do in an earlier system? Close the window, probably, and see where it zooms to as it closes so you can figure out where its folder is. And, since it might be inside another folder (or several others), you might have to open several windows before you can grab the original one to throw it away. But in 8.5, you can skip all that: grab the icon on the title bar and drag it to the trash. That's all.

To drag the icon, click on and hold the mouse button down until you see the icon highlighted (if you have sounds turned on, you'll hear something, too, when the icon is ready to be moved). This takes only a fraction of a second, but the delay is important: without it, you'd sometimes accidentally drag the icon when you meant to move the window.

Dragging out the title bar icon.

Special drags for the icon. You can use special as-you-drag keyboard combinations on title bar icons the same way you use them on standard icons: hold down Option to make a copy of the folder, or ⌘ Option to make an alias, as you drag the icon off the title bar.

Drag a folder into itself! As I was working on this section, I found a terrific use for the title bar icon. Since I'm working with a beta copy of the software, the system isn't set up the way I usually work—including the Apple menu. After opening the System Folder for the umpteenth time to check something, I realized I should stick an alias of it into the Apple Menu Items folder. Since the System Folder window was open with the Apple Menu Items folder visible inside it, all I had to do was hold down ⌘ Option and drag the window's title bar icon right into the Apple Menu Items folder!

Icons and Folders

Icon Items

Shaded titles. Icon names are no longer surrounded by a white space on the desktop. Instead, the name is against a pastel shade that coordinates with the colors in the background pattern you've chosen.

The alias clue. There's a tiny but noticeable—and handy—change to alias icons in 8.5. The icon titles are still in italic, but the icons themselves have a little curved arrow added to the lower left of the icon—the same arrow you get added to the cursor when you're ⌘ Option-dragging an alias out of an icon. (The significance of the arrow? An alias *points to* the original item.)

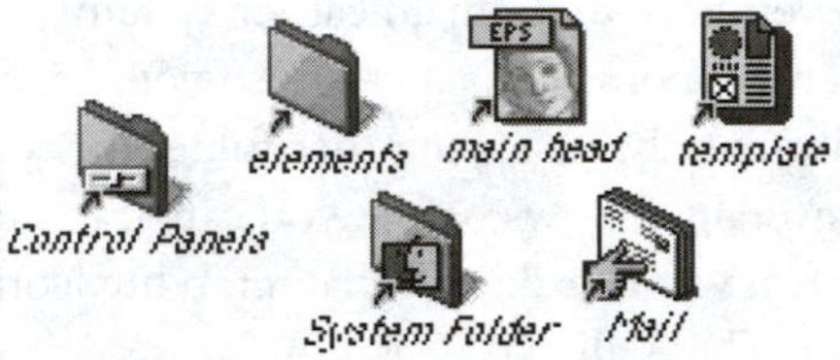

Locked icons. When OS 8 moved the "locked" icon closer to a file's name in a window's list view, it was a welcome improvement, but it wasn't enough—you still couldn't tell at a glance whether a file was locked when a window was in an icon view. But now, locked files have altered icons: a little padlock is added.

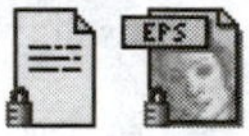

Get mo' better info. OS 8.5 introduces the giant-size Info window in response to the Get Info command. The window is multilayered, with a pop-up menu that lets you choose General Information, Sharing (the same as the File menu command), and, for applications, Memory. And there's new, welcome, function inside the Get Info window: you can rename the item without going back to its icon on the desktop, and even apply a label from the handy, built-in Label menu.

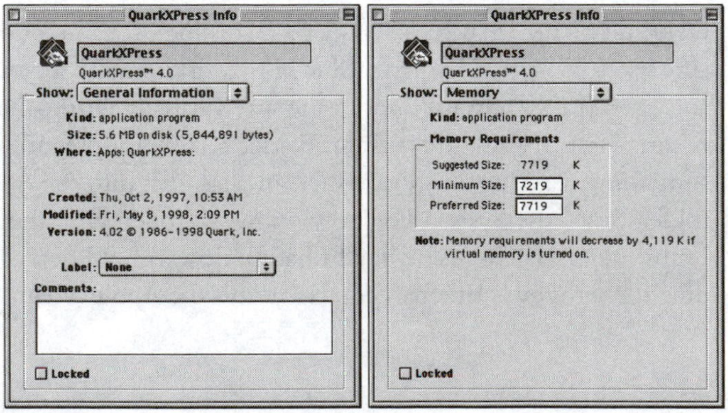

Two screens of the new Get Info window for applications.

> *The whole concept and attitude towards icons and hieroglyphs is actually counterrevolutionary—it's a language that is hardly "user-friendly."*
> *John Dvorak, San Francisco Examiner, 1984*

Playing favorites. There's a new system subfolder, the Favorites folder, marked with a ribbon; an alias of it is automatically placed inside the Apple Menu Items folder. It's meant to provide quick and easy access to any item—an application, a document, another folder—by letting you select it from a Favorites submenu in the Apple menu.

So what, you say? You already do that with your own Apple Menu Items subfolders? Well, here's one big difference: there's a built-in shortcut to getting aliases into the Favorites folder: Control-click on any desktop item and select Add to Favorites from the pop-up menu!

The other big difference is that the list of Favorites is available from other places, too—like Open and Save dialogs (eventually, when application programmers catch up with OS 8.5) and Choose dialogs (described a little later).

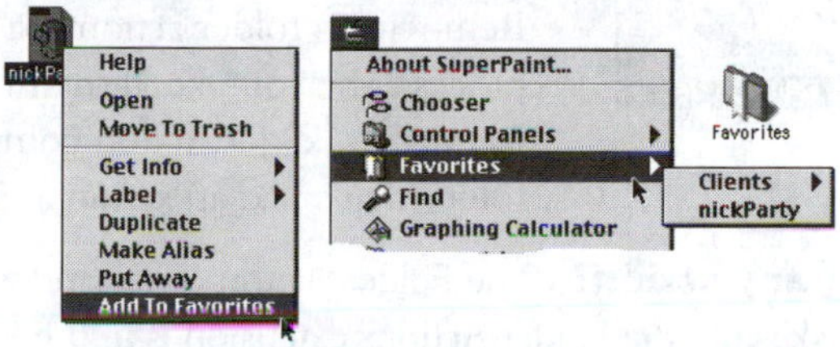

Using the Add 1to Favorites command will put an alias of the item into the Favorites folder.

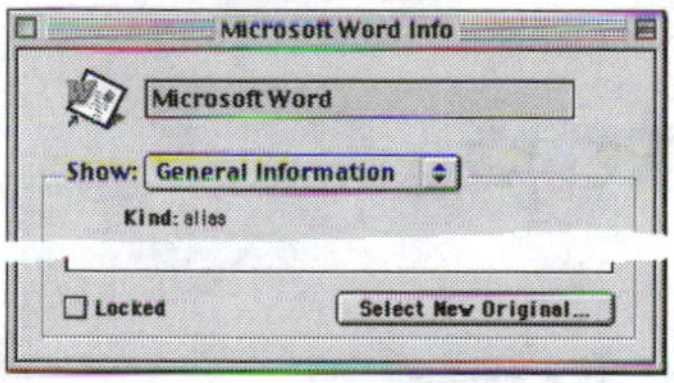

Click the Select New Original button to fix an alias that's been detached from its original item.

Rewiring aliases. When an alias loses its connection to its original item, there's an easy way to connect them again: use the Get Info command, and click the Select New Original button. You'll get the new Choose dialog (described a little later) that lets you find the original—if it's around—and reunite it with its alias.

Folder Actions

No lights, no camera, just actions. The Mac's programming language (oh, all right, *scripting* language), AppleScript, has a new job in OS 8.5: handling *folder actions.*

What's a folder action? Well, it's something that happens when you interact with an opened folder window in the Finder. If, for instance, you drag a file into the window, it could be automatically duplicated in another, backup, folder. Or if you drag something out of the window, you could get a dialog that says you can't remove the item from the folder. Folder actions can be triggered by opening or closing a folder window, too; you might for instance, have an "open folder" action triggered by closing the window—which means you can't really close the window!

A folder action is an AppleScript that's attached to the folder. You can tell if a folder is an action folder because it gets a little AppleScript "badge" attached to its icon.

Where actions are stored. You can store folder action scripts anyplace, but where they really belong is in a special system subfolder: the Folder Action Scripts folder in the Scripts folder inside the System Folder. (Read that second clause again. I dare you.) That's where the system's default action scripts are stored, and you should keep them all together.

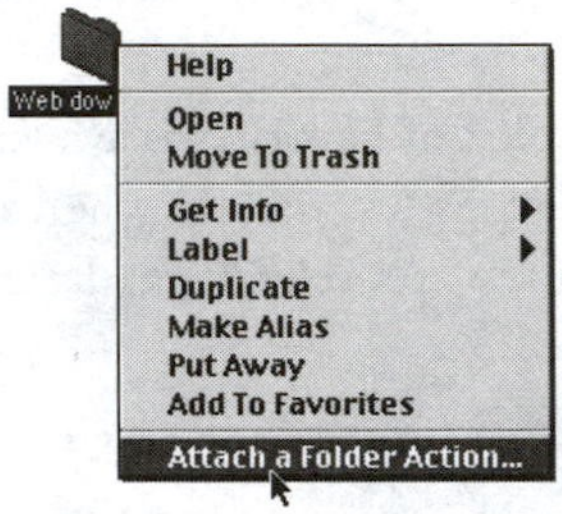

Attaching an action to a folder. It's easy to attach an action to a folder: Control-click on the folder to get the contextual menu, and choose Attach a Folder Action. In the dialog that opens, select a folder action from the list and click OK. Removing a folder action is a single-step process: the contextual menu will have a Remove a Folder Action command in it for a folder that's had an action attached.

Not getting any action? If the Folder Action command isn't in your contextual menu, make sure the Folder Actions extension is in the Extensions folder.

Beyond the Desktop

The Application Switcher

The sliding Application menu. In 8.5, you don't have to guess what application's running by its icon in the Application menu: you actually get the name of the application in the menubar, too.

But if it's taking up too much room in your menubar, you don't have to leave the application's name there: just grab the dotted gray bar and slide it to the right (and back again) to show only a portion of the application's name, or to show just the icon.

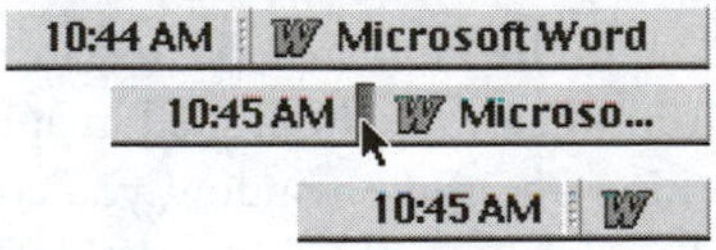

Changing the size of the Application menu's "title."

Clicking on the dotted gray bar in front of the Application menu toggles the menu "title" between the icon-only and icon-and-full-name versions.

The Application Switcher palette. You can turn the Application menu into a floating palette that lists all the currently open applications by simply dragging it off the menu bar—slide the cursor through to the bottom of the menu and, with the mouse button still down, keep dragging. The menu turns into a palette called the *Application Switcher.* (You can drag off the palette no matter what application you're in—you don't have to be in the Finder.) The Application Switcher floats on top of all other windows so it's always visible. To move to one of the applications in the list, just click on it.

The buttons in the Switcher work just the same way the commands do in the Application menu. So, for instance, if you Option-click on an item, you'll hide all the windows of the current application as you move to the new one. Hidden applications have dimmed icons in the palette, and the current application's button is darkened.

Dragging off the Application Switcher palette. Microsoft Word is currently active; the Quark and Help Viewer icons are dimmed because their windows are currently hidden.

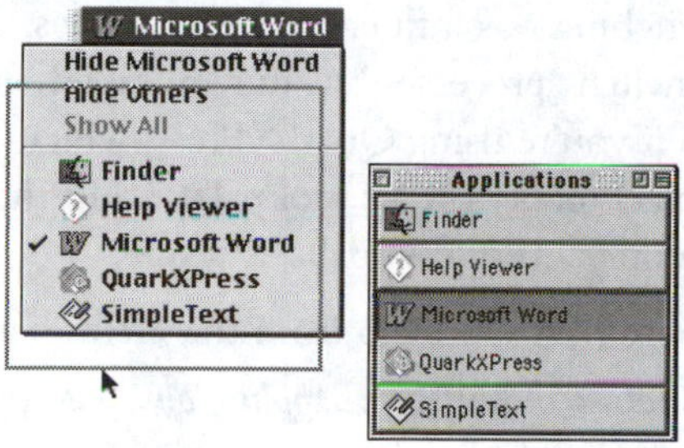

Although it feels like you're ripping the Application menu off the menubar, the Switcher palette is only a special version of the menu; you can leave out the palette and still use the Application menu if that's easier at any given point in your work.

Open document. If you want to open a document in one of the applications in the Switcher, you can just drag the document's icon into the Switcher button, the same way you would drag it into the program's icon.

A large-icon version of the Switcher.

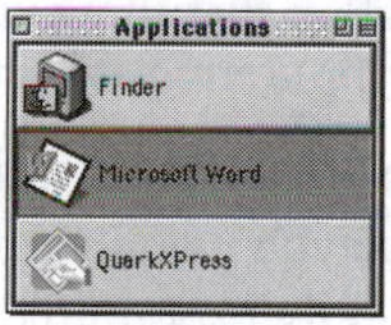

Changing the icon size. The Switcher provides two different sizes for its icons. Toggle between them by Option-clicking in the Zoom box.

The icon-only palette. The Switcher's zoom box has a special function: it toggles you between the standard full view that includes the names of the listed programs, and one that shows only their icons. This works for both small and large icons.

Changing the palette's orientation. If you prefer a horizontal orientation for your Switcher so you can stick it at the bottom of the screen, just Option Shift-click in its zoom box. You can use the horizontal version with small or large icons, and with or without the program names, but you can see by the pictures here what a difference your choices will make when it comes to the palette's size.

Changing icon size and dropping the icon name affects the length of the horizontal Switcher palette.

Keyboard commands for application switching. You can cycle around opened applications by pressing ⌘-Tab to move in one direction, and ⌘-Shift-Tab to move in the other. These keyboard commands work whether or not the Application Switcher is open.

Altering the keyboard commands. The choice of the ⌘-Tab combination for application switching was influenced by Windows, which uses the same combination to switch "processes," as they're called on the other side. This can be a problem if you're using QuarkXPress, which uses those keyboard commands to select tools from its tool palette, but the key combination is changeable, albeit in only a very roundabout way:

1. In the Finder, choose Mac OS Help from the Help menu.
2. At the top of the Help window, type *Application Switcher*, and click the Search button (or press Return).
3. Click the *Switching between open programs* item in the list of found items.
4. Scroll towards the bottom of the window, until you see the underlined phrase *Help me modify the keyboard shortcuts,* and click on it.
5. Follow the prompts in the series of dialogs that show up, and reassign (or turn off) the keyboard commands for application switching.

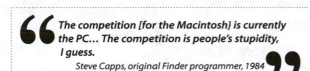

> ***The competition [for the Macintosh} is currently the PC… The competition is people's stupidity, I guess.***
>
> *Steve Capps, original Finder programmer, 1984*

Whoops! I lost the zoom box. I hope you won't need this tip, and that the only reason I did was that I was using a beta version of 8.5 to write this chapter. But I found that whenever the title bar was too small on the palette (in a small icon-only view, or for horizontal orientation), the zoom box disappeared. Without the zoom box available, you can't change the icon's size, orientation, or get back the applications' names if you're in the icon-only view. Restarting, even after trashing the Finder's preferences file, doesn't help.

But if you get stuck like this, here's how to get out: Open the Help system and go to the section on the Application Switcher, as described in the last entry. At the very bottom of the window, you'll find an underlined command: *Restore the default display settings for the Application Switcher for me.* Click it and you're back in business.

Advanced palette manipulation. The Application Switcher is fully controllable by AppleScript. You can, for instance: put the icons in order according to when they were opened instead of alphabetical; stick the palette in a corner of the screen and "glue" it there; or, even get rid of the palette's window controls so the application icons are just in a row at the bottom of your screen instead of in a floating palette. But you don't have to know any AppleScript to reap some of its benefits. You'll find a few palette manipulation tricks wired into the Help system. So, if you look up information about the About the Switcher (as described two entries ago), you'll find a few options under the Advanced Application Switcher Features section; click on the description, and it will be applied to your palette.

The New Help System

The new Help Center. The new "Help Center" help system in 8.5 is miles ahead of the Apple guide approach we've been stuck with for the last several systems. It's fast, it's intuitive (at least, for anyone used to clicking on blue, underlined text to go from place to place), and even the beta version I'm working with offers complete and helpful information in many areas. To access the help system, choose Help Center from the Finder's Help menu, or press ⌘? while at the desktop; the main window is shown here. You can access the help information by drilling down through topics—all you have to do is click on underlined text—or by typing in a word or phrase and clicking the Search button.

After the main Help Viewer screen, you'll find major topics listed on the left; click on one and its subtopics are listed on the right. Once you get to the topic information, you'll find links to related information, as well as do-it-for-me links that will, say, open the control panel that's under discussion.

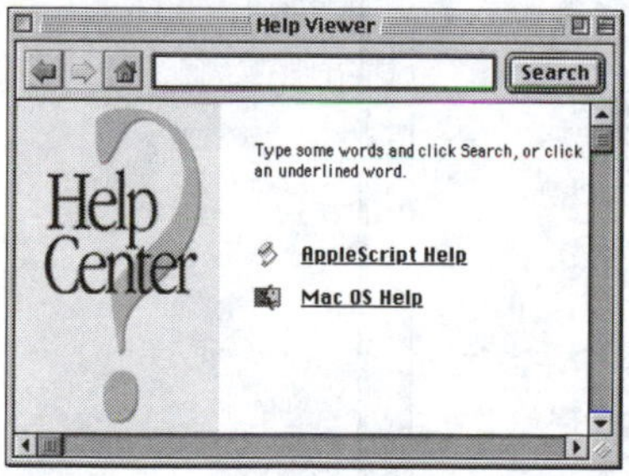

The new Help Center help system starts you out with a choice of two main topics. Or, you can go directly to a search.

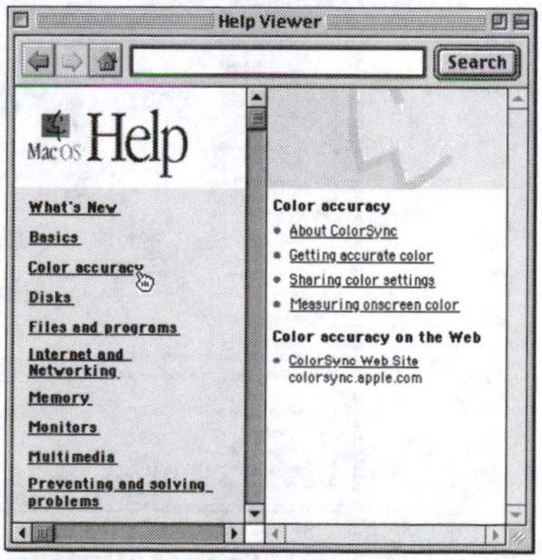

Clicking on the Color Accuracy topic on the left gets a list of topics and subtopics on the right.

Context-sensitive help. You don't have to open the Help Center from its menu and then find the information you want if you're looking at something that's linked to the Help system. Any time you see a Help button in a dialog or window, you can click it and the Help system opens displaying information about that subject.

Special search characters. When you use more than a single word in the Help Center's Search field, you can use special symbols to define the relationship between the words. With a little forethought, you can narrow down the search to just what you need.

Symbol	*Meaning*	*Example*	*Finds*
+	and	alert + sound	pages that include both *alert* and *sound*
|	or	alert | sound	pages that include either *alert* or *sound*
!	not	alert ! sound	pages that include *alert* but not *sound*
()	for grouping	(alert | sound) ! dialog	pages that include *alert* or *sound*, but not *dialog*

And Also...

Apple System Profiler. Among the improved utilities with OS 8.5 is the Apple System Profiler, whose beefed-up capabilities and improved interface make it quite a workhorse. In the picture here you can see the System Profile tab that covers the basics of hardware and system software; each category in a tab can be collapsed or expanded to hide or show its information.

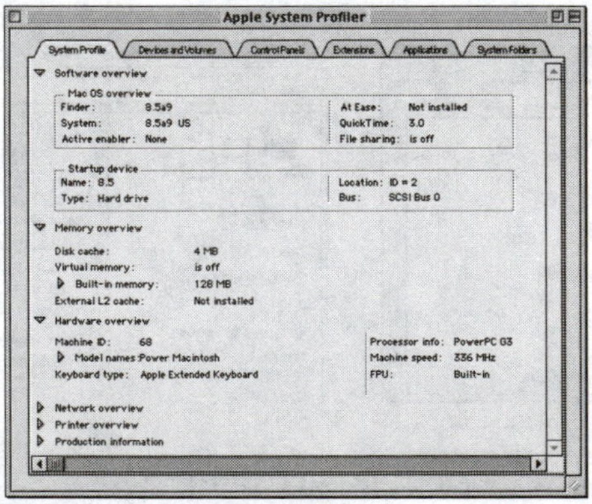

System Installation. The new System Installer boasts one improvement that cuts out a lot of install-stopping dialogs when you're working on a custom installation. Instead of dealing with an awkward, not-quite-hierarchical set of install screens for each of the system components you want to install, you get a more sensible Customize setup. Once you click the Custom button, each component in the list has a pop-up menu that lets you choose from Recommended Installation, Customized Installation, and Customized Removal. Selecting Customized Installation from the menu lets you go through the usual dialog to select options, but when you dismiss the dialog, you're back at the Custom Install screen. This lets you keep track of all the options you've chosen, and when you're finished selecting everything the installation can proceed without needing your input along the way.

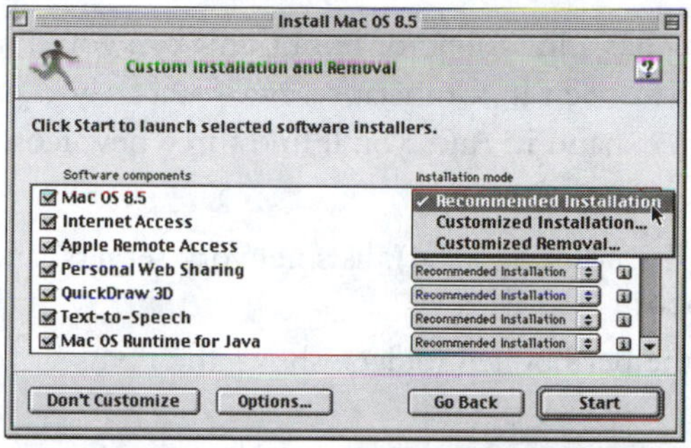

The Internet control panel. Although the Internet Config utility included with OS 8 gave you a central place to input all your internet-related information that various telecom programs could then read, it was an awkward, cobbled-together approach that left something to be desired in the interface department. The new Internet control panel offers a much cleaner approach to the same situation, and includes the ability to build "sets" of information for different needs or locations. The picture here shows the shortened and full version of the control panel window; you toggle between them with the Edit Sets arrow. As you can see, the full window provides four tabs for information, including, on the Web tab, your default browser and home page.

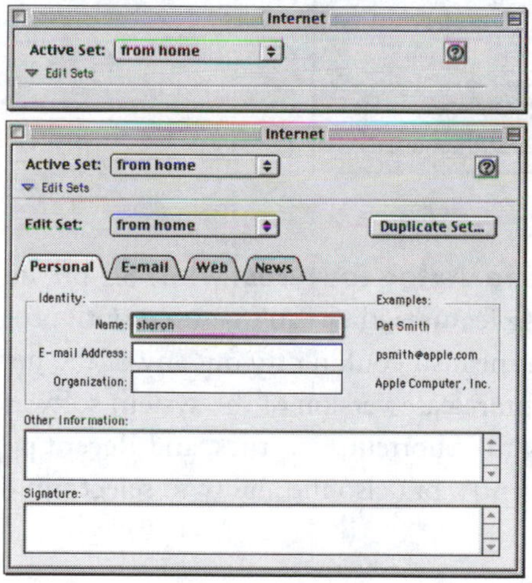

The Internet control panel serves as a central place for all your telecom information.

The Choose dialog. In Chapter 12, which, because of the way things work, I wrote months before I wrote this one, I point out how awkward it is when you have to "select" a folder from an Open dialog instead of actually opening it. Utilities that want you to choose a folder for, say, storing special files, need a folder *chosen* but not *opened*—and each program seems to alter the Open dialog for this purpose in a different way. The engineers at Apple are so good that they responded to my complaint before this book was even published: 8.5 includes something called the Choose dialog that is available to any program that cares to use it.

In the Choose dialog—the picture below shows the one you get when you click the Select New Original button in an alias's Info window—you can navigate through folders, either opening them or selecting the one you want. The Open and Choose buttons clearly differentiate between the two operations.

A Choose dialog has a lot going for it: not only can you double-click on a folder in the list to open it, for instance, but you can also just click on its leading arrow to expand it. And, you'll find three new icons that provide pop-up menus:

- Shortcuts (the pointing hand): lists network servers, and lets you log onto them
- Favorites (the beribboned folder): shows the items in your Favorites folder
- Recent (the clock): lists recently opened or saved documents

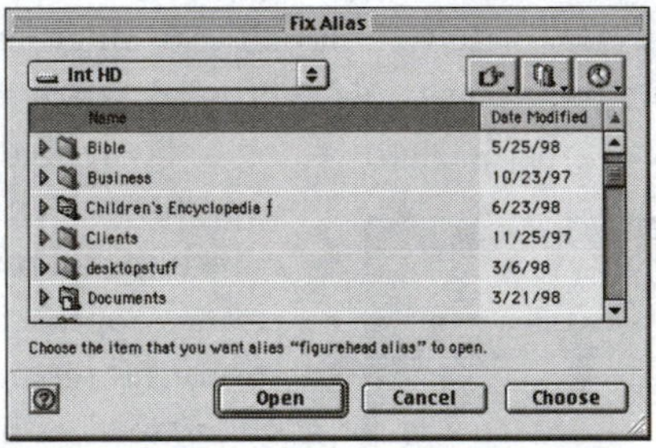

The new Choose dialog design.

New Open and Save dialog features. While 8.5 provides some new Open and Save dialog features, they can't be used until programs are designed to use them—which means I couldn't try out any of the new features, since I'm working with a prerelease version of the system software. But what's promised is not only the Shortcut, Favorites, and Recent pop-up menus as described in the last entry, but also the ability to select multiple items in an Open list.

PART 4

Other System Elements

Part 4 At a Glance

12

Applications and Documents

Buying and Installing Software

Applications

Documents

Document Interchange

In This Chapter

Buying and Installing Software

In General

You don't own the software you buy. You don't actually buy the software that you purchase: you pay for a *license to use* it. And the licensing agreement—to which you agree just by opening the package—usually allows you to run a single package on a single Mac. That sounds reasonable, but it's easy to start running into problems. What if you own a desk Mac and a PowerBook? Sometimes you need the software on one, sometimes on the other, and it's ridiculous to have to buy two copies of a $600 word processor just so you can keep typing no matter where you are. But some licensing agreements are more reasonable, being *single-user* instead of *single-machine* licenses; that lets you legally run the software on any machine you happen to be using.

Maybe you beta not. When a program is in its earliest stage of development, it's referred to as *being in alpha,* or being an *alpha version.* The second stage, when the interface and functions are pretty much pinned down but not necessarily working smoothly, is referred to as *beta.* Some companies release beta versions of new products to the public (through web site downloads) so they can have the benefit of lots of feedback about bugs that crop up in real-world usage. Remember that beta software, almost by definition, doesn't work correctly. It often causes repeated crashes, which in turn might cause corrupted system files on your hard drive. Many beta versions of software keep a *b* or *ß* character in their version numbers; if you're dying to try some, wait for something like a *b3* or *b.v3* release.

Betaware is something else, though: a sarcastic label for software released before its time, making unwary consumers into unwilling beta testers.

Version numbers. As software programs develop in response to customer's comments (and complaints, and to competitor's products), they get assigned *version numbers.* When a product is totally reworked, it gets a whole-number advance (like LetterSmith 1 to LetterSmith 2) if not a whole new name. But minor changes for bug fixes or for compatibility with other programs or new system software get decimal numbers, like PaintBucket 1.2 or 1.01 or 1.1.1. (Some companies like the double-decimal system, others don't—there's no strict rule for this stuff.) Whether the number is a tenth or a hundredth is usually indicative of how many changes were made, whether they were minor or major—and how much you'll pay for the upgrade.

But Roman numerals aren't the same as version numbers. Roman numerals are part of the name; so, you can have ScriptMaster Pro II 2.0, where one number's the name, and the other is the version.

Piracy hurts everyone, matey. Piracy is copying and distributing software, cheating the publisher of its profits. One attitude is that the cost of duplicating disks is so low that all software is way overpriced. But there are costs associated with the research and development of a product; without profits from one version, development on the next version suffers. Some experts estimate that for every legal copy of a popular piece of software, there are five illegal copies being used.

To put software piracy in perspective, try using piracy rationales in regard to hardware: "I shoplifted this new PowerBook because… it's only one (copy)… it's overpriced… I don't use it that often… no one will ever know… it doesn't work all that well, anyway."

> ***Lotus's Jazz, which could eclipse Lotus 1-2-3 as the greatest piece of personal computer software yet, will fuel the Mac's growth.***
> *Macworld, August 1985*
>
> ***We shipped 40,000 units [of Jazz] that very first month. Within a few months, 41,000 came back. Even the pirated copies were returned.***
> *Jim Manzi, president of Lotus*

Copy protection. *Copy protection* is a scheme used by a software company to prevent piracy. Back in the early days, some schemes included a special piece of hardware (called a *dongle)* that was attached to one of the computer's ports; if the hardware wasn't there, the program didn't run. (And, I'm sorry to report, there is at least one package that still does this.) Or, every time you ran the program, it asked you to insert a master floppy disk just to check on you.

Consumer complaints finally registered, thank goodness, so few programs have restrictive copy-protection schemes. The most popular, and least intrusive, approach for single-machine users is that of serial numbers. Each copy of a program has an individual serial number that you have to type in when you install the software on your hard drive. You don't need the number unless you call in for support or install an upgrade. But if you're on a network, the program might not run if another copy with the same serial number is already running (while that seems fair, the fact that it continually checks the network for other copies of itself adds traffic to the network and can slow things down or cause other problems).

An approach that's popular for games is having you type in something from the documentation (*"the third letter of the fourth word in the eighth line of page 28"*). This sounds benign at first—until you've told the kids to put away that booklet for the zillionth time, or they've lost it. (And it's not as if you can't make a copy of the usually very slim documentation.)

The native isn't restless. Software can be written to take advantage of the PowerPC chip's capabilities, in which case it's referred to as *native* code. Programs not in native code run in a special *emulation* mode on a PowerPC Mac; it emulates a 68000-based machine, which can slow things down considerably. That's why you'll see many installation programs offering to install one or the other version of an application.

Some programs come in a combo version known as *fat binary,* or simply *fat,* which contains instructions for both types of processors so it runs wherever you install it.

Don't emulate—upgrade. If your old 68K version of a program is running just fine on your newer PowerPC-based machine (and it's likely that it does), you should still switch to the PowerPC version of the program if there's one available. When a program runs in 68K emulation mode on a PowerPC, it runs slowly because of the background translation going on. Your zippy PowerMac will run the old program at about the same speed as a Quadra would do it.

Choosing Software

Review reviews. Check the reviews of the product you're planning to buy: in major magazines, in a user group newsletter, in an on line forum or web site. Gathering facts about the program's features and opinions about its performance can help you choose which product to buy.

There's a general assumption that major magazines have to pull their punches when reviewing products because they might otherwise risk their advertising revenue from the manufacturer. As an insider, I know that's just not true. I've written for all the major magazines, including Macworld in its first year of existence and MacUser from its very first issue to nearly the last one. Not once in eleven years of reviewing products have I ever, ever, *ever* been asked to change comments or temper my criticisms—and I can be quite critical.

The editorial and advertising ends of professional magazines are completely independent at reputable publications. And you have the added benefit, in reviews from major magazines, of the usually higher level of expertise and exposure that the professional writers have—it's hard to do a good review of a program if you're working in the vacuum of not having used other, similar, programs, too.

Where can you find reviews if you don't have back issues of a good magazine? There are the magazine and other Mac web sites (a few suggestions are listed here), but also check the manufacturer's web site: you'll often find links to the favorable reviews of its products. (You're unlikely to find links to *unfavorable* reviews, so keep looking!)

- Macworld: macworld.com
- MacAddict: macaddict.com
- MacHome Journal: machome.com

- MacWEEK: macweek.com
- MacinTouch: macintouch.com
- TidBITs: tidbits.com

Other places to find information. What can you do besides track down product reviews before you shell out for the perfect software product?

- Talk to other people—in person or online. See what they're using, how they like it (or not). Go to a user group and ask around.
- See if the manufacturer has a demo version of the product available; most larger companies have downloadable demo software on their web sites.
- Find a friend (or make a new one) who's using the software. Ask for a personal demo, or for some hands-on time on her computer.
- Find a book about the product. A major program may have several how-to books written about it; you'll get more information about the product's features than can be squeezed into a 2500-word magazine review. If you're considering the purchase of a $600 program, a $20 book can be a wise investment.

Compatibility. Make sure that all your products will work with all your other products. This goes for both hardware and software, especially if you have some non-standard hardware like an accelerator card. Make sure you know what you have, and check reviews and with the vendor to see if everything is going to work together (not that the reviews or the vendor will always address your particular issue).

Sometimes upgrading one item means you'll just have to upgrade some of your other stuff, too—there's no way around that. When it comes to software, you have to check what hardware it can run on (some may be limited to PowerPCs, or '040-or-better machines—which means '040's and PowerPCs) and what operating system it runs under. And you have to be careful: a package that says something like "Needs system software 7.1 or later" may in fact *mean* "or any later version of *System* 7." When there's been a major operating system update since a software package was released, don't assume the "or later" label actually includes the latest operating system update.

Bandwagon buying. Sometimes it's important to jump on the bandwagon and buy what everyone else is using, just so you can get the advantages of being in the majority. (You shouldn't apply that philosophy to *computers,* of course—we're talking software here!)

Say you run into problems with WebMeister, or just want to learn how to use its more subtle features. Who you gonna call? The company's too small to provide telephone tech support, the product isn't popular enough to have its own newsletter, or books in the book store, or hints and tips in a Mac magazine. Not even anyone else in your user group has the program. Don't underestimate the importance of these kinds of resources.

Buying Software

Let your fingers do the walking. Even before buying Mac software at an actual computer store became an exercise in frustration due to shrinking shelf space, mail-order buying was an economical way to go, with great prices and large selection. Now, of course, there's also the web-based versions of catalogs, as well as web-only ordering spots. I've been buying software through catalogs for years; I've also always bought memory and peripherals like modems and hard drives by phone or, more recently, through the Web. I've never yet had a problem as a result.

The most important thing to remember is to deal with a reputable company—the lowest price won't always be the best deal in the long run.

macconnection.com
macwarehouse.com
cybout.com
smalldog.com

The mail/web-order companies with the best reputations in the Mac community are MacConnection, MacWarehouse, and the web-only Cyberian Outpost. One of my personal favorites is Small Dog Electronics. You'll also find that you can order directly from some manufacturers, and you'll find links from their sites to places where you can order their products.

Buy the old version, quick!. As soon as a major new version of a program comes out, rush out and buy the older version. Because here's what can happen: BitDiddler 1.0 sells for $99. The 2.0 version comes out at $195, with a $50 upgrade for current users. You buy the old version and upgrade it—for a savings of about $50. Sometimes an offer like this is good only for people who bought the older version within weeks of the new program's coming out, so keep a receipt. (And check that there *is* such an upgrade policy before you buy that old one!)

Upgrade in haste, repent at leisure. When the latest and, presumably, greatest version of your software applications come out, you don't have to be first out of the gate in the upgrade rush. Even if you succumb to a "limited time only" upgrade offer—which often makes financial sense—that doesn't mean you have to replace your old version immediately.

Let the two versions live side by side on your drive for a while, until you're sure the new version is reliable, both internally and in its dealings with things like file exchanges with other programs that you use.

What version you already have. You can't count on the name of a program to tell you what *version* you're actually using: FileMaker Pro 3 had several minor revisions before FileMaker Pro 4 came out. While there was no FileMaker Pro 3 2.0, there might have been—and it wouldn't be in the title.

There are two places to look for the real version number of a program. The best way is to run the program and check its About box, the first item under the Apple menu. Or—and this works most, but not all of the time—select the program's icon on the desktop and use the Get Info command; the version number should be listed in the Info window.

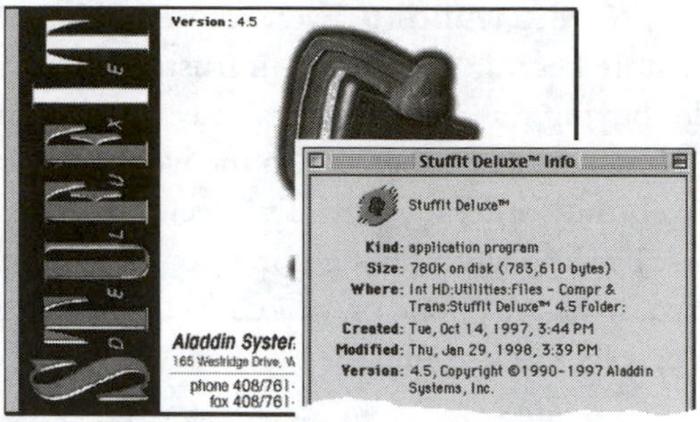

You can usually find a version number in a program's About box (left); sometimes the version number is in the icon's Info window (right).

The sidegrade approach. A *sidegrade* is an "upgrade" to a program from a competitor's product. Sidegrades are sometimes offered by publishers for new or upgraded programs—you send them the documentation or the master disk from the rival product DoctorDisk, and they'll send you their new SectorSurgeon software for half price. You can get some great deals this way—as long as you were going to switch allegiance anyway.

IN THE BEGINNING

You can probably name the top sellers in today's software market without thinking too hard. Microsoft Word. QuarkXPress. FileMaker. Photoshop. But do you even recognize all the top-ten sellers from the early Mac years?

	Dec 85	Apr 86	July 86	Sept 88
1	Jazz	Excel	Excel	Word
2	Word	Jazz	Word	PageMaker
3	Multiplan	Word	File	Excel
4	File	Multiplan	MacDraw	FullWrite
5	Chart	File	MacProject	MacProject
6	Dollars & Sense	MacDraw	PageMaker	TOPS
7	MacDraw	Dollars & Sense	Jazz	MacDraw
8	MacProject	Helix	Omnis 3	PowerPoint
9	Back to Basics	pfs:file	Multiplan	Cricket Presents
10	pfs:file	MegaForm	Chart	4th Dimension

Shareware

Public domain, shareware, and freeware. *Public domain* is an oft-misused phrase, since it means the author of the piece has given up all rights to it; it's commonly, though mistakenly, used to refer to *shareware* and *freeware,* great concepts that got started in the computer community.

Shareware is a program that you obtain for free (from a friend, user group, or on-line) so you can try it out. If you like it, you pay for it by sending the author a small fee, usually five to twenty-five dollars. *Freeware* is just what it sounds like—there's no fee involved at all. If you use shareware, make sure you pay for it—that's what keeps programmers upgrading that program and creating others in their spare time. Some shareware programmers release versions that are less than fully functional, missing something like printing capabilities; this category is sometimes referred to as *crippleware.* Other shareware works only for a limited time.

Getting shareware from the web. Shareware is available all over the place: on disks that come with books and magazines, through user groups, and, of course, on various web sites.

One of the best places to find shareware on the web is through c|net's *shareware.com*. You can use its search capabilities to browse through the latest shareware posted for the Mac, or for shareware that's connected to specific topics (fonts, desktop enhancements… whatever), or for a specific package.

Here's how easy it is to get the shareware you want. (Let's say you're looking for something called *StuffCM):*

1. Use your browser to go to shareware.com. As you can see from the first picture here, there are several choices on the main page for finding software, including browsing through lists of the latest arrivals or the most popular downloads.
2. On the main page, type *StuffCM* into the Quick Search box.
3. Select *Macintosh* from the pop-up menu beneath the text box.
4. Click the *search* button. You'll get the Search Results page, with a list of items that match what you asked for (you may be surprised at the list if you're not accurate in what you ask for!).
5. Click on the link for the item you want. You'll get a list of places from which it can be downloaded.
6. Click on one of the archives in the list to start the download.

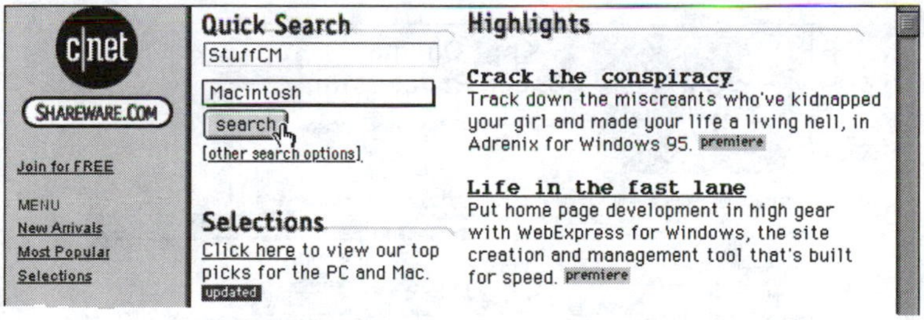

Type in the name of the software you're looking for on shareware.com's main page and click the search button.

Shareware.com also provides a "power search" form that you can get to by clicking the *[other search options]* link on its top page. This lets you search by topic, keywords, dates, and so on—especially handy if you don't know the actual name of the software you want.

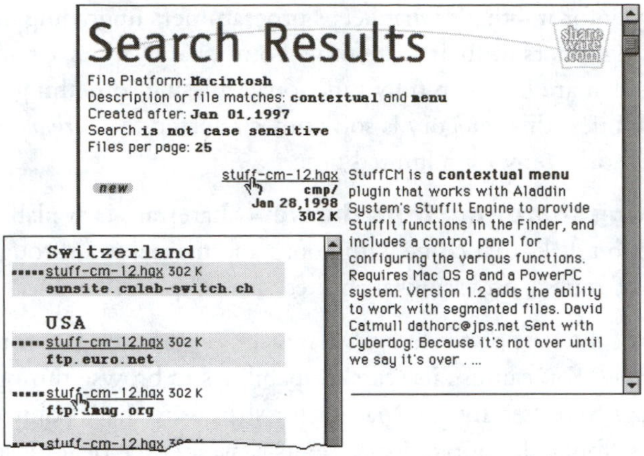

In the Search Results window (top) click on the software you want to download. In the downloadable list (bottom), click on the software at one of the locations.

If you find yourself using the search options more often than the quick search option on the top page at shareware.com, you can go directly to the Power Search page with this address: *shareware.com/code/engine/Power*—which is easy to use if you make it a bookmark in your browser.

Browsers, bookmarks, addresses
Chapter 28

Paying for your shareware. You don't need to be told that you should pay for your shareware. If it's handy enough for you to want to use it, the author deserves payment. Sometimes, however, the bother of writing out a check and mailing it (though nothing compared to the time the author put in, or probably even to the time you're saving by using the program) keeps you from actually getting around to paying for the software.

Most shareware today can be paid for online, and to make it even easier for you, many of the shareware programs provide a button that automatically launches your browser and sends you to a central site that collects payments for shareware authors; you get to pay with a credit card.

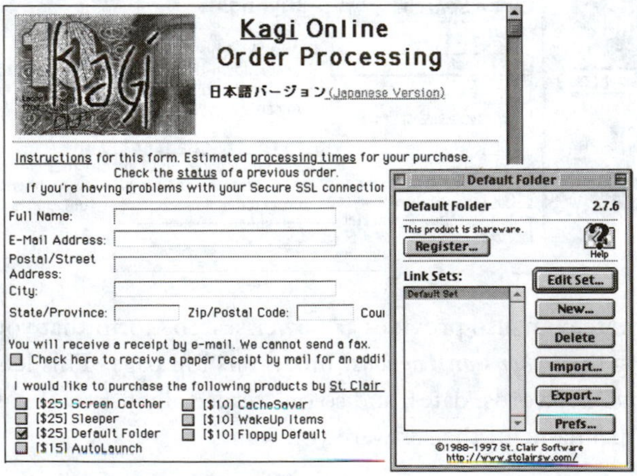

Clicking the Register button in Default Folder's control panel sends you to the Kagi web site where you can pay for your shareware.

"You don't need to be told that you should pay for your shareware." Did I write that at the beginning of this entry? Well, maybe *you* don't, but most people do, and it's the software itself that usually tells you. Most shareware utilities show you reminders at startup; the one shown below, from Window Monkey, provides a variety of opening remarks to goad you into doing the right thing. (I purposely tortured the poor creature for about two months just to get these pictures for you.)

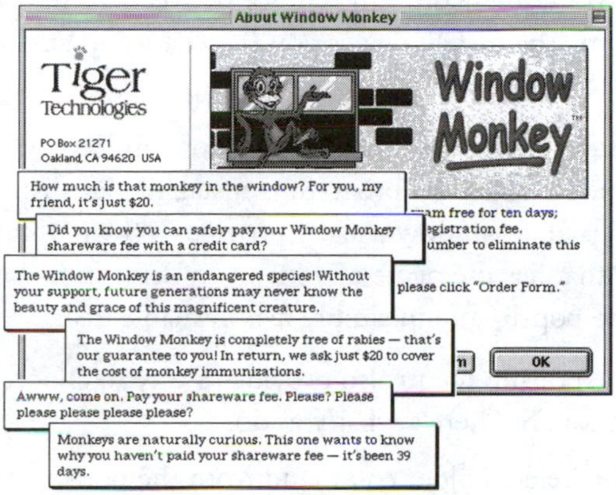

Window Monkey's ever-changing startup comments encourage you to pay your dues.

Installing Applications

The support staff. While an application is only a single file on your disk, the fancier the program is, the more support files it will have. At a minimum, there's a preferences file tucked into your System Folder's Preferences folder. But the possibilities are seemingly endless: dictionaries, translators, plug-ins, special fonts....

Support files often have to be in the same folder as the application, or in subfolders inside the application's folder. Sometimes you can put the support folder anyplace and just "show" the application where it is the first time you launch it. Companies like Claris coordinate the support files for their products so that a single folder (usually placed in the System Folder) can be shared by all the company's products.

Read me first! There's a reason files with this name make their way onto software installation disks. A printed manual goes to production before the software does; if something changes at the last minute, the only place to make note of it is on the disk. These files, generally referred to as *read me* files, might have important information about the product, or the installation process, that didn't make it into the printed instructions. So if there's a file that says Read Me on your disk, do yourself a favor and read it. All you have to do is double-click on it to open it, and quit the reader program (usually it's SimpleText, included with your system software) when you're finished.

Use the installer. If a program comes with an installer, use it. An installer takes care of all the details for you, placing support files in the proper places. Other reasons to use the installer (if "easier" isn't good enough): some applications are condensed to fit on a master disk, and the installer returns it to its full, usable version; sometimes a copy-protection scheme is carried out during the installation process, and you have to "stamp" your name on the product and input a serial number that proves you're an official user.

And, since most installers offer the choice between an Easy and a Custom installation, using the installer gives you the chance to customize the items that are installed along with the main program.

Choosing the location. Whether you choose an Easy or a Custom install, you can still choose *where* the program is installed. This isn't obvious to a lot of people: an installer window usually provides a Switch Disk button and a pop-up menu that has the name of your main drive in it—and many people assume that the pop-up menu simply lists available disks.

But, in fact, the pop-up menu also provides a way to choose a specific folder for the installation. So, here's what you do:

1. Choose the Select Folder command from the pop-up menu at the bottom of the Install window.
2. Navigate through your drive(s) and folders to find the folder you want the *program's folder* installed in. (Use the New Folder button if you want to create a subfolder for it.)
3. When the folder you want is showing in the list, click on it and click the Select button.

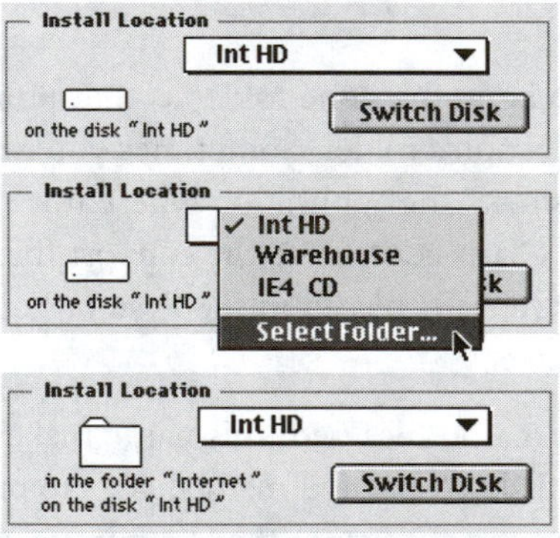

Choose a location for an installation by using the pop-up menu in the Location area of the Installer window.

You'll find the folder you've selected is identified in the Location section of the Installer window, with a folder icon instead of the original disk icon.

Keep in mind that an installer creates a folder for the program it's installing, so you don't have to. You pick the folder where the new application folder will be placed, but you don't create the folder yourself.

Easy versus custom installs. You should always take the time to do a custom installation instead of the "easy" one. When Easy Install is selected in the pop-up menu, you'll see a general list of what's going to be installed; switch to Custom Install, and you'll see a more specific list of the items that come with the program. The list is often hierarchical, so clicking on a leading arrow (as for *Internet Explorer Options* in the picture here) displays a list of sub-items.

You can click in any box to include items in the installation; clicking in a top-level item selects or excludes all its sub-items. If you don't know what an item is, try clicking its Information button (although some descriptions aren't particularly helpful).

Specific options vary from one installation to another, but in general, you'll be able to choose from these options:

- Installing a specific version of an application: for a PowerPC or a 68K Mac, or the "fat" version that runs on both. Some installers simply default to the fat version, which wastes disk space, since the combined code is much larger than either of the specific ones. Some installers are smart enough to choose the version of the program you need.
- Include or exclude special fonts. Some applications need special fonts to "look" their best: a dictionary application, for instance, might include a special font that's used for pronunciation guides. Other applications include bonus fonts which you may want to add to your collection—or, you might already have them installed.
- Include or exclude special tutorials and sample files.

The Easy Install option (top) lists what's going to be installed; the Custom install option (bottom) lets you control all the details.

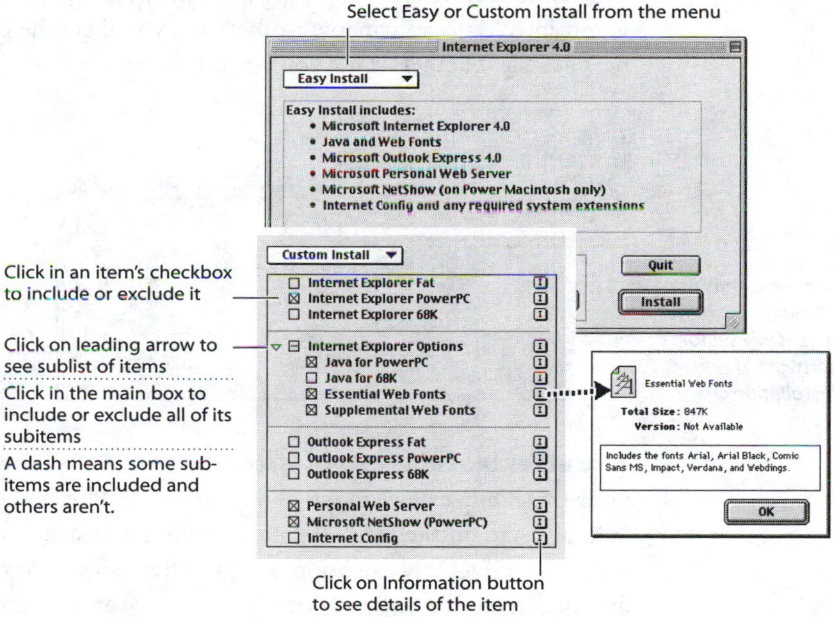

Turn off your extensions. Most software installers insist that you turn off all your extensions before you install the new software; some just tell you that virus-protection software running in the background might cause a problem. I've seen some strange, hard-to-believe results from ignoring this injunction, even when virus protection wasn't included in the extensions that were running, so it's best to follow it. (Is most of this paragraph gobbledygook to you? Chapter 9 explains all about extensions.)

Installing from a CD. If you follow everyone's advice and turn off all your extensions, it's going to be extremely difficult to install any software that's on a CD, since the Mac doesn't know how to access a CD unless the CD-ROM extension is running. The solution is to make a CD-only extension set with the Extensions manager so you easily can turn off everything except that one necessary extension:

1. Open the Extensions Manager.
2. Select New Set from the File menu.
3. Select All Off from the Edit menu.
4. Scroll through the list to find the extension named Apple CD-ROM, and click in its checkbox to turn it on.

That's all: any time you want that set to be used, you select it in the pop-up menu in the Extensions Manager window, then restart the Mac. If you're not going to be using it for a while, make sure you select your standard set (the name defaults to *My Settings*) from the pop-up before you close the Extensions Manager window—otherwise, you'll get the CD-Only set at your next startup whether or not you want it.

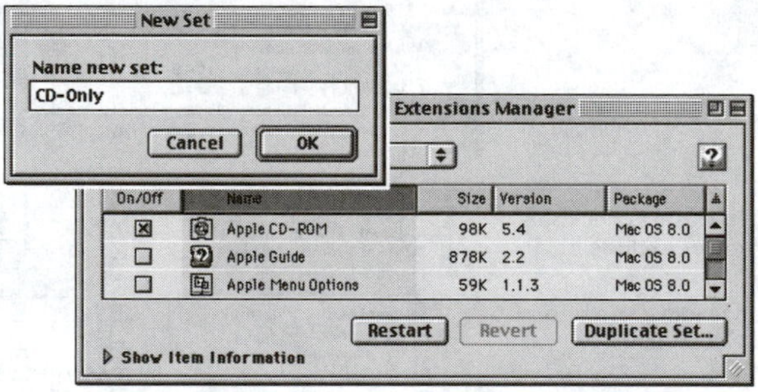

Use the Extensions Manager to create a CD-Only set for software installations.

The all-extension restart. Here's the problem: you're working with your CD-Only extension set while you're installing some new software. When you're finished with the installation, the installer restarts the Mac—with your CD-Only extension set still active. So you have to restart it *again* after using the Extensions Manager to reset your full set of extensions.

Sometimes you can get out of this because some installers let you just quit the installer and return to the desktop; this gives you a chance to re-set your extensions before restarting the Mac. But here's a sure thing: when you've first restarted with the CD-Only set, *before* running the installer, use the Extensions Manager to select your full extension set. Then, if the installer automatically restarts the Mac for you, the full set of extensions will load.

And here's an almost-sure thing, in case you forget to set up the sure thing: when the Mac restarts, hold down Spacebar. If you get it down early enough (and hold it down long enough), the Extensions Manager window opens, and you can select your full extension set and click the Restart button.

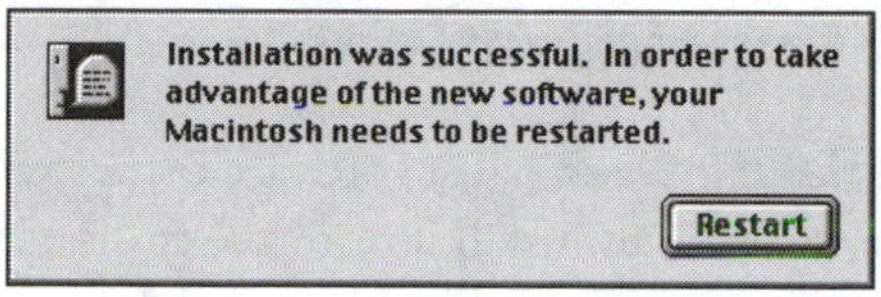

Some installers force you to restart as soon as the installation is finished.

Partial installs. When you're dealing with large (one might say *cumbersome)* programs, you might not install everything the first time around if you use a custom install option; you might, for instance, decide to forgo the tutorial and its files to save space on your drive. But what if you wish later that you had installed the tutorials—and they're not in a format that you can just drag to your hard drive because they have to be "processed" by the installer? And, the original installation took an hour or more and you *really* don't want to go through all that again?

Relax. If you did a custom install before, you can do it again. But this time you can customize it to install *only* those tutorials (or dictionaries, or whatever) instead of everything but.

Uninstallation. If you're finished with an application—you can't use it with your new system software, perhaps, or you have a replacement program—just erasing the application isn't the best approach, unless it's a very small, uncomplicated program. All those support files scattered around your drive, in the application folder and in the System Folder and its subfolders, need to be erased, too.

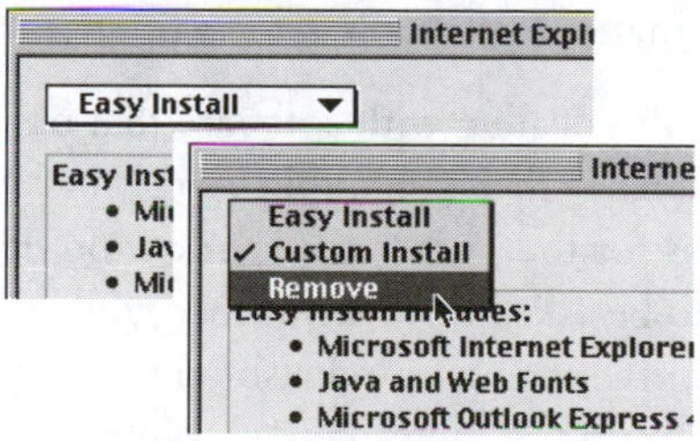

Use the program's installer to remove it and its support files.

If the program used an installer, see if it has uninstall option that will erase all the support files for you. (Sometimes, in an upgrade to a new version of the same program, the installer takes care of this for you.) In the standard installer, the same pop-up menu that provides the Easy/Custom option usually has a Remove command in it.

The desktop rebuild. If you've just installed an updated version of a piece of software, you should rebuild the desktop after the installation: restart the Mac while holding down ⌘ Option, and click OK when you get a dialog asking if you want the desktop rebuilt. This updates the information in the invisible desktop file that keeps track of which documents belong to which application. Without a rebuild, you may find problems when you try to launch a program by double-clicking on a document icon; for instance, the older version of the software, if it's still on your drive, may launch instead of the newer version.

Other Install Considerations

Name, no rank, serial number. Most software comes with a serial number that you have to type in either to install it or to use it the first time. The number might be on the package, on a card inside the package, or affixed to the manual. Here's what you should know about serial numbers:

- Serial numbers prove you're a legitimate user of the product (presumably, since of course you can install someone else's copy and use their number, too). For some products, presenting a valid serial number is the only way you can get tech support or an upgrade.
- Some programs need the serial number or you can't install or run the program at all; others ask for it at installation or the initial run only for your later convenience.
- Some programs need a specific serial number for each copy of the program; others look for only a pattern of numbers, letters, and spaces, but which serial number is used with which copy of the program is not important.
- Once the number's been entered, you can usually access it in the program itself, most often through the About command under the Apple menu.

Keep track of the serial number. Sooner or later you'll have to reinstall your software or something will happen (like its preferences file's being corrupted and erased) that makes the software think it's just been installed. Either way, you'll need that serial number. And you won't be able to access it through the program's About command if you can't get the program to run.

Here's what I do anytime I'm dealing with software that has a serial number. First, I write the number on the disk (a Sharpie works fine even on CDs); if there's a set of floppy disks for the installation, write it on the *second* disk of the set because you're likely to be asked for the number while the first one's inserted. Then I write it in the manual. And also on the box. Oh, and in a little desk accessory, too—you could use the Note Pad. No matter how disorganized you get, you should be able to find the serial number when you need it.

Entering the serial number. Programs coded with serial numbers ask you to enter the number either during installation or when you first run the program. If the Installer or the application itself doesn't want to accept the serial number, keep these guidelines in mind:

- Double check that you haven't substituted zeroes for capital O's, and vice versa.
- Follow uppercase and lowercase conventions exactly; make sure that Caps Lock isn't down, since that will change lowercase letters to capitals.
- Type in all spaces and hyphens. Make sure no handy-dandy extension you use to help you type things like em dashes (long dashes) is substituting characters when you try to type the hyphen.
- Sometimes it's not the serial number at fault. If the program is asking for your name, company, and the number, it might not accept incomplete information—try putting in a company name even if you aren't with a company. (I have a lot of software stamped with "me" as the company name.) You can try typing just a space if you don't want a company name to show.
- If your serial number starts with "No." or "#" you shouldn't include it in what you're typing. Usually. I did have a stupid package once that wanted the pound sign typed in with the number.

Mark update disks. It's not unusual to have three or four—or more—floppies or CDs for the same piece of software as updates come out. And their labels seldom have the actual version number (4.03.87v10, or whatever) on them. But *you* can put the version number and/or the date you received the disk on the label. It saves a lot of disk-swapping when you need to figure out which disk has the most recent version of the disk on it.

Installing from disk images. When a program comes on multiple floppies, installation and re-installation can be a pain. And floppies, while sturdy, are not the most stable of media available for your use. But you can, in effect, store the disks—in fact, the install disks for many different programs—on a single Zip cartridge or other removable medium.

Use the Disk Copy utility that comes with your system software (it's described in Chapter 4) to make *disk images*, and store them on a Zip disk. When you need to reinstall the program, mount the images and run the installation from the images. Not only do you cut down on the floppies you have to store within easy reach (although you should keep the originals *someplace)*, the installation process will go faster from the images: you won't have to swap disks, and the information will be fed in from something that's faster than a floppy. (For full speed, you can drag the image files to your hard drive instead of mounting them from the removable media.)

An important caveat: *most* floppy-disk installs can work from disk images, even when they're copy-protected in some way. But you should do a test run before counting on the image files to the extent that you lose the floppies!

Spring cleaning—maybe next year. For a utility that purports to provide some very needed support for Mac users, **Spring Cleaning** ($50, Aladdin) is quite a disappointment. Its main purpose is to uninstall an old application and its support files. Sounds great, doesn't it? But the design is clunky, the approach is slow, and it doesn't seem to understand the difference between versions of the same program.

I wanted, for instance, to simply uninstall another of Aladdin's products—StuffIt 4.0, since I had already installed the 4.5 version separately. But you can't tell Spring Cleaning to find a specific program; every time you run it, it reads through your entire hard drive to compile a list of information. Then, I accidentally clicked on the wrong program in the list and couldn't get Spring Cleaning to forget that one so I could choose something else—I had to quit and restart the program. Finally, when it showed me the list of files it considered related to StuffIt 4.0, it also included the newest ones from the 4.5 version—and every stuffed file on my drive (which means that if you're uninstalling an old PageMaker version, all your PageMaker documents will come up in the list). Every time you want to do something, it seems that another dialog box pops up asking if you want to do it—right after you *said* you wanted to.

Spring Cleaning is so slow, and the interface is so uncomfortable, you're better off using the Finder's Find command, and Apple's System Profiler, to round up information about what's on your disk, and then manually removing the old stuff.

Keeping track of extensions, etc. If you've read about installing system software in Chapter 8, you might recall that I suggested you "stamp" all the extensions and control panels with a label immediately after installation so you can always tell the Apple pieces.

Here's a variation: mark all your extensions and control panels (and maybe even fonts) just before you install any new software so you can easily see what the new product adds. If you want to coordinate this idea with keeping the Apple items marked separately, here's how you do it inside each folder you want to mark:

1. Add the label column to a list view with the View Options command.
2. Sort according to Label to separate the previously "stamped" Apple items from the others.
3. Optional: Use the Finder's Preferences command to rename one of the standard labels to something temporarily useful, like *Already in here*.
4. Select everything that's *not* labeled and apply the new label to it.

Everything in the folders will be labeled as either Apple items or "already" items, so anything without a label after your program installation is new. Once you're familiar with what's been installed, you can remove the *Already* label from the non-Apple things, or apply it to the new arrivals.

It's too bad we're limited to only seven different labels; with more, we'd be able to stamp everything according to the package it came with. You might consider, though, setting aside a label or two for companies or products that really fatten up your System Folder's subfolders, like Microsoft or Photoshop.

Making the Most of Your Software

Register now! You'll see that plastered on your software instruction manual—and it's advice you should follow. As a registered user, you may be eligible for several perks:

- Notice of upgrades, bug fixes, and so on.
- Special deals on upgrades, and/or other products from the company
- Free or trial subscriptions to a newsletter about the product.
- Free telephone support—sometimes for a limited period of time.

Most major software packages and utilities offer online registration, so you don't even have to fill out that little card and mail it in. But if you *do* fill out the little card—make a copy of it to keep, just in case.

Learn your software. Different people have different learning styles; some learn best by doing things, some can glean everything they need from a book, and others do much better with a teacher—even one on videotape. In reality, however, most users buy their software and learn it on their own no matter what their "best" style of learning is, and only turn to others when there's a problem. Here's what you can do to get the most out of your software:

1. Use the tutorial provided in the manual, following it step-by-step on your computer.
2. Read the manual. Give it a full read-through right away even though many of the features or procedures may not be entirely clear to you until you've used them. Even if you don't remember how to do a specific procedure, you'll remember that it's possible, and you can look up the details.
3. Use the program. *Really* use it, for real projects. Or on a made-up but realistic project.
4. Explore the program: look at, and use, each command in every menu and submenu—especially if you don't know what it does!
5. Read magazine articles that describe how to use the program's more advanced features, or subscribe to a newsletter devoted to it, or get together with other people who use the program. (Or all three.)
6. After you've used the program for two or three months, or even a few weeks of intensive work, go back and read the entire manual again. You'll understand all the references to the program's features, and you'll pick up all the little details this time around.

RTFM. This is a well-known acronym in the computer world; it stands for *Read the manual.* Right, I left out a word, but you can fill in the blank.

It's not just a gentle, well-intentioned piece of advice. It's a knee-jerk reaction to someone who asks how to do something that's plainly spelled out in the program's basic instructions. (I fondly recall one user group member who called my husband at his office to ask for help and said, "I know it's probably in the manual, but I don't have time to read it." My husband's reply is unprintable.)

apple.com/usergroups

User Groups. I've mentioned "user group" several times in this chapter, and in other spots throughout this book, too. What's a user group? Simply a group of Mac owners who get together to share information and learn more about the Mac and its applications. If you don't know about one near you, check out Apple's special "help line": the User Group Locator at its web site.

Applications

Launching Applications

Three, two, one... The basic way to open, or "launch" an application has remained the same since the dawn of Macintosh: you double-click on its icon. Then there are the basic variations: select an icon and use the File menu's Open command or press ⌘O. Then there's the alias approach, which lets you do anything to the alias that would normally open the original icon. And there's the Apple menu… and starting with a document… oh, and the Startup Items folder…. You get the idea: there are plenty of ways to open an application, with some more favored than others depending on the user and even on the situation. Here's a quick round-up of the basic ways to get an application going:

- **From a desktop icon**: double-click or select and use an Open command.
- **From the Apple menu** or a submenu that you set up: select it to open it.
- **From the Recent Applications** submenu in the Apple menu: select it to open it.
- **Automatically** at startup: put the application or its alias in the Startup Items folder.
- **With an alias**: Open the alias in any of the ways you'd open the original.
- **From the Launcher**: a single click on a Launcher button opens the program.
- **Through a document:** open a document in any of many ways (double-clicking on it, for example), and its parent application opens.

Add-on launch methods. Most contextual menu add-ons (covered in Chapter 6) provide the handy capability of launching an application from a pop-up submenu; FinderPop, PowerMenu, and CMTools all let you create a launching submenu that launches a program or lets you move to it when you select it from the menu. I've always used a macro editor (it's QuicKeys now) to let me launch my most-used applications simply by pressing one of the function keys at the top of the keyboard. I like this better than the pop-up approach because I don't have to reach for the mouse, and because I don't have to be in the Finder to use it.

Clean up after yourself. If you're launching an application from the Finder, hold down Option while double-clicking on the icon to close the window that it's in.

Macros and macro editors

Chapter 10

Launch multiple applications. You can launch more than one application at a time if you can get at their icons at the same time. If you always run, say, Photoshop and PageMill together when you're working on a web-page design, you can keep their aliases together on the desktop or in a pop-up window for easy access; select them both and use then the Open command.

If you have multiple icons selected, double-clicking on one will open all of them.

Canceling the launch. In the old, slow days, you could cancel a program launch by pressing ⌘. right after the launching process started. I haven't been able to do this in years, though I'm told it's still a function in the system software. I don't think I've slowed down all that much (at least when it comes to keyboarding), but I sure am using faster Macs. So the question is: does the feature still exist if nobody can use it?

The Launcher

Basic use. The Launcher control panel lets you launch an application, and open a folder or document, by clicking on a button. That doesn't sound like much of an improvement over double-clicking on one of those items, but you can have a Launcher button for an item that's otherwise buried several folders deep. And while that doesn't sound like much now that any window can be set to buttons instead of standard icons, the Launcher does have several options that make using it more convenient than setting up your own launching window.

To open the Launcher window, open the Launcher control panel, either from the Control Panels folder inside the System Folder, or from the Apple menu's Control Panel submenu. To create a button, all you have to do is drag an icon into the Launcher window; the icon itself actually stays in its original location, and a button for it appears in the Launcher.

When you drag something to the Launcher window, an alias for the item is created and placed in the Launcher Items folder inside the System Folder. You can change the buttons in the Launcher window by manipulating the contents of the folder: place aliases in it, or take them out, and the next time you activate the Launcher window, its buttons will update to reflect the changes.

The Launcher works for more than just launching applications: it works for opening anything that can be aliased (which is anything on your desktop). You might want buttons (in different folders) for things like: disks and the trash; the System Folder and its most-used subfolders; folders of documents that you use for current projects; documents (like a calendar or To-do list) that you use often.

You can horizontally scroll the buttons in the Launcher window if they're not all displayed at once, but it's more convenient to resize the window so you can see all the buttons at the same time.

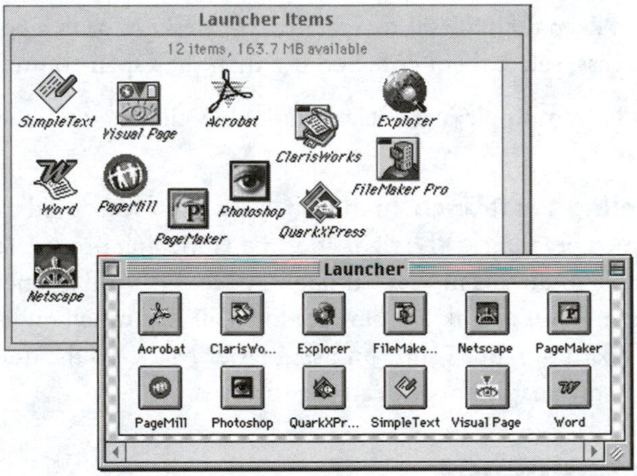

The buttons in the Launcher window are based on the aliases in the Launcher Items folder.

Launch the Launcher at startup. To have the Launcher window open automatically at every startup, open the General Controls control panel and check the *Open Launcher at system startup* option. The Mac puts an alias of the Launcher control panel in the Startup Items folder when you check this option.

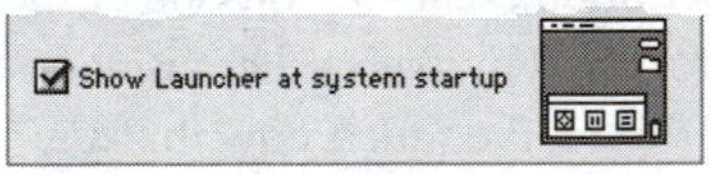

Renaming buttons. Buttons in the Launcher default to the same names as their original items, and they're organized alphabetically. To rearrange the order of buttons, change the names of the aliases in the Launcher Items folder; as with arranging items in Finder windows and the Apple menu, using a space or other special leading character bumps names to the top of the list.

But you'll also want to rename the aliases for another reason: shorten them so you can see the whole name, since there's limited space under the small button sizes; you don't really need anything named *Adobe® PageMaker 6.5* when *PageMaker* or even *PMaker* can identify it.

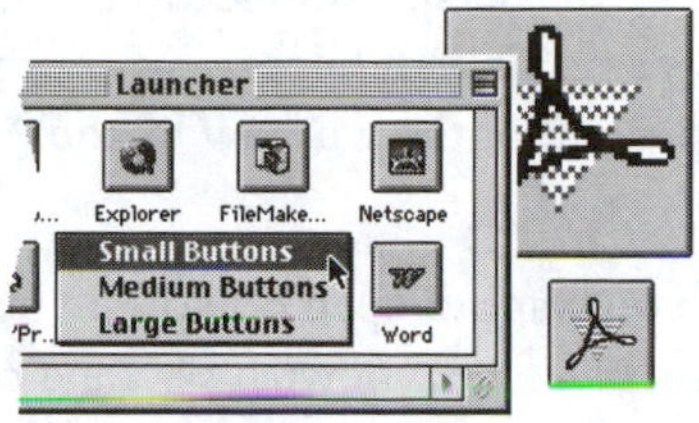

The Launcher window displays small buttons; the large and medium buttons are at the right.

Change the button sizes. You have three choices for Launcher button sizes, cleverly categorized as Small, Medium, and Large. To change the button sizes, hold ⌘ and press the mouse button, then select the size from the pop-up menu.

Removing buttons. To remove a button, hold down Option and drag the button out of the window, directly into the trash. If you let go of the button someplace other than the trash, it stays in the window; in fact, even a trash alias isn't good enough—it has to be the honest-to-goodness original trash can. The strange cursor (with the plus sign on it) that you see as you Option-drag is simply the one that normally indicates that an Option-drag makes a copy of a file in another location.

You can also open the Launcher Items folder and drag an alias out of it to remove its button from the Launcher window; the window is updated the next time it's the active window.

Launcher layers. Make subsets of your Launcher items by creating folders inside the Launcher Items folder, giving each a name that begins with the bullet character (•) on Option 8. Each of the folder names (minus the bullet) appears at the top of the Launcher window as a button; click on a button and the window displays the contents of the folder. Each button gets its own color for its window background.

If you leave any items loose in the main Launcher Items window, they'll appear as a group under a default Applications button, even though you haven't made an •Applications folder—and even if they aren't applications!

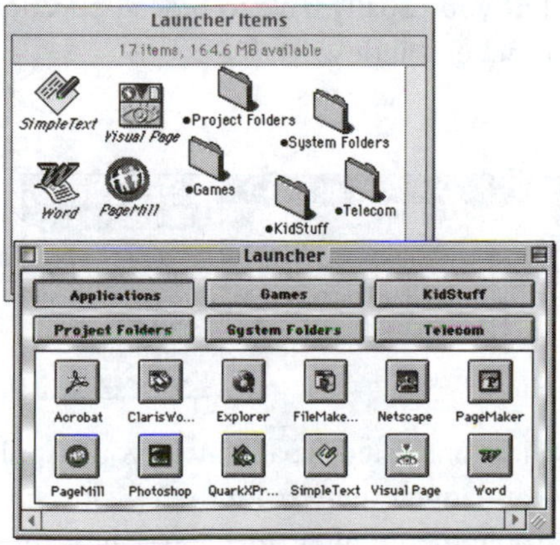

Bulleted folders appear as buttons at the top of the Launcher. A default Applications button appears for the loose items in the main level of the Launcher Items folder.

Eight is enough. There's a limit of eight buttons for the Launcher window; if you create folders beyond that limit, they'll appear as buttons on the main level of the Launcher window—the default Applications button used for loose items in the window. (And, as a result, you'll lose *another* of your folder/buttons, because it will be bumped out of the window by the Applications button.)

Getting to the folders. If you want to open one of the bulleted inner folders in the Launcher Items Folder, hold down Option and click on the folder's button in the Launcher window (the cursor changes to a folder cursor when you're hovering in the right spot). This is especially convenient when you want to get into the folder to simply rename some of the buttons you're looking at.

The folder cursor appears over a button when you hold down Option.

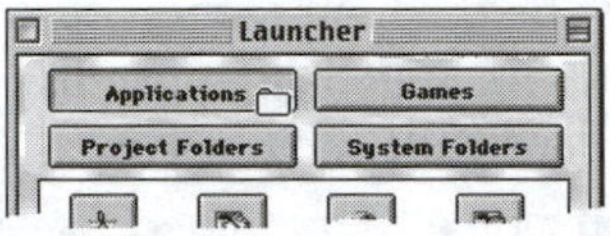

Getting to the Launcher Items folder. If you combine the information in the last few tips, you can make a shortcut for opening the Launcher Items folder itself. Instead of creating an *•Applications* subfolder for a button, leave the applications loose in the main folder; this automatically creates an Application button. Then, by Option-clicking on the button, you'll open its folder—the Launcher Items folder.

Who ya gonna call? Hold down ⌘ Option and click anywhere in the empty background area surrounding the folder buttons (or around the outer edge of the main button area if you have no folder buttons set up) to see a screen of credits.

Launcher in the Apple menu. The Launcher is handy when you're on the desktop, but it's not so convenient when you're in an application and want to launch another one to run at the same time. Not only do you have to move back to the desktop, but you usually have to hide application and Finder windows to get to the Launcher window.

Using the Launcher Items folder from the Apple menu.

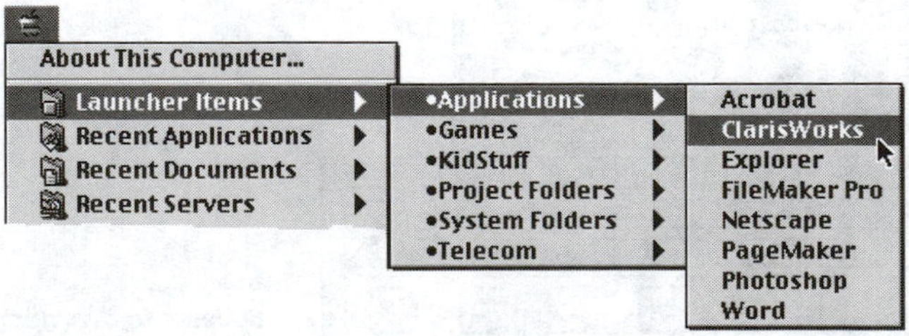

If you don't have applications listed separately in your Apple menu or one of its submenus so you can launch them from there, you can just put your Launcher list in the Apple menu: place an alias of the Launcher Items folder in the Apple Menu Items folder. You'll get a submenu of the items in the Launcher Items folder; if you have inner folders, they'll have submenus, too, and you can select from them.

Bringing the Launcher back. I always set up beginners' machines with the Launcher window in the lower left corner of the screen. But when it's closed accidentally, the user is confused—it's not so easy to explain (over the phone, usually) how to go through an Apple menu submenu or through the System Folder to get to the Launcher control panel to open the window again.

The solution for beginners is handy for everyone: I make an alias of the Launcher control panel, and hide it behind the Launcher window. If the window is closed, the alias is right there so you can double-click on it to open the window again. (I even name the alias *Bring back Launcher.)*

Drag and drop works. It doesn't feel as though it would work, but you can drag an item and drop it onto a Launcher button the same way you'd drop it on a standard icon; if the button item can open the dragged icon, you'll launch the application and open the document. If your button is a folder, you can drop something into the folder the same way.

Make a launch pad. For opening applications and documents you use often, the Launcher window is a handy approach since it lets you group things and launch items with a single click. But, since it's not a Finder window, you can't turn it into a window tab at the bottom of the screen. You can, however, create your own launcher window from a standard Finder window:

1. Create a new folder on the desktop, and name it *Launcher* or *Launch Pad.*
2. Open the folder and set the window to a small button view.
3. Create aliases for the items you want to launch by ⌘ Option-dragging them into the launching window. (This creates the alias, drops the *alias* suffix, and leaves the original icon in its original spot.)
4. Turn the window into a tab by dragging it to the bottom of the screen or by using the As Pop-up Window command from the View window.

When you want to launch something, click the window tab, then click the button; if you Option-click on the button, the window will pop back down automatically as the program launches.

This approach has several advantages over the standard Launcher window besides the neat little tab: you can arrange the buttons in any order, and you can size the window to any proportions.

If you want the launch window to open automatically when you start your Mac, you could try to remember to leave it open each time you shut down. Or, you could put your launching folder (the original or an alias) in the Startup Items folder so it opens at each startup.

Duplicate Launcher aliases. When you're working with the Extensions Manager control panel, adjusting the items that will be on or off, you'll eventually run into notices that there are duplicates of "Launcher," and you'll be asked which you want to keep.

Here's what's happening: the Extensions Manager keeps track of not only the Extension and Control Panel folders, but also the Startup Items folder. If you use the General Controls control panel to set the Launcher window to be displayed at startup, an alias of the Launcher control panel is placed in the Startup Items folder. When you use Extensions Manager to turn off all extensions and startup items, the Launcher alias is moved into a Startup Items (Disabled) folder.

On the next startup that includes the General Controls control panel, it not only opens the Launcher window, it also puts a new alias into the Startup Items folder. The *next* time Extensions Manager turns off all your startup items, it tries to move the new alias into the Disabled folder—but there's one already in there. So, it asks you if you want to delete one of the aliases; you delete one, but you're left with the other inside the Disabled folder. Guess what? On the next startup, you get a new alias, and the next time you turn off the startup items, you go through the whole rigmarole again.

There's no way around this if you use the Launcher at Startup setting and also mess around with turning extensions on and off. But it's reassuring to know what's going on and that you can just delete either of the Launcher aliases when you're asked.

Handling Multiple Applications

Juggling multiple applications. You can run more than one application at a time; if you have enough memory, you can run more than a dozen at a time if you want. (Chapter 13 covers memory allocations.) But only one application is the *active* application at any one time: its windows are on top of all the others, and its menus are on the menubar. If all its windows are closed, you can usually tell which application you're in by the menu titles. If that doesn't do it for you, check the icon at the far right of the menubar: it belongs to the current application. And if *that* doesn't help, click on that icon, because it opens the Application menu, where the current application is listed with a checkmark.

Juggling multiple open applications involves two basic working issues: moving from one application to another, and handling the multiple-window clutter that results from having so many things open at once. Luckily, the Application menu can help with both, since it not only lists opened applications but also provides window-hiding commands.

Moving to an opened application. Switch to an open application by:

- Choosing it from the Application menu.
- Clicking in any exposed part of one of its windows. Sometimes the window you clicked in will become the active window in that application; sometimes, depending on the application, whatever window you were working in last is the one that's activated no matter which one you clicked on to get there.
- Using any of the methods that would normally launch it, such as selecting it from the Apple menu or double-clicking one of its document icons. You can even double-click on the application's icon in the Finder, even though the icon is dark because it's already open.

More ways to move. Some of the most convenient ways of moving from one opened application to another aren't built into the system at all, but come from add-on utilities. Any procedure that normally launches an application (covered a little earlier in the chapter) will also move you into the already opened program, although some utilities work only from the Finder.

- Contextual menu add-ons like **FinderPop**, **PowerMenu**, and **CMTools** that let you launch programs also let you move into them. Their usefulness is limited, however, because their menus are available only from the Finder.
- The contextual menu available from the Finder's About box contains an Open command; point to the icon of a listed program and you can use the Open command. This, of course, is limited to those rare times you're actually looking at the About box.
- **Window Monkey** (covered in detail a little further on), since it provides a menu of all opened windows in all applications, also always has a list of open applications in it. One of its options is to place the menu with the application's menus rather than at the right end of the menubar; since I have a 20-inch screen, this puts it in the middle of the menubar—a much shorter trip than to the far right end, in most cases.
- If you've created a launch macro with something like **QuicKeys** or **KeyQuencer**, you can use it to send you right to the opened program.

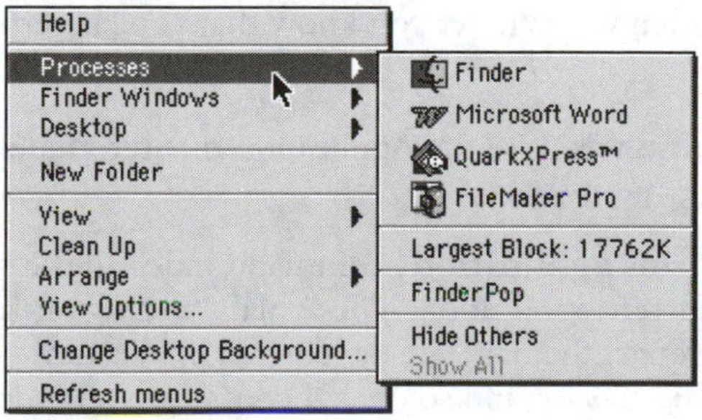

FinderPop's Processes menu has a techie name, but handily lists all currently running applications so you can move directly to the one you want.

The Application menu. The Application menu at the far right of the menubar lists all open applications (and desk accessories). Its "title" is a miniature icon of the application you're in (for the Finder, you get a mini OS logo); every item in the menu gets a mini-icon, too. If you're running only a single application, all you'll see in the list is that application and the Finder.

The way an item is displayed or marked in the menu tells you its status:

- The active application is checked.
- An application whose icon is normal has all its windows showing—they haven't been hidden to stay out of the way. Even if they're totally obscured by other windows, they're there and you'll see them if you move the windows that are in the way.
- An application with a dimmed icon is open, but its windows are currently hidden from view because one of the Application menu's hiding options was used.
- An application marked with a diamond is asking for attention (see the next entry).

To move to an application, select it from the menu; you can select it even if its icon is dimmed.

The Application menu: Word is the active application (it's checked, and its icon is the current menu "title"); ClarisWorks windows are hidden (its icon is dimmed); the Finder is clamoring for attention (it's marked with a diamond).

The attention getter. When an item in the Application menu is marked with a diamond, that means it's asking for attention. Something else usually gets your attention first: a blinking Application menu icon with or without an alert sound. This happens most often with the Finder and the Print Monitor. The Finder may be waiting to tell you that a background application has quit; Print Monitor often wants to let you know that your LaserWriter has run out of paper.

The Hide commands. Use the Application menu to hide and show windows for running applications:

- The **Hide [this application]** command hides all the windows belonging to the current application. The actual wording of the command changes to reflect the name of the current application—*Hide Word, Hide Photoshop, Hide Finder*, and so on. Of course, if you hide the application's windows, you can't do any more work in it. So, choosing the Hide command also moves you to another application—the last one you were using before you moved to the current one. This command is dimmed if all the other applications are already hidden.

- The **Hide Others** command hides everything *except* the current application.
- The **Show All** command displays all the windows for all running applications.

Hiding a window is different from *closing* it. When you close a window in an application, you have to save its contents or lose them; hiding a window means it's just temporarily out of sight. (Floating windows and palettes are always hidden for background application even when you leave their regular windows showing.)

Automatic window hiding. Hold down Option as you move from one application to another (by selecting from the Application menu or by clicking in an exposed background window), and windows belonging to the application you're leaving are all hidden.

The hidden Finder. When you "hide" the Finder, there's no dropcloth effect behind the current application—the Finder windows disappear, but you can still see desktop itself and any icons that are out on it.

If you want icons to disappear, too, uncheck the *Show Desktop when in background* option in the General Controls control panel. This will hide the Finder—its windows and its icons—whenever you're in another application. You'll still see the desktop pattern or background picture in the background, but clicking on it won't move you into the Finder.

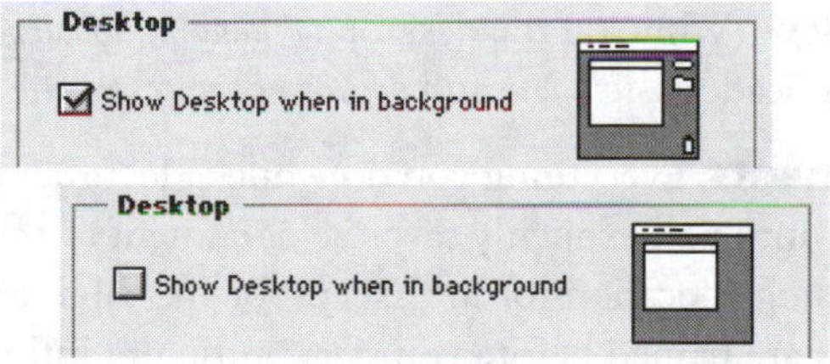

Unchecking the Show Desktop option in the General Controls control panel hides not only its windows but also its icons, as you can see by the sample desktop in the control panel.

Moving to the Finder. You can move to the Finder by clicking on any part of the desktop you can see: you don't have click on a Finder window or icon, as was the case before System 7. If you Option-click on the desktop to move the Finder, you'll hide the windows of the application you're moving from.

Window Monkey

Monkeying around. When I first tried out the shareware **Window Monkey**, ($20 shareware) I thought that its main purpose was to colorize the dreary gray OS 8 Finder windows. But, in fact, it's much more useful than that: Window Monkey keeps a menu of open windows and recent folders in the menubar no matter where you're working. The top section lists the open windows in the current application. The middle section—the handiest part—

tigertech.com

lists all the other open applications (including the Finder) and the windows that are open in them: select a window from the submenu, and you're moved right to that window in the application. It's much handier than simply moving to the application and then having to activate a window other than the one that the application activates for you. But wait, there's more! There's also a list of recently used folders so you can move to one easily without clicking your way through things on the desktop. *And*, the menu stays active when there's an Open or Save dialog on the screen (except in a few uncooperative applications, like Microsoft Word), so you can jump to the folder of your choice without having to navigate through the dialog's menus.

Documents

Handling Documents

Creating a document. A *document* is the file you create with an application. Most applications start you off with an empty window—a blank document. Some require you to specify that you want to create a new document; almost all applications provide a New command in the File menu to make a new document. In some cases, you have to provide information before you even start on the document: in a database, for instance, you usually have to name the document before you get to do anything with it, while many graphics programs will ask you what size you want the document to be before they can give you a new window. (While on the desktop *window* and *folder* are practically synonymous, in applications, *window* and *document* are often the same thing.)

Saving documents. Everything you do while a document is open is merely stored in RAM until you explicitly save the document to the disk, giving it a name and choosing a location for it. (Except for special documents like database files, which are named before you start putting in information, and are saved automatically at intervals.) The application's Save command opens a dialog box—cleverly referred to as the Save box—that lets you name the document and choose a location. There are some limitations as to what you can name a document; not surprisingly, they're the same limitations as described in Chapter 6 for desktop icon names:

- The name can't be longer than 31 characters.
- You can't use a colon in a file name.
- Two files in the same folder can't have the same name.
- There's no difference between capitals and lowercase in file names, so *Memo, memo,* and *MEMO* are all considered the same and can't coexist in the same folder.

Save versus Save As. When you first save a document, the Save and Save As commands work identically. Once a document's been named and saved, however, the commands work differently.

For an existing document, the Save command saves the changes you've made since you last saved it. You don't get a dialog: the file is saved under the same name and in the same folder as the last time—with the edited version replacing the earlier version. With Save As, you get the standard Save dialog so you can save a *copy* of the edited document in a different location and/or under a different name. Remember that when you do this, the original has none of the edits saved in it—only the Save As version contains the changes.

Some programs, written by programming purists, dim the Save command until you've saved the document initially; and other purists insist (and rightly so) that the dialog is a *Save As* dialog, not a Save dialog, since you don't ever see a dialog on a regular Save operation.

When to save. You should save the same way the old joke says you should vote: early and often. If the computer crashes before you've saved your document, or before you've saved the changes you've made, you'll have to do it all over again. (Experts everywhere agree that neglecting to save a document at frequent intervals somehow increases the chances of your computer's crashing—something to do with cosmic balance.)

Some applications let you set an auto-save interval; every ten minutes, say, your work is saved to the disk without your having to do anything. If you need reminders for saving documents, try any or all of these:

- Before printing.
- Before switching to another program that's running.
- Before making a major change that can't be undone.
- Before pasting a large item from the Clipboard.
- Before making a global change in the document (with a Search and Replace operation, or by changing a master page definition).
- Before opening a control panel or desk accessory.
- Before doing anything that has made your computer crash recently.
- Before putting the system to sleep.
- Before walking away from the computer.
- Any time the phone rings.

Opening documents. The basic ways to open a document are:

- Use the application's Open command.
- Double-click on the document icon on the desktop.
- Drag the document icon onto the application icon.

But there are at least a dozen other ways to open a document, most of which mirror the ways you can open an application. You can, for instance, put an alias of a document on the desktop, in a window, in the Launcher, or in a menu; and, if you're using the Apple Menu Options control panel, recently used documents appear in the Apple menu's Recent Documents submenu.

Apple Menu Options
Chapter 9

When you open a document, it still exists on the disk: a *copy* of it is placed into memory and the original file isn't altered until you use a Save command. (Except for special cases, like most databases, where changes are immediately written to the disk.)

The "Application not found" dialog. A Mac document keeps embedded in its information the name of its parent—the creator code of the application that created it. When you double-click on a document, the Finder checks the creator code and opens the correct application.

If the application isn't available, you'll get a dialog that says "The application that created this document can't be found." Depending on which system components you have installed, the dialog may be a dead end or it may suggest an application in which you can try to open the document. The next section, *Document Interchange,* discusses the details.

The drag-launch. The drag method for opening a document in an application seems less convenient than the double-click method, but the advantage is that you can drag a document onto an application *other* than the one that created it. If the application knows how to interpret the information, it will open the document. So, you could drag a plain text document onto your word processor's icon, or onto a spreadsheet's icon, and have it open there instead of in SimpleText, where it would normally open.

SimpleText
Chapter 10

Handling multiple documents. When you have more than one document open in an application, basic window rules apply: only one window can be active at a time, and clicking in any window activates it.

Some applications provide a Window menu or submenu that lists the open documents and lets you move from one to another; some even provide keyboard commands for moving from one window to the next. Window Monkey, a shareware utility described earlier, provides a menu that lists, among other things, the currently open documents in the active application so you can easily move from one to another.

IN THE BEGINNING

In the Dark Ages of Macintosh, folders were merely a figment of the Finder's imagination. You'd create and use folders on the desktop, but once you were in an application and used an Open dialog, all the files on the disk were listed as if there were no folders at all.

This wasn't as bad as it sounds, since the only disks available were 400K floppies. By 1986, with the introduction of the Mac Plus and its 800K disks, "real" folders became a part of the Mac file structure.

Locked documents. You can lock any document to protect it from inadvertent changes by selecting its icon on the desktop, using the Get Info command, and checking the Locked box.

The Get Info command
Chapter 6

What happens when you open a locked document depends on both how you open it and which application you're using. When you double-click on a locked document on the desktop, you always get a dialog (shown here) that informs you the document is locked. If you open it from within an application, however, you may or may not get a similar dialog. Some applications, like Word just open the document with no further ado but append the document's name in the title bar with a parenthetical *(Read-Only).* Other programs may warn you when you open the document but give no further indication of the document's special status. Still others may not tell you anything when you open the document or give any interface feedback, but when you try to edit the document you'll get a dialog telling you it's not modifiable.

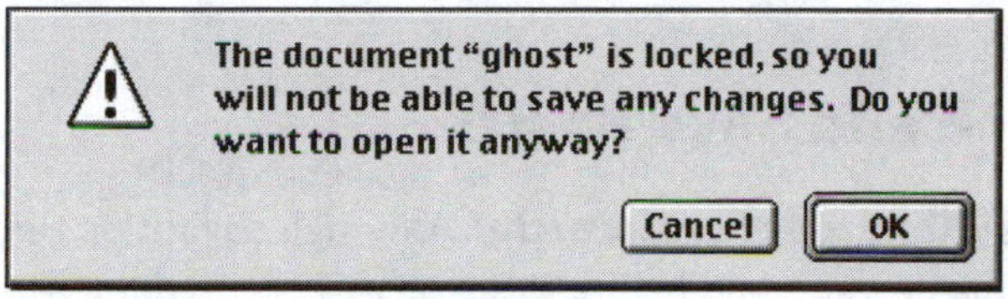

Stationery. The concept of *stationery* comes from the real-world practice of tearing a piece of paper from a pad of pre-printed stationery: each piece is blank except for the pre-printed items like a letterhead. Mac stationery is a document that you can use as a template for other documents. If you open a piece of stationery, you get an untitled document with the same formatting and contents as were in the original stationery document. You save the new document under any name you want, and the original stationery is left untouched to serve as a template for yet another document.

The Document and Stationery buttons in ClarisWorks' Save dialog.

But how do you get that original piece of stationery? In applications that support the stationery concept (they're few and far between), there are buttons in the Save dialog that let you save a document as a standard document or stationery. Stationery documents get their own special icons, usually a variation of the application's standard document icon that indicates multiple pages. Some programs offer stationery capability under a different name, like the templates provided by Quark, PageMaker, and Microsoft Word.

Forcing stationery. If you like the concept of stationery (which is actually a pretty good idea) but your favorite program doesn't provide the option, you can make your own: save a "form" document from your application, get Info on its icon on the desktop, and click the Stationery Pad box. The icon changes—both in the Info window and on the desktop—to a stationery document, and when you open the document, it opens as untitled in its parent application. Although the Stationery Pad checkbox was also available in System 7, the way applications handled such a document varied—sometimes you'd have to name the new document before you opened it, for instance. OS 8 has ironed out those wrinkles, so you'll always get a new, untitled document based on the stationery document.

Creating stationery on the desktop.

Open and Save Basics

The path through a hierarchy. Although navigating through Open and Save dialogs is second nature to anyone who's used the Mac for a long time, the less-than-intuitive interface has always boggled beginners. Even users who've had Macs for quite a while are sometimes flummoxed when presented with anything beyond what they're used to doing in Open and Save dialogs—perhaps always using a Documents folder, or always saving in the same folder as the application they're using. The problems are seldom connected with clicking buttons, or even switching disks; it's that folder hierarchy that gets to most people—especially when where you want to go is not just up or down through the current series of folders, but "across" to something else.

So, this section is a step-by-step tour of navigating folders in Open and Save dialogs. (The Open dialog is used as the example, but the Save dialog works the same way.)

First, take a look at a folder hierarchy on the desktop, in two different views (in the figures on the next page). There are two different ways of following the same "path" to the StuffIt Read Me file: through a series of open folder windows, and in a single-window hierarchical view. It's pretty easy to see the relationship between the two, and find the "target" Read Me file we're going to be working with.

Then, look at the illustration of the actual path that was taken from the top-level drive to the target document, ignoring other items (and possible paths) along the way.

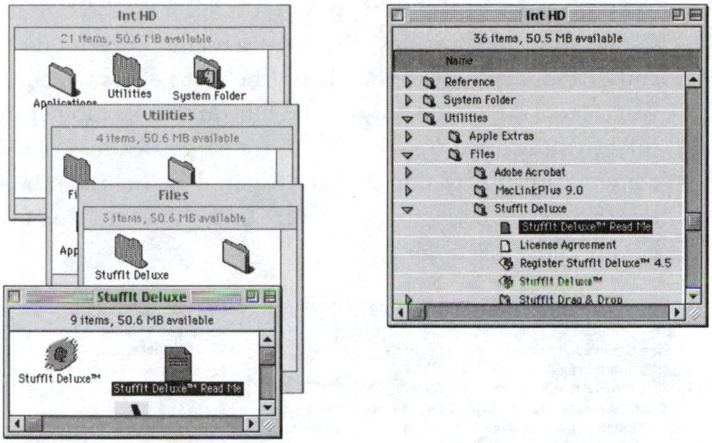

A Folder hierarchy, and a path to a file, in icon-view windows (left) and in a list view (right).

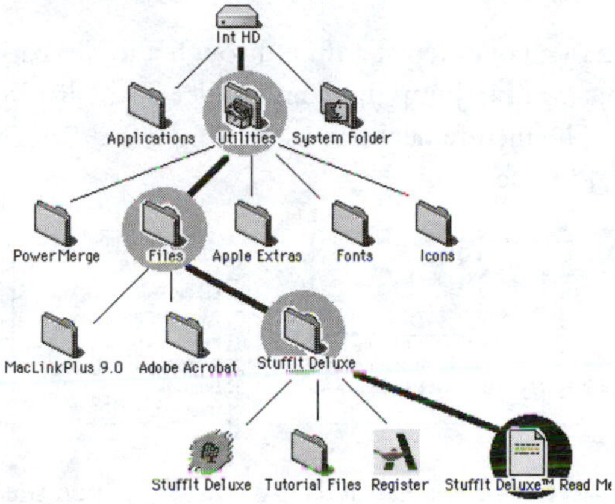

The path from the drive to the document.

Traveling down in the dialog. Inside an Open/Save dialog, you'll see a list of folders and files topped by a pop-up menu. The menu indicates which folder you're looking in, or it shows that you're looking at the main level of the disk or the desktop itself. Moving "down" through a series of folders is a simple matter of selecting a folder in a list and clicking the Open button. The folder you select appears in the pop-up menu and its contents are displayed in the list. The picture here shows the path from the hard disk to the ReadMe document illustrated in the last entry.

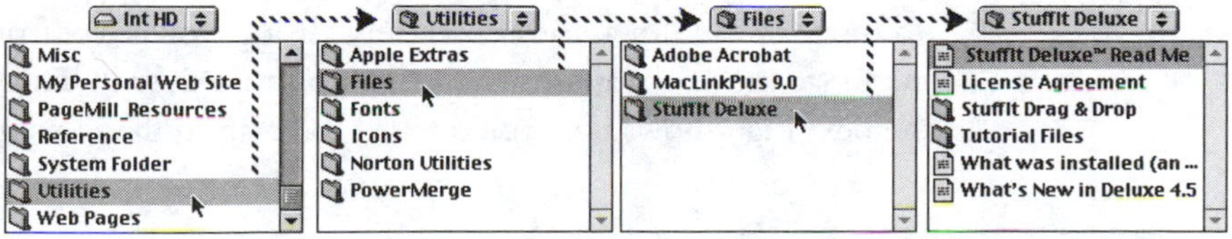

Traveling down through a series of folders.

Traveling up in the dialog. To move back up through the hierarchy of folders in a dialog, you use the pop-up menu. Press on the menu so it opens, and drag down to the second item (the first item is the current folder). When you release the mouse button, you'll be in the next folder up in the path; the folder you selected from the menu is now the "name" of the menu, and its contents are displayed in the list. (Right: drag *down* to move *up*—the Mac interface is not perfect.) The picture here shows moving from the original target up to the next folder.

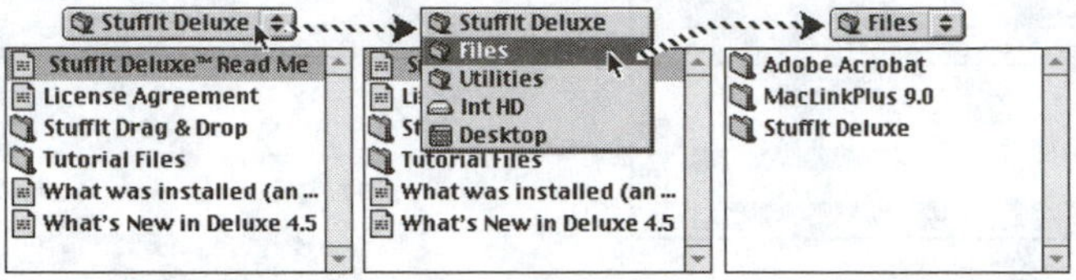

Moving up one folder in the hierarchy.

You don't have to go one step at a time through a folder path to get up towards the top. You can jump up to any folder in the list by selecting it in the pop-up menu. The picture here shows moving from the original target back to the disk level in one step.

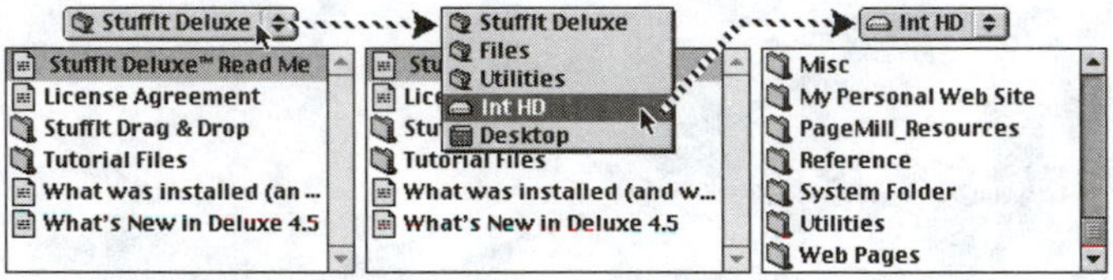

Skipping steps in the hierarchy.

The path less traveled. Okay, let's say you've opened the StuffIt Deluxe Read Me file that you've excavated from its nested folder, but now you want to read the MacLinkPlus ReadMe file while you're still in SimpleText, the program you used to read the first file. You close the first file and use the Open command to open the second one. But how do you get to it?

The illustration on the next page shows the original path (the thick dark lines) you took to the first file. You can see that you have to move back "up" a folder and down through another one (the gray lines) to get from where you are to where you want to be. Unfortunately, there's no way to move "across" in the hierarchy except by going up where you came from, and then back down a different path.

To move up, and then back down, in a dialog, you select from the pop-up menu (to move up) and from the list (to move down). The second picture on the next page shows how you'd travel the path in the previous illustration.

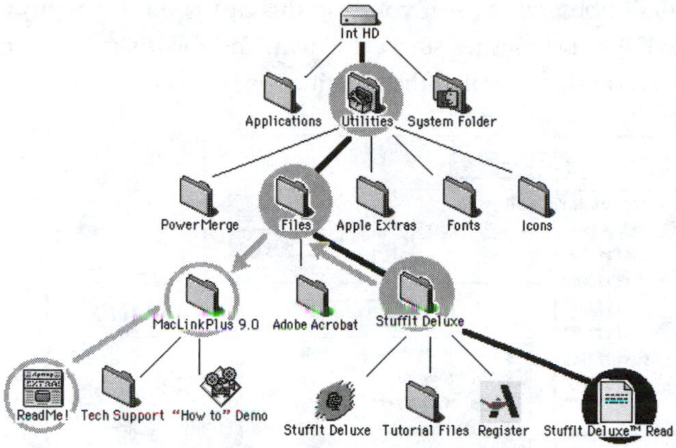

Moving "across" in the hierarchy involves moving back up, and then down again.

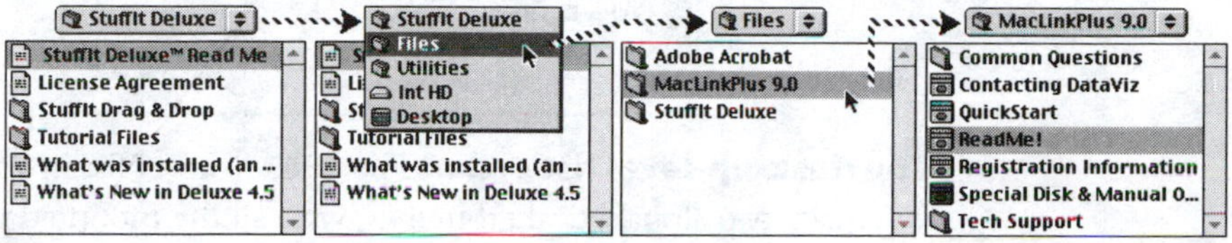

Move up by selecting from the pop-up menu, then back down by selecting from the list.

Dealing with the Desktop Level

The desktop level. Before System 7, the topmost level you could see in an Open/Save dialog was the system disk (usually the internal hard drive). Items scattered around on the desktop—loose files and folders—were included in the list of things on the main level of the drive. Now the topmost level is the more logical desktop level, which shows everything on the desktop: mounted disks, loose files and folders, and even the Trash (which is dimmed so you can't select it). There are several ways to jump to the desktop level in the dialog:

- Select *Desktop* from the pop-up menu
- Click the Desktop button
- Press ⌘D
- Press ⌘Shift

That last option doesn't seem to make much sense, but it's perfectly logical in the overall Mac interface: it's the same key combination that activates the desktop itself when you're in the Finder.

The shared desktop. Just as the Finder's desktop is shared by all mounted volumes in the Finder, so is the desktop-level list in an Open/Save dialog. If something was dragged out of a floppy disk onto the desktop, for instance, it's listed on the top level along with items that belong to your internal hard drive.

If you're observant (or if you read this tip) you'll know how to tell what disk a listed item belongs to: select the item, and the disk icon in the upper right of the dialog shows which disk the item is stored on.

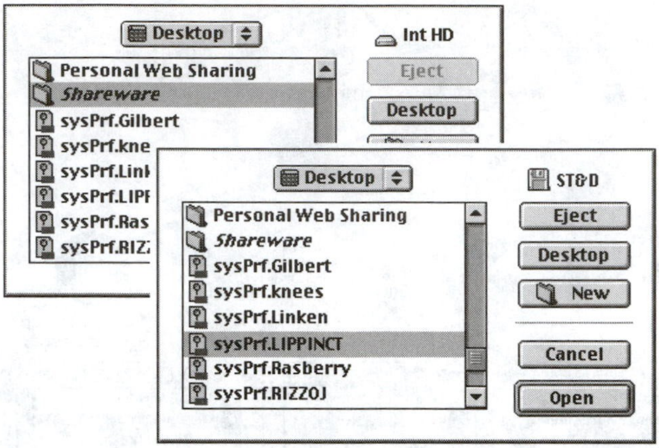

On the Desktop level, you can tell which disk an item is stored on by selecting it in the list and checking what disk icon is displayed in the upper right corner.

The desktop-level list order. The desktop-level list in an Open/Save dialog is actually two alphabetical groupings, with all the mounted volumes first and then the items that are out on the desktop (with the dimmed Trash can at the bottom). Selecting an item by typing its first letter or two is sometimes awkward because of the groups. If you're looking at the top of the list, as in the picture here, and type S expecting to select the *ST&D* disk, you won't get it—you'll have selected the folder *Shareware* instead. On the other hand, if you're somewhere in the middle of this list and type A to jump back to the top, expecting to get the first disk, you'll wind up at the *cardfonts* folder instead.

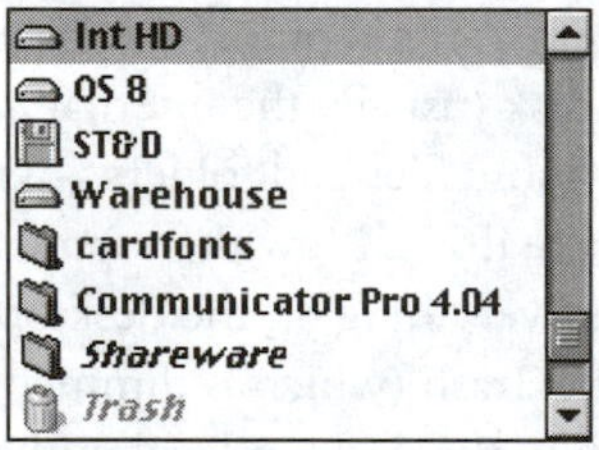

Saving a document to the desktop. When you want to save a document directly to the desktop so you can't forget about it, you move up to the desktop level before doing the save. But what disk is the file actually being saved on, since the desktop level is shared?

The disk whose icon is displayed in the dialog is the one where the document will actually be saved. Which brings me to another point:

Using any of the standard methods or shortcuts to get to the desktop level in the dialog (clicking the Desktop button, selecting Desktop from the pop-up menu, or pressing ⌘D) moves you to the desktop level *and* selects the startup disk (usually, the internal hard drive)—even if you started out buried in a nested folder on a Zip disk.

If you want to save a document out on the desktop but have it stored on a disk other than the startup, go up to the desktop level, then click on the target disk's name in the list; its icon will appear over the buttons. As long as the disk is selected while you're on the desktop level, the saved file will go to that disk.

Desktops on shared volumes. Shared volumes on a network don't share their desktops the way standard mounted disks do. A shared volume displays a folder named *Desktop Folder* on its root level; open the folder, and you'll see the things on that volume's desktop.

Open and Save Dialogs

The default Open/Save folder. The folder that's displayed when you use an Open or Save dialog in an application depends on what you've done so far, what application you're using, and the Documents setting in the General Controls control panel.

Most applications display their own folders the first time you use an Open or Save command after you've launched the program. Once you've selected a folder for opening from or saving to, the program uses that location as the default the next time you use Open or Save during that work session; the current folder continually changes to match whatever you used last. When you're running multiple applications, each application remembers its own last-used folder. (That wasn't always the case—in the earliest systems that let you run multiple applications, the system kept track of a single last-used folder, which was very frustrating as you moved from one application to another.)

Set a default Open/Save folder in the General Controls control panel.

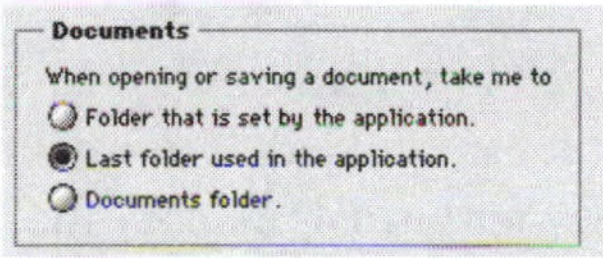

You can override this normal course of events by using the General Controls control panel. Its Documents settings provide these choices:

- **Folder that is set by the application**. This matches the normal default, which uses the application's folder as the first stop for an Open/Save dialog.
- **Last folder used in the application**. This sets the initial folder for the first Open/Save to match whatever was used the last time you used the application.
- **Documents folder.** This sets the default folder for Open/Save to a special Documents folder on the main level of the drive. If you don't have one, it creates the folder for you.

The Save lists. There are two text boxes in a Save dialog: the one where you type the name of the document, and the one that lists the folders inside the folder you're looking at. Only one can be active at a time, since typing could be naming the file or using the keyboard to select from the list.

To activate one box or the other, click in it or use Tab to move back and forth. When the text box is active, either the text cursor is blinking in it or text is selected; when the list box is active, there's a dark frame around it.

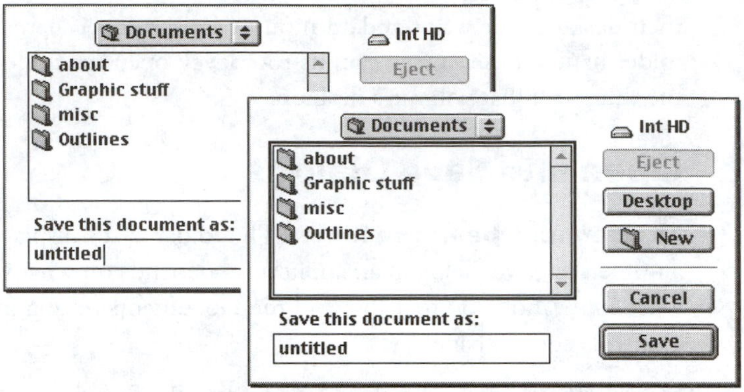

There's a frame around the list box when it's active.

Odd items in the list. Most applications filter out certain items from the list in the Open dialog. You won't, for instance, see other applications in the list even if they're in the folder you're looking at (although you'll probably see them, dimmed, in a Save dialog). And you'll usually see only the documents that you can actually open—why have a Photoshop document showing in a SimpleText list? Some applications let you control the filters by selecting from a pop-up menu or buttons; ClarisWorks, for instance, lets you specify just word processor documents, just spreadsheet documents, and so on.

The most disconcerting thing to see in a list, however, is something you normally don't see at all—invisible files and folders. You might run across *VMStorage,* for instance, which is your virtual memory file. But the one that

IN THE BEGINNING

When you're in a Save dialog, you can see the other files that are in the current folder, although their names are dimmed because you can't select them (since you're saving something, not opening something). But it wasn't always like that.

Early Mac systems displayed only folders in the Save dialog list, not documents. This made some sense, since you weren't going to be opening a document but you had to be able to open folders. But without knowing the names of documents already in the current folder, you often re-used a name and had to deal with a "Do you want to replace?" dialog—an extra step that was a life-saver, but shouldn't have been necessary.

Another change: originally, the icons in front of items listed in an Open or Save dialog list were generic ones, indicating only whether each item was a document, an application, and so on. System 7.1 was the first to provide miniature versions of the actual desktop icons for each item.

puzzles most users is the *Move&Rename* folder that sometimes shows up in a list, and sometimes doesn't, seemingly at random, and with funny leading characters in the name, too. This is simply an invisible folder used for file sharing; if you have sharing turned on through the File Sharing control panel, the folder is created on the main level of your system disk.

The mystery folder.

Eject button leaves the ghost. The Eject button is activated when you're using a removable disk; you can use it for the current disk whether you're on the desktop level or down several folders. But the ejection doesn't remove the disk's icon from the desktop; it leaves the "ghost" discussed in Chapter 4, and sooner or later you'll be asked to reinsert the disk unless you go back to the desktop and get rid of the ghost.

Tidbits. Some odds and ends about Open and Save:

- Which documents are listed in an Open/Save dialog depend on the application you're using. Some applications display only their own documents, some show all the documents in the current folder (even though you won't be able to open them), and some let you choose which documents should be listed.
- The Save button in the Save dialog changes to an Open button when you've selected a folder in the list. This makes sense, since you're opening the folder, but early Mac systems left the default button as Save even when its function was to open a selected folder.
- Aliases are italicized in lists. "Opening" the alias opens the real thing, whether it's a folder or a document.
- Names that are too long to be displayed in the list are truncated, with an ellipsis added to show the displayed name is incomplete.
- When you create a new folder with the New Folder button, make sure you're in the right spot: the new folder will be placed inside the folder that's currently displayed in the list box.
- When you insert a disk—a floppy, CD, or any removable media—while an Open/Save dialog is open, the dialog automatically displays the contents of the newly inserted disk.

The alias Option option. The niftiest trick for Open/Save dialogs is the alias Option option. Hold down Option while you "open" an alias in the list, and you're transferred to the folder that holds that item (the file isn't opened). This works whether the alias is for a file or a folder. You can add Option to any of the ways you'd normally open an item in the list: press Option while you click the Open button, add it to the ⌘O combination, hold it down while you press Return to trigger the default Open button, or keep it down while double-clicking on the item in the list.

Creating aliases
Chapter 7

Shortcuts in the Save and Open dialogs. Because you use the Open and Save dialog boxes all the time, there are plenty of shortcuts available to get you through them quickly: for "clicking" buttons, moving through folders and disks, and moving through items in a list. They're rounded up in the following table.

Open and Save Dialog Shortcuts

To "click" buttons:	
Cancel	⌘. or Esc
Desktop	⌘D or ⌘Shift
Save	Return or Enter or ⌘S
Open	Return or Enter or ⌘O or double-click item in list
New Folder	⌘N
Eject	⌘E
To move through folders and disks:	
To the next available disk	⌘→
To the previous available disk	⌘←
Up one folder level	⌘↑ or click on the disk icon
Down into the folder selected in the list	⌘↓ (or Return or Enter to trigger the Open button)
To move through the list:	
To select the previous or next item in the list	↑ and ↓
To select a specific file	Type as many letters as necessary to differentiate the file from the ones before and after it alphabetically
To view the previous or next group in the list (equivalent to clicking in the scroll bar)	Page Up or Page Down
To view the top or bottom part of the list (equivalent to dragging the scroll box to the top or bottom)	Home or End
For the Save dialog:	
To activate the list or the text box	Tab to alternately select, or click in the list or box

The Go To folder. Create a folder and name it *Go To* (or something similar), but make sure you put a space as the first character in its name so it always percolates to the top of a list. Leave it on the desktop.

Put aliases of the folders you use the most inside the Go To folder—your projects, the System Folder, whatever. No matter what application you're working in, and no matter where the Open/Save dialog puts you, it's simple to get where you want to go:

1. Type ⌘D to get to the desktop.
2. Press Spacebar to move to the Go To folder.
3. Press Return to open the folder.
4. Type a letter that will select the folder you want.
5. Press Return to move to the folder.

It seems like a lot, but it takes less time to do it than to read about it. I find this setup incredibly convenient because no matter what I'm doing, the places I need to be most often are readily accessible.

Select, but don't open. Sometimes a program or utility wants you to indicate what folder should be used for a special purpose—where to save special files, or where to retrieve them from, for instance. The Open dialog is normally used for this procedure, even though you're going to *select* a folder, and not *open* it. Unfortunately, there's no set way to do this: sometimes the folder you're selecting has to be opened and showing in the pop-up menu, sometimes it has to be just selected in the list; and sometimes there's a special button provided and sometimes you just have to use the Open button (even though you're not opening the folder).

The sort of generic approach used by many applications is shown in the first picture here: a Select button is added to the list of standard buttons in the Open dialog. But QuicKeys handles the situation very nicely: click on a folder in the list, and a button beneath the list makes it very plain that you can select that folder, while using the standard Open button would open it.

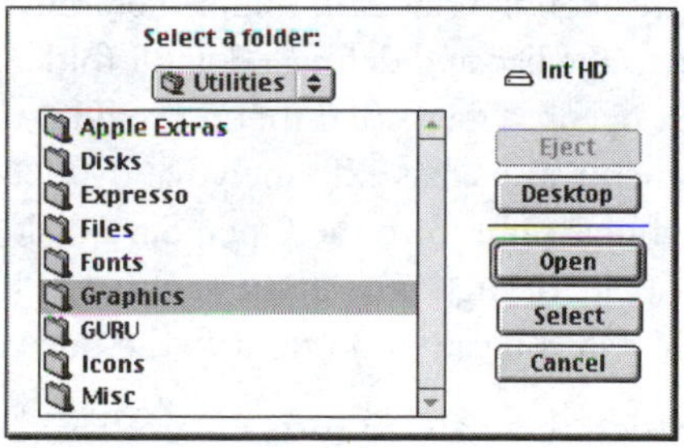

Some dialogs just add a Select button.

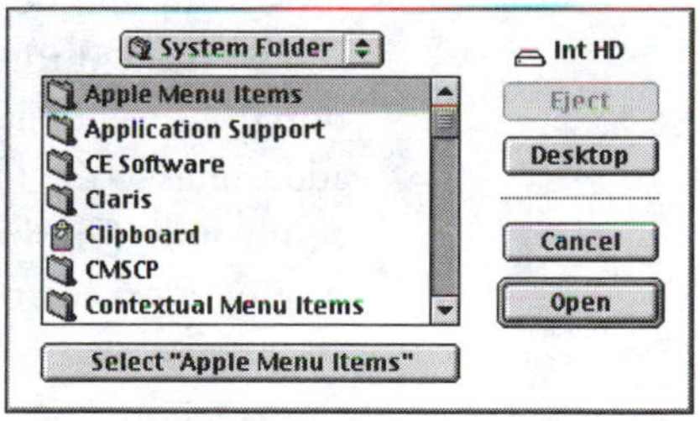

QuicKeys' folder selection in the Open dialog.

Adobe's PageMill, on the other hand, isn't quite as friendly. The pictures here tell the story: you're supposed to choose a location, so you select a folder and have no choice but to click the Open button. You go into that folder, and the first item is automatically selected (which is standard for Open dialogs everywhere); but because the first item is a folder, the Open button is still active. It's not until you think to click on a dimmed item in the window to deselect the folder in the list (and why in the world would you think of that?) that the Open button changes to In Here, indicating that you can select the currently opened folder.

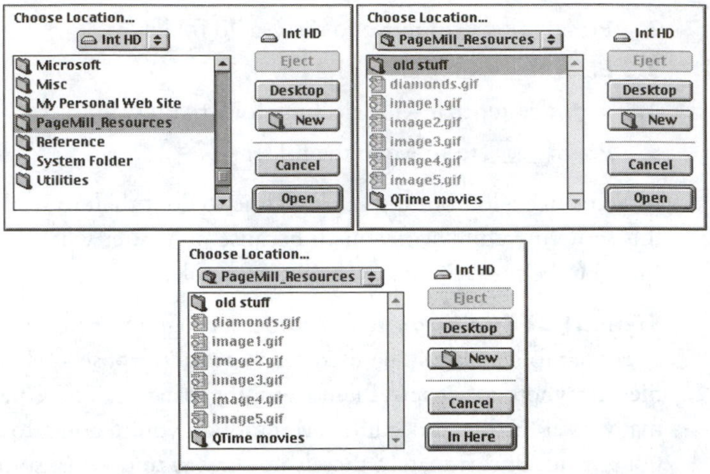

PageMill's method for folder selection in an Open dialog is unfriendly: unless you click to deselect the folder in the list, you'll never see the In Here button.

Enhancing the dialogs. A shareware product that puts commercial products to shame (not to mention that it should embarrass Apple for not having built more controls into the Open and Save dialogs), **Default Folder** ($25, shareware) adds a few little things to your dialogs—but it's the little things that mean a lot.

Default Folder

Default Folder puts three little icon menus where the icon of the current drive usually appears (although you can set the icons to appear only when you put the mouse cursor in the area). The menu you'll use the most is the one that lists folders you've visited lately, so you can jump right back to them without moving up and down through the standard folder hierarchy. You also get to add permanent folders to the list, and define a default folder for each application to use when it first opens. The second menu provides the commands to add things to the first menu, as well as extremely handy Get Info and Trash commands. (Trashing things right from the Open/Save dialog—we've been waiting for that from Apple for nigh unto 15 years now!) The third menu lists all the mounted volumes so you can jump right to the one you want.

In addition to these basics, there are all sorts of niceties. Can you see an open desktop window in the background? Just click on it and the dialog lists it as the currently open folder. Can't see the background because the dialog is in the way? Default folder lets you move the dialog. In all, this is a can't-live-without-it utility.

shareware.com

Another handy enhancement is **Dialog View** (shareware, $25) which lets you modify the Open/Save box in several ways: make the list longer (and the box wider); change the font and size for the list; set folder names to show in bold; and change the size and style of the icons in the list—or remove them completely. These are nice enhancements, but compared to the functionality Default folder offers, the price is a little high.

Then there's **Window Monkey** ($20, shareware), described earlier in the chapter; its menu stays active while Open and Save dialogs are open, listing recently used folders for you to choose from (except in some snobby programs, like Microsoft Word, where the Window Monkey menu is dimmed when a dialog is open).

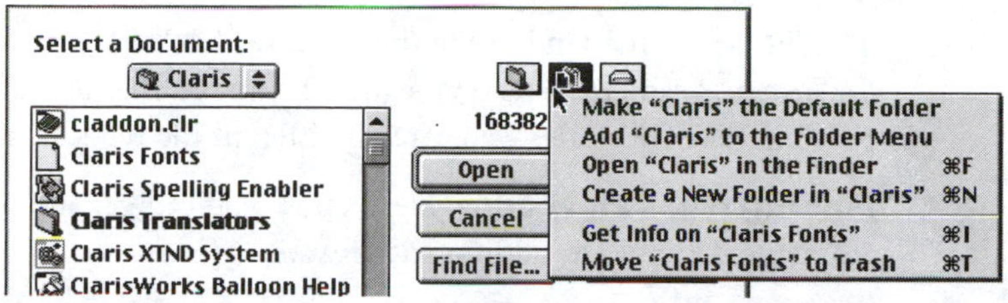

Default Folder adds three menu icons to the Open/Save dialog that let you quickly navigate to target folders as well as trash or Get Info on selected files.

The Dialog/Default combo. If you use both Dialog View and Default Folder, rename one or the other to force Dialog View to load first, or you'll wind up with clashes and crashes. I've renamed Default Folder to Diefault Folder to prevent the problem.

Document Interchange

File Formats

About file formats. Text is text, right? Why can't you open a word processed document in any word processor?

Well, if the file contained just text, you could. Most English-language programs use a standard code called ASCII to spell out the letters of the alphabet and basic punctuation. Unfortunately, most word processing files don't contain just ASCII text characters: they also include special codes that tell the program how to display and print the information with the formatting you've applied. These codes vary from program to program. As a result, each program is said to have its own *file format,* or *native format*.

Trying to open a file in a program other than the one in which it was created can cause problems. In some cases, you won't be able to open the file at all; in others, you'll be able to open the file but it will be full of all sorts of extra characters that'll look like gibberish. —DD/JB

File types and creator codes. Every file has two four-letter codes attached to it: a *creator code* and a *file type*. Both codes are always four letters; if you see one that looks like it's only three letters, there's a leading or trailing space that's an important part of the name.

The creator code tells the Mac which application created the file—it's how the Finder knows which application to open when you double-click on a document. (An application's creator is itself.) Creator codes are registered with Apple, so no two programs can have the same code.

The file type is the kind of file (boy, that really clears it up, doesn't it?). Word, for instance, can create its own native document files as well as text files, support files like Glossaries—they're all different file types from the same creator.

Finding types and codes. Here's how you can get any file's type and creator code without any additional software:

1. In the Finder, open Find File.
2. Select *file type* from the first menu.
3. Click the More Choices button.
4. Select *creator* from the first menu in the second row.
5. Drag the icon of the file you want to know about into the Find File window.

The file you drag actually stays in its original location, but when you let go of the mouse button you'll see the two codes in the window. The picture here shows a ClarisWorks word processor file.

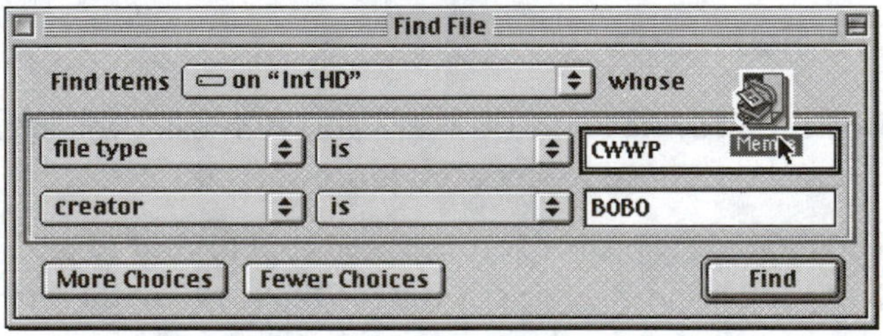

Getting a file type and creator code from Find File.

Changing types and codes. Several utilities can not only check creator codes and file types, but also let you change them. These two are the best:

DiskTools

- The $20 shareware **DiskTools Collection** includes DiskTools itself, an ever-handy utility that's been around (with appropriate improvements) for a decade. It can find things with a sophisticated combination of commands, show you invisible items, and let you see and change file types and creator codes. (It also comes with the PhonePad utility and two calculators.)
- The $10 shareware **More File Info** is a contextual menu extension that lets you get info like the file and creator type when you point to something on the desktop—and, while you're there, you can change it, too.

Fork it over. All Mac applications, and many documents, consist of two parts: the *data fork* and the *resource* fork. For applications, the data fork contains the code that makes the program work; for documents, the data fork contains the text of the file and the formatting commands. An application's resources are the pieces that are reused at different points of the program, like icons and dialog boxes; the dialogs themselves are made with other resources, like icons and buttons. For a document, the resource fork contains things like the file type, creator code, and created/modified dates. Apple's infamous **ResEdit** program is a *resource editor* that lets you change items in a file's resource fork (that's covered in Chapter 10).

ASCII Files

ASCII. *ASCII* ("ask-key") is an acronym for the American Standard Code for Information Interchange, which is a universal system of numbering characters. Every text character, tab mark, paragraph mark, punctuation mark, and other common text symbol has its own ASCII number, which all computers understand.

All computers support at least the original 128-character standard ASCII set; the Mac uses an extended, 256-character version. That's why some characters you can create in a Mac text editor, like é or ©, may not be displayed if you paste the text into an online message window, which usually accepts only the 128 standard ones. The characters in the extended set, shown in the table on the next page, are numbered from 0 to 255; the characters 0 through 128 are common with the original ASCII standard. The first 32 numbers are reserved for non-printing characters like tabs, newlines, and returns, so they aren't shown in the chart.

Most applications use ASCII to code the text you type in, adding their proprietary formatting and layout codes around it. If you want to share files between programs, ASCII is always a safe way to get the raw text (and nothing else) across. —SZA/JB/HN

Text files. For exchanging text information, ASCII is a sure bet: it can be read by any text-processing program. If all you need is the text, but no formatting (not even bold and italic styles, although tabs and returns are preserved in basic ASCII), it's as good as any other format, and its small file size is a bonus.

Most non-graphics Mac programs (word processors, spreadsheet, databases) offer a text-only save option, which might be referred to as *text* or *ASCII.* If you're going to save a text version of a document, you should first save it in a standard format so you have a copy that has all the formatting; then, do a Save As to save the text version. —SZA/DD/HN

ASCII Codes

32	spc	64	@	96	`	128	Ä	160		192	¿	224	‡
33	!	65	A	97	a	129	Å	161	°	193	¡	225	·
34	"	66	B	98	b	130	Ç	162	¢	194	¬	226	‚
35	#	67	C	99	c	131	É	163	£	195	√	227	„
36	$	68	D	100	d	132	Ñ	164	§	196	ƒ	228	‰
37	%	69	E	101	e	133	Ö	165	•	197	≈	229	Â
38	&	70	F	102	f	134	Ü	166	¶	198	∆	230	Ê
39	'	71	G	103	g	135	á	167	ß	199	«	231	Á
40	(	72	H	104	h	136	à	168	®	200	»	232	Ë
41	)	73	I	105	i	137	â	169	©	201	…	233	È
42	*	74	J	106	j	138	ä	170	™	202		234	Í
43	+	75	K	107	k	139	ã	171	´	203	À	235	Î
44	,	76	L	108	l	140	å	172	¨	204	Ã	236	Ï
45	-	77	M	109	m	141	ç	173	≠	205	Õ	237	Ì
46	.	78	N	110	n	142	é	174	Æ	206	Œ	238	Ó
47	/	79	O	111	o	143	è	175	Ø	207	œ	239	Ô
48	0	80	P	112	p	144	ê	176	∞	208	–	240	
49	1	81	Q	113	q	145	ë	177	±	209	—	241	Ò
50	2	82	R	114	r	146	í	178	≤	210	"	242	Ò
51	3	83	S	115	s	147	ì	179	≥	211	"	243	Ú
52	4	84	T	116	t	148	î	180	¥	212	'	244	Û
53	5	85	U	117	u	149	ï	181	µ	213	'	245	ı
54	6	86	V	118	v	150	ñ	182	∂	214	÷	246	ˆ
55	7	87	W	119	w	151	ó	183	∑	215	◊	247	˜
56	8	88	X	120	x	152	ò	184	∏	216	ÿ	248	¯
57	9	89	Y	121	y	153	ô	185	π	217	Ÿ	249	˘
58	:	90	Z	122	z	154	ö	186	∫	218	⁄	250	˙
59	;	91	[	123	{	155	õ	187	ª	219	¤	251	˚
60	<	92	\	124	|	156	ú	188	º	220	‹	252	¸
61	=	93	]	125	}	157	ù	189	Ω	221	›	253	˝
62	>	94	^	126	~	158	û	190	æ	222	ﬂ	254	˛
63	?	95	_	127	none	159	ü	191	ø	223	ﬁ	255	ˇ

Text with layout. Microsoft Word offers another option in its Save dialog to turn a formatted file into ASCII text without losing all of its spacing: *Text with Layout.* With this option, Word saves the file as text, inserting spaces to re-create spatial formatting like indents, tabs, tables, and line and paragraph spacing. This makes it possible to have a plain text file with the white space that was present in the formatted document. —DD/HN

Spreadsheet and database formats. ASCII is also a standard format for transferring information from spreadsheets and databases, but these programs need more information than just the text. They need to be told what text goes into each field and how to separate groups of fields into records. The standard way to do this is to place either tabs or commas between the fields (or columns), and returns between the records (or rows), in a format called *tab-delimited text* or *comma-delimited text*. Nearly all spreadsheet and database applications, including personal information managers, let you import and export data in these formats. —RSR/HN/JB

Inter-Application Exchanges

Built-in translation. Many programs have built-in translators for files created by other applications. If the translator you need is present, you'll be able to open the file with all the information and formatting intact. All you need to do is open the file from within your application; sometimes the program's Open dialog provides a pop-up menu to display the file formats the program supports. —ML

Interchange formats. While text can be read by almost any program, and native formats can be read by their creators and some other major players in the same categories, there are some intermediate or *interchange* file formats that are recognized by many different programs. Not all the information is carried in an interchange format, but what's lost is usually formatting that's easily reapplied. Most programs offer at least one interchange format as a Save option.

The basic text-based interchange formats are:

- **RTF (Rich Text Format):** Supported by many word processors and page layout programs; preserves formatting like fonts and styles, and sometimes even style sheets.
- **SYLK (Symbolic Link):** Primarily for spreadsheets, also used by some databases; preserves formatting like commas and column widths along with formulas.
- **DIF (Data Interchange Format):** Primarily for databases, also for spreadsheets; field names and data are preserved, but not formulas or text formatting.
- **DCA (Document Content Architecture):** More popular in the PC world, where it's supported by many word processors; can be translated by MacLinkPlus (which comes with the system software) for Mac programs.

Graphics don't have similar interchange formats, although certain file types (like PICT, TIFF, and EPS) are so common that many programs handle them, obviating the need for an interim format.

Easy does it. The Mac OS Easy Open control panel (known as simply Easy Open) doesn't actually open or translate any of your documents. What it does is replace the "Application not found" alert with a dialog box that lets you choose an alternate application to open a document when the parent application isn't available.

You configure Easy Open with the options in the control panel. There are three Translation Choices Dialog box options, which control what happens when Easy Open is triggered:

- **Always show dialog box.** If you turn this on, you'll get an application selection dialog *every* time you try to open a document whose creator isn't on your Mac. Turn it off, and the dialog appears only the first time you open a document with a specific creator code; after that, Easy Open will open all documents with that same creator code in whatever application you picked the first time.
- **Include applications on servers.** With this on, Easy Open will laboriously search all mounted disks, including file server volumes, for applications which can open the document type. This takes a *long* time, so you'll usually want to keep this unchecked.
- **Auto pick if only 1 choice.** Although this seems like a logical option, if the only choice is a bad one and *Always show dialog box* is turned off, you'll be stuck with the bad choice every time you try to open a document with that creator. —SZA/DC/ML

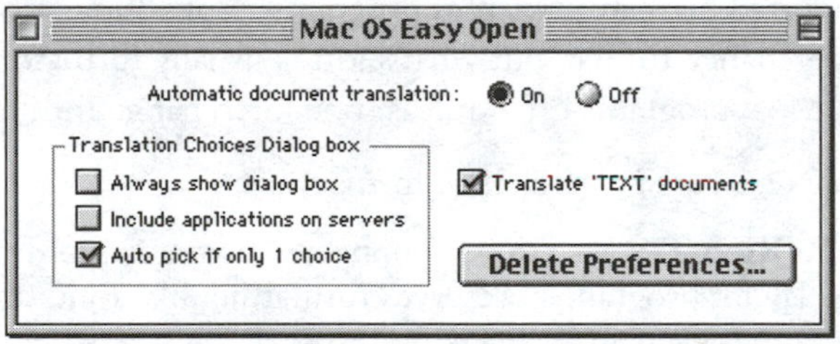

Easy Open provides only a few options, but can be a great help, especially when used in combination with MacLinkPlus.

Not so easy, but not impossible. As you use Easy Open, you build up a list of document/application relationships that are used automatically. Unfortunately, you can't edit this list, and it may become outdated as your applications and needs change.

If you use the control panel's Delete Preferences button, your entire list of relationships is thrown out and you have to start from scratch. But if you turn the *Always show dialog box* option on in the control panel, you'll be asked, every time you open an "orphan" document what application you want used—and changes are recorded in the list.

dataviz.com

MacLinkPlus. Once a separate program from DataViz, **MacLinkPlus** is now included with OS 8. MacLinkPlus is a file-translation utility that uses special filters to translate one file format to another so you can open a document in an application that didn't create it, yet preserve formatting and other non-text information. The translators work not only with MacLinkPlus, but also with Easy Open, Claris products, and Microsoft products. So, with the translators installed (they go in a DataViz folder in the System Folder), you get more Save and Open options in Easy Open and in some application programs, too. **MacLinkPlus/PC Connect** ($200) is still a separate product; it includes both hardware and software so you can connect a Mac and a PC to each other and transfer files back and forth.

MacLink Minus. If you get a notice that "MacLinkPlus has expired: This product is a demo version." when you're using it or Easy Open (which uses it), don't worry: it's not a demo version, and it hasn't expired. It generally means, however, that you've got a corrupted MacLink file someplace or the install was incomplete (or just messed up) or your desktop needs to be rebuilt.

Rebuilding the desktop
Chapter 24

Try the easy thing first: rebuild your desktop by restarting and holding ⌘ Option down. If that doesn't work, you'll have to do a clean re-install of MacLink Plus from your system CD:

1. Trash MacLinkPlus Setup (from the Control Panels folder), MacLinkPlus for Easy Open (from the Extensions folder) and the DataViz folder (from the System Folder). You won't be able to empty the trash if the control panel and extension were loaded on the current startup, but you can just leave them in the trash for now.
2. Insert your system CD. (The CD doesn't have to be the startup; you can still be running from your internal hard drive.)
3. Open the Software Installers folder.
4. Open the MacLink Plus folder.
5. Double-click on the Installer icon.
6. Run the Easy or Custom Install option.

After installation, the Mac is automatically restarted and its desktop is rebuilt.

For graphics. Adobe Photoshop is a champ at handling all sorts of file formats because it has so many built-in file translators. But when that's not enough—or if you don't *have* Photoshop—there are standalone products that let you translate graphics files from one format to another. (These products are covered in Chapter 19.)

- **DeBabelizer Toolbox** ($400) and **DeBabelizer Lite** ($140) from Equilibrium Technologies supply dozens of translation filters for more graphics formats than you can name. The Toolbox, of course, offers more filters, and while both programs can work on folders full of files in one fell swoop, the Toolbox version offers full batch-processing scripting and some image editing capabilities as well.
- **Transverter Pro** ($400) from TechPool lets you manipulate Postscript files, converting them to TIFFs or EPS format that you can edit and/or place in your programs.
- **GraphicConverter** and **GIFConverter** are great shareware translation utilities that handle most basic graphics translation needs.

Electronic publishing. Electronic publishing tools like **Adobe Acrobat** let you create a document that's readable on another computer without worrying about applications, fonts, or translators. Using the utility's driver in the Chooser, you "print" a copy of the document to the disk, and anyone with the correct "reader" (which is distributed for free) can access the contents of the document. But this doesn't offer editable documents to the recipient, which is the thrust of this chapter.

OLÉ! As you might expect, Microsoft wasn't satisfied with Apple's Publish and Subscribe *[Neither was anyone else!—SZA]*. So, it developed its own way to share information between files: *Object Linking and Embedding* (OLE). OLE is similar to Publish and Subscribe (described in Chapter 10) in that it lets you maintain a live link between documents. But rather than making part of a document available as a separate file, OLE lets you embed an entire document inside another one. The embedded document, called an *object*, can be an existing file or a new document you create from within the destination application.

Here's an example. Say you're creating a report with Microsoft Word and you want to include a Microsoft Excel worksheet within it. You position the insertion point where you want the worksheet to appear and select Object from the Insert menu, and choose an existing file or create a new one. A worksheet grid appears in the Word document and the menus and toolbars change to offer Excel commands; clicking outside the spreadsheet grid lets you work with the Word document.

The main benefit of OLE over Publish and Subscribe is that OLE doesn't require an intermediary file. In addition, simply double-clicking the embedded object opens it with the application that created it, if that application is installed on your Mac and you have enough available memory. But like Publish and Subscribe, OLE is only available within programs that support it—such as all Microsoft applications. —ML

PC File Exchanges

Internal differences. Here's a roundup of the things that cause problems when you try to share files between Macs and PCs:

- **Text characters.** PC text files often include additional characters such as *line feeds* at the beginning of lines. These characters may appear as little boxes when the file is viewed with a Mac text editor. Line feeds must be stripped out of a document for proper word wrap.
- **Special characters.** Macs and PCs use different character sets: Macs use an extended ASCII character set of 256 characters, including symbols and accents not normally available on PCs. If you use special characters in a Mac document, they may not display properly when the document is opened on a PC.

- **File formats.** A document usually includes information understood only by the application that created it. This information may confuse other programs, just as it does when incompatible file formats are used between Mac programs.
- **Mac file forks.** Most Mac documents consist of two parts—the *resource* and the *data forks*. PCs don't have the same kind of file structure, so they don't know how to deal with it.
- **DOS file extensions.** Macs and PCs use different schemes to associate data documents with applications. PCs just ignore the four-letter type and creator codes on Mac documents. The Mac has no built-in way of interpreting the three-character filename extensions that identify the creating application in the PC world. —SZA/RSR/ML/HN

Cross-platform applications. Most major applications are available for both Macintosh and Windows users. In most cases, these programs have similar (if not identical) feature sets and file formats on both platforms, so the Mac version can read PC-created files, and vice versa. Choosing the same application on both the Mac and the PC makes sense if you plan to share files across platforms.

There are some caveats, however. First, sharing features and file formats does *not* guarantee that documents will look precisely the same on both platforms. Font differences that foul up the formatting of a word processor document is just one example of the kind of problem you might encounter. And cross-platform sharing isn't always as easy as just opening the other file; you may have to use a special intermediate file format, which makes going back and forth from Mac to PC much less convenient.

Still another complication is that there are often long lags between Mac and Windows releases of new versions of the same product. The user with the newer version may have to save files in the older format—and therefore may not be able to take advantage of the newest features—if the document has to be portable. If you're running a cross-platform operation, it might be worth holding off on upgrading one side until the other side catches up. —RSR/ML/HN

Translation. Many of the same translation utilities that work for intra-Mac documents work for cross-platform documents. Some are built into popular applications (like Word and Photoshop), and others work as stand-alone: MacLinkPlus, DeBabelizer, and Transverter Pro all handle PC-to-Mac (and back) translations. —RSR/HN

PC Exchange. The PC Exchange control panel works in the background, letting you mount PC-formatted disks on your desktop (it also provides a PC formatting option when you initialize or erase floppy disks). But PC Exchange's primary function is to let you double-click on a PC-formatted *file* and have it open automatically in the Mac application of your choice. Any PC file that has a three-letter *extension* (a period and three letters following the

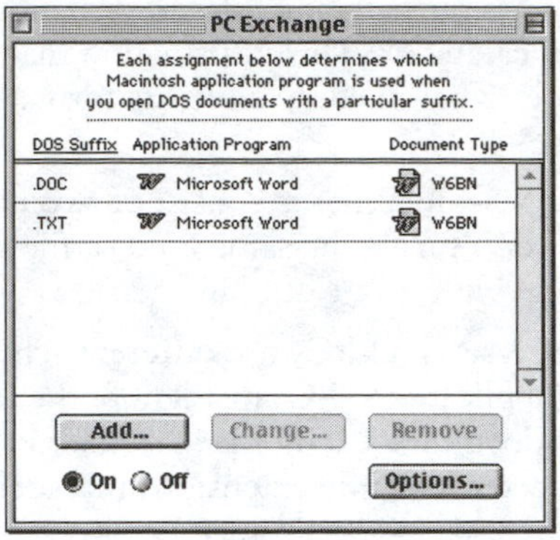

This setup will open two different DOS extension files into the Mac version of Microsoft Word.

basic file name) can be "mapped" to a specific application through the control panel. So, double-clicking on a .TXT file can open SimpleText or the word processor of your choice; double-clicking on a .DOC file can also open into your word processor. All you have to do is use the control panel's Add button, type in the extension letters, and select the application and document type of your choice with the buttons and menus provided in the window.

PC Exchange doesn't do any file *translations* (as does MacLinkPlus), so this mapping isn't a guarantee that you'll be able to use the file—it simply means you can try an automatic open into an application rather than having to use the application's Open command.

For word processing. Word processing files are probably the easiest types of files to share, formatting intact, because so many of the popular programs are cross-platform and allow their documents to be saved in formats that can be read by other popular programs on either platform.

If your word processor doesn't acknowledge the rest of the world, or the person you're getting a PC file from has an unfriendly program, you'll probably be able to export in RTF (Rich Text Format, described above under Mac file formats) and then import that format, with the word processor doing all the necessary interpretation to preserve both the text and the formats.

Spreadsheet and database information. Tab- or comma-delimited text is a standard format for transferring information from spreadsheets and databases; nearly all such applications let you import and export data in one or both of those formats. The data is stored as ASCII text, the delimiter character separates fields or columns, and return characters normally mark the ends of records or rows. All spreadsheet and databases let you export and import text files, so you can always be sure of being able to get information from platform to another as well as from one platform to another, when you're using spreadsheets and databases—even if you have to give up some formatting. —SZA/RSR/HN

The SYLK and DIF interchange formats described above in regard to Mac file formats also work on other platforms, so even formulas and some formatting can usually be transferred from one platform to another.

Graphics formats. A good way to transfer graphics files between platforms is to rely on applications that read and write multiple formats, like Adobe Photoshop and Deneba Software's Canvas. Another approach is to turn to a utility such as DeBabelizer, Transverter Pro, or GraphicConverter (described earlier in the chapter). As for the three most popular Mac graphics formats:

- The PICT graphics format is not widely supported in the PC world, although a few PC programs can read it and most conversion utilities can translate it into something more universal.
- Tag Image File Format (TIFF), the standard for scanned images and bitmaps, is platform-independent but subtle differences exist between the Mac and PC versions. Photoshop, MacLinkPlus, and **FlipTIFF** (freeware) can help when you are translating TIFF files between platforms.
- The EPS (Encapsulated PostScript) format allows Mac and Windows users to save preview images along with PostScript files. Those previews don't travel well across platforms, so don't include them if you'll be handing them to a Windows user. —RSR/HN

Compression standards. As with other products, the Mac and the PC have different standards when it comes to compression. **PKZip** ($50 from PKWare) is the most popular PC equivalent to Aladdin Systems' StuffIt family on the Mac.

If you receive a file with the suffix *.zip,* it has almost certainly been compressed with PKZip and you'll need to decompress it before you can use it. **StuffIt Deluxe** has an Unzip command in its Translate menu. **ZipIt** ($10 shareware) is unique in its ability to create as well as decompress Zip archives.

If you don't have ZipIt and need to compress a file before sending it to a PC user, there's a version of **StuffIt Expander** that works on PCs. —RSR/HN

13

Using Memory

In This Chapter

Your Mac and Its Memory

Memory Basics

RAM basics. When someone refers to a computer's memory, they're generally referring to RAM, its *random access memory.* It's called "random access" because you can get to any piece of it without having to go through the information in order. (A brief informational side trip: in the stone ages of computers, any information storage was referred to as *memory*—including disks. Before disks, there were tapes that stored information, and that "memory" was read into a computer serially—from beginning to end. Hence the *random access* phrase to describe non-serial access to stored items.)

What's in RAM is there only as long as the computer stays on. If you turn off the computer or something interrupts the power supply, everything in RAM disappears. That's why it's so important to save your work at frequent intervals.

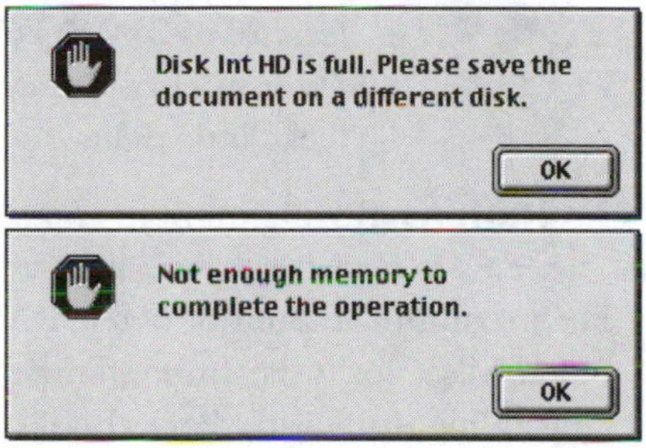

Memory versus disk space. Just a helpful reminder: when you get a *Not enough memory* message, that's referring to RAM, not to space on your disk.This often causes confusion among beginners. There's a big difference between the two dialogs here—with one, you're out of disk space; the other means you really don't have enough memory.

K, bytes, megabytes and more
Chapter 2

How much memory do you have? To find out how much memory you have (well, not *you*, but your computer—you can assume your memory is diminishing with age), choose About This Computer from the Apple menu when you're in the Finder. You'll get a full report on not only how much memory you have, but how it's being used. The part labeled Built-in Memory is the RAM you have in your computer; the part labeled Virtual Memory is the standard RAM plus whatever amount of virtual memory is turned on. (All of this is detailed later in the chapter.)

The first line of information in the About box tells you how much RAM is in the computer.

How much memory do you need? As much as you can afford, and then some. Luckily, the cost of RAM is peanuts compared to what it once was, so load up—it's the cheapest but most effective upgrade around. You can run multiple programs, and everything will run faster when there's lots of RAM available. But more specifically, what's bare minimum and comfortable minimum when it comes to RAM? The operating system eats up quite a bit; you need room for at least one program to run along with the Finder, and high-end programs need very large chunks, too. Later OS's use more than earlier ones, and PowerMacs need more than 68K machines.

A lean OS 8 system takes around 10MB of memory just for itself. If you have 16 megs of memory, that's *barely* enough room to run a large application—and many applications won't run under such constraints. While there are various tricks to get beyond the physical RAM limitations (like virtual memory), nothing is as fast as standard RAM, and upping the RAM in your machine is the best way to go.

> ***Wouldn't it be great if the Mac had 4 megabytes of RAM? Going from 512K to 4 megabytes on a Macintosh would be like trading in a Volkswagen for a Ferrari.***
>
> *David Bunnel, Macworld July 1985*

Think of 16MB of RAM as your absolute minimum. For running a very large program, or two small-to-medium applications, you'll need at least 20 to 24MB. For high-end graphics or multimedia, even 48MB might feel a little tight.

RAM chips, SIMMs, DIMMs

Chapter 2

Macs have memory limitations. Buying more memory for your Mac isn't always the neat solution it seems to be: Macs have a limit as to how much memory they can use. The maximum amount of usable RAM varies from one model to another. The oldest Macs, for instance, are limited to 4MB of RAM; some middle-aged ones, including many early PowerBooks, have 8MB limits. The limits of each model are listed in Chapter 2. But note that the limitations are for *physical* memory—the RAM that you install. Using virtual memory (described later in the chapter), each Mac can break its RAM barrier and go a little further.

More About Memory

The Memory control panel. There are three basic tools and procedures you use for controlling how your Mac's memory is being used. The first is the About box, where you can see how much memory you have and how it's currently allocated. Another is the Info window of every application you run, where you can set minimum and maximum memory allocations; that's covered a little later. The third basic tool is the Memory control panel, where you control basic memory features: the disk cache, virtual memory, and the RAM disk, all of which are covered later in this chapter.

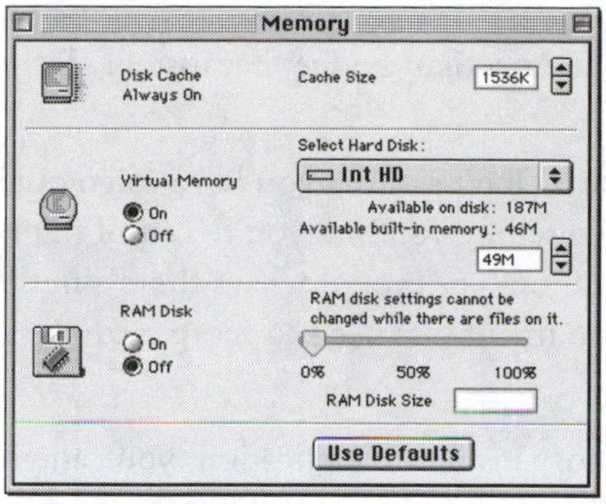

The memory control panel lets you set memory-use basics.

The Shift effect. Turning off extensions at startup by holding down Shift also turns off the memory control panel, so if you turn off extensions, you won't have any virtual memory on, the disk cache will be either turned off (on older Macs) or set to the 96K minimum (for newer Macs), and no RAM disk will be created. But the settings in the control panel aren't affected, so at your next startup with extensions on, all the Memory settings will be used again.

Subtle low-memory warning signs. Some problems that crop up as a result of tight memory situations just won't trigger a helpful dialog telling you that more memory would solve the problem. Here are some of the things that could be due to low memory; some of them can be cured by re-allocating existing memory or by buying more memory for your Mac.

- Applications quit unexpectedly.
- The Finder says you have to close some windows.
- You can't save a document.
- It takes a long time to do something that is normally speedier—opening windows on the desktop, making changes in any document, and so on.
- Documents print slowly or not at all.

Sure fixes for memory shortages. If your system seems chronically short of memory, here are some possible solutions (most of which are detailed later in the chapter):

- Trim down the amount of memory the **system** is using by getting rid of unneeded extensions and control panels.
- Change the allocations for the **applications** that you run so they won't use so much memory.
- Use **virtual memory**; it uses space on your hard drive as if it were RAM. It's free, since it comes with the system software. It can be slow, especially on older machines, and it takes up drive space that may be at a premium on older machines.
- Use **RAM Doubler** (described later in the chapter); it's cheaper than real memory and faster than the Mac's virtual memory, a solid product that works with almost everything except Photoshop.

- Buy more **real memory**. It's a great investment, and may be well worth it even for someone on a tight budget because of all the time and grief it saves in the end.

Out of memory (not). Don't assume you have to go out and buy more RAM if you get a dialog telling you that you're out of memory and can't do something in an application—or even if it says there's not enough memory to run the application. You might just need to reorganize the memory that you do have.

If you run out of memory inside an application, you can give it more memory from the total available on your Mac. Details appear a little later in the chapter, in the section *Memory Allocations.* If there's not enough room to launch an application, it might be just because you've got too many others running and have to quit some or simply shuffle them around, so to speak. That's covered a little later, too, under *Memory Fragmentation.*

Then again, sometimes you really are out of memory and do have to buy some more.

The not-so-modern memory manager. In early versions of System 7, there was a special setting in the Memory control panel for something called the Modern Memory Manager, which improved memory performance for PowerPC-based Macs. It's been rolled into OS 8, so you won't find the setting in the control panel anymore.

The 32-bit problem. Solved. This is of only historic interest to owners of current and recent Macs. But if you have an older Mac, or ever trouble-shoot for someone who uses one, it's good to know.

The Mac's operating system was designed right from the start to accommodate 8 megs of memory. Every spot in memory has an "address" that the computer uses for referencing; the highest number originally available is, in binary, a string of 24 ones—which allows for 8 megs worth of memory addresses (24-bit addresssing). Starting with System 7, the Mac added another byte for memory addressing; with 8 bits to the byte, that means it went from 24- to 32-bit addressing, letting it track 4096MB of memory addresses—more than it can physically accommodate.

At first, the system software provided a setting in the Memory control panel to let you turn 32-bit addressing on and off because some programs couldn't run with it on. Later, you didn't have a choice, because the system *always* turned it on, and didn't let you turn it off. This is still the case with OS 8.

But there was one other 32-bit problem. Macs up through the IIcx couldn't see more than 8 megs of memory even if you tried turning on 32-bit addressing because of a problem in their ROMs (these are generally referred to as *dirty ROMs).* For those models, you also had to add an extra extension from Apple or Connectix, variously named *Mode32* or *32-bit Enabler*. Those capabilities are also rolled into OS 8, so all these problems should be things of the past.

RAM Doubler

RAM Doubler can triple your memory. Connectix's **RAM Doubler** ($55) is one of the utilities that a large majority of Mac owners use. With it, you can double or even triple the amount of memory your computer has—or at least trick the Mac into *thinking* it has more memory.

connectix.com

RAM Doubler does its magic in the background using a combination of amazing tricks. It compresses the information going into RAM and decompresses it on the way out; it grabs memory that's been allocated to other things but is not currently being used; and, when necessary, it uses part of the disk instead of RAM to store some information. All this happens in the background, so you don't have to do a thing once you set it up.

There is, of course, a penalty, and it's the usual one in the computer world: your Mac slows down. But if you're not too greedy in adding this "fake" memory to your total, the five-to-ten percent performance hit it extracts is easy to live with. Also, keep in mind Connectix's recommendation: have at least eight megs of physical memory before using RAM Doubler.

PRAM

The PRAM. *PRAM* ("P-ram," not "pramm") is *parameter RAM,* a small portion of memory that stores some basic but important information—the *parameters* that your Mac users. (Don't get me started on the misuse of this word by the general populace. *Parameters* means *variables,* not *limits.* Even the holographic doctor on Star Trek Voyager defined it wrong for his simulated family when his "daughter" asked what it meant.)

Information stored in PRAM includes many items set through control panels:

- date and time
- insertion point and menu blink rates
- keyboard repeat rate
- mouse tracking and double-click speed
- volume setting
- modem and printer port settings
- startup disk setting
- virtual memory and RAM disk settings

Time and date problems
Chapter 24

PRAM is special not because of what it holds, but because it lives through shutdowns and even the unplugging of your Mac. Like regular RAM, it needs constant electrical refreshing, but it gets power from an internal battery which lasts for years. (That's why the time and date can remain set even when your computer's unplugged.)

More about zapping
Chapter 24

Zap! Pow! Sometimes the information stored in PRAM gets corrupted (that is, just generally confused) so you have to clear it and reset the parameters; the procedure is known as *zapping.* To zap PRAM, restart the computer and hold down [⌘][Option][P][R] while it's starting up. You'll hear your usual startup tone, the screen might flash, and the system will restart all over again with the startup sound. Keep those keys down through another round or two—Apple used to recommend a single zap, but for some systems, it's suggested that you wait until the third try before you release the keys and let the system start up.

For an older, NuBus-based Mac, you can zap the PRAM on a restart. For newer Macs, you have to shut down the Mac and then start up again with the keys down. That's because PCI-based Macs store some settings in NVRAM—*non-volatile video RAM,* which also has to be zapped. You can do that only at a startup, and you have to get the keys down *immediately.* You also have to then drag out the Display preferences file from the Preferences folder and then restart once more!

This procedure resets all the options in PRAM to their defaults, except for the time and date, which remain set. You'll have to open a lot of control panels and reset your options.

IN THE BEGINNING

A PRAM zap used to reset the time and date as well as other control panel settings. On early Macs, the date defaulted back to January 1, 1904.

What's so special about that date? It makes the date calculation easier from the Mac's point of view. The year 1900 was not a leap year, despite the fact it's divisible by four. By not starting at 1900, but four years later (in the leap year), the Mac and its programmers didn't have to worry about convoluted calculations to figure out how many days in a given month or on what day of the week a certain date falls. It's the earliest date in this century that could be used without running into mathematical problems.

Memory Allocations

Memory for the System

How much your system needs. Since you don't assign or adjust the memory allocated to the system, in one way you don't have to worry about how much it needs—it will take what it needs from what's there. The only thing you have to worry about is that you have enough RAM in your Mac to run the system and an application or two.

I installed OS 8 on three different machines in one week and the system used 9.5 to 11.5 megs of RAM in each—even without enabling all of Apple's extensions and control panels, never mind any third-party products.

Find out how much your system is using. Use the About this Computer command under the Apple menu in the Finder to see how much RAM your system is using. You'll probably get an unpleasant shock.

Why does the system use so much? It takes a lot of memory to do all the things the system does for you. But it's not just the basic System file that takes all that memory—other things are allotted memory from the system's total:

- The Finder
- Extensions and control panels
- The disk cache (as set in the Memory control panel)
- An active RAM disk

Trimming extensions to save memory. Most extensions, and many control panels, use small amounts of memory—but when you have lots of extensions and control panels, those small amounts really add up. A quick look at my own extension use shows the top five memory hogs: AppleShare, QuicKeys, ATM, Apple Menu Options, and the Appearance extension. Three of those are system components, while the other two are among the most-used utilities on the Mac. Together, they take up nearly 2 megs of memory.

While the average memory usage by most extensions is probably on the order of 20K or so, the average number of extensions is well over a hundred—pushing most standard systems into including at least 3 megs of memory just to accommodate standard system pieces.

Move extensions and control panels that you don't need to a disabled folder or delete them from your drive.

Conflict Catcher's memory report. Although Casady & Greene's **Conflict Catcher**, covered in Chapter 9, was meant to manage extensions and conflicts, one of its features is a description of each extension, which helps you figure out whether or not you need it. More germane to this chapter is that the report includes the memory usage for each extension—which is how I knew the numbers for the last entry. In fact, I was amazed to find that the top memory-user of all was a control panel I'd forgotten that I'd installed: Close View. I put it in my system to demonstrate it for someone, and just left it there. Guess what? It was taking up *4 megs* of memory! I disabled it, restarted, and, sure enough, my system memory use went down a full four megs.

When your system eats up new memory. If all the new memory you put in your computer is taken up by the system when you check in the About box, you're using an older Mac and system that need 32-bit addressing turned on manually. Use the Memory control panel to turn it on, then restart the Mac.

> ***A megabyte of memory provides a flexible environment to tailor to your own work habits and style.***
>
> *Macworld, April 1986*

If you zap the PRAM (a trouble-shooting procedure described earlier) it resets all the control panels to their defaults—including the Memory control panel. You'll have to reset the 32-bit addressing every time you zap the PRAM on an older Mac.

Memory for Applications

The Application partition. Every application needs its own chunk of memory, called its *partition*, or *allocation*. It has to be large enough to hold both the application itself and any documents you open in it, although applications vary as to how much of a document they hold in memory at any one time.

The amount of memory an application takes when you open it depends on what's set in its Info window, which lists three sizes:

- The **Suggested Size** is the allocation recommended by the manufacturer. It may allow for either minimum or optimum performance, depending on what they're trying to prove: *Hey! We can run in less than a meg of memory!* or *Wait till you see how fast this runs even in just the standard memory allocation!* You can't change this number.

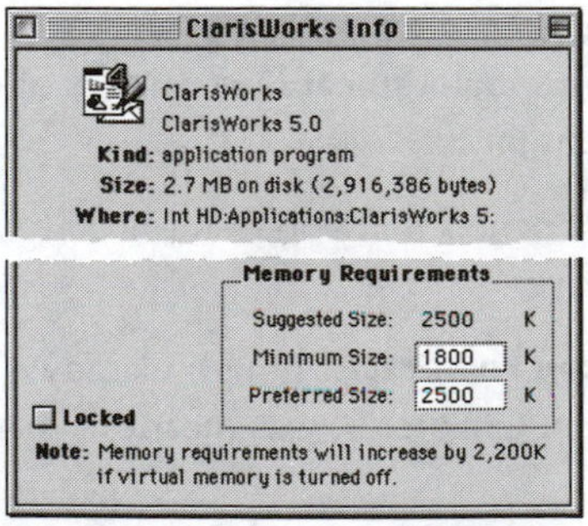

An application's Info window shows its suggested memory allocations.

- The **Minimum Size** comes pre-set to the manufacturer's recommended minimum allocation for decent performance. You can change this number to something higher or lower if your minimum performance requirements differ from the company's.

- The **Preferred Size** also comes pre-set to what the manufacturer considers the right allocation for good performance for an average user. You can change this number, too.

To change the Minimum or the Preferred size, just type in the new number and close the Info box. (While you can look at an application's Info window while the application's running, you won't be able to change any of the numbers until you've quit.)

The PowerPC less-is-more approach. For programs that were written specifically for PowerPC-based machines, the numbers in the Minimum and Preferred size boxes change based on whether or not you have virtual memory turned on.

Before the PowerPC chip was born, Mac applications were designed to load partially into memory, and run back to the disk when they needed information that they didn't think you'd use right away (say, loading a spell-checker function). This meant they could use less memory, even though it also occasionally slowed things down. But applications written for the PowerPC environment interact differently with the Mac's processor. They load completely into memory (that's why they take longer to launch) so everything's there when you need it (and, of course, even when you don't need it). Do they work faster? Sure they do, if you have room to load them at all.

Luckily, you can get PowerPC "native" programs to behave like non-natives, leaving parts of themselves behind on the disk: Just turn on virtual memory. Even a little bit—like 1MB. What kind of difference does it make? With virtual memory off, PageMaker's requirements go up by 4767K, Word's by 3918K, and even ClarisWork's modest needs balloon by 2200K.

And *that* explains the mysterious note at the bottom of a PowerPC-native application's Info window which says its memory requirements will increase if you turn off virtual memory. Or, if virtual memory is off, the note says how the memory requirements will go down if you turn it on.

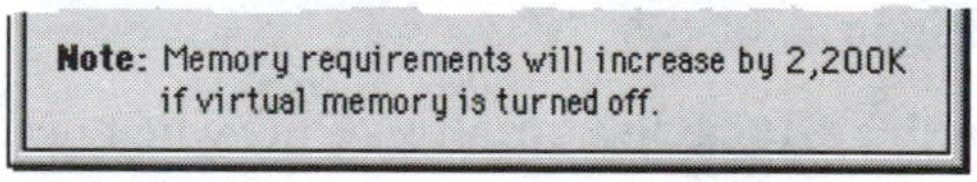
Note: Memory requirements will increase by 2,200K
if virtual memory is turned off.

Memory requirements change for PowerPC-native applications based on whether or not you're using virtual memory.

Which number does the application use? When you launch an application, it looks to see if there's enough memory available so it can use the allocation listed in the Preferred Size box. If there isn't enough around, it will settle for less, as long as it's at least as much as is set in the Minimum Size box. You won't know if it's working in its full allocation or not unless you check the About command in the Finder, where you can check all the current memory allocations.

In the About box, you can see how much memory is allocated to each program; the overall length of the bar represents the size of the partition. The colored part inside the bar shows how much of that partition is currently in use. This amount changes as you use the program, depending on what you're doing, how many documents you have open, and how large the open documents are.

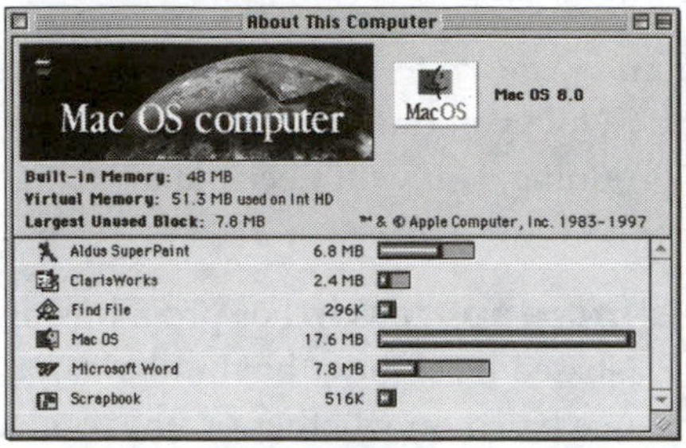

The Finder's About box shows how memory has been allocated to the programs that are running. The colored part of each bar shows how much of an application's partition is used.

When to make the allocation larger. Whenever possible. Oh… you want details. Okay.

- The first rule of memory allocation is the same as for deserving charities: give as much as you can. If you've got plenty of RAM, be generous and up the Preferred size by 50 to 100 percent of the pre-set one. Most programs run faster with more memory.
- Check the Finder's about box when you're working, especially with large or multiple documents. If the colored "in use" segment is most or all of the allocation bar, you should be giving the application more breathing room.
- There are some pretty obvious clues in some dialog boxes that show up when you're in an application that needs more memory. You might get the mild *Not enough memory to complete the operation* or the uncomfortable *Not enough memory to undo this procedure, proceed anyway?* or the dire *Memory is running low; Save your work immediately*.
- There are also more subtle signs that there's not enough memory for an application: it may be working sluggishly, especially with large documents. You may have trouble printing. Or, the program may up and quit on you with or without the little farewell message *The application [name] has unexpectedly quit.* (Not that quitting without your say-so is subtle; it's just not obviously connected to a low memory situation.) While the sudden quit can be caused by several things, it's quite often just a too-small memory partition.

When to make the allocation smaller. Only when necessary. When you just absolutely have to run another program along with whatever's already running, it might be necessary to lower the allocations for all the programs you're trying to run simultaneously so there's room for them all. (On the other hand, you may have enough total memory but it's all chopped up into unusable pieces: that's covered a little further on).

When there's not enough memory to launch. When you try to launch a program and there's not enough memory to accommodate it, the dialog you get depends on the situation; the three possibilities are shown here.

- If there's another application running in a partition large enough to accommodate the new program, and it has no windows open or all its documents are saved, you'll be asked if you'd like to quit that application and open the new one—and you'll get a Quit button to facilitate matters.
- If there's an application running in a partition large enough to accommodate the new program, but it has unsaved documents, the Mac will suggest that you quit that program.
- If there's no single program using a large enough memory partition to accommodate the new program, you'll just get a wimpy suggestion about closing windows and desk accessories. (Don't even bother.)

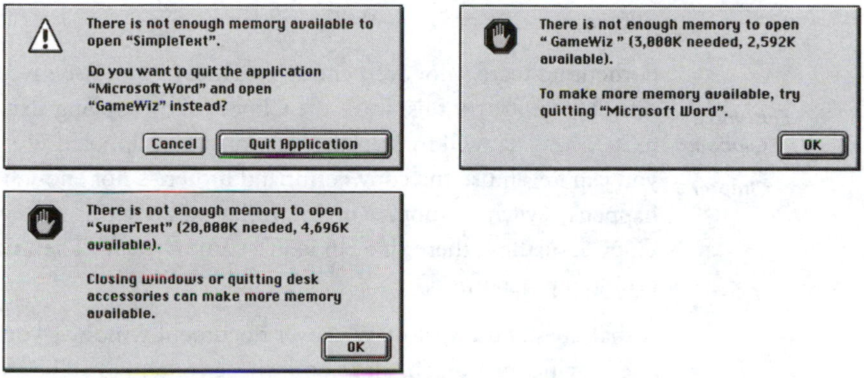

The three "not enough memory to launch" dialogs.

If you get the final dialog, you may have to quit more than one already running application to make room for the new one—although, if your problem is not lack of total memory, but memory fragmentation (covered below), you'll be able to re-launch those applications and use everything at once.

Launching works, but other things don't. An application uses more of its allocation as you work with it, especially when you're working with large documents. So, you may have no trouble launching an application in the memory you've allocated in the Info box, yet run into problems later. Sometimes you can adjust to the tight space by closing extra document windows. Other times, the only solution is to quit the program, allocate more memory to it, and start again.

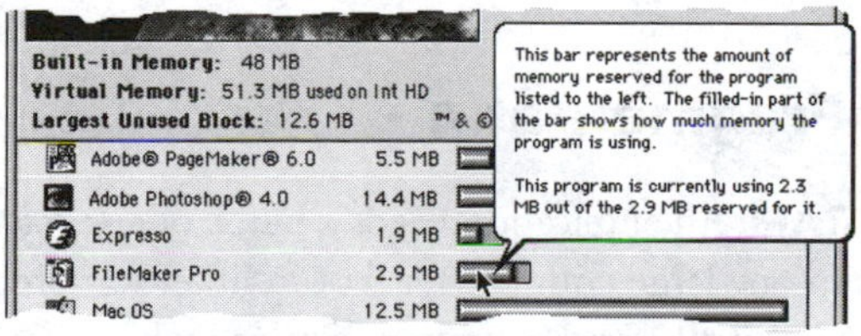

Use Balloon Help to see exactly how much of a memory partition is in use.

About the About box. An application doesn't always use all the memory you allocate to it. To see how much of the partition is being used, check the

Finder's About box. The colored area of the partition bar indicates how much of the allocation is being used. If you want the exact number, turn on Balloon Help and point to one of the listed applications.

Houston, we have a problem. If you're merrily working along and suddenly get out-of-memory messages inside your application, here's what to do: SAVE! Right away. If you have multiple documents open, save the most important one first. Then close the documents and quit the program. Launch it again when you can give it more memory. (You might have to allocate more in its Info window; or, the problem might be simply that there wasn't enough memory available for it to get its full allocation, which means you'll have to quit some other programs before re-launching.)

Flushing the Clipboard
Chapter 5

Sometimes there's not even enough memory to let you save a document. In that emergency, try this: flush the Clipboard by copying a single letter or word to it, *twice.* That will free up any memory the Clipboard was using. Sometimes you can't even use the copy command if there's not enough memory. If that happens, switch to another program (if one's running) or even to the desktop. Copy something there (like an icon's name)—*twice.* Then move back to the problem program.

If that doesn't do it, close whatever document windows you can that don't need saving. In a pinch, close one whose contents you haven't saved, sacrificing your work there in order to save other documents instead. (Isn't this getting a little dramatic?)

IN THE BEGINNING

Programmers used to take pride in writing programs that didn't use a lot of memory. But that was when memory was expensive and there wasn't all that much in the average computer. Here's how the recommended memory requirements have changed for some programs over the years.

	1986	1991	1994	1997
PageMaker	256K	1500K	1500K	5200K
Word	160K	512K	1024K	6000K
Excel	304K	900K	2048K	10000K

Memory Fragmentation

Contiguous RAM. An application needs a block of *contiguous* RAM to work—memory that's in one large chunk instead of in little, scattered pieces. As you work on your Mac, it allocates memory when and where needed; when the memory is no longer needed, it's "released" back for general use. But you can wind up with those chunks of memory in non-adjacent spots, so they can't be added together to be used for a large program. That's called *memory fragmentation.*

Think of your computer's memory as one long curb for parking. A compact sedan slides into place at the first spot. A Jeep parks behind it, followed by some gas-guzzling oversized luxury car, and then a classic Beetle; the curb is full. Both the Jeep and the Beetle pull away, leaving the second and fourth spaces open. Another luxury car shows up, but it can't park: while the total space at the curb is enough (in fact, it's longer than the car), it's split into two parts that the car can't use. The Beetle comes back, and it parks in the Jeep's vacated spot. Now there's extra space behind the Beetle, though not enough for any car to use, and there's still the Beetle's first space that's open—once again, the total space is enough for, say, another Jeep, but it's unusable because it's split into two segments.

Okay, you're probably ahead of me here: the curb is the Mac's memory, and those cars are applications, with their sizes controlled by how much memory they need. The first program you launch always takes the first parking space at the curb—I mean, the first block of memory; subsequent launching take the following spaces. When you quit a program, it frees up its block of memory but sometimes that block is unusable. Launch a large program, and it can't add together unconnected freed-up memory spaces; it needs a contiguous block of memory.

With all that behind us, now it's easy to understand the information given in the Finder's About box. The picture here shows three things running that together use under 26 megs of memory. There's a total of a little over 51MB of memory (it's the virtual memory figure that gives the overall total available).

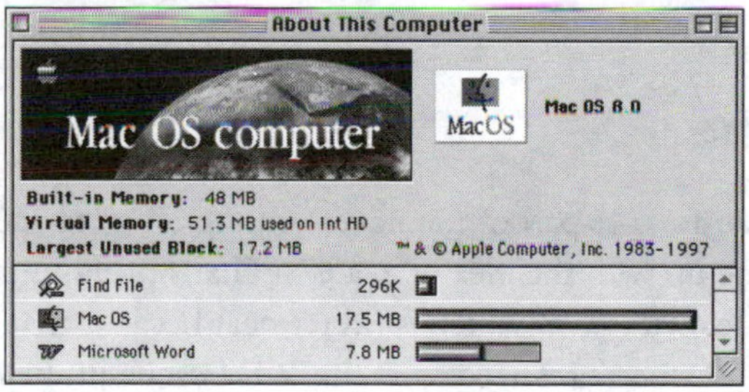

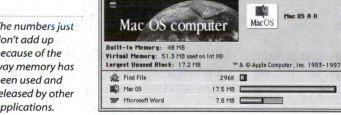

The numbers just don't add up because of the way memory has been used and released by other applications.

That means there's at least 25MB of memory not being used, yet the Largest Unused Block report is 17.2 megs. That's because it's just what it says: the largest unused *block* of memory that's available for use. So many other applications have been opened and closed during the course of a work session that the memory's been chopped up into pieces. (Not that 17.2MB is an unusable piece of memory. With the situation shown in the picture, it would be very easy to launch another, or even several other programs without much problem.)

Avoiding memory fragmentation. You can avoid fragmenting your memory by paying attention to the order in which you launch and quit programs. The program you use the most should be launched first because it's less likely you'll quit it, leaving a "hole" and fragmenting memory. Then you can launch and quit other applications as necessary with fewer problems. If you use two programs a lot, launch them both to start with and use the remainder of the space to launch and quit other things.

Defragmenting memory. To defragment memory, you don't have to restart the computer. Just quit all the applications that are running, and then start them up again. If you know in what order you originally launched them, you can quit them in reverse order until you're down to the first one or the first few that are in the first, contiguous memory allocations.

Unfortunately, the About box lists items in alphabetical order rather than in launch order. However, if you keep the window visible while you're quitting programs, you'll see the Unused Block report change, so you'll know what's going on.

Please release me, let me go. Some programs, like some children, just aren't as polite and well-behaved as they ought to be. In some cases, this means that they won't release any or all of their memory allocation when they quit. In those cases, you'll have to restart the Mac to get all the memory back to where it's supposed to be. How will you know when this happens? When you've quit all running programs so that only the Mac OS is reported in the About box, but the Largest Unused Block total is still much smaller than it should be.

Special Memory Considerations

The Cache

The cache bonus. As part of the never-ending effort to speed up computing, engineers came up with the idea of a *cache.* (That's pronounced *cash,* not *catch* or *cashay*; it rhymes with *stash,* which is pretty neat because that's pretty much what it does.) Formerly referred to as the *RAM* cache in the Memory control panel, this function is now called the *disk* cache. Either one is technically correct, because it's really a transfer of information between the disk and RAM.

Retrieving something from memory is hundreds of times quicker than getting it from a disk. So, a cache sets aside a portion of memory to store things that you've just retrieved from your disk. Statistically speaking, if you just got it from your disk, you're likely to want it again soon; if it's in RAM, you can have it almost instantly. When the cache is full, it dumps some of the stuff that's already stored and puts the new stuff in.

The disk cache is controlled through the Memory control panel. Starting with System 7, you no longer had the option to turn off the cache; this is just fine,

Adjust the cache size by clicking on the arrows.

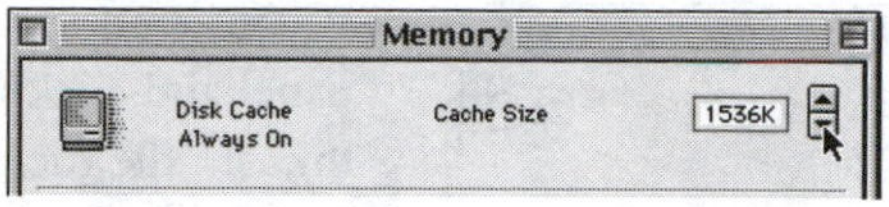

because PowerMacs need a cache to perform well, and you can't run a PowerMac on less than System 7 even if you want to. Although you can't turn it off, you can adjust the size of the cache by clicking on the little arrows next to the disk cache size. The control panel doesn't note it, but you do have to restart the Mac for it to be able to use the new cache size.

When a cache helps the most. A disk cache works most efficiently when you're dealing with data that doesn't change a lot, or at all. If you're working mostly in one program, the procedures you use the most can all be stored in the cache, significantly increasing the speed. A large cache can help when you're retrieving data from a CD-ROM, since its contents are static.

On the other hand, if you switch around among several programs while you're working, you may not see much difference in any of them—by the time you repeat an operation in one program, it may have already been knocked out of the cache to make room for instructions from another program. (Although the switching process itself might be a little faster.) Another example: working in a database that constantly changes the disk file as you change records might slow down with a cache because every time something is changed on the disk, corresponding information in the cache has to be purged.

The new and improved cache. Prior to System 7.5, there were some very strict guidelines as to how to set the best cache size: 32K for every meg of RAM, but no higher than 512K. The caching system that was used in earlier systems actually slowed things down if you gave it *too* much, since time was wasted looking for things that might not be there.

But since System 7.5, the operating system is a lot smarter in this regard. The more cache you set aside, the faster things are going to happen. So, go ahead and up that cache setting to at least 1500K if you can spare it. (And if you want to see what a difference the cache makes, try running with a minimum 96K setting and then again with around 1500K—you won't need a stopwatch to see the difference on the desktop when you open a crowded folder like the System Folder.)

Part of system memory allocation. The disk cache allocation is lumped into the general allocation given to the system software. So, when you change the cache allocation you'll see a change in the amount of memory the system uses, as reported in the About box.

The default setting and the default setting. This is so ridiculous I'm embarrassed, on Apple's behalf, to have to explain it. When you install OS 8, the disk cache is set to 96K in the Memory control panel. You'll almost certainly find that your desktop operations are a little sluggish; it's especially noticeable when you're opening a window with lots of items in it.

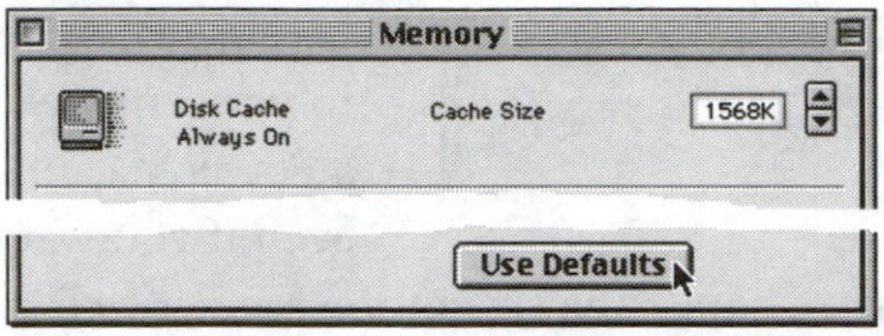

Click the Use Defaults button to set the cache size to its true default.

If you open the Memory control panel and click the Use Defaults button, the cache size will jump up based on how much real memory is installed on your machine. How crazy is that? Isn't *default* what you get when you don't specify something else? Why doesn't the amount default to the default setting from the very beginning?

Setting your disk cache to its true default is the best way to optimize your computer's desktop speed.

The obligatory Photoshop warning. Since Photoshop uses its own virtual memory scheme to speed the way it works, making heavy use of disk-to-memory swaps, anything other than a minimal 96K cache might can actually slow down Photoshop operations.

But that doesn't mean you can't set a higher cache and still use Photoshop. First of all, low- to mid-level use of Photoshop won't clash with the cache; the slowdowns only occur when you're making intensive use of Photoshop. And even then, you may still be able to use a higher cache if you're doing intensive work. I asked several graphic designer friends to set their minimal caches higher (around 1600K) for a while, and no one had any Photoshop problems—but everyone got a faster Finder.

Zapping the PRAM zaps the cache. Zapping PRAM (if you don't know what that is, you sure will after you've read this book or used your Mac for a while) resets the disk cache to its 96K minimum, so don't forget to reset it.

Temporary cache reset. If you start up with Shift down to turn off extensions, the disk cache will be turned off (on older Macs) or reset to the 96K minimum (newer Macs). The setting remains where you have it so it will be restored to that setting at the next startup, so there's no way to really tell that the cache is off.

Hardware caches are a different currency. You'll see the word *cache* used in other ways besides for the disk cache in the memory control panel, particularly in reference to a *hardware cache* that's built-in to some processors or can be added separately. You'll find this coverage:

- The cache in PowerPC processors, and a description of Level 1 and Level 2 caches, are in Chapter 2.
- The Cache Switch control panel for '040 Macs—and the hardware caches built into these machines—are covered in Chapter 9
- The cache card for the IIci is mentioned in Chapter 2.

Virtual Memory

Not exactly real memory. Virtual memory is a way of using space on your hard drive as if it were RAM. (If you think that's a little confusing, just wait until we get to RAM disks, which is a way of using RAM as if it were a disk!) The major benefit of this approach is that hard drive space is a lot cheaper than RAM, and new Macs have plenty of extra drive space. The major drawback is that accessing a hard drive is *lots* slower than accessing RAM, so once you fool the Mac into thinking it has more memory, you might not want to use it after all!

Virtual memory, or VM, is turned on and off through the Memory control panel. It comes pre-set to on, since PowerMacs work much more efficiently if there's a little virtual memory running.

VM is faster than it used to be. VM is not an island unto itself—other facets of the Mac that speed your work don't stop working when you turn on virtual memory. Since *those* components are much faster these days, a virtual memory setup of reasonable size doesn't cause the noticeable slowdown that used to make it a when-all-else-fails option.

What other components? First of all, there's the hard drive: access and transfer times are getting faster all the time, so the major bottleneck is wider than it used to be. Another important but often forgotten factor is the caching used in PowerMacs: special high-speed memory chips keep track of the things you do the most so they can be retrieved from there instead of from regular RAM. If the Mac's not looking to regular RAM for something, it's not going to be grabbing it from virtual memory either. With larger, faster caches these days, the things you do the most won't slow down when you turn on VM.

Using the Memory control panel. New Macs come already set to use 1MB of virtual memory as a default. You may want to raise that, or even turn it off under certain circumstances, and then, of course, you'll need to turn it back on. In the memory control panel:

1. In the Virtual Memory section, click the On button; this plumps up the little Mac icon and activates the Hard Disk menu.

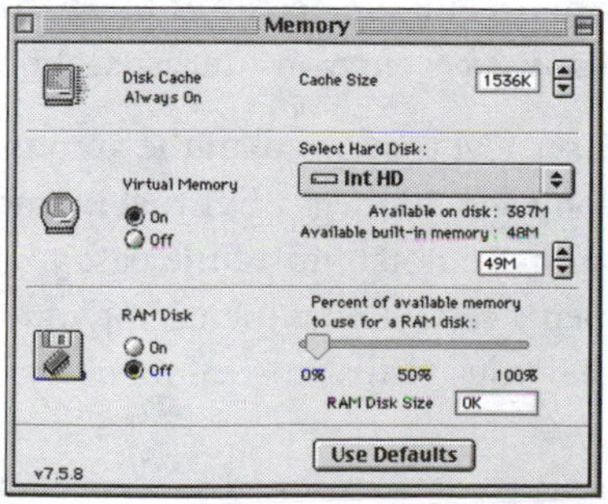

2. If you have more than one hard drive, select the fastest one you have—or at least the one with enough room on it—from the pop-up menu.
3. Set the *total* amount of memory you want by clicking the little arrows. You have to add together the amount of physical RAM that's in your machine plus the amount of virtual

memory you want. If you have 16 megs of real memory and want 5 more of virtual memory, you'd need to set this number to 21MB.

4. Restart the Mac to activate virtual memory.

You lose more disk space than you think. The disk space set aside for virtual memory is not the amount of virtual memory that you've asked for: it's the virtual amount *plus* the real RAM amount—that number that you set in the control panel. This doesn't hurt too much when you're adding, say, 5 megs of virtual memory to your 16-meg system because you lose 21MB of space; but when you've already souped up your memory to, say 48 megs of RAM and then turn on a measly 1 megabyte of virtual memory for the sake of efficiency on a PowerMac, you lose nearly 50 megs of drive space! Good thing that a gig drive is standard these days!

How VM works. Basically, VM puts absolutely everything that's in memory (real memory plus virtual memory) onto the hard drive in something called a *swap file.* There's a spot on the disk for every spot in memory, which means the Mac can look up something on the drive very quickly. Information is constantly swapped from the drive to real memory (and back) so what you need is accessed only from real RAM, since that's how applications are programmed to work.

QuickTime can be NotSoQuicktime. QuickTime movies need lots of speed to play without being choppy. Some of that speed comes from the processor, and the rest comes from the fact that QuickTime movies load into RAM as much as possible and play from there. If you're using virtual memory, that RAM is disk-based; that slowdown, especially added to an older Mac's slower processor, can result in movies that look more like flip-card animation than movies.

The same holds true for extended sounds and music—with VM on, disk access during playback can break up the flow. (This doesn't apply to audio CDs you might be playing on your Mac, since they use an entirely different sound channel, and no memory.)

How much VM to set. For a PowerPC where you don't need any extra RAM because you have plenty, set VM to 1MB. (This means that applications will actually use less memory overall; the details of this particular quirk are described in the *PowerPC less-is-more* entry in the last section.)

In normal situations, never set VM to more than the amount of physical RAM you already have—don't add 10 megs of virtual memory to a system with 8 megs of real RAM. You can notch up a little past your real memory total if you *really* need to open a certain document, but you won't want to run that way as a rule. The higher your virtual-to-real memory ratio is, the slower your Mac will run.

Lots of little things, but not a BIG THING. Virtual memory works best when you use it because you need to run multiple applications and move around from one to the other. Using VM because you want to allocate a humongous amount of memory to a single program so you can work on a billboard-size document doesn't work—you'll get so much of a slowdown that you might as well break out the Crayolas and do the job by hand. (On the other hand, for a temporary solution to the problem of not being able to open a document at all, an occasional slow-as-molasses document is not so bad.)

Another obligatory Photoshop warning. Adobe's Photoshop uses its own virtual memory scheme, which is incompatible with the system's VM setup. At worst, you'll get system crashes; at best, your Photoshop work will slow down to a crawl. (Actually, at very best, you can use Photoshop with the system VM on—if you're working on very small pictures with basic tools, so Photoshop's virtual memory never really kicks in.)

PowerBook virtual memory. Virtual memory on a PowerBook can be a real problem: since it uses the disk, and using the disk means eating up battery power, using VM means shorter battery life. If you use a lot of VM, try to stay plugged in.

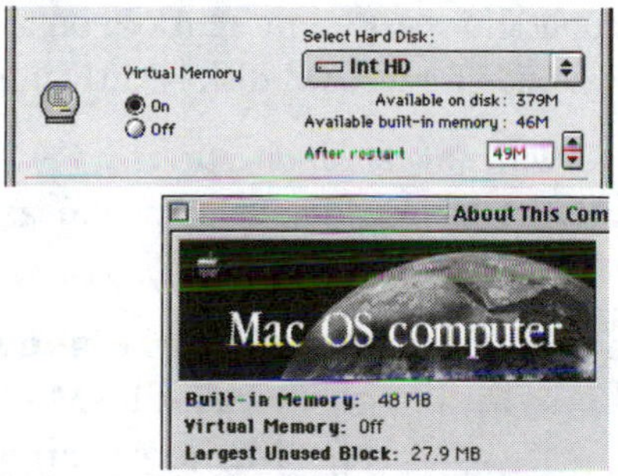

Although the On button is clicked, virtual memory is currently off; the "After restart" label is the vital clue (top). But it's easier to check the VM status in the Finder's About box (bottom).

Some older Macs don't do VM. Unless you have an '030 or better Mac, you can't use virtual memory at all. The only exception is the '020-based Mac II, which can handle virtual memory if it's had a PMMU upgrade along the way. If you have an older Mac and you're not sure what processor it uses, check the memory control panel: if the Mac can't do VM, there won't be a VM section in the control panel.

HFS Plus formatting
Chapter 4

VM, '040's, and HFS Plus. An '040 Mac using 8.1 or later can't save its VM file on a disk that's been formatted with the HFS Plus, or Extended, format.

Temporary turn-off on purpose. You can turn off virtual memory temporarily by holding down ⌘ during the startup procedure. This is temporary because the settings in the control panel don't change—VM will be back on at the next startup. But it is turned off for the current startup, which you'll notice if you check the About box in the Finder. In the control panel itself, the only clue to the current situation is the subtle *After restart* note in the window.

Temporary turn-off behind your back. If you start with Shift down to turn off extensions, virtual memory will also be turned off, although the settings remain where you had them so that they'll be turned on at the next startup.

RAM Disks

RAM masquerading as a disk. Now that you know all about virtual memory, where part of the disk masquerades as RAM, it's time to deal with the opposite concept: a RAM disk, where a portion of RAM behaves like a disk.

The advantage of working from a RAM disk is that it's lightning fast—RAM access can be hundreds of times faster than disk access. The main disadvantage has always been that the RAM disk contents disappear if there's a power interruption. Then there's the problem of losing from available RAM anything you apportion to a RAM disk.

The practical disadvantage is that it's really difficult to fit anything really useful on a RAM disk these days. A relatively lean (if not totally stripped-down) OS 8 System Folder takes about 100 megs; even if you could cut that in half, can you afford to put aside 50MB for a RAM disk to hold it? It's dangerous to leave documents on RAM disks (although it's such a pleasure to work with them from there). And large applications eat up more room on a disk than they used to—putting 15 to 20 megs aside for a RAM disk is fairly impossible, too.

But when you're working with smaller applications, a RAM disk is still a nifty approach to speed things up; setting aside one or two megs of memory for a RAM disk isn't so difficult.

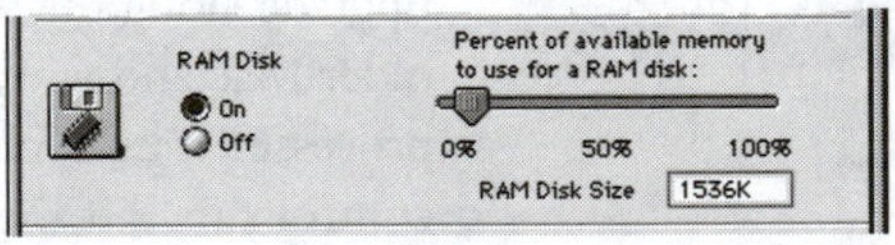

Setting up a RAM disk in the Memory control panel.

How to make a RAM disk. You create a RAM disk with the Memory control panel: click the On button, and set the size of the RAM disk either with the slider control or by typing in a number. Then restart the Mac, and you'll see a floppy-type icon on the desktop that represents your RAM disk; the centipede-like image on the icon is a RAM chip.

To put something on the RAM disk, just drag it there as if it were a real disk—while the "read" end of the copy procedure (as the information is read from a physical disk) takes as long as usual, you'll be amazed at how quickly the "write" part of the copy flashes by. From then on, just use the RAM disk as if it were a real disk.

Where the RAM comes from. The RAM you've set aside for a RAM disk gets dumped into the system allotment. If you check the About box after creating a RAM disk, you'll see that the system memory allocation has jumped by the amount of the RAM disk.

How to get rid of the RAM disk. Getting rid of a RAM disk isn't exactly intuitive. Here's what you're likely to do: you copy anything you need from the RAM disk to your hard drive, and then you drag the RAM disk icon to the trash, figuring that "ejecting" it should get it off the desktop. Nope—it can't be trashed. Okay, so you go to the Memory control panel to turn the RAM disk off. Nope again. The *Off* button is dimmed, so you can't even click it.

These stumbling blocks are actually safety nets: Apple didn't want you to unintentionally get rid of a RAM disk when it might have important information on it. You have to first get rid of the RAM disk *contents* before you can get rid of the RAM disk. Drag the contents to the Trash and use the Empty Trash command, or use the Erase Disk command. Then go to the Memory control panel and turn off the RAM disk. You'll see that it disappears from the desktop.

Gone but not forgotten. When you turn off the RAM disk in the Memory control panel, it's pretty much gone but not forgotten. That is, while it disappears from the desktop, the memory that was allocated for it remains in the system allocation until you restart the Mac. So, if you dumped the RAM disk because you needed the RAM, you won't get it back until you restart.

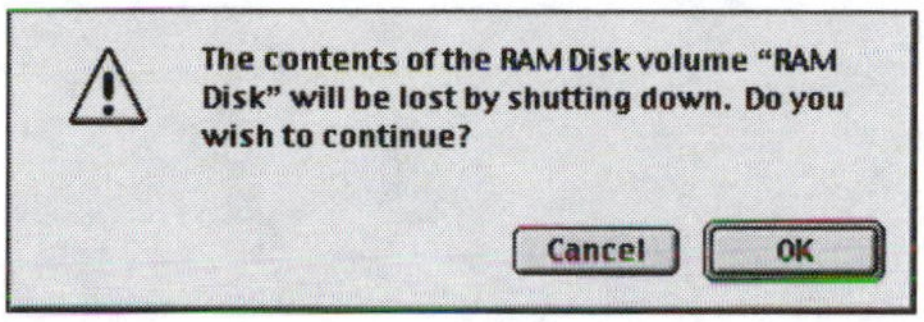

Survival of the RAM disk. On some Mac models, if you shut down, the contents of the RAM disk will be gone when you start up the next time, but the disk itself will be there. This isn't really as odd as it seems if you realize what's going on behind the scenes: the RAM disk wasn't just purged of its contents, the disk itself was wiped out along with its contents. What you see when you start up again is a new RAM disk that was created at startup. You'll get a special dialog when you try to shut down with a RAM disk on your desktop. On other models, the contents of the RAM disk seem to survive the shutdown. What's actually happening, however, is that the contents are written to the hard drive at shut down and back onto the newly created RAM disk at startup. When the contents are considerable, this can cause a noticeable delay on shutdown and at startup.

On Macs manufactured after 1992, the RAM disk contents survive a restart procedure; so, you won't have to redo the contents if, for instance, you change a control panel setting and restart to get the changes to take effect.

RAM disk contents also survive a system crash that requires a restart, as long as you don't lose power to the Mac during the crash.

Running an application from a RAM disk. If you run an application from a RAM disk, remember that the RAM you allocate to the disk is still just imaginary *disk* space to hold the program; you still have to allocate regular

RAM for the program to run in. You can, however, allocate less RAM for the program partition than you usually do without running into the slowdowns that a smaller partition normally causes.

Zapping a RAM disk. While a restart leaves a RAM disk intact, that's only if you do a plain old restart. If you zap the PRAM during the restart, that resets everything in the Memory control panel, turning the RAM disk option off, wiping out the existing one and its contents.

14

Fonts

Font Formats

Type and Typography

Managing Your Fonts

Using Fonts

System Software Fonts

Your Font Collection

In This Chapter

Font Formats

Bitmapped Fonts

Multiple formats. Back at the dawn of Macintosh, there was a single type of font (no pun intended), used by both the Mac's screen and its ImageWriter printer which, by no coincidence, both displayed things at a resolution of 72 dots per inch (dpi). The letter designs that looked good on the screen also worked for the printer, so a single font format served both purposes.

But while printer technology advanced to provide 300 dpi (in the first LaserWriters), then 600 (on today's standard LaserWriters), and even higher (on more expensive printers), the screen resolution has stayed pretty much the same. And so the problems started. Why waste the capabilities of the printer just because the screen was limited in its display capabilities? But if you design a font to look good at 300 dpi or better, it's rarely legible on the screen; and, the information the Mac needs to display something isn't the same information a LaserWriter needs for its high-resolution printing.

So, we wound up with several font technologies, some catering to the screen display, some to the printer resolution, and some trying to provide the best of both worlds in a single package.

Bitmapped fonts. A *bitmapped* font is designed and displayed as a series of dots. (The name comes from the fact that each dot in a letter takes a single *bit* of memory, and it's *mapped* to that spot in memory.) That's all the Mac had at the beginning, and it was revolutionary, since no other computer could display letters that had been designed dot-by-dot for legibility. And, since the Mac display used *square* pixels instead of *round* ones like other computers, letters and other forms were even more legible because the points of contact from one dot to the next are larger with adjacent squares than with adjacent circles.

The number of dots available for a bitmapped character's design is limited by the point size of the font. (For our purposes, we can assume that a *dot* is the same as a *pixel* is the same as a *point.)* A standard 12-point font is 12 dots high—but it has to include room for the tallest capital letters and the "tails" (descenders) on some of the lowercase letters. That's why it's hard to design readable bitmapped fonts at small point sizes.

A font in a particular point size has to accommodate both tall capitals and the descenders on some lowercase letters.

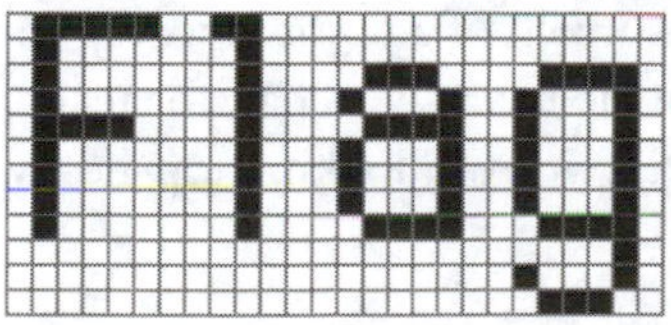

The jaggies. A bitmapped font is designed not only for a specific typeface, but also for a specific *size*. If you don't have a specific size installed when you ask for it, the Mac takes an existing size and scales it up or down to the best of its abilities.

When you enlarge a bitmapped font, you create distortions. Making a 24-point font from a 12-point original means every dot in the original becomes four dots in the new one (because you double both the horizontal and the vertical size). Creating a 48-point font from a 12-point design means every single dot is now a block of 16 dots. While these enlargements don't matter for horizontal and vertical lines, angles and curves become a series of stair-step blocks known as the *jaggies*. The distortions are even worse when you try to display a font that's not a multiple of the original. If you want a 30-point font and have only a 12-point design available, every dot has to be turned into a block two and half pixels tall and wide; since there's no such thing as a half-pixel, sometimes a pixel is added and sometimes one drops out, resulting in varied line thicknesses and blobs around the curves.

Fonts derived from a smaller size (12 points, top) are increasingly jagged as they get larger (24 points, center, and 48 points, bottom).

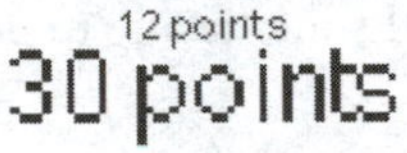

Using a size that isn't a multiple of the original creates uneven lines and blobs.

Shrinking a bitmapped font isn't any better than enlarging it; dots stay or drop out at unpredictable spots even when you cut a size in half (making a 12-point font from a 24-point original, for instance).

Hand-tooled bitmapped sizes. Even if larger fonts could somehow be neatly scaled up from the smaller installed sizes, you'd wind up with some problems. Consider the first picture here, which shows two sets of 24- and 48-point letters; on the left the letters are scaled up from 12-point size, while on the right they've been designed in the larger size to begin with. The designed larger fonts have smooth curves—in fact, much smoother than the original 12-point font in its original state, because there are lots more dots to work with in the design of a larger font size. The picture on the next page illustrates that: it's a magnified view of the two 24-point letter sets, the one scaled up from a 12-point design, and the one that was designed for the larger size. It also illustrates another point, an important one when it comes to good-looking fonts: the larger point sizes aren't just *larger*, they're *different*. The large *A*, for instance, doesn't have as much of a point at its top as the small *A* did. And, while the small *B* was divided exactly in half for its curves, the large *B* is has a larger bottom curve to keep it from looking top-heavy.

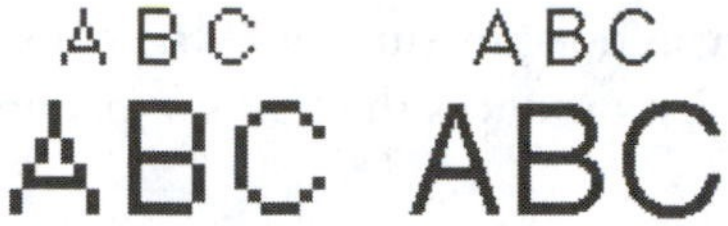

24-point and 48-point letters scaled up from a 12-point design (left) and created in the larger sizes (right).

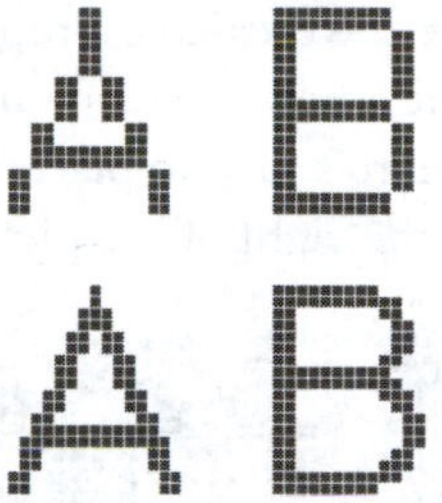

An enlarged 12-point design (top) and a true 24-point design (bottom) illustrate design differences.

PostScript Fonts

PostScript outline fonts. When the LaserWriter arrived on the scene a year after the Mac's release, everything about fonts changed. The LaserWriter included Adobe System's *PostScript* font format—fonts were described mathematically as *outlines*, which the *interpreter* in the printer drew and filled in at its 300-dpi resolution. With this approach, it didn't matter what font size you chose: small fonts were readable because 300 dpi provides such tiny dots, and large fonts weren't jagged because the mathematical description of the shapes were more than just scaled-up dot patterns.

The PostScript interpreter draws an outline as instructed, but the outline isn't filled in the way you'd pour paint into a frame because the LaserWriter still works with dots—albeit tiny ones (that are getting tinier all the time). The letter outline is placed on a grid of dots, and any dot inside the outline is used for the letter; this process is called *rasterization*. Of course, curves can still get a little jagged, but the dots are so small that you don't usually notice the rough edges.

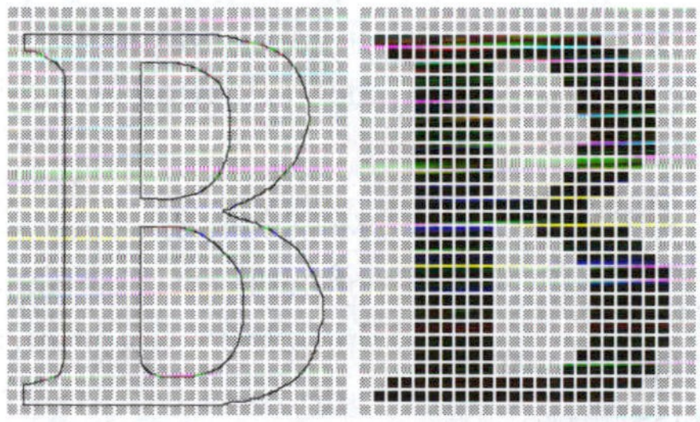

The outline laid on a grid (left) and the pixels that finally get included in the letter (right).

For PostScript printers only. Because PostScript fonts come as files of information sent to the printer's interpreter, they won't print correctly on a non-PostScript printer, which doesn't have the interpreter built in. Unless you have a special utility that interprets the PostScript separately, on the Mac's end of things, you won't get the high-resolution output that PostScript can provide. But you do have a special utility available—ATM, which is included with the system software, and is covered in detail later in the chapter.

PostScript hinting. The near perfection of PostScript fonts lies in a concept called *hinting:* a way of embedding special-circumstance information in each font description so that the font appearance is the best as possible at any size.

With a letter's outline laid against a square grid, there are bound to be times when a good fit just isn't possible—especially when it's a small font size. Take the lowercase *f* example here (please). No matter where it's placed on the grid, there are some important dots missing, or extraneous ones added. There's just no placement that produces the best dot pattern, the one shown at the right of the picture.

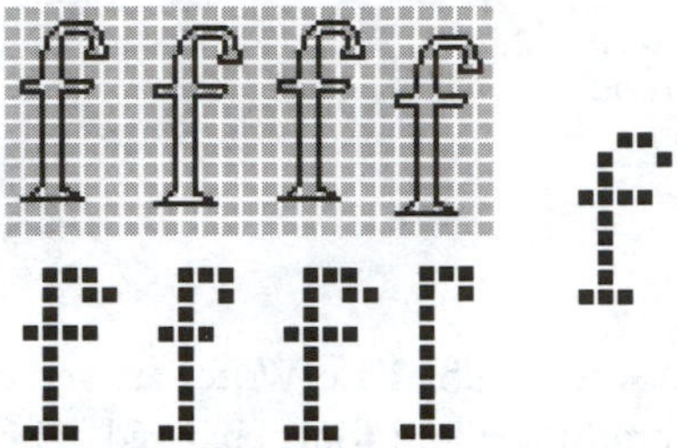

Various outline placements on the grid (top) produce unacceptable letter shapes (bottom). There's no placement that produces the best shape for the letter size, shown at right.

Hinting instructions included in the font file take care of situations like this, always ensuring that the best possible letter shape is used for the resolution of the output device, whether its a 300-dpi LaserWriter (which is considered low-resolution for PostScript) or a 2540-dpi imagesetter.

Type 1 and Type 3 PostScript. Adobe worked with two different PostScript font formats, Type 1 and Type 3 (Type 2 never got off the drawing board). Type 1 included the hinting technology that provides superb printing; the technology could be licensed, for a fee, by anyone who wanted to create Type 1 fonts. Type 3 fonts didn't require a licensing fee—and didn't include the hinting technology, so it produced fonts of a lesser quality. After a few stubborn years, Adobe finally shared the specs for Type 1, so the only Type 3 fonts you might find today are ones that have been floating around for years.

A *Type 3 font* is not the same as *Level 3 PostScript:* the latter is the latest revision of the PostScript language that's built into PostScript printers to interpret information coming from the computer.

Screen fonts and printer fonts. If you are an alert and discerning reader—which of course you are, because you bought this book—you probably noticed a minor problem among all these font details: bitmapped fonts were designed for the screen and work on printers (although not all that well), while PostScript fonts work only for printers. What do you see on the screen if you're using a PostScript font? PostScript fonts come as a set of two files:

In the Beginning

Unless you were there at the beginning, it's hard to understand the thrill of the earliest Mac days when almost anything led to a new discovery. Knowing nothing about character sets for fonts, and especially that different sizes for bitmapped fonts had different designs, we were pleased to find a picture hidden in every font on Shift Option ~ and puzzled by the fact that the picture changed when you changed the font size. Geneva provided a sheep, a rabbit, and a bird; New York alternated between a heart and robot; Athens had bear-paw prints; San Francisco had a car; London had a flower; Monaco hid a candle. The characters are preserved for posterity here.

- The *screen font* is used for the screen display, and also lets the system know to put the font's name in font menus. The screen font is either that old standby, a bitmapped font designed dot-by-dot for screen display, or, more likely these days, a TrueType font (described in the next section). Screen fonts are stored in suitcase files, whose icons look more like skinny briefcases.
- The *printer font* is the file that holds the PostScript information that goes to the printer so it knows how to draw the high-resolution letters. Its icon depends on its manufacturer (the Adobe icon is the one shown here).

The screen font (left) and the printer font (right) icons.

For all intents and purposes, *bitmapped font* and *screen font* are interchangeable, although the latter usually implies that it's the screen companion to a printer font. *Printer font*, *outline font,* and *PostScript font* are generally interchangeable terms, too.

Basic PostScript printer fonts are AWOL. Your system comes set up with the screen versions of some basic PostScript fonts, like Helvetica, Times, and Palatino. Yet, while there are no companion printer fonts, they're printing just fine on your LaserWriter.

Built-in PostScript fonts
Chapter 15

Is this miraculous? No, but it sure is handy. The LaserWriter comes with a certain number of fonts built its their ROM, to save download time (it also makes some PostScript printers more expensive than others, since the fonts have to be licensed from Adobe). Just how many fonts? Well, the counting method varies—but that's covered later in this chapter.

Printer font names. The names of printer fonts are usually pretty silly-looking, and occasionally next to impossible to translate. There's a formula that's used to name most printer fonts: the first five letters of the family name, with three letters for each descriptor. So, Helvetica becomes *Helve*, Garamond Bold becomes *GaramBol*, Gill Sans Ultra Bold Condensed becomes *GillSanUltBolCon*, and so on. (My favorites are the Book versions of fonts that get *Boo* added to their names, like *QuoruBoo*.)

Abbreviations for printer file names
Later this chapter

The majority of abbreviations refer to weights or styles; these are the most common:

Bol	bold	Kur	kursive
Boo	book	Lig	light
Bla	black	Med	medium
Con	condensed	Obl	oblique
Com	compressed	Reg	regular
Dem	demi, demibold	Rom	Roman
Ext, X	extra, extended	Sem	semi(boldf)
Hea	heavy	Thi	thin
Ita	italic	Ult	ultra

If you rename a printer font to something resembling its real name, the Mac won't be able to find it when it's time to send it to the printer, so don't succumb to the temptation.

The ATM advantage. The terrific **Adobe Type Manager** (ATM) is a utility that uses the information in a printer font file (for Type 1 PostScript fonts) to create a screen version of the font. Of course, you already *have* a screen version of the font—but in only a limited number of sizes. And if you use a different size, or have to zoom in on text in a layout program until the magnified letters are about 5 inches tall, you'll encounter the jaggies. With ATM, you get smooth-looking fonts at any size. Since it knows how to make that bitmapped version for the screen, ATM can also create a good-looking bitmapped version of any size that can be sent to a non-PostScript printer.

ATM comes with your system software—if you know where to find it! There's a section on ATM later in this chapter.

Multiple Masters. An outline font is defined with certain common attributes for all its characters, like the thickness of its lines, or the angle for oblique letters, or its overall width (standard, condensed, expanded). Adobe—the people who invented PostScript—also introduced a special type of font that contains several definitions, or *master designs*, which define the extremes in one or more categories, such as weight or width. These fonts are called *multiple masters.*

It's easy to identify a multiple master font: it has MM in its name. When you use a multiple master font in a program that "understands" multiple masters, you get to manipulate the look of the font from one extreme to the other of any of its controllable attributes. The picture on the next page, for instance, shows how you can manipulate Tekton MM in Adobe Illustrator, altering its weight and width by sliding controls in a special window. As you create new fonts, you get new fonts listed in the Font menu (or, in some programs, in a submenu); the name is simply the font's name appended with the numbers that indicate the adjustment to the font's attributes. (The second picture here shows how the font descriptions are handled in an Illustrator submenu.)

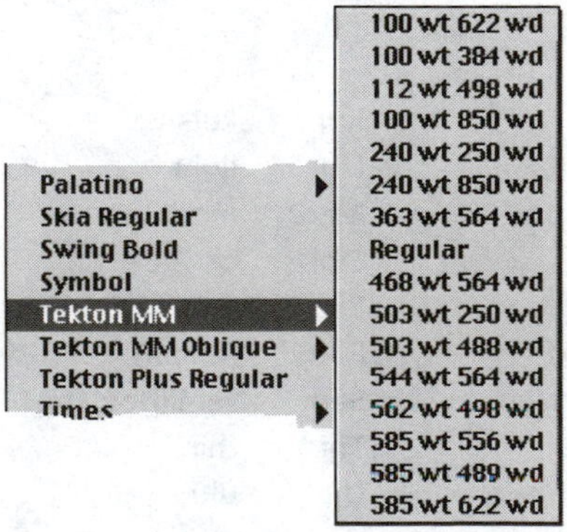

Using multiple masters creates new fonts for a Font menu or its submenu.

In most programs, you wind up creating a dozen fonts you don't need, because they're created as soon as you let go of the controls—even if you're only experimenting. The only way you'll be able to get rid of the umpteen font versions cluttering your menu is to go to the font's suitcase and drag out the unwanted versions.

Various weight and width adjustments for a multiple master font.

AFM files. An AFM file *(Adobe Font Metrics)* contains information that describes certain font dimensions. Very few programs actually need or use this information (Interleaf comes to mind, but it probably doesn't come to very many minds these days), but you may find font collections that include AFM files in the folder that holds the screen and printer fonts. You don't need them.

Outline, outline, and outline. The word *outline* is used three different ways in relation to fonts. One is the what we've been describing here: mathematical descriptions of the letter outlines in a font. Another is the simple outline style that looks like this. And, finally, some outline fonts come with *character outlines,* or *font outlines*: individual files of editable characters that you can use as graphics, and alter if you have the right program.

TrueType Fonts

TrueType. Apple introduced its TrueType font technology in 1991 as a direct result of the high licensing fees (about $700 *per printer)* it had to pay Adobe in order to include the PostScript interpreter and basic fonts in LaserWriters. TrueType was a joint venture with Microsoft, who, of course, wanted to both get out from under the Adobe yoke and also take over every aspect of computer use. TrueType has been unable to replace the entrenched PostScript standard for printed output—especially for professionals—but it has turned into a viable alternative for many users and uses. And it's a must for Web designers and surfers.

TrueType is, like PostScript, an outline font format: its files contain mathematical descriptions of the shapes of letters that can be drawn at any size and any resolution. One of TrueType's advantages is that the interpreter (called the *TrueType scaler)* is in the computer's operating system rather than in the printer. So, the Mac can figure out how the font is supposed to look—at any size—for the screen. For a printer like the StyleWriter, it can send the screen renderings for good print at any size—just as if you had a bitmapped version of every possible size of the font. For a LaserWriter, it first downloads the

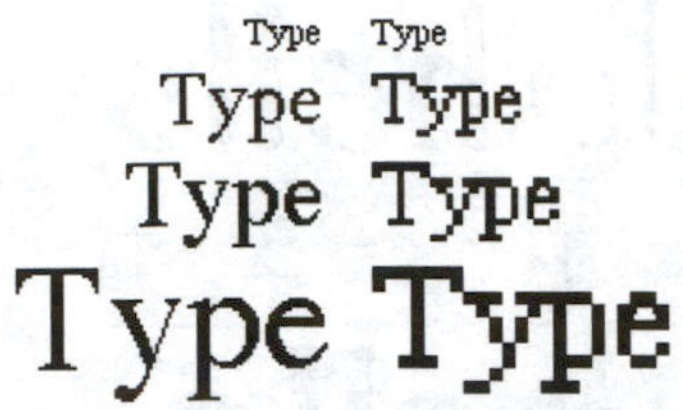

The smooth TrueType version and the bitmapped rendering of a font for uninstalled sizes.

scaler and then sends the font information, freeing up the Mac sooner since the LaserWriter will do the font figuring.

The picture here shows the TrueType and bitmapped displays of the same font, when only a single bitmapped size is available.

Never mind print—it's the Web! While TrueType will never replace PostScript as a standard for print material, it's already a standard someplace else—the Web. Because, of course, Web information is delivered directly to users' screens. Luckily, since the TrueType joint venture included Microsoft, the standard has been embraced and furthered by all computer users.

But it can be a complicated situation. You can't just design a web page using a TrueType font and have it show up on a user's screen; the specific font can be specified for the web page, but the font itself has to reside on the user's machine, or some other font will be substituted. Toward that end, Microsoft has set some Web font standards by including a small TrueType font collection with its Internet Explorer application. The fonts are also downloadable from Microsoft's site for free; but since Explorer comes with OS 8, you already have the fonts. (There's more about them later in the chapter.)

The hefty TrueType file. A TrueType font file takes more room on a disk than a PostScript font file—at least double the space (say, 70K versus 35K), and sometimes more. Even when you add the necessary bitmap font to the PostScript total (because you need something for the screen and the Font menu), the TrueType file is much bigger. In all though, TrueType takes less room, because you almost always have four PostScript files for each font (standard, bold, italic, and bold italic) and, just to make things even, you'll need ATM to make the PostScript fonts more readable on screen.

Telling TrueType apart. We're jumping the gun a little bit here, since font files and suitcases are covered in the next section. But it's easy to tell TrueType from bitmapped fonts when you're looking at their files. For one thing, the names differ: bitmapped versions include the point size in their names (like *Geneva 14*). But their icons are also different: bitmapped fonts have a single A on the icon, while TrueType icons have multiple A's in different sizes. The picture here shows the Geneva suitcase with its single TrueType file and six bitmapped files. (It also shows a relatively rare italic "cut" for a system bitmapped font: it's the one used by default for desktop aliases, so it's important that the letters be especially legible.)

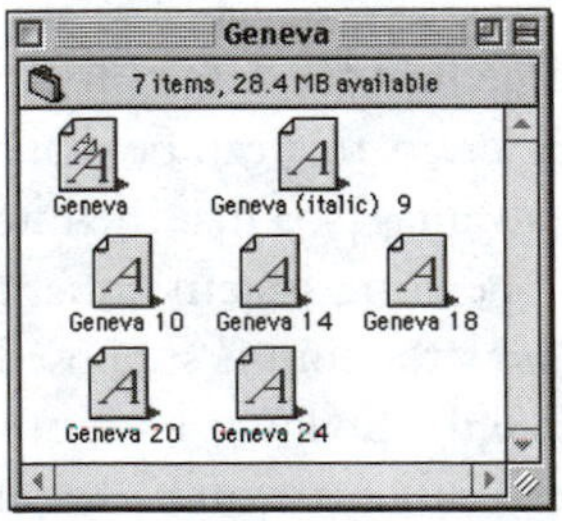

Bitmapped is better. Most of the basic fonts you get with your system software (Geneva, New York, Helvetica, and so on) come in suitcases that contain both a TrueType and several bitmapped versions of the font, as you can see in the picture for the last entry. Why bother with the bitmapped versions at all if TrueType works for both the screen and the printer? Because a bitmapped version hand-tooled for a specific size is always better-looking on the screen than anything else. The enlarged samples here tell the story. In the TrueType version (top), the serifs drop out at the smaller point size and the *o* is squared in the larger size. Considering the size of hard drives these days, there's no reason to dump the multiple bitmapped versions of a font just to save space.

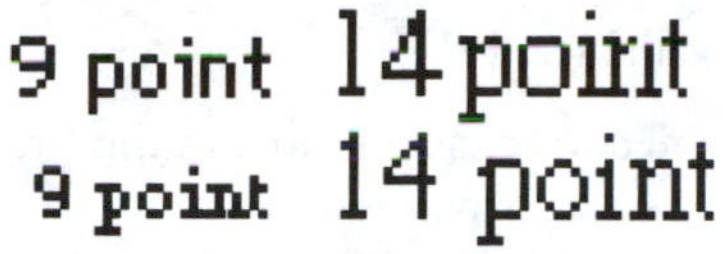

Enlarged views of TrueType (top) and bitmapped (bottom) versions of the same font.

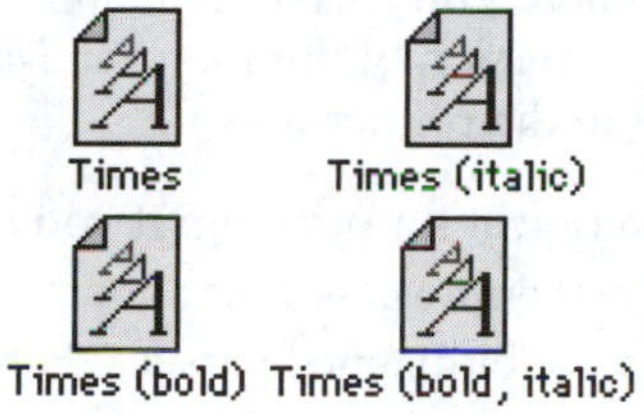

TrueType families. Most TrueType fonts come as a single file that's used no matter what style you apply. Others come in families, just like PostScript fonts. The Times font in your system, for instance, comes in four versions.

A memory hog. TrueType uses more printer memory on a LaserWriter than does a PostScript font. The TrueType files are larger not only on disk, but also in the amount of memory needed in the printer to hold their information. In addition, for most LaserWriters, the TrueType scaler is sent to the printer first, followed by the font information; the scaler itself takes a chunk of memory, which puts a severe strain on older, low-memory LaserWriter models.

QuickDraw GX fonts. QuickDraw GX and QuickDraw GX fonts were supposed to have made the Macintosh font community stand on its ear. Instead, they were ignored by the bulk of Mac users. The idea behind QuickDraw GX fonts was that they were supposed to remove the limit of 256 characters per font, providing 16,000 characters. This would allow fonts to contain fractions and small caps and other special characters that don't fit into a single font in the other technologies. Developers and users alike were slow to move toward this new format, possibly due to the confusion that already exists between using TrueType and PostScript fonts. Apple hasn't totally abandoned the platform, but isn't pushing it anymore, either. —TA

Mixing Formats

They all just get along. You should realize, right up front, that you have at least two different font technologies on your Mac when you first set it up. The system comes with both bitmapped and TrueType fonts; in some cases, certain fonts come in both versions. And if you use a PostScript printer, you've got the third one mixed in already.

You don't have to worry about any of this. In every case, the Mac will choose the correct technology for the situation so that you'll get the best screen output and the best printer output.

This is the priority the Mac uses for screen display, moving to the next technology when the first isn't available:

1. The bitmapped font of the correct size is always the first choice, since that provides the best screen display.
2. The TrueType version of the font is the next choice. If there's, say, only a 12-point bitmap of the font, and you're using 12-point text with 14-point headings, the TrueType version will be used for the 14-point size, and the bitmapped version will still be used for the 12-point text.
3. With ATM installed, when there's no correct bitmap for a specific point size, and there's no TrueType version of the font, the Mac will let ATM draw the screen font based on the printer font file.

Using ATM
Later this chapter

The Mac does the same quality control for printing. If you have a PostScript printer, it gives priority to the PostScript version of a font, then to the TrueType version, and, finally to the bitmapped version. For a non-PostScript printer, the priorities are the same as for the screen.

TrueType versus PostScript. While it's easy, painless, and necessary to mix font technologies, there is one major choice most users have to make: TrueType or PostScript for high-quality printouts?

If you're a graphics professional, I don't have to tell you that PostScript is what you need, since it's the industry standard. And if you're not a professional but you're preparing files for high-resolution output at a service bureau, you should be using PostScript fonts because that's what the "big boys" use.

But nonprofessional users have always been persuaded by the "professionals use it" statement into thinking that PostScript is "better" than TrueType—even to the extent of using a utility that translates PostScript font information for printing to a non-PostScript printer. But that's just not the case. TrueType offers superb output, and can be the technology of choice, with no penalty, for anyone. In fact, TrueType offers several advantages over PostScript: it works on any printer; it's simpler to use because everything you need is in one file; it provides good print at any size, for screen and printer, with no additional utilities; and the fonts are less expensive than PostScript equivalents. In fact, even professionals can stick with TrueType for jobs that are "in-house" rather than being sent out to a service bureau, since compatibility is the main reason the industry has settled on a standard at all. So, if you have no pressing need for PostScript fonts, consider TrueType a viable alternative, not the second-best choice.

Sometimes you don't want TrueType. Bitmapped, TrueType, and PostScript fonts work together pretty harmoniously. But, while you can't "turn off" TrueType, you can remove a specific TrueType font from your system, in the one situation where you might want to. If you have both a TrueType and a PostScript version of a font, the PostScript version displayed with ATM will more accurately represent the final printed output—but if the TrueType version is in the system, that's the one that will be used for the screen display. When you're tweaking a layout, you'll want the PostScript version rendered on the screen.

OpenType: another standard. Sometime towards the end of this book's shelf life, OpenType should be a standard; at this point, the new format—sponsored by Adobe and Microsoft—is just being hammered out. It promises to solve cross-platform font problems as well as web-based problems (like what happens when the surfer doesn't have the font that the designer really, really wants specified for the page). Some of the points we can look forward to: a single file for the screen and printer, with TrueType and PostScript Type 1 versions packed together; the same characters showing up on all platforms, and a single font containing definitions for things like two styles of numbers and its small caps version.

Type and Typography

Typography

Fonts and families. Alphabets come in different designs: skinny, fat, formal, casual, ghastly, gorgeous. An alphabet (including numbers, punctuation marks, and so on) with a particular design is called a *typeface*. Strictly speaking, a typeface and a *font* are not the same thing. In traditional typography, each size and style of a typeface design is considered a separate font. So, 12-point Times, 14-point Times, and 12-point italic Times are actually different fonts. This made perfect sense when the cast letters for each "font" had to be physically separated for easy handling and quick access, but in today's common usage the terms are interchangeable.

A *font family* is a group of typefaces designed with similar features; like most families, font families use a single family name, such as Times or Helvetica. A typical font family consists of four members: a regular version, sometimes referred to as the *book* or *Roman* version; a heavier, bold version; a slanted, italic version; and a bold-italic version. When you get "a" font, as a rule you usually get four fonts, one for each major family member. In fact, that's the only time computer-based font terminology reverts to the true definition of *font*—when someone's trying to impress you with the number of fonts included in a package they want you to buy!

Many basic families of four keep the plain/italic/bold/ bold italic relationship among themselves even when those aren't the true weights and styles in the family. For instance, here are two examples from the built-in LaserWriter fonts:

	Bookman family	***Avant Garde family***
(plain)	Bookman Light	Avant Garde Book
(bold)	Bookman Demibold	Avant Garde Book Oblique
(italic)	Bookman Light Italic	Avant Garde Demibold
(bold italic)	Bookman Demibold Italic	Avant Garde Demi Oblique

Font families aren't limited to four members: some have a dozen members, some have upwards of fifty. But they're usually divided into small groups—sort of different "branches" of the family so you can buy a few at a time. You might, for instance, add to your basic Garamond family by getting the condensed version of the font, and wind up with Garamond Condensed, Garamond Condensed Bold, Garamond Condensed Italic, and Garamond Condensed Bold Italic, so you still have the basic gang of four. Later you might add the Light Condensed branch of the Garamond family. —SZA/JF/EF

Basic type terms. The most important features that are part of a font's design are its *baseline, x-height, cap height, ascender, descender,* and *counter;* they're "defined" in the picture here. There are, of course, many more terms (like *arm* for the little branches on the letter *k*) and tons of details (like the ascender can be taller or shorter than the cap height), but these basics are enough to get you through.

The other basic term you need to know is *point*—the unit of measurement for fonts. You're already somewhat familiar with this: the sizes you choose from a Font or Size menu are in points. A point is about 1/72 of an inch (.0138 inch); not coincidentally, that's about the size of a single dot on the original Mac screen.

Monospaced and proportional fonts. A *monospaced font*, or *monofont,* is one where every character takes up the same amount of horizontal space no matter how wide it actually is: skinny letters like *i* get built-in white space on either side to match the width of a relatively fat *m.* Monospaced fonts look awkward—somewhat typewritten, or old-style computer-generated (you know, from when computer printouts were on

Letters from a monofont (left) and a proportional font (right).

green-and-white striped paper with holes punched along the side for feeding into a printer). The Mac's Monaco font is monospaced (Aha! You just realized how it got its name!).

When a font's letters are adjusted so they take only the room that they need, the font is a *proportional* one.

Serif and sans serif faces. The typeface you're reading now is a *serif* face; it has small counterstrokes, called serifs, at the ends of the main strokes. Serifs are a holdover from type's predecessor, calligraphy, in which letters were capped with flourishes from the calligrapher's pen. Serif faces are often used for long passages of text, since most people find serif type easy to read.

A *sans serif* ("without serif") face doesn't have flourishes at the end of its strokes. Unlike serif faces, sans serif characters tend to have a uniform stroke width, making them appear more modern, but also making them harder to read in long passages. (Some people set books or magazines in sans serif type, but this is the exception in the United States.) Most publishers like to use sans serif faces for headings, captions, or other relatively short elements of a publication. —EF

serif

sans serif

Size and Style

What's the point? It's difficult to predict the overall look of a font at a specific point size, both for an individual font and in comparison to other fonts. Yes, 12 points is 12 points, but the way they're distributed makes a visual difference.

The Bookman and Garamond samples shown here, for instance, are both 12 points, and you can see that the overall size from the tops of the capital letters to the bottoms of the descenders is the same. But the fact that Bookman has a greater x-height in relation to its capital letters makes it seem much bigger than the Garamond sample; and, of course, there's the overall width of Bookman, which also makes it look larger although top-to-bottom point size isn't affected at all by characters' widths.

12-point Bookman Old Style
12-point Adobe Garamond

And here's another example. The samples of Helvetica and Zapf Chancery here are the same point size, although Helvetica looks much larger—after all, its lowercase letters are nearly the size of the other's capitals. But if you measure them, top to bottom, they're the same size. The optical illusion is due to several design factors in both fonts: Helvetica has a tall x-height and short descenders; Zapf Chancery has tall ascenders (the tall lowercase letters are even taller than the capitals) and long descenders, which doesn't leave much in the way of x-height. And, since the eye tends to "measure" a font by its x-height, you have the visual discrepancy although, as you can see in the second example, the actual measurements are the same (we slapped in a character with a descender for Helvetica so you can see how much room it takes).

Helvetica y *Zapf Chancery*

These samples are the same font size, although Helvetica looks much larger, because of its high x-height and short descenders

Bold and italic, designed and derived. You might be wondering why you need a family that includes bold, italic, and bold-italic members when the Mac itself can just apply those styles to the base font. Well, here's why: the *designed* version is always better than the *derived* one—the one the computer creates from a basic font design.

A derived bold font merely thickens every vertical line in a character, usually an extra pixel's thickness. There's no thickening of the horizontal lines in a character set, or changes in serifs or counters, or adjustment to the overall width of different letters. You can see from the picture here that the designed bold font (at the bottom) has fine detail changes like the knob for serif in the lowercase *f*, and a rounder, larger dot for the *i*. It's also obvious that a derived bold takes much less space on a line, and is easier to read despite its thicker letters.

The derived bold font is in the center; the designed one is on the bottom.

A sample of Times
A sample of Times bold
A sample of Times bold

You have the same situation for derived and designed italics. A derived italic is merely slanted, with the top parts of the letters shifted to the right and the bottom parts shifted to the left. A designed italic is barely slanted—it's just "curlier" than the derived one. You can see in the sample here that, for instance, the designed font keeps bottom serifs on only the right side of most characters, gives the *f* a descender, and provides an entirely different design for the lowercase *a*.

The derived italic font is in the center; the designed one is on the bottom.

A sample of Times
A sample of Times italic
A sample of Times italic

And, of course, when you put bold and italic together, the differences between the derived and designed versions are multiplied. The difference is so obvious, in fact, that I'm not even going to label the last picture for you!

A sample of Times bold italic
A sample of Times bold italic

Weighing in. If you venture into the world of fonts beyond the basics, you'll soon discover that it's not just a matter of standard versus bold: there's bolder than bold, and darker than that, and thicknesses in between standard and bold, and things even thinner than the standard. These variations are referred to as *weights*, and fonts often include a weight in their names, like Helvetica Light or Quorum Heavy. Here are the names you're likely to see, in order from lightest to heaviest:

ultra light
thin/extra light
light
roman/book/regular/plain
medium
demi bold
bold
black/heavy/extra bold
ultra bold

Applying Bold to different weights
Later this chapter

But there's no strict definition of how heavy demi bold is, say, or how thick the lines of an extra bold font are. One font's *medium* might be heavier than another's *demi bold*. But within a family with lots of variations, you can trust this list. Pretty much.

Italic versus oblique. In general use, *italic* and *oblique* are often used interchangeably, but they are different styles. Italic, as mentioned earlier, is more of a curly variation on a font than a slanted one. But an oblique font *is* a slanted font, with the tops of the characters leaning towards the right. Sometimes what you see on the screen looks oblique (because it's a derived font) but the printout will be a true italic; sometimes, though, a font is designed as an oblique font—but you get it by choosing Italic from a style menu. (There's more about choosing styles versus choosing fonts in the Using Fonts section.)

This is oblique
This is italic

Designed styles versus custom styles. If you have a Style menu or submenu in an application, you'll find many more choices than just bold and italic; there are choices like underline, outline, and shadow, and sometimes even underline variations (words only, double underline, dotted underline), condensed, expanded, small caps, and "strikethru."

Although some fonts are designed for some of these styles (condensed, expanded, and small caps), there's a big difference between the basic bold and italic designed styles for fonts and all these other styles. Bold and italic are, for the most part, designed for each font; the other styles are simply superimposed on the basic font design—with varying degrees of success—by the program you're working with. The interactions between designed fonts and the Style menu are covered in the *Using Fonts* section later in this chapter.

Typesetting

Leading. Leading ("ledding") is the space between lines of type, measured from the baseline of the type on one line to the baseline of the type on the next. It's usually automatically set at 120 percent of the type size; for 10-point type, for instance, the leading would be set at 12 points. Word processors usually refer to this as *line spacing* rather than leading, and default to an *auto spacing* that accommodates the tallest character in the line (in case you insert a 15-point character in the middle of 12-point text).

Although the standard 120-percent setting works fairly well in most cases, it's often worth experimenting to determine what looks best for the typeface and line length you're using. Typefaces with small x-heights generally need less leading than do faces with comparatively large x-heights; pages with short lines of text need less leading than do pages with long lines. (The white space between lines serves as a highway for your eyes to follow when moving from the right-hand margin back to the left.)

The relationship between the font size and the leading is written as 10/12 or 11.5/13, and referred to as "ten on twelve" or "eleven-and-a-half on thirteen." — SZA/AJ/DD

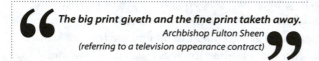

> ***"The big print giveth and the fine print taketh away."***
> *Archbishop Fulton Sheen*
> *(referring to a television appearance contract)*

Justification. People often consider a justified right margin (making all the lines exactly the same length) the hallmark of professionally typeset text, probably because this feature was all but impossible to achieve with a typewriter. The truth is, though, that when you ask your Mac to justify your type it has no choice but to mess with the spaces between the letters or between the words in each line, making for inconsistent spacing that can make reading a chore. Often you'll wind up with large white gaps in different spots on different lines that form what's called a "river" of white meandering through a paragraph. Many page layout programs allow you to control the maximum and minimum amounts you'll allow the program to stretch or compress the spaces, but the best amount is none at all. Remember that if you must justify the right margin, you'll need to spend some time adjusting line breaks—and even rewriting sentences if necessary—to get your lines to set smoothly, with consistent-looking spacing.

The basic justification options are:

- **Justified:** Words line up along both the left and right edges of the paragraph; also referred to as *fully justified*.
- **Flush left:** Words line up at the left edge of a paragraph, with the right edge breaking wherever necessary to accommodate the words on the line; occasionally still referred to as *ragged right.*
- **Flush right:** Words line up at the right edge, leaving the left edge ragged.
- **Forced justification:** A line of text, no matter its length, stretches to reach from the left edge to the right edge of the paragraph; usually used for headlines, and often difficult to read. —SZA/AJ/DD

Kerning. Kerning is adjusting the space between individual letters. Since each letter is designed within its own little "box," there's always a wall between letters. This isn't an issue when the letters themselves are pretty boxy, like a *D* and an *E* next to each other. But put a *W* and *A*, or an *A* and a *V* next to each other at a large type size, and they'll look like they're keeping each other at arm's length.

WAVE
WAVE

Before and after kerning.

Some fonts have *kerned pairs* built-in: information that automatically nudges pairs like *Wa* or *To* together at print time. (The number of kerned pairs in a font varies; generally speaking, the more the better!) But having the information built into the font helps only when you're using an application that "understands" kerned pairs: all page layout programs know what to do with them, while most word processors don't. And all upscale layout programs let you kern any letter combination manually.

Tracking. Kerning is an art. *Tracking,* on the other hand, is a coarse but occasionally necessary approach: it squeezes together (or moves apart) *all* selected letters by adjusting the spaces between them. Rather than trying to adjust the relationship between special pairs of letters, tracking is usually used just to fit whatever needs to get onto a single line. Used judiciously, tracking is a handy layout tool. And it's also a function you don't find in word processors, where the same result is obtained by using condensed or expanded "styles" for a font.

Tracking is used in page layout programs to squeeze or spread letters on a line. It's called character spacing in some word processors, and in some programs the same function comes from extended or condensed "styles."

Tracking is used in page layout programs to squeeze or spread letters on a line. It's called character spacing in some word processors, and in some programs the same function comes from extended or condensed "styles."

Tracking is used in page layout programs to squeeze or spread letters on a line. It's called character spacing in some word processors, and in some programs the same function comes from extended or condensed "styles."

Tracking is used in page layout programs to squeeze or spread letters on a line. It's called character spacing in some word processors, and in some programs the same function comes from extended or condensed "styles."

Tracking is used in page layout programs to squeeze or spread letters on a line. It's called character spacing in some word processors, and in some programs the same function comes from extended or condensed "styles."

Top, unadjusted text. Left, slight and very tight tracking; right, slight and very loose tracking.

On the beaten track. Both tracking and kerning affect letterspacing, with tracking applied to several characters, or full lines of text at a time. If your text needs both tracking and kerning, it is wise to do the tracking first, and then do the touch-up with kerning. —RT

Ligatures. *Ligated* characters, or *ligatures*, are not the same as kerned pairs, although they share the same philosophy of keeping certain letters together. Unlike kerned pairs, however, ligated characters actually touch each other. You can see in the picture here the difference ligatures make, although the picture doesn't illustrate the subtlety that comes into play when you're reading body text and the ligatures help the words flow by.

Ligatures tie certain letters together.

fi fl ff
ﬁ ﬂ ﬀ

Most fonts have the *ﬂ* and *ﬁ* ligatures included in their option-character set (on Shift Option 5 and Shift Option 6), so you can specifically type them if you need them. But if you're that picky about your type, you'll be using a high-end program like QuarkXPress that lets you simply specify that ligatures be used where possible.

Font Creation and Design

Fontographer. Fontographer ($500, Macromedia) lets you create your own PostScript, TrueType, or Multiple Masters fonts, letter by letter. If you don't want to start drawing from scratch, Fontographer offers many automatic creation tools (including autotracing of printed or hand-drawn artwork) and allows you to import an existing font and modify the character outlines individually or en masse. You can even create a font by interpolating between two fonts or two weights of the same font. It offers excellent automated production tools for adjusting font metrics (which define the way the characters fit together), *hinting* (to make the type clear and readable on the screen and on low-resolution printers), and building extensive kerning tables. —SZA/KT

macromedia.com

Special effects. You don't always need just the right font: sometimes you can create it yourself.

For words or phrases that serve as the focal point of a page, you can alter an existing font in Illustrator or Freehand. These programs let you turn text into editable PostScript outlines which can be manipulated in various ways to achieve all sorts of unusual and fantastic effects. You can do anything to the outlines that you can do to any other artwork in either program. For instance, you can use FreeHand's Paste Inside command or Illustrator's Mask feature to place a full color TIFF image within a series of characters. Or maybe you want to give your type a rough look; use Illustrator's Roughen filter, or a third-party filter like Doodle Jr. to make jagged or rounded, bumpy text.

When it comes to changing the font of lines and lines of body text, you don't want to edit the outlines—but you can alter the font right in a program like QuarkXPress. You can stipulate that the height or width of a font be a percentage of its original design; the definition can be used on selected text, or as part of a style definition so it will be automatically applied to all the text.— SZA/RT

You can alter a font with commands in QuarkXPress.

This is all the same font, with
various scaling options applied.

Managing Your Fonts

Font Files and Suitcases

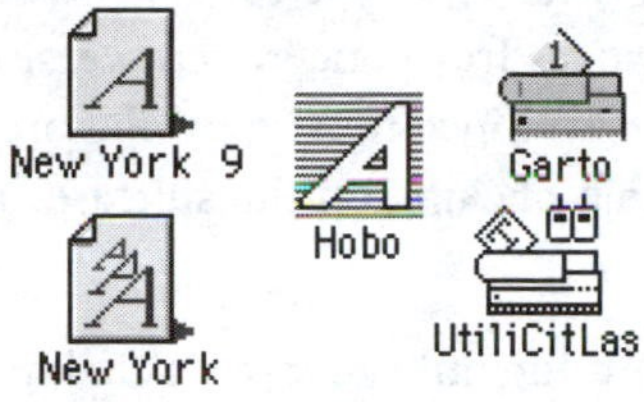

Font file icons. There are three different kinds of font file icons, for bitmapped fonts, TrueType fonts, and printer fonts. A truetype font has a single A on its icon, and a TrueType font has multiple A's. Printer font icons vary according to their manufacturers; three different ones are shown here.

But if you look in your Fonts folder, it's unlikely that you'll see any bitmapped or TrueType file icons, because the files are usually combined into a *suitcase,* a special type of file with a distinctive icon.

Suitcases. A suitcase is similar to a folder in that it holds other items, you drag things into and out of it, and you can double-click on it to open it. But a suitcase is actually a *file*, not a folder, and the components you see when you open a suitcase are not separate files but *resources* that make up the suitcase file.

A suitcase window is branded with a little—what else?—suitcase in its upper left to remind you you're not working with a folder. Although bitmapped and TrueType font files can exist on their own as separate files, once you put them in a suitcase they become part of the suitcase file—they're the resources in the suitcase.

What this means on a practical level is that if you drag a font icon out of a suitcase, you actually get a copy dialog on the screen as a new file is created to hold the font you're dragging, since it didn't exist independently inside the suitcase the way a document exists inside a folder. (And that's also why searching for fonts with Find File doesn't work when they're inside suitcases!) The font you drag out comes out as a separate font file, not as another suitcase—although you could drag it directly into another suitcase.

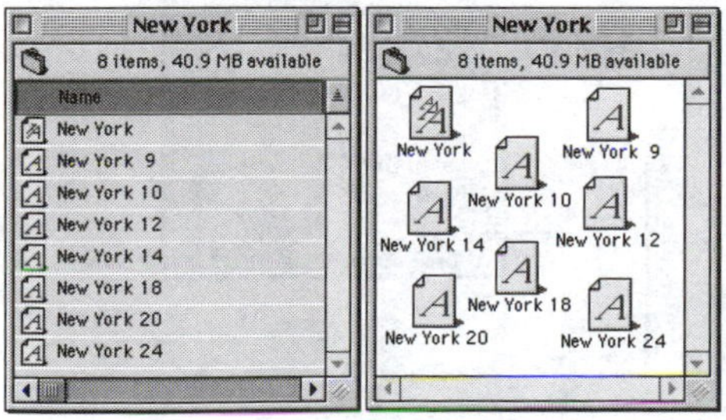

Two views of an open suitcase; note the suitcase icon in the window's upper-left corner.

Putting the font file away. When a font file has been created by dragging it out of its suitcase, you can select its icon and choose the Put Away command from the Finder's file menu—and the font will zip right back into the suitcase from whence it came.

Change the sentence used in the sample
Chapter 1

Seeing font samples. You can see a sample of a font by double-clicking on the bitmapped or TrueType font file; TrueType fonts provide samples in three sizes. (The sample sentence changes from one system version to the next; the ones shown here are from OS 8.1.) Since most font files are stored in suitcases, that means you'll be double-clicking on the suitcase, and then on the font file.

Double-clicking on a printer font file only gets you a dialog telling you what it's for.

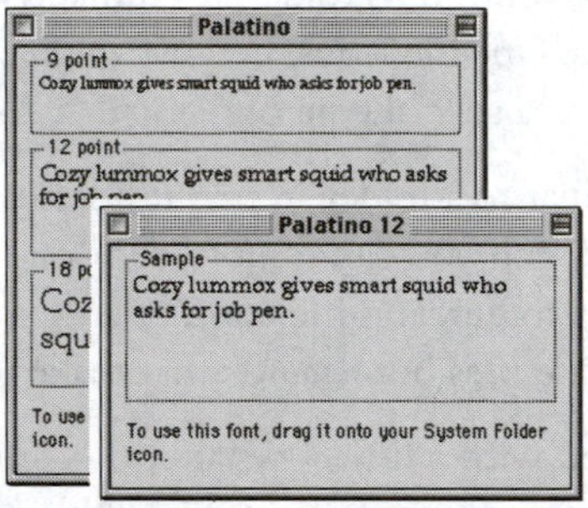

Double-clicking on a font file opens a font sample; TrueType (top) shows three sizes, while a bitmapped version shows the size you clicked on.

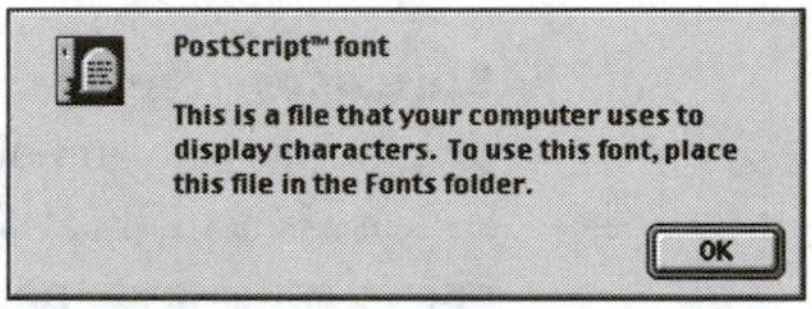

Double-clicking on a printer font doesn't get you much of anything.

Packing suitcases. You can combine suitcase contents without ever opening a suitcase or touching an individual font file. Just drag one suitcase into the other; the dragged suitcase dissolves into nothingness and its contents are added to the first suitcase. Depending on which suitcases you're combining, you might want to change the title of the suitcase that's left.

Font and suitcase manipulation are limited when they're in the Fonts folder and applications are running; this is covered in the next section.

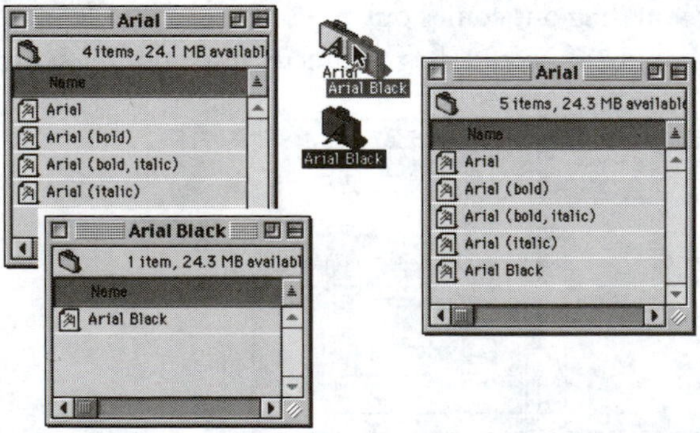

Drag one suitcase into another to combine their contents.

Project suitcases. If you're working on a special project that requires a bunch of special fonts that you don't normally use, there's no reason to keep all those fonts cluttering your Font menus, especially if you're working on the project sporadically instead of every day.

For special projects, make special suitcases: a project suitcase to hold all the bitmapped and TrueType fonts you need for a single project (excepting those that are part of your usual Font menu). You can drag just the single suitcase in and out of your Fonts folder.

What about the companion printer fonts if you're using PostScript? You could apply a label to the project suitcase and all its related printer fonts to make it easy to gather them up when the project's over. But in between uses, there's no need to move the printer files out of the Fonts folder, since they don't use up any memory or put their names in Font menus.

If you're constantly shuffling fonts in and out of suitcases and your Fonts folder, however, you should consider getting font management software like Suitcase, Master Juggler, or Adobe Type Manager Deluxe, all described later in the chapter.

Making an empty suitcase. There's still no New Suitcase command anywhere in the system software, so you can't just make an empty suitcase and start putting fonts in it. If you want to start with an empty suitcase when you're making a special combination of fonts, you have to take an existing suitcase, open it, empty its contents, and change its name.

You can cut out many of these steps by making an empty suitcase and tucking it away in, say, a utilities folder. When you want an empty suitcase, duplicate the "master" empty one, and save yourself some steps.

Installing Fonts

Installing fonts. All fonts—bitmapped and TrueType (loose or in suitcases), and printer files—go in the Fonts folder inside your System Folder. You can drag any of these items into the closed System Folder, and they'll be automatically routed to the Fonts folder.

You can add fonts to your Fonts folder at any time, but they won't appear in the Font menus of any applications already running because Font menus are "built" when a program first runs (although some high-end graphics and layout programs know how to rebuild their Font menus while they're running). You'll get a dialog reminding you

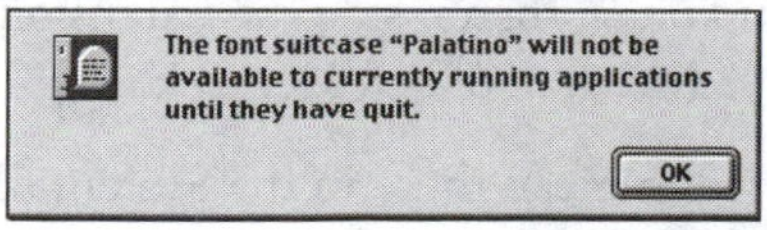

of the situation after the font's been placed in the folder; if you want to use the new font in a current application, you'll have to quit and relaunch it.

Removing a font from the Fonts folder is a simple matter of dragging it out of the folder, or out of one of the suitcases in the folder. But you won't be allowed to do it until you quit all the open applications. In fact, even if you're only trying to move a font from one suitcase to another when they're both in the Fonts folder, you won't be allowed to do it unless there are no applications running.

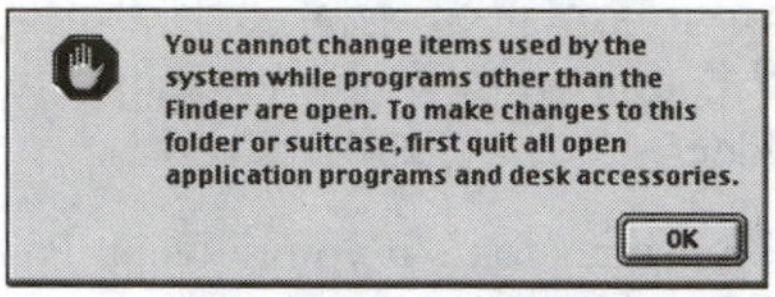

If you want to override this restriction, you can: drag the Fonts folder out of the System Folder, then drag the font out of the folder or its suitcase, and then put the Fonts folder back in place. But you're courting disaster doing this, since the font you removed will still be listed in Font menus of running applications, and selecting its name could bring the whole system crashing down.

You can't have too many fonts. But you can have too many fonts in your Fonts folder and in your Font menu.

There's a limit to the number of suitcases the system can access at once: 128. (This is usually described as a limit on how many suitcases can be "open," but don't confuse that with the suitcases' windows being open on the desktop: any suitcase the system is using is considered an open file—and you're unlikely to have over a hundred windows open on your desktop.) But since you can have dozens or even a hundred fonts in a suitcase, there's no practical limit on the number of fonts you can have on your system at one time.

Memory and disk space concerns aren't as important as they were, what with multimegabytes of memory and gigabytes of storage space on modern Macs. But the more fonts you use at one time, the more sluggish things become: every application takes longer to launch because it's building its Font menu, and it takes a long time to scroll through a never-ending Font menu of 200 choices.

So, move suitcases that contain groups of fonts for specific projects into and out of your Fonts folder as you need them, or use a utility that lets you manipulate which fonts are open at any given time.

What's an "installed" font. In the early days, fonts were resources stored directly in the System file; printer fonts, when they were invented, were first stored loose in the System Folder, then inside the Extensions folder. Since System 7.1, however, we've had the Fonts folder to keep things a little neater.

The phrase *installed font* used to mean those in the System file; now it refers to all the bitmapped and TrueType fonts in the Fonts folder. But the phrase also usually includes any font that's available to your application; so, if you use a font management utility like Suitcase, an installed font may not even be on your startup drive—but if it's in your Font menu, it's considered installed for most purposes.

System fonts and system font. The phrase *system fonts* can refer to the group of fonts that are installed with your system, or strictly to certain sizes of Charcoal/Chicago and Geneva that are used by the system for menus, dialogs, and desktop icons. But *the* system font is the one you select, through the Appearances control panel, as the one to be used for menus.

All these fonts, and where to find them
Later this chapter

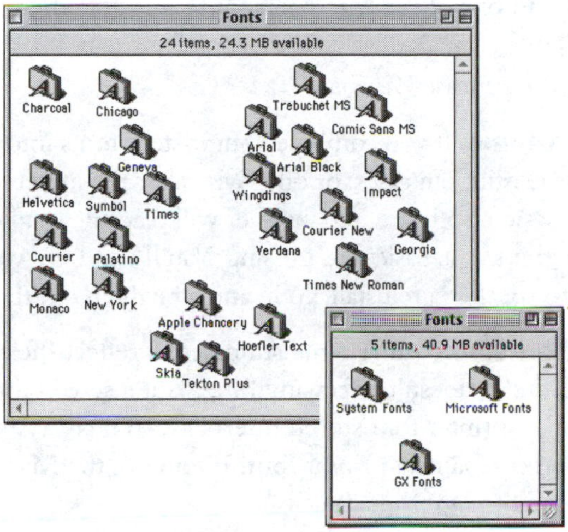

Before and after organizing the fonts that come with your system.

Organize your system fonts. Depending on what you included in your original system installation, you have at least ten font suitcases (the basic system fonts), possibly four more (from QuickDraw GX), or even ten or twelve others (from installing Microsoft Explorer). But whether you have ten or twenty-four suitcases from the installation, you don't need them all around. In case you have them all but don't know which are which:

Basic System	***GX***	***Microsoft***
Charcoal	Apple Chancery	Arial
Chicago	Hoefler Text	Arial Black
Courier	Skia	Comic Sans MS
Geneva		Courier New
Helvetica		Georgia
Monaco		Impact
New York		Minion Web
Palatino		Times New Roman
Symbol		Trebuchet MS
Times		Verdana
		Webdings
		Wingdings

Rather than put them all into a single suitcase, which you might prefer to do, I keep each of these groups in their own suitcases named *SystemFonts, GXFonts,* and *WebFonts.* You can handle everything in six steps:

1. Select nine of the ten basic system fonts and drag them into the tenth's suitcase.
2. Rename the suitcase *SystemFonts.*
3. Select the three GX fonts and drag them into the fourth suitcase.
4. Rename the suitcase *GXFonts.*
5. Select all but one of the Microsoft fonts and drag them into the one suitcase.
6. Rename the suitcase *WebFonts.*

Reinstall problem. If you combine your system fonts into a single suitcase, or rename the existing suitcases, or otherwise alter the initial setup and then reinstall your system software, the installer will place new suitcases in your Fonts folder since it thinks the basics are missing. You'll wind up with two copies of all the basic fonts; so, after a reinstall, go in and straighten out the mess!

Renaming fonts. You can rename suitcases to reflect their contents, or even your attitude, and it doesn't affect anything. But a screen font keeps the name of its companion printer font stored internally, so it always knows what to look for; so, *never* rename a printer font. If you do, the Mac won't be able to find it when it's time to print.

adobe.com
symantec.com
alsoftinc.com

Juggling suitcases. If you've got just a handful of fonts installed on your Mac, you don't have to read any further. But if you're a font junkie, and you need a way to handle your font collection, moving groups of fonts in and out of service according to the projects you're working on (or just according to whim), there are three utilities that can help: Alsoft's **MasterJuggler** ($50), Symantec's **Suitcase** ($65), and **Adobe Type Manager (ATM) Deluxe** ($70).

Each of these font management utilities lets you store the fonts you don't need all the time someplace other than the Fonts folder. You can access fonts from any mounted volume, activating them when you need them and disabling them when they've served their purpose. By defining *sets* (a collection of fonts, usually grouped by project), you can shuffle fonts in and out of service as a group even if they aren't in the same suitcase. The programs keep track of where all the fonts are, so you don't have to keep all the printer fonts in the Fonts folder, either.

Some Mac programs, like PageMaker and QuarkXPress can even recognize fonts that have been switched on or off, and update their font menus accordingly without your having to quit and relaunch them. —SZA/GS

The Font Menu

True fonts come shining through. Some applications are nice enough to supply a font menu whose font names are displayed in their own typefaces instead of the standard Charcoal. Of course, that becomes a problem when you have picture fonts installed, since some of them are *very* difficult to read. There's a little bit of a tradeoff, since true Font menus take longer to draw than plain ones; this is especially true of the first time you use the menu after launching the program, and is especially noticeable on older Macs. Nice programs let you choose plain or fancy on a click-by-click basis by, say, holding down Option when you want to see the true fonts in the menus. Several utilities, like Master Juggler and MenuFonts, let you add true-font menus to all your applications.

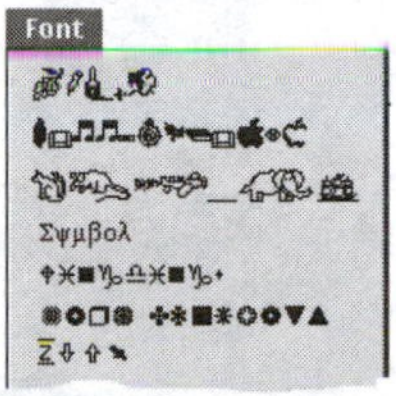

Some true-font menus are difficult to read.

Font style shorthand. When you buy a family of fonts, you'll see several to many printer fonts and usually a single suitcase. You put that suitcase in your Fonts folder, and *wham!* there are twenty new fonts suddenly listed in your Font menus because there were so many in the suitcase. Worse than that, the simply named suitcase has little to do with the odd names you see: you thought you installed Univers, but you get eight different listings, only one of them beginning with U, as shown in the "menu" here. (The real menu is much worse, because these font names are interspersed among all the others.)

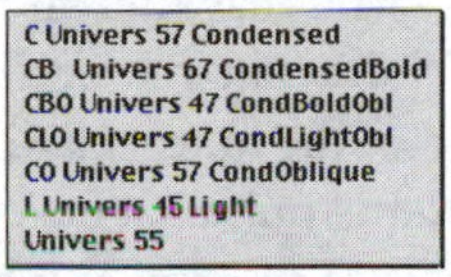

Because so many programs display fonts not only in menus but also in scrolling lists in dialogs, and those lists are generally of fixed width, multiple-member font families caused a problem: you'd get a half-dozen or more listings of a certain font, but you couldn't see the difference between, say, Garamond Bold and Garamond Semibold, because all you could see of each was the first word.

Unfortunately, the solution was to put descriptors in *front* of the name, causing the menu-listing problem. Here are some of the initials you'll see, and what they stand for (they can be used in combination, as you can see in the picture):

B	bold	H	heavy	P	poster
Bk	book	I	italic	S	semi
Blk	black	K	kursiv	Sl	slanted
C	condensed	L	light	U	ultra
D	demibold	N	narrow	X	extra
E	extended	O	oblique		

These abbreviations are not the same as the ones used for printer fonts names, which were described in the section *PostScript Fonts;* printer fonts almost always have the first five letters of the family name in the beginning of their odd names.

Playing the numbers. You may have noticed, in the figure on the previous page, that many of the Univers fonts in the menu include numbers. Univers, in fact, has twenty-seven versions, numbered 39 (ultra condensed thin) through 83 (extra black extended). Other large font families, like Helvetica and Frutiger, include numbered versions, too. You might guess the numbers are somehow related to what the fonts look like, and you'd be right.

For numbered fonts, the first of the two digits refers to the weight, with 3 being light, 9 being very heavy, and 5 the medium. The second digit refers to a different aspect of the font: —JS

Number	*Stands for*
3	extended
4	extended oblique
5	roman (plain)
6	oblique
7	condensed
8	condensed oblique
9	ultra condensed

Managing the Font menu. If you have more than a couple dozen fonts installed—and these days, who doesn't?—you may find yourself taking a very long scroll down the Font menu to select the font you need; you may even give up on using Zapf Chancery because of the long trek to its spot at the bottom. Dealing with the multiple entries for family members, and trying to remember what fonts look like in a plain-font menu… in all, the Font menu isn't always a nice place to visit.

But there are several utilities that make the experience much more pleasant, allowing you to organize all those family members and/or display fonts in their own styles.

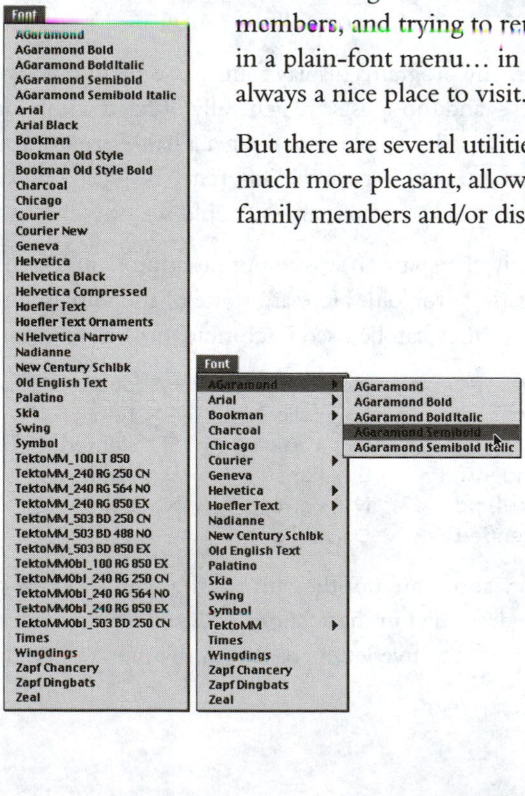

The original menu (left), and the version created by a utility that groups family members.

- Adobe's **Type Reunion Deluxe** ($40) shortens your Font menu by organizing fonts into families, placing all the styles for each family into a submenu. It can display fonts in their own typefaces and, as a crowning touch, lists the most recently used fonts at the top of the menu.
- Impossible Software's **TypeTamer** ($60) consolidates font families into submenus, making your Font menu easier to navigate. TypeTamer performs a few other handy tricks as well. It places an icon beside each font name, indicating whether the font is PostScript, TrueType, or bitmapped. It lets you zip to a font in the menu by typing the first few letters of its name. Best of all, the program's TopFonts feature places the names of the fonts you're using at the top of the Font menu, allowing you to reselect them without scrolling down the menu. TypeTamer also lets you create your own font categories for the Font menu, based on the way you work. For example, you might want to place all your script fonts in a category, or maybe divide fonts up by vendor or publishing project.
- Dubl-Click Software's **MenuFonts** ($40) is a control panel that groups fonts by family in the Font menu and displays them in their own type styles. It includes a number of other nifty features as well. It puts a bar along the edge of the menu that lets you access samples of a font in different sizes. It lets you know whether a font is PostScript, TrueType, or bitmapped by placing *Ps*, *Tt*, or *Bm* next to the name. And, to save you time when you have a long Font menu, MenuFonts lets you jump to any letter in the Font menu simply by pressing a key on the keyboard (press Z and you're whisked to Zapf Chancery, for example). MenuFonts has trouble displaying Multiple Master fonts in its submenus, but that won't be a problem for the majority of users.
- **Suitcase** and **MasterJuggler**, font-management utilities described earlier in the chapter, provide true-font menus as an added benefit. —SZA/EF

adobe.com
impossible.com
dublclick.com

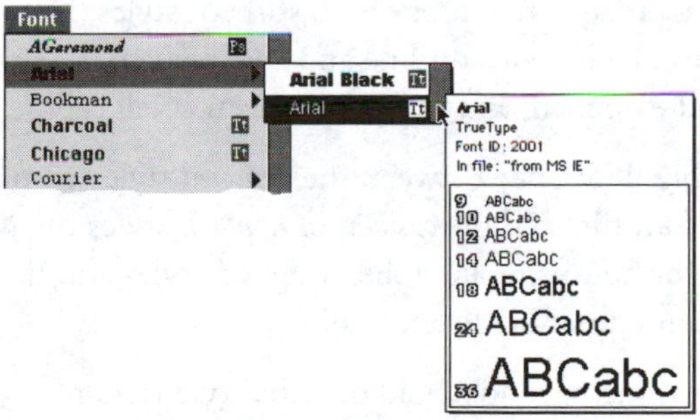

MenuFonts organizes fonts by family, marks the type of font, and provides samples and basic information about the font.

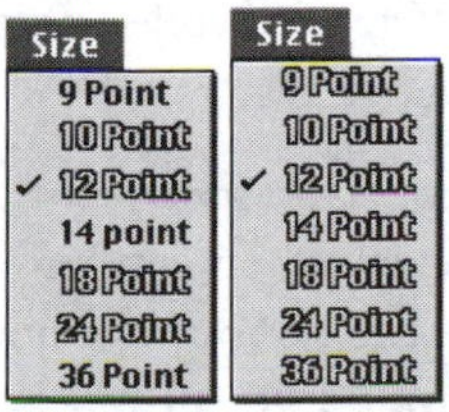

Point sizes in menus. A Size menu or submenu not only lets you choose the size for the font, but also indicates which screen sizes are available as bitmapped fonts by outlining them in the menu; the menu at the left in this picture shows four sizes are installed. If all the point sizes are outlined, you either have *lots* of bitmapped sizes installed or, more likely, you're working with a TrueType font. You can, of course, select a nonoutlined (uninstalled) size; you'll just have to put up with distorted type on the screen.

If you're using ATM to handle screen display, the bitmapped sizes are still the only ones appearing outlined.

IN THE BEGINNING

In the earliest Mac days, adding something to a Font menu took considerable effort. First and foremost, you had to *find* some fonts, which were few and far between—and strictly bitmapped affairs, of course. Then there was the problem of actually installing them, because the Font/DA Mover hadn't been invented yet.

If you tracked down some fonts and a font-adding utility (no easy feat, seeing as how there was no Web and little or no online support of any kind for Macs—in fact, there were no *modems* for Macs, or telecom software!), you still faced the final problems: a Font menu was limited to a nonscrolling list of 20 fonts. Which were listed, not in alphabetical order, but in reverse order of their installation.

Using Fonts

Working With Styles

Designed and custom styles. You've got your basic gang of four for most fonts: regular, bold, italic, and bold-italic. (We discussed all this early in the chapter.) But your style menu offers all sorts of styles, like the handy underline and the usually hideous outline and shadow variations; then there's condensed and extended, and sometimes even small caps.

But there's a big difference between the *designed* styles whose descriptions are included in a font file, and the *custom*, or *applied,* styles the Mac draws on the fly. And it can be confusing how the designed styles and the applied ones interact—or sometimes fail to act at all.

In general, anything beyond a bold or italic style is going to be applied by the Mac—unless the special style is in the font's name, like WhiteHorse Small Caps or Hothouse Condensed. Using an applied style—if it works at all—can have unexpected and sometimes unattractive results.

Use the Style menu. Using the Bold or Italic style from the style menu is the best way to apply a style to a font—even when you know you have a separately designed bold or italic style for that font. You may not have a choice, since usually the different cuttings of a font don't all appear in the menu. But if they do, don't worry about choosing, say, Cowboy Bold—just choose

Cowboy as the font and apply the bold style; Cowboy Bold will be automatically substituted for the printout.

This approach also has the advantage of letting you work with stylesheets in your application without switching fonts in the middle of a paragraph just to get a word bolded. For instance: You're using a stylesheet that's using Bookman Old Style as body text. You want to bold a phrase in the middle somewhere, so you select it and apply Bookman Old Style Bold from the Font menu. Everything's okay until you decide to redefine the style to use Century Schoolbook for the body text. But the phrase in the middle is no longer a bolded body font because you manually applied a different *font* there, not just a bold style—it remains Bookman Old Style Bold.

Applying styles
Chapter 16

Don't use the Style menu. If you have a font designed in a heavy weight, or designed as italic or oblique, don't add bold or italic to it from the Style menu. Sometimes adding an applied style on top of the same designed style won't change anything at all; but if it does, it's not going to change it for the better!

Underline. An applied underline style (and it's almost always applied, since underline formatting went out with typewriters and few fonts are *designed* as underlines) looks very different on the screen and in a printout. On screen, the underline is elegantly broken for descenders and swashes, and even shows up in the middle of a descender's bowl—in all, a rather nice look. But in the printout, you'll get a solid line for the underline, in a different thickness than what you saw on screen, and usually at a different distance from the baseline of the font. No WYSIWYG here! If you needed any further reason to avoid underlining things, this is it.

Underlines on-screen (left) and in printouts (right).

Minding your p's and q's! Minding your p's and q's!
Minding your p's and q's! Minding your p's and q's!

Small caps. The Small Caps style available in many Style menus gives you all capital letters, with the shifted ones larger than the unshifted ones. The Mac derives this style by using the uppercase letters from one size of the font for the unshifted characters, and using them from a different size of the font for the shifted, taller characters. As a result, the shifted, taller letters always look thicker than the unshifted, shorter ones—a very amateurish look.

But there are fonts designed as small caps, which keeps all the letter strokes at the same thickness. An added benefit of designed small caps is that the taller letters stay the right height in relation to the shorter ones. In derived small caps, the height difference depends on what size you're using; for some sizes, the difference is too exaggerated and at others the difference is barely discernable.

THIS IS A DERIVED SMALL CAPS FONT.
THIS IS A TRUE SMALL CAPS FONT.

Condensed and extended styles. The Condensed style you find in some Style menus isn't the same as a font designed as condensed, or compressed. The picture here shows the difference: the standard type is at the top; the second line is a condensed style applied by the Mac (most programs let you specify the amount of "condensation"); the bottom line is a true condensed font. You can see that while the second line has letters squeezed closer together, the letters in the last line are designed differently—the O's, for instance, are no longer round.

Top, the base font; middle, the applied condensed version; bottom, the designed condensed version.

An open mind—or a hole in the head?

An open mind—or a hole in the head?

An open mind—or a hole in the head?

When you choose a condensed style from a Style menu, there's no font substitution at print time, as there is for bold or italic/oblique fonts. A condensed font is an entirely different font family, usually with its own members, like Helvetica Condensed, Helvetica Condensed Bold, Helvetica Condensed Italic, and so on.

An *extended* or *expanded* font is the opposite of a condensed one, but all the issues are the same. The Mac can apply an extended style, but all it does is stretch the letters out on the line (the second line in the picture here); a font that's designed as extended has its letters designed differently (look at the rounder O and G in the bottom sample. And, as with condensed fonts, there's no font substitution at print time.

Top, the base font; middle, the applied extended version; bottom, the designed extended version.

STEPPING STONE, OR STUMBLING BLOCK?

STEPPING STONE, OR STUMBLING BLOCK?

STEPPING STONE, OR STUMBLING BLOCK?

The condensed and extended styles you find in some word processors have the same effect as does the tracking function in most page layout programs.

Sometimes bold, sometimes italic, sometimes not. Conventional wisdom says that unless you have a printer font for a particular style, it can't print that style at all. Sometimes that's true: the picture here, for instance, shows what's on the screen, and what's printed out, for the Hobo font with styles applied to it. Try other fonts, and you might find that bold or italic, or both, work even if the results are not exactly attractive.

There's information in each font that tells the printer whether it's allowed to alter the basic printer font to get the styles you've chosen. So, for instance, it can forbid the obliquing of a font when you use the italic style; it can allow a bold derivative through smearing the existing font a little or by using a slightly larger font size than is called for; it can specify that an outline style be white against a black shadow or an outline of the font character shape. The only way you'll know if your font will print with the style you see on your screen is by printing out a sample.

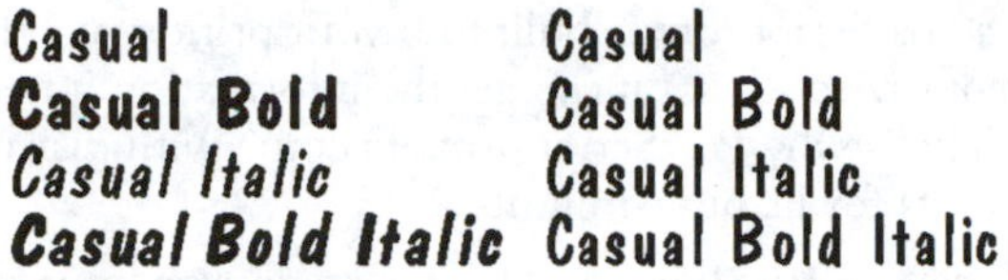

The screen display (left) and the printout (right).

Bolder than bold, blacker than black. When you apply a bold style to a basic font, the Mac substitutes a true bold font for printing whenever possible. But things get really tricky when you're working with more than just two weights of a font.

Consider one of my favorites: Quorum. I have five different weights in printer files: Light, Book, Medium, Bold, and Black. But only three screen fonts came with the family: Light, Book and Medium. Using the Bold style on the Book version gets the Bold font printed; bolding the Medium weight of the font is how you get the Black font printed. (Using bold on the Light weight does *nothing!*) But while the true-weight fonts are used in the printout, the document shows only that the original base font has had bold applied to it. Without a lot of experimentation, you might conclude that you're just missing certain screen fonts in this family and that you can't get at the two other weights. And you're going to have to experiment, because the interactions differ from one font to another.

Using ATM

ATM. ATM (Adobe Type Manager) is a program whose capabilities and availability seem to morph over time. Its main purpose in life is to give you smooth text from PostScript fonts: on screen, and on non-PostScript printers. And, with a feature that used to be in a product called SuperATM but is now rolled into plain ol' ATM, it can create a "fake" font to imitate one that's missing from your system but was originally used in a document that you're looking at or printing.

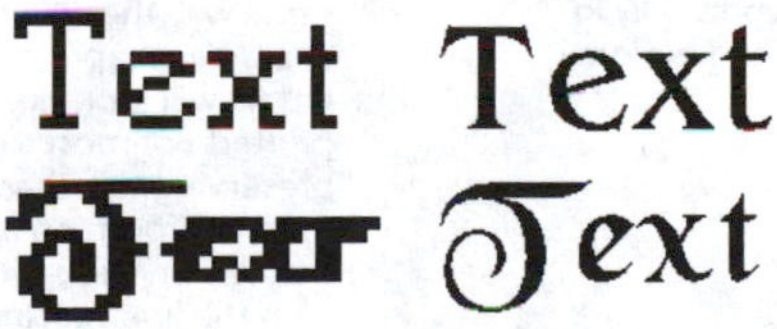

The ATM difference: smooth type at any size without a TrueType or matching bitmapped available.

You have ATM, even if you don't realize it, because it comes with your system software. If you have the OS 8 CD, you have to do a custom install of the QuickDraw GX component, ignoring QuickDraw GX itself and just installing ATM and the couple of extra fonts you'll find in the same section. If you have OS 8.1, you'll find an Adobe Software folder on the CD, with the ATM installer inside.

Partial custom installations
Chapter 8

ATM and font files. ATM uses the information in a PostScript font file to draw a smooth-looking font on the screen at any size, or to send to a non-PostScript printer. This simple fact has two corollaries:

- Even if a PostScript font is built into your printer, you'll need the printer file on your Mac so that it can get the information it needs for the screen display. That's why PostScript printers come with disks providing the printer fonts for its built-in fonts.
- You still need a TrueType or at least a single-size bitmapped version for any font you want ATM to render for the screen, because that's the only way you'll get the font into your font menu.

The slight blurring around letter edges (left) produces smoother-looking fonts.

The ATM control panel. The ATM control panel (its name is *~ATM* to make it load last) provides several options for controlling the appearance of text on the screen.

This gives you smooth text on the screen and on non-PostScript printers. If it's turned off, all the other options are dimmed.

The more fonts you use, the higher this should be set. If you find that fonts are succumbing to the jaggies on-screen or in printouts (and you're sure they're PostScript fonts), that's a clue that you need a larger cache.

Turning on this option smoothes letter edges by using colors that fade gradually from the text color to the background color, fooling the eye into seeing a smoother edge; you can disable it for fonts being used at sizes for which a screen font is installed.

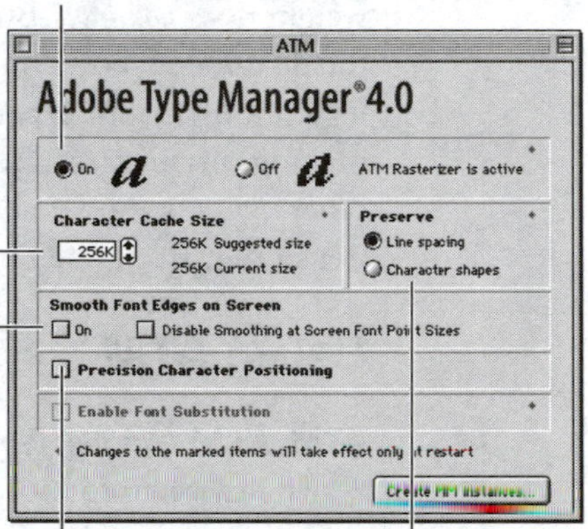

The 4.0 version of ATM can position characters along a line of text more accurately than earlier versions when you check this option; it works only in applications that can support it or "fractional character widths."

You can't have both. Line spacing shows line breaks on the screen the same way they'll be printed out; character shapes shows what the letters will look like when they're printed. For most fonts and styles, preserving the character shapes takes up more room on a line than will actually be used on the printout. Stick with the line spacing option.

The preemptive strike. The fonts you see on the screen when ATM is running aren't always the ATM-rendered PostScript fonts. If there's a TrueType version of the font available, the Mac uses that instead; and, if there's a bitmapped version of that particular size (which is unlikely for a large size), that's given first preference for screen display.

Since TrueType wins out over ATM display for *any* point size, you'll probably want to get rid of TrueType versions of fonts where you can if your font design and layout is super-important; this is getting difficult to do, since so many fonts come with a TrueType version as the only screen font.

Fake fonts. Besides rendering smooth type for screen display, ATM can substitute a faked font in any document you open that was created with fonts not on your system. It does this by using two special multiple master fonts, *Adobe Sans MM* and *Adobe Serif MM*, installed into your Fonts folder when you install ATM or Adobe Acrobat or the Acrobat Reader; companion printer fonts, *AdobeSanMM* and *AdobeSerMM* are also installed so you can print the faked fonts.

I had a very weird problem with these fonts when I first launched Adobe Acrobat 3.0, which also uses them. It wouldn't run at all because it said the fonts weren't around, although they were in the Fonts folder. I dragged them out and put them in again; Acrobat still couldn't see them. I got rid of them and ran the Acrobat installer again, which put new copies in my Fonts folder. It *still* couldn't see them, and wouldn't run. I dragged them out of the Fonts folder again, and then dragged them into the closed System Folder, which routed them to the Fonts folder. And, finally, Acrobat could see them. (I'm only sharing this, not explaining this, because some things are beyond explanation.)

Now you see it, now you don't. If you haven't installed ATM but you're using Acrobat or its Reader and everything's working fine with its fonts substitution, that's because a special "personal" edition of ATM is installed along with Acrobat or the Reader; it's personal to the Acrobat programs and runs only when one of them is running. You may find ATM in the Acrobat folder, but putting it in with your control panels won't do you any good on a system-wide basis.

Miscellaneous Issues

Where's that font? Sometimes you know you have a font installed, but it doesn't appear in the Font menu. The first thing to do is not be so sure of yourself: double-check to see that the font is really installed correctly (this is the most common source of the problem). Remember that a font won't appear in an application's menu if you installed it (or opened it with Suitcase, ATM Deluxe, or MasterJuggler) when the application was already running.

Fonts and printing. The way a font is printed depends on both the font and the printer—and, for that matter, the contents of the Fonts folder, and your system setup. You might be using a TrueType font on a PostScript printer, or a PostScript font on a non-PostScript printer; you might be using a PostScript font but you have only the screen font for it on your machine; you may or may not have ATM running. All these issues are covered in detail in Chapter 15.

WWYTINWYG. That's: *when what you type is not what you get.* This usually happens when you're working with a picture-type font of symbols or ornaments:

you type a certain character, but the one that you think is coming out of your fingers just isn't the one that appears on the screen. You check the characters set in Key Caps, you're sure you've used the correct key combination, you type it again—and right before your eyes, the wrong character shows up again. Here are a few of the things that can cause this uncomfortable phenomenon:

- You don't realize that the Caps Lock key is down, effectively replacing your unshifted character with the shifted one.
- Your application is set to replace straight quotes and apostrophes with their curly equivalents.
- The software you're using makes certain automatic corrections, like capitalizing the beginning of a sentence or a single letter *i*.
- Your application or some utility watches as you type and replaces certain consecutive keystrokes with another character—like using an em dash (normally on Shift Option -) when you type two hyphens in a row.
- The text is formatted for Small Caps, which substitutes shifted letters of a smaller size for the unshifted letters you type.

In most cases, if you switch out of the pictorial font and into a plain text font, you'll notice the character substitution and be able to correct it.

Design guidelines. While most beginners succumb to the temptation of using as many fonts as possible on a single page, most settle down to more reasonable approaches after a little while. Here are a few basic guidelines to help you settle down in the right direction:

- Use a serif font for body text; they're generally easier to read in a large block of type.
- Use a sans serif font for large-type headlines; serifs in large print are very distracting.
- Mixing a serif font for body text with a sans serif for headlines is fine; mixing different fonts in the body text, or as headline fonts, is something best left to professionals.
- Use fonts from the same family when you can to achieve an overall unity of design. Since families come with members in a range of weights and styles, you can get variety yet be sure that everything works well together.
- Use a single style option for emphasis: **bold** or *italic*, for example, but ***not both***. Leave underlining to typewriters, and avoid using ALL CAPITAL LETTERS for emphasis within text.
- The size of the font for a block of text should be related to the width of the column; the narrower the column, the smaller the font. The rule of thumb is that a column should hold an alphabet and a half (A through Z plus A through M, typed with no spaces) of the font.

For faxing. For fax documents, whether printed for standard faxing or sent directly from you computer's modem, be careful about which fonts you choose. The font should be a little larger than what you might normally use for a printout; at least 12 points, and 14 points for some fonts. Avoid fancy, especially script, fonts; a sans serif font is most likely to come out clear at the other end. The font should have large counters (the round areas inside a lowercase g, for instance) so they won't bleed closed at the other end of the fax transmission.

More font utilities. You might have your font menus straightened out, with families bunched together and everyone appearing in their actual fonts instead of Charcoal, but your font-wrangling tedium isn't over; luckily, neither is our list of font utilities. These take care of overall font chores like checking for corrupted fonts, looking for "orphans" (printer files with no screen fonts and vice versa), and corralling duplicate files on one or more volumes.

theinside.com
diamondsoft.com

- **Font Box** ($80, Insider Software) scours your hard drive and other attached volumes, cataloguing your fonts and checking for duplicates, corrupted files, and orphan fonts. Most people I know who've used it love it, but I ran into some problems. Although I chose, in a dialog, that certain duplicate fonts should be renamed, they were actually deleted; the ones that were renamed were named to odd things like *M* (for *MT Extra)* and the ones mistakenly deleted were taken from my system disk—so I returned to a desktop devoid of Charcoal, Chicago, and Geneva. (Good thing there's a version of Chicago in the ROM!) Still, people who use it more often have few or no problems, so it's still on my recommended list.

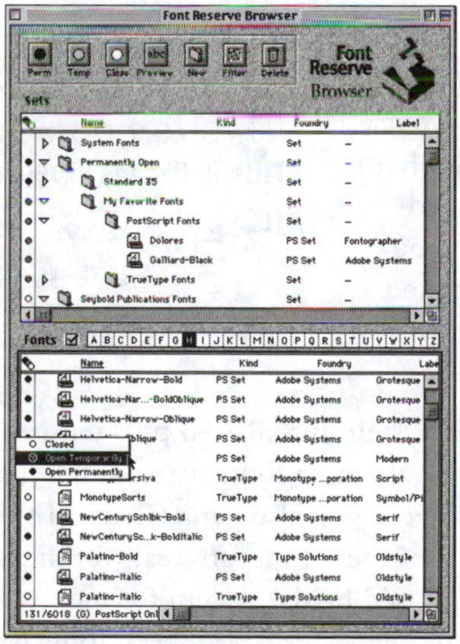

Font Reserve takes an entirely new approach to handling font files, working with its own database.

- **Font Reserve** ($120, DiamondSoft) takes an entirely different approach to font handling, as you can see by the picture here. It searches through your font suitcases and compiles a database of their contents; you manipulate the database rather than the fonts or suitcases themselves. Font Reserve checks for corrupted fonts and orphans, lets you search for a font, and preview typefaces.

Whatever happened to ID conflicts? Unexplained phenomena involving fonts used to occur regularly because of font ID conflicts. The conflicts stopped suddenly (even before Mulder and Sculley could investigate).

Each font on a Mac has to have its own Font ID number, and there used to be only 256 available—with Apple reserving the first 128 for its own use. With hundreds of fonts available in the first few years of the Mac's existence, you'd wind up with a few using the same ID, causing all sorts of trouble. In 1988, Apple replaced a critical resource (FONT) with another one (NFNT), which could accommodate 16,000 different font IDs. Occasionally there are still some conflicts, but they're rare. —SZA/RT

System Software Fonts

Roundup

You have more fonts than you think. When you install your system software, you get nine basic fonts installed in your Font menu (Chicago, Geneva, Times, and so on). But OS 8.1 comes with twenty fonts that can be installed from three different places; in addition, if you have an Apple printer—*any* Apple printer—it came with another twenty fonts; and, finally, if your printer is a PostScript printer, you get another dozen or so along with the printer. So, you probably have at least 40 or 50 fonts at your disposal if you know where to look. (And that's font *families*—I'm not counting the different styles that each font might come in.)

IN THE BEGINNING

The Mac's original fonts were all bitmaps, of course, but many of them were redone as TrueType when the time came. Others didn't make the cut, and dropped out of the system software a long time ago. I thought you'd like to see what they looked like (that's Cairo in the middle).

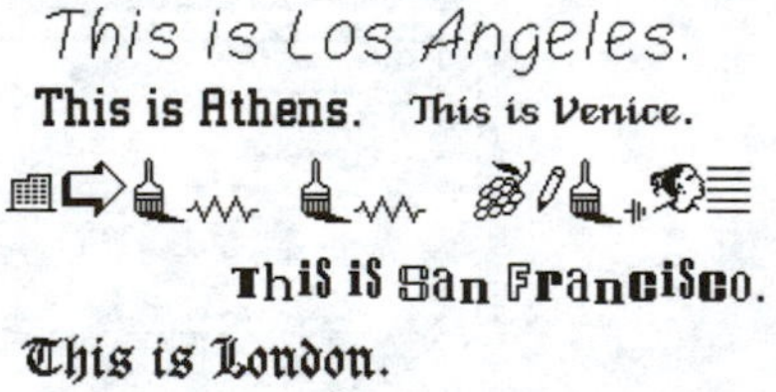

This is Los Angeles.
This is Athens. This is Venice.
This is San Francisco.
This is London.

The basic fonts. A basic system installation puts ten suitcases in your Fonts folder; in addition to the nine fonts listed in the installer (if you customize down to that level), you also get a Charcoal suitcase—the OS 8 default system font. Most of these fonts are real workhorses: Chicago, Charcoal, and Geneva are used by the system for menus and desktop items; New York and Geneva are highly readable screen fonts (one serif, one sans); and Times, Helvetica, and Palatino are the basic PostScript triumvirate (with Palatino providing some welcome relief from the narrow Times).

Of the final three, you get two monofonts (one serif and one sans), and Symbol, an overlooked collection of mathematical symbols that can also serve other purposes.

Basic System Fonts

Charcoal, the alternate system font introduced with OS 8.

Chicago, the original system font, designed for great screen legibility at 12 points.

Courier, in case you want your computer to pretend it's a typewriter.

Geneva, the Mac version of the classic Helvetica font. The Swiss name for Switzerland is Confoederatio Helvetica. Get it?

Helvetica, the classic sans serif font selected as *the* sans serif for PostScript printers. But it's difficult to read on the screen, even when there are specific bitmapped versions available.

Monaco, monofont. What else would you call it when all the original bitmapped fonts were named for cities?

New York, a pun gone awry. The Mac version of the staid Times font used by the newspaper of the same name-but it was the *London* Times that used it.

Palatino, similar to Times but more readable with its wider characters.

Symbol,τηισ ισ τηε σψμβολ φοντ.

Times, the staid newspaper font chosen as "the" PostScript serif font in the early days despite its poor screen presence.

The hidden fonts. There are four additional Apple TrueType fonts on your system installation disk that get installed if you install QuickDraw GX. However, since most people don't need QuickDraw GX itself (and we recommend against installing it), you're missing those extra fonts. You can, however, simply run the Installer—either the main Installer or the QuickDraw GX installer—and customize an installation so you can get at the fonts and bypass QuickDraw GX itself. (Customized installations are covered in Chapter 8.)

The four extra fonts are shown here—although you'll get only three additional suitcases, since the two Hoefler fonts are in one suitcase.

The GX Fonts

Apple Chancery is a near-copy of Zapf Chancery, with a larger x-height for more readability, and differently styled numbers.

Skia is a neat little informal font that's easy to read at small sizes. Custom-made for tiny or crowded Help windows.

Hoefler Text straightforward text font with old-style numbers: 123.

Hoefler Text Ornaments

The Microsoft collection. An installation of Microsoft Internet Explorer adds ten or twelve font suitcase to your Fonts folder: an install with the OS 8 CD give you ten, while an install from a Microsoft CD provides two extra—Minion Web and Webdings. Even if you're not going to use or install Explorer, you should add the fonts to your system: they're used by a majority of web page designers, so keeping them available means the pages will look better on your screen. Besides, why ignore ten or twelve fonts?

microsoft.com

You won't even have to run an installer to get at the fonts. On the OS 8.1 CD, the fonts are loose in the Explorer Install folder: use Find File to look for them (*"kind is font"*) and you won't have to find them yourself. If you don't have the CD and want the fonts, they're free for the downloading from Microsoft's web site.

The Microsoft Fonts

Arial is one of the most commonly used fonts for body text on web pages.

Arial Black isn't used quite as often on web pages, but makes a nice coordinating font.

Comic Sans MS is a breezy informal font.

Courier New is nearly indistinguishable from the old, standard Courier; but, while Mac users all have standard Courier, the same can't be said of PC users, so Microsoft leapt into the gap.

Georgia is nothing special, but its tall x-height does make it readable at smaller font sizes.

Impact doesn't have much of one although its minimal descenders for letters like g and y give it some character.

Minion Web is a typewriter-style, but not monospaced, font; guaranteed to cause confusion with standard Minion font files.

Times New Roman is just a Times font for the rest of them (see the Courier New comments).

Trebuchet MS is a sweet little font whose best design details (like the bottom of the l and open-descender g) are lost at some sizes.

Verdana is another high x-height font, like Georgia, but sans serif.

Webdings ▲◆▮ ⚲▮?▲ ▲◆ⓘ●■ ✓⚲▲◉▲ ⓘ▲ ⓘ? ⓘ▲? ●✓!▮

Wingdings ✋↗ ⌧☐◆ ♎♏♍☐♎♏ ◆♒♓⬩⌧ ◆♏●● ❍♏ ♋◆ ◆♒♏◆♓☐⬩◆♏☐✍♍☐❍

The PostScript collection. Most PostScript printers come with a set of PostScript typefaces built into their ROMs; the screen fonts are also usually supplied on disk so you can get them in your font menu. Five of the fonts (Courier, Helvetica, Palatino, Times, and Symbol) also come with your basic system software. The chart here shows the other six.

Basic PostScript Fonts

Avant Garde is a clean, no-fuss sans serif font.

It's hard to see Bookman, know its name, and not think "children's books."

Helvetica Narrow is just what the name says-a narrow version of the old stand-by.

New Century Schoolbook is very similar to Bookman, with lower x-height and narrower character widths.

Zapf Chancery is over-used but still elegant, the first script font the Mac ever saw.

Zapf Dingbats ❂✳❍❑▲◆❖◗✡✢✦✧✪✫✰✱✲✁✂☎✾✆☛✈✉✿☞➾➻✓✔✖✗✘✚✐✍†

But wait, there's more! The **Apple Font Library** of TrueType fonts comes bundled with Apple's printers—every kind of printer. The collection includes TrueType versions of fonts that were previously offered only in one or two bitmapped sizes as screen fonts to match built-in LaserWriter fonts. The set includes all the fonts listed in the last entry, as well as the ones shown here. It's a surprisingly good collection, offering a little of everything in the way of font types: serif, sans serif, script, text, and pictures.

The Apple Font Library

DELPHIIAN IS AN ALL-CAPS FONT THAT NEEDS TO BE OF A CERTAIN SIZE (NOT THIS ONE) TO BE APPRECIATED.

Garamond Narrow, a highly readable narrow font for when you need to squeeze more info onto a page.

Helvetica Black is the heavy-weight member of this popular sans serif family.

Helvetica Compressed: Yet another family member.

Lubalin Graph is a typewriter-style but not monospaced font with a very tall x-height.

Lucida Bright is eminently readable with its extra-large x-height.

MACHINE IS ANOTHER ALL-CAPS FONT; WE DON'T KNOW WHAT "MACHINE" IS INVOLVED.

Nadianne is an informal handwriting font.

Old English Text-the name pretty much says it all; think calligraphy.

This is what Onyx looks like there's not much to say about it.

Oxford is an interesting semi-caligraphic font that seems to confuse its upper- and lowercase letters.

There's Swing, just in case you need another handwriting font.

ZEAL IS HALF TEXT ⇧ ⬋ ⬂ ◁ ⬁ ⇩ ⬋ ▷ ✹ ⬇ ⬀ ⬅ ⬊ ▷

Of character sets and option characters. Every font has a character set: all the characters available through various keyboard combinations. But we tend to think of the full set as separate sets, available with certain modifier keys; so, there's an unshifted set, a shifted set, a set available with Option and yet another one available with Shift Option. It doesn't matter how you define "character set" as long as you're aware that a font's characters aren't all on the surface.

IN THE BEGINNING

The first LaserWriters had only four built-in fonts: Courier, Helvetica, Times, and Symbol.

The Mac also lets you type accented characters, a combination of an accent and another character already in the set, by typing a special sequence of keys: you press, for instance, Option E and don't see anything on the screen, but then you press E again and you wind up with *é*. In picture fonts, these option characters aren't combinations of other characters, but entirely different characters usually unavailable any other way from the keyboard.

There's lots more about character sets and typing accents in Chapter 16—including how to use Key Caps to see what's available in a font. But many of the font illustrations in the rest of this section show character sets and option characters for various fonts, so it's important that you know at least the basics of the terminology.

Charcoal and Chicago

The same difference. Chicago was retired after a decade of service as the default Mac system font, replaced by Charcoal in OS 8. (You can set the system font in the Appearances control panel.) They're very similar, although easy to tell apart for anyone who's stared at Chicago menus for years: Charcoal looks both "rounder" because of the way it treats some of its counters (the round parts of letters, like the two in *B* and the one in *g*) and capital letters (like *O*, which is definitely an oval in Chicago), and a little more "angled" because of its relatively flat approach on the tops and bottoms of letters like *C* and *S*, and the true points on letters like *A* and *V*.

But the character sets are—with one exception—the same for both fonts, so there's only one character chart here, for Charcoal. The one exception: the zero in the Chicago font is slashed—something not present in the original bitmapped Chicago, but added when the TrueType version came out. Both fonts have a full complement of accent characters, although it's unlikely you'll need them, since neither lends itself to particularly attractive printouts.

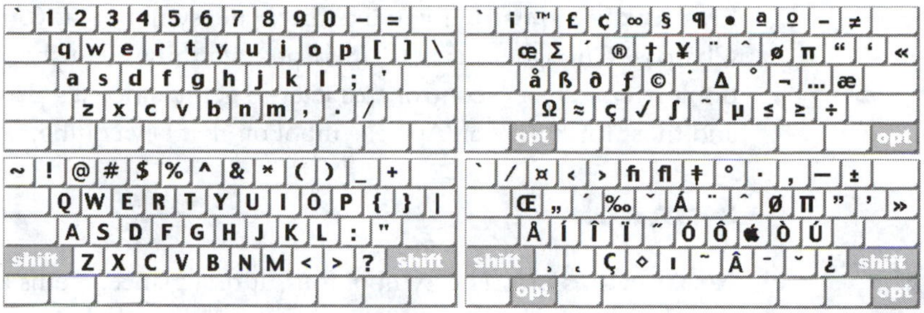

Charcoal's character set.

Control characters. Charcoal and Chicago are the only fonts that I know of that have an extra character set accessible through the Control key (although this will hold true for any system font—there are others planned for 8.5). The symbols include all sorts of things that are used in menus, like symbols for: the modifier keys (Shift, Option, ⌘ and so on); other keys that might be referenced in menus (like Tab and Enter); special markers like the checkmark and diamond; and odds and ends which I've yet to see in any menu, like *Page down* and *Rotate.*

Charcoal's control characters.

It's likely you'll find these special characters in any font that's designed to serve as a system font (there are bound to be more choices eventually). It's just as likely that you won't be able to use them, because you can't type characters with the Control key: Mac programs just aren't set up to acknowledge a Control key combination as a typed character. There are, however, two ways to access them.

First, you can use the Key Caps desk accessory, which interprets Control key combinations: type the characters in Key Caps, then copy and paste them where you need them. Alternatively, if you're using a utility or program that lets you enter characters according to their ASCII codes, you can just use the numbers shown in this chart.

Control Character ASCII codes

	Type	Name	ASCII		Type	Name	ASCII
⇥	Control B	Left tab	2	✓	Control R	Check	18
⇤	Control C	Right tab	3	◆	Control S	Diamond	19
⌅	Control D	Enter	4		Control T	Apple	20
⇧	Control E	Shift	5	⌦	Control J	Forward delete	21
^	Control F	Control	6	⌫	Control W	Delete	23
⌥	Control G	Option	7	⇠	Control X	Left arrow	24
↩	Control K	Return	11	⇢	Control Z	Right arrow	25
↪	Control L	Return right	12	⇡	Control Y	Up arrow	26
⇣	Control P	Down arrow	16	⟲	Control [	Rotate	27
⌘	Control Q	Command key	17				

The Apple symbol. If you like the Apple symbol that you see in the Charcoal/Chicago fonts here, there are two things you should know: you don't need to type a control character to get it, since it's also on Shift Option K; and most fonts have an Apple symbol on that key combo.

Symbol

It's Greek to me. The Symbol font, at first glance, seems to be a Greek alphabet, but in fact it's a set of mathematical symbols (that and the four card suits, for some reason!). You'll see what seem to be a lot of vertical lines on the Option and Shift Option character sets, but they are slightly different, as you'll see in a later entry.

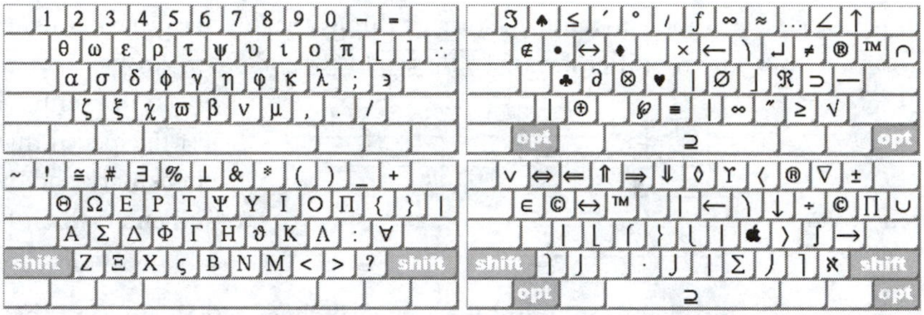

Symbol's character set.

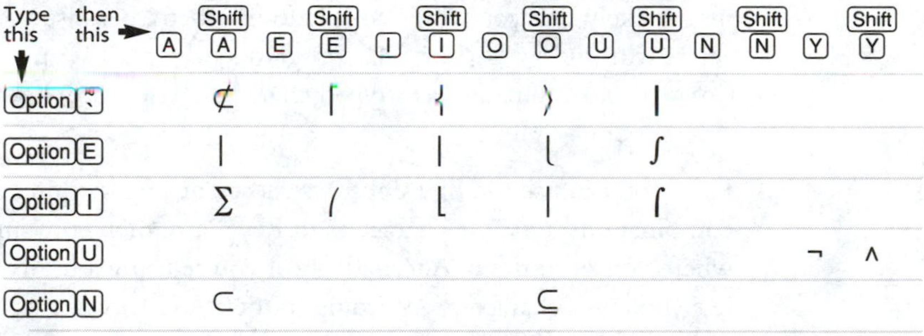

Symbol's option characters.

Braces and brackets. Many of the symbols in Symbol are actually pieces that you can type on top of each other in adjacent rows of text to make tall braces and brackets for formulas. You can type a small right bracket with the] key; you can type a larger one by typing the top half of a right bracket with Shift Option ., moving down a line, and typing Option K for the bottom half; make an even larger one by adding an extension in the middle with Option H; if you need something even larger, you can type multiple extensions in the middle. All the vertical line characters in the Option and Shift Option character sets are used for extensions with the various bracket and brace pieces; there's a variety because of the way they line up with the characters above and below them. The bracket pieces, and their key combinations, are shown on the next page.

left bracket	⎡	Option ~, Shift E
	⎢	Shift Option S
	⎣	Shift Option D
right bracket	⎤	Shift Option .
	⎥	Option H
	⎦	Option K
left brace	⎧	Shift Option F
	⎨	Option ~, Shift I
	⎪	Shift Option J
	⎩	Shift Option H
right brace	⎫	Shift Option Z
	⎬	Shift Option G
	⎪	Shift Option J
	⎭	Shift Option X
left parenthesis	⎛	Option I, Shift E
	⎜	Shift Option Y
	⎝	Option U, Shift E
right parenthesis	⎞	Shift Option I
	⎟	Shift Option N
	⎠	Shift Option ,
integral	⌠	Option I, Shift U
	⎮	Option ~, Shift U
	⌡	Shift Option B

In summation... There seems to be two *sigma* characters in Symbol, on Shift S and again Option I-Shift A. But the latter one (the one that's harder to get at) is actually the mathematical symbol for *summation;* it's the same Greek letter, but at the same point size it's a little bigger both because it's taller and its bottom drops below the baseline used for the rest of the font.

sigma Σ summation ∑

Zapf Dingbats

Zapf, and dingbats. The "first" name of two basic LaserWriter fonts—Zapf Dingbats and Zapf Chancery—is the last name of their designer, Hermann Zapf (who also designed other familiar fonts that don't have his name—like Palatino and Optima). The dingbat part of the font's name is simply a term that has long been used in typography to refer to little symbols or ornaments.

Zapf Dingbats has the distinction of being used incredibly often without being overused, because by its very nature it's used in only bits and pieces. Need some circled numbers? Arrows or checkmarks? How about a pointing finger?

The only problem is that it's hard to find and remember where characters are, since there's no obvious pattern. The charts in this chapter should help you find everything you want in the font (and find out what exactly is in there to begin with), but you might be comforted to know that there *is* some logic to the arrangement of the symbols in the font and their corresponding keyboard positions: the symbols are arranged according to the code numbers the computer uses to represent letters. (There, I told you it was comforting.) Arrange the symbols by code—alphabetically, more or less—and you'll see everything beautifully grouped: four scissors, four hands, three pencils, all the stars and arrows. Of course, that doesn't help much when you're looking for a specific character, but it's so comforting to know. And the charts in this chapter will help you find the characters you need.

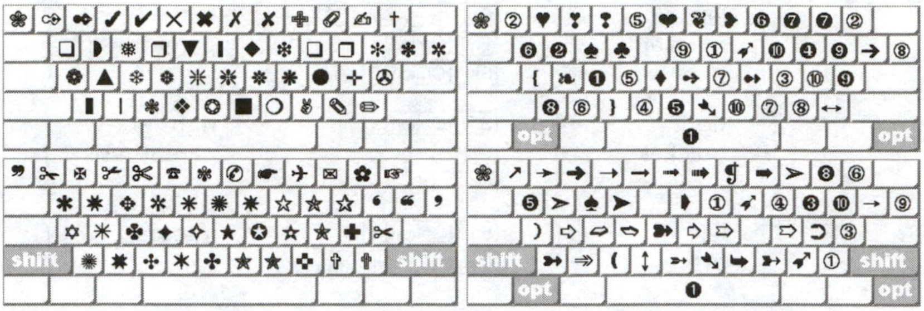

Zapf Dingbats character set.

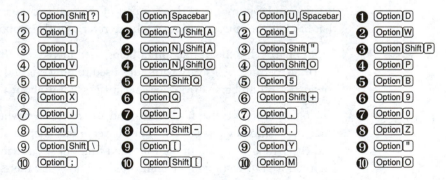

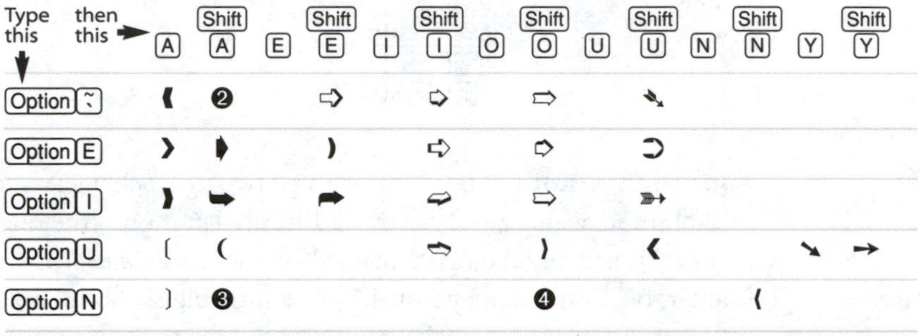

Zapf Dingbat's option characters.

The numbers. There are four sets of circled numbers, 1 through 10, in the Zapf Dingbats character set: serif numbers in black and in white circles, and sans serif numbers in black and in white circles. It's not easy to see the difference between the serif and sans serif characters until after you've printed them, so be extra careful if you're working with them.

①	Option Shift ?	❶	Option Spacebar	➀	Option U, Spacebar	➊	Option D
②	Option 1	❷	Option ~, Shift A	➁	Option =	➋	Option W
③	Option L	❸	Option N, Shift A	➂	Option Shift "	➌	Option Shift P
④	Option V	❹	Option N, Shift O	➃	Option Shift O	➍	Option P
⑤	Option F	❺	Option Shift Q	➄	Option 5	➎	Option B
⑥	Option X	❻	Option Q	➅	Option Shift +	➏	Option 9
⑦	Option J	❼	Option –	➆	Option ,	➐	Option 0
⑧	Option \	❽	Option Shift –	➇	Option .	➑	Option Z
⑨	Option Shift \	❾	Option [	➈	Option Y	➒	Option "
⑩	Option ;	❿	Option Shift [	➉	Option M	➓	Option O

Store the numbers. If you're using one of the Zapf Dingbats circled number sets throughout a document, there's always an approach that can make life easier. In Microsoft Word, for instance, I keep an Autotext entry that consists of the numbers 1 through 10 in the circled set I always use; with two keystrokes, I can insert the entire string of numbers in the document, and then cut and paste or drag and drop them where I need them. You can do the same in any program that lets you store formatted text in a glossary or library; depending on how you're using the numbers, it might be easier to store them in shorter groups of three or five digits.

If the program you're using doesn't provide this kind of special storage and recall, you can create the string of numbers (or substrings, like the numbers 1 through 3) for any or all of the circled sets and store them in the Scrapbook. Just copy them out when you need them. You can even store them in the Note Pad, although they'll revert to whatever font you've set for it; you can just reapply Zapf Dingbats after you paste them back into your document.

Hoefler Text Ornaments

Hoefler Text Ornaments. The Hoefler Text Ornaments font (an oxymoronic name!) gets installed if you install QuickDraw GX, or if you go back and specifically install the TrueType fonts available from the GX installer. The Hoefler Text suitcase that gets placed in your Fonts folder includes both the text and the ornamental font.

Hoefler Text Ornaments has a very small character set, with plenty of empty spaces on even the unshifted and shifted character sets; there are no Option or Shift Option characters (except for the obligatory apple on Shift Option K) or accents.

The majority of the ornaments are swirly swashes, with solid black versions on unshifted keys and outline or half black/half outline versions on the shifted keys. There are also a few whimsical icons thrown in, including left- and right-pointing hands with jester-like cuffs instead of the usual shirt cuff design.

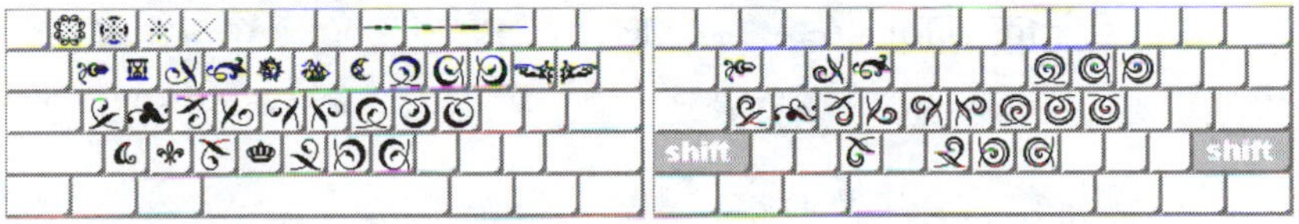

Hoefler Text Ornament's character set.

Made for each other. Many of the figures in Hoefler Text Ornaments are matched to make larger figures when used in pairs (you may have noticed that a few of the characters seem to be missing a left or right edge). There are some characters that work together in triplets, and some are meant to be used in long, decorative lines.

Some of the Hoefler Text Ornaments are meant to be used in continuous lines.

Many of the Hoefler Text Ornaments are designed to work in pairs or triplets.

Zeal

Over zeal-ous design. The core of Zeal is its uppercase-only letters with bars above and below the letters. The bars extend beyond the letterforms so that when you type, they form unbroken lines above and below the letters. But Zeal is also the third picture font that Apple has included with its products (the original bitmapped Cairo was first, followed by Zapf Dingbats), and it has among its characters sets of arrows (with and without shafts), astrological and zodiac symbols, and clocks.

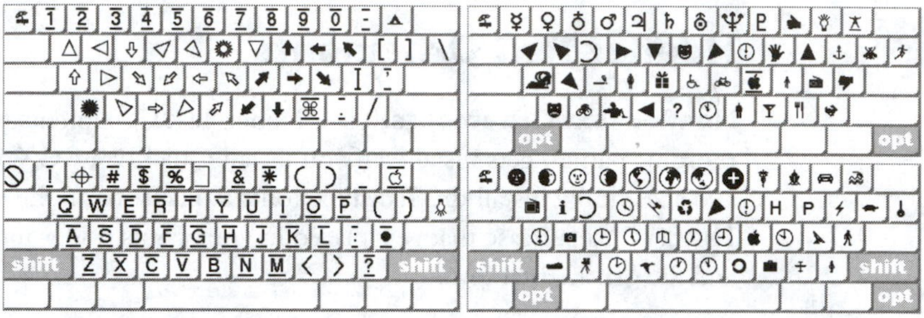

Zeal's character set.

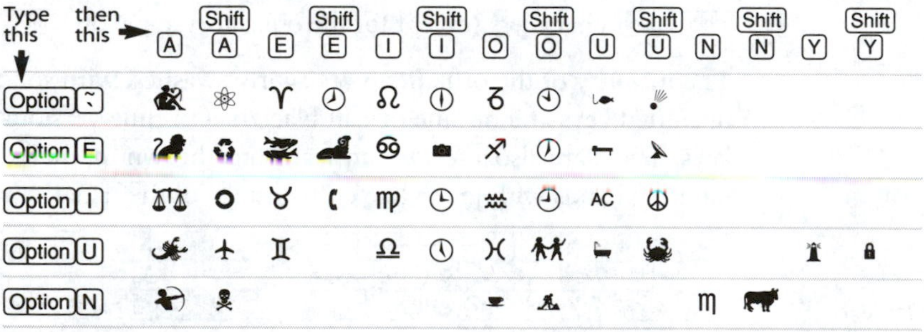

Zeal's option characters.

Bridge over troubled spaces. Typing a space between Zeal words breaks the bars; to avoid this, type Shift - , as you would to normally get the underline character.

THIS IS ZEAL ZEAL WITHOUT BREAKS

The print-over characters. There are three special characters in Zeal—a square, a circle, and a slashed circle—that will print over whatever character you type before them. So, you can type a letter from some font and then put it in a circle or square; or, use a picture from a font (Zeal or something else) and use the slashed circle to indicate "forbidden." It's very strange to work with overprinting characters, since, for instance, when you backspace over one the text insertion point doesn't move but the character disappears.

To combine characters, first type the character you want inside the Zeal shape, then switch to the Zeal font and type the character. The square is on Shift 6; the slashed circle is on Shift ~; to get the circle, type Option E and then Spacebar.

Wingdings and Webdings

The Wingdings character set. Microsoft's Wingdings is quite a collection of symbols: arrows (a very full quiver), zodiac signs, clocks, circled numbers, mailboxes, pointing fingers, stars, boxes, and even happy (and unhappy) faces. Like Microsoft's other fonts, it doesn't have the usual Apple symbol on Option Shift K, but it does have the command-key symbol (go figure).

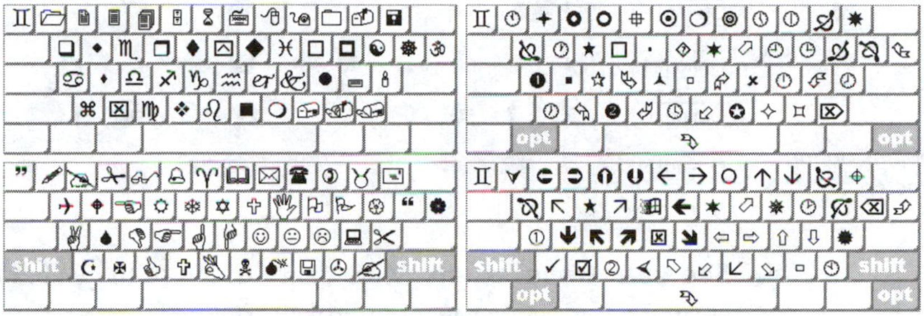

Wingdings' character set.

Wingdings' option characters.

Wingdings numbers. Wingdings offers two sets of circled numbers (to Zapf Dingbat's four), but it's even worse when it comes to keyboard placement, with almost all the numbers being accented characters. It does, however, offer zeroes in the number set, if you can think of a use for them.

The Webdings characters. Its name may be more clever than its character set, and it has a way to go before becoming the Dingbats of the Web, but Webdings gets installed when you install Microsoft Explorer from a Microsoft disk (rather than from your system disk). So much of it is heavy black, with thick lines and silhouettes, that one assumes it was designed for use with the colorized text available for web pages.

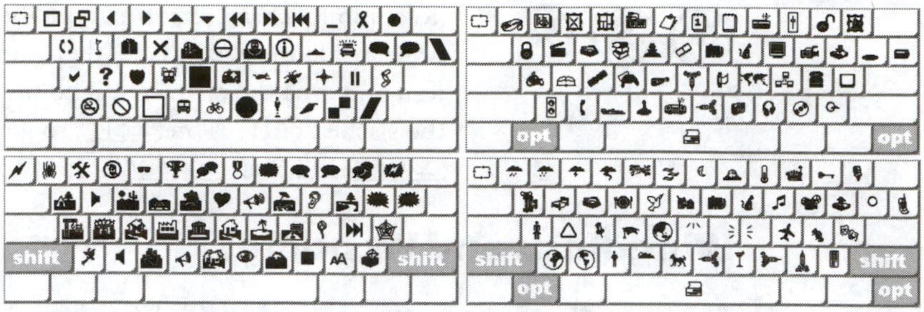

Webdings' character set.

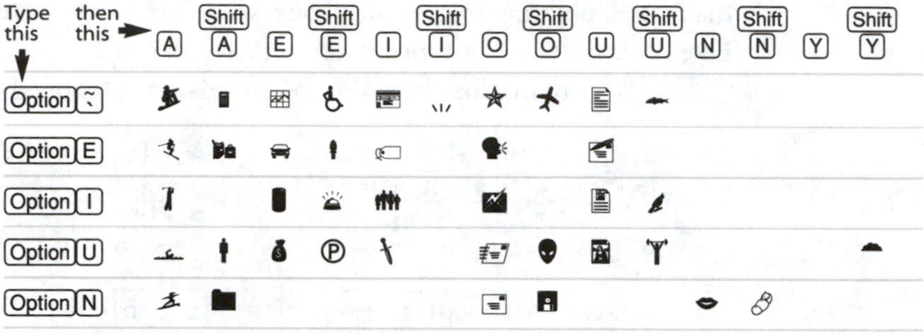

Webdings' option characters.

See your travel agent. More than a dozen of the Webdings characters were created to fit together in an unbroken panoramic view of… well, of no place you'll ever see all these things together. The picture here shows fourteen characters strung together.

Your Font Collection

Choosing and Collecting Fonts

Types of fonts. When you start collecting fonts, you should try and keep your collection balanced. There are four basic categories of fonts:

- **Text fonts**: For body text, of course—the kind that comes in paragraph upon paragraph of information. A good text font is relatively invisible: that is, the reader doesn't *notice* the font itself.
- **Display fonts**: Designed to look good at large point sizes (18 points and over, say); used for headlines.

- **Decorative fonts**: Designed to catch your eye, evoke a mood, convey an attitude; from elegant handwriting to grungy mud-spattered blobs and everything in between.
- **Specialty fonts**: Foreign-language characters or pictures.

Start your collection. Okay, so maybe you do have about fifty fonts that came with your Mac and printer (as described earlier). But fifty just aren't enough—especially when there are tens of thousands of fonts out there just waiting for you. You can buy PostScript or TrueType fonts; you can get *free* fonts, for that matter. But just where do you start?

First, decide what *type* of fonts you need. Is TrueType enough for you? Do you need PostScript? Can you use mostly TrueType and get a few PostScript for special situations?

Next, decide what *kind* of fonts you need, based on the documents you're producing: text fonts, display fonts, decorative fonts… remember, try to keep the collection balanced.

Then it's time to consider your budget. There's lots of free fonts out there, but sometimes you get what you pay for. Free and shareware fonts are often missing the Option and Shift Option characters that you may need—but maybe you only need a brief headline or picture caption and not a full character set. And the majority of free and inexpensive fonts are TrueType, not PostScript; once again, however, that may suit your needs.

Not as easy as 1-2-3. Count fonts. Or count families. But know what you're counting when you're comparing font packages or prices. If you buy a package that offers sixty fonts, don't be surprised if you wind up with only a dozen or two: as discussed early in the chapter, Times and Times Italic and Times Bold are three different fonts, and vendors tend to count the way that sounds the best.

A font by any other name. Since font names and designs aren't trademarked, fonts with the same name may look alike but not be identical (they might also look alike but have totally different names). This is further complicated by the fact that fonts from a single *manufacturer* may be sold by different *vendors* under their own labels.

The possibility of similar-but-not-quite-identical fonts, and the havoc they can wreak on a print job is one of the main reasons professionals stick with the Adobe version of a PostScript font wherever possible; if you deal with a service bureau for high-quality output, you'll probably want to do the same. If not, you'll have to bring copies of your own fonts to the printing site—a violation of your licensing agreement with the font vendor. (You didn't think you actually *owned* those fonts, did you?) Practically speaking, if you bring your fonts to the printer and make sure he erases them from his systems after the print job's done, no one's going to be giving you a hard time about it. —SZA/DD/KT

Expert sets *Expert sets,* or *expert collections*, are companion fonts for certain typefaces that provide special characters such as small caps, fractions, old-style numbers (the kind that dip below the baseline), and ornate alternate letters. Unfortunately, they exist for only a handful of fonts. —EF

The accidental collection. You'll be adding to your font collection without even knowing it: lots of programs come with fonts that they need, and when you install the program, you get the fonts. Microsoft Explorer adds about a dozen fonts, but Microsoft has always slid a font or two in with its programs—notably the MT Extra font; ATM and Acrobat add *Adobe Serif* and *Adobe Sans*. Reference CD's like encyclopedias and, especially, dictionaries usually come with their own fonts for good screen display; utilities like calendars also add their own; MacIntax uses a different font approach seemingly every year. One day you open your Fonts folder and there are thirty mystery fonts.

Sometimes you can identify the program that installed the fonts (*TaxFont,* or *Comptons* is pretty much a giveaway). But the only way you can be sure is to visit your Fonts folder before you install any software, select all the fonts already in there, and give them a label. After you've installed the new software, check the Fonts folder again; any unlabeled item belongs to the new software. If the name of the font alone won't help you remember where it came from, you can put a note in the Comments area of its Info window.

Printed samples. As you add to your font collection, it will be difficult to keep track of which font looks like what; double-clicking on a font file for a sample in a Finder window is not only awkward, but gives a wimpy single sentence with few uppercase characters. There are several ways you can create font sample printouts that you can look at and throw away, or catalog for future reference. Note that the "manual" approaches require that the fonts actually be installed, while certain utilities can just look inside suitcases no matter where they are and extract the information.

- Create a template. Use any word processor or page layout program, type all the characters in a font (including Option and Shift Option characters if they're significant for the font) and a few sentences; copy and paste a few copies, setting them to different point sizes. To use the template, just do a Select All and change the text to the target font. Don't forget to put the name of the font on the page!
- Use a premade template. PageMaker, for instance, comes with a nicely designed document named *Character Set* that you can use for your font samples.
- You can print samples of the fonts your printer "knows" about: the ones in ROM, the ones downloaded to its memory, and the ones stored on an attached hard drive. The sample is simply a single line of text for each font, but sometimes that's all you need. Use the Apple Printer Utility's Print Font Samples command.

- FontCharter is a simple but handy utility that comes with Dubl-Click's MenuFonts utility (described earlier in the chapter). It prints a single page of all the characters in a font, including the ASCII codes for each. It works with the installed fonts from its Font menu, but you can also open any font suitcase and access its files.

FontGander

- I've saved the best for last: **FontGander** ($20, shareware) provides everything you could ask for in a font sampler utility. It provides various on-screen displays that you can even trigger by dropping a font onto the Gander icon in case you just want a quick sneak. But for printouts, you can choose from several page setups, including a single font to the page (the Gander view shown in the picture here) and several multicolumn, multifont pages. You can work with installed or uninstalled fonts. Best of all, you don't have to pick or print the fonts individually: you can select an entire folder-full of fonts at once and get printed samples.

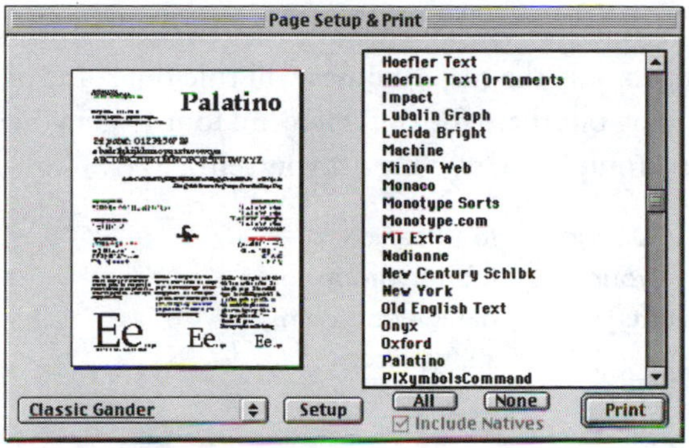

FontGander offers several different printout options, and multiple font selection.

Font Sources

Shopping around. You can buy fonts from all sorts of places; you can even buy the same fonts from several different places, since many retailers can license fonts from their original makers. In fact, font design companies often license fonts from other houses, so you might wind up buying a Monotype font from Adobe.

How can you find out who offers what kind of fonts? If you make a living doing graphics and layout, there's nothing that beats a printed version of a font vendor's choices: most are available for a fee (of $25 to $100) directly from the vendors. But for less intensive work, or for starters, nothing beats checking things out on the web (where you can usually order the printed catalog, too—and often download a free font while you're there). Indicative of how the ever-changing computer world has affected even staid old

> ***What businessman knows about point sizes on typefaces or the value of variable point sizes? Who out there in the general marketplace even knows what a "font" is?***
>
> *John Dvorak*
> *San Francisco Examiner, February 19, 1984*

foundries is that a catalog like FontHaus's *x-height*, previously published traditionally, is now a Web-only publication.

Here's where you can find the major font houses on the web:

Adobe	adobe.com
Agfa	agfa.com
Bitstream	bitstream.com
Font Bureau	fontburea.com
FontHaus	fonthaus.com
Image Club	adobe.com
ITC	itcfonts.com
Letraset	letraset.com
Linotype-Hell	linotype.com
Monotype	monotype.com
URW	urwpp.de

But sticking to only the major houses will rule out some of the best new designs waiting out there for you. Here are four to get you started (you should surf around to add to the list yourself!):

Fonthead Design	fonthead.com
Foundry Group	foundrygroup.com
GarageFonts	garagefonts.com
Shift	shiftype.com

Font freebies. Free is not bad. Free is good—both as a concept, and also often in the design of the free font. Some major houses offer a free "font of the month" or one for registering for their printed catalog. Others just offer them with no strings attached, building brand loyalty and so on. There are two terrific spots on the Web that can let you know about free fonts. The Font Fairy (*ourworld.compuserve.com/homepages/kayhall/*) offers pointers to the sites that offer free fonts; the Fontz site (*indigo.simplenet.com/fontz/*) offers nearly 1000 downloads directly from its site.

Package deals. In addition to selling fonts singly, most of the major manufacturers offer package deals that significantly reduce the cost per font. Adobe sells its **Type Basics** pack (the 35 basic PostScript printer fonts plus 30 more faces "specially chosen to complement the 35 printer fonts") for $200. Adobe's Value Pack, including 30 text, script, decorative, and display faces, sells for just $60, which works out to a couple of dollars per font. And those are the list prices: You can get these packages and similar ones from other vendors through mail-order companies for about 40 percent less. —RT/KT/EF

I can't believe I bought the whole thing. Adobe, Monotype, Agfa, and the other vendors with large libraries also offer their entire libraries on CD-ROM. The CD itself is available for a nominal cost (Adobe's Type on Call is included free with most of their major software packages), and most of the fonts are encrypted (unreadable unless you have a code) until you call the manufacturer with your credit card number. In return, the vendor tells you the codes that unlock the fonts you want. Most of the font vendors offer bargains to customers who buy fonts this way, charging $25 or so for fonts that may normally retail for $100 or more. Most also offer unlocked CDs, giving you access to an entire library on your desktop. Other font libraries, such as FontHaus and URW, offer their entire libraries for as little as 20 cents per font. —RT/KT/EF

Clip art addendums. Humongous inexpensive font collections—usually a mix of PostScript and TrueType fonts, with more of the latter—are often thrown in as a bonus with clip art collections; if you're a font freak, it might be worth buying the clip art just to get the fonts. The two packages I happen to have within arm's reach as I write this are Nova Development's **Art Explosion 125,000**, which includes 1500 fonts, and IMSI's **MasterClips 150,000**, which has 2,000!

15

Printing

In This Chapter

About Printers

Printer Technologies

Dot-matrix printers. A dot-matrix printer (like those in Apple's old ImageWriter line) has a *printhead* that moves back and forth across the width of the paper; groups of pins poke out of the printhead, pressing against an inked ribbon. The grid of pins in the printhead gives the *dot-matrix* printer its name; the alternative description, *impact*, comes from the way it functions. The number of pins in the printhead can vary, with a higher number of pins giving better print quality.

Dot-matrix printers are slow, averaging as little as a half-page per minute, and very noisy. Their advantage, which makes their unavailability frustrating, is that you can send multiple-part forms through them and get all the layers printed at the same time.

Inkjet printers. An inkjet printer like Apple's StyleWriter creates little dots on paper by spraying tiny jets of ink from its printhead. The dots start out very small, but spread a bit as they soak into the paper; instead of creating a splotchy output, however, the slight smear means each dot comes in contact with the ones next to it, creating a continuous, smooth line even around curves.

Inkjets not only provide better output than impact printers, they're also faster and quieter; it's not surprising, then, that the impact-printer market faded away.

Laser printers. A laser printer like Apple's LaserWriter prints images with the same technology used by a copy machine. It beams flashes of laser light onto a photoelectric drum; a dry ink powder called *toner* sticks electrostatically to the imaged portion of the drum. The toner particles are transferred to the paper, and a hot fuser roller melts the toner onto the paper.

Laser printers are bigger and more expensive than inkjets, but they're faster and quieter, and provide output generally judged as higher-quality. —SZA/RS/BW

Thermal fusion. A thermal fusion printer uses tiny heated elements in the printhead to push a ribbon against the page, bonding a waxy ink to the paper. Desktop and portable varieties of thermal fusion printers compete with black-and-white inkjet printers. Cost per printed page is generally higher than for inkjet printing, but there's no liquid ink to run or smear. —RS

Color printers. Some color printers use technology based on black-and-white printer technology, while others take an entirely different approach. Regardless of the technology, however, a color printer has to handle the actual "coloring process" in one of two ways. In the *pigment* approach, the color is created by mixing basic colors either before they're applied to the paper, or on the paper itself (as when a blue dot is overprinted with a yellow one to make green). In the *dithering* approach, different-colored dots are printed in clusters so the eye sees them as a combined color.

- It didn't take long for the **inkjet** approach to include color: either separate printheads, or separate ink cartridges in a single printhead, squirt dithered colors onto the page. In more expensive *phase-change* models, the "ink" starts as separate colors of wax, and the correct proportions are melted together and then sprayed onto the paper as a single color instead of a dithered one.
- A **thermal-wax transfer** printer uses rolls of plastic film coated with four different colors of wax-based pigments; heating elements melt the wax and transfer it to the paper, dithering the correct color from the limited range of colors on the transfer ribbon. Phase-change versions first melt the wax pigment to mix it, then apply it as a single color. Both types require multiple passes of the page.
- A **dye-sublimation** printer works in much the same way as a thermal-wax printer, but the pigments are heated by the printhead so they turn gaseous; the "sublimed" dye then penetrates the paper's special coating. Dye-sub printers don't have to use dithering or halftones to create different colors or shades of colors; they can blend the correct amount of each primary color (cyan, magenta, yellow, or black) to create just the right color at each printed dot. That's why they're called continuous-tone printers.
- A color **laser printer** uses the same basic technology as a black-and-white laser printer but has a four-chamber toner unit that holds cyan, magenta, yellow, and black toner. For each color in the document, the parts of the image for a single color are etched onto the drum and the paper passes by to pick up the color; four passes are required to get all the colors. Some (very expensive) laser printers can print continuous-color images because they use transparent toner; others (like Apple's models) use opaque toner so continuous-tone images are printed as halftones. —SZA/RS/BW

Color inkjet cartridges. There are three approaches to color inkjet printing:

- Single-cartridge systems can accommodate only one cartridge in the printer at a time: either the all-black ink or a three-chamber cartridge for cyan, magenta, and yellow ink. If you want the black ink for text, you have to swap cartridges, or settle for a "composite black" from the color cartridge that's not as black as a true black ink, and generally doesn't look as crisp. This need for swapping for text output might be acceptable, but there's no working around the fact that some graphics won't print well because many colors include some level of black—and there's no way to swap cartridges to add black to the color printing.
- Dual-cartridge systems keep both a black and a three-color cartridge mounted in the printer so you don't have to manually swap one for the other. The printer automatically switches to the black cartridge for text or when color graphics need a shot of true black; both text and graphics look better for it.

- A four-cartridge system, as you've probably already guessed, provides a separate cartridge for each color. It's not only more convenient, but it's also more efficient since it provides more individual jets for each color, getting more ink onto the paper each second. Four-cartridge systems are, of course, the most expensive type of inkjets. —SZA/BW

Imagesetting: no dots here. An *imagesetter* is a super-high-resolution output devices that differs from any printer you might have in a more important way than just its resolution (and its cost). Imagesetters don't work with dots; unlike on even the best laser printer, where a line is actually just a series of dots, on an imagesetter a line is actually a line. And, instead of paper, an imagesetter draws its images on film, which is then used to print the paper version of the document.

More Printer Points

PostScript printers. The terms *PostScript printer* and *LaserWriter* and *laser printer* are often used interchangeably, but they are not the same.

- *Laser printer* is the generic term for a printer that uses laser technology to create an image on a page.
- *LaserWriter* is Apple's brand name for its laser printers.
- *PostScript printers* use a built-in chip to interpret PostScript commands.

Most, but not all, LaserWriters and laser printers are PostScript printers; in this chapter, most of the LaserWriter information applies to the PostScript models.

The nonexistent QuickDraw printer. There's no such thing as a QuickDraw printer, even though you'll find the phrase used occasionally in this book, in other publications, and even in Apple's literature. QuickDraw is the "language" that the Mac uses to create images, both letters and pictures, on the screen. These "QuickDraw" images can be easily sent to a printer, but the printer itself doesn't contain or understand the QuickDraw routines the Mac uses. So, a "QuickDraw printer" is just a positive way to label a "non-PostScript" printer.

PostScript versus QuickDraw. QuickDraw is cheaper and slower; PostScript is faster and more expensive. That's it in a nutshell, but if you want a few more details…

The reason QuickDraw is slower is not because of some inherent flaw in the design of the language. It's slower overall for printing because the *rasterizing*—the translation of the font information into actual bitmaps that will be printed—is done in the Mac, where the processor has other demands on its time. For PostScript printers, the rasterizing is done in the printer, by the printer's chip. But speed is not PostScript's only benefit: it also provides high-quality and high-resolution graphics capability that QuickDraw can't match.

A PostScript printer can do everything a QuickDraw printer can do, since the QuickDraw printer isn't really doing anything but reaping the benefits of the Mac's brain. QuickDraw printers can't do PostScript jobs, though: they can't print PostScript graphics at all, and they can print PostScript fonts only with the help of ATM (covered in Chapter 14).

One more in-a-nutshell: If your printing needs are primarily text, a QuickDraw printer is perfect for you. If you're a graphics professional, or a wannabe, you need PostScript output.

They're all dot matrix. Despite the differences in underlying technology and output, all printers are, in the end, dot-matrix printers: they all—including laser printers—draw letters and images by using dots. The better resolution in more expensive printers comes from their ability to use smaller, and sometimes variable-size, dots.

Higher printer resolution comes from smaller dots, but even LaserWriters use dots to print.

Printer resolution. Subjective judgments aside, we usually rate print quality in terms of *resolution*. Printers use tightly packed arrays of dots to create the shapes we see on paper. The tighter the array of dots—that is, the more dots per inch (dpi)—the higher the resolution, and the finer the images appear. Inkjet printers typically produce 300 to 720 dpi, a respectable resolution that rivals laser printing quality.

Laser printers originally kicked out a mere 300 by 300 dpi; the standard now is 600 by 600 dpi, but there's also a growing market in affordable graphic arts laser printers that boast 1,200 by 600, and even 1,800 by 1,800 dots per inch, many of which also offer various forms of enhanced resolution. —BW

> ***"Many Mac users have yet to come to grips with the fact that their PostScript printers, far from being simple output devices, are separate computers of labyrinthine complexity, and that the printer's internal page description language is understood completely by only three people, all of whom work at Adobe Systems."***
>
> *David Ramsey, MacWEEK columnist*

Resolution enhancement. Vendors such as Apple, LaserMaster, NewGen, and Xante sell printers with controller circuitry that manipulates the laser beam to create a higher apparent resolution, beyond the 600 dpi of a standard laser engine. For comparative purposes, enhanced resolutions are hard to quantify because different vendors use different electronic techniques. One vendor's "800 by 800" enhanced resolution may look as good as another's "1,000 by 1,000." If you're looking for better text quality, start by looking at Hewlett Packard's LaserJet printers, which combine true 600-by-600-dpi resolution with resolution enhancement technology, and compare it with higher-resolution models from Xante, LaserMaster, NewGen, and so on. (Resolution enhancement that improves text and graphics doesn't always improve grayscale images, which needs a different type of enhancement technology, like Apple's PhotoGrade).

But remember that 1,200 dpi on a toner-based printer doesn't compare with the sharpness of a 1,200-dpi imagesetter. The laser-drum-toner process produces a rather sloppy, nonuniform dot in comparison to the photo-chemical process of imagesetters. —RS/BW

PostScript clones. Some printer manufacturers felt shut out of the PostScript printer market because of Adobe's initially stringent licensing policies. Others wished to add features (like resolution enhancement) that Adobe's PostScript hardware/software designs had failed to address. As a result, they developed or licensed PostScript-compatible interpreters that performed like Adobe's patented PostScript. Over the years, these clones have become pretty reliable, but since Adobe's lightened up its licensing policies in the same time span, fewer vendors feel compelled to employ clone PostScript. —BW

teletype.com
birmy.com
infowave.com

Faking it. There is a way to get a QuickDraw printer to pretend it's a PostScript printer: through emulation software. This can really slow things down, but if you only need it occasionally (if, for instance, most of your printing needs are text-based so QuickDraw alone works fine most of the time), you can get PostScript graphics printed on your QuickDraw printer. Check the latest reviews of programs like **StyleScript** ($100, Infowave), **T-Script** ($145, TeleTypesetting), and **PowerRIP** ($200, Birmy Graphics).

For printing PostScript fonts, however, you don't need an emulator: you already have all you need, in the ATM control panel that comes with your system software—that's all covered in Chapter 14.

Label printers. Sometimes all you need is a quick label or two to slap on an envelope or package—and it's a real pain to put in a partially-used sheet of labels and make sure you set up the print job so it hits the labels that are left and not any of the blanks. But a separate label printer solves the problem.

costar.com

CoStar's **LabelWriter XL** and **XL Plus** print quietly on thermal paper. They're both about $160; the XL prints standard skinny address labels, while the XL Plus prints wider labels for shipping, floppy disks, video cassettes, and so on. A roll of 700 address labels, available from CoStar and through general computer and office outlets is under $20. The bundled software stores up to 1,600 addresses, and the addresses can even include PICT graphics. It also generates and prints a postal bar code for each address. —KF/JK

Plug 'n' Print

Setting up. Most printers come with a cable for connecting to your Mac, and most connect to the printer port on the Mac's end of things, although the modem port can be used in some cases. For a straightforward serial printer like the ImageWriter, you can use either port; for networkable printers, you have to use the printer port (even if you don't consider your Mac and your printer a real, live, network).

Networks Chapter 26

If you're connecting a printer (usually a LaserWriter) to your printer port, the instructions will tell you to use network wire and cabling; this means you need two network connector boxes, one each for the Mac and the printer, and the phone-wire cable that connects them. But that setup is for when you have more than one Mac connected to the printer, because the network connectors let you hook up several devices at the same time. If it's just you and your LaserWriter, however, you can use the basic serial cable that was made for the ImageWriter (generically, it's an 8-pin serial cable) to connect your LaserWriter directly to the Mac's printer port.

Juggling act. What if you have, say, a serial-interface inkjet printer, a LocalTalk-interface laser printer, a modem, and an Apple QuickTake camera? The LocalTalk printer has to go on the printer port, leaving the three other peripherals to share the modem port. A manual switch box that lets you keep everything plugged in and turn a knob to select a device. Prices range from $20 to $60, depending on how many ports are provided. For around $100 you can snag Momentum's four-connector **Port Juggler**, a small box that automatically switches to the correct device depending on which application you're using. —BW/RS

Adapting PC printers for the Mac. You can use a PC printer with a Mac; you just need the Macintosh driver software and a serial-to-parallel converter cable. GDT Softworks' **PowerPrint** ($100) includes a serial-to-parallel converter for printers that have only a PC-standard Centronix parallel port. The PowerPrint software has print drivers for just about every dot-matrix, inkjet, and laser printer; it includes support for a built-in spooler, grayscale capability, color printer support, multiple feeder trays, text rotation, scaling, and multiple paper sizes. —RW/RS

Color Printing Comments

Color printing on black-and-white printers. There's lots to be said for eye-catching color, but a color printer isn't always necessary for final color output: Just get the right kind of paper. Previously a specialty item through catalogs, wonderful laser paper is now available from your local office supply store—and the bigger the store, the bigger the selection. You'll find colors from pastel to neon; textures like speckled granite, marble, and rain-spattered silk; and preprinted items like certificates, bordered announcements, and even tri-fold brochures.

Another approach, for laser printers only, is using special transfer ribbon—a colored film that melts against the toner on the printed page. You print the page as usual, using black where you want to add the color, tape a little piece of the film over the part you want colored, then send the page through the laser printer a second time (without printing anything on it this time); the heat of the LaserWriter bonds the colored film against the previously printed black area. You peel off the excess, unmelted film and you have your spot color where you need it. The film comes not only a variety of colors, but also in metallics which can add a nice touch to a special document when used correctly.

> *"Obviously, color images should be our ultimate goal" was one of Steve Jobs' earliest quotes concerning:*
> *a) The video screen of the Macintosh*
> *b) The printing mechanism of the ImageWriter*
> *c) The first Macintosh T-Shirts*
>
> *Andy Ihnatko, February 1989, The Active Window*

Thermal-wax solid blacks. Sometimes the straight black from a thermal wax transfer printer may have a matte texture or tiny gaps in coverage. You can get a glossier, more solid-looking black by specifying 100 percent of cyan, magenta, and yellow, in addition to black (provided your software lets you specify colors that way). —BW

Odd colors from an EPS file. When you save an EPS file, the PostScript settings for the printer in use at the time are stored with the file. When you print from another device, there may be minor or even major color changes. You can avoid this either by choosing the final output device's driver before creating the EPS file, or by saving the file as a TIFF image.

Rough-edged color text. When you're printing color text in small point sizes, you're better off using a single color ink: cyan, magenta, or yellow. Most other colors use a halftone or dither pattern made of different-color ink dots, which makes small type look unacceptably coarse. —BW

StyleWriters and ImageWriters

Models

ImageWriter models. The Mac started out with a trusty sidekick, the dot-matrix ImageWriter printer. You can't buy ImageWriters any more, except as used models, but they were so sturdy there are many still in service. ImageWriters are slow (a half-page per minute at highest quality output) and noisy (those firing pins are whiny little buggers). There were four ImageWriter models:

- **ImageWriter I:** The original, which received its number only retroactively when the ImageWriter II came out. (In fact, its name was actually *Imagewriter*, with a lowercase *w*.)

- **Wide-carriage ImageWriter:** You probably never heard of this because not too many people bought it, so it didn't stay in the lineup long. But those who bought it *really* needed the extra width of the carriage.
- **ImageWriter II:** Although it wasn't any quieter than its predecessor, the II was faster, used smaller pins in the printhead for better output (although it has the same number of pins), and provided an option for a network card so it could be shared. It also introduced something we've forgotten all about at this point: an add-on cut sheet feeder. A *cut sheet feeder??* Originally, you had to use those continuous fan-fold paper that needed to be torn apart (and have their feeder strips torn off the sides) or hand-feed a single sheet of paper to the printer at a time.
- **ImageWriter LQ:** Another one you've never heard of unless you're an old Mac hand. It offered more pins in the printhead for better printing (LQ stood for *letter quality*) but was plagued by problems from the start and never had a chance when LaserWriters hit the market.

StyleWriter models. Apple's inkjet line of StyleWriters has developed from a simple, slow, black-and-white model to speedy color models. Along the way came other improvements, too, like higher resolution and ink that didn't smear at the slightest hint of dampness. Despite the great printouts and good prices, StyleWriters, and inkjets in general, are often ignored because of their lack of PostScript capabilities.

Here's a quick roundup of the StyleWriter line; you'll find more detail in the StyleWriter Specs chart.

- **StyleWriter I:** Apple's first effort at a low-cost, high-resolution (300 dpi) printer; like the ImageWriter I, this printer got its numeral only in retrospect.
- **StyleWriter II:** A ton of small improvements over the original model, including a smaller case, the ability to hold 100 sheets of paper at a time (instead of 50), and the ability to be shared by multiple Macs.
- **Portable StyleWriter:** Not a StyleWriter at all, but a repackaged Canon BJ10•EX to satisfy early PowerBook users.
- **StyleWriter 1200:** The last black-and-white-only StyleWriter upped the standard 360-dpi inkjet resolution to 720x360.
- **Color StyleWriters:** Starting with the Apple Color Printer and its 360-dpi color output, color printing became affordable for almost everyone. The Color StyleWriter Pro quadrupled the speed of the Color Printer, and subsequent color StyleWriters have improved even more.

Since StyleWriters can print in different *modes,* you might see different speed ratings in charts or specs: draft mode can be four or five times faster than "best" mode; our chart shows the number for best-mode printouts. For color StyleWriters, both the page-per-minute speed rating and the dots-per-inch resolution depend on whether you're using black-and-white printing or color; both numbers are in the chart.

StyleWriter Models

	Resolution (dpi)		Pages per Minute	
	B&W	Color	B&W	Color
Color StyleWriter 6500	600x600	600x300	8	4
Color StyleWriter 4500	600x600	600x300	5	4
Color StyleWriter 4100	600x600	600x300	5	1.5
Color StyleWriter 2200	720x360		5	.3
Color StyleWriter 2500	720x360		5	.66
Color StyleWriter 2400	360		3	.3
Color StyleWriter 1500	720x360		3	.3
Color StyleWriter Pro	360		2	.5
Apple Color Printer	360		.5	.29
Portable StyleWriter	360		1.5	-
StyleWriter 1200	720x360		2	-
StyleWriter II	360		1	-
StyleWriter	360		.5	-

StyleWriter and Inkjet Tips

Testing. 1, 2, 3, testing... You can print a test page on your StyleWriter by holding down the On button after you've pressed it to turn on the printer.

Inkjet paper. With their improved ink formulations, the current crop of color inkjets look better than ever when printing on (cheap) plain ol' paper. That said, printouts look even better when you use special coated papers that keep the ink on the paper surface. Uncoated papers let the color ink sink in, leaving the surface slightly uncovered, producing a somewhat washed-out look. —BW

Cartridges. Printing with inkjet ink costs more per page than using laser printer toner. An ink cartridge for Apple's StyleWriter 1200, for example, costs around $25 and prints about 466 pages of text. That's more than five cents a page, compared to about two cents a page for a $90 LaserWriter printer cartridge. Printing high volume or lots of high-ink-coverage graphics could empty a cartridge every two or three days.

Mail-order ink-cartridge pricing is typically about 20 percent less than list. For the nimble-fingered and damn-the-warranty, full-cartridge-ahead user, it's possible to buy inks and refiller tools to get about ten uses out of each cartridge, saving about $10 a cartridge. If you want someone else to deal with the mess, you can buy "remanufactured" (refilled) cartridges at less than the usual price. —SZA/BW/RS

Keep those cartridges wrapped. Avoid opening a new ink cartridge if you know you're not going to be using your printer for a while; the ink may dry up before you get a chance to use it. A friend of mine let a newly opened ink cartridge languish for six months, and he then ran out of ink after only 50 pages—instead of the normal 300 pages on a cartridge. Take his advice and change the cartridge *after* your vacation! —ND

When the one-color well runs dry. Sometimes ink clogs some of the fine holes in inkjet printheads, so you may get either no print at all from one of your colors, or blank stripes where the partially blocked ink isn't making it to the paper. There are three things you can do to unclog the printhead's pores:

- When you're printing, click the Options or Utilities button in the Print dialog (the button depends on which printer you're using) to get a dialog like the one shown here. Click the *Clean ink cartridge* checkbox, and the StyleWriter will blow through the accumulated crud before it starts printing. You won't have to turn off the option; it's turned off automatically after a single use.

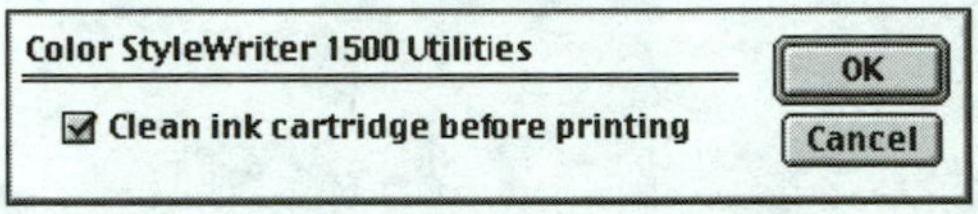

- Heavy use of the clogged nozzle sometimes breaks the dry dam. Try printing a heavily inked page one or more times. You can make a suitable page by going into a graphics program, drawing a box that fills a whole page, and filling it with a solid color or a dark pattern.
- If the nozzle really blocked with a dried-out clump, you can try soaking just the print head (not the whole cartridge) in some alcohol. —SZA/ND

Accommodating thick paper. For thick paper stock or envelopes on most StyleWriters (check your StyleWriter or its manual to see if yours is one of them), there are two physical adjustments you have to make. One lever is on the paper tray; move it so that it points to the envelope icon. The second adjustment is trickier: open the printer's cover and move the lever on the ink cartridge to the envelope icon. You should flip both levers back to the normal positions when you're going to use regular paper again.

Speeding up a 2400. The Color StyleWriter 2400 uses two cartridges, a black one and a tri-color. If you're not using color, you can take out both cartridges and replace them with Apple's **High-Performance Ink Cartridge**. It will really speed up print jobs because it has more ink nozzles than the smaller cartridges, so more ink hits the page on every pass.

Share and share alike. A StyleWriter connected to a Mac can be shared by other Macs on a network. (Of course, the StyleWriter will be connected to the first Mac's *modem* port because its printer port will have the network connection.) To set up the sharing:

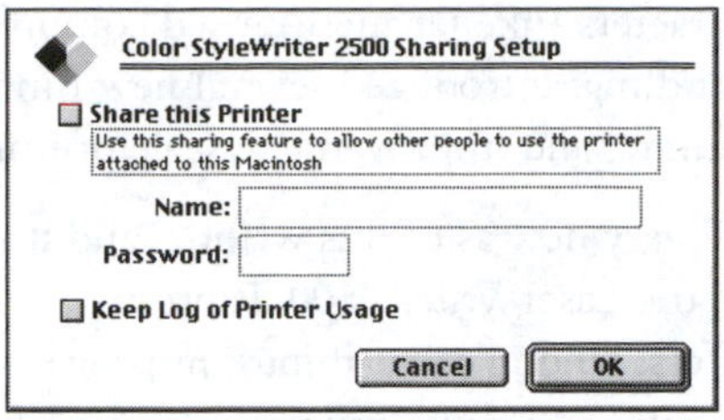

Setting up sharing for a StyleWriter.

1. Open Chooser.
2. Select the StyleWriter driver.
3. Click the Setup button.
4. Turn on sharing with the Share this Printer checkbox in the next dialog; you can also give the printer a name and set a password for it.
5. Click OK.

If you can't get the sharing dialog to show up, or get at all its controls, you may be missing the PrinterShare extension that you need; it comes with both the system software and the printer software, so it's easy enough to find another copy.

Sharing a StyleWriter means sharing your Mac. The StyleWriter doesn't have a brain to figure out how a page should look; the Mac always does that end of a job. On a shared StyleWriter, the Mac that the StyleWriter is connected to gets to do all the thinking, no matter which Mac sent the print job, and that slows down the "host" Mac considerably.

LaserWriters

Features and Models

It's the PostScript, stupid. No, I'm not calling *you* stupid—it's just a tag line (or a campaign slogan). As mentioned earlier, not all LaserWriters are PostScript-capable. The information in this section, and other sections of the chapter, refer to LaserWriters as if PostScript were the norm (which it is now). Some of the information applies to LaserWriters in general, too. The non-PostScript LaserWriters are: LaserWriter IISC, LaserWriter Select 300, and Personal LaserWriters 300, LS, and SC.

Leveling on the printing field. Not all PostScript interpreters are created equal. The original LaserWriters had the original PostScript built in; it's been retroactively labeled PostScript Level 1 to differentiate it from its descendants.

PostScript Level 2—standard in LaserWriters since the IIf and IIg—added many capabilities to PostScript (and therefore to the printers in which it lived); for most users, the most important difference was that Level 2 handled memory better, so there were fewer out-of-memory messages, Courier print-outs, and just plain choke-ups. Level 2 also: speeded printing by being able to cache elements used on more than one page; allowed "composite" fonts that need more than 256 characters (like Japanese); used compression and decompression to speed file handling; introduced several new functions to make color printing more accurate; and improved grayscale printing capabilities.

Level 3 PostScript is still very new as of this writing, and it's included in only one LaserWriter to date, the LaserWriter 8500. It promises faster, better printing, of course; it also offers, among other things, improvement in printing grayscale photos, colors, and 3-D items and provides for a larger set of ROM-resident fonts.

The speed factor(s). A printer's performance is usually rated in *pages per minute (ppm),* but that's misleading because it refers to how fast a page can be churned out once it's ready to go—how fast the "print engine" performs. But before the mechanical end of things can take over, the page has to be "imaged": all the information has to be processed, with a full page being "designed" from the instructions that came to the printer, before it can be printed at all. The imaging end of things is taken care of by the LaserWriter's processor chip; and, as with Macs, the type of chip and its clockspeed control just how fast it can do things.

Chips and clockspeeds

Chapter 2

There have been only a few different chips used in LaserWriters, and they can be easily divided into two groups: the Motorola 68000-series chips (as in the early Macs), and the more advanced RISC (*reduced instruction set computing*) chips. In the chart on page 590, any processor that's not a 68-something is a RISC chip. Within each group, more advanced chips (the ones with higher numbers) are faster; and for each chip, a faster clock speed means faster performance.

So, a LaserWriter's two speed factors combine to set its overall speed: the processor is in charge of the imaging process, and the print engine is in charge of printing the pages. A 12-ppm LaserWriter could outperform a 16-ppm with a slower processor if a document is complex and needs a lot of processing time.

Which speed factor is more important depends on the kind of work you do. If you print mostly text, and often do multiple copies of a document, a faster engine is your concern. If you work on complex graphics and layouts, usually printing a single copy at a time, the processor speed is much more important.

Resolution. Even the oldest of the LaserWriters have a resolution of at least 300 dpi; the standard has been 600 dpi for several years now (some models can do either), and some printers offer even higher resolution.

For text, the difference between 300 and 600 dpi printing isn't that big a deal except at the smallest font sizes: the 300-dpi text is a little thicker than the 600 dpi, but you seldom see any jaggies or poorly formed letters. For graphics, though, the difference practically slaps you in the face, since the jaggies on 300-dpi curved and angled lines disappear at 600 dpi.

Resident fonts. Laser printers come with "resident fonts" contained in their ROMs to speed printing—if the fonts are already there, they don't have to be sent from the Mac or retrieved from a printer's drive. But how many fonts are there depends on two things: which printer you're talking about, and how you count fonts. (The whole issue of just what *is* a font is discussed in Chapter 14; traditionally, each size and "cutting"—italic, bold, and so on—counts as a separate font, but we generally refer to the "family" as a single font.)

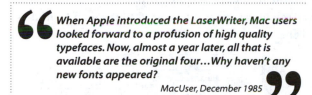

> ***When Apple introduced the LaserWriter, Mac users looked forward to a profusion of high quality typefaces. Now, almost a year later, all that is available are the original four…Why haven't any new fonts appeared?***
>
> *MacUser, December 1985*

The first LaserWriter was touted as having 13 fonts, but they belonged to four families: Courier, Helvetica, Times, and Symbol. The first three came in plain, bold, italic, and bold-italic—which adds up to 12 fonts (if you're trying to brag). All subsequent LaserWriters (and PostScript laser printers in general) had 35 fonts, or so they wanted us to believe; there were only eleven font families—seven beyond the original LaserWriter:

- Courier: (plain), Oblique, Bold, Bold Oblique
- Helvetica: (plain), Oblique, Bold, Bold Oblique
- Helvetica Narrow: (plain), Oblique, Bold, Bold Oblique
- Times: Roman, Italic, Bold, Bold Italic
- Palatino: Roman, Italic, Bold, Bold Italic
- Bookman: Light, Light Italic, Demibold, Demibold Italic
- Avant Garde: Book, Book Oblique, Demibold, Demi Oblique
- New Century Schoolbook: Roman, Italic, Bold, Bold Italic
- Zapf Chancery: Medium Italic
- Zapf Dingbats
- Symbol

Some LaserWriters have one other font built-in: the *Emulator font* used to—what else?—emulate the printing available on some non-Apple laser printers.

Fine Print and PhotoGrade. FinePrint and PhotoGrade are built into some LaserWriters by means of an *ASIC (application-specific integrated circuit)* chip. One is meant to produce better text, and the other improves grayscale printing for photos and graphics.

FinePrint improves printed output of text by printing dots of different sizes (or, more accurately, *partial* dots) when necessary to round out a curve. How much of a difference does it really make? Little to none. I printed out various size samples from two different LaserWriters (a Pro 630 at 300 dpi and a 12/640 at 600 dpi) and neither I nor anyone I showed them to could see a difference between the FinePrint and non-FinePrint versions.

PhotoGrade, on the other hand, makes an incredible difference, letting a LaserWriter print using 91 levels of gray instead of the usual 33. (Of course, in both cases it's really printing only black dots, but it's the size and arrangement of the dots that make us see grays instead of black dots on white paper.)

For many printers, you can't use either option, or sometimes just not both at the same time, unless you've added extra memory to the printer. Once you have enough memory, there are two places you control whether FinePrint and PhotoGrade are on: set the default through the Apple Printer Utility (in the Imaging Options level), and override it if you need to through Print dialog's Imaging Option screen.

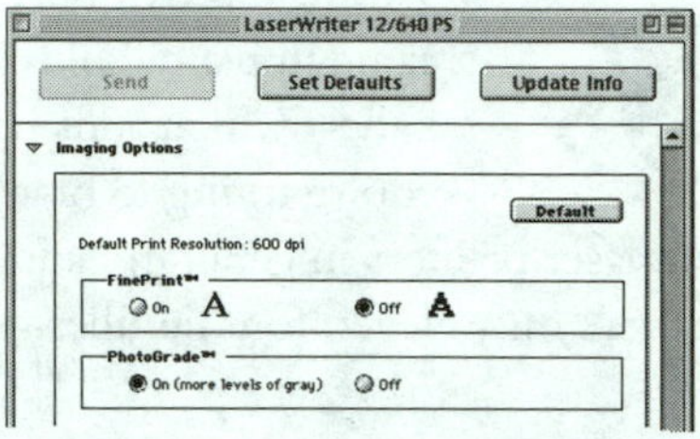

Set the defaults for FinePrint and PhotoGrade in the Apple Printer Utility.

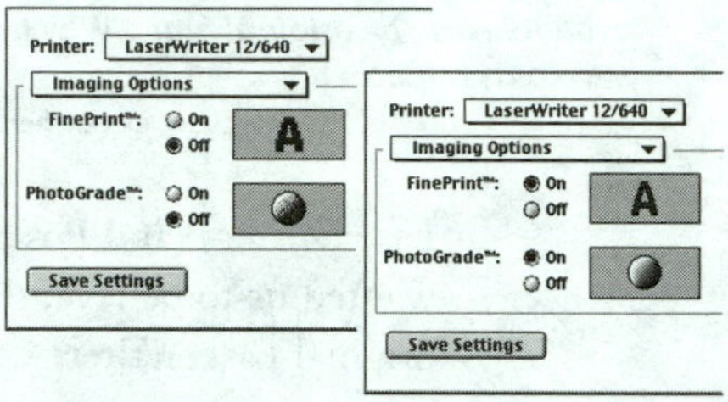

Override the default settings for FinePrint and PhotoGrade in the Print dialog.

Memory. PostScript printers need a lot of memory. They need almost a meg to hold the image of a none-too-fancy page before it's printed and nearly another half-megabyte to do the calculations that create the page image. Any leftover memory is used for storing fonts and for caching images of letters it has already drawn, so it won't have to create them from scratch again the next time they're needed. That means a 2MB printer has less than 400K available for font storage—enough for perhaps ten typical PostScript fonts. Some printers use additional RAM for double-buffering, wherein one page gets ready while a previously processed page is fed to the print engine, and technologies like PhotoGrade and FinePrint are RAM hogs. And, of course, complicated graphics and layouts need more memory than a basic text page.

For anything but basic printing, you'll want to add memory to your LaserWriter to speed up printing or, in some cases, to make printing possible.

It's easy to add memory to a LaserWriter, and it's a cheap upgrade, too, since SIMM prices are so low. But what's not easy is deciding where the SIMMs should go if you have multiple slots. There's no easy formula if you're using SIMMs of different sizes (which you can do); where the larger one goes sometimes depends on what size SIMMs you're working with. You're actually going to have to pick up your printer manual when it comes to this one!

The LaserWriter family. While there are nowhere near as many LaserWriter models as Mac models, there have been quite a few in Apple's printer-production history (which, as I write this, seems to be coming to an end, with Apple indicating they won't be making any more printers). But the models out there (I know of dozens of originals still turning out basic text copy) can be loosely classified into groups:

- **LaserWriter and LaserWriter Plus:** The originals, retroactively referred to as LaserWriter I's, can still handle basic text output but their limited memory and use of Level 1 PostScript limits their functionality.
- **LaserWriter II family:** This line improved upon the originals with a different print engine that worked faster and produced blacker blacks; each one also, of course, had better and faster processors. The later models in the line included Level 2 PostScript.
- **Personal LaserWriters:** The low-cost alternative in their time, they were slower than the models in the II line; in keeping with the *personal* idea (as opposed to business or network), there were cutbacks in other ways, too, like smaller-capacity paper trays.
- **LaserWriter Select:** Three models that seemingly have nothing in common except their names: one (the 300) has no PostScript, another (the 310) has a RISC processor but only 13 resident fonts instead of the usual 35 and doesn't have FinePrint or PhotoGrade, and the last (the 360) has triple the speed and memory capacity and Level 2 PostScript. Go figure.
- **LaserWriter Pros:** These LaserWriters introduced 600-dpi resolution and multiple paper trays, along with ever-faster processing. The monster 810 has the most advanced processor (even better than later LaserWriters), a whopping 750-page paper tray, and lets you print tabloid-size (11 by 17) paper.
- **Color LaserWriters:** Unlike their StyleWriter counterparts, the resolution of LaserWriter output doesn't change as you switch from black and white to color; however, the number of pages it can print per minute drops to a rate lower than any other LaserWriter (even the first)—but if you need color output, that hardly matters.
- **LaserWriters by-the-number:** The last round of LaserWriters were simply assigned numbers instead of any special names. When there's a pair of numbers (like 12/640 and 16/600), the first number refers to the page-per-minute rating (but that's the *engine* rating, not the *imaging* time, as described earlier). In this crowd, the 8500 stands out not just because it has a single number after its name, but because it can churn out 20 pages after speedily processing them with its 60MHz processor.

LaserWriter Specs

	Processor	Speed	DPI	PPM B&W	PPM Color	Hard Drive Ext	Hard Drive Int	Memory Max	Memory Slots	Memory Type	Memory Speed	Postscript Level
LaserWriter	68000	12	300	8	-	-	-	1.5	0	-	-	1
LaserWriter Plus	68000	12	300	8	-	-	-	1.5	0	-	-	1
LaserWriter IIf	68030	20	300	8	-	-	●	32	8	30-pin	80ns	2
LaserWriter IIg	68030	25	300	8	-	-	●	32	8	30-pin	80ns	2
LaserWriter IINT	68000	11.16	300	8	-	-	-	2	0	-	-	1
LaserWriter IINTX	68000	16.67	300	8	-	-	●	12	12	64-pin	120ns	1
LaserWriter IISC	68000	7.45	300	8	-	-	-	1	4	-	120ns	-
Personal LaserWriter 300	-	-	300	4	-	-	-	0.5	0	-	-	-
Personal LaserWriter LS	-	-	300	4	-	-	-	1	4	30-pin	100ns	-
Personal LaserWriter SC	68000	7.275	300	4	-	-	-	1	4	30-pin	120ns	-
Personal LaserWriter NT	68000	12	300	4	-	-	-	8	2	30-pin	120ns	1
Personal LaserWriter NTR	AMD 29005	16	300	4	-	-	-	4	1	72-pin	80ns	2
Personal LaserWriter 320	AMD 29205	16	300	4	-	-	-	8	1	card	-	2
LaserWriter Pro 600	68030	25	600	8	-	-	-	32	2	72-pin	80ns	2
LaserWriter Pro 630	68030	25	600	8	-	●	●	32	2	72-pin	80ns	2
LaserWriter Pro 810	Weitek 8200	7.25	800	20	-	●	-	32	3	card	-	2
LaserWriter Select 300	-	-	300	5	-	-	-	4.5	1	30-pin	80ns	-
LaserWriter Select 310	AMD 29205	7.25	300	5	-	-	-	5.5	1	72-pin	100ns	1
LaserWriter Select 360	AMD 29200	16	600	10	-	-	-	16	1	72-pin	80ns	2
LaserWriter 4/600 PS	AMD 29200	16	600	4	-	-	-	6	1	card	-	2
LaserWriter 12/640 PS	AMD 29040	30	600	12	-	-	-	64	2	72-pin	70ns	2
LaserWriter 16/600 PS	AMD 29030	25	600	17	-	-	-	32	2	72-pin	80ns	2
LaserWriter 8500	AMD 29040	60	600	20	-	-	-	48	1	72-pin	60ns	3
Color LaserWriter 12/600	AMD 29030	30	600	12	3	-	-	40	2	72-pin	60ns	2
Color LaserWriter 12/600PS	AMD 29030	30	600	12	3	-	-	40	2	72-pin	60ns	2
Color LaserWriter 12/660	AMD 29030	30	600	12	3	-	-	40	2	72-pin	60ns	2

Using a Hard Drive

The font express. It was a great disappointment to me that when I replaced my LaserWriter Pro 630 with the more advanced 12/640, I had to give up a great convenience: the internal hard drive the 630 accommodated for font files. (I also miss the little window in the paper tray that told me at a glance if the supply was getting low.)

If a LaserWriter has its own hard drive, it can retrieve fonts from that drive instead of from the Mac's; this saves lots of time (transfer from the printer's drive is much speedier than the network transmission of font information), and frees up your Mac a lot sooner in the course of a print job. The LaserWriter chart on the previous page shows which models can have SCSI drives attached internally or externally for font storage.

Special formatting. You can't use a drive that's formatted for the Mac on a LaserWriter; the drive has to be connected to the LaserWriter first, and then formatted through the Apple Printer Utility:

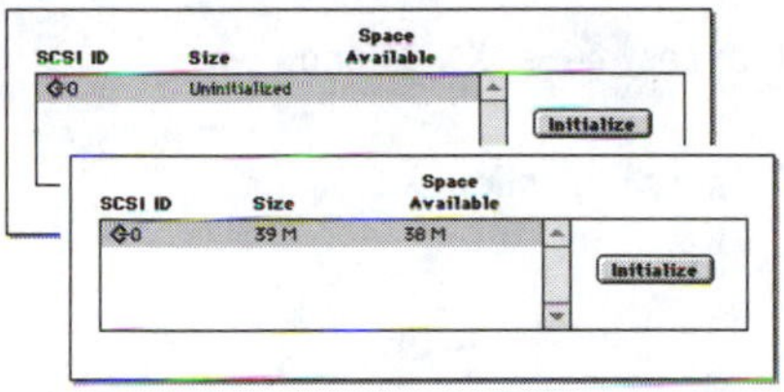

The Disks level before and after initializing an attached drive.

1. Open the program, select the printer in the Printer Selector window, and click the Open Printer button.
2. When the printer window opens, click on the arrow in front of the Disks category.
3. Select the drive in the dialog window, and click the Initialize button.

If you swap a printer disk from one type of LaserWriter to another, you'll have to reformat the disk, since different LaserWriter models use different formatting schemes.

Downloading fonts. To download fonts to the drive, you use the Apple Printer Utility. The procedure is the same as downloading fonts to the printer's memory (described later in the chapter), except that you have to choose the disk's SCSI ID number from the pop-up menu at the bottom of the window.

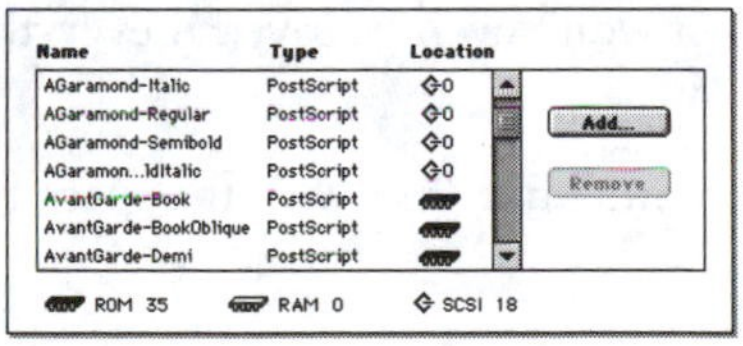

The Fonts dialog in the Apple Printer Utility's window after downloading fonts to the drive, showing the total of 18 fonts on the drive.

The storage setup. Only about 20 percent of a printer's hard drive is used for font storage; the rest is used as a *font cache.* When you store font files on the drive, they're still only the files of information needed to create a font. When you use the font in a document, the printer figures out how the letters should look and creates a bitmapped font of the right size to use for the printing (remember, even LaserWriters use bitmaps as final output). That information is flushed out of the LaserWriter's memory when more room is needed. But when you have a hard drive, it's used to store the rasterized font information so it won't have to be recalculated—that's the font cache.

The fact that you can't use the whole drive for font file storage isn't a big deal; font files are small—a hundred of them easily fit in about three megs of drive space.

What's on that drive? You can easily get a list of fonts that have been downloaded to the printer's hard drive by using the Apple Printer Utility, described later in the chapter. But that doesn't tell you how much of the drive is filled.

Here's a PostScript program that will tell you about the hard drive's capacity, although it doesn't differentiate between the font files and the font cache portions.

1. Type this program *exactly* as it's printed here, in a word processor or SimpleText:

```
/Helvetica findfont 14 scalefont setfont
statusdict begin
30 100 moveto
(*A page is 1024 bytes -- a K. ) show
30 115 moveto
(Total number of pages: ) show
diskstatus
10 string cvs show
30 130 moveto
(Number of pages free: ) show
10 string cvs show
showpage
```

2. Save the file as a text file.
3. Launch the Apple Printer Utility.
4. Use the Send PostScript File command to send the text file to the printer.
5. You'll be asked where you want to save the PostScript Log for the download. Put it anywhere—it won't even be saved if everything goes well; it's only for error reports.

Postscript files and downloading
Later this chapter

Your printout will look something like this, with the space reports given in kilobytes:

Number of pages free: 34235
Total number of pages: 39991
*A page is 1024 bytes -- a K.

Fonts for ATM. Adobe Type Manager (covered in Chapter 14) can't access the font files on a printer's hard drive. So, if you want good screen text, you'll need two copies of each printer font—one on the Mac for the screen display, and one on the printer's drive for speedy printing.

Toner Tips

Dense and denser. You seldom need full-strength toner on your printers for good printing; using more than you need means only that you'll run out sooner. While the lowest settings might give type a slightly grayer look, a light setting is fine for text, and just-below-middle setting works fine for solid black areas when the cartridge is new. (As it ages, you up the print density to get more on the paper.)

Apple Printer Utility
Later this chapter

Older LaserWriters have manual settings for print density adjustment; on the very early models, the dial's on the outside, while models in the II line have the dial inside, under the lid. For all the manually set models, the number settings go from 1 to 9, with 9 being the lightest (really!). All recent and current LaserWriters have software-controlled density settings. Use the Apple Printer utility to set the density.

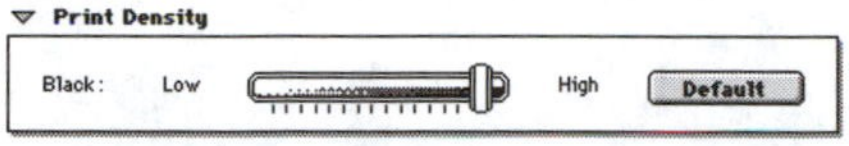

Good to the last drop. As your toner cartridge approaches the end of its useful days and the LaserWriter light indicates you're low on toner, you can extend easily the cartridge's life for a hundred, or sometimes several hundred, more pages. Remove the cartridge and give it a few brisk shakes from end to end to jog the remaining toner around. Don't turn the cartridge upside down; just make motions like you're sifting flour. You should be able to do this a dozen times or more before the "low toner" light refuses to turn itself off and the cartridge is really getting empty. (In the meantime, just ignore the light.) And, be careful in there; a just-used cartridge is hot to the touch. —SZA/JF

Buying toner cartridges. It's easy to go through over $500 a year in toner cartridges if you do a reasonable amount of printing, but you can cut that cost considerably with some careful shopping.

- You don't need Apple-brand LaserWriter cartridges. All laser printers are based on only a few different interior designs and can share cartridges. The chart on the next page shows which LaserWriters use which cartridges, so don't let the hapless help at the local superstore tell you, as they tell me where I live, that they just don't carry cartridges for Apple printers.
- Buy at a superstore or web/mail order, not at a computer store or a small office-supply store. You can save up to 25 percent of the cost of a new cartridge when you buy from a high-volume source.
- Consider a *remanufactured* cartridge, which costs about 40 percent less than a new one. In remanufacturing, the cartridge is thoroughly inspected and completely rebuilt, including a new imaging drum if needed (the drum needs to be replaced, on average, every third time the cartridge is re-used). The expertise with which this is done makes a difference to the performance life, so all vendors are not alike when it comes to this savings plan. Avoid *recharged* cartridges which are merely re-filled with toner (a "drill and fill" job) with no inspection or replacement parts.

LaserWriter Toner Cartridges and Substitutes

Apple LaserWriter	Comparable Printer	Laser Engine	Apple Toner Cartridge	Hewlett Packard Cartridge	Canon Cartridge	Other
LaserWriter, LaserWriter Plus	LaserJet II, IID, III, IIID	Canon CX	M0180	HP92285A	EP	
LaserWriter II, IISC, IINT, IINTX, IIf, IIg	LaserJet, LaserJet Plus, LaserJet 500 Plus	Canon SX	M6002	HP92295A	EP-S	
Personal LaserWriter SC, LS, NT, NTR	LaserJet IIP, IIP Plus, IIIP	Canon LX	M0089LL/A	HP92275A	EP-L	
Personal LaserWriter 300, 320, 4/600PS	LaserJet 4L, LaserJet 4ML	Canon PX	M2045G/A	HP92274A	EP-P	Xerox 113R0005
LaserWriter Select 300, 310, 360	Xerox 4505, 4510	Fuji Xerox XP10	M1960G/A			
LaserWriter Pro 600, 630, 16/600PS	LaserJet 4, LaserJet 4M, 4M Plus, 4 Plus	Canon EX	M2473G/A	HP92298/A	EP-X	
LaserWriter 12/640PS		Fuji Xerox P893	M4683G/A			
LaserWriter Pro 810 (11-micron toner)	Compaq Pagemarq 15/20, Dataproducts LZR 1560	Fuji Xerox XP20	M1853G/A			Xerox 113R00110 Dataproducts 299275-502
LaserWriter Pro 810 (7-micron toner)	Compaq Pagemarq 15/20, Dataproducts LZR 1560	Fuji Xerox XP20	M3602G/A			Xerox 113R00110 Dataproducts 299275-602
LaserWriter 8500	Xerox 4520	Fuji Xerox XP20	M5893G/A			Xerox 113R00110
Color LaserWriter 12/600/660	Canon Color LBP 360P	Canon HX LBP				
Cyan			M3757G/A		R74-3019-150	
Magenta			M3760G/A		R74-3018-150	
Yellow			M3758G/A		R74-3017-150	
Black			M3756G/A		R74-3020-150	

It's easy being green. Don't throw your laser cartridges away. They're not exactly biodegradable; they'll be sitting in a landfill somewhere till the end of time, or thereabouts. Most cartridge manufacturers provide a mailing label for returns right inside the box you get the cartridge in-with postage prepaid. Use it!

LaserWriter Tips

Stop the printer test page. Each time you turn on your LaserWriter, it spits out a test page with all sorts of important information on it. But if you don't need a reminder about its capabilities or a report on how many pages it's printed so far in its life, you don't need to waste the time, paper, and toner every day. Use the Apple Printer Utility to turn off the test page: under the Startup Page category, just uncheck the startup page option.

LaserWriters default to having a startup page printed, but you can turn it off through the Apple Printer Utility.

If you want a single test page (but you don't want it on all the time), you don't have to reset the Startup Page option and restart the printer; you can just use the Print Configuration Page command in the Apple Printer Utility.

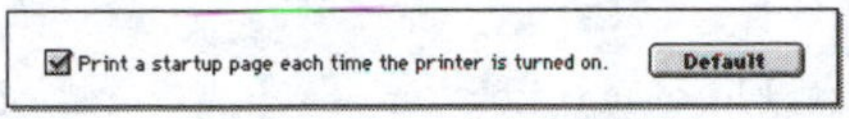
Print a startup page each time the printer is turned on.
Default

The first-page delay. Does it seem to you that your first printout after a long lunch takes longer than other print jobs? It's not a psychological problem. Many later-model LaserWriters have built-in energy-saving circuitry that decreases the power draw when the printer's not being used; the rest state kicks in after an hour or so of idle time, and it takes up to a full minute for it wake up completely when the Mac clamors for attention.

Too many fonts spoil the broth. LaserWriters with small amounts of memory have a hard time handling documents with lots of fonts. If you can't print a document, or it's coming out with Courier for some areas, try turning on the Unlimited Downloadable Fonts option: you'll find it through the Page Setup dialog, using either a button or a pop-up menu that says PostScript Options.

Other printing problems
Chapter 24

Ways to speed up laser printing. Here are a few ways you can speed up that output; most are explained elsewhere in the chapter, but I thought you'd like a quick roundup.

- Use the LaserWriter's built-in fonts.
- Add a hard drive to the LaserWriter (if it can handle one) to store fonts.
- Manually download fonts to the printer before the print job.
- Use a black-and-white printing option instead of color/grayscale when you don't need the latter.
- Add more memory to the printer.
- Uncheck the *Unlimited Downloadable Fonts* option through the Page Setup dialog's option button or menu.

Laser-proof media. If you're going to send envelopes or labels through your LaserWriter, make sure they're meant for laser printing. The heat inside the printer can melt glue not made to stand up to higher-than-usual temperatures; at the least, you'll wind up with unusable envelopes/labels; at worst, labels will peel off inside the LaserWriter and gum up the works.

And if you want to print overhead transparencies, make sure you get laser-proof ones, because the standard ones may melt as they go through the rollers—don't ask how I know!

Ill-legal on Color LaserWriter. If your Color LaserWriter has less than 16MB of memory, it can't use the same high resolution for color printing as it does on standard-size paper. Instead, it uses a special compression technique when imaging the page, using only cyan, magenta, and yellow, which can result in missing pixels or the dreaded jaggies. If you up the memory to 16MB or more, the printer can use the same imaging for the larger page sizes, adding in the black ink.

Older-model tidbits. Here's a quick list of what you should know if you have an older LaserWriter:

- If you're using an older LaserWriter with Level 1 PostScript—especially one that has little memory—you may have trouble printing a document with multiple master fonts in it: you get a "processing" notice but then nothing happens, and the printer returns to its idle wait state. There's really no way around this; you'll have to change the font in your document to a standard PostScript or TrueType font.
- The LaserWriter II line models have an ADB port, but it's totally unusable. It was meant for later expansion (multiple cut-sheet feeders, for instance) but no add-on devices were ever developed.
- The IIf can print legal-size pages only if it's been upgraded from its original 4 megs of memory to 5; it need the extra meg to image the larger page.
- The LaserWriter IIg, for some reason, didn't have Zapf Dingbats included in its ROM, as did all the other LaserWriters. It also had some networking problems that were addressed by a (free) ROM upgrade. The new ROM included Dingbats, so if you have a IIg and it has Zapf Dingbats built in (you can check with the Apple Printer Utility), you have the replacement ROM.

Printing Software

The Chooser

Good choice. The Chooser desk accessory is for letting you *choose* items like printers and file servers, and then set options regarding the item you chose.

Clicking in an icon in the left panel lists options on the right. The Chooser also lets you turn AppleTalk on and off (since many printers are connected through AppleTalk) and, in some cases, it lets you turn background printing on and off. Once you set choices in the Chooser, they remain until you change them, although some general trouble-shooting procedures (like zapping the PRAM) can reset it to defaults.

The awkward thing about using the Chooser is that there's no OK button; things happen when you select them, even though you seldom get feedback.

There are a few keyboard shortcuts available in Chooser:

- Pressing Tab alternately activates the left or right pane.
- In the active pane, you can type a few letters to select the item you want.
- In the active pane, you can use ←→↑↓ to select the item adjacent to the currently selected item.

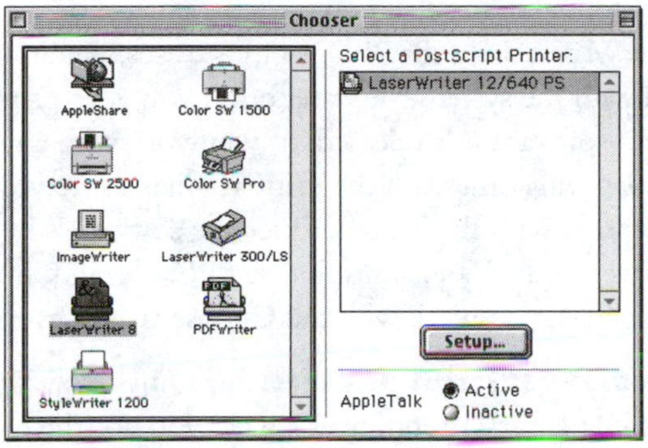

Drivers. The printer icons in Chooser are the *printer drivers* that are in your Extensions folder. A printer driver is special software that translates printing information coming from an application into instructions that a printer can understand. This saves the application from having to know about all the different printers available; it can work with sort of generic information and let the driver take care of the specifics.

Your system software comes with drivers for all of Apple's printers; third-party printers usually come with their own drivers that you install separately.

PPD files. PPD files? What kind of computer is this, anyway? (Sigh…)

Somewhere during System 7's reign, the LaserWriter 8 driver came out and introduced a new concept: *PostScript printer descriptions*, or *PPDs*. These files go in the imaginatively named Printer Description folder in your Extensions folder. (These files are also sometimes referred to as *printer page description* files; they were also originally called *printer description files,* or *PDFs,* but that acronym's been shanghaied by *portable document format.*)

Okay, but what *are* they? Since there are so many LaserWriter models around with so many different capabilities, a single driver can't take care of them all; all the driver itself does now is get at the common capabilities, like image scaling and font substitution—the items that have always been in Page Setup and Print dialogs. The PPD file describes what a specific LaserWriter model is able to do, like use multiple trays, or print both sides of the paper, or use 600 dpi, or print in color. So, you choose the LaserWriter driver, and then select the PPD file that goes with your printer. Of course, since this *is* a Mac, you don't have to worry too much; you can tell it to find the correct PPD file for you once you tell it which printer you have.

Setting up a new printer. When you get a new printer—or when you've installed OS 8 and have to start again with printer connections—you have to set up a few things so the Mac and the printer understand each other, and so that you'll get a desktop printer icon for a LaserWriter.

First, you have to make sure that you have the correct driver for the printer; and, for a LaserWriter, the right PPD. In most cases, you'll have everything you need installed with the system software; but if you get a printer that comes out after the system software was released, or you work with a non-Apple printer, the required files will come with the printer—make sure you run the installer software that comes with the printer. Once the software's in your System Folder (the driver in the Extensions folder, PPD files in the Printer Descriptions folder), you work with the Chooser to get everything going.

Setting up non-PostScript printers. For QuickDraw-based printers (inkjets, and some LaserWriters), here's what you do (the exact choices depend on the printer you have, since they offer different options):

1. Open the Chooser and click the printer's icon in the left panel.
2. If you're offered a choice of ports in the right panel, click on the one you're using—the printer or the modem port. The way the choices are presented varies from one printer to another: sometimes you get icons labeled *printer* and *modem*; sometimes you get icons labeled *serial port;* sometimes you get icons without labels.
3. If there's a Setup button, your printer is able to be shared with any other Mac that you're connected to; if you're going to share it, click Setup to name the printer and set any passwords you want to use.

That's all there is to it; the Mac now knows where to send the printer information, and which driver to use for formatting the printed output.

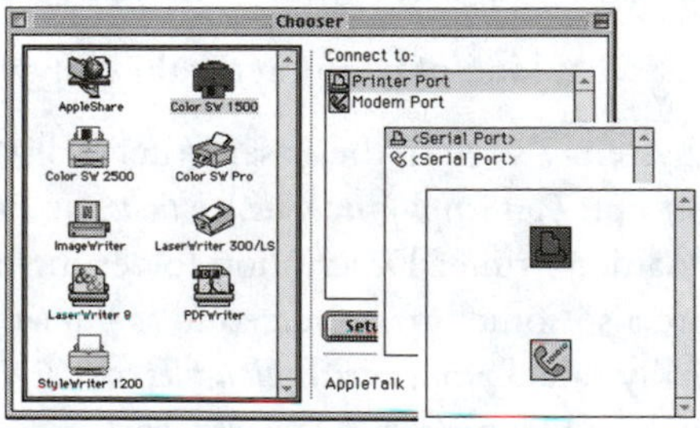

The representation of the printer and modem ports varies with the printer driver you select.

Setting up a LaserWriter. The setup for a LaserWriter isn't incredibly difficult, but there are certainly more steps and more choices than for non-networked printers.

1. Open the Chooser and click the LaserWriter 8 icon.
2. Select the LaserWriter in the right panel.
3. Click the Create button (it's a Setup button if you've worked with the printer before).
4. Use the Auto Setup button for the PPD to be selected automatically or, use the Select PPD button to do it yourself. With Auto Setup, certain other printer options are also registered (see the next entry).
5. This step's optional: use the Printer Info button to retrieve any specific printer information you may not be sure of (like how much memory is installed); use the Update Info button in the dialog that opens so the Chooser checks with the printer for the latest info.
6. Use the Configure button to tell Chooser what special hardware options you've added to your printer if you've selected the PPD yourself. The choices are based on the printer's possibilities: envelope feeder, special high-volume paper cassette, double-sided printing, memory upgrades, and so on.
7. Click all the OK buttons you see to get back to the Chooser.

When you're finished, there'll be a little icon next to the printer's name in the Chooser list, and a desktop icon to match.

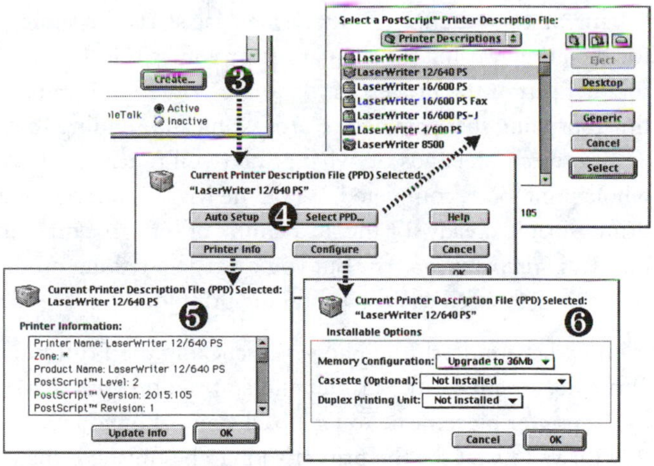

The dialog that opens (center) when you click the Chooser's Create button has many options.

For a new or upgraded printer. The PPD files for each printer can describe only certain basic options that are built in, and provide information about *possible* options, like extra memory or special paper trays. If you've added optional extras, you may not be able to use them because they won't show up in Page Setup and Print dialogs without your letting the system know that they're available.

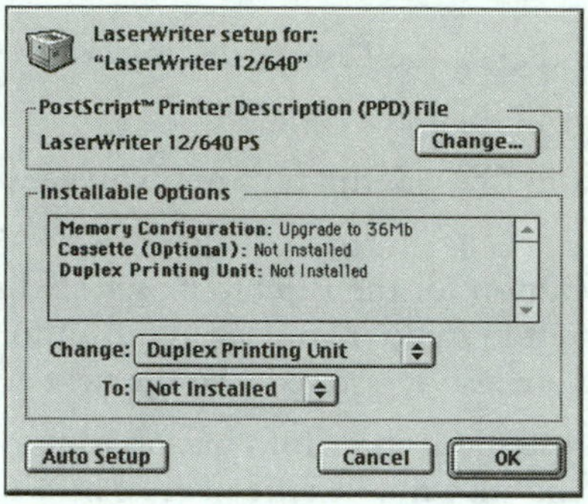

You can make simple setup changes through the Change Setup command from the Finder's Printing menu.

The easiest way to get this taken care of is to select the printer in Chooser, click the Setup button, and then click the Auto Setup button in the next dialog. If you've done a simple, single upgrade, like a RAM upgrade, you can change the setup manually from the desktop: click on the desktop printer icon, choose Change Setup from the Printing menu, and use the pop-up menus to indicate the changes.

No PPD. If you can't find a PPD for your laser printer, click the Generic button in the PPD dialog; this will give you the basic laser printing options and create a desktop printer for you. (Check with the printer's manufacturer to see if there's a special one available, especially when you upgrade your system software.)

Background printing. The next few sections deal with background printing issues, but you should know what background printing's all about. And it's easiest to understand background printing if you first know what happens *without* background printing.

When you click the Print button, the Mac starts processing your document for the printer, using the printer driver you've selected in Chooser. It sends the first part of the processed file to the printer and waits for the printer to finish printing that part before processing and sending the next piece. (How large a "piece" depends on what printer you're using.) This continues until the whole print job is completed. While the Mac is waiting for a signal from the printer that it's ready for the next chunk of information, you get a dialog box that says *Printing in progress*. But you can't do anything on the Mac because its attention is focused exclusively on the print job.

With background printing, however, clicking the Print button processes the entire document for the printer and stores it on your disk instead of sending it to the printer piecemeal. You get back control of your Mac sooner, since you don't have to wait for the printer's job to be finished; the communication between the printer and the Mac, and the feeding out of parts of the processed document, are done in the background.

On older Macs, background printing slows down the Mac's responsiveness. On newer ones, the slowdown is perceptible during the actual download of parts of the document to the printer but doesn't necessarily interfere with what you're doing. But you should avoid disk-intensive procedures while background printing's going on, since then you and the Print Monitor will be arguing over disk access and you'll both be slowed down.

Desktop Printers

The desktop printer. Desktop printing was ushered in with System 7.6 and is now the crux of Mac printing. It was originally touted as a great way to send a document to the printer—drag a document icon onto the printer icon—but I could never understand how that could be convenient: most people print from within their applications, and if you're on the desktop, it's likely that your document is going to be nested down several folders deep. How convenient is that? But even if you do most of your printing from your applications, the desktop printer approach does provide a few options more convenient than the old way of doing things, especially for background printing.

You can print everything you need to without touching the desktop printer, since it functions in the background. But you can use it to get a print job started and to access the Desktop PrintMonitor to control the job once it starts. First, some basics:

- A desktop printer icon, which is usually the icon of its printer type, changes to reflect its current status: a dark frame around it means it's the current printer; when a print job is in the queue, waiting to be sent, there's a document icon superimposed on the printer icon; during a print job, the document icon gradually fills with gray to show the status of the job; when you stop the print queue, preventing anything in the list from being printed, there's a stop sign on the printer icon; and, if there's an X through the icon, the printer belongs to a different system's desktop (you probably have multiple startup drives).

Left, the standard desktop icon and the framed default printer; center, documents waiting in the queue (top) and a document being printed; right, a stopped queue and an inactive printer.

- You can rename the desktop printer without affecting its performance—the actual name of the printer, as it appears in Chooser, isn't changed. The name of the desktop printer icon, however, is the one that appears in the pop-up menu Print dialogs.
- You can print a document by dragging its icon and dropping it on the desktop printer. The application will open so you can use the Print dialog to set options, and the print job starts.

- Double-clicking a desktop printer icon opens the PrintMonitor.
- A desktop printer is a necessity: if you try to trash the one you have, a new one is created automatically.
- Selecting a desktop printer icon puts a Printing menu in the Finder's menubar.

The good, the not-as-good, and the ugly. While many different pieces of the system software work together to provide printing capabilities, there are two extensions that let you create and use desktop printers: Desktop Printer Spooler and Desktop Print Monitor. Without them, you not only can't use desktop printers, but if you've already created one, it reverts to a folder (of all things!).

If you turn off these two extensions, you can still have full printing capabilities, including background printing (sometimes desktop printers and background printing are confusing for beginners), which is provided through the Print Monitor extension and accessed through the Chooser (just as in previous systems).

As for the ugly: If you still have System 7's Desktop Printing Extension hanging around in your Extensions folder, it's not only unnecessary but it also could cause your system to freeze on startup under OS 8.

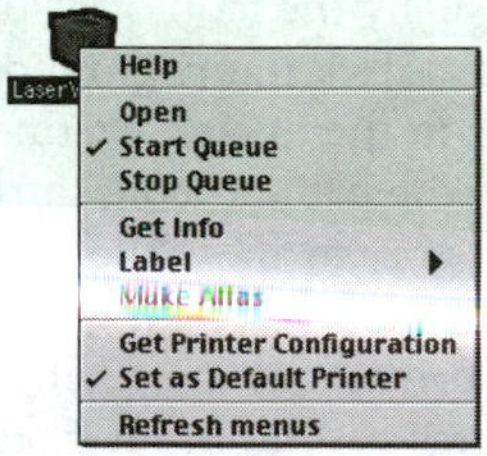

The contextual printer menu. Accessing the Finder's Printer menu is a two-step process, since a printer icon has to be selected in order for the menu to be added to the menubar. But you can do it in one step by Control-clicking on the desktop printer icon: the menu that appears has all the Printer menu commands in it.

Multiple desktop printers. If you have more than one desktop printer, you select the one you want to be the current one and use the Set Default Printer command from the Printing menu, or press ⌘L. The default printer is the one that shows up by default (duh!) in Print dialogs, where you can select a different printer instead for any print job if you have more than one desktop printer available.

The desktop printer without the desktop. If you find yourself going to the desktop to open a desktop printer to get at the PrintMonitor—which means you have to hide your application windows, and maybe even close Finder windows just so you can see the icon—you can set things up so you don't have to go to the desktop at all.

Create an alias of the desktop printer and put it in your Apple menu; selecting it from there gives you the Print Monitor window without your having to find the desktop printer itself. You get two additional bonuses with this trick: The printer's icon in the Apple menu changes with a print job just the way

The icon in the Apple menu changes the same way the desktop printer does.

the real one does, so a click on the Apple menu means you can tell at a glance how far along the print job is because you'll see the page graying as the job progresses. And, when there are any print jobs in the queue, they all appear as the printer's submenu items; selecting any item is a waste of time, since it's like trying to open one from the Print Monitor window (you get a dialog telling you that it can't be opened)—but you can see the list without having to open the monitor.

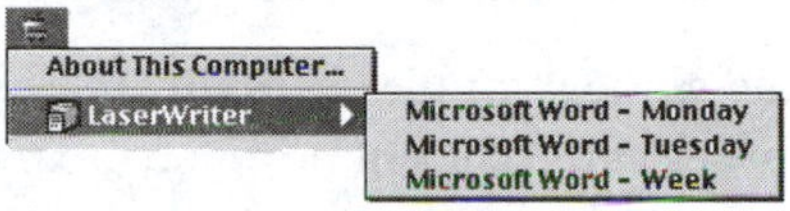

Items in the queue appear in the printer's submenu.

Look, it's a folder… it's an application… it's… …a desktop printer. The icon is more than just a drag-and-drop station for print jobs and a shortcut to the Print Monitor window. It's an application—sort of; it's so intertwined with the system's printing capabilities that you can Get Info on the printer icon and allocate more memory to it (which you should do if you're running into problems with big print jobs).

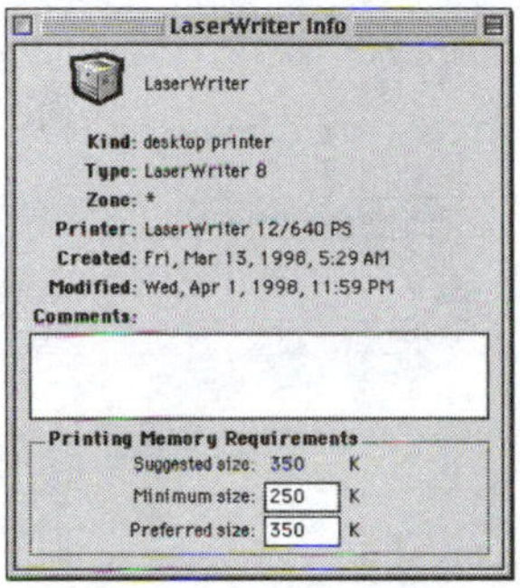

You can allocate more memory to the Print Monitor by using Get Info on a desktop printer.

On the other hand, the desktop printer is a folder—sort of. The print jobs that get spooled to it are stored as files inside the printer icon, just as if it were a folder; if you use Find File to find one of the print job files, you'll see the desktop printer represented as a folder in the list. Of course, double-clicking on the icon doesn't open it and display the files as a folder normally does: you just get the Print Monitor window. And if you start up without the desktop printer extensions running, you'll see the desktop printer icon show up as a standard folder, and double-clicking on it opens a normal window with the print files inside it.

The desktop printer, when it's opened, is also a Finder window: you can turn it into a pop-up window at the bottom of the screen; you might find it easier to open from a window tab than by double-clicking on its icon.

The Desktop Print Monitor

The Print Monitor. Okay, it's the *Desktop* Print Monitor, but we don't have to be so formal; it's unlikely you'll get it confused with the standard Print Monitor used by non-PostScript printers.

For PostScript LaserWriters, the default printing setup is a desktop printer and background printing, although you can override either or both when you need to. All you do is use the Print command as usual, and the document is processed for the printer, saved on the disk, and then sent out in pieces to the printer as a background process controlled by the Desktop Print Monitor. Since print jobs are first sent to a holding area before they go to the printer, you get to intercept them and change their handling before, or even during, the time they're actually printed.

To access the Desktop Print Monitor, double-click on the desktop printer icon. You'll get a window that shows you the status of the current print job in the upper area, and information about any of the other print jobs waiting.

To do something with one of the print files, select it and then use a button or menu command. You can select the current print job or any one in the queue; Shift-click to select multiple items.

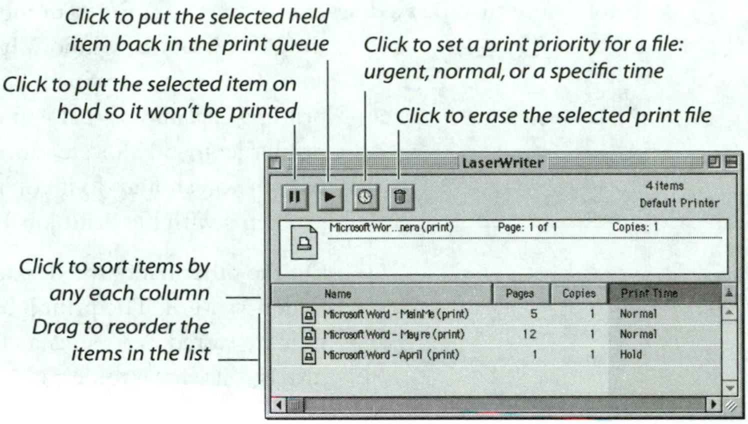

Prioritize. When you send a job to the printer, it just gets in line after all the others already there, but you can change the print order inside the Print Monitor window by assigning a priority with the Print Time button or by manually reordering them. Individual priorities are noted in the Print Time column.

The printing priorities (three of which are assignable by clicking the clock icon) are:

- **Urgent:** This puts the file ahead of all the other items in the print queue—except for those also labeled *urgent*.

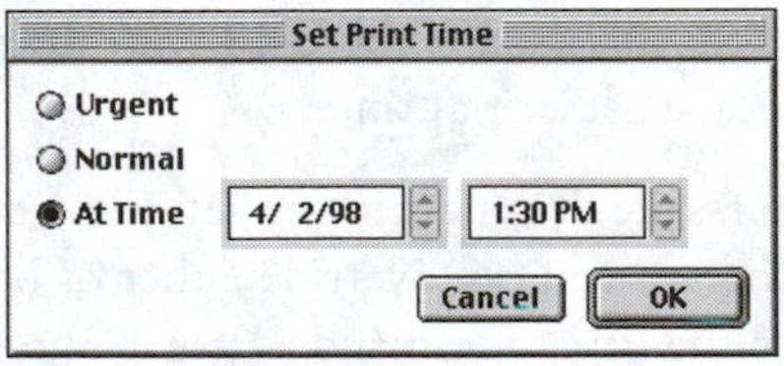

The Print time dialog.

- **Normal:** The default, this keeps a file in its place in line so that it gets printed in turn, after all the others in front of it.
- **Time:** Set a specific printing time for a file in the Print Time dialog. This is handy if you know you're

going to a meeting, say, and you can print time-consuming files when you're not fighting for the Mac's attention. Or, if you set your Mac to turn on automatically in the morning before you get there, you can set it to print things out for you that you didn't need right away.

- **Hold:** Put a file on hold by selecting it and clicking the Hold button at the top of the Print Monitor window. It doesn't ever get printed until you select it and hit the Resume button—at which point you can tell it from what page it should resume printing.

While you can click any of the column headers to change the sorting order, that's only for your viewing convenience; the print order doesn't change. But when items are sorted according to the Print Time column, you can drag them around in the list to change their priorities. If everything is set as Normal, all you'll see is a changed list order. But if you've set some individual priorities, you'll see the dragged document change its priority label: if you drag a Normal file to the top, above an Urgent file, its label changes to Urgent; dragging an Urgent file beneath a Normal file changes its label to Normal, and so on.

The Print Monitor menu(s). Bet you didn't notice it had one (never mind more than one)! When you use the Print Monitor, you're on the desktop and the Finder's Printing menu (the one that shows up when you click on a desktop printer) is active; you can use it in conjunction with the Print Monitor window.

The menu commands apply to the whole queue rather than to each print file: the Stop Printing Queue command, for instance, keeps every file in queue from printing until the queue is restarted, at which point the files are printed in their priority order.

The other menus available for the Print Monitor are the contextual menus you get if you Control-click somewhere in the window. The menu commands are an odd assortment: some are from the Printing menu, some apply only to the files (if you're clicking on the file instead of elsewhere in the window), and some, like Close, apply to the window itself. But there's no logic to which ones show up where sometimes: the Start and Stop Print Queue commands, for instance, show up only if you're clicking on one of the print jobs, even though the commands apply to the whole queue.

The hidden buttons. You can issue the Stop Printing Queue and Start Printing Queue commands without using the Printing menu: hold down Option Shift and the Hold and Resume buttons change to Stop and Start buttons. I like this because I keep the Print Monitor window on my second monitor, and the Printing menu is way over on the other monitor, quite a mouse trip away.

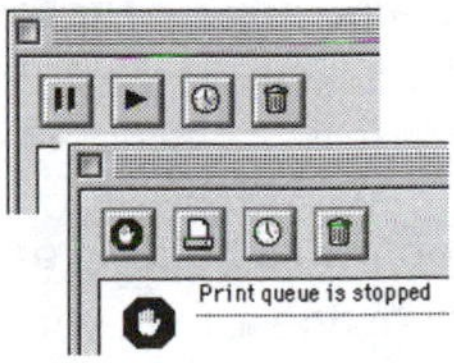

Multiple printers, multiple monitors. If you have more than one printer available on your network, you'll have more than one desktop printer, too. Here are some multiple-printer pointers:

- You can select a printer without making it the default if, for instance, you want to check or change its configuration. Just click on it once to select it the way you'd select any desktop icon, and then use the Printing menu commands on it.
- You can open more than one Print Monitor window at a time. Even if a printer isn't the default, you'll see the list of items in its queue and be able to manipulate them.
- You can drag a print file from a Print Monitor window to another desktop printer (its icon or its Print Monitor window) to redirect a print job.

Before-the-fact control. If you're using a PostScript printer, you can set printing priorities, and even bypass the background printing option, through the Print dialog.

In the Print dialog, the pop-up menu includes a Background Printing item. Select it and you'll get pretty much the same dialog you get in the Print Monitor window for setting printing priorities. In addition, you get to completely override the background printing option and send the document directly to the printer; this ties up your Mac, but it ensures that you get to print the current document ahead of all the others, even urgent-labeled items.

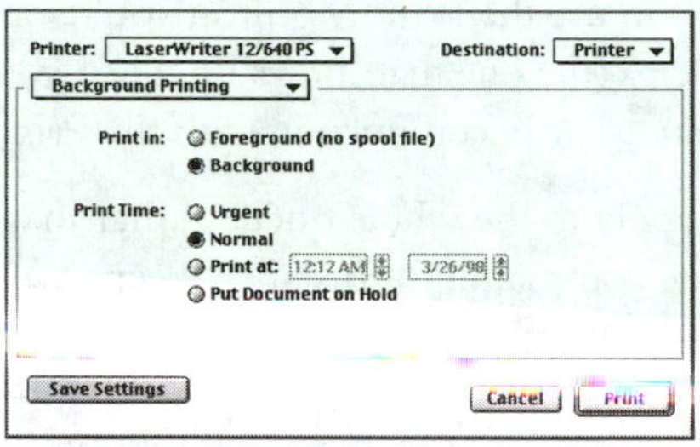

Delayed printing gratification. If you want to process a printing job but not have it printed until later:

1. Use the Print command as usual.
2. Immediately open the Print Monitor.
3. Select the print job and click the Set Print Time button.
4. Set a specific print time, or click Postpone Indefinitely, in the dialog.

If you want to delay *all* printing, use the Stop Printing command in the Print Monitor's File menu. You can do this before you send any print jobs by double-clicking on the Print Monitor icon to open it. When you want the print jobs to start again, use the Resume Printing command.

Resume *where?* If you spool a print job into a holding pattern and later tell the Print Monitor to print it, you'll get a dialog asking you if it's okay to "resume printing at page 1." This can come as quite a surprise when you've spooled a job that's supposed to print from page 5 to page 10! But the PrintMonitor page numbering refers to the physical page of the job you sent, so in this case, page 5 would be page 1—if you know what I mean.

The Standard PrintMonitor

The PrintMonitor. If your printer doesn't provide background printing through a desktop printer, you can still get background printing (except for an ImageWriter): select the printer driver in Chooser and click the On button (you also have to turn on AppleTalk). After that, you print in the normal fashion from an application and the Print Monitor takes over all the processing. It processes the document for the printer and stores the processed version in the Print Monitor Documents folder inside your System Folder (if it can't find the folder, it creates a new one); then it feeds the information out to the printer in pieces.

Although it's in your Extensions folder, the Print Monitor is actually an application, and you can interact with it while you have print jobs lined up; you'll find it listed in the Applications menu at the far right of the menubar whenever it's working on a print job.

Close the document. You can close a document as soon as it's been sent to Print Monitor, because the print job comes from the file that's been saved in the Print Monitor folder, not from the document file.

Stack 'em up. One of the handiest benefits to background printing is that you don't have to wait for one document to print before you use the Print command on another. Send as many documents you want to the printer and let Print Monitor feed them out one at a time.

Canceling a print job. If you press ⌘. while the document is being processed for printing, the operation is cancelled and the printing process dialogs disappear from the screen. But you may be fooled: the dialogs may have disappeared because the document's been processed and stored in the Print Monitor Documents folder before the Mac "heard" you press the cancel keys—and in a few minutes the print job's going to start rolling out of the printer against your wishes. To stop it, you'll have to use the Print Monitor.

Working in the Print Monitor. When the Print Monitor is working, it's listed in the Applications menu so you can open its window. You'll see a status report for the current print job (how many pages are left to print, for instance) and all the waiting print jobs listed. Here are the things you can do in the Print Monitor window:

- Cancel the current print job by clicking the Cancel Printing button or by pressing ⌘. while the Print Monitor window is active.

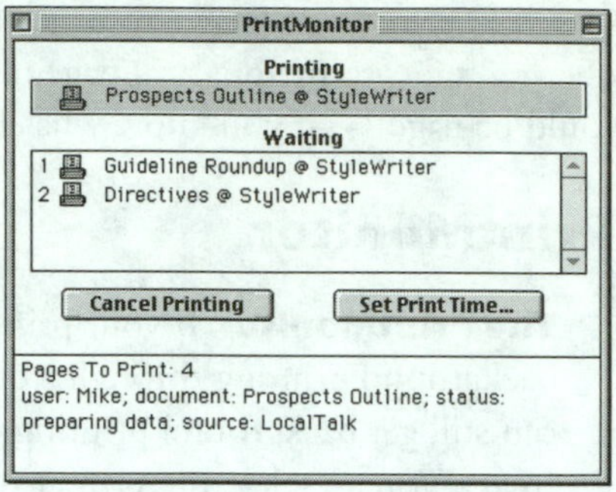

The PrintMonitor window.

- Remove a waiting item by selecting it and clicking Remove.
- Reorganize the list by dragging an item up or down by the little printer icon. (You won't be able to move an item that has been set to print at a specific time.)
- Get information on a waiting document by selecting it in the list; you'll see how many pages it is, what application created it, and when it was spooled to the PrintMonitor.

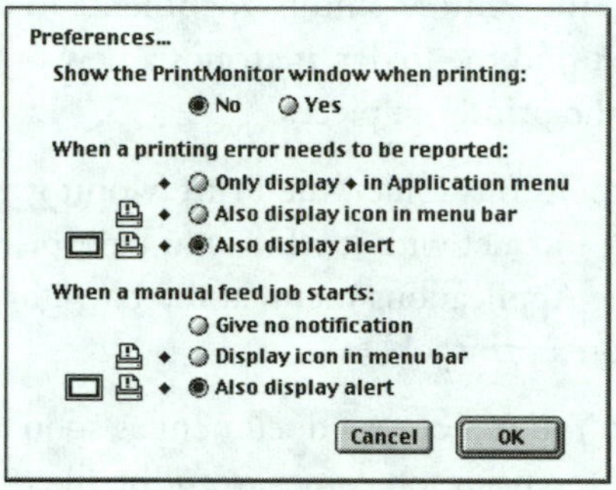

PrintMonitor preferences. There's a Preferences command for the PrintMonitor that everyone ignores because it's in the File menu that everyone ignores. But you can use it to set all sorts of handy options, including things like automatically showing the Print Monitor window when it's working, and how to report printing errors.

The Apple Printer Utility

Take control over your printer. The Apple Printer Utility has replaced the older LaserWriter Utility as the basic tool to control your printer. It's included with system software, as well as with the printing software that comes with Apple printers. With it, you can set and check printer defaults, check built-in information like fonts and memory, download fonts and PostScript files, and even print font samples.

The Printer Utility has an extra step that the older printer utilities didn't: when you first run it, you have to specifically open the printer you want to work with by selecting it in the Selector window and clicking the Open Printer button. After the information is retrieved from the printer, you get a window for the printer, listing all the items you can control.

The Printer Utility has an odd interface: one long, scrolling window with categories of information; click on the arrow in front of a category, and a dialog-box-like area is revealed. The categories that show up depend on your printer: items like Disks, for instance, show up only for those printers that have hard drives attached.

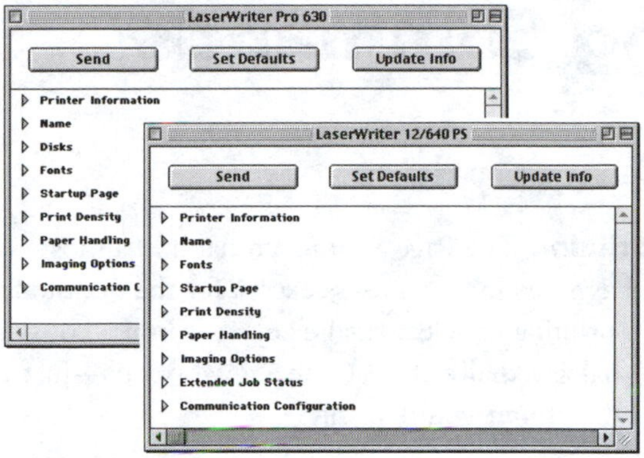

The list of options differs slightly for different printers, based on their capabilities.

Registering changes. The most important thing to remember when you're working in the Printer Utility is that you have to click the Send button at the top of the window after you've made changes to any of the categories; otherwise, the changes won't be made to the printer setup.

Category options. Some of the categories in the Printer Utility window are described elsewhere in this chapter, in context; here's a few of the others available for all models:

- **Name**: Your printer's name defaults to the same as its model name/number. You can rename the desktop printer icon, but the original name still shows up in the Chooser. If you have more than one printer on a network, model names aren't very friendly, since it's difficult to remember, say, which one's set up for envelope printing, or which has the legal-size paper tray. Use the Name category in the Printer Utility to officially rename your printer.

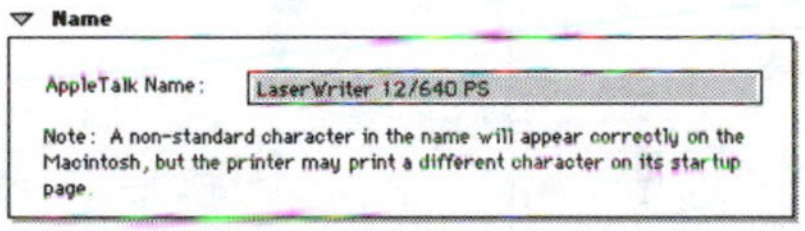

- **Paper Handling**: Set the default size for a multipurpose tray (if you have one) and enable or disable the automatic tray switching for when one tray runs out of paper. There are occasionally some odd interactions between the size setting and the Page Setup dialog for some applications: with PageMaker, for instance, unless you set the legal size paper option here, it will be ignored at print time.

- **Imaging Options**: Set the defaults for resolution (if the printer has a choice) and for FinePrint and PhotoGrade; the availability of the latter options—especially whether they can be used at the same time—often depends on how much memory's in your printer. You can override these default settings for any print job through the Print dialog's Imaging Options settings.

The Printing Commands

Page Setup Options

The basic dialog. The Page Setup command in almost every application's File menu is ignored by most users except for the occasional trip there to set up sideways printing or select legal-size paper instead of standard. But the Page Setup dialog actually offers quite a few options—just which ones depends on the printer you're using.

Whatever printer you're using, there are four basic options in the Page Setup dialog available for most printers; as you change settings, the picture on the sample page changes to demonstrate the effect of the change. (The picture is the famous *dogcow,* Clarus.)

- **Paper Size**: A pop-up menu of various paper sizes. When you change the paper size, margins and page breaks change in your document.
- **Orientation**: Standard (portrait) or sideways (landscape). Landscape is a great way to get wide tables and spreadsheets printed on a single page.
- **Scaling**: Scaling down (or, sometimes, up) from the document size you've been working on.
- **Layout**: Printing multiple pages on a single paper. (For PostScript printers, this option is in the Print dialog.)

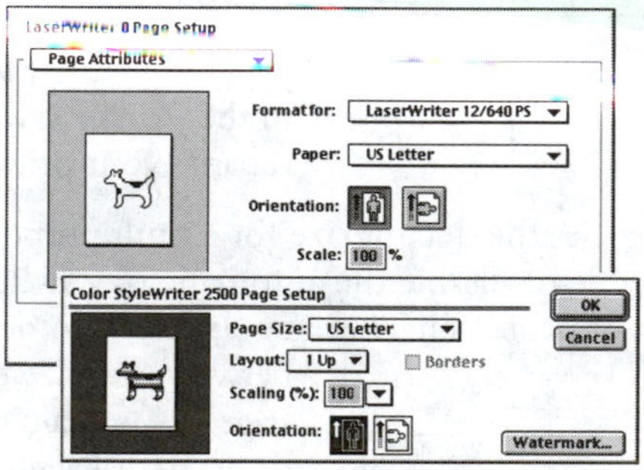

Page Setup options depend on what printer you're using.

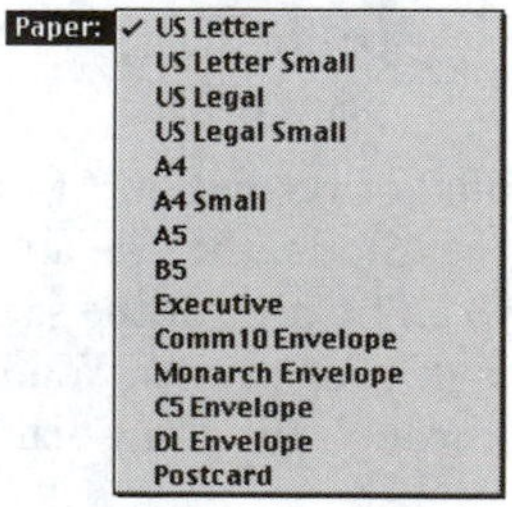

How small is small? Three of the basic paper sizes appear twice in the menu for some printers, once each with *Small* appended to the name. The size of the paper doesn't change, however, as you can see in the chart on the next page. What does change is the margin area that won't be printed to: the Small sizes have larger margins, and therefore smaller printing areas.

Paper sizes. Just what size are all those paper sizes?

Description	*Size (inches)*
US Letter, US Letter Small	8.5 x 11
US Legal, US Legal Small	8.5 x 14
A4, A4 Small	8.3 x 11.7
A5	5.83 x 8.27
B5	7.2 x 10.1
Executive	7.25 x 10.5
Comm 10 envelope	9.5 x 4.13
Monarch Envelope	7.5 x 3.88
C5 Envelope	6.38 x 9.02
DL Envelope	4.33 x 8.67
Postcard	3.94 x 5.82

Scaling. The *printout,* or *image,* size isn't the same as the *page* size. You can control the size of the image separately from the paper size by using the scaling command in Page Setup. Shrinking the image doesn't give you multiple miniature pages on a paper (there's another command for that); it shrinks the image and prints it starting in the upper left corner of the page.

The amount of scaling you can do for a printout and still get a decent image depends on the printer you're using. You can type in any number you want (within some limitations for each printer—generally, 5 and 400 percent are the outside limits). But QuickDraw-based printers do poorly when you change an image size unless the change is a certain proportion to the original; for these printers, you'll find a pop-up menu of suggested sizes in the dialog.

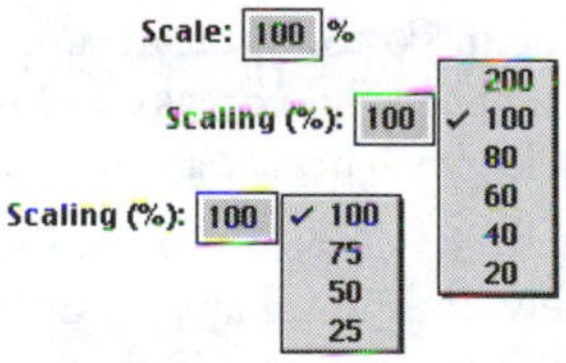

Scaling results vary according to the printer you're using. Top, a PostScript lets you type in almost any number; middle, a StyleWriter 1200's suggested size; bottom, the suggestions for a LaserWriter 300.

Keep in mind that the percentage figure is a *reduced to* percentage, not a *reduced by* number: a picture reduced *to* 75 percent is three-quarters of its original size, while a picture reduced *by* 75 percent is only a quarter of its original size.

But even getting that concept down pat mathematically doesn't always prepare you for what you're going to get as a printout. Reducing an image size to 50 percent doesn't give you something that covers half a page: it covers a *quarter* of the page because both the horizontal and vertical measurements have been cut in half. And, doubling the size of a full-page image gives you not two, but *four* printed pages.

Multiple pages on a page. The Layout option in most Page Setup dialogs (it's an option through the Print dialog for PostScript printers) lets you print more than one page on a page—that is, you can print miniature "thumbnails" of your pages, which is a great way to do a quick review of your layout and content. PostScript printers, of course, let you choose even more options, like 12 or 16 pages to a paper, and arranging them either in rows or columns on the page. Almost all printers let you choose whether or not you want a border around the miniature pages.

Specifying which pages to print in a Print dialog refers to the *document's* pages, not the pages the printer is working with; so, asking for a printout of pages 1 through 4 when you have 4-up layout means you'll get a single piece of paper with the four miniature pages on it.

50 percent = 65 percent. You might assume that using a 2-up layout would cut each page image by about 50 percent, but you'd be wrong. The page image is shrunk to fit on a half-page in the opposite orientation, which makes it about 65 percent of its original size. So, a 12-point font in the printout won't look like a 6-point font; it will be a very readable 7.8-point font.

PostScript options. PostScript printers provide a list of special printout options through their Page Setups; for some printers, there's a button that accesses the options, while others have a pop-up menu that let you get to the options. Here's what they are, and what they do:

- **Flip Horizontal, Flip Vertical, Invert Image:** These are straightforward options that are demonstrated by Clarus the dogcow.
- **Substitute Fonts:** This substitutes PostScript fonts for certain bitmapped fonts in your document: Times for New York, Helvetica for Geneva, and Courier for Monaco. This is a vestige of the early days, and it can cause a mess: yes, you should be printing in PostScript fonts and not in bitmaps, but switching the font at print time changes line breaks and page breaks. (And since it's done behind users' backs, it's hard for a novice to track down.)
- **Smooth Text:** This is another archaic option: it smoothes the lines of bitmapped fonts by adding a few dots along any 45 or 90-degree lines. But it doesn't affect PostScript fonts, and won't work on TrueType fonts, either—and nobody prints in just bitmapped fonts anymore.
- **Smooth Graphics:** This smoothes the edges of bitmapped images by adding a few extra pixels where there would otherwise be a jagged edge. If you're using bitmapped images for their textural feel, you don't want to turn this on; on the other hand, if the bitmap is composed mostly of lines, turning this on is a good approach.
- **Precision Bitmap Alignment:** This shrinks bitmapped images by about 4 percent for printer's printing at 300 and 600 dpi so that the image size will match the printers capability. With a standard bitmapped image at 72 dpi, a 300-dpi printer has to provide about 4.17 dots in the printout for each dot in the image; most image dots are therefore replaced with four printed dots, with every fifth or sixth image dot getting 5 dots in the printout. The result is a distorted image or pattern. By reducing the image

by 4 percent, the computer sends a 75-dpi image to the printer, a number that can be easily quadrupled to the printer's 300-dpi capability.

- **Unlimited Downloadable Fonts:** The printer normally retains downloaded font information until the entire document is printed, in case you need the font later in the document. Sometimes this doesn't leave room for all the fonts you're using, and you'll wind up with Courier being used in the printout instead of what you planned. By checking the Unlimited Downloadable Fonts option, font information is flushed from the printer's memory more often, making room for new ones. (Some programs take care of this themselves regardless of the Page Setup setting.)

A few more. There are still more options available through Page Setup, specific to different types of non-PostScript printers. The most common are:

- **Watermark:** Printers that provide watermark capability let you choose from among a list of watermarks (like Draft and Confidential), scale it, place it on the page, and set the density.

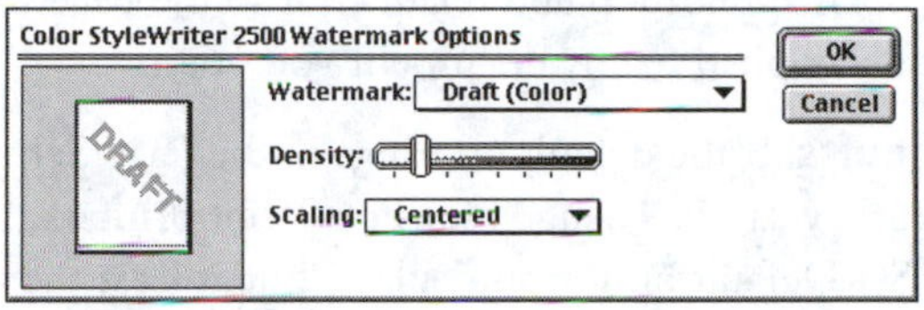

The watermark option dialog for the StyleWriter 2500.

- **Larger Print Area, Larger Page Area:** This reduces the margins around the edge of the page so you can print more on a page.
- **Precision Bitmap Alignment:** This option is described in the last entry, since it's found mostly on PostScript printers, but it's available for some other high-resolution printers, too.

In addition to the options provided for Page Setup by the system software, some applications add other items to the Page Setup dialog; they're accessed either through buttons (on non-PostScript printers) or a pop-up menu (on PostScript printers).

Printing recipe. Watermarks. Booklets. Mailing labels on partially-used sheets. Sophisticated print previews. You can have it all ("all" being far too much to actually list here) with **PrintChef** ($50, MindGate). PrintChef allows so much control over printing options, hooking into both Page Setup and Print dialogs, that you'll think you have a new OS to play with! No matter what you need printed, or how, PrintChef seems to handle it, providing extra attention to details like the "creep" you have to allow for on margins for folded, stapled or stitched booklets.

mindgate.com

Page Setup Pointers

Document-specific settings. The changes you make in Page Setup are for the document that's active when you choose Page Setup. The settings are stored with the document, so that the next time you open it, the Page Setup dialog will show the same settings. For a new document, Page Setup offers its default settings.

The Page Setup update. If you switch printers in Chooser, you'll get a dialog (shown here) that most Mac users have seen but simply dismiss and go on their way without thinking about what it means.

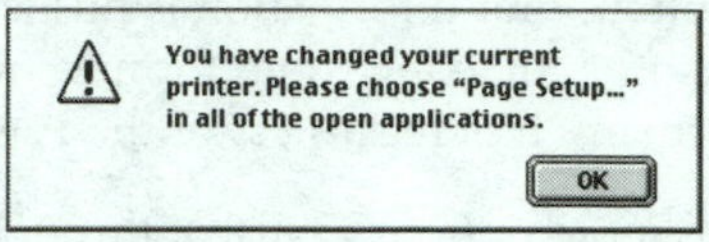

Since different printers have different capabilities, the same document sent to different printers can look quite different—not only because the resolution of the printout changes but because the resolution change and a possible change in the “printable area” of the page affects line breaks and sometimes even page breaks. In order to see those changes reflected in your documents, you have to open the Page Setup dialog and click its OK button. Sometimes it's easier to just quit any open application and relaunch it so the page setup changes will be automatically applied to any document you open.

Setting defaults. If the default offerings in the Page Setup dialog don't work for you, they can be changed for PostScript printers. It would be nice if there were a Set Default button someplace, but at least there's a trick: change the settings to where you want them and then click the OK button while holding down Option. You'll get a confirming dialog, and then the new defaults will be used.

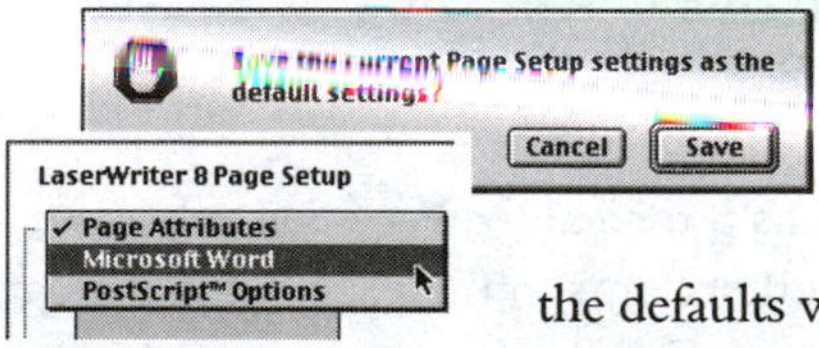

You can, in fact, set either global defaults or application-specific defaults. Use the pop-up menu at the top of the dialog; if you leave it at Page Attributes, the defaults will be global, but selecting the current application's name before you Option-click OK uses the settings as defaults only for that application.

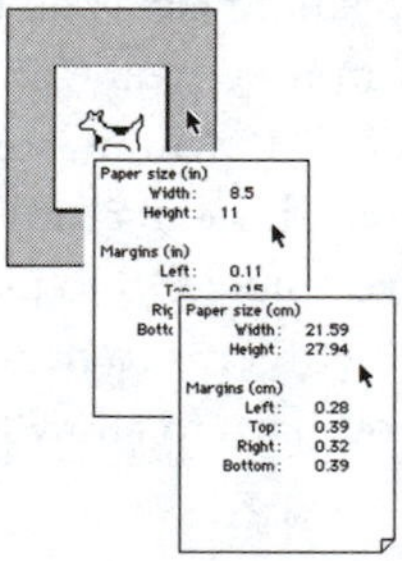

Sizing it up. Clarus the dogcow does more than just change position to show you how you're paper's going to be printed: he can actually tell you the dimensions, and the margins, for each of the standard paper sizes. Just click on the sample page for the measurement in inches; click again for the centimeter version; click once more to get back to the dog.

The OS 8 shrinkage. Most upgraders to OS 8 found that documents previously set to the standard US Letter size opened set to US Letter Small after the upgrade. (Well, actually, what they found were messed-up layouts and page breaks; *then* they found the setup problem.) There's no way around this problem: you just have to reset the setup option in Page Setup for each document.

But if you find that even new documents created under OS 8 are defaulting to US Letter Small instead of US Letter, reset US Letter as the default.

The Print Command

In the Print dialog. The Print dialog changes according to the printer you're using; the only basics in common are the number of copies, and which pages to print.

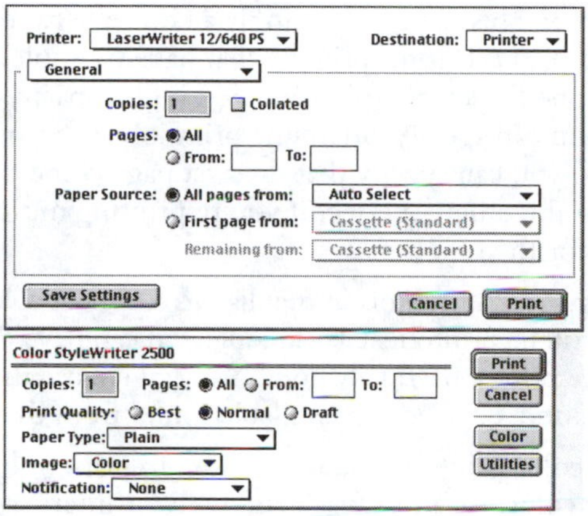

The Print dialog differs depending on what printer you're using.

Page count. As befits the only options common to all printers, there are several shortcuts in regard to using the controls for page number and copies:

- Use Tab to move from one text box to the next and Shift Tab to move to the previous text box for the three numbers.
- You don't have to click the From button if you're specifying pages to be printed; just entering a number in the From box automatically selects the button.
- If you want a single page printed, type that page number in both the From and the To box.
- If you want to print from a certain page all the way to the end of the document, you don't have to check the last-page number; you only have to enter the starting page in the From box and leave the To box blank.

Now you see it, now you don't. You don't have to wait for the Print dialog to appear. If you know you want two copies of the first four pages of the document, you can hit ⌘P for the Print command, but then go ahead and type 2, Tab, 1, Tab, 4 and Return for the Print button just as if the dialog were open. The dialog will open briefly to register the keystrokes, then go away just as quickly.

Quality is option one. QuickDraw printers offer several options in their print dialogs (even if the number of choices is put to shame by the gazillion offered for PostScript printers). Exactly which ones you get depend on the printer, but here are the ones that show up for various models:

- **Print Quality:** StyleWriters offer two print qualities, *Faster* and *Best.* The Faster mode prints at about 180 dpi; Best uses the top dpi available and can slow down the print job considerably. ImageWriters offer *Best*, *Faster*, and *Draft* modes. The first two offer the same trade-offs you find in StyleWriter jobs: one is quicker but rougher (at 72 dpi) and the other is slower but better (at 144 dpi). The Draft option prints with a built-in font that's oddly spaced in order to preserve the line breaks that the real font uses, and it doesn't print graphics at all.
- **Paper Source:** This used to be simply a choice between automatically or manually fed paper. But for printers that have multiple paper sources—say, an envelope feeder, a legal-size tray, a high-capacity paper cartridge—you can specify where the print job is coming from. If there are two trays, you can specify that the first page come from one tray, and the rest from the other—perfect if you're printing multi-page letters with a letterhead for the first page.
- **Notification:** You'll find this in the dialogs for most color printers, especially StyleWriters; printouts take so long, you can have the Mac beep to let you know the print job's finally done. You can choose the standard system alert as the sound, or select any available sound from the pop-up menu.
- **Image:** For color printers, you can choose to print in black and white, grayscale, or color; for most black and white printers, you can choose black and white, grayscale, or PhotoGrade printing.
- **Paper Type:** Some printers, like the Color StyleWriter 2500, can adjust the amount of color that's going to be applied to the page; some types of paper need less color than others. Use the pop-up menu to identify the type of paper you're using.

The collating option. The Collate button prints a multiple-copy job so that each copy is printed start to finish instead of five copies of page one followed by five copies of page two, and so on. Here's what you should know about collated print jobs:

- Collating takes a lot longer than printing it uncollated because each page has to be reimaged when its turn comes around again.
- If your application provides its own collate option, it might clash with the Print dialog's collate option. You'll have to experiment with only one of them on, or with both of them on; the results vary from one application to another.
- If you're on a network and choose to collate a print job, you may find other print jobs are printed in between your multiple copies because of the way items are spooled to the printer.

The Print dialog provides many different screens for PostScript printers.

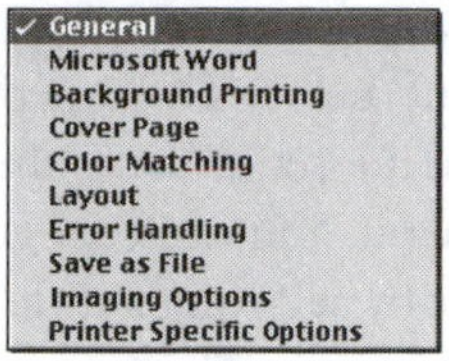

Now playing on ten screens. If you use a LaserWriter printer, you get a Print dialog with so many choices they're divided into (at this point) ten screens, each available through the pop-up menu in the dialog. Luckily, you'll only need one or two of them all the time, although you may find some of the other choices extremely handy for certain print jobs. You can click the Print button in any one of the screens and the printing will start with the settings in all the screens.

Most of the Print dialog screens are covered elsewhere in the chapter, in context of their subject matter, but here's a roundup:

- **General:** These are the basic settings, for the number of copies, which pages you want printed, and so on.
- **Application:** The second menu choice is always specific to the application you're using, and the options provided depend on the application. The picture here shows Microsoft Word in the menu, and its options include printing only the current selection, printing or ignoring hidden text; for FileMaker Pro, the choices include printing all records, the group being browsed, or a single record.
- **Background Printing:** Background printing is the system default, but you can override it here, and tag a file as Urgent or Normal, or put it on hold, without going to the Print Monitor.
- **Cover Page:** Print an identifying page before or after your document to separate it from other print jobs on a shared printer.
- **Color Matching:** Set black-and-white printing instead of grayscale, or grayscale instead of color, depending on your printer's capabilities; also, set up Color Sync options.
- **Layout:** A Page Setup dialog on steroids—not only can you set how many pages per sheet you want for thumbnails, you can set the layout direction and choose from a variety of borders around the miniature pages.
- **Error Handling:** Set what you want done if there's a PostScript error, or if the current paper tray runs out of paper during the print job.
- **Save as File:** "Print" a file to the disk as a PostScript file instead of sending it to the printer.
- **Imaging Options:** Turn options like FinePrint and PhotoGrade on and off, overriding the printer's default settings.
- **Printer Specific Options:** Depending on the printer, options like selecting the resolution of the printout, or printing double-sided pages.

Skip the menu. You can move from one Print dialog screen to another without using the menu: just press ⌘↑ or ⌘↓ to move to the previous or next screen.

Choosing without the Chooser. If you have multiple printers available, they'll all show up in a menu in the Print dialog. The one that's selected by default is the one you've chosen in the Chooser or set as the default desktop printer through the Finder's Printing menu. You can change the default printer by selecting a different one in the pop-up menu. This not only changes the printer for the current print job, but also sets it as the default for subsequent jobs.

Setting Print dialog defaults. If the standard defaults in the Print dialog aren't the ones you need, create new ones: go through all the screens and make your selections, then click the Save Settings button on any screen to save its settings.

Redefining Print dialog defaults on a temporary basis can be a real time-saver. Say you're working on redesigning the table on page five of your Word document; you want to try several changes to the fonts, size, border width, and cell shading to see what you like best. Each time you want to print it, you issue the Print command and have to move to the Word screen and type 5 in the From and To boxes. But if you do it once and click Save Settings, you'll always get page 5 until you reset the defaults.

Canceling a print job. The old standby of pressing ⌘ . to stop a print job after you've clicked the Print button still works—usually. Some short print jobs are processed so quickly that you can't stop them in time by just pressing a couple of keys.

But if you're working with background printing on, which is the system default, you do have another chance to cancel the job: move to the Print Monitor and cancel it there.

Stop the presses! Okay, so you've sent the print job and can't stop it even from the Print Monitor because it's only a single page and it went to the printer too quickly for you to catch. The only problem is that you thought you were typing the numbers 4 and 5 in the From and To page boxes but you mistakenly typed a 45 in the Copies box—and you hit the Print button before you could stop yourself.

In these cases, the only way you can stop 45 copies from coming out of the printer is to shut the printer off in the middle of its efforts. You'll probably wind up with at least one page at least partially through the path it takes through the printer, which means you'll have a paper jam register when you turn the printer back on. So, while you're there to shut it off, open it and take any stuck paper out.

Other Printing Issues

Fonts

Fonts on QuickDraw printers. If you're printing on an ImageWriter or StyleWriter, or a non-PostScript LaserWriter, you should make sure that all the fonts you use in your documents are TrueType fonts so that they'll be scaled smoothly for the printout.

You can use PostScript fonts if you've installed ATM; because it creates QuickDraw-based font displays for the screen, it doesn't take much more effort to send the information to the printer. But make sure you have the PostScript printer file available and not just the TrueType screen version, or you'll still get the TrueType-based output. With ATM running, if you have both a PostScript font and a TrueType font, the PostScript version "wins" for the printout.

More about ATM
Chapter 14

Fonts on PostScript printers. Between your Mac and your LaserWriter, you may have three different types of fonts (PostScript, TrueType, and bitmapped) in any of several places (the Mac's drive, the printer's drive, the printer's memory, and so on). Because of the high level of cooperation between your Mac and its printer, you're shielded from the worst of it, but you should know where things are and how they're used in case you run into trouble. When the Mac send a print job to the LaserWriter, the printer first checks what fonts are going to be needed for the page, and then starts looking for their font files, in this order:

1. In the printer's ROM, since this is the fastest place to get the font information.
2. In the printer's RAM, in case the font's been used recently and the information is still there.
3. On the printer's hard drive, if there is one.
4. On the Mac's hard drive, in the Fonts Folder, where the original file is usually stored (although font-management software like Suitcase lets fonts be stored elsewhere on the drive and remain available to the printer).

If it hasn't found the proper printer font at this point, it asks the Mac for the TrueType font information which is, in all likelihood, in a suitcase in your Fonts folder because otherwise it wouldn't have displayed on the screen. If the suitcase contains only a bitmapped version of the font, the printer will settle for that as a last resort. For both TrueType and bitmapped fonts, the Mac does the actual font processing and sends the results to the printer.

When there's no such font. In most cases, a LaserWriter can print *something* close to what you see on the screen because it can at least find a screen font that it can use to print with. But if you try to print a document that was created on another Mac, you may not have its fonts anywhere on your printer or on your Mac.

When there's just no font to be found, a LaserWriter will default to a Courier printout. (That's also its default for when it has run out of memory and can't print all the different fonts on a page, so be sure you stop to figure out which problem is causing the Courier substitution.)

If you're using ATM, however, it will fake a font for the LaserWriter to use if you have the multiple master fonts *Adobe SerifMM* and *Adobe SansMM* installed; the fake won't look the same as the original font, but its general size and weight will match, and all the line breaks and page breaks will remain intact.

Manually downloading fonts. You can save some time in the printing process by manually downloading PostScript fonts to the printer. This keeps the font information in the printer's memory so the Mac doesn't have to send it each time a document uses those fonts; it stays in memory, packed in more efficiently than the fonts that are downloaded automatically by the Mac at the printer's request, until you turn off the printer.

Use the Apple Printer Utility to download fonts:

1. Open the program, select your printer in the Printer Selector window, and click the Open Printer button.
2. When the printer window opens, click on the arrow in front of the Fonts category to display the font information.
3. Click the Add button.
4. Select RAM from the Destination pop-up menu at the bottom of the Add dialog.

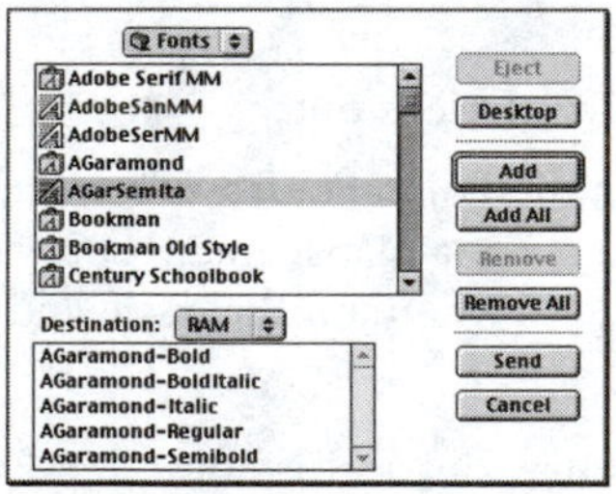

The Add dialog for font downloading; note that the download list at the bottom uses full names for fonts instead of the printer file name.

5. Select the printer files in the list that you want to download (you can select only one at a time); click the Add button, or just double-click on the font name to add it to the list. If you add the wrong one to the list, select it and use the Remove button.
6. When you have all the fonts you want in the list, click the Send button.

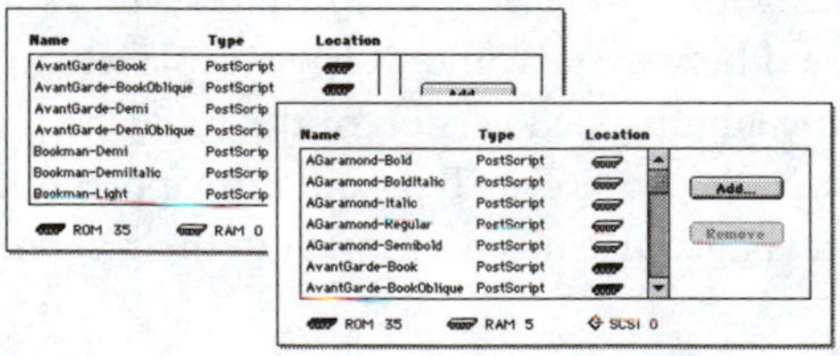

The Apple Printer Utility Fonts dialog, before and after font downloading; note the reported number of fonts along the bottom of the dialog.

The better downloader. OS 8.1, and ATM and some other Adobe products, come with the Adobe Downloader utility, which makes downloading fonts easier because of just a few friendly little advantages over the Apple Printer Utility. First and foremost is the fact that you can select multiple fonts in the list before adding them to the download list—a minor but greatly appreciated ability. You can even just drop font files on the Downloader's icon and they'll be sent to the current printer. Scour your hard drive with the Finder's Find command and see if you already have this utility. And use it!

Tip within a tip: Use the drag-and-drop capability to download a set of fonts for a specific job when its something you have to do, say, at the beginning of every day. Label the PostScript fonts files for the job in the Fonts folder and sort the folder's window by label in a list view so you can select all of them at once. Then, just drag the whole pile onto the Downloader icon.

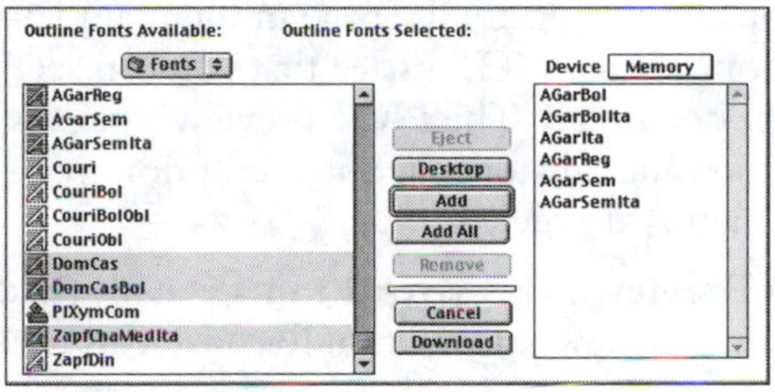

Adobe's Downloader lets you select multiple font files to be added to the download list.

PostScript Files

PostScript files. PostScript, as we've pointed out many times throughout this and the Font chapter, is a *page description language.* You may think you're sending a beautifully designed page to the printer, but what's really being sent is a description of how the page should look—and the description is in the PostScript language, which is made up of English words and symbols. So, a PostScript file is, actually, a text file.

You can create a single PostScript file that contains everything the printer needs to reproduce a document, including even the font information. Most people use this capability when they want to bring something to a service bureau for output because it means bringing a single file instead of, say, a Quark document, twenty graphics, and twelve fonts. It won't matter if the bureau even has QuarkXPress, never mind the fonts—the printer will be able to work with just the PostScript file. (The downside, of course, is that if something goes wrong with the print job, you can't just open the file and fix the document.) Another use for "postscriptability" is for turning a document into something that can be placed in a page layout program—a document that wouldn't normally be accommodated as a placed file (like, say, an Excel spreadsheet section).

Here's how you create a PostScript file from any document:

1. Use the Print command to open the Print dialog.
2. Choose *File* in the Destination pop-up menu.
3. Choose *Save as File* from the main pop-up menu.
4. From the Format pop-up, select the appropriate file format:
    - **PostScript Job:** This saves the entire file as a standard PostScript file that will later be sent to a printer.
    - **EPS Mac Standard Preview:** This saves a single page of the document (you should specify the page in the main level of the Print dialog) along with a 72-dpi image that you can see if you place the file in another document. If you try to resize the placed preview image, the onscreen representation will be very distorted.
    - **EPS Mac Enhanced Preview:** This saves a single page of the document (you should specify the page in the main level of the Print dialog) along with a PICT image that you can see if you place the file in another document. The PICT preview image is scalable onscreen without too much distortion, but this option makes the file bigger than the Standard preview.
    - **EPS No Preview:** This saves the image with PostScript information only and no preview information for onscreen use.

EPS file format
Chapter 19

5. Select a PostScript level compatibility level: Level 1 for eventual printing on older LaserWriters, Level 2 for everything else.
6. Select a data format: ASCII or the more compact Binary form.
7. Define the font inclusion:
    - **None:** You'll need to supply the fonts with the file for printing, but it keeps the file size smaller.
    - **All:** Every font in the document will be embedded in the PostScript file, preventing missing-font problems but increasing the files size.
    - **All But Standard 13:** This embeds font information in the file for any font except the thirteen font families built into PostScript printers.
    - **All But Fonts in PPD file:** Most PPD files list the 13 standard fonts, so in most cases this choice is the same as the last. If you're using a printer that might have a different set of fonts in its ROM, you can use this—but you have to have that PPD selected through the Page Setup command before you create the PostScript file.

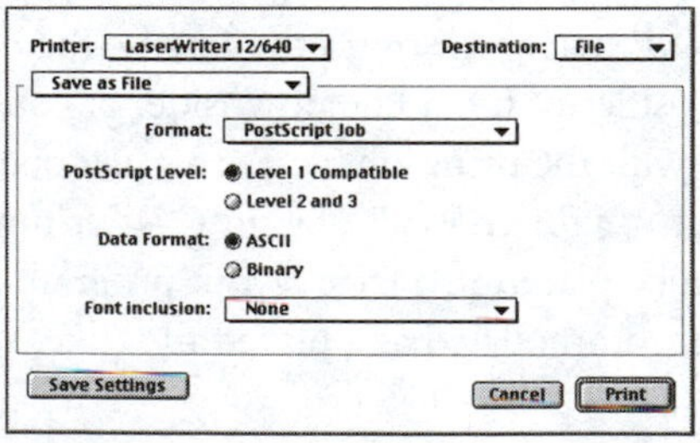

The Save as File option in the Print dialog.

8. Click the Print button (which actually works as a Save button, since the file is "printed" to the disk).
9. In the next dialog, give the print file a name and choose a location for it as you do for any file that you save on the Mac.

IN THE BEGINNING

Before the relatively recent version of the LaserWriter driver, you could print a PostScript file to the disk—but only if you belonged to the small group of people in the know, because the capability was *really* hidden. First, you'd prepare the document and use the Print command. Then you'd click the Print button. Then, you'd have to press ⌘K or ⌘F—one of them included the fonts and one didn't; I'd like to think the ⌘F was the one that included the fonts, but I don't remember, and I wouldn't swear to it, considering. Oh—and if you didn't press the keys quickly enough after clicking the Print button, the document would just be printed regularly.

Downloading a PostScript file. If you're placing a PostScript file inside another document, you don't have to worry about anything else when it comes to printing, except that the file is available at printing time—the same way you need a placed graphics file available.

But if you want to send a PostScript file directly to the printer, you can't just print it by opening it in an application or dragging it to a desktop printer: what you'll get is the text of the PostScript file printed out. To get a PostScript file to print a page image, you have to *download* it to the printer, using the Apple Printer Utility:

1. Open the program, select your printer in the Printer Selector window, and click the Open Printer button.
2. Choose the Send PostScript File command from the Utilities menu.
3. In the next dialog, select your file from the list and click the Add button (you can add more than a single PostScript file to the Send list).
4. Click the Send button.
5. You'll be asked to name the PostScript Log file and choose a location for it. You have to save the log file, because clicking the Cancel button cancels the download; save it anywhere, since the log is created only if something goes wrong with the print job.
6. Click the Save button and the download begins.

If everything goes all right, you'll get a dialog that seems to indicate that something's wrong: it says something about a file not being created because no output was returned from the printer. That's referring to the PostScript log file, which is only created when something goes wrong, so you'll be getting your printout in the printer just about the same time you get that dialog on the screen.

Sending a PostScript program to the printer. There are times you might want to send a PostScript *program* to the printer—like the one described earlier in the chapter that finds out how much room is used and left on a printer's drive. You download a PostScript program the same way you download a PostScript file—because a PostScript file *is* a program, with instructions in it as to how to draw the page.

The big difference between a PostScript program and a file that's a page image comes before the download: the program is saved not as a PostScript file (through the Print dialog, as described above) but as a plain text file.

No PostScript printer necessary. You can create a PostScript file even if you don't have a PostScript printer; this comes in handy since you might want to give the file to someone else for printing. Just choose the LaserWriter driver in the Chooser and then work with your document; the Page Setup and Print commands reflect the Chooser setting, not what's actually connected to your Mac.

PART 5

Productivity Software

Part 5 At a Glance

16

Word Processing

In This Chapter

The Basics of Text Handling

Text Entry and Selection

The primary rule of text processing. Entering text is just a matter of typing, keeping in mind this basic rule: *Everything happens at the insertion point.*

The *insertion point* is the vertical bar that blinks on and off in the text you're working on. Typing or using Delete takes place at the insertion point; if you paste text, it appears at the insertion point. Clicking with the mouse repositions the insertion point, although for small moves using the arrow keys (→←↑↓) is more convenient.

Selecting and deselecting. The basic way to select text is to simply drag across it. Take the shortest route from the beginning to the end of the selection, dragging down across lines of text. Keep in mind that you can drag backwards, too.

To select large, irregular segments of text, click at the beginning of the text block and Shift-click at the other end. Just as on the desktop, a Shift-click also modifies an already made selection, adding to or subtracting from it.

To deselect text, click someplace that won't select anything, or select something else. Typing to replace the selection leaves you with unselected text, too. But often the most convenient way of deselecting text is pressing ← or → to move to the beginning or end of the selection.

Selecting in units. Double-clicking selects a whole word; depending on the application, it may also select the trailing space so that if you press Delete, you're not left with two spaces between the adjacent words that are left

This word selection is pretty much built into the Mac, so you'll find it almost everywhere—even on the desktop and in most dialog boxes. But applications that handle text also provide their own selection capabilities: for lines, sentences, paragraphs, and so on. Make sure you explore the selection capabilities of your word processor or layout program, because unit selection saves a lot of time when you're editing.

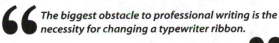

> ***The biggest obstacle to professional writing is the necessity for changing a typewriter ribbon.***
>
> *Robert Benchley, 1949*

The Shift-click origin. When you use Shift-click to change a selection, you might be surprised when you mean to extend the selection and it actually shrinks. What you get on a Shift-click depends on what you selected to start with. Say you drag from the middle of a sentence towards the end, and then decide you want a few more words near the beginning. You Shift-click at the beginning of those two words to add them to the selection, but what you get is *only* those two words. A Shift-click actually selects *from the original click point* to the Shift-click spot. (If you had dragged backwards, from the end of the sentence towards the beginning, the Shift-click would have added the earlier words to the selection.)

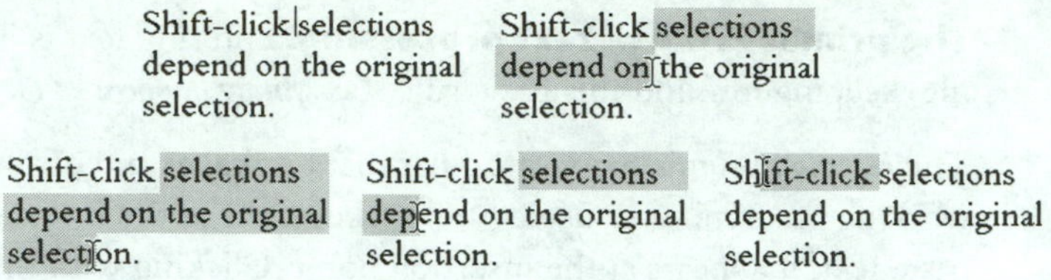
Shift-click selections depend on the original selection.
Shift-click selections depend on the original selection.
Shift-click selections depend on the original selection.
Shift-click selections depend on the original selection.
Shift-click selections depend on the original selection.

Top, the original selection Shift-clicked or dragged from the insertion point to the middle of the second line. Bottom: left, a Shift-click beyond the original point; center, Shift-clicking within the original selection; right, Shift-clicking in front of the original selection.

Shift-click units. Using a Shift-click to extend a selection (that is, holding down Shift and clicking at a spot in the text to add to the original selection) usually works in the "unit" of the original selection. So, if you double-click to select a word, Shift-clicking someplace else selects up to and including the nearest whole word, even if the Shift-click spot is in the middle of a word.

A simple drag operation for the original selection doesn't define a "unit" for this Shift-click operation. But if you use a special function to select another unit of text (Cmd-clicking for a sentence works in some word processors, for instance, or triple-clicking for a paragraph), a Shift-click will select to the end of that unit.

Unit select-and-drag. If you double-click to select a word, but keep the mouse button down on the second click and start dragging, you'll add whole words to your selection.

In most word processors that allow other unit selections with clicking (for sentences or paragraphs, for instance), if you keep the mouse down and start dragging after the initial unit selection, you'll continue selecting in that unit.

Caps Lock is not Shift Lock. On a typewriter, locking down Shift gives you the shifted character for every key, so that if you hit 8, for instance, you get an asterisk. But the Shift on a keyboard is just that: it locks for *capital* letters, and all other keys you hit still type their unshifted characters.

Caps Lock isn't All Caps, either. If your word processor has an All Caps style that changes lowercase, or mixed-case, text to all capitals, that's not the same as if you had typed in shifted characters or used Shift to type them. When you apply All Caps, you can take it off later and return the text to its original lowercase or mixed case, but you can't do the same with characters that are true capital letters.

Control panels and text. Basic text-entry settings are scattered through three different control panels:

Delay and repeat rates, the Keyboard control panel
Chapter 5

- Set the blink rate for the insertion point in the General Controls control panel.
- Set the key repeat rate (how fast repeated characters are typed when you keep a key pressed down) and the repeat delay (how long you have to hold down a key before the repeating starts) in the Keyboard control panel.
- Choose the highlight color in the Appearance control panel.

The Don'ts of word processing. Typewriter skills just don't cut it in the computer age—except, of course, that the letters and numbers are still in the same place (most of the time). Here's what you absolutely shouldn't do:

- Don't press Return at the end of a line unless you're ending a paragraph.
- Don't use double spaces after a sentence (or a semicolon). That spacing requirement—which made things easier to read in the days of typewriting monotype—is unnecessary with word processors.
- Don't press Tab to indent the first line of a paragraph. Instead, set a *first line indent* for the paragraph so that it's automatically indented.
- Don't use tabs to center a title on the page; use a center paragraph alignment.
- Don't use multiple spaces instead of tabs. If you change the size or font of the text, the size of the spaces also change, disrupting the alignment you wanted. (And repositioning tabbed text is so much easier than working with spaces!)
- Don't use multiple tabs to get somewhere on a line: set a tab where you need it. The only exception: When you've set tabs for columns of text and you have to leave a blank in one of the rows, you use two tabs to get past the blank column.

Formatting and Special Characters

Character and paragraph formatting. *Formatting* characters means applying a font, a size, and a style (like bold, underline, or italic) to text. You can apply formatting "after the fact" to selected text, but the easiest way to format small chunks of text is on the fly, using keyboard commands to turn character formatting on and off as you type.

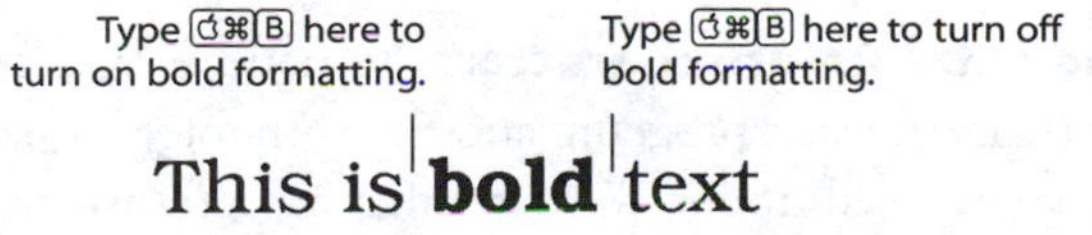
Type ⌘B here to turn on bold formatting.
Type ⌘B here to turn off bold formatting.
This is **bold** text

Using keyboard commands to turn formatting on and off as you type is the easiest way to format small chunks of text.

Formatting a paragraph means setting all the options that affect the text in a paragraph, like margins, indents, line spacing, and tab stops. Depending on your word processor, a paragraph format can also include things like extra space before the paragraph, or preceding each paragraph with a number. When applying paragraph formatting to a single paragraph, you don't have to select the paragraph first—whichever paragraph contains the insertion point is considered selected.

Hyphens and dashes. A *hyphen* should be used only as a character that either splits a word or joins multiple words. An *em dash* is what people normally call a dash—there's one right there. An *en dash* is half the length of an em dash and is used as a minus sign or to indicate ranges of numbers. (They get their names from their widths: more or less that of a capital *M* and lowercase *n.)*

Here's a comparison of the three, and how to type them. You'll find that the length of the hyphen in relation to the en dash varies from one font to another.

hyphen	-	-
en dash	–	Option -
em dash	—	Shift Option -

Hard spaces, hard and soft hyphens. Most programs interpret the Option Spacebar character as a *hard space,* which glues together the words on either side of it so they won't be split at the end of the line. (Most picture fonts, though, like Zapf Dingbats, have a character for the Option Spacebar keystroke.) The *hard,* or *nonbreaking, hyphen* is a related concept: you use it when you don't want the words on either side of it to be separated at the end of a line. The *soft,* or *optional, hyphen*, on the other hand, is used to show where the word should break if it falls at the end of a line—but it shows up only if it's needed. The key combinations you need to type these characters can vary from one program to another, but you'll usually find the hard hyphen on ⌘ Shift -, and the soft hyphen on ⌘ -.

Smart quotes and inch marks. All word processors let you automatically type "curly" or "smart" quotes and apostrophes—the ones that actually curl towards the right or left to surround text. But remember to turn them off when you're typing something like 6' 10" for six feet, ten inches—which needs straight apostrophes and quotes. (And we'll see if, by the time what I typed goes through several computers and programs for editing and layout, if some clever Mac program "fixes" those straight symbols by substituting curly ones when no one's looking.)

Removing extra Return characters. Sometimes you'll wind up with a document (from another program, another computer, or pasted in from something you copied from a Web site) that has a return character (a paragraph marker) at the end of every line, and two return characters to mark a true paragraph break—one for the end of the line, and an extra one leaving a blank line before the next paragraph.

You can do a quick, global search-and-replace in your word processor to change each of those end-of-line returns to spaces; the trick is to first mark the spot where the double returns are, because that's where you still need a return character when you're finished. Here's how:

1. Replace every double paragraph mark with something not used elsewhere in the document, like ## or */*; this marks the spots where paragraphs begin and end.
2. Replace every paragraph mark with a single space; just removing the paragraph mark will combine the last word of a line with the first word of the next line.
3. Replace every ## or */* (or whatever you used as a marker) with a single paragraph return to restore the paragraph breaks.

Typing Special Characters.

The Option(al) character sets. Seemingly without conscious thought, everyone's aware of the fact that every alphanumeric key on the keyboard provides at least two characters: the upper- and lowercase versions of a letter, a number and a punctuation symbol, or two different punctuation symbols. There are two full character sets: one for shifted keys and one for unshifted keys.

But the Mac actually allows for four full character sets, with four characters accessed from each key; the third and fourth are accessed with the [Option] key and a [Shift][Option] combination. Just as you type [Shift][8] to get an asterisk, you type [Option][8] to get a bullet. The actual characters available depend on the font you're using. While there's no guarantee of extra characters in every font, or which ones are where, there's some standardization as to what characters are stored on what key.

Typing accents. In addition to providing all sorts of characters that you can type, the Mac also lets you add certain accents to some letters: you type the key combination that provides the accent and nothing appears on the screen, but then you type the letter to be accented, and—*voilá!*—the letter and the accent appear together. (To type that accented *a,* I typed [Option][E], then [A].

There are five basic accent marks available in most fonts (three of them are available just by typing regular keys, but then they're printed by themselves, and not over the next letter):

Name	*Symbol*	*Keys*	*Example*
acute accent	´	[Option][E]	é
grave accent	`	[Option][~]	è
circumflex	^	[Option][I]	ô
umlaut	¨	[Option][U]	ü
tilde	~	[Option][N]	ñ

Not all accents can go over all letters; the tilde, for instance, won't go over an *e,* and the circumflex won't go over an *n.* You can see which letters work with which accents—and where the basic accents are (in case you don't have this book at hand)—by using the Key Caps desk accessory, which gets its own section coming up next.

What's where, and how to remember. Understanding why certain special characters are placed on certain keys can help you remember where they are. For instance: the bullet (•) and the degree symbol (°) resemble the asterisk; all three are on the 8 key. (If the logic isn't obvious, look for a connection that means something to you.) There's a chart on the next page showing some of the special characters, and how you can remember where they are if you need them. (You can use Key Caps to see what's where on the keyboard; that's covered in the next section.)

Typing fractions. When you're typing fractions and want them to look better (but you don't need to do a professional graphic designer's job of getting them perfect by using a special font), there's a multi-step way of getting decent-looking fractions.

1. First, make sure you use the special *virgule* character on Shift Option 1 (for most fonts) instead of the normal slash; the virgule's angle is better for fractions. (How effective this is depends on what font you're using.)
2. Superscript the numerator and set its size to about three-quarters of the text point size (about 8 points in 12-point text).
3. Change the denominator's size to the same as the numerator, but *don't* subscript it.
4. If the application you're in lets you kern characters, nudge the characters closer together—or further apart, if that's what you want.

Here's a before and after: 1/2, ½.

Key Caps

Key Caps. The Key Caps desk accessory is a simple but useful tool when you're trying to figure out just where a certain elusive character is stored. With Key Caps open, select a font from its menu; the Key Caps keyboard displays the main characters in the font. To see the other characters, press Shift, Option, or Shift Option, and the keyboard changes to show you the available characters.

You can enter sample text in Key Caps by typing or by clicking on the keys in window. If you want to use a modifier key—Shift or Option—you have to use the keyboard, since the keys don't stay "down" when you click them. You can copy the sample text into a document, saving you the trouble of remembering a keystroke combination for a special character. (The pasted text won't appear in the font you chose in Key Caps, but you can change the font once you're back in your document.)

Key Caps knows what keyboard you're using; when you open it, it uses a keyboard layout that matches your keyboard—a full extended keyboard, a PowerBook layout, an older keyboard with no numeric keypad. I've faked most of the screen shots in this section to save room—the full keyboard layout includes all the cursor control keys and the numeric keypad, too. —SZA/EF

Special Characters, Special Keys

Character	Type	Logic
•	Option 8	Asterisk is on 8 key; it's sort of round, too
°	Shift Option 8	Shaped like bullet and asterisk also on 8 key
º	Option 0 (zero)	Looks like underlined zero
®	Option R	On the R key
∞	Option 5	Looks like a flattened %; percent symbol also on 5 key
…	Option ;	Same key as colon, which has two dots
¿	Shift Option /	Same key as question mark.
¨	Option U	The umlaut, which starts with U.
√	Option V	A basic V-shape.
◊	Shift Option V	Two V's together.
¬	Option L	Looks like an L lying down
– (en-dash)	Option -	A short hyphen
— (em dash)	Shift Option -	A long hyphen
≠	Option =	The *does not equal* sign, same key as equal sign
±	Shift Option =	Plus-or-minus symbol, same key as plus sign
≤, ≥	Option , , Option .	These keys also have the < and > symbols on them.
÷	Option /	The slash is used for division
¡	Option 1	Like upside-down exclamation point (on this key)
ƒ	Option F	Looks like a lowercase f
¢	Option 4	Dollar sign also on 4 key
†	Option T	Looks like a T
¥	Option Y	Looks like a Y
ﬁ	Shift Option 5	"Five" starts with the first two characters of the ligature
å, Å	Option A, Shift Option A	Special A's
ç, Ç	Option C, Shift Option C	Special C's
ø, Ø	Option O, Option Shift O	Slashed circles
π, ∏	Option P, Shift Option P	P for *pi*, lowercase and upper
µ	Option M	*Mu* starts with M

Keyboard resources
Chapter 11

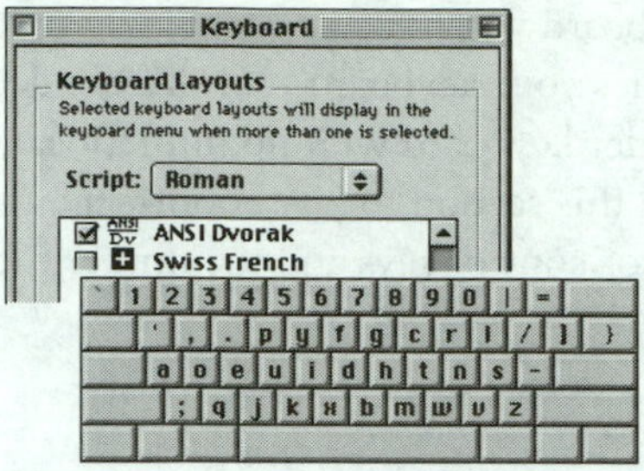

Key Caps and keyboard resources. Key Caps—and almost any utility you use to find keyboard characters in a font—is tied to the keyboard resource you've selected in the Keyboard control panel. If you've selected a special keyboard, such as for a foreign language or for a different key arrangement, the new key arrangement is shown in Key Caps.

Out, damned box! When there's a box on a key in Key Caps instead of a character, that means there's no character for that key (or key combination) in the font you've selected from the menu. Some fonts have a character for every key combination, while others don't have much beyond the standard upper- and lowercase letters.

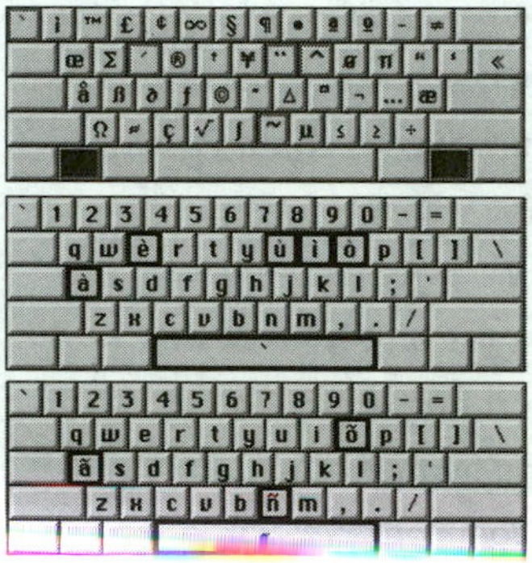

The Key Caps accents display. Top, pressing Option shows the accent keys. Middle, after pressing the grave accent in the upper left; bottom; after pressing the tilde accent in the N key.

Accent characters in keycaps. Key Caps can show you the special accent characters in a font, and which letters the accents go with, so that you can learn how to type them (or just copy them out of Key Caps).

First, press Option. You'll see five keys framed with a dotted border; these are the keys you use, in combination with Option, to put accents over letters.

With Option still down, type one of the framed letters, or click on it in the Key Caps keyboard; then, release the Option key. The Key Caps display changes to show which letters can take the accent, by framing the keys in black.

Key Caps in the background. Key Caps works in the background: size a document window so you can still see the Key Caps window, and you'll see each letter you type into your document highlighted on the Key Caps keyboard. What good is that? If you're working with a symbol or picture font at some point in your document and you don't know where the characters are that you need, you can set Key Caps to that font and then work in your document. Then, when you need a special character, you can glance at the Key Caps window to see where it is. When you press Shift, Key Caps shows the shifted characters; press Option and it shows the option characters. You'll even be able to see the accented characters as you type (or look for) them.

Better than Key Caps. Key Caps is free, and it's right there when you install your system software, but it has its limitations. For example, you may have trouble seeing the characters for some fonts, since Key Caps displays them in only a single size.

BigCaps, a utility that comes with Dubl-Click Software's MenuFonts (described in Chapter 14), takes care of this problem. As its name implies, BigCaps can display fonts at a larger size than Key Caps, in a resizable window. It has a few additional features: its window is resizable, and it can display fonts even if you're not using them and they're not in the menu.

Impossible Software's **TypeTamer**, also discussed in the Font chapter, provides a way to quickly view and insert special characters. It displays a window that contains all the special characters in a font; you simply click on a character to insert it into your document. Unlike Key Caps, TypeTamer inserts the character in the correct font, saving you the trouble of changing it in your document. —EF

Writing Tools

Word Processor Features and Programs

Styles. A *style* is a collection of character and paragraph formats that you can apply in one fell swoop. You can, for instance, define a *Title* style that applies three character formats (Palatino, 14, bold) and two paragraph formats (centered, blank line after) at one time.

The great thing about styles is that if you change a definition, every paragraph tagged as that style changes automatically. You want those subtitles in 12-point Schoolbook? You don't have to find each one—you just change the style definition.

Styles can also be based on other styles, letting you change all the related styles in your document just by changing the primary style. You can also define which style should be applied automatically to a following paragraph, which lets you format as you write—press Return and the new style is automatically applied.

A *style sheet* is the collection of styles used in a document. Some programs confuse things by calling the definitions for a single style its style sheet. And, to muddy the waters a little further, some programs have separate *character styles* and *paragraph styles.* And some programs that claim they offer styles give you only character styles, which lets you apply a combination of character styles in one action—handy, but nowhere near as convenient as paragraph-based styles. —SZA/EC

Outlining. Good writing means putting your thoughts in order; since they seldom come out in the correct order, re-ordering is what outlining is all about. But outlining isn't just a straight roster of items that you drag into various positions until they make perfect sense. An outline is a hierarchical listing that lets you use headings and subheadings and sub-subheadings as far as you need to sort things out. And, with the capability to collapse or expand headings to hide or show what's beneath them, you can concentrate on one section of your outline at a time or get a quick overview of the whole thing any time you want.

Macros. A macro lets you string together a series of commands that can be played back with a single keystroke. A macro might be as simple as one that combines the Save and Close commands, or it can perform more complicated editing combinations like finding every graphic in the document, resizing it, formatting the line following it as a caption, and saving the changes.

Nisus, ClarisWorks, and Word all provide some macro capability. But since Word incorporates Microsoft's Visual BASIC programming language for its macros, it is both more complicated (beyond the simple recording level) and far more powerful than the macro abilities you'll find in other programs.

IN THE BEGINNING

Every word processor has an outliner now, but outlining was a new invention, and a separate product, when ThinkTank was first released by Living VideoText. But the smaller, desk accessory outliner Acta had one of the best ads ever, showing how Julius Caesar might have used it (read that last line carefully).

THINGS TO DO TODAY

> Come, see, conquer
> Make salad for toga party
    > *Something different…romaine, garlic, eggs, anchovies and croutons?*
> Send thank you to Cleo for pyramid tour
> RSVP to Senate for Ides of March event
> Invade Carthage
> Take chariot in for tune-up
    > *Remember to have wheel hubs greased*
> Set date for next bocce game
> Series stands at 8-2 Brutus

Grammar checking. Let me be blunt: there's not a good grammar checker available anywhere yet in this universe. English grammar is much too complicated and subtle to be helpfully analyzed by some computer program—at least, by any program yet invented. Sure, it can flag problem words for you—but how many times do you want to be queried as to whether you meant to use *to, too,* or *two?* I even had one grammar checker, a long time ago, ask me, at every instance of the word *the,* if perhaps, just maybe, might I have meant *thee,* the archaic form of *you?* Give me a break! (And how might *that* sentence be interpreted?)

Of course, you can train most grammar checkers to ignore certain things and look for others, but then you can train yourself to do that, too. Grammar checkers that also check *style* can be useful—letting you know, for instance, that all your sentences are *way* too long—but nothing even approaches the skills of a real-life editor.

I used to use five test sentences on any grammar checker to see if it could catch common errors (using *that* instead of *who,* and *between* instead of *among,* for instance), but I'll spare you the full test. Instead, let me share with you the single test sentence that Word 98 caught:

I was impressed by him refusing the reward.

The *him* should be *his.* But Word 98 decided to flag the passive-voice construction instead, and suggested this:

He refusing the reward impressed me.

I rest my case.

Word processing programs. There's no use providing a separate section to cover word processors any more, since the field has narrowed so drastically. We're going to forego any feature roundup, since programs are constantly updated and this book has a relatively long shelf life; check recent reviews in magazines or online for the nitty gritty. Here are your choices:

- **ClarisWorks** ($100, Claris): If the word processor in this integrated package is enough for you, it's a bargain: reasonable power, a beautiful interface, a great price, and a bundle of other applications tied into it.
- **Microsoft Word** ($400): The word processor users love to hate. The Word 98 arm of Office 98 is a more polished version of Word 6 with a few extra capabilities and still enough quirks to remind you that it's a Microsoft product. (There's a $150 fee to upgrade from Word 6; for only $150 or so more than the price of Word alone, you can get the whole Office suite that includes Excel and PowerPoint—and there's a variation on the package that includes Microsoft Bookshelf, a good collection of reference works.)

claris.com
microsoft.com
nisus.com

- **Nisus Writer** ($140, Nisus): The third entrant in this field. Indicative of its struggle to stay out there is the fact that the 5.1 version added features and still cut its price practically in half. Its strong point has always been its PowerFind feature that lets you define search-and-replace options a million different ways.

If ClarisWorks doesn't provide enough power for you, Nisus Writer could be the word processor of your dreams—as long as you work pretty much alone. If you're sharing files or working in an office environment, you'll have to join the rest of us hammering away in Word.

Other Tools

About standalone tools. Back in the early days—as hard as it is to believe now—word processors didn't have spell checkers built in; they didn't have outlining capabilities, either; layout programs lagged behind in the spell-checking department even longer than the word processors. But so much is built into any program that handles text that standalone tools like spell checkers, dictionaries, and thesauruses (thesauri?) are either disappearing or dropping their prices; Big Thesaurus, described below, was $100 when we described it in the last edition of this book, and now it's $30.

The only advantage to a separate tool that provides a function which already exists in one of your programs is if you also need it for some program that doesn't have that capability.

A standalone program is traditionally one that you run as a separate utility, showing it which documents you want spell-checked or otherwise processed. But the extra steps of saving a document, launching a utility, and using it to check the document, makes it unlikely you're really going to use it all the time. So, look for one that interacts with the programs you use.

Spelling Coach and Big Thesaurus. Deneba's **Spelling Coach Professional** ($50) comes as close as any spelling checker to doing it all. Batch-check selections or let Coach Pro watch for errors while you type; a pop-up menu gives you options for correct spellings, and if none seems appropriate, you can ask for phonetic guesses. It includes a 95,000-word main spelling dictionary (about 90 percent with definitions) and legal, technical, and medical supplements.

It includes the seamlessly designed **Big Thesaurus** (also available separately for $30) which has a menu that automatically appears in all your programs. Highlight a word, and a keystroke or a menu click opens the thesaurus window; you can easily open additional windows for any words you see in the first window. This multiple-window scheme comes close to Roget's index in that when several windows are arranged to be simultaneously visible, glancing from one to the other increases your chances of finding just what you need. —RC

> “***Word 3, Users 0***
> *Robert Wiggins, MacUser magazine, July 1987*
>
> ***Word 4, Mice 5***
> *Robert Wiggins, MacUser magazine, August 1989*
> *(5 mice is MacUser's highest rating)*”

Spell Catcher

Spell Catcher. Previously incarnated as Thunder 7, **Spell Catcher** ($55, Casady & Greene), is one utility I absolutely can't live without; years ago I delayed moving to System 7 until a compatible version of Thunder 7 was available, and I would've done the same in regard to OS 8. Spell Catcher's menu stays on the menu bar no matter where you're working, so it's always available.

For me, the crux of this program's usefulness is its watch-as-you-type approach: Spell Catcher is always in the background keeping track of your keyboard activity. You can set it to beep or flash immediately for all sorts of typos (misspellings, double words, no capital at the beginning of a sentence); it can make corrections automatically or wait for your approval. Spell Catcher's glossary function lets you “teach” it the correct spelling for common misspellings; so, *hte* changes to *the* as soon as it leaves your fingertips, casadyg.com

and something like *amif* expands to *Apple Menu Items folder.* You don't have to do anything special to trigger the corrections and expansions—as soon as you type the space that signifies the end of a word (or a punctuation mark), Spell Catcher jumps into action. (Microsoft Word gives me this capability, too, but Spell Catcher makes it available everywhere.) Spell Catcher can also check spelling in an after-the-fact "batch" mode.

While the spell-checking and glossary expansion functions are enough to keep this on my top-ten utility list, there's more. Spell Catcher's Thesaurus is expansive and includes lots of synonyms as well as related words, and even antonyms—all grouped by meaning and with definitions; all you have to do is click on the word you want substituted for what you typed, and it's automatically entered in your document.

Could you ask for anything more? You don't have to ask: there's more. There's a group of little "extras," like curly quote substitution and em-dash insertion when you type a double-hyphen. And there's GhostWriter, which saves every keystroke you make so that if you crash without saving a document, you can reconstruct it from the separate file GhostWriter compiled.

All these functions come in a smooth, unobtrusive utility with an elegant interface that's totally customizable—you can have it on or off in any application, and you can define which functions work in which program. It's an absolute must-have for anyone who does anything more than the most casual of writing on the Mac.

shareware.com

Type it for me. The shareware program **TypeIt4Me** ($30), like SpellCatcher, provides a watch-as-you-type anywhere and everywhere capability. You teach it your shorthand abbreviations, and it expands a few letters into full words or phrases. It's a terrific program, but decide what it is you need in the way of help, because while Spell Catcher costs about twice as much, it does more than twice as much with its built-in spelling dictionaries, thesaurus functions, and GhostWriter capability.

Zillion Kajillions.

If you write in iambic pentameter
But can't find a rhyming parameter,
If you wish you were nimble and quick
In completing a new limerick,
You can find what it is that you need
With ease and incredible speed
One, two, or a million times
With a Zillion Kajillion Rhymes.

nisus.com

Eccentric Software (now part of Nisus), offers **A Zillion Kajillion Rhymes** ($30), which contains an extensive dictionary of common, technical and slang terms. **A Zillion Kajillion Clichés** ($30), its companion, makes finding just the right (if trite) expression as easy as… pie, falling off a log, duck soup, taking candy from a baby, A-B-C, 1-2-3, shooting fish in a barrel…. *(Duck soup??)*

ClarisWorks Tips

These tips were tested for ClarisWorks 5; most of them work in the previous version, too. The first section, General Tips, applies to ClarisWorks in general, no matter which module you're working in.

ClarisWorks may have been renamed "AppleWorks" by the time you read this!

General Tips

The double-click split. Instead of dragging the little black "split bar" at the top and left of the scroll bars to split a window, you can just double-click on the bar to split the window in half. And no matter where the split bar is positioned, double-clicking on it will unsplit the window.

Document windows Path menus. If you press ⌘ while clicking on the title of a window, you'll get a Path menu like the one in Finder windows, which tells you what folders the document is stored in. You won't be able to select anything from the menu—everything is dimmed—but it does let you check what folder you're working from.

Menu options. There are several places where holding Option while opening a menu changes the menu in one way or another:

- In the File menu, Close changes to Close All.
- In the File menu, Print changes to Print One Copy, a change that lets you bypass the print dialog.
- In the Font menu, the font names get listed in the standard system font instead of in their own fonts.
- In the Edit menu, Insert Date and Insert Time change to Insert Fixed Date and Insert Fixed Time. (The "unfixed" date and time change when you open the document later, to match the current date and time.)
- In the Edit menu's Writing Tools submenu, Edit Word Services is added to the bottom of the submenu.

Selecting a type for a new document. When you use the New dialog, you don't have to click on the type of document you want and then click the Open button. Instead, you can just double-click on one of the choices. Or, even simpler, type a single letter to indicate which module you want to work in: W for Word Processing, P for Painting, and so on. As for Drawing and Database, D selects Drawing, and DA selects Database. Then just hit Return to trigger the OK button.

Keyboard equivalent for dialog buttons. In almost every ClarisWorks dialog, you can use ⌘ and the first letter of the button name to trigger the button: ⌘D for Discard, for instance, or ⌘R for Replace. In some cases, two buttons might start with the same letter, but that's no problem: pressing ⌘ changes the button names to include their keyboard commands.

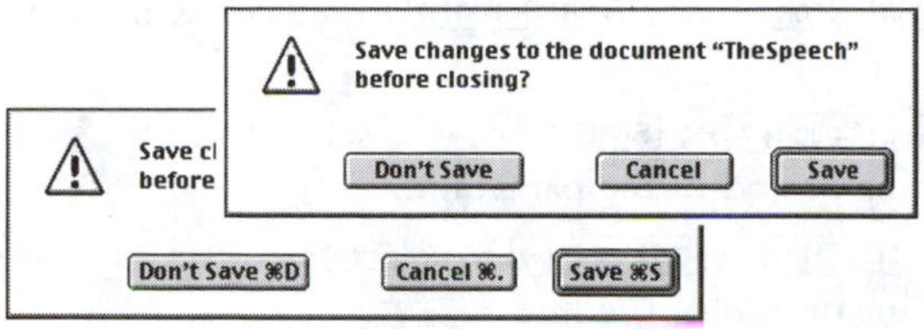

Holding down Command displays the keyboard equivalents for dialog buttons.

Drag information from one module to another. You don't have to export and import information to move it around among the word processor, database, and spreadsheet modules. Open both documents, select the information, and just drag it from one window to another. (To select the information in the database, you have to be working in the List view.)

As you move from one module to another, information is distributed in very logical ways: tabs in the word processor are column dividers in the spreadsheet and field separators in the database. A row in the word processor is a row in the spreadsheet and a record in the database.

When you're dragging information into a database, it will create as many new records as it needs to accommodate the data (the number of rows you're dragging). But you have to have enough fields defined to hold the information, or you'll lose some. Drag five columns of information into a database with only three fields defined, and the information from the last two columns disappears.

Rearrange button bars. To rearrange the buttons on a button bar, just ⌘ Option-drag buttons to new spots. If you ⌘ Option-drag a button off its bar, the button is removed from the bar completely.

Selecting and Editing Text

You're really moving now. You can move the blinking insertion point in big jumps instead of the little steps that ←→↑↓ provide:

- Use Option ← or Option → to go to the beginning or end of the current word, or the next word if you're already at the beginning or end of a word.
- Use Option ↑ or Option ↓ to go to the beginning or end of the current paragraph.
- Use ⌘← or ⌘→ to go to the beginning or end of the current line.
- Use ⌘↑ or ⌘↓ to go to the beginning or end of the document.

Selection shortcuts. ClarisWorks has lots of selection shortcuts; you might notice that many of them add Shift to the insertion-point moves listed in the last entry.

- Double-click to select a word.
- Triple-click to select a line (not, unfortunately, a sentence).
- Quadruple-click to select a paragraph.
- Use Shift Option ← and Shift Option → to select a word at a time in either direction.
- Use Shift Option ↑ or Shift Option ↓ to select from the current spot to the beginning or end of the paragraph.
- Use ⌘ Shift ← or ⌘ Shift → to select from the current spot to the beginning or end of the line.
- Use ⌘ Shift ↑ or ⌘ Shift ↓ to select from the current spot to the beginning or end of the document.

Canceling a selection. Because of ClarisWorks 5's drag-and-drop editing support, when you place the cursor over selected text you'll see the drag-and-drop cursor. If there's a selection and you want to edit in the middle of it, it seems that you have to first click somewhere to deselect the text and then click where you want to edit. But you can skip the separate deselection: clicking in a selection will place the insertion point where you clicked, despite the drag-and-drop cursor that you're using.

Selecting bullet lists and checkboxes. You can select an entire bulleted item by simply clicking on its leader character—you don't have to triple-click, as you do for standard paragraph selection.

Selecting a checkbox item is a little trickier, since clicking on the leading box alternately checks and unchecks it. But if you click right in *front* of the checkbox, that selects the entire item.

Miscellanous Word Processor Tips

Toggling invisible characters. There's a Preferences setting that lets you turn invisible characters, like tabs and paragraph symbols, on or off. But you don't have to go through that dialog: pressing ⌘ ; toggles the invisibles on or off, no matter how you have the general preference set. —SZA/CS

Quick-click text box. You can create a floating text box even in a word processor document, and there's a really quick way to do it: just Option-click anywhere in the document for the box to appear, and start typing. (You'll want to set a text wrap afterwards, of course, or the text in the text box will be superimposed on the background text.)

Double-click shortcuts. Double-clicking on items in the Ruler opens appropriate dialogs:

- Double-click on a tab (already set on the ruler, or the button on the ruler) to open the Tab dialog box.

- Double-click on the line spacing or justification controls to get the Paragraph Format box.
- Double-click on a column number or icon to get the Section dialog.

Inserting graphics. If you add a graphic to a word processor document by merely using Paste, it will appear as a (usually) large character in the line where the insertion point is blinking.

Instead, with the Tools showing at the left of the window, select the Pointer tool, and *then* choose Paste from the Edit menu; your graphic will appear as a completely separate object from the text. You can then choose Text Wrap from the Options menu and wrap the text around your graphic. —CS

Superior versus superscript. There are two pairs of character formatting options in the Style menu that seem to describe the same thing: superscript and superior, and subscript and inferior. The difference? Superior and inferior change the point size of the selected text as well as move it above or below the baseline; superscript and subscript merely shift the text, leaving the point size intact.

This is superior text
This is superscript

Find/Replace

Finding and replacing invisibles. You can specify invisible characters (like tab and return) in a Find/Change dialog by typing a backslash (that's a *backslash,* not the forward slash on the ? key) followed by a letter that represents the character:

Tab	\t
Return	\r
Line break ("newline")	\n
Page break	\b
Column break	\c
Section break	\§ (Option 6)

Quick-type invisible codes. The most common invisibles you'll be looking to find or change are the tab, return, and line break characters. You don't have to remember their codes (although the line break is the only one you might forget), because you can type them into a Find or Change box by holding down ⌘ and then pressing the key you use to put the character in a document: Return, Tab, or Shift Return (for line breaks).

Find it again, Sam. If you want to find another instance of the last thing you looked for, you don't have to open the Find dialog again: just press ⌘E.

Drag and Drop

Drag and drop original or copies. When you use drag-and-drop editing, you get to simply drag a selection from one spot in a document to another. But if you want to drag a copy instead of the original, hold down Option as you drag.

You can also drag selections from one document to another; for inter-document drag-and-drops, it's always a copy that's dragged, even if you don't hold down Option.

Drag and drop with paragraph styles. When you drop a selection into another part of the document, the newly placed text takes on the paragraph style of its new location. So, if you move a checkbox style line of text in between two Body-style paragraphs, the checkbox line will revert to Body style—in fact, it won't even be a separate line/paragraph any more, and will append itself to the paragraph where you drop it. But you can keep paragraph styles intact as you drag and drop, as long as you make sure you select the entire paragraph (including the invisible, trailing paragraph marker) before you drag it.

Styles

Redefining the default text. ClarisWorks word processor documents default to using Helvetica, which is very difficult to read on the screen. If you redefine the Body style to, say, Geneva, that works only for the document you were working on when you redefined the style.

To change the default font for *all* new documents, use the Preferences command; in its Text screen (use the pop-up menu), set Geneva (or whatever) as the default font.

Setting the default font in Preferences alters style definitions like Body to include Geneva instead of the original default Helvetica as part of the definition.

The defined-in-advance style. If you've created a particular combination of formats that you want to use as a style, you can quickly define a style using the already formatted text as the definition. Select the text, open the Stylesheet window, and click the New button; in the next dialog, name the style, check the *Inherit Style from Selection* option, and click OK.

Stylesheet window basics. The list of styles in the stylesheet window provides visual clues about the styles and about the selection in your document. The styles are sorted by type: Basic, Paragraph, Outline, and Table, and each type is labeled with an icon, except for Basic, which has no icon.

The stylesheet window has three views: the basic one, an expanded Edit view that shows the style definition, and one that includes a sample of the selected style. Clicking the Edit button expands the window; clicking Done collapses

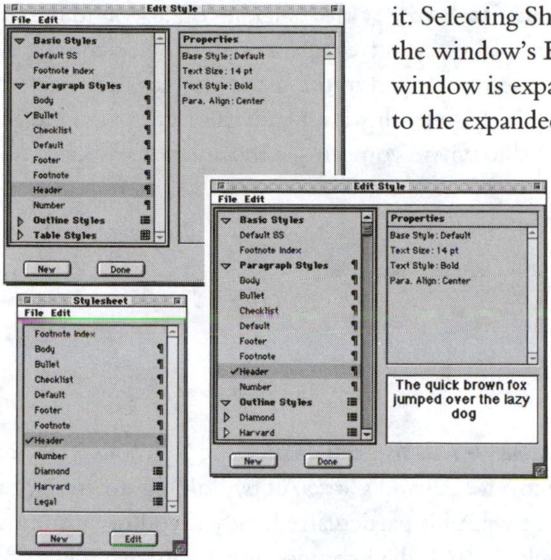

Three views for the Stylesheet window.

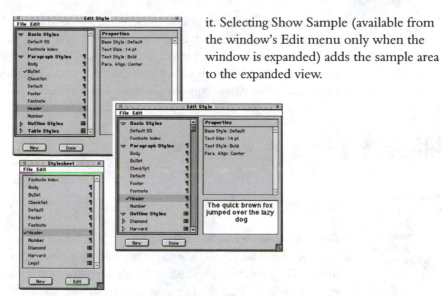

it. Selecting Show Sample (available from the window's Edit menu only when the window is expanded) adds the sample area to the expanded view.

Stylesheet window shortcuts. There are many hidden keyboard and click shortcuts for the Stylesheet window:

- Pressing Tab alternately selects the style list or the edit pane in the expanded view.
- Using ↑↓ selects the item above or below the currently selected item in the active pane.
- Pressing Page Up or Page Down lets you see the top or bottom of the list in the active pane (but it doesn't change the selected item).
- Option-clicking directly on a style name opens the Edit view.
- You don't need to use the size box in the lower right corner to change the window size; you can drag on the bottom or right edge to of the window to resize it. (When the cursor is in just the right spot for the drag, it changes to a double-headed arrow.)
- If you click in the sample area, you'll get various types of samples for the selected style—how it looks on the overall document page, for instance.

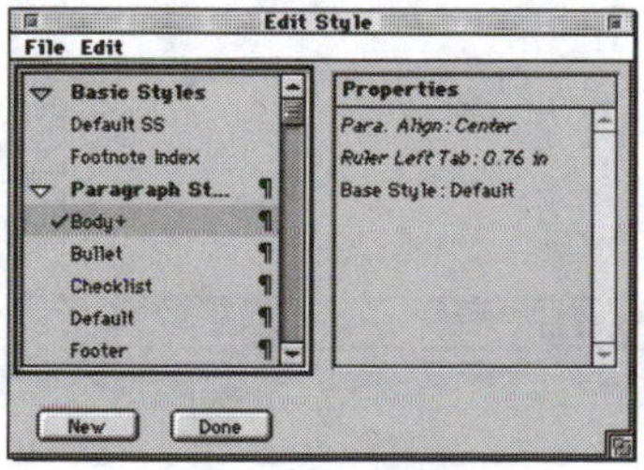

The + sign on the style name means there's additional formatting beyond the style definition; the Edit pane shows the additions in italic.

Styles plus. When there's a plus sign next to a style name, that means the current selection was defined as that style, and then edited to include something that's not in the style definition. Even a very minor change, like setting a tab in a paragraph, for instance—counts as a change to the style.

You can see what additional formatting has been added to the base style by clicking the Edit button; the additions are shown in italics in the Edit pane.

Quick return to Body style. Clicking on a style in the Stylesheet window applies that style to the current paragraph or selected text. But clicking on the style that's already selected in the list re-defines the selected text in the document as the Body style; this is a handy shortcut when the Stylesheet window list is scrolled to where you can see the current style, but not the Body style.

Word Tips

These tips were tested for Word 98, but most work (sometimes with minor variations) in Word 6, too.

Basics

Close and Save All. You can change the Save and Close commands in the File menu to Save All and Close All by holding down Shift as you open the menu. The Save All is particularly handy if you're quitting Word and don't want to cycle through the open documents to save them or be asked, for each one, if you want them saved before Word quits.

Double-click shortcuts. Word's document window and status bar have several "hot spots" that you can double-click to get dialog boxes or perform actions, as shown in the following picture.

There are hot spots all over, although some of them depend on the view you're using. When the window's split, for instance, you don't have to use the Remove Split command or drag the split bar up into the top of the window to get rid of it—you can just double-click on it, if you have the Document Map showing, double-clicking on the vertical divider bar closes it. So, just click away wherever you are and see what happens.

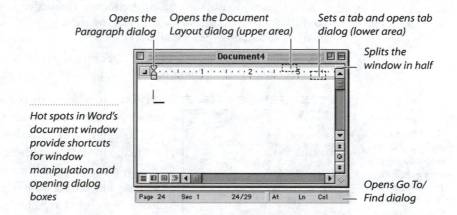

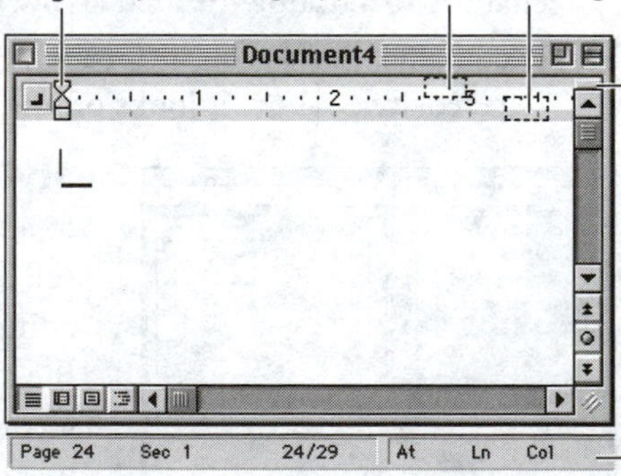

Hot spots in Word's document window provide shortcuts for window manipulation and opening dialog boxes

Keyboard control. You can control everything from the keyboard if you want to in Word; this is no big surprise in a program that was created for the Windows world, but sometimes it really is convenient to ignore the mouse.

To activate the keyboard control, press ⌘-Tab. For menus, you'll see that every title will have a single letter underlined; press that letter (no ⌘ key necessary) and the menu drops down. Every menu command will have a single underlined letter; press the letter, and the command is executed. You can use ← and → to move from one menu to another once a menu's open; ↑ and ↓ move you up and down inside an opened menu.

Dialog boxes that open after you've pressed ⌘-Tab will have all their controls marked so that you can press the ⌘ key and the underlined letter to choose the option.

The keyboard control mode turns off automatically after you've used it for a command or dialog box. You can cancel it manually by pressing Esc.

In addition to all this, there's a simple approach for simple dialogs: for dialogs with only buttons in them, pressing the first letter of the button name triggers the button (*Y* for *Yes*, *N* for *No*, and so on). As a special bonus, pressing N also triggers the *Don't Save* button for when you're closing a document because it used to be a No button.

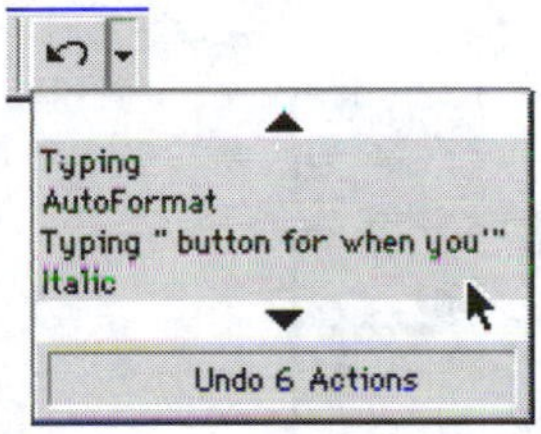

Selecting multiple undos. When you want to take advantage of Word's multiple Undo feature to move back through several editing changes, you don't have to repeatedly use the Undo command either from the keyboard or the menu. Instead, use the Undo menu in the Formatting toolbar: select as many of the listed undoable items as you want, and they'll all be done at once. This works for multiple redos, too—of course, you have to use the Redo menu.

Now, where was I? When you first open a previously saved document, you can jump to the spot you last were working on by pressing ⌘-Option-Z.

Slide rules. When you have Rulers turned off in any view that allows Rulers (not the Outline view, for instance), you'll see a light gray bar along the top, or the top and side, of the document, where the Ruler would normally be displayed. If you move the mouse cursor over the gray bar and hold it there for a second or two (without the mouse button down), the Ruler slides out of the window's edge so you can check or change its settings. A second or two after you move back into the document, the Ruler disappears again.

Character and Paragraph Formatting

Quick-format for words. You don't have to select a word before you apply a font, size, or style to it: if the blinking insertion point is in the word (including at the beginning or end of it) formatting is applied to the entire word.

Keyboard commands for font switching. Since Word allows you to create character styles as well as standard paragraph styles, and it allows you to assign keyboard commands to styles, that means it's possible to call up a font at a keystroke.

But it's even easier than that, because you don't have to create a style first. Word lets you assign keyboard combos directly to a font:

1. Choose Customize from the Tools menu.
2. Click the Keyboard button.
3. Scroll through the Categories list and select *Fonts.*
4. Scroll through the Fonts list and select the font you want.
5. Click in the *Press new shortcut key* box and press the key combination you want to use for the font.
6. If you want the keyboard command to work only in the current document, or only in the current template, use the *Save changes in* pop-up menu to indicate that; leaving the menu at *Normal* puts the keyboard assignment in the Normal template so that it's always available.
7. Click the Assign button.

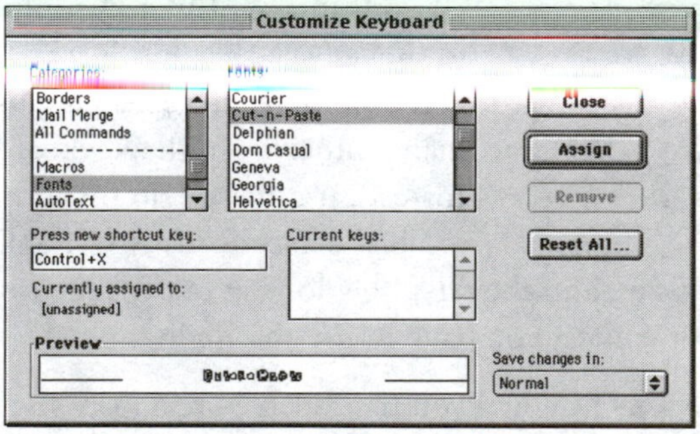

Assigning a keyboard command to a font.

Using the Paintbrush. Okay, the tool is actually called the *Format Painter*, but, as descriptive as that is, nobody calls it that. It's incredibly handy once you get the hang of it, especially after you figure out how to differentiate between painting a character format and paragraph format.

To use the Paintbrush, first you click in or select the text *whose format you want copied,* then you click the Paintbrush tool. The mouse cursor changes, not to a Paintbrush, but to an special I-beam text cursor with a plus sign on it. Anywhere you click or drag with this special cursor is reformatted to match the original selection (which was sort of "loaded" onto the Paintbrush when you clicked its button in the toolbar). Here are the things to keep in mind:

- Character formats only are picked up by the Paintbrush if the insertion point is blinking in text or if the selection is text. To pick up paragraph formats, you have to first select an entire paragraph, including the trailing (usually invisible) paragraph marker; the easiest way to select an entire paragraph is by double-clicking on it from the selection bar at the left edge of the window.

- The picked-up formats are applied wherever you click or drag the special cursor. If you've picked up only character formats, a single click of the special cursor applies the format to the word you clicked on. If you've picked up paragraph formats, a single click applies the formats to the entire paragraph you click in; dragging across even partial paragraphs (say, the end of one and the beginning of the next) applies the paragraph formats to the entire paragraphs.
- If you want to "paint" more than one spot, double-click on the Paintbrush tool in the toolbar; the cursor remains "loaded" so you can click and/or drag in several spots. To get rid of this semi-permanent setup, either click the Paintbrush button again or just start typing in the document.

Quick style definition. Here's the quickest way to create a new style—you won't even have to open a dialog box: format a paragraph to conform to your new style requirements, select it by double-clicking on it from the selection bar, type the new style name in the Style menu in the Formatting tool bar (just select, then type right over whatever's there), and press Return or Enter.

Unfortunately, Word 98 still didn't fix a little bug that's a corollary of this capability. If you press ⌘ Option S to activate the style name in the toolbar and type the name of the style you want to apply to the current paragraph, then press Return, the style is applied. If you misspell the style name, Word figures you're creating a new style—and it creates a new style with the misspelled name.

Quick redefine of styles. You can quickly redefine a style without using the Style definition dialog. First, apply the style to an existing paragraph and then make the changes to it. Select the entire paragraph by double-clicking on it from the selection bar. Next, click in the Style menu in the Formatting toolbar (which selects the text there), and press Return twice: the first time opens a dialog box, and the second okays the redefine option.

Multiple style deletion. If you've imported parts of other Word documents (or entire documents, through the Insert command), you may wind up with lots of styles in your document that you just don't want or need. Working through the Style dialog box to delete them means you have to select and delete them one at a time. But there is an easier way (of course, or this topic wouldn't have an entry!).

Start with the Style command in the Format menu, but click the Organize button in the Style dialog. In the Organize dialog, you can select multiple styles in the left pane: Shift-click to select styles listed next to each other, or ⌘-click to select non-contiguous styles. Then click the Delete button. You'll get a dialog confirming the deletion of the first style in the list that also offers a Yes To All button so you won't have to confirm the deletion of every style you selected.

Odds and Ends

The Repeat command. The Repeat command (⌘Y) repeats the last editing command, your last edit, or the last thing you typed. If you've just applied a style to a paragraph, you can click in another paragraph and use Repeat to apply the style there, too.

If you want to use Repeat for a group of character or paragraph formats (bold, outline, and italic, say, or justified, indented and double-spaced), use the Font or Paragraph command to apply all the formats at once instead of using keyboard or toolbar commands to apply them individually. That way, the Repeat command will include all the formats, instead of just the last one you applied.

Uncurly quotes. If you have automatic curly quotes (for both apostrophes and quote marks) turned on through the AutoCorrect dialog, how do you get straight quotes for inch or foot marks? As soon as you type the character, press ⌘Z for Undo: it won't undo the typing, but it will undo the change from straight to curly quote.

Selecting interior blocks of text. You can select any rectangular part of text by holding down Option as you drag. This is useful if you have tabbed columns because you can actually select a column of information. You can apply formatting to the selection, or even cut or copy it, although the success of cutting or copying depends on what exactly you had selected (including or excluding leading or trailing tabs, for instance).

Footnote shortcuts. The Footnotes command in the View menu splits the document window so you can review the text of the footnote entries, but there are two other ways to open the footnote "pane." Hold Shift while you drag the window's split bar, and you'll get the footnote pane instead of a regular split window. Or, simply double-click on a footnote reference mark and the window splits to display that footnote.

To close the footnote pane, you can drag the split bar back to the top of the scroll bar, or press ⌘ Shift S. But to close the pane and jump to a specific footnote reference at the same time, double-click on the reference mark next to the footnote itself in the lower pane.

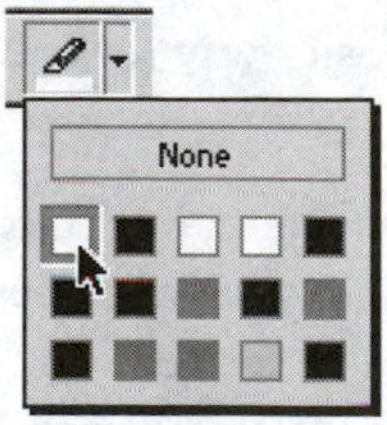

Selecting a highlight color. "None" is used to erase existing highlights.

The Highlighter tool. Word 98 is driving me crazy with its combination of great new tools and power, and brain-dead interface and operation. But on the great new tool side is the Highlight tool, which works just like its real-world counterpart—except that you can erase these highlights. It's wonderful to just mark things with different colors in a document while I'm working on it instead of having to use asterisks or bold-italic formatting so I can easily find them later. I hope this idea is picked up by every application under the sun.

- To access the different colors, or the None "color" for removing highlights, you have to click on the little arrow next to the highlight button; clicking on the button only triggers the current highlight color or lets you pick up the tool.
- To highlight text, you can grab the Highlighter from the toolbar and drag it across the text; or you can select text first and then click on the highlighter button (or select a color from its drop-down menu.)
- Once you have the Highlighter, you can put it down by clicking on its button again; or you can click where you want to type and just start typing—the highlight won't be applied to the new typing.

Find and Replace

Finding again. To find another occurrence of the last item you searched for, you don't have to open the Find dialog again: just press ⌘ Option Y. Combining Find Again with Repeat (⌘ Y) lets you find something, apply a format to it (if that's what you did to the found text), find the next occurrence, apply the format to it, and so on, all without a dialog box in the way.

Replace formatting shortcut. You can specify character or paragraph formatting for the Find or Replace text, but it's a multi-step process: Select the category (font, paragraph, styles, and so on) from the dialog's Format menu, then specify the formats in the dialogs that open—and do it separately for each category. But you don't have to do all that. First, click in either the Find What or the Replace With box—wherever you're defining the format. Then use the Formatting tool bar to define the format (click on the Bold button, select a style, choose a font and/or size), and the formatting selections go into the Format definition in the dialog.

Tied up in nots. You can specify a search or replace format for text that is *not* something: not Bold, for instance, or not All Caps. With the Find or Replace dialog open, click in the Find What or Replace With text box, and click *twice* on the toolbar button that does the formatting. The first click adds the formatting to the definition (as described in the last entry), but the second click adds the *Not* to the definition. A third click in the button removes the formatting definition from the dialog entirely.

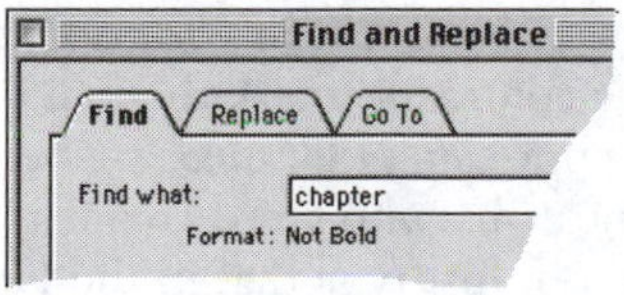

If there's no toolbar button for the format you want to specify, select Font from the dialog's Format pop-up menu, and click in the style's checkbox until it's empty (it starts as a dash, then goes to a checkmark first).

Finding and replacing for format. If you simply want to find and replace for character or paragraph formats (like changing all the blue double-underlined text to red dotted-underlined text), set up the Replace dialog for the formats without putting any text in the Find What and Replace With boxes.

If you want to find specifically formatted text and return it to whatever is normal for the paragraph style that contains it, leave Replace With blank but set the format for the Replace to *Default paragraph font*, which you can select from the Style menu on the toolbar.

Curling up those straight quotes. If you import a document that has straight apostrophes and quote marks instead of curly ones, it's easy to curl them—you don't even have to worry about the difference between opening and closing quote marks (which are different characters). Just use the Replace command and type a single apostrophe in both the Find What and Replace With boxes; although they'll be straight marks in the dialog, Word will do all the replacements with curly apostrophes. For quote marks, just type the quote mark in both the Find and Replace boxes; once again, it will be the straight quotes in the dialog, but the replacements will be curly—and the correct-facing marks will be inserted in the appropriate places.

Finding and replacing with highlights. You can use the Highlight tool in conjunction with the Find and Replace dialogs to do all sorts of nifty things, even though you can't specify the color of the highlight you're looking for. Here are three handy basics:

- It's easy to find highlighted text as you scroll through a document, since it's really eye-catching. But sometimes, especially in long documents, it's easier to jump from one instance of highlighted text to the next using the keyboard. To do this, use the Find command, leaving the Find What box blank but clicking the Highlight tool to add that as the format for the Find text. Click the Find Next button to find the first instance of highlighted text (of any color), and put the Find dialog away. From there, all you have to do is press ⌘ Option Y, the Find Again command, to jump to the next area that's highlighted.

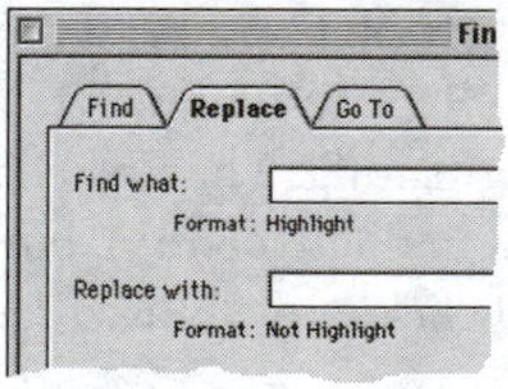

Remove all highlighting with Search and Replace.

- You can remove all the highlights from a document in one fell swoop by using the Replace dialog. Leave both the Find and Replace text boxes empty, but set the Find format to Highlight by clicking once on the Highlight tool button, and the Replace format to Not Highlight by clicking on it twice. Then click Replace all.

- You can highlight certain instances of text in your document for later review by letting the Replace command mark them. Say you're looking for every occurrence of the phrase *the faculty and staff* because you realized almost too late that sometimes what you were saying applied only to one or the other rather than to both. Just type that in the Find box (with no formatting indicated) and type the same thing in the Replace box, adding the Highlight formatting to the replace. Click Replace All and you'll have every occurrence highlighted. And here's a great tip-within-a-tip: select a highlight color on the toolbar before you open the Replace dialog, and that's the color that will be used for the operation.

Tables and Columns

Selecting a table. Select a row or column in a table by putting the pointer at the top or side of the table, where it will change to a thick arrow, then click.

To select an entire table, double-click anywhere inside it while pressing Option, or press Option Clear (on the keypad) when the insertion point is anywhere in the table.

Creating uneven columns. When you drag the column markers on the ruler, you don't just change one column, you change them all. How do you create two columns that have different widths? In the Columns dialog box, check Left or Right for the automatic settings, or click Two or Three Columns and uncheck Equal Column Width. Then enter the widths you want for your columns. Now when you drag the column markers in the ruler, it will affect only one column.

There's a visual clue on the ruler that lets you know if the columns are set for equal or unequal sizes: the area between the columns is plain gray when columns are equal, but has a grid icon in the gray when columns are set to be unequal. —SZA/EC

Avoid the pencil and eraser. The new pencil and eraser tools for drawing tables and merging cells (by erasing their divider lines) are cute and clever, but not particularly useful; after all, this is a computer—why should a I draw umpteen lines for a five-by-twenty-cell table?

To create a table, stick with the Insert Table menu command or button to get started; the pencil can be used to quickly divide a cell or two where you need it.

The eraser, unfortunately, has to be dragged across the lines you want to erase; it would actually be useful if you could just click on a line to delete it. As it is, it's still much quicker to merge cells—especially three or more—by selecting them and using the Merge Cells command, which is a single operation; the eraser has to be dragged across every divider individually.

Customizing

Tool bar tricks. Here are four quick tips for working with toolbars:

- Control-click anywhere on a toolbar to see a list of other toolbars; select one from the menu to open it.
- Reposition a button on a toolbar by holding down ⌘ while you drag it.
- To remove a button from a toolbar, hold down ⌘ and drag the button off. Let it go on another toolbar to move it there; let it go anywhere else, and it just disappears.

- To make a copy of a button, hold down Option while you drag it. Let it go over another toolbar to put the copy on that toolbar. Let it go anywhere else on the screen, and you'll get a new toolbar holding that button.

Creating and changing keyboard commands. To change an existing keyboard equivalent or create a keyboard combination for a command that doesn't have one:

1. Choose Customize from the Tools menu.
2. Click the Command tab.
3. Click the Keyboard button.
4. Find the command you want in the Commands list, using the Categories list to narrow the search (although most of the time, selecting All Commands in the Categories list is the only thing that will let you get to the command you want).
5. To remove an existing keyboard command, click on it in the Current Keys list and then click the Remove button.
6. To add a keyboard command, click in the Press New Shortcut Key box and press the key combination you want. You'll be informed if it's already in use for another command.
7. Click the Assign button.

Using the Work menu for documents. When you work on certain documents over and over, even for a relatively short period of time, it's easier to get at them from a menu than through the Open dialog—you can't count on their always being in the File menu's recent list.

Word 98 comes with a Work menu that lets you easily add items to it: simply select the Add to Work Menu command from the menu, and the active window is added to the list. Unfortunately, it's added to the list with its entire path name, so you'll get something like: *Internal Drive: Documents: WorkStuff: Meetings: May: Memo* as the document name in the menu. You can edit the name, although the method is incredibly clumsy (even for Microsoft); read through the next entry to see how it's done.

Creating your own documents menu. If you prefer separate document menus for different types of documents, you can create your own, through a process that was apparently designed by someone with a deeply ingrained hatred of the Mac and its users—and it's an all-new approach just for Word 98.

First, you have to create the menu itself:

1. Choose Customize from the Tools menu.
2. Click the Toolbars tab, and click on Menu Bar in the Toolbars list (right, the menubar is a toolbar!). The list isn't alphabetical, so you'll have to scroll through to find it. You can press M to jump from one item that starts with M to the next, but you can't type a second letter to specify what you want.

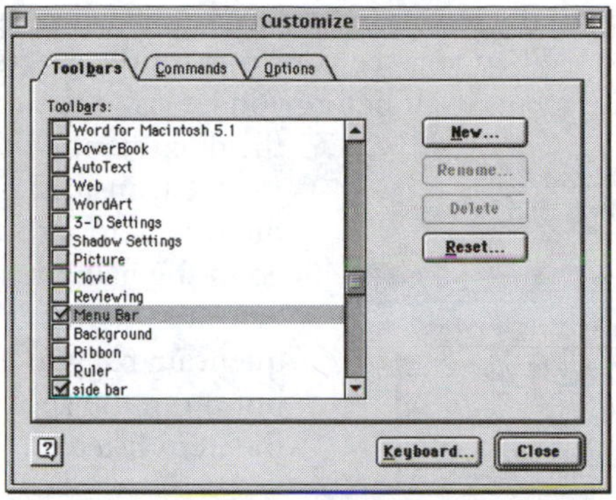

You can edit menus and menu items if you turn on the Menu Bar "toolbar" first.

When you find Menu Bar, you have to click on the checkbox in front of it, not just on its name, to truly select it. With that accomplished, you'll get a second menubar on your screen, just beneath the "real" one.

3. Click the Commands tab.
4. Select the New Menu item at the bottom of the Categories list.
5. Select the New Menu item that appears in the Commands list, and drag it up into the fake menubar, dropping it where you want it placed.
6. With the dark frame still around the New Menu title in the title bar, click the Modify Selection pop-up in the Customize dialog. A single click will keep the menu open (because of the OS8's sticky menus), which is easier than if you have to keep the mouse button down for this procedure.

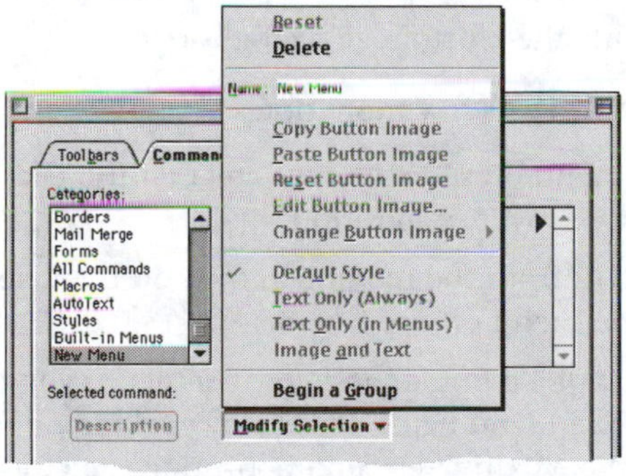

Using the Modify Selection menu to name the new menu.

7. At the top of the popped-up menu, edit the name of the menu to Documents (or something more specific); click outside the menu or press Enter to close it.
8. Click the Close button.

Okay, so now you have a new menu in the menubar, but it's empty. You think adding items to it will be any more elegant than creating it to begin with? First, open the document you want to add to the menu. Then:

1. Use the Tool menu's Customize command to turn on the fake tool bar again: in the Toolbars tab, click on Menu Bar.
2. Click the Commands tab.
3. In the Categories list, click the All Commands category.
4. In the Commands list, select the FileOpenFile item. If you click anywhere in the Commands list to activate it, you can press F to jump to the first command that starts with that letter. You'll get FileClose, and FileOpenFile isn't too far beyond that.
5. With FileOpenFile selected, the pop-up menu at the bottom of the dialog will list the names of all your open documents; select the one that you want added to your menu.

6. Drag the FileOpenFile item from the Commands list up to your menu in the fake menubar. When you see your menu title selected, make sure you slide down to the menu itself before you let go of the mouse button, or the document will wind up in the menubar instead of in the menu. For the first item into the menu, you let go in the blank box that drops down beneath the menu name; for subsequent items, you let go of the mouse button in the spot where you want the item listed.

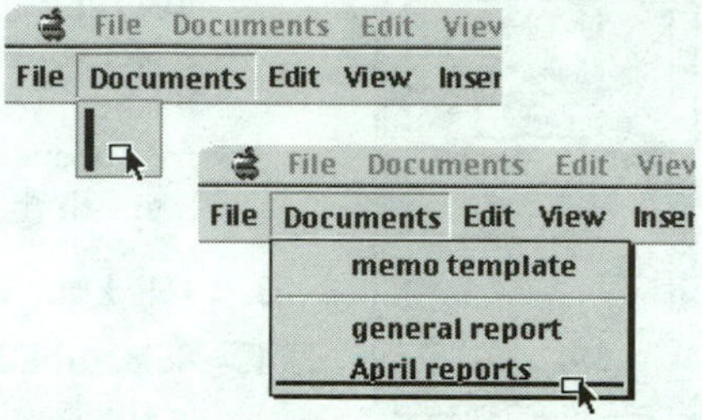

Putting an item in an empty menu (top left) and into an existing menu (bottom right).

7. You get the entire pathname of the document cluttering up your menu. To edit it, keep it selected, and click the Modify Selection pop-up menu; edit the name of the document at the top of the pop-up, the same way you did for the menu name itself. Click outside the menu or press Enter to close it.

All these gymnastics are worth it to have quick selection of documents that you use often. Cut down on the hassle by adding as many items to your menus as you can at one time—open them all so you can add them (even to different menus) while the Customize dialog is open.

More menu-wrangling. A few more notes about altering Word's menus:

- To reposition a menu on the menubar, turn on the fake menubar and just drag the menu title to a new position.
- To remove a menu from the menu bar, turn on the fake menubar and then just drag the menu off the fake bar.
- To alter the name of a menu or an item in a menu, you turn on the fake menubar, select the menu name or item by clicking on it in the *fake* menu, and then using the Modify Selection pop-up in the Commands tab.
- To add a divider line, turn on the fake menubar and move to the Commands tab in the dialog. Select the item you want just beneath the divider, and choose Begin a Group from the Modify Selection pop-up.
- To get the Work menu back if you've removed it, first turn on the fake menubar. In the Commands tab, select Built-in Menus from the Categories list, and Work from the Commands list, dragging the Work menu into the spot you want (on the *fake* menubar, of course).

17

Spreadsheets

In This Chapter

About Spreadsheets

The Joy of Spreadsheeting

What's a spreadsheet? A spreadsheet is a grid of *cells* arranged in rows and columns. The columns are identified by letters, and the rows by numbers; a cell is identified by its column/row position: A1, B12, AB56, and so on.

You put numbers into some cells, formulas into others, and have the spreadsheet perform all sorts of nifty calculations. (Of course, you can also put text into some cells to serve as labels.) Since formulas refer to cells (like *C2*15*), when you change the contents of a cell, the results of all the formulas change instantly.

The little spreadsheet pictured here shows four basic living expenses over a period of six months. By using the spreadsheet's built-in functions, the total for each month is calculated across the rows, and the totals and averages for each expense over the six months are calculated in the columns; the overall total is also included in the lower right of the grid.

	A	B	C	D	E	F
1		Rent	Heat	Electric	Phone	Total
2	January	750	35.26	22.36	56.23	863.85
3	February	750	42.69	32.65	45.89	871.23
4	March	750	31.26	35.69	42.31	859.26
5	April	925	15.36	38.36	38.59	1017.31
6	May	925	12.89	42.12	44.88	1024.89
7	June	925	8.56	48.64	37.19	1019.39
8	Total	5025.00	146.02	219.82	265.09	5655.93
9	Average	837.50	24.34	36.64	44.18	

The "what if" experience. Not every formula you write or spreadsheet you create will be as simple as a household budget. By combining simple formulas and more advanced functions, you can create more complex spreadsheet models, like the loan amortization table on the next page. And then you can play with the most powerful spreadsheet feature, and the one that made the whole category take off (and, in fact, really launched the personal computer as we know it): the *what if* analysis. You change a value and see the instant recalculation, answering the question, "*What* happens *if* this number changes?"

You set up a loan amortization table, and then wonder: what if you decide to buy a cheaper car? Or change the loan term? Or find a better interest rate? It's easy to see how these changes will affect the monthly payment. Just change the information in the appropriate cell and—presto!—your change is reflected throughout the spreadsheet.

The picture here shows a good example of what-iffing. The design includes an area at the top where you enter the amounts you already know: the amount of the loan, the interest rate, and the loan term. The monthly payment formula in cell D5 uses the formula *PMT(D3/12,D4*12,D2)*, which says to find the periodic payment for a loan based on its interest rate, number of periods, and principal—the numbers stored in cells D3, D4, and D2 (with adjustments to calculate months instead of years). The rest of the table calculates and displays the interest, payment, and ending balance for each month of the loan.

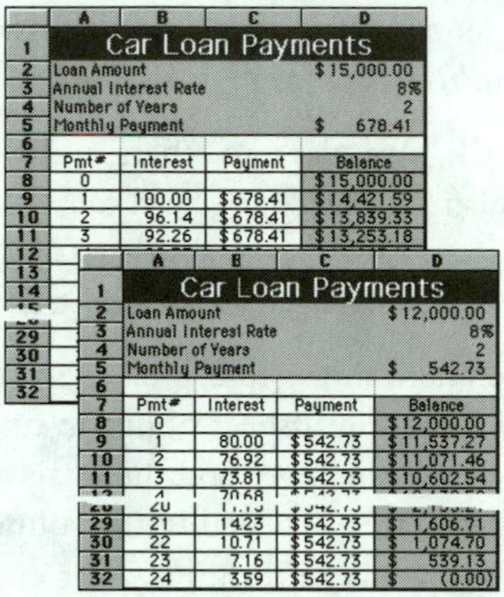

Since all the information in the table is based on the numbers in the three cells at the top of the table, changing one of the numbers changes the entire table. You can see that in the picture, which shows two different loan amounts; the single change for the loan amount affected everything else. —SZA/EG/ML

Charting. Sometimes a picture is worth a thousand numbers. Spreadsheets include charting capabilities that let you—and others—understand your numbers at a glance. The charts here are just two of many that can be made from the sample budget spreadsheet shown at the beginning of the chapter. Charts are stored with the spreadsheet and stay linked to the numbers that created them, so changing the numbers instantly changes the charts.

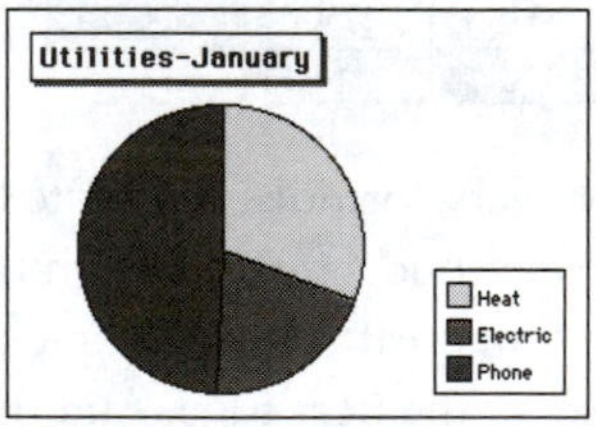

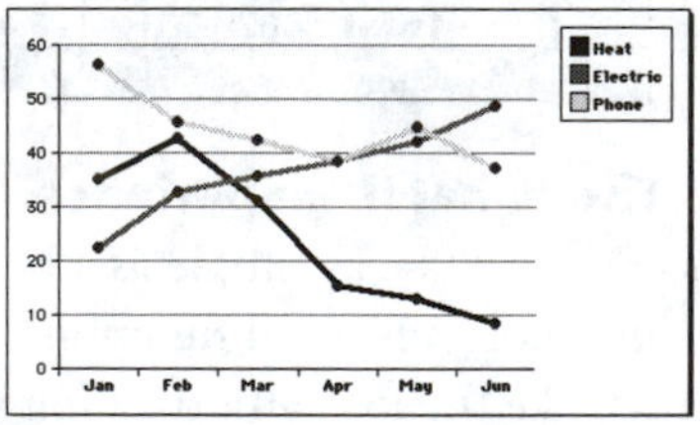

Macros. Most spreadsheets give you the ability to write and use *macros* that automate repetitive tasks or create custom functions. Say you've been keeping track of the scores for your bowling league. Each week, you create a stacked bar graph that puts each bowler's scores into a bar and color codes the scores for each game. Rather than go though the steps to create the chart manually each week, you can create a macro to do it automatically.

System-wide macros Chapter 10

When you first get started with macros, use the software's macro recorder to have it write the macro for you. This is a nice—although limited—use of macros that can help familiarize you with the macro language. —EG

Database management. Spreadsheets are also useful for simple database functions. By setting up columns for different categories of information (the *fields)* and using rows for the data (the *records)*, you can organize, sort, summarize, and otherwise analyze data. Excel provides the capability of defining areas of a spreadsheet as a database for easier manipulation. But keep in mind that a database can perform reasonably sophisticated mathematical functions and analysis within and across records, and except for very complex data, a database will usually work better for many kinds of data manipulation. —SZA/DC/ML

Databases
Chapter 18

Spreadsheet programs. There are three spreadsheet programs available for the Mac: the Microsoft Excel powerhouse, the elegant and reasonably powerful spreadsheet module in ClarisWorks, and the "think different" approach of Spreadsheet 2000.

If you have **ClarisWorks**, or are going to get it for its other modules, it will probably provide everything you need for spreadsheeting. **Excel's** power comes at a cost—money, learning time, disk space, and RAM—so make sure you need its special features before you decide to go with it. (In fact, even if it comes with the Microsoft Office suite you've purchased because you want Word 98 and some bonuses, you still might want to use a different spreadsheet program if your needs are less than extensive.)

claris.com
microsoft.com

Spreadsheet 2000. ($110, Casady & Greene), originally marketed as K.I.S.S.—Keep It Simple Spreadsheet—takes an entirely different approach to handling numbers and charts. You work on a blank layout page, where you drop separate grids for different types of information. When you want to setup calculations, you draw lines from one grid to another, through whatever "operator" relates them. It's sometimes awkward and annoying, and sometimes simple and powerful. The drag-and-drop approach to everything—from the background document pattern to cell formats to the operators for "formulas"—is simple and elegant, but in the end it's more time consuming than simply clicking on a toolbar button without having to drag anything back into the document window. There's a tool palette for almost everything (over 20 basic palettes), so the screen tends to get cluttered quickly. In all, it just makes you wish that you could have some of SS2000's capabilities grafted onto your other spreadsheet software, or a little more of the traditional spreadsheet approach buried in SS2000.

casadyg.com

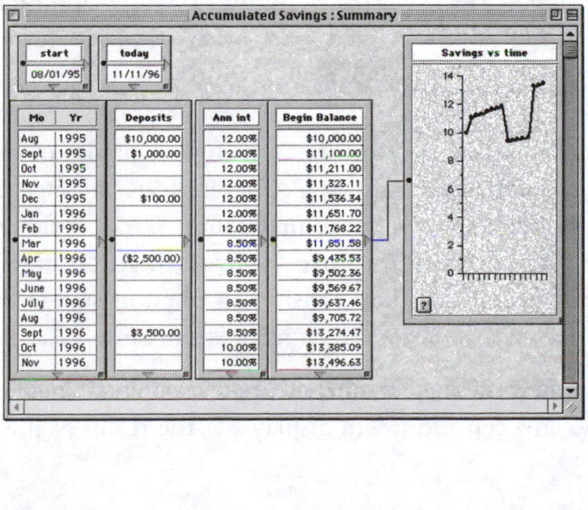

A Spreadsheet 2000 document window, with its separate but interdependent grids.

Spreadsheet Basics

Data entry. To enter information in a spreadsheet cell, you select the cell by clicking in it, and then type the information into an area at the top of the screen variously called a *formula bar* or *edit bar.* To actually enter the information into the selected cell (which is framed with a special border so you can keep track of it), you press Enter or click an Enter button, or just move to another cell. You can enter the data and move to an adjacent cell at the same time by using various keys:

This key enters data and...	*...moves from the current cell to:*
Tab	the cell to the right
Shift Tab	the cell to the left
Return	the cell below
Shift Return	the cell above

Editing entries. You can change the contents of a cell in two ways:

- Select the cell and type something different in it.
- Select the cell, click in the *formula bar* at the top of the window where the cell's contents are displayed, and use standard text editing techniques to change what's there.

No matter how you edit an entry, don't forget to press Return or Enter or click the Enter button to complete it. —CB

Three types of data. There are three types of data you can enter in a cell: text, numbers, and formulas. A spreadsheet automatically recognizes text as anything that's not a number—even strings that are combinations of numbers and text. But you have to specifically indicate when something's a formula, by typing the equal sign as the first character of the formula.

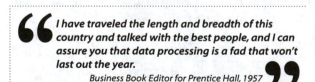

> ***I have traveled the length and breadth of this country and talked with the best people, and I can assure you that data processing is a fad that won't last out the year.***
> *Business Book Editor for Prentice Hall, 1957*

Cell ranges. Cells have names based on their column/row positions: A1, A2, B3, and so on (although there are other ways to refer to single cells, too). But so many formulas depend on groups of cells, called *ranges,* that there's a special way to refer to them, using the names of the cells at their beginning and end. Traditionally, a colon indicates a range, so that A1:A5 describes the first five cells in the first column, A2:G2 describes a section of the second row, and A1:E5 is a five-by-five-cell grid in the upper left corner of the spreadsheet. ClarisWorks insists on the non-standard double period to define a range (A1..A5), but the concept is the same.

Building a formula. A formula can be as simple as an addition problem: enter *=5+2* in a cell and it will display a 7, the result of the formula. But most formulas refer to other cells: if you want to add the numbers that are stored in cells A1 and A2, your formula would be *=A1+A2*. That way, if you change the contents of A1 or A2, the formula result would also change.

But you don't have to type the names of cells in a formula—all you have to do is click on the cell while you're building the formula, and its name is entered into the formula. This is not only fast and convenient, it helps prevent typographical errors, too. When you want to refer to a cell range in a formula, all you have to is drag the mouse from one end of the range to the other, and the range reference will be filled in.

Priority of operations. When you punch numbers into a calculator—a real one or the Mac desk accessory—the numbers are processed in the order you enter them, so 5+3*2 is 16. But in a spreadsheet, certain operations have priority over others and are performed first in a calculation regardless of their position in the formula: exponents have top priority, followed by multiplication and division, and then addition and subtraction. When operations have equal priority, like two division operations, or an addition and a subtraction, they're performed from left to right. In a spreadsheet, 5+3*2 is 11.

You can change normal priorities by using parentheses: operations inside parentheses are performed first. This shows (in bold) which operations are performed for each step of a problem.

Innermost parentheses	5 + (10 + (**6-1**) * 4) / 2
Parentheses, multiplication	5 + (10 + **5 * 4**) / 2
Parentheses	5 + **(10 + 20)** / 2
Division	5 + **30 / 2**
	5 + 15 = 20

It's not all relative. When you refer to a cell in a formula by using its column/row name, the spreadsheet knows that cell's spatial relationship to the current cell (the one with the formula in it). If your formula's in cell B4 and it refers to the range B1:B3, the spreadsheet knows that you've asked it to look at the three cells immediately above the formula. This comes in handy when you copy the formula to cell C4, and it automatically changes to reference C1:C3, the three cells above the new location.

But this standard type of cell referencing, called a *relative reference*, isn't always what you need; sometimes part of a formula needs to refer to a specific cell no matter where you put the formula. For that, you use *absolute referencing* in the formula so the cell reference won't change. Using a dollar sign in the cell's name makes it an absolute reference: \$A\$5, for instance. You can make a cell reference "half" absolute so that the row never changes but the column stays relative, or vice versa: \$A5 or A\$5.

Filling in. The same formula, with only relative cell reference changes, is often used in adjacent cells in a spreadsheet. The little budget spreadsheet shown at the beginning of the chapter, for instance, totals and then averages each of the four columns, and also totals each of the six rows.

There's no need to copy and paste, or drag and drop, formulas that you want to repeat in adjacent cells. Spreadsheets provide Fill commands so you can select a cell with a formula in it, along with a group of cells to its right or below it, and have the formula slapped into every selected cell, with relative cell references in the formula automatically altered along the way. With Fill commands, it takes barely longer to set up sums for 100 columns than it does to do a single column.

Functions and arguments. You don't have to create formulas for everything you want the spreadsheet to calculate. If you want the average of cells A1 through A5, you could use the formula *(A1+A2+A3+A4+A5)/5*—or you could use a built-in spreadsheet *function.* Functions are pre-designed calculations that perform mathematical (and other) operations on the data you supply; the data items, placed inside parentheses, are the function's *arguments.*

So, instead of *A1+A2+A3+A4+A5,* you can add those five cells with the SUM function like this: SUM(A1:A5). And if you want the average, you don't have to sum the cells at all—you just use the AVERAGE function, like this: AVERAGE(A1:A5).

You'll see function names spelled in all caps throughout this chapter, because that's how a spreadsheet displays them. But you don't have to type the capitals: type the function name in lowercase, and it's automatically capitalized when you enter the formula into the cell. (And if it doesn't switch to all caps, you've misspelled it!)

These tips work for both Excel and ClarisWorks, and are likely to work in any other type of spreadsheet software you use. References to the "formula bar" just need to be translated to "edit bar" for use in ClarisWorks.

Generic Spreadsheet Tips

Pay attention to the mouse cursor. Spreadsheets change the mouse pointer to provide visual clues about things you can do. The basic cursors are:

- A white cross (or plus sign) in the spreadsheet area: click to select a cell, row, or column; drag to select multiple cells; or click to add a cell to a formula if the formula bar is active.
- A standard I-beam when it's in the formula bar; click to edit the contents of the formula bar.
- A black, double-arrowed bar when it's between column or row headings; drag to change the width of the column or height of the row.
- A standard arrow pointer when you move it out of the spreadsheet window; use it to work with the window or menus.

In addition to the old standards, Excel and ClarisWorks provide their own special cursors for special procedures. Excel, for instance, has a split-bar, double-arrowed cursor (sounds like a good name for a cattle ranch!) for

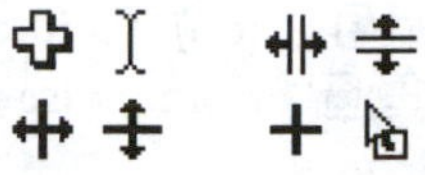

Standard cursors (left) and special ones (right).

opening up hidden rows and columns, and a solid cross for dragging fills for cells; ClarisWorks has a hollow arrow and miniature cell to show when you're going to drag and drop cell contents. —SZA/CB/ML

Working within a selected block. When you select a block of cells, they're all highlighted, but the active one is framed so you can see which one you're actually working with. Using Tab or Return (with or without Shift) will move you around only within the selected area, bouncing you to the beginning of the next row or column in the selected block instead of moving to outside the selection.

I can't believe I entered the whole thing. The cell width and the contents of the adjacent cells determine what's displayed in a cell. A long text entry spills over to the next cell if that cell is empty; otherwise, the text display is truncated to fit in the cell (although the complete text is stored). Long numeric entries in narrow cells are displayed as a series of pound signs (#####).

Quick adding. When you want to add the contents of a cell to a formula, you don't have to type the plus sign and then type the cell's name or click on it for its name to be entered: click on a cell while you're building or editing a formula, and the spreadsheet assumes you want its contents added in, and will enter the plus sign automatically. If you want to add a range to the formula, click in the first cell and then drag to the end of the range; once again, the spreadsheet enters the plus sign for you.

IN THE BEGINNING

There wasn't much software around when the Mac started. It came with MacWrite and MacPaint, and... that's all. But it wasn't long before Microsoft came out with its killer spreadsheet: Multiplan, a Mac-only application.

Multiplan had 63 columns and 255 rows, all identified by numbers. So, a cell's name had two numbers in it, one for the row and one for the column, like this: R4C3. To this very day, Excel offers that as an alternate cell-naming scheme, for users *really* pining for the old days!

Watch out for active formulas. When there's a formula in the selected cell and the formula bar is active, it's all too easy to accidentally alter the formula when what you wanted to do was move to a new cell: you click in the cell where you want to go, and its name gets added to the formula.

If you forget to enter a formula or the changes you've made to it, and you mess it up by mistakenly clicking around, there are two ways to handle it. Using Undo works if you've added only a single cell reference, since it undoes the last thing you did. But clicking the Cancel button in the formula bar (the big X) cancels *all* changes to the cell contents since they first went into the formula bar. (Pressing Esc also works to cancel the changes in both programs, and in Excel you can use ⌘., too). Neither Undo nor any of the cancel options will work if you hit Enter or otherwise enter the altered formula first.

Turn a formula into a text value. If your formula just isn't working, you don't have to delete the whole thing just because the spreadsheet keeps beeping at you, not letting you enter the incorrect formula. Remove the equal sign from the beginning of the formula so that the cell will store it as text until you have a chance to come back to it and figure out what's wrong.

Transposing rows and columns. Spreadsheets have always offered special ways of pasting data, manipulating it slightly from what you copied, through the Paste Special command in the Edit menu. Although Excel offers all sorts of special pastes, ClarisWorks also provides one of the handiest: Transpose.

When you choose the Transpose option in the Paste Special dialog, the row and column information you copied to the Clipboard is pasted so that rows become columns and columns become rows. This is handy when you've filled in the months of the year in column A and then realize you really want them in row 1, across the first twelve columns. But you can also copy a block of cells and transpose the paste so that the entire grid is reversed, as shown in the picture here.

	Heat	Electric	Phone
Jan	35.26	22.36	56.23
Feb	42.69	32.65	45.89
Mar	31.26	35.69	42.31
Apr	15.36	38.36	38.59
May	12.89	42.12	44.88
Jun	8.56	48.64	37.19

	Jan	Feb	Mar	Apr	May	Jun
Heat	[illegible]	42.69	31.26	15.36	12.89	8.56
Electric	22.36	32.65	35.69	38.36	42.12	48.64
Phone	56.23	45.89	42.31	38.59	44.88	37.19

Left, the original data; right, the transposed paste.

May the best width win. Size a column to accommodate its largest entry by double-clicking on the right edge of the column header (the letter at the top of the window). To do this to multiple columns at one time, select them by dragging across the header titles and double-click on the right edge of any one of them.

This works for rows, too, for situations where you may have larger font sizes in some cells across rows: double-click on the bottom edge of the row's name.

Moving formulas. When you use Copy and Paste, or a Fill command, to copy a formula to other cells, the relative references in the formula change, as they're supposed to. But if you use drag and drop (or ClarisWorks' Move option) to move a formula to a new location, the cell references remain as they were in the original. But they're still not absolute references: they don't have dollar signs in their names, and if you copy or Fill them from the new location, the relative references will change as they should.

Naming cells. Every cell in a spreadsheet has a "name" that defines its position in the grid of columns and rows, like A1 in the upper left corner, B2, C3, and so on. But you can give cells, or ranges of cells, names, too, which makes several things easier. For one thing, you can use a Go To command or work with a list of names to jump right to a cell—and it's easier to remember a group of data named SecondQuarter than to remember that it starts at cell J72. And, you can use your cell names in formulas, which makes them both easier to write and easier to read later. (Named cells referenced in formulas are absolute references.)

Basic chart types. With spreadsheets offering a wide range of chart types and styles, it's tempting to go crazy. The colors and styles might be a matter of taste, but keep in mind that certain types of charts are for certain types of data. Here are the four basics:

- A line chart shows how something changes over time, with multiple lines charting multiple items.
- A bar chart is useful for comparing differing items either with no time component or sharing the same time component.
- A pie chart is for showing how the whole (whatever) is apportioned to the components; it shows the components in relation to each other and to the whole, but gives absolutely no indication of how large the "whole" actually is.
- The stacked bars in a stacked bar chart are each somewhat like a pie chart because they show you the relationship of the parts to the whole; but stacked bars also let you compare different "wholes" and see the overall size or numbers of each. But stacked bars can be misleading because each component starts only where the last left off. In the picture here, for instance (the stacked bar chart is in the lower right), the middle segments of the first and last bars end at approximately the same spot, but the value of the segment in the third bar is about twice that of the one in the first bar.

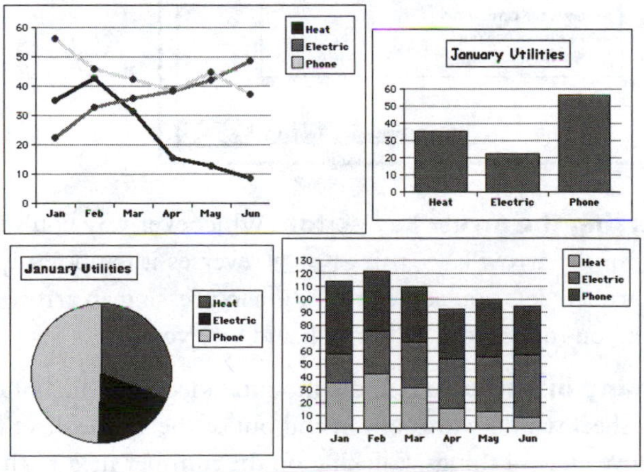

The same basic information presented in different types of charts.

ClarisWorks Tips

These tips were tested for ClarisWorks 5. Most will work in the previous version, too.

ClarisWorks may have been renamed "AppleWorks" by the time you read this!

Moving Around and Selecting Things

Selecting all and almost all. A shortcut for selecting the entire spreadsheet is clicking in the blank box at the top left, where the row and column headers intersect; this is handy if you're working with the mouse instead of the keyboard (when you could just use ⌘A for Select All).

There's also a selection option named Select All Data: Option-click in the blank box, and everything from cell A1 to the farthest cell that contains data is selected. Holding down Option also changes the Edit menu's Select All command to Select All Data.

General ClarisWorks tips ... Chapter 16

Setting the arrow key action. By default, using the arrow keys moves you around in the entry bar for editing cell contents. But you can change that through the Edit menu's Preferences command, and make the arrow keys move you from one cell to another instead. (While you're in there, you can change the action of the Enter key, too.)

Despite the fact that the Preferences window's title refers to the current spreadsheet, the preferences are set for the entire program.

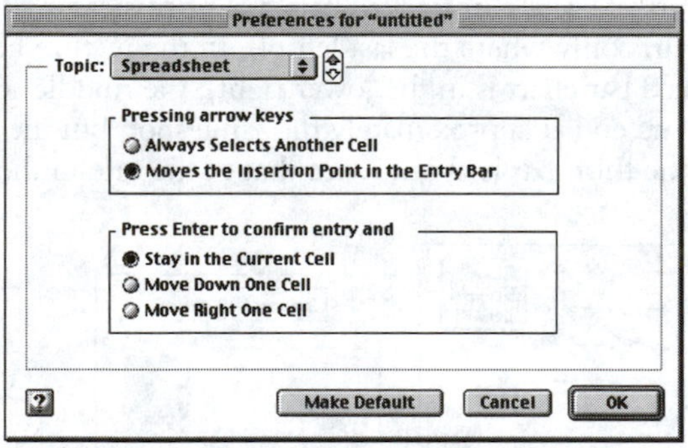

Reversing the arrow key action. Whichever way you've set the preferences for the arrow keys, using Option reverses it temporarily. So, if an arrow key normally lets you edit in the edit bar, pressing an arrow key with Option will let you move from cell to cell, and vice versa.

Zooming in and out. Use the mountain icons in the bottom left of the spreadsheet window to zoom in and out of the spreadsheet for a close-up or birds-eye view of things. Clicking on the number next to the icons gives you a pop-up menu that lets you select the size you want without having to work your way up or down to it.

Using the Other item from the zoom pop-up lets you specify any percentage you want. If you type in a number other than one on the original list, it's usually used as the basis for the zoom increment for the next few clicks of the zoom icons. So, enter 10 as the percentage and click "zoom in" and you'll get a 20 percent view, and then 40 percent, then 80 percent, and so on.

Entering and Editing Data

Activating the edit bar. If you're working from the keyboard and have selected a cell, you don't have to reach for the mouse to click in the edit bar to activate it so you can edit the cell contents. Pressing Option→ or Option↑ puts the insertion point at the end of the cell contents in the edit bar, while Option← or Option↓ puts it at the beginning of the contents.

Auto-enter absolute references. If you're clicking or dragging on cells to enter their names into a formula, you can make the references absolute by ⌘Option-clicking or dragging on the cells.

Use Fill Special. Need to enter a series of days or months, or even numbers, into adjacent cells? Click in the cell that contains the first month of the series and drag to the right or down as far as you want to go. Then choose Fill Special from the Calculate menu, and select the series that you want; ClarisWorks is usually able to figure out which one you want and suggests it as the default. —SZA/CB

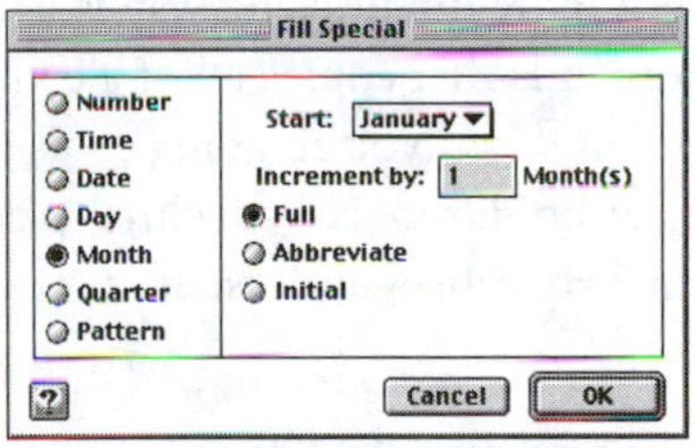

The Fill Special dialog.

Moving without drag and drop. You can move a selected cell (or block of cells) by ⌘Option-clicking wherever you want the selection moved. As with a drag-and-drop move, this doesn't change any of the cell references in formulas you may be moving.

Editing the formula. When the edit bar is active, and the arrow keys are set to work for editing instead of for cell selection, it's pretty obvious that you can use ←→ to move a character at a time in the editing area. But you can also use ↓↑ to jump to the beginning or end of the formula.

Paste function shortcut. When the Paste Function dialog is open, you can jump to the function you want by typing the first few letters of its name.

Here are a few other tidbits relating to the Paste Function command:

- Open the Paste Function dialog with the command in the Edit menu or by clicking the *fx* button in the tool bar.
- Use ↓↑ to select the next or previous function in the list.

- Use Page Up Page Down to scroll up and down in the list, and Home End to jump to the top or bottom of the list; none of these keys changes the currently selected function.
- If you're not exactly sure of the function you need, narrow down the list by using the pop-up menu at the top of the dialog.

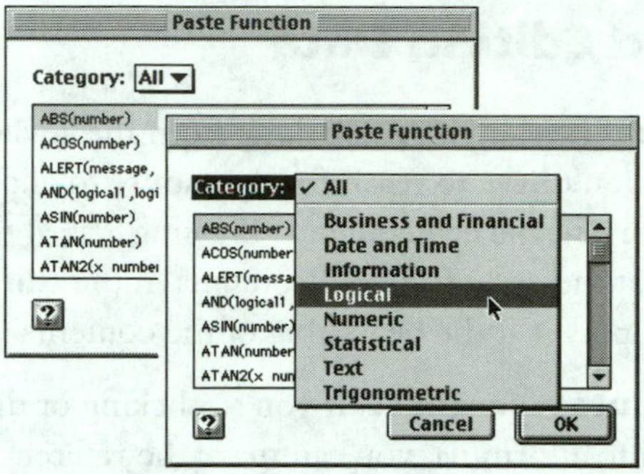

Use the Paste Function menu to narrow down the list when you're not sure of the function you need.

Formatting

Quick formatting. There are two ways to apply formats to cells that are much faster than applying them individually. One way is to use the Copy Format and Paste Format commands that copies all of a cell's formats so they can be pasted into other cells. But when you're going to use a certain group of formats over and over again (say, bold, red, two-decimal-place numbers), create a style that can be stored in a stylesheet and use it on any cells that need that formatting.

Stylesheet palette tips
Chapter 16

Splitting windows. The split bars work in ClarisWorks spreadsheet windows the same way they work in almost any window that provides them: drag the black bar above the vertical scroll arrow (or to the left of the horizontal scroll arrow), and the window splits into panes with their own scroll bars. It's a great way to compare data in rows or columns that are far apart under normal circumstances. Drag the split bars back to their starting positions to unsplit the window.

There are two splitting shortcuts: double-click in the split bar in its original position to split the window exactly in half. To unsplit the window, you can double-click in the split bar or anywhere along the split line itself.

Locking row and column titles. When you split a window using the split bars, all the panes you create can still scroll, although some are interdependent and scroll together when you're using four panes instead of two. But when you want to "freeze" some rows or columns in place so that you can scroll the rest of the spreadsheet and keep the titles in view, you don't have to split the window at all. Instead, select the row(s) or column(s) you want as titles, and choose Lock Title Position from the Options menu. The gridlines will change from dotted to solid for the titles—and you can still split the window in either direction.

And there's a bonus: when you lock title positions on a multi-page spreadsheet, the titles will appear on every printed page.

Hide and seek. Hiding a column is a good way to get something out of your way temporarily—and it's an even better way to get a group of columns out of your way; it's a good alternative to splitting the window in many situations.

To hide a single column, grab the right edge of the column header and drag it to the left, into its left edge. When you want to hide multiple adjacent columns, it's easier to select them all and use the Column Width command to assign a width of zero to all of them at the same time.

You can show a column again by dragging the column header divider (the one where you initially dragged to hide the column) back out to the right. To show multiple hidden columns, you don't have to resort to the Column Width command or drag repeatedly: select the columns before and after the hidden ones and then re-size either one of them by dragging; that will resize all the selected columns, including the hidden ones, to the new width.

Rows can be hidden, too, by dragging the bottom edge of the row title up into its top edge. All the other details work, too, except that you'll be using the Row Height command instead of Column Width to work with multiple rows.

Your only clue to the fact that there are hidden rows or columns in the spreadsheet is that there will be missing letters or numbers in the headers.

Charts

Reversing the axes. I don't know about you, but it seems to me that more often than not, the numbers in my spreadsheet are arranged the way I want them but a quick chart comes out backwards, with the X and Y axes the opposite of what I want.

You don't have to copy your spreadsheet data and paste it transposed to switch the rows and columns, and then make another chart. Just edit the existing chart, using the General screen in the Chart Options dialog, clicking either the Rows or Columns button under "Series in."

Transpose the X and Y axes of a chart by using the "Series in" buttons in the Chart Option dialog's General screen.

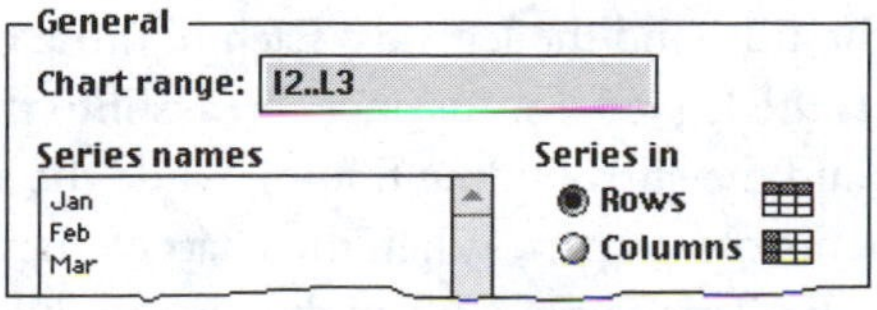

Shortcut to chart edits. When you want to edit an existing chart, you can select it and choose Chart Options from the Edit menu, or you can just double-click on the chart itself. As a bonus for all that effort, you can go directly to the part of the Chart Options dialog you need by double-clicking on the right spot in the chart: double-clicking within the charted information takes you to the Series screen; double-clicking on the title or series legend takes you to the Labels screen; double-clicking on the labels for either axis takes you to the Axis screen—with either the X or Y axis button already selected, based on which axis you clicked on!

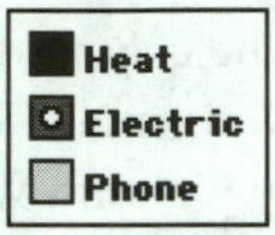

Adjusting colors. To change the color used in a chart element, click on the color sample next to the series name in the legend. You'll see a little bullet in the sample that indicates it's selected. Open the tool panel and use the Fill palette (by the paint bucket) to select a new color.

If you're going to print the charts in black and white or grayscale, stick with shades of gray as your chart colors so you can be reasonably sure what's going to be printed: you may find a color like yellow drops out entirely and "prints" as white, and you can't predict what shade of gray red will turn out to be. If there are more than three different colors in the chart, consider using patterns as fills for pie or bar charts to further differentiate the elements; for line charts, try changing the thickness of lines or the shape of the data points.

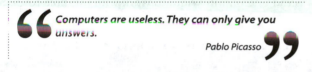

> *Computers are useless. They can only give you answers.*
>
> *Pablo Picasso*

Editing a chart as a picture. You can make really major changes to a chart by turning it into a picture and editing it as a drawing. Keep in mind that the *picture* of the chart is no longer linked to the data, so make sure your data is set before you spend a lot of time on editing the visual end of things.

First, turn the chart into a picture: Select the chart window and use the Copy command. You can then paste the chart into a new document, or just as a floating window that's stored with the spreadsheet the same way the original is stored. If you want the picture floating in the same spreadsheet, it's even easier to just Option-drag a copy out of the original chart window.

Once the chart is a picture, use the Ungroup Picture command to separate the elements of the chart. You'll have to use it at least twice, because the first ungrouping merely separates the major components like the grid background, the bars (or slices), the title, and the legends. Each of those components can be broken down further: the legend, for instance, breaks into the text and the little sample color boxes (and the surrounding frame), while the slices of the pie or the stacked bar elements come apart. When the chart elements are separated, you can edit them with ClarisWorks built-in drawing tools.

If you've turned your basic chart into a thing of beauty and then realize you need to change the data behind it, you won't always have to re-do everything: change the data and the original chart, make a picture out of the changed chart, copy the changed element, and paste it into the chart you've already edited, making further changes as necessary.

Creating a pictogram. It's easy to create a pictogram—a chart where little pictures are used to form the "bars" that normally stand for the amounts in a series (although it's not easy to create a *good-looking* pictogram). First, find the picture you want to use for the pictogram and copy it to the Clipboard. Then:

1. Select the data in the spreadsheet.
2. Press ⌘M to open the chart dialog.
3. Click on the pictogram chart type.
4. Click the Series button.
5. Click in the Sample box.
6. Paste your artwork into the box.

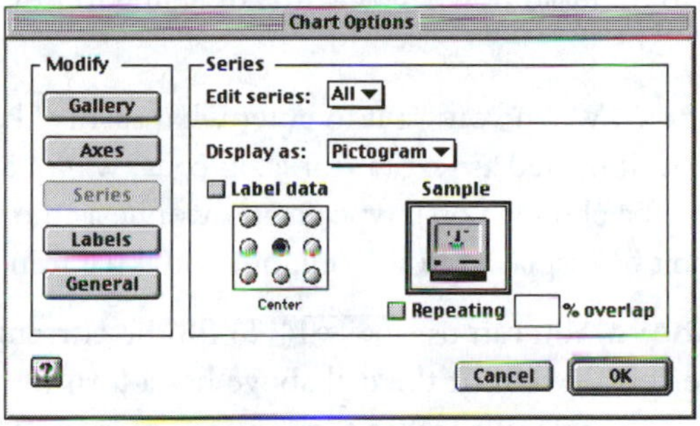

Paste your own image in the Sample box for a pictogram.

The picture will be stretched to fit the height and width of what would normally be a bar in the chart. You can adjust for some of the distortion by changing the overall size of the chart: just grab a corner of the chart window and drag it to resize the chart.

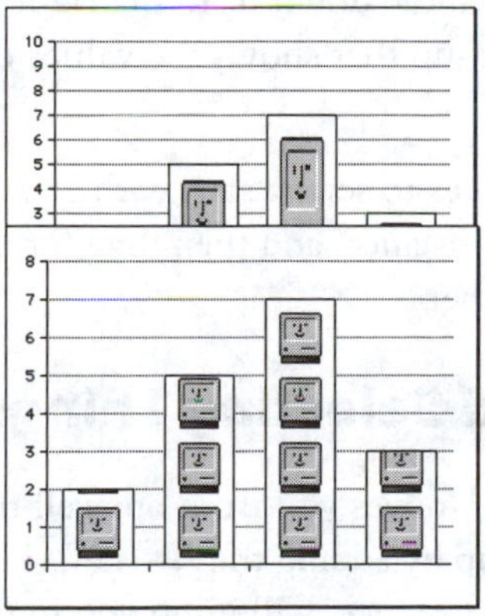

The picture is distorted to fit the size of the bar (top). A picture can be repeated inside the bar, but the number of pictures has nothing to do with the number that the bar represents (bottom).

If you use a small picture, you can use it as a repeating element in the chart bar instead of having it stretched to fit: click the Repeating checkbox beneath the sample picture in the Chart Options dialog. But that has its own problems. First, the width of the picture is still distorted inside the bars unless you size the chart to accommodate the width of the picture. More importantly, the image is used as many times as necessary to fill the bar size—the number of little pictures has nothing to do with the number the bar represents, which adds up to a very misleading chart. Use ClarisWorks pictograms with great caution!

Excel Tips

These tips were tested for Excel 98.

Entering and Editing Information

Edit directly in the cell. You don't have to reach for the mouse after you've selected a cell from the keyboard and want to edit its contents: press ⌘U to activate cell for editing, with the insertion point placed at the end of its contents. If you know you want to edit the cell contents and you're selecting it with the mouse instead of the keyboard, double-click on it to both select it and activate it for editing.

Move cells with drag and drop. You can drag a cell or a range by its border to move it to a new position. Hold down Option while dragging to copy it to the new location. Hold down Shift while dragging to insert it between other cells. —SZA/EC

Numbers as text. When you want to enter what seems like a number or calculation but want it treated as text (as for a zip code, where a leading zero would otherwise be chopped off), type an apostrophe as the first character. The apostrophe won't be displayed in the cell, but you'll see it in the formula bar.

Copy from above. You can use Control " to fill the current cell with the contents of the cell above it. If the cell above has a formula in it, you can copy the *result* of the formula rather than the formula itself by pressing Control Shift " instead.

Use AutoFill. Whenever you need a "series" in your spreadsheet—numbers, days, months, and so on—you can enter the first item and let Excel auto-fill the rest. Put the information into the first cell, pressing Enter to enter it, and then drag the fill handle down or to the right as far as you want the series to go. You'll get a pop-up that shows the values of the cells you're dragging across.

Excel is really smart when it comes to series: start with two selected cells whose contents are 1 and 3, for instance, and then drag for a fill, and it will suggest 5 and 7 as the next numbers.

Moving Around and Selecting Things

Leapfrogging. Using ←→↑↓ moves you from one cell to another, but you can leapfrog from group to group by adding the ⌘ key, skipping over blank cells. The first use of ⌘↓, for instance, will jump you to the bottom of the block of used cells you're currently in. The second press of ⌘↓ will jump over any blank cells and land you in the next used cell in that row.

For really big leaps, you can use the Home and End keys, which jump you to the first (upper left) and last (lower right) cells of the worksheet without changing the selected cells. If you want to select the first or last cell, use ⌘-Home and ⌘-End instead.

Noncontiguous selections. You can select cells or blocks of cells that aren't next to each other (in order to apply formatting, say) by selecting the first cell or block, and then holding down ⌘ while you select subsequent cells.

> *Computer: One who computes.*
>
> *Webster's Collegiate Dictionary, 1929*

Moving a selection block. If you've selected a block of five cells in a row to apply some formatting, and then want to select another five cells two rows down to apply some more formatting, you don't have to reach for the mouse, because you can move a selection block without affecting cell contents. Option-Tab moves the block to the right and Shift-Option-Tab moves it to the left, while Shift-Option-Return and Option-Return moves it up and down.

Selecting referenced cells. If the current cell has a formula in it, you can select all the cells to which the formula directly refers by pressing ⌘-[. Pressing ⌘-Shift-[instead will select all cells even indirectly referred to in the formula.

Formatting Cells and Sheets

Basic formatting from the keyboard. You can apply all the basic number formatting choices to a cell by using keyboard commands. All the commands start with Control-Shift and most use a key that's easy to remember for the format:

Number format	**Control-Shift *and...***
General	~
Currency	$
Percentage	%
Exponential	^
Date	#
Time	@
Two decimal places, 1000 separator, and - for negatives	!

Copying cell formats. A cell's format includes text formatting (like font, size, and style), alignment (like left or centered), and number formats (like dollar signs and the number of decimals). It's easy to copy a cell's formatting to other cells:

- Use the Format Painter tool (the paintbrush): click in the cell whose format you want to copy, click on the paintbrush, and click in the cell (or drag across multiple cells) with the paintbrush.

- To paint non-contiguous cells with the paint brush, double-click on the tool button so the formats "stick" to the brush after using them on the first group of cells. To "let go" of the brush, click the button once more.
- Skip the Format Painter tool completely: press Control C to copy a cell's format, and Control V to paste the format anywhere else.

Hide and seek. Hiding a column or row is a good way to get something out of your way temporarily—and it's an even better way to get a group of columns out of your way. It's a good alternative to splitting the window in many situations. The description here applies to columns, but you can do the same things with rows.

To hide a single column, grab the right edge of the column header and drag it to the left, into the left edge. When you want to hide multiple adjacent columns, select them all and drag the right edge of any one of the headers.

The only way you'll know that there are hidden columns is if you notice some letters missing in the header. Excel's visual clue to a hidden column—a slight shading in the header divider—is so subtle as to be nearly useless. But you don't need the Unhide command in the Format menu's Column submenu to show the columns again—you can just use the mouse.

To show a single column again, just drag the divider where the hidden column is to open it up again. You can't drag directly on the divider, or you'll change the width of the showing column; but if you place the cursor to the right of divider, you'll see it change to a split bar with double arrows, and you can drag at that point to reveal the hidden column.

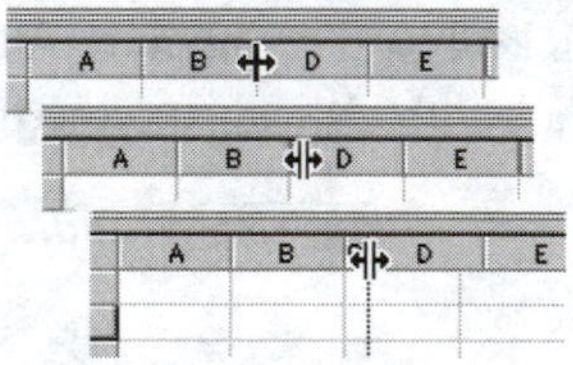

Top, the normal cursor means you'll be changing the width of column B; middle, the special cursor means you can show the hidden column; bottom, dragging open the hidden column.

The quickest way to reveal multiple hidden columns is to select the columns on either side of the hidden group, place the cursor to the right of the center divider, and drag when you get the special cursor: all the columns will open.

Inserting cells. You can insert cells individually, in groups, or as full rows or columns just by clicking in the right spots—no Insert dialog necessary:

- Option-click in a cell to insert a new cell above it, shifting all the others in the column down by a row.
- Shift Option-click the last cell in a selection to insert as many cells as are in the selection.
- Select an entire row or column by clicking in in its header and press ⌘I to insert a new row or column above or to the left of the selected one.
- Option-click on a row number or column letter to insert a new row or column above or to the left of where you click.

Seeing red (or green, or bold or...) You can apply conditional formatting to any cell so that, for instance, if a number dips below a certain point it will appear in red—and you don't have to write a formula in the cell to get the formatting. Simply use the Conditional Formatting command from the Format menu and define the conditions that should trigger the format change that will override the cell's basic formatting. The picture here doesn't look like much because this book isn't printed in color, but the definition changes the color of the font in the cell to blue if the value is in the range -10 to 10 (the "between" definition is actually inclusive of the end values you define), and uses red if the value is below -10.

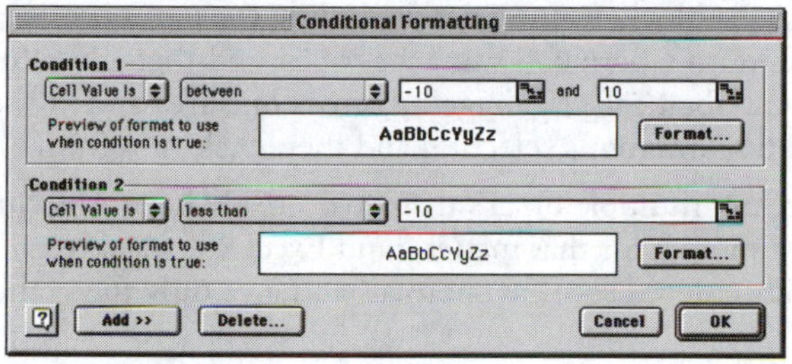

Formulas

Reversing references. If you've already entered a cell reference in a formula and want to change the reference type, select the cell reference and press ⌘T until Excel places the absolute reference dollar signs where you want them; it will cycle through applying it to just the row, just the column, and both row and column. —SZA/EC

Don't argue with me. When you forget which arguments come in which order for a function, start the formula with the equal sign and the function name, then press Control Shift A: all the argument names will be filled in, as if you had used the Paste Function command. So, type *=PMT*, press Control Shift A, and you'll get *=PMT(rate,nper,pv,fv,type)* in the formula bar, with the first argument selected so you can fill in a value or cell reference.

If you need more help than just the argument list, press Control A after you type the function name and you'll get a Wizard that explains the function.

Edit a range in a formula. When you're editing a formula that refers to one or more cell ranges, the range names are color-coded in the formula bar to match special frames around the ranges in the spreadsheet (the frames appear only when you're working on the formula). To change a range, grab the handle on the outline and change it to encompass more or fewer cells—the formula automatically changes to reference the new range.

Use AutoSum to add columns or rows. Select a cell at the bottom of a list of numbers and click the AutoSum button (the one with the Σ on it), and

Excel will create a SUM formula for you, usually guessing correctly as to which cells you want summed. A single click of the button will display the formula so you can check it or edit it, while a double-click will simply enter the formula and display the answer. (Or, press ⌘Shift T to trigger a "click" of the button.)

That's the basic AutoSum function, but you can take it a little further:

- Select more than one cell (in your Totals row, for instance) and click AutoSum to enter the SUM formula in all the rows instead of your having to fill it across.
- AutoSum rows and columns at the same time in either of two ways. select the block of numbers, including the empty cells to the right and at the bottom where you want the totals, and then click AutoSum. Or, select just the Total cells by dragging across one area and ⌘-dragging the other for a discontiguous selection and then click AutoSum.
- AutoSum multiple blocks that have already been AutoSummed (or manually summed, for that matter), and Excel knows enough to ignore the already entered sums as subtotals and give only the grand totals. —SZA/EC

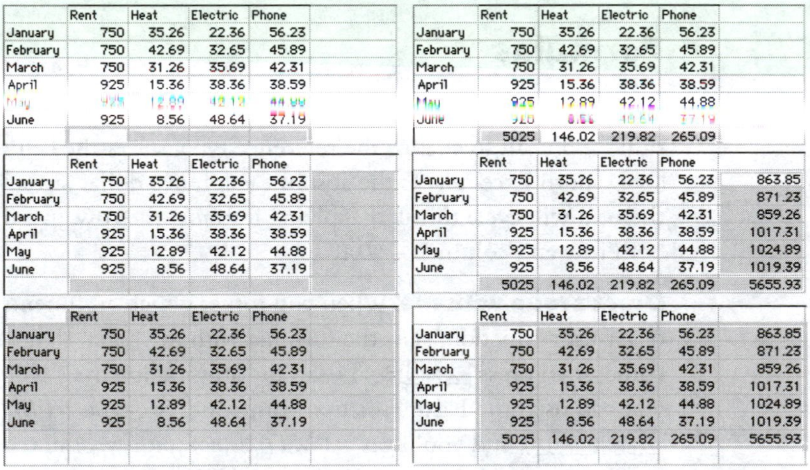
Rent Heat Electric Phone
January 750 35.26 22.36 56.23
February 750 42.69 32.65 45.89
March 750 31.26 35.69 42.31
April 925 15.36 38.36 38.59
May 925 12.89 42.12 44.88
June 925 8.56 48.64 37.19
5025 146.02 219.82 265.09
863.85
871.23
859.26
1017.31
1024.89
1019.39
5655.93

Before and after AutoSum. Top, selecting the cells for the column totals; middle, a discontiguous selection; bottom, selecting an entire block.

Miscellaneous

Contextual menus. Excel 98 provides a wide array of contextual menus that pop up almost anywhere you summon them; you can get the menu by holding down Control and clicking someplace (as you can almost anywhere in OS 8) or by using the traditional Excel combination of holding down ⌘Option while you click. Because the menus are contextual, they'll change based on where you click: in an empty cell, a filled cell, a row or column label, the toolbar, and even on the title bar of the active window.

> **More memory is on many a Mac owner's wish list. When you use Excel a sizable portion of the Mac's 512K of RAM is taken up by the program.**
> *Macworld, February 1986*

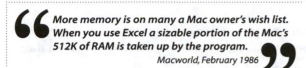

Changing the scope of a chart. When you select a chart on your worksheet, the area that contains the charted data is surrounded by a special frame. To quickly change the contents of the chart—say, add or delete a row or column of data—just grab the handle in the lower right of the frame and drag it to surround a different range of cells.

If you select specific parts of the chart, the cells that define those parts are framed and can be adjusted in the same way.

Cycle through workbooks. If you have more than one workbook open, you don't have to use the Windows menu to go from one to another: pressing ⌘M takes you to the next workbook window and ⌘Shift M takes you to the previous one.

Localized and general scrolling. When you use a window's scroll boxes, they work in relation not to the whole worksheet, but to the *used* area of the worksheet. So, if the outermost cells you've used are in row 100 and column Z, dragging the vertical scroll box to the center of the scroll bar will move you to row 50, while centering the horizontal scroll box will let you see row M.

If you want the scroll boxes to relate to the entire worksheet instead of the used area, hold down Shift while you drag them.

Tear-off palettes. When you use a toolbar button's drop-down menu by clicking on the little arrow next to it, and the drop-down has a gray pattern along its top or side edge, that means the drop-down can be torn off as a separate palette: with the mouse button still down from pressing on the arrow, just drag away from the tool button to free the palette.

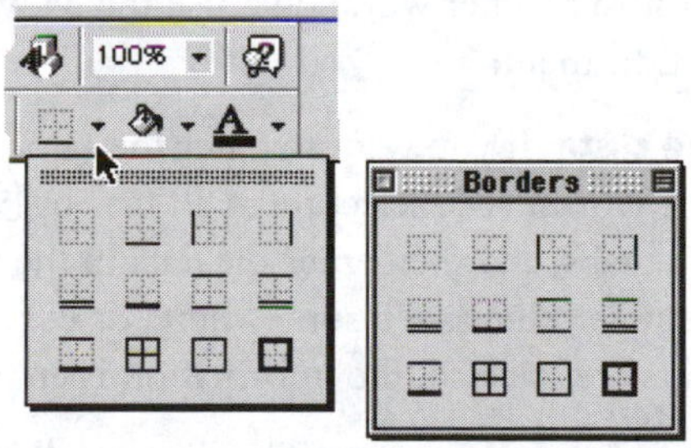

Tearing off a palette from a toolbar button.

The hidden Copy command. You can copy a selected section of the spreadsheet to the Clipboard as a PICT graphic (which will include gridlines, and row and column headings) that can be pasted into any program as a graphic. Just hold down Shift when you open the Edit menu, and the Copy Picture command will be in the menu.

Worksheets

Rename sheets. You can change the name of a worksheet in an Excel workbook by double-clicking on the tab for the sheet to select its name, and then typing the new name in the tab.

Flipping through worksheets. You can go from one worksheet to another without reaching for the mouse: use Option→ and Option← to move to the next and the previous worksheet.

Selecting multiple worksheets. You can select more than one worksheet at a time to perform certain global operations like deleting the worksheets, running a spell check, or turning off all the gridlines. (A selected tab gets a white background, which is a little opposite of what you'd expect, but they're gray in their normal state.)

- To select multiple worksheets, click on the tab of any one, and Shift-click on another; all the worksheets in between those two will also be selected.
- To select noncontiguous worksheets, ⌘-click on their tabs.
- To select all worksheets, Control-click on any tab and use the Select All Sheets command from the pop-up contextual menu.

Inserting multiple worksheets. You can insert more than one new worksheet at a time by selecting several existing worksheets and then using the Worksheet command from the Insert menu; it will insert as many worksheets as you already have selected.

Moving and copying worksheets. You can re-order worksheets by simply dragging them by their tabs to their new positions. You can make a copy of a worksheet by holding down Option as you drag the tab.

To copy a worksheet into another workbook, use the Move or Copy Sheet command from the Edit menu.

Entering the same data. If you want to enter the same information in the same cell for multiple worksheets, select them all first by Shift-clicking or ⌘-clicking on their name tabs, and then enter the data in the top worksheet. You can type data into a single cell, paste it somewhere, or use a Fill command; as long as multiple sheets are selected, the information is entered on every one.

Using the worksheet scroll arrows. The four scroll arrows at the bottom left of each workbook window control the worksheet tabs when you have so many that they're not all displayed at the same time. (Although you can use the special split bar to split the bottom area of the window between the tabs and the window's scroll controls.) You can scroll one tab at a time with the inner arrows, or jump to the beginning or the end of the group of tabs with the outer arrows.

But there are also two hidden tricks with these scroll arrows. Shift-click on either of the inner arrows to scroll the tabs forward or backward in a group (the group is the number of tabs that you can see at one time). Control-click on any of the arrows to get a pop-up list of all the worksheets; select one to jump to it.

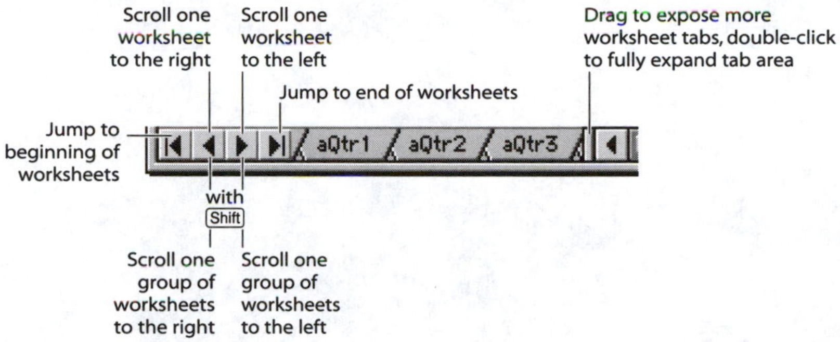

18

Databases

In This Chapter

About Databases

Database Basics

Basic concepts and terminology. A database is basically an electronic version of an index-card filing system. Every index card is a *record;* every discrete piece of information on the card—what you'd put on each line of the card—is a *field;* the complete collection of cards is a *file*, or the database itself. (Sometimes "database" gets a little muddy, since it's both the file and a term for the database *program,* as in "FileMaker is a database.")

Database programs let you print *reports* that make lists of the information on all the records, even tallying numbers and statistics. And they provide a special kind of field you can use on records, called *calculated fields*, that perform calculations based on the contents of other fields on the record.

Flat-file versus relational. The difference between a flat-file and a relational database program is in the way information is shared between the database files the program creates. Flat-file databases create independent database files that aren't linked to any other files; a relational database can look up information from another file to use it in the current file, and even alter the data in some other file based on the one you're working with.

Say you're making a list of products we mention in the Bible in a flat-file database. If there are five products from Microsoft, you have to make five records, and each time, you'd be entering the basic Microsoft information (name, address, email, phone, and so on) all over again. It takes lots of time, and the file size is bigger because of the repeated information. Then, when you want a list of all the companies that were mentioned, you wind up with Microsoft listed five times. If you work solely in a company-based file, you'd have one record for each company but some will have a single product listed, some will have a half-dozen or more—and then the products are difficult to list or look up.

With a relational setup, though, you'd have one file for companies and another one for products. You'd set it up so that if you entered the name Microsoft on a record in the Product file, the database would look in the Company file where Microsoft's information is stored, and import the address, email, and so on automatically so you could see it on the product's record. And, if you set it up right, you don't have to go to the Company database to enter a new company—entering it on a product's record would automatically create a new record in the other database.

FileMaker Pro. There's no doubt about it: **FileMaker Pro** ($200, FileMaker, Inc.) is the most popular Mac database around, and with good reason: it's easy to use, has a beautiful interface, and yet there's incredible power lurking just below the surface, in its relational and script capabilities.

FileMaker Pro

For the most mundane of database tasks—a name and address file, say—FileMaker's a cinch even for beginners. You create a few fields, drag them around in layout mode, and then work with them in Browse mode. The Layout tools include just enough graphics tools that you can make an attractive layout for screen or print purposes, and you'll find grids, guides, and alignment commands to help everything line up.

filemaker.com

As you move up from simple databases, you'll find flexible, powerful features before you even get to scripting or relational capabilities: "container" fields for sound, graphics, and even movies; global fields that contain the same information on every record; an incredible range of functions for calculated fields; easy-to-set-up reports with all sorts of summaries and subsummaries available; and layout buttons that you can assign specific actions to without any scripting.

Another of FileMaker's advantages is that so many people use it: it's easy to find help, whether on-line, in person, or in magazines, books and newsletters. Don't let its ease-of-use and elegance fool you: this is a heavy-duty database that can satisfy the vast majority of business and personal users.

claris.com

The ClarisWorks database. If **ClarisWorks** ($100) came bundled with your Mac, or you bought it for its word processor or other functions, you already have a database that might be all you need. It's a straightforward, flat-file database that's easy to use, although, it doesn't have as much in common with FileMaker Pro as you might expect, considering their common parentage. (Although currently they come from different companies, since some Claris products, including ClarisWorks, have been sucked back into Apple, and others spun off into the re-named FileMaker, Inc.)

The ClarisWorks database offers plenty of input controls: checkboxes, radio buttons, and pop-up menus and lists. There are lots of different approaches to finding things, and you can store search criteria for searches that you do often. It's easy to make lists, labels, and reports.

acius.com

4th Dimension. ACI US's **4th Dimension** ($275) is a full-featured, cross-platform relational database that is well suited for even the most demanding applications. Users can start by creating basic databases with limited functionality and have plenty of room for change as their needs and proficiency grow. For experienced users and developers, there's a wealth of tools and features—including a high-powered programming language—for creating sophisticated custom applications. The **4th Dimension Desktop** package ($475) includes a compiler to turn a database into a standalone program.

Relationships in 4D are drawn (using a connect-the-dots metaphor) and displayed graphically, making them easily understood. You can also create subfiles (a separate file that is associated with a particular record) to keep track of performance reviews, revisions, or other data that may be present on some records but absent on others.

It's telling that in the last edition of this book, we reported that this powerhouse program was $875; now it's $275. In an arena dominated by the ever-more-powerful yet sleek FileMaker Pro, users just aren't willing to pay big bucks for a program whose advanced features are difficult to learn. That 4th Dimension isn't a program for novices isn't necessarily bad; a program with the power to handle complex data requirements often suffers in ease of use. —SZA/JL

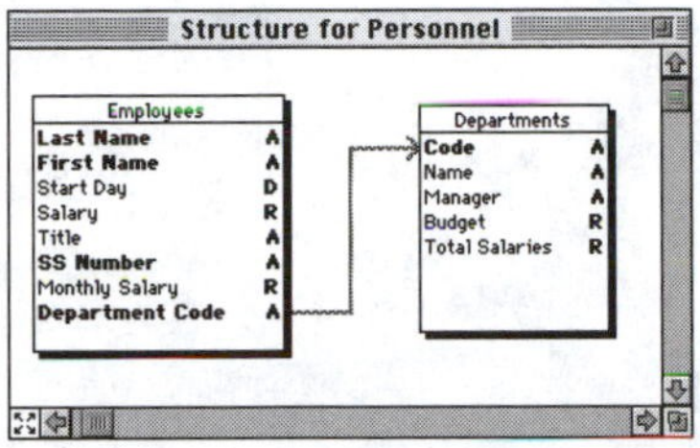

You can create and display relationships graphically in 4th Dimension.

Panorama. ProVue Development's **Panorama** ($400) takes a spreadsheet-style interface and adds full multiuser capabilities, an integrated word processor, a snappy forms generator, real security, AppleScript awareness, and a programming language that includes a much-needed interactive debugger. Panorama's long-standing claim to fame is its speed, which comes from loading the entire database into RAM, even though it's a fully relational program.

Each field can be edited with the program's word processor; you can format and style text to your heart's content. This makes it easier to build meaningful forms and reports, as well as fancier interfaces. Interfaces are further improved thanks to an interface engine that ProVue calls SuperObject. You can use it to create lists, menus, scalable text and pictures, buttons, and matrix objects (like schedules, multiple column lists, or calendars) without having to program. —SZA/DC

provue.com

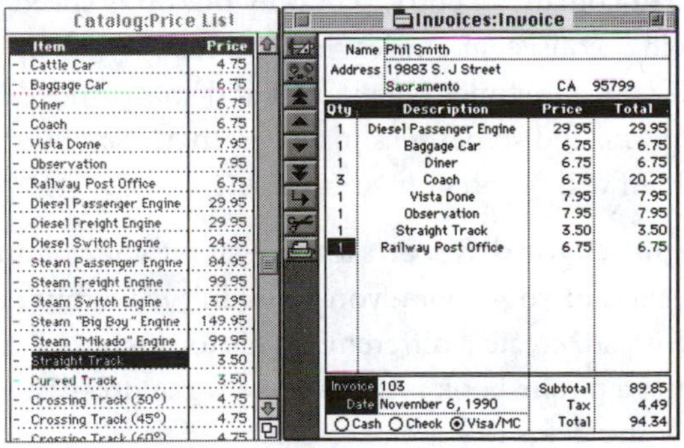

While not a relational database program, Panorama can link databases via procedures. Clicking on an item in the price list (left) automatically generates a new line item in the current invoice in the Invoices database (right).

Visual FoxPro. Long known as the speed demon of Mac database programs, FoxPro's current incarnation, **Visual FoxPro** ($500, Microsoft), is a cross-platform, high-end, heavy-duty relational database manager with full object-orientation and integrated client-server capabilities. (How's that for an opening sentence?)

microsoft.com

But it's hard to understand why Microsoft continues to offer this product, since its Access database is included in the Windows version of its Office suite; as yet there's not only no indication of its being dropped but evidence of its continued development and support. However, considering its price and the level of expertise needed to get at its potential, this is a product for only a tiny fraction of the Mac market. —SZA/SS

General Tips

Database Design

What's coming out, not what's going in. In the database consulting I do—sometimes clients just need some help, sometimes they want me to develop the database myself—I always advise users to start by thinking what information they want to get *out* of the database. Focusing on what you want out of it, and *how* you want it out, helps define what you need to put in.

If, for instance, you're going to want a list of people's names alphabetized by last name, then you'd better plan to put the names in with first and last names in separate fields. Or, if you do bulk mailings, the zip code needs to be in a separate field, which is not necessary in a smaller database of names and addresses.

Use all the data entry control available. Almost all databases offer some help in keeping your data accurate and consistent. Use data-entry control options to let you select values from a list, mark checkboxes or radio buttons, automatically enter default data, restrict data to a certain value or range, or insist that a field contain an entry. Not only does this speed up the data entry, but you'll avoid inconsistent entries that will really mess up search and sorting procedures. If you sometimes type in *MA* and sometimes *MASS* and sometimes *Massachusetts,* and sometimes maybe even *Massachussetts,* finding things and sorting them will be a nightmare. —SZA/EC

Different layouts for different uses. Even if your monitor is so big it touches both sides of your room, you shouldn't try to put every single field in each layout. Instead, create a different layout for each use—one for data entry, one for creating a phone book printout, one for address labels, and so on—and show only the fields that are necessary.

If you do have many fields in a layout, use background colors (or gray shades) to distinguish different areas; framing related fields in a rectangle or rounded rectangle is another way to make a potentially confusing layout easier to deal with. —SZA/EC

Field Definition and Manipulation

Input fields and formatted fields. It's so much easier to just type in 10 digits for a phone number and let the database format them into something like 123/456-1234. Not only do you save input time, you'll have consistency, with spaces, dashes, and slashes in the same spots on each record.

If your database doesn't let you define an "output" format for a field—and some of the most popular ones don't—it's easy enough to create a work-around: create one field for the input (PhoneIN, for instance), and another, calculated field (PhoneFMT) that takes the information from the first field, formats it correctly, and displays it on the screen.

Formatting ZIP codes. Make sure that ZIP code fields are defined as text rather than number fields. A numeric ZIP code field will strip the leading zero from ZIPs like 07461 and may perform a subtraction on 07461-8976. Since text fields can contain text *or* numbers, you don't have to worry that leading zeros will disappear, either. (The same caveat goes for telephone fields, where 555-1212 might be treated as a math problem.)

Use the Date format. If your database offers a special DATE field definition, use it for dates. In addition to providing simple formatting advantages (like accepting *4/1* as input but displaying *April 1*), using a special date field lets you sort and calculate correctly. Without a date format, fields that seem to hold dates but in fact are text fields will sort April before January because of the alphabetization. And if you want to use dates in calculations (as when checking, say, how many bills are more than 60 days overdue), a field must be defined as a date field for the calculation to work.

ClarisWorks Database Tips

These tips were tested for ClarisWorks 5; many will work in the previous version, too.

ClarisWorks may have been renamed "AppleWorks" by the time you read this!

In General

Going by the book. The status area not only keeps you apprised of which record you're looking at, how many records you have, how many are visible, and whether or not they're sorted, but also lets you move from one record to another by using the "record book":

- Click on the upper or lower page to move to the previous or next record.
- Drag the lever up or down to move to the general area you want: with the lever in the center of the book, for instance, you'll see a record from the middle of the file.

- Select the number immediately below the book (it tells you which record you're looking at) and type the number of the record you want, then press Return or Enter.

You can also use ⌘-Return or ⌘-↓ to go to the next record or ⌘-Shift-Return or ⌘-↑ to go to the previous one.

The number used on the record book to refer to a record has nothing to do with a specific record. As you show and hide records, and sort them by different fields, record "number 1" is just the first one of the current batch.

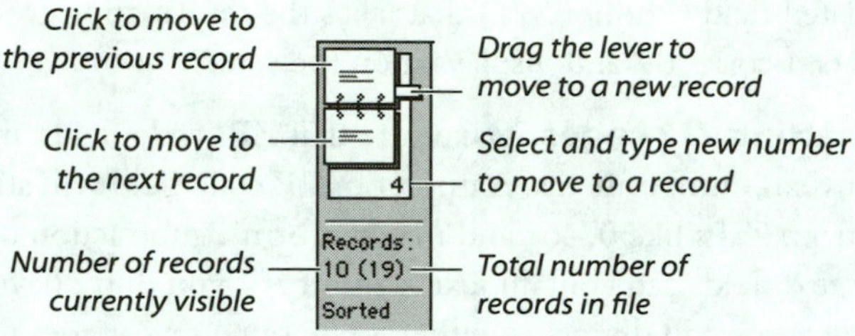

The view from here. One of the frustrating things about creating layouts is that you constantly have to switch back to Browse mode to see the effects of your changes. That's where the New View command comes in handy. Next time you change a layout, select New View from the View menu for a second window for the same database; select Tile Windows to arrange the two windows on the screen. Make sure that a filled-in record is displayed, and then switch to Layout mode in one of the two windows. As you change the layout—by moving and resizing fields, changing field formatting, and so on—you can instantly see the effects of your modifications in the other window. —SZA/SS

You can use New View for more than two windows, and for more than just the Layout and Browse modes of a single layout: browse two different layouts; browse the same layout in list and standard views; look at the layout and browse mode for three different layouts at the same time.

If you simply want to look at two different records at the same time and they're not adjacent in the list, use the split bar just above the top vertical scroll arrow to divide the window so it has panes with separate scroll controls; you'll be able to view different records in the upper and lower panes.

Cross-file drags. ClarisWorks' highly developed sense of drag and drop lets you drag a record from one database window to another. The only information that's actually transferred, however, is whatever's stored in identically named fields in both databases. If you drag a record from one database to another and there are no fields in common, all you wind up with is a new, blank record in the target window.

In Layout Mode

Automatic text tool. To edit an existing text box in Layout mode, you don't have to switch to the Text tool: double-click on a text box with the Selection tool to activate the text box and automatically switch to the Text tool. A triple-click activates the text box, switches to the text tool, and selects the word you clicked on; a quadruple-click will wind up selecting the entire contents of the text box.

Resizing multiple fields. With multiple fields selected, resizing one resizes all of them—but proportionately, not to the same size. If, for instance, you select a small, a medium, and a large field, and drag the end of the small one so that you change it from one inch in length to two inches, the other two fields will increase their lengths not by an inch, but to double their initial sizes.

Deleting a part. There's no yang for the yin of the Insert Part command in the Layout menu, but that doesn't mean you can't get rid of a part when you redesign a layout. Just remove all items from it—by deleting them or moving them to another part—and then drag its border up into the border of the part immediately above it (for the top-most part, just drag the border into the top of the window). When you let go of the mouse button, the part is gone.

IN THE BEGINNING

Are you so used to the name of your computer that you always spell the name of the apple wrong? How did the Mac get that name, with that spelling?

In Apple's early days, code names were given to projects in one of two categories: female names and apples. In addition to the Mac's precursor, Lisa, there were also an Annie and a Sara. Then there were Pippin and Golden Delicious, and then came… well, then came Jef Raskin, who originated the Mac project and named it after his favorite type of apple. He's responsible for misspelling it—but then, look how he spells his name! (Maybe we should blame his parents.)

Checkboxes and Radio Buttons

The checkered checkbox. The ClarisWorks database checkbox is an odd creature. First, it doesn't work the way checkboxes do on a Mac, providing a list of options from which you can choose as many as you want. A ClarisWorks checkbox is always single, not grouped, so it can stand for only a single value which is checked or not.

But the name you give the checkbox is just that: the checkbox's name. It has nothing to do with the "contents" of the checkbox field, as it does in big-sister program FileMaker, where clicking a checkbox puts the checkbox's name into the field. When you're dealing with checkbox fields for searching, sorting, calculations, or exporting, keep these points in mind:

- If you refer to a checkbox field in a calculation, the checkbox field is a 1 if the box is checked, and zero if the box is unchecked.

- If you use a checkbox field in a Match criterion, the checkbox value is either *true* (for checked boxes) or *false.* So, you have to use something like: '*Field*' = *true* (with no quotes around the *true).*
- If you export information or copy multiple selected records and paste the information elsewhere, the checkbox field will be exported as text: either *on* (for checked ones) or *off.*

Radio button fields. The content of a radio button field is not what you'd expect—it doesn't default to the value of the button name, but instead is simply the number of the button: if the first button of the group is selected, the field holds a 1, for the second button, the field holds a 2, and so on. If you export the information or copy it out of the database, you'll get numbers where you thought you had text entered.

Since it's difficult to create and modify calculations and match criteria where you have to remember which values were assigned to which buttons in a field, use the NUMTOTEXT function when you're dealing with radio button fields. So, for instance, in a match dialog you could see if the button labeled *married* is selected in the *status* field by using:

```
NUMTOTEXT('status')="married"
```

Radio frames and titles. A group of radio buttons defaults to being framed in a thin gray line with the title of the field used as a label for the group. This is generally a good approach, but there may be times you'll want to alter the frame or label, or get rid of one or the other entirely.

- To reformat the frame, select the radio button group in the layout and use the "pen" controls to change the frame: its thickness, color, and even a pattern (if you want a dotted or striped effect). Selecting None as the line thickness will get rid of the frame completely. (Selecting white as the frame color also usually gets rid of it—unless it's on top of a colored background.)
- To change the button label, you have to go back through the Define Fields dialog, select the field, and click Options. In the area *Label for control*, type the new name for the label.

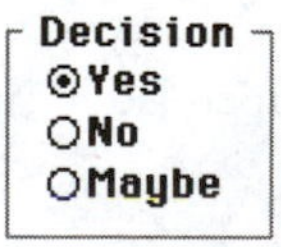

The default radio button format.

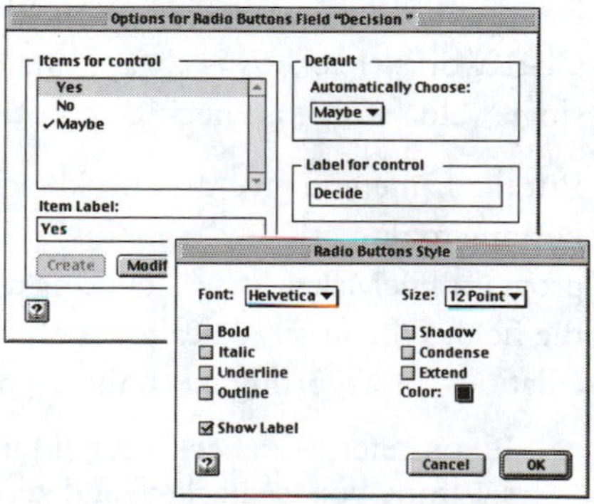

Control the radio button label through the Define Fields dialog (top) or the Style dialog (bottom).

- To get rid of the label completely, you can leave the *Label for control* area blank. Or, you can double-click on the radio button group in the layout, and uncheck the *Show Label* button in the Style dialog that appears.

Searching and Sorting

Three different approaches. The ClarisWorks database offers three distinct ways to find things, and it's important to understand the differences—not only with regard to how information is found, but what happens to the found records.

	Looks for	***Looks at***	***Looks in***	***Result***
Find/Change command in Edit menu	Simple text and numbers that you type in (as in a word processor's Find command)	Current (unhidden) records	All fields	Shows match on first available record (and subsequent records with Find Next button); provides Change option
Match Records command in Organize menu	Text, numbers, or formulated criteria ("AmountDue>500")	Current (unhidden) records	Specified field only	Matching records are selected (highlighted) but hidden/unhidden groups are not affected
Find mode from Layout menu	Simple or formulated criteria; multiple criteria ("AmountDue>500" AND "CustType <> VIP")	All records	Specified field(s)	Matching records become the current set, with non-matches hidden

There are four Match Records shortcut buttons on the ClarisWorks toolbar: *equals*, *does not equal*, *is less than*, and *is greater than*. Instead of using the Match Records command and then building your match criterion, you can simply click in a field on a record and then click one of the shortcut buttons; ClarisWorks will use the name of the field and its contents as the match criterion. So, it's a cinch to find all the records in the visible set that have the same value in a certain field as does the current record.

There are two additional Match buttons available—*is less than or equal to* and *is greater than or equal to*—that are just waiting to be added to the Button Bar.

1. Choose Edit Button Bars from the pop-up menu at the left of the button bar.
2. Keep *Default* selected in the dialog box's list and click Modify.
3. Select *Database* from the pop-up menu in the next dialog.
4. Select each of the new buttons in turn by clicking on it and then clicking the Add button.
5. Click the Done button.

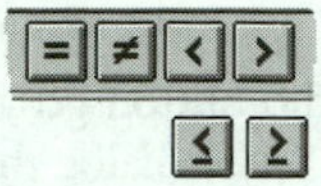

The default Match buttons and the two you can add.

Reposition the new buttons on the button bar by holding down ⌘ Option as you drag them.

Re-search assistance. If you use certain search criteria repeatedly, you don't have to continually recreate them. To save a search:

1. From the status area while in Browse or Find mode, click the magnifier icon to see the Search pop-up menu, and choose New Search.
2. Name the Search in the dialog that opens, and click OK.
3. You'll be in the Find mode at this point, so enter the search criteria. The button in the status area that's usually Find will instead be Store; click it to store the search criteria and perform the search, too.

Using a stored Search.

When you want to re-use the Search, just select it from the Search pop-up menu.

You can create and store Sort procedures the same way you do for Search criteria, using the Sort icon and menu in the status area.

The Name-type field. ClarisWorks offers a special field type named *Name*, which works as a text field with one special exception: if you sort by a Name-type field, the sort is done according to the *last* word in the field. That means you can type a person's full name in a single field and still sort by the last name.

Of course, this also poses a few problems: *John Jones Jr* will be sorted under *Jr* and *Microsoft Corporation* will be alphabetized by *Corporation*. To get around the first problem, type Option Spacebar between *Jones* and *Jr* to have it treated as a single word. In the second situation, type the @ symbol as the first character in a Name field and it will be sorted according to the first word in the field. But—and this is a big but—the @ won't show on the screen or in printouts; it only shows when you're actually editing the field.

Calculations

Last name first. One of the most common text calculations in a database is converting separate first and last names into a field that presents the last name first, followed by a comma and the first name. Creating a separate field for this calculation (I always name it LastFirstName) is lots easier than trying to set up a layout where the last and first names slide together with a text-object comma between them. The calculation itself is simple, too (make sure you include the space after the comma in the quotes:

Rich	Wolfson	Wolfson, Rich
Hochreich	Doffie	Doffie, Hochreich
Luttropp	John	John, Luttropp
Aiton	Carol	Carol, Aiton
Szubin	Jerry	Jerry, Szubin
Marilyn	Rose	Rose, Marilyn

Using a "LastFirstName" calculated field.

```
'LastName' & ", " & 'FirstName'
```

Formatting phone numbers. As pointed out in the *General Tips* section, formatting certain data, like phone or social security numbers, can cause a problem when you do it on entry: it increases both input time and the chance of using slightly different formats (slashes instead of hyphens, for instance) from one record to the next. The solution is to have one field serve as the input field, where you type nothing but the numbers, and use a calculated field to format and display the numbers.

This formula takes the 10 digits in a *phone* field and formats them like this: 123/456-1234.

```
LEFT('phone',3) & "/" & MID ('phone',4,3) &"-" & RIGHT(',phone',4)
```

There's no check here to see if there are, indeed, only ten digits in the field to start with. The easiest way to ensure that is to use the Options button in the Define Fields dialog for the input field. In the Verification section, check the *Must Be In Range* button and fill in 1000000000 and 9999999999 as the lower and upper ranges; that makes sure that there are 10 characters, all numbers, in the input field.

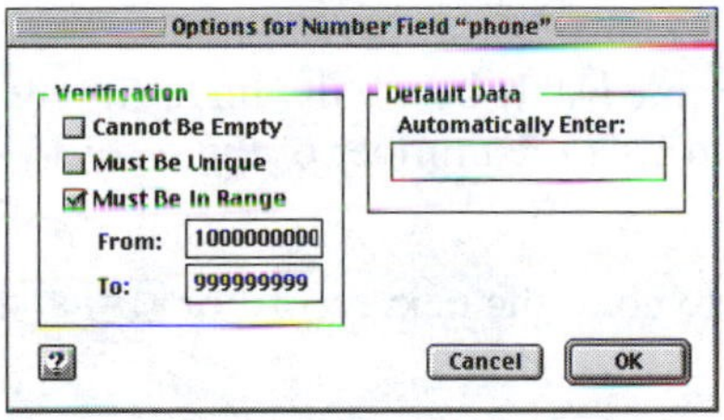

Making sure the Phone input field has the correct number and type of characters.

Creating compound serial numbers. Unlike FileMaker, which automatically creates serial numbers with embedded letters and symbols (BN-K1, BN-K2, and so on), ClarisWorks' Serial field deals solely with numbers, although you can specify both the starting number and the increment. You can, however, use a calculated field to put together the straightforward serial number and whatever other characters you want. Using a formula like this:

```
"BN-K" & 'Serial'
```

results in the BN-K1, BN-K2, and so on.

You can embed other identifying information in a serial number; using various date and time functions is one way to include special information. The NOW() function, for instance, gets the current date and time from the Mac's clock; the DAYOFYEAR *(date)* function returns a number that tells which day of the year (day 1, day 17, day 332, and so on) a given date is. Combining the two functions—DAYOFYEAR(NOW())—returns a number for the current day. Embed that in a serial number calculation like this:

```
"BN/"&DAYOFYEAR(NOW())&"-"&'Serial'
```

and you'll have records with serial numbers like BN/59-8 where the final number is absolutely unique to each record but the number after the slash indicates the day on which the record was created.

For FileMaker Pro

Theses tips were tested for FileMaker Pro 4; many of them also work with the previous version.

Browsing

Getting around. The numbers in the status area at the left of each FileMaker window tells you how many records you've created, how many you're currently browsing as the result of a Find command, and which record of the current set you're looking at. The little book lets you move from one record to another:

- Click on the upper or lower page to move to the previous or next record.
- Drag the lever up or down to move to the general area you want: with the lever in the center of the book, for instance, you'll get a record from the middle of the file.
- Select the number immediately below the book (it tells you which record you're looking at) and type the number of the record you want, then press Return or Enter.

You can also use ⌘Tab to go to the next record or ⌘Shift Tab to go to the previous one.

All these methods for moving around also work for moving between requests, layouts, and report pages.

The number used on the record book to refer to a record has nothing to do with a specific record. As you show and hide records, and sort them by different fields, record "number 1" is just the first one of the current batch.

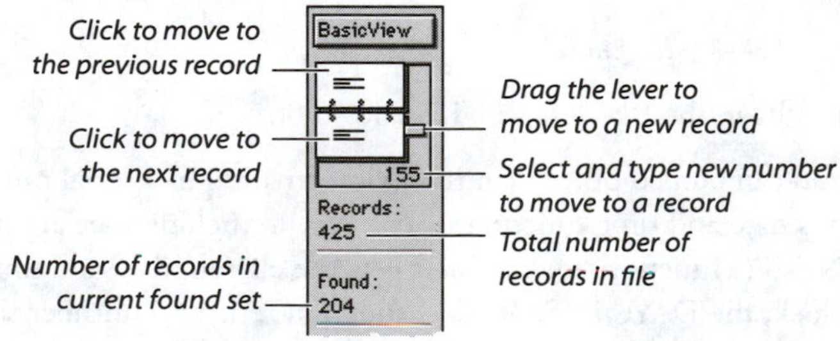

Bypassing the Delete alert. When you use Delete Record to remove a record from your file, FileMaker asks you if you're sure you want to delete it. This is a normal Mac touch—giving you a chance to change your mind before an irreversible operation is performed. But if you're *sure* you want to delete the record, ⌘ Option E will avoid the dialog box.

Layout Basics

Holding on to a tool. Generally, after you use a tool in Layout mode, it automatically switches back to the Selection tool (the arrow). You can hang on to a tool indefinitely by double-clicking on it instead of single-clicking when you select it. If you want tools to be locked with a single click:

1. From the Edit menu, select Application from the Preferences submenu.
2. Select Layout from the pop-up menu in the Preferences dialog.
3. Check *Always lock layout tools.* —SZA/EC

Automatic text tool. To edit an existing text box, you don't have to switch to the text tool: double-clicking on a text box with the Selection tool activates the text box and automatically switches to the Text tool. A triple-click activates the text box, switches to the text tool, and selects the word you clicked on; a quadruple-click will wind up selecting the contents of the text box.

What a drag it is. When you drag to select multiple items in a layout, only objects completely surrounded by the drag are selected. But press ⌘ while you drag, and anything the selection marquee touches will fall into its grip. —EC

Selecting like items. To select all items of the same type (all fields, all labels, all lines, and so on) in a layout, select one and then press ⌘ Option A. Clicking on a tool and using Select All also works to select all the items created with that tool, but since there's no "tool" for fields, it's a more limited approach.

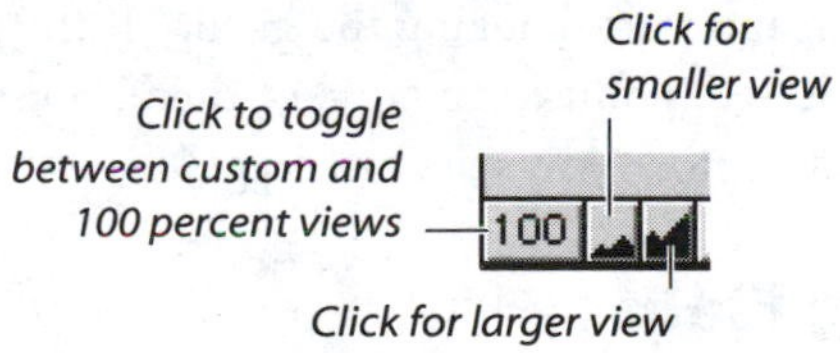

Changing the zoom level. Click on the zoom in or out icons to change the magnification one level at time. But clicking on the number next to the zoom controls toggles you between the standard 100 percent view and the last magnification used.

Duplicating a layout object. There are three ways to duplicate an existing layout item (a field, label, button, or graphic):

- Select the item, then copy and paste it.
- Select the item and use the Duplicate command in the Edit menu.
- Hold down Option and drag out a copy of the item.

In the case of fields, the last two options open the Select Field dialog so you can add a label or even switch the field name; using Copy and Paste doesn't open the dialog.

Quick-set defaults. To use any settings as a default for a layout item, set them while nothing in the layout is selected. This works for text settings such as font, size, and style, as well as for line, pattern, and color settings for graphics tools.

If you've formatted an item with a combination of formats that you want to use as defaults, ⌘-click on the object (field, text box, or graphic object) and its formats will be used as the defaults for other items of its kind.

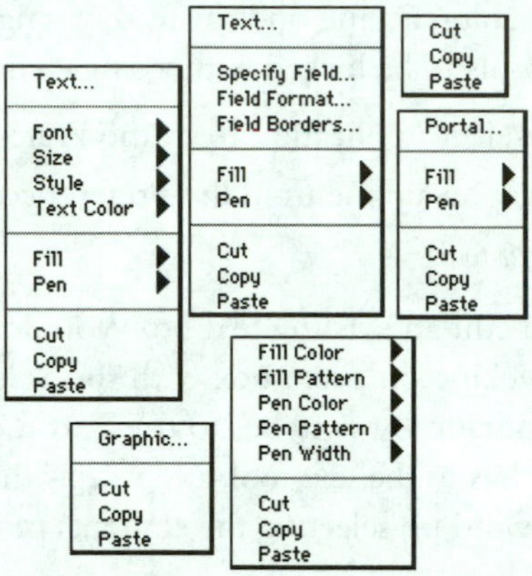

Just some of FileMaker's contextual menus that you'll see in Layout mode.

Contextual menus. Holding down Control and clicking on just about anything in a FileMaker window pops up a contextual menu (a feature that predates the Mac's contextual menus) that provides formatting and editing commands tailored to the item you're pointing to. While this works in any mode—Browse, Layout, Find—you'll find it handiest when you're working in Layout.

Shift-drag. Using Shift as a movement constraint seems to present a problem when you're moving a group of selected objects: hold Shift and click on one of the items to drag the group, and the item you click on is deselected from the group, since that's what a Shift-click does, just as on the desktop.

There are two ways around this problem. If you're going to Shift-click on the final item to add it to the group before you move everything, just don't release the mouse button after you click on the item: keep down both the Shift key and the mouse button, and start dragging the group. If the group of items is already completely selected, point to any one of them, press the mouse button, and *then* press Shift, before you start the drag.

Manipulating Fields

Adding a field label. If you want to add a label for a field (because you didn't when you started, or because you mistakenly deleted it), just double-click on the field. The Specify Field dialog opens with the current field selected. Check the Create Field Label button and click OK—it's lots faster than creating the label with the Text tool.

Adding a field to match another's formatting. If you've tweaked the format of a certain field to just the way you want it (say that, in a lapse of good taste, you have a field whose text is formatted for 15-point red, bold, shadowed and italic, with a dotted green border and a pale pink background), you don't have to go through all that formatting again to make another field match it. Select the formatted field, and use the Duplicate command. The Specify Field dialog opens with the field selected; select a different field and click OK. The new field will match the formatting of the original.

Opening the format dialog. To format the contents of a field, you don't have to select it and then choose a command from the Format menu. Instead, hold down Option and double-click on the field. This opens the appropriate formatting dialog for the field: Text Formats for text fields, Number Formats for number fields, and so on.

Resizing multiple fields. With multiple fields selected, resizing one resizes all of them—but proportionately, not to the same size. If, for instance, you select a small, a medium, and a large field, and drag the end of the small one so that you change it from one inch in length to two inches, the other two fields will increase their lengths not by an inch, but to double their initial sizes.

Working with Parts

Click on the icon, or Command-click directly on a part label to toggle the label orientation.

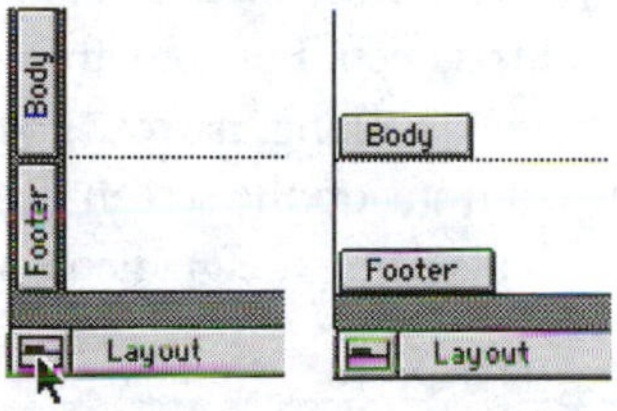

Working with part labels. Clicking on the part icon in the bottom of the window frame is not the only way to toggle between horizontal and vertical part labels: you can ⌘-click directly on a part label to switch all the label orientation.

Background color. To color the background of a part, you don't have to draw a box and fill it with color, sending it to the back of all the fields and labels. Instead, click on the name of the part in the layout (the little tab at the left of the window), and choose a color from the Fill color palette.

Get rid of the body. When you're creating summary reports—say, to count your baseball cards to check how much the collection is worth—don't forget that you don't need a body. The body contains information about each card that may distract you from the totals that the report is designed to show (like the fact that your Topps collection is worth $26,457). —EC

Shifting parts. To reorder parts on a layout, Shift-drag a part label to the new position. This only works on parts that *can* be shifted, like subsummaries, but you can drag them from the top to the bottom of the layout (or vice versa) to change them from trailing to leading summaries (or, again, vice versa.)

Deleting parts but not pieces. You can delete an empty part in a layout by dragging its bottom border up to the next part or by selecting the part's label and pressing Delete.

If the part contains objects or fields, pressing Delete gets you a dialog asking if you want to delete the part and all its items. But selecting the label and pressing

Option Delete deletes the part and shifts its items to the part immediately below it. (So you can't do this to the bottom-most part on a layout.) —SZA/EC

Layout Design

List-view dividers. When you're planning a list view, it's important to put a visual divider between records, whether they're single rows of information or something "taller." Draw a light-color line at the bottom of the body part to get a line between every record in Browse mode.

Adding a line to the bottom of a body part visually divides the records in browse view (right).

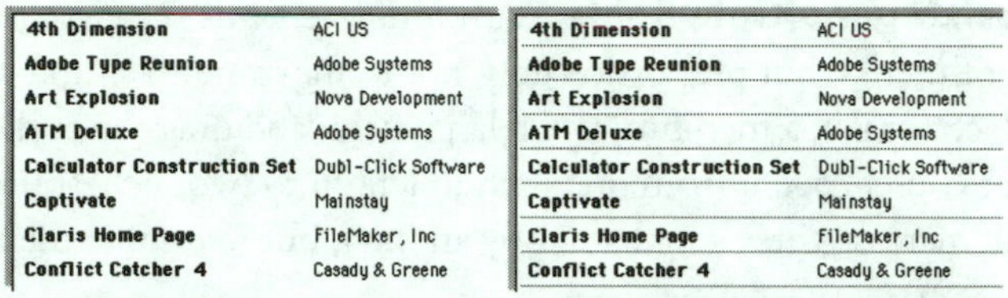

4th Dimension	ACI US
Adobe Type Reunion	Adobe Systems
Art Explosion	Nova Development
ATM Deluxe	Adobe Systems
Calculator Construction Set	Dubl-Click Software
Captivate	Mainstay
Claris Home Page	FileMaker, Inc
Conflict Catcher 4	Casady & Greene

Shaded columns. To divide columns of information in a list view, you could use a vertical line, but along with the recommended horizontal divider, that will give you a spreadsheet-like grid on the screen. For something a little more subtle and elegant, but just as effective, create a long, narrow graphic with repeated gray gradients that are sized to the columns on the screen. Paste the graphic at the back of the body and place the fields using the gradients as dividers.

Using a multi-gradient graphic to visually divide columns.

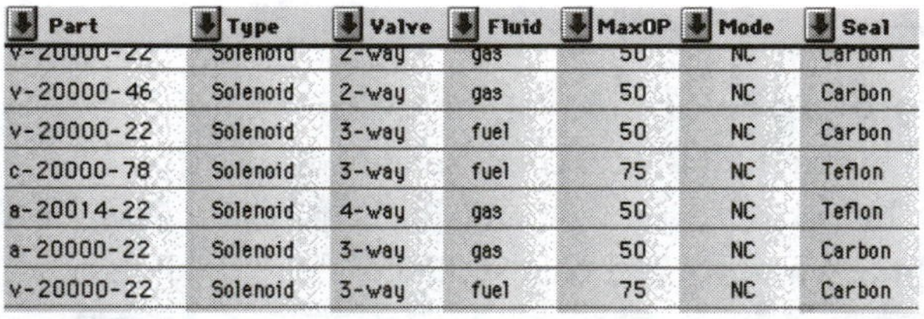

Part	Type	Valve	Fluid	MaxOP	Mode	Seal
v-20000-22	Solenoid	2-way	gas	50	NC	Carbon
v-20000-46	Solenoid	2-way	gas	50	NC	Carbon
v-20000-22	Solenoid	3-way	fuel	50	NC	Carbon
c-20000-78	Solenoid	3-way	fuel	75	NC	Teflon
a-20014-22	Solenoid	4-way	gas	50	NC	Teflon
a-20000-22	Solenoid	3-way	gas	50	NC	Carbon
v-20000-22	Solenoid	3-way	fuel	75	NC	Carbon

Do not enter. You can't enter information into a calculated field, but you *can* click or tab into it, and if you hit any key when the field is selected, you get a dialog that tells you the field is not modifiable. To avoid that waste of time, always format calculated fields so that they can't be entered: use the Field Format command and uncheck the *Allow entry into field* option.

Click the new tab order. When you want to change the tab order of the fields on the layout, clicking *Create new tab order* in the dialog after selecting Tab Order from the menu blanks out all the arrows that store the tab-order numbers. But you don't have to type in new numbers: simply click in an arrow, and the next available number will be automatically entered in it.

Layout menu divider. If you have a long list of layouts in the layout pop-up menu and would like to group them, reorder them with the Set Layout Order command in the Mode menu. But a divider line in the pop-up menu helps organization lots of layouts into logical groups.

Add a divider line by creating a new, blank layout and naming it with a single hyphen; the hyphen will appear as a full-width line in the menu. Since you can use duplicate names on layouts, you can make more than one divider, and place them with the Set Layout Order command.

You won't be able to select the blank line from the menu, so you won't wind up in the blank layout accidentally. But it's hard to get there on purpose, too, since you can't select the line even when you're in Layout mode. To move to the blank layout so you can delete it (I can't think of why else you'd want to move to it), use the "book" control in Layout mode: click the pages, drag the lever, or type the number of the layout to get there.

Button rows. When you switch from one view to another, the currently selected record remains the same. Switching from a list view, where you can see rows of information for multiple records to a "form" view for a specific record is usually a two-step process: you first click on the row (record) you want, and then switch to the other layout with a built-in or scripted command. Wouldn't it be more elegant if you could just click on a row and be switched to that record in the form view?

This is very simple to set up:

1. In the list layout, use the Button tool to draw a long, skinny button that covers the body part.
2. When the button dialog opens, assign the Go To Layout command to the button, using the name of the layout you want to switch to.
3. Use the Bring to Front command to keep the button on top of all the fields.
4. Make the button invisible by assigning no line and no fill to it.

That's it. In Browse mode, when you click on a row in the list view, the click is passed through to select that record before the Go To Layout command is executed, so you wind up looking at the selected record.

Of course, this assumes that your list view is for viewing only, since you can't click in a field in a row. If you want to edit data in the list view but still want the convenience of one-click jumping to a record in another view, create a little button—visible or not—and put it at the far left of the body part, in front of all the data. In browse view, there'll be a button on every row.

Input

Validating field entry. While using buttons and menus as input devices prevents misspellings and other erroneous data from being entered, it limits what can be entered. When you want to make sure that the right kind of data is being entered but you want to let the user enter anything within the correct

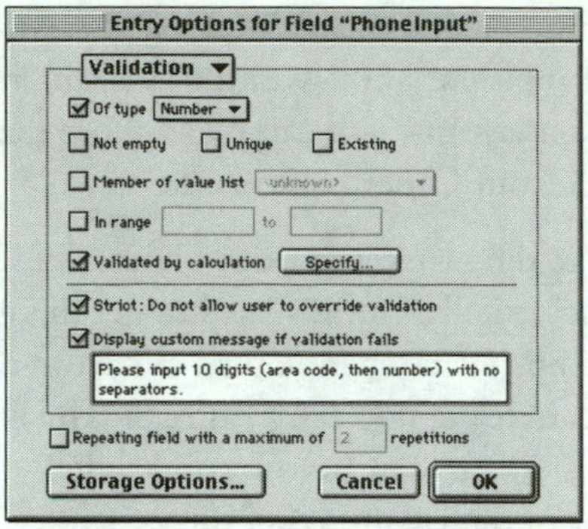

The validation setup for phone-number entry.

parameters (like the right number of digits for a social security number), make the validation part of the field definition.

You can set up validation for a field which will take only 10 digits for a phone number, to be later formatted with separators:

1. Select the field in the Define Fields dialog.
2. Click the Options button.
3. Select Validation from the pop-up menu.
4. Check the first box, and set the type to Number.
5. Check the Validate by calculation option, and specify this calculation in the next dialog: Length(PhoneInput)=10.
6. Turn on the Strict option.
7. Type in a message for the dialog that will appear if invalid data is entered.

Auto format. It's a great disappointment that FileMaker Pro 4 still doesn't provide some sort of auto-format on input to take care of things like phone numbers, social security numbers, and other things you'd like to be able to type in without worrying about separators. You can fake it, though, by using one field for input and another for display.

Take a simple example of inputting a 10-digit phone number by just typing the numbers, but displaying it with separators like this: (123) 555-1234. You use a calculated field to work on the contents of the input field, with a calculation that looks like this:

```
"(" & Left(PhoneInput, 3) & ") " & Middle(PhoneInput, 4, 3)
& "-"&Right(PhoneInput, 4)
```

A similar formula would work for social security numbers:

```
Left(SSInput, 3) & "-" & Middle(SSInput, 4, 2) & "-" &
Right(SSInput, 4)
```

If you're creating the database for someone else to use, you'll have to get fancier because you'll have to allow for the possibility that the user will type in numbers with separators (although they may be the wrong separators). One approach is to use an IF statement to check on how many characters are in the input field, which will tell you whether or not separators were used; another is to validate the field contents on entry (as described in an earlier entry).

Invisible auto-formatting. The double-field approach for auto-formatting, where one field is used for input and one for display, is a little clunky from an interface point of view: not only do you see two fields in the layout, but when you mistakenly try to edit the formatted field, you find it's a calculated field that doesn't allow entry or edits. Here's an elegant solution to both problems.

Give the display field an opaque fill (white, or a color to match the rest of the layout). Turn off the *Allow entry into field* option in its Field Format dialog. Make the input and display fields exactly the same size, and put the display field on top of the input field, using the Bring to Front command if necessary.

When you're in Browse mode, clicking on the tandem field activates the input field because the display field, though on top, has *Allow entry* turned off. You input the information to the input field, and as soon as you click or tab out of it, it disappears beneath the opaque display field—which is displaying the formatted version of what you just typed or edited.

Pop-up Menus, Buttons, and Checkboxes

Use a divider line in a pop-up menu. To put a divider line in a pop-up menu or list, type a hyphen on a separate line in the value list. This is particularly useful to separate the main choices from options like Other and Edit List at the end of the menu.

If you use the same value list for radio buttons or checkboxes, you'll get a blank line at the hyphen (or extra space, depending on how you orient the buttons).

Deleting contents from a pop-up menu field. When you use a pop-up list, it's easy to make a field blank (after you've mistakenly entered information) because you can select the contents and use Delete. But for a pop-up menu, there are no choices other than what's already in the menu, and you can't empty a field once you've put something in it. You can add the Other option to the bottom of the menu, and then use the Other dialog to delete the current contents, but there's an easier way: add a blank line to the value list for the menu, and it shows up as a blank in the menu. Select the blank to empty the field. (Make sure you make a blank line with Return; don't type a space.)

What's the "other" value? When you use the Other option with a menu or pop-up list, the value you enter is shown in the field even when it's not part of the original list. When you make an Other button or checkbox, clicking it brings up the dialog for your entry, but all that shows on the record is a selected Other button, with no clue as to the actual data.

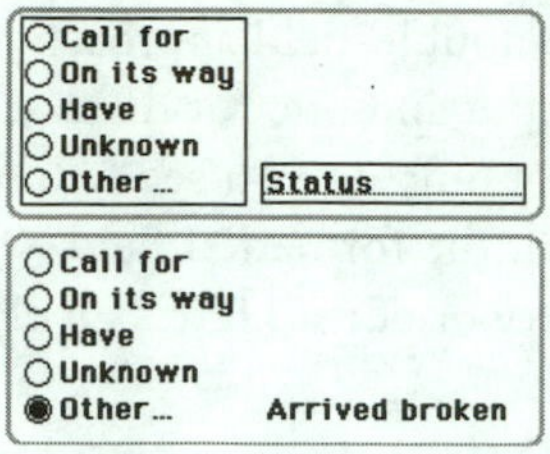

Using two versions of the same field on a layout lets you see what "Other" stands for: the Layout view (top) and the Browse view (bottom).

To display the data, duplicate the field on the layout and format it as a standard field; uncheck the box in the Field Format dialog that allows data entry for the field so that it can display but can't be used for input. As the figure here shows, the "other" contents will be printed next to the "Other" button when you put both versions of the field on the layout.

Of course, the second copy of the field will display the contents even when it's one of the named buttons, so you might want to go a step further. Instead of putting a duplicate of the field (the Status field, in our example) next to the buttons, create a calculated field that will check the contents of the Status field; if the contents don't match any of the button names, then it should display the contents—otherwise, it should stay blank. The general approach of the IF statement is:

```
If (Status=[any buttonname], "", Status)
```

This formula checks the contents of Status against the names of the buttons. When there's a match, an "empty string" is the result; if there's no match, it uses the contents of the Status field as the result.

Because you have to allow for all the button names in the match, you have to use OR's in the IF statement, like this:

```
If (Status="Call for" or Status="On its way" or Status="Have" or
Status="Unknown","",Status)
```

The easiest way to put this together is to copy the list of button names from the Value List dialog and paste them into the Calculation definition, adding the quote marks and other parts of the statement, so you can be sure you typed everything correctly.

This works fine, and is fairly straightforward—and therefore easy to understand. But there's an even better way to create the calculation, one that involves a lot less typing (and makes things easier when there are even more items in your button list). Use the PatternCount function to check the contents of the Status field against a string that includes all the button names, and put it inside the IF statement, like this:

```
If (PatternCount ("Call for On its way Have
Unknown",Status),"",Status)
```

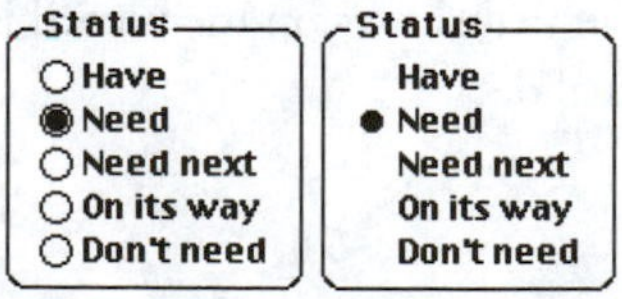

You can skip the standard radio buttons and use a bullet approach.

Radio button bullets. The picture here shows the standard radio button look, and an alternative bullet approach. To achieve the latter, all you have to do is select the field in Layout mode, and set the line thickness to None—that gets rid of the circle around the button.

You can do some similar things with checkboxes. If you get rid of the line thickness, you'll have X's in front of the choices, but they won't be in boxes (and they'll look overly large because they'll include the pixels that would normally be seen as the corners of the box). Or, you set a thicker line that gives a thick border to an empty box, and fills the box in completely when it's checked.

Checkboxes contain lists. When you use checkboxes for input, clicking a checkbox is like typing the button name into the field; clicking multiple buttons puts all the button names into the field, separated by return characters.

The same checkbox selections (left) can result in different field contents (right) because the order of the checkboxes themselves doesn't count.

☒ Vanilla Scoop ☒ Chocolate Scoop ☒ Syrup ☐ Bananas ☐ Nuts	Vanilla Scoop Chocolate Scoop Syrup
☒ Vanilla Scoop ☒ Chocolate Scoop ☒ Syrup ☐ Bananas ☐ Nuts	Chocolate Scoop Syrup Vanilla Scoop

But the order of items stored in the field isn't related to the order of the checkboxes. Text is entered in the field in the order in which you check and uncheck boxes: checking a box adds its label to the bottom of the stored list, and unchecking the box removes the its label (and closes any gap that was left).

Finding and Sorting Things

Looking for empties and nonempties. The easiest way to find records with blank fields is to type an equal sign (=) in the field in Find mode. To find non-empty fields, type an equal sign in the field, check the Omit box, and then click Find. Or, you can find either the blanks or nonblanks and then, in Browse mode, choose Find Omitted from the Select menu to take a look at the group of records that *weren't* selected by the Find operation.

On the other hand, the fastest way to find empty *records* is to sort your file in order of a field that should never be empty—such as a client's name. All the empty records will appear at the top of the list. —SZA/EC

Finding non-alphanumeric characters. When you do a find or a lookup, FileMaker ignores non-alphanumeric characters in a field. So, if you look for records with, say, an A+ in a field, you'll also get all the A's and A-'s along with them. And if you were to do a Find for records with a certain field empty, you'll still get fields that have, say, just an @ symbol in them.

To force FileMaker to really look at the contents of fields beyond the basic alphanumeric characters, you have to alter the field definition slightly—either when you create the field, or afterwards:

1. Open the Define Fields box and create or select the field.
2. Click the Options button.
3. Click the Storage Options button in the next dialog.
4. In the next dialog, select ASCII from the pop-up menu for the default language.

ASCII characters
Chapter 12

Click OK as many times as necessary to put all the dialogs away, and you'll find that searching, sorting, and lookups all pay attention to all the characters in the field.

Some things are more equal than others. The equal sign as a special symbol in FileMaker searches has always been defined as an "exact match" for whatever you type after the symbol in Find mode. (That's why it's used, as described in the last entry, for finding empty records—used all by itself, it means "equals exactly *nothing.")*

But it never works quite as expected, because "exact match" actually means: "find records that have *a separate word* in this field that exactly matches...." So, while a search for *John* would find records for *John, James John Jones,* and *James Johnson*, an "equals" search finds both *John* and *James John Jones* because *John* is a separate word in both those records.

FileMaker Pro 4 introduced another operator, awkwardly called the *field content match.* Its symbol is a double equal sign, and it works the way you probably expected the other operator to work: it finds records that truly exactly match whatever you type in the field as the find criterion.

This...	***Finds...***
John	John, James John Jones, James Johnson
=John	John, James John Jones
==John	John

Sorting with non-alphanumeric characters. Fields with non-alphanumeric characters will sort ignoring everything except the alphanumerics. To get them to sort correctly, define the field with the ASCII storage option described in the previous entry.

Or, if you don't want the field defined for a storage option, you can trigger the ASCII sort at the time of sort: in the Sort dialog, click the *Override field's language for sort* and choose ASCII from the pop-up menu.

Special sort orders. You can define a special sort order for any field so that, for instance, records can be ordered according to some priority instead of alphabetically.

Say you have a radio button field with buttons labeled *Top Priority, Special Attention,* and *Standard,* and you want records sorted according to those priorities.

1. Choose Sort from the Mode menu.
2. Move the field (in the picture here, it's named *Priority)* to the Sort list.
3. With the field selected in the Sort list, click the *Custom order based on value list* button.
4. Choose the appropriate value list from the pop-up menu.

Since this sort is defined through the Sort dialog, not through a field definition, you can just set it up at any time for a single sort operation or make it part of a Sort script to have it always available.

In this example, the field used its own value list, and both had the same name, but that's not necessary. You might have a value list, for instance, consisting of *yes, no,* and *maybe.* The value list might be used for more than one field and, of course, have a name not related to any of those fields. But the list can be used to define the sort order for any of those fields (or any other field, though it's unlikely other fields would have only those values ready for sorting).

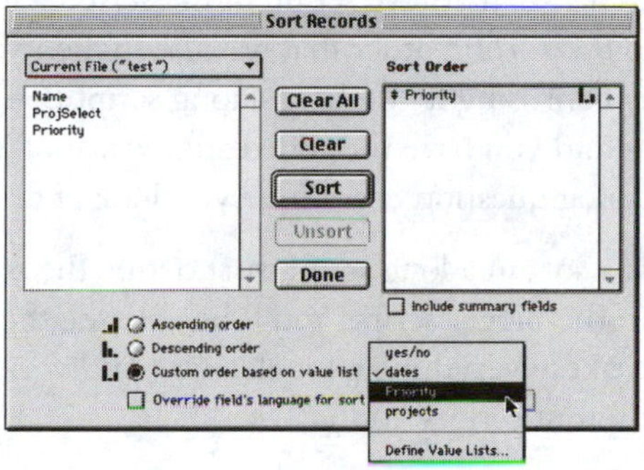

Setting up a special Sort order.

Creating automatic serial numbers with letters. If you need serial numbers that include letters or other non-numeric figures, you can still get FileMaker to create the number automatically. In the Define Fields dialog, select the field (it has to be a Number field), and click Options. In the Auto Enter section of the dialog box that appears, type the starting serial number, such as An-BT-1. When a new record is created, only the numeric portion of the number will be increased, producing An-BT-2, An-BT-3, and so on. —SZA/SS

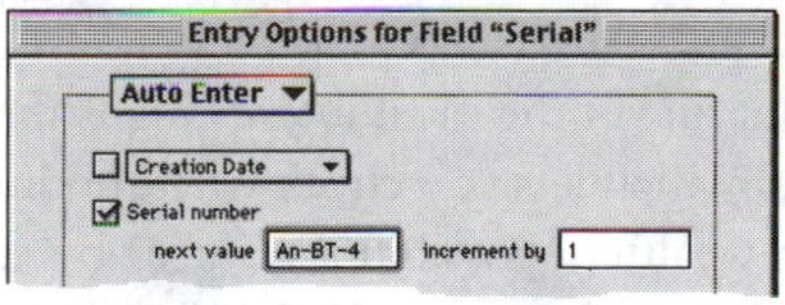

Scripts

Keyboard controls in the script window. When you're working in the Script window, you can do lots of entry from the keyboard instead of with the mouse:

- Pressing Tab alternately selects the left or right panel.
- Pressing Spacebar sends the currently selected command from the left pane into the script panel.
- Using ↑ and ↓ selects the previous and next lines in the active panel.
- Select commands in the activated left panel by typing a few letters (capitals are ignored). You can't type a space, though, since that triggers

moving a command to the right panel. So, there's no way to type *set field* so you can select it instead of *set error capture,* which comes before it. But if you type *set* to select *set error capture,* pause a second, and type *set* again, you'll get *set field.* (Pause and type it again, and you'll get *set zoom level*, and so on.)

- When you put a command in the list (by double-clicking, using the Move button, or using Spacebar), its default position is the bottom of the script. To put a command elsewhere in the script without having to reposition it, select a line in the script first; when you add the new command, it will be inserted beneath the selected one.

Naming sorts for long scripts. FileMaker still doesn't indicate, in a script, what the sorting order is that you've set up in the script—all it says is *Sort [restore]*, referring to the sorting order that was used when you created the script. It's especially confusing if you have a long script that does more than one sort operation—and you have the added annoyance of having to deal with the Keep/Replace dialog question every time you look at or edit the script.

Whenever you have a sort in a long script, first define the sort as a separate script, then call it in the bigger script. You'll be able see the name of the sort script, which makes everything a lot clearer. (And you'll be able to use the same sort in different scripts, too.)

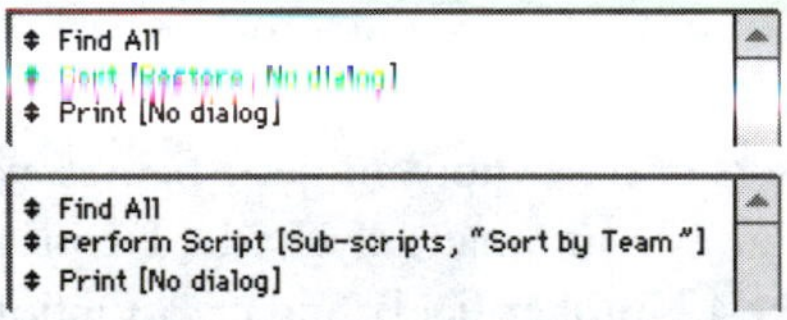

The standard Sort command in a script (top) gives no clue as to what kind of sort it is. Calling the Sort as a subscript (bottom) keeps thing clearer.

Detecting modifier keys. FileMaker 4 added a long list of Status functions for scripting purposes, but one of the most interesting is the *Status(CurrentModiferKeys)* which lets you check what modifier keys are being held down. This opens a wealth of possibilities, since you can script a button to do one thing if it's clicked, and something else if it's Option-clicked, or ⌘-clicked, or clicked with the Shift, Control, or Caps Lock down, or any combination thereof.

So, you might have a button perform a sort in ascending order if clicked, or descending order if Shift-clicked; you can proceed to a confirming dialog when a Yes button is clicked in a dialog, or bypass the confirmation if the button is Option-clicked; you can forego setting up a password for "expert" access to some part of the database (data entry, or layout design) and use a key combination with a click on a hidden button.

The Status(CurrentModiferKeys) function returns a number that indicates which key is down:

1	=	Shift
2	=	Caps Lock
4	=	Control
8	=	Option
16	=	⌘

To check for a combination of keys, you simply add their numbers together: ⌘Option would return 24, for instance, and ⌘ShiftControl is 21.

To actually respond to key presses, you have to check for them inside the button's script; in most situations an IF statement (with ELSE or ELSE IF's) will suffice, though for more complex choices, you might consider using the CASE statement instead.

Say, for instance, you have previously defined two sort procedures for a field—SortUp and SortDown—for ascending and descending sorts. You want a button click to do the SortUp, and a Shift-click to trigger the SortDown. You have to create a script for your button that will choose between the two subscripts based on the modifier key, like this:

```
If ["Status(CurrentModifierKeys)=1"]
    Perform Script [Sub-scripts, "SortDown"]
Else
    Perform Script [Sub-scripts, "SortUp"]
End If
```

Create a button for the layout, and attach this script to it.

Checking the status of modifier keys doesn't have to occur only when someone clicks a button: the check, and some branching, could occur in the middle of a long script. But that would mean the user would have to press the keys at just the right time, so it's not a very reliable approach unless it's inside a loop (and even then, it's questionable).

Relationships

A self-relationship. Since neither this book nor this chapter purports to actually teach basic techniques, this tip assumes you know the basics of setting up and using relationships between FileMaker files. But what you might not know is that you can set up a relationship in a file *to itself*—which opens up a wealth of possibilities.

For instance: I have several databases relating to this book project. One is a file of hardware and software companies; another is a database of products. They are, of course related to each other, providing several advantages: as I add an item to the Product database I don't have to enter the specifics of the company if I've already done that in the other database; when I'm in the Company database, I can see a list of products for each vendor, culled from the other database; and, if I'm in the Company database, I can create new records in the Product database just by adding to the list displayed on the company's record.

But what I really wanted was a list of products on every record of the *Product* database, showing what other items were available from the same company—so when I was looking at the record for DeBabelizer, I'd see that there were three other products from Equilibrium. That's where the self-relationship comes in—and once you know it's possible, you can probably figure out how to set it up yourself. But I'll describe it anyway.

1. Define the relationship. When you're prompted to choose a file to relate to, choose the current file. Set the relationship to be based on a logical field—in my example, it's based on the CompanyName. I usually name this type of relationship "me"; if I need more than one within the same file, I name them "meCompany", "meChapter", and so on.
2. In Layout mode, draw a portal for the *me* relationship. Format it for as many lines as works for your layout and situation; add the scrolling capability, and choose a color for the alternating lines to make it easy to read.
3. Put the appropriate fields in the first row of the portal. For my example, it's simply the Product field. But be sure you choose the *related* field, and not the original one; there's a pop-up menu at the top of the Field dialog that opens when you drag a field onto the layout—select the relationship from the pop-up. (Related field names begin with double colons.) So, on a record, you have the field *Product* on the current record, but also a field labeled *::Product* inside the portal.

That's all you need for a scrolling list of related records inside a file. When I create a new record and input the name of the company that publishes a specific piece of software, all the other items from that same manufacturer are listed.

Calculations based on a self-relationship. The self-relationship you set up to see a list of related fields within a file as described in the last entry doesn't have to be limited to a simple list. You can perform calculations on the items in the list, too, to keep track of totals, averages, and so on, without setting up summary fields or making reports.

My company/product list doesn't lend itself to much in the way of calculations, but it's handy to just get a total count of products available from one company so I don't have to scroll through the list to count them. All I had to do was create a calculated field (PrdTotal) to hold the total number of products, using the COUNT function to count the records. The trick is to make sure that you choose the *related* field in the Calculation dialog. The pop-up menu above the list of fields lists the current file as well as related files; you have to choose the related file (which is the previously defined self-relationship) from the menu, and then select the related field from the list, as shown in the picture on the next page.

With this approach, you can use functions like SUM and AVG to keep track of information within a single file, displaying the results on each record in Browse mode. Note that you don't have to put this calculated field inside the portal in order for it to work.

Left, the calculation definition using the relationship's Product field. Right, the layout (top) and the browse versions (bottom) of the results; note that the calculated field isn't inside the portal.

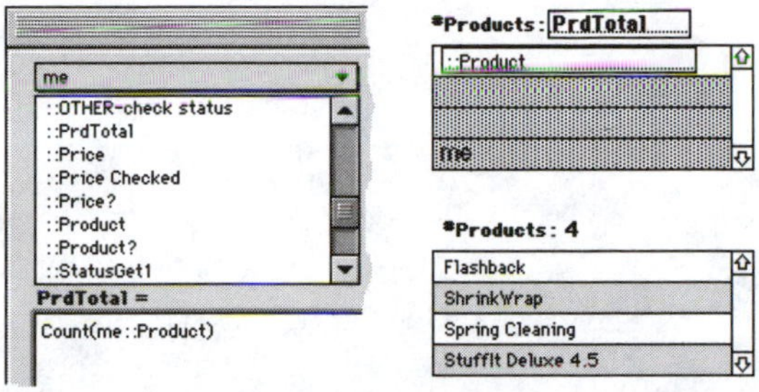

The jump-to button. The handiest trick of all when using a self-relationship list is also the easiest to set up. Once you have a list on each record of the other related records, you can make a button to let you quickly jump to any of the records in the list.

In Layout, use the button tool to draw a tiny button in the first row of the portal, at the far end of the row. Define the button function as *Go to Related Record*, making sure to select the *me* relationship from the pop-up menu in the button definition box. For the button label, you can just type < and format it to an appropriate size; you can color the button to match the stripes in the scrolling list. That's it: you'll get a button on every row in the list, and clicking it takes you right to that record, in the same file.

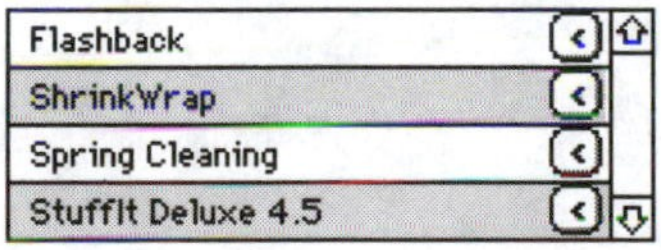

PART 6

Creativity Software

Part 6 At a Glance

19

Graphics

In This Chapter

Graphics on the Mac

Basics

Bitmapped graphics. A bitmapped graphic is made up of individual dots. Picture a sheet of graph paper: if you color in some of the squares, you can make a picture. A bitmap is simply a collection of tiny dots—on your Mac's screen or on a printout—that have been filled in with black, white or colors to make a picture.

Each dot on the screen corresponds with, or is "mapped" to, bits in the computer's memory—hence the phrase *bitmapped graphic.* Bitmapped graphics are also sometimes referred to as "paint" graphics because the Mac's first graphics program, MacPaint, worked with bitmaps.

Working with bitmapped graphics is a little like working with an oil painting: the only way you can change what you first put down is to either paint over the parts you want to change or scrape off some areas and paint in something else. Suppose you paint a bitmap image of a square, and then you paint a circle overlapping it. What looks like a square and a circle to you is just a collection of colored pixels to the computer. If you want to move the circle an inch to the right, you'll find it very difficult to select, because it's not a separate "object." And even if you did succeed in moving it over, you'd find that there's a blank where it used to be—not the piece of the square you thought was there! Similarly, if you wanted to resize the square without changing the circle, you'd find it impossible. —SZA/AB

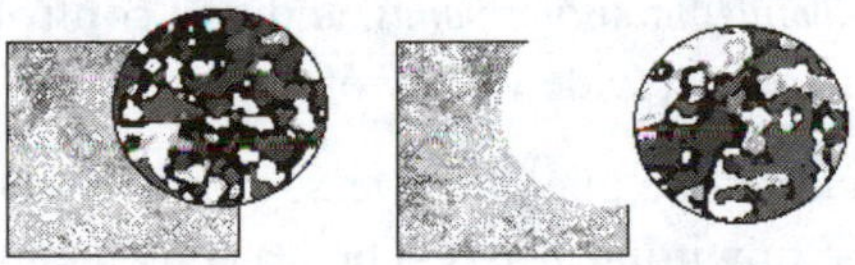

Since bitmapped graphics are a collection of dots, there's nothing "behind" the circle if you move it.

Vector graphics. Vector graphics, the alternative to bitmaps, arrived on the Mac with MacDraw in 1986, and have been around ever since in programs Illustrator and FreeHand; they're also referred to as *draw* or *object-oriented* graphics.

With vectors, you have objects that can be manipulated separately. Vector graphics are like Colorforms™—those thin little shapes that you stick onto a background to make pictures. Instead of working with a collection of pixels, you make pictures from geometric shapes, lines and curves. The shapes stay separate, so you can pick them up and move them around later if you want to. And (unlike with Colorforms), you can change an object's attributes, like its overall size, proportions, and color —SZA/AB

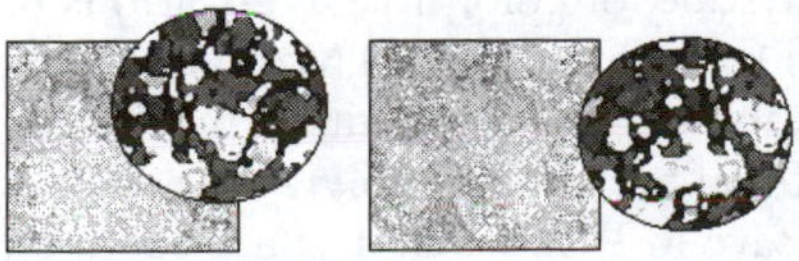

"Objects" exist separately in a drawing and can be manipulated singly.

Bitmapped versus vector graphics. Bitmaps are easy to make and easy to understand, but they have their limitations. For one thing, they're hard to edit. For another, when you look closely—or when you enlarge a bitmap—you can see that "curved" edges are actually jagged because they're made up of individual, square pixels.

Vector graphics are not only easy to manipulate, they take lots less disk space to store. And they have the edge on bitmaps in another way: vector graphics are *resolution independent,* which means you can zoom in or resize them as much as you want, and they'll never look jagged. And if you print a vector graphic, it will look as sharp and detailed as your printer can make it. (By contrast, a bitmap will always print out at its own built-in resolution—so even if you have a 1,440-dpi printer, you could still end up with coarse, 72-dpi output from a bitmap.) Of course, vector graphics can't do everything. For one thing, they're not good for photos. They don't do things like random textures (like tree bark) very well, either. —SZA/AB

PostScript graphics. A "PostScript drawing program" is still a vector-based draw program as described in the last entry. What makes it a *PostScript* drawing program is that the information about your drawing is stored so that a PostScript description of it can be sent to a PostScript output device.

Bézier curves. One of the toughest concepts to master regarding drawing in PostScript programs is the *Bézier* (bez-ee-ay) *curve*. Created by French mathematician Pierre Bézier to streamline the process of cutting car parts with automated machines, Bézier curves provide an inventive way to control curves. Using two *endpoints*, or *anchor points*, and two control handles for each line segment, you can create a wide variety of curves.

Unfortunately these curves are one of the least intuitive aspects of drawing ever to be loosed upon unwitting artists. The learning, er, *curve* is so steep it seems unclimbable at first. Eventually, after some practice, the magic of Bézier curves becomes apparent. —RT

File formats. While bitmaps and vectors are the two types of graphics, there are many different ways to save them, so there are more than two kinds of graphics file formats. Fortunately, fewer than a half dozen formats account for the vast majority of the graphics files you'll run into.

- **TIFF** (*Tagged Image File Format*, pronounced as a word): This is a bitmapped format that's pretty common in the publishing business. TIFF files often turn up in the form of scans or stock photos. They can contain black and white, grayscale, or color images at various resolutions. Just to complicate things, TIFFs come in both Mac and PC flavors. Most Mac graphics programs can deal with both kinds, but PC software is not usually so bright—so if you're planning on giving a TIFF to a PC-using friend, be sure you save in PC format if your program offers that option.

- **PICT** (*PICTure*, pronounced as a word): Can't decide between bitmaps and vectors? PICT, the Mac's native graphics format, lets you have either one, or even both, in the same file. A few programs, like ClarisWorks, can work with both vector and bitmap PICTs.
- **GIF** (*Graphics Interchange Format*, pronounced as a word with a hard *g*): A compressed file format; images stored this way take up less space, which makes them useful for web pages where you want to minimize download times. GIF images can only have 256 colors, though—so this format is much better for line art and cartoons than for photographs.
- **JPEG** (*Joint Photographic Experts Group*, pronounced "jay peg"): Another compressed format, but this one lets you have millions of colors, which is what you need to make photos look realistic. You can also get much higher compression with JPEG than with GIF, but you have to watch it: unlike GIF files, JPEG-compressed images lose some quality when they are expanded again—and the more compression you apply, the worse they look.
- **EPS** (*Encapsulated PostScript*, pronounced as separate letters): These vector graphics are the elite of the publishing industry. They can be scaled up or down without losing quality, and they take best advantage of any printer's resolution. The *encapsulated* part refers to the fact that the file stores the PostScript information for the printer as well as QuickDraw information for screen display. (Technically, you can also store a bitmap image in an EPS file, but EPS is very inefficient with bitmaps—file sizes can balloon dramatically—so it's seldom done.)

So how do you know which format to use? Here's a brief rundown:

- **Publishing:** Use EPS for line art and TIFF for scanned photos.
- **Web pages:** Use GIF for line art (logos, decorative graphics, and so on) and JPEG for photos.
- **Personal artwork:** Use your graphics program's native format, or use PICT. If the image is one you don't plan to modify any further and you're just archiving it, use JPEG at a high quality setting. Important: Don't store images you're actively working on in JPEG format! Every time you open and re-save a JPEG image, a little more quality is lost. Keep images you're working on in PICT or Photoshop format until you're sure you're finished, then you can file them in JPEG format if you need to save space. —SZA/AB

Programs and Utilities

The big three. The big three graphics programs on the Mac (and, in fact, in computerdom-at-large) are Photoshop, Illustrator, and Freehand. But make no mistake: these are—in price, complexity, and results—tools for the professional; if you want to get into Mac graphics, you don't have to start here.

Adobe's **Photoshop** ($600) is, as its name implies, the perfect place to edit photographs, but it's also the profesional tool of choice for from-scratch artwork. Version 5, just being released as this book goes to print, has finally added text-handling features as well as a solution to my personal Photoshop pet peeve: the lasso can finally shrink automatically around a selection.

The illustration tools **Illustrator** ($375, Adobe) and **Freehand** ($400, Macromedia) take an entirely different approach to creating and editing graphics, since they were developed specifically to produce PostScript output. Instead of photographic-type artwork, these programs concentrate on high-quality PostScript output of text and illustrations. Professionals keep both programs around, and for the most part, they offer equal power and elegance. When pushed to state a preference for one of the programs, most designers finally opt for Illustrator, so if you're looking to try one, that's the best place to start.

> ***Question: How many designers does it take to screw in a light bulb? Designer's answer: Does it have to be a light bulb?***

The big painting programs. When the gamut of painting programs ran from the inexpensive (about $100) MacPaint and SuperPaint to the high-end (around $1000) Photoshop, there was room for an in-between approach, which both Deneba's **Canvas** ($400) and MetaCreation's **Painter** ($275) fulfilled. Both are beautifully executed programs, with Canvas leaning towards the illustration end of things, and Painter mimicking a real (non-digital) artist's approach to painting better than any other program.

The only hesitation in recommending either of these programs is what I think of as the price/benefit ratio. To go with the non-mainstream Canvas, despite its excellence, when it's the same price as Illustrator and not that much less than Photoshop, is not the best move for a beginner. With the amazing Painter, the price comparison is not against the higher-priced programs, but the beginner programs: if you want to learn Mac painting techniques, you can start out with packages under $100 and then graduate to a more expensive approach—at which point you might decide you need Photoshop.

For the rest of us. You want to do a little artwork for your web page, or for a newsletter, or just for your pleasure and further edification. You *don't* want to spend around $500 to paint on-screen in your leisure time. Who ya gonna call? Luckily, many of the big programs have "lite" versions:

- **Photo Deluxe** ($50, Adobe) is a baby Photoshop, perfect for home and business, especially when coupled with the cheap digital imagery available through digital cameras and CD-ROM-based storage of traditional photos. Whether you're putting up the new baby's picture on your web site with Mom's dark-circled eyes freshened up, creating a family-reunion montage, or cropping personnel photos for a database, Photo Deluxe lets you have the basic photo-manipulation tools at less than ten percent of Photoshop's price.

- **Painter Classic** ($90, MetaCreations) is a subset of Painter, but definitely isn't just a crippled version of a larger program. It uses the real-world-artist approach, providing familiar tools and special effects.
- **Art Dabbler** ($50, MetaCreations) is just that: a program that lets you dabble in the world of computer painting. But don't let the name or the price fool you: there's lots to this program that will keep you—and any older kids in the family—busy for a long time. You can even create animations to be played back in flipbooks or as QuickTime movies.

adobe.com
metacreations.com
deneba.com

- **ArtWorks** ($50, Deneba) offers a double-barrel approach, combining drawing and painting capabilities in one package—accompanied by 500 fonts and 8,000 clip-art images!

And don't forget: **ClarisWorks** includes both paint and draw capabilities along with its word processor, database, and spreadsheet, for only $100—although if you don't need any of its basic productivity modules, don't buy it just for the graphics capabilities, which are nowhere near the sophistication (or fun) of any of the other packages described in this entry.

DeBabelizer. In case you're not up on your biblical references, this product refers to the Tower of Babel, whose construction led to the splintering of the then sole human language. And, so went the communication between computer programs as more and more graphics formats were created to serve various needs.

Equilbrium's **DeBabelizer** ($400) handles—reading and writing—more than a hundred different graphics file types, changing one to another as needed. It supports scripting and batch processing; it can even extract graphics from references in an HTML file and work on them as a batch. You can optimize graphics files: reduce or increase color depth, remap the colors to any built-in or custom palette (web designers take note!), and improve dithering when you're reducing the color bit depth. **DeBabelizer Lite** ($140) offers a little more than half the number of filtering capabilities for less than half the price; you don't get CYMK handling, or some of the more advanced features, like scripting and palette manipulation.

equil.com

GIFConverter. While it doesn't approach the sophistication or power of DeBabelizer, the shareware **GIFConverter** ($30) may supply all you need in the way of graphics file conversions—and the price is right.

Clip Art

About clip art. The concept of clip art has been around in the traditional graphics arts community for a long time: you buy a book of pre-drawn art that you can use in your artwork any way you see fit. Why waste your time drawing a light bulb, for instance, when someone else can do it better and faster and your time is better spent concentrating on, say, the layout of your Bright Ideas newsletter?

As with almost everything, the available computer clip art runs the gamut from so-so to terrific. Most professionals turn up their noses at the "One Hundred Gazillion Images!" packages, but they are (the packages, not the professionals) life-savers for the less artistically endowed among us.

When you buy a package of clip art, you're allowed to use the images any way you want: you can use them as-is or alter them, put them in a book or in a newsletter, or print them out for your children to color. What you *can't* do is turn around and sell them for someone else to use—a reasonable enough limitation.

Here are some things to keep in mind when you shop for a clip art package:

- Know what kind of images you need for the job you're doing. EPS graphics, for instance, are perfect for print jobs, but not for the Web.
- Most packages are updated every year or so—sometimes every six months. Yesterday's 60,000 images is today's 100,000-image package. But that almost always (I've yet to see an exception) includes the original 60,000 images, so you're getting only (*only??*) 40,000 new ones if you buy the same brand. You're probably better off buying one brand the first time, from another manufacturer the second, and then maybe back to the first vendor for your third purchase—at which point, the package may have tripled in size, enough to make it worth the purchase price despite some repeats in the content.
- The majority of clip art is colorful—not exactly what a person with black-and-white/grayscale printing capabilities from a LaserWriter can use. In many cases, the lighter colors in a graphic will drop out, the middle-range colors will all look the same, and the darker ones all print as black, ruining the image. If you expect to make use of most or all of a package and it's primarily color, make sure you have a program like Illustrator that will let you go in and change the fill colors—or a late-model LaserWriter that provides top-notch grayscale capability.
- Most of the photographs included with big clip art packages are not top quality. I have one package with three photos of the Statue of Liberty included—and not one of them shows the entire crown in the shot. Photographs are difficult to print well, too, and unless you're lucky enough to find *just* the right picture, you'll need a photo-manipulation program to make any use of them.
- The best clip art is designed so you can alter it, taking apart what are essentially grouped images. If, for instance, there's a cornucopia of fruit, you should be able to pull out the apple at its mouth and find that both the apple and the cornucopia (and its other contents) are still complete images unto themselves.

- Most important of all: make sure your clip art comes with a reference book of the images—preferably with a decent index, although you won't have much choice there. Online catalogues and search engines just aren't enough, and no match for browsing through a book of miniature images to familiarize yourself with the clip art collection.

novadevcorp.com

Clip art for the Web
Chapter 21

Nova's Latest Explosion. Nova Development's **Art Explosion** ($90) just keeps growing, having started at 40,000 images, jumped to 125,000, and now settled for a while at 250,000 (the name of the package includes the number of images, so you can keep track of which one you're buying). On the 21 CD-ROMs, you'll find that a little more than half are vector art; you'll also find TIFF and JPEG images, photos, backgrounds, borders… with 250,000 items, you'll find a little of everything, including web-oriented graphics, short animations, and a few thousand fonts.

The ClickArt Collection. The first ever clip art package for the Mac was T/Maker's ClickArt, a line that has grown exponentially and is now available through Broderbund. The **ClickArt Image Pak** started as a collection of 45,000 images, went to 65,000 and then 125,000 and is now at the 200,000 mark. For Windows, that is. It's especially sad that the first Mac clip art seems to be abandoning the platform, especially in an area where it's so easy to do two versions of a product. I'm listing it here anyway, with the high hope that they'll come to their senses and put out the Mac version of their humongous package. In the meantime, the **Incredible Image Pak** of 40,000 images is available for $15 (although compared to a few hundred thousand in other packages, that's not so incredible), and various smaller packages, like **ClickArt Newsletter Art, ClickArt Parties & Events, ClickArt Christian Illustrations,** and **ClickArt Beastly Funnies** are available for $18-$30.

adobestudios.com

The Adobe Image Library. What better company to provide clip art images than the one that provides the top-notch graphics programs? Of course, Adobe sort of cheated by buying out the Image Club line of graphics to jump-start their library, but that only means that you can get both the old Image Club products as well as new ones through Adobe. The Library (which is a category of products, not a product itself) includes both photographic and illustration collections.

The top-notch photographic collections, with titles like Animals, Business Essentials, Action Sports, Active Women, Endless Skies and Floral Focus, are priced at $300 and include about 100 images each. Adobe's attention to the needs of the graphics professional means that each image is supplied in four formats: CMYK high-res, RGB high-res, RGB "optimized" (for screen viewing for presentations or web use), and RGB low-res for comps.

The **DigitArt** clip art collections are $100 each for one to two hundred images. Available collections include: Businessville, Hoopla! Cuts, Nifty

Fifties, Law & Justice, Technology Then & Now, and Neo Retro. (Samples from the first three packages are shown here.)

Art Parts Fonthaus refers to its **Art Parts** collection as "wacky clip art," and perhaps that's a good description of the style. There are 65 different Art Parts sets that are $35 each on disk, or 13 sets together on a CD for $170; as I write this, their newest CD set, called **Cheap Parts**, is priced at $99.

fonthaus.com

MasterClips. Up from the previous 101,000 and 202,000 versions, the MasterClips 303,000 package ($70, IMSI) is an excellent package offering terrific images of several types: vector, fine art (classic paintings and illustrations); masterphotos (photographic images); web images (buttons and other 3-D objects); and "classics," from the traditional Dover clip art collection. It also includes about 200 animation clips, almost 5000 sound clips, and 2000 TrueType fonts. In all, bargain price without the sometime bargain quality penalty!

imsisoft.com

MEGA Gallery. The **Corel Mega Gallery** ($40, Corel) offers 50,000 vector clip art images—the first 15,000 coming from the superseded Gallery 2 package—as well as 60,000 photo images (low-res, for web use), 1,000 fonts (mostly TrueType, but some Type 1 PostScript), and a few hundred sounds and animations. It doesn't really deserve the *mega* prefix, seeing as how other packages offer hundreds of thousands pictures, but it's a decent price for good, extremely usable art.

corel.com

Clipables. The **Clipables** packages have always received good reviews, though not much name recognition. Now they're available in a single collection, **Clipables Master CD** ($150, C.A.R. and Neuconcepts)—and it's been available at a "special" price of only $50 for quite some time, so you may find the actual price has been lowered by the time you read this.

clipables.com

The collection of four original Clipables packages—Main Library, Statements, Travel and Vacation, and Editions—provides over 2000 different EPS images. Each is rendered in full color, but the original black-and-white versions are also included; as a bonus, each image was rasterized in Photoshop to create a PICT file, saving you the trouble of converting it for other uses.

WetPaint and WetSet. The **WetSet Collection** ($350, DublClick) is a ten-volume collection of the **WetPaint** clip art products ($30 each). This has always been a favorite of mine—way back when the Mac could barely handle color, the black-and-white bitmap approach could be just what you need for some projects. But the collection, though convenient, is overpriced in today's clip art market. You're better off sampling (from their web site) and then perhaps purchasing some of the better packages—the ones best served by the bitmapped approach, like For Publishing, Printer's Helper, and Industrial Revolution.

dublclick.com

ClarisWorks Paint and Draw Tips

These tips were evaluated for ClarisWorks 5, but most work in the previous version, too.

ClarisWorks may have been renamed "AppleWorks" by the time you read this!

Painting and Drawing

Quick copy. Make a quick copy of any selection (painting) or selected object (drawing) by holding down Option as you drag it.

Quick eye dropper. Pressing Tab while you're using any tool will select the Eye Dropper; pressing Tab again gives back the tool you were using. If you've actually selected the Eye Dropper in the toolbox, Tab alternates between it and the last-used tool.

Polygon sides. The Polygon tool lets you draw regular polygons from triangles to forty-sided objects (that don't have an official name). But the way you adjust the tool is different in the Paint and Draw modes. For painting, you simply double-click on the Polygon tool to get the dialog where you enter the number of sides you want. In the Draw layer, you click on the tool to select it and then choose Polygon Sides from the Edit menu.

Tear-off palettes. All the palettes that pop out from items in the tool panel—like the line and fill colors, line width, and patterns—can be dragged out onto the screen, where they turn into stand-alone palettes.

Styled lines. You can change the line you draw with the line tool by adjusting its width and color, but you still get a solid line. There are two ways, however, to get styled lines.

The first is to use the pen pattern palette; select a pattern, and the line tool will use it; changing the width of the line gives different effects with patterns.

The second way works only in a paint document, not for drawing. Forget the line tool entirely and instead edit a paintbrush: double-click on the paintbrush tool, select an existing brush shape, click the Edit button, and create a new brush shape. Painting with a brush that has "gaps" in it makes styled lines (hold down Shift to paint a straight line).

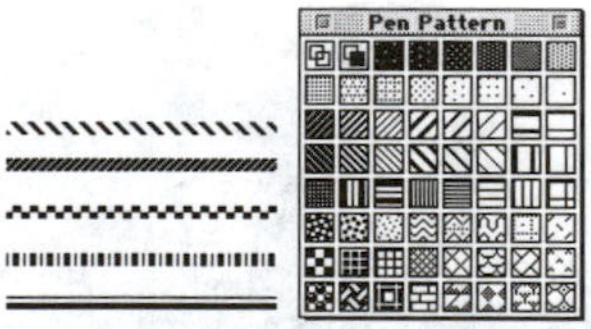

Changing the Pen pattern affects the line tool, letting you paint styled lines.

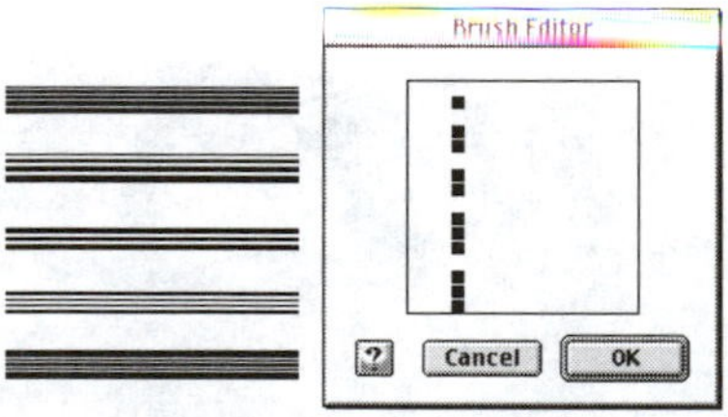

You can paint styled lines by editing the Paint brush.

More colors. The default color palette provides 81 different colors for fills and lines, but you can up that to 256. In the Preferences command for the document, select Palettes from the dialog's pop-up menu, and click the *Editable 256 Color Palette* button under the Colors button. In addition to giving you more colors, you'll find that the larger palette also lets you use the basic Mac Color Picker to change the selection of colors in the palette.

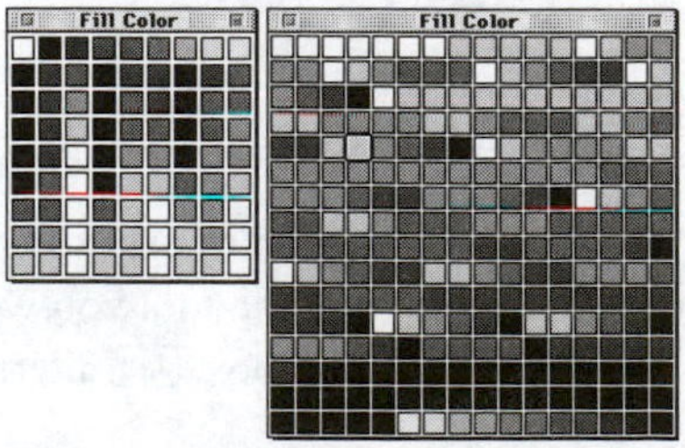

Switch from the default, smaller Color palette to the larger one with a Preferences setting.

Editing colors, patterns, and textures. The colors, patterns, textures and gradients that are in their respective palettes can all be edited if you want to change them. Just tear off the palette so it's a separate window, then double-click on the item you want to edit. The editing window that opens, and the tools it provides, depends on what you're editing.

Drawing

Hang on to a tool. When you click on a tool and then use it to draw a shape, the tool is automatically unselected as soon as the shape is finished—the Selection Arrow is activated again. If you'd like to use a tool for more than one item, double-click on the tool; it will remain selected until you click on another tool. ClarisWorks provides some visual feedback for this, too: a single-time tool is inverted to gray in the palette, while a multiple-use tool is inverted to black.

Shape edit shortcuts. You can change some of the attributes of a rectangle, rounded rectangle, or arc by simply double-clicking on the object itself in the document, which opens a dialog where you can set the changes. You can change a rectangle to a rounded rectangle of any "roundness" on the corners; a rounded rectangle can be changed to a rounded-end rectangle; and an arc can have its starting angle and total angle changed, as well as have the sides framed (to look like a pie slice).

IN THE BEGINNING

Xerox filed a copyright infringement suit against Apple in 1990 because Apple derived the Mac interface from programs developed at Xerox PARC (Palo Alto Research Center). The suit asked to have Xerox declared the sole owner of the graphical user interface. In the response, Apple acknowledged Xerox's pioneering role but said that ideas can not be copyrighted.

In June of 1993, Apple lost its five-year copyright-infringement case against Microsoft and Hewlett-Packard for copying the Mac's graphical interface. An Apple spokesperson declared: "We think it is important that innovative graphical computer works receive the protection to which they are entitled under the copyright law."

Shift for moving multiple objects. Holding down Shift when you move an object constrains the movement to a vertical, horizontal, or 45-degree angle. Holding Shift while you click on an object adds it to or subtracts it from a group of selected objects. So, if you select three objects, then hold down

Shift while you click on one of them to "grab" the group to drag it in a straight line—you wind up only deselecting that one from the group!

It's not impossible to constrain the movement of a group. After selecting the group, just click on any one of the items and, *after* the mouse button is down, press Shift and then start dragging. Alternatively, you can press Shift before clicking on the last item you want to add to the group, and once you Shift-click on it, keep the mouse button down and start dragging.

Rotating multiple objects. If you're going to rotate more than one object at a time, you'll probably be surprised at the outcome unless you group the objects first. The picture here shows what happens to the two objects (on the left) if you rotate them 90 degrees as separate objects (center) or as a grouped object (right).

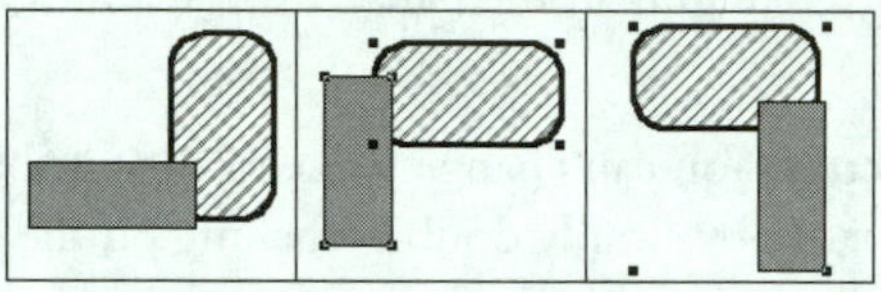

The result of rotating multiple objects (left) varies according to whether the objects are separate (center) or grouped (right).

Painting

Repeating copies. Holding down Option while you drag a selection pulls out a copy of that selection, but adding ⌘ lets you leave multiple copies behind as you drag; the number of copies you leave behind depends on how fast you move the mouse. The picture here shows the effect from a simple striped circle, but by using different shapes or colors, you can, in effect, paint with any kind of "paintbrush" you care to design.

The repeating copy trick also lets you "Band-Aid" holes in regular patterns by just dragging over them. The second picture here, for instance, shows how a mistaken erasure can be repaired by simply ⌘Option-dragging a selection across the "damaged" area.

Holding down Command-option creates multiple copies as you drag a selection; the top figure was a slow drag, while the bottom one was faster.

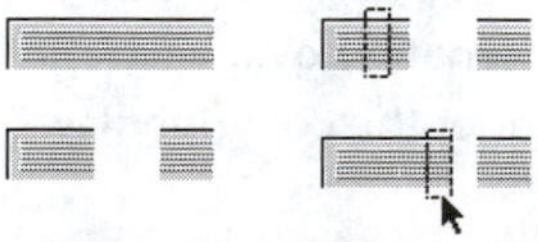

Left, the original figure and the mistaken erasure. Right, drawing a selection rectangle and Command-option dragging the selection to repair the hole by repeating the pattern.

Embossing. "Embossing" text or graphics shapes is a great way to get some subtle texture into a background graphic or border; and, while it's a multi-step process, it's easy to do. The main goal is to have the shape (or text) the exact same shade as the background, and provide a slightly darker edge on one side and a slightly lighter edge on the other.

1. Choose your background color and make a block of it by drawing a filled-in rectangle.
2. Create the shape you want to emboss, or paste it in or drag it in from a Library. (If you make the shape—both the outline and the fill—the exact same color as the background, you can skip the next step.)
3. For any figure that's not the same color as the background, lasso the shape and drag it onto the background. Use the Pick Up command from the Transform menu to pick up the background color and drag the altered shape out of the color block.
4. Lasso the color-matched shape, hold down Option, and drag out a copy of the shape.
5. Select a color one or two shades lighter than the background and pour it into the second shape with the Paint Bucket.
6. Lasso either shape, drag out a copy, and pour in a color that's a shade or two darker than the original.
7. Lasso the lightest shape and drag it onto the background.
8. Lasso the darkest shape and drag it onto the background, exactly on top of the light shape. While it's still selected, nudge it three pixels to the right and down by pressing → three times and then ↓ three times.
9. Lasso the original shape (the one with the color that matches the background), and drag it onto the other shapes, aligning it exactly with the lightest shape. Nudge it one pixel over and down by using the arrow keys.

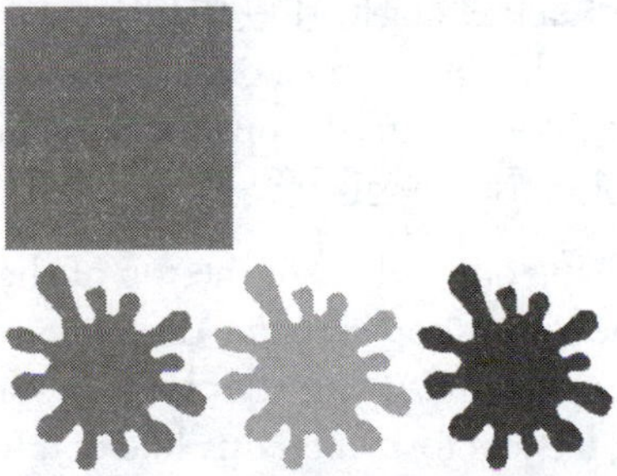

For embossing, start with a block of color, and three copies of a shape: one that matches the background color, one that's lighter, and one that's darker.

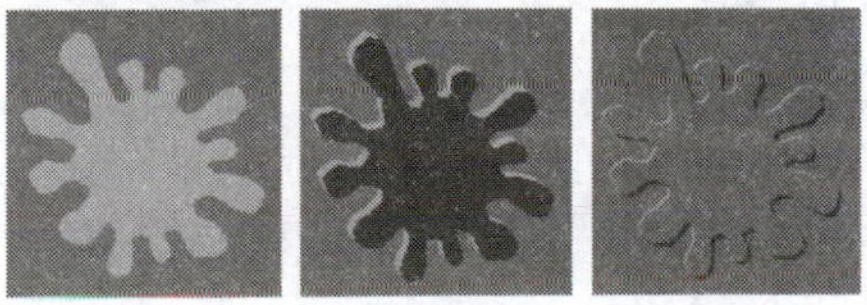

The three-step process: start with the lightest color, offset the darkest color on top of it, and place the background-colored shape on top, positioned between the other two.

Automatic lasso. The cinching effect of the lasso is one that you often need when making a paint selection, but dragging it around the image you want is, well… a drag sometimes. If there's enough clear space around the image, you can use the selection rectangle instead, holding down ⌘ while you drag; when you release the mouse button, the selected area shrinks down to lasso whatever is inside the rectangle.

Selecting the entire document. When you want to select the entire document, just double-click on the Selection Rectangle; a rectangular area the size of the document (regardless of the size of the image) will be selected.

To lasso everything in the document, you can double-click on the Lasso, or ⌘-double-click on the Selection Rectangle.

Photoshop Tips

My "graphics team" helped collect and evaluate the tips in this section, with Jerry Szubin being the official collaborator on most entries.

These tips were written for Photoshop 4, since version 5 came out just before the book went to print. Almost all these tips work in the new version, with the exception of some tool palette keyboard shortcuts and the "easter egg" in the About box.

General

Plugging in. To select a plug-in location other than the default on program startup, hold down ⌘ Option on launch.

Reset dialog opens. You can reset most dialog box settings to what they were when the box first opened by holding down Option, which changes the Cancel button to a Reset button, and the clicking the Reset button. This conveniently leaves the dialog box open for a different set of changes if that's what you need. For a keyboard-only method of resetting the dialog, press Option Esc.

Delete key color tricks. Pressing ⌘ Delete fills a selection with the background color. To fill only the opaque area of a selection with the background color, use ⌘ Shift Delete. If you want the opaque areas in the selection filled with the foreground color, use Option Shift Delete.

Beyond credits. Clicking on the logo at the top of the toolbox gets you the expected, formal Adobe Photoshop credits—the same ones you get by selecting About from the Apple menu. If you wait long enough, the text begins to scroll, and you'll see some less formal credits like den mother (I know that feeling), babysitter (I know that feeling) and the all-important Legal Mumbo-Jumbo.

If you ⌘-click on the toolbox logo or hold down ⌘ while choosing About, you'll get a different—a *very* different—logo in the About box. And if you ⌘-click on the nose… well, I'm not going to tell you what will happen—you'll have to try and see.

Auto-size a new document. There are three ways to "automate" the sizing of new document:

- If there's something on the Clipboard, the size in the New dialog defaults to the size of the Clipboard contents in case that's what you want.
- To match the size that you last used in the New dialog, hold down Option as you select the New command, or press ⌘ Option N.
- The Window menu remains available when the New dialog is open. To match the size of any opened document, select it from the Window menu when the New dialog is open.

The contextual menus. If you Control-click with almost any tool anywhere in your document, you'll get a contextual menu whose commands, of course, depend upon the tool you're using. So, with a selection tool active, you'll get commands including Select All and Load Layer; with the Paintbrush, you'll get Next Brush, Previous Brush, and all the layer modes listed.

Two of the most convenient pop-ups are for the Eraser and the Move Tool. For the Eraser, you get a menu with Next, Previous, First, and Last Brushes, and the four eraser tools. Best of all is the contextual-ness of the menu for the Move Tool: the menu lists all the layers, but *only* the layers, that have an opaque pixel at the spot that you click.

Tools and Palettes

Hide and seek palettes. Pressing Tab alternately hides and shows all the open palettes and the toolbox. To hide/show only the palettes, leaving the toolbox where it is, press Shift Tab.

Auto-open tool palettes. It's easy to open the Options palette for a specific tool, without having to go up to the Window menu for the Show Options command: just press Return while a tool is selected, and its palette opens.

Collapsing palettes. You can collapse a palette window by double-clicking on its title bar; even though there's no title in it, it's still a title bar as far as the Mac's concerned (you use it to drag the window around). But then you get nothing but a blank title bar, which, while it clears up the screen, doesn't help much when you need something and can't tell which palette's which. Instead, double-click on the palette *tab*, which collapses the window down to just display the tab(s).

When you want to expand a palette again, you can double-click on the frontmost tab or single-click on any background tab. You can tell the difference even when the palette's collapsed because the frontmost tab is white and the others are shaded.

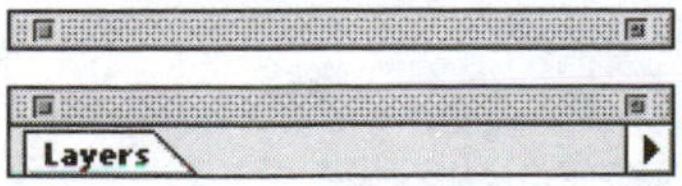

Collape a palette by double-clicking on the title bar (top) or one of its tabs (bottom).

Join and separate palettes. You can combine any of PageMaker's palettes into single windows that have tabs for accessing each individual palette: just drag the tab of the palette from one window to another. To separate palettes, drag the tab out of the window and drop it anywhere on the screen.

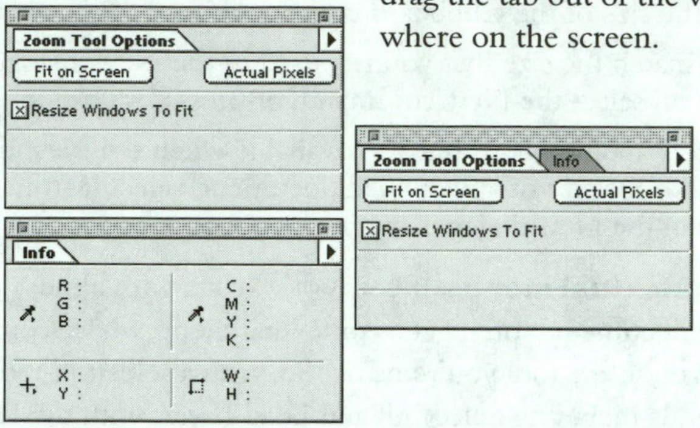

Two palettes (left) combined into one (right).

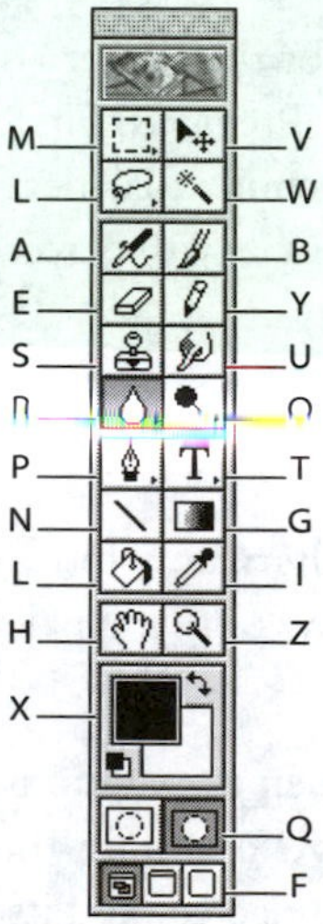

Pressing a letter on the keyboard selects various items in the toolbox.

Keyboard selection of tools. Everything you see in the toolbox, and even some things you can't see, can be selected from the keyboard, so you won't have to move the mouse from the section of the document you're working on.

The multiple tools accessed through pop-out menus from the toolbox can also be accessed from the keyboard, by multiple presses of the letter key, which cycles the spot through all its available tools.

Swapping foreground and background colors. You can swap the foreground and background colors showing in the Tool palette by pressing X. To return both swatches to the default, press D.

Skip the pop-out. Instead of selecting a tool from a Tool-palette pop-out menu, you can Option-click on the tool to cycle to the next item.

Temporary tools. No matter which tool is active, you can switch to a few important ones temporarily by holding down certain keys:

Hand tool	Spacebar
Move tool	⌘
Magnify tool	⌘ Spacebar
Minimize tool	⌘ Option Spacebar

Precise, and not, pointers. You have a choice of two or three different cursors for each of the tools you use. Every tool offers a *standard* cursor, which usually is the shape of the tool itself. Every tool also has a *precise* cursor, a light crosshairs with a dot in the middle that shows the cursor's "hot spot." In addition, the "painting" tools (eraser, pencil, airbrush, paintbrush, rubber stamp, smudge, blur, sharpen, dodge, burn, and sponge) also have a cursor referred to as *brush size*, which is the size and shape that you've set for that tool.

You set the preferences for the two groups of tools (Painting and Other) through the File menu's Preferences command, in the Display & Cursors dialog. But you can override the default settings with Caps Lock. If you've set the preference to Standard or Brush Size, keeping Caps Lock down will give you the Precise cursor, and vice versa.

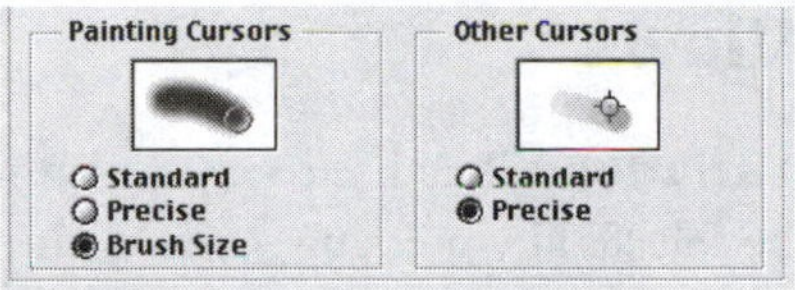

The cursor settings in the Display & Cursors dialog.

Off to see the wizard. Hold down Option and select Options from the Layers palette menu. For some reason, this results in the adorable little window shown here.

The palette trash can. In earlier versions of Photoshop, you had to drag an item (a layer, for instance) to the little Trash can at the bottom of the window to delete it. Starting in Photoshop 4, however, just clicking on the Trash can deletes the currently selected layer. (Both methods of sending something to the Trash are undoable.) The only difference: when you click to delete, you'll get a confirming dialog as to whether you really want to throw the item away.

Tip within a tip: to use the click method of trashing something and bypass the confirming dialog, Option-click on the trash icon.

Info window shortcuts. When you want to change the measurement or color readout modes in the Info palette, you can use the palette menu (click in the menu arrow at the right of the palette) to open a dialog that lets you take care of all the settings. But to change only one setting, it's faster to use the individual pop-up menus: click on the eyedropper or crosshairs cursors in the palette for a menu of choices.

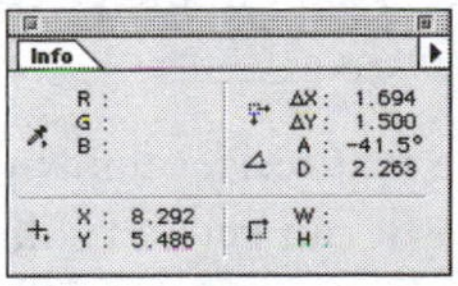

The palette menu opens a dialog for setting all options, but you can set individual options by clicking in the palette itself.

The invisible tape measure. When you're using the Line tool, the Info window tells you how far you've moved from the original click spot horizontally (ΔX) and vertically (ΔY). It also shows you the line's angle (A) and length (D, for *distance)*.

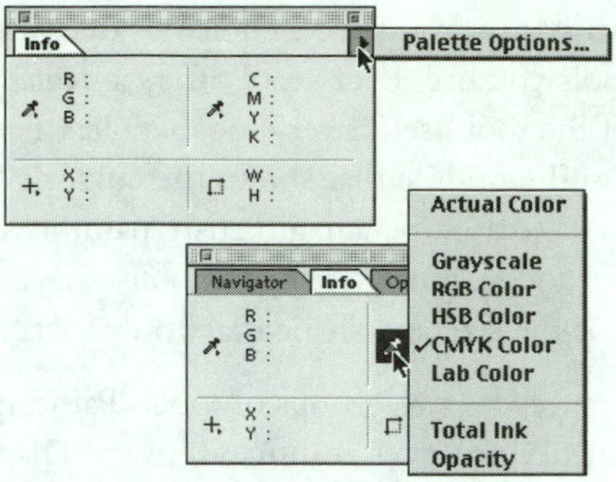

Use the readouts in the Info window as a measuring tape.

If you want to simply measure something but not draw anything, set the line width to zero, and drag the invisible line across the area you want to measure.

Windows and Views

Basic zooming, and variations. The basic way to zoom is to use the Zoom tool (which can be selected by pressing Z) to click anywhere on the document to increase its size. Here are some handy basic variations on the zoom theme:

- Hold Option to change the tool so it zooms out instead of in.
- Use ⌘ Option + and ⌘ Option - to zoom in and out.
- Double-click the Zoom tool icon in the palette to go directly to a 100 percent view.
- Drag the Zoom tool over an area to magnify the dragged area to the full size of the window.
- No matter what tool you're using, you can press ⌘ and drag a rectangle in the Navigator window to enlarge that area in the real document—a great way to jump to a portion of the document that isn't showing in the window.

Hold that zoom. You can type a zoom percentage directly in the lower left corner of either the document window or the Navigator palette; pressing Return or Enter applies that percentage to the view. But if you hold down Shift while pressing Return or Enter, the percentage stays selected so you can immediately type in a different one if the first doesn't meet your needs.

Full size versus full window. There are several ways to view your work at actual size: double-click on the Zoom tool icon in the palette, use the Actual Pixels command in the View menu, or press ⌘ Option 0 (zero).

But there's another "full-size" view, one that resizes the window to the full size of the screen—or, at least, as large as it can get and still keep the correct proportions for its contents. So, the result of using this full-window view depends on the size of your screen, and the size of your artwork. To get the full window, double-click on the Hand tool icon in the palette, choose Fit on Screen from the View menu, or press ⌘ 0. (Clicking a window's zoom box merely sizes the window to display as much of the artwork as possible at its current zoom size.)

The screen background. If your artwork isn't as large as the screen (or larger), the surrounding screen items can be distracting, and various surrounding colors can be misleading. Press F to center the artwork on the screen and change the screen background to black; press it again to change the surrounding area to gray; press it once more to return to a standard window view.

Selecting

Moving the selection shape. You know you can move the active selection shape by simply grabbing and dragging it. But you can actually shift the shape while you're still drawing it, in case you see that you've started at the wrong spot: just press Spacebar without lifting the mouse button, and the shape will start moving along with the mouse. Let go of the key, and you can continue drawing the selection shape.

Selection shape constraints. Holding Shift while you use the selection rectangle or oval constrains the shapes to squares or circles. But this works only for the first selection, because after that, Shift adds to the selection rather than constrains the shape.

Constraining shifting selections. As you drag an active selection shape to a new position, you can constrain it to vertical, horizontal, or 45-degree movements by holding down Shift. This is a little tricky, because if you press Shift before you click the mouse button, you'll be adding to the selection when you start dragging. So, make sure you press the mouse button *before* you press Shift.

Moving the shape with arrow keys. You can move the selection shape without dragging it: using ↑↓←→ shifts it by a pixel. You probably already knew that, because using those keys to move an object on the screen is pretty much second nature to Mac users. But you might not know this: using Shift with any of the arrow keys moves the selection in 10-pixel increments.

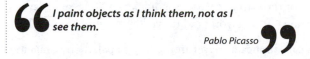

> ***I paint objects as I think them, not as I see them.***
>
> *Pablo Picasso*

Altering a selection. There are lots of ways you can alter a selection after it's made, using different keys in combination with a selection tool:

- Shift-drag to add to the current selection; the addition can be "attached" to the current selection, or in a totally different area.
- Option-drag to remove part of the original selection.
- Shift Option-drag a new selection, and you'll wind up with only the parts that are in common to the original selection and the new one.

You can use the Shift-Option method to make an entirely new selection inside an existing one without deselecting first. If, for instance, you used Select All to select the entire layer, you can simply Shift-Option-drag a new selection anywhere in the layer; because that actually selects only the area in common to both selections, you wind up with the smaller selection in the end.

Layers

Merging a layer. Pressing ⌘-E merges the current layer with the one beneath it—it's the same as the Merge Down command in the Layers palette menu. Just make sure, before you use it, that your layers are in the order you *think* they are so that the current layer is merged with the correct layer.

Because pasting something creates a new layer, when you want something pasted onto an existing layer, pressing ⌘-V,E will, in effect, paste something to the current layer—just make sure it's in the right spot before you merge the layers! (That's holding down ⌘ while pressing V and then E—a tiny time saver over pressing ⌘-V and then ⌘-E.)

Merging multiple layers. The Merge Visible command combines all the visible layers into one; its keyboard command is ⌘-Shift-E. But here's a terrific variation on that capability: create a new, empty layer and then press ⌘-Shift-Option-E. All the visible layers will be *copied* onto the new layer, so you have a merged layer but all the original layers are still there.

Swapping and selecting layers. As noted in the Arrange submenu, ⌘-[and ⌘-] move the current layer forward or back, and adding Shift to either combination jumps the layer to the top or bottom of the pile. But a variation on those keyboard combinations can select a layer without moving it in the hierarchy: Option-[and Option-] select the previous or next layer, while Option-Shift-[and Option-Shift-] select the first or last layer.

New layer option. When you create a new layer through the Layer menu, you get a dialog that lets you set options for the layer—including that all-important layer name so you can keep track of things. Clicking on the New Layer icon at the bottom of the Layers palette is a quick way to create a layer, but you don't get the dialog—unless you hold down Option while you click!

Quick duplicate. You can duplicate a layer in the Layers palette by dragging the layer you want into the New Layer icon at the bottom of the palette. Holding Option while you drag it in opens the New Layer dialog.

20

Page Layout

In This Chapter

About Page Layout

Basics

About layout. Even the simplest of word processors these days lets you set up multicolumn pages and wrap text around graphics. But for detailed work or large files, there's nothing like a page layout program for giving you complete control over the design of a printed page.

There aren't so many products in the field that we need to talk about the features you should look for; they all offer the same basic features, although the implementation often differs. Most people need PageMaker or QuarkXPress, with the majority opting for Quark (see the next entry); if you do single-page ad layouts, you should take a look at Multi-Ad Creator, and for special high-end jobs you might want to consider FrameMaker.

IN THE BEGINNING

Adobe PageMaker began life as *Aldus* PageMaker, from a company named for Aldus Manutius, a fifteenth-century printer and font designer who created one of the first italic font faces. He printed the first small, almost pocket-sized books, cheaply enough so that many people could afford to buy them. When he died, he was buried surrounded by books.

Aldus (the company) was bought out by Adobe years ago. Where did that name come from? It's the name of a dry creek that runs behind the Northern California home of the company's founder.

PageMaker and QuarkXPress. There's no sense in spending a few pages on the differences between these programs. Each has the undying loyalty (or, for XPress, the grudging respect) of its users who refuse to switch. And both programs change often enough that a book like this, with a relatively long shelf-life, can't hope to be current beyond the first few months of publication.

Adobe's **PageMaker** ($500) was the first heavy-duty layout program for the Mac. Even as its power has evolved, its interface has remained as elegant as ever. **QuarkXPress** ($700) took over the lead years ago, however, being first to offer extraordinary control over type and then color separations. Sometimes referred to as simply *Quark*, other times just *XPress*, it is now the industry standard. Adobe has stated that the next PageMaker (the current one, at this writing, is 6.5) will be so different—and modeled after rival Quark—that it won't be getting just a new number, but a new name to go with its brand-new look.

adobe.com
quark.com

If you do any but the lightest of layout chores that a word processor might satisfy, you need one of these programs.

Creator and Creator2. The best-kept secret in professional Macintosh publishing has long been **Multi-Ad Creator** ($650, Multi-Ad Services) While it's used by a zillion newspapers, magazines, and in-house ad departments, Multi-Ad's marketing is so bad that most people still don't know about this excellent program. Multi-Ad Creator is clearly designed to make ads, but you could make any one-page piece with it. Some favorite features:

- Importing graphics is a snap, and you can easily make 1-bit TIFFs transparent or colorized.
- A Mask palette with Illustrator-like pen tools lets you easily auto-mask any imported image or trace areas in an image.
- The Starburst tool has no peer, even among drawing programs.
- Powerful text handling, especially the style sheets, go beyond—far beyond—anything you've ever seen, including not only character styles, but also algorithmic styles ("the first line of the paragraph should be in Helvetica, then change to Palatino; put a Zapf Dingbats bullet at the beginning of the paragraph," and so on).
- Controlled export of an entire ad (or just a portion of it) as an EPS or DCS (separated EPS) file for inclusion in a multipage layout program.

multi-ad.com

For Multi-Ad's multipage approach, there's **Creator2** ($1000). It "feels" like QuarkXPress in many ways, with its box-based layout system. But if you thought Quark gave you great control over your layout, how does kerning at 1/1000-em sound?

Both programs have downloadable demos available at the vendor's site, so you've got nothing to lose but some download time if you want to try them out. —SZA/RA

Multi-Ad Creator is great for single-page layout.

FrameMaker. Standard page layout programs can produce most types of documents, but if you need to include lots of tabular material or footnotes, want to build cross-references into your file, or need files that flow seamlessly not just between Macs and PC's but possibly to Unix as well, you should consider **FrameMaker 5** ($900, Adobe), which was designed for just that sort of work.

You could use FrameMaker for short documents and brochures, but it's meant for documents that have a fairly consistent layout from page to page. It can handle graphics and rules, but it doesn't have the typographic and graphics-oriented bells and whistles of PageMaker or XPress. It really comes into its own for long documents like technical manuals or in-house guides—jobs you might start out by producing in a word processing program (which is what FrameMaker most feels like). FrameMaker's built-in word processor has an excellent spelling checker, extensive find-and-replace features, automatic index and table of contents generation, footnotes, and so on.

adobe.com

FrameMaker has the best table-handling of any program for the Mac, plus unique features such as automatic cross-referencing and conditional text (that is, *insert if…,* which lets you include or exclude certain text in different versions of a document). It also has an impressive equation editor for doing math texts. Because FrameMaker is available on so many different platforms—including Windows—it's also great for large corporations that need to move documents around among Macs, PCs, and Unix-based systems. You can even use a Reader utility to read FrameMaker files over networks or on CD-ROMs. —KT/DB

These tips work with both PageMaker 6.5 and QuarkXPress 4.

Generic Tips

Work with style. If you don't use stylesheets, learn how and then *use* them. There's nothing that makes text formatting and editing easier than using stylesheets. (See Chapter 16 for more about stylesheets.)

Temporary grabber hand. You can move a page around in the window with the Grabber hand, but you don't have to get it from the toolbox: hold down [Option] and you automatically get the hand as a temporary tool. Quark does this right, with the mouse cursor changing to the hand as soon as you press [Option]; in one of PageMaker's few interface bumbles, you won't see the hand until you press the mouse button.

Seeing what you're moving. When you drag something in a layout, what you see is an *outline* of the item; when you stop dragging and let go of the mouse, the item itself appears in the new position. But when you're trying to align something carefully, or when it's a graphic whose frame outline doesn't match the shape of the graphic, moving the outline isn't good enough.

To move the object itself instead of its outline, hold down the mouse button until the cursor changes to the "drag" cursor, and then drag the object. In Quark, you can set the delay for the change in the Interactive tab of the Application Preferences.

Setting global defaults. Setting document defaults while a document is open applies those settings to the current document. When you want to set defaults to affect all new documents, set them while no documents are open.

Serial deletions. If you hold down the Delete key while clicking on items with the Item tool (Quark) or the Selection tool (PageMaker), each item will be deleted as you click on it. (But Quark annoyingly beeps at you while the key is down and the mouse button isn't.) —SZA/RR

Font styles, not styled fonts. If you need to apply bold or italic formatting to some words in a paragraph, use the Bold or Italic text style commands; don't apply the bold or italic variation of a font to the selected text.

When you use the standard style commands, the styled font is used for printouts, but you can still change the base font at any time by changing the paragraph style or text style definition. So, if you bold a word in the middle of a paragraph that's been defined as Dom Casual, Dom Casual Bold is used in the printout. But if you redefine the paragraph's style to use Bookman Old Style, the bolded word will print in Bookman Old Style Bold.

That's just what you'd expect, of course, so it doesn't seem like any big deal. But if you originally selected text and changed it to Dom Casual Bold and later changed the paragraph definition to be Bookman Old Style, the local formatting for the bolded text would still be Dom Casual Bold—the font wouldn't change to match the new base font.

Editing styles safely. Suppose you need to edit a paragraph style, but you're not sure what other styles might be based on it. Since the same change might be undesirable in the subordinate styles, here's a way to check which styles will change along with the one you're altering.

Assign a weird color, like magenta, to the style you're editing before you make any other changes. The color change will ripple through to the dependent styles, and a quick perusal of the document will show you which based-on styles will be affected. You can then decide if you want to unlink the dependent styles from the parent, or simply redefine them slightly to avoid an unwanted change. (And don't forget to take off the magenta!) —SZA/JW

Unfast saves from Word. If you're importing a Microsoft Word file for your layout, make sure that it was saved normally, and not as a "fast save," which often causes problems once it's in PageMaker or Quark because editing changes were simply appended to the end of the Word file instead of incorporated where they belong. The best approach is to do a Save As from Word to create a fresh file for the layout program; that way, even if the Fast Save option is turned on, it can't be used for the new file.

PageMaker Tips

These tips were tested for PageMaker 6.5.

Documents, Windows, and Pages

Flipping pages. The scroll arrows on either side of the tiny page icons at the bottom of the window let you scroll through the pages if they're not all displayed at once. You can jump to the first or last page by ⌘-clicking on the left or right arrow. Holding Shift while you click one of the arrows moves the pages in groups of six.

Use the page icon scroll arrows to flip through the pages.

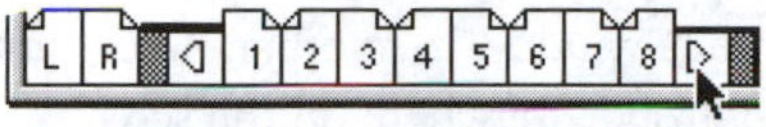

Scanning through the pages. You can sit back and watch a slide show of your entire layout by holding down Shift and then choosing Go To from the Layout menu.

The click-zoom toggle. You don't need the Zoom tool to change the View size of the document. You can, instead, ⌘ Option-click anywhere in the document to toggle between standard and 200 percent view. A ⌘ Option Shift-click zooms you to 400 percent view.

IN THE BEGINNING

Many layout programs have come and gone since the Mac arrived. You might recognize the name Ready, Set, Go! as one of the hangers-on, although we finally dropped it from this Bible edition. But do you remember the one that was touted as the "page layout program to replace all others"? Scoop. Yes, Scoop. Or how about these integrated/layout programs (for some reason, musical names were popular): Jazz, Ensemble, Harmony, Quartet, Ragtime, and Executive Office.

The nonparallax view. The zoom view you have for each page (or spread) is stored separately for each page. So, as you page through your document, you might be jumping from a 50 percent view to a 400 percent view to a normal-size view. To make every page or spread normal size as you move to it, hold down Shift while you click on the page icon.

To set all pages to the same view, hold down Option as you select a Zoom To size from the View menu.

Switching documents. With multiple documents open in PageMaker, Option-clicking on a title bar switches you to the next document. Open windows in the story editor are also included in the rotation, so with a single document and one story open, this is a handy way to switch from layout view to an open story editor window. —RR

Shrinking files. A PageMaker file gets bigger every time you save it, even if you haven't added any pages or material, because the program appends changes to the existing file rather than replacing it with the new, edited version (which might be smaller).

You can avoid this by changing the Save Option in the Preferences dialog from the default *faster* to *smaller.*

Tools and Palettes

Joining and separating palettes. You can combine any of PageMaker's palettes into single windows with tabs to access each individual palette: just drag the tab of the palette from one window to another. To separate palettes, drag the tab out of the window and drop it anywhere on the screen.

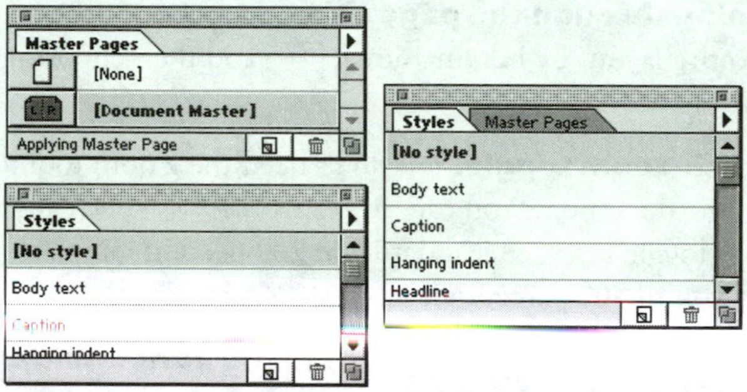

Two palettes (left) combined into one (right).

Showing and hiding all palettes. To show or hide all the palettes at once, just press Tab when there's no text active. Use Shift Tab to hide everything except the Tools palette.

Showing and hiding individual palettes. You can show and hide palettes through quick keyboard commands. (The only way you'll remember them, though, is through constant usage—there's little rhyme or reason to key assignments.) Here are the basic palette "toggles":

Colors	⌘ J
Styles	⌘ B
Control	⌘ '
Layers	⌘ 8
Master Pages	⌘ Option 8

If you've combined palettes so that previously independent palettes are tabs in a joint palette, using a "show" key combination will open the joint palette if necessary, and bring forward the correct tab.

Collapsing palettes. You can collapse a palette window by double-clicking on its title bar; even though there's no title in it, it's still a title bar as far as the Mac's concerned (you use it to drag the window around). But then you get nothing but a blank title bar, which, while it clears up the screen, doesn't help much when you need something and can't tell which palette's which. Instead, double-click on the palette *tab*, which collapses the window down to just display the tab(s).

When you want to expand a palette again, you can double-click on the frontmost tab or single-click on any background tab. You can tell the difference even when the palette's collapsed because the frontmost tab is white and the others are shaded.

Collapsing a palette by double-clicking on the title bar (top) or one of its tabs (bottom).

Shortcuts from the Tools palette. Double-clicking on most tools in the Tool palette opens certain dialog boxes, as shown here. Double-clicking on the Hand changes the view to Fit in Window, and double-clicking on the Zoom tool makes it 100 percent view.

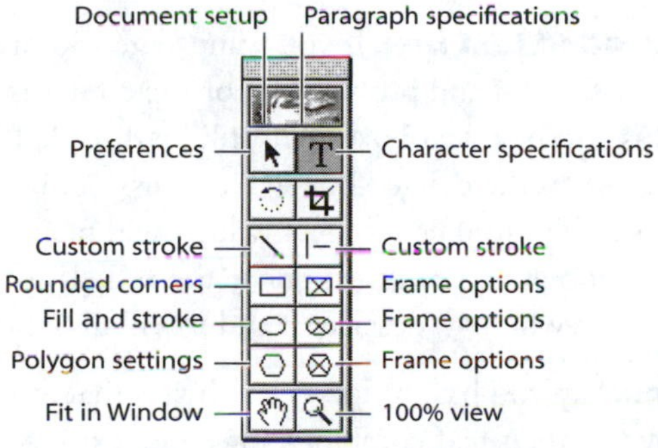

Deleting items from a palette. To delete an item from a palette, select it and either drag it to the trash icon at the bottom of the palette, or just click the trash icon. Either way, you get a confirming dialog. If you want to bypass the dialog, hold Option as you click or drag.

Text and Text Boxes

Flowing text. When you place text in a PageMaker document, whether through the Place command or by clicking on the end of a text box to "load" the cursor, there are three ways to flow the text: manually, automatically, or semiautomatically.

- A **manual** flow lets you drag a new text box to the size you want; or, if you click for a manual flow, the text box will be drawn to the width of the column defined on the page and stretch vertically from the click spot to the bottom of the page. The cursor reverts to the selection arrow at the end of a manual flow.
- An **automatic** flow pours all the text from the spot where you click or drag until there's no text left; the text boxes are drawn automatically on

the pages according to the margins or columns you've set, and new pages are added automatically as necessary to accommodate the text.

- A **semi-automatic** flow works like a manual flow except that the cursor remains loaded after the first page or column is filled so that you can click or drag in another spot for the next text box.

You can easily switch from one type of flow to another: pressing ⌘ changes the default manual flow to automatic, and Shift changes it to semi-automatic.

The loaded text cursors: manual, automatic, and semi-automatic.

And it's easy to tell what mode you're in, since the cursor changes to reflect what will happen.

Homeless text. If you want to enter text without picking a spot on a page for it, just open the Story Editor (⌘E) while no text is active and type or paste the text into the Editor. When you close the Editor window, you'll be asked if you want to place the text. Agreeing loads the cursor so you can pour the text; saying no makes the text disappear.

Deleting a threaded text box. If you want to get rid of a threaded text box, you can't just select it and press Delete, or the contents will also disappear; the previous and next text boxes will still be threaded to each other, but the material that was in the deleted box will be missing. Instead, roll up a text box until the top and bottom edges meet, which will push the contents to the following box. Although you can then delete the rolled-up "box," you don't have to: just click anywhere to deselect it and it will disappear.

Quick combine. Say you have a dozen text boxes that aren't threaded, but you'd like to have all their text combined into one text box. Cut and paste? (And cut and paste, and cut and paste…?) Nope, it's easier than that.

1. Put all the text boxes on the same page or on the pasteboard so you can see them all at once; you can roll them up to show only a line or two of text.
2. Select all the text boxes.
3. Choose the Cut or Copy command.
4. With the Text tool, draw a box or click somewhere on a page.
5. Choose Paste.

All the text boxes' contents will be combined in the new spot.

Miscellaneous

See what's installed. Losing track of which plug-ins you've plugged in? ⌘-click on the logo at the top of the tool palette to get a list of what's installed.

Getting out of nested dialogs. Whenever you're in a secondary or tertiary dialog and faced with clicking several OK or Cancel buttons to get rid of all them, you can Option-click the OK or Cancel in the topmost one, and they'll all close. Or, add Option to what you'd normally do from the keyboard:

Option Return clicks the OK button for all the dialogs, and ⌘ Option . cancels all the dialogs.

Selecting layered objects. When you have overlapping objects, ⌘-click on the top one to select the next one down. If there are more than two overlapping, continue ⌘-clicking until you've selected the one you want.

Don't misapply master pages. It's easy to mistakenly apply a master page definition to the current page because simply clicking on a master in the Master Page palette immediately redefines the current page for that master. To avoid this particular slip of the mouse, select Prompt On Apply from the palette menu; you'll be asked before the master page definition is changed.

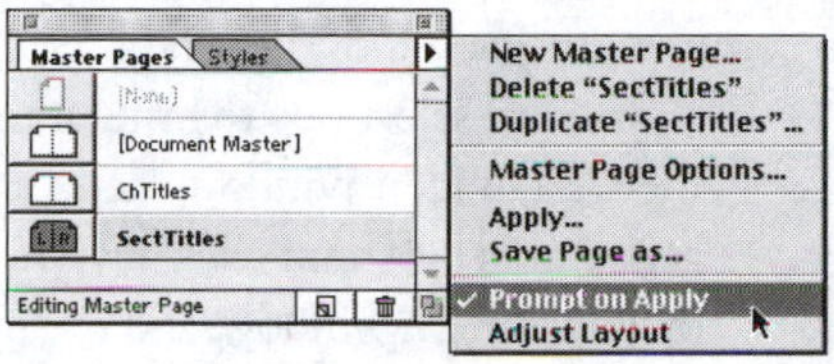

Selecting near guides. When there's a guide—or several guides—across an object you're trying to select, you often get the guide instead of the object when you click. But if you ⌘-click, you'll get the object every time.

New styles based on existing ones. There are two ways to create a new style from within the Styles palette: you can click on the New Style icon while an existing style is selected, or you can drag an existing style to the New Style icon. Both let you create a new style that starts out with the attributes of the current style, but one is a *duplicate* of the current style.

What's the difference? For a new style, the Based On and Next Style defaults are the general defaults; a duplicated style copies the Based On and Next Style options from the original.

Clicking on the New Style icon starts a new style with the current style's attributes; dragging a style into the icon duplicates it. (These actions echo the two commands in the palette's pop-out menu, New Style and Duplicate Style.)

Crop before importing a graphic. When you place a graphic in PageMaker and then crop it, the entire graphic is still included—not just the part you can see, and even including the "empty" space around a small figure, which is actually a collection of white pixels. Crop your pictures in your graphics program before importing them to PageMaker.

Temporary full-res. If you want to see a compressed image temporarily displayed at full resolution, press Control when the page is being redrawn.

New-color shortcut. Instead of selecting New Color from the Colors palette pop-out menu, you can ⌘-click on any one of the first three colors

(None, Paper, Black) to open the Color Options dialog. A ⌘-click on a color usually opens the dialog so you can edit a color, but since the first three aren't editable, you can create a new color in the dialog.

QuarkXPress Tips

These tips were tested for QuarkXPress 4.

Windows and Pages

The hidden Window menu. The Windows item in the View menu is a submenu that provides two commands (Stack and Tile) and lists all the open windows so you can select one to bring it to the top. But there's a hidden Window menu that's much easier to get at: hold Shift and click anywhere on the title bar of a document window, and the menu pops up with the two commands and a list of open windows.

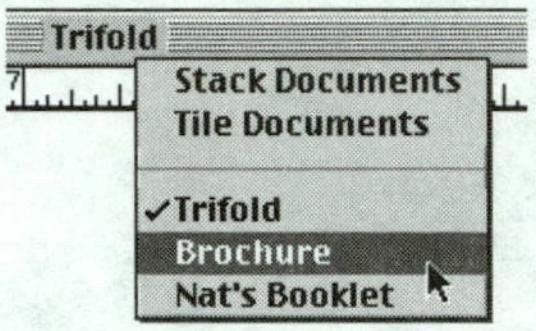

Hold shift and click on a window's title bar to get a Window's menu.

Some zooming shortcuts. Zooming in and out of various-size views is something you do constantly while you're working on a layout. Luckily, there are lots of ways to shrink and magnify the view.

- Use ⌘1 and ⌘0 to jump to Full (100 percent) and Fit in Window views.
- With the Zoom tool, click in the document to jump up to the next preset size. Option-click in the document with the tool to go down incrementally.
- Temporarily switch to the Zoom tool for enlarging a view by holding down Control. For zooming out, hold down Control Option.
- Drag the Zoom tool across an area of the document to enlarge that area to the full size of the window.
- When using the Item or Content tool, ⌘ Option-click anywhere in the document to toggle between 100 and 200 percent views. (In Quark 4, unlike in previous versions, this works even if Caps Lock is down.

Keyboard percentage zoom. You can jump to any specific percentage view strictly from the keyboard: press Control V to activate the View Percent field in the lower-left corner of the window, type a number for the percentage and press Return or Enter to activate it.

Tip within a tip: Type a T in the field to go to a thumbnail view.

Inserting multiple pages. If you're inserting a page by dragging a master page icon into position in the Document Layout palette, holding down Option while you drop the icon into position will trigger the Insert Pages dialog so you can insert multiple pages at that spot.

Tools and Palettes

Collapsing palettes. The Document Layout palette is the only one with a zoom box, and none of the palettes has a collapse box. But you can still collapse them, just by double-clicking on the title bars.

Selecting tools. Use ⌘-Tab to cycle through the tools in the Tool palette; ⌘-Shift-Tab, of course, selects tools in the reverse direction.

Keep the tool. A single click on any tool except the Item or Content tool selects it for a single use: as soon as you use the tool (draw the picture box, or the text box, or rotate an item, for instance) you're bounced back to the Item or Content tool—whichever one you were using before you clicked on the new tool. To select a tool and keep it for further use, Option-click on it.

IN THE BEGINNING

There was no program that took advantage of the LaserWriter's PostScript capabilities, until Just Text was released. It's hard to believe it received favorable reviews—but the product was more important than the process at that point.

Just Text gave a great deal of control over the size and exact placement of text, and even graphics, in a document. But it did it all in a window that showed only 9-point Geneva, and could hold only 32K of information. And it did it with commands like this:

- For an em dash (a long hyphen), you'd type *{md}*
- For italics, you typed *{f6}* at the beginning and *{f4}* at the end of the italicized word.
- To begin a new paragraph, you typed *{ql}* (for *quad left*) at the end of the previous paragraph. For a little extra spacing, you'd use something like *{ql}{a6}*.

So, to get a line of text like this:

You *like* this—this *program*?

you'd type something like this (including some initial commands for where the text begins on the page, and the font and size):

{il9}{ir9}{p12}{l213}You {f6}like{f4} this{md}{f6}program{f4}?

But that's not the worst of it. Once you finished typing the gibberish, you couldn't just print it. First it had to be *compiled,* which is the process of taking "raw" code that humans use and turning it into a language that the computer understands; in this case, the language was PostScript and the computer was the LaserWriter. If the compiler program found any errors (and you can imagine how easy it was to make a few mistakes), it told you where they were. Or it just crashed. Once you managed to get the compiled PostScript code, which was a text file, it had to be downloaded to the printer with yet another utility, since downloading a file isn't the same as simply printing it. And if you were very, very lucky, the page that came out was what you meant print.

Default tool attributes. It's easy to set the default attributes for any tool in the tool palette. You might want to, for instance, make the line tool always start out with a 1.5-inch thickness, or have text boxes always start with a None background instead of White.

Some defaults (like, say, a setting for a 4-point, dotted straight line) make sense only within the context of a single document. Others make sense as an application default so that, for instance, all your text boxes in all your documents start out defaulting to a None background. To set a default for a specific document, open the document and make sure it's the active window before you set the default. To set the default for all new documents, close all document windows before setting the defaults.

1. Select Document Preferences from the Edit menu's Preferences submenu.
2. Click the Tool tab.
3. Find and select the tool you want in the scrolling list.
4. Click the Modify button and set the default attributes you want.

You can select more than one tool at a time in the Tool tab's list to set their defaults the same way:

- Click one tool and then click the Select Similar Types button to automatically select its companions: all the text boxes, for instance, or all the line tools.
- Shift-click to select a group of tools starting at the selected one and ending with the one you Shift-click on.
- To select noncontiguous tools in the list, ⌘-click on the ones you want.

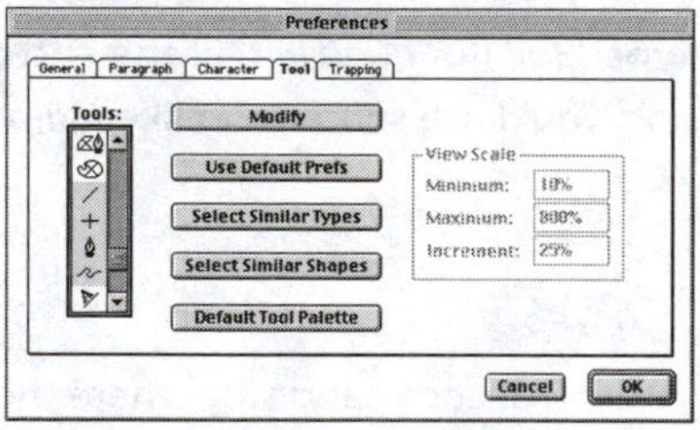

Setting Tool preferences (the Select Similar Types button was clicked after selecting the line tool).

Keyboard control for the Measurements palette. Use ⌘ Option M to activate the Measurements palette (it will also open it if it's not already open). Once the palette is activated, you can use Tab and Shift Tab to move from one field to another, and type numbers or letters to activate the field contents.

To activate/open the palette and jump right to the Font field, press ⌘ Shift Option M. You can type the first few letters of a font's name to go to it in the list and then press Return or Enter to select it.

To deactivate the palette from the keyboard, press ⌘ . or Esc.

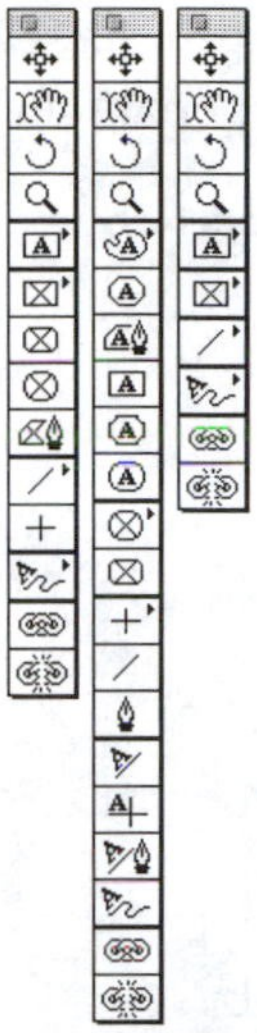

The default tool palette (left) and two customized palette designs.

Customizing the Tool palette. You can customize your Tool palette to some extent, adding and deleting tools based on what you use the most.

To add a tool that normally appears in a pop-out menu, hold down Control while you select the tool from the pop-out. To delete a tool from the palette, Control-click on it. You can't delete any of the four top tools, or the bottom two (Link and Unlink), or a tool that's serving as access to a pop-out menu.

Shortcut to the Tool tab. You can jump right to the Tool tab of the Preferences dialog by double-clicking on any of the "creation" tools (the tools that make or draw things).

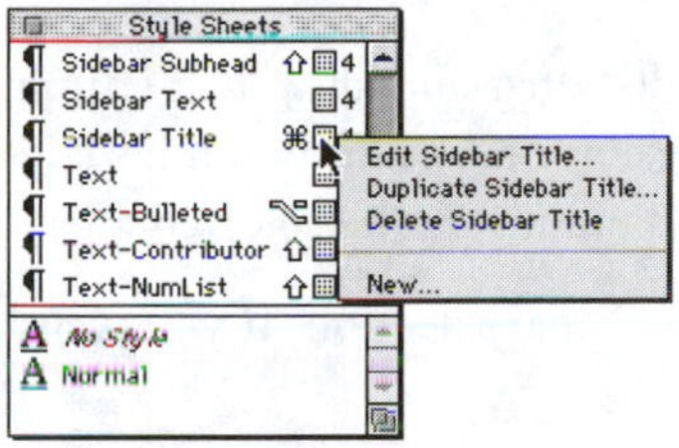

Hold down Control to get a Styles palette pop-up menu.

Styles palette pop-up. To get a quick little pop-up menu with four important commands in it, hold down Control and click on one of the styles in the Styles palette: you can edit the style, duplicate it, delete it, or start a new style.

Working with Text and Styles

Deleting text. Using Delete, of course, deletes the letter before the current text cursor position. To delete the letter to the right of the blinking cursor, you can use ⌦ or Shift Delete.

To delete a whole word at once instead of a letter at a time, you can press ⌘ Delete. That deletes the word you're in, or the word to the left of the cursor if it's between words. ⌘ Shift Delete also deletes the word you're in, but it deletes the word to the right of the cursor if it's between words.

Click selections. You can select increasingly large chunks of text depending on how many times you click the mouse:

Clicks	*Select*
2 clicks	the word
3 clicks	the line
4 clicks	the paragraph
5 clicks	the story

Moving around in and selecting text. You can move the text insertion point from the keyboard in various increments (a word, a line, a paragraph), and, by adding the Shift key to the combination, you can select the same unit. But there's *still* no way to easily select that all-important unit, a *sentence!1*

Unit or destination	***Move insertion point***	***Select from current spot to***
Next character	→	Shift →
Previous character	←	Shift ←
Next line	↓	Shift ↓
Previous line	↑	Shift ↑
Next word	⌘ →	Shift ⌘ →
Previous word	⌘ ←	Shift ⌘ ←
Beginning of current paragraph	⌘	Shift ⌘ ↑
Beginning of next paragraph	⌘ ↓	Shift ⌘ ↓
Beginning of line	⌘ Option ←	Shift ⌘ Option →
End of line	⌘ Option →	Shift ⌘ Option ←
Beginning of story	⌘ Option ↑	Shift ⌘ Option ↑
End of story	⌘ Option ↓	Shift ⌘ Option ↓

Dragging text. Quark 4 added drag-and-drop text editing. Turn it on in the Application preferences (Interactive tab), and you'll be able to drag selected text by grabbing it from anywhere inside the selected area.

Dragging the text moves the original selection. If you want to drag a copy, hold Shift while you drag it.

There are two little problems with Quark's implementation of drag and drop. First, there's no feedback when you click on a selection to drag it; the cursor doesn't change until you move the mouse. Second, if you drag a double-clicked word—which gets selected without its surrounding spaces—into a new spot, spaces get added correctly around the word in the new spot, and the multiple spaces you left behind are automatically deleted. But if you drop the word in the wrong spot and drag it to another spot, you'll get an extra space added after it. Drag it again and get another space. And so on—one extra space for every drag!

Copying paragraph formats. You can copy all the paragraph attributes of one paragraph to another by first putting the cursor in the paragraph you want to change, then Shift Option-clicking the paragraph you want to copy from. If you're using style sheets, the style is copied from one paragraph to the other; but even without styles, the paragraph attributes—like justification, indents, and tabs—are copied. —SZA/DB

Keyboard kerning and tracking. Kerning and tracking tighten and loosen text by adjusting the space between letters. Kerning changes the space between a pair of letters, while tracking applies a more sweeping transformation, usually to entire lines or paragraphs of text at a time. There are kern-pair values built into fonts, and tracking can be part of a style sheet definition, but both can be applied manually, too.

For kerning, start with the text insertion point between the two letters you want to kern; for tracking, select the line(s) you want to adjust. Then, use these keyboard commands:

Decrease 1/20-em	⌘ Shift-[
Increase 1/20-em	⌘ Shift-]
Decrease 1/200-em	⌘ Option Shift-[
Increase 1/200-em	⌘ Option Shift-]

Using the kern controls in the measurement palette uses the 1/20-em unit. If you want the smaller unit, Option-click on the kerning arrows.

Add the Option key to a click of the kerning controls to use a smaller unit for kerning or tracking.

Fine-kern from the Measurements palette. Clicking on the kerning controls in the Measurements palette decreases and increases the kerning by 1/20-em. To make the controls work in the tiny 1/200-em unit, hold down Option while you click them.

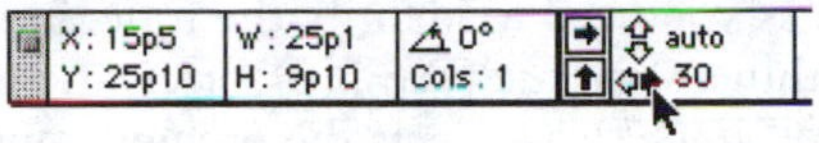

Temporary drag and drop. If you leave the drag-and-drop option off, you can still use it temporarily: hold down ⌘ Control Shift and you can drag selected text to a new spot.

IN THE BEGINNING

A long, long, time ago in a town not so far away (from me), original Mac programmer Andy Hertzfeld gave the Princeton User group a demo of his new program, Switcher, which let you (gasp!) run more than one program at a time on your program. Nearly as interesting as the program, and the programmer, were some of his anecdote about the early days; one in particular stands out in my memory

Head Macintosh development honcho Steve Jobs had spurts of creative enthusiasm (interspersed, by all accounts, with rants and rages) and rushed into the programmers' den one day with a great idea: the Mac Man. At a random interval—every thousandth or so menu pull-down, for instance—a little Mac man could appear on the screen waving at you.

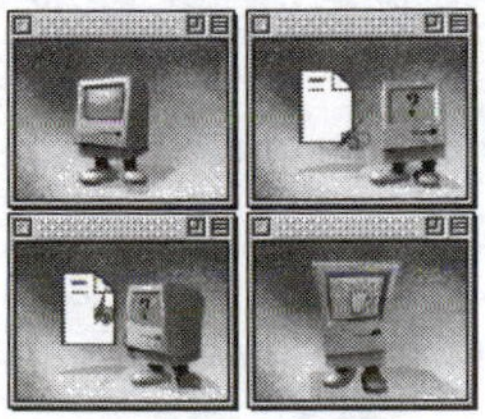

The Mac Man didn't make the cut, but I have the uncomfortable feeling that the people at Microsoft remembered him when they put together that stupid animation for their help system in Office 98.

Changing local formatting. If you have *local formatting* on some text in a paragraph—say, bold or italic (or even a different font or size) applied to certain words—it's preserved when you apply a style to that paragraph. The rest of the text will change to match that of the style definition, but the locally formatted text will keep its manually applied formatting. You can force local formatting to change to the formatting defined by the paragraph style by holding down Option while you click on the style's name in the Style palette (or while you select it from the Style menu's Paragraph Style Sheet submenu).

Applying a font from the keyboard. There are several ways to choose a font without reaching for the mouse:

- Define a character style, assign a keyboard command to it, and use it to change the font whenever you want. (You also get to define other character attributes—like size and color—this way.)
- Use ⌘ Shift Option M to activate the Font area on the Measurements palette. Type only as much as you need to identify the font, and press Return or Enter. (Shortcut within a shortcut: Option F9 selects the next font in the pop-up menu, and Option Shift F9 selects the previous one.)
- To type a single Zapf Dingbats character, press ⌘ Shift Z and then type the character.
- To type a single Symbol character, press ⌘ Shift Z and then type the character.

Redefining a style by example. There's no easy way to redefine multiple aspects of a paragraph's style sheet. Say you have a style called BodyText that you're using for the body of the document. You know you're not too happy with it, so you work on a single paragraph, changing the font, the size, the leading, the indents, adding the tabs you forgot in the original definition, and tightening the tracking just a tiny bit. Aha! Perfect! But all you have in your Style palette is the selected BodyText style, and it has a little plus sign in front of it to show there's additional formatting in the current paragraph. There's no way to say: "See this? This is the new definition for BodyText!"

Here's a multistep but easy way of achieving that result. With the text cursor blinking in the paragraph that was defined as one style but formatted with the new attributes:

1. Click on the No Style option at the top of the Style palette to "undefine" the current paragraph.
2. Control-click on any style in the Style palette to get the pop-up menu and select the New command.
3. Give the new style a name (I use the soon-to-be-changed style's name and an equal sign: *BodyText=*). Set the Based On and Next Style options to match the original's options and click OK.
4. Control-click on the old style name in the palette and choose Delete from the pop-up menu.

5. Select the new style as the one to replace the deleted style.
6. Alter the name of the new style to match the old name.

Miscellaneous

Active apply button. When you're making multiple changes in a dialog box like the one for paragraph or character formatting, it's helpful to see the changes as you make each one instead of all at once—and it's especially nice to see them made interactively so that as you drag a margin marker, for instance, the margins of the current paragraph change. You don't have to keep clicking the Apply button after each edit. Instead, press ⌘ Option A while the dialog is open and the Apply button remains selected, and all changes are made to the document as you work in the dialog box.

Live scrolling. Quark 4 introduced the option of "live scrolling": as you use the scroll box in either scrollbar, you can see the pages go by so you don't have to guess what page you'll be on when you let go. Turn the option on (or off) in the Application preferences dialog, in the Interactive tab.

Find first. Pressing Option while the Find dialog is open changes the Find Next button to Find First—a very handy option because otherwise Quark starts the search from wherever in the text you last edited.

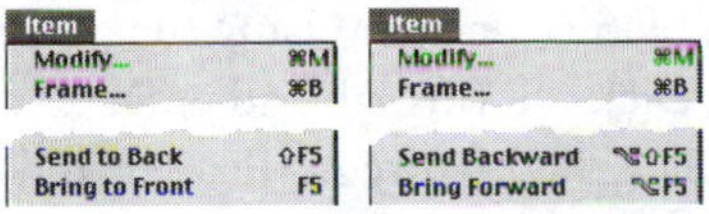

Backward and forward. The Send to Back and Bring to Front commands in the Item menu move a selected item to the back or top of the layered order of items on a page. But if you hold Option when you open the Item menu, the commands change to Send Backward and Bring Forward, and the selected item will move back or forward only a single layer.

The Option option works with the keyboard commands, too. The menu lists Shift F5 and F5 as the keyboard equivalents for the basic commands; adding Option to either keyboard command changes its function the way holding Option changes the menu command.

Selecting stacked objects. If you have items overlapping or stacked (a text box, say, with a picture box on top of it and a rule slashed across both), you can hold down ⌘ Option Shift while you click and each item will be selected in turn.

Single- and double-page guides. When you're working with facing pages, dragging a guide out of the top ruler puts it only on the page you dragged it onto. If you want a guide that spans both pages, you have to drag the guide down at the far left or right of the layout, on the pasteboard, so you're not touching either page while you drag.

The special Delete Item function. Try this when you want to delete any item from the layout: Click on the Item tool, and select the item. Then press ⌘-Option-Shift-Delete. Trust me—try it right away!

Begone! You probably already know that you can get rid of a guide by dragging it back into the ruler from whence it came, or off the opposite end of the screen, into the vertical or horizontal scroll bar.

But what you probably didn't realize is that you can drag any guide—horizontal or vertical—into either ruler (or scroll bar). No more dragging something from the middle of a double-page spread on a double-page monitor *all* the way over to the edge of the screen. Grab the *edge* of a guide and drag it to the nearest ruler: move the top edge of a vertical guide into the top ruler, or the left edge of a horizontal guide into the vertical ruler. A half-inch or one-inch trip instead of a ten-inch drag!

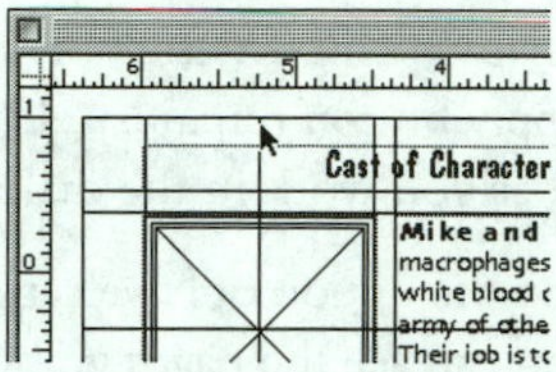

Dragging this rule straight up into the top ruler will make it disappear.

Want to get rid of *all* the horizontal or vertical guides at once? Option-double-click on either ruler, and all the guides in that orientation disappear (including the ones from the Master Page).

Rotate the box but not the contents. By setting opposite angles for both a box and its contents, you can rotate the box without rotating the final orientation of the picture or text. Using the Modify command for the item, click the Box tab and enter an angle for the box; then click the Picture or Text tab and enter the reverse value for the picture. (So, enter a 30-degree angle for one, say, and use -30 for the other.) The picture here shows what happens when you do it with a text box with 45-degree angles.

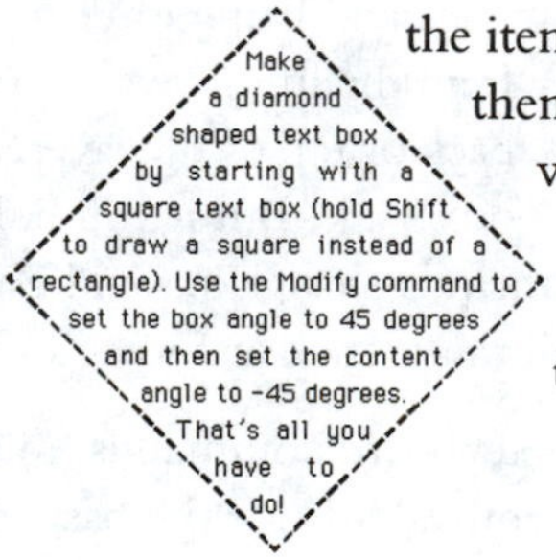

Make a diamond shaped text box by starting with a square text box (hold Shift to draw a square instead of a rectangle). Use the Modify command to set the box angle to 45 degrees and then set the content angle to -45 degrees. That's all you have to do!

21

Web Page Design

In This Chapter

Designing Web Pages

Design Software

What do you really need? All you really need to create a web page is a word processor that can save a text file that will later be opened inside a browser. Since the HTML (Hypertext Markup Language) is strictly text, there's no reason you can't just type the text—no reason except, perhaps, preserving your sanity. Automating the entry of opening and closing tags for every HTML element is a job for an HTML editor, and if you're going to do any serious work, you need an editor rather than a word processor.

The more you want to do on a web page, the more you need. You'll need graphics, and something to edit them in. You might want sound; you might want some simple animations. Luckily, all the basic tools have shareware versions for beginners or basic design, so you don't have to spend a fortune to get started.

Oh, and you need both Netscape Navigator and Microsoft Explorer to make sure that your web page behaves correctly in both browsers! Luckily, those, too, are free.

HTML editors. There are quite a few HTML editors out there, differing in approach, price, and power (with, of course, the price/power items advancing pretty much hand in hand). Here's a roundup of products that goes pretty light on their actual features; more than any other category of software, these programs are evolving and leapfrogging each other in terms of capabilities, so you'll have to check current reviews for details.

Visual Page

The category of visual editors, where you can work on your page elements while the HTML code is written for you (but where you can directly edit the HTML at any time) is pretty neatly divided into three duos of comparable prices. On the low end, there's **Visual Page** ($80, Symantec) and **Home Page** ($90, Claris). Both are easy to get started in and provide plenty of elegant power for beginning-to-intermediate page design; Visual Page is my personal favorite. For about twice the price, there's **PageMill** ($150, Adobe) and **FrontPage** ($150, Microsoft). Adobe ought to be ashamed of itself when it comes to PageMill—it was the first out of the gate and could have taken over the web-page design category, but even the 2.0 version was filled with annoying (almost crippling) quirks—and the Mac version is still languishing at 2.0 as I write this, months after the 3.0 version is available for the PC. And FrontPage? It generally gets favorable reviews, but I find the interface confusing and unfriendly—and I'm strange enough to love the power Microsoft

symantec.com
microsoft.com
claris.com
adobe.com

Word provides, so it's not just an anti-Microsoft attitude that makes me say that. Stick with either of the lower-end products instead of either of these mid-range offerings! On the high end of the visual-editor category are **Dreamweaver** ($300, Macromedia) and **CyberStudio** ($350, GoLive). While Dreamweaver has more cutting-edge features, you might not be able to use them if you're trying to serve surfers with less than cutting-edge browser capability; CyberStudio is a delicious mix of power and performance. If you're starting out on page design, you don't need either of these tools, but when you move up, CyberStudio is the better bet at this point.

macromedia.com
golive.com
bare-bones.com

Every hardcore web designer in the world disdains the visual-only approach and swears by **BBEdit** ($120, Bare Bones Software), a text-based editor with all sorts of features that make HTML coding (and, especially, search-and-replace editing) a snap. But if you want to try the text-editing approach, start with the shareware **Alpha** ($30) along with the freeware plug-in **HTML Mode.** There's also **PageSpinner** ($25, shareware) which, unlike BBEdit and Alpha, started out as an HTML editor and not a text editor; it's a little less powerful, but in many ways much more convenient.

> ***The web of our life is of a mingled yarn, good and ill together.***
> *Shakespeare, All's Well That Ends Well*

Utilities. In addition to an HTML editor and the graphics program of your choice, there are several programs that, while not absolutely *necessary*, can make web-page design easier.

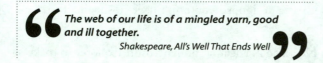

- The freeware **GIFBuilder** is so good at what it does, I can't imagine its staying free forever. You create your still-frame GIF files somewhere else and then drag them into GIF builder, which lets you set the necessary animation options.
- The shareware **GraphicConverter** can change almost any kind of graphic file into a JPEG or GIF for the web; it also lets you set transparency and interlacing.
- If you want an environment where you can both create your graphics and animate them, try **WebPainter** ($90, Totally Hip Software). You get the basic painting tools and the ability to duplicate (and then adjust) individual frames; then you can put together the animation with pauses, timing adjustments, and loops. The ability to "onionskin" the previous and next frames over the current one helps you create smooth animations. You can even view your animation as it would be seen at various modem speeds. And WebPainter comes with a bonus of over 500 ready-made GIF animations that you can use or alter. When you're ready to step up from GIFBuilder but not shell out for a full-fledged animation studio, this is the one to get.
- If you use Photoshop to prepare your web graphics, **PhotoGIF** and **ProJPEG** ($35 each, BoxTop Software) plug-ins let you slim down and spiff up your GIF and JPEG images for web pages.

totallyhip.com
boxtop-soft.com
shareware.com

Web clips. Okay, so you're not an artist. If you were working on a newsletter destined for print, you'd be buying clip art. Well, you can do the same for your web pages, but you need clip art designed for web pages. Why? Because web-page art should include: images optimized for the web (GIFs that use the web-safe colors, for instance); buttons for common web-page functions (Home, Next, Previous, and so on), preferably in at least two states (active and inactive); bullets to use for lists; bars to use as dividers instead of HTML's gray option; and small background patterns that tile correctly. Luckily, there are a few collections of web clip art that meet these criteria—and, I'm sure, many more on their way.

novadevcorp.com
artbeats.com
totallyhip.com

- Nova Development, known for its humongous collections of standard clip art, also offers a modest (in comparison), excellent collection of web art: **Web Explosion 20,000** ($50) that includes 10,000 buttons, 500 bullets, and 750 backgrounds.
- If you need animations, Nova's **Animation Explosion** ($50) fits the bill: over 5000 animated items from generic buttons to 3-D items.
- **Artbeats Web Stock** ($50, Artbeats) offers over 2000 items, heavy on the animation end of the things, and high on the quality.
- **Hip Clips** ($55, Totally Hip Software) is a handy collection of 250 ready-made animations. (But you might want to spend a little more and get the company's WebPainter, described earlier—which includes two Hip Clip collections.)

w3.net

HTML versions. HTML is a language of sorts, and as such, it continually evolves. To keep track of what's in, what's out, what's hot, and what's not, check in with its sanctioning body, the World Wide Web consortium (known as W3).

But remember that although you might be cutting edge, most surfers aren't—and if you want them to experience your site, you have to provide it at a level that their machines and browsers—and their modem speeds—can handle.

Beginner Basics

About HTML. Web pages are "written" in *HTML—Hypertext Markup Language.* It's not a programming language at all; it's merely a way of embedding formatting instructions in a plain-text file. The text is sent across the Internet to a user's machine, where browser software looks at the instructions in the file, formats the information accordingly, and displays it on the user's screen.

HTML is, in fact, reminiscent of the earliest word-processing software, which was unable (before the Mac!) to display simple formatting like bold or italic characters, or centered text, on the screen. You'd type in your text with special, cryptic definitions before and after certain words or paragraphs to format the text when it was printed.

HTML uses special definitions called *tags* to tell a browser how to display information in its windows.

Tag, you're it! The *tags* that HTML uses to define the look of a page come—with a few exceptions—in pairs referred to as *opening* and *closing* tags. The opening tag is placed before the text you want formatted, and the end of the formatting is indicated with the matching closing tag.

Both kinds of tags use brackets like <this> to set them off from other text. The tags themselves are often single letters, like <I> for italic, although some can get quite involved because they can include *attributes* that further define a format (like how big a picture should be). A closing tag uses the same characters, but with a slash: </I> is the closing italic tag.

The HTML document tags. Every HTML document begins with the tag <HTML> and ends with </HTML>. There are two major divisions within those tags: first, the head (<HEAD>), and then the body (<BODY>), which use opening and closing tags, too. Inside the HEAD section, you use the <TITLE> tag to put a name in the document's title bar. So, the basic structure of every one of your web pages will be:

```
<HTML>
<HEAD>
<TITLE>My Web Page</TITLE>
<BODY>
  The body of the document contains everything
  the user will see in the browser.
</BODY>
</HEAD>
</HTML>
```

Tag attributes. Some tags can have *attributes* included in them to define something beyond a basic, default appearance or function. Attributes go inside an opening tag; the name of the attribute is followed by an equal sign, followed by the attribute information inside quotes—*straight* quotes, not the curly ones that word processors use. So, for instance, the background color attribute appears inside the BODY opening tag like this:

```
<BODY BGCOLOR="#FFFFFF">
```

Character-formatting tags. The basic character-formatting tags are for bold and italic text. You simply use the opening and closing tags around the text you want formatted, so this:

```
<This is <B>bold</B> text, this is <I>italic</I>, and this
  is <B> <I>bold italic</I> </B>.
```

turns into this:

This is **bold** text, this is *italic,* and this is ***bold italic***.

Many "paragraph" formats include special formatting for the text, so you don't always have bold words and phrases for, say, "headlines."

Paragraphs and heads. An HTML "paragraph" is basically the same as one in a word processor: any text that's between presses of Return is a paragraph, even it's a single line, or a single word.

HTML provides for several basic types of paragraph formatting. The paragraph format itself (the <P> tag) defines separate paragraphs on the screen, automatically separating them with extra space; this is usually referred to as the *Normal* paragraph formatting. There are six levels of heads (tags <H1>, <H2>, and so on) that format the text with various combinations of size, bold, and italic to represent importance. So, with the following HTML, you'd get the results shown in the picture below.

```
<H1>My Home Page</H1>
<H2>How I Started</H2>
<P>It didn't take long to get started with my first HTML project
because I know how to follow directions, and I have a very ordered
mind.</P>
<P>I'm also very intelligent, and I read the instructions in the
Macintosh Bible to get me started.</P>
```

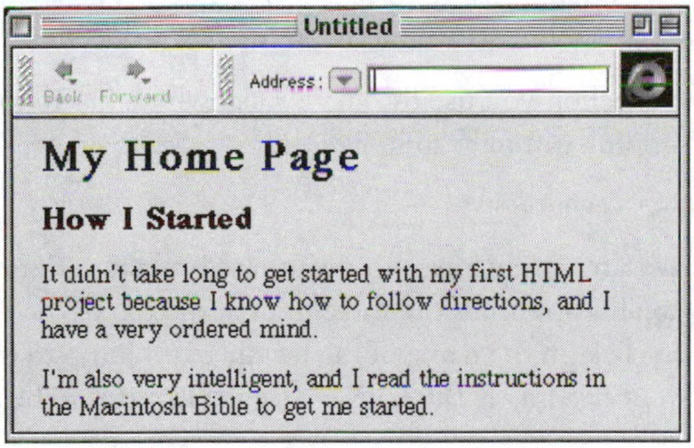

It's all relative. Always keep in mind that the user gets to define, through the browser software, certain aspects of a web page. Your HTML document might define basic paragraphs of text with first and second-level heads on it that look perfectly fine in both browsers. But a user may have re-defined what a basic paragraph, or headlines, should look like from his end, throwing off all your careful formatting.

Lists There are various types of list formats available, divided into two groups: *ordered*, where the items in the list are numbered or "lettered" in order, and *unordered,* where each item in the list is preceded by a special character, like a bullet or a square. They're informally referred to as number and bullet lists.

Both types of lists use nested tags: an outer set (<OL> for *ordered list*, <UL> for *unordered list*) to define the list itself, and inner tags to define the separate items in the list. The inner tags (<LI> for *list item*) need opening tags only, at the beginning of each line. Here's the HTML, and the results, for numbered and bulleted lists:

1. first
2. second
3. third
4. fourth
	`<OL>`
	`  <LI>first`
	`  <LI>second`
	`  <LI>third`
	`  <LI>fourth`
	`</OL>`

• first
• second
• third
• fourth
	`<UL>`
	`  <LI>first`
	`  <LI>second`
	`  <LI>third`
	`  <LI>fourth`
	`</UL>`

Anchors away. The crux of a web page is its *links:* colored or underlined text or graphics which, when clicked on, can take you to another document, or another spot in the same document. To jump to a specific spot in a document, the document must have an *anchor* defined. The anchor itself is invisible—it just serves as an internal reference point.

To create an anchor, you use the anchor tag, which has to include a name attribute so a link can refer to it, like this:

```
<A NAME="anchorName">
```

Say you have a relatively long text document broken into three sections with H1 heads. You'll want to list the three titles at the top of the document so that the user can click on the name of the heading and jump to that area of the document. If your heading is *Part One*, it's tagged like this to be a first-level head:

```
<H1>Part One</H1>
```

You can insert an anchor immediately in front of the heading in the document by embedding the anchor tag within the head tag. The anchor is named *firstpart* here instead of the more logical *Part One* so you can see which is the anchor information and which is the heading text:

```
<H1> <A NAME="firstpart"> </A>Part One</H1>
```

Creating a link. A link can jump you to another spot in the same page by referring to an anchor, or to another page entirely by referring to the URL of the other HTML document. Referring simply to another document links the user to the top of that page; you can refer to an anchor in another page if you want to go somewhere other than the top.

To create a link, you use the anchor tag, with an HREF (*hypertext reference*) attribute inside it. Say the top of your page has a bulleted list for the sections of the page, like this:

```
<UL>
   <LI>Part One
   <LI>Part Two
   <LI>Part Three
</UL>
```

Assuming you've created an anchor named *firstpart* at the Part One heading, as described in the previous entry, here's how you'd turn the first item in the bulleted list into a link to that anchor (the pound sign indicates that the anchor is in the same document as the link):

```
<LI><A HREF="#firstpart">Part One</A>
```

Defining text as a link usually turns the text into blue, underlined text, although you can specify a different style—and a user can override the definition from the browser end.

Adding graphics. There are two types of graphics used on web pages: GIF for simple drawings, and JPEG for photographs. The Mac's native PICT format that so many programs produce has to be translated to GIF before it can be displayed by a browser.

Once you have your graphics prepared, however, it's relatively simple to refer to them in the HTML document, using the IMAGE tag, and the SOURCE attribute that names the graphics file and its location:

```
<IMG SRC="ImageFolder/PartPicture.gif">
```

The "path" (the series of nested folders—or, on the PC side, the subdirectories) to the image comes before the image name, and everything has to be *exact*, including upper and lowercase letters. The example here shows a "local" path—the image is inside a folder that's in the same folder as the HTML document itself.

Design Tips

General

What's in a name. The name you give your HTML document when you save it is the file's name. But an HTML document also has a *title*, and that's not the same thing as a name. Use the <TITLE> tag inside your document to give it a title which will appear in the browser's window, and also in a user's menu if she chooses to bookmark your page.

The blank GIF: a designer's best friend. Designing a web page isn't like laying out something for print. You not only don't have control over the final look (because the surfer gets to set preferences, and even override your specific settings), you are limited in the commands you can use to place things on a page.

One of the biggest helps is a "blank" GIF: a small, single-color GIF that you've made transparent. (Since the transparency is applied to a single color, not an actual background, a block of color becomes invisible when you make its "background" transparent.) No matter how many different size blanks you need, you only have to make one, and then re-size as necessary. Keeping the original one small keeps download time brief, and re-using it means no repeat downloads. (How small? Try one-by-one pixel!)

Use the GIF to nudge things in one direction or another, or to space them correctly when you're not using a table. Don't use the SPACER tag instead of a real graphic: it's supported only by Netscape, not Explorer.

Test runs early and often—times two. As you work on your web page, keep checking how it looks from a browser's point of view. Every HTML editor gives you a shortcut command to switch immediately to a browser in case you want to check your page there instead of just in the editor's preview mode.

But check it in both Navigator *and* Explorer, to make sure there aren't some subtle changes that might affect how your page is viewed. There's no excuse not to use both browsers for this—no matter which you use for your personal surfing—since they're both free.

Here's what to keep in mind as you move back and forth between your editor and the browser(s):

- You can make changes in the editor and then switch to the browser—but unless you save the changes to the disk from within the editor, you won't see any changes in the browser, which interprets only what it can read from the disk.
- You can save the changes to the disk but they still might not appear in the browser because it's still working with the last version it read from the disk. Click the Refresh or Reload button in the browser to make it read the file all over again.

Stay a step behind. Every time an update to a browser comes out, you update your software right away. A new addition to the HTML standard, and you're on it. A nifty new helper application is invented, and you're there.

Most users are not like you. Most users stay a conservative step (and sometimes two) behind, updating software only when it's been around for awhile. If you design cutting-edge web pages, you'll narrow your audience to only those who have the latest and greatest. So, learn the new stuff, but don't use it right away; let the world catch up with you.

Size it right. You may have a super-duper extra-large monitor, but the majority of people don't. There's nothing more annoying to a reader than having to scroll horizontally to see an extra inch or two of text or graphics—and then, of course, having to scroll back again before moving down the page. Keep your design within the boundaries of a standard screen, allowing for the scroll bars on the browser window—and don't forget, not everyone's fortunate enough to have a Mac, either!

Your target area is 640 by 480—the resolution of a standard monitor—to start with. But the browser window itself takes up some of that space, especially at the top of the screen, where most people leave on at least the navigation buttons. So, your design area is actually about 595 by 350. *Unless* you expect people to print the page, in which case the maximum horizontal measurement is 535 pixels. (Why are we dealing with the vertical measurement at all, since pages can scroll ad infinitum? Because your first page, at least, should be designed so that the user can see *all* the important stuff at one time, without having to scroll.)

Background check. There are many ways you can make sure that your page design works within the 595 by 350 target area described in the last entry. But one of the easiest is to make a background with a perfectly sized frame in it: make a GIF that's simply a 595 by 350 black frame around a white area. Load it as your background graphic temporarily any time you want to make sure you're working in the right area. This is particularly important for designers with humongous screens—even when they remember to keep the "little people" in mind, it's difficult to go back and measure things and resize windows.

There's no place like home. Make sure you always provide an easy to get back to the top of the current page, and to the top of your home page no matter where your reader might be; it's really annoying to have to click a Back button a half-dozen times to retrace a route.

Target practice. This sly trick will help keep visitors from wandering off exploring the links on your page, never to return. Insert the "target=window" tag inside your pointer anchors like this: <A target=window href="targetname" </A>. This opens the target site in a new window, keeping your original page waiting patiently in the background. —SZA/JH

Check that spelling. Your HTML editor doesn't have an integral spell checker? Tough! Spell check your web page contents someplace else; nothing shouts "AMATEUR!" or "CARELESS!" as loud as misspelled words on a web site. An HTML document is, at heart, only a text document, so it can be opened in a word processor, spell-checked, and saved as text for use as a web page again. Or, use something like Casady & Green's Spell Catcher, described in Chapter 16.

Backgrounds

KISS. That's an acronym used in design and programming fields that stands for *keep it simple, stupid!* And it's really important to keep a background simple—in this case, that means *subtle*—so that it won't detract from the overall page design or make the superimposed text difficult to read. Keep the colors light for the most part, and keep textures and patterns to only a few, preferably light, shades. Remember: it's a *background*. Leave it there!

Colors versus graphics. There are two distinctly different approaches to putting a background on a web page. One is to simply make it a solid color, using the BGCOLOR attribute at the beginning of the BODY tag, like this:

```
BGCOLOR="#FF3300"
```

A colored background takes absolutely no time to load in the browser, because there's nothing to load: the browser simply sets the color on the user's machine. An HTML editor will let you simply select from a palette of colors and insert the color's number in the code.

The second approach is to use a graphic as the background. A graphic used as a background is repeated indefinitely (or infinitely?) in both a horizontal and vertical direction on the web page; the size of the graphic, and how well it "tiles" against itself, matching the edges, can make or kill a page design. The BACKGROUND attribute is used in the BODY tag for a background image:

```
BACKGROUND="[pathname]/bckgrnd1.gif"
```

A background image is transmitted to the user the way a standard image is although, of course, it has to be sent only once and not repeatedly for the tiling. Even if the user has images turned off, the background image is displayed on the page.

Border edge. One of the most effective page designs is also one of the simplest to achieve: a border of some sort down the left edge of the window. This can be a narrow border for looks only, or a wider one that can accommodate buttons, text, or graphics.

A vertical border is simply a repeated background graphic that has color or texture only along its left edge. But in order for it to become a border and not a tiled small graphic, the image itself has to include a lot of white space so that the whole thing stretches across the width of a window. (In fact, if you widen or horizontally scroll a web page with a vertical border graphic, you'll see that's it's repeated way off to the right sooner or later.) If you're using a texture or something other than a straight edge on the border, you have to make sure that it blends seamlessly when it's stacked.

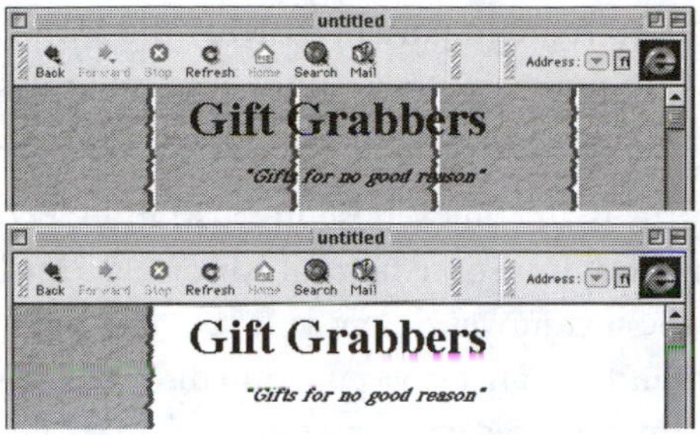

Top, a background graphic from an image that doesn't include white space to its right. Bottom, using the same graphic with the white space.

Also: make sure that there's plenty of white space (or background pattern) to the right of the border so surfers with large monitors who like to keep the window wide won't see the border repeat.

Double border. You can create a border for both sides of a page, like the one shown here (it's a real site—stop by *thetipster.com)* by making a standard border graphic with a narrower-than-usual white space so that the graphic is repeated before the right edge of the browser window.

Using a double border.

Layout on top of borders. Once you start using borders, you have to be more careful of all the text on the page, nudging it over so it won't print on top of the border itself. You can just indent all the text (the `<BLOCKQUOTE>` tag does the trick, but editors just provide indenting buttons you can click on), but that's not always the best solution—and it won't work at all if you need some text or graphic appearing on the border itself.

Once you've decided to use a background border, you've pretty much committed yourself to using tables to format the page content. At the very least, you need a two-column table, with the leftmost column fixed to the width of the border to keep things on or off the border of the page.

Text

Break out. Paragraphs of text presented as *Normal* text have an empty space between them, which makes it easier to read. If, however, you have paragraphs consisting of single lines that you don't want spaced like that—and for which you can't use another pre-defined format—use a *line break* instead of a *paragraph break* at the end of each line.

In an HTML editor, you enter a line break by typing Shift Return instead of just Return. In the HTML code, the tag is <BR>, which doesn't need a closing tag.

Watch the white space. I've been preaching "no multiple spaces" in word processing for as long as there've been word processors—and people who type multiple spaces instead of creating and using tabs.

On a web page, it's even more important to avoid the temptation of putting in an extra space or two to nudge things around, because browsers ignore multiple spaces—even though the preview mode in most editors acknowledge them.

Using multiple returns is also an exercise in frustration, because they're ignored by browsers, too. But some helpful editors can mislead you: you hit Return a few times, the text moves down, you save it—and it appears correctly inside the browser window. That's because an editor like Visual Page automatically translates multiple presses of Return into multiple line breaks, entering as many lines of <BR> as you typed Return.

Using multiple spaces after all. Although multiple spaces are ignored by browsers, there's a special kind of space—the *nonbreaking space*—that has several handy properties: it "glues" words together so they won't be split at a line break; it's a little wider in any font than the standard space; and, you can use as many as you want next to each other and browsers will interpret them correctly.

To insert a nonbreaking space in your text, you have to type the code ` ` wherever you want the space. (Some HTML editors let you type Option Spacebar or Shift Spacebar and interpret the key combination as the nonbreaking space code.

Relative font sizes. When you're assigning a font size to text, you don't work with the point sizes that you're used to on the Mac. Instead, you get numbers like +1, +2, 0, -1 and -2. Since the user can set a desired size for the fonts in a paragraph, what you get to do is simply assign a *relative* size, larger or smaller, than the default that the user has set.

Text control with spacers. Use the GIF spacer (described earlier) for controlling text. A normal paragraph of text is predefined for its line spacing, a space between paragraphs, and no first-line indent. All of these can be altered with spacers.

- For a first-line indent, put a horizontal spacer in front of the first word of the paragraph.
- For larger spaces between paragraphs, put a vertical spacer in the first line of text—make sure it's early in the first line, so it won't wrap down to the second line if someone changes the width of the browser window. Use the spacer instead of typing a space between words so that the word spacing stays reasonably accurate. (If you're indenting the first line of the paragraph, a single spacer can take care of the indent and the paragraph spacing.)
- To adjust the line spacing, put vertical spacers in the text every few words so that there'll be at least one in every line even if someone changes the width of the browser window or the size of the text. Use the spacer instead of a space between words—otherwise, the text space and the graphic space make too large of a gap.

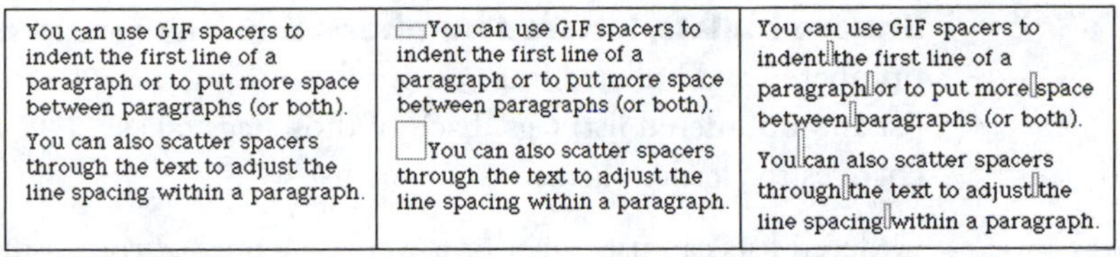
You can use GIF spacers to indent the first line of a paragraph or to put more space between paragraphs (or both).
You can also scatter spacers through the text to adjust the line spacing within a paragraph.
You can use GIF spacers to indent the first line of a paragraph or to put more space between paragraphs (or both).
You can also scatter spacers through the text to adjust the line spacing within a paragraph.
You can use GIF spacers to indent the first line of a paragraph or to put more space between paragraphs (or both).
You can also scatter spacers through the text to adjust the line spacing within a paragraph.

Using blank GIFs to space text.

ASCII text — **Chapter 12**

Curly quotes. Most web pages display straight apostrophes and quote marks because they're included in the basic list of ASCII characters and the curly, printer's quotes are not. But even straight quotes have to be "passed" to the text symbolically, since they mean something else in HTML. To indicate quote marks, for instance, you have to use the code `"` (including the closing semicolon). For other special characters, you use a number code between the ampersand and the semicolon, including the pound sign to indicate a number. The four you need for curly single and double quotes are:

single open quote	‘	‘
single close quote	’	’
double open quote	“	“
double close quote	”	”

To get this:

This is a "straight" quote and this is “curly.”

you'd use:

```
This is a &quot;straight&quot; quote and this is &#147;curly.&#148;
```

Set a friendly font. The basic font used for text is controlled by the browser—and, therefore, the user (although many users don't realize they can set this preference). With versions 4 of Netscape and Explorer, you can specify the font you want to be used on your page—but the trick is that the user has to have that font on his system, or everything goes back to the default, anyway. Luckily, the FACE attribute lets you list more than one font, so if the first is missing, the second, and then the third, will be looked for before going back to the default:

```
<FONT FACE="arial, geneva"> Hello, surfer! </FONT>
```

Many HTML editors won't show the font you've specified, but the browsers will; this makes design a little awkward, since you have to open the page in a browser to see what it looks like.

Microsoft's Web fonts — **Chapter 14**

Which fonts should you use? The TrueType fonts from Microsoft Explorer, provided with both its programs and the Mac system software—as well as being downloadable from Microsoft's site—are fast becoming standards on both platforms.

Square bullets, lettered numbers. You don't have to stick to the default numbered and bulleted lists you get from using the <OL> and <UL> (ordered list and unordered list) tags. Each of those tags takes a TYPE attribute that changes the leader characters for the list.

Ordered lists can use upper or lowercase letters or roman numerals; you simply use a type of A, a, i, or I, like this: `<OL TYPE="a">`. For unordered lists, the TYPE choices are *disc* (the standard bullet), *square,* or *circle:* `<UL TYPE="square">`

The results of the disc, square, and circle TYPE attribute with the <UL> tag.

● Monday	□ Monday	○ Monday
● Tuesday	□ Tuesday	○ Tuesday
● Wednesday	□ Wednesday	○ Wednesday
● Thursday	□ Thursday	○ Thursday
● Friday	□ Friday	○ Friday

Graphics

The browser-safe palette. Since all but a relatively few monitors can display at least 256 colors at a time (that's 8-bit color), web design has settled on 256 colors for most uses—sort of. The problem is that while an 8-bit Mac monitor can display 256 colors, and a PC monitor can display 256 colors, they're not the same 256 colors. But they do have 216 colors in common, so basic web design uses those 216 colors—the *browser-safe* colors the platforms have in common. If you use something not in the "palette" on one or the other platform, that computer will try to match the color by dithering two others together, combining dots to approximate the right shade; this adversely affects the look of many graphics. (This doesn't apply to photographic images, but only to the colors used in backgrounds, text, and GIF images.)

How do you make sure you're using the right colors? Most graphics programs let you specify a Web palette from which to work, some utilities convert colors for you, and HTML editors let you just apply font and background colors and do the grunt work for you. But if you want the specific RGB (red, green, blue) value for a color so you can use it in your code like this:

```
COLOR="#FF3300"
```

you can look it up in the Mac's Color Picker. You can open the Color Picker only indirectly: the easiest way is to open the Appearance control panel and choose Other for the highlight, which opens the Color Picker. Move the sliders on the three color-value bars (keep *Snap to Web color* checked to make sure the slider stops only on the notched numbers) and see what the HTML number is for the color you create.

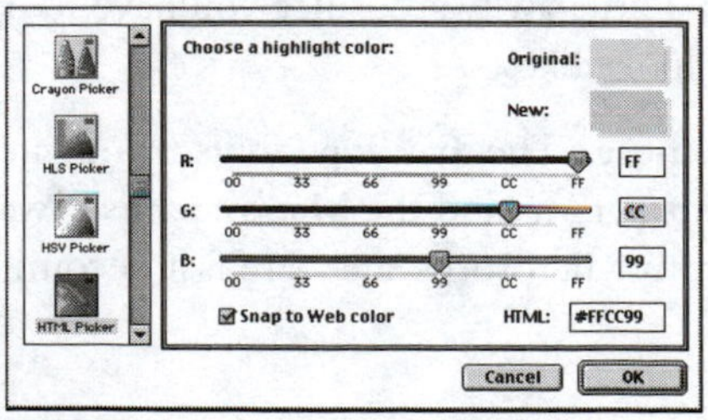

Using the Color Picker to find the code for a web-safe color.

The table. You can download a table of color values, and ready-made palettes that can be used in programs like Photoshop and DeBabelizer, directly from a site built and maintained by the very person who coined the term "web-safe colors," Lynda Weinman. The picture here shows just a piece of one of the tables (the original, of course, is in color); each shade's color value, and proportions of red-green-blue is noted in its colored cell.

33CCFF R: 051 G: 204 B: 255	00CCFF R: 000 G: 204 B: 255	99FFFF R: 153 G: 255 B: 255	66FFFF R: 102 G: 255 B: 255	33FFFF R: 051 G: 255 B: 255	00FFFF R: 000 G: 255 B: 255	00CCCC R: 000 G: 204 B: 204
003333 R: 000 G: 051 B: 051	00FFCC R: 000 G: 255 B: 204	33FFCC R: 051 G: 255 B: 204	33CC99 R: 051 G: 204 B: 153	00CC99 R: 000 G: 204 B: 153	66FFCC R: 102 G: 255 B: 204	99FFCC R: 153 G: 255 B: 204
99CC99 R: 153 G: 204 B: 153	66FF99 R: 102 G: 255 B: 153	33FF99 R: 051 G: 255 B: 153	33CC66 R: 051 G: 204 B: 102	00CC66 R: 000 G: 204 B: 102	66CC99 R: 102 G: 204 B: 153	009966 R: 000 G: 153 B: 102
00CC33 R: 000 G: 204 B: 051	33CC33 R: 051 G: 204 B: 051	66FF33 R: 102 G: 255 B: 051	00FF00 R: 000 G: 255 B: 000	66CC33 R: 102 G: 204 B: 051	006600 R: 000 G: 102 B: 000	003300 R: 000 G: 051 B: 000

A piece of the color table.

Through a GIF, darkly. The GIF images you place on your web page need transparent backgrounds so they won't be surrounded by a blotch of white. If you set the background of the page to white, you won't see the blotch, but a browser might allow the user to override the background color setting—and *he'll* see the blotch.

If the GIF image wasn't originally saved with a transparent background color, you can change it in your HTML editor. Although accessing the editing window itself varies from one program to another, they all provide a "magic wand" that lets you click on the background of the image to make it transparent. Although you'll see the change in the image on your page immediately, you have to explicitly save the change to the image file while the editing window is still open, or it will revert to its former state.

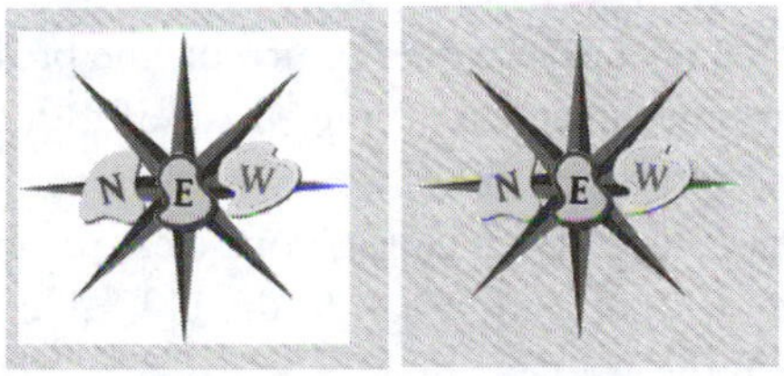

An image on a textured background page before and after setting the image background to be transparent.

The background *color*, not the background When you set the background of an image to be transparent, you're not really setting the *background* to be transparent: you're selecting a specific *color* to be transparent. Usually, you don't see the difference between these two concepts because you click on the surrounding white area of a graphic and it disappears—you think it's the background that's been changed. But if you use a graphic that has internal white areas, like the dove icon shown on the next page, you'll see that when you make the "background" transparent, all the other parts of the image that have the same color as that background also become transparent.

To get around this problem—when you don't want the background showing through parts of the image—you have to change the color of either the surrounding background space or the interior areas of the image. It's usually easier to change the background color: in your graphics program, surround the original image with a rectangle of a solid color—a color that's not in the image itself. When you place it on your web page (or when you're still in the graphics program) make that background color transparent, and the interior of the image will be safe.

Making the surrounding white area for this image transparent makes all its white areas transparent.

Top, before and after editing the outer background. Bottom, before and after applying transparency.

Orientation with the text. When you work with text and graphics "flat" on a page—without using a table to keep things in place—the graphic is treated the same way "inline" graphics are treated in word processors and layout programs. In effect, the graphic is a single, giant character that's plopped in the line of text—throwing off the spacing of the lines above and below it.

When you put a graphic on a page with a return or line break before and after it, there's no problem, since it sits on a "line" by itself. But when it's not separated that way, you have to be careful of how you align the graphic within the text. (To set alignment in an HTML editor, you select the graphic and choose the alignment from a menu or button bar. In the HTML code, the alignment is the `ALIGN` attribute in the `IMG` tag.)

For any image larger than a line of type set with more than a single line of type, the first three alignment choices—top, middle, and bottom—are unacceptable, although there are occasions when the bottom alignment can work. Each of these options puts a single line of the text with the graphic and bumps the rest of the text underneath the graphic. The left or right alignment is what you need to wrap text around a graphic.

The top, middle and bottom alignments keep a single line of text on the same line as the graphic (top). Defining left or right alignment for an image wraps the text to its side (bottom).

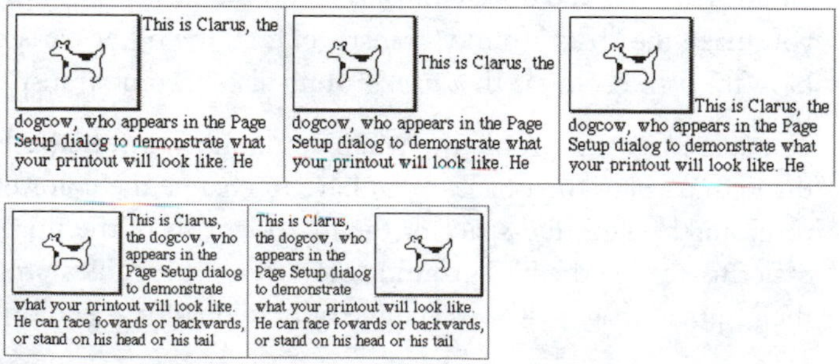

Breathing space. When you wrap text around a graphic, the text bumps up against the edges of the graphic. If you're not using a table to separate the two, you can easily space them by using a single, well-placed spacer—a transparent GIF rectangle.

Put the spacer directly after the image (for a left-aligned image), between it and the text, and set it for left alignment, too. Make it as wide as you want the space to be, and make it long enough to bump down the first full line of text to keep it away from the bottom of the image.

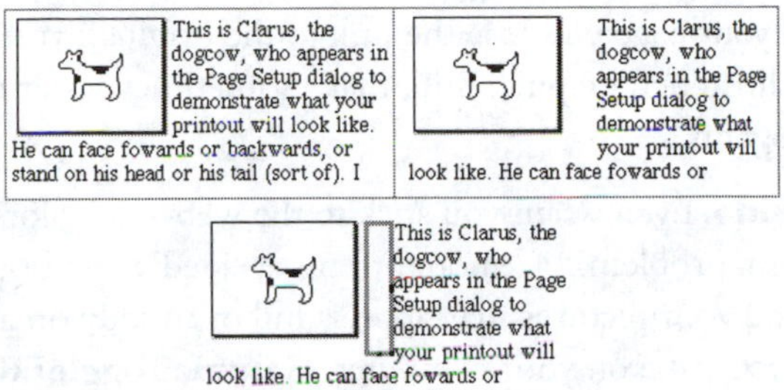

The difference between the too-tight wrapping (top left) and the good spacing (top right) is a single transparent spacer GIF (bottom).

The no-image test. Turn off the automatic image loading in your browser and take a look at your page. Can you still figure out what's going on? Don't depend solely on images for navigating your site; many people surf without images getting downloaded at all. There are two things you can do to accommodate these people and, in fact, you should do both.

First, assuming the top of your home page fits entirely into a single screen (as it should, for good design), provide small text links at the bottom that echo whatever graphic links appear elsewhere on the page.

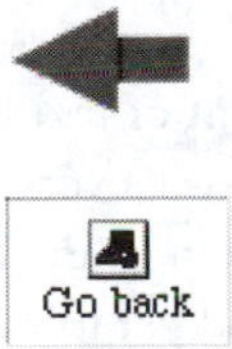

Top, the image; bottom, the appearance of the alt label when images aren't downloaded

Second, provide an *alt label* (alternative label) for every graphic on the page, like this: `<IMG SRC="Images/back.gif" ALT="Go back">`. That way, each image icon will have a label when someone's doing image-less surfing.

Specify the graphic size. The only thing just as important as the name (and path) to the graphic in an image tag is its size. Why, when the image will load without the size specified? Because if you define the height and width inside an image tag, like this:

```
<IMG SRC="arrow.gif" WIDTH="84" HEIGHT="59">
```

the text on the page knows where it has to go and can load before the image does.

> ***Pages that take a minute or more to load just don't cut it with the average Web surfer whose attention span for new sites has been measured at only about eight seconds.***
>
> *Paul Bonner, Windows Sources Magazine, September 1997*

Auto-convert GIF. Most HTML editors will let you simply paste a graphic onto a page and automatically create a GIF file for you, so you don't have to worry about a separate utility or art program to convert anything if you can get onto the Clipboard. You'll wind up with a few extra steps, though, because the new GIF file will be named something like *image2.gif* and when you rename it to something more descriptive, your page will lose the link to the original; you'll have to re-place the newly christened graphic. Still, that's sometimes faster than running a separate program.

The dark side. Even when you stick to the web-safe colors, you've got a cross-platform problem: PC monitors are decidedly less bright than Mac monitors, and your pictures may appear dull or muddy on a PC when they looked perfectly fine on your computer. **GammaToggleFKey** is a nifty piece of freeware that can toggle your monitor into a mode that mimics the PC screen (*gamma* being the brightness and color tones on a monitor).

shareware.com

Links and Anchors

Use real names. Name your anchors! If you stick with your HTML editor's default anchor name (something clever and descriptive like #2312), you'll have a heck of a time editing your page as the design grows.

In addition, the anchor's name is usually displayed by a browser when the user places the mouse pointer over the link, and the extra feedback about where the link goes can be very useful.

Bullet links. If you use graphics as bullets in front of text links, make sure you define both the bullet *and* the text as the link—it's very annoying to click on a nice chunky, buttony-looking bullet and have nothing happen! With both defined as the link, the user can click on either and get to the destination.

Tables

The layout tool. Tables are a web designer's best friend. They're the only way you can keep elements on a page in the right places when a user starts resizing the window. When you set the table's lines to be invisible, there's nothing on the web page that indicates there's actually a table: instead, all you see is well-placed text and graphics that behave no matter what happens to window. Learn how to handle tables, and you've got half your web-design problems solved.

And don't forget: you can put a table *inside* another table cell, which lets you solve all sorts of tricky layout problems.

Let the borders go south. When you're using tables for layout, turn off the borders: `<TABLE BORDER="0">`. Even if you think framing different parts of the page is an "effect" you want, you're probably wrong. The rest of the page design should "frame" the important parts of the page. Borders should be on only for very specific reasons; if, for instance, the page (or a section of it) is, say, a calendar of events.

Fixed-width only. The width of a table can be defined in two ways: relatively (as a percentage of the width of the browser window) or absolutely (in terms of pixels):

`<TABLE WIDTH="100%">` or `<TABLE WIDTH="600">`

Always, always, *always* define your tables in pixel widths; otherwise, when the user resizes her window, she'll be resizing your table cells, too, wrecking the whole purpose of tables—layout control!

The amoeba table. *Amoeba??* That's a single-cell creature, and a single-cell table can be a very handy design tool. Why? Because if you've defined a fixed-width table (as described in the last entry) and put everything inside it, the width of your page won't change if the user re-sizes the width of the window (which usually re-flows text).

Excel. Some HTML editors (FrontPage and Visual Page, for two), understand the difference between Clipboard contents coming from Excel and text coming from anywhere else. If you paste information in from Excel, it will be automatically formatted into a table by the editor!

GIF Animations

The minimalist approach. When it comes to animations on a web page, a very little goes a very long way. It's a design challenge (to put it mildly) to get something that adds interest to the page without distracting the viewer.

Your GIF animation doesn't have to repeat endlessly. You can often make your point with just a few repetitions (making sure that the final frame is one that you want left on the page). Another approach is to define the image to loop endlessly, but to put a long delay on the first or last frame so there's a considerable time lapse between loops, cutting way down on the annoyance factor.

Implied motion. Well, of course, in animation you might say that all motion is merely *implied,* but that's not what I mean here. Since the number of frames in an animated GIF affects the file size (and therefore the download time), it's important to use as few frames as possible to achieve the animation you need. There are times when you can replace several frames of something changing position with a single "blur" frame that makes it look like the object has moved.

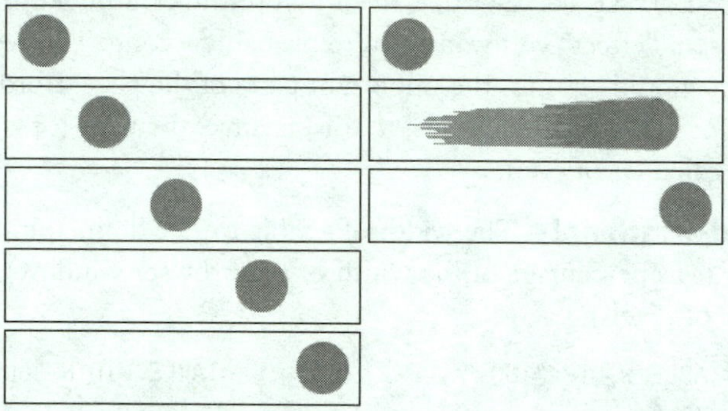

Left, the original five-frame animation. Right, the three-frame replacement.

Eyeball to eyeball. When it comes to the <BLINK> tag, which makes the text it surrounds blink on and off, take the advice printed on a banner hanging in my friend Michael's office: "Thou shalt not blink."

Frames

Sparingly. Avoid using frames unless you're very, very good, and very, very careful. Frames introduce lots of design and navigation problems: their borders take up precious screen space; it's seldom clear to the user what the Back and Forward buttons will affect; framed pages take longer to load; there are problems for a user who tries to print a framed page.

A good use of frames is to keep navigational buttons on-screen—along the left side or top—while the main part of the page scrolls. But make the button area stationary, not scrollable.

Spare. The more frames you use, the less space you have; and if you make each framed area scrollable, you'll lose even more space. Remember that you can not only suppress the scroll bars for each frame individually, but also get rid of the dividing borders, too.

22

Music, Movies, and More

In This Chapter

In General

QuickTime

QuickTime: more than you think. When you say "QuickTime," most people think of movies and videos on the computer. While it's true that QuickTime started off as a digital video format, it has become much more than that: it's a way of storing and playing back all kinds of still images, sounds, video and even interactive programs. QuickTime isn't just for Macs, either—you can play QuickTime files on PCs and other computers as well. A great source of information is the QuickTime FAQ (Frequently Asked Questions), which you can find on the Web; the author, Charles Wiltgen, is Apple's QuickTime Evangelist. —AB

quicktimefaq.com

QuickTime extensions. QuickTime's many capabilities are made possible by a whole constellation of files, including a slew of System Folder doodads. If you go poking around, here's what you're likely to find:

- **QuickTime**: The master extension on which everything else depends. It contains the *codecs* that encode and decode many different kinds of digital video and audio.
- **QuickTime Musical Instruments**: Contains the digitized "voices" of musical instruments that are used by QuickTime's built-in synthesizer when playing back MIDI files.

- **QuickTime PowerPlug**: Speeds up QuickTime functions on PowerPC Macs.
- **QuickTime VR**: Makes it possible to view QuickTime Virtual Reality files (panoramas and "object movies") that give the illusion of 3D images. A QTVR "pano" acts as a window on a 360-degree view; you can turn around and see what's behind you, or move closer to an object of interest. Some panos even let you click on objects in the scene to interact with them. Object movies, on the other hand, let you spin a seemingly solid object around and view it from any side, top or bottom.
- **QuickTime MPEG Extension**: Lets you play back movies and sound files encoded with the MPEG-1 standard (but only on PowerPC Macs). These movies can be found on the Web and on MPEG-1 CD-ROMs, also known as Video CDs. (These are not to be confused with the similar-looking DVD movies, which require a DVD-ROM—not *CD*-ROM—drive, as well as special MPEG-2 decoding hardware.)

- If you own a digital camera, you may also have the extensions **QuickTime IC** and **QuickTime IC Extras**, which let you download images directly from cameras such as Apple's QuickTake models. —AB

The QuickTime Settings control panel. The QuickTime Settings control panel lets you control autoplay for audio and multimedia CDs, tell QuickTime how fast your internet connection is (for better playing of QuickTime movies in your browser), set what kind of synthesizer to use for MIDI music files, and use other custom settings. There's a considerable difference between the QuickTime Settings control panel version 2.5 which shipped with OS 8 and 8.1, and the QuickTime 3.0 version released afterwards (which you can download, for free, from Apple's web site). The first offers two "panels," one each for CD autoplay and synthesized music; the update offers five panels, with a major change to the Music panel.

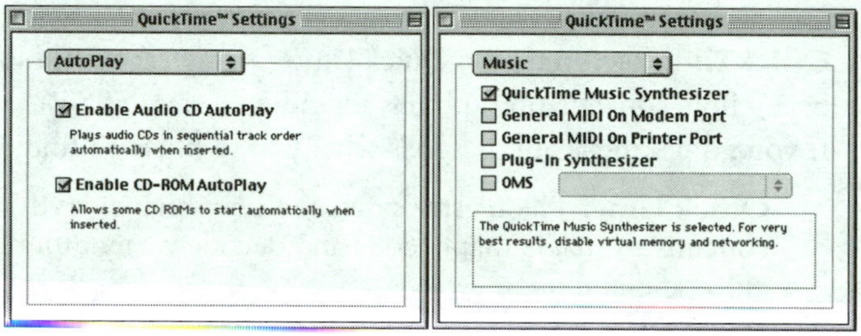

The QuickTime Settings control panel options for version 2.5.

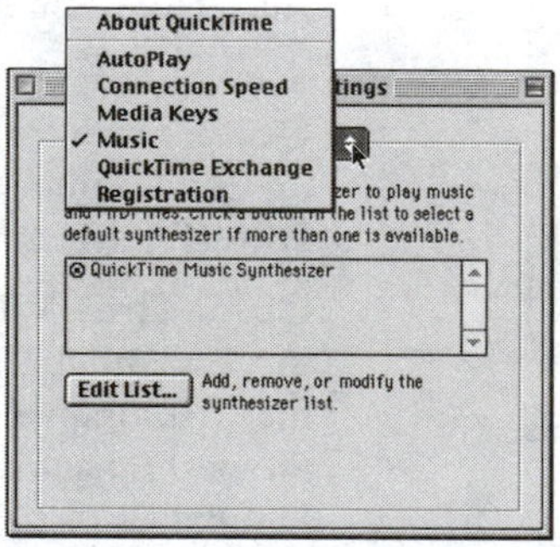

QuickTime Settings 3.0 has many more options available.

Foreign exchange rates. Keep the "Enable QuickTime Exchange" option turned off in the QuickTime 3.0 control panel. This feature is meant to let you double-click QuickTime files that originated on non-Mac computers, but it does this by altering a file's type and creator—and that can wreak havoc with Mac programs, leading to all kinds of weird error messages. Unless you have a very specific reason for needing this feature (if you're dealing with batches of QuickTime files created on a Sun workstation, for instance), it's safest to turn it off. —AB

When the worm turns. The relatively virus-free world of the Mac did acquire a special kind of virus—a *worm*—known as the AutoStart 9805 worm, connected to the use of the QuickTime Settings control panel. This self-replicating program will intermittently slow down your computer and destroy some of your disk files, but it can attack only if *Enable CD-ROM AutoPlay* is turned on in the control panel (that's not the Enable *Audio* CD AutoPlay). Since few if any Mac CD-ROMs are set up to autoplay anyway, you have nothing to lose by turning this off. —SZA/AB

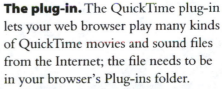

> ***I like a film to have a beginning, a middle, and an end, but not necessarily in that order.***
> *Jean-Luc Goddard, film director*

The plug-in. The QuickTime plug-in lets your web browser play many kinds of QuickTime movies and sound files from the Internet; the file needs to be in your browser's Plug-ins folder. When you install the QuickTime update, the plug-in is automatically installed, too, but you have to move it to the right folder. —SZA/AB

The QuickTime bonus applications. QuickTime comes with two applications: MoviePlayer and PictureViewer. **MoviePlayer** is a simple program that lets you open any QuickTime file—video, audio, MIDI, still image, whatever. You can also get information such as the file's pixel dimensions, running time, frame rate and so on. **PictureViewer** lets you open still images (not movies) and look at them. Period. Since you can do this just as well with MoviePlayer (any version), this seems like a waste. —AB

QuickTime Pro. The basic QuickTime is free with the system software and/or for the downloading. But for a measly thirty bucks, you can get QuickTime Pro, which comes with MoviePlayer Pro and PictureViewer Pro.

MoviePlayer Pro lets you do a lot more than the free version: edit, splice, and resave movies. You can even apply some interesting filters—there's one that simulates old, scratched black-and-white film, for example, including an occasional hair popping up in the frame. And MoviePlayer Pro isn't just for movies: it can play MIDI music files, and can read in the music tracks from an audio CD and convert them to AIFF (audio interchange file format) files you can play on your computer. (Make sure you read the next entry about this program!)

As for **PictureViewer Pro**, it lets you convert and save an image in any of five—count 'em—*five* formats. Wow, impressive! Seriously: if you need to convert graphics files, get the shareware application GraphicConverter, which supports over three dozen different formats. —AB

The free MoviePlayer Pro. MoviePlayer 3.0 is free, but the Pro version comes with the thirty-dollar QuickTime Pro. Unlike PictureViewer Pro, MoviePlayer Pro actually provides useful extras, as detailed in the last entry. But hey—why pay extra for all these goodies? Apple's dirty little secret is that MoviePlayer 3.0 Pro is exactly the same as the older MoviePlayer 2.5.1, which is still free! —AB

QuickTime compression. QuickTime supports IMA (Interactive Multimedia Association) compression, a multimedia industry standard which allows relatively high-quality sound to take up much less disk space. IMA compression, while not perfect, sounds much better than any compression previously available on the Mac. —FB

Controlling the MoviePlayer. When you play a movie back in any version of MoviePlayer, you can control many of its functions. The pictures here tell the story.

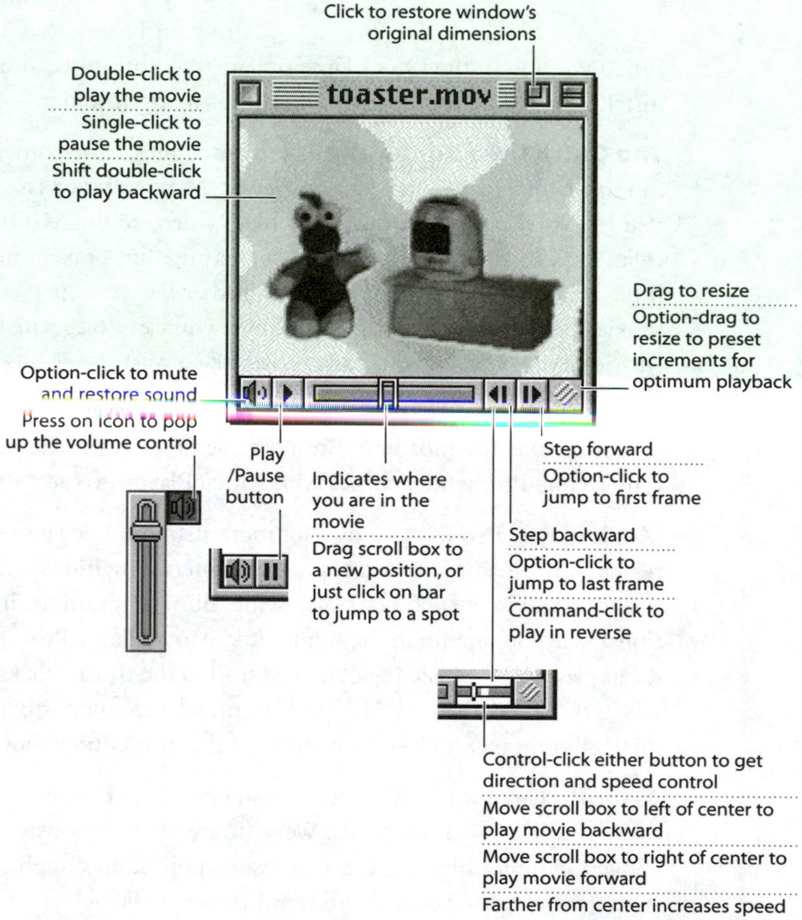

QuickTime synchronization. One of the wonderful things about QuickTime is that it allows audio and visual data to play back in synchronization. That may not seem like a big deal, but it has been problematic in the past to get visual and audio events to play back in sync. If, for example, you

have a sprite dance across the screen while you play an audio file, it will probably dance at a different speed on a PowerMac and on a Quadra; the audio, however, will play back at the same speed on both computers. This presents a major problem if you want music to reach a climax at a certain point in an animation. QuickTime helps solve this problem because it keeps the different events running in sync, no matter what Mac is playing it back. —FB

Keyboard control of MoviePlayer. There are also several keyboard shortcuts for MoviePlayer:

To:	*Press:*
Play	[Spacebar] or [Return] or [⌘][→]
Pause	[Spacebar] or [Return]
Play backward	[⌘][←]
Step forward	[→]
Step backward	[←]

Multimedia

Making multimedia. Making multimedia tends to require considerably more computing power and resources than does playing it back. Image-editing programs, for example, benefit from lots of RAM and fast CPUs; video and audio editing are virtually impossible without copious disk storage as well. If you plan to make multimedia titles on a regular or even semi-regular basis, you will want some serious computing horsepower:

- **Memory:** Lots of it. Luckily, it's cheap, so load up. For a beginner, 64 megs; double that for serious work.
- **CPU:** Nothing less than a PowerPC even for a beginner. For serious work, the top-speed PowerPC chip is a minimum, a G3 chip is recommended.
- **Storage:** Gigabytes upon gigabytes on one or more hard drives; as with memory, prices have dropped precipitously, so this isn't too much of a burden. Opt for the faster SCSI drives if your Mac has two different busses.
- **Slots:** You'll need room for special boards for video digitizing or sampling. Unfortunately, at this point no G3 model comes with more than three slots—which are quickly used up by, say, a digitizing board, an extra monitor, and a card for extra-fast storage connections.
- **CD-ROM drive:** You might not want the fastest model available, since you have to make sure that you won't be misled as to how your multimedia title might play back on most users' systems, but you won't want an old, sluggish one, either.
- **CD-R:** If you're authoring CD-ROM multimedia titles, you'll want to be able to make your own CDs for test and archival purposes.

- **Monitor:** Get a large screen because it's much easier to work on—you can see both the work you're doing (in a window sized for playback on a standard monitor) and all the tools you need to do the work. Get enough video RAM to run the big screen in millions of colors. —SZA/MEC

Ingredients of multimedia. The name says it all: there are multi media in multimedia.

- **Text:** While at first glance, text may seem to be boring and low-tech, it can actually be a powerful addition to a multimedia work. It's good for lots of things, and has at least one powerful advantage over some other forms of media: it's very compact—the text of an entire book takes up less room than, say, a medium-fidelity rendition of one top-40 song.
- **Graphics:** Multimedia titles usually rely very heavily on graphics, using them as background "frames," user-interface elements like buttons, illustrations of subject matter, or even *as* the subject matter. But graphics take up disk space, and the larger the picture and the more colors it uses, the more space it takes up. Displaying pictures requires RAM, too, with larger pictures needing more memory.
- **Sound:** You can use sound in a variety of ways in your multimedia title, from simple sound effects to high-fidelity music. Remember, though, that a sound effect can go from interesting to boring to downright annoying the more often a user hears it. Use sound effects only when they're needed, and not just when they're possible.
- **Video and animation:** Video can liven up almost any presentation, but it has its drawbacks: it's expensive to produce, takes up lots of disk space, and even with QuickTime's sophisticated assistance, it can still task the processing speed of many machines. —SZA/MEC

Doubled RAM isn't multimedia RAM. RAM-stretching tricks like virtual memory or Connectix's RAMDoubler tend to give multimedia titles fits—as in fits and starts, especially on older machines and with slower drives.

RAMDoubler and virtual memory
Chapter 13

Playing audio or video requires the constant attention of your Mac's CPU. Utilities like RAMDoubler, however, use compression schemes to pack temporarily inactive portions of your Mac's memory into smaller spaces, and compressing and decompressing memory uses CPU time. While your Mac is doing that, it can't also be decompressing the video from a CD-ROM. Virtual memory also ties up the CPU, and then aggravates the problem by using the Mac's hard disk; hard disks are *lots* slower to access than RAM, and this interrupts the smooth playback of a video. —SZA/MEC

Bit depths. Most multimedia titles require a minimum 8-bit depth, for 256 possible colors—nowhere near the number of different colors the eye can see. It takes at least 16 bits (which can show thousands of colors) or more before the number of colors available is sufficient to rival photographic quality. But multimedia authors want to reach the widest possible audience, and, for now, staying with a 256-color limit is the best means for reaching that audience, since so many computers still have monitors limited to 256 colors at a time.

Multimedia developers cope with the 256-color limit by using two techniques to make 8-bit pictures seem to show more colors than they can. The first method is called *dithering*, which uses more than one pixel to represent a single point in the picture: a bluish pixel and an adjacent reddish pixel will be blended by the eye to form a larger, purplish pixel. Dithering can fool the eye to some extent, but at the cost of making the picture look less sharp. The second method is to choose the right set of 256 colors that best shows the picture; this is called using a *custom color palette*. —SZA/MEC

Authoring Tools

Authoring tools? We all know what programming is: writing line after line of cryptic code in C, Pascal, or BASIC in order to create a computer program that serves some useful or entertaining purpose. And then there's this thing called "authoring." Authoring systems like HyperCard can also create useful programs. So what's the difference, anyway?

In a nutshell, people who use authoring systems get things done a lot faster than programmers, because authors use "higher-level" tools—tools that do more of the work for them. Some of these tools don't even require you to write any code, and all of them feature more or less English-like scripting languages that make life a lot easier. A SuperTalk command like "play movie 'Fred's Birthday' at the location of card graphic 'Frame'" can take the place of scores of lines of programming code.

This section provides an overview of today's most popular authoring tools. Most of these programs are available as downloadable demo versions, so you can try before you buy—always a good idea when you're considering something as complex and (potentially) expensive as an authoring tool. Check the vendors' web sites for the latest versions, prices and availability. —AB

HyperCard. The first tool that made it really easy to create programs with a more or less complete Mac-style look and feel was **HyperCard** ($100, Apple Computer). It's inexpensive, requires little in the way of RAM, hard disk space and processor power, and you can do quite a lot with it. Its stack-of-cards metaphor makes it particularly suitable for small database projects. Unfortunately, HyperCard has seen little improvement since its 1987 debut, and as of version 2.4 (current at this writing) it's showing its age. Support for color is poor, there are no vector ("draw") graphics, and some basic interface elements such as menus are very cumbersome to work with. And HyperCard has no PC version, so your HyperCard stacks are strictly Mac-bound.

However, Apple has big plans for HyperCard 3.0: it is to be fully integrated into the QuickTime system extension. HyperCard stacks should then be able to run on any machine that has QuickTime installed, just as QuickTime movies and sound files now do. Of course practically every Mac has QuickTime; the big news is that this will supposedly also work on PCs, making it possible to bring your HyperCard stacks to a vast new audience. (In theory, stacks should also work with web browsers that use the QuickTime plug-in, making HyperCard applications web-deliverable at a stroke.) Apple has been working on this for years, and no ship date has yet been announced—but when it finally happens, it will mark a major change in the low-cost authoring tools arena. —AB

SuperCard. Designed to remedy HyperCard's shortcomings—like lack of support for color, layers, and vector graphics, and HyperCard's limited one-card-at-a-time authoring environment—**SuperCard** ($145, IncWell DMG) was a tremendous improvement in most respects, and quickly garnered a small but devoted following among educators and corporate developers. Although it has consistently gotten rave reviews, the product was never marketed well, and it passed through several companies before coming to its present owner, IncWell. —AB

Version 3.5 of SuperCard is a powerful general-purpose application development tool. It shares HyperCard's easy-to-understand scripting language (and indeed can import HyperCard stacks), while greatly expanding its capabilities. A browser plug-in makes it possible to deliver SuperCard projects over the Web, and the SuperCard package also includes internet-savvy features that let projects send and receive e-mail, ftp files, and do other Internet tasks. SuperCard's one major drawback is that there is as yet no version available for PCs. —AB

Director. Of all the authoring tools described here, **Director** ($1000), Macromedia) is probably the least suited to general-purpose application development—yet it's easily the best known. Macromedia's marketing muscle has pushed to the fore a program whose filmstrip metaphor, while ideal for slideshows and presentations, is poorly suited for many other tasks. Many applications that have been created with other products described here simply can't be built—or can only be built with great difficulty—using Director.

Make no mistake, though: Director is a powerhouse when it comes to time-based tasks such as animation, presentations (with limited interactivity) and the like. It's probably the single most often used system for authoring multimedia CD-ROMs, where its ability to work with multiple onscreen "actors" and precisely synchronize their actions to a soundtrack makes it the best tool for the job. Director "movies" can run on both Macs and PCs, and they can be delivered via the Web to browsers equipped with one of Macromedia's "ShockWave" plug-ins. —AB

Authorware. An oldie but in some ways a goodie, **Authorware** ($2,999, Macromedia) was originally developed for educators who were thought to be afraid of programming—hence in Authorware, everything is done by dragging symbols around on a flowchart. The system is comprehensive (when you buy Authorware, Macromedia basically throws in a copy of every other program in its catalog), but its awkward interface and multi-thousand-dollar price have kept it from achieving widespread use. It does run on PCs as well as Macs, and over the Web via a plug-in. —AB

DreamWeaver. Although sold as an HTML editor, **DreamWeaver** ($299, Macromedia) is the first (and currently the best) of a new generation of tools that makes it feasible to build serious multimedia applications using the new web technologies: dynamic HTML, JavaScript, and cascading style sheets. Because this approach by definition lets you deliver applications on multiple platforms as well as across the Web, tools like DreamWeaver are likely to supersede products like HyperCard and Director for an increasing number of projects in coming years.

DreamWeaver offers a WYSIWYG environment that lets you drag text and graphics into position and then easily assign behaviors (including animation) to them without having to write any code. Pop-up menus let you choose actions for each object, and DreamWeaver then writes the necessary JavaScript code for you automatically. The program also includes tools for managing a web site. Because DreamWeaver's output is HTML, it works on Macs, PCs and other computers. And the program itself is available in both Mac and PC versions. —AB

Presentation programs. A traditional presentation program—as opposed to a multimedia authoring tool—is basically a slide-making tool for business presentations. If you're doing the presentation from the computer itself (as opposed to just preparing the slides and handouts), you'll be able to add basic effects like sounds, "wipes" from one slide to the next, and even QuickTime movies. A presentation program lets you create master slides with backgrounds that repeat from one slide to another, and outliner that lets you create and manipulate your presentation information, and an easy way to reorganize the slides you've created. Most importantly, it lets you easily print the presentation material to make handouts for your talk (as well as speaker notes!).

The standard for presentations is from steamroller Microsoft: **PowerPoint** ($300), which has the advantage of near-perfect cross-platform compatibility. **Astound** ($150, Gold Disk) is a good alternative—at half the price!—but the Mac version is currently two version numbers behind the PC version, so there may be less-than-enthusiastic support and development from the manufacturer.

Sound and Music

Audio CDs

Music to your ears. If your Mac has a built-in CD-ROM drive, you can play standard audio CDs with it, for your own personal music station. Even Macs without special audio enhancements have surprisingly good fidelity (although nothing to rival a separate stereo setup) even with just the internal speaker—good enough for some background music while you're working.

Your Mac can just play CDs automatically when you insert them, or you can use the AppleCD Audio Player desk accessory to control the play list.

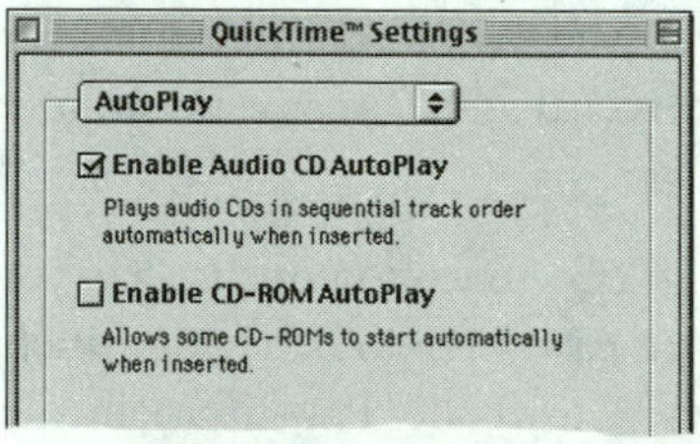

AutoPlay on insert. If you'd like an audio CD to play when you insert it, use the QuickTime Settings control panel and check the Enable Audio CD AutoPlay button.

Double-click on insert. If you don't have a CD set to play automatically, you can open its icon when you insert it; you'll see tracks on it, represented by ugly old black-and-white icons. Double-click on one and the AppleCD Audio Player opens, and that track starts playing.

Tracks on an audio CD are represented by black-and-white icons.

Setting the volume. Set the volume for your audio CD in the Monitors & Sounds control panel: the system sound volume setting affects the CD's volume. In fact, if you click the Mute button so your computer won't beep, you won't be able to hear CDs, either.

The volume setting in Monitor & Sounds interacts with the one in the Audio Player: the Player's top volume value is the one that's set in the control panel, so it can't get any louder than what you've set for the system.

The Player. The AppleCD Audio Player is a desk accessory that's installed in your Apple Menu Items folder; if it's not in your Apple menu, you can use the Find command to scour your drive to see where you might have moved it.

The Player has two basic modes: the small version, which supplies the basic controls you'd expect from a CD player, and a fuller version that lets you create a play list for each CD. Toggle between the two versions by clicking the little triangle at the bottom left of the small version. (And don't ignore the customizing command in its Options menu, which lets you change both the background and readout colors.)

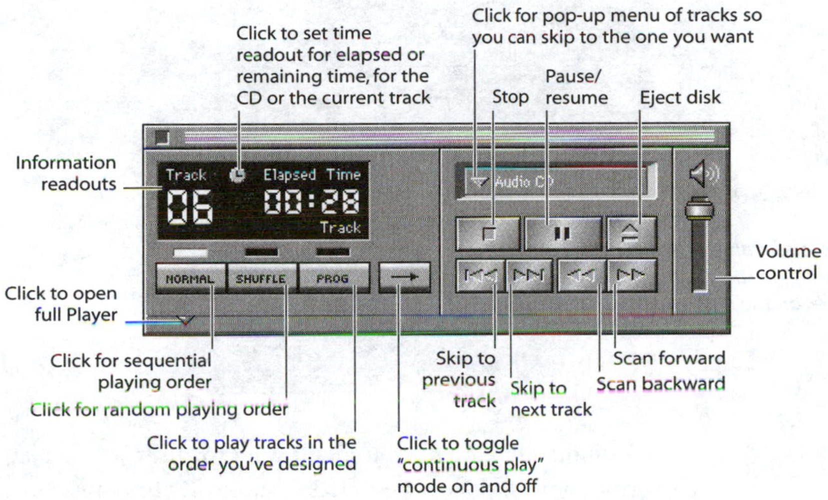

Keyboard shortcuts. The main buttons in the Player have keyboard equivalents (which work only when the Player is the active window):

Stop	Delete or Clear
Pause/Resume	Spacebar or Enter
Eject	⌘E
Previous Track	←
Next Track	→
Volume adjustment	↑ and ↓

No-strain strains. When the Mac plays a CD for you, you're not losing any computing power. Playing a CD is not like performing a background task that requires CPU attention and slows down other things you're doing; it's an independent operation that won't affect any of the work you're doing on the Mac.

Creating your play list. In the full version of the Player, you can create your own play list for whenever you use that CD. The first thing you'll want to do is name the CD and the songs, since there's no way the Mac can read that information from the disk—all it can do is identify separate tracks and their playing times. You click on the "name" of any track to edit it, or press Tab and Shift Tab to move from one track title to another. If you edit a name, pressing Return enters the changed name and moves you to the next title. You can play a track (so you'll be able to identify it) by double-clicking on the track number. Don't worry—your Mac *will* recognize the CD the next time you use it, so you don't have type this information in again!

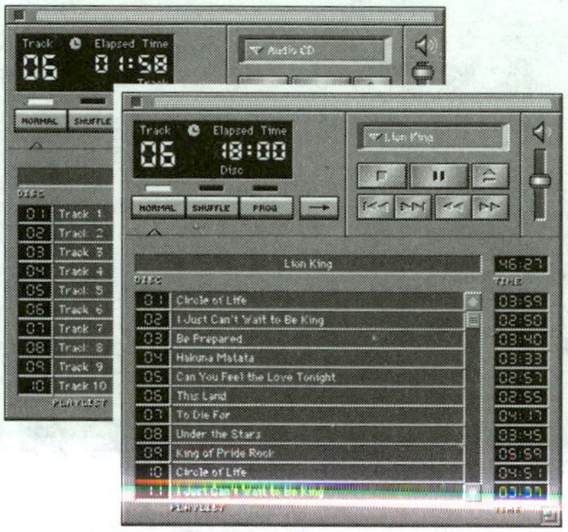

Before and after identifying the songs on the disk.

Once the titles are in, you might want to create a new play list. (Purists will cringe at this, since a well-crafted audio CD has music in the proper musical order already!) Just click the PROG button in the upper part of the player to switch to the play list mode. On the left is the normal order; on the right will be your custom order. Just drag items from the left and deposit them in slots on the right. You can insert a track between ones you've already put in the list, and reorder the list by dragging things up or down in it.

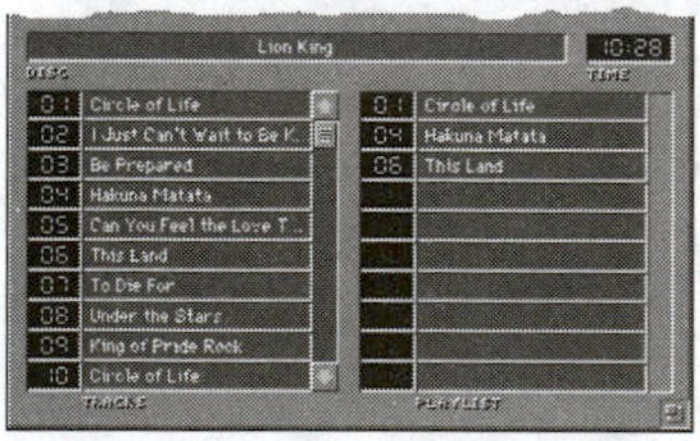

Working with the play list.

Where is all this information? All the information you enter about a CD—its title, its track titles, and the play list you create—are stored inside your Preferences folder in a file named *AppleCD Audio Player Prefs.* If you store lots of information there, you may want to add the file to your list of miscellaneous backup items so that if it becomes corrupted you won't have to enter all the information again. And when you reinstall a clean system, don't forget to copy this file to your new System Folder.

In the Beginning

It's long been a piece of movie/computer trivia that HAL, the schizo computer in 2001: A Space Odyssey has a very interesting name. Shift each of its letters to the next one in the alphabet, and what do you get?

But here's a more subtle piece of trivia: When HAL starts really breaking down, he starts singing "Daisy, Daisy, give me your answer, do." What's happening is that HAL is regressing to his "childhood," and author Arthur C. Clarke is paying homage to early computers and their programmers. At Bell Labs, back in 1932, the first tune ever played by a computer was... you guessed it. Then, carrying on the tradition, Bill Gates programmed the first microcomputer, the Altair, to hum the same tune.

Grabbing sound from an audio CD. Here's how to record a snippet of music or other sound from an audio CD to use as an alert sound:

1. Click the Sound button in Monitors & Sound.

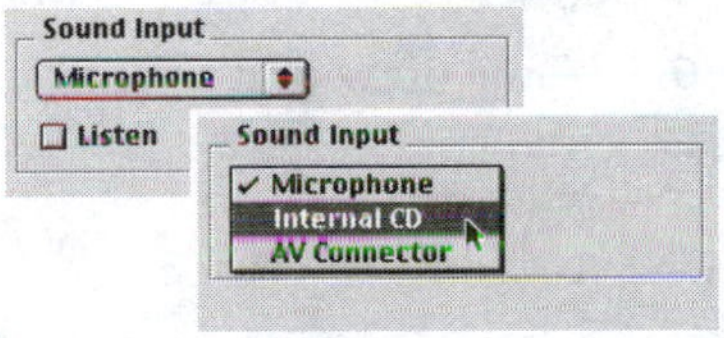

Setting the Sound Input option.

2. In the Sound Input section, select Internal CD from the pop-up menu. Click the Listen button so you'll be able to hear what's going on when you're recording.
3. Insert the CD; if you're system is set up to play CDs, it will just start playing. Use the AppleCD Audio Player utility to find the section of the CD you want to record.
4. Click the Alerts button in Monitors & Sound.
5. Click the Add button.
6. Listen to your CD. When it gets to the spot you want to record, click the Record button. (If you can't hear the CD after you click Record, you forgot to check the Listen button back in step 2.)
7. If you want to grab two different spots for the total sound, use the Pause button after the first snippet. When the second sound begins, click Pause again to continue the recording.
8. After you've stopped the recording, use the Play button to see if the sound recorded exactly the way you wanted it. If everything's fine, save and name the sound.

Don't forget to go back to the Sound area and reset the input option to microphone, because it's easy to forget, and one day you'll be wondering why your microphone isn't working.

Another sound-grab procedure. You can also use the MoviePlayer application to grab sound from an audio CD. (You need either MoviePlayer 2.5 or MoviePlayer Pro that comes with QuickTime Pro; the MoviePlayer 3.0 that comes with the free QuickTime 3.0 was stripped of its Import command.) With MoviePlayer, you can grab sounds of any length and save them in a format that can be used with multimedia presentations, not just with the system software. Here's how:

1. Insert the audio CD, run MoviePlayer, and choose the Import command from the File menu.
2. Select the track you want from the audio CD. (They'll be listed simply by number, not by name.)

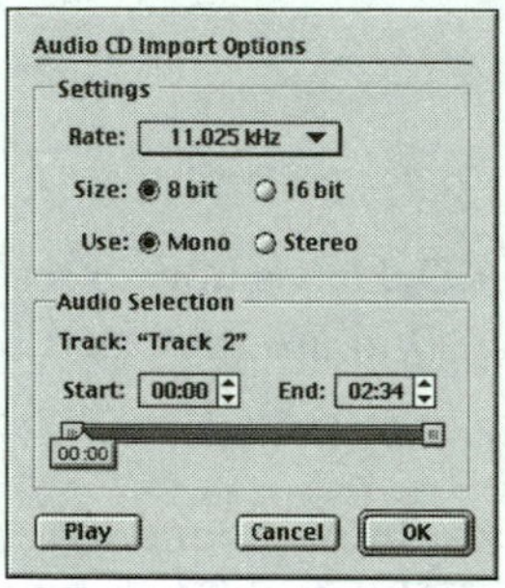

The MoviePlayer's Import Options in the MoviePlayer application.

3. Click the Convert button.
4. In the next dialog, click the Options button.
5. In the Audio CD Import Options dialog, select the sampling rate you want, the size (8- or 16-bit), and Mono or Stereo. Use the Audio Selection controls to find the part of the track you want, and click OK when it's all set.
6. Name the sound file and save it.

Digital Audio

Digital audio. You can produce audio on the Macintosh in one of two ways, either through the use of MIDI (covered in the next section), or through the use of digital audio. *Digital audio* is recorded audio waveforms that are stored as bits and bytes like all other forms of digital media.

You can digitize sound—that is, change it from its natural analog-based form to a digital form that can be stored, manipulated, and played on the computer—very easily. Your Mac comes with a microphone and the Monitors & Sound control panel lets you record up to ten seconds of sound; you can grab sounds from audio CDs through the MoviePlayer application, too—both these techniques were covered in the last section. And most Macs also have input for other audio sources.

macromedia.com
opcode.com

When you get serious about working with sound, you'll need more than the nifty little tools that come with your system software or those that can be downloaded as shareware. Check the latest features and reviews regarding **SoundEdit 16** ($280, Macromedia) and **Audioshop** ($100, Opcode Systems). —SZA/FB

A little bit better. Digital audio is commonly found in 8-bit or 16-bit formats. The *bit rate* refers to the number of possible values used to describe the *dynamic range* of an audio file (that is, the range between the loudest and softest sound). The 8-bit files have 256 possible values, while 16-bit files have 65,536 possible values, which results in a marked difference in sound quality; 16-bit files are the standard for high-quality audio and are used for audio CDs.

But 16-bit files are twice as large as 8-bit files, and older 68K Macs can't play them without additional hardware (although the Sound Manager extension can interpret 16-bit files and play them back in 8-bit format for these Macs). If your project is designed to be played back solely on a high-end Power Mac, go nuts and use the best quality audio you can. —FB

Sample rates. The process of recording sound onto a computer is often referred to as *sampling* because when you record audio onto a computer, it samples that audio signal thousands of times per second to re-create the waveform digitally. The sample rate determines the frequency range at which the digitized audio can be reproduced. For example, audio CDs are sampled 44,100 times per second—at 44.1kHz. Digital audio plays back at half the sample rate, so 44.1kHz plays back at a maximum of 22.050kHz, which is well beyond the range of human hearing.

Much as we would all like to have CD quality audio on our multimedia projects, the reality is that it takes far too much computer overhead to play 16-bit, 44.1kHz audio while playing an animation or displaying a high-resolution graphic file. —SZA/FB

File Sizes for One-Minute Audios

	8-bit Files		16-bit Files	
Sample Rate	**Stereo**	**Mono**	**Stereo**	**Mono**
44.1kHz	5.3MB	2.65MB	10.59MB	5.3MB
22.254kHz	2.67MB	1.34MB	5.34MB	2.67MB
22.050kHz	2.65MB	1.32MB	5.3MB	2.65MB
11.127kHz	1.34MB	0.67MB	2.67MB	1.34MB
11.025kHz	1.32MB	0.66MB	2.65MB	1.32MB

Audio formats. Like text or graphics, audio can come in a variety of different formats. The most common generic audio format on the Mac is *AIFF* (Audio Interchange File Format); on the PC, the most common format is Microsoft's *Wave,* or .WAV. On the Internet, it's common to see audio files in Sun Microsystems's *uLaw* format. The main thing to remember is that when you're using audio files across platforms, you should use a format that the target platform can read. Most audio programs can save audio files in a wide variety of formats, and there are plenty of shareware programs available on the Internet that can do this. —FB

MIDI

MIDI basics. *MIDI* stands for *Musical Instrument Digital Interface*; it's a protocol that's used for passing digital musical data between electronic musical devices. With the right hardware and software, computers can also understand MIDI data. On computers, MIDI is typically used to play music: rather than store a digital recording of the music itself, you use the MIDI protocol to store information about the musical *performance* and let the playback device (usually a synthesizer or sound card) take care of producing the actual sounds. Because MIDI is only sending performance data, it takes very little CPU overhead.

A *MIDI sequencer* is a program that lets you write music using the MIDI protocol; a song played back using MIDI is referred to as a *sequence.* MIDI uses the serial port on a computer to transmit MIDI data to a synthesizer, which plays the data it receives using its own internally generated sounds. A MIDI *channel* supports a single musical part with a unique musical voice, and a serial port provides 16 channels. On a Macintosh, without using additional hardware, you can get 32 channels of MIDI if you use both serial ports (most Mac models have two ports).

You should realize that MIDI isn't only used for music. Because it's merely a protocol for sending data, MIDI can be used for other, nonmusical purposes—like sound effects. For example, MIDI is often used to synchronize sound effects to a video source. —FB

General MIDI The original MIDI specification let each musician decide which sounds he could use for which program numbers. *General MIDI* was created to make it possible for musicians to create sequences that would sound the same on different systems. It defines a standard *instrument bank* so that if a sequence sends out a program-change message, the instrument that's chosen is predefined. For example, General MIDI specifies that program 0 is a piano and program 12 is a vibraphone. In order for a General MIDI sequence to play correctly, the synthesizer that plays it back must support the General MIDI standard. General MIDI has become very popular in the PC world for game and multimedia applications because just about every PC sound card currently sold supports General MIDI. Because MIDI data takes so little CPU power, it's very appealing to developers, although it's not used nearly as commonly on the Mac as is digital audio. —FB

Creating MIDI. General MIDI is a great way to get started creating music on your Mac. In addition to your Mac, you'll need a MIDI sequencing program, a MIDI interface to connect your Mac to your synthesizer, a synthesizer (this doesn't have to be General MIDI-compatible), and a MIDI controller, which usually takes the form of a piano-like keyboard. There are many manufacturers of MIDI hardware; *Keyboard* and *Electronic Musician* magazines often have good articles about buying synthesizers, so I recommend looking there as a place to start.

opcode.com
motu.com

As for software, there are several manufacturers that address the needs of musicians at all levels. Two vendors with a long history in the Mac world are Opcode Systems, with products like **MIDI Translator II** ($45) and **MIDI Translator Pro** ($100), and Mark of the Unicorn, with its **Freestyle** ($175) program. —SZA/FB

Musical notation. Another area for MIDI software is applications that are designed for music notation. While many sequencers have notation features, composers who wish to write complicated music scores need to explore programs that are designed for that purpose. **Finale** ($550, Coda) is considered by many to be the final word in notation programs. It supports almost every conceivable type of notation but has a steep learning curve.

codamusic.com
ars-nova.com

On the much lower end, there's **SongWorks** ($125 Ars Nova) which has a frustrating interface but might be worth the effort if all you need is simple single- or multiple-part (up to eight parts) sheet music. —SZA/FB

Animation and Video

Animation

Computer animation. Traditional animation (Disney, Warner Bros., and so on) has always been frame-based, with individual frames drawn on clear *cels* (sheets of transparent celluloid), overlaid onto a background, and then photographed frame by frame.

Animation on the Mac is both easier and more complex than traditional methods. Easier, because you don't have to draw every single frame of your animation. In most cases, you can simply create *keyframes* at important points in your animation, and your animation software will use a process called *tweening* to create the intermediate frames. (Tweening refers to creating the "in-between" frames to produce a smooth transition between keyframes.) On the other hand, digital animation is sometimes more difficult than traditional animation simply because of the sheer number of parameters that you can control. Digital animation offers multiple light sources, sophisticated motion paths, motion blurs, and other techniques which would be impossible to replicate using traditional methods. —SF

2-D animation. Computer 2-D animation is basically the same as traditional animation: you create a background, and use ever-changing foreground images to create the illusion of motion. If you want to just try your hand at a few cartoon-type projects, try MetaCreation's **Dabbler** ($45) or **WebPainter** ($90, Totally Hip Software). The next step up would be **CinemationCD** ($150, Vividus) or its big brother **Cinemation** for about a hundred dollars more.

metacreations.com
totallyhip.com
vividus.com
macromedia.com

The top-of-the-line animation program on the Mac is **Macromedia Director** ($650, Macromedia), which can create stand-alone animations to be played back on the platform of your choice, or clips to be integrated into a presentation or even played on the Web, with the help of the ShockWave browser plug-in. You can even create interactive animations, with clickable areas on the screen.

3-D animation. Although some 2-D animation work still starts with pencil and paper drawings, 3-D animation is almost completely created on the computer. The two main stages in creating 3-D art are *modeling* and *rendering*.

In the modeling stage, you start by making a *wireframe* image on the screen (so called because the picture is made with a series of lines that look like a wire framework, which require much less processing time than generating a filled-in image); you then fine-tune the image to simulate real-life characteristics and movements. You apply a surface, textures, and lighting effects to the image, often using the same software that you used to generate the wireframe. The character or scene can be modeled from various angles, allowing you to create different versions of the same image.

The rendering process takes the choices you've made about surfaces, textures, motions, and lighting effects and turns them into a finished 3-D image. The rendering process also saves your images on disk, using one of the standard file formats (such as PICT, PICS, or QuickTime) that a multimedia application can use. Rendering, however, can take a long time and it requires your Mac to do a lot of highly complex math work, so you really should use the fastest Power Mac that your money can buy.

metacreations.com
strata.com

3-D packages range vastly in price and sophistication. On the one end of the spectrum, many developers use **StudioPro** ($950, Strata) or **Infini-D** ($500, MetaCreations). Macromedia's **Extreme 3D** ($400) offers time-based 3-D animation capabilities in addition to good 3-D modeling and rendering. —SZA/JK

Digitizing Video

Video connectors. Attaching a video source to your Mac requires some sort of cable and connector. There are two different connector types for video: a high-quality *S-Video connector* (which looks a lot like an ADB connector) and a *composite video connector* (which looks like the RCA connectors on the backs of most stereo amplifiers). Different Mac models offer one, the other, both, or neither; unfortunately, the first few rounds of G3 Macs don't offer any handy video import. —SZA/MEC

Video sources. Getting the Mac set up to capture video is one thing; getting the video captured is quite another. (Note: unless you are doing all this merely for your own amusement, you don't want to capture video from commercially produced videotapes, television broadcasts, cablecasts, or laser disks—you'll be violating copyright laws and leaving yourself open to a very expensive legal education.) Your video source will probably be some sort of videotape: VHS, Hi-8, or, if you are verging on the professional, Beta-SP. Whatever your source, make sure that it is the highest quality possible; the more video "noise" in your original, the harder it will be to compress well. Furthermore, as the Mac's video capabilities improve, you may eventually want to recapture your video, and you will be grateful for a high-quality original when you do. —MEC

> ***"Although the Xerox Star had icons, the Lisa [Mac's predecessor] was the first product to let you drag them with the mouse, open them by double-clicking and watch them zoom into overlapping windows... It was the first to feature the menubar, the one-button mouse, the Clipboard, and the Trash can."***
>
> *Larry Tesler, Lisa development team*

Quick! The cam! Tired of looking at QuickTime movies you downloaded from the net? Feel like making some of your own? Well, you could get a video camera and a video input board (or an AV-equipped Mac), but why spend big bucks? You can shoot your own QuickTime movies for as little as $200 with Connectix's **QuickCam**, a golf-ball-sized video camera that plugs into any Mac's modem, printer or the new USB port. (An older grayscale model can still be found in some stores for under a hundred bucks).

Sitting on its tiny pyramidal stand, the eyeball-like QuickCam grabs color video and feeds it into your Mac without any need for special video boards or AV inputs. You can create QuickTime movies of anything you can point it at (and it focuses down to an inch!) or grab still pictures for insertion into your web page or newsletter. With the freeware program CU-SeeMe from Cornell University, you can even use QuickCam for videoconferencing. —AB

Compressing video. The still pictures that make up a video take up a lot of room: a single 16-bit picture measuring 320 by 240 pixels is over 150K. At thirty of those pictures a second, a single minute of video would take over 250MB! Luckily, there are ways to compress video files, and the compression schemes also allow the compressed video to be decompressed quickly enough to be shown on screen.

The most practical types of compression schemes are *lossy*; that is, they deliberately discard some of the video information, which reduces the picture quality of each frame. A good lossy compression scheme throws away information that least reduces the picture quality. One type of lossy scheme uses something called *frame differencing*. In this scheme, key frames are chosen and stored periodically. Non-key frames contain only those pixels that differ significantly from those in the key frame. This sort of compression works well for video that doesn't contain a lot of motion. Another scheme reduces the number of pixels stored in each frame by collecting adjacent pixels of similar color and making them all the same color, which can make the picture look blocky and less distinct. In practice, both schemes are usually used when compressing video. It takes a certain amount of experience and experimentation to balance these different compression methods for the best results. —MEC

Tips for capturing video. A number of video editing programs support video capturing, which is not surprising, since the bulk of the work of capturing is handled by QuickTime itself. In most cases, the process is no more elaborate than choosing "Record" or "Capture" from a menu or dialog box. Before you do, though, you should set your frame rate and compression choices from QuickTime's standard dialog box. The menu which brings up the box is not standard; it will vary from program to program. You also want to set the capture window size. Once you have these things set, you can start capturing. After that, sit back, relax, and watch the free space on your hard disk start to disappear!

- *Capture your video without any compression if your hardware supports it and you have the room.* Most codecs (compressor/decompressor) are just too slow to compress video in real time, and besides, you will want to play around with compression settings to get the best possible results.
- *Capture video in short segments.* The longer the segment, the longer it takes to compress, the more disk space it uses, and the greater the chance that something will go wrong in the process, forcing you to recapture.
- *Defragment your hard disk before you capture video.* If your Mac has to search all over your hard disk looking for empty sectors, it takes precious processing time away from the video capture, and will almost certainly result in your losing some frames.
- *Turn off CPU-hungry extensions and network connections.* Some extensions work continually in the background, taking small chunks of processing time away from the capture process. Also, if you have AppleTalk turned on, the Mac will be checking the network periodically and, while it's doing that, it won't be working on your video.
- *Capture your video at the final frame size you wish to use.* If you're planning to show your video in a 180-by-120 window, it doesn't make sense to capture it at a larger size; this will merely consume disk space and processing time. Worse, if you plan to show your video in, say, a 320-by-240 window and you capture it at 180-by-120, it will look terrible when scaled up.

- *Capture your video at the final frame rate you wish to use.* The television standard in America (NTSC) shows frames at about 30 per second (actually, it is 29.97 frames per second…go figure). You should capture video at some even fraction of this rate for the best playback: 15 frames per second is usually a good choice. Capturing at an uneven fraction of the standard rate can result in jerky motion, dropped frames, and other oddities.
- *Put a floppy disk in your floppy disk drive (and a CD in the CD drive, and a cartridge in your removable drive).* Seriously. Every so often your Mac likes to check all attached drives to see if something has been put in them. This check takes a little time, and time is something you don't have to spare when capturing video. Once a disk is in a drive, the Mac doesn't check anymore until the disk is removed. —MEC

QuickTime video compression. QuickTime manages video compression through *codecs*, (compressor/decompressor), software that handles the compression and decompression of video, graphical, and audio data. Some codecs are built into the QuickTime extension itself, while other, more specialized, codecs are separate extensions managed by QuickTime. The standard QuickTime Compression dialog box includes a pop-up menu that lets you choose which codec to use:

- **None:** Use this to convert video from one bit depth to another, and for capturing video that you want to compress later.
- **Animation:** Use this for animations as opposed to video—material that's made up of a sequence of still images.
- **Apple Video:** The first video codec for QuickTime, it provides fast enough decompression for many video playback needs, (seven times faster than its compression speed). The relatively fast compression speed makes it useful for doing editing experiments before final editing and compression.
- **Cinepak:** Most commonly used for video in multimedia titles, it compresses even more tightly than Apple Video and decompresses much more quickly. It lets you specify the data rate for your video, particularly useful for video that will play from a CD-ROM, where the maximum data transfer rate may be relatively low. Compression is very slow, however, often taking the better part of an hour to compress a mere 30 seconds of video. —SZA/MEC

Editing video. The field of video editing packages runs the price gamut from free to extremely costly. Nearly all video editors have certain interface elements in common: a time line that lets you select portions of the movie and places to insert clips, a clip palette that lets you choose from the unedited clips you wish to use, and a window to play back the current state of your movie.

- **MoviePlayer**, Apple's video viewer doesn't have a real editing interface, but you can do rudimentary video editing with it by using the traditional cut, copy, and paste commands that are standard on the Macintosh. You simply hold down the Shift key as you move the slider to select part of the movie, then choose Cut, Copy, or Clear from the Edit menu. When you finish editing, choose Save As from the file menu and make sure to select the *Make Movie Self-contained* option in the dialog; otherwise, it will simply save a tiny file that points to the original movie, and if you move that file to a different disk, you'll lose your edits. As described earlier in the chapter, you can use the 2.5 version that came with OS 8 and 8.1 for editing, or MoviePlayer Pro (which you have to buy), but *not* MoviePlayer 3.0 that comes with QuickTime 3.0.

apple.com
strata.com
adobe.com

- In **Videoshop** ($250, Strata), you can trim individual clips and layer multiple video tracks. It has a storyboard as well as a time line so you can see which clips, in which order, are currently in your movie, and it has a more robust set of effects, transitions, fades, and filters.
- **Premiere** ($540, Adobe) is probably the standard of multimedia video professionals, as well as having a place in the world of broadcast video editing. It has a huge number of standard transitions and effects, supports batch compression, lets you "matte" one video onto another, and much more. Its weakest feature may be its manual, which is skimpy and sometimes misleading, but if you can afford to buy it, you should have it. —SZA/MEC

PART 7

Special Areas

Part 7 At a Glance

23

PowerBooks

In This Chapter

The Hardware

Richard Wolfson was the associate editor for this chapter. You won't see his initials throughout, but many of the entries are the result of his contributions.

Displays

Screen technology. The big division between types of PowerBook displays is not color versus black-and-white, as you might expect, but between two types of *LCD* (liquid-crystal display) technologies: *active* and *passive matrix.*

Active-matrix screens provide crisp, sharp images at wide viewing angles, and react immediately to cursor moves and screen changes. Passive-matrix screens are less bright and sharp, must be viewed almost straight-on and are relatively slow to react. Drag an object on the screen, or just move the cursor at a normal speed, and you might see a trail of images left behind; move the cursor too quickly, and it totally disappears for a few seconds (this is known as *submarining* because the cursor seems to have dipped beneath the surface of the screen in its travels).

Active-matrix displays are far superior, but they have two major drawbacks: they're heavy, and they're expensive (about $1000 more for a color active-matrix display). Passive-matrix technology has improved: *dual-scan* passive-matrix displays redraw the top and bottom halves simultaneously, for double the refresh rate. And, with processors getting faster every year, *everything* happens faster.

> ***"Where a calculator on the ENIAC is equipped with 18,000 vacuum tubes and weighs 30 tons, computers of the future may have only 1000 vacuum tubes and perhaps weigh 1.5 tons."***
>
> *Popular Mechanics 1949*

The first PowerBooks were strictly black-and-white, regardless of the screen technology. Later models offered four, and then sixteen shades of gray. Finally, color showed up on PowerBooks, first on the washed-out 165c passive-matrix screen and then in the superb 180c active-matrix one.

Screen size. PowerBook screens range from 8.4 to an incredible 14.1 inches on a diagonal measurement, but, as with desktop monitors, the measurements can be deceiving. The screen's *pixel resolution* is the more important factor, since the number of pixels it uses horizontally and vertically determines how much information is displayed. A standard desktop monitor has a pixel resolution of 640 across and 480 down. The majority of PowerBooks have the same resolution; the screen measurement is smaller because each pixel is smaller. The oldest PowerBooks are limited to a 640x400 (instead of 480) resolution, while others can go as high as 800x600 (though you may find yourself squinting at those tiny dots). Some models offer a choice of resolutions; in most cases, the higher resolution (with more pixels displayed) can be used only with fewer colors showing at a time.

Unfortunately, the latest PowerBooks (the 3400c and all the G3's) can use their own displays and an external monitor for mirroring the display, and not as two different monitors (making one big screen) the way desk Macs can.

Video output. With the exception of the PowerBook 100, every black-and-white and grayscale PowerBook still "thinks" in color, and can provide color information for an external color monitor, although the models of the first round (140, 145, 170) and the I/O-impaired 150 have no video port to accommodate a monitor hookup. For PowerBooks with video ports, the level of support (how large a monitor, or how many colors) varies from model to model. The Duos, of course, can support a monitor when inserted into a Dock or when attached to a mini dock.

Other Components and Capabilities

Batteries. The continuing quest for inexpensive and lightweight, but long-lasting, batteries for laptop computers has resulted in four distinct battery technologies for PowerBooks.

- **Lead acid,** the same type of battery as in your car, was used only for the PowerBook 100.
- **Nickel-cadmium (NiCad)** batteries are used by the 100-series PowerBooks.
- **Nickel-metal-hydride (NiMH)** were introduced with the Duos, and proliferated into several different varieties. NiMHs recharge faster and last longer than NiCads.
- **Lithium-ion (LiIon)** batteries are the latest and greatest, and are the batteries for all current PowerBook models.

The expansion bay. Starting with the 5000-series PowerBook (and including the 190) most PowerBook models include an *expansion bay*, which comes with a floppy drive in it. Pop out the floppy drive and insert something else: a hard drive, memory modules, a Zip drive, or a CD drive. The specs on the expansion bay changed from the first models that offered it to more recent and current models, so make sure whatever you order as an add-in will actually fit in your model.

PCMCIA cards. The 500-series PowerBooks introduced a new type of slot: *PCMCIA*, for *Personal Computer Memory Card International Association.* Although the 500's need a "card cage" (Apple's **PCMCIA Expansion Module**, originally priced at $200) that replaces the left-hand battery, later models have built-in, accessible PCMCIA slots.

The PCMCIA acronym is such a mouthful that the cards for the slot are commonly referred to as simply PC cards. They come in three sizes: Type I,

Type II, and Type III, with the difference being their thicknesses. The PCMCIA slots usually come in pairs, but can accommodate only one Type III card because its girth blocks the second slot.

An amazing amount of functionality can be built into a PC card: modem, memory, Ethernet connections, and combinations thereof are all on PC cards for PowerBooks.

Handy-dandy PowerBook products. Several PowerBook products, hardware and software, are mentioned in context throughout this chapter. But here are a few items that we want to bring to your attention:

newertech.com
apstech.com
vsttech.com
iomega.com
3com.com
globalvillage.com

- Newer, faster, better **PC card modems** ($200-$300) are available from old hands like Megahertz (now 3Com) and Global Village.
- If you're using an external **Zip drive** with your PowerBook, you may need a **battery pack** for it ($50, Iomega).
- VST Systems has engineered an **internal Zip** drive for your 190, 1400, 3400, 5300, or G3 PowerBook ($330).
- Instead of plugging and unplugging three to five wires every time you hook up your PowerBook to your desk machine or network, use **BookEndz** ($180-200, depending on model, Newer); this mini docking station holds all the cables in place so you can just slide the PowerBook in and out (you'll want a second set of cables for the most convenient setup).
- **Batteries**, **chargers**, and even **car adapters** are available for various PowerBook models from both VST and BTI.
- The **PowerDoor** ($15, APS), a replacement I/O door for the one that constantly breaks off the back of 140-180 models.

PowerBook Models

Gee whiz, G3. What's faster than a speeding bullet? Or at least almost twice as fast as the former "fastest portable in the world" (the PowerBook 5300)? It's a G3 PowerBook with the PowerPC 750 chip. The original PowerBook G3 was superior in every way: the largest PowerBook screen yet, lots of fast memory, fast internal bus, 5GB drive, zippy modem, 2MB of on-board video RAM, 20x CD-ROM unit… the list goes on. Superior in price, too: its introductory sticker of $5700 could cover the cost of the next-fastest PowerBook (a 5300) *and* a G3 desktop machine.

Other G3 PowerBooks followed (it's the only kind of PowerBook you can buy now), with prices currently ranging from $2300 to $6000, screen sizes from 12.1 to 14.1, and speeds from 233MHz to 292MHz (the processor is on a daughtercard, which bodes well for upgrades).

The 3400 series. The PowerBook 3400c models are a closely related group of four (the 3400c/180 model comes in two configurations) that all offer a 12.1-inch active-matrix color screen and a collection of features that, at their release, were standard PowerBook options: PC card slots, expansion bay, floppy drive unit, CD-ROM drive unit, and infrared capability. The minor details that separate the models are not all items that are included in the PowerBook chart at the end of this section, so here's a quick reference chart.

The 3400 PowerBooks

	3400c/180	3400c/180	3400c/200	3400c/240
Processor (603e) speed	180	180	200	240
Hard drive	1.3GB	1.3GB	2GB	3GB
CD-ROM speed	-	6x	6x	12x
10BASE-T Ethernet	-	●	●	●
Built-in modem	-	●	●	●

The 2400 lightweight. The 2400c/180 is the only model in the 2400 "series"; at 4.4 pounds, it's the lightest non-Duo PowerBook ever made (in fact, it's lighter than some of the Duos). How did they manage that? Well, there's no floppy drive, and no room for one, either: it comes with an external floppy drive (a totally different design from the one made for the Duos). Another way to shave weight was to keep the screen size at 10.4" rather than boost it to over eleven or twelve inches to match the size of its contemporaries. And then there's the even-smaller-than-usual keyboard. But many buyers avoided this model because CD access is a must these days.

The 1400 series. There are two basic machines in the 1400 series: the passive-matrix 1400cs and the active-matrix 1400c. The 1400cs has two variations, with the slower 133MHz model coming with an 8x CD-ROM drive, and the 166Mhz model having a 12x CD-ROM drive. All the "modern" PowerBook options are included on this series: expansion bay, PC card slots, and infrared capability.

The 5000 series. The four models of the 5000 series got off to a bumpy start: Consumers complained about the absence of a CD-ROM drive, almost a standard already at that time in the PC world, and a few early problems with lithium-ion batteries cast a pall over the new lineup. The supply nonetheless fell far short of demand: the 5000-series machines started the PowerPC-based PowerBook genealogy, offered larger screens, PCMCIA slots, infrared capability, an expansion bay, and 64MB RAM expansion.

The 500 series. The 500-series PowerBooks (four models offering different types of screens) provide '040 power in an all-in-one laptop design. The 68LC040 chip used in these PowerBooks (and in the Duo 280 and 280c) is a special low-power version of the chip so it uses less battery power; it's missing some of the built-in FPU functions of the standard '040 chip. The 500 PowerBooks introduced the double-battery approach, and use special "intelligent" batteries that keep track of the charge and time that's left. One of the batteries can be replaced by a PCMCIA adapter (described earlier).

Duos and Docks. The Duos introduced a new concept in take-it-with-you computing. For traveling, you have a lightweight laptop, but back at the desk, it slips into a docking station and performs as the brains of a desktop system that includes a standard monitor and keyboard, and even slots for expansion. To keep the Duo small and light, the design called for no internal floppy drive and few ports—in fact, there's only a single serial port (for an external modem or printer), a connector for a dock, and the option of a phone jack for an internal modem. To hook up anything else to a Duo when it's not in its Duo Dock, you need a mini-dock that provides extra ports. So, the thrill of traveling light is often mitigated by the necessity of schlepping a bag full of extras for either planned activities (a presentation, say) or in case of emergencies (you need the Floppy Adapter and an external floppy drive to reinstall a corrupted system from floppies).

The Duo Dock turns a laptop Duo into a desktop Mac. The Duo slides in the front of the Dock, creating a setup that includes an internal floppy drive, a complete set of I/O ports, NuBus slots, and a connection for an internal hard drive.

The **Duo Dock II** was introduced to accommodate the thicker, color Duos (although you can upgrade the original with a new top). Additional features included a math coprocessor (optional on the original), a 32K memory cache, an Ethernet port, and support for a 20-inch monitor (the original was limited to a 16-inch monitor). Then there's the **Duo Dock II+** which really should be called a "minus" instead of a "plus" because it doesn't have the math coprocessor—it was made for '040 and PowerPC Duos, which don't need an FPU.

If you don't need a full Duo Dock (and you don't *want* it when you're traveling), you should be using a mini dock that lets you hook up a floppy drive, hard disk, and so on. Unfortunately, neither the mini docks nor the full size ones are available as anything but used equipment, so you may have trouble finding what you need if you didn't get everything along with your Duo.

The 100-series models. The 100-series PowerBooks (with the exception of the 100 itself) were referred to as "all-in-ones" because they include an internal floppy drive; all but the 190 and 100 use the 68030 processor, and all but the 100 use NiCad batteries.

- The **PowerBook 190,** released at the end of 1995, was the last of the 68K PowerBooks. While it uses the low-power '040 chip, it shares most of its design with the 5000-series PowerBooks released at the same time: infrared capability, PCMCIA slots, and an expansion bay. The 190c and 190cs were the color versions.

- The **PowerBook 150** was positioned as an entry-level PowerBook at a point when the first PowerBook models were out of production and the price tags of current models were prohibitive. At heart, it's just a 145B with a 40MB RAM limit and four levels of gray in a 600x480 screen—and a severely limited set of I/O ports, not even including video out.
- The **PowerBook 160** introduced the grayscale passive-matrix screen; the **165** is its twin except for a faster processor. The **165c** was the first color PowerBook, but its passive-matrix screen displayed washed-out colors. The **180** was the first PowerBook to use the standard 640x480 pixel proportions of a desktop monitor, in a grayscale active-matrix screen; the **180c** had a tiny but beautiful active-matrix color screen. All these second-round PowerBooks have a 14MB RAM limit.
- The **PowerBook 140** and **170** were in the original group of PowerBook offerings. The 170 was the top-of-the-line, with its active-matrix screen, a faster '030 processor, and an FPU. The **145**, with its faster clock speed, replaced the 140; the **145B** is identical, just redesigned internally for cheaper manufacturing. All these models have black-and-white displays and are limited to 8MB of RAM.
- The **PowerBook 100,** one of the three original models, stood out not only because of its light weight and the lack of an internal floppy drive, but also because it used the 68000 processor, a chip that had long been abandoned in desktop models. Its display is a slow passive-matrix one; it's the only PowerBook to use a lead-acid battery.

IN THE BEGINNING

All Macs have code names during development, of course; but sometimes the code names are used in software and then forgotten. The balloon help for the Caps Lock extension in System 7.1 is a case in point; *TIM* and *Derringer* were two of the PowerBook code names.

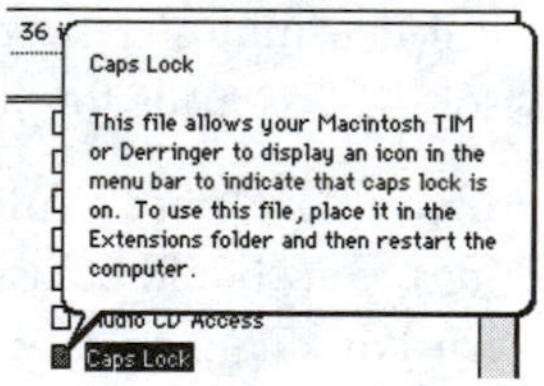

The Portable. The fifteen-pound Mac Portable was Apple's humorous first entry into the portable market; it had a full-size keyboard, a trackball off to the right, and a beautiful active-matrix screen (although only a few late units came with backlighting).

Upgrading. When you're deciding whether you should upgrade your PowerBook, the issues are the same as those for upgrading a desk machine (discussed in Chapter 2). Consider carefully the cost of the upgrade, especially for an older PowerBook whose inherent limitations (in addressing memory, for instance) might still keep you from having a machine that can do what you need it to do. Also consider whether the cost of the upgrade is worth it compared to the cost of a new machine or that of a used machine that is more advanced than yours.

Additional memory and a larger hard drive are almost always effective upgrades, no matter which PowerBook you're using. Other than that, the reasonable upgrades at this point are those that move a 68K machine into PowerPC territory or change a "plain" PowerPC machine into a G3. Newer Technology offers both. Its **NUpower 500/167** ($550) puts a 603e processor into an '040 500-series PowerBook. For the 1400, there's a 167MHz 603e upgrade for $500 that's just not worth it when you consider there are various-speed G3 upgrades for that unit starting at $690. There's also a G3 upgrade for the 2400 ($830). By the time you read this, there will no doubt be other upgrades available, so be sure to check their web site.

newertech.com

Using PowerBooks

Conservation Efforts

Unplugged is for MTV. The best battery-saving tip of all: stay plugged in whenever possible. When you're plugged in, you don't have to worry about the rest of the tips in this section.

Perchance to dream. The PowerBook sleep mode drastically cuts down on battery drain. You can put a PowerBook to sleep manually with the Sleep command in the Finder's Special menu, or from the Control Strip, or by pressing the Power button on models that have one; later models go to sleep when you close the cover. Or, you can have your PowerBook go to sleep automatically after a specific period of inactivity.

In sleep, the screen goes blank and the hard disk stops spinning, but those are only the most obvious results; all sorts of internal components are also powered down during sleep. A touch of a key wakes up a sleeping PowerBook instantly.

Where has all my power gone? Quick: What eats up the most battery power on your PowerBook? A colorful, brightly lit screen? Keeping the hard drive spinning? It's hard to conserve battery power if you don't know where it's all going.

- The biggest drain on the battery is something you have little control over: the CPU itself. And the more powerful the processor, and the faster its clock speed, the more power it uses.

- Next in line for biggest power draw is the hard drive, but *keeping* it spinning is not necessarily the greatest evil: getting it to spin up from its sleeping stillness takes more energy than having it rotate at speed for a few minutes. On the other hand, an unused spinning hard drive wastes energy. The best sleep interval for a hard drive depends very much on how you work; just keep in mind that letting it go to sleep at short intervals, when you'll have to spin it up every few minutes, might be wasting more power than it's saving. A spinning CD just about matches the drain of a spinning hard drive.
- The third big power drain is an in-your-face option: the screen backlight.

The quick conservation guide. Keeping the power drain to a minimum lets you work longer on a single battery charge. Here are some things you can do to maximize your battery life (some are detailed further in other entries):

- Keep *processor cycling* turned on in the PowerBook control panel.
- Keep hard disk access to a minimum: stick to the minimum necessary virtual memory allocation and allow *lots* of memory for an opened application so it won't go to the disk so often.
- Avoid using a CD or floppy disk.
- Keep the backlight turned down as far as possible.
- Keep AppleTalk turned off.
- Put the PowerBook to sleep whenever you're not using it for more than a few minutes.
- Keep the settings in the PowerBook control panel at maximum conservation settings.
- If yours is a original model that lets you run the CPU at two different speeds, set it to run at the slower speed.

Keeping track. The Control Strip provides a way to keep track of both the current charge level and the current use level; you can choose to have either or both displayed in the Control Strip at any time.

The Control Strip
Later this chapter

For a full battery, the battery-level bars are all dark; they start fading, from the right, as the battery goes down. The battery consumption gauge reflects the current amount (get it?) of power use. If you think you're working conservatively but that gauge is all the way to the right, it's time to check all your settings—and perhaps review your work habits.

The Control Strip's battery readouts. Top, a full charge, and top usage; bottom, a slightly depleted charge and more conservative usage.

The occasional shut down. Don't shut off your PowerBook—just put it to sleep. The only times you really need to turn off a PowerBook are when you are:

- Connecting a SCSI device to it
- Connecting it to another Mac in SCSI disk mode
- Connecting a monitor directly to an all-in-one PowerBook
- Connecting an external floppy (except to the 2400)
- Inserting a Duo into the Duo Dock or connecting it to a mini dock
- Opening it for repair or upgrade
- Not going to use it for more than a few days

Processor cycling. Not exactly awake, not exactly asleep—the PowerBook has a twilight zone between the two called, reasonably enough, a *rest* state. Through a process called *processor* or *power cycling,* the processor chip in the PowerBook catnaps whenever it hasn't been used for a few seconds; as soon as you do anything, it wakes up. (You might notice that a blinking text cursor blinks *verrry slowly* if you're not typing for a few seconds). Because the processor is the biggest single source of battery drain, cutting its needs every few seconds, for seconds at a time, adds up to great savings.

Processor cycling is used by default, although it's an option you can turn off—but it's a hidden option so you can't just turn it off by mistake or through curiosity. This is covered below, in the PowerBook Control Panel section.

> ***One needs more rest if one doesn't sleep. That's why I go to bed early.***
>
> *Evelyn Waugh*

Why would you turn that gem of a power-saving function off? Because it interferes with some game software. Just make sure you turn it back on again!

Color and contrast don't count. Color PowerBook screens eat up more battery power than do their grayscale and black-and-white counterparts. But it's not the color itself that's drawing the power—it's the extra backlight needed to get through the multi-layered color screen that eats up power. So, running a color PowerBook in black-and-white won't conserve any battery power, and changing the contrast settings makes no difference on any screen. But turn down the screen brightness whenever you can.

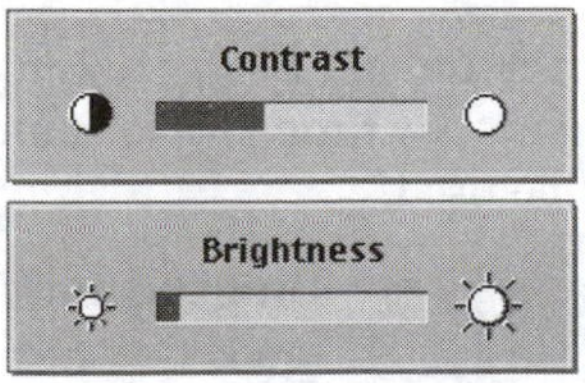

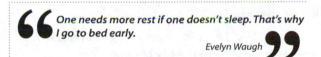

The minimal dialogs for later-model PowerBook brightness and contrast controls.

Stop talking. When AppleTalk is turned on, it continually checks the serial port for signs of network activity—even if there's nothing connected to the port. Of course, the way it checks is by sending a signal and seeing what comes back, and that takes electrical power, which, of course, is coming from your battery.

The silent modem drain. You've probably realized that using your modem drains battery power (or maybe you never thought about it). But the modem is sucking power sometimes even when it's not in use: some basic general telecom packages (not specialized software for accessing online services) open the modem port when you launch the program, and that starts draining the power.

The PowerBook Control Panel

Controlling sleep cycles. The PowerBook control panel lets you set the automatic battery conservation options: screen dimming, hard disk spindown, and system sleep. But it lets you set them in a very easy way: with a single slider control whose extreme positions are *Better Conservation* and *Better Performance.* Just reposition the control and all the settings are taken care of for you.

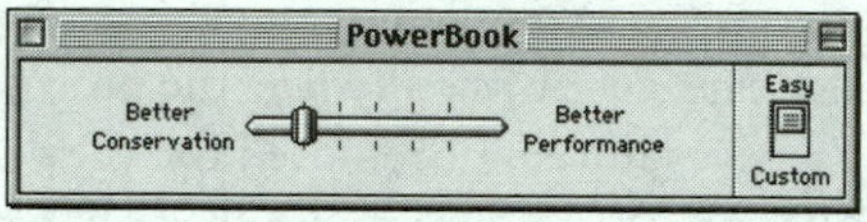

For control freaks. You can change the three conservation settings separately if you want to tweak your PowerBook's behavior. Flip the Easy/Custom button in the upper right to move between the easy and custom controls, by either dragging the switch to the other position (which is a little difficult) or just by clicking in the *empty* spot in the switch.

Set the three conservation settings to where you want them; the numbers by the controls indicate the minutes for the interval. You'll see that the "easy" control slider changes in response to your settings.

Sleep sets. Because there's a tradeoff between power conservation and your PowerBook's performance (as noted even in the label on the control panel's top slider), you'll want extremely different settings for when you're running just on battery and when you're plugged in. Luckily, the bottom panel of the PowerBook control panel lets you make up two sets of settings, and override either one at any time.

- **Battery:** With the *Auto* button active and *Battery* selected in the pop-up menu, change the slider controls. Any time you're running on battery, these are the settings that will be used.

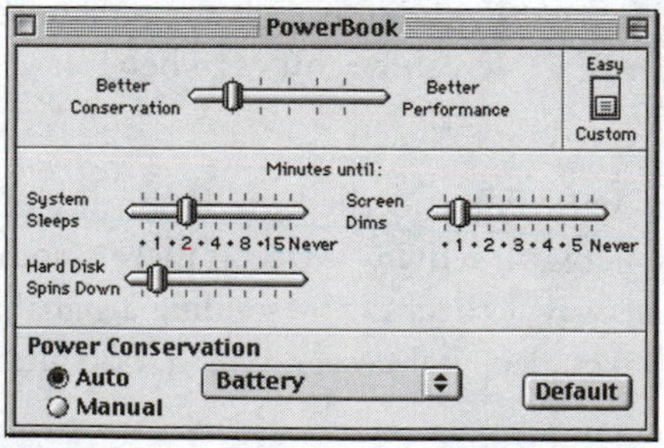

- **Plugged in:** With the *Auto* button active and *Power Adapter* selected in the pop-up menu, change the slider controls. When you're plugged in, these are the settings that will be used.
- **Override:** When you want to work with temporarily different settings (you're on battery, for

instance, but need to up the performance factor for a while), click the *Manual* button and change the slider settings. If you change the settings before you click the button, you'll wind up changing one of the Auto sets you've created.

Note that both Auto sets are just that: *auto*. You don't have to select either one to use it—the PowerBook knows if it's plugged in or not and uses the appropriate set.

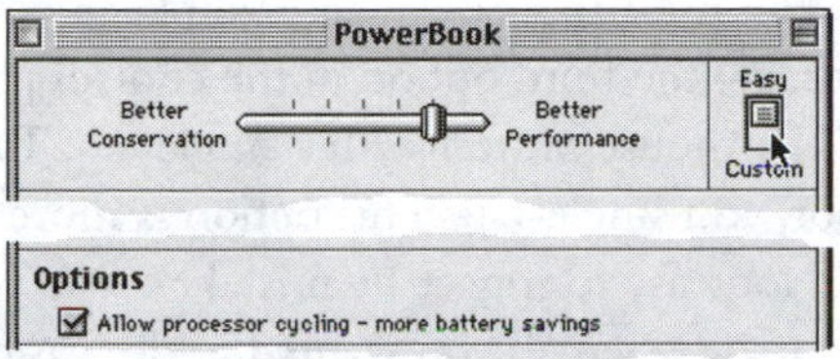

The hidden option. To control the processor cycling setting (keeping it on saves power but might interfere with some game software), you have to find the hidden panel in the PowerBook control panel.

You have to start from the collapsed, easy version of the control panel (which is a pretty silly requirement), and hold down Option while you click or drag the switch to open the control panel to its fullest. You'll get a new section, with a checkbox that lets you turn the cycling on and off.

System Software Specials

The Trackpad control panel. The first trackpads were simple trackball replacements (which, in turn, were simple mouse replacements) with no special powers of their own. But later PowerBook models offered smarter trackpads, and all recent trackpads let you use the trackpad to click, double-click, and even drag things without keeping the "mouse" button down.

The Trackpad control panel lets you set those trackpad options, as well as the tracking speed.

- **Tracking Speed:** This is similar to the mouse tracking speed, discussed in Chapter 5. While the Mouse control panel offers a separate *Very Slow* option, for the trackpad you're offered a special 1-to-1 setting so that the distance you move on the pad is translated to exactly the same distance on the screen.

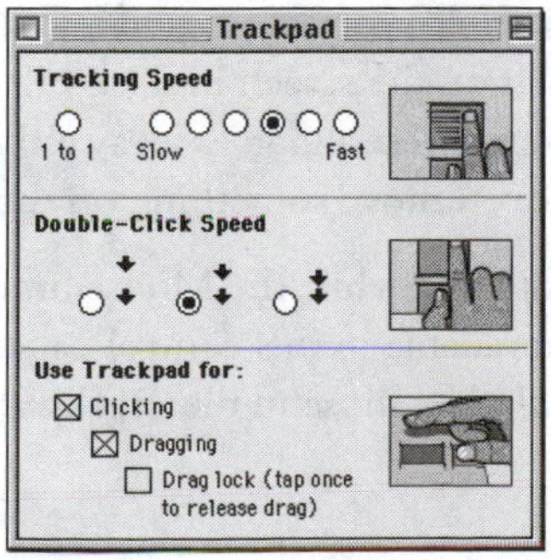

- **Double-Click Speed:** This is really the double-*tap* speed; if you tend to drum your fingers while they're resting on the PowerBook, keep it at the slowest setting! But double-tapping is a much more natural motion for trackpad users than having to use the button.
- **Clicks and drags:** You can't turn off the double-click/tap option, but you can select or ignore the single-click/tap option as well as the options that let you drag things without using the "mouse" button.

Drag versus drag-lock. The click and drag options in the bottom part of the Trackpad control panel aren't exactly intuitive; and you'll find that they're connected so that unless you choose the "lesser" one(s) you can't turn on the next one or two.

The dragging option uses a double-tap to start a drag: tap once regularly, than tap the second time but keep your finger on the pad instead of lifting it, and you can drag something around as if the mouse button were down. Since this doesn't echo the way you use a mouse—where you keep your finger down on the *first* click to do a drag—the third option in the control panel, Drag Lock, lets you "lock down" the mouse button with a single tap. To unglue the item from the mouse cursor, you single-tap. This option is more awkward than the default because it's far too easy to trigger by mistake—you wind up with things stuck to your cursor when all you wanted to do was click on them.

Date & Time—and battery power. On PowerBooks, the Date & Time dialog that lets you set options for the menubar clock also allows you to turn on a battery charge indicator in the menubar; you can tell the relative battery charge at a glance, and see if the battery is charging. But for a better at-a-glance check, use the battery module in the Control Strip, which can tell you which charge mode the battery is in, and also indicate the strength of your current usage.

The Mouse addendum. The Mouse control panel has an extra section in PowerBook systems (which is a little strange for a computer that doesn't use a mouse). The addendum lets you control *Mouse Tracks,* a cute term for leaving a little trail of cursors behind you as you move the cursor around (which is *much* more hygienic than what a mouse might leave as a trail). You can choose how long a trail to leave, and whether or not to leave one at all. On screens where a cursor disappears when you move it too quickly, leaving a trail is a good way to see where you've been—which is usually a clue as to where you are. You can also thicken the I-beam text cursor to make it easier to see.

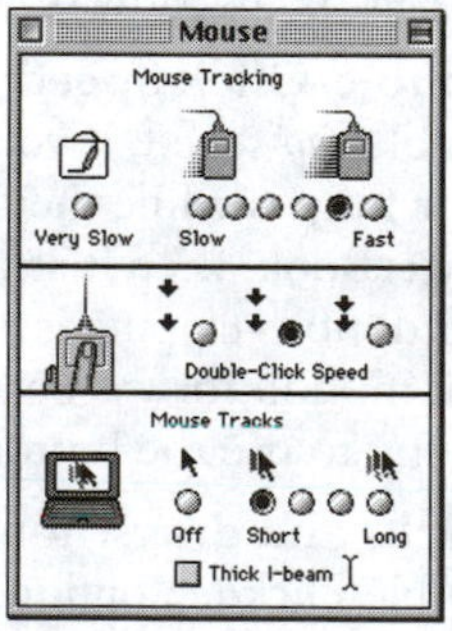

Keeping mouse tracks on sometimes interferes with Balloon Help: you might find a few blank help balloons left on the screen here and there. But it's only a temporary effect and goes away either by itself or as soon as you move something on the screen.

Also note that while the Mouse Tracking section is always available in this control panel, its settings are overridden by those in the Trackpad control panel.

Control Strip modules. The Control Strip (covered in detail in Chapter 9) provides several modules specifically for PowerBooks, and a few that, while not PowerBook-only items, are especially important to PowerBook users.

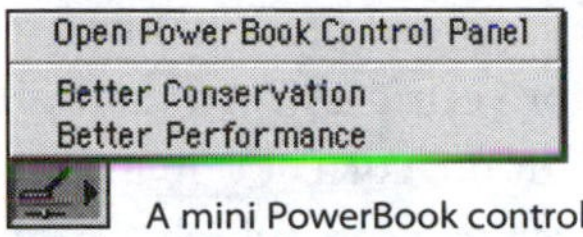

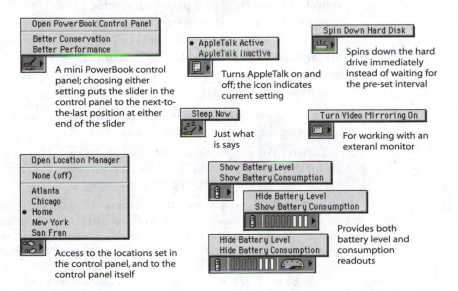

A mini PowerBook control panel; choosing either setting puts the slider in the control panel to the next-to-the-last position at either end of the slider

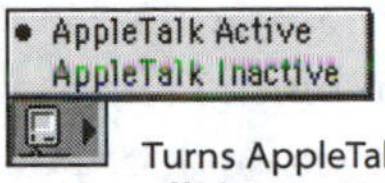

Turns AppleTalk on and off; the icon indicates current setting

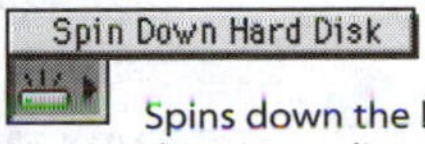

Spins down the hard drive immediately instead of waiting for the pre-set interval

Just what is says

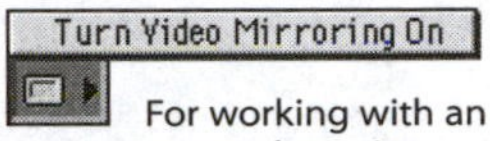

For working with an exteranl monitor

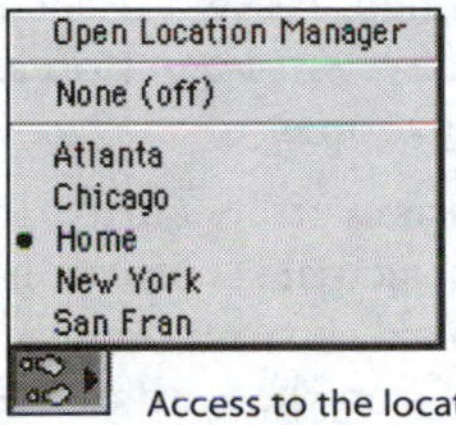

Access to the locations set in the control panel, and to the control panel itself

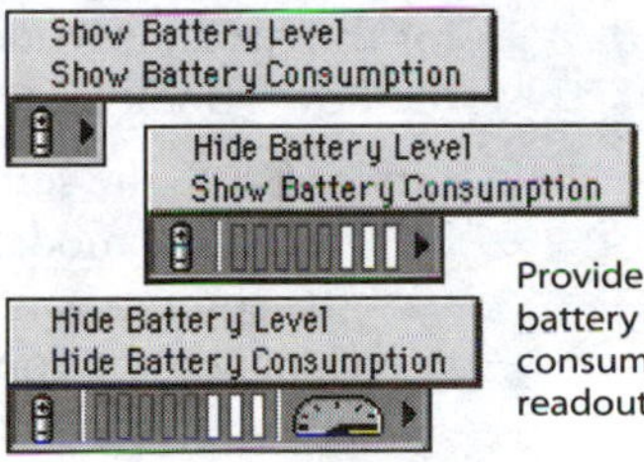

Provides both battery level and consumption readouts

There are shareware Control Strip modules available that offer functions beyond those provided by the ones that come with the system, as described in Chapter 9. **Jeremy's Control Strip Modules** ($10, shareware) are strictly for PowerBooks, and include improvements on the Apple offerings as well as some originals. Many are handy for older PowerBooks, like the ones that check and let you change the processor speed, and the ones that deal with the 500's smart battery; others, like Power Countdown (which displays the time left before certain power conservation features are activated) are for any PowerBook.

The Location Manager. The Location Manager control panel lets you create groups of settings (hmm... sounds like the PowerBook control panel, and Extensions Manager) from different control panels and system settings; the sets are referred to as *locations*, and you can choose one based on, of course, where you're working at any given time. Unfortunately, its usefulness is limited because it doesn't address one of the most important resettings travelers face: internet and other online access options.

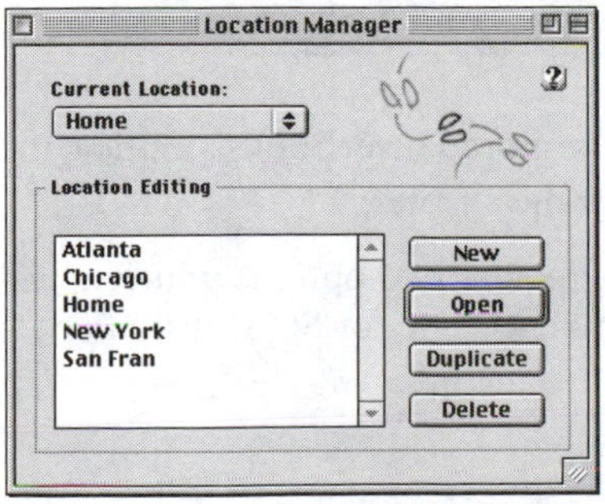

If you used the Location Manager in a pre-OS 8 system, make sure you reinstall it with your OS 8 or 8.1 installation, since previous versions won't work under the new OS.

Password Security and its breaches. The Password Security control panel provides security against casual snoops, asking for a password when the PowerBook is turned on or, optionally, when it comes out of sleep. Use the control panel to set up your password, provide a hint if you think you're going to forget it, and to turn the password protection on and off. You get a simple dialog at startup that asks for your password (and provides your pre-programmed hint); failure to type in the correct one in three tries either shuts down the PowerBook or puts it back to sleep, whichever state it started from. Keep these points in mind:

- If you're going to use the PowerBook in SCSI disk mode, make sure you turn off the password protection first.
- When a PowerBook drive is partitioned, Password Security kicks in only for the startup partition; if there's a System Folder on another partition, the PowerBook can start up from that one.
- Under OS 8, the setup portion of Password Security doesn't work on 2400 and 3400 models, although the actual security portion does. If you start the computer with a Disk Tools disk from previous system software, you can open the control panel that's on the hard drive, turn it on or off, and set the password; when you restart from the PowerBook, the settings will be used. (I hope this tip becomes obsolete *very* quickly!)
- At the release of OS 8.1 and its option of Extended format for disk, Password Security didn't work with extended-format drives. There's no word at this point if it will be updated for use (although we can assume it will be); if you format your drive with the Extended option, don't use Password Security unless you have a version that Apple explicitly states works with HFS Plus.

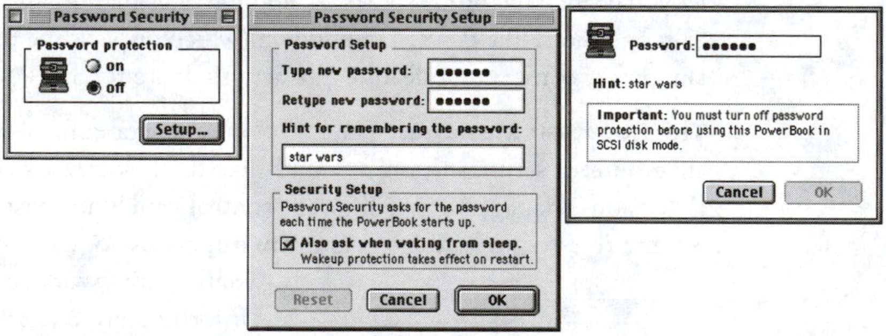

The Password Security control panel, the setup dialog, and the Password request.

And also... Here are a few more PowerBook-specific control panels that aren't covered elsewhere in the chapter:

- **PowerBook Setup:** Provides two options which apparently had nowhere else to go: the ID number setting for SCSI disk mode, and the time/date setting for an automatic wake up. The settings show up only on models capable of those functions.

- **AutoRemounter:** Automatically remounts network devices when the PowerBook wakes up.
- **PowerBook Display**: Contains settings for working with an external monitor; with some models, you can use the PowerBook display and the monitor as one virtual screen, the way a double-monitor setup is used on desk machines, or you can set them up for mirroring so that the monitor shows the same thing as is on the PowerBook display—perfect for demonstrations. (Other, more recent models, work in mirror-mode only.)
- **Infrared control panel:** Sets up options for infrared use—if you actually have some other device that uses infrared connections.

General PowerBook Tips

No burn-in. Although screen burn-in was never an issue for PowerBook screens, as it was for early phosphor-coated monitors, a PowerBook screen is subject to a "shadowing" effect if you leave it on and unchanged for, say 24 hours. To cure the shadowing, put the PowerBook to sleep or turn it off; the longer the screen was on, the longer it needs to be off to cure the shadows.

Finger-lickin' good. If your cursor is jumping around erratically in response to trackpad use, it might be because your finger's damp. Stay dry! Try placing a small piece of paper on the trackpad surface; if the jumping goes away, the problem is your finger, not the trackpad.

Another reason for erratic cursor movement is touching the pad in two places at the same time, so make sure you're not resting a second finger against the surface unless you're doing it on purpose (to achieve the effect described in the next entry).

The two-finger trackpad trek. When you want to take a shortcut across your screen, use two fingers on the trackpad: you can make the cursor jump across the screen or stop halfway, depending on where it is and where your fingers are.

Say the cursor is near the left edge of the display. Put your index finger on the left edge of the trackpad. Then, put your middle finger down on the opposite edge of the trackpad; the cursor will jump about halfway across the screen. Lift the first finger, and the cursor will jump to the right edge of the display. You can also just switch from one finger to the other without the middle step as long as you get the second one down a fraction of a second before you lift the first—try it a few times and you'll get the hang of it.

Using an external monitor. All but the earliest PowerBooks can drive an external monitor, and the monitor can be used instead of, or in addition to, the PowerBook screen. Keep these points in mind:

- Nothing shows up on the external monitor the first time you turn on your PowerBook after connecting it. Open the Monitors or Monitors and Sound control panel to activate the monitor.
- The PowerBook won't go to sleep if a video cable is attached—whether or not the monitor is on, and whether or not there's even a monitor at the other end of the cable.
- Although the monitor has its own power source, running a monitor is a significant drain on the PowerBook battery because it's juicing the video card. Stay plugged in when using a monitor.

Playing around. Note that many games assume a 640x480 display, so older PowerBooks, even if they're capable with their memory, hard drive, and processor speed constraints, may not be able to run many games because of the dimensions of the screen. —JK

Killing the startup sound. Changing the volume or clicking the Mute button in the Monitors & Sound control panel doesn't affect the startup chord. If you want to dampen it, you have to plug something into the audio port on the back of the Mac. If you use earphones (to keep your coworkers from realizing you're playing CDs or games!), that will keep the startup chord from being audible. If you just want to get rid of the sound, get a "miniplug" from an electronics store—it's the little plug that's at the end of earphones—and plug that in to the audio port. But then you won't hear *any* sounds, including alert sounds.

The 500 single-port storm. The 500-series PowerBooks have a single serial port that's used for both external modems and printers. Keep these points in mind:

- For a serial printer like the Portable StyleWriter, turn off AppleTalk so the port will work for the printer.
- Selecting a printer in Chooser can get confusing. Selecting an ImageWriter gives you a single combined port icon, but selecting a StyleWriter driver gives you a choice of the modem or printer port, as if you had two. Use the modem port setting.

The Duo Dock as a recharging station. You don't usually insert a sleeping Duo into a Dock, since pressing the Power On key on the Dock's keyboard ejects a sleeping Duo. But if you're not planning on using the docked Duo, you can insert a sleeping unit anyway: the Dock serves as a handy recharging station for a sleeping Duo. It also keeps your Duo safely locked in the Dock when it's not with you.

Batteries and Power Adapters

Battery bits. Here are some basic guidelines for almost any kind of PowerBook battery:

- Batteries are made of toxic materials. They should be handled with reasonable care, and recycled rather than thrown out. Most battery manufacturers accept old batteries—not for credit, but for proper disposal; even Radio Shack accepts discards.
- Leaving a battery charging for weeks at a time reduces its lifespan; unplug once in a while even if you're working at home.
- When a battery is really run down, you might not be able to wake your PowerBook even when you plug it in. Leave it plugged in for about 20 minutes and try again.

Rechargeable, not immortal. Rechargeable batteries have a limited *life-cycle*—the number of times the battery can be drained and recharged. NiCads, for instance, have an average of 500 life cycles, which translates to two to three years of use. If your battery just won't recharge anymore, it may be really and truly dead.

Keep that bunny banging the drum. There are several things you can do to encourage your battery to last through as many cycles as possible:

- Don't leave it inside an unused, unplugged PowerBook for more than a month; batteries drain even when the PowerBook's not in use. (The PowerBook 100's lead-acid battery shouldn't be left alone for more than two weeks.)
- Keep it in a cool, dry place when it's not inside the PowerBook.
- Charge it fully before storing it (outside the PowerBook).
- Don't leave it in storage for more than three months or so without giving it a full recharge.
- Discharge NiCad and NiMH batteries completely at regular intervals. (See the *Reconditioning* entry a little further on.)

Trickle me, Elmo. PowerBook batteries are charged in two different modes: they charge relatively quickly to about 80 percent capacity in *fast charge* mode, then charge the rest of the way at a slower pace, in *trickle* mode. So, you can charge a battery most of the way in about two hours and then need almost twice that much time to finish charging. This method strikes a nice balance between getting a usable charge as quickly as possible and avoiding ruining a battery by overcharging it.

It's not actually the battery, of course, switching modes, since the battery itself doesn't do the charging; but the charge circuitry in the PowerBook, and external chargers, handle the chore with aplomb.

The trickle clue. You can easily tell whether your inserted battery is being charged in fast or trickle mode by checking the battery monitor in the Control Strip. If there's a lightning bolt going through it, it's in fast mode; if there's a plug across it, it's in trickle mode. (If it's plain, then you're not plugged in.) The battery icon in the menubar, if you've turned it on in the Date & Time control panel, registers only the fast-charge mode; when in trickle mode *or* unplugged, the icon is a plain battery.

Stuck in trickle. If you charge a battery long enough so that it's in trickle mode and then swap it with another, more depleted battery, the charger (external or in the PowerBook) won't know the difference and will remain in trickle mode. It takes a *very* long time to charge a battery in only trickle mode. If you're going to swap batteries, unplug the power cord for a moment and plug it back in to reset the charger to fast mode.

Don't get shorty. For batteries that have exposed contacts, it's important to keep them covered with a cap (for the batteries that come with one) or case (shoe-shine mitts from better hotel rooms work well). If something metallic, like a paper clip or key, bridges the contacts, they'll short—ruining the battery and possibly causing burns or even a fire.

Reconditioning. If you continually charge a NiMH or NiCad battery, use it for a while, and recharge it, without ever totally draining the charge, you won't be able to ever really fully charge it. These batteries need occasional *reconditioning* in order to hold a complete charge.

Running a battery down to the point where you get low-battery warnings and the PowerBook shuts off isn't really a complete discharge. If you have an external charger/reconditioner, that's the best way to recondition the battery. But the system software comes with a software-based reconditioner named, in a flight of fancy, *Battery Recondition.* You'll find it in the Portables folder inside the Apple Extras folder.

Plan ahead if you're going to use this utility: it takes about two hours to run, and then you'll need another two to four hours to completely charge the battery again. Letting it go overnight is the painless way.

The secrets of NiMH. The variety of NiMH batteries, and which machine uses what, can be confusing. Here's the rundown of NiMH types:

- There were four types of NiMH batteries used with Duos, each providing a little more power than the last. They're referred to as Type I, II, III, and High-Capacity Type III.
- The 500-series PowerBooks use a special "intelligent" battery that includes a special chip to help the PowerBook manage its power needs

more efficiently and provide a more accurate charge reading than is available from other, "dumb," batteries.

- The 190 and 5300's share a common battery (as they do so many features).
- A 30-watt-hour version is used for the 1400 PowerBooks.

And here's a quick chart of what uses what, including the Apple part number so you can order the right one or figure out which one's already at hand.

Kind of NiMH	*Used in...*	*Part number*
Type I	Duo 210/230	M7782
Type II	Duo 250, 270c, 280	M1499
Type III	Duo 280, 280c	M1499
Type III High-Capacity	Duo 2300	M2780
Intelligent battery	500's	M1908
NiMH	190 and 5300's	M3254
NiMH	1400	M2538

Mix and match. There are three batteries with the same shape, made for three different types of PowerBooks; they're interchangeable to some extent. The three are: the LiIon for the G3 models; the LiIon for the 3400; and the NiMH used in the 190 and 5300.

Both the PowerBook G3 and the 3400 can use, and charge, all three batteries; but the time you'll get on a battery charge will be significantly shorter with anything less than the battery made specifically for those models. The PowerBook 190 and 5300 can recognize only their own battery, the NiMH model.

Need 8.1 for 3400's better battery. If you want to use a G3 LiIon battery (the 47 watt-hour model) in a 3400, you have to move to OS 8.1. With a lower system, the 3400 won't recognize or be able to charge the battery, and you'll get an X through the battery indicator icon.

Back-and-forth for 500 batteries. You may be using two batteries in your 500, but the 500 is using only one of them—one at a time, that is. The one in the left bay is drained completely before the 500 starts sucking at the other one. Occasionally swap which battery is in which bay so that you're not constantly depleting the one battery.

The Duo switcheroo. The Duo battery has a little switch on it that doesn't do anything. Really. It's there so you can flip it back and forth to remind yourself, say, that you just took it out of the external charger and it's ready to go.

Later and adapters NiCads better. NiCad batteries went through two subtle revisions, each one providing longer-lasting power. The original one, model number #5417, is a 2.3 amp-hour model labeled 140/170. The second-generation NiCad is 2.5 amp-hours, model #5653; the third one is #5654, a 2.9 amp-hour version. When you buy a new battery, make sure you get that last model.

The power adapters for the 100-series PowerBooks were quietly improved over time, with the later ones able to recharge your battery in a shorter time. The first model (#M5140) is a 15-watt version with a dangerous propensity: The black ring at the tip of the plug was prone to hairline cracks which could result in serious damage to the motherboard. The second version is a 17-watt model (#M5651); the best is the third model (#M5652), a 24-watt version.

SCSI Connections

SCSI connections. PowerBooks have a different type of SCSI port from desktop Macs because there's not much room at the back of a PowerBook; it's called the *HDI-30* (for *high-density interface*, with 30 pins). To connect a standard SCSI device, you need the HDI-30 SCSI cable, which plugs into the back of the PowerBook and provides a standard 25-pin male SCSI connector at the other end.

There are two PowerBook SCSI cables used for two very different purposes. The *HDI-30 SCSI System Cable* is used for connecting SCSI peripherals to the PowerBook; the *HDI-30 SCSI Disk Adapter Cable* is used to connect the PowerBook *as* a SCSI device to another Mac. These two cables are often confused, but there are several differences between them:

	System Cable	*Disk Adapter Cable*
PowerBook connector:	HDI-30	HDI-30
Pins (on HDI-30):	29	30
Second connector:	50-pin male	50-pin female
Length:	18 inches	10 inches
Color:	light gray	dark gray

In addition to these two PowerBook-specific SCSI cables, there are two others, standard for desktop Macs that you may wind up using. The *SCSI system cable* has a 25-pin male connector at one end and a 50-pin male connector at the other. The *SCSI extension cable* has a 50-pin connector at each end, one male and one female.

Attaching a SCSI device. Adding a SCSI device to the Mac—like an external hard drive, CD-ROM drive, or Zip drive—is basically the same as attaching one to a desk Mac, except that Apple recommends you add a terminator both at the end of the chain *and* before the first device "for optimum performance." That means you have to do it only if you're having problems. I always start without the extra terminator, and only occasionally—about five percent of the time—have to add it after all.

If you do add the "before" terminator, it goes on the far end of the HDI-30 SCSI cable; and, of course, it has to be a pass-through terminator so you can hook up the next device or cable.

SCSI disk mode. All PowerBooks except the 140, 145, 145B and 170 provide a unique feature called *SCSI disk mode*, where you can use the PowerBook itself as an external SCSI drive. (The transfer of files across a SCSI connection is much faster than using an AppleTalk network connection.)

You need two cables for this hookup: the HDI-30 SCSI Disk Adapter cable for the PowerBook end, and the standard SCSI system cable on the desktop end. Miraculously enough, the free ends of each cable—50-pin male and 50-pin female—fit together. You attach the shut-down PowerBook to the shut-down desk Mac, turn on the PowerBook and then the Mac, and voilà: The PowerBook's internal drive shows up as an icon on your desk Mac.

Of course, there are a few more details for a successful hookup:

- **Termination**. As with any SCSI chain, proper termination and termination power are necessary. And, as with any chain, it's sometimes hard to figure out what's the proper setup. Depending on the PowerBook model and the desktop model, you may need one or two terminators (they'll fit between the two 50-pin connectors) or perhaps none.
- **Other devices in the chain**. If you have multiple devices, the PowerBook will usually wind up at the end of the chain: it's the one you'll be taking on and off the most often—and it has only a single SCSI port anyway. With multiple devices, termination requirements will probably change, and you'll probably need the SCSI extension cable (with its two 50-pin connectors) instead of the system cable.
- **The SCSI ID**. A PowerBook is pre-set to use 1 as its SCSI ID number in disk mode. If you already have a device assigned to 1, change it or use the PowerBook Setup control panel to change the PowerBook's number.
- **Battery power.** Don't run a PowerBook on battery power in SCSI disk mode; the constant spinning of the disk and the extra power to the SCSI port will eat up the battery in no time.
- **Password protection.** Turn off password protection if you have it on through the Password Security control panel.

PowerBook-to-PowerBook connection. You can't just connect one PowerBook in SCSI mode to act as an external hard drive for another PowerBook, even if you have all the right cables. A PowerBook in SCSI mode doesn't provide any termination *power*, usually provided by the desk Mac on a normal hookup. To make a reliable PowerBook-to-PowerBook SCSI connection, you need this chain:

1. The first PowerBook
2. HDI-30 SCSI System Cable
3. Pass-through SCSI 50-pin terminator with power supply
4. HDI-30 SCSI Disk Adapter Cable
5. PowerBook in SCSI mode

SCSI Sentry

APS Technologies' **SCSI Sentry** ($30) is the perfect product for the center of this chain: it works as an end-of-chain or a pass-through device that detects and solves many SCSI signal problems. You can get a separate termination power supply ($20) for situations like this PowerBook chain; or, get SCSI Sentry II, which includes the termination power supply, for $45.

SCSI Pro

What's up,Doc?If you're connecting SCSI devices to the PowerBook, the best way to go is something called **SCSI Doc** ($30, APS Technologies). It plugs into the HDI-30 connector on the PowerBook and provides a standard 25-pin SCSI connector on the other end—with a switch that lets you choose standard SCSI or SCSI-mode connection. The **SCSI Pro** version ($20) is for standard SCSI hookups, with no SCSI-mode option. You can get both for $35; PowerMerge Limited, a "lite" version of a highly recommended file-synching program comes with each package.

File Synching

That synching feeling. When you have two versions of a file, one on a desk Mac and one on your PowerBook, it's not too hard too keep track of which is most current. If you have two versions of *lots* of files, however, you've got a problem. Which one is the most recent? Have they *both* been changed, with different information in them? Synchronizing files in multiple locations—*synching* them—can be time consuming if you don't plan ahead.

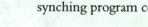

If you sync files manually, you have to look at their modified dates to see which is the most recent version, and copy files back and forth accordingly—presumably across the network that's set up between your PowerBook and a desk machine. The modified date on a file serves as a time and date "stamp" for the file.

A file-synching utility (like File Assistant, which comes with the system software) saves a lot of the drudgery, but can't resolve the problem of updating information within a file, or combining changes if both files were changed—although it can alert you to the problem.

Out of sync. Since any synching procedure is based on a modified date of a file (and has nothing to do with the file's contents), keep these points in mind:

- Make sure the time and date is set correctly on both your PowerBook and your desk Mac. If you change the clocks *after* you've created files, the modified date of the files won't reflect their true modification times.
- If you're traveling with your PowerBook and change the clock to match a new time zone, you may return to find your most recent files are stamped as older than the original files. It's seldom worth changing the PowerBook clock because of this problem.

- If the PowerBook is taken apart for upgrades or repairs, its battery is removed—resetting the clock. If you don't reset the correct date and time, your files will be stamped incorrectly.
- Some files are date-stamped as modified even if you only *look* at them—just open and close them. If you're doing read-only operations, lock the file on the desktop (in the file's Info window) so its date can't change.

The forgotten files. Your documents aren't the only things you might want to sync on a regular basis; it's easy to forget about "background" files when you're working on more than one machine. There are all sorts of peripheral files we use every day that we don't think about too often, since they're not actually documents that we create and save in the normal way. For instance:

- **Support files:** Custom dictionaries and glossaries for word processors, spell checkers, and thesauruses.
- **Macros:** Have you ever tried to call up a macro on one machine that you actually created on the other? Sometimes it's easier just to record a fresh one on whatever machine you're on, but synching the macro file would take care of the problem.
- **Desk accessory files:** Whether it's Scrapbook pages or a rolodex-type accessory, desk accessory files contain information that need to be updated. (Make sure you sync the desk accessory *files,* not the desk accessories themselves.)
- **Telecom files:** How you ever saved someone's address during an online session and then tried to retrieve it when you're on your other machine? Or saved an entire message or thread to review later, but it's on the other drive when you're ready to read?

The File Assistant. The dorky little guy on the File Assistant utility does basic, nothing-fancy file synching between your PowerBook and another volume. You can do strict folder-to-folder and/or file-to-file synching, creating

matched pairs with one-way or two-way synching (for folders). You can't manipulate folder contents—in fact, you can't even *see* folder contents.

When you first run File Assistant, you'll get nothing but a blank screen; you have to start with the Show Setup Window command to get things going. Once you select the pairs of files or folders, you define which way the sync should go, and then double-click the arrow between their icons to actually start the process.

File Assistant is just limited and clumsy enough to make it not worth the effort if you're setting up one-way synching: it's easier to just drag the target folders from one volume to another. If you're updating both volumes, though, it's a little easier to automate the process. But if that's something you do reasonably often, it's time to read the next entry.

PowerMerge

PowerMerge. Of all the stand-alone file-synching programs that came out soon after the PowerBooks were released, only **PowerMerge** ($80, Leader Technologies) remains—and rightly so, in an atmosphere of "may the best program win." You can use a variety of controls to define which files, folders, and disks should be synchronized, and when. You can include or exclude a specific file from a sync run, or any file that meets certain criteria. You can set the sync to run at a specific time, or in reaction to a certain event (like mounting a volume or logging on to a network). PowerMerge is so smooth and easy to set up that I use it all the time for backing up my desktop work (by setting up a one-way sync).

The Problem Clinic

In General

Insomnia. If your PowerBook isn't automatically going to sleep when it's scheduled to, check out these possibilities (after you've double-checked your settings in the PowerBook control panel):

- Opened applications may be doing background processing that keep the PowerBook from going to sleep.
- Timed events in open applications or extensions may be kicking in at intervals, constantly resetting the "clock" that's keeping track of how long the PowerBook's been idle.
- The PowerBook won't go to sleep when certain peripherals—some monitors and SCSI devices, for instance—are connected.
- Network access may be triggering activity on the PowerBook.

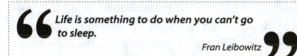

> ***Life is something to do when you can't go to sleep.***
>
> *Fran Leibowitz*

Don't forget that drive driver. When upgrading to OS 8 or 8.1 on a PowerBook in which you've installed a non-Apple drive, make sure you've updated the hard drive's driver. This is a recommended, and even necessary, step for any system upgrade (as described in Chapter 8) but it can be even more important on a PowerBook. Many users, too anxious to wait for third-party driver updates, found that the system software worked just fine, as did their PowerBooks, with one exception: the hard drive would never spin down for sleep.

Resetting the power manager. Resetting the power manager is a panacea for all sorts of ills on a PowerBook—much like zapping PRAM is for all Macs. When your battery isn't charging, or it's not lasting too long, or the PowerBook thinks you didn't even put a battery in, try resetting the power manager. For most models, resetting the power manager consists of many small steps, and some of them differ from one model to another.

Resetting the Power Manager

For 100-series PowerBooks (except the 190) and Duos

Shut down the computer, and remove the AC adapter and the battery (or batteries). Then:

For the 100	Hold in the reset and interrupt buttons for 15 seconds.
For the 140, 145, 145B, and 170	Press the reset and interrupt buttons simultaneously by pushing them in with a paper clip bent into a U-shape; hold the buttons in for 30 seconds.
For the 150	Hold in the reset button for 30 seconds. (Note the special later step for this model, below.)
For the 160, 165, 180, and 200 and 2300 Duos	Hold in the rear power button for 30 seconds.

After the appropriate procedure listed above, do these steps in this order (which is *not* the order you'd normally follow!):

1. Reconnect the AC adapter to the PowerBook.
2. Plug the adapter into the wall outlet.
3. For all but the 150: Turn on the PowerBook. For the 150: Briefly press the reset button again. You might hear a pop from the speaker, and the PowerBook may start up. If it doesn't, press the main power button in back.
4. *Now*, reinsert the battery.

For the 500-series PowerBooks

1. Shut down the PowerBook.
2. Hold down [⌘][Option][Ctrl] and Power On for a few seconds.
3. Turn the PowerBook back on.

For the 190, 1400, 2400, 3400, 5300, and G3 series

There are several ways to reset the power manager on these PowerBooks, but the easiest is to zap the PRAM, since that also resets the power manager for these models:

1. Shut down the PowerBook.
2. Start up while holding down [⌘][Option][P][R]. You should hear two startup chimes before you let go of the keys.
3. If the computer shuts down at this point instead of starting up, use the power button to start it.

Ignore the internal clicks. A slight clicking sound from your PowerBook at irregular intervals is nothing to worry about: the sound circuit is shut down periodically to save battery power, and the click you hear is the circuit shutting off. Some internal hard drives also make a clicking sound when the drive arm parks and unparks.

Serial port in use (not). If you get an erroneous "serial port in use" error when you try to establish a PPP connection, open the Infrared control panel and change the setting to IRTalk.

Some PC-drive deaths under 8.1. Some third-party PC card drives won't work under OS 8.1 without their drivers being updated. You'll find some updates in the CD Extras folder on the system CD, but you may have to contact your card vendor for the one you need.

Model-Specific Problems

Blank screens after OS 8 install. If you install OS 8 or 8.1 on your 190 or 5300 PowerBook and the display is blank when you restart, or after you reset the PRAM, this is a "normal bug"; a second restart should take care of it. But to shut down safely (because, although you can't see anything, the PowerBook probably started up), press the Power button once to bring up the shutdown dialog; you won't be able to see it, but then pressing Return will trigger the Shut Down button.

The AppleTalk/Open Transport clash. When you restart a 2400 after installing OS 8 or 8.1, the serial port may be in use by AppleTalk. If you've also installed OT/PPP you need to release the port for Open Transport's use: turn off AppleTalk, restart the PowerBook, and select the modem/printer port in the OT/PPP control panel.

No Video Player on the 1400. The 1400-series PowerBooks can't use the Apple Video Player; Apple has provided an alternative, the MoviePlayer, which you'll find in the Apple Extras folder.

The brain-dead 500 battery. The "intelligent battery" in the 500-series PowerBooks has a chip whose memory is easily corrupted, especially when left uncharged for a long period of time. Symptoms of this stupidity include: the battery can't be charged in the PowerBook or externally; the battery isn't recognized by the battery icon; the battery completely discharges in a sleeping PowerBook in a day or two (instead of a week); the battery is *extremely* hot to the touch when removed from the PowerBook.

vsttech.com

There are two cures for a dumbed-down smart battery. Apple provides a free fix with its later system software, Intelligent Battery Reconditioner; **EMMpathy** (the Energy Monitoring Module controller in the battery is what's at fault), put out as freeware from VST Systems, also fixes the problem.

The 500-series loose screw. The screws underneath the hinge endcaps on the 500-series PowerBook tend to come loose. If you don't keep them tightened, the screw, the hinge mechanism, or even the screen can be damaged when the screw actually comes loose.

The key to success. Early Duo 210 and 230 models had some significant keyboard problems: keys that repeated and a spacebar that wouldn't work at all; these need total keyboard replacements. But if the Duo's been opened for memory or modem installation, the problem may be simply from a too-tight screw at the bottom of the case: Turn your Duo over and loosen the screw that's at the center of the case.

shrevesystems.com

You can check if you have the best of the Duo keyboards if you can open your Duo. Check the last letter of the serial number on the bottom of the keyboard; F is the last keyboard revision. Keyboard replacements are still available through certified Apple repair persons and "parts" companies like Shreve. (If you're in New York, check out Tekserve, my particular favorite; they're at 212-929-3645.)

The 100-Series PowerBooks

The NoCharge NiCad. If you can't get your 100-series PowerBook to run on the battery alone, but it runs when you plug it in, that probably means the battery isn't charging at all. If your battery stays so low it might as well be dead even after hours of being plugged in—or, you've noticed, it charges in an external adapter but not while in the PowerBook—you've got a blown fuse on the PowerBook's motherboard, which effectively disconnects the battery while it's inside the PowerBook.

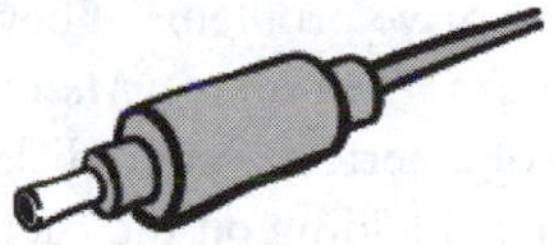

There are several ways this can happen, but the cruelest one is because of a defective adapter. The 17-watt adapters with part number M5140 on the "brick" are especially prone to this problem: look for a break (even a hairline crack) in the black ring around the end of the adapter.

Old solders sometimes die. Here's a problem that every PowerBook 100 encounters sooner or later: the battery won't charge when it's in the PowerBook, and the PowerBook won't work on AC power—but the it runs on a battery that's been charged externally. The problem is due to a broken solder joint between the motherboard and the AC adapter socket. If you can get a repair center or Apple to handle it, they'll give you a $400 motherboard replacement. Or, you can grab a soldering iron (or a knowledgeable friend who has a soldering iron) and do it for free.

Once the motherboard is out, you'll see a hairline crack on the underside of the solder connection between the AC receptacle and the board. A simple reheating and reflowing of the existing solder usually works, but the best thing to do is wick out the existing solder and replace it with high-quality solder.

Trackball improvement. Improve the trackball performance on the 100 with this simple adjustment:

1. Take out the trackball by removing the retaining ring and then taking out the ball.
2. Locate the shafts to the left and bottom of the trackball well; each has a blue roller on it.
3. Slide the blue roller on the left shaft down from its original position. Move the blue roller on the bottom shaft further to the right.
4. Return the ball to the well and replace the retaining ring.

By moving the rollers this way, the ball comes in contact only with their edges and there's less movement of the rollers and the shafts while you're using the trackball; as a result, you get smoother trackball action.

Display cables on 140 and 145. A problem screen on an early-production 140 or 145 might be due to a too-thin cable inside the PowerBook, an acknowledged problem on the early production models. If the display works correctly when you squeeze the right side of the frame around the screen, you've probably got the cable problem. The fix is a simple shim that's easy for a technician to install.

PowerBooks with serial numbers later than CK121xxx or higher, or F2208 or higher, or any number beginning with FC, already have the shim installed.

This is *so* a Macintosh disk! The earliest production models of the 140 and 170 had some significant floppy drive problems. They're very finicky when it comes to reading disks, and the *This is not a Macintosh disk* dialog is the frequent response to insertion of a perfectly good disk. The problem was apparently caused by inadequate shielding on the backlight converter, a problem attended to later in the production runs of both models—first with a shield, and later with a new, less sensitive, floppy drive. These models had shielding installed at the factory:

- 140's with serial numbers higher than F2150xxx
- 170's with serial numbers higher than CK205xxx

These models had the improved (rev B) drive:

- 140's in any configuration other than 4/40 or 4/80 (4 megs of RAM and 40MB or 80MB hard drives)

- 140's in a 4/40 configuration and serial numbers starting with or higher than F2211xxx
- 140's in a 4/80 configuration and serial numbers starting with or higher than F2212xxx
- 170's with serial numbers starting with or higher than FC213xxx or CK213xxx

Disk problem work-around. Disk-reading problems on a 140 or 170 may be due to inadequate backlight shield as described in the last entry, but you might be able to work around the problem if you can't get the PowerBook fixed. When you get a *This disk is unreadable* dialog, eject the disk, turn the backlight off, and reinsert the disk; this often makes the disk readable. If the problem disk is one that was mass-produced, try making a copy of it at a desk Mac; the PowerBook might be able to read the copy when it can't read the master.

On the Road

Travel

X-ray away. You can't damage your PowerBook by putting it through the x-ray machine at an airport. Honest. X-rays are a form of light; it's magnetic waves that might erase your disk or otherwise damage something in your computer. I've actually x-rayed several PowerBooks (including my own and Sharon's—but I did Sharon's first) at a friend's medical office just to prove the point; nothing happened! The magnetic field from the motor that runs the conveyor belt for the airport x-ray isn't a problem, either—there's just not a strong enough field to affect the data on the hard drive.

Sleep it to save time. Once you've passed your PowerBook through the security x-ray, you might be asked to open it and start it up to prove it's a computer and not a terrorist device. How long does your PowerBook take to start up? A minute? Two and a half minutes? That's a long time when you're heading for the gate. Keep your PowerBook in sleep mode, and a single press of any key will start it up instantly.

Sit right down and write yourself a letter. Here's a great way to make sure you'll have backups of important files when you get to where you're going: e-mail them to yourself before you leave. Then, if something happens to the copies you're working with, you can retrieve fresh copies.

Phoning (away from) Home

The other online toolkit. "Online toolkit" usually means software, but I'm talking about the equipment you might need just to hook up to a phone line in an unfriendly hotel room. (Data-friendly hotels have phones with data jacks in them that you can simply plug into.)

You may need any or all of these:

- A length of **phone wire** to connect your PowerBook to a phone jack. A short one will do when you're in a data-friendly room, but you'll need a longer one when you might have to snake it around and below an attached-to-the-wall desk that's over the only phone jack in the room.
- An **extension cord**, because the room's phone jack and power outlet might not be in close proximity.
- A **RJ-11 duplex adapter** lets you plug in both a phone and a modem to a single wall jack.
- A second length of **phone wire** and a **coupler** (also known as a *splice adapter)* provides an extra-long phone wire if you need it.
- **A small screwdriver** to remove the plate that covers a phone jack.
- An **RJ-11 clip adapter** lets you connect directly to phone wires in a room that doesn't have phone jacks at all because its phone is hard-wired into the wall.

TeleAdapt adapters

teleadapt.com

Teleadapting. If you travel outside the country, you'll be boggled by the wide variety of phone jacks used around the world; but you can stay online if you choose one of TeleAdapt's hundreds of international phone-plug adapters. They're available individually ($30) or in multipacks ($50-$450) for various geopolitical regions. And if you don't know what you need, don't worry—TeleAdapt seems to know it all! Check out their web site before you take off, especially the terrific Destination catalog, which details telephone and power supply information for countries you've never heard of (along with the ones you need to know about).

Tapping a phone line. No, not that kind of tapping! If you're someplace that doesn't offer modular phone plugs—an older or out-of-the-way hotel—you can connect directly to phone wires by using an RJ-11 clip adapter, which gives you the RJ-11 connector for the modem on one end and alligator clips on the other to attach to the phone wires. (You can buy the clip adapter, or make your own—described in the next entry).

Where can you find the wires you need? First of all (assuming you're in the U.S.), you're looking for the red and green wires of the bunch that you'll find. The easiest place to get at the wires is usually behind the wall plate where the phone wire goes into the wall; the plate is usually just attached to the wall with one or two screws. (Remember, your online toolkit includes a screwdriver—but a room-service knife or other bladed implement will do in a pinch.) When you take the plate off, you'll be able get at the wire terminals, where the wire is attached; attach the clips to the terminals. If there's no hope at the wall plate, you can try removing the bottom of the phone, or at least loosen it, and follow the wires to their terminals, where you can attach your clips.

With one clip on each of the necessary wires, stick the other end in your modem jack, and you're set.

Don't forget to put everything back together the way you found it; you're not on the men's hockey team at the Nagano Olympics.

Roll-your-own clip adapter. The main piece of equipment you need for phone systems hard-wired into a wall (beyond a screwdriver to remove the wall plate) is an RJ-11 clip adapter that provides a standard connector on one end for your modem and two wires with clips on the other to tap into the two phone wires you need. I've only ever seen this item for sale as part of a larger collection of tools and equipment, but you can easily make one yourself for only a few dollars. Here's what you'll need:

- An RJ-11-to-spade adapter (Radio Shack part #279-391)
- Two insulated alligator clips
- A piece of 3/16-inch heatshrink tubing

Here's how to put it together:

1. Cut off two of the adapter wires, leaving the red and green ones.
2. Cut off the spades from the red and green wires; strip a half-inch of each wire.
3. Slip the heatshrink tubing over the wires, pushing it all the way down to the clip.
4. Remove the insulating covers from the alligator clips and slide one each onto the red and green wires.
5. Attach the wires to the alligator clips (soldering makes the most reliable connection).
6. Slide the insulating covers back up over the alligator clips.
7. Slide the heatshrink tubing to the V where the red and green wires split apart. Shrink it by holding a match under it for a few seconds.

Digital PBX. Many offices and hotels have digital phone systems (PBXs) that are incompatible with your modem (which is analog); trying to use your modem incorrectly on a PBX line can fry it. Since many PBX systems use standard RJ-11 jacks, it's easy to inadvertently connect. Luckily, it's also fairly easy to identify digital systems in those instances where the hotel workers don't even understand the question you're asking. Here are the giveaways:

- The phone has a data port. You can be fairly sure the system is digital, but that's why the data port is there—so you can plug your modem into it.
- The phone has an LCD display with the time, the number you're calling, and so on.
- The phone has more than the standard keypad numbers: one-touch buttons for the front desk, housekeeping, room service, and so on.
- The underside of the phone may have warning stickers that say something like: *"Not for direct connection to telephone lines / hotel use only."*

I carry a cheap single-line phone tester (a few dollars at your local electronics store); when connected to a properly functioning analog phone line, its LED glows green.

The pause that refreshes. You have a phone card for voice calls because it's cheaper than dialing direct from a hotel room and paying surcharges on the call; you want to use it for online calls, too. We can't give you exact directions because the exact solution depends on the phone companies involved: which is making the call, which is receiving it, and which one issued the card. But we can give you directions as to how to figure out what to do.

First, analyze how you use the card for voice calls. Here's a typical setup for an AT&T card (the examples, of course, use fake numbers):

1. Dial 0 plus the area code and number you want to reach. If the local carrier isn't AT&T, start the sequence with 10288: 02125551234 or 1028802125551234.
2. Wait for the tone and AT&T acknowledgement to start (about 7 seconds).
3. Dial the calling card number: 12341231234.
4. Wait for the next acknowledgement (about 5 seconds).
5. Dial the personal identification number: 9999

The entire sequence looks like this:

02125551234 (wait) 12341231234 (wait) 9999

To translate that into a number the modem should dial, you use a comma to indicate a pause; most programs are set up to translate a comma as a 2-second pause, so your dialing string looks like this:

02125551234,,,,12341231234,,,9999

Your own situation may call for (no pun intended) an entirely different sequence, with the PIN entered earlier, and different places for pauses, but the basic approach will be the same.

The phone duet. Here's another solution to the calling-card problem that works if you have a modular phone system in your hotel room. Set things up so you have both the voice phone and the modem connected. In some cases this will be a cinch: if there's a data port on the side of the phone, just plug in the modem, and the phone is still available. If there's only a single phone in the room but it's modular *and* you have the duplex adapter described in the "online toolkit," you can plug the adapter into the wall jack and connect both the phone and the modem to it.

When you have to make a calling card call, you can use both the modem and the phone's number pad to punch everything in. Make sure you let the modem take the first round, though: it's set to wait for a dial tone before it does any dialing, and if you punch in the first few numbers from the phone, the modem won't be able to take a turn.

PowerBook Models and Specifications

	PROCESSOR		DISPLAY			
	Chip	Speed (MHz)	Size (in)	Type	Depth	Resolution
PowerPC Models						
G3/250	233/250/292	250	12.1/13.3/14.1	active	color	800x600
3400	603e	180/200/240	12.1	active	color	800x600
2400c	603e	180	10.4	active	color	800x600
1400c	603e	166	11.3	active	color	800x600
1400cs	603e	133/166	11.3	passive	color	800x600
5300/100	603e	100	9.5	passive	grays	640x480
5300c/100	603e	100	10.4	active	color	640x480
5300ce/117	603e	117	10.4	active	color	800x600
5300cs/100	603e	100	10.4	passive	color	640x480
'040 Models						
540c	68LC040	66	9.5	active	color	640x480
540	68LC040	66	9.5	active	grays	640x480
520c	68LC040	50	9.5	passive	color	640x480
520	68LC040	50	9.5	passive	grays	640x480
190cs	68LC040	66	10.4	passive	color	640x480
190	68LC040	66	9.5	passive	grays	640x480
Duos						
Duo 2300c	603e	100	9.5	active	color	640x480
Duo 280c	68LC040	66	8.4	active	color	640x480
Duo 280	68LC040	66	9	active	grays	640x480
Duo 270c	68030	33	8.4	active	color	640x480
Duo 250	68030	33	9	active	grays	640x400
Duo 230	68030	33	9	passive	grays	640x480
Duo 210	68030	25	9	passive	grays	640x400
'030 (and under) Models						
180c	68030	33	8.4	active	color	640x480
180	68030	33	10	active	grays	640x400
170	68030	25	10	active	b&w	640x400
165c	68030	33	9	passive	color	640x400
165	68030	33	10	passive	grays	640x400
160	68030	25	10	passive	grays	640x400
150	68030	33	9	passive	4 grays	640x400
145, 145B	68030	25	10	passive	b&w	640x400
140	68030	16	10	passive	b&w	640x400
100	68000	16	9	passive	b&w	640x400
Portable	68000	16	10	active	b&w	640x400

	MEMORY Max	On-Board	Speed (ns)	Int. drive	Battery	Weight (lbs)	PCMCIA	Bay
PowerPC Models								
G3/250	192	32	60	IDE	LiIon	7.7	●	●
3400	144	16	70	IDE	LiIon	7.2	●	-
2400c	80	16	60	IDE	LiIon	4.4	●	-
1400c	64	8	70	IDE	NiMH	6.7	●	●
1400cs	64	8	70	IDE	NiMH	6.7	●	●
5300/100	64	8	70	IDE	NiMH	5.9	●	-
5300c/100	64	8/16	70	IDE	NiMH	6.2	●	-
5300ce/117	64	16	70	IDE	NiMH	6.2	●	-
5300cs/100	64	8/16	70	IDE	NiMH	6.2	●	-
'040 Models								
540c	36	4	70	SCSI	NiMH	7.3	-	-
540	36	4	70	SCSI	NiMH	7.1	-	-
520c	36	4	70	SCSI	NiMH	6.4	-	-
520	36	4	70	SCSI	NiMH	6.3	-	-
190cs	36/40	4/8	70	IDE	NiMH	6.3	-	-
190	36/40	4/8	70	IDE	NiMH	6	-	-
Duos								
Duo 2300c	56	8	70	IDE	NiMH III	4.8	-	-
Duo 280c	40	4	70	SCSI	NiMH III	4.8	-	-
Duo 280	40	4	70	SCSI	NiMH III	4.2	-	-
Duo 270c	32	4	70	SCSI	NiMH II	4.8	-	-
Duo 250	24	4	70	SCSI	NiMH II	4.2	-	-
Duo 230	24	4	70	SCSI	NiMH I	4.2	-	-
Duo 210	24	4	70	SCSI	NiMH I	4.2	-	-
'030 (and under) Models								
180c	14	4	85	SCSI	NiCad	7.1	-	-
180	14	4	85	SCSI	NiCad	6.8	-	-
170	8	2	100	SCSI	NiCad	6.8	-	-
165c	14	4	85	SCSI	NiCad	7	-	-
165	14	4	85	SCSI	NiCad	6.8	-	-
160	14	4	85	SCSI	NiCad	6.8	-	-
150	40	4	70	IDE	NiCad	5.8	-	-
145, 145B	8	4	100	SCSI	NiCad	6.8	-	-
140	8	2	100	SCSI	NiCad	5.1	-	-
100	8	2	100	SCSI	lead acid	6.8	-	-
Portable	8	1	100	SCSI	lead acid	15.8	-	-

24

Problems and Preventions

Prevention and Preparation

Troubleshooting

Common System Problems

Disks, Drives, and SCSI

Applications and Documents

In This Chapter

Prevention and Preparation

Your Hardware

General environmental protection. As a general rule of thumb, if you're comfortable, so's your computer: it doesn't like extreme heat or cold, or excessive humidity; if you're in a very dusty environment (or one with animal hair around), you'll have to clean the components more than otherwise.

Surge protectors. Everyone recommends surge protection as an easy way to protect your Mac from sudden voltage swings. A surge protector—basically a power strip with the surge protection built-in—runs about $50 for a good one, a small price to pay for protection. But I don't use one, and never have—and that includes more than a decade of computing up in the country, where power outages and voltage swings were very much a way of life. I've always found that the Mac itself could put up quite well with the vicissitudes of electric life. But I'm not quite willing to tell you *not* to bother with a surge protector and then get blamed if something goes wrong! But I will tell you that the importance of surge protection, for most situations, is exaggerated.

And a surge protector won't provide any safety from a lightening strike, so don't just turn off, but *unplug* your system in severe thunderstorms.

The Mouse pad. A mouse pad stakes out an area of your desk that's specifically for the mouse, provides an excellent rolling surface (with just the right amount of traction), and keeps dust and dirt to a minimum in the mousing area. Your mouse won't need cleaning as frequently if you give it a pad to run around on.

Cleanliness is next to mouseliness. You need to give the insides of your mouse a cleaning every once in a while. The roller ball picks up dust, lint, and general gunk, which gathers on the rollers inside that actually control the movement of the cursor on screen. When the cursor starts moving erratically, that's usually a sign that the mouse needs cleaning.

Remove the ring at the bottom of the mouse by turning it, and drop the ball out. You'll see two or three rollers inside—some might be plain black bars, and some black bars with thicker white rings around them (it depends on your mouse model). The point of contact between the ball and the rollers or rings is what gets really dirty and needs to be cleaned off.

You can usually just scrape off the gunk, although tough jobs call for dipping a cotton swab (that's a generic Q-Tip, of course) in alcohol and holding it against the gunk stripe to soften it. A stiff but not sharp object works well for the scraping—a toothpick is a good tool. Get the rollers clean, clean the ball with a soft cloth (with some alcohol if it's really dirty), and put it all back together.

Keyboard protection. If you work in a dirty environment (or if you're a natural slob, and eat and drink at your keyboard) you can get a special keyboard cover, called a "skin," (about $15) that you can keep on the keyboard while you work. The skins are strong, but very thin and don't interfere with the working of the keys.

Working inside the Mac We've come a long way, baby—the original Macs were practically sealed against a user's efforts to open it. But these days, almost everyone opens a Mac sooner or later, at least to put in some new memory. As with surge protection, the issue of working around an open Mac has probably been exaggerated (although it's better to err on the side of caution).

When you open your Mac, you expose its delicate innards to the possibility of a static shock, which could fry some of its components. That shock's going to come from *you*, so be careful. Basic precautions include leaving the Mac plugged in, because that provides some grounding, and touching something *else* metallic before handling any components, in order to discharge any static charge you may have built up. (And, for heaven's sake, stop shuffling your feet on that carpet!)

Hard drive maintenance. You can prevent serious problems by catching them when they're not so serious. Practice some preventive medicine for your hard drive (only the last involves software that you actually have to buy!).

- Rebuild the desktop (by holding down ⌘ Option at startup). This speeds up the appearance of the disk on the desktop, purges the invisible desktop file of outdated icons, and repairs broken alias links.
- Run Disk First Aid to nip minor problems in the bud.
- Run Norton Disk Doctor or TechTool Pro to examine the disk, and its files, for any problems.

How often you should do these things depends on how much you use your Mac. For light-to-average use, every two months or so is fine. If you use your Mac most of the day, every day, every two weeks is not too often!

In addition, do an annual wipeout: every year or so, back up all your work and totally reformat the drive. This also gives you a chance to do general housekeeping, getting rid of files you no longer use or need.

Backing Up

To go forward, you must back up. That's one of my favorite advertising slogans, used for years by Retrospect, one of the premier Mac back-up utilities. Backing up is the single most important disaster-prevention procedure there is. There's an almost trite, but true expression: There are only two kinds of computer people—those who've lost data, and those who are about to.

You might lose a file because it becomes corrupted and you can't open it. Maybe you threw it in the trash by mistake. Or you might lose an entire disk or hard drive to some physical disaster. But if you have an extra copy of your important documents, you can use the backups if you lose the originals.

Backing up can be as simple as dragging important files to a removable disk and sticking it on a shelf, or as complicated as making incremental backups of everything on your hard drive with special software and then storing the backup copies off-site in case of major disaster.

Back up onto what? What do you back up your information onto? As files get larger, floppies seem to get smaller. And if you're thinking of backing up an entire hard drive, those floppies are *miniscule*—you'd need about 1500 of them for everything on a 2-gig drive! But when your choice is between no backup and floppy backup of selected important files—copy to the floppies!

Luckily, the cost of high-capacity removable media is within everyone's reach these days, so there's no excuse not to get yourself a separate setup to help with backups. For about $150 you can get a system that provides around 100 megs of storage on each removable cartridge; for under $300 you can get a system that handles a gig on every cartridge. (Iomega's Zip and Jaz drives are the most popular, SyQuest offers a great bargain; both are discussed in Chapter 4.) There's also the old standby of tape backup systems, which offer huge capacity and speed benefits at, of course, a price. And, if your Mac has more than a single hard drive, you might consider backing things up from one drive to another.

Archival problems. For active files, you make backups so you can get right back to work if something happens to the original file. But there's another kind of "backup," too—an *archival* backup, which means the file is no longer active but you want to keep it around—just not on your hard drive where it's taking up room. Most people realize that long-term storage has the extra consideration of the longevity of the storage medium itself; a CD-ROM, for instance, will stay viable longer than a magnetic-based medium.

But here's what most people forget: you might preserve an old file only to find you can't access it. Maybe by the time you need an old file, the application that created it might not be around. Most applications can open documents only one or two versions back—so how will you open that booklet you made in the first version of QuarkXPress? Keeping the application itself around isn't the solution, because older versions of programs often won't run under new systems on new hardware.

There are only two approaches, both ungainly, that take care of the out-of-date archive problems. You can either keep an old hardware setup around so you'll always be able to open older applications and their documents, or you'll have to, every year or two, open old documents in newer versions of the parent application, and re-save them in an updated format.

Backup software. You can manually back up files or folders, but if you do it on a regular basis (as you should), that method quickly becomes tedious. There are several software solutions:

- On the high end, there's **Retrospect** ($150, Dantz Development). It's the only choice for tape backup setups (and it's bundled with many backup drives), and works with any other medium you use, too. For network setups, there's the **Retrospect Network Backup Kit** ($300).
- For the rest of us, Dantz has two other packages, **DiskFit Direct** ($30) for backups to removable media, and **DiskFit Pro** ($75) for file-server-based operations.

dantz.com
leadertech.com
aladdinsys.com

- Although **PowerMerge** ($80, Leader Technologies) is a "file-synching" program to keep files updated between a PowerBook and a stationery Mac, you can set it for "one-way synching," which is backing up; that's what I use all the time. **PowerMerge Lite** is only $15 and may be all you need—and you can download a free trial from Leader's web site.
- Don't forget **StuffIt**. It's not backup software, but it will let you squeeze down the size of files before you move them to another disk for storage. Sometimes it will be the only way you can fit something on a floppy, or even on a 100-meg Zip! A free copy comes with almost every telecom program. **StuffIt Deluxe** ($80, Aladdin Systems), described in Chapter 28, offers lots more features as well as the ability to split a large file across two or more disks.

The forgotten backups. If you do piece-meal backups (instead of a whole-drive backup), you'll probably remember all your important documents. And, since you can always reinstall your system software and applications, it's not so important that they be backed up. But here are some of the files most people, to their eventual dismay, often overlook:

- **Preference files:** These are easily corrupted and often cause both application-specific and system-wide problems. Some preference files hold lots of information that you'll hate to have to reenter after you reinstall an application or just trash a corrupted version of the preferences file.
- **"Desk accessory" files:** Any little utility you use that really has only a single file you work with a lot (like the Scrapbook or some Note Pad replacement) probably has *lots* of information in it that you don't store elsewhere. The file may be in the utility's folder, or in the System Folder or one of its subfolders.
- **Bookmarks:** Your browser stores these in a separate file or folder.

- **Dictionaries and glossaries:** If you've been entering a few words a day into your word processor's dictionary or glossary, that adds up to a lot of words over a period of months.
- **Macros:** A macro utility stores your macros in one or more files in its folder or in one of the system folders.

Troubleshooting

Diagnosing Problems

Before you call. If you're going to call anybody's tech support (even that guy you met at the user group), the person at the other end is going to want to know what your hardware and software setup is: which Mac model, how much memory, which system software, what extensions, and so on. The easiest way to get this information is to run the **Apple System Profiler** (included with your system software, and detailed in Chapter 9) which will gather up all the information for you.

The next thing you should do is try a few basic troubleshooting procedures yourself; the first question out of your support personnel's mouth is likely to be, "Have you tried it without extensions?" and you should have the answer ready. (And the answer *shouldn't* be "No, not yet.")

Isolating the problem. If you've just added a piece of hardware to your setup, or installed a new piece of software, and things start falling apart, it's a good bet that the new item is causing or at least contributing to the problem. But most of the time figuring out what's actually causing the problem isn't so easy. The most important step in troubleshooting is figuring out what the problem *is*—from there, it's relatively simple to figure out the solution.

Say you're having trouble printing a document. Is it the document, or some small part of it—a single graphic or font? Is it the printer, or the network? Is it the printer software, or something else in the system software? Maybe it's something about the application and the way it's interacting with the printer software.

When you run into a problem, try to isolate the different variables involved. With a printing problem, for instance, check if the application can print another document; if it can't, see if *anything* prints from *any* application. That helps determine whether the problem is bigger than your document, or smaller than your printer! If it's only that document that won't print, you can try printing part of it, or changing its fonts, and so on.

The isolation factor works for more general problems, too: you can try working without extensions if you're having general system crashes, or detach all your external SCSI devices if you suspect a SCSI problem.

Fix-It Procedures

Rebuilding the desktop. There are several invisible files on your hard drive that keep track of things like where files are stored, how icons look, which documents belong to which applications, and how aliases are connected. It's occasionally necessary to replace these invisible files because the information in them can get corrupted; this is called *rebuilding the desktop.*

To rebuild the desktop, hold down ⌘ Option at startup (actually, pressing the keys just before the desktop shows up is soon enough). Just before the disk is mounted on the desktop, you'll be asked if you really want to rebuild the desktop on the volume; click the OK button. If you have multiple volumes that mount automatically at startup, you'll get the "Do you want to rebuild?" dialog for each volume in turn. You can rebuild any or all of the volumes.

Apple says that a reliable desktop rebuild occurs only with extensions off, so you have to hold Shift at startup until you see the Extensions Off dialog, then press ⌘ Option for the rebuild. Most people don't bother and the desktop seems to be rebuilt reliably in most instances. If you skip the extensions-off option and the rebuild doesn't help, go back and do it the more thorough way.

The freeware **TechTool**, described in the next section, forces an even more complete desktop rebuild.

The rebuild effect on aliases. Rebuilding your desktop solves some alias problems and can cause others. If your aliases seem to continually forget where their originals are, a desktop rebuild might solve the problem. But a rebuild sometimes affects aliases left out on the desktop—you might not be able to drag and drop things on to them anymore because they'll refuse to highlight. If that happens, just make new aliases.

Zapping the PRAM. The PRAM ("pea-ram")—*parameter RAM*—is a small amount of memory (about 24K) that retains its contents even when the computer's shut off and unplugged. Most of your control panel settings are stored in PRAM, as are the time and date, and things like the status of the serial and ADB ports. Sometimes the information in PRAM gets corrupted and causes all sorts of weird problems, like your losing control panel settings, your communications program not being able to find your modem, and unstable network connections. To solve the problems, you have to reset the contents of PRAM to their defaults, a procedure known as *zapping the PRAM.*

To zap the PRAM, start up the Mac while holding down ⌘ Option P R. You'll hear the basic startup chimes, then you'll hear them again. And again. After the third time, let go of the keys and let the Mac start up the rest of the way.

For an older, NuBus-based Mac, you can zap the PRAM on a restart. For newer Macs, you have to shut down the Mac and then start up again with the keys down. That's because PCI-based Macs store some settings in NVRAM—*non-volatile video RAM*—which also has to be zapped. You can do that only at a startup, and you have to get the keys down *immediately.* You also have to then drag out the Display preferences file from the Preferences folder and then restart once more! —SZA/HN/TL

The PowerBook 500/5000 zap. For PowerBook 500 and 5000 series models, hold down the zapping keys for only two startup chimes. If you go for a third round, you won't be able to start up the machine unless you hold in the power switch on the back of the PowerBook for about 30 seconds.

A more thorough zap. Zapping the PRAM at startup actually resets only a little more than half the PRAM contents—the half prone to corruption. But that doesn't mean that your problem can't stem from the other half, so you should use **TechTool** (freeware, MicroMat) to do a thorough zap through software rather than as a startup trick. As a bonus, it can save your PRAM settings in a disk file. Save them when everything's going fine, and take a look at them again when things are falling apart, and you'll have a good idea as to whether PRAM settings are the root of your problem.

The forced quit. Sometimes an application freezes up so that it won't respond to the keyboard or the mouse. But if you have other things open, you don't want to have to restart the Mac from that frozen state if you can just get out of the current, choked application. That's what a *forced quit* is for.

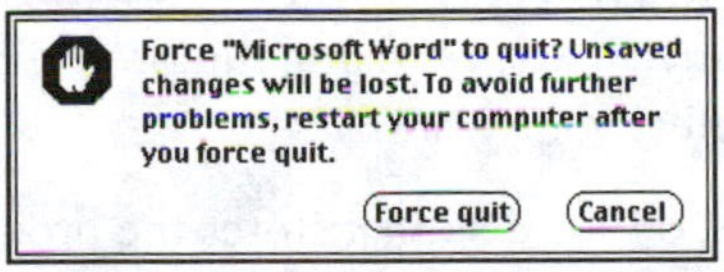

To force-quit a balky application, press ⌘ Option Esc. You'll get a dialog asking if you really want to force the quit, with buttons labeled Force Quit and Cancel (it's a really primitive dialog, with no platinum look, and squished buttons). There's no sense canceling, since you can't do anything in the frozen program, so click Force Quit. If you're lucky, the button will work and the program will quit (taking your probably unsaved document with it). If you're not lucky, the Force Quit button will also be frozen and you'll have to move on to the hard restart, described in the next entry.

If you're able to force quit a program, quit all your other opened applications normally and restart the Mac right away.

The hard restart. When things really freeze up—a "hang," when no keyboard commands work at all—you have to do a *hard restart*, or *reset*, losing everything in any document you haven't saved. Press ⌘ Control and the Power key together to reset the Mac.

On the very rare occasion that this doesn't work, you'll have to press the reset button on the Mac itself—all models in recent years have one somewhere on the CPU case. If your model doesn't, flip the Mac off and back on again—or even unplug and re-plug it—if that's the only way to get out of the freeze.

IN THE BEGINNING

MacsBug is a debugger—a program that tracks down and displays what's going on in another program—used by Mac programmers. But the *Macs* in Macs bug doesn't stand for Macintosh: it stands for *Motorola Advanced Computer Systems.*

Updating the disk driver. As detailed in Chapter 4, there's a piece of software on your hard drive called the *driver* that lets the Mac communicate with it. Sometimes the driver becomes corrupted and needs to be replaced; sometimes it needs to be updated to match a system update. If you're using an Apple internal hard drive and Apple's **Drive Setup** formatting utility, updating or replacing the driver is as simple as running the utility from a different startup and clicking the Update Driver button. Third-party software is just as easy to use, but you have to make sure you have the most recent version of the utility. This procedure is recommended for moderate-to-severe disk problems.

Reinstalling system software. Corruption of various system files can cause intermittent crashes, so reinstalling system software is a basic (though lengthy and hated) trouble-shooting procedure. Make sure you do a *clean install,* as outlined in Chapter 8.

Fix-It Software

The First Aid station. Disk First Aid is a disk-diagnostic and repair utility that comes with your system software. You can use it to fix many disk problems, and run it as a preventive measure, fixing minor problems before they turn into major ones that affect your work.

You can't run Disk First Aid on the disk that stores the program. So, if you need to run it for your startup disk, you'll have to start up on another disk (use your system CD) that has Disk First Aid on it.

Create an emergency startup. If you always have an alternative startup disk around—whether it's a second hard drive, your system CD, or a Zip disk—you'll be able to start up your Mac (probably) when something goes wrong with the system on your main startup drive. But when there's something wrong with the original startup disk, you need more than just another startup disk—you need an "emergency" disk that has some disk-repair utility on it.

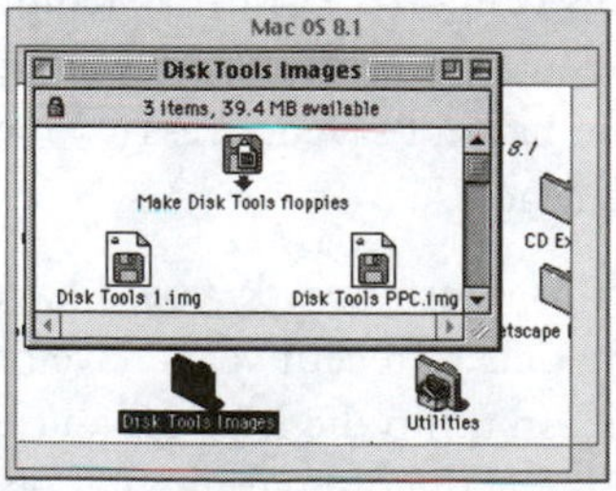

Use the disk images on your system CD to make an emergency startup floppy.

The simplest approach is to just use your system CD, which will act as a startup and give you access to Disk First Aid, the first line of defense against disk problems. But the best approach if you have a Zip drive or other large-capacity removable is to make an emergency disk that has a complete system on it, including Apple's disk utilities, as well as a disk-mounting utility like SCSIProbe, a disk-recovery utility like Norton's Disk Doctor, and the formatting software you used for your now-comatose internal drive (if you didn't use Apple's formatting software). This gives you access to all your tools—something you can't do with the basic system CD.

But the system software also provides another startup tool—or, at least, it provides the tool to make the tool! In the Disk Tools Images folder on the system CD, you'll find two Disk Tools disk image files; one is for 68K Macs, the other for PowerPC Macs. You can use the image to make a floppy (as described in Chapter 4) so you have an emergency floppy on hand.

Think you'll *never* need a floppy startup? Hah! If you've got major SCSI woes, you won't be able to see your hard drive, the CD-ROM drive, *or* any Zip drive! Make that floppy now.

Formatting software. If you're not using an Apple drive, or you have an Apple drive but you used a different formatter on it, make sure you keep an updated version of the drive formatter handy. (Formatting software is covered in Chapter 4.) You never know when you might have to reformat the drive, or at least replace the driver software.

Norton Utilities

symantec.com

The Doctor is in. Norton Utilities ($100, Symantec) has long been both the first and last name in disk diagnostics and repair. At various spots in this chapter, you'll run across the phrase "run Norton's"; what that means is that you should run the Norton Disk Doctor portion of Norton Utilities. The Disk Doctor is used as both a preventative (fixing little disk problems before they become big ones) and a fixer (after things go south). The package includes the *really* handy UnErase utility to retrieve things that were accidentally erased, as well as the System Info utility that tests and reports on various system components. This is a must-have utility for any but the most casual of Mac users.

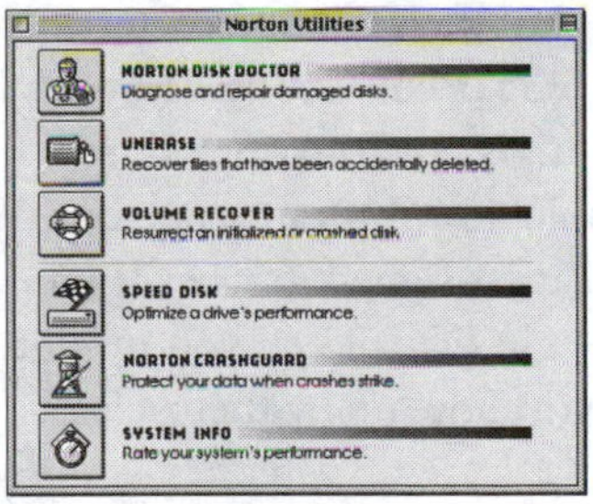

The little TechTool. The freeware TechTool from MicroMat started out as a one-trick pony: it let you rebuild the desktop file more completely than the ⌘ Option on startup trick could do. (That built-in option merely rebuilds the existing desktop files, which usually clears up desktop-file-based problems; TechTool erases the old desktop file completely, forcing a complete rebuild from scratch, which would solve a more deep-rooted desktop-file

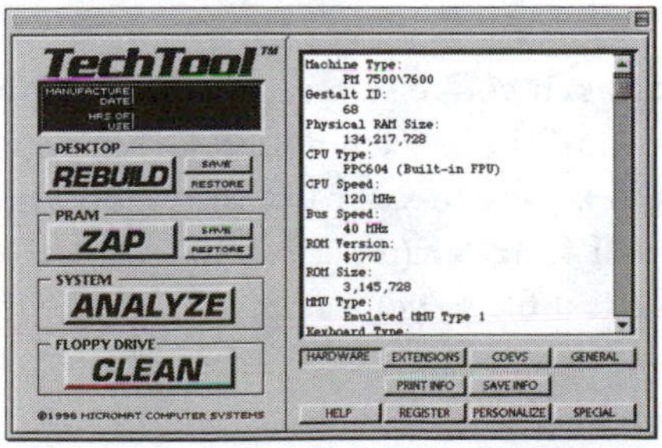

TechTool's basic screen.

problem.) The current version offers not only a better desktop rebuild, but also a more thorough PRAM zapping, as described in an earlier entry. You can also use it to poke around and get more information about your hardware than you'll know what to do with.

micromat.com

The big TechTool. Most software tends to bloat over time as its designers add more and more features. Usually this leads merely to "featuritis," a disease whose symptoms include useless features that require extra memory and disk space. But sometimes growth is good, as with TechTool's spawning of **TechTool Pro** ($150, MicroMat). This commercial product from the long-trusted makers of the freeware utility is going up against Norton's Utilities, offering disk diagnostics, repair, and recovery tools in addition to its very thorough hardware-probing utilities (*fourteen* different ways to test your modem!). It's too early to rate the product, but by the time you read this it will have been out for at least many months, and you can check the current reviews. I'm betting it'll be a winner.

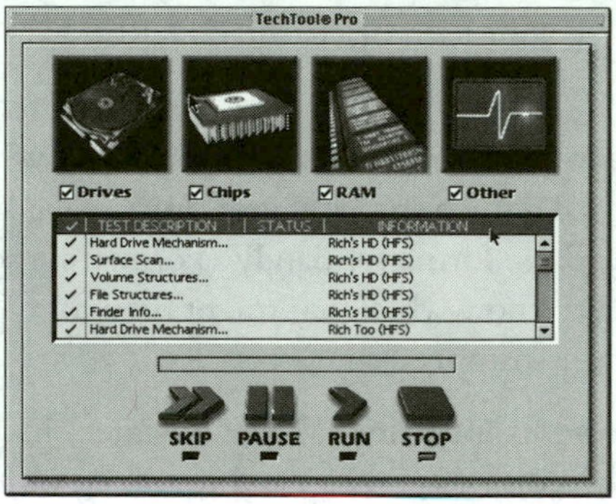

TechTool Pro provides many high-end testing options.

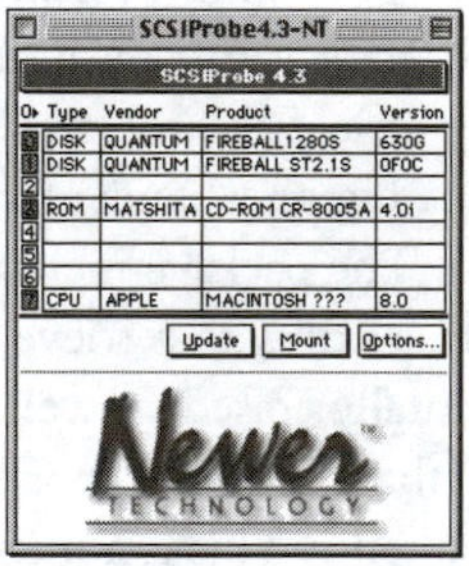

SCSIProbe. There may be no such thing as a free lunch, but there's still free, terrifically useful software. **SCSIProbe**, long a favorite Mac freeware program, is now distributed (still free) by Newer Technologies. You can scope out your SCSI bus and see what's assigned to what ID number, but it's main purpose in life is to let you mount SCSI devices that refuse to show up by themselves.

CanOpener

CanOpener. Abbott Systems' **CanOpener** ($65) is another utility that's been around a long time, and it can be invaluable in extracting text and pictures (and even sounds and movies) from damaged files that can't be opened by any application.

Save those keystrokes. If you're suffering from intermittent crashes, you may be saving your document every ten minutes—but you can do a lot of typing in ten minutes. A keystroke-saver like the Ghostwriter module in Casady & Greene's **Spell Catcher** (described in Chapter 16) keeps all your keystrokes in a separate text file so you can piece together that last ten minutes of typing.

Common System Problems

Crashes and Freezes

Freezes and crashes. There are two types of serious problems that bring your computer to a screeching halt. It's a *freeze* when everything is visible on the screen, but you can't do anything—the mouse cursor might still be moving (or not), but nothing responds to clicking or dragging. A *crash* is even worse; most of the time you'll get an apologetic dialog ("Sorry, a system error has occurred"), but you'll never be able to recover any of your unsaved work. Some really bad crashes skip the polite notice and just shut down or restart the computer by themselves. A crash is also known as a *bomb* because the dialog used to always have a bomb icon in it; it's also an umbrella term, so a freeze is a type of crash.

Thawing out. If your Mac freezes, it's often an application-based problem rather than a system-wide one. Although you'll lose your unsaved work in the application that freezes up, you should be able to get out of the freeze and save your other work. Here's what to do on a freeze:

- Wait a few minutes. I've waited out a few assumed freezes in some software applications only to find that the application was actually thinking *very sloooowly* for a minute or more, and everything returned to normal. (Microsoft Word, of course, was usually the application in question.)
- Double-check that the keyboard and mouse are plugged in correctly!
- If the Mac is truly frozen, force quit by pressing ⌘ Option Esc.
- Assuming the Force Quit worked and quit you out of the frozen program, save your work in other programs and restart the Mac.
- If the Force Quit doesn't work—either clicking the button froze the mouse, or the mouse wasn't working so you couldn't click the button to start with—you'll have to move on to the Reset (press ⌘ Control and Power), missing the chance of saving your work in other programs.

Avoiding the freeze. Continual freezes that don't seem to be limited to a single application can come from hardware or software problems, so it's difficult to make a definitive list of what to do to prevent them. Even the hardware causes are vague and/or complicated—like the wrong control panel setting for a newly installed card, or memory that's the wrong speed for an upgrade, and so on.

But, assuming you're having non-specific freezes and you haven't added anything new to your system, or otherwise changed system configurations (like memory allocations, or virtual memory) lately, here are some things you should try:

- Check for extension conflicts (especially, but not only if, the crash is during startup).
- Allocate more memory to the applications you're using.
- Get rid of the preferences files for the applications in which you freeze, and for the Finder and other system components like control panels.
- Check for SCSI problems (there's almost always activity on the SCSI bus, so random crashes can start there).
- Reinstall system software.
- Replace the hard drive's driver.

About error codes. When you get a system crash or an unexpected quit, you'll often find that the accompanying error message lists a code number (like "error Type 1"), and you may well wonder: What the heck does all of this mean?

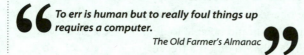

> *To err is human but to really foul things up requires a computer.*
>
> *The Old Farmer's Almanac*

More printer's ink has been wasted answering this question than any other troubleshooting question about the Macintosh. I've seen books devote dozens of pages listing the meaning of almost every imaginable error code number. The information in these tables typically isn't any easier to understand than the error codes themselves. And they almost never contain any useful advice as to what to do if you get a specific error. The plain truth is that these messages are meant to be used as guides to programmers who routinely get these messages while debugging their software; they have little usefulness for the rest of us. —TL

The improper shutdown message. There's nothing like adding insult to injury. Actually, the "improper shutdown" message is very much like adding insult to injury. If the Mac crashes and you have to reset it with ⌘ Option-Power, you may get the message shown here on restart. It's a little slap in the face when you know darn well how to shut down properly but the Mac didn't let you! Turn off the warning in the General Controls control panel (and don't worry—you don't have to use the Power key to shut down properly anyway; you can use the Finder's Shut Down command).

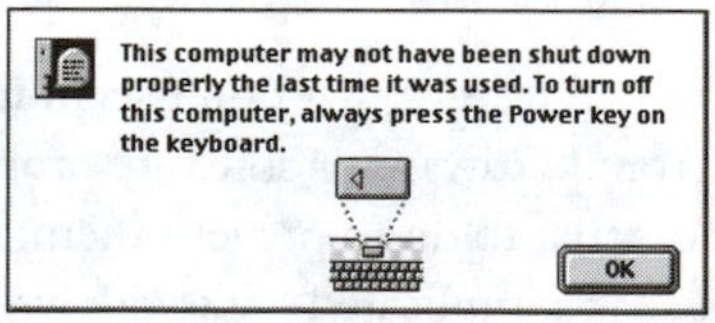

This computer may not have been shut down properly the last time it was used. To turn off this computer, always press the Power key on the keyboard.
OK

Check the trash. After a "bad" restart (from a forced quit or a reset), check your trash—you may find a Rescued Items folder in it. The files inside the folder are the temporary files an application makes while you're working; if the Mac crashes, the temporary files get dumped into the Rescued folder in the trash. Sometimes (though not often) you can open these files and recover some of the work you perhaps forgot to save before the crash.

Corrupted system software. Corrupted system software can cause intermittent system crashes. Unfortunately, continued crashes can cause system corruption. You may have actually fixed the original crashing problem (say, by getting rid of some bad preferences files) but you won't know it because now you're crashing from the corrupted system. Unfortunately, reinstalling the system software becomes part of many solutions no matter what the original problem.

The 5xxx and 6xxx crash problem. If your Mac is from the PowerMac or Performa 5200, 5300, 6200, or 6300 series and you're experiencing continual freezes, there's a special utility on your system CD that you should run. You'll find it in the CD's Utilities folder; it's called the 5xxx/6xxx Tester. You run the test, and if a message tells you a problem was found, you call Apple and they do a free repair. (Of course, your problem could be just software-based, in which case the Tester won't diagnose anything.) The 6360 model (PowerMac and Performa) is exempt from whatever problem seems to plague the others in the family.

At Startup

No sign of life. You should hear your Mac's startup chimes and hard drive running when you start up your Mac. You should also see the green power light come on. If you see no sign of life at all:

- Check if your power strip or surge protector is off.
- Try plugging your Mac into a different wall outlet.
- Check for disconnected or incorrectly connected cables to all components of your system.
- Consider swapping power cables to see if this helps your Mac start up.
- See if any other system components can start up separately (a monitor or external drive) to check the power situation.

Doing all this will help isolate whether the problem is just with your Mac (a bad motherboard, power supply, or hard drive), with your power connection (to the wall outlet or surge protector) or is perhaps not even a hardware problem at all. —LL

Dead battery, dead Mac. A totally dead Mac when you try to start up might be, for some models, due to the internal battery's having died (the one that keeps your PRAM alive, and also helps bring the Mac to life when you press the Power key). If your Mac seems to forget the time and date between shutdown and startup, the battery is probably at fault.

The blinking question mark. When you start up and get nothing but a disk icon with a blinking question mark in it, the Mac can't find a startup

disk—one with a good System Folder on it. Or, sometimes there's a minor or major problem with the disk that has the System Folder on it (rather than the problem being the System Folder itself).

- First, check the obvious: if the startup is an external volume, make sure it's connected properly and turned on.
- Try restarting the Mac by pressing ⌘ Control and the Power key.
- If that doesn't work, try to start the Mac with your system CD or an emergency startup disk. There shouldn't be a problem with the startup, but the question at that point is whether or not your hard drive will mount on the desktop after the Mac starts up.
- If the hard disk shows up, run Disk First Aid, update the hard disk driver, and reinstall the system software.
- If the hard disk doesn't show up, follow the suggestions later in the chapter to try to mount the drive, *then* fix the drive and its system folder.

The Sad Mac and the Chimes of Doom. If your Mac starts up (if it can be called a startup) with a dark screen, an unhappy Mac icon (known as the Sad Mac) and a scary-sounding chord (known as the Chimes of Doom), you've got *real* problems. Most Sad Macs are hardware problems, although some system software problems can cause them, too. On later models, you may stay at a blank screen instead of seeing the Sad Mac icon, and the sound, instead of a dark chord, is a cross between a car crash and breaking glass (*somebody* has a sick sense of humor). If you still can't start after zapping the PRAM and trying with extensions turned off:

- If you've recently installed new memory, cheer up: the problem is most likely a faulty installation (rather than faulty chips). Open the Mac, remove and then reseat the memory DIMMs or SIMMs and start again.
- Check all the SCSI cables and termination, and try again.
- Start up with the system CD or an emergency disk. If the system starts up, assume the problem is on the startup drive. Try reinstalling or updating the driver software; if that doesn't work, reinstall the system software.

68040 and CD startup. Talk about strange problems! If you try to start a 68040 Mac from a CD-ROM by holding down C at startup, or by using ⌘ Option Shift Delete to bypass the internal drive, it won't work if the CD-ROM drive is set to ID 5. (Internal CD-ROM drives are set to ID 3.) But you can start up from a CD by starting up with something else first and selecting the CD as the startup in the Startup Disk control panel, then restarting the Mac.

Choking on a partition-based startup. If your Mac is choking somewhere in the startup process, and you've set a drive *partition* as the startup device through the Startup Disk control panel, the problem might be that you forgot to set that partition to automatically mount at startup. Bypass the startup setting by using a startup disk or CD, or zapping the PRAM to reset the startup to the default internal hard drive. After that startup, use your drive formatting software to set the partition in question to automatically mount.

No HFS Plus startup for '040 Macs. OS 8 and its descendents won't run on any 68K Mac except for those with '040 chips, like Quadras. But an '040 machine can't start up from an Extended format drive, nor can they store virtual memory files on one. But when running OS 8.1, they can access other HFS Plus volumes.

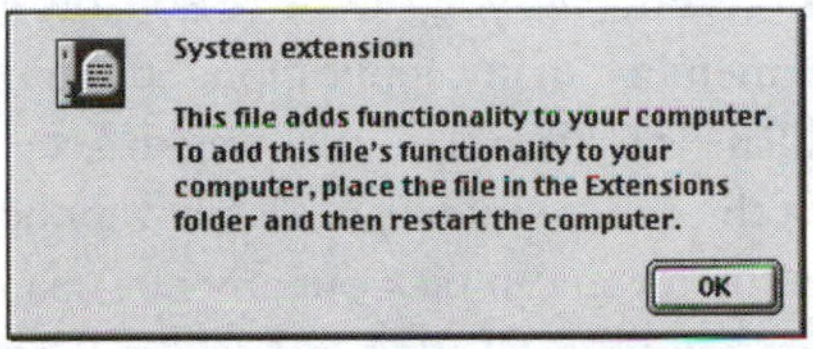

Not the startup folder. If you see this dialog at startup, you've mistakenly dragged a system extension into the Startup Items folder (inside the System Folder) instead of into the Extensions folder. It's the same dialog you get if you double-click on an extension icon.

The enabler startup screwup. Let's say that for some reason you have multiple devices attached to your Mac, and some have System Folders on them, but only one System Folder has the "right stuff": it has the enabler your Mac needs to start. If the Mac looks at another System Folder first (because of the rules about startup order), it won't keep looking for a usable System Folder: you'll get a dialog that says *This model Macintosh requires a newer version of the system software.* So, make sure that the disk that has the complete System Folder on it is the one that comes first in the startup order.

Flashing screen. On some Mac models at startup, the screen may flash, then go blank, and then come back on. This is normal in some situations; usually the video driver in ROM, which starts the monitor at first is being replaced by a newer on in the System Folder.

Another start-up freeze. If you've upgraded to OS 8 or its successors from System 7.x, you may still have the old Desktop Printing Extension in your Extensions folder. It's not only no longer necessary, it may cause freezes at startup.

Extension Conflicts

Extension conflicts. Extension conflicts are probably the biggest cause of problems on the Mac. Sometimes a single extension causes the problem because it conflicts with the system software; sometimes it's a combination of two or more extensions that, although they work by themselves, just can't get along with each other. The results of an extension conflict can be as obvious as a freeze during startup, or as mysterious as random freezes or crashes—or anything in between. (We're using "extensions" as a general term here, which includes control panels that load at startup.)

In one way, extension conflicts are easy to diagnose: if you can start up with extensions off (by holding down Shift at startup) and things are working fine, but things don't work when the extensions are loaded—that's it: it's an extension conflict. On the other hand, tracking down the culprit isn't always easy—especially when it's a combination of culprits rather than a single one.

The latest isn't the greatest. If you've added new software and then have what seems to be extension conflicts, you can be reasonably sure the newest software is the culprit; remember, many applications add items to the Extensions and Control Panels folders. The best way to keep track is to make sure that everything in both of those folders has a label applied to it before you install any new software; then, you can pick out any new extensions and control panels that were added during an installation by looking for unlabeled ones.

Oh say, it's the last one you can see. If you're freezing on startup, as the extension icons march across the screen, in all likelihood you have an extension conflict. And the problem extension is probably the last one that shows up on the screen before things grind to a halt—*or,* it's the one loading immediately *after* the last one you can see, and it just doesn't even make it to the screen.

You might not be able to identify the icon on the screen, but you can start up with extensions off (hold down Shift), and look in the Extensions and the Control Panels folders to find it. You can find the one that is probably loading after it by clicking on that last one you saw to select it, then pressing Tab to select the next icon alphabetically. With those two suspects collared, you can try some restarts with and without them to narrow down the problem.

Finding the culprit. If you're pretty sure you have an extension conflict, that's when the real fun begins, because you have to figure out just which one is the culprit. You'd think that, at worst, you could just try extensions one at a time and see when things break down, but that wouldn't necessarily find the problem. Extension conflicts can be much more subtle than that, because sometimes extensions that are no problem by themselves don't know how to play nicely with others; sometimes the conflict can be caused by a combination of, say, three specific extensions; sometimes it's "merely" a matter of which extension loads into memory before its rivals get there.

However, no matter how complicated things get, you *are* going to have do the extension shuffle, continually moving extensions in and out of the Extensions folder, the Control Panels folder, and the System Folder, restarting each time to see if things work.

The Extensions Manager that comes with your system software helps this process considerably, since you don't have to manually move things around. But the premiere utility for this operation is **Conflict Catcher** ($80, Casady & Greene), since it can do automatic shuffling, testing, and restarting. (It's described in Chapter 9.)

If you're going to do the job manually, remember that you don't have to test the extensions one at a time. Split them in half, and if things work, add half of the remaining ones, and so on, until the system starts crashing again.

Forcing the reorder. Sometimes extensions can work together as long as certain ones load before or after other ones. Extensions (and the extension component of control panels) load alphabetically, in three different groups: first come the items in the Extensions folder, then come those in the Control Panels folder, and finally the ones loose in the System Folder. By renaming or relocating an extension or control panel, you can change the loading order. (There's more about this in Chapter 9.)

Viruses

What's a virus? A virus is a computer program designed to sneak onto your hard drive as a separate file, or embed itself in another file, all behind your back. It might be as benign (though annoying) as something meant to put a happy face on the screen at random intervals, or as lethal as something meant to erase your hard drive. The term *virus* was settled on because the nasty little program copies itself from one place to another, "infecting" machines and files.

Viruses are not much of a problem in the Mac world, though there have been a few—just enough to warrant a few anti-virus programs being written. In fourteen years of heavy Mac use, I've only had to deal with one virus, picked up through a floppy disk used in a college computer lab. Your greatest exposure to viruses is in downloaded files from the internet or an online service, since you have little knowledge, and no control, over where the file's been before you get it. But, again, in all these years of online activity, I've never downloaded an infected file.

So, be aware of the problem, but don't sweat it. (And don't believe an "expert" or tech support person who "diagnoses" a problem with this answer: *It must be some sort of virus.)*

> ***"Here in Canada, we don't have nuclear weapons. We are not allowed to own guns. Not like in the United States, where people are nasty… Perhaps because I am a Canadian, I don't do nasty things."***
>
> *Creator of the first Mac virus (the "Peace" virus), in MacUser magazine interview.*

Diagnosing a virus. Unfortunately, your Mac won't start sneezing and coughing if it's infected, and a virus can cause a wide range of problems: simple or complex, application-specific or system-wide, benign or disastrous. But problems on a Mac are rarely caused by viruses, so that should never be your first assumption when you run into a problem that's not easily identifiable; extension conflicts and corrupted system software cause the most "mysterious" problems.

There are two ways to identify a virus problem: keeping in touch with the Mac community so that if a virus does show up, you'll know the symptoms; and running an anti-virus program to check for an infection.

symantec.com
drsolomons.com

Virus protection. The fight against viruses is a two-prong one: preventing infection, and "disinfecting" if the prevention hasn't worked. The premier protection utility is **Norton AntiVirus for the Mac** ($70, Symantec), formerly SAM—Symantec AntiVirus for the Mac; there are continual updates available at the web site. It checks any inserted disk, watches downloads and e-mailed files. In case something slips by, it works in the background or foreground to scour the drive for infected files. Terrific product, no doubt, but I've always had a copy around and never used it; I don't care for the constant scanning slowdown for a problem that's relatively rare. Also on the commercial end is **Virex** ($70, Dr. Solomon's Software), which sports most of the same features as Norton's, and a great interface.

Turn it off for installs. If you use a virus-protection program, make sure you turn it off before installing any new software. Virus protection running in the background (on-going protection can be provided only with an active extension) can interfere with the program's being installed correctly.

White title bars. If you install OS 8 and find that the title bars of windows are white, you may have the MBDF virus, one that's been around for about a decade—you just never realized it! Any virus program should be able to remove it.

When the worm turns. Just as we were laying out this chapter, a new Mac virus showed up—a special type known as a *worm*, and this one called the AutoStart 9805 worm. This self-replicating program will intermittently slow down your computer, cause a lot of disk access, and destroy some of your disk files, but it can attack only if Enable CD-ROM AutoPlay is turned on in the control panel (that's *not* the Enable Audio CD AutoPlay). Since few if any Mac CD-ROMs are set up to autoplay anyway, you have nothing to lose by turning this off.

Word macro viruses. When Microsoft Word first included WordBASIC as part of its features, it became possible to program a virus just for Word and its documents. One that quickly surfaced turned every Save into a Save As, and let you save documents only as templates instead of regular documents. (It's simple to write a macro that behaves like a virus because macros can be embedded in a document, activated on opening that document, and automatically transferred to Word's Normal template and from there to every document it opens.) Microsoft quickly jumped on the clever little virus—which surfaced on both Macs and PCs when Word 6 came out—offering a fix downloadable from its web site. A word to the wise.

Trash

Problems deleting fonts. If you're trying to delete a font file, the Mac may refuse to let you drag it out of the System Folder. If this happens, drag the entire Fonts folder out of the System Folder and restart. Now delete whatever fonts you want. Then return the Fonts folder to the System Folder, replacing the new one that was just created, and restart again.

When the trash won't empty. The Trash can is bulging, but when you go to empty it, it refuses to cooperate. Calling your local sanitation department won't help you. However, one of the following solutions is almost certain to fix this glitch.

- If the problem is that the file is simply locked, the Macintosh informs you of this when you try to delete it. It should also suggest the simplest solution: hold down Option when choosing the Empty Trash command.
- If a message says that the file/folder can't be deleted because there is not enough memory to complete the operation, just restart your Mac and try deleting again.
- If a message says that the file/folder can't be deleted because it is "in use," quit all your open applications and try deleting it again. Otherwise, restart and try again.
- Start up with another startup disk and try to delete the file.

Whether or not you finally succeed in deleting the file/folder, you may still have underlying corruption of your disk's *directory*, which is the underlying cause of the problem. Left alone, the problem may return or get worse. To fix things, run Disk First Aid from an emergency startup disk and make repairs as needed. If you have **Norton Disk Doctor** or **TechTool Pro**, use it, too. —TL

Miscellaneous

Date and time mistakes. Is your Mac all of a sudden telling you that it's 1904 or 1956? Has it lost all track of time, so that when you start it up its clock is wrong—even though you set it during the last work session when you noticed it was off?

There's an internal battery that keeps the date and time current when the Mac is off or even unplugged. It dies eventually, and can take the time and date with it. For most models, this is an easy fix (although you have to open the Mac case), and the battery can be purchased at a local Radio Shack store.

There are three different batteries. The oldest, compact, models use something that looks like a standard AA battery (but it's not); others use a half-AA battery (it's half-height) that's on the motherboard either in a little cage or secured by Velcro (or its generic equivalent). If you need more information—or a battery, try the *halfaa* web site.

halfaa.com

The molasses Finder. If things in the Finder are really slow—opening and closing windows, and copying things, for instance—try upping the Disk Cache in the Memory control panel. It comes set to only 96K, but if you click the Use Defaults button, it will jump to a size more in keeping with the total amount of physical RAM you have. Giving the cache 1.5 to 3 megs of memory speeds the Finder considerably, although you may find some compatibility problems between a high cache and Photoshop's virtual memory demands (as discussed in Chapter 13).

If it's just your desktop picture that's being slowly redrawn when you close a Finder window, you may be a little low on Finder memory. Switch to a pattern instead of a picture (with the Desktop Pictures control panel) to speed things up.

Mouse misery. When your mouse cursor behaves erratically, it could be a hardware or software problem.

- If the cursor jumps around, or moves in only one direction, the mouse probably needs cleaning.
- If the cursor doesn't move at all but the Mac responds to keyboard commands, check the connection from the mouse to the Mac or keyboard.
- If the cursor isn't moving at the correct speed, check the Mouse control panel settings; zapping the PRAM resets them to their defaults and you have to change them back.
- If the cursor is moving, and in the right directions, but just moving very slowly, that's probably because you attached the mouse cable after the Mac was up and running. Using the Mouse control panel won't help; you have to restart the Mac.
- For general mouse and cursor problems, try zapping the PRAM, which will reset the ADB ports.

Colors going crazy. If you quit from a game or kiddie CD, or sometimes from a graphics program like Photoshop, and you return to a desktop where the colors are all wrong (the inside of windows are dark blue or the menubar is green, say), the application you were using has probably adjusted the monitor settings behind your back, either changing the number of colors displayed (usually, down to 256 from a higher setting) or the "system palette" (the specific group of colors in use at any given time). Just open the Monitors & Sound control panel and reselect your usual setting to straighten things out.

Losing an alias link. When you use an alias for an item that's been deleted from a disk, you'll get a dialog telling you the original can't be found. This occasionally happens even when the original is still around; sometimes it's because you've rebuilt the desktop and some links broke, sometimes rebuilding the desktop *fixes* the broken links. (Hey, I only report the news.) In any case, don't panic, assuming that you've actually lost the original—use the Find command to track it down.

Generic icons. If some of your desktop icons have lost their individuality and reverted to their generic versions, try rebuilding the desktop. If this fixes everything, don't worry about it. But if it fixes only some of the icons, or the problem keeps coming back, it's time to run Disk First Aid and Norton's.

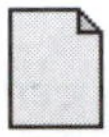
generic

Can't rename an icon. When you click on an icon's name but the editing rectangle doesn't appear, it's usually because the icon is locked (through its Info window)—locking a file keeps you from changing both the contents and the name. This applies to locked disks and to CDs, which are by definition locked from any changes.

The system also prevents some icons from being renamed—a shared volume on a network, for instance: just think of the mess it would cause if you tried renaming a disk or folder after it's already been mounted on someone else's desktop on a network! You don't actually have to be on a network to run into this little problem: if File Sharing is on (in the File Sharing control panel) and a disk or folder is set to be shared (with the Finder's Sharing command), you won't be able to change the icon's name.

Disks, Drives, and SCSI

Floppies

This is *so* a Macintosh disk! If you insert a floppy disk and the Mac says it is unreadable and offers you the option to initialize it, don't panic—and don't initialize it. As long as you don't erase the data on the disk, the odds are generally good that you can recover the data, even if the disk itself turns out to be unsalvageable.

- Eject the disk, slide the metal access shutter back and forth a few times, and reinsert it, two or three times. If the disk mounts, grab the files from it *immediately* and get rid of the floppy.
- Reinsert the disk while holding down ⌘ Option to rebuild its desktop.
- Eject the disk and try it in another Mac if you can. If another drive can read the data, copy the files to the hard drive and then to a new floppy.

- Maybe it's really not a Macintosh disk. Make sure PC Exchange is installed (and turned on) and try it again.
- The disk may really be damaged. Try running Disk First Aid and then inserting the floppy. Ditto with Norton's. If neither can read the disk, see if you can use Norton's disk copy utility to make a copy of the disk, which might be readable.

If you get unreadable-disk problems with many, many floppies, the problem is probably your drive, not the disks. —SZA/TL

Stuck on you. Since the dawn of Macintosh, there's been a special emergency-eject tool for stuck floppies, although it doesn't come with the Mac. A straightened paper clip pushed into the tiny hole near the floppy drive will mechanically eject a floppy that won't otherwise come out. You have to push the wire in straight, and apply quite a bit of pressure sometimes, but it usually works. (CD-ROM drives have the same emergency hole.)

It's possible that a *really* stuck floppy has a bent shutter (with, maybe, even the inner spring popped out) that's caught on the inner mechanism of the drive, and only dismantling the drive itself will get the floppy out.

The "minor repairs" offer. If you insert a disk and get a dialog that says something like: *This disk needs minor repairs. Do you want me to repair it?*, go ahead and click the OK button. If you don't, you won't be able to read the disk contents; if you do, the process won't erase anything on the disk.

Other floppy problems. If you get read or write errors with a floppy, do what you can to get your material off the disk, and then reformat it. If there's any trouble at all in formatting it, get rid of the disk—it's not worth the risk of losing information to save a few dimes' worth of media.

Hard Drives

Mounting a hard drive that won't. If your Mac won't start up normally, but you get it to start up with a system CD, emergency disk, or a second startup device, and then you don't see the internal hard drive on the desktop, there are two things you need to do: get that drive to mount and fix the drive so it behaves in the future.

First check for basic hardware problems: disconnect any external SCSI devices and see if the computer starts up normally. If that doesn't work, here are the procedures for mounting a reluctant drive:

- First, try, try again. Just try restarting a few times—from the reluctant drive or from another startup. Sometimes you'll get lucky (but don't assume you'll *stay* lucky, and find and fix the problem!).
- If you're working from a second startup disk and you have the SCSI Probe utility, use it to mount the drive.

- If SCSI Probe doesn't mount the drive, run Disk First Aid from the system CD or emergency startup (or from the second startup drive if you have one). Sometimes Disk First Aid can see the disk even if it's not mounted, and running the utility will mount and fix the drive.
- If Disk First Aid doesn't work, try using Norton's or TechTool Pro; they also can usually work on an unmounted drive.

After mounting a problem disk. Once a balky drive is mounted, you need to fix the problem that caused it. There are several reasons for a drive's refusing to show up on the desktop and/or serve as a startup drive, ranging from system software to driver software to hardware problems. If the non-mount is a single incident that wasn't preceded by other problems (like lots of system crashes), I usually just do the first two steps here. If it wasn't a single-incident problem, I do all four steps without even bothering to test in between to see if the disk is working better.

- Replace the drive's *driver*. If you forgot to update the driver when you updated your system software, this is most likely the problem and it should be the only thing you have to do to keep things working again. But sometimes the driver gets corrupted and has to be replaced, so run your disk formatting utility and replace it if you're having problems.
- Run Disk First Aid to fix any problems. If it reports problems found and fixed, you can assume things are okay and try working again without trying the other disk-fix operations. (The assumption might be wrong, of course.)
- Run Norton's Disk Doctor or TechTool Pro to take care of more serious disk problems.
- If it's the startup drive, reinstall the system software.

No startup, but mounts okay. If your internal hard drive won't serve as a startup disk but mounts without a problem when you use a different startup, the problem is most likely the system software, which needs to be reinstalled.

Rescue that information. If you've managed to mount a hard drive that earlier refused to show up, don't assume it will behave from then on. In fact, don't assume you'll *ever* be able to mount it again, and copy any important material to another disk *immediately,* while you still have access. Then you can attend to the drive itself.

Bypassing the internal drive. Sometimes a serious problem on the internal startup drive, like a corrupted driver, can keep the entire SCSI chain from working, which means you won't be able to start up with another device (except for, perhaps, an emergency floppy). You can make the Mac ignore the internal hard drive by holding down ⌘ Shift Option Delete at startup. If it starts from an alternative startup, you can try mounting the internal drive with SCSIProbe or just go ahead and use Disk First Aid or Norton's on it. Try replacing the driver as soon as you can access the drive.

Recovering erased files. When you empty the trash, your file isn't actually erased from the disk. Instead, the *disk directory*, which serves as a table of contents for the disk, is altered. The sectors in which your document were stored (they can be scattered all over the disk) are marked as available for reuse. But the information is still there, just waiting for the right utility to extract it. Norton Utilities and TechTool Pro both have modules that recover "erased" files from disks; sometimes part, but not all, of a document can be recovered.

To maximize your changes of file recovery, don't put *anything* on the disk, because it might over-write the sectors holding the "erased" file. Now is not the time to install Norton's on your drive! Don't even work on existing documents, because editing them can make them larger, and they might be stored in those marked-for-reuse sectors where your old document lived.

Just don't do *anything* until you recover the file. One person I know did almost everything right when he realized he had mistakenly erased a large folder of important files. He didn't use his Mac at all; he went out and bought Norton's. He didn't install it on his drive; he ran it from the CD. But when he first launched it, it told him there wasn't enough memory, so he turned on Virtual Memory. Which wiped out some 20 megs of his drive for the virtual memory file—including, of course, the files he was trying to recover.

Tip within a tip: I've occasionally received a "zero percent" chance of recovering report from Norton's UnErase and told it to try anyway—and it worked. So don't give up until the really bitter end.

The really dead end. Sometimes a drive is misbehaving so badly or so often that there's nothing you can do to fix it other than totally reformat it, wiping out its contents and starting again.

If you're lucky, the reformatting will be in response to continual problems that may have wreaked havoc but that didn't kill the drive or make it unmountable. Because that means that you'll be able to get all your data off it before you erase it with Drive Setup (for Apple drives) or the formatter that came with the drive.

Files replaced by a strange document. An Extended format disk can be read only by OS 8.1 and later. Hook up an HFS Plus disk to an earlier system, and you won't be able to get at its contents. All you'll see is a single file named—well, you can see in this picture what it's named. It's a SimpleText document that explains to the uninitiated (that's not you, since you've been initiated here) that the disk can be read by OS 8.1 and later systems.

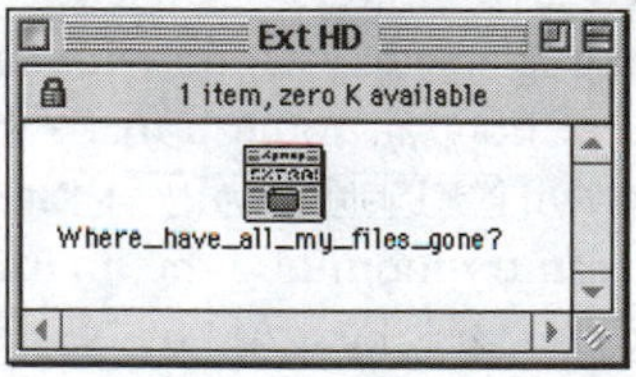

Heavy-duty recovery. When your corporate records—or maybe those personal records the IRS wants to see—have been erased or are on a dead drive, and you can't do anything, look into a data recovery service like DriveSavers. Professional recovery is expensive, with a charge per meg of drive space (not per meg of data recovered), but sometimes it's worth every penny.

drivesavers.com

IN THE BEGINNING

I've known about, and written about DriveSavers for many years. Once, when doing some research for a magazine article, I was talking to the owner of the company. I made an offhand remark about the significance of their phone number (800-444-1904) to Macophiles and was met with first a moment of silence, then laughter and congratulations. It seems that the number, with its significant final four digits, was chosen on purpose, and a little prize put aside for the first person who noticed and commented upon it. In several years of business, I was the first to say anything! I soon received a DriveSavers mug filled with—what else—Life Savers.

SCSI Chains

SCSI symptoms. SCSI-chain problems can cause everything from preventing startup to random crashes while you're working to problems saving and opening files to… well, here's a list of some problems that may indicate you've got SCSI woes ("disk/drive" in this list refers to any SCSI volume):

- The icon of a drive doesn't show up on the desktop.
- The icon of a disk shows up intermittently on the desktop.
- You get multiple icons for the same drive on the desktop (and you haven't created partitions!).
- The Mac refuses to start up at all, displaying either the Sad Mac on a dark screen, playing the Chimes of Doom, or not getting past the blinking question mark icon.
- The Mac crashes at startup, or soon thereafter, or unexpectedly during use, especially when trying to access an external device.
- The Mac starts up, with or without some problems, but the desktop and its contents blink out and back on again repeatedly.
- There are continual read-write errors with a SCSI device.

Basic SCSI trouble-shooting. When you suspect a SCSI problem, it's time to do some detective work. If things go wrong after adding a new device to the chain, you've at least got a starting place although you still won't know if it's a conflict with another device, something wrong with the new item, or "just" a cabling problem. Here are some things to try:

- Make sure all the SCSI devices in the chain are turned on.

- Detach all external SCSI devices to see if the problem goes away.
- If you have more than one device on the chain, test each device alone with the Mac to make sure each works.
- Check the ID numbers on each device.
- Swap the order of the devices in the chain. (Strange, but true: sometimes a different order works even with all the same devices, cables, and termination.)
- Double-check the termination of each device—you may have something in the middle of the chain that's internally terminated.
- Add or remove terminators, even if you're already following the basic termination rule of one at the beginning and one at the end of the chain. Keep in mind that the terminator device itself might be defective.

apstech.com

- Get an active terminator like **SCSI Sentry** from APS (described in Chapter 4.)
- Remove and reattach all the cables, in case one wasn't seated properly the first time. (Do this with all devices *off*.)
- Replace or swap cables to test that each cable you're using is working properly. Check that all the pins in the connectors are straight and clean. (Minor oxidation on connectors can be rubbed off with a pencil eraser.)
- Change the way cables go in and out of the devices: if the "in" cable is in the top port, put it in the bottom, and put the "out" cable or the terminator in the top port. (Strange, but it has made a difference for some people!).
- Try to shorten the overall length of the SCSI chain by using shorter cables from one device to another.

It might be the driver. There are times when all symptoms seem to point to a SCSI problem when, in fact, it's the hard drive's driver that's at fault. This is a simple fix, so you should try it before spending too much time playing with SCSI cables.

Removables

Removable drivers on the disks. Just as a hard disk needs a driver installed in order for it to mount on the desktop, so does a removable disk; the removable's driver is installed when you format the disk. Occasionally you'll find an old removable disk or cartridge with a driver that's much older than the mounting software or the system software expects to find. Sometimes that means the disk just won't show up on the desktop. But you can usually mount it either with something like SCSIProbe or with the utility that came with your removable drive; the drive utility can also usually update the driver on the disk.

After-mount. If you insert a removable disk and it doesn't show up on the desktop, you may be missing the proper extension, or the extension might be incompatible with the system software you're using. Several utilities can mount SCSI-device disks after they've been inserted, but you can't beat the free **SCSIProbe**.

Auto-mounting removable media. If you don't have the right driver for a removable disk to be mounted on your desktop, and you don't have a utility for after-the-fact mounting, restart the Mac with the disk already in the drive—it will be mounted like any other SCSI disk. You'll have to shut down the Mac to remove the disk.

Applications and Documents

Applications

Stay up-to-date. Some software-based problems aren't due to buggy software, but to incompatibilities between older programs and newer system software (or vice versa). It's never a good idea to update the minute new software comes out, but you'll have to update your programs and system software in tandem sometimes in order to keep things running smoothly. So, keep track of application updates by checking with the manufacturer's web site occasionally. And, if you register your product when you get it, you'll probably get a direct notice about updates and bug fixes.

Who ya gonna call? If you have a problem with a specific program and you are in desperate need of immediate help, call the vendor's technical support line. You'll find the number somewhere in the documentation that came with your software. But before you call, make sure you read through the manual to see if the problem is a known one, and then check their web site to see if the problem has already been addressed there.

If you are not in a panic for an immediate answer (which may not be so immediate anyway, as many technical support lines are notorious for keeping you on hold indefinitely), your software's documentation probably lists online locations where you can leave messages or check for technical support tips. User-supported Mac forums and newsgroups are also a good place to leave requests for help. —SZA/TL

Not enough memory? Sometimes when you try to launch a program you'll get a dialog telling you there's not enough memory for it. You might occasionally get a message while you're in an application that there's not enough memory to complete a procedure. Neither of these messages is necessarily accurate: you may indeed have plenty of memory but it's just not available to the application at the time. Chapter 13 covers all these issues in the Memory for Applications section.

Unexpected quits. When a program "unexpectedly quits," you usually get a dialog from the Finder telling you so. But you'll already know, because you'll have been working along and all of a sudden, the program—and the document you were working on—disappears. Sometimes there's not even a dialog waiting for you in the Finder.

First, quit all other applications and restart your Mac. An unexpected quit leaves everything else in an unstable condition, and you don't want to lose any more work. Next, allocate more memory to the application in its Get Info dialog (detailed in Chapter 13) and try again.

While most unexpected quits come from low-memory situations, other culprits include extensions conflicts, clashes between old and new applications and system software, and corrupted preferences files.

IN THE BEGINNING

Legend has it that the first bug was a true bug, a moth that blocked a relay switch in a Harvard Mark II computer. But that's the only legend. There's a logbook which was for years on display at the Naval Surface Warfare Center with an entry dated September 9, 1945: *"Relay #70 Panel F (moth) in relay. First actual case of bug being found."* It's obvious that from the wording that the word *bug* for computer glitch was already in use. The unfortunate moth was, by the way, taped to the logbook.

And, one more legend-buster: the bug wasn't discovered by Admiral Grace Hopper, the developer of the COBOL language—she just liked telling the story a lot and so it became associated with her.

Houston, we have a problem. If you're merrily working along and suddenly get out-of-memory messages inside your application, here's what to do: SAVE! Right away. If you have multiple documents open, save the most important one first. Then close the documents and quit the program; launch it again when you can give it more memory. (See the "Houston" entry in Chapter 13 for further suggestions about saving documents whose lives are in danger because of an out-of-memory problem in an application.)

When a program doesn't work. There are dozens of explanations for why a program, or some features in a program, won't work the way they're supposed to—or at all. The problems can range from freezing or automatically quitting on launch to frequent crashes (especially when trying to use a particular feature) to problems opening, saving, or printing documents. There are three major problem areas, so try any or all of these:

- Allocate more memory to the program (covered in Chapter 13).
- Trash the preferences file that belongs to the application or utility: you'll find it in the Preferences folder inside the System Folder, or in an application-specific folder inside the Preferences folder.
- Start with extensions off (except any that are crucial to the running of the program) to see if the program runs without extensions that might be clashing with it.

Documents

No application available. If you have to open a document for which you don't have the parent application, there are several thing you can try:

- Drag and drop it directly on the application icon of another application that might be able to open that type of file.
- Launch a related program and try to open the document from within the application.
- See if a related application has an Import command that can open the document.
- Make sure your MacLink Plus software (included with your system software) is installed and running, and see if it can translate the document.
- If you need some elements in the document, try CanOpener to extract the text or pictures.

Application, but not found. If you double-click on a document and get an "Application not found" message, but you *know* you have the application, try dragging the document icon onto the application icon to open it, or try running the application and opening the document from inside the application. Then use Save As to save a copy of the problem document and throw the first copy away.

If you have continual problems with erroneous "Application not found" messages, it's more likely a system problem than a document problem. Rebuild the desktop; if that doesn't help, run Disk First Aid. If you still have the problem, bring out the heavy artillery—Norton's or TechTool Pro—and give the drive a once-over.

Wrong version of the application opening. When you update an application, double-clicking on its older documents should open the newer version of the application. If you get the old one opening (or, if you've trashed the older one and *nothing* opens), try rebuilding the desktop.

Of course, when we started laying out this book, I ran into the opposite problem: double-clicking on a Quark 4 document launched Quark 3, which then told me it couldn't open that version of a document! Nothing fixed that weird problem. Since I didn't want to get rid of Quark 3 yet, I stuffed it so that the Mac wouldn't know it was still around, and now double-clicking on Quark documents opens Quark 4.

Corrupted files. If you get a dire dialog when you try to open a document—that the file is corrupted or damaged or that a disk error has occurred, don't despair. You might still be able to save the contents of the file. Try any or all of these:

- Make a copy of the file by duplicating it on the desktop or by dragging it to another disk, and try to open the copy.
- Copy the file to another disk and try opening it from there.
- If you couldn't open the document by double-clicking on it, try launching the application first and using its Open command.
- Open the file in another application that can handle its file type.
- Use a utility like Norton's Disk Doctor to try to recover the file.
- Assume it's a disk problem rather than a document problem, and run Disk First Aid, or Norton's Disk Doctor; then try opening the document again.

Another corrupted-file problem. Sometimes a document opens but continually causes problems—refusing to print, or freezing the Mac when you try and scroll the document. This kind of problem usually boils down to one of three things: an embedded, corrupted graphic; a font problem (either corruption or missing); or, in Word, some kind of bogus style sheet definition. As the computer gods would have it, the only document corruption I ran into while working on this books was *this* chapter! The chapter started out with material extracted from the Quark files from the last edition and a zillion notes I had made while working on other chapters. I worked exclusively in Word's outline view, in both Word 6 and Word 98 when it came out, until it was time to actually pull the chapter together. Then, I found that if I scrolled toward the end of the chapter in a normal view, or in a completely expanded outline view, the computer would freeze. Repeatedly. (It was a corrupted graphic pasted in towards the end; all my backup copies had the same problem.)

When you have some internal corruption in a document (so you can open it but just can't manipulate it) and you can't just redo it from scratch, here's some things to try:

- Try and pinpoint the area of the document that's the problem. If you always get a PostScript printing error on page 10 of your PageMaker document, it's probably an element on that page. Delete the elements one at a time, or try moving them to the pasteboard, and see which one's keeping you from printing (or whatever).

- Do a Save As from within the application and see if the new file works.
- If the application provides an Export command, see how much of the document you can export.
- Try copying out chunks of document into a new, blank document. Divide it up into pieces, save each piece as a separate document, and see which documents behave and which one doesn't. Then break up the problem document into smaller pieces, and so on, until you've isolated the problem.
- If you suspect it's some weird formatting problem—like a Word style sheet—do a Select All and apply a single style to everything.
- Try extracting the important parts of the document with a utility like CanOpener, and put the document back together again.

Printing

When the printer won't behave. When your printer mysteriously refuses to cough up your output, or doesn't provide the usual options, the fault almost always lies with the Macintosh, not with the printer.

- Check the Chooser, and select your printer icon. If your printer doesn't show up:
  - Check that the printer is on.
  - Check all the printer cables: disconnect and reconnect them.
  - Make sure you have the printer driver software in the Extensions folder.
- Give a LaserWriter time to warm up after you turn it on.
- Check the setting in the AppleTalk control panel: should you have Printer Port, Modem Port, or Ethernet selected?
- If you're using PrinterShare to print to a non-network printer that's attached to another Mac, make sure that the host Mac is on.
- For LaserWriters, find and trash the LaserWriter Prefs file from the Preferences folder.
- If you're running with extensions off, you won't be able to use many of the special features of desktop printers (you'll see an X through the desktop printer icon).
- Zap the PRAM to reset the serial ports (and, after restarting, re-choose the printer in the Chooser).
- Try reinstalling your printing software.

—SZA/TL/HN

The AWOL desktop printer icon. If you find that, after you set up your printer through Chooser, there's no little icon next to the printer name and there's still no desktop printer appearing, there are several possible explanations:

- You're using a printer that doesn't support desktop printing.

- You haven't installed all the necessary printing software; there are several extensions needed besides the printer driver. Install printing software either from your system CD or from the disks that came with your printer (whichever is more recent).
- The correct software is installed, but you have certain extensions turned off.
- You didn't answer the OS setup questions for the assistant that ran automatically after you installed the system. Networked printers like the LaserWriter are very fussy under OS 8, and I've found that in some instances, unless you complete the information through the Setup Assistant, the Mac refuses to create a desktop printer—even if you manually set all the control panels that the Assistant seems to alter. You can run the OS Setup Assistant again without reinstalling it, since it's placed on your hard drive when you install the system.

Thanks for the memory. Some repeated printing problems, especially for larger or more complicated documents, might be due to a lack of thinking room for the desktop printer's Print Monitor. Do a Get Info on the desktop printer icon and allocate more memory to it. I found this solved some occasional freezing problems when pressing ⌘ Option Esc for a forced quit from an application that I thought was frozen actually brought up a dialog that asked if I really wanted to quit the Desktop PrintMonitor.

Allocate more memory to the desktop printer to avoid general printing problems.

PostScript errors. PostScript errors while printing are almost always due to either some corruption in the document or lack of memory in the printer.

If you think it's the document, you have to figure out where the problem is by printing only a little of the document at a time (if you can). Sometimes the problem is a corrupted font, sometimes it's a problem with an EPS graphic placed in a layout—and sometimes it's a corrupted font that's embedded in the EPS graphic! Working with a piece of the document at a time (say, a page at a time in a multi-page layout) should help narrow down the problem.

For memory problems, printing part of the document at a time is also a solution (which leads, of course, to some problems in diagnosing the problem!), as is using fewer fonts on a page. Memory is cheap, so it pays to fill your printer with more memory just as a matter of course.

The non-PostScript PostScript error. My LaserWriter 12/640 continually reports a PostScript error on the screen when the only "problem" is that it's out of paper; refilling the drawer makes the dialog go away.

Time out! If your PostScript printer bows out of a print job with a "timeout" error (-8993) when printing multiple copies of large or complex documents, try printing either one copy at a time, or select Foreground Printing in the Print dialog (in the Background Printing section) .

Missing printer drivers after OS install. When you do a clean install of OS 8, you may find there's no icon for your older StyleWriter printer in the Chooser. Use the StyleWriter 1500 driver for a StyleWriter, StyleWriter II, or StyleWriter 1200. Use the Color StyleWriter 2500 driver for any Color StyleWriter. If you have a non-Apple printer, reinstall its printer software from the original disks or drag it over from your old System Folder. (Check with the printer manufacturer to see if there's an update to coordinate with new system software.)

Lib is missing. If your Mac refuses to print and gives you a dialog saying that something-or-other *Lib* is missing (that's short for *library,* and there are several extensions with *lib* in their names), you'll probably find that the "missing" file is, indeed, in your extensions folder. Restarting the Mac usually solves the confusion.

Switch-printing. If you move back and forth between a LocalTalk network printing device and a serial printer, you might have trouble accessing the serial printer after turning off AppleTalk. You'll have to restart the Mac to get at it.

Paper jams from multipurpose tray. If your paper continually jams when being fed from the multipurpose tray, you might have the wrong paper size specified in the Page Setup dialog. For a LaserWriter 8500, you should leave the access door open to avoid misfeeds from the multipurpose tray.

Light bands on laser prints. Even though toner cartridges look light-tight, they're not. Stuffing them back into their light-proof shipping bags when you take them out of the printer temporarily will prevent damage to the photoelectric drum inside. Once overexposed to light, the cartridge may start showing one or more bands of overly light printing across the page, caused by exposure lines on the drum. All you can do then is buy a replacement. —BW

Problems with printing Finder windows. The HP DeskWriter's printing software won't let you print a Finder window or the desktop (using the Finder's Print Window command) without a freeze or crash. Check with HP for an updated driver sooner or later. (Maybe.)

25

Facts and Fun

In This Chapter

Reference Works

In General

The computer advantage. The advantage of quick searches through tons of material puts computer-based reference works miles ahead of their paper-bound counterparts. Some CD-based references rely on this fast-search capability alone to get you to switch from the volume on your bookshelf, while others take more advantage of the medium, bringing words and concepts to life with graphics and animations. And a CD-based multimedia dictionary can not only pronounce words for you, it can let you look up words you don't even know, based on what's in the definition (like looking for the word for a twelve-sided figure by using *twelve sides* as the search term)!

Some CD tips. If you use reference CDs frequently (or plan to), there are several points you should keep in mind—only some of which the CD's documentation or ReadMe file will bother to tell you.

- Most multimedia CDs need the monitor set to 256 colors; you may get "out of memory" errors or crashing otherwise. Most change the monitor settings automatically, usually letting you know about it first; most also forget to set it back to thousands or millions afterward, so you'll have to do it manually through the Monitors & Sound control panel.
- Some multimedia titles need Virtual Memory turned off in the Memory control panel.
- Most programs on CDs create and maintain a Prefs file in your Preferences folder (inside the System Folder); if you don't use a CD any more, you can get rid of the Prefs file.
- Many multimedia titles have Install programs on the CD that put all sorts of things on your hard drive. Most of the installers aren't all that smart: they often, for instance, replace a newer system file (like a QuickTime extension) that's on your drive with the older one that's on the CD. Whenever possible, use the "Custom" option in an installer and disable the older extension installation; sometimes you can skip the installation completely if you already have the extensions you need. Here's what a typical installation for a multimedia CD might drop in your System Folder:
  - QuickTime extension
  - QuickTime PowerPlug extension (needed only for PowerPC Macs)
  - Sound Manager extension
  - QuickTime Musical Instruments extension
  - Special fonts that the program uses for display

Lots of reference CDs require that you copy some portion of the program to your hard drive and run it from there, although you'll still need the CD; the main program, which runs much faster when it's on your hard drive, then accesses information on the CD.

The .com table. There are so many companies mentioned in this chapter, and so many of them are mentioned several times, that there was no use sticking a web icon in the margin for every one, every time. So here's a table of the companies mentioned in the chapter, and their URLs.

The .com Table

Berkeley Systems	berksys.com	Learning Tech	learntech.com
Broderbund	broderbund.com	LucasArts	lucasarts.com
Bungie	bungie.com	Macally	macally.com
Casady & Greene	casadyg.com	MacPlay	macplay.com
CH Products	chproducts.com	Maxis	maxis.com
Davidson	davd.com	MECC	mecc.com
DK Multimedia	dkonline.com	Microsoft	microsoft.com
Edmark	edmark.com	Mindscape	mindscape.com
Eidos Interactive	eidos.com	MultiEducator	multieducator.com
Graphic Simulations	graphsim.com	Parsoft	parsoft.com
Grolier Electronic Publishing	grolier.com	Simon & Schuster	simonandschuster.com
GT Interactive	gtinteractive.com	Softkey	softkey.com
Harper Collins	harpercollins.com	The Learning Company	learningco.com
InterPlay	interplay.com	ThrustMaster	thrustmaster.com
Knowledge Adventure	jumpstart.com		

Encyclopedias, Etc.

Grolier Multimedia Encyclopedia

Grolier Multimedia Encyclopedia. From the minute you launch the **Grolier Multimedia Encyclopedia** ($35 standard, $50 deluxe, Grolier Electronic Publishing), you know you're looking at something that was designed for the computer. You can choose from six basic types of information presentation (Articles, Gallery, Atlas, Timelines, Guided Tours, and Interactivities); a pop-up menu provides subcategories for each. When you're viewing information, it's easy to move to related topics because all you have to do is click on a tab like Picture, Media List, or Related Articles. Although the setup encourages you to browse, finding specific information in the more than 35,000 entries is made easy by a good search engine and a filter option that lets you browse through materials within a certain subject area.

The "multimedia" part of the encyclopedia is its extensive support in the way of photographs and music clips, and a few well-done animations. Printed reference material seems almost archaic when you look up the entry on "animation" and then get a movie to see how it's done, or check on skeletons and see how a ball and socket joint moves.

The world according to Microsoft. It's hard to love an encyclopedia that lists *Microsoft Windows* as the first, default topic when you look up *computer*, but I was willing to give **Microsoft Encarta** ($80) a chance, anyway. Encarta finds a good balance between breadth and depth for a general encyclopedia, although it needs more memory and disk space than any other CD reference. And while I'd like to be enthusiastic about the wealth of material included, it's difficult to get past what is, finally, a terrible interface. I'm not condemning it because it has a Windows look and feel, although it is hard for a dyed-in-the-wool Mac person to work with that inelegant approach; the real problem is the hard-to-read screen font, and lines of text that are cut off at the top, bottom, and even sides as you scroll through it.

But **Microsoft Bookshelf** ($50), a compendium that comprises a great collection of reference tools, including an encyclopedia, dictionary, thesaurus, almanac, atlas, and a book of quotes is a terrific product. Everything's easy to find; the interface, though Windows-inspired, is easy to work with; and, although each edition is labeled with a year (Bookshelf '98, for instance), only the "year in review" section is time-sensitive. The whole package strikes a good balance in the breadth-versus-depth dilemma and deserves a spot in any home with school-age children.

The Complete National Geographic

National Geographic. National Geographic magazine, as a cultural icon, has two traditions associated with it: adolescent boys looking through the issue for pictures of bare-breasted females, and subscribers saving years' worth of back issues for reference. Well, cable TV and the web has no doubt made the first custom obsolete; and Mindscape has made the second unnecessary.

The **Complete National Geographic** ($175, Mindscape) is every single issue of the magazine—from the very first one (in 1888!)—on a collection of 30 CDs. The equivalent of 185,000 pages of text (thank goodness for the Search feature) includes all the articles that have fascinated millions of people over the more than 100 years of publication. And, since it's the *Complete* magazine, you get all the product advertisements, too. It would be a perfect package if it weren't for the fact that every time you launch the program you're "treated" to a full-fledged TV-style commercial for a certain brand of film. (Tip: click to stop the ad in its tracks). Despite the tacky opening, it's wonderful addition to any home library.

Back talk. The **American Heritage Talking Dictionary** ($30, Softkey) answers the question I've had about other computer-based dictionaries: Why should we have to figure out those arcane pronunciation symbols when we're using a computer? And it answers the question out loud—because this dictionary, true to its name, does indeed speak more than a third of its 200,000 entries. It provides links to similar words and synonyms, and includes lots of pictures and a sprinkling of QuickTime movies. The main dictionary resides on your hard drive for speed (it comes in both 68K and PowerPC versions), while the multimedia elements stay on the CD for space reasons; you don't need the CD to run the basic dictionary. Like any good dictionary, this one includes place names and biographical data; extras include a word-hunt feature using wildcards for when you don't know the proper spelling of the word you're looking for, and an anagram maker.

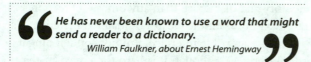

> **"*He has never been known to use a word that might send a reader to a dictionary.*"**
> *William Faulkner, about Ernest Hemingway*

Science and So On.

The Way Things Work

The Way Things Work. David Macaulay's wonderful book **The Way Things Work** ($40, DK Multimedia) has lost nothing in the transliteration to CD—in fact, it has gained a little (if that's at all possible). This volume is a guide to "machines, inventions, and technology" suitable for a wide range of ages (from about ten years on up). There's a wealth of wonderfully illustrated diagrams for items from dishwashers to telescopes; there are lots of links between related items and you'll find an animated sequence every time you need one.

A.D.A.M. and Eve. Mindscape's anatomy primer, **A.D.A.M. The Inside Story** ($30), is suitable for students in junior or senior high school, or any family member who's curious about the structure of the human body. While most of the program merely identifies components of various systems (like skin, organs, and skeletal), it also includes four hours' worth of video and animation demonstrating many bodily processes. Looking up information about a specific body part is frustrating, and sometimes fruitless: the organization of the program is very hierarchical (you have to move up and down through topic branches instead of directly where you want to go), and sometimes there just isn't the depth of information you're looking for. But it's a captivating piece of work that invites exploration by anyone even mildly interested in anatomy. With the configurable body on the screen—you can choose male or female, or white, black, Asian, or Hispanic features and skin tone—these packages are both anatomically and politically correct.

The **Nine Month Miracle** ($20), however, is a disappointing effort that covers conception, pregnancy, and childbirth from a myriad of directions, resulting in a choppy presentation of facts, figures, pictures, and video. To view a developing fetus, for instance, you have to suffer through a "family album" with a sappy scenario of a couple expecting their first baby; there's a section for each month, and to get to the good part, you have to listen to boring, stilted dialog first. There's lots of information here, and even a section for very young children, but even the most advanced of medical information is often buried in a package suitable for a junior-high sex ed class.

Encyclopedia of Nature. The Eyewitness series of encyclopedias (the printed version) has always been a staple at my house, and I've added to the collection over a period of years. I was skeptical about these excellent volumes being translated well onto CD, but, based on the **Eyewitness Encyclopedia of Nature** disk ($35, DK Multimedia), the computer series is even better than the paper versions. The graphics are crisp and clean, and the interface is intuitive, designed so that you can delve deeper into the subject at hand or go off in a tangent exploration. All the text can be spoken aloud if you wish, and there's a selection of movie clips that demonstrate things like jellyfish locomotion. Other volumes in the series include **History of the World** and **Encyclopedia of Science**, and **Children's Encyclopedia**. DK has also started a Virtual Reality line (cats, dinosaurs, and so on), where you can wander around a "museum" looking at exhibits and go off on special side trips (like a dinosaur dig).

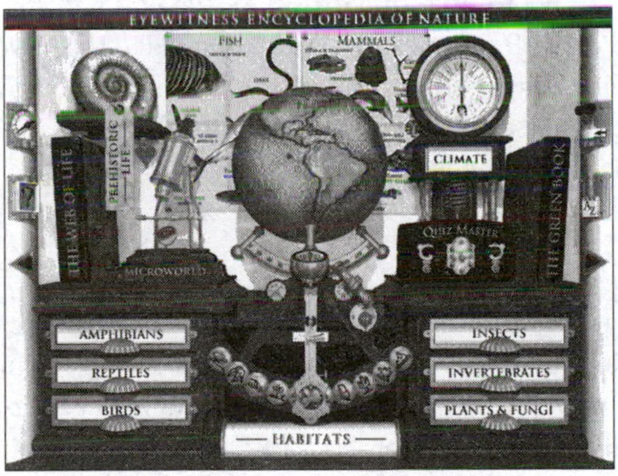

The inviting opening screen of the Eyewitness disc has the same feel as the book series of the same name.

On Evolution. After years (oh, all right, *decades)* of being a Stephen Jay Gould fan, I finally know what he looks and sounds like because 's "expanded book" **On Evolution and Natural History** ($40) includes a QuickTime video of one of his lectures, along with the complete text of one of his essay collections, *Bully for the Brontosaurus.* In addition, the CD boasts the illustrated text of Darwin's *Origin of the Species* and *The Voyage of the Beagle*. If you need to research this subject or these texts, the Find function and the links between them would certainly be helpful. But if you're reading for enjoyment, I recommend the traditional paper copy, and a comfortable chair.

Music and Poetry

Musical voyages. Learning Tech's Voyager line of CD Companions are HyperCard stacks that let you listen to an entire composition as a text commentary scrolls by; you can click to bring up a glossary of music terms and theory, or to read about the life of the composer. Titles ($40–$60) in the series include **Ludwig van Beethoven: Symphony No. 9, Igor Stravinsky: The Rite of Spring, Antonin Dvorák: Symphony No: 9 "From the New World"** and **Franz Schubert: The Trout Quintet**. The three titles in the **So I've Heard** series ($15 each) are designed to be music samplers, offering you commentary and sound clips from an array of composers. **Volume 1: Bach and Before** takes you from the music of ancient Greek rituals to Bach; **Volume 2: The Classical Ideal** is an earful of the work of 18th century composers such as Mozart and Haydn; and **Volume 3: Beethoven and Beyond** explores Beethoven's impact on the classical music scene.

The great thing about all of the offerings is their interface: You'll find the screens easy-to-read, punctuated with elegant illustrations, and designed with search tools and icons that make it a pleasure to explore the topic at hand. —CG

Poetry. For literary commentary in an interesting and interactive form, check out Learning Tech's **Poetry in Motion** ($20), a CD-ROM with audio, graphics, and over 90 minutes of QuickTime video that gives 18 modern poets (including Allen Ginsberg, William S. Burroughs, and Tom Waits) a chance to recite/perform their work and comment on it (interviews with some of the authors are also included). —CG

Pop Culture

People. What could be more representative of pop culture than Learning Tech's **People: 20 Years of Pop Culture** ($20) from People magazine? It provides plenty of low- to mid-brow fun through its twenty years of cover stories as well as diversions like Face-To-Face (with like-minded covers morphing into one another. This certainly isn't a must-have for your reference library, but it's fun and would make a good gift, too.

The fab four. Even a die-hard Beatle fan who spent her adolescent years in love with John Lennon can't find Learning Tech's **A Hard Day's Night** ($30) particularly enjoyable. You get a tiny QuickTime window that plays the entire movie while you can read through some mildly interesting but overblown commentary (it states, for instance, that the opening of the movie was as cinematically ground-breaking as that of "2001: A Space Odyssey"). Yes, you can read the script of the movie, and play around with its QuickTime controls, and pick up fascinating little tidbits, but there's just not enough here to keep you at your computer. If you want a trip down memory lane, or into rock and roll history, rent the movie.

A home run. Get yourself some peanuts and Cracker Jacks to go with **Baseball's Greatest Hits** ($30, Learning Tech), an enjoyable collection of well-presented player and game stats, photos, sound bites, video clips of disappointing quality, and, of course, a trivia challenge. You won't find anything on Cal Ripkin's record-breaking game streak because the most recent "footage" is of Joe Carter's game-clinching three-run homer for the Blue Jays in the '93 World Series, but baseball nuts seem to prefer their facts and trivia slightly aged. I'm not a big baseball fan, but I've raised one, and he'll be happy with this CD for a long time anyway.

Comics as history and art. If you think of Superman when you think of comics, or if Archie and Veronica are more comic book characters than Internet buzzwords for you, you may be disappointed in **Comic Book Confidential** ($30, Learning Tech). Some of the most famous comics—published as books or in newspapers—are never mentioned here, presumably because of copyright and permission problems. But even if you don't know or care about many of the comics covered here, you'll still find some of the accompanying information utterly fascinating—like the Congressional hearings in the fifties that "proved" the link between comic books and juvenile delinquency (I think it was a separate commission that proved the link between juvenile delinquency and rock-and-roll). Although you could wish for wider coverage, what's here is enjoyable and well-presented. —RW

Kids and Computers

Issues and Equipment

Where to put the computer. Not many families buy a computer *just* for the kids, and even fewer buy separate ones for them. So, most setups are centrally located in a family room or living room where everyone can access it.

But if you do have a "kids" computer, I'm adamantly against putting a computer in a child's room (I wouldn't put a TV in there, either). I prefer to draw my kids out of their rooms rather than give them more excuses to shut their doors on the rest of the family, especially since they became teenagers. For the youngest children, you'll want the computer more centrally located, anyway, since they both need help and always want to share the experience ("Look, mom!") anyway.

QUIET!! To have kids, software, and sanity all at the same time, you need earphones; standard Walkman-style work just fine. When you've heard "Find the letter A" in a cloying tone for the umpteenth time, or had to listen to preschool background music for hours on end, you'll be glad to spend a few dollars on sound insulation. (You'll also appreciate it if you have older kids, or a spouse, who's into noisy games.)

How old is old enough? I'm not suggesting that if a child doesn't start early enough on a computer, he'll forever lag behind his peers educationally. Nor am I recommending that you get a computer specifically for a young child. But if you have, or you're getting, a Mac, and you happen to also have a child, you'll find that most three-year-olds have the motor skills necessary for pointing and clicking, and the cognitive skills to know that what they're doing with the mouse is affecting what's happening on the screen. Two-and-a-half isn't too early to let them play with the simplest of programs; although purposefully maneuvering a mouse and using its button is beyond many two-year-olds, most can be taught to press one key at a time to get some feedback from the screen.

The care and not feeding of a computer. The computer area should be taboo for certain combinations—like kids and food, or kids and drink. The potential problem with liquids is probably obvious, but cookie crumbs can sift down into the keyboard, too. The youngest kids need to be taught that while the computer is something you can play on, it is *not* a toy, and needs to be treated gently—the same way you might teach a young one to press piano keys one at a time and not just bang away at it.

Educational, shmeducational. Hey, for a four-year-old, *everything* is educational. So, although there's educational software covered later in this chapter—things that foster specific learning skills or cover particular subject areas for young children—don't get hung up on educational software just because you're embarrassed to admit you're letting a preschooler *play* on a $2500 machine. There's nothing wrong with playing; in fact, psychologists will tell you that playing is a child's job.

Data protection. Because few families can afford multiple computers, it's important to keep your grown-up stuff from being messed up by the youngsters in the family. For older kids, it's a simple matter of designating some folders off-limits. But for the younger ones, who behind your back might accidentally move from a program to the desktop, and then have fun dragging lots of little pictures into the cute little garbage can, you need to set up a "fire wall" (as it's called in big business). There are several approaches, with different levels of security:

- If your child isn't an explorer, setting up the Launcher control panel with her program icons in it, and keeping other desktop folders closed, is probably sufficient protection against software accidents.
- Use the General Controls control panel settings to lock the System Folder and your Applications folder when the kids use the machine. You

can even store your documents inside a subfolder in the Applications folder to protect them.

- Turn on the Simple Finder option in the Finder's Preferences dialog (through the Edit menu). This gets rids of all keyboard equivalents for menu commands.
- Edmark's **KidDesk** ($25) is a Finder replacement. You can choose from several desk styles; each comes with a collection of useful little gadgets like a calendar, note pad, and calculator—and even a private mail system that sends messages to the desks of other family members! Application icons appear on the desk surface, and the only way to access the real desktop is through a password.

Creating and using aliases

Chapter 7

Ejecting CDs. Even young kids catch on quickly—before you know it, they'll be clicking their way out of a program and getting the CD out of the drive. But if they do it incorrectly, leaving the ghost icon of the CD on the desktop, they'll be asked to insert the CD at annoying intervals. First, make sure your child knows how to quit out of every program—"officially," not just by clicking on the exposed desktop if it's available. Next, set up a way to eject the CD properly. Unfortunately, one of the "proper" ways is to drag it to the Trash—not a habit you want the little ones to get into. So, make an alias of the Trash, change its icon to something more appropriate, and teach the kids to use it for ejecting CDs. (See Chapter 7 for more information about creating and using aliases.)

Spit It Out!

Make an alias of the Trash and edit its icon to create a CD-eject icon.

Creativity and Fun

Kid Pix. From a black-and-white shareware program to a full-color multi-activity CD, **Kid Pix Studio Deluxe** ($30, Broderbund) has come a long way—and it's a must-have for ages three to twelve. Activities include a fun paint program that uses tools that have plenty of weird options and make strange noises, a puppet show where pressing different keys makes various body parts move, and a stamp-your-own scene builder where the stamps are animated. This will hold any child's interest for a very long time.

Creative writing. Children can make up stories and illustrate them with MECC's **Storybook Weaver** ($45) and **My Own Stories** ($35 each). The programs provide elementary word processing and hundreds of images and background scenes, as well as dozens of sounds. Storybook Weaver draws its images (knights, trolls, treasure chests) from folklore; My Own Stories offers contemporary symbols (shopping malls, Frisbees, fire trucks). —CS

Ye Olde Print Shoppe. The **Print Shop Publishing Suite** ($50, Broderbund) is a classic that keeps growing in capabilities. Create and print greeting cards, posters, calendars, certificates—just about anything, within a simple interface. This CD version includes more than 20,000 pieces of clip art and a few dozen fonts, too. Terrific—and not just for kids, either.

Child labor? Davidson's **Kid Works Deluxe** ($30) is mildly disappointing but still worthwhile. Write your story on one side, illustrate it on the other, occasionally using "stickers" instead of words. It's a confusing design for the younger end of the four-to-nine target age range; the stickers, for instance, are presented in small groups and you have to open a sticker book to change the group. For the older half of the recommended age range, this program is very close to being very good.

All aboard! Each title in the **Imagination Express** series ($20 each, Edmark) provides a theme (ocean, neighborhood, castle, and so on) and related pictures and information for a child to write a story about. The approach is wonderful, but far too complicated for the lower half of the recommended Kindergarten-through-eighth-grade range. It would be great in a classroom where a project could be worked on over a period of months, but probably wouldn't work very well at home.

Thinkin' Things. Edmark offers three **Thinkin' Things Collections**, numbered 1 through 3 for age groups three to seven, six to eleven, and eight to thirteen. They're all terrific CDs that offer four or five interesting activities that foster such important learning areas as critical thinking skills, memory, problem solving, logic, and spatial dexterity. Sounds like heavy-duty stuff, but the kids will never notice because they'll be enjoying themselves too much. The programs are $25-$40; but if you have more than one kid to please, the $50 **Thinkin' Things 3CD Gold Collection** is the way to go.

Animaniacs. Whether or not your kids are familiar with Warner Bros.' Animaniacs cartoon characters, they can enjoy the **Animaniacs Game Pack** ($20, Davidson), a collection of five simple but interest-holding games in a wacky but nonviolent environment (in Smoocher, you help Dot blow kisses at the bad guys to knock them down). Fine for seven through preteen (although my mid- and late-teen sons admit they still like the silliness of the games).

For the Youngest

Living Books. The interactive storybooks from Broderbund ($20–$35) are terrific for the young set (from 2 to 7 years). You can choose between "read to me" and "interactive" modes; in the latter, the words on each page are read, but then you can click on something on the page to get some sound, music, and animation, or just click to go to the next page. Each package comes with a paperback version of the book,

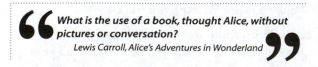

> ***"What is the use of a book, thought Alice, without pictures or conversation?"***
>
> *Lewis Carroll, Alice's Adventures in Wonderland*

Dr. Seuss's ABC's, of course.

for that all-important cuddle-time reading. The line includes Dr. Seuss titles like **The Cat in the Hat** and **Dr. Seuss' ABC's**, selections from the ever-popular **Berenstain Bears**, and miscellaneous titles like **Arthur's Birthday**, **Harry and The Haunted House**, and **The Tortoise and the Hare**. The best way to get started, though, is with the **Three For Me Library Volume 1** ($40), which includes Sheila Rae, the Brave and two of the best-ever storybooks: Just Grandma and Me (with Little Critter, and with the best click-on-it animation in any storybook), and Mercer Meyer's Little Monster at School.

Three For Me

Fisher-Price. Cross one of the most trusted names in young children's toys with one of the most trusted names in children's software, and you get Davidson's Fisher-Price collection (about $20 a title), aimed at children as young as 18 months old.

Wild Western Town (ages 3-7) provides seven different activities within the western theme. So, for instance, you can make a Wanted poster by selecting from a wide variety of features (as well as odds and ends like fishing poles, bugs, and frames), or try to match a guest with his belongings at the hotel's front desk. There's a confusing "background" game going on the whole time, with gold bars hidden around and Bandit Bob lurking in the shadows, but few children will be able or willing to keep track of that when they're playing the other games. Getting from one spot to another can be mildly frustrating, but the individual activities are charming and will keep the kids busy for a long time.

Build a wanted poster from the hundreds of parts available.

Pirate Ship (ages 4-8) takes the same approach as Wild Western Town: a generous handful of separate activities with a background game (looking for the pieces of the lost treasure map). Instead of the Wanted poster, you get to build a ship in a bottle from various pieces. In the most amusing section, you get to fire items from a canon: any item you see in the picture, including, say, the chicken sitting on the barrel. You can aim the canon and adjust the force of the shot by how far you pull back the plunger.

The **Little People's Discovery Farm** is recommended for ages 18 months to 3 years. (I cringe a little at software for babies. But there's nothing wrong with it; what is wrong is the notion that it's *necessary!)* This is an utterly charming package with four activities: matching the baby animals with their mothers, feeding the animals, growing things in the garden, and a version of Old MacDonald where you get to click on the animal who will be in the song (and do the singing). If you insist on getting software for the youngest member of the family, this is the one to get.

Educational Software

The most important educational tool. Do yourself a favor: Learn to type! No more hunt-and-peck, no matter how fast: Do it the right way and everything's faster, from word processing to e-mail. And as soon as the kids' hands are big enough, make them learn touch-typing, too. There are lots of packages out there, and some are even aimed at kids:

- **Typing Tutor** ($30, Simon & Schuster)
- **Mario Teaches Typing II** ($35, InterPlay)
- **Mavis Beacon Teaches Typing** ($40, Mindscape) and **Mavis Beacon Teaches Typing for Kids** ($20)
- **Jumpstart Typing** (for kids: $30, Knowledge Adventure)

A subtle learning tool. The perfect educational tool on the Mac is one that's never claimed to be one: **Spell Catcher** from Casady & Greene. This interactive spelling checker, described in detail in Chapter 16, watches as you type and immediately alerts you to a misspelled word. You can backspace and retype, or press a key and get a list of suggestions as to the correct spelling. (Not that there's a question as to how to spell each word, but there might be a question as to just what that word was supposed to be: Type *accomodate* and you'll get *accommodate,* type *mispell* and you'll get *misspell*—but type *ontoward* and you'll have to choose from *untoward, on toward,* and *onto ward.)*

While Spell Catcher is meant as a writer's tool, it's the perfect spelling teacher for kids. From an educational point of view, there's nothing better than immediate feedback—and Spell Catcher's menubar flash or beep is instant. If your child spells something incorrectly, she can try again by backspacing to the mistake in the word and typing again from there or by double-clicking to select the word and then retyping it. After a second try, or if she's stymied the first time around, she can open the Spell Catcher window that displays both the misspelled version and the correct one—exactly what an attentive, patient teacher would do in the same circumstances.

Reading and math skills. If you want to give your child some extra experience in two of the three "R's":

The Learning Company's Reader Rabbit was one of the first educational games on the Mac; it has been continually upgraded and improved. Now on CD, **Reader Rabbit Deluxe 1** (ages three to six), **2** (ages five to eight), and **3** (ages six to nine) concentrate on building reading skills with simple but colorful and fun activities. Even within each package ($35 each), you can set the skill level that's appropriate for your child—and change it as your child grows. So, a three-year-old can play Word Train concentrating on sounds that words begin with, but a year later can work with ending sounds, or even vowel sounds in the middle. You can't go wrong with this series. And, as with most rabbits, this one has multiplied. There are **Reader Rabbit Math** titles, grade titles (**Preschool**, **Kindergarten**, **1st grade**, **2nd Grade**), **Reader Rabbit's Interactive Reading Journey**, **Math Journey**, and more, ranging in prices from $25 to $40 dollars.

The only thing more prolific than rabbit software is Davidson's Blaster series, one of the longest-running educational titles around. It all started with Math Blaster, an arcade shoot-'em-up takeoff. Now there are **Math Blasters** for three different age groups (encompassing 4- to 12-year-olds), for **Pre-Algebra**, **Algebra**, and **Geometry**, as well as Blaster math mysteries and **Math Blaster Jr**.; most are $30, from Davidson. There's a **Reading Blaster Jr**. program ($40), too, and a **Kindergarten Blaster 3CD Set** ($45) that covers math, reading, and science basics.

Knowledge Adventure started with three titles in its **Jump Start** series: **Preschool**, **Kindergarten**, and (predictably) **First Grade.** Each offers a collection of activities that help develop necessary learning skills, starting with counting, letter and number recognition, shape identification, and the concepts of "same" and "different." By the time you're in the First Grade package, you've progressed to science concepts, language arts basics, and telling time. But, as with the aforementioned rabbits, the line has multiplied, adding packages at both ends: through **Fifth Grade** at this point, and down through **Pre-K**, **Preschool**, and, yes, even **Jumpstart Baby**. Along the way are some specialized math packages (like **Jump Start Second Grade Math**). Most packages are $30.

Davidson's **Kid Phonics** and **Kid Phonics 2** ($35 each) provide practice in basic reading skills through clever and interesting games like the Silent Letter Stagecoach and the Homonym Hotel. We could quibble about some of the choices made for the target audience of six to nine years (most wouldn't be able to recognize *mail* and *room,* and *night* and *stick*, as words that make compound words together), but in all they're terrific packages.

Math for the Real World

In **Math for the Real World** ($30, Davidson), you and your band are traveling around the country playing gigs, accumulating money for a studio session that will let you hit the big time. Along the way, you have to answer questions and solve puzzles based on math skills—all the while keeping track of your gas gauge and food supply. While it's not exactly the real world (at least we can hope not, for the 10-and-up target audience), it's an engaging combination of work and play.

Geography and Social Studies. Can your child sing the classic "Don't know much about history, don't know much geography," and *mean* it?

The software program that spawned a TV Series—Broderbund's **Where in the World is Carmen Sandiego?**—also includes titles that take Carmen (and your kids) to Europe, through the USA, and even space. You learn about geography and history as you track Carmen and her band of thieves. You have to collect enough clues to get an arrest warrant and find the suspect, using information offered by witnesses and informants. If you find that the suspect stole something from Francisco Pizarro, you'd have to travel to 16th century Peru—and if you didn't just happen to know that, you'd be able to look it up in the standard reference book that comes with the software. (Depending on the package, you might get a paperback edition of the *World Almanac and Book of Facts, Fodor's U.S.A.* travel guide, the *New American Desk Encyclopedia*, or *What Happened When*.) Titles are about $35 each. And, for the jealous younger sibling, there's **Carmen Sandiego, Junior Detective** ($30), a program aimed at five-to-eight year-olds with minimal or no reading skills. A "case" is in a single country, the clues are all visual, and there's plenty of on-line help at hand.

MECC has taken to heart the saying: "The journey is the reward." The company offers educational games for ages 10 to adult in which players "travel" a route packed with adventures, information, and colorful characters. In **The Oregon Trail** ($45), players follow the covered wagon route pioneers trekked in 1848 from Missouri to Oregon's Willamette Valley. After "stocking up" on supplies, they head west, dealing with difficulties such as river crossings and wagon breakdowns as well as day-to-day decisions like how much food to consume. Players can stop along the way to trade, buy supplies, or hunt. It's top-notch edutainment, with geographical and historical information skillfully interwoven throughout. **The Amazon Trail** ($35) is a canoe trek up the Amazon River. The scenario: A mysterious disease has afflicted a hidden Inca village and a secret medicinal plant hidden in the rainforest is the villagers' only hope for salvation. You must find the plant and then the people, along the way stocking up on other items the Inca king might desire. The trip weaves in and out of time, allowing the traveler to meet up with explorers, scientists, and others who shaped the development of the Amazon. The color animations are absolutely stunning, and digitized photographs and speech and authentic South American music provide nice touches of realism.

Grolier's **How Would You Survive?** ($35) is a superb package based on the book of the same name. While the title might imply some sort of action adventure, it actually covers the daily life of three ancient cultures: Aztec, Egyptian, and Viking. You can see how women were treated, what children did, what kinds of food were eaten, and what monetary system was used. You can explore a single culture in depth, or go back and forth and compare certain facets of each society. There's no built-in game here, but that's no drawback; it's a wonderful reference book brought to life that will fascinate the ten-to-fourteen age group.

How Would You Survive isn't a game of survival, but a cultural living experience.

MultiEducator puts out a series of history CDs that focus on different periods and areas. **American History** is without a doubt the ugliest piece of software I've ever seen. It looks as if it had been designed by a ten-year-old (and one without any taste, at that); it's also rife with typos and grammatical errors. It's impossible to get past these factors to learn anything from the actual content of the CD. **World History: 20th Century** has a different design, but it's no better. It's amateurish, hard to read, and, overall, a very bad experience. **Civil War: America's Epic Struggle** is only a slight improvement over the others—if you don't mind glaring red text on a bright blue tweed background (which is better than the areas where there's blue text on blue background!), and buttons and lists that aren't aligned. But it's just as well that you can't quite read it, because if you could, you'd find things like "Dredd-Scott Decision," with its egregious double D and hyphen. If the graphics, design, and spelling in an educational product are so poor, how could you possibly depend on the quality of its content?

Who Built America? ($40, Learning Tech's Voyager line) is a thoughtfully designed CD-ROM put together by the American Social History Project. It explores, through words and pictures, the people and events that shaped U.S. history from 1876 to 1914. With its background audio and stylized photographs, this presentation has the look and feel of a PBS documentary—a good one. —SZA/MT/CS/CG

Science and Nature. Most science and natrue packages are aimed at the junior and senior high schoolers.

The blurb on **The Cartoon Guide to Physics** ($20, Harper Collins) says it's for "anyone with a passing interest in physics—or with an interest in passing physics." That pretty much sums up the attitude of this fun yet mildly educational CD. The title itself might ring a bell, since cartoonist Larry Gonick has been at this on paper in the pages of *Discover* and other magazines for years. I could do without the guide, Lucy, doin' her rap thing during some explanations, but she's easy enough to ignore. Oh, and in case you don't think about physics much—or much about physics—don't forget that its rules keep planes up, and roller coasters going, and apples falling on people's heads; it's not just dry formulas. Through interesting interactivities where, for instance, you get to set the starting point and initial force of a ball in a winding tube, you get a feeling for how potential and kinetic energy work in a roller coaster.

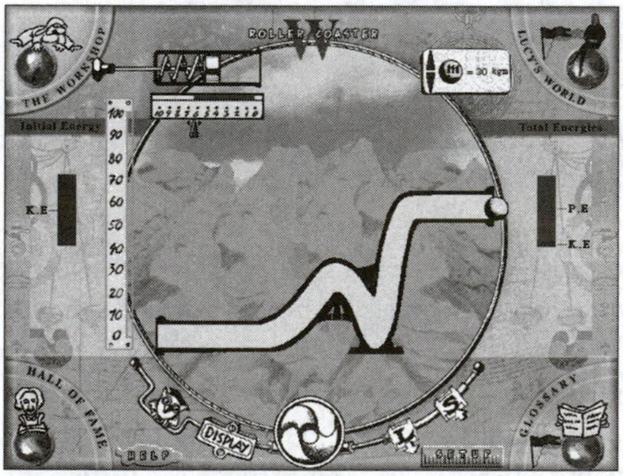

You can play with a roller-coaster tube in ***The Cartoon Guide to Physics****, but you're really learning about kinetic and potential energy.*

The **Eyewitness Encyclopedia of Space and the Universe** ($35, DK Multimedia) covers space exploration and technology, and the solar system and beyond, from several different angles. Whether you're exploring the moons of Jupiter or the rings of Saturn, reviewing the Apollo moon shots or checking out Russian space history, this software keeps you interested with succinct descriptions and fascinating graphics. And when you think you've absorbed enough information, you can play QuizMaster, where you can choose the number of questions, the categories, and the time limit—and play by yourself or against an opponent.

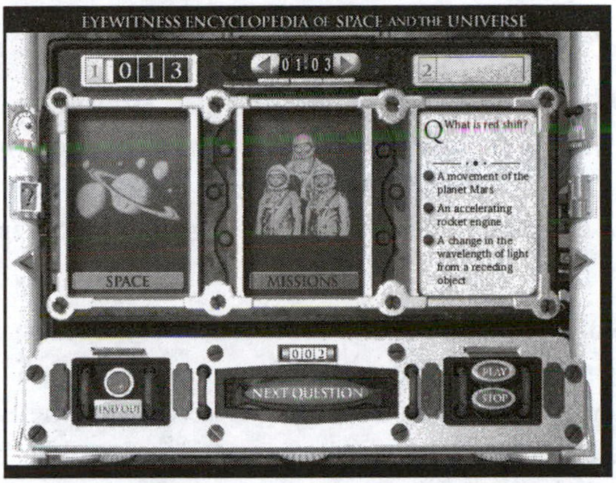

Do you know the answer?

Douglas Adams, an author best known for his Hitchhiker's Guide to the Galaxy books, teamed with naturalist photographer Mark Carwardine to write a terrific environmentalist book called **Last Chance to See.** The software version is also terrific (Learning Tech, $40), offering a sobering view of the species disappearing from earth. Make sure you check out "Dr. Sutherland" from the Sidebars menu. The interview with this poison-snake expert, who says he developed his snake bite kits so that people would stop interrupting his gardening, is a stitch. When asked what to do when bitten by a deadly snake, he replies: "Well, what do you think you do? You die, of course. That's what *deadly* means."

Testing, 1, 2, 3, Testing... Practice may not always make perfect, but it can certainly make you better. For those standardized tests that get us to various educational stages—the SATs, GREs, GMATs, and so on—a little practice can boost the score just enough to make a difference—often as much as 100 points. Many companies provide test-practice software for your highschooler to practice those SAT questions, or for grad school wannabes, including:

- **Personal Trainer** series (**ACT**, **SAT**, and **GRE**; $40 each), Davidson
- **SAT I** ($20, Cliffs Studyware)
- **Score Builder for the SAT/ACT** ($40, The Learning Company)
- **Higher Score on SAT, ACT, and PSAT** ($20, $30 for deluxe version, Kaplan/Simon & Schuster) and **Higher Score on GRE, GMAT, and LSAT.**
- **Inside the SAT and ACT Deluxe** ($35, Mindscape/Princeton Review)

—RW

The Game Room

Arcade and Action Games

Prince of Persia I and II. Ever since the days of Dark Castle—a wonderful game effort from Silicon Beach, who brought us SuperPaint to move beyond the beautiful, but limited world of MacPaint—Mac gamers have shown a proclivity for catapulting their digital alter egos off high perches and across deep chasms.

The **Prince of Persia CD Collection** ($20, Broderbund), which includes both the original game and its sequel, is a superior example of the run 'n' jump genre. You'll find yourself gasping as you propel the Prince across seemingly impassable voids and through apparently impossible situations. —SZA/CB

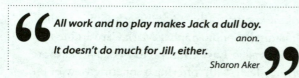

> *All work and no play makes Jack a dull boy.*
> *anon.*
> *It doesn't do much for Jill, either.*
> *Sharon Aker*

Another kind of toy story. Breaking out of the computer-game world of senseless violence with **Power Pete** ($20, MacPlay), the cuddliest arcade game going. You're Power Pete, a battery-operated protagonist stuck in a toy store full of evil teddy bears, gingerbread men, heinous cavemen, and nasty little candies that want nothing more than to drain your batteries. Although this game contains some elements of violence, it is restricted to toothpaste guns and exploding birthday cakes. All in all, it's a great deal of fun. —SZA/BF

Dark forces in a doomed marathon. When it comes to first-person perspective shoot-'em-ups—and it often does—there are some outstanding packages that became instant classics when they were released.

- The big daddy of this genre is Bungie's **Marathon**, which uses high-res graphics and smooth 3-D scrolling to produce fantastic gameplay. There are several in the series: **Marathon 2** (which excels in network gaming, $20), **Marathon Infinity** ($40), and a **Trilogy** ($45).
- The classic **Doom** is generally unavailable, but its follow-ups **Doom II** ($15, GT Interactive), **Ultimate Doom** ($40), and **Final Doom** ($50) have the same engrossing and hyperkinetic action, as well as the same particularly violent and disturbing themes.
- All the awesome technical achievements of the Doom titles are featured in **Dark Forces** ($20, LucasArts) and **Jedi Knight: Dark Forces II** ($50) but the violence is kept at a more acceptable level, consistent with the Star Wars movies. Speaking of Star Wars, LucasArts also has **Rebel Assault** ($25) and **Rebel Assault II** ($20), games that blur the line between game and interactive movie. —SZA/BF

ShadowWraith. The best top-down view shoot-'em-up—by a mile—is **ShadowWraith** ($10, StarPlay Productions). It includes ultracrisp graphics, speedy gameplay, and a CD-quality (audio CD, that is) soundtrack. ShadowWraith also comes bundled with **Souls in the System**, a networkable game, for $40. —SZA/BF

Simulations

Sim City 2000. Maxis has—and probably always will—dominated the sim genre of gaming. The crowning achievement is **Sim City 2000** ($30), which allows you to micromanage a city literally from the ground up. Dealing with the complexities of supplying housing, power, and water will pale in comparison to the headache you'll get with your first bona fide earthquake. Additional "scenarios" are available for about $12 each. **Sim Farm, Sim Tower, Sim Earth, Sim Isle, Sim Town** and **Sim Ant** offer up varying levels of sim gaming, though none of these games have been able to capture the glory of the flagship products Sim City ($20) and Sim City 2000. —SZA/BF

Pinball wizards. I have a pinball machine in my family room, and there's nothing like the physical, analog pleasure of a real game. Well, actually, there is something *like* it: pinball simulation games have been around for quite a while. And while none will have you thinking you're Tommy or even Elton John, they're a pleasure to play. StarPlay's Mac classics are **Crystal Caliburn** and **Loony Labyrinth** ($30 each); either will keep you enthralled for hours at a time and let you do everything but tilt the table.

Flight Unlimited. Modern computers have brought the average person incredibly close to the realities of flight. From a World War II dogfight to an imaginary mission in an A-10 Warthog, today's flight simulators offer a spectacular experience. If going for a casual flight in a private plane without the worries of getting shot down is more your speed, then check out **Flight Unlimited II** ($30, Eidos Interactive). This flight enthusiast's nirvana includes multiple aircraft, your choice of airport destinations (leaving from San Francisco), 3-D photorealistic landscapes, "adventures" like dangerous weather, and real-world physics. Flight Unlimited should permanently unseat the anemic-in-comparison Microsoft Flight Simulator as the leading noncombat flight sim. —SZA/BF

A-10 Attack! and F/A-18 Hornet. There are currently two excellent combat sims coexisting in the Mac market. **A-10 Attack!** ($50, Parsoft) is easily the most complex of the current sims, and the graphics and physics of gameplay are the best available. The new Cuba missions should propel A-10 to the forefront of combat gaming. Not far behind is **F/A-18 Hornet** ($15, Graphic Simulations). Hornet is an order of magnitude simpler to fly, and the excellent networking features and fabulous graphics make it a better alternative for flight enthusiasts who don't have rudder pedals. There's also the **F/A Hornet Korean Crisis** ($10) and the **Hornet Bundle** ($25) that includes both Hornet 3.0 and the Korean Crisis. Star Wars fans will be thrilled with **X-Wing: Collector's CD** ($20, LucasArts) which is superior in every way to its DOS counterpart. This is the cream of the crop in spaceflight simulations. The force is with us! —SZA/BF

Gaming hardware. For years Mac users had to attack their favorite games with a keyboard or a measly mouse. Anyone who has had to play an arcade game with a mouse knows this is no way to go through life.

CH Products has an impressive line of Macintosh peripherals. The **Flightstick Pro** ($80) is probably the best all-around stick on the market; its two-button **Jetstick** ($50) is, as CH's ads say, for the "gun-shy." Another good low-end joystick is the **Macally Joystick** ($40). For hard-core flight simulator junkies there's the **MFCS**, the Macintosh Flight Control System ($100, ThrustMaster), with its military-style grip and four buttons. If you're into driving simulations, there's the **Formula 22** ($180), with its cushion-grip steering wheel that clamps to your desk, a gear shifter, and, yes, acceleration and brake *pedals!* —SZA/BF

And Also...

Myst and Riven. We've come a long way, baby—from the first text-based adventure, Zork, to the breathtaking **Myst** ($20, Broderbund), and its long-awaited sequel, **Riven** ($45). Instead of typing in commands and keeping a map in your head, you get to wander around a beautiful, mysterious world, mousing your way from one spot to another. The graphics are stunning, the music worthy of more than a computer game. What's the point of the game, and its rules? Ah, that's part of what you have to figure out. How much direction do you get from the company's descriptions? In Myst, you're unraveling "a chilling tale of intrigue and injustice." In Riven, "nothing is as it seems."

You Don't Know Jack

Do you know Jack? It's not your father's *Jeopardy.* It's more like the Comedy Channel's *Win Ben Stein's Money* (which must have been inspired by the original **You Don't Know Jack**). It has spawned several packages, like **YDKJ Movies, YDKJ Sports, YDKJ Television,** and three volumes of general questions and the **YDKJ Pack** combo package ($20–$40, Berkeley Systems).

This game, for one to three players, puts you in the middle of a TV quiz show with a sarcastic, manic, and occasionally smarmy host. When the multiple-choice question appears on the screen, you buzz in by hitting "your" key on the keyboard. A wrong answer elicits a snide comment from the host (as does a right answer, sometimes). The categories are cleverly named, and often double-entendred, perfect for any age from young teen to adults. The questions aren't throwaways; you really have to know stuff to play this game. And you have to know a wide variety of stuff, too—sometimes just for a single question. For instance, you're asked which of four people, including Hawkeye Pierce and Steve Austin, outranks the others. You have to know the television characters (from M*A*S*H* and The Six Million Dollar Man), remember their military status, and also know the relative levels of military officers.

The You Don't Know Jack series is a perfect computer game that offers something unique beyond the game itself—it's a *social* activity centered around the computer, accommodating up to three players at a time and enough fun left-over to provide amusement for a small audience, too.

PART 8

Connections

Part 8 At a Glance

26

Networks

In This Chapter

About Networks

Rich Wolfson is the associate editor for this chapter. Most of the non-initialed entries are the result of his contributions.

Basics

You may already be a network. Do you have a Mac and a LaserWriter? Do you have a network? If you've answered yes to the first question, then the answer to the second one is also *yes*.

A network made up of a single Mac and a printer isn't the kind of network this chapter's all about. But if you have two Macs connected to a LaserWriter—a relatively common setup for old Mac hands who've handed down their originals to other family members as they've tried to keep on the cutting edge—you do have the kind of network we're talking about in this chapter, albeit a very tiny one. But once both those Macs are connected to the printer, they're also connected to each other and you can pass files back and forth between them.

Peer and peerless networking. There are two ways to set up network services. In a *peer-to-peer* arrangement each Mac is capable of sharing files with others on the network. In a *server-based* setup, files to be shared are kept on a central file-sharing computer.

The Mac's system software has built-in peer-to-peer networking; it's called *file sharing* and is a cinch to set up. It's often all a small office needs, and if you have more than one Mac in your home, it's a convenient way to exchange files.

For a server-based Mac network, you need Apple's separate networking software, **AppleShare**, which comes with its Workgroup Servers. It's available separately (version 5 is current as of this writing) for $750 for a five-user license, and $470 as an upgrade to the previous version. With it, you dedicate a single Mac as the *file server,* a centrally managed depot for storing and sharing files. The server's hard disk appears to everyone on the network as an icon on their desktops. (AppleShare is also a system component that lets you do peer-to-peer file sharing; you'll have an AppleShare icon in Chooser even if you never bought the big product by the same name.)

In both setups, certain files and folders can be assigned *privileges,* defining who on the network can access them, and what can be done with them (viewed only, copied, changed, and so on).

Open Transport. *Open Transport* is a group of extensions that updates the network system software the Mac used for the first decade or so of its life; it offers the speed necessary to keep up with today's heavier networking demands.

Before Open Transport, AppleTalk was the Mac's networking language, and everything else was just an add-on. That even goes for TCP/IP, the networking protocol used over the Internet: even though you could (and still can) install MacTCP, AppleTalk had privileged access to the operating-system resources. Open Transport reverses this situation, making every protocol—whether TCP/IP, Netware, or DecNet—an "equal-opportunity" protocol. It uses industry-standard *API's* (Application Programming Interface), so that an application that's written for Open Transport or for APIs can use any network protocol. Previously, network software developers had to crank out their own software for each protocol they wanted to support. Now they only have to write one interface to Open Transport, and it will handle the different protocols. (In fact, Open Transport comes with TCP/IP network protocols.) —RW/JR

Network protocols. In local area networks, computers share a sort of "party line" over which all the digital communication takes place. That saves on cabling, but it creates the potential for incredible chaos. Imagine if all the phones on your block were connected in a single, huge party line. Picture the interruptions, the eavesdropping, the total jam you'd be in. Sooner or later you and your neighbors would start developing rules and procedures (let's call them *protocols*): hang up if the line is busy and try again later, keep calls short, hang up if an incoming call is not intended for you, and so on—to guarantee at least a semblance of orderly communication.

Solving this "party line" problem is the crux of networking. Although you can see and touch network cabling, it's the invisible sets of complex rules and digital procedures—the protocols—that really make a network run. In fact, for any network there may be dozens of separate protocols at work, many operating in different ways at the same time. —RC/BW

The layered look. Network folks tend to think of different parts of a network as occupying separate "layers," based on their functions: wiring and raw signaling capability is one functional layer, protocols that organize those signals into a meaningful data flow form another distinct functional layer, and protocols that ensure reliable data transmission across the network form yet another discrete layer, and so on.

Terms like Ethernet, AppleTalk, and 10BaseT that are generally used to describe "a" network could actually be describing different parts of a single network. 10BaseT, for example, is a wiring scheme, using twisted-pair cabling similar to phone wire. Ethernet, on the other hand, is a somewhat broader term, defining how computers and other devices should access the wiring—another distinct layer; Ethernet can and does run on other types of wiring, not just 10BaseT, or 100BaseT. And AppleTalk refers to an entire group of protocols created by Apple that governs almost every other aspect of networking—that is, how computer messages are organized and sent so that they arrive where they're supposed to without error.

If you've got a Mac-only network, you can pretty much safely stick to AppleTalk (lucky you). If you've got to connect with other kinds of computers, however, you'll need to know about—and coexist with—other protocol suites. —RC/BW

Shared printers. There's more to computer networks than sharing files; you can also share equipment like printers; in fact, AppleTalk's main task in the early Mac days was connecting expensive LaserWriter printers to several Macs.

Most Mac-compatible printers have the same LocalTalk ports as do Macs, so when you connect a printer to your Mac with LocalTalk, it appears in Chooser, ready to use, even if it's down the hall. With LocalTalk circuitry built-in, your printer becomes a print station: it sits by itself informing everyone that it's there, ready for service to anyone on the network who selects it in the Chooser. For more recent-model Macs and LaserWriters, Ethernet is built-in.

A level above a simple shared printer on a network is a *printer server.* Apple's AppleShare file-server software includes print service: when you print to a printer connected to the server, your print job is sent to the server, which stores everyone's print jobs, automatically feeding each job to the printer. If a printer doesn't have network circuitry, such as LocalTalk, built-in, connecting the printer to a print server is one good way of sharing it over the network.

A level *below* a shared network printer of the kind we've been discussing is the GrayShare/ColorShare-controlled StyleWriter that, when connected to any Mac on the network, is also available to other Macs on the network. But in this setup, everybody's print jobs get sent to the Mac that's connected to the StyleWriter, which then feeds the job to the printer—resulting in a sometimes unusable host Mac. —RW/BW

Plug-and-pray. The plug-and-play beauty of the Macintosh makes it easy to start building a small network of from two to 20 Macs (or even 40 with basic Ethernet setups). Beyond that, it becomes more like "plug-and-pray," because you'll need to know more about the inner workings of your network—the very things that AppleTalk has been handling automatically—and you'll need to purchase additional products to keep it humming. Example? Imagine that your 10-person organization grows to 40 people. All this time your network has been slowing down, and some people regularly find that it doesn't work at all! Unless you hire a network consultant, you'll have to learn about AppleTalk *zones* and *network numbering*. You'll need to know what *routers* are, and how they can reduce network traffic jams. —RW/BW

AppleTalk

The AppleTalk protocol. In the early days of the Mac, the built-in network circuitry as well as the required inter-Mac cabling was called AppleTalk. That made people think the wiring *was* the network, when in reality it's just a minor part of the whole. As described earlier in the chapter, when we say "AppleTalk protocol" we're really talking about a large group of protocols that govern AppleTalk networks.

The low-speed network circuitry and wiring that used to be called *AppleTalk* is now called *LocalTalk*, to distinguish it from the other types of wiring and transmission schemes over which your Mac's AppleTalk protocols can operate. Ethernet is another transmission/wiring scheme over which AppleTalk protocols operate—one that you simply can't ignore these days, since Ethernet circuitry has been built into Macs since the Quadra.

The AppleTalk protocol breaks some real ground by merit of its plug-and-play nature, automatically handling a lot of techie things like assigning workstation and network addresses, and routing messages between networks. Instead of dealing with cryptic numbers, you can assign names to workstations, or to sections of your network, called *zones*, which are unique to AppleTalk and part of why it's so easy to use. —BW

The LocalTalk chain. Look on the back of any Mac since the Mac Plus, and you'll find a connector marked with a printer icon. That connector does more than connect printers: it's also a LocalTalk network port. You can connect Macs and other LocalTalk-equipped devices (like printers) by connecting LocalTalk connectors to the ports and then stringing special cabling between them.

You could, actually, connect two Macs printer-port-to-printer-port and they'd still be networked—but all you'd have on the network is the two Macs. A LocalTalk connector is a Y-connector that lets you have one connection coming into and one going out from each device on the network. Because of the way the connections are made, from one device to the next rather than radiating out from some central point, the setup is referred to as a *daisy chain.* —RW/BW

No loop-de-loop. A LocalTalk network can't be set up as a loop, so there will always be two open connections, one on each end of your daisy-chained devices, because only one of the two connections on those devices will be in use. For small networks, the empty connector seldom causes a problem. In many cases, you need to insert a *terminator*, or *terminating plug*, in the open socket of the LocalTalk connector to reduce signal reflections along the wiring. —RW

LocalTalk imitators: better than the original. Early on in Mac networking, Farallon bettered Apple's LocalTalk connectors with its PhoneNET substitute: it was so much better that even Apple switched

> *Although the Macintosh…was unarguably inspired by research done at Xerox PARC…Apple deserves recognition for being the first to bring a graphic user interface to market in a personal computer.*
> Fred Davis, MacUser, November 1988
>
> *In science the credit goes to the man who convinces the world, not to the man to whom the idea first came.*
> Sir William Osler (1849-1919)

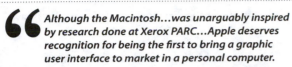

to PhoneNET and LocalTalk connectors haven't been available for years. PhoneNET ($15 per connector) and its imitators let you use standard phone wire with phone (RJ-11) connectors between the network connectors instead of the more expensive LocalTalk shielded cabling. It also extended LocalTalk's overall wiring limit, as described in the next entry

farallon.com

If you already have LocalTalk cabling, just switch over to PhoneNET-type hardware for any additional needs. Farallon makes an adapter for connecting LocalTalk to PhoneNET systems, so you won't lose whatever you have invested. —RW/BW

LocalTalk limitations. The original version of Apple's LocalTalk cable supported only up to 1,000 feet of total wiring with a maximum of 30 *nodes* (connected devices). PhoneNET-type connectors extend the total wiring limit to 3,000 feet; and, with quality wiring and *star repeaters* to boost signal strength it's possible to put 50 or 60 nodes on a PhoneNET network without too much distortion. —RW/BW

Ethernet

About Ethernet. Once you start adding dozens of busy people to a network, you'll need a faster network. Even folks in small offices and at home are scanning photos and shuttling QuickTake images around. LocalTalk, with a maximum transmission speed of 230.4Kbps (kilobytes per second) is just too slow in many situations.

Enter *Ethernet*, which boasts a transmission speed of 10 megabits per second; the newer FastEthernet hits 100 megabits per second. That's like moving up from a cow path to a multilane freeway! Graduating to Ethernet entails getting the right hardware to connect to the Ethernet cabling, and installing Ethernet driver software. —RW/BW

Hubba hubba. Ethernet networks traditionally need a *hub*, a central piece of hardware to which all the nodes on the network attach; a very different approach from LocalTalk's daisy-chain, this type of setup is usually referred to as a *star* topology. Farallon's EtherWave adapters (which hooked to each Mac, like a PhoneNET adapter) used to be an alternative to hubs for a small network, but the price of hubs dropped so drastically that the connectors aren't being made anymore.

Two ports in the storm. All recent and current Macs have Ethernet ports built into them. There are two types of Ethernet ports, and many Macs have one of each.

The basic Ethernet port built into most Macs is called an *AAUI* (Apple Attachment Unit Interface), specific to the Mac. To use that port, you plug in a small, $40 transceiver box between the AAUI and the specific kind of wiring you're using. Think of the AAUI port as kind of general-purpose port that lets you plug into several types of Ethernet cabling, provided you buy the type of transceiver that corresponds to your network cabling. If you get a 10BaseT transceiver, you can plug into a 10BaseT-wired network; with a 10Base2, transceiver you can plug into a 10Base2 (thin-net) network.

Most PCI-based Macs have two Ethernet connectors, an AAUI *and* a built-in 10BaseT connector, for which you need no transceiver. You simply plug the standard RJ-45 10BaseT plug (which looks like a fat phone plug) straight into the 10BaseT connector on the Mac. It's fairly plug-and-play Ethernet at that point—even more so than LocalTalk because you don't have to buy anything extra, except, of course, for the cabling. —RW/JR

Custom installs
Chapter 8

Ethernet drivers. Once you have all the hardware, you need an Ethernet *driver* to get things to work. OS 8 comes with the *Ethernet (Built-in)* extension for Macs with built-in Ethernet. If it wasn't installed when you installed your system, go back and do a custom install of the networking software component so you get the items you need. If you add an Ethernet card, the proper driver will come with the card. With the software installed, Ethernet shows up as a selection in the AppleTalk control panel.

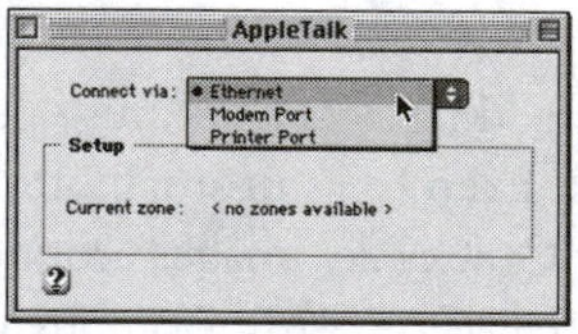

Apple's Ethernet driver works with most Ethernet cards, but not all; sometimes the card manufacturer says that you must use the driver provided with the card. This can cause a problem if you're a network manager installing network software on dozens of Macs. If you go to install a new Apple Ethernet driver on all the Macs, for example, and you're not aware that some cards in some Macs won't work with that Apple driver, you'll soon be getting calls from folks who suddenly can't get on the network.

Some vendors' drivers may offer a performance boost for their cards. For that reason it's probably a good idea to use the card manufacturer's Ethernet driver. Some manufacturers actually just give you the Apple driver; but for a particular piece of hardware, the vendor's own specialized driver will do a better job. —RW/JR

FastEthernet. Ethernet's ten megabits per second sounds like a lot of data under the bridge but it may work out to be less than you think. About a third of that is carrying the network protocols that keep data messages organized. And, of course, it's shared with other systems on the network, further cutting into what *you* get for your actual data. In short, even Ethernet bogs down, which is why a lot of folks are moving to 100-megabit-per-second Ethernet: *100BaseT*, or *FastEthernet*.

To move on up to FastEthernet you'll need:

- **A good reason**. If your conventional Ethernet setup is serving you well, why upgrade?
- **A 100BaseT network adapter card** for your Mac. You can't move up without one.
- **A 100BaseT** hub.
- **Macs that can make use of the extra network speed**. That generally means PCI-bus Power Macs. NuBus expansion slots generally can't move data fast enough to take full advantage of a NuBus 100BaseT interface.
- **Open Transport system software**. Older network extensions just can't keep pace.

If you currently have a 10BaseT network installed and you have to buy an Ethernet card for any of your Macs, you should consider one of the dual-speed 10/100BaseT cards on the market. They go for around $250 and can operate at both 10BaseT and 100BaseT speeds. Buy one now, and when you upgrade to 100BaseT wiring and hubs, you won't have to replace your card. Most 10/100BaseT cards can sense whether you're connected to a 10BaseT or 100BaseT hub, and will downshift or upshift as needed. —RW/JR

asante.com
dayna.com
apple.com
farallon.com

Add-on Ethernet. For older Macs without Ethernet circuitry built-in, you'll need an Ethernet card for Ethernet capability. They're pretty cheap these days, generally under $100. The major vendors are Asanté, Dayna, Farallon, and Apple. Some simply provide an AAUI, others a specific connector for 10BaseT or 10Base2. Still others provide several different kinds of Ethernet ports on the same card, so you can use the one that best applies to your current cabling, and still be able to use the same card if your cabling changes. —RW/JR

PowerBooks

Connecting PowerBooks. You rove with your PowerBook, creating reports and lots of other fresh data, all of which need to get onto your company's file server back at the office. You'll also want to tap directly into the office e-mail when you're back in town. Basically, you want that PowerBook to feel right at home with a network connection of its own. Fortunately there are many ways to do that, for every make and model of PowerBook.

- **LocalTalk**: Every PowerBook has LocalTalk networking built-in, so you can hook it to a LocalTalk (or PhoneNET) network just as you would any

Mac. Once you've got a LocalTalk connector in place along the daisy chain, you disconnect and reconnect the lead between the connector and the PowerBook, leaving the connector itself in place along the daisy chain. When you return to the office, plug the LocalTalk connector lead into the printer port on the PowerBook and fire up the computer; you'll be on the network.

- **Ethernet**: You've got several options for connecting to an Ethernet network, depending on the model of PowerBook you own—although the options have narrowed, since so many products were available for only a short time.
  - The Duo Dock II, 500-series, and later PowerBooks have built-in AAUI ports, just like most Macs. All you need is the appropriate transceiver to link the AAUI to the specific form of Ethernet cabling installed at the site.
  - For a Duo, you might be able to buy a used **MicroDock** (originally sold by Newer Technology) with its 10BaseT connector (and ADB port).
  - For 100-series PowerBooks, there were SCSI Ethernet adapters for providing Ethernet capabilities, at only about half the speed of a standard Ethernet adapter: Focus Enhancements' **EtherLAN SC**, Asanté's **Mini EN/SC**, and the **DaynaPort Pocket SCSI/Link**. (Right after you find any one of these products, you're ready to set out for the Holy Grail.)
  - For any Ethernet-challenged PowerBook, you can use serial-port-to-Ethernet adapters such as Farallon's **EtherMac PowerBook Adapter** ($199). It's slower than a straight Ethernet connection, but convenient.
  - You can get Ethernet on a PC card for PowerBooks with PC slots: Farallon's **EtherMac PC Card** is $110. —RW/BW

PB, phone home. One thing about a good network: it's awfully hard to leave behind. Whether you're roving with your PowerBook or handling some office business from home, you can still reach your company's file servers, printers, and e-mail over the phone lines. AppleTalk dial-in access has been around for years: You establish a modem connection between your remote Mac and another Mac or a black-box device on the office network, and the two Macs use the regular AppleTalk network to pass data back and forth. The telephone connection basically substitutes for the network cabling, though at much slower modem speeds. Early products used proprietary drivers to send AppleTalk protocols over the wires via modem. Apple set the standard with the Apple Remote Access protocol, which finally integrates dial-in access at the Mac system level. Originally shipped with the early PowerBooks, **AppleTalk Remote Access** ($125 for the server, $55 for a client) is now a separate product. Farallon's **Timbuktu Pro** ($140) goes one better: it provides remote access over the internet. —RW/PH/BW

Tips

Mac-to-Mac connect. You can connect two Macs directly to each other without any networking connectors or cables. A standard Mac-to-printer cable (also called an ImageWriter cable or, more formally, the Macintosh Peripheral 8) goes from the printer port on one computer to the printer port on the other; after that, you can use file sharing software as if they were both connected to a networked printer.

If you want to connect two newer Macs through their Ethernet connectors, you need a special cross-over cable, where the receive and transmit wires at one end are swapped. (The cross-over is performed by a hub on a regular network setup.)

Limits for different types of cable. Network cabling and transmission schemes vary in speed, maximum cable length, and in the number of devices you can connect on a single run of cable. The table below tells you what to expect from the predominant types of Mac network cabling. (Note that for 10BaseT and 100BaseT Ethernet, one device per cable run is optimal; you can increase the number and decrease reliability.) —JR/BW

Cable Limits

Cable type	Maximum nodes per segment	Maximum cable run without repeaters	Maximum transmission speed
Apple LocalTalk	30	1,000 feet	230.4K/sec
PhoneNET LocalTalk	30	3,000 feet	230.4K/sec
10BaseT	1*	300 feet	10MB/sec
10Base2	30	550 feet	10MB/sec
10Base5	100	1500 feet	10MB/sec
100BaseT	1*	250 feet	100MB/sec

* One device per cable run is optimal

At your service. Because "service" is the raison d'être of computer networking, whether it's print spooling, file sharing of centralized databases or documents, or e-mail, your network is likely to require at least one type of server. Although you can run several services from a single Mac if you have to, matching the right Mac with the right server software is a tricky business. You need to consider the number of people accessing the server at any one time, how many and what kind of services you've installed, the kinds of files you're sharing, and the speed of your cabling (LocalTalk versus Ethernet, for example). Given the number of interrelated factors, we'll just list a few considerations in no particular order:

- If you store thousands of 100K or smaller files on a file server, then the server should be able to complete file requests quickly. If, on the other hand, you're storing multimegabyte image files, you'll want a dedicated Mac with a fast CPU and faster network cabling than LocalTalk. Still, if people don't use the server a lot, then you won't need the fastest CPU. Get the idea?
- Use the latest version of AppleShare, add extra memory to the server machine, and get the biggest, fastest hard drive you can afford—you'll never regret it.
- You usually know your server setup is too slow when users consistently complain about it. If only a few complain, find out whether they're inadvertently slowing themselves down. Launching applications from a server will definitely slow you down over LocalTalk, as will double-clicking a Word document from a mounted server drive or sharing font suitcases. LocalTalk just can't take it. It's good practice to always copy files to your desktop before opening them.
- Different types of server software can often work together on the same Mac. For example, you can run Apple's Apple Remote Access on the same machine as your AppleShare file server, no problem. (And that way, ARA can just tap into the AppleShare user list, so you don't need another utility to create a user's account for the ARA server.)
- You're better off upgrading (for example, purchasing faster drivers or CPU accelerators) the server hardware you already own and handing the newly purchased Macs over to individual users. Any network—whether it's five users or 5,000—is only as good as the people on it. The real work is done by the workers, and it is done better with better tools. —BW

Ethernet naughts. On the whole, moving to Ethernet is pretty painless. When something goes wrong you've usually made one or more of the following mistakes:

- You didn't use the manufacturer's Ethernet driver and the card works only with that driver, not with the Apple-supplied Ethernet driver.
- You're plugging 10BaseT wiring directly between Macs without going through a hub.
- You're not using a transceiver along with the AAUI port, or using the wrong type of transceiver for the kind of Ethernet cabling that's installed. —JR

Truly twisted, sister. You can buy preassembled, modular PhoneNET-style cabling from many sources, and in many lengths, with the connecting jacks already attached at each end. But the pairs of wires in many of these modular cables aren't twisted around each other. That can be a problem once you get past 30 to 50 feet because it's the twist in twisted-pair wiring that helps cancel out the electrical interference to which unshielded cabling is vulnerable.

For longer runs, purchase *Category 5 twisted-pair* phone wire (the cabling that's round, instead flat like the wire that runs from your phone to the jack in the wall); you'll probably have to attach RJ-11 jacks yourself. —RW/BW

IN THE BEGINNING

What's in a Name? Apple's developers get monthly disks these days with straightforward names like "SDK" (software development kit) and the date. But in the old days, developer disks were named after movies and TV shows (some of which were current at the time). Names like:

The Byte Stuff	The Postman Always Clicks Twice
The Hexorcist	The Hound of Bitmapsville
Disky Business	Gorillas in the Disc
Lord of the Files	Hex, Drives, and Videotape
Code Warrior	ROM in Holiday
Hack to Future	Night of the Living Disc
A ROM With a View	2000 Leagues Under the CD
A Disc Called Wanda	The Winter of Our Disc Content
Northern Hexposure	The Silence of the ROMs

Plant printers properly. Printers with built-in LocalTalk or Ethernet circuitry can theoretically plug in anywhere on the network. I've known some folks though, who've insisted on locating the network printer physically closer to the boss's office on the assumption that she'll thereby gain both priority and speed in printing. But networks don't work that way. In fact, you don't even have to directly connect a network printer to the Macintosh that's functioning as its print server, since the server can also find it on the network and send it spooled jobs.

However, many large networks use devices known as *routers* to subdivide a network into separate physical subnetworks. The router device stands between the two subnetworks it connects, and you must make sure to locate a network printer and the print-server Mac on the same side of the router—within the same subnetwork. Otherwise, the router will get clogged with the constant print traffic that's forced to hop through the router. —BW

Your house is prewired for a network. So, your daughter finally got her own Mac in her bedroom, but you drew the line at getting a second LaserWriter. Now she needs to print from her bedroom to the printer in your den, and you're *really* tired of that wire running through the hallway and down the stairs almost every evening. There's an easier way, because every house has built-in AppleTalk network wiring!

This description assumes many things, but you should be able to take the basics and run. The basic assumptions are: your house has standard two-pair/four-wire wiring; you have only one phone number (which uses a single pair of wires); and you're using PhoneNET-type connectors that work with standard phone wires (they use the "outer" pair of wires, the ones not used by the single phone line).

Your Mac and the LaserWriter already have network connectors on them. On each connector, there's a wire that's connecting the Mac and the printer, and an empty jack with (probably) a transistor in it. Ignore the blank connector on the Mac, but remove the resistor from the unused jack on the printers' connector. Run a phone wire from that jack to the telephone jack in the wall. (Use a duplex adapter if you want to keep the phone plugged in!)

Meanwhile, upstairs, put a network connector on the Mac; put a transistor in one of jacks, and run a phone wire from the other to the phone jack on the wall. That's it: the two Macs are connected to the printer and to each other.

As long as your phone wiring has an empty pair of wires, you can use it for your network. Newer homes have six-pair phone wires, so you're likely to have an empty set, but you'll need some advice as to which wires are unused and how to tap into them. (You can't use a phone-enabled pair of wires because they always carry a dial tone.) We rewired our house with six-pair cabling because we have five—yep, count 'em, *five*—different phone numbers; but that leaves the sixth pair free for the network, just as we planned it. (We also ran Ethernet cabling so we'll be ready when all our Macs are.)

Small Networks and File Sharing

File Sharing Setup

Before the software. You need the hardware setup. It's all been covered in the first half of the chapter, but you might find the information a little too general or theoretical when all you want to do is connect two Macs (say your desk Mac and your PowerBook, or your Mac and the kids') to the same printer.

For a two-Mac, one-LaserWriter network, here's all you do: get three Farallon PhoneNET connectors and put one in each device (in the printer port on the Macs). Get two lengths of phone wire, and connect each Mac's PhoneNET

Connecting two computers to a printer with PhoneNET connectors.

connector to the one on the printer. This leaves an open connection on each of the Macs, which shouldn't present a problem; but, you should insert the little terminating transistor that probably came with the connector into the open hole.

The rest of this section assumes you have a very small network—two or three Macs and a printer. (Over the years, this has become a common home setup as older Macs are handed down to the kids for their own use while Mom or Dad—or Mom *and* Dad—get a new one.) But the basics are the same for larger networks that have peer-to-peer sharing enabled.

File-sharing software. File-sharing capabilities are built into your Mac, but you do need to install the system software components that let you use it. If you didn't install everything the first time around, you can do a custom install of just the parts you need, which are in the Networking and Connectivity section of the custom install (see the chart *The No-Thinking-Necessary Custom Install Guide* in Chapter 8).

Before you worry about installing anything, it's easy to check if you already have what you need: in the Chooser, you need the AppleShare icon in the panel along with your printer icon; and see if you have the File Sharing and the Users & Groups control panels.

Share and share alike. Setting your disk, or specific files or folders, to be shared is a two-step process. First, you turn on file sharing itself:

1. Open the File Sharing control panel.
2. Put in your name, a password (which is optional and, on a home network, usually unnecessary), and a name for your computer. These will probably already be filled in, since they're items the Setup Assistant insists on having right after you install OS 8.
3. With the information in the top section completed, click the Start button in the center section.
4. Ignore the bottom section: linking a program so it can be shared over a network causes incredibly slow performance.

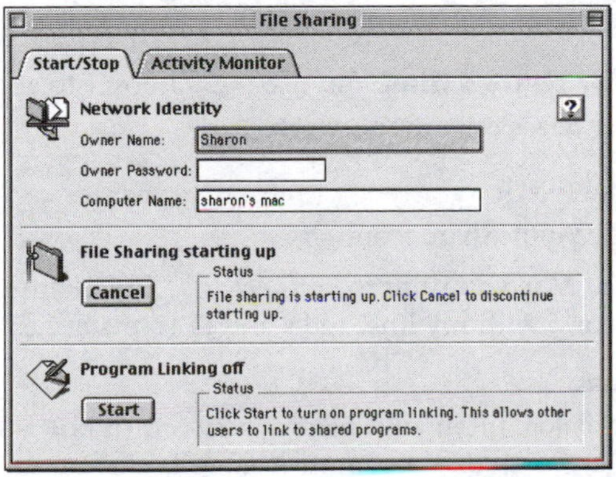

The File Sharing control panel.

Next, you have to set items on your computer to be shared; you can share the entire hard drive, or just certain folders or files.

1. Select the item (the disk or folder) on your desktop.
2. Choose Sharing from the File menu.
3. In the sharing window, click *Share this item and its contents.*
4. Set the *privileges* in each of three areas: for the owner (in case you log in from somewhere else); for defined Users & Groups (defined through another control panel); or for "Everyone." There are four levels of privileges, available from a pop-up menu, for each group.
5. If you've selected to share a disk or a folder, use the Copy button to specify the same privileges for all the enclosed folders.

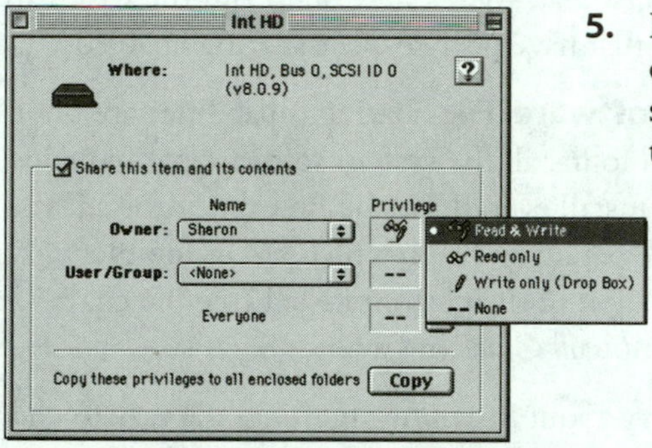

The sharing window, with the pop-up privileges menu.

Setting up users and groups. If you want to assign different degrees of access to different users, you'll have to register each user's name (and give them passwords if you want) in the Users & Groups control panel. You can also organize users into Groups, so you can set access privileges for several of them at once. The File Sharing Monitor control panel lets you keep track of who's using which of your shared items.

The Activity Monitor. It sounds like a Fisher-Price gadget for new parents, but the Activity Monitor is a tab in the File Sharing control panel that lets you see who's accessing the shared items on your Mac.

There's also a list of the shared items, and a Privileges button; select an item and click the button to change its access privileges—this is easier than finding it on the desktop to change them. —JK/CR/SH

Logging on for shared files. You use the Chooser to access files set for sharing on other Macs on your network.

1. Open the Chooser.
2. Click on the AppleShare icon.
3. Click on the Mac you want to connect to. (The picture here shows my home network, with my husband's and kids' machines in the list.)
4. Click OK.
5. In the next dialog, fill in your name, password (if one is necessary, based on the privileges set up on the remote Mac's file sharing setup), and click OK.

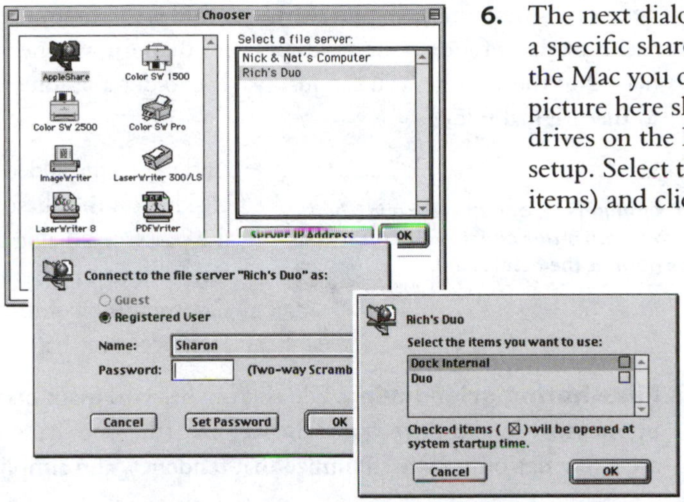

Accessing a shared volume through the Chooser.

6. The next dialog lets you select a specific shared item that's on the Mac you connected to; the picture here shows the two drives on the Duo and Dock setup. Select the item (or items) and click OK.

Once you're finished logging on, the other Mac's hard drive appears as an icon on your desktop, the same way it looks on its own Mac. The big difference is that if you open the remote drive, you'll see a folder named Desktop Folder that holds the items that are out on the other Mac's desktop.

Accessing the shared files. How much access you have, and what you can do with accessed items, depends on the privileges that were set on the remote Mac. Since folders can be set for read-and-write, read-only, and write-only, your options may be limited. A folder that's been defined as write-only (it's subtitled "drop box") lets you do nothing but copy or save things into it—you can't even open it to see what else is inside; it gets a special icon to let you know its status.

Logging off. There are two simple ways to log off from a shared volume: drag it to your trash, or select it and press ⌘Y (the Put Away command).

Tips

Quick log-ons. There are two ways you can get a shared item back on your desktop without having to go back through the Chooser and its dialogs:

- Keep the Recent Servers option turned on in the Apple Menu Options control panel. Each time you log onto a shared volume, it's added to the Recent Servers submenu; select it from the submenu to go directly to the dialog that asks for your password.
- While the volume's mounted on your desktop, make an alias of it. Double-clicking the alias after the volume's been unmounted will take you directly to the password dialog.

Direct access. If you need access to a specific folder on a shared volume, you don't have to log onto the main volume and then find the folder you need every time. Instead, find the target folder the first time you log on, and make an alias of it on your desktop. From then on, whenever you're connected to the volume, you can just use the folder alias on your desktop to get to the original folder.

And here's the added advantage: double-clicking on the aliased folder will open the password dialog so you can log onto the volume without touching Chooser, the volume's alias, or the Recent Server list.

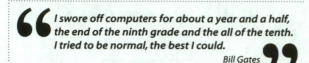

> ***I swore off computers for about a year and a half, the end of the ninth grade and the all of the tenth. I tried to be normal, the best I could.***
>
> *Bill Gates*

File-sharing grief-saving. File sharing has two main disadvantages: It uses up memory in and slows down the *host Mac* (the one that's sharing files). Here are a few tips on how to minimize that tendency, and simplify its use overall:

- **Consolidate shared items:** You can share up to ten separate items (files, folders, or disk volumes), but unless you're setting up different access privileges for each of them, it's much easier to gather everything you're sharing into one folder and share it.
- **Ask those you share with to be considerate:** The fewer people with whom you share files, the less time your Mac will spend responding to their requests. Ask the people with whom you share files to free up your Mac by disconnecting as soon as they've copied what they need.
- **Limit number of shared files:** Share as few files as possible. The fewer files you share, the fewer opportunities there will be for someone else to accidentally delete or rename your files or see something they shouldn't.
- **Use as little security as possible:** You should be able to control access to your sensitive files by being careful about which folders you share. As soon as you start creating users and groups and setting privileges for them, you'll find yourself tangled in a web of security that you'll constantly be asked to change. A lot of people will forget their passwords, and there's no place to look them up—you can only create new ones.
- **Keep the names the same:** If you do register users, make sure all owners of file-sharing Macs on the network register users with the same names. If Margaret registers as Meg on one Mac, Peggy on another, and Maggie on a third, she'd have to remember which Mac knew her by which name.
- **The need-to-use basis:** Encourage users to mount volumes only when necessary, not automatically at startup (unless, of course, *that's* necessary.)

—RW/BW

Instant messaging. The Mac's file-sharing capability includes a hidden instant-message system that you can use to send a message to anyone who has logged onto your machine.

1. Open the File Sharing control panel.
2. Click the Activity Monitor tab.

3. Option-double-click on the name of the user you want to message.
4. Type your message in the dialog that appears, and click OK.

Your message will appear on the screen of the user you selected.

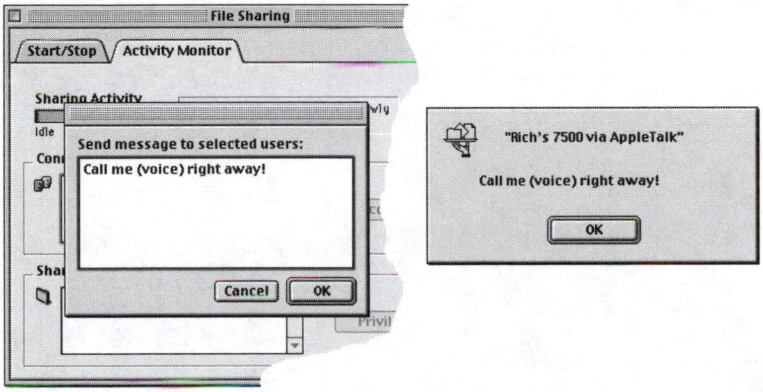

Message somebody logged onto your computer through the File Sharing control panel (left) and she'll get a message box on her screen (right).

27

The Online Universe

Modems

Getting There from Here

E-mail and Other Online Activities

Online Services and Providers

The Internet

In This Chapter

Modems

Rich Wolfson was the special research assistant for this section. Most of the tips here are the result of his contributions.

Hardware Basics

Modems. To connect your computer to the rest of the world, you need a *modem*, which connects your Mac to a phone line. It takes the digital signals that the computer uses and changes—*modulates*—them into the analog signals (sound) that can be transmitted on phone lines. It also, of course, translates—*demodulates*—incoming analog signals into digital computer-speak. (Hence the word modem, from its original title-by-function: *modulator-demodulator.)*

You connect your Mac to the modem, the modem to the phone line, and voila: you've got a pipeline to the outside world. Modems can be external or internal; for some PowerBooks, they can be on a removable PCMCIA card.

Although there are lots of different modems out there, you don't have to puzzle through all the specs to figure out what you need. When you get right down to it, you'll be making your buying decision on three basic factors: transmission speed, price, and manufacturer reliability. The rest is bells and whistles: size, shape and color, LED readouts or little status lights, and so on. Although there are other important inherent modem features, if you buy a new modem you'll pretty much get the latest in those features. So, although we attempt to be thorough by presenting all sorts of hardware information in this section, don't let yourself get bogged down in the details; few people need to know the details of v.90 or MNP10 modem protocols.

Error correction. Even when modems were slower, *error correction* and its partner, *error detection* were an important part of telecommunication. WYSIWTOEG (what you send is what the other end gets) is an important communication concept, and with all those blips of information whizzing back and forth, it's easy for something to go wrong. But if you don't *know* that something went wrong in the early part of, say, a file transfer, you might spend a half-hour transmitting the whole thing only to have an unusable file at the end of the procedure.

Error detection/correction, which was included in telecommunication software early on, works something like this: The sender divides the overall transmission into smaller blocks. It takes a block, analyzes it, and sends both the analysis and the block to the other end. The receiver analyzes the block it received, and compares that to the analysis that was sent; if they match, it signals for the next block. If they don't match, it asks for that block to be resent.

The modems you buy today (or any time in the last several years) incorporate error detection and correction as part of their hardware, so you don't have to rely on slower, software-based procedures.

As with so many features of telecommunicating, however, this whole setup works only if the modems on each end of the transmission understand the same procedures, or protocols. Luckily, as new modems come out with more advanced features, they incorporate the older features as well.

Data compression. If you can squeeze your data down to a smaller file size before transmitting it, the transmission will take less time—saving you time, money, and probably some other important stuff, too. We cover software-based file compression utilities briefly later in this chapter, but most modems include hardware-based compression in case you don't compress your files from the software end of things.

The hardware approach is certainly easier, because neither the sender nor the receiver has to do anything to reap the savings of compressed file transmission. On the other hand, since it works only when the modems at both ends understand the compression scheme, you may wind up doing software-based compression anyway—because you seldom know what's on the other end. (In fact, you may not be entirely clear as to what's on your own end, either, in terms of hardware compression capability.)

If you've already compressed your files, sending them through a modem with hardware compression won't get you any extra benefit—most modems won't try to compress an already compressed file, and if they do, you'll see only a tiny further compression, because a file can be squeezed down only so far.

And, if you're concerned that your modem will compress a file and make it unusable at the other end of the transmission because that modem isn't as capable as yours—don't. The modem is smart enough to check the other modem's capabilities before it does anything like that!

Protocol standards. The agreed-upon standards among modem manufacturers are identified by arcane labels beginning with a *V.* followed by a number, and sometimes the word *bis* or *ter* (Français for *second* and *third*). Here are the ones you're likely to see:

Standard	*Maximum bps*
V.22bis	2,400
V27ter	4,800
V.32	9,600
V.29	9,600 fax
V.32bis	14,400
V.17	14,400 fax
V.32terbo	19,200
V.34	28,800
V.34 plus	31,200 and 33,600
V.42bis	33,600
V.80	(video-phone ready)
V.90	56,000

(In case you actually need to say some of these out loud: V.32bis is *"v dot thirty-two biss."*)

Hayes compatibility. Way back when, Hayes Microcomputer Products developed protocols for computers and modems to talk to each other about basics like dialing, answering the phone, and hanging up. This *Hayes command set* (also referred to as the *AT command set,* since commands start with *AT*, calling the modem to pay ATtention) is used by almost all modems today for their core set of commands. You'll find most modems are advertised as being Hayes compatible.

> ***This "telephone" has too many shortcomings to be seriously considered as a means of communication. The device is inherently of no value to us.***
> *Western Union internal memo, 1876*

Additions to the command set have been made by various manufacturers over the years, so if you decide to delve into this arcane area, make sure you check the manual that came with your modem so that you know how to talk to it. (How do you send those commands, even if you know them? If you're using a general communications program, covered below, you can type the commands in the program and they'll be sent to the modem.)

Fax modem. Every modem's a fax modem these days. You should be aware that no matter the speed of your modem, its fax capabilities will be, at best, only half that speed. There are pros and cons to using your modem for faxing, and, of course, some tips and techniques, so we have a small section later in the chapter that covers faxing issues.

megahertz.com
supra.com
globalvillage.com
hayes.com

Modem models. With standard modems having pretty much reached their highest speed potential, there aren't a lot of differences from one model to another, and the differences are mostly superficial: an LED display with letters or little lights over labels, or the kind of fax software that comes with it. (Most fax software is specific to the modem: Supra has FAXcilitate, Global Village has GlobalFax, and USRobotics and Megahertz cards use FaxAction.)

Three of the best-known and most reliable brands for Mac users are **Supra**, **Global Village**, and, for PowerBook PC card modems, **Megahertz** (from USRobotics, recently subsumed by giant 3Com). I've used all three for years and have never been disappointed. **Practical Peripherals** and **Hayes** (which now owns Practical Peripherals!), are also dependable companies.

Those modem reports. Do you have an LED readout on your modem, but the only signals you understand are OK (it's ready and waiting) and 28 (it's transmitting at 28,800 bps, more or less). Or does the modem have little labels whose lights blink during the course of your telecommunicating—but you might as well be looking at the helm of the starship Enterprise (in any of its incarnations)?

Here's a quick guide to those little signals:

TX	data is being sent out
RX	data is coming in
OH	the modem has taken the telephone line "off hook"
AA	auto-answer is turned on
CD	a connection has been made with a remote modem

Beyond modems: ISDN. The problem with computers and telephones is that they speak different languages—digital and analog—and information has to be translated back and forth by modems. The phone lines themselves are capable of carrying digital signals, although they're not optimized for it. In all, though, it seems to make sense to provide digital-only capabilities over phone lines for computer communications. That's what ISDN—Integrated Services Digital Network—is all about. Since it actually provides two data channels, you can use one for data transmission while simultaneously using the other for voice, fax, or standard modem transmissions. Or, the channels can be combined to carry data at twice the speed of the single-channel transmission. An ISDN channel carries data at 64K; most people use a double channel, for 128K speed—more than twice as fast as the best modem (56K) under ideal conditions.

But all this speed comes at a cost. For hardware, although you won't need a modem anymore, you will need an ISDN terminal adapter, which costs twice as much as a modem. Then there's the cost of the service itself. The installation is upwards of $500, and monthly fees range from $30 to $100—and there's a per-minute cost of about a penny per minute on top of that.

Beyond modems: cable. Wouldn't you be interested in having something that costs a small fraction of ISDN's cost (say, about $20 a month) and is about 20 times faster? Get a cable modem if your cable company offers it. A cable modem uses that same line that's pouring cable-TV data into your home—and you know how fast *that* stuff comes in! It's so fast that it's not measured in bits per second, the way most modem speeds are; instead, its theoretical maximum speed is 10 *megabits* a second—about 175 times faster than the fastest modem performing at its very best.

Cable modems use *asymmetric data transmission,* providing super-fast incoming data but standard-modem outgoing information (sometimes as slow as 14,400 bps). But the outgoing information is normally a little text and a few mouse clicks for a web page, not data-heavy sound and graphics, so it's a great setup for anyone who can get it. (I'm still waiting, anxiously, although the for-one-computer-only restriction of a cable modem is going to cause problems here at home where we have to accommodate three desk machines and two PowerBooks that at this point can hook up to the modem line in the office, living room, family room, or, yes, even the bedroom—although *I* know who's going to get priority!)

At the Speed of Data

Modem transmission speed. There are several factors that will affect your actual data transmission speed once you start using your modem (see the *File transmission speed* entry), but the first concern is the modem's speed rating.

A modem's speed is usually measured in *bits per second*, or *bps;* the use of the term *baud,* and the related argument about the difference between the terms, is rarely heard anymore. Also seldom seen these days is the *cps (characters per second)* ratings; the difference between cps and bps is a factor of 1000, so that a 28,800 bps modem is the same as a 28.8 cps modem—which makes the verbal reference "twenty-eight eight" handy, since it covers both pretty neatly.

When Macs were first able to use a telephone, the standard modem speed was 300 bps; it jumped to 1200 in a couple of years, then multiplied to 2400, 4800, and so on to the current low-end standard of 28,800. There are two speeds beyond 28.8 that are generally available—33.6 and 56K—but how much speed you'll actually get out of them is debatable (and the debate is described in the next few entries).

28.8 versus 33.6. Look at those numbers, and you'll think there's no debate at all—just get the top speed that you can, and it's worth dumping your current one to move up to the next. But it's not that simple.

First, the issue of 28.8 versus 33.6. The latter model achieves its greater speed (about 15 percent more) by using special built-in compression techniques. But if files are already compressed (through software like StuffIt), a modem's hardware compression schemes don't work. If the bulk of your modeming is transferring files, you won't benefit much, if at all, from the faster modem, so it's not really worth moving from 28.8 to 33.6. Of course, if you're buying a new modem, then get the 33.6 to start with!

The 56K standard. We're lucky to be able to label an entry "56K standard," because until recently there were two competing standards: the X2 technology from modem giant USRobotics, and the k56flex, or k56Plus, from the even bigger giants Rockwell and Lucent Technologies. The two technologies were (and are) totally incompatible; everyone finally agreed on a compromise referred to as V.90 (or occasionally as V.PCM). Most modem manufacturers are offering free upgrades from their X2 or k56flex models. But whether or not you can get the full, or even *almost* full speed from one of these demons depends on a lot of factors. And, like the cable modems discussed earlier, these models are *asynchronous,* working faster in one direction (to you) than the other (from your Mac).

Information in your Mac is digital to start with; it's translated into an analog signal by the modem for your local phone lines, and when it reaches a central place in the phone system, it's translated back into digital form again. The translation introduces some noise, and it's that noise that keeps your modem to barely more than 30K at best. But when a service provider has a direct digital connection, it can use a greater speed to send things because the signal won't degrade as much. So, your 56K modem might let you approach that speed for incoming information, but you'll be limited to the 25K to 33K standard modem speed for transmissions in the other direction.

File transmission speed. There are several things that affect the actual transmission speed of a file; some of them are in your control, but others are entirely out of your hands.

- **The modem speed:** The speed rating on your modem may not always be the speed at which you travel, but it represents the upper speed limit for everything you do online.
- **The file size:** Larger files take longer to transmit. (Duh.) You can make the files smaller before you send them by using a compression utility. (Some telecom software, like AOL's, includes compression software and lets you access it from within the main software.)
- **The phone line:** If the line is noisy (and modem transmissions are more finicky about noise and static than you are), the transmission will take longer because some blocks will have to be sent more than once until there's an error-free transmission.
- **The service you're using:** If the commercial service or BBS you're using is crowded at the time you're doing a download, it might be splitting its attention among many users, making your modem wait for its turn.
- **Your Mac's serial port:** Older Macs have slower serial ports and won't be able to handle the speed of a super-fast modem.

Speaking at different speeds. A fast modem can speak slowly when it has to—when it's talking to a computer with a slower modem. So don't worry when your friend says you won't be able to telecommunicate directly with him any longer because your blazing fast new modem won't jibe with his 9600 antique: a fast modem can always slow down.

Modem Strings and Dialing Strings

Stringing along. The least friendly aspect of Mac computing (Microsoft notwithstanding) has always been something called *modem strings,* or *initialization* or *init strings*. (These are not the same as *dialing strings*, covered a little later in this section.)

Telecom software, especially on the Mac, generally tries to protect us from the nastier aspects of what's going on behind the scenes, but sometimes you need to know how to deal with out-of-the-ordinary circumstances. For the most part, you won't ever have to create, edit, or otherwise touch a modem string. You install your software, pick the name of your modem from within some dialog box in the software, and go on from there. But when you run into problems and some helpful soul tells you to edit your modem string to solve your problem, you might as well be at least *mildly* comfortable with the whole idea.

Whenever you use your modem, your software first sends information to the modem telling it how to behave for the rest of the session (or until it's told otherwise), using cryptic shorthand that looks something like this:

```
ATS0=0 X4  Q0 V1 &C1&D2\N0&K4^M
```

That's a modem string: a series of letters and numbers that stand for modem commands. These strings tell the modem all sorts of things, like: whether or not to display its status in a window ("Busy" "Dialing…" "Connecting" "Connected at 28000 bps"); whether it should stand by to receive a call, and how many rings to wait before it answers; and to go ahead and dial even if there's no dial tone available.

When you're using the right software, you can also send commands directly to the modem instead of embedding them in the modem initialization string. Because all the commands are prefaced by AT (for *ATTENTION! I'M TALKING TO YOU, MODEM!),* they're generally referred to as AT commands.

Normal people shouldn't have to worry about AT commands in "command mode," but sometimes we have to work with them in the modem strings.

Creating and editing modem strings. How do you control a modem string? In a general telecom software package (covered later in the chapter), you can usually just type the string into a window and press Return for it to be sent to the modem. In service-specific software like that for AOL or one of CompuServe's packages, you have to poke around Preferences and Settings dialogs until you see a likely prospect labeled *modem string* or *init string* or *initialization* or *configuration,* and that's where you can do your editing.

In CompuServe's Information Manager software, for instance, you have to use the Edit menu's Preferences command, and then click the Define Modem button to access the Modem Setting dialog, where you'll see the modem string. For AOL, you use the Setup command, and click the Edit Modem Profile button; the string goes in the Configuration box.

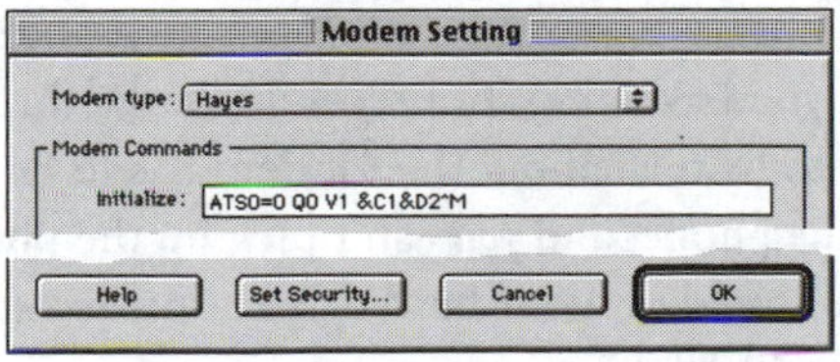

Accessing CIM's modem string.

Blind dialing. Modems usually wait for a dial tone before dialing. This seems perfectly reasonable, since it's what you do, too, but a dial tone isn't always available when you're traveling out of the country, or dealing with a local PBX system that uses something besides the standard dial tone.

To make your modem work without waiting for the dial tone—known as *blind dialing*—edit the modem string to include *X1,* the blind-dialing command. If there's already an *X4* command in the modem string, edit it to *X1,* and remember to change it back to *X4* when you're working with a standard phone line again.

Dialing string. A *dialing string* is not the same as a modem string. The modem string sends a commands to the modem. The dialing string is simply the phone number you're "dialing." In the down-and-dirty days of telecommunicating, the dialing string would be part of a command (starting with ATDT), but now all software provides a place for you to put the phone number, which gets sent as a command. The dialing string has to include the same numbers you use when you dial; so, not only is the number and the area code part of the string, but also any prefixes before the area code, and outside-line access numbers.

By, the, way. A comma in a dialing string makes the modem pause, usually for two seconds by default. The PowerBook chapter describes how to make a credit card call through a modem set up; the dialing string requires several pauses strung together, like this:

```
02125551234,,,,12341231234,,,9999
```

Some telecom software has a limit on the number of characters that can be entered in a dialog as the dialing string. If you're stuck, you can redefine the length of the pause by adding S8=6, for instance, to the initialization string to make the comma trigger a six-second pause. Then your dialing string would look like this:

```
02125551234,,12341231234,9999
```

Faxing with Your Modem

Your computer as a fax machine. All modems are fax modems these days, and almost all of them work for both sending and receiving faxes. It's a great convenience to not have to print out a document and then fax it from a standard machine (if you have one), but receiving faxes through your modem means your Mac has to be turned on, the modem has to be set, through its fax software, to answer the phone, and *you* can't pick up the phone. To top it all off, received faxes are stored on your hard drive as images (a picture of text rather than the text itself) which take up a lot of room and print very slowly.

So, if you need incoming faxes on anything approaching a regular basis, make sure you get yourself a real fax machine.

The fax software. You have to install fax software to use your modem's fax capabilities. The features offered by fax software vary from one package to another, but include things like a phone-number list, an option to "collect" documents for later faxing, automatic generation of cover pages, keeping track of documents that were sent (and to whom), and so on.

stfinc.com
symantec.com

Modems sold as Mac modems usually come with Mac fax software: Global Village modems, for instance, come with **GlobalFax**, while Supra modems are bundled with **FAXcilitate**. If you want something with more (or different) power, there are third-party programs like stf Technologies' **FAXstf Home** ($40) and **FAXstf Pro** ($80).

Just another output device. Once the fax software is installed, configured, and running, it's a cinch to use. All you have to do is keep in mind that the fax machine you're sending a document to is just a remote printer. You'll find a fax icon in the Chooser that you can select the same way you would if you were choosing another printer. From then on, your File menu sports a Fax command instead of a Print command; instead of a Print dialog, you get a fax dialog where you can put in the telephone number, and so on. Most fax software provides a shortcut to temporarily access a fax instead of your having to use the Chooser—holding down Option or Shift or some other modifier combination temporarily changes the Print command to a Fax command. Some fax software even provides a separate fax menu in the menu bar.

Watch out for art. If your fax is going to include artwork (on a cover page, for instance), forget about EPS art. Printing to a fax is like printing to a non-PostScript printer, only worse: not only is there no PostScript, but the resolution of a standard fax printout is about 200 by 100.

Modem Tricks and Tips

Get a separate phone line. The best tip of all isn't free—it'll cost you a few dollars a month—but it will save *lots* of grief. Get a second phone line, just for the modem. While one family member is online, the others can still make and receive calls; and, no one will accidentally pick up an extension while you're online and interrupt the transmission—*just* as you get to the end of a 45-minute download. Even if you live alone, you may find the convenience of a separate modem line well worth the cost.

Closing the serial port. Sometimes when you switch from one communications program to another, or even if you try to start the same program after a crash while it was online, you get an error message that the modem port is in use and that the program you are launching cannot use it; under some circumstances the program may even crash. That's because the first program told the Mac operating system it was using the port, and the system, for obvious reasons, won't let two programs try to send data out the same port at the same time. Restarting your Mac, or using the free utility **CommCloser**, will solve the problem. —RS/HN

Disable call waiting. If you have a call-waiting feature on the line you're using for a modem connection, make sure you disable it before using the modem—a beep for an incoming call will ruin your transmission. Most phone services let you dial *70 to disable call waiting throughout the next call that you make. You can add it to your dialing string; typing an asterisk dials the star on the phone pad.

Getting There from Here

Making Connections

Open Transporting. Open Transport is now the standard networking software for Macs—and networking is actually used for Internet access. But you need at least a 68030 machine to use Open Transport, so older machines have to stick with AppleTalk-based networking. A PCI-based Mac *must* use Open Transport, while non-PCI 68030-or-better Macs can use either. If you're in that either-or group, go for Open Transport: it's easier to set up, and is faster on PowerPC Macs.

With Open Transport, you use the TCP/IP and PPP control panels to take care of Internet configurations; this is the setup we've covered in most of this section. Without Open Transport, you have to use the MacTCP control panel, which is a little clunkier.

Easy does it with savvy service providers. If you're lucky, you'll never have to touch most of the control panels and settings that control your telecom connections. Install the software from your service or service provider, and everything is taken care of for you, except perhaps the actual telephone number you have to use for access. Software from AOL is notoriously easy to set up, and CompuServe is not that far behind; most large ISP's (Internet service providers) also have simple setup operations, with an installer that does all the work for you.

If your software does have an installer, use it! There are so many bits and pieces that need be stored in various spots that you're bound to forget one; besides, many installers ask you to input information during the installation process, which means you won't have to do it later.

But you should have at least a passing acquaintance with some of the background utilities that are used in making online connections, so they're rounded up in this section.

Modem scripts. Modems are pretty much the same on the hardware end of things, but can differ widely in minor ways for hardware, and major ways in software. Instead of each telecom program having to deal with how it will communicate with a specific modem model, your system software takes care of all that, much the same way it handles communication between applications and printers. And, just as you have to pick a printer description file for some printers so the Mac will know about their special features, you have to indicate just which modem you have, too.

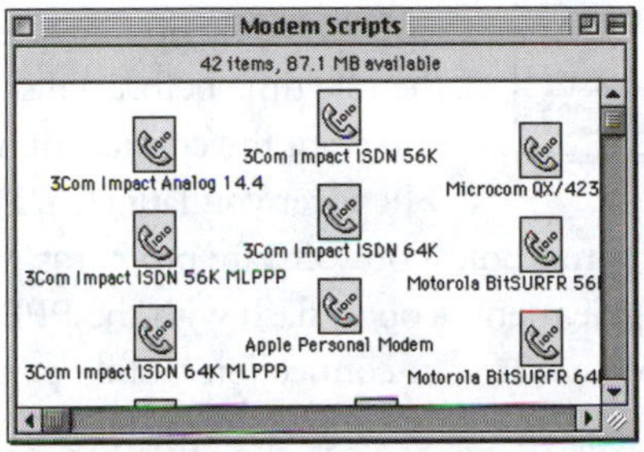

Modem scripts tell your telecom application how to communicate with your specific modem.

When you install your system, it creates a Modem Scripts folder inside the Extensions folder; the "scripts" inside the folder are named for the modem models they describe. If your modem isn't among the collection, its script probably comes on a disk with the modem, so you can add it to the folder.

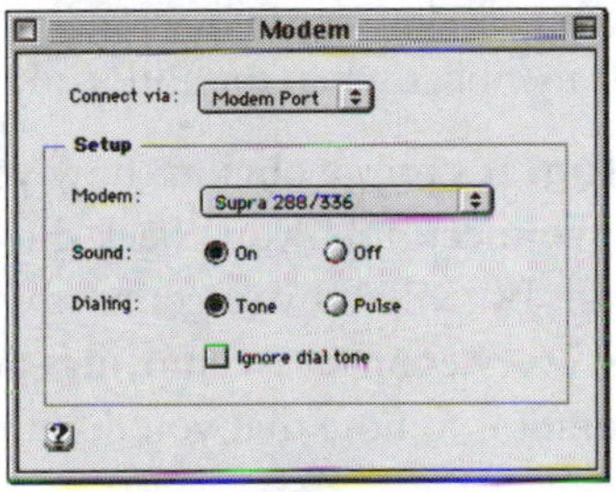

Set up your modem through the Modem control panel.

The Modem control panel. The Modem control panel is the easiest of any system software settings you have to take care of: choose Modem Port or Printer Port from the first pop-up menu, and select your modem from the second pop-up (the list comes from the files in the Modem Script folder).

The TCP/IP control panel. To manually setup the TCP/IP control panel, you'll need a crib sheet from your ISP. On it you should find your *dial-in number* (don't hesitate to ask for a list of numbers—the one the ISP selects may not be optimal); a *nameserver address* or two (same kind of numbers); and a *domain name*. Be sure you've been set up with "dynamic server addressing"; some ISPs may suggest "manual addressing," which is faster connecting, but will ultimately fail you as traffic builds.

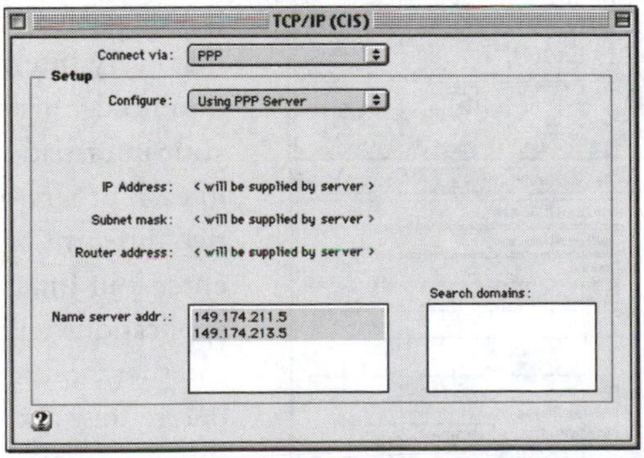

If your software doesn't set up the TCP/IP control panel, you'll have to enter some of the information manually; other information is provided by the remote computer when you log on.

If you use more than one service, you can save a set of configurations for each one, and easily switch from one to another. —SZA/SB

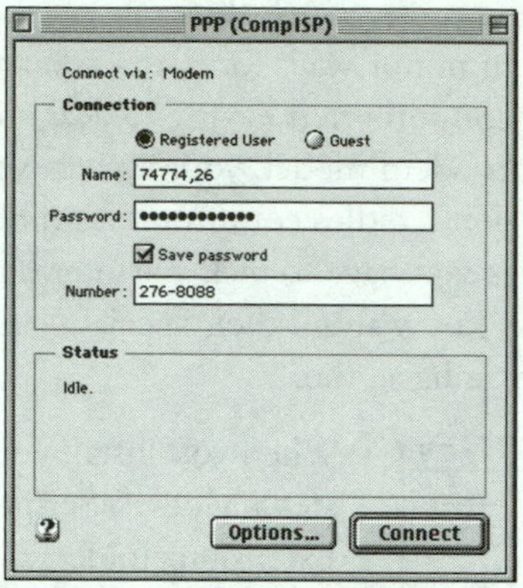

The PPP control panel. The PPP control panel is one of the most basic of your telecom controllers: it stores your basic connection information, like your username and password for the service you're connecting to, and the number to dial to log on.

The Options button in this control panel opens a multitab dialog box where you set all sorts of handy preferences, like the length of the idle time before a disconnect, whether you want the connection made automatically whenever you launch a TCP/IP application (that's the setup in most communication software programs these days), and whether you want the Apple menu icon to flash with the PPP icon while you're connected (a nice visual clue that your connection is still open).

The PPP control panel provides shortcuts to the other two control panels you need for your setup—TCP/IP and Modem: just choose either, or both, from the PPP menu that's added to your menubar when the PPP control panel is open.

Bypass the password dialog. It's pretty obvious how you can avoid constantly typing in a password at connect time: you check the Save Password option in the PPP control panel. But what if you connect without a password? Being asked for a password on every connect is annoying, but there isn't anyplace you can set your configuration to note that you don't need a password.

Just check that Save Password box even if you don't have a password: it saves the (blank) information from the password text box, which serves as the nonpassword.

Central configuration. The freeware **Internet Config**—which a standard system installation puts inside the Internet folder it creates on your hard drive, so you don't—serves as a central repository for all the information that every Internet-related application needs. Instead of entering your information and preferences in each program (maybe you use two different browsers), you can enter it in Internet Config; most applications will look for the Internet Config information before they ask you to fill in things in their own dialogs.

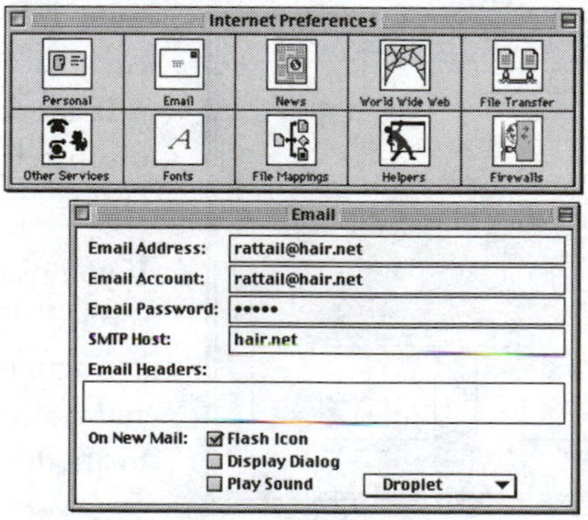

Using General Telecom Software

General-purpose software. If you use AOL or CompuServe, you also use the software made to access those services. If you have a direct Internet provider, you use a browser to do your surfing. But there are still a few general-purpose telecom programs around for when you need to just access another computer through its modem.

stfinc.com

- **Microphone Pro** ($100, STF Technologies) is a powerhouse, and is indispensable for anyone with midlevel to intensive telecom needs. MicroPhone's best feature has always been its scriptability, which lets you automate almost any available task. That said, however, unless you intend to work with its scripting capabilities, you'll probably be satisfied with a lesser package.
- The shareware **ZTerm** ($30) has been around a long time, and provides all the basic functions you need to communicate directly with another Mac or access a bulletin board.
- The **ClarisWorks** ($100) package provides a telecom module that is smooth, trouble-free, and provides everything you need—and it has a word processor, spreadsheet, database, and graphics capabilities.

> ***"If you want to see a speed demon in action, load a 512K RAM disk with the System, the Switcher, and... MultiPlan and MacTerminal."***
>
> *Macworld, April 1986*
>
> *[MacTerminal: the first telecom program for the first Mac, which wasn't designed to accommodate a modem.]*

Manually setting up a connection. Because of multiple telecommunications standards a general communications application must offer an array of configuration choices; that's what makes telecommunications one of the most difficult computer tasks to master. You'll need to understand these basic settings:

- **Bits per second:** Modems can connect not only at their top speed but also at any slower speed. When two modems connect, they negotiate to determine the highest transfer rate they have in common, dropping down automatically to a lower rate for a noisy line. But no modem can use a higher speed than your software is set for, so be sure your software is set even higher than the speed you want, to make use of the modem's compression.
- **Flow Control:** Modems generally can't transmit data over the phone line as fast as your Mac can push it out, and sometimes your Mac can't keep up with the incoming data from the modem. *Handshaking,* or *flow control* lets either device tell the other to pause the data flow until it catches up on the processing. Modems support *hardware handshaking*, a scheme that uses dedicated wires in the serial cable for signaling.
- **8-1-No:** Depending on the program you're communicating with, you may need to send and receive data in chunks of either seven or eight bits; your software should offer a choice under the heading *data bits*. The end of one byte and the beginning of another is marked by a *stop bit*. Finally, *parity* is an old-fashioned way of checking that the other computer

received exactly what you sent. Far and away the most common setting is eight data bits, one stop bit, and no parity, nicknamed *8-1-no*.

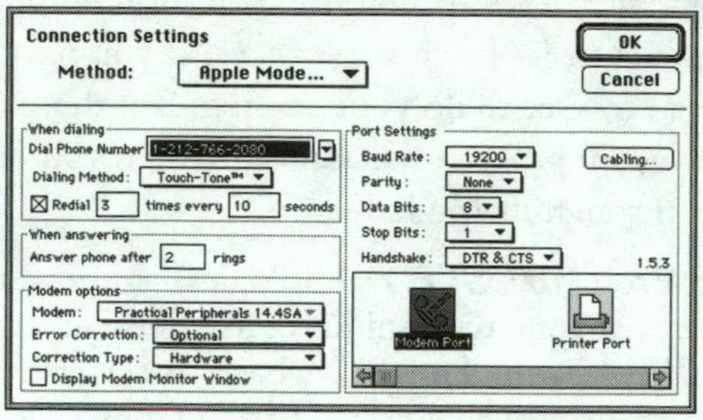

In the Apple Communications Toolbox, under "Port Settings," you'll find the common settings for parity, data bits, and stop bits. Here, flow control is called "Handshake." The dialog box may look different depending on the application you're using.

- **File-Transfer Protocols:** You can send plain-text (ASCII) files via modem as if you were typing it out, but there are lots of problems with text transfers, with characters getting dropped or garbled. To send anything but plain text, or even if you just want to make sure a text file arrives intact, you need to use a *file-transfer protocol*—a set of conventions for how much data will be packaged, sent, and verified. These protocols are independent of the computer, the modem, and even the communications software you are using. (Basic file-transfer protocols are described in the next entry). —SZA/HN

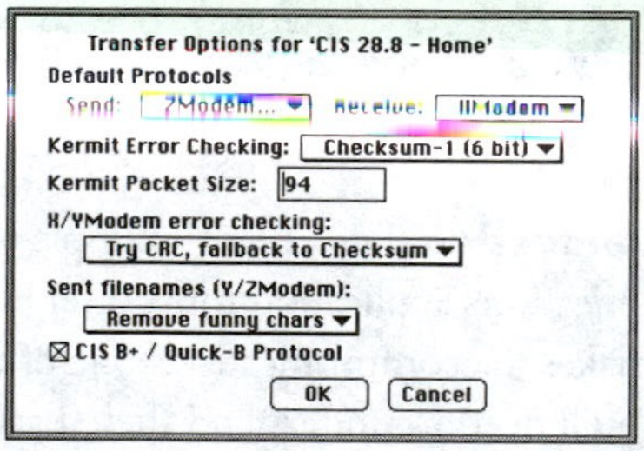

This dialog from ZTerm allows you to set various aspects of file transfer protocols, but the only areas you need to bother with are the two menus under Default Protocols, and the check box for CIS B+, which you need to check only when using CompuServe.

X, Y, Zmodem. Here's a guide to some commonly used transfer protocols (in order of preference):

- **Zmodem** should be your choice whenever possible. It's the fastest, can send multiple files in a batch, includes the files' names and other information about them, and can resume interrupted transfers right where it left off.
- **Ymodem** (and an even faster variant called Ymodem-G) also supports batch transfers and file names but contains no error-checking protocol. It's a very fast way to transfer files, but use it only with modems that do hardware error correction.
- **Xmodem** is an older protocol that is still widely used, in part because it's supported by virtually all communications programs, while its Y and Z cousins are not. It's relatively slow because it sends smaller packets and waits for one to be acknowledged before sending the next. It uses an error-detection technique called *checksums;* some implementations

offer a CRC *(cyclical redundancy checking)* option, which you should use if available.

- **Kermit** works with a wide range of computers and telecommunications equipment, including mainframes that don't support newer protocols. It's still a favorite among many government and university users. But it's generally slower than the alternatives, and it's not supported on most services. —HN/RS

Being There

IMHO, you should LOL ;-). People can't talk and write online like they do in the rest of the world. They *emphasize* words _one way_ or >>another<< because there's no accepted standard for bold or underlining in the primitive world of telecom. Other online expressions fall into three categories: emoticons, acronyms, and emphasis/actions.

Emoticons, also referred to as *smilies*, are unbearably cute little faces created from standard typographical characters, used to show an emotion that isn't otherwise obvious. It's sometimes important, for instance, to show that you're only kidding: Don't be an idiot! :-). (To see the face, look at the figure sideways). Sometimes the basic smiley face doesn't have a nose :), or it has a different nose or mouth, like this : ^ >. Here are some basic combinations:

:>)	different nose	:^	different nose
:-(	frown (bummer!)	:-<	frown
:-D	laughing	:-*	kiss
;-)	winking	:-X	keeping mouth closed
:-P	sticking tongue out	:-o	surprised
:-(0)	yelling	~ :-(	very angry (steaming)
8-)	wearing glasses	B-)	wearing sunglasses
O:-)	innocent (halo)	]:-)	guilty, sneaky (devil)
\:-)	wearing beret	*=:-)	wearing chef's hat
o-)	cyclops	)	Cheshire cat

There seems to be an infinite number of online acronyms, but here's a sample of the most common:

BTW	by the way
IMO	In my opinion
IMHO	in my humble opinion
OTOH	on the other hand
LOL	laughing out loud
ROFL	rolling on the floor laughing
ROTFLOL	Rolling on the floor laughing out loud
MorF	male or female? (popular in chats)
GR&D	grinning, running and ducking
RTFM	read the #@%$&! manual
PMFJI	pardon me for jumping in

You can also express emotions by setting off words in brackets <blush>; you'll often see <grin> or, among experienced onliners, the abbreviated <g>. Actions and sounds can be conveyed by setting them off in brackets, so if you're <whistling a happy tune> to show that you're not afraid, or you ran to your keyboard in a rush to get online ::whoosh!::, you can let others know. And, of course, you can send a {hug} like that or like this {} to someone who needs it. —SZA/JH

Online etiquette rules.

- DON'T TYPE IN ALL CAPS! It's hard to read and it looks like YOU'RE SHOUTING!
- Make messages easier to read: Break up long ones into separate paragraphs, using Return twice after a paragraph for a blank line.
- Quote a short, relevant piece of a message to which you're replying.
- Don't delete messages to which you reply. In a public message forum, the original message helps others follow the conversation.
- Reread your messages before you post them. You'll be surprised how often you reconsider and decide to either tone down the language, or polish it up, or rewrite a section for clarity.
- Use smilies and emoticons, but sparingly. It's sometimes important to give readers a clue to your state of mind, but you might try writing so that the clues aren't needed.
- Stay on the topic.
- Disagree with the message, not the messenger. If you don't agree with what someone said, state your case—don't call him names or point out grammatical errors.
- Give as much as (or more than) you take. Seek help, but don't forget to help others.
- Stay out of flame wars (flaming being angry online exchanges). Life's too short and nothing ever—not *ever*—gets settled.
- Give the clueless newbies a break. We all have to start somewhere, sometime. —SZA/JH

Spam. *Spamming* refers to electronic mass mailings, whether posted to a newsgroup or sent directly to a zillion individual e-mail addresses. The word does indeed come from Hormel's canned meat, but indirectly—it really comes from a Monty Python sketch which used the refrain *Spam, Spam, Spam.*

There's not much you can do about spam; it's in the category of unsolicited sales phone calls and junk mail, although the majority of spam is from sex sites and for "business opportunities" for making money. If you get any, you can notify your online or service provider of the sender, because efforts are being made to block this kind of misuse of the electronic bandwidth.

E-mail and Other Online Activities

About E-mail

My dear friend UserName. Whenever you join any online service, you'll pick a *user name* (also known as a *user ID* or *screen name*) to identify yourself. Your user name doubles as your e-mail address, so pick something short that will remind people of you, and try to use something similar on every service you join. Though services such as America Online allow wild (and even stupid) screen names, contain yourself.

If you join more than one service, you'll have a different e-mail address for each service. Pick one service—the service you access most often or that you're likely to keep the longest—as your main public e-mail receptacle; then you'll have one address to give out or put on a business card. If you get a lot of e-mail, or if you get e-mail on several services, you should look into e-mail management software (see the *E-mail managers* entry below). —JH

E-mail between online services. Within a service like AOL or CompuServe, you can send mail to another member by using simply the member's "address," which is either a name, a number, or some combination thereof. But you can send mail to either service through the Internet, from either service to an Internet address, and even between the two services, using the Internet as the go-between.

To reach a CompuServe or AOL address through the Internet, from a standard Internet e-mail address or from the other service, use: *username@AOL.com* or *username@compuserve.com.*

If a CompuServe address is a number instead of a name, the number will have a comma, which needs to be changed to a period: *72245,345@compuserve.com* becomes *72245.345@compuserve.*

And, if you're sending something through the Internet *from* your CompuServe account, you prefix the address with *internet:* *(internet:jerry88@aol.com);* if you're using CIM (CompuServe Information Manager), the "internet:" prefix is automatically added if you choose *internet* as the type of address from the pop-up menu when you're putting things in your address book.

Getting a head(er). Every online service implements e-mail in a different way, but they all have some things in common. Mail always has a header filled with information including who sent the message and when. You must supply the *subject*—a descriptive title—the addressees' correct e-mail addresses, and of course the body of the message. When you reply to a message, everything is supplied automatically except the body. Some software automatically appends the word "Re:" to the subject, the date and time are updated, and lists you as the sender. —JH

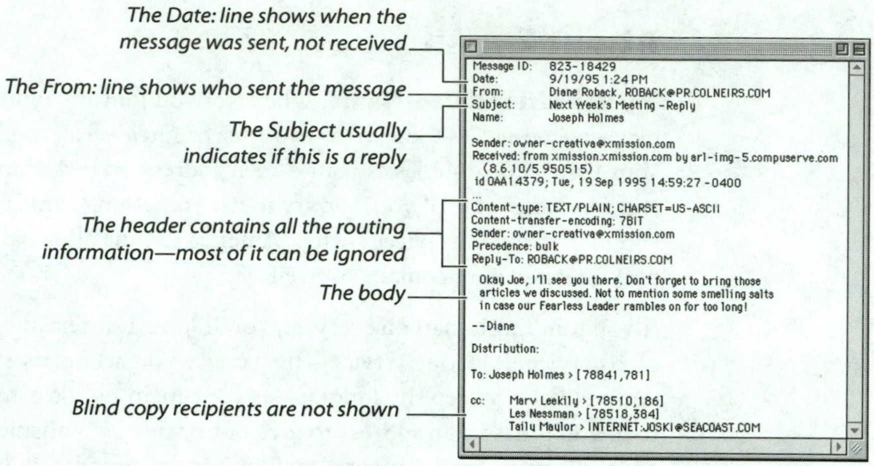
The Date: line shows when the message was sent, not received
The From: line shows who sent the message
The Subject usually indicates if this is a reply
The header contains all the routing information—most of it can be ignored
The body
Blind copy recipients are not shown
Message ID: 823-18429
Date: 9/19/95 1:24 PM
From: Diane Roback, ROBACK@PR.COLNEIRS.COM
Subject: Next Week's Meeting - Reply
Name: Joseph Holmes
Sender: owner-creativa@xmission.com
Received: from xmission.xmission.com by arl-img-5.compuserve.com (8.6.10/5.950515)
id OAA14379; Tue, 19 Sep 1995 14:59:27 -0400
...
Content-type: TEXT/PLAIN; CHARSET=US-ASCII
Content-transfer-encoding: 7BIT
Sender: owner-creativa@xmission.com
Precedence: bulk
Reply-To: ROBACK@PR.COLNEIRS.COM
Okay Joe, I'll see you there. Don't forget to bring those articles we discussed. Not to mention some smelling salts in case our Fearless Leader rambles on for too long!
--Diane
Distribution:
To: Joseph Holmes > [78841,781]
cc: Marv Leekily > [78510,186]
Les Nessman > [78518,384]
Taily Maylor > INTERNET:JOSKI@SEACOAST.COM

The format of a typical e-mail message. We've abbreviated the "header" in this message, which was originally three or four times larger.

E-mail managers. If you send or receive only a few e-mail messages a day, your online service's software will suffice. But if you get lots of e-mail, or if you need to sort it into categories, and store and retrieve it easily, you should consider an e-mail manager, an application which automatically goes online to send and retrieve all your mail, letting you read and reply to it at your leisure.

Eudora began life as a free e-mail manager, and later spawned an expanded commercial version, **Eudora Pro** ($90, Qualcomm). Eudora Pro sends and retrieves e-mail through a TCP/IP connection. It will check for mail on demand or at regular intervals, filing the messages in user-created "mailboxes," filed according to content through a special filtering system. Eudora Pro is well-designed and powerful, if a tad quirky. There's no address book, for example; instead a "nickname" system allows a short name to stand for a full e-mail address or a group of addresses. Still, for those who rely on a TCP/IP-based service for e-mail, Eudora Pro is easy to use and stable. The free Eudora Light is still supported; it lacks filtering, spell checking, and other features, but it makes a terrific first e-mail manager.

qualcomm.com

Claris E-mailer ($90, also part of ClarisWorks Office), is the best all-round e-mail manager, less powerful than Eudora Pro at filing messages, but covering most other areas better. E-mailer will retrieve e-mail from CompuServe, America Online, and an Internet service provider, on demand or on days and times you preset. It's is a natural choice for those with accounts on more than one service, but it has several slick features that make it a terrific utility even if you retrieve e-mail from just a single service—like automatically sending a prewritten reply ("I'm on vacation."). —JH

Transferring Files

Sending files. It's always been easy to send a file to someone else on the same service by "attaching" it to a message. But for awhile there, sending stuff *between* services, or across the Internet, was an arcane art: you translated the file into plain text by *binhexing* it, and sent the text. On the other end, the recipient would decode the binhexed file (recognizable by its *.hqx* suffix) and get the original back. Now, all you have to do is tell your software to send an attached file in *MacBinary* format (see the next entry), and everything gets transmitted correctly.

But you'll still want to *compress* the file to make it smaller and save transmission time for both you and the recipient. Most online software comes with some form of **StuffIt**, *the* compression utility, but you might want to use **StuffIt Deluxe**, available separately. Again, your software probably has decompression built in or tied into **StuffIt Expander**, which you can also use separately. Usually the compression and decompression are done automatically by the software, so you won't have to do a thing.

StuffIt Deluxe
Chapter 28

Oh—and if you really need to manually binhex something, StuffIt Deluxe can do both that and the decoding end of things.

The MacBinary imperative. Virtually every Mac telecommunications program has a setting for enabling something called *MacBinary*. It should be on by default, and you should leave it on unless you have some very special reason to turn it off.

MacBinary is not a protocol but a file format. It was devised by Mac telecommunications pioneers to deal with some unique Mac features, including the fact that the Mac divides files into two segments (called the *data fork* and the *resource fork*) and stores some information about files, such as type and creator codes, creation and modification dates, and icons, in the Finder rather than in the file itself. MacBinary solves these problems by combining both forks in a single block and adding a 128-byte header with the Finder information; when receiving a file, MacBinary-aware applications recognize the header, decode the file, and restore it to standard format.

When MacBinary is turned on and you initiate a file transfer, your software will convert the file into the MacBinary format. If it's sent to a PC or a mainframe, it will stay in MacBinary format, but if it reaches a Mac via a Mac communications program, it will automatically be converted back to its original format. —HN

Plain binary files. If another Mac user sends you an attachment as a standard binary file instead of MacBinary, you probably won't have to get another copy of it, as long as you know what kind of file it was supposed to be. If you know the file type and creator code of the original file and have a utility, like Drop•Info that lets you reset the file type and creator code of the transmitted file (since it was lost in the plain binary transfer), in almost every instance you can just open the file after the codes are redefined.

Virus checkers *Chapter 24*

Don't worry, be happy. No matter what you hear, computer viruses can't be transmitted by an e-mail message; but viruses *can* hop onto your hard drive when you download files. All the commercial services do an excellent job of keeping their libraries clean, but bulletin boards aren't always so safe. Invest in a good virus detection utility. —JH

Other Activities

Discussion forums. *Forums* are where public discussions occur. Also known on various services as *message boards*, *SIGs* (for special interest groups), or *conferences*, each discussion forum is devoted to a topic and divided up into subsections on subtopics. CompuServe's show business forum, for example (GO SHOWBIZ), is divided into 24 subsections, including Recent Films, Classic Films, Cult TV/Films, Soap Operas (one section for each network!), and Daytime Talk Shows. Forums are run by *sysops* (SYStem OPerators), *forum leaders*, or *moderators*, who stir up conversations, enforce the rules, and answer questions. For many people (including yours truly), discussion forums are the heart and soul of online services.

Forum discussions don't occur in real time; instead, you compose a message, give it an informative title, address it to a specific person (or to "All"), and *post* it in the appropriate forum and section, where everyone who drops in can read the message and comment on it. The original message and the string of replies and replies to replies, all keeping the same subject, make up a *thread*. (As powerful and useful as message threading is, not all services use it.)

These forum discussions sometimes take on the character of religious debates, and some especially inflammatory messages become known as *flames*. But for the most part, forum discussions are civil, and often lively and informative. They can go on for days and even weeks. —JH

Libraries. All the services offer software you can download. The online universe is simply bursting at the seams with games, utilities, reading material, fonts, system updates, demo versions of commercial software, and Frequently Asked Questions (FAQ) documents, stored in the *libraries* of online services.

Of course, you don't need an online service like CompuServe or AOL to download software, because you can also get almost everything from someplace on the Web. —SZA/JH

Chatty Cathy... and Kelly and Kevin and... America Online didn't invent the "chat" concept, but it certainly brought both the word and the activity to the forefront of American consciousness. The concept: dozens of people are typing at their computers at the same time; everything everyone types appears on everyone else's screen, prefixed by the typist's name. Confusing? You bet. You type a comment, press Return, and anywhere from seconds to a minute or more later, everyone else can see it—but by then the statement you were replying to has scrolled off the screen, and a dozen other, perhaps totally unrelated, comments have appeared. In addition to the conversation itself, participants type in all sorts of "signals" that indicate emotions or actions. Some software offers helpful conversation-tracking features, like keeping the "words" of a conversation in a different color from side comments for emotions or actions. But even with the most helpful of software, chatting is a great mental exercise.

Unfortunately, the mental exercise sometimes comes only from keeping track of who said what. The actual conversation in many chat rooms runs the gamut from juvenile to banal to singles-bar-in-the-seventies-repartee. You can still sometimes find a good, moderated conference on CompuServe's Mac forums and in certain Web chats—where people take turns talking in full sentences and meet to discuss specific topics that don't have anything to do with sex or calling each other names.

(Chat rooms seem particularly addictive to teens. One recent afternoon, my younger son was trying to get in touch with a friend of his, whose phone line was constantly busy. He said he knew why—she dropped into a particular chat room almost every day after school. So, he went online, dropped in, and asked her to get off the computer and call him. Which she did.)

Mailing lists. E-mail is a nifty way to sign up for mass mailings on various topics, everything from exotic music to technical support to Apple Computer press releases. Some lists mail out all the messages, or digests of them, contributed by all the folks who subscribe to the list, making a sort of e-mail based discussion forum. Other lists are little more than electronic junk mail.

Signing up typically involves sending a message to a list server (not the mailing address) with a subscribe command in the body. (Lists usually include unsubscribe instructions at the end of every mailing.) Here's one to get you started: for the Apple EvangeList, e-mail *macway-request@solutions.apple.com* with any message in the body. —JH

Online Services and Providers

Commercial Services and ISPs

America Online. America Online (AOL), as a result of blanketing Mother Earth in free sign-up disks, boasts the largest collection of members of any online service. It was the first to offer a graphical interface (modeled after Apple's own AppleLink) to all users. It even bought its chief (though ailing) rival, CompuServe, which it promises to keep alive as a separate entity doing its own thing.

Although so many former "content vendors" have moved to the Web, AOL provides hundreds of special-interest areas. It also, of course, serves as a gateway to the Internet. It lets you have several "screen names" for identification and e-mail on the same billing account—perfect for families and small organizations (and split personalities). For the kids, you can set "security levels" that block them from certain areas, from the Internet, and/or from getting attachments with their mail.

These are only the main "channels" that AOL offers in its wide world of information.

CompuServe. CompuServe (or CIS, for CompuServe Information Service) was dragged kicking and screaming into the age of graphical interface, hemorrhaging members left and right along the way, and finally being sold to America Online (some said the deal was strictly because AOL needed more dial-in nodes *right away* due to class-action law suits by subscribers whose chief membership benefit was a busy signal).

CompuServe is positioning itself as a "business resource" and offers, in addition to hundreds of free areas, many for-pay information services; of course, it too is an Internet gateway. What's still unique about CompuServe—and what will keep me there until its dying day—is its *threaded* discussions. When someone posts a message, and someone else replies, and others reply to the original or to the replies, it's easy to follow the "thread" of comments and reply to any of them. This is eons ahead of the "drop it in this folder" method of having an online conversation.

The other best thing about CompuServe is its Mac support. It's the only place that offers Mac experts officially hanging around in the Mac forums, answering questions as well as keeping things generally humming along.

There are several ways you can access CompuServe. The main software is **CIM—CompuServe Information Manager**, the graphical approach to CompuServe's content. The second tool, indispensable for frequent visits to certain forums (as opposed to the wandering around you can do through

CIM) is **CompuServe Navigator**, which you can set up to automatically get your e-mail, respond to any mail you picked up previously, and zip through any forum to gather recent postings (and post your messages).

CompuServe's Information Manager offers the long-awaited graphical connection to the service.

Local bulletin boards. Bulletin boards—small, usually inexpensive, specialized, and local online services—were once the only destination for a modem user. As the major commercial online services grow more enormous and the Internet becomes a household word, bulletin board systems (BBS's) are fading from view—or moving to the Web. Most boards use graphical interfaces, the most popular of which is SoftArc's **First Class**. After downloading the First Class Client software (available from any First Class BBS by logging on with any standard communications software), you can dial in to any First Class BBS and use easy icon- and menu-based navigation. —JH/SB

Internet service providers. The Internet service provider market is probably one of the most volatile markets in existence. Everyone—from garage-based small companies to multinational cable and telephone companies—is clamoring to be your *ISP (Internet Service Provider),* your conduit to the Internet.

Fee structures are usually similar to those of commercial online services; typically, $10 to $20 a month gets you basic software, unlimited access, and an e-mail address.

Using a large, nationwide ISP like Earthlink rather than a local provider has its pluses and minuses. You should expect to get better customer support and reliable performance from a national ISP, but you may have to make a long-distance call to connect to the service, which can quickly add to the cost. Luckily, the number of *POPs* (local telephone call *points of presence*) for large service providers is growing. This means that if you are located near a metropolitan area, you should be able to connect via a local telephone call. —SZA/JH

CompuServe Tips

Recent uploads. To check for the recently uploaded files on CompuServe, you have to check each library individually. Using CompuServe Information

Manager, go to a forum, select Search from the Libraries menu, leave the text fields blank, check the One Week Ago radio button, and click Search. —JH

Auto-mail retrieval. CIM has Send/Receive All Mail and Get New Mail commands (in the Mail menu), but CIM stays online after checking for mail. Hold down ⌘ while selecting Send/Receive All Mail, or ⌘ Option while selecting Get New Mail, and CIM will do its thing and then log off automatically. —JH

CIM's auto-lookup addresses. When you start a new mail message and the cursor is in the Name field, just type the first few letters of the person's name, the same way you stored it in your address book. As soon as you type, CIM fills in the rest of the name, changing its suggestion as you continue typing. Press Return when it's showing the right name, and the address is automatically filled in for the next box.

Right back atcha. If you want to quote something from a message when you reply to it, just select it in the original message and then click the Reply button. Your message box will open with the selected material in it, set off by dashed lines and labeled as coming from the original sender.

The browser of your choice. When you access the Internet through CIM, you can make it launch any browser (I guess that should be *either* browser) by setting your choice through the Preferences command, using the General icon.

For CompuServe Navigator. Three quickies for your "Nav session":

- Copy Table, found in the Edit menu, acts like a normal clipboard copy except that every series of spaces is converted into a tab. This is very useful when copying text that has been formatted with spaces substituted for tabs and indents.
- Shortcut: Highlight the thread subject in the Session View window and—avoiding the Summary menu—type E to retrieve the entire thread so far, O for this one message, B for this Branch, and T for all new thread messages next session only.
- If you need a CompuServe local access number when you're traveling, use Navigator in terminal mode (or any telecommunications application) and dial 1-800-346-3247. At the Host Name prompt, type PHONES and then follow the prompts. —JH

AOL Tips

Buddy Lists. The Buddy List is one of the best online ideas ever. You create a list of your friends on AOL—you can categorize them as friend, family member, or colleague—and then you're notified automatically whenever any one of them logs on while you're online (in case you want to send them an instant message).

The way to get the darn Buddy List window open, however, is anything but intuitive. There are two routes (one only a little better than the other): use the keyword BuddyView to open the window, or use the Buddy Lists command from the Member menu and then click the View button. You can also set it to open automatically whenever you log on, through the Buddy List command—click on the Buddy List Preferences icon.

I wanted to do a screen shot of a Buddy List, so I asked one of my sons to log on; what you see here are a few of his forty-seven closest friends.

Instant Messenger service. This is not the same as the Instant Message service that keeps AOL members in real-time touch with each other! The Instant Messenger service lets people who aren't on AOL send you instant messages from the Internet. It's a free service for both of you, so use the keyword *Instant Messenger* to get more information.

I just vant to be alone. AOL was created to keep you in touch—with the world, with your family, friends, and colleagues—but sometimes you just don't want them all to be in touch with you! While instant messaging may be great when you want to send something, and your Buddy List keeps you in touch with your inner circle, sometimes you've got to get some work done or just otherwise surf and skim with no interruptions. (Or maybe just no interruptions from the guy you met in the chat room who thinks you should be joining him in a business venture that sounds curiously like a pyramid scheme.)

AOL's most important dialog box is the Privacy Preferences dialog, where you can choose to remain invisible from individuals or groups, or everyone in the online world. You may not be aware of its existence, because access to it is buried in the Buddy List dialog, which has a Privacy Preferences button. But you can see by the picture here that the choices it presents as to who can see that you're online and who can instant message you lets you block everyone or only a select few.

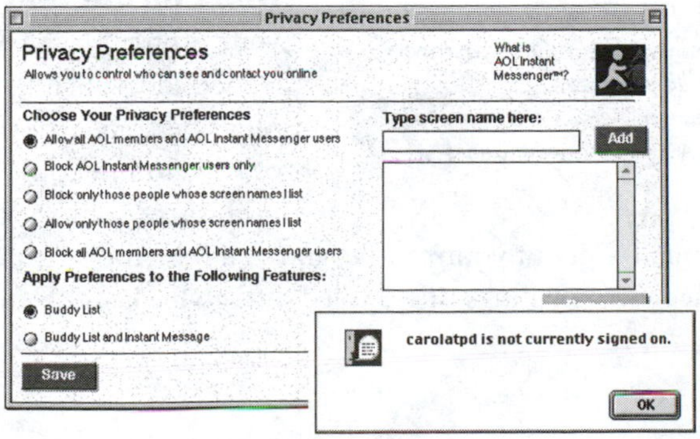

Set your privacy preferences through the Buddy List dialog and you'll be invisible to the people you've specified.

Once you've blocked someone, what do they see if they search for you or try to instant message you? A dialog that says you're not even logged on—that way they're not insulted that you've blocked them from seeing you.

Temporary turn-off. If you want to stay generally available to instant messages but occasionally need to hang out the equivalent of a "Do Not Disturb" sign when you're trying to get some work done, you can temporarily block messages that you don't have time to attend to:

1. Select Send an Instant Message from the Member menu.
2. In the To box, type *$im_off*. Upper or lowercase doesn't matter, but it's important to include the underscore.
3. In the message area, type anything, as long as it's at least a single character—even just a space.
4. Send the message.

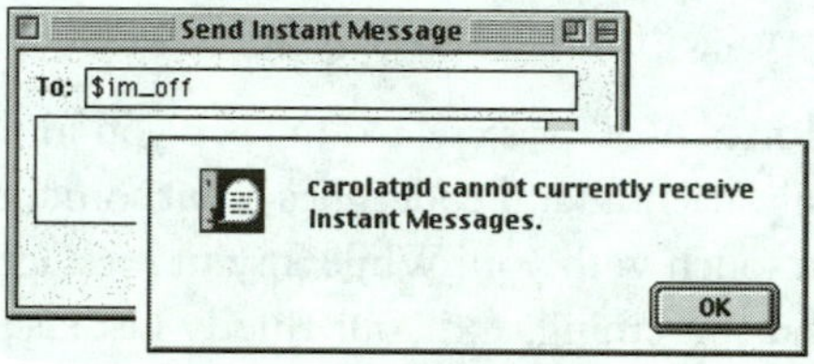

The magic message.

If anyone tries to message you while you're in this mode, they'll see a dialog that says you're not currently able to receive instant messages. To turn the instant messaging back on, just do the same thing again, but with *$im_on* in the To box.

Stop that graphics delay. If you're really tired of waiting for America Online to send graphical elements to your hard drive just so the splash screens look pretty, locate and install a copy of ArtValve. It's a control panel that stops AOL from performing that annoying interruption; it substitutes a generic icon for the missing graphics. You can find it on America Online. —JH

Web site shortcut. If you're in AOL and heading for the Web, you don't have to access the Internet and then go to the site. Instead, you can use the standard Keyword dialog (in the Go To menu, or ⌘K) and type the URL of the web site you want, like: *http://www.thetipster.com*. (Browsers let you skip all the introductory stuff, but you can't in the Keyword dialog.)

> ***"If you can't make money with 8 million customers, how many customers do you need?"***
> *Marc Andreesen, Netscape founder, regarding AOL's financial difficulties*

Don't fill out that profile! Leave your profile blank. What started out as a good idea—listing your hobbies and other personal information so people of a like mind could contact you—has been turned into a tool for those of a warped mind. Fill out your profile, and you'll be the target of all sorts of unsolicited mass mailings. If it's filled out, go back and blank it out.

The Internet

The Basics

What *is* the Internet? The incredibly complex structure that is the Internet is actually pretty easy to describe. A network is a group of computers connected so that they can share information. The Internet is networks, and single computers, interconnected so they can share information. What started as a military and educational quasi-experiment has turned into a necessity of everyday commerce and communication.

Okay, then, what's the Web? The World Wide Web (by English grammar rules, that should be World-Wide Web, but by convention there's no hyphen) is not so much a separate entity in the vast Internet universe as it is a way of accessing much of the Internet. Access is Mac-like no matter what computer you're using: point and click to move from place to place.

All about the Web
Chapter 28

Eternal accolades to Tim Berners-Lee, who became famous but not rich from "inventing" the Web. He suggested, in a 1989 paper, that the display of Internet information could be graphical in nature and navigating from one place to another could be accomplished by a series of *hyperlinks,* or more simply, *links.* The approach was totally platform independent because everything could be described in a simple text document that would be easy to transfer to any computer. The document, using HTML (HyperText Markup Language), would be translated into pictures and formatted text on the user's end. Within two years, HTTP was being used on the net, and within five, it seemed to have taken over the world.

Alphabet soup. As befits an arena that started with computers before they became personal, Internet-related terms are very much a collection of arcane acronyms and initials. (Lots of them include a P for *protocol,* which, as in its standard English definition, is just a set of rules.) With a few exceptions, noted in the descriptions below, the letters are pronounced separately, not as words. Many of these items have fuller explanations and more information later in the chapter.

- **IP:** *Internet Protocol*. A standard code used to identify individual computers in a network, or on the Internet. You might already have run across something called an *IP address*. You certainly have seen it if you've "manually" set up your Mac for Internet access.
- **TCP/IP:** *Transmission Control Protocol/Internet Protocol.* (You don't acknowledge the slash when you're spouting off this string of initials—just say "t-c-p-i-p.") These are the network protocols for the Internet and for some non-Internet multiplatform networks, especially those that include Unix machines.

- **SLIP:** *Serial Line Internet Protocol.* (This one's pronounced as a word.) A protocol for using TCP/IP over phone lines; pretty much replaced by PPP (next entry).
- **PPP:** *Point-to-Point Protocol.* Another protocol for dial-up TCP/IP connections. It's considered better than SLIP, and has become the standard.
- **FTP:** *File Transfer Protocol.* You guessed it—protocols for sending files from place to place, used for uploading and downloading files. An *FTP site* is one that stores files ready for download (although basic Web sites might also include downloadable files). In the laid-back world of computer jargon, the initials are also used as a verb: *You can FTP to this site to get the files you need.*
- **SMTP:** *Simple Mail Transfer Protocol*. A protocol for zapping e-mail around the Internet.
- **POP:** *Post Office Protocol.* (Pronounced as a word.) A protocol for storing and retrieving e-mail. This usually has a number after it, for the evolving protocol, and programs are referred to in terms of *compliance* with the protocol: "That mail package isn't POP3-compliant."
- **URL:** *Universal Resource Locator.* An Internet "address," describing where specific information resides.
- **HTTP:** *HyperText Transfer Protocol.* The method used to describe, in text-only documents, how a graphical web page should look on a user's screen.
- **ISP:** *Internet Service Provider.* (Aha! A *P* that doesn't stand for *protocol!*) A company that lets you hook up to the Internet; it can be small and local, or large and nationwide.

The Duke of URL. Every accessible resource on the Internet has its own unique address—its URL (which, despite the musical reference in this entry's title, is pronounced as separate letters, not "earl"). You can learn a bit about what a URL points to by reading it piece by piece; this is a distinctly useful talent.

Gopher and FTP
Later this chapter

The URL starts with the *protocol*, a few letters followed by a colon that tell you what sort of address it is: *http:* indicates a World Wide Web page; *ftp:* is an FTP site from which you can download a file; and *gopher:* is a gopher site. The protocol is followed by a double-slash (//) separator.

Next come the *domain* and *subdomains,* which identify the host computer or network; when there's a list of subdomains, they're separated by periods, referred to as *dots* when saying the address. Web site domains usually begin with *www.;* FTP sites start with *ftp.* One of the subdomains is usually the name of the company or organization.

Finally (or, not so finally, as we'll see in a later entry), there's a three-letter *domain type* or *top-level domain* that tells what kind of organization you're dealing with: *.com* is business (commercial), *.org* is nonprofit organization, and so on. Here's a typical address: *http://www.thecompany.com.* —SZA/JH

Top-level domains. There are six basic top-level domains, or domain types:

com	commercial
edu	educational
gov	government
mil	military
net	network or internet
org	organization (nonprofit)

At least, that's how it started. But it was a very U.S.-centric system, and as the internet spread, two-letter top-level domains were introduced, to identify the country of origin: *us* for United States, *uk* for the United Kingdom, *jp* for Japan, and so on. You'll seldom see the *us* domain name, but you'll often see the codes for other countries. (You can find a complete, ever-growing list of country codes at *http://uci.edu/WebSoft/wwwstat/country-codes.text.)*

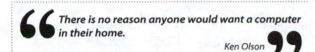

> ***There is no reason anyone would want a computer in their home.***
>
> *Ken Olson*
> *Digital Equipment Corporation founder and President, 1977*

But that's not all. The proliferation of sites on the World Wide Web has everyone pushing for additional domain names. But the issue that should have been settled the year before this book went to print is still up in the air as it goes to press. The wrangling is among the internet specialists, commercial ventures, and the government (that alone is enough to drag out the process; the issues are not only what the domain names should be, but also who *decides* what the names should be, who gets to register and keep track of them, and, of course, who's going to make money doing so.

Address paths. Using an address that ends with the domain type will get you to some main or top-level page of information for the organization you're contacting. From there, many sites offer ways to follow paths to specific information. If you know what you need and where it's stored, you can use the resource's *path name* as part of the address to jump right to the spot. A path name is the route you need to get to an item through its host computer's directories (similar to the Mac's folders).

Path names start after the domain type, with a slash (/) and sometimes also a tilde (~) that indicates you're looking at a home directory. The words in the path that list the subdirectories you're going through (like going through nested folders on the desktop) are separated by a slash. The final item, after the last slash, is the resource itself.

```
http://www.thesite.org/~joiners/membership/signup.html
```

While case, upper or lower, doesn't matter through most of the URL, it *does* matter in the path name. That's the first thing to examine when you get a "404 Not Found" error in your Web browser. —SZA/JH

Registering a domain name. You can't just pick a domain name and start using it. You have to register a domain name through the proper organization; right now, that's InterNIC.

internic.net

Although InterNIC started out taking care of all domain names, and doing it for free, now you have to pay for a domain name ($100 for the first two years) and there's quite a move to break InterNIC's monopoly in the area. But, along with the establishment of new domain names (as described in an earlier entry), the whole thing is up in the air at this time. —SZA/JH

Features and Functions

E-mail addresses. E-mail addresses on the Internet are easily recognizable: the @ ("at") sign gives them an instantly recognizable difference from commercial-service addresses which, when used internally, are simply names consisting of words and/or numbers.

The first part—the part in front of the @—of an Internet e-mail address is the user's name: *sharon,* or *JohnDoe*, or *WrthCmdr1.* The part after the @ is the *domain name*, followed by a period (called "dot" when you're saying the address out loud) and then a three-letter code for the *domain type.* You don't have to worry about upper- and lowercase letters in e-mail addresses.

Permanent e-mail address. The "permanent" e-mail address is an interesting concept. As ISPs come and go, many of us switch. But that means a new address with many attendant hassles. A group called **PO Box** offers addresses that can be aliased to whatever your current real address is. It's cheap, and it works. Check out http://www.pobox.com. —SB

I heard the news today, oh boy. *Usenet news groups* are the Internet's discussion forums, despite the misleading word "news" and the fact that posted messages are confusingly called *articles*. Because most news groups aren't supervised, they're seldom as focussed and civil as commercial-service forums; pick your news groups carefully if you're easily offended. And because millions of users have access to the groups, they lack the intimate feel of the best forums on the commercial services.

The news group address can tell you a bit about what you'll find there. The address is organized into hierarchies, from the broadest to the most specific, separated by periods. The first part specifies the general category. The most common are:

alt.	the alternative—often wilder and weirder—groups
biz.	business
comp.	computers
k12.	kindergarten through 12th grade
misc.	miscellaneous

rec.	hobbies and recreation
sci.	science
soc.	social, cultural, religious
talk.	controversial topics

There are many others, including geographical ones like "ca." for California and "ba." for Bay Area.

Read the remainder of the address for a clue about the specific contents: *comp.newton.misc*, for instance, contains miscellaneous discussions of the Newton MessagePad; any group name ending with ".binaries" includes uuencoded (specially coded for transmission over the Internet) images, sounds, or even applications. (Your news reader or Stuffit Expander can decode these for you.) —JH

News readers. There are a few fine news readers, but the best is John Norstad's free **NewsWatcher**. It's beautifully implemented, and so simple to use that you probably won't need to crack open the instructions. (One clue: John has implemented drag and drop very nicely—make use of it.) Its only serious disadvantage is that it doesn't let you read and reply off-line. A commercial news reader, **NewsHopper** ($60; Landware), has one big advantage: it's the only one that allows off-line reading. For the terminally lazy, a browser like Netscape Navigator will read news groups too, though without the bells and whistles of the best stand-alone readers. —JH

demon.co.uk/sw15

Just the FAQs, ma'am. Almost every news group posts a current *FAQ*, a *Frequently Asked Questions* document (pronounced "fack"), which contains guidelines and rules for the news group, and often a FAQ covering the subject of the group as well. (A list of FAQs is kept at *cis.ohio-state.edu/hypertext/faq/usenet/*.) Read the FAQ before posting messages or risk looking like a *newbie*. —JH

FTP(ing). The *File Transfer Protocol* that defines how files can be sent over the Internet is also an adjective used to describe a site that stores files for download ("an FTP site"), and a verb that refers to both getting to the site ("If you FTP to this site...") and getting the file ("FTP the file to..."). You can FTP (in any sense of the word) with any browser, or with FTP-specific software.

You get to an FTP site the same way you get to any site on the net: use your browser (or specialized software) and the FTP site's address (its URL). After you get to the site, you'll probably have to look for the file. Most FTP sites are organized in nested *directories*, similar to the Mac's folders, so you can go up and down the hierarchy to look for files.

With the ubiquitous Web and its two browsers, most people never need an FTP-specific piece of software. But if you do, use the shareware classic **Fetch** ($25). —SZA/JH

ftp.dartmouth.edu/pub/software/mac/

IN THE BEGINNING

Picture this favorite trade-show T-shirt in the early days. Large letters on the front: IBM. In smaller print, following the letters:

I
Bought
Macintosh

Gopher. Before the World Wide Web, people moved through hierarchical menus of resources by way of *Gopher*, a slick and still useful method of creating a directory of resources. Your Web browser makes a fine Gopher application, though the old standby **Turbo Gopher** is fine. For a sample, you can visit the "mother of All Gophers" at *gopher://gopher.umn.edu*. You can also use keywords to search all gopher databases using an application called **Veronica**, which you can get from *gopher://futique.scs.unr.edu/11/veronic*>. —JH

Telnet. Telnet is a primitive but sometimes necessary method of remotely logging onto another computer. Telnet will usually plop you at the remote computer's command-line prompt, at which point you'll need to enter a username and password, but from there you can, for instance, join in a MUD, search for resources, or use a few Unix commands to maintain your Web pages. Check out NCSA Telnet at ftp://ftp.aloha.net/pub/Mac/. —JH

irchelp.org

IRC. The Internet version of an AOL chat room is *Internet Relay Chat*, or *IRC*, in which live conversations take place over *channels*. Unlike chats on the commercial services, IRC is often thrilling for immediate news of world-shaking events. Eye-witness accounts of the Oklahoma City bombing and the Gulf War were first transmitted over IRC. For Internet chat, you need your basic connection, a program (or *client*) that lets you chat, and a place to "go." You can get a stand-alone chat client, or one that works with your web browser. **Homer** (*ftp://ftp.aloha.net/pub/Mac/*) and **Ircle** (*alf8.speech.sc.cmu.edu/~ircle/*) are shareware chat programs. If you use Netscape Navigator, you can download netscape's **iChat** client from Netscape's home page.

Most IRC channels start with a #, and most IRC servers have a channel called *#newbie*, which is a good place to start. To find channels, try *www.dal.net*, *www.undernet.org*, *www.another.net*, and Netscape's home page. —JH

Ping pong. A ping is how long it takes (measured in seconds) for your text to reach another user in the chat room. Type */ping nickname or /ping/#channel-name* to ping everyone on the channel to see what your ping is. —JH

28

The World Wide Web

In This Chapter

The World Wide Web

Basics

The World Wide Web. For years, the Internet was little more than text, text, and more text. Then the World Wide Web changed everything. It was as if the telegram had been followed directly by the invention of glossy color magazines. And because it's so simple to compose a personal Web site, web content has grown tremendously quickly. Imagine what cable TV would be like if every person with a video camera could schedule a TV show—that's the Web in a nutshell. (Yes, it sounds like it could be a nightmare!) You can read a history of the World Wide Web at *w3.org/hypertext/WWW/History.html*.

There's still plenty of text, of course, but the Web presents it in formatted *pages*, with color illustrations, backgrounds, and even animation and sound. The Web's most revolutionary innovation, however, is its use of *hyperlinks,* or, more simply, just *links*—click on linked text or pictures and you're whisked off to some spot on that page or elsewhere on the Web. It's as if the entire Web is just one enormous—if slow—multimedia magazine. —SZA/JH

The browser. The program that lets you access the Web is a *browser*, an application that efficiently scoops up the text "behind" the web page you see, and then, after reading the special *tags* embedded within the text, does all the heavy-duty formatting locally, on your Mac. This method gets the information to you much more quickly than if the fully formatted page had to be downloaded through your modem.

HTML tags only tell your browser how text should look and where things are placed on the page; all sorts of extra attractions—sound, QuickTime movies, animations—have to be handled by other applications. Some of these are modules called *plug-ins* that let the browser do things like play a QuickTime movie. Others are *helper applications* that automatically handle certain types of files that you download from the Web. —SZA/JH

Web technologies. The Internet is fertile ground for new technologies. Here's a rundown on hottest:

- **Java.** The hot Web technology of the moment promises to turn the Web from glossy magazine to interactive TV. A Java-enhanced Web browser downloads tiny platform-independent applications associated with web pages. These *applets* can do amazing things on the web page. For instance? Time will tell. Cool-but-forgettable demos of the technology abound. Play Tetris, do a crossword puzzle, gaze at 3-D modeling, or read a live stock ticker tape.

A game of Tetris—er, Quatris—played live over the Internet (including sound effects) with the help of the plug-in ShockWave.

- **ShockWave for Director**. Macromedia Director creates multimedia for the Mac, and Macromedia's free AfterBurner software will convert and compress those files so you can add them to web pages. Drop the free ShockWave plug-in into your browser and you can experience slick interactive animation over the Web.
- **RealAudio**. Radio over the Internet, piped live into your Mac. No more waiting through a five-minute download just to hear a single 20-second sound sample. From a growing list of RealAudio Web sites you can listen to sports and concert coverage, news broadcasts, and rebroadcasts of archived speeches and music. Don't expect FM-quality sound—the fi isn't yet hi—but it's improving. The RealAudio client software for listening is free.
- **CU-SeeMe**. It's not a hot new technology. It's a hot *old* technology, developed in 1992 at Cornell University. CU-SeeMe is video conferencing over the Internet—videophone!—using an inexpensive Mac video camera like the $100 Connectix's QuickCam and the video digitizing capabilities of an AV Mac or a video digitizing card. You'll actually see live pictures of everyone in the conference, though it's more like a slide show than video.
- **VRML** (Virtual Reality Modeling Language). This programming language can set the user down in a three-dimensional environment. VRML browsers and viewers are in the works. Check out the latest developments: *http://rosebud.sdsc.edu/SDSC/Partners/vrml/software/browsers.html.* —JH

macromedia.com
realaudio.com
cu-seeme.cornell.edu

JavaScript. While Java is a programming language that can build platform-independent applications, *JavaScript* is a scripting language whose instructions can be embedded in the HTML code of a web page. As your browser encounters the JavaScript commands while it's building the page on your Mac, it executes the instructions (assuming your browser understands JavaScript).

JavaScript could have taken over web-page design if the usual nonsense hadn't erupted between its developer, Sun Microsystems, and Microsoft. Instead of supporting Sun's version of JavaScript, Microsoft added its own bells and whistles, that only Explorer (and not Navigator) could interpret. In the one-upmanship that Microsoft seems to engender with so many of its "colleagues," the situation soon escalated so that Navigator could support certain JavaScript features and Explorer others. That left many web developers sticking with either the most basic of JavaScript functions (and what fun is that?) or having to choose which browser to support—or writing two versions of every page. Or ignoring JavaScript entirely. Stay tuned.

C is for Cookie—that's good enough for me. (If you've had a kid—or been one—any time in the last twenty years, you know the tune for this entry title.) Internet cookies have been getting a bad rap. Yes, they can be mis-used—as can so many technologies—but they certainly serve a purpose. A cookie is simply a special file that a web server sends to your hard drive. The next time you visit the same site, the server can identify you. It can use this information to, for instance, personalize the page you see when you come back based on the things you did at the site on your last visit.

Home sweet home. There are three different meanings for the term *home page:*

- The page your browser goes to automatically when you first start it, and when you click the Home button.
- The main page for any multipage site.
- An "about me" personal page (these proliferated when AOL offered free Web space to its members).

Misinformation on the Web. One of the Web's great advantages is also one of its weakest points: anyone can publish on the Web. What's the problem with that? Case in point: one of my sons was doing a paper on Isaac Asimov's works. We surfed around looking for information. One of the "Asimov" pages started out with this statement: "Although I've never actually read any of Asimov's books…" Really! The author went on to give his opinion of other people's opinions of Asimov's works.

Caveat surfer.

Browsers and Other Software

Browser wars. There are two main browsers available for surfing the Web: Netscape's **Navigator** and Microsoft's **Internet Explorer**. The rivalry between the two has resulted in a game of leapfrog that has led to feature enhancements and version number increments that changed faster than for any other software I can think of. Each has settled in at version 4 for awhile as of this writing, but they'll probably continue to advance in tandem.

netscape.com
microsoft.com

Oh… did I mention that they were both free? You'll find an option to install Explorer with your system software; some system versions supply Navigator, too. Both are available for download from the Web, too. (There's some irony involved if you use the one browser to get to a site where you can download the other one.)

After years of preferring Navigator over Explorer—both on merit and on general principal—Explorer 4 is my browser of choice. It's a Mac product that Microsoft did right, and edges out Navigator in several of its niceties. Still, the products are so close there's no clear winner at this stage. Which is no big deal, since you can easily try out both of them.

The biggest helper of all. Because bigger files take longer to transmit, *file compression* has long been a staple of the telecommunicating world: a file is

> ***...we've had a very in-depth involvement. Whenever you get involved with prototype machines that early on, you are essentially part of the engineering team ... Microsoft has been an extension of the internal Mac software team for the last few years.***
>
> *Bill Gates, 1984*
>
> ***I've noticed that Microsoft's taken a lot more credit than they deserve.***
>
> *Bruce Horn, (Finder programmer), 1984*

squeezed down to a much smaller size, transmitted, and then reconstituted at the other end. How is this miracle wrought? The most basic of tricks for compressing text files is to represent the most-used letters of the alphabet with fewer bits of information (instead of the standard computer-based approach of needing eight bits of information for every character). On the graphics end, the basic trick stores information about pixel *changes* in the picture rather than for every single dot in the picture; visualize a landscape photo which is two-thirds blue sky and you can see that it would take less room to say "make this and the next 2,000 pixels sky blue" than to store the color values for each pixel individually. Compressing a text-based file (including formatted word processor documents) can save twenty to eighty percent of the file size; compressing graphics can save from five to forty percent, depending on both the file type and the individual graphic. Because the first Mac compression utility was named *StuffIt*, compressed files are generally referred to as *stuffed* files in the Mac world.

In addition to file size, transferring files on the Web presents another hurdle, discussed in the last chapter: you can send only text over the Internet. With a method called *binhexing*, any Mac file can be translated into text characters, and then translated back into a real document of text or graphics, or sound, or whatever it was originally.

None of this is a big deal: compression and binhexing, and the restoration of the files after being transferred, is usually handled automatically by your browser. But it's Aladdin Systems' **StuffIt Expander** that's doing all the work in the background, first de-binhexing the file if necessary and then unstuffing it. This is the "biggest helper of all" referred to in the entry title. Aladdin made this freeware a long time ago, and it's included with every browser, commercial-service software, and general telecom software package; it's also available for downloading from almost anywhere on the Web. The companion shareware utility, **DropStuff**, is available at Aladdin's site (as well as elsewhere); you can use it to compress files that you want to send someplace.

StuffIt Deluxe

The commercial route. If you do any but the simplest of stuffing and unstuffing, get Aladdin's **StuffIt Deluxe** ($80). It includes things like: a choice between using faster or more efficient compression; the ability to split compressed files into multiple disk files (for when even the compressed version won't fit on a disk); a wider range of file types for both compression and decompression operations; and the ability to create self-extracting archives. (A self-extracting archive, identifiable by the *.sea* suffix, is a compressed file that doesn't need a utility to decompress it: double-click on the file, and it extracts the original file automatically.)

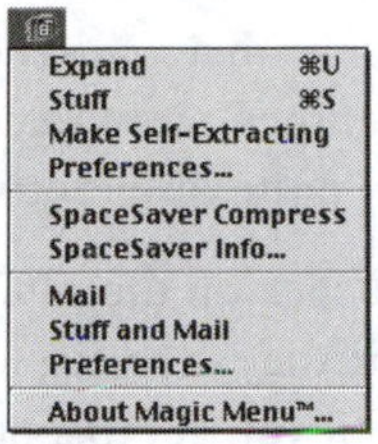

The StuffIt Deluxe Finder menu.

With **StuffIt Deluxe** (version 4.5 is current as of this writing), you get a Finder menu with commands that can be carried out on selected desktop items, and a pop-up contextual menu with the same commands. Best of all is the feature that has made everyone to whom I've shown it run out and buy the program: in the Finder, alter a file's name by adding *.sit* to it (the suffix used to denote a stuffed file), and it's automatically compressed as soon as you hit Enter to enter the name change. Delete the *.sit* suffix from a stuffed file, and it's automatically decompressed. The same thing works for self-extracting archives (the *.sea* suffix). No muss, no fuss, no bother.

aladdinsys.com

If you have StuffIt Deluxe, you can set it to be your browser's "helper" instead of Expander.

Acrobatics. Adobe **Acrobat** started out as a utility for electronic publishing: something that could take a mixed text-and-graphics document and preserve its contents and layout, and display it on any computer platform. PDF (portable document format) files are everywhere you look: you'll find them as read-me's on disks and as downloadable files on commercial services and the Web.

adobe.com

The freeware Acrobat reader is included in your system software—it's also downloadable from almost anywhere on the Web, including, of course, Adobe's site. With it, you can open and read any PDF, and even search through its contents. To create a PDF file, you need the Acrobat application.

Which brings us to Acrobat (the reader) as a helper application. When the reader is defined as a helper application in your browser (which it usually is by default), linking to a PDF file on a web page will launch the reader and display the PDF in the browser window.

I seem to be the only person who hates this. (I used to feel I was the only person who didn't like John Wayne, or watch Dallas.) But it's just not all it's cracked up to be. First of all, most PDF files were designed for printed materials, not for the Web. The fonts are wrong, the pictures aren't great, and the layout stinks when you put it in a browser window. The pages are relatively large, and therefore slow to load and to move around in. The Reader loads inside the browser window, and its controls leave even less room for the actual document, which you can read only by scrolling back and forth horizontally. As a final insult, when you quit your browser, the Reader is left open in the background (and you never even realized it existed separately from the browser), taking up, oh, maybe eight megs of memory. There, I feel better for getting that off my chest!

Searching on the Web

Search engines versus directories. There are two main ways to find something on the Web: through a *directory* or with a *search engine.* The line between these two gets a little muddy sometimes, since many sites offer both capabilities, but their functioning is actually quite different.

A directory provides lists of categories. You click on the category and see subcategories. Click on one of those, and get further subcategories, drilling your way down to the information you need, until you get to a point where there's actually a list of related sites instead of just categories. A search engine lets you type in a few words and finds sites that include those words as basic topics.

Most search sites are a combination of directory and search engine, so you can use the best approach: drill down to a certain level of category to narrow your search, and then type in what your keywords for the search.

Here are some directory/search sites to try (many are interlinked so you can move from one to another—sometimes you won't even have to reenter your search criteria):

yahoo.com altavista.com
excite.com infoseek.com
lycos.com

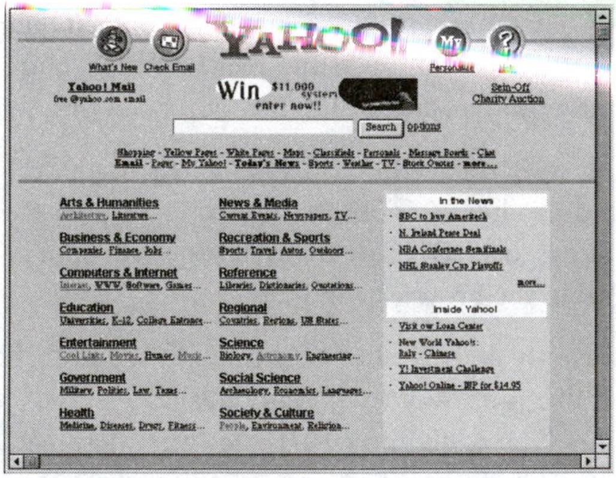

The original famous Web directory, Yahoo! You can click on a category to drill down, or use the Search option at any time.

The Search button. The Search button at the top of Navigator takes you to a site that lists several search engines; if you want to go directly to a specific site, you should set up a bookmark for it. In Explorer, the Search button is set to take you to (what else?) a Microsoft site. But you can set it to take you to the search site of your choice, through the Home/Search category in the Preferences dialog.

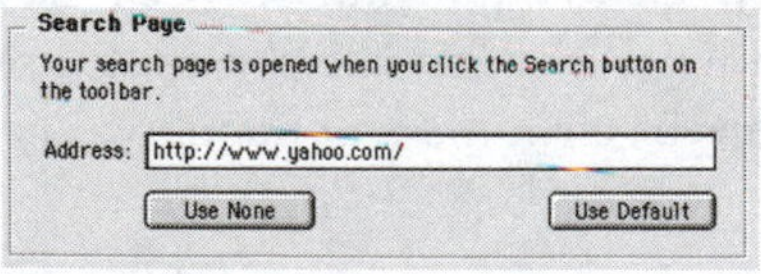

Set the default search site in Explorer's Preferences dialog.

Advanced search screens. Search engines provide advanced searching capabilities in two ways: through a special *syntax* for the keywords you enter (see the next entry), and through a separate page that lets you narrow the scope of the search. Look for a button or link on the main page that lets you access the advanced search options.

The picture here shows the Lycos search engine's advanced search screen (the inset is the pop-up menu at the top of the screen). You can see how, by using the various criteria available, you'd be able to increase the chances that the pages found in the search will be the ones most likely to help you.

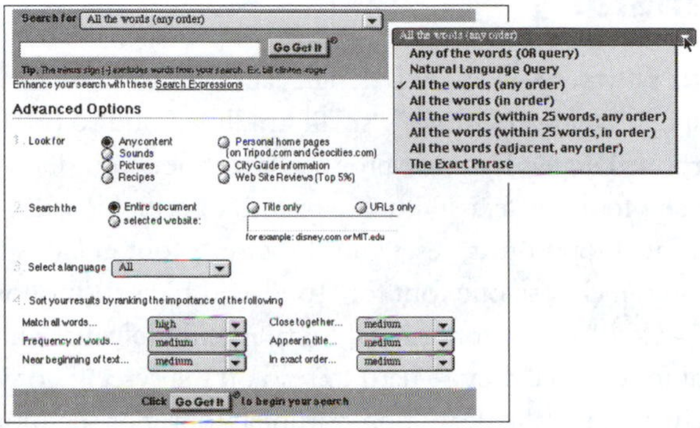

Advanced searching in Lycos.

Search syntax. When you enter keywords for a search in a search engine, be careful if you're using more than one word for the search. Most engines default to something known as an OR search, which means that any site with *either* keyword (one OR the other) will be listed. So if you enter *George Washington,* you'll get "hits" that contain the name George (anybody) or the word Washington (for a person's name, the capital, or the state).

You can be much more explicit with your search keywords without going to an advanced search screen, by using the *search syntax* that the search engine uses. The syntax "operators" (symbols like + and - and quote marks) let you set up things as simple as "both these words have to be on the page" to the more complex "both these words should be on the page, in this order, within 25 words of each other, but don't show me any pages that also include the third keyword I've typed in."

Unfortunately, the syntax varies from one engine to another. In Yahoo, for instance, you use a plus sign to indicate that each word should be included in the found pages (*+Simon +Garfunkel)* and a minus sign to exclude pages that contain that word *(python -monty)*. In Lycos, that second search would be phrased *python NOT monty.*

Search syntax is a very powerful tool, so you should learn the basics of the engine you use the most. You'll be able to find the "rules," and download them, from the search engine's site.

The Find command. The Find command in your browser's Edit menu is different from the Search button: it's for finding specific text on the current page. Explorer is a little more specific about this function, using *Find in Page* as the name of the command.

Surfing Tips

These tips work in both Netscape Navigator and Microsoft Explorer. They were tested with version 4 of each program.

In General

Set your fonts. Basic HTML design calls for text to be simply labeled as "paragraph," "largest headline," "small headline," and so on. How those labels are interpreted depend on *your* browser, which lets you define the font, size, and color of text for basic text styles. So, instead of cringing at 24-point text or squinting at 10-point text, reset your browser's font defaults for basic web pages. You can choose one font for "fixed-width" text (monofont) and one for "variable-width" text (proportional font). Avoid Helvetica and Times as the proportional fonts, since they're hard to read on the screen; go with a legible screen font like Geneva as the default proportional font. For the monofont, Courier usually works better than Monaco because it's more legible at smaller sizes.

In Explorer, use the Language/Fonts category in Preferences to choose the fonts. You can't set the default size, but the handy Larger and Smaller buttons at the top of the window automatically change the size of all the fonts on the current page. Navigator's Fonts category in its Preferences lets you set both the font and the size for the two defaults. It also provides an option to override fonts that are explicitly defined in a web page (the topic of the next entry).

Get your fonts. As HTML standards have evolved to allow more control over the look of the page, designers have been able to designate specific fonts for a page rather than just letting your browser apply the styles based on the basic paragraph definition.

If you have the fonts that designers use, your pages will be more legible. And you do have the fonts—or you can get them. As detailed in the Fonts chapter, TrueType fonts are not only Mac standards, but Web standards. The most-used ones are supplied with Internet Explorer (which comes with your system software) and are also downloadable from Microsoft's web site. Of the dozen or so fonts supplied, the ones used the most are Arial, Comic Sans, and Trebuchet, so make sure that these, at least, are installed on your Mac.

Real estate. Both Navigator and Explorer offer toolbars at the top of the window that can be pretty handy, but also take up a lot of screen space. The toolbars can be turned off, but also manipulated in other ways to take up less space—check the Navigator and Explorer sections later in the chapter, since the methods differ from one program to another.

Through a background, darkly. Some backgrounds are terrible for text—too dark, or too patterned, for you to see the text comfortably, or at all. Just drag across the text to highlight it and you'll be able to read it: the highlight color obliterates the background. For large bodies of text, use the Select All command in the Edit menu (⌘A).

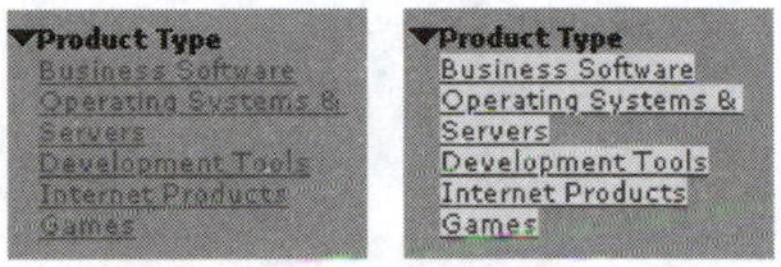

Before and after highlighting to make the text more readable.

Form fitting. The buttons and text fields on a web page form don't act entirely like Mac controls, although there are some similarities.

- You have to click on the circular part of a radio button to select it, not anywhere along its title, as you can on a Mac radio button.
- Pressing Return sometimes triggers a single push button (like Go or Search) on a page, but not reliably so.
- You can almost always Tab from one text box to another, and Shift Tab backwards through them. You can also cut or copy text from one box and paste it into another.

Avoiding the link on a copy. If you'd like to copy the text of a link but not trigger the link itself, you can't just drag across the link to select it for copying—when you release the mouse button, you'll have activated the link.

But you can copy the link if you select a little text before or after it along with the text of the link itself. If all you want is the link, press the mouse button instead of clicking it; both browsers offer Copy Link to Clipboard commands in a pop-up contextual menu.

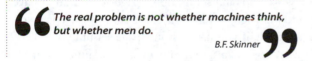

> ***The real problem is not whether machines think, but whether men do.***
>
> *B.F. Skinner*

Take an educated guess. If you're looking for a particular company's web site and you don't know the URL, you don't always have to go through a directory or a search process to find it. It's often faster to take a few guesses at the address—it doesn't take long to get the *URL not found* report.

Start with the name of the company: *apple.com, microsoft.com*, and so on. If there's more than one word in the company's name, try the main word in the title, or all the words together: *robotics.com* or *usrobotics.com*. Sometimes words are separated by hyphens or underscores (*outa_site.com* or *outa-site.com*) but *never* by spaces. Certain words, like *systems* and *technology/technologies* are often abbreviated, as in Aladdin Systems' *aladdinsys.com* and Newer Technologies' *newertech.com*.

After a few logical but failed tries, you can always hit the search engines.

Weird JavaScript error dialog. I ran into this odd JavaScript error recently. The error report window (top figure) stretched across the full width of my 20" screen, had no close box, didn't accept a Return or Enter to dismiss it, and wouldn't go behind the main browser window. It just sat there, having taken over the screen, and wouldn't budge. Just before giving up and pressing ⌘ Option Esc to quit the browser, I scrolled across another 15 inches of window, to find an OK button which, when clicked, dismissed the window. So, don't give up!

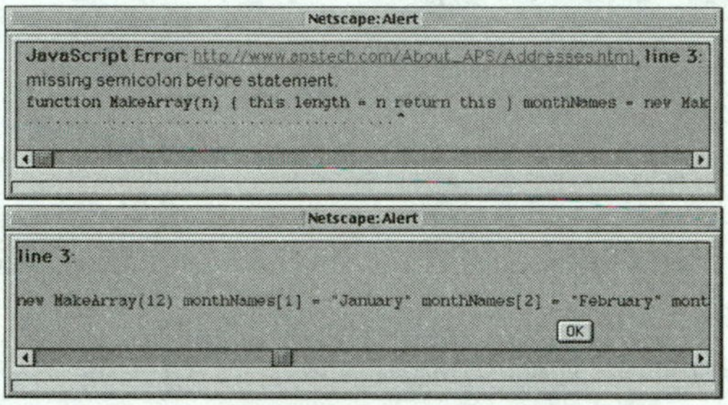

Top, the window that took over the screen and refused to be dismissed; bottom, the far right of the same window, after scrolling, offered a button for escaping.

Getting On and Around

Set a home page—or not. Your browser lets you decide what home page it should start with—where it goes when you first launch it. Explorer usually defaults to a Microsoft page, and Netscape to one of its pages; when you install Explorer with the system software, the default home page is one of Apple's.

Set your home page to the one *you* want—the one you use most often. If you always start out with a fix of current events, set your home page to a news page; if you always log on to search for something, set it to one of the search engines; if you're a Mac junkie, set it to one of the many Mac-centric pages out there. Or, you can do what I do, and set no home page at all. I don't have any place that I always go to first, so downloading some starting page is just a waste of time for me. In addition, if you have a home page set but your connection isn't open (and doesn't open automatically when you launch your browser), you'll get a dialog on every launch that tells you the page can't be found because your connection isn't open.

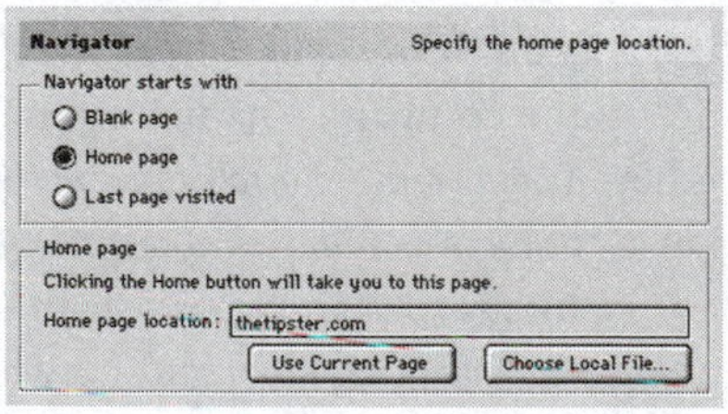

Setting the home page in Navigator.

To set the Home page in Navigator, select Preferences from the Edit menu. Click the Navigator category to see the Home page options; type in the URL of the page you want in the Home Page Location box. (You can, if you're at the page, just click the *Use Current Page* button.) If you want no page at all, click the Blank Page button.

In Explorer, start with the Preferences command. Click the Home/Search category, and fill in the URL of the page you want in the Address box. If you don't want a home page, leave the Address box blank.

Bookmarks. Using a *bookmark* is a quick way of getting back to site or page that you like: you add it to a list of bookmarks, then simply select it from a menu or other list. Microsoft insists on calling these *favorites,* but "bookmark" is the accepted generic term (and it's used in this chapter except in the Explorer-only section).

It's easy to add a bookmark when you're on a page you like: Use Add to Favorites (from Explorer's Favorites menu) or Add Bookmark (from Netscape's Bookmark menu).

There's more about organizing your zillion bookmarks in each program, later in their individual tips sections.

Skip the main page. You don't have to bookmark the main page of a site you visit often. There are several sites that I use where I never hit the top page at all, as a matter of fact; at shareware.com, for instance, I always use the Power Search option, so I've bookmarked *shareware.com/code/engine/Power.*

Adding a bookmark from a link. If you see a link that you'd like to add to your list of bookmarks, you don't have to copy the URL and paste it someplace, or go to it and then use the Add Bookmark command. Hold down the mouse button on the link in the current page, and use the Add Bookmark for This Link (Navigator) or Add Link to Favorites (Explorer) command.

Spelling counts! While case, upper or lower, doesn't matter through most of the URL, it *does* matter in the path name. So, while *shareware.com*, *Shareware.com*, and *ShareWare.com* will all get you to the same place, there is a difference between *shareware.com/code* and *shareware.com/Code*. (This is the first thing to examine when you get a "404 Not Found" error in your Web browser.)

Go forth! (and back, and forth). Once you've been surfing around, the Forward and Back buttons at the top of the browser window seem the quickest way to move back and forth to places you've been, but they're neither the only way to get back nor always the most efficient. Don't forget these options:

- Use a bookmark to jump back to a spot.
- Use the Go menu, which keeps track of where you've been.
- *Press* (don't click) on the Back button for a list of places you've been.
- Use the History list to see where you've been; use [⌘H] in either browser to open it. In Explorer, you can specify how many places should be stored in the History window through the Advanced screen of the Preferences dialog.

- In Explorer, click the arrow next to the Location box at the top of the window to get a pop-up menu of recent pages.

The Open Location dialog. Although a browser lets you type a URL at the top of the window and then press Enter to go there, it's a pain to click in the narrow text box; at least Navigator automatically selects the contents of the box when you click there, but Explorer won't go that far. But it's often reaching for the mouse at all that slows you down, so don't bother: press ⌘L to open the Open Location dialog, type the URL, and press Return.

Go-to shortcut. You don't have to type in the *http://www.* prefix or even the *.com* suffix when entering a URL with the Open Location command or at the top of the browser window. Typing just *thetipster,* for instance, will take you to *http://www.thetipster.com*.

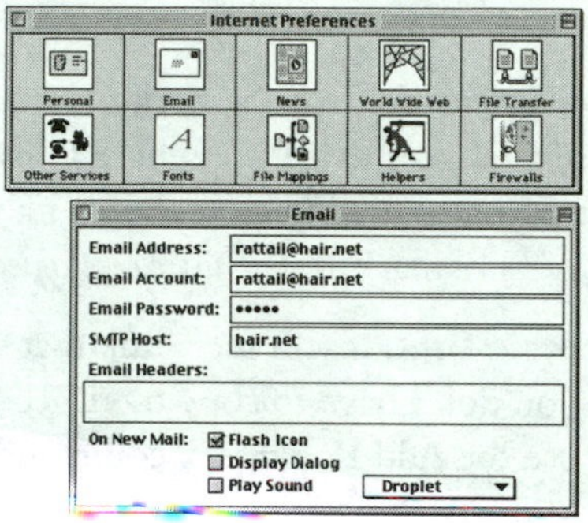

Internet Config is a central repository for your internet-related information.

Central repository. Do you use more than one program that accesses the internet? Are you tired of configuring each one with the same information? The Internet Config utility that comes with your system software lets you enter all the information in one spot; most "polite" internet programs will check there for the information before they bother you to fill in their blanks.

Don't get disconnected (or do). If your PPP connection turns itself off while you're staring at a particularly engrossing web page, or you were distracted by a short telephone call, you may have your idle time set too short for the way you work. On the other hand, if you tend to walk out of the room during a download and forget to walk back in within a reasonable time frame, and your PPP connection is open an hour later, your idle time is set too high.

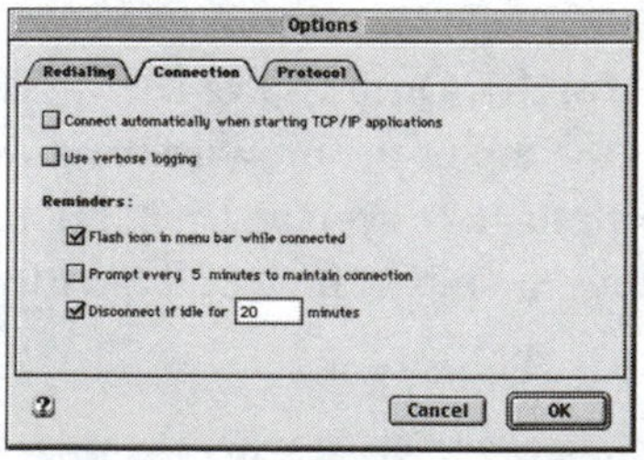

Set the disconnect idle time through the PPP control panel.

This auto shut-off or stay-on isn't a browser program setting: it's in the PPP control panel. Click the Options button in the control panel, and click the Connection tab in the dialog. Check the Disconnect box if it's not checked, and put in a reasonable (for you) idle time.

Connect to... What *is* that silly little Connect To thingy in your Apple menu? It's a very tiny AppleScript application that puts up a single dialog that defaults to showing one of Apple's web sites; clicking Connect launches your browser and goes to the site named in the dialog.

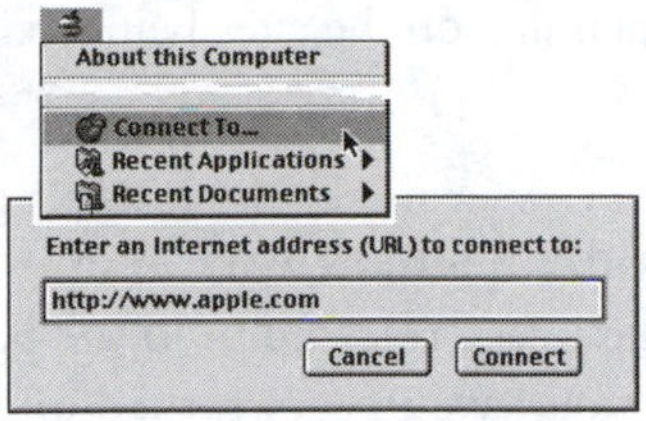

Believe it or not, this can actually be useful. If your browser is set to go to a certain home page at launch, but you want to go someplace else, you don't have to start the browser, stop the home page from loading (or wait for it to load!), and then go where you want. The Connect To script overrides the home page setting and takes you directly to your destination.

Speed

Leap before you finish looking. You don't have to wait for an entire page to load if you see a link on it that you want to move to: just click the link and the current download stops and you go to the next place. (I love those quick escapes).

Halt! You can stop a page in the middle of a download by clicking the Stop button at the top of the browser window. Using ⌘. also works, and Esc sometimes works, too (depending on the browser and the version you're using). When you want the page to load completely, use the Refresh button (Explorer) or Reload button (Navigator).

Open a second window. You can use more than one window at a time in your browser. If you have a list of "hits" from a search, you might want to leave that window the way it is and open its links in another window so that you don't have to reload the hits list to try another link. The contextual menu you get when you press on a link includes an Open Link in New Window (Explorer) or New Window With This Link (Navigator) command.

But Explorer provides a neat shortcut: click on a link while holding down ⌘, and the link automatically opens in a new window.

Skip the Images

Turn them all off. The text of a web page comes through relatively quickly, no matter what speed modem you're using. And, since the HTML code behind the page—the instructions for how things should be placed on the page and what the text should look like—is all text, the basic page and its layout can show up on your screen in a surprisingly short time. It's those pictures that choke up the bandwidth.

So, when you're in a hurry, turn off the graphics. In Navigator, simply use the Show Images command from the View menu; when it's unchecked, the image downloads are stopped. In Explorer, you have to through Preferences, checking or unchecking the Show Images button in the Web Content category. (This is very inconvenient if you work the way I do, turning the images on and off quite frequently depending on the sites being visited; I've created a macro for it.)

When images are turned off, a browser marks the image's place with an icon and a label. (An image icon with a question mark in it, though, indicates that the server couldn't find the image referred to in the page—it has nothing to do with whether or not you have images turned on.) A well-designed page (like the one shown here) has all its images labeled so you can still tell what they are even if you can't see them; when they're not labeled in the HTML, they'll be stamped "Image" on your screen—not exactly helpful. Navigator uses large desktop-style icons to hold the places, while Explorer uses much smaller icons that interfere less with the overall look of the layout of the page when images are turned off.

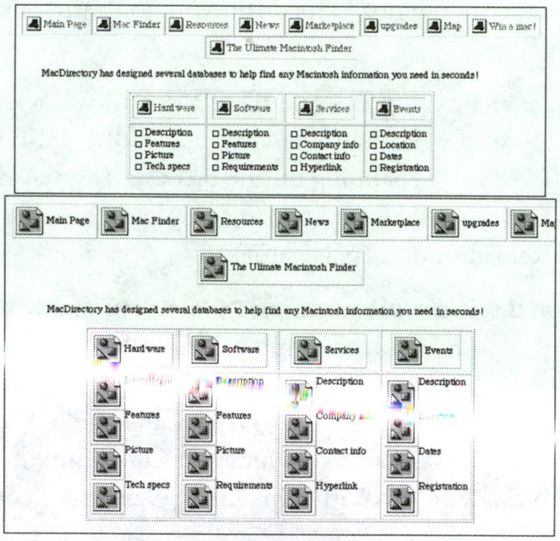

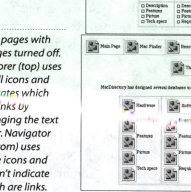

Web pages with images turned off. Explorer (top) uses small icons and indicates which are links by changing the text color. Navigator (bottom) uses large icons and doesn't indicate which are links.

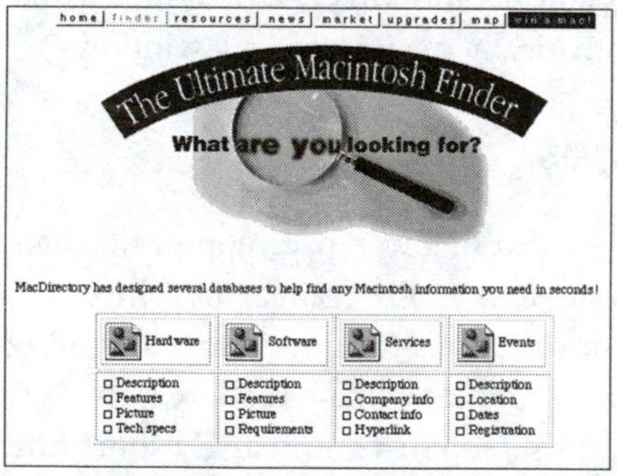

The same page, with most of its images loaded.

Turn on an image. When you're faced with a page full of image icons and want to see one of them, it's easy to load just that image: point to it, hold down the mouse button, and select Load Missing Image (Explorer) or Load This Image (Navigator).

You can also load an image by just clicking on its icon: a single click in Navigator does the trick, while Explorer requires a double-click.

If you load an image that's repeated elsewhere on the page (a button icon, for instance), the single load will put the image in every spot that it belongs.

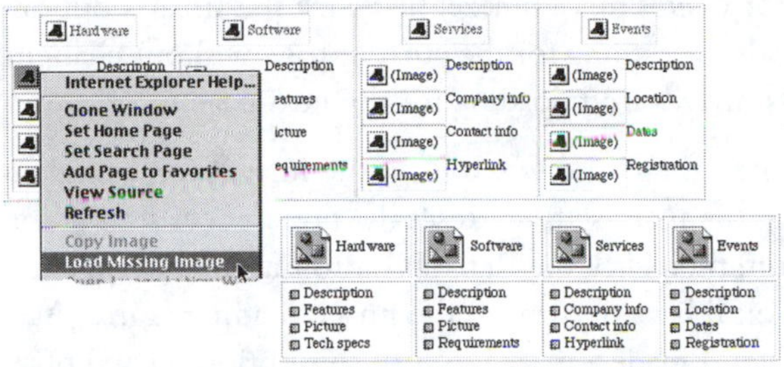

Loading a single image (upper left) that's repeated on the page fills it in wherever it's used (bottom).

When an image is a button. So many images serve as links that often a click or double-click to load the image will trigger a link instead of load the image. If you want to get the image and use the link, make sure you use the pop-up menu Load command instead of the click option.

How can you tell ahead of time which images are links and which are just images, since they all look the same? Explorer is much more helpful in this situation. An image's label indicates whether or not it's a link; the label for a link image appears in the same format (usually in blue, with or without an underline) that a text link uses. In addition, moving the mouse pointer over a link image changes the cursor to a hand, and shows the destination in the status toolbar at the bottom of the window. In Navigator, you'll just have to check the pop-up menu to see which of its commands are active, since there's no clue as to the status of a missing image.

IN THE BEGINNING

The top-end system in mid-1986 was the Mac Plus with its incredible full megabyte of memory, and an 800K floppy disk drive. The new 20-meg external hard drive, at $1500, was finally available. Buy the computer, the drive, and the new, improved ImageWriter II for a total of only $4700.

Only $4700? It was a bargain compared to *upgrading* to that setup. The original Mac and ImageWriter were $3000 together. Add $500 for a second, external floppy drive (each drive handled only 400K disks). Another thousand to upgrade the original 128K of memory to a full megabyte. Then came $300 to upgrade the internal hard drive to 800K capacity, $600 for a new logic board to match the Mac Plus's capabilities, and $130 for the new keyboard (which came to about $45 for each cursor key). No upgrade path for the printer, so just buy the new one ($600, with another $30 for the different cable) along with the hard drive. Just under $8000 in a short 18 months of computer ownership.

Turn on the images for a page. There are times when you'll go to a page and won't be able to figure out anything without the images turned on. Instead of loading the images one at a time, you can turn them all on for the entire page.

Navigator makes this a breeze: just click the Images button in the toolbar. That loads everything for the current page without changing the setting that prevents images from loading for the next page.

In Explorer, there's no way to load the images for a single page without changing the main setting. Reset the preferences setting for Load Images to turn it on, then click the Refresh button in the button bar to reload the page. Then, you'll have to turn off the image-loading again. (As I mentioned a few entries ago, I made a macro to turn this option on and off.)

Downloading

Setting a download folder. One of the things you'll do a lot on the Web is download files; each browser lets you set a folder to act as the default place for downloads.

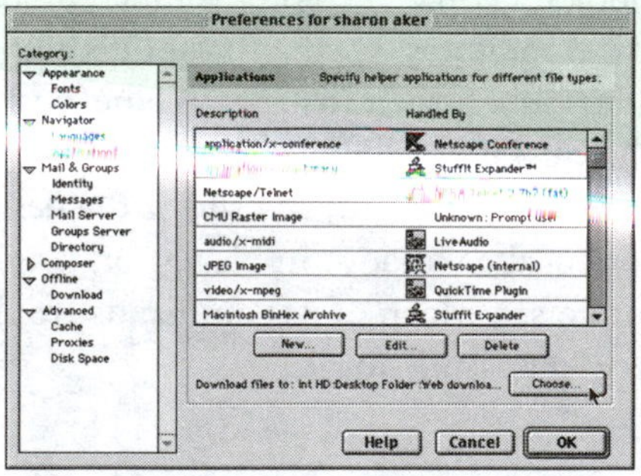

Navigator hides its download-folder setting.

Netscape has always liked to make setting the download folder like a treasure hunt; version 4 is different from, but no less puzzling than, its predecessors. Use the Edit menu's Preferences command, and click the Applications category under the Navigator category. On that screen, click the Choose button and select the download folder you want.

Explorer is a little more direct: use the Preferences command, select Download Options in the Receiving Files category and use the Change Location button in the Download Folder section. Explorer also provides options for multiple download folders, keyed to the helper application doing the download; so, stuffed or binhexed files can go one place, sound files another, and so on. You set these separate download folders through Preferences; in the File Helpers category, select the type of file and click the Change button, which opens a dialog that lets you set the download file for just that application and file type.

Background and multiple downloads. If you've hopped on the Web to grab a little shareware utility, you don't have to watch the download progress dialog and wait until it's finished before you go off to another page. Go to whatever page you have next in mind and let the download complete in the background. Things will slow down a little—for both the download and the next page you're getting—but it's better to move more slowly than not at all!

And, if you need a few little utilities downloaded, you don't have to wait for one to finish before you start the next: pretend the first one's finished, and download the second—and a third and a fourth if you want. They can all download at the same time.

Multiple downloads won't save you any time, since your bandwidth doesn't magically widen to accommodate them, but it means that you can set up the downloads and move to the next place you want to be.

Grabbing graphics. You don't have to download a graphic that you see on a web page; in fact, you can't "download" it in the usual fashion because it's not designed to be downloaded. But you can easily put it on the Clipboard or save it as a file on the disk. Just click on the image, holding down the mouse button, to get a contextual menu with Copy and Save commands. In Navigator, you can also just drag an image from a page to the desktop, and the image will become a separate disk file.

(Mandatory comment: many web-page elements are copyrighted, so watch what you do with anything you grab from a page.)

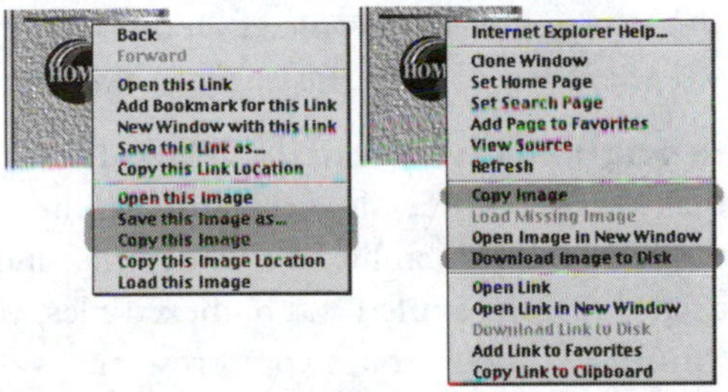

Netscape (left) and Explorer (right) both have pop-up menus that let you copy or save images.

Auto-unstuff (or not). If you're downloading a single file, it can be pretty handy that your browser takes care of the background work involved in unstuffing it—especially since it's often a two-step process, first converting it from a binhexed file (the .hqx suffix) and then from its compressed form (the .sit suffix).

But when you're setting up multiple downloads, the auto-unstuff option can slow things down: not only are you having things written to the disk as they come in as files, but you've got another application accessing the disk as it reads the downloaded file and writes the converted one. It looks like everything's happening at the same time, but it's not: everybody's taking turns with the disk access. So, for multiple downloads, it makes more sense to just let the binhexed or stuffed files be stored on the disk so you can decode them later.

To stop the automatic unstuffing and decoding of files in Navigator, you have to break their links to the helper application that does the work, which defaults to StuffIt Expander. In Preferences, click the Applications subcategory under Navigator. There are three file-type links you have to break: *Macintosh BinHex Archives* (with .hqx suffixes), *Macintosh StuffIt Archive* (with .sit suffixes), and the lesser-used *Application/X-MacBinary* (with .bin suffixes). To break the links, find the file types in the list and click the Edit button. In the next dialog, click the Save to Disk button.

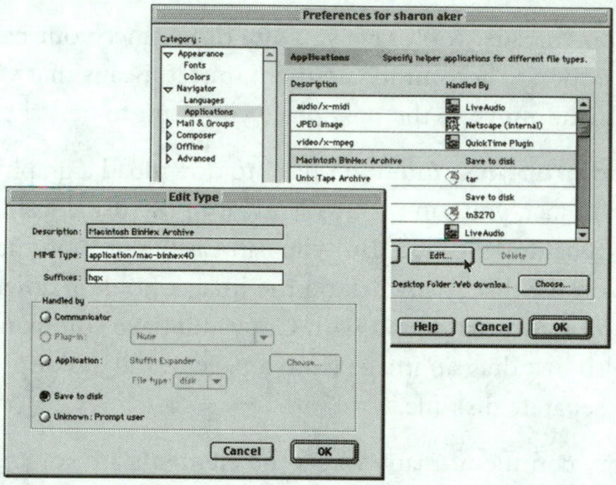

Breaking a helper-application link in Navigator's Preferences dialog.

Explorer makes it a little easier to prevent automatic processing of downloaded files. In Preferences, select Download Options, and uncheck the *Automatically decode MacBinary files* and *Automatically decode BinHex files* options.

Auto-erase the original. In most cases, you'll find that files that you download eventually become three files on your disk: the original stuffed file, the secondary unstuffed but still binhexed encoded file, and the final decoded file. To automatically erase the stuffed and binhexed files, you have to work with settings in StuffIt Expander, not in your browser.

First, you have to find Expander. It's usually stored by default in the Internet folder that the system installation puts on your hard drive; inside that is an Internet Utilities folder, then an Aladdin folder and, finally Expander. If you can't find it, use the Find command in the Finder to look for it.

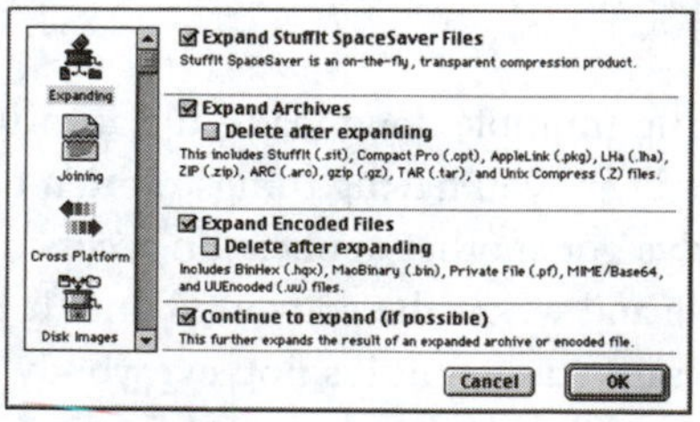

Set the automatic erase for stuffed and encoded files in Expander's preferences.

Double-click on the Expander icon and choose Preferences from the Edit menu. In the Preferences dialog, shown here, check or uncheck the *Delete after expanding* options under Expand Archives and Expand Encoded Files categories, depending on whether or not you want the originals erased or preserved.

If setting the preferences doesn't work, or only works sometimes, you probably have several copies of Expander on your hard drive. Use the Find command to find them and delete all but the most recent one. Don't forget to tell your browser (and other software, like AOL's) the location of the single copy of Expander that's left.

Navigator Tips

These tips were tested for Netscape Navigator 4.

Manipulating the toolbars. Navigator's tool bars can be altered, moved, or removed entirely to give you more screen space.

- To remove either or both toolbars, use the Hide Navigation Toolbar and Hide Location Toolbar commands from the View menu; they change to Show commands so you can get the toolbars back.
- To change the amount of vertical space the Navigation Toolbar uses, use the Appearance category of the Preferences command and choose Pictures Only or Text Only instead of Pictures and Text.
- To change the positions of the toolbars, grab one by its "handle"—the dotted area at its left edge—and drag it up or down to swap its position with the other one's.
- To temporarily collapse either toolbar, click on its handle (you don't have to click on the handle's arrow—anywhere on the handle will do).

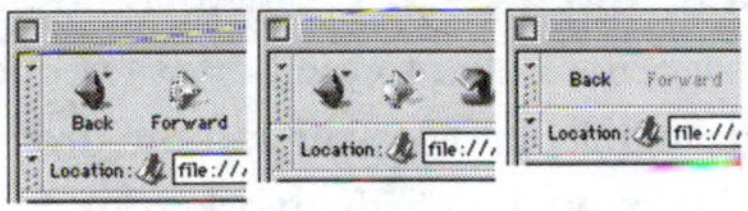

The Navigation toolbar with pictures and text, just pictures, and just text.

The toolbars swapped from their default positions (top), the Navigation toolbar collapsed (middle), and both toolbars collapsed (bottom).

The Bookmark menu. Although adding a bookmark to the menu is as simple as using the Add Bookmark command when you're at a page, a long list of locations is inefficient. You can control the organization of your Bookmark menu through the Bookmark window, which opens when you press ⌘B.

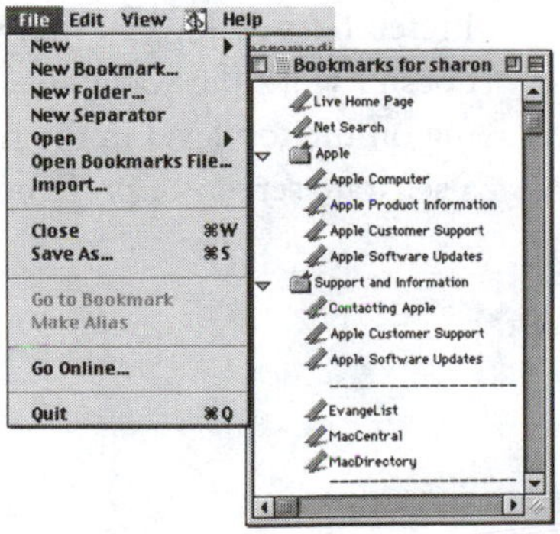

The New Bookmark, New Folder, and New Separator commands are available in the File menu when the Bookmark window is open.

In the window, you can reorder the items by dragging them around. The folders act as menu items, and their contents are the submenus. You can put something in a folder by dragging its icon into the folder icon. To create new bookmarks, folders, or separators, use the special commands in the File menu that are available only when the Bookmark window is open.

Nested folders. If you put folders inside other folders, you'll get multilevel submenus in your Bookmark menu. The picture here shows two different approaches to listing the two groups in the Support and Information menu. At the upper left is the sub-submenu approach, using folders within folders in the Bookmark window. In the lower right is the default setup, where all the items are in a single submenu divided into two groups.

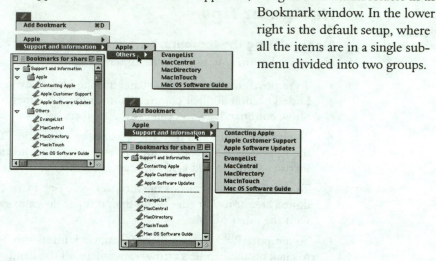

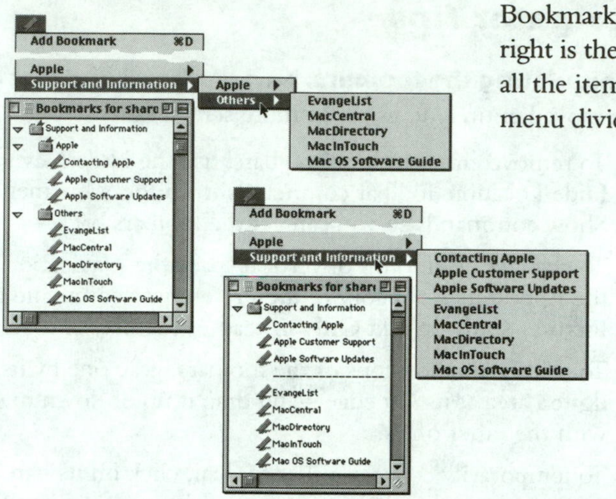

Adding a bookmark in a specific spot. When you use the Add Bookmark command for the current page, it's added to the bottom of the Bookmark menu. Since Netscape didn't deign to give the Mac version the drop-into-the-menu ability that it gave to the PC version, here's the workaround. When you want to add a bookmark for the current page but want it somewhere other than the bottom of the menu, press ⌘B to open the Bookmark window, and then drag the little bookmark icon in the Location bar (it's called the Page Proxy icon!) into the window, dropping it into the spot you want it to appear in the menu.

Info on a bookmark. To get the details about any bookmark (and to enter comments of your own about it), select it in the bookmark window and press ⌘I to Get Info.

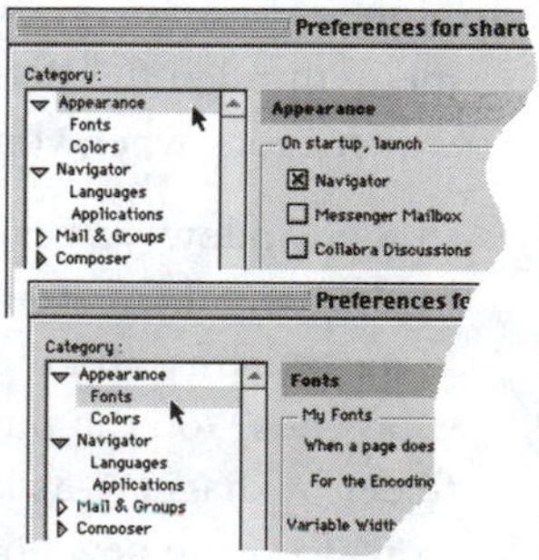

A top-level preference is more than just a container for other preferences: it has its own preferences settings.

Top level category in Preferences. The hierarchical structure in the Navigator Preferences dialog can fool you because it doesn't work the way you'd expect it to: clicking on the top level in the hierarchy gives you a separate screen of preferences settings.

> **“So we went to Atari and said “Hey, we’ve got this amazing thing, even built with some of your parts, and what do you think about funding us? Or we’ll give it to you. We just want to do it.” And they said “No.” So then we went to Hewlett-Packard and they said “Hey, we don’t need you. You haven’t got through college yet.”**
>
> *Steve Jobs, about his and Steve Wozniak’s project—the first personal computer.*

Save the URL. If you want to save the URL of the current page someplace other than in Navigator, you don’t have to Copy and Paste it: you can drag the little bookmark icon in front of the Location box at the top of the window into any drag-and-drop enabled application.

Mo’ zilla. When you have a few free seconds, try typing *about:mozilla* in Netscape’s Go To field and pressing Return.

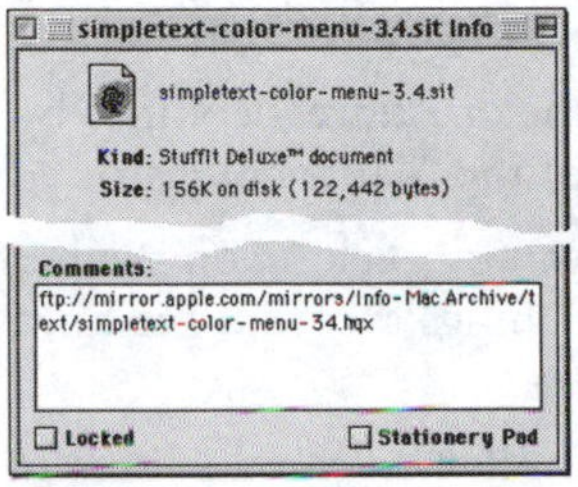

A file retrieved through Navigator keeps its URL origin in the file’s comments.

Where’d that come from? When you download or save something from Navigator, it stores the URL of origin in the Comments section of the disk file. Do a Get Info from the desktop, and you can see where you found the file originally.

Explorer Tips

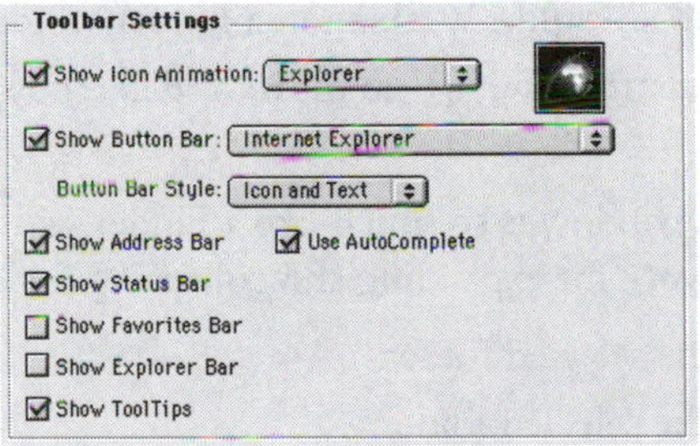

Control the toolbars from the Browser Display screen of the Preferences dialog.

Tool time. Explorer has three toolbars at the top of the window, one at the bottom, and one along the side. They can be turned on and off individually, and most can also be modified to some extent. Use the Preferences command to turn the various toolbars on or off; you’ll find them in the Browser Display category.

Manipulating the top toolbars. If you want the convenience of all three toolbars at the top of the window without losing all that screen real estate, combine them into two rows, or just one. You can drag a toolbar by the striped gray handle at its right, moving it up and down in the toolbar area at the top of the window. You can plop it right in the same row as another toolbar, and then use the handle as a slider to change how much of the row is given to each toolbar.

Quick add to the Favorites bar. The basic way to add a favorite item to the Favorites toolbar is to work in the Favorites window, dragging the item into the Favorites folder.

But there's a quicker, better way when you want to add the current page to the Favorites bar: hold down ⌘Shift as you select Add To Favorites from the Favorites menu.

Organizing favorites. You can organize your favorites by working in the Favorites window, accessed through the Open Favorites command in the Favorite menu or by clicking the Favorites button in the toolbar. (It also opens automatically under other circumstance, such as when you use the New Folder or New Favorites command.)

The Favorites window is much like a Finder window, and you'll be comfortable creating new folders (which are, of course, the submenus in the Favorites menu), working with the folder hierarchy, and moving items in and out of folders. You can also:

- Change the width of the Name or Address column by dragging the striped gray area at the right of the Name column.
- Sort according to either column by clicking on the headers (although you'll probably want to order things according to how often you use them, not alphabetically).
- Rename an item by clicking on its name and editing it.
- View the full name in a short column by clicking on it; its name will spill over to the Address column while it's selected.
- Reorder the items in the menu by dragging them around in the window's list (this part is *totally* unlike working in a Finder window!).
- Select multiple items in the list (to move or delete) by Shift-clicking on them.

In fact, the Favorites window is so much like a Finder window that the same keyboard shortcuts work for expanding and collapsing folders inside it:

- ⌘→ expands the selected folder.
- ⌘← collapses the selected folder.
- ⌘Option→ expands all the levels in the selected folder.
- ⌘Option← collapses all the levels in the selected folder.

Keep it brief. Keep the names of your favorite places brief (you can rename them in the Favorites window). With long names, it takes a lot of mousing to get into a submenu.

Keep it unique. The name you assign to a location is the one that's used by the Location text box and dialog. As you start typing in either of these, Explorer guesses which location you want based on what you've typed so far. With names that all start the same (like the defaults *Apple Computer, Apple Customer Support, Apple Product Information*) you have to type quite a bit before getting the right guess, so rename locations with differences early in the name.

Creating sub-submenus. You're not limited to a single level of submenus in the Favorite menu. Put a folder inside another folder in the Favorites window, and you'll get a second-level submenu.

Deleting a favorite. The Favorites window has a nifty relationship with the Finder: you can drag an item directly from the window—which belongs to Explorer—directly to the Finder's trash (if you can *see* the Trash).

But there's an easier way to delete a favorite: select it in the Favorite window and press Delete. You have to click on the icon in front of the favorite's name, not on its name or address; otherwise, the text will be deleted, but the item will remain.

Drag in and out. You can drag an item out of the Favorites window into any drag-enabled application. Perhaps more importantly, you can drag stuff *into* the Favorites window: either selected text from a document window, or even documents directly from the Finder.

Where *is* that file? If you know you downloaded a file—because you absolutely positively remember doing so or because you checked the Download manager and it's listed there—but it's not on your disk where you thought it was, the Download manager can tell you where it was stored: double-click on the item in the Download manager and you'll get the location of the stored filed—as well as information like where you downloaded it *from*. And, if you want to move the file, use the Change button in the dialog, and the file will be moved to the folder of your choice.

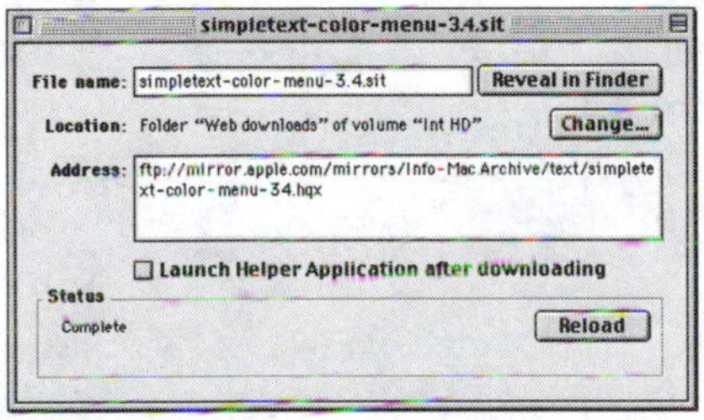

Double-clicking on a file in the Download Manager tells you where it came from, and where it went—and lets you move it, too.

> ***Years it took radio to gain 50 million domestic listeners: 40.***
> ***Years it took television to gain 50 million domestic viewers: 13***
> ***Years it took the World Wide Web to get 50 million domestic users: 4***
>
> *Time Magazine, July 1998*

Download management. When you delete something from the Download Manager window, the file itself isn't deleted from your hard drive. The Download Manager is merely a list of what you've done (combined with, sometimes, what you're going to do), even though it looks a lot like a Finder window.

PART 9

Appendices

Part 9 At a Glance

Appendix A

The Tipster List

Top Tipsters

Above and beyond the call of tipstering

Doffie Hochreich
Jerry Szubin
Binky Melnik
Carol Aiton
Rich Wolfson

Special Tipsters

Special contributions by some very special people

Marilyn Rose
John Luttropp
Andy Baird
Tommy Riccota

Chapter Contributors

Chapter 2
JK John Kadyk
RT Rob Teeple

Chapter 3
BB Brad Bunnin
AC Andreu Cabré
JC John Christopher
JK John Kadyk
JM Joe Matazzoni
AN Arthur Naiman
DR David Ramsey

Chapter 4
JC John Christopher
HN Henry Norr
RS Randy Singer
RW Rich Wolfson

Chapter 7
NL Nicholas Lavroff
CR Charles Rubin
JS Jerry Szubin

Chapter 10
EC Elizabeth Castro
JK John Kadyk
CR Charles Rubin

Chapter 12
JB Jamie Brown
DC Dennis Cohen
DD Darcy DiNucci
ML Maria Langer
HN Henry Norr
RS Randy Singer

Chapter 14
TA Ted Alspach
DD Darcy DiNucci
JF James Felici
EF Erfert Fenton
AJ Alastair Johnston
GS Gene Steinberg
JS Jerry Szubin
KT Kathleen Tinkel
RT Rob Teeple
The "Graphics Team"*

Chapter 15
ND Nancy E Dunn
KF Karen Faria
JF James Felici
JK John Kadyk
RS Randy Singer
BW Bob Weibel
RW Rich Wolfson

Chapter Contributors (continued)

Chapter 16
RC Rick Casreen
EC Elizabeth Castro
EF Erfert Fenton
CS Carolyn Said

Chapter 17
CB Christian Boyce
EC Elizabeth Castro
DC Dennis Cohen
EG Eve Gordon
ML Maria Langer

Chapter 18
EC Elizabeth Castro
DC Don Crabb
JL Jay Lee
SS Steve Schwartz

Chapter 19
AB Andy Baird
The "Graphics Team"*

Chapter 20
RA Randy Anderson
DB David Blatner
RR Ray Robertson
KT Kathleen Tinkel
JW JB Whitwell
The "Graphics Team"*

Chapter 21
JH Joe Holmes

Chapter 22
AB Andy Baird
FB Fletcher Beasley
MEC Michael E Cohen
SF Steven Frank

Chapter 23
JK John Kadyk

Chapter 24
JK John Kadyk
TL Ted Landau
LL Lisa Lee
HN Henry Norr
BW Bob Weibel
RW Rich Wolfson

Chapter 25
CB Chris Breen
BF Bart Farkas
CG Connie Guglielmo
CS Carolyn Said
MT Mary Toth
RW Rich Wolfson

Chapter 26
RC Ron Colvin
SH Stephen Howard
PH Paul Hurley
JK John Kadyk
JR John Rizzo
CR Charles Rubin
BW Bob Weibel
RW Rich Wolfson

Chapter 27
SB Steve Bobker
JH Joe Holmes
HN Henry Norr
RS Randy Singer

Chapter 28
JH Joe Holmes

**The "Graphics Team": Carol Aiton, John Luttropp, Tommy Ricotta, Marilyn Rose, Jerry Szubin*

Web Site Tipsters

Thanks to everyone who dropped by

Nick Aker
Nat Aker
Diego Akerman
Douglas Anderson
Lyle Anderson
Shane Anderson
Duncan Baird
Adam Barisoff
Eric van Beest
Joshua Blake
Ilyse Blazar
Jonathan Blazar
Martijn Broeders
Natalie Buongiorno
Nicholas Burbules
Mark Burgess
Jesse Carneiro
Rames Creel
Mary Saige Decker
Carolyn K Dotzenrod
Tonya Engst
Glenn Feldstein
Karyn Feldstein
Neil Fiertel
Jared Finck
Dan Frakes
David Gavin
Michael Geraci
Marcelo A Ferreira Gomes
Mike Gould
Arthur Greenwald
David Grothe
George Gunderson

Web Site Tipsters (continued)

Kent Hayden
Michael Hetelson
Ron Holmes
Tim Holmes
Philip Hurst
Craig Isaacs
JP Kang
Michael Korican
Mark Kriegsman
Mike van Lammeren
Artemy Lebedev
Ted Lippincott
Amber Lunch
Mark D Matthews
Marilyn Matty
Paul McGrane
Derek K Miller
Al Monaro
Rich Morin
Glen A Mortensen
Chelsea Muehe
Lori Myers
Matt Neuburg
Tom O'Grady
Tony Ochoa
Alissa Ostrove
Max Ostrove
Ernst J Oud
Eric Prentice
James Procopio
Lydia Raspberry
Barry L. Ritholtz
Steve Rittner
Adam Rose
Daniel Rose
Isaac Rose
Larry Rosenstein
Aaron D Ruiz
Robert Sandler
Chris Sargent
Andrew Sasaki
Adam Scinto
Mark Showalter
Mike Simmons
Bill Soucy
Eric Staak
Richard Sucgang
Nick Triantafillou
Lorene Turner
Skip Via
Amanda Volker
Jennifer Volker
Keely Volker
Vincent Volker
Adrian Walls
Alan Warner
Christopher Weuve
Curt Wiederhoeft
Eric Wilson

Appendix B

Vendor Contact Information

3COM
5400 Bayfront Plaza
Santa Clara CA 95052
800•638•3266, 408•764•5000
fax: 408•764•5001
3com.com

A

Abbott Systems
62 Mountain Rd
Pleasantville NY 10570
800•552•9157, 914•747•4171
fax: 914•747•9115
abbottsys.com

ACI US
20883 Stevens Creek Blvd
Cupertino CA 95014
800•384•0010, 408•252•4444
fax: 408•252•0831
acius.com

Adaptec
691 South Milpitas Blvd
Milpitas CA 95035
408•945•8600
fax: 408•262•2533
adaptec.com

Adesso
100 Corporate Pointe
Suite 230
Culver City CA 90230
310•216•7777
fax: 310•216•7898
adessoinc.com

Adobe Systems
345 Park Ave
San Jose CA 95110
800•833•6687, 408•536•6000
fax: 408•537•6000
adobe.com

Aladdin Systems
165 Westridge Dr
Watsonville CA 95076
408•761•6200
fax: 408•761•6209
aladdinsys.com

Alps Electric
3553 North First St
San Jose CA 95134
800•825•2577, 408•432•6000
fax: 408•432•6035
alpsusa.com

Alsoft
PO Box 927
Spring TX 77383
800•257•6381, 281•353•4090
fax: 281•353•9868
alsoftinc.com

America Online
8619 Westwood Center Dr
Vienna VA 22182
800•827•6364, 703•448•8700
fax: 703•448•0760
aol.com

Apple Computer
1 Infinite Loop
Cupertino CA 95014
800•776•2333, 408•996•1010
fax: 408•974•6726
apple.com

APS Technologies
PO Box 4987
6131 Deramus
Kansas City MO 64120
800•235•8935, 816•483•1600
fax: 816•483•3077
apstech.com

Ars Nova
PO Box 637
Kirkland WA 98083
800•445•4866, 425•889•0927
fax: 425•889•8699
ars-nova.com

Artbeats
PO Box 1287
Myrtle Creek OR 97457
800•444•9392, 541•863•4429
fax: 541•863•4547
artbeats.com

Asante
821 Fox Lane
San Jose CA 95131
800•662•9686, 408•435•8388
asante.com

Astound Incorporated
710 Lakeway Dr
Suite 230
Sunnyvale CA 94086
408•720•0337
fax: 408•720•1011
astound.com

ATTO
40 Hazelwood Dr
Amherst NY 14228
716•691•1999
fax: 716•691•9353
attotech.com

Autodesk
111 McInnis Pkwy
San Rafael CA 94903
800•964•6432, 415•507•5000
autodesk.com

B

Bare Bones Software
PO Box 1048
Bedford, MA 01730
781•687•0700
barebones.com

Beale St Group
PO Box 820001
Memphis TN 38182
901•751•9333
fax: 901•274•0853
beale.com

Berkeley Systems
2095 Rose St
Berkeley CA 94709
800•877•5535, 510•540•5535
fax: 510•540•5115
berksys.com

Binary Software
2118 Wilshire Blvd 900
Santa Monica CA 90403
800•824•6279, 310•449•1481
fax: 800•555•7217
binarysoft.com

Birmy Graphics
250 East Dr
Suite H
Melbourne FL 32904
407•768•6766
fax: 407•768•9669
birmy.com

Boxtop Software
10960 Wilshire Blvd
Suite 1550
Los Angeles CA 90024
310•235•3900
fax: 310•235•3999
boxtop.com

Broderbund Software
500 Redwood Blvd
Novato CA 94947
800•474•8840, 415•382•4400
fax: 415•382•4419
broderbund.com

Bungie Software Products
350 West Ontario
7th Floor
Chicago IL 60610
800•295•0060, 312•563•6200
fax: 312•563•0545
bungie.com

C

C.A.R./Nueconcepts
4661 Maryland Ave
Suite 200
St Louis MO 63108
800•288•7585, 314•454•3535
fax: 314•454•0105
clipables.com

Caere
100 Cooper Ct
Los Gatos CA 95030
800•535•7226, 408•395•7000
fax: 408•354•2743
caere.com

Casady & Greene
22734 Portola Dr
Salinas CA 93908
800•359•4920, 408•484•9228
fax: 408•484•9218
casadyg.com

CE Software
1801 Industrial Circle
West Des Moines IA 50265
800•523•7638, 515•221•1801
fax: 515•221•1806
cesoft.com

CH Products
970 Park Center Dr
Vista CA 92083
619•598•2518
chproducts.com

Cliffs Studyware
PO Box 80728
Lincoln NE 68501
402•421•8324
fax: 402•477•9898
cliffs.com

Coda Music Technology
6210 Bury Dr
Eden Prairie MN 55346
800•843•2066, 612•937•9611
fax: 612•937•9760
codamusic.com

CompuServe
PO Box 20212
Columbus OH 43220
800•848•8199, 614•457•8600
fax: 614•457•0348
compuserve.com

Connectix
2655 Campus Dr
San Mateo CA 94403
800•950•5880, 650•571•5100
fax: 650•571•0850
connectix.com

Corel
1600 Carling Ave
Ottawa ON
Canada K1Z 8R7
800•772•6735,
fax: 613•761•1295
corel.com

CoStar
599 West Putnam Ave
Greenwich CT 06830
800•426•7827, 203•661•9700
fax: 203•661•1540
costar.com

Creative Solutions
7509 Connelley Dr
Suite D
Hanover MD 21076
800•367•8465, 410•766•4080
fax: 410•766•4087
creative-solutions-inc.com

Cyberian Outpost
3300 State Route 73 South
Wilmington OH 45177
800•856•9800, 860•927•2050
fax: 860•927•8375
outpost.com

D

Dantz Development
4 Orinda Way
Building C
Orinda CA 94563
800•225•4880, 925•253•3000
fax: 925•253•9099
dantz.com

Datadesk International
9524 SW Tualatin-Sherwood Rd
Tualatin OR 97062
800•994•6788, 503•692•9600
fax: 503•691•1101
datadesk.com

DataViz
55 Corporate Dr
Trumbull CT 06611
800•733•0030, 203•268•0030
fax: 203•268•4345
dataviz.com

Davidson & Associates
19840 Pioneer Ave
Torrance CA 90503
800•545•7677, 310•793•0600
fax: 310•793•0601
davd.com

Dayna Communications
Sorenson Research Park
849 West Levoy Dr
Salt Lake City UT 84123
801•269•7200
fax: 801•269•7363
dayna.com

DayStar Digital
5556 Atlanta Hwy
Flowery Branch GA 30542
770•614•0070
fax: 770•614•0500
daystar.com

Deneba Software
7400 SW 87th Ave
Miami FL 33173
305•596•5644
fax: 305•273•9069
deneba.com

Diamond Multimedia
2880 Junction Ave
San Jose CA 95134
800•468•5846, 451•967•2450
fax: 541•967•2401
diamondmm.com

DiamondSoft
351 Jean St
Mill Valley CA 94941
415•381•3303
fax: 415•381•3503
diamondsoft.com

DK Multimedia
95 Madison Ave
New York NY 10016
212•213•4800
fax: 212•213•5240
dkonline.com

DriveSavers
400 Bel Marin Keys Blvd
Novato CA 94949
800•440•1904, 415•382•2000
fax: 415•883•0780
drivesavers.com

Dubl-Click Software
20310 Empire Ave
Suite A102
Bend OR 97701
541•317•0355
fax: 541•317•0430
dublclick.com

E

Eccentric Software/Nisus
PO Box 2777
Seattle WA 98111
800•890•3030, 619•481•1477
fax: 619•481•6154
nisus.com

Edmark
PO Box 97021
Redmond WA 98073
800•691•2986, 425•556•8400
fax: 425•556•8940
edmark.com

Eidos Interactive
651 Brannan St
Suite 400
San Francisco CA 94107
415•547•1200
eidosinteractive.com

Equilibrium Technologies
3 Harbor Dr
Suite 111
Sausalito CA 94965
800•524•8651, 415•332•4343
fax: 415•332•4433
equil.com

Extensis
55 SW Yamhill St
4th Floor
Portland OR 97204
800•796•9798, 503•274•2020
fax: 503•274•0530
extensis.com

F

Farallon Computing
2470 Mariner Square Loop
Alameda CA 94501
800•485•5741, 510•814•5100
fax: 510•814•5020
farallon.com

FileMaker, Inc
5201 Patrick Henry Dr
Santa Clara CA 95052
800•325•2747, 408•727•8227
fax: 408•987•3932
filemaker.com

FontHaus
1375 Kings Hwy
East Fairfield CT 06430
800•942•9110, 203•367•1993
fax: 203•367•1860
fonthaus.com

FWB Software
2750 El Camino Real
Redwood City CA 94061
650•482•4800
fax: 650•482•4858
fwb.com

G

Global Village
1144 East Arques Ave
Sunnyvale CA 94086
800•736•4821, 408•523•1000
fax: 408•523•2407
globalvillage.com

GoLive
525 Middlefield Rd
Menlo Park CA 94025
800•554•6638, 602•774•0991
fax: 650•463•1598
golive.com

Graphic Simulations
15400 Knoll Trail Dr
Suite 214
Richardson TX 75248
214•699•7400
fax: 214•699•0972
graphsim.com

Grolier Electronic Publishing
90 Sherman Turnpike
Danbury CT 06816
800•285•4534, 203•797•3500
fax: 203•797•3835
grolier.com

GT Interactive/Humongous
3855 Monte Villa Pkwy
Bothell WA 98021
800•499•8386, 425•486•9258
humongous.com

Gyration
12930 Saratoga Ave
Building C
Saratoga CA 95070
800•316•5432, 408•255•3016
fax: 408•255•9075
gyropoint.com

H

Harper Collins Interactive
10 East 53d St
New York NY 10022
212•207•7000
harpercollins.com

Hayes
PO Box 105203
Atlanta GA 30348
404•840•9200
fax: 404•441•1238
hayes.com

Humongous Entertainment
3855 Monte Villa Pkwy
Bothell WA 98021
800•499•8386, 425•486•9258
humongous.com

I

Impossible Software
PO Box 52710
Irvine CA 92619
800•470•4801, 714•470•4800
impossible.com

IMSI
1895 Francisco Blvd East
San Rafael CA 94901
800•833•8082, 415•257•3000
fax: 415•257•3565
imsisoft.com

IncWell DMG
PO Box 6761
Chandler AZ 85246
530•647•8157
fax: 530•647•8157
incwell.com

Infowave (GDT Softworks)
4664 Lougheed Hwy
Suite 188
Burnaby BC
Canada V5C 6B7
800•663•6222, 604•473•3600
fax: 604•473•3699
infowave.com

Insider Software
6540 Lusk Blvd
Suite 161
San Diego CA 92121
800•700•6340
theinside.com

Insignia Solutions
41300 Christy St
Fremont CA 94538
800•848•7677, 510•360•3700
fax: 510•360•3701
insignia.com

InterPlay Productions
161815 Von Carmen Ave
Irvine CA 92606
800•468•3775, 949•553•6655
fax: 949•252•2820
interplay.com

Iomega
1821 West Iomaga Way
Roy UT 84067
800•697•8833, 801•778•1000
fax: 801•778•3748
iomega.com

K

Kaplan Interactive/ Simon and Schuster
888 7th Ave
New York NY 10106
800•527•4836, 212•492•5800
kaplan.com

Kensington Microware
2855 Campus Dr
San Mateo CA 94403
800•280•8318
fax: 650•572•9675
kensington.com

Keyspan
3095 Richmond Parkway #207
Richmond VA 94806
510•222•0131
fax: 510•222•0323
keyspan.com

Knowledge Adventure
1311 Grand Central Ave
Glendale CA 91201
800•542•4240
fax: 818•246•8412
jumpstart.com

L

La Cie
22985 NW Evergreen Pkwy
Hillsboro OR 97124
800•999•1455, 503•844•4500
fax: 503•844•4501
lacie.com

Landware
PO Box 25
Oradell NJ 07649
201•261•7944
landware.com

Leader Technologies
4590 MacArthur Blvd
Suite 500
Newport Beach Ca 92660
714•757•1787
leadertech.com

Learning Tech/ Voyager products
361 Broadway
Suite 600
New York NY 10013
212•334•2225
fax: 212•334•1211
learntech.com

Logitech
6505 Kaiser Dr
Fremont CA 94555
800•231•7717, 510•795•8500
fax: 510•792•8901
logitech.com

LucasArts Entertainment
PO Box 10307
San Rafael CA 94912
888•532•4263, 415•472•3400
fax: 415•721•3394
lucasarts.com

M

MacAddict
PO Box 58251
Boulder CO 80328
888•771•6222, 415•468•2500
macaddict.com

MacConnection
528 Route 13
Milford NH 03456
800•800•0009, 603•335•0009
fax: 603•446•7791
macconnection.com

MacHome Journal
612 Howard St
Sixth Floor
San Francisco CA 94105
415•957•1911
fax: 800•800•6542
machome.com

MacMall
2645 Maricopa St
Torrance CA 90503
800•222•2808,
fax: 310•225•4000
macmall.com

MacPlay
17922 Fitch Ave
Irvine CA 92714
714•553•3521
macplay.com

Macromedia
600 Townsend St
San Francisco CA 94103
800•470•7211, 415•252•2000
fax: 415•626•0554
macromedia.com

MacWarehouse
PO Box 3013
1720 Oak St
Lakewood NJ 08701
800•255•6227, 908•370•4779
fax: 908•905•9279
macwarehouse.com

MacWEEK
301 Howard St
15th Floor
San Francisco CA 94105
609•786•8230
macweek.com

Macworld
501 Second St
San Francisco CA 94107
800•288•6848, 303•604•1465
fax: 415•604•7644
macworld.com

Mainstay
591-A Constitution Ave
Camarillo CA 93012
805•484•9400
fax: 805•484•9428
mstay.com

Mark of the Unicorn
1280 Massachusetts Ave
Cambridge MA 02138
617•576•2760
fax: 617•576•3609
motu.com

Maxis
2121 North California Blvd
Suite 600
Walnut Creek CA 94596
800•245•4525, 510•933•5630
fax: 510•927•3736
maxis.com

MECC
6160 Summit Dr North
Minneapolis MN 55430
800•685•6322, 612•569•1500
fax: 612•569•1551
mecc.com

MegaWolf
1771 Grasso Blvd
New Haven CT 06511
203•562•1243
megawolf.com

MetaCreations
6303 Carpinteria Ave
Carpinteria CA 93013
805•566•6200
fax: 805•566•6385
metacreations.com

MicroMat Computer Systems
8868 Lakewood Dr
Windsor CA 95492
800•829•6227, 707•837•8012
fax: 707•837•0444
micromat.com

Microsoft Corporation
One Microsoft Way
Redmond WA 98052
800•426•9400, 425•882•8080
microsoft.com

MicroSpeed
2495 Industrial Parkway West
Hayward CA 94545
800•438•7733, 510•259•1270
fax: 510•259•1291
microspeed.com

Mindgate
164 Oliver Smith Road
Flintville TN 37335
800•648•6840, 931•937•6800
fax: 931•937•6801
mindgate.com

Mindscape
88 Roland Way
Novato CA 94945
415•895•2000
fax: 415•897•8286
mindscape.com

Momentum
7 Waterfront Plaza
500 Ala Moana Blvd
Suite 400
Honolulu HI 96813
808•543•6426
fax: 808•522•9490

Monotype Typography
150 South Wacker Dr
Suite 2630
Chicago IL 60606
800•666•6897, 312•855•1440
fax: 312•855•9475
monotype.com

Multi-Ad Services
1720 W Detweiller Dr
Peoria IL 61615
309•692•1530
multi-ad.com

Multieducator
244 North Ave
New Rochelle NY 10801
800•866•6434, 914•235•4340
fax: 914•235•4367
multieducator.com

N

Netscape Communications
501 East Middlefield Rd
Mountain View CA 94043
800•638•7423, 415•528•2600
fax: 415•528•4120
netscape.com

Newer Technology
4848 Irving St
Wichita KS 67209
800•678•3726, 316•943•0222
fax: 316•943•4515
newertech.com

Nisus Software
PO Box 1300
Solana Beach CA 92075
619•481•1477
fax: 619•481•6154
nisus.com

Nova Development
23801 Calabasas Rd
Suite 2005
Calabasas CA 91302
818•591•9600
fax: 818•591•8885
novadevcorp. com

O

Opcode Systems
3950 Fabian Way
Suite 100
Palo Alto CA 94303
800•557•2633, 650•856•3333
fax: 650•856•3332
opcode.com

Orange Micro
1400 North Lakeview Ave
Anaheim CA 92807
714•779•2772
fax: 714•779•9332
orangemicro.com

P

Parsoft Publishing
710 East Park Blvd
Plano TX 75074
972•379•4462
fax: 972•379•4463
parsoft.com

Port
66 Fort Point St
Norwalk CT 06855
800•350•7678, 203•852•1102
fax: 203•866•0221
port.com

PowerLogix
8760A Research Blvd #240
Austin TX 78758
888•769•9020, 512•795•2978
fax: 512•795•2981
powerlogix.com

Practical Peripherals/Hayes
PO Box 921789
Norcross GA 30092
800•225•4774, 770•840•9966
fax: 800•225•4774
practinet.com

Pre-Owned Electronics
125 Middlesex Tpke
Bedford MA 01730
800•274•5343
preowned.com

ProVue Development
18411 Gothard St
Unit A
Huntington Beach CA 92648
800•966•7878, 714•841•7779
fax: 714•841•1479
provue.com

Q

Qualcomm
6455 Lusk Blvd
San Diego CA 92121
800•238•3672, 619•587•1121
fax: 619•658•2100
qualcomm.com

Quark
1800 Grant St
Denver CO 80203
800•676•4575, 303•894•8888
fax: 303•894•3649
quark.com

S

Shreve Systems
1200 Marshall St
Shreveport LA 71101
800•227•3971, 318•424•9791
fax: 318•424•9771
shrevesystems.com

Simon and Schuster (Kaplan)
888 7th Ave
New York NY 10106
800•527•4836, 212•492•5800
simonandschuster.com

Small Dog Electronics
RR#1 Box 171-1
Prickly Mountain Road
Warren VT 05674
802•496•7171
fax: 802•496•6257
smalldoggy.com

SoftKey International
One Athenaeum St
Cambridge MA 02142
800•227•5609, 617•494•1200
fax: 617•494•1219
softkey.com

StarPlay Productions
PO Box 217
Greeley CO 80632
800•203•2503, 303•447•9562
fax: 303•447•2739
starplay.com

STF Technologies
629B Mock Plaza
Blue Springs MO 64015
800•771•6208, 816•220•1772
fax: 816•220•1778
stfinc.com

Strata
2 West Saint George Blvd
Suite 2100
Saint George UT 84770
800•678•7282, 801•628•5218
fax: 801•628•9756
strata.com

Strider
1605 7th St
Menominee MI 49858
906•863•7798
stridersoftware.com

Supra/Diamond Multimedia
2880 Junction Ave
San Jose CA 95134
800•468•5846,
diamondmm.com

Symantec
10201 Torre Ave
Cupertino CA 95014
800•441•7234, 408•253•9600
fax: 408•253•3968
symantec.com

SyQuest Technology
47071 Bayside Pkwy
Fremont CA 94538
800•245•2278, 510•226•4000
fax: 510•226•4100
syquest.com

T

TeleAdapt Inc
2151 O'Toole Ave
Suite H
San Jose CA 95131
408•965•1400
fax: 408•965 1414
teleadapt.com

TeleType
311 Harvard St
Brookline MA 02146
617•734•9700
fax: 617•734•3974
teletype.com

The Chip Merchant
4870 Viewridge Ave
San Diego CA 92123
800•426•6375, 619•268•4774
fax: 619•268•0874
thechipmerchant.com

The Learning Company
1 Athenaeum St
Cambridge MA 02142
800•852•2255, 617•494•5700
learningco.com

ThrustMaster
7175 NW Evergreen Pkwy #400
Hillsboro OR 97124
503•615•3200
fax: 503•615•3300
thrustmaster.com

Total Impact
295 Willis Ave
Suite E
Camarillo CA 93010
805•987•8704
fax: 805•484•9469
totalimpact.com

Totally Hip
201-1040 Hamilton St
Vancouver Canada
604•685•6525
fax: 604•685•4057
totallyhip.com

U

U.S. Robotics/3 Com
5400 Bayfront Plaza
Santa Clara CA 95052
847•262•5000
3com.com

V

Visioneer
34800 Campus Dr
Fremont CA 94555
800•787•7007, 510•608•6300
fax: 716•871•2138
visioneer.com

VST Technologies
125 Nagog Park
Acton MA 01720
978•635•8200
fax: 978•263•9876
vsttech.com

W

Wacom Technology
1311 SE Cardinal Court
Vancouver WA 98683
800•922•9348, 360•896•9833
fax: 360•896•9724
wacom.com

WestCode Software
15050 Avenue of Science
Suite 112
San Diego CA 92128
800•448•4250
westcodesoft.com

Index

A

B

E

F

I

J

K

L

M

N

O

P

Q

R

S

T

U

V

W